SEARCHING FOR GOD IN AMERICA

SEARCHING FOR GOD

IN AMERICA

The Companion Volume to
◆
the Acclaimed Public
◆
Television Series

HUGH HEWITT

WORD PUBLISHING

Dallas · London · Vancouver · Melbourne

SEARCHING FOR GOD IN AMERICA

A complete list of sources, copyrights, and attributions for works excerpted in this edition of *Searching for God in America* may be found on page 504 of this book.

While every effort has been made to trace all present copyright holders of this material, whether companies or individuals, any unintentional omission is hereby apologized for in advance and we will be pleased to correct any errors in acknowledgments in any future printing of this book.

Published in association with Sealy M. Yates, Literary Agent, Orange, California.

Text design, typesetting, cover art, photo selection, and editorial services—Koechel Peterson & Associates, Inc., Minneapolis, Minnesota.

Library of Congress Cataloging-in-Publication Data

Hewitt, Hugh, 1956-
    Searching for God in America / Hugh Hewitt.
        p. cm.
    Includes bibliographical references (p.) and index.
    1. United States—Religion—1620-   2. United States—Religion.
I. Title.
    BL2525.H48   200'.973—dc20
ISBN 0-8499-1308-X   96-7791
                                                  CIP

Printed in the United States of America

6 7 8 9 RRD 9 8 7 6 4 3 2 1

FOR

◆

Betsy, Diana,

William, and James

"Do not be afraid to search for God.

Then it will truly be the land of the free

and the home of the brave.

God bless America."

———◆———

POPE JOHN PAUL II

October 7, 1995
Central Park, New York

Contents

Introduction

HUGH HEWITT

When did many of us begin to believe that most of us had ceased to believe?

The first "us" includes the chattering class—the editorial writers, the TV producers, the professionally opinionated, and a large swath of the Academy. But it includes much more as well. Perhaps the "overclass" of recent years is coextensive with the first "us."

The second "us" is simply all Americans living at the end of the millennium.

And it seems to me—a television talker and voracious consumer of high-brow intellectual products—that the overclass is laced with a deep-seated assumption: that Americans generally do not really believe in God anymore, at least not a present, active, startlingly real God. A God who commands. A God with an agenda.

Do you disagree with this? The culture-defining class manifests its belief in American disbelief in a hundred ways, subtle and not subtle. Some are obvious. The entertainment fare served out by the television and film industries rejects God as real by simply not dealing with Him.[1] And this nearly total removal of God from the vast amount of media we consume has an effect of gradually diminishing the relevance of the Divine to ordinary life. Think of it as the practice of shunning—an apostate is not exiled, but simply and completely ignored. At first, those doing the shunning must be obliged to practice *not* noticing the target. But after a while, it must become routine, indeed, second nature. The shunned is still there, still breathing, still living, still feeling, but invisible. And the shunned one is ready to return—passionately eager to return, in fact—but without an invitation has learned not to press. Mind you, the original hostility of those doing the shunning probably drains away, but even if all the anger or disgust burns away, the disappearance is no less complete.

So because of the attitudes and practices of many of us in the chattering class—the overclass—Americans have generally put on an attitude toward God that resembles nothing so much as the attitude of everyone but Jimmy Stewart toward Harvey. We are amused by belief, but perhaps we suspect that not even Jimmy Stewart really believes in the rabbit.

Note thus far the complete absence of absolutes in my opening paragraphs. I don't

---

[1] In this book, He gets the capital letter I believe He deserves.

believe there's a "war" on religion in the U.S. Far from it. There is simply a tyrannical uniformity among the overclass that consistently treats belief as somehow just not very smart. Or serious. But it would be tacky to say so. So God is segregated from ordinary life and routine communication.

Belief does have its protected zone: the Saturday religious pages appear in almost all major newspapers; some cable television is exclusively given over to religious broadcasting; the occasional George Burns takes a turn as God the Father. And the political power of belief is always a hot and recognized issue, whether it's the Catholic bishops denouncing nuclear arms or Ralph Reed exhorting the Christian Coalition. And Bosnia has launched a thousand essays on ancient religious strifes rising again. In fact, the political dimension of faith is a convenient substitute for a searching look at believers' beliefs.

Real belief, though, that's a different subject, a parallel universe. Outside of some theological seminaries, does anyone ever think about belief?

Well, yes, they do. All the time. By the tens of millions.

But "we" don't talk about it much outside of faith's zone of protection—retreats, Sunday church, the Promise Keepers rally. Certainly not at Saturday night's dinner party or the partners' meeting, or the PTA, or the barbershop, or the swim-team meet. Even Gallup's regular inquiry into the religious practices of America does not inquire as to the specifics of America's collective faith. Rather, for poll-takers the questions about religion are on the order of those involving material goods: How many days of vacation for you annually? How many visits for Sunday services? Do you have one, two, or three television sets?

I hosted a talk-radio show in Los Angeles from 1990 until my retirement from the medium in the fall of 1995—a retirement brought about because of many factors, including my desire to focus on this book and the television series by the same name. In the last year of that show's life, I increasingly set aside an hour of time to talk about faith.

My approach was unconventional, especially for a broadcast on KFI, the "Big Foot" of West Coast radio—a fifty-thousand-watt, clear-channel behemoth that dominates L.A. AM radio ratings. Rather than search out the cutting edge, hot-button controversies, I highlighted everyday faith issues. One memorable show in that year of O.J. raised a simple theological question: Is it right to pray for the dead? My little question lit up the board. "A full board" is a term of art in radio land. It means all incoming lines are jammed with callers. I had a full board.

I interviewed an Israeli rabbi, Adin Steinsaltz, whom Orthodox Jews will recognize as the author of a historically significant Talmud commentary. Full board, despite the rabbi's intense accent.

I interviewed Greg Laurie, one of the country's rising superstars of evangelical Christianity. Full board.

I spent six weeks reading—just reading—C. S. Lewis's *Mere Christianity* over the airwaves. Full board times six. And when I retired, I was reading—just reading—Richard Foster's classic book *Celebration of Discipline*. Full board.

In my television job, we'd noticed the same phenomenon. We are in the fifth season of *Life & Times*, the nightly news and public affairs show of the PBS Los Angeles affiliate,

KCET. Among the very few shows that have soared above our average nightly ratings is the one-on-one interview I conducted with Robert Funk, the organizer of The Jesus Seminar. Other interviews with religious leaders have followed, and my questions are usually limited to the ideas and issues of belief. And the audience always responds.

I have to conclude that a great many Americans want to hear about, talk about, think about God in a serious way. And thus this book and thus the show.

The audience for such a conversation is not infinite, though the stakes may be. The public falls into three distinct groups. First, there are the convinced and the convicted. And they are millions. These men and women have mature and rich relationships with God. They know what they know, and they are confident they know the truth. They are "convicted." And they practice their faith. These folks enjoy the conversation because it takes seriously what they take seriously. In America, the vast number of these convinced and convicted are Christians of one sort or another, but the numbers of convicted Muslims, Jews, Buddhists, and others are huge and growing.

There are also the disbelievers. These are not legion in number, but when I have encountered them, they have been vocal. A disbeliever differs from a non-believer in that their disbelief *is* their belief. Not content to put the issue of God into their own box of other legends, they in fact are anxious to evangelize disbelief. People of faith find this group a challenge, for its members are stuck endlessly on issues of proof. Faith is quintessentially extra-rational. Those who demand evidence are not really interested in a serious conversation about the rationality of extra-rational reasoning. You can guess at the quality of this conversation.

Finally, among believers and non-believers alike there is a huge number of the spiritually restless. Aware of the pressing nature of the first question, Is there God? the restless hover around what others have named the gates of faith. Some are just outside the gates, others just inside. But the whole issue of crossing to-and-fro leads to extraordinary curiosity. These are the hungriest of all. And their dilemma is intense in modern America.

The edge effect of crowds has always fascinated me. Any speech, any public performance that draws a crowd also draws an edge of folks drawn toward but not into the tumult. One minute these individuals are all for diving in, and the next minute they are retreating.

There are quite simple explanations for hesitating at the edge of any crowd. Fear of the unknown, the uncomfortable newness of novelty, and basic shyness are all ingredients. When Jesus preached His Sermon on the Mount, I can only imagine that He could see on the far fringes of the masses a few people neither coming nor going and certainly not in a hurry to sit or draw closer.

In America the centrifugal forces pulling people away from a serious conversation about faith are huge. Nervous laughter and sidelong glances will greet any water-cooler talker who broaches even as ordinary a subject as prayer. And in an age of Monumental Frauds—not just the TV preacher who has tumbled, but celebrities of all walks and professions—the twin defenses of distance and skepticism are well and necessarily developed.

So what's a genuinely curious searcher to do? I've asked my friend Mark Roberts to pen an introduction that answers that question. Mark is a rare combination of pragmatic pastor and serious scholar. He's Dr. Roberts to his colleagues in academia. A Harvard Ph.D. as well as his commentaries on the biblical Books of Ezra and Nehemiah establish his scholarly credentials. He's also Pastor Mark to a congregation of four hundred families. And while his ministry is now suburban, it's been urban as well. Mark's seen a lot of searchers in his day, and he's answered thousands of questions. If you live somewhere near the gates of faith, his introduction will provide you with a guide book to getting on with your inquiry.

And I suspect you do in fact live somewhere near these gates. Why? Because you have picked up a book with a wholly unambiguous title. In so doing, you have by your action declared yourself to be a "seeker." Welcome to a group that stretches as far back as the first man who asked whether or not there was an Order and an Orderer—whether or not there is God.

The American family of seekers is not so old, of course, but its history is rich. The European colonization of the North American continent is a story of religion—sometimes alone, sometimes in partnership with the desire for wealth. No one can seriously contest that from the writing and signing of the Mayflower Compact forward, the history of America is in large part a history of millions of individuals seeking God.

That search has not been systematic. It has not been orderly. It has been beautiful and terrible, majestic and squalid, inspiring and dreary. The search has brought untold numbers to a belief in God—to faith. But large numbers have dismissed the enterprise quickly and conclusively. For those in the former category, the faith they have found defies quick summary. The differences among their beliefs are too numerous even for a lengthy catalog. Some of those beliefs are wholly and irreversibly incompatible with each other. Still others gradually evolve across a theological spectrum so nuanced and subtle that a precise parsing, while possible, is an exercise without a reason.

Stepping back from this huge accumulation of history, it is possible to see, very clearly in fact, an awesome collection of testimony to the vigor of Americans' search for the Almighty. Imagine the size of the room necessary just to hold one copy of every sermon delivered in the past seven days. And the accumulation of Americans' spiritual treasury has been an on-going and energetic activity for nearly four hundred years.

The reasons are obvious. There are just two.

First, Does God exist? is the most critical question imaginable if the answer is yes. Most folks know that. They intuitively understand the stakes. If God exists and He cares whether or not you believe—that He will act toward you as you act toward Him—then your decision about faith is pretty clearly a large one.

Second, more than any other country, America has allowed its people the freedom to search for God. That freedom has been pinched at times, but always present. Especially in the modern era, there is nearly unlimited license to pursue God (or be pursued by Him). As a result of this freedom, there is a rich legacy of personal accounts of people's search for communion with the Divine. Orthodoxy has existed at times and places in our land—sometimes a fierce orthodoxy, a killing orthodoxy. But the past three hundred seventy-five years here have been incredibly free relative to anywhere else on the globe. The search has been an uncontrolled and uncontrollable parade of zeal in a thousand different directions.

What to do with this legacy? Well, mine it, of course. This book is a modest borrowing from the American spiritual treasury as well as a marker from 1996 as to the state of faith in America. The marker comes via the interviews conducted for PBS's series with the same title as this book. Read those transcripts, and you will have been immersed in deep wells of faith that are uniquely tied to this year and this country. We set out to show you some of the country's beliefs via conversation with individuals who appeared to us to be models of faith-filled lives. They did not disappoint.

To focus exclusively on people of faith in 1996 would be to impoverish ourselves. Americans have been praying and thinking, preaching and debating God from the country's beginnings. In this book we recover and showcase some of those centuries-long conversations.

I have selected each entry with these guidelines in mind.

I wanted serious thought, though not necessarily seriously conveyed. The writing might be light or poetic or brief, but in each instance it is produced by an individual whom the record suggests was quite serious about the question of faith. So Mark Twain easily coexists with Jonathan Edwards, Thomas Jefferson with Lily Tomlin. The thread that binds the selections together is a purposefulness on the authors' part to convey either the story of their own belief and how that belief sprang into being and changed their lives, or some commentary on religion in America.

I am particularly taken with conversion narratives. There is no category more dramatic than a conversion story, and usually these real-life dramas are themselves radioactive with genuine spirituality. Yes, the book you hold also contains excerpts from writers or talkers whose search led them into a box canyon wherein there was no God or even a sign out. But the terrors of such conclusions are more than offset by the wondrous bounty of reflective writing on God's immense presence in, and operation on, the most gifted communicators of the past few hundred years. I have not been put off by length. Where a classic exists—*The Baltimore Catechism*, for example—but is not generally available even in libraries, I have reproduced it in its entirety for the convenience of the curious.

I hope the book inspires you. That is a frank admission of my own evangelical design. In his classic *The Screwtape Letters*, C. S. Lewis had the senior devil instruct the younger tempter to keep the human target focused on anything except the eternal questions, counseling that a soul goes in harm's way—from Satan's point of view—the moment the mind turns to questions involving the Divine.

Not that I'm an evangelist. Far from it. I'm a television host. But I am aware of the power of words, especially the words of individuals convicted of faith. Any serious review of the texts herein is a dangerous thing for non-believers who cherish their non-belief.

For thirty-five years I practiced a fairly rigorous Roman Catholicism. I am still a member of the Catholic tribe. No third grader obliged to commit the Latin Mass to memory ever wholly sheds the church, nor do I want to. But I made a choice to read Luther six years ago, and then Calvin, and so on. I set up my tent on the Protestant side of the river, but I didn't burn the bridge. Augustine, Kempis, and Nouwen are camping on the far side. They may be right. My own crossing has made me sympathetic to others wondering about God. The show and this book are the results of that sympathy.

I will be satisfied if this collection brings you even a series of postcards from—for you—the faraway land of faith. Whether Yahweh, Allah, Jesus Christ, or some other "Higher Power" speaks to you, you will find some pioneers who heard the same voice some time in the past. And their language is American.

God knows you have picked up this book. That's what I believe. And the agencies and instruments of an omniscient, omnipotent, and omnipresent God defy human understanding. It may well be that some text herein has lain dormant for two or three centuries, ready to take hold of one individual's mind now, in the last few years of the millennium. My job is to pick a few dozen of the best spiritual grappling hooks and leave them lying around. Rush in where angels love to tread, and you may get caught. Even the brave atheist should enjoy running the course. There are a few safe zones within which he or she can rest awhile.

But give yourself the time and the opportunity to ask the big question. The overarching crisis of modern America is the evisceration of the opportunity for reflection. Very few can survive the deluge of three-minute music videos and twenty-five-minute happy meals, ten-minute lube jobs and one-minute managers to sequester for themselves a period of quiet prayer or inquiry. The Mayflower Compact emerged only after a month-long sea voyage without any means of communication with anyone but the shipmates around— a dangerous voyage to a dangerous land. "When a man knows he is to be hanged in a fortnight, it concentrates his mind wonderfully," concluded Dr. Johnson. When the Pilgrims were tossed about on lonely seas, their collective mind fashioned the Compact. And when modern Americans carve for themselves some quiet from among five hundred channels and ten thousand bulletin boards on the Net, they may fashion, one by one, an inner life of faith. The comings and goings of that life, and its qualities, are described within. I hope one or more of them acts either as a prompt to go forward or a glue that binds.

The Search for God: A Christian Perspective

REV. DR. MARK D. ROBERTS

It is the best of times; it is the worst of times, for those who seek God. Religious options have never been more plentiful; religious confusion has never been more prevalent. Interest in spirituality abounds, as does widespread embarrassment about religion among members of what Hugh Hewitt calls "the chattering class." Our pluralistic society claims to welcome people of all faiths to the cultural party, yet it often kicks out those who believe that their faith is actually true in reality.

So what's a genuinely curious searcher to do? As a Christian, and a pastor, I can only offer a Christian answer to this question. Not a generic religious answer, but an answer that reflects my own faith experience and theological convictions.

How can I expect to offer one particular answer to life's central questions when so many other answers are available? In his book, *A Generation of Seekers*, Wade Clark Roof observes that today we can embrace "creation spirituality, Eucharistic spirituality, Native American spirituality, Eastern spiritualities, Twelve-Step spiritualities, feminist spirituality, earth-based spirituality, eco-feminist spirituality, Goddess spirituality, and men's spirituality, as well as what would be considered traditional Judeo-Christian spiritualities."[2]

Is it unkind, then, to represent only one spiritual tradition and to speak as a committed Christian or a committed *anything* in such a pluralistic world? No, I don't think so. Even most relativists I know unapologetically preach the absolute rightness of their relativism, and I appreciate their ironic proclamation. Moreover, my own experience suggests that true seekers after God long for honest answers about faith, even if they choose not to accept these answers for themselves. When we who have faith say only what we think others will find acceptable, we do them and our faith a sad disservice.

As a pastor I frequently talk with people about matters of faith. Rich conversation comes from open dialogue. I am no longer simply the preacher, but also the listener, and often the learner. I remember many seekers I have known in my life, especially two men who both happen to be named "Bob." They are like many other people I have met who are on a spiritual pilgrimage.

---

[2] Wade Clark Roof, *A Generation of Seekers, The Spiritual Journeys of the Baby Boom Generation* (San Francisco: Harper San Francisco, 1993), p. 243.

I met the first Bob in college. As freshman roommates, we struggled together to find ourselves, not to mention God, in the intimidating world of Harvard University. Bob and I began arguing about religion almost the moment we met, after he noticed the abundance of Christian literature in my bookshelf. But soon our discussions left the safe world of reason and entered the unprotected zone of the heart. We shared our faith and our doubts, our hopes of heaven, and our fears of life without meaning.

Raised a Catholic, Bob found his childhood faith lacking in many ways. He wanted to believe, but just couldn't. His struggle with faith was especially poignant in light of a promise he had made to his dying father. On his deathbed, Bob's father had asked him never to abandon his Christianity. Of course Bob had said, "Yes." So, a few years later, he found himself torn between his spiritual integrity, on the one hand, and his promise to his father, on the other.

Bob's search for God ultimately led him away from his Catholic roots into explorations of Buddhism, vegetarianism, and other spiritualities. Though we lost personal contact along the way, when I last heard about Bob he had found deep meaning through his family life and through caring for people with AIDS.

I met the second Bob in his office. My wife and I were interviewing him among several obstetricians as we looked for someone to help deliver our first child. We liked this doctor, but were most surprised by his answer to our question about his views of circumcision.

"You're asking me this?" he wondered in his strongest Jewish accent. "You're asking me?" he inquired ever more loudly. Reaching into his desk drawer, he produced a yarmulke. After donning it he queried once more, "You're asking *me*?"

Our choice of Bob number two as our doctor proved to be an excellent one. But, beyond his medical expertise and professional compassion, he freely offered various opinions about religion. He seemed fascinated by my role as a pastor, especially in light of my academic background. After consultations on pregnancy, we'd end up talking at length about religious matters, often about the Dead Sea Scrolls and their relationship to Christianity. We did understand that such conversations were not helpful to my wife while she was in labor, thank God!

Though loyal to his religious upbringing, Bob's search for spiritual meaning took him beyond Judaism. His fascination with Christianity was not simply intellectual. More than orthodoxy, he strove for authenticity in matters of faith. Not merely satisfied with belief, he sought to live out his convictions in tangible ways like starting a program to help impoverished women in Africa fight cervical cancer.

Both of these Bobs, though different in many ways, share much in common. Both have keen intellects, with doctorates earned in America's finest universities. Both have strong moral convictions, demonstrated in sacrificial care for others. Both have embarked upon spiritual pilgrimages that have taken them beyond the clearly defined traditions of their youth. Both have a deep hunger for God, in spite of the fact that they are precisely the kind of people who are not supposed to be religious, according to cultural pundits.

I am writing this introduction for Bob number one. And for Bob number two. And for the scores of "Bob-like" seekers I have met in my pastoral ministry. And for all who deserve to understand how one might seek God in a Christian way. And, I hope, for you.

Our Hunger for God

The American overclass may be shocked by today's widespread yearning for spiritual meaning, but those who observe life from a biblical vantage point aren't surprised. From the opening chapters of Genesis through the closing chapters of Revelation, the Bible teaches that human beings exist to be in relationship with their Creator. Even if our rebellion against God, which theologians call sin, muddles our creative yearnings, we nevertheless sense a profound need for relationship with some Higher Power. As the fourth-century theologian Augustine prays to God in his *Confessions*, "You have made us for Yourself, and our hearts find no peace until they rest in You."

Augustine's prayerful sentiments echo the Psalms of the Hebrew Scriptures. One of these ancient poems reads, "As a deer longs for flowing streams, so my soul longs for you, O God. My soul thirsts for God, for the living God. When shall I come and behold the face of God?" (Psalm 42:1, 2).[3] Don't you relate to that kind of soul-level longing for God?

Admittedly, there are seasons of life in which we overlook our soul's need for God. Sometimes we forget our soul altogether. When we're young and strong we can focus on achievement, success, and status. We invest ourselves in careers and relational adventurism. But inevitably life's realities explode our denial. Divorce, death, and discouragement call us to hear the cries of our soul. Sometimes even the emptiness of success pries open our hard heart. We wonder, *Where is God? When shall I come and behold the face of God?*

When we begin to feel a hunger for God, we get in touch with our created purpose: "to glorify God and to enjoy Him forever," in the classic expression of seventeenth-century British Protestantism. From this vantage point, eras of disinterest in spirituality should be the exception, not the rule. Indeed, both world history and this book prove that point.

In 1993, television producer Norman Lear, not generally known for his religiosity, spoke to the National Press Club about a "tidal wave" of spiritual sentiment in our culture. He testified to "a buzzing, disconnected eruption of spiritual reaction to our times, operating without the sanction of the popular culture or organized religion." And, he continued, "it is available to any groper."[4] Whether intentionally or not, Mr. Lear echoed the insights of the first-century Christian missionary known to us as the Apostle Paul. In his address to the intelligentsia of Athens, Paul stated: "From one ancestor [God] made all nations to inhabit the whole earth, and he allotted the times of their existence and the boundaries of the places where they would live, so that they would search for God and perhaps grope for him and find him though indeed he is not far from each one of us" (Acts 17:26, 27).

---

[3]All biblical quotations are from the New Revised Standard Version, unless otherwise indicated.
[4]Normal Lear, Address to the National Press Club, December 9, 1993, text from Federal News Service.

According to this text, human groping for God is part of God's created design. Our search for God flows, not only from our individual createdness, but also from the very structure of the universe. Once again, searching, even groping for God is part of the plan.

If you've ever experienced the futility of trying to feel around for a light switch in a dark and unfamiliar room, this aspect of God's design seems rather nasty. Indeed, if you've ever struggled with doubt, desperately wanting to believe in God but finding faith elusive, then you've probably already accused God of meanness. For reasons we don't always understand, God sometimes allows those who seek Him to wander around lost in the wilderness for what seems to us like an unfair length of time.

But the good news in Paul's Athenian address is that God intends gropers to be finders. Paul affirms that God "is not far from each one of us." The word "us" here refers not to Christians or Jews, but to Greeks who had simply shown a modicum of interest in Paul's message. They represent the majority of religious seekers today, whom Norman Lear calls "unaffiliated gropers." Even and especially to such as these, God is near.

That means God is near to you. Sometimes it doesn't feel that way. Often God seems to us to be light years away at best. As a pastor, I regularly find myself reassuring people who don't sense God's presence at all that, in fact, He is near. I don't expect them to feel better instantly, though sometimes God's light shines into someone's soul as I offer words of faith. Nor would I encourage anyone to deny his or her feelings of divine abandonment. The discovery of God's closeness often comes when we finally embrace our doubts and fears, even our anger with God. But no matter what we feel, the biblical good news remains: God is near!

God with Us

In fact, God is far more than near. Believers in the God of Abraham, Isaac, and Jacob have for several millennia confessed that God has actually acted in human history. God spoke to Abraham, calling him to go to an unknown land and promising to bless all people through him (Genesis 12:1-3). Through Moses God gave the Torah, the Law of the Jewish people. Some Jews even believed that the Torah was the very presence of God's divine Wisdom on earth (Sirach 24:19-23).

Early Christians affirmed that Jesus was the incarnation of God's Wisdom and Word (John 1:1-18). The word *incarnation* means "becoming flesh." In other words, Jesus is not simply a good teacher who shows us the way to God, or a person in which there is a spark of divinity, but God in human flesh in a unique sense. Jesus is "Immanuel," "God with us," in a way unlike any other person (Matthew 1:23).

Those who find this Christian belief hard to stomach stand in good company. Many of the earliest Christians, who had a hard time imagining that a good God would become mixed up with evil matter, denied the reality of the incarnation. In fact, the classic Christian message becomes far less plausible by proclaiming that the incarnate God also died on the Roman cross. The scandal of the crucifixion eclipses even the reproach of the incarnation.

It's certainly not easy to believe such things. And I don't have space here to explain why I think it's right to do so. Yet God's becoming human in Jesus means that God is not only near, but with us in a profound way. The New Testament says that because Jesus became like us "in every respect," He can sympathize with our weaknesses and help us in times of trial (Hebrews 2:17, 18; 4:14-16). That means that God knows what it's like to be us on the inside. When you feel spiritual hunger, God knows that feeling. When you feel despair, God understands. When you struggle with doubt, God has been there and is there with you.

Moreover, Christians believe that, in Jesus, God has taken on the very thing that keeps us away from knowing God—our sin. In the mystery of God's salvation, Jesus became sin so that we might have a restored relationship with God (2 Corinthians 5:21). In Jesus, God not only has drawn near and become like us, but God has also overcome that which would keep us away from Him. Jesus is "God with us" so that we might be "us with God" forever. If this is true, it's very good news! But it's still not the end of the story.

One of the scariest movies I saw as a boy was the horror classic *Creature from the Black Lagoon.* I still get the willies when I think about it. As the film begins, Dr. Maya, a scientist in Brazil, discovers a fossil that looks like a combination of a human hand and a giant claw. Excited by the implications of this discovery, Dr. Maya recruits a team of scientists to explore the Amazon jungle in search of more fossil remains.

The search leads the team up the River of the Black Lagoon and ultimately into the mysterious lagoon itself. There they discover a giant creature that looks like a cross between a lizard and a human being. Their search has succeeded far beyond their wildest dreams!

In their zeal for fame, the scientists attempt to kill this "Gill Man," as they call him, but their failed attempt only arouses the creature's anger. Now he will seek them, or their lives actually. He isn't interested in friendship, except, of course with the attractive female assistant whom he seeks to capture as a life partner. The hunted creature has become the hunter; the seekers are now the "seekees," as they try to escape from the enraged creature from the Black Lagoon. This shocking reversal propels the movie to its conclusion, which, of course, leaves room for a sequel.

The biblical story of the human search for God follows a similar plot line.

One of our very first scriptural pictures of God shows Him seeking His fallen people. In Genesis 3, the man and the woman eat the fruit that God commanded them not to eat. So when God comes to the garden, they hide in the woods. Yet God does not ignore them or expose them. Rather He calls out, "Where are you?" (Genesis 3:9). Already in the third chapter of the Bible we find a "seeking God."

Through the prophet Hosea, writing in the eighth-century B.C., God offered a moving demonstration of His seeking. Hosea's wife had committed adultery and was living with her illicit lover. God commanded Hosea to redeem his wife, to seek her, and to bring her back. In spite of her sin and failure, Hosea was to seek his wife as an illustration of God's redeeming, seeking love for Israel (Hosea 3:1-5).

Early in the sixth-century B.C., the prophet Ezekiel foretold the coming fall of Jerusalem and the complete devastation of the nation in 586 B.C. But he also envisioned a future restoration of God's people through the gracious power of the Lord. In Ezekiel 34, God rebukes the so-called "shepherds" of Israel. These leaders have not cared for their flocks, but have instead used their power for personal advantage. Even when God's people were scattered throughout the world, the shepherds failed "to search or seek for them" (34:6).

But after condemning the false shepherds, God speaks surprising words of promise: "I myself will search for my sheep, and will seek them out. I will rescue them. . . . I will bring them out from the peoples and gather them. . . . I will feed them. . . . I will seek the lost, and I will bring back the strayed, and I will bind up the injured, and I will strengthen the weak" (34:11-16). God will not allow His people to languish forever in exile, but will become the Good Shepherd who searches for His sheep, who tenderly nourishes and heals them.

In Luke 15, Jesus reinforces Ezekiel's picture of God as the Good Shepherd. "Which one of you, having a hundred sheep and losing one of them, does not leave the ninety-nine in the wilderness and go after the one that is lost until he finds it? When he has found it, he lays it on his shoulders and rejoices. And when he comes home, he calls together his friends and neighbors, saying to them, 'Rejoice with me, for I have found my sheep that was lost.' Just so, I tell you, there will be more joy in heaven over one sinner who repents than over ninety-nine righteous persons who need no repentance." The Good Shepherd in this parable not only searches for sheep, but specifically for the *one* that is lost. God's search for us reaches new levels of extravagance in the ministry of Jesus.

I cannot overemphasize how important it is for us to grapple with the biblical picture of a God who seeks us, but how easily it can be overlooked. The dogma of our culture simply assumes that it is our freedom and responsibility to be the seekers in matters of religion. But the Bible teaches that spiritual seeking begins with God, not with us. Even before we begin to yearn for God, God yearns for us. Our seeking is always a response to God's gracious invitation.

In addition to our cultural bias, even our religious conditioning might cause us to miss the fact that God seeks us before we seek Him. Too much preaching and church growth strategy has assumed the American cultural model of seeking rather than the biblical model. Even much well-intentioned Christian outreach takes as its foundation our search for God, not God's search for us.

About twenty years ago a prominent Christian organization launched its national evangelistic outreach called the "I Found It" campaign. Across America billboards, bumper stickers, and banners proclaimed enigmatically: "I Found It." The purpose, of course, was to intrigue people so that they would want to find out about "it," which was new life through Jesus Christ. At that time a number of theologically concerned Christians objected to the "I Found It" effort. "It's wrong to say, 'I Found It,'" they complained rather piously. "We should rather say, 'I Found *Him.*'"

But from a fully biblical perspective, both "I Found It" and "I Found Him" miss the good news. They get the order backwards. The biblical gospel is not "I found" anything, but "God found me!" I am found by God through Jesus Christ. And God can find you, too!

John Newton got it right two centuries before "I Found It" happened on the American scene. In his moving hymn "Amazing Grace!" Newton writes:

> *"Amazing grace! how sweet the sound*
> *That saved a wretch like me!*
> *I once was lost, but now am found,*
> *Was blind, but now I see."*[5]

Newton, whose despicable life as a slave trader was turned around by God's amazing grace, did not think in terms of his successful search for God. Rather, he who was lost had been found by God. How sad, given the popularity of "Amazing Grace!" in our society, that the image of a seeking God who finds us is so foreign to our way of thinking.

Even as those who sought the creature from the Black Lagoon were shocked to discover that they were now being sought, so we may be startled by the fact of God's seeking us. We are so accustomed to thinking in terms of our seeking after God that the reversal of agency is unexpected. Nevertheless, the Bible is clear. Even before you begin to seek God, God is seeking you.

How Can I Be Found by God?

God is first and foremost the genuine searcher. In Christian perspective, God not only has drawn near, become human in Jesus, and taken away the penalty of our sin, but also God is seeking us. I actually believe that God is seeking you. Depending on where you are in your spiritual pilgrimage, you may not believe that God is seeking you. You may not even believe that God exists or that God is personal enough to seek anything. But at least you know that God *may* be seeking you, if there is a God and if that God is revealed in the Bible. There's a start. You may want think about how the mere possibility of God's search for you impacts your spiritual quest.

If you do consider the Bible as a guide to truth about God, then you are in a position to have your consciousness of spiritual seeking radically transformed. You may have spent your whole life trying to find God, trying to be good enough for God, or trying to earn God's elusive pleasure. Your heart may even fight to reject the image of God the seeker. It seems too good to be true. But that is, in fact, the essence of God's grace.

The idea that God is seeking you will transform not only your search for God, but also your sense of self. Have you ever been sought by someone? Perhaps a company pursued you for a new job. Do you remember how great that felt, even if you didn't take the job? I remember how surprised and honored I was when I first discovered that Irvine Presbyterian Church was interested in me to be their pastor. How much more would your sense of personal worth grow if you came to believe that the God of the universe was seeking you!

As a young child, my brother had a security blanket, his "blankee." Years of loving virtually destroyed this "blankee," until it had absolutely no practical value, even as a rag. Yet it had immense value because my brother loved it. Whenever his "blankee" was lost, the whole family would have to search for it until it was found because it mattered so much.

---

[5]Emphasis mine. John Newton, "Amazing Grace!" (1779).

And so it is with you. You have inestimable value because God loves you and searches for you when you are lost, even when you feel like a worthless rag.

Your spiritual yearnings not only reflect your created need for God, but also reveal God's search for you. Although it may feel as though you are alone in your spiritual journey, in fact God is drawing you near. Those who feel their need for God intensely are those in whom God is greatly and graciously at work.

But we often quench our own flames of spiritual passion. Sometimes we do so by belittling our souls. Generally, however, we douse the fire of faith through benign neglect. Our lives are so full already. Who has time for God? Yet most of us can think of times and places where God has found us in the past. These locations and occasions vary as much as people do. God finds me most often when I'm hiking in the mountains or listening to Beethoven's *Missa Solemnis.*

One man in my church is a marathon bicyclist who rides for hundreds of miles at a stretch. When asked why, he answered: "Because that's where God can find me. When I'm out by myself on a ride my spirit is available to God." I would not recommend that you go out and ride a bike for a hundred miles to be found by God. Most of us would see God face-to-face before we finished the ride! But I would urge you to make time in your life for whatever makes you available to God's grace.

Even if you're not sure that God is there or that God listens to prayer, I'd encourage you to give prayer a shot. After all, what do you have to lose by praying? At most, you risk embarrassment, some wasting of valuable time, and more seriously, significant disappointment. But if a God who hears our prayers does in fact exist, surely communication with this God is something we ought to do in our spiritual search.

You might consider the suggestion to pray so obvious that it hardly deserves attention. Surveys show that the vast majority of people do pray, at least in times of crisis. But I have found that believers struggling with doubt and seekers struggling with faith find prayer to be one of the hardest things to do. Over and over again I have heard, "I just don't know how to pray!"

We find a model "seeker's prayer" in a touching story from the Gospel of Mark. A father brought his son to Jesus for healing. The father explained that his boy suffered from an evil spirit that prevented him from speaking and would throw him to the ground without warning. As the boy writhed in the dirt before Jesus, the man pleaded, "If you are able to do anything, have pity on us and help us." Jesus replied, "If you are able! All things can be done for the one who believes." In desperation the father cried out, "I believe, help my unbelief!" (Mark 9:14-29). Now, that's an honest prayer!

I sat with Tony many times as he prayed that way. Though growing up Christian, he found himself drowning in the quicksand of doubt. Again and again Tony would begin his prayers with this preface, "God, I don't even think You're there. I don't even like praying. But if You are there, please help me." Through several months of spiritual anguish Tony's prayers were answered. He was found by God, a God who prefers a doubter's honest, halting prayer to the articulate spewing of false religiosity.

If you struggle to pray, you may find encouragement in Psalm 145:18: "The Lord is near to all who call on him, to all who call on him in truth." Sometimes calling on God in truth involves freely confessing our doubts, our fears, our disappointment with God. But God promises to draw near to *all* who call on Him honestly, including you.

Americans have a peculiar tendency to go it alone in matters of religion. In their landmark study of American culture, Robert Bellah and his colleagues found one woman named Sheila who actually named her religion, quite aptly, "Sheilaism." In a recent survey, *eighty percent* of Americans agreed that "an individual should arrive at his or her own religious beliefs *independent* of any churches or synagogues."

It's tempting to critique the arrogance of our religious individualism, but at the moment I'm more concerned about its foolishness. If we want to learn how to play the piano, we go to someone who plays well. If we want to improve our golf game, we meet with the local pro. Wouldn't it make logical sense, then, to listen to people of faith if we want to grow in our faith?

Needless to say, this book provides a convenient entrance into the listening process. As you read, you will have every opportunity to learn about faith from those who have gone ahead to blaze the trail. At times you'll be challenged by those whose faith differs from what yours may be. Don't be put off by that challenge. Usually we discover what we believe most clearly in dialogue with those who see things differently. Of course, every now and then we learn something from them, too!

Beyond your reading of this book, I'd urge you to find a community of faith in which your search for God will be nurtured and through which God may find you. In spite of our American tendency to keep faith a personal matter, God often finds us through His people and even through those religious institutions which we often disdain.

Responding to God's Invitation

Throughout the Bible God invites us to come to Him even as He draws near to us. The prophet Isaiah presents God's invitation in language that is ever so timely, even though it is centuries old: "Ho, everyone who thirsts, come to the waters; and you that have no money, come, buy and eat! Come, buy wine and milk without money and without price. Why do you spend your money for that which is not bread, and your labor for that which does not satisfy? Listen carefully to me, and eat what is good, and delight yourselves in rich food. Incline your ear, and come to me; listen, so that you may live" (Isaiah 55:1-3).

How often we hunger and thirst for God, yet feel that we lack the spiritual resources to be satisfied! How often we spend our very lives for that which does not satisfy! Yet God invites us to come, to eat and drink that which we cannot afford. I would be remiss, however, if I left the impression that once you have found God, or better, been found by God, your seeking is over. In their zeal to draw people to Christ, Christians have too often neglected the extent to which a genuine relationship with God involves a lifetime of seeking.

We who claim to know God through Jesus Christ have found something wonderful that we want to share with others. To hoard it would be a selfish travesty, not to mention disobedience to God. But though we believe that we have found in Christ the answer to life's greatest questions, we err if we suggest that we have all the answers or even if we think that our version of the answer is the definitive version. In my experience, just when I think I have God neatly boxed in, He shatters my foolish box with an exception to the rules that I have established for His behavior.

That has been true for me in my understanding of those who seek God. I once assumed that seekers are those who don't know God but are looking. If you study all the biblical passages on seeking God, however, you'll find that almost every one of them assumes that seeking is something one does *after* one has a relationship with God. Seeking is, biblically speaking, something believers do. The life of faith is not a game of finders keepers, but finders seekers. True finders don't sit on what they already have, but continue to seek more. Once we have found God, our search continues as we grow in our knowledge and love of God.

Sometimes we who claim to know God through Christ are catapulted back into the wilderness of doubtful seeking. Almost every Christian I know has gone through seasons of doubt, in which what he or she believes seems very fragile. The experience of seeking God in these times feels more like the search of the unbeliever than the believer.

At many points in my life I have struggled to maintain my faith in a God who seems to vanish into thin air. Several years ago my father slowly, painfully died of cancer. Though he was a man of great faith who believed in God's power to heal, he did not experience healing on this side of heaven.

My father's extended illness rattled my faith. Here I was, serving as a pastor, proclaiming the power of God over life's challenges, praying for the sick, some of whom were miraculously healed. Meanwhile my own father was wasting away as cancer destroyed his body. Where was God in all of this? Why would God answer my prayers for complete strangers, and not for the dad whom I loved so dearly? Was God really there? Was He there, but unconcerned with my needs, or simply unloving?

During my struggle with doubt I took some of my own advice. I made time to be in places where God could find me. I spent many hours hiking by myself, calling out to God. My prayers were like the father who brought his son to Jesus: "I believe, help my unbelief!" I continued to seek the Lord, though He seemed very far away at times.

What happened? All I can say is that somehow God found me. He didn't solve my theological riddles. I still don't have fully satisfying answers to the problem of human suffering. I still don't know why God didn't heal my father, when He certainly could have. But what I know is that in my grief, God found me. I knew that my God, who became human in Jesus, truly shared my father's physical pain and my emotional suffering. I felt embraced by God's love. For me it was grace, amazing grace.

And so I continued on the journey, moving along in a life of seeking God and in the ministry of helping others in their search. As you embark upon a new leg of your spiritual journey by reading this book, may I wish you *Bon Voyage*!

CONVERSATIONS ABOUT FAITH

SEARCHING FOR GOD IN AMERICA

Searching for God in America

A Conversation with
Charles Colson

He was President Nixon's "hatchet man" in the White House inner circle, a master of political dirty tricks. But when Watergate
finally toppled the Nixon Administration, Charles Colson—Special Counsel to the President—found himself in a federal penitentiary sentenced
to one to three years for obstruction of justice. At the lowest moment in his life, Charles Colson turned to God. Today, one of the darkest
figures of the Watergate era has risen to become one of the leading evangelical voices in the nation. For more than twenty years,
Colson has headed Prison Ministries Fellowship, a nonprofit organization with more than a million volunteers in seventy countries.
Colson founded Prison Ministries to help mend the lives of prisoners and their families and to work for prison reform. Charles Colson is
interviewed at the Prison Fellowship Ministries in Reston, Virginia.

A CONVERSATION WITH
CHARLES COLSON

He was President Nixon's "hatchet man" in the White House inner circle, a master of political dirty tricks. But when Watergate
finally toppled the Nixon Administration, Charles Colson—Special Counsel to the President—found himself in a federal penitentiary sentenced
to one to three years for obstruction of justice. At the lowest moment in his life, Charles Colson turned to God. Today, one of the darkest
figures of the Watergate era has risen to become one of the leading evangelical voices in the nation. For more than twenty years,
Colson has headed Prison Ministries Fellowship, a nonprofit organization with more than a million volunteers in seventy countries.
Colson founded Prison Ministries to help mend the lives of prisoners and their families and to work for prison reform. Charles Colson is
interviewed at the Prison Fellowship Ministries in Reston, Virginia.

A CONVERSATION WITH
CHARLES COLSON

Charles Colson founded Prison Fellowship Ministries, which has touched the lives of thousands through prison evangelism. The former White House special counsel was once an inmate himself, jailed for seven months for obstruction of justice in connection with the Watergate scandal. It was during that prison stay that he first began to help others come to Christ, organizing Bible studies and telling fellow prisoners about his feelings for Christ. Since then, he has preached to multitudes and authored many books, including the best-selling *Born Again* and a more recent effort, a first novel entitled *Gideon's Torch*. He is also the recipient of the Templeton Prize, an award honoring great achievement in the field of religion. Colson continues his work today, traveling to prisons all over the world, providing a ray of hope where often there is no hope at all.

HUGH HEWITT: Chuck Colson, thank you for joining us.

CHARLES COLSON: I'm delighted to be here. Thank you.

HUGH HEWITT: Let's go back to 1973. A lot of people in our audience will not even remember 1973. Some remember the summer of Watergate, but it was really the year of Watergate. The Senate Watergate Committee was meeting, the White House was in disarray, and the entire country was drawn into this scandal. What happened to you in 1973?

CHARLES COLSON: Well, my life was changed forever. I had come out of the White House and was going back to my law firm. I had decided to leave before Watergate began, and I was a fellow who had really accomplished everything I ever set out to do in life. I mean, my story was the American dream fulfilled: poor kid grows up in the Depression years, scholarship to Brown University, academic honors, youngest company officer in the Marines, youngest administrative assistant in the United States Senate. I'd succeeded at everything I'd ever done, and I ended up in an office next to the President of the United States. And in the spring of 1973, when I left that to go back to my law firm, there were clients waiting at the door, a yacht in Chesapeake Bay, limousines, everything a person could want.

HUGH HEWITT: Big bucks.

CHARLES COLSON: Big bucks. But I felt absolutely dead inside. And I kind of thought I was just burned out from, you know, four years in the White House, beeper on my belt all the time, a telephone by my bed and the President waking me up in the middle of the night, and Henry Kissinger walking into meetings saying, "Mr. President, today we changed the whole future course of human history." I mean, caught up in that for four years, I thought I was just tired. But that emptiness, that deadness inside, persisted. And Watergate was beginning to shake the foundations of the Nixon presidency.

HUGH HEWITT: And it grabbed you as well.

CHARLES COLSON: No; actually, I really wasn't told I was going to be a target until the fall of 1973. In fact, the first prosecutor said I would not be. So I wasn't personally quite so involved as I was worried about the country, worried about Richard Nixon, worried about what would happen to the presidency.

In any event, in March of 1973, as the Nixon presidency was crumbling with Watergate, I walked into the office of a client (I was about to be counsel once again for the Raytheon Corporation) and met Tom Phillips. He was a businessman, engineer, and president of the company at age thirty-six. I mean, a dynamic fellow. I walked into his office (I hadn't seen him in four years), and he was completely different. He was at peace. He was smiling. His desk was clear. And he started asking me questions about me. This was a fellow who was always in a hurry, always racing, always driving. And this day he was so changed that about fifteen minutes into the conversation, I said, "Tom, what's happened to you?" And he said, "I have accepted Jesus Christ and committed my life to him." I almost fell off the chair. I had come from the vast spiritual wasteland of the Northeast, not from the Bible Belt; I had never heard anybody talk that way. Here was a businessman/engineer talking about Jesus Christ as if he knew Him! I mean, I'd gone to Sunday school, studied about Him as an ancient historical figure. So, I nervously changed the subject.

HUGH HEWITT: Well, just pause here for a second, because I remember reading that in your book. Did you conclude that Tom Phillips was weird?

CHARLES COLSON: I thought this was the strangest thing I ever heard a man say. And I thought, *I don't know what's happened to him, but I want to get out of this conversation quick.* But it wasn't so much what he said that got my attention; it was the difference in him, the change in his life.

Over the next several months the Watergate scandal spread, and I found myself drawn into it more personally. I used to wake up in the morning and there would be reporters and camera crews outside of my home, and I was hauled before grand juries and Congressional investigations. All through this time, Washington became a very ugly place. But Tom Phillips was kind and decent and caring and civil—everything Washington wasn't.

And so, one summer evening in August I went back and said, "Tom, you've just got to tell me what happened to you. I need to know." That was the night that he shared his own experience. He was a fellow who, like myself, had been a success at everything he'd ever done and was at the top. He was head of the largest corporation in New England, had a Mercedes in the driveway and kids in the best schools. And he would wake up in the middle of the night, and he'd look at the stars and the planets and the galaxies. And as a scientist, as an engineer, he knew that we're not here as the result of some cosmic accident. He knew there was something beyond. And he started studying Eastern religions and everything he'd get his hands on.

Finally, one night when he was in New York on business, he stayed in a hotel, saw there was a Billy Graham crusade at Madison Square Garden. He went, sat in the upper deck. And that night, the head of the largest corporation in New England heard the gospel that Jesus Christ is fully God, fully man, wants to live in our lives, is knocking at the door of our lives. And my friend was drawn forward as Billy Graham preached that night, and he gave his life to Christ. He told me he walked outside that night, and the sky was kind of dark and overcast, but it looked beautiful to him. And he said his whole life changed that night.

He told me this beautiful story and actually wanted to pray with me. And I said no, I'd never prayed except in church by rote. But he made me listen to a chapter out of a book written by C. S. Lewis—one of the great scholars and intellects of the twentieth century, a Christian professor at Cambridge and Oxford. Lewis wrote a book called *Mere Christianity*. And that night, Tom Phillips read the chapter called "The Great Sin, Pride." And as he read, it was like my whole life parading before my eyes. I realized that Lewis had written that chapter for me. I thought I had done all these things with government and positions of power and influence because I was idealistic. Actually, I was trying to show how good I was. It was like a torpedo hitting midship.

And that night, I took that little book. (I had promised I was on my way for a holiday with my wife on the Maine coast.) Took the book and promised I would read it. Said good night to Tom and went out to the driveway and got into my automobile, but I couldn't drive it out of the driveway because I was crying too hard.

HUGH HEWITT: Why?

CHARLES COLSON: Maybe partially relief that I found the belief that there was a God that I could call out to. And repentance for what I had missed in my own life, for the things I had done—not Watergate, but the sins in my own heart which were much greater than any of the things that get paraded about in newspapers. And deeply convicted emotion in my own soul. And I sat in that car for maybe an hour. Alone, crying, but not alone at all. (I was the guy who never cried, never showed any sign of weakness, wouldn't even admit it to myself.)

I woke up the next morning with the most marvelous feeling that I was free. I thought maybe that was just a temporary thing. We went off on our holiday, and I read *Mere Christianity*. I took a yellow pad like you're holding and like all of us lawyers hold, and I put two columns: there is a God; there isn't a God.

Jesus Christ is God; He isn't God. I read that book, studied it. And I was certain—more certain than I've ever been about anything in my life—that Jesus Christ is exactly who He says he is, the living God, and He came into my life. That was twenty-three years ago this year, and nothing has been the same in my life since.

HUGH HEWITT: I want to focus on the moment in Tom Phillips's driveway for a second. Here you are, the toughest guy among a bunch of tough guys. That's how the Nixon White House was staffed.

CHARLES COLSON: Ex-Marine Captain. White House hatchet man. *Time* magazine said "the toughest of the Nixon tough guys."

HUGH HEWITT: And so, you're sobbing. Did it occur to you, you might have had a breakdown?

CHARLES COLSON: No, because I knew exactly what was going on. I sensed what was going on in my life, and I really sensed that I wanted to know God . . . in the worst way. I really sensed that He was real and that He was hearing that prayer. I'd prayed before, you know. Before landing, one night in the Marine Corps, I remember looking out at the stars and praying. Once with my second son sailing and I spoke to God; I said, *Thank You for giving me this child.* I guess a lot of us have experiences like that, but we always think God is too busy and too powerful to hear us. That night I knew He was hearing me. I was just convinced of it. It was an experience that I probably could not find the right words to describe, but an absolute certainty that the God of the universe in the person of Christ, the person of Jesus, was hearing that prayer.

HUGH HEWITT: Did you feel something?

CHARLES COLSON: I think I felt a tremendous sense of relief that night. An emotional release. Years of pent-up pride and ambition and envy. And, I mean, take the deadly vices; they were all in me. Suddenly to feel that Christ really died on the cross for my sins, that it is a real historical fact, that I could be forgiven, that I could have a new life in Christ, that I could have the peace and joy and contentment that I saw in the life of my friend, Tom Phillips; that's a magnificent discovery. That's the greatest discovery in life. There's nothing like that.

HUGH HEWITT: It's twenty-three years later now, and people still doubt the authenticity of your conversion. Does it bother you?

CHARLES COLSON: Of course it does.

HUGH HEWITT: Does it surprise you?

> ...if I'm right; if Jesus Christ is who He says He is; if He'd come and live in my life; if He'd take the toughest of the Nixon tough guys, the White House hatchet man; if He could take Chuck Colson and turn his life around, then He could turn anybody's life around.

CHARLES COLSON: No, not a bit. Of course people are gonna doubt it. Because if I'm right; if Jesus Christ is who He says He is; if He'd come and live in my life; if He'd take the toughest of the Nixon tough guys, the White House hatchet man; if He could take Chuck Colson and turn his life around, then He could turn anybody's life around. The problem is a lot of people are running away and don't want their lives turned around. A lot of people know that if I'm right, they've missed the boat.

I mean, I had a guy come up to me one day at the National Prayer Breakfast. I saw him coming in the distance, and he looked angry. He walked up to me, and he chewed me out. This was in 1977 or 1978. He called me every name in the book. He said, "You're the biggest phony. You're a fraud. You're just trying to get sympathy." He was a state senator from Maryland; and, oh, this guy was angry. Three years later, I was in exactly the same place—at the National Prayer Breakfast at the Washington Hilton Hotel. I was walking across the lobby, and I saw the same fellow coming at me. And I thought, *Oh, no, here we go again.*

But this time he came up and threw his arms around me, and he started crying. He said, "Thank you for your witness because you convicted me." He said, "I wanted to believe you were a phony because I didn't want that. But," he said, "I knew that if you were real, then I had to deal with my own problems." And he said, "Because of you, I've become a Christian and my marriage has been reconciled." I mean, this was a great story. But a lot of people feel like he used to, and I still run into it today, mostly in your profession.

HUGH HEWITT: Does it matter?

CHARLES COLSON: No. I'm doing what I know is true. I know there is truth—that it is Christ, that the revelation of God in Scripture is true. And that's the way I'm going to live my life. And all I care about is pleasing Him. Nicest thing about being out of politics. The most refreshing thing about being out of politics. In politics I had to worry about pleasing fifty percent of the people—at least fifty percent—in order to get re-elected. Now I just have to worry about pleasing my Lord.

HUGH HEWITT: What about the comment from Bob Woodward, the journalist who was central to Watergate? He was featured in a film by Prison Fellowship, your ministry. He said Colson was the trickster, the booby-trap hatchet man who needed to destroy and incapacitate his enemies. Of course he'd go to Jesus Christ; he needed to believe one hundred percent in something. Richard Nixon crumbled, so Colson turned to God. What about that criticism?

CHARLES COLSON: Well, that isn't what Woodward says today. He just did an interview for Billy Graham, as a matter of fact, in which he said that Colson's real: "At first I didn't believe it. But now I've seen what he's done with his life; I see the tremendous ministry that he has in the prisons. And I believe he's very sincere." He's said some very generous things. So maybe there's one skeptic who got converted.

HUGH HEWITT: Let me ask you about Watergate again, because some in our audience don't even know what Watergate is. It's been twenty-five years since the break-in.

CHARLES COLSON: Sure, I have kids come up to me today and say, "Mr. Colson, can I have your autograph? You're in my history book."

HUGH HEWITT: Yeah. (laughs)

CHARLES COLSON: (laughs) Doesn't do much for you.

HUGH HEWITT: What were you convicted for?

CHARLES COLSON: I pleaded guilty to disseminating derogatory information about Daniel Ellsberg when he was awaiting trial for his role in stealing the Pentagon papers and publishing them. To put out defamatory information in the press is obstruction of justice. I didn't feel that I could plead guilty to being part of the Watergate cover-up, because I didn't think I was, and the evidence later showed that I wasn't. But I had tried to defame Ellsberg. I really pleaded guilty because, after a Mike Wallace interview on *60 Minutes,* I couldn't be open and up-front about my own faith. Wallace said, "If you're really a Christian, what are you going to say about Nixon's language on the tapes?" And I couldn't say anything, because I was going to go on trial. And I went home that night and I said to my wife, "I think to be free, I've got to go to prison. I think I've got to make the decision to plead guilty to something I've done in order to live my Christian life. I don't want to go through two years of trials and three years of appeals. I can't do it."

HUGH HEWITT: How long were you sentenced for?

CHARLES COLSON: One- to three-year sentence, which was cut short to seven months. I spent seven months in prison.

HUGH HEWITT: How tough were the seven months?

CHARLES COLSON: Well, the toughest thing wasn't so much the physical environment. I'd been in the Marines and lived in foxholes and aboard ship, and I had grown up in kind of modest circumstances. So, prison as a physical experience was not that terrible. I was worried a little bit about my life; my life was threatened by an ex-Chicago policeman. But the awful thing was the isolation from my family . . . and the fact that I was inside that prison and controlled. I was told what to do, day in and day out. When I arrived, I was in a bare-walled receiving room. I stood there naked, and they threw me a pair of undershorts that had five numbers stencilled on them. I knew I was the sixth person putting them on. I was in a dormitory at night, jammed with all kinds of people who had tough experiences in their lives. There were a lot of racial tensions. It was the sense of helplessness. It was the sense I was cut off. If my family needed me, there was nothing I could do. And I didn't even know what was going on outside. It was that sense of awful isolation and helplessness that every prisoner feels. It was such a sensation for me that I've never been able to forget it. And it's one of the reasons I keep going back to prison.

HUGH HEWITT: Everyone thinks that the Watergate people who went to jail, including you, just sort of did time—played a little golf, played a little tennis, looked at television. That doesn't come through in your book.

CHARLES COLSON: (laughs) No, I was in a minimum-security prison for a good part of the time, and then I was in a holding facility where they had a lot of Mafia kings.

Prison is not very glamorous. I mean, you don't find many people trying to get in. You find most people trying to get out of any prison because of the loss of freedom and the dehumanizing effect. I ran the prison laundry. I was next to the former chairman of the board of the American Medical Association. He ran the dryer; I ran the washer. Some days we'd trade off for variety. It was tedious. And there was a lot of human suffering around me. And because I was a lawyer, just about everybody in the prison came to me for help. So I was busy. Plus, I was trying to write a little book that I hoped might help a few people. It was called *Born Again*, and it came out a year after I got out of prison. I started writing it in prison.

> Contrary to what a lot of people have written, there were many times when I told him we shouldn't do something, argued with him. But ultimately he was the fellow elected, and I was there to serve him. So, we got the job done.

Prison was a tough experience . . . with all the mind games that the prison officials played with me. I mean, it was very difficult. Very tough to come out of the office next to the President of the United States and end up in a prison cell.

HUGH HEWITT: We'll come back to the prison experience in a little bit. I want to go back to the preconversion Chuck Colson and the postconversion Chuck Colson. How bad were you?

CHARLES COLSON: (laughs) Well, we never know how bad we really are ourselves. I guess the fairest thing is to read the accounts of people who knew me. Some people who worked for me wrote glowing defenses, saying I was a great guy. Somebody who worked for me once wrote, "Chuck Colson was brilliant, wonderful to work with. But be careful; he's so tough, he'd run over his own grandmother." And then, about a month later a newspaper said Chuck Colson boasted he'd run over his own grandmother. I never said it. I called all of my friends in the press—both of them—and I said, "Hey, I never said that." But it was already a legend in the morgues of newspapers all across America. And to this day, people write articles and say, "Chuck Colson, who said he'd run over his own grandmother. . . ."

But maybe it wasn't too inaccurate a description. I was an ex-Marine Captain. If the President of the United States, who was the Commander-in-Chief, said, "Do this," and there was a war going on, I did it or looked for a way to get it done. Contrary to what a lot of people have written, there were many times when I told him we shouldn't do something, argued with him. But ultimately he was the fellow elected, and I was there to serve him. So, we got the job done. All my life I've hated to take no for an answer. If something needs to be done, I'm gonna get it done. Nixon once said on one of the tapes, "Chuck Colson's the guy who'll walk through a door without opening it." So maybe that wasn't too inaccurate.

HUGH HEWITT: Tom Phillips, the night of your conversation with him, the night of your conversion, read you the riot act about the Nixon White House.

CHARLES COLSON: He sure did.

HUGH HEWITT: Did he pinpoint it accurately, and what did he say?

CHARLES COLSON: Yes, he pinpointed it accurately. He said, "You know, if you guys in the Nixon White House, instead of resorting to all those dirty tricks, had just trusted that God would reward you for doing what was right, you wouldn't be in this mess." And, you know, when he talked that way I think that convicted me of my own sin and made me feel unclean. You asked how I felt in the driveway. For the first time in my life, I really felt unclean. I'd always been a success. People had always said, "Isn't Chuck Colson great," so I could insulate myself against my own inner feelings. I think what happens when somebody's converted to Christ, all those outward layers, all those protective mechanisms are stripped away. And the defenses are stripped away. And you see yourself the way you really are, and you don't like what you see. Up until that time I thought that God, like any good college professor, would grade on a curve. That night in the driveway, I came to the realization that God holds us to a standard of righteousness—to be like Him. And none of us makes it. We all fall short of the glory of God. And the only hope we have is the forgiveness that we find in Christ, who thereby reconciles us to God.

HUGH HEWITT: Did you feel forgiven in the driveway?

CHARLES COLSON: Yeah, I did. I honestly did. I felt like two hundred pounds were taken off my shoulders (laughs). And I've been through some pretty tough times since. I know people think about jailhouse conversions and foxhole religion . . . and that people only get converted under great stress and pressure. That's not so. I mean, ninety-nine percent of the conversions are not dramatic like mine. They're just that people suddenly come to realize who they are, who God is, and the fact that they can have a personal relationship with Him. It's the most marvelous discovery. And some people find it under very ordinary circumstances. For me, I must say, it was dramatic. But, in the twenty years since that night, I've had all kinds of experiences. I mean, I had seven months in prison. And I had major surgery and almost died—cancer surgery. I've had some pretty down moments. I've had some scary experiences in prison where they almost rioted. I mean, you don't suddenly become a Christian and all your problems go away.

HUGH HEWITT: Less than a year after the driveway experience, your conversion, you're in Maxwell Prison. And you're smuggling clothing into the prison. And you say to yourself, *The old Colson is back.*

CHARLES COLSON: (laughs) Sure. The old Colson often comes back. The Apostle Paul writes in the First Epistle to the Corinthians, "I die daily." I have to die daily. I'm still a strong-willed person, still very determined. I have lots of drive, lots of energy. And I have to stop and say, *Now, wait on the Lord,* and get my priorities straight each day. Luther once said, "We are at one time sinner and at the same time saint." Each of us is a combination. Solzhenitsyn put it best: "The line between good and evil passes not between principalities and powers, but through the human heart, every human heart." It oscillates back and forth, and that's true in believers. I mean, the believer is not suddenly perfect. A believer is struggling, day by day, to live the Christian life and come closer to the standards of Christian living that God has called us to. That's what the Christian life is all about. And I think you do that until the day you hop into your coffin.

HUGH HEWITT: A couple of times you've commented in your writings and in your speeches that Watergate and its unraveling convinced you of the factual accuracy of the resurrection of Christ. How so?

CHARLES COLSON: Well, it's a great analogy, actually. If anybody really looks at what happened in Watergate, they would discover that Nixon did not know the full scope of the Watergate cover-up until March 21. John Dean, his counsel, paraded into the office and said, "Mr. President, there's a cancer growing on your presidency." And if you look at the tape of that day, you'll see that was when he laid out everything that had gone on and Nixon suddenly knew there was a criminal cover-up. Haldeman called me a couple of days later. I did not know about that meeting, but he told me some things. And I said, "Bob, you'd better get a lawyer." I think everybody at that point knew that it was serious and that the White House was involved.

John Dean went off to Camp David to write a report, began to think that he was in trouble. And he wrote in his own memoirs with refreshing candor that on April 4, less than three weeks later, he went to the prosecutors to make a deal, as he put it, to save his own skin. The moment he did that, Jeb Magruder went to the prosecutors. And a whole string of guys went to the prosecutors. I took a lie detector test. Here we were, the twelve most powerful men in the world. We were surrounding the President of the United States. And we couldn't keep a lie for three weeks!

The truth of the gospel depends upon the fact that Jesus Christ was bodily raised from the dead. How do we know that? We have the eyewitness testimony of five hundred people, according to the Apostle Paul. We have eleven apostles who were with Him and who saw Him raised from the dead. There was Thomas, who put his finger in the wound because he doubted Jesus. And all of the apostles were with Jesus after He was bodily resurrected from the tomb. Now, if He was bodily resurrected, that is the most convincing evidence of the divinity of Jesus Christ. And there's the testimony of the apostles for forty years. And they had no power like we did in the Watergate. They were persecuted. They were crucified upside down. All but one died a martyr's death. They were stoned, beaten, and not once did they deny that they had seen Christ risen from the dead.

I believe that men will give their lives for something they believe to be true. They will never give their lives for something they know to be false. If Christ hadn't risen, the Apostle Peter would have been just like John Dean. He would have gone and turned state's evidence to save his own skin. Not one of them denied the resurrection of Christ, which to me means that they had to have seen the risen Christ, God in the flesh. Otherwise they would have saved their own skins just like we did in Watergate.

HUGH HEWITT: You mentioned John Dean. You spent time in the holding facility with John Dean, with Herb Kalmbach, with Jeb Stuart Magruder. All of these men had religious experiences. Was it all genuine?

CHARLES COLSON: I don't think John Dean ever professed to have had a religious experience. I would be delighted if he did. And he actually did study as a divinity student before Watergate; that's kind of ironic. But, no, he has never said he had a religious experience. Herb Kalmbach did. And I used to help Herb with his Bible, and Jeb Stuart Magruder did, too. Interestingly enough, today Jeb remains in faithful ministry of the gospel. So his was a real experience, I'm certain.

HUGH HEWITT: Let me ask you about the people around you after your conversion, Chuck, because the week before, you were the high-powered Washington lawyer. And I see those people all the time, and you see them all the time; they're directed, successful, big moneymakers. Suddenly you're going down on your knees, you're forming Bible groups. Did this knock your wife, Patty, for a loop?

CHARLES COLSON: Yeah, it did. It was probably harder on my family than it was on me when I went to prison. And Patty was raised Catholic, and she was a faithful church-goer, and she believed in Christ. All of a sudden I said, "Wow! I've had a tremendous experience." She said, "Well, I've known about Jesus all the time."

Then we got to a living room of a Congressman, and soon we were all down on our knees praying. And in the Catholic tradition, praying that demonstratively in public is rare, so there was some momentary strain. But we kind of got used to that. I can say that through that prayer and fellowship, through the prison experience that followed, and through Patty's spiritual growth, our marriage has become much stronger than it ever was before. Our relationship with the kids is much better than

> I believe that men will give their lives for something they believe to be true. They will never give their lives for something they know to be false. If Christ hadn't risen, the Apostle Peter would have been just like John Dean. He would have gone and turned state's evidence to save his own skin.

it ever was before. And I think one of the things that becoming a Christian does is set your priorities straight. My old priority was success, getting ahead at any cost. Postconversion, my wife and family became the second most important thing in my life. The first most important thing was my relationship with Christ. And Patty is now a Bible study leader in the community.

HUGH HEWITT: How bad was the Nixon White House in terms of good and evil? And did you have to go back and make a lot of amends after your conversion?

CHARLES COLSON: I went back and made a few. The thing I felt worst about was having defamed Arthur Burns, who was the chairman of the Federal Reserve Board. I knew the Eisenhower White House, which was a benign bunch of fellows in a kind of a peaceful, quiet era in American life. I knew the Kennedy White House. I mean, we all talk about Nixon stealing the Constitution and we blow up all the sins of Watergate. We forget that it was Bobby Kennedy who sent the FBI in the middle of the night to wake up the steel executives to break the steel strike. So, you know, as a Washington lawyer in the sixties I saw abuse of power by Kennedy and by Johnson. We figured, when we got in the White House, it was our turn.

HUGH HEWITT: It wasn't really your turn, was it?

CHARLES COLSON: No, it was not our turn. That's right. But that was the way we looked at it. And that was the mistake. Eventually somebody had to bring the cycle to an end. But I have also been exposed to White Houses after the Nixon White House. And I would have to say that what the Bible says about human beings applies to all White Houses; all have fallen short of the glory of God. I wouldn't heap all the sins of the past on the Nixon presidency, because there are plenty to go around in other presidencies as well.

HUGH HEWITT: During your time in prison, you had an experience with the Holy Spirit, as distinguished from your conversion. A lay minister came and preached on the power of the Holy Spirit. Now that confused me. It's not in my tradition. What was that all about?

CHARLES COLSON: When I was in prison, a Campus Crusade worker came in and gave us the little Campus Crusade book on appropriating the Holy Spirit, a very simple little book. He was explaining how we should be able to feel the presence of the Holy Spirit. And I had an actual physical experience of feeling the presence of the Spirit. Now, that isn't like what some Christians call the baptism of the Holy Spirit. I think we have one baptism, and the Holy Spirit is with us from the moment of conversion. Part of Christian growth is becoming aware of how God is working in our lives. And that was a night in prison when I really became aware of the presence of the Holy Spirit.

> …the wonderful thing about becoming a Christian is that it gave me a new mind, a new intellect, a new sense of curiosity. Becoming a Christian was a moment when I made that act of faith, when I was declared righteous by God, and when I began a new life.

And I do think the Holy Spirit at times deals in my life, to convict me of things. When I had been out of prison for a year and had some wonderful offers in business and law, I felt a deep conviction that I had been in prison for a purpose and that God wanted me to spend my life working in the prisons. I think that was the visitation of the Holy Spirit, convicting me of what I needed to do.

HUGH HEWITT: And is that experience distinct from your surrender discussed in your book *Born Again*?

CHARLES COLSON: Yes. Let me be absolutely clear. There is a moment in which you are converted, when God regenerates you. And that's a moment in which you have a new life that begins in Christ. From that point forward, God's going to be with you in a lot of ways. I mean, even today I will pick up the Bible, read a verse that I've read maybe twenty times, and suddenly I'll say, *Wow!* The Lord kind of gives you an insight, gives you an understanding.

I was just in South America and had devotions with a marvelous man by the name of Henry Bryant. And I understood something about the peace of Christ that I had never understood before. And the wonderful thing about becoming a Christian is that it gave me a new mind, a new intellect, a new sense of curiosity. Becoming a Christian was a moment when I made that act of faith, when I was declared righteous by God, and when I began a new life. And then I have had lots of experiences along the way.

HUGH HEWITT: Let me ask you about that—about becoming a Christian. In one of your books, you wrote that if there are so many darn Christians running around, how come the world isn't better than it is?

CHARLES COLSON: (laughs) Well, George Gallup put it very well: "Religion is up; morality is down." Why is it that forty-four percent of this country is in church on any given Sunday morning, and one third of the country claims to be born again, and yet we are in a downward spiral in terms of the degeneracy of our culture? And the simple answer to that is that Christians aren't taking the Christian faith seriously. Gallup also found that where ethics are concerned, only six to ten percent of Christians behave differently from non-Christians.

Maybe what we have to conclude from that is that a lot of people have had spiritual experiences and then figured they were for their own gratification, and they've kept on living the way they lived before. Maybe some had an experience and walked away from it. Maybe some were perfectly content just to go to church on Sunday morning to have their ears tickled and feel good enough to survive the rest of the week.

But that's not Christianity. Christianity is when Jesus Christ saves us and transforms us—not so that we will feel good the rest of our lives, but so that we'll serve Him. Dietrich Bonhoffer, the great German martyr who was killed in a Nazi concentration camp, said that Christ bids a man to come and die—to follow Him in the radical act of giving his life for Christ. I don't think I could go back, ever. I'm too grateful to God for what He has done in my life. I want to live for Him. And that's a rather radical decision, because I start reading the Bible and it goes contrary to lots of things in human nature. There are lots of people I don't like and I would like not to have to love them, but I have to love them.

HUGH HEWITT: This is a question I've asked everyone in this series of conversations, and now I'll ask you. Why doesn't God just get this done? Just short-circuit this conversion process? Go out and touch everyone on the shoulder? Why doesn't He just turn people to whatever tradition is appropriate for them, make them Christian, whatever, just get it done?

CHARLES COLSON: (laughs) Well, all anyone can do, Hugh, is to speculate about that. None of us is God. None of us knows the mind of God. God obviously has a plan, which is revealed to us in the Scripture, in which He calls people to Himself. But there is also a battle going on in every human soul between good and evil. And that battle continues, even as we are sanctified in Christ or are being sanctified.

Why doesn't God just choose *for* us? I think that this earth is a testing ground. I think life is part of a challenge to see how well our faith develops. And He said that one day we will stand before Him, and He will separate the sheep from the goats—those who cared for Him while He was naked, in prison, hurting, suffering. And of course they'll all say, "But Lord, when didn't we come to You?" And He will say, "That which you have not done to the least of these My brethren, you have not done unto Me." I think life is a testing process.

HUGH HEWITT: That does seem a little unfair when you have had Tom Phillips, the president of Raytheon, to help bring you to the Lord. And then a marvelous group of men gathered around to nourish you and get you through your prison experience. Some people don't have anything.

CHARLES COLSON: Well, the job of the church is to rescue people who are sinners, bring them in and let them know the love of God and then work with them. I mean, we do that in our ministry. We worked with two hundred thousand inmates last year. And our job is not just to come in and say, "Hey brothers, here's the gospel. Be saved." Our job is to lead them to Christ and then help them, and that's what the church should be doing. And that's what the church does do. The church disciples people. Ideally, the church is supposed to help people grow in their faith and experience the love and caring I did.

HUGH HEWITT: Is the church really doing its job?

CHARLES COLSON: In some respects, yes; in some respects, no. In terms of having an influence on the culture, no. I think the church in America is weak because it has been caught up in a marketing mentality, which puts a higher premium on recruitment than on repentance. This mentality brings people in because bigness must be good, then feeds them a sugar-coated message and leaves them as stillborn Christians. But then, many parts of the church do an absolutely marvelous job. I happen to belong to a great church that really disciples people; it's doing marvelous things in the community, great stuff with evangelism. It's like any other enterprise. I mean, some parts of the church are doing a wonderful job, but not enough of the church is doing what it ought to be doing.

HUGH HEWITT: One of the striking comments in your readings is that most Christians do not know how to love God. So I thought, *Well then, if most Christians in Chuck Colson's opinion don't know how to love God, what's wrong with the church? Why isn't it teaching people how to love God?*

CHARLES COLSON: (laughs) Early in the eighties I had this hunger to know what it means to love God and Jesus said if you love Me, you'll keep My commandments. Obedience is loving God. Living the way Jesus teaches us. And so I went around and did a little survey, and I said, "What does it mean to love God?" And people would say, "I have a good feeling in my heart toward God." Or, "I go to church regularly." Nobody had a very good answer. And so I wrote a book called *Loving God*, which turned out to be one of the best that I've written. It was reprinted thirty-some times and is being re-issued. Billy Graham just used it in a crusade.

I have a passion to have people love God, and then come into the body. See, Christianity is not an individual effort. It isn't just Jesus and me. When we are converted we become part of a new community, and the church is that new community. It is the bride of Christ becoming pure and holy and righteous. And it is to be an influence in society. The job of the church is to take people in, to equip them to be ministers of the gospel themselves in their communities. And I think that's where we are short-circuiting the process today.

HUGH HEWITT: Well, how do you love God?

CHARLES COLSON: We love God by being obedient to His commands, by taking the Scripture and saying, *This is the blueprint for my life. This is the Bible. This is what I'm going to live by.* And we read it, we study it, and then we have the guts to do what it says.

Living the gospel is not easy . . . because it's counter-cultural. One of the things that people say is, "Oh, Christianity was made up. Years ago, people got together and wrote this Bible to give people a good way to live. They invented this Jesus, who was a great moral teacher." Well, no one would make up a religion like Christianity. It goes against every single one of our natural human instincts. Nobody's going to invent a religion that tells us to love our enemies, turn the other cheek, overcome evil with good. Nobody's going to do that. The gospel is a radical message that could only have come from God.

HUGH HEWITT: Hasn't it been watered down? Other guests who've sat in your chair during this series have said they've backed away from the parable of the rich young man who went up to Christ, in the Gospel of Mark, and said, "I've kept all the commandments. What do I do?" And Christ said, "Well, sell everything you have and follow Me and give the money to the poor." And the rich young man didn't do that. It seems to me that a lot of people fairly object to the fact that the church in America just doesn't do that.

CHARLES COLSON: Well, that's right. But the church has never been perfect. Lots of people short-circuit the gospel message, but that doesn't deny the truth of the message. People just find it difficult to live by.

HUGH HEWITT: This series is called *Searching for God in America*. People are out there looking around right now. They're opening every cupboard. What do you make of that? Why is that happening?

CHARLES COLSON: Well, I think I'll give you two answers to that, Hugh. Number one is they've always been looking for God. The *imago Dei*, the image of God, is in every single human being. People watching us on television right now are saying to themselves, *Oh, I don't want to listen to this religious talk.* Deep inside they're saying, *I know that's true.* They know it's true, because that's the way we're made. We are God's creation, and we know it. And we're like a puppy dog who's running around in circles, and we can't wait to feel the tug of the master's hand on the leash and know that we're connected with the God who made us. We know that. It's in us; it's part of our very nature.

But that search for God is being intensified today because we live in this high-tech, fast-moving information age. If one thing is settled in our lives today, it becomes unsettled tomorrow. You work for AT&T for years and years, and all of a sudden the company down-sizes and you're out of a job. There's tremendous insecurity.

We are seeing the fruits of thirty years of radical individualism and relativism in American life—that there are no absolute values. Our culture is being poisoned with pornography and banality, and people are losing their sense of connectedness. I mean, what makes a society is the belief that we have certain values that we all share and that we inherit these from the past. All of that is crumbling in American life today.

There's moral disintegration going on, and people feel uncertain about their safety. They fear crime. Look at what's happened to the crime rate in America. Violent crime has gone up five hundred and sixty percent since the sixties. Any day, any of us could have a gun held in our face by a juvenile criminal—a predator fourteen to seventeen years old. I mean, the numbers in the juvenile crime rate are swelling.

The old sense that we're all in this together, that this is a community of people trying to get along, has been shattered. And so there is anger among the races. There's xenophobia toward new immigrants, yet this country is a collection of immigrant descendants! In the midst of all this anger in America, people are saying, "Is anything true? Could it be that we can know God? Is there something more? Is there something real? Is love possible in a loveless era?"

HUGH HEWITT: And how do you answer that for the people who are listening to you right now?

CHARLES COLSON: Oh, the answer is yes. There is a positive answer.

HUGH HEWITT: But I mean, how can you persuade them of that?

CHARLES COLSON: First of all, all of us need to confront ourselves. What are we like, really? In our culture, we have a myth that we're really good. (I talked about this in the Templeton Address.) And that all that we need is more knowledge and we'll be better. That's one of the great myths of the twentieth century. We really aren't good. We're sinners. We aren't morally neutral inside. Left to our own devices we will choose evil. And so if we really look at what's inside of us, we won't like what's there.

Then we need to look at the historic fact that Jesus Christ actually was on that cross. He was nailed to that cross as a sin offering. He took that suffering for me, as my substitute. He took my sins upon Himself, and He died on that cross so that I could be forgiven. And forgiveness is possible.

When I go into prisons and talk about the fact that people can be forgiven, the people I talk to know that they are sinners. I mean, there's no pretense in prison. I love to preach in a prison. I'd rather preach there than in any of your best churches in this country, because the people in prison understand that they need God's grace and forgiveness. They need to know if it's possible to have a new life.

> If it's true for me, I can do what I want. Which is a perfect prescription for moral chaos. That's exactly the reason people are searching for God. Our society is crumbling because we don't believe there are any absolutes. But there are.

I would say to the skeptic out there, You've got nothing to lose. It's almost Pascal's wager theory. If I'm right, then that is the greatest news you will ever hear.

HUGH HEWITT: People are going to be mad at you, Chuck Colson. You're violating the great American principle of never claiming something to be absolutely true. You're claiming that Christianity is absolutely true.

CHARLES COLSON: That's right. People are saying that there are no absolutes except that there absolutely is no absolute. Christianity is an affront to the culture; it always has been.

HUGH HEWITT: That claim is also an affront to other religions, isn't it?

CHARLES COLSON: Yep. It's called the scandal of the cross, the scandal of the Star of David. It's the assertion that there is the God of Abraham, Isaac, and Jacob; there is the God of Jesus; there is one true God. That has always been an offense. And particularly so in American society today, when the ultimate virtue worshiped is tolerance. Anything goes. If it's true for you, that's fine; you do that. If it's true for me, I can do what I want. Which is a perfect prescription for moral chaos. That's exactly the reason people are searching for God. Our society is crumbling because we don't believe there are any absolutes. But there are.

HUGH HEWITT: Well, then, what is going to happen? What's your understanding of what's going to happen to the devout and holy Muslim, the devout and holy Buddhist, the devout and holy Hindu? They may be working alongside your ministry in the prisons, or they may be some of the people in prison who have been forgotten.

CHARLES COLSON: I can't judge that because I'm not God. All I know is what Jesus said: "No man comes to the Father but through Me." So I believe that the only way to God is through Jesus Christ.

Now, don't take offense at me. I'm quoting the Scripture of the Christ I know. And I know Him because He has come into my life and lives in me. I know Him because the historical evidence is absolutely overwhelming that He died on the cross and was raised again. So I believe His Word.

I fully respect the Muslim who believes something else. Although Muslims *do* believe in Jesus. They believe that instead of being bodily resurrected, He was somehow assumed into heaven. The Buddhist really does not believe in one God. But Jews, Muslims, and Christians all believe in one true God. The question is how to get to Him.

HUGH HEWITT: And do you believe there are consequences for not believing? Eternal consequences?

CHARLES COLSON: Oh, yeah. I believe there's heaven and hell. I believe that there is an actual hell. I do not believe that when we leave this earth, we get a pass. I don't believe we're mercifully and peacefully annihilated. I believe that there is eternal damnation for those who have heard the gospel and turned away.

HUGH HEWITT: So you're a throwback to Jonathan Edwards. There is a hell, and it's not a pleasant place.

CHARLES COLSON: That's right. Jonathan Edwards is one of my heroes. I suppose it also makes me a throwback because I believe in someone who lived two thousand years ago.

HUGH HEWITT: How does a viewer, who's just been touched by what you've said and wants to know God, do that?

CHARLES COLSON: If I were that viewer, I would go to a pastor of a Bible-believing, Bible-preaching church and ask him. I would call up Campus Crusade, which is a wonderful evangelistic ministry. If I were a Roman Catholic, I would go to my parish priest. If I were Greek Orthodox, I would go to the priest and say, "I've just heard a man on television who said people can have a personal relationship with Jesus Christ. Tell me about that." Or, I'd write a letter to Chuck Colson. Anybody can do that. Write to me and I'll certainly be more than happy to answer your letter.

HUGH HEWITT: Okay. Now, Chuck, what does a personal relationship with Jesus Christ mean to you? As opposed to some of the other understandings of religion.

CHARLES COLSON: Well, some people look upon Christianity and religion as a set of creeds and beliefs. I don't believe that. I believe that Christianity is Jesus. Jesus says, "I'll knock on the door. And if you open the door I will come in and live in your life. I and the Father are one." It is not my life I live, but it is Christ who lives in me. I have been crucified with Christ. Christianity begins as a personal relationship with Jesus Christ, the living God, who actually lives in our lives. And it is the most personal and intimate relationship there is. Out of that flows the new community of believers. I mean, my brothers and sisters around the world are all those who have had that kind of an experience, where Christ has come to live in their lives.

> The great drama of the relationship between Christ and man is that while man is searching for that something more, Christ is reaching out to him. The object is to turn around, face Him, and come to Him.

HUGH HEWITT: Your writings are pretty strict. Let me quote something to you. You wrote, "We aren't interested in reducing religion to a form of therapy. We want to respond to the God who exists objectively."

CHARLES COLSON: That's correct. I mean, religion may be a therapy, but Christianity is not a therapy. Christianity is truth, and it's true whether we believe it to be true or not; it's objectively true. And it reflects the ultimate reality that there is a God who created this. He is the Alpha, the starting point of everything else. All things are held together by Him and through Him; the Scripture says that about Christ. And so I believe there's absolute objective reality, and much of life is spent running away from it. The great drama of the relationship between Christ and man is that while man is searching for that something more, Christ is reaching out to him. The object is to turn around, face Him, and come to Him.

Christianity is not something that just makes people feel good. C. S. Lewis said something about that. He's my favorite author, and his book *Mere Christianity* was influential in my own conversion. C. S. Lewis said, "If you're looking to be happy or to feel good, I don't recommend Christianity. That won't make you feel good. That's liable to upset your life dramatically. If you want to feel good, I recommend a bottle of port wine."

HUGH HEWITT: There are a lot of people out there that are not very good people, Chuck. In the old days, you may have considered yourself to have been one of them. Why would God want to save everyone? Why would He want to do that?

CHARLES COLSON: I think He wants everyone He created to come to Him. I think His Son went to the cross to die so that whoever would believe would have eternal life and not perish. God is obviously anxious to have us come home, to return to him. That's the great drama of life.

I mean, we are free. We are not automatons. We are not puppets. God created us with a free will, and we make choices all of the time. From the day we're born to the day we die, the most important questions we can ask ourselves are *Do I want to know God? Do I want to be at peace with God?* and *Do I want to have a relationship with Him?*

HUGH HEWITT: Anyone too far gone to experience that?

CHARLES COLSON: No, of course not. Nobody.

HUGH HEWITT: How about if they were converted and then fell away? A few people you spent time with in prison had that reaction: "I was there. I lost it. I sinned again and again and again."

CHARLES COLSON: Yeah, sure. A lot of people do that. One of the people I wrote about in prison fell, was arrested, and went back to prison. I just heard from him quite recently. He's out of prison, and he's got his life together. It's a struggle. Life is not easy. Particularly for guys getting out of prison. It's really tough. They don't have any friends. Nobody likes them. I mean, when I came out of prison, I was a celebrity. So I was accepted. Fame—that's all that matters in American life. But the average guy getting out of prison, he doesn't have many people to go to. That's one reason this ministry reaches out to people like that; they don't have anywhere else to turn. Simply because of that a lot of them are going to slip. And a lot of people slip because the flesh is weak.

HUGH HEWITT: Does God ever stop forgiving?

CHARLES COLSON: No. Not if you come to Him in genuine repentance. No. The Bible says that only the sin of blasphemy against the Holy Spirit cannot be forgiven. I don't think a true believer can commit blasphemy against the Holy Spirit.

HUGH HEWITT: Let me go back again to your strict theology. You enjoin people to "ground faith in the objective Word of God and Scripture, for if we ground our faith in experience, we open ourselves to every wind of mysticism." You're a literalist as to the Scripture? Is it all authentic?

CHARLES COLSON: Well, *literalist* is not really the right word. I believe that the original autographs of Scripture were dictated by the Holy Spirit and are without error. I don't believe that the Scripture can be in error, because the Holy God who is perfect and righteous cannot err. We have translations. We have gone back with great effort and enormous investment of scholarship to try to find out if we have the exact words of the original autographs. We don't have the original autographs, but we keep finding earlier and earlier copies.

The Bible is the only document that I know of that has virtually contemporaneous copies, that actually can be dated. Copies of the New Testament go back to 125 A.D., within fifty years of the time they were written. Or less, in some cases. Some scraps in Oxford are even older than that. The Dead Sea Scrolls are extraordinary discoveries. But, all I can say as a Christian is that I believe that the Bible is God's inspired Word.

HUGH HEWITT: The Creation story—seven days—do you believe that?

CHARLES COLSON: The Bible is not like any other book, but you have to read it like any other book. Parables are parables. Poetry is poetry. Metaphors are metaphors. Allegories are allegories. Where you have to be very careful (and scholars spend a lot of time on this) is reading a didactic teaching as didactic teaching, reading historical accounts as clearly historical accounts, and reading parables as parables. When it says that the heavens declare the glory of God, well, we know that the heavens don't speak. We use the same kinds of expressions in modern American language. We say the mountains clap their hands. We say that the sun rises. You say that on your television show. But the sun doesn't rise. Obviously. We know that. But that's a figure of speech. And the Bible is replete with figures of speech that people could understand. And they have to be read as figures of speech.

Now, you asked specifically about the seven days. No, I believe that those are seven ages. Actually, I don't think it matters whether it was seven literal days or not.

HUGH HEWITT: Then what did you mean when you wrote, "The world may scoff, but can call me a fundamentalist anytime"?

CHARLES COLSON: Because if you go back to the early part of the twentieth century, there was a great split in the church between the fundamentalists and the modernists. The modernists were so-called higher critics of the Bible. And they strayed from the fundamental beliefs that had been historic orthodoxy going back to the earliest church councils. The earliest church held these truths to be fundamental, such as the Apostles' Creed. The fundamentalists came along and published little books called *The Fundamentals* in the early part of the twentieth century, in which they said they were not going to let the modernists tell them that there wasn't really a bodily resurrection of Jesus. They believed in the virgin birth. They believed in the deity of Christ. They believed in His coming return. They believed in the inspired, authoritative Word of God. And they believed in Christ's substitutionary death on the cross.

Those are the fundamentals of the faith. I believe in those. If that makes me a fundamentalist, I am a fundamentalist. *Fundamentalist* is now more of a cultural term in modern American life, but it's actually one of those words, like *gay,* that has been stolen. And the meaning has been changed. It now means a sort of narrow-minded, bigoted separatist. Well, historically it has simply meant someone who asserts and believes in the fundamentals of the faith and is orthodox. And I'm orthodox.

HUGH HEWITT: The most common question that people want me to ask all my guests, Chuck, is this: Why is there suffering? Why are children born diseased? Why are they born blind? Why do innocents suffer? Why are innocents killed?

CHARLES COLSON: I don't know. The only thing that I know is that I live in a sinful world and the consequences of that sin are manifest in people. There is suffering, and inexplicable acts take place.

Why would a loving God allow this? Well, the only other choice for a loving God would be to control human nature, to take away our free will. He created us in the Garden, perfect. In Paradise. And then we sinned. Now we're living with the consequences of that sin. We feel them systemically, institutionally, in terms of disease and chaos. The Bible predicted that would be the case. But for everybody there is the possibility of ultimate redemption. I mean, that's all that really matters as you go through life. Maybe the rich young ruler you were referring to earlier had a harder time seeing that truth than a beggar like Lazarus did. Mother Teresa argues that the poor can see better. Through all their pain and suffering, they see the reality of God in a way that those of us who live comfortable, upper-middle-class lives cannot.

HUGH HEWITT: Clearly you believe in Satan.

CHARLES COLSON: Yes, indeed.

HUGH HEWITT: Why? Why would God allow Satan to run around? He could have given us free will without putting an adversary on the globe at the same time.

CHARLES COLSON: Oh, I think it's part of the drama in Scripture—that Satan is still here, tempting us. I suppose God could have given us free will without him, but He didn't. And Satan's temptations test our faith.

HUGH HEWITT: Chuck, that leads to another question. How do you explain the American obsession with angels in the last couple of years?

CHARLES COLSON: People are looking for answers. The growth of the New Age religion is rampant because people are spiritually hungry. New Age isn't new, either; it's a do-it-yourself form of first-century Gnosticism—that people can find God on their own terms, define Him themselves. And in this individualistic era, many don't want to humble themselves before God. They prefer to have their own guardian angels, their own mystics, their own gurus, and to find their own religion in whatever ways suit them and make them happy. So the angel mania that is going on in America is perfectly understandable. It's part of the search that is going on for something more, some meaning to life.

HUGH HEWITT: Have you ever experienced any doubt since your conversion?

CHARLES COLSON: Yeah. And if anybody tells you that they haven't doubted, they'll lie about other things as well. Everybody has moments of doubt, sure.

HUGH HEWITT: When did it happen to you?

CHARLES COLSON: Oh, it happens periodically. But I must tell you this: it's simply the normal process of life. Particularly when I see suffering and I wonder, *How can God allow this? Could all this be true?* And what Christ has done for me is almost too good to be true, and so I have had weak moments. But God has manifested Himself to me in unmistakable ways.

HUGH HEWITT: How so?

CHARLES COLSON: I'll give you one illustration. We had a prison event going on in Oregon, and fifteen hundred inmates came out for it. And

> …in this individualistic era, many don't want to humble themselves before God. They prefer to have their own guardian angels, their own mystics, their own gurus, and to find their own religion in whatever ways suit them and make them happy.

Kathy Troccoli was singing. She's a wonderful gospel singer, a wonderful performing artist, both secular and gospel. After she sang "My Life Is in Your Hands," a man came up to her and said, "Kathy, thank you for singing that song. It touched me in the deepest part of my heart. I was really in need today, really in distress, and that song helped me. You see, my wife wrote me to say she was going to divorce me. And I didn't think I could get through this day. But because of that song, I can."

Five days later and two thousand miles away from Oregon, Kathy Troccoli was in Chicago with me at a Prison Fellowship rally. She sang the same song for this rally of volunteers, "My Life Is in Your Hands." And afterward, a woman walked up to Kathy and said, "Thank you for singing that song. It touched me in the deepest part of my heart. I've been going through a very tough time, and I've decided to divorce my husband, who's in prison."

Kathy said, "Where is your husband?" She said, "Salem, Oregon." Kathy said, "I talked to him," and she told her the man's name. And the woman couldn't believe it, and Kathy couldn't. And they stood there crying and praying. That couple is now reconciled. Now, you can say that was a coincidence, but you could never convince that couple of that. With a song, God reached a man in a prison in Oregon and five days later reached his wife in a rally in Chicago, and He brought the two people together. He mended their relationship. I have to say that's the work of a sovereign God.

HUGH HEWITT: Why don't people believe stories like that?

CHARLES COLSON: That's the battle that's going on between the rebellious self that says, *I am the master of my own destiny,* and the little child inside that says, *I want to know God.* That battle goes on and on. It's happening day in and day out. It may happen while this program is on.

HUGH HEWITT: Quite clearly you believe in miracles. How often do you see them?

CHARLES COLSON: Well, you're looking at one right now. For God to have changed my life is a miracle. And every time He changes a life, that's another miracle.

HUGH HEWITT: Let me ask you to pause for a moment, Chuck. In one respect, people are going to think of you as a Watergate figure, as a convicted obstructor of justice in the Ellsberg case. In another respect, they'll think of you as well-off, Brown University-educated, with all the tools and talents to find your way out of that mess. Why didn't you get out of it?

CHARLES COLSON: Oh, come on. I could have gotten out of prison. A guy in Texas said, "Come with me and I'll make you a millionaire. I'll have a million dollars in your capital account at the end of two years, and that'll be after taxes." I had some really good offers when I got out of prison, too. Old clients said they'd be back and give me a hundred thousand dollars a year to represent them. I could have done a lot of things instead of Prison Fellowship. But, I have taken every book royalty I've received and given it to this ministry. I haven't kept a speaking fee in twenty years. I received a million dollars—the Templeton Prize—and gave it to Prison Fellowship. I mean, if I were working in prisons because I wanted something out of it, I've been pretty dumb.

> I've never forgotten the hopelessness and despair in the prison dormitory I was in. I mean, guys with nothing to live for. They'd lie on their bunks, looking up at the sky. Their bodies were literally corroding, atrophying. Their souls were being sucked out of them.

HUGH HEWITT: I had read that, and I was going to ask you about that. The Templeton Prize is a great honor, but it's also a great benefit. It's a million bucks. And your books have made hundreds of thousands. Why does all this money go to Prison Fellowship? You make fifty-nine thousand dollars a year.

CHARLES COLSON: Right. Because I don't believe that it's mine. If I thought it was mine, I could keep it. But I didn't earn the Templeton Prize. The Templeton Prize was given to me for the ministry of Prison Fellowship, the work that God has done through my life. It belongs to God.

One time when I was writing one of my books, I had one of those experiences we were talking about, where I really believed God was nudging me to do something. And I remember saying, "Everything I have is Yours." If I write a book about what God's done in my life, is that really mine? I don't think it is; I think it belongs to God. So, I'm not being a hero, and I'm not trying to win brownie points, and I'm not trying to impress people with how good I am. To me, it is the only reasonable response.

HUGH HEWITT: Do you understand how that kind of story might literally scare the hell out of someone? If you give away all this money, are you suggesting that everyone has to make the same kind of commitment?

CHARLES COLSON: No, no. Everybody should deal with their own conscience in their own way. And I don't ever try to make judgments for other people. And lots of people have very different circumstances. I'd been successful before I went to the White House. I'd had a very successful law practice and made some good investments, and I am able to afford it. Maybe if I couldn't afford it I wouldn't have done it. So I don't ever want to be self-righteous about that.

HUGH HEWITT: Okay, let me turn to Prison Fellowship. It's big now. Two hundred and eighty people work in the surroundings where we are. You have fifty thousand volunteers. You've been in prisons all over the world. Why do you care?

CHARLES COLSON: I do what I do out of gratitude to God for what He has done in my life. And I have a passion to see the gospel invade the prisons. I guess I've never forgotten what it was like to be a prisoner. I've never forgotten the hopelessness and despair in the prison dormitory I was in. I mean, guys with nothing to live for. They'd lie on their bunks, looking up at the sky. Their bodies were literally corroding, atrophying. Their souls were being sucked out of them. And it was a horrible thing to watch: men with nothing to live for, no families, nobody caring about them. And so I do have a passion to bring the gospel, the good news, into those prisons. But I also know it's God's call in my life. So I have to do it out of obedience.

As long as I've got the strength and energy and the mental abilities. And as long as I can do it, that's what I'm going to do.

HUGH HEWITT: Tell me about Sam Caselvera.

CHARLES COLSON: Sam Caselvera is a prisoner in Delaware. Still is. Still in prison. Life without parole. I've tried to get him out many times but probably won't be able to. Sam Caselvera is a big, rough, mean-looking guy who committed some serious crimes. He was justly sentenced, although I think that now he would be safer to have on the streets than you or I would be. When I went over to the Delaware prison on one of my visits, Sam Caselvera wrote a poem. I happen to love poetry, but I don't know that I've ever been quite so touched by a poem. And the thrust of the poem was that I had said I would come back and I did. And I was there when this big, burly inmate stood up at a breakfast on an Easter Sunday morning and read that poem and couldn't get through it. He started to break down and cry. And I always think about Sam Caselvera and the guys who are on death row in prisons all across America. They're depending on us to come, to be there. And we're not going to let them down.

HUGH HEWITT: Bessie Ship is another person you wrote about. She found the gospel after a Prison Fellowship visit four weeks before she died of AIDS. Did it matter that she found the gospel?

CHARLES COLSON: Oh my, yes! I think of the great eternal consequences. I went into that prison on Christmas morning. It was the first time I'd ever met an AIDS patient. I have to tell you that I didn't want to do it. I had gotten into Raleigh, North Carolina, the night before and turned on the television, and Mother Teresa was on with her arms around some AIDS patients coming out of prison in New York. And I looked at her, this little ninety-pound Albanian nun, and I thought, *Chuck Colson, you're twice her size. You're an ex-Marine captain, a tough guy, and you couldn't do what she does.*

I went to sleep that night thinking about Mother Teresa and thanking God I'd never had to see anybody with AIDS. The next morning I went to the North Carolina State Prison for Women. I preached, and after the service the warden said, "Would you come see Bessie Ship?" I said, "Who's Bessie Ship?" She said, "She's our AIDS victim." And I started to say, "No, I'm too busy. I have got to go to the men's prison." I mean, this was back in 1985, when people didn't know how people got AIDS.

But I went over to death row, and there was this frail little woman sitting there in a nightgown and a bathrobe, and she was cold. She was in a death-row cell. She had the Bible in front of her. I said, "Bessie, do you know the Word?" And she said, "No." She said, "I would like to." The chaplain led me in. And I grabbed her hand and prayed, and she received Christ.

Then I went outside and had a press conference. Governor Jim Martin, whom I knew, set her free the next day. So she went home. She was baptized in her home, in her bed. And an ex-convict fixed up her home for her, got her a television set. We had Bible studies in her house. And two days before she died, she turned to Al Lawrence, the area director for North Carolina at the time, and said, "I'm the happiest I've ever been in my life, because now I know people love me. God loves me, and you and Chuck Colson love me." So, it was worth it to her for eternal consequences. It sure was worth it to me.

HUGH HEWITT: There are prisons all over the United States. They're filling up at record pace. Do people understand what goes on in the prisons? Do they care?

CHARLES COLSON: No. They don't care any more than I did. Before I was converted, when I was in the White House, I could go anywhere. I could visit a military installation. I'd just call up and have a four-engine Lockheed Jet Star waiting for me. I'd never go to a prison. I mean, who'd want to go to a prison? My idea of a prison was a place where you locked up rotten criminals, threw away the key, left 'em there, and forgot about 'em. That's what most American people think.

But as Christians, we shouldn't feel that way, because Jesus Himself told us that what we do for the least of these, we do for Him. And so when we visit a prisoner, we're visiting Jesus. We should have the greatest compassion for those who have sinned the most and who therefore most need to hear the gospel. One of the things that's counter-cultural about Christianity is following God's call to do something that most people don't care a whit about. And that's what I'm doing. A lot of people would just as soon I'd go away and not upset their conscience.

HUGH HEWITT: Another question, Chuck. Are you really critical of "three strikes and you're out," the latest fad in justice systems? You seem to be a softie on crime.

CHARLES COLSON: (laughs) No, I'm hard on crime. I just think you have to deal with it in an intelligent way. "Three strikes and you're out" has never worked. Anywhere. I mean, locking up guys with three minor offenses, locking 'em up for life, it's ridiculous. It's not a deterrent. No one has ever been able to establish that prison is a deterrent. If it was a deterrent, I'd be all for more of it. If prison was a deterrent, then I think crime could be stopped, and I want to stop crime.

I just don't think it has been approached intelligently. Since 1972, when I got out of prison, the prison population in this country has quadrupled. During that same period of time, there's been an almost a five hundred percent increase in violent crime. So violent crime has gone up as the prison population has gone up. And every study shows that there's no correlation between prisons and crime. Prisons do *not* stop crime. They keep criminals locked up and away from society, and that's important . . . but it's effective only as long as they're locked up. We're crazy if we think prison is gonna stop crime.

HUGH HEWITT: What do you do about it?

CHARLES COLSON: I go to the root causes. Now, I'm a conservative. And for years, conservatives have criticized the liberals for talking about root causes—poverty and the environment and racism. The liberals have pointed out the wrong root causes, but just because they have the wrong root causes doesn't mean that there aren't root causes. There are. Crime is caused by the lack of moral teaching and training during the morally formative years.

We know that crime is a moral problem. So we've got to start rebuilding the family. We've got to start doing something about the cultural influences of the rot that comes across television and popular culture and music. We've got to start doing something about teaching absolute truth in schools. Value-free education produces value-free students.

> The church will come alive when it really starts to do what it's supposed to do—make disciples and equip them to live as Christians in the world. If every American who claims to be a Christian lived the way the gospel taught, this society would be dramatically transformed.

We've got to do something about reaching kids early, which is why the most exciting thing Prison Fellowship does is Angel Tree. At Christmastime, prison inmates give us the names of their children, and we pass that information along to churches. People in those churches buy gifts and deliver them to the kids. They actually go into their homes and give them illustrated Bibles and gospel comic books. Four hundred and sixty-five thousand kids received Christmas gifts through Angel Tree last year. And those are the kids who are most at risk.

And so if we can get the people in church out of the pews and into the streets and doing kinds of things like Angel Tree, then we can do something about crime. That's going to the root cause.

HUGH HEWITT: Are you alarmed by the recidivism rate among Prison Fellowship prisoners? Forty percent. That's significantly less than usual, but it's still high.

CHARLES COLSON: Sure.

HUGH HEWITT: What's that say to us?

CHARLES COLSON: We are dealing with thousands of inmates. We're not going to have a perfect score. Although, I must say, Hugh, for twenty years we've run a prison in South America called Humana, and we've been able to track the inmates who get out of that prison. We know where they go. We keep in touch with them. And so we have an absolutely foolproof statistic.

When the prisoners enter that prison, their chains are taken off and the guard says (and there he's called an inmate, not a guard), "In this prison, you're constrained—not by chains and steel, but by the love of Christ." They go to chapel and character-building classes. I mean, it's like a spiritual retreat center. The recidivism rate there is four percent . . . compared to seventy-five percent in Brazil. So I know that the gospel transforms those prisoners' lives, and I know that what we are preaching works. And I know that we could do that in the prisons in America if it weren't for the ACLU.

HUGH HEWITT: So you'd like to have the key. You'd like to take an entire prison.

CHARLES COLSON: We're thinking about it right now. I mean, a couple of states want to try it because it's been so successful in Brazil and Ecuador. In a couple of cases, they say we'll get sued. But let's see what happens.

HUGH HEWITT: Let me ask you about the downward spiral that you've referred to a number of times. America is in a serious dilemma regarding crime and moral problems. Was this inevitable? There are not a few Christians out there who believe that this is a mark that is clearly called for—that we're at the end of the last millennium. Do you put any credence in that?

CHARLES COLSON: I don't ever play the end-time game of speculating on when the world is going to come to an end and when Jesus is going to return. I think that game is counterproductive. When you start speculating on that, you start not doing the things you're supposed to do. I don't get into that business. I don't know whether this is the end time or not. I do know that history is cyclical. There's a period of moral decay, and then there's a great spiritual movement and moral renewal in society. I think we're reaching the bottom of a downward spiral of of an extreme decadence caused by the abandonment of truth. Out of that will come one of two things: the collapse of American culture, as Rome and other societies throughout history have collapsed, or a period of renewal when the church comes alive. If there's a renewal and rebirth of moral values, people will start to live differently.

HUGH HEWITT: What do you mean by "when the church comes alive"?

CHARLES COLSON: The church will come alive when it really starts to do what it's supposed to do— make disciples and equip them to live as Christians in the world. If every American who claims to be a Christian lived the way the gospel taught, this society would be dramatically transformed. It's happened many times. There have been great revivals in this country. There was the Oxford movement in England, the Welsh revival in the early part of the twentieth century.

HUGH HEWITT: Well, depending on how you count, America's had three or four great awakenings.

CHARLES COLSON: That's true.

HUGH HEWITT: Are we on the cusp of one?

CHARLES COLSON: Well, there's a professor in Illinois who says we are. Professor Fogel says that we're in the beginning of what he calls the Fourth Great Awakening. I'm not quite that optimistic. I would like to think that's so. I'd love to think that's so.

HUGH HEWITT: What would be the marks of a new great awakening in America?

CHARLES COLSON: We would see a lot of repentance in churches. We have seen a wave of repentance break out on college campuses and in some churches this year. There have been spontaneous movements of the Spirit of God.

HUGH HEWITT: Expand on "repentance."

CHARLES COLSON: Well, we see kids up all night praying and confessing sins, and a deep sense of worship. We've seen that happen in some churches lately. So, yeah, there are some signs that it could be happening.

Promise Keepers is one great movement. The *Washington Post* called it "misogynist" and said the religious right is trying to take over, and that is absolutely nonsense. It's just men saying they want to keep their promises as men—to God and to their families. And that's a wonderful thing. I'll be speaking at several Promise Keepers conventions this year. If you go, you'll see seventy, eighty thousand people in a football stadium. And they're on fire. They want to live their lives differently—not the way this culture is teaching, that people can hop from bed to bed, live any way they want, do anything they want, and indulge in every kind of degenerate lifestyle. They're saying, "No, we're going to live by God's promises, and we're gonna keep our commitment to our families." That's a wonderful movement and a great sign of revival.

If a revival were to come in this country—an awakening, a spiritual movement—we would see people beginning to behave differently. We would see people turning off the television. We'd see cultural tastes and habits change. Tocqueville talked about habits of the heart. A society is shaped not so much by its laws as it is by its music and customs and conventions and form of community. The animated structures of society really move a culture. And so we would see a fresh movement. We'd see a lot of shelters going up in the inner cities to take care of the poor and the homeless. We'd see a passion for justice. And we'd see righteousness in the way people live out their lives. Tastes would change. Some of the garbage that is now being fed to America would change, and we'd see kids coming out of school knowing the difference between right and wrong. We'd see schools teaching abstinence instead of handing out condoms.

HUGH HEWITT: What would you see in prisons if an awakening was to begin?

CHARLES COLSON: Well, I've seen it in a Texas prison. We had an incredible experience last Easter. There were four hundred men on death row, and many of them were converted. In a North Carolina prison three quarters of the inmates turned out for our rallies. Fifteen thousand out of twenty thousand prisoners in the state came out, and a couple thousand came to Christ. So, things like that would be breaking out in the prisons. We are seeing some signs of that. I'd like to see the cultural forces in America turn around much more dramatically than they have. By most indicators we are still in a period of cultural decline. But there are some signs of the church coming alive.

HUGH HEWITT: Would the way that government governs change too?

CHARLES COLSON: Sure.

HUGH HEWITT: You've been there. You've been in the White House. You know what it's like. Would this paralysis in Washington be eliminated?

CHARLES COLSON: Oh yes, because the people who are governing us would get it in their heads that the public won't tolerate this political nonsense. If a mood of righteousness swept this country, people would be driven out of Washington. Maybe that's going to happen. I think of the 1994 elections and some of the anti-incumbent sentiments. I think of some of the pressures for term limits. I think of people's disillusionment with what I call the political illusion that government can solve all of our problems. These may be signs that the people want to take control of their own lives again.

HUGH HEWITT: That phrase you just used, "a mood of righteousness," could be a book title. But wouldn't a mood of righteousness scare a lot of people? Doesn't that sound somewhat threatening to our friends who may not belong to any church or any faith?

CHARLES COLSON: Well, it shouldn't frighten them because they would live better lives. Let's face it. Whenever Christian influence has been on the ascendancy, people have lived better. There was less crime. And if you are married and someone comes along and takes your spouse, that doesn't make you very happy. If a mood of righteousness affected this nation, lives would suddenly be safer and happier and more fulfilled. Even if not everyone rushed off and joined a church or was converted, the level of public contentment would still be lifted. Because it's always happened. That has happened in every revival.

HUGH HEWITT: Let's get more in-depth about your particular ministry to help bring about this revival. Describe Prison Fellowship for us. Just what is it?

CHARLES COLSON: Prison Fellowship is an interdenominational ministry. It cuts right across all the denominational lines. We're largely volunteers. As I've already said, we go into prisons. We put on three-day seminars in which we teach inmates how to live as Christians, how to survive in the prison environment, and how to adjust when they get out of prison. We also do Bible studies in the prisons.

Angel Tree is a program in which we go into the homes of the inmates at Christmastime. We give gifts to their children, tell them the real meaning of Christmas, provide gospel comic books, Bibles, and illustrated children's Bibles. It's a wonderful program, and now we're starting to pick up and mentor those kids year-round. We got a thousand into camp last summer. I want us to get a half million into camp.

And we do biblically based criminal justice reforms; we work in about half the states. We've also started a Neighbors Who Care ministry to crime victims; church groups try to help victims with their needs and, of course, minister to them with the gospel.

Prison Fellowship is a Christian outreach to inmates and their families, a biblically based reform movement in criminal justice, and an effort to work with victims.

HUGH HEWITT: You have become an evangelist. I don't know if anyone calls you that, but you've become an evangelist. At least that's how we identified you for this show. Is everyone called to evangelism?

CHARLES COLSON: No. Evangelism is proclaiming the gospel, and I do that in prisons. Although I speak to audiences all over the place, my primary calling is to the prisons. So, yeah, I'd be a prison evangelist. Some people are called to be pastors to congregations. Some people are teachers, some are prophets. The Bible says that there's a whole variety of tasks to be performed. Not everybody's an evangelist, but everybody should be able to share the faith with someone else and help lead that person to Christ.

HUGH HEWITT: Do you see that Christians are too often embarrassed by what they believe? Even at the moment of your conversion and throughout your books, there's this element of being a little bit embarrassed by it all.

> Most so-called value-free education courses teach kids that they'll find their values themselves. And those kids are lost. I mean, their parents'll never get 'em back. Those are the kids that we're running into in prison.

CHARLES COLSON: Oh, yeah. It's hard when you're brand new to go out and show your faith. After the first headlines about my conversion and all of the publicity and cartoons, Richard Nixon called me in one day to the White House. I went to meet him in the Lincoln Sitting Room, and he started asking me some questions. I had the feeling he was alone, and he looked kind of beleaguered and depressed. He was an old friend, and I had the feeling I really should have talked to him about Christ, but I didn't because I was so new. And when I got out of prison I made up for that. But yeah, it's hard; it's one of those things I've had to grow into.

HUGH HEWITT: I always considered President Nixon a believer in God and Christianity. Have you?

CHARLES COLSON: He wrote in his memoirs, in *RN*, that as a child he had believed as his mother taught him to believe, that Jonah was actually in the belly of the whale and that Jesus was bodily resurrected from the dead. He now believed that those things were simply metaphors, stories to take as examples or illustrations.

Well, if you don't believe in the bodily resurrection of Christ, you're not a Christian. On the other hand, Billy Graham had some tremendous experiences with him. Billy told me about that. And I did, too. So I don't know. Who's to judge? I'd like to believe he was despite what he wrote in *RN*.

HUGH HEWITT: In recent years you've spent a lot of time talking about juvenile crime, about the new kind of youngster out there, the hardened criminal. Really, it's scary. What ought parents do about their children that they haven't been doing?

CHARLES COLSON: I think that we forget that the family's the first school of human instruction; it has been through the centuries. It's a pre-Christian notion that the family is where children are civilized. That concept goes back to Plato and Aristotle, even earlier; I think we've lost that.

We've got the two-wage-earner families. Parents are so busy that they leave their kids parked in front of the television set for seven hours a day. They don't sit around the dinner table at night talking about what's right and what's wrong. The most important lessons I learned in my life, I learned from my dad, sitting on his lap. He would say, "Chuck, never lie."

I don't think parents are investing that kind of effort and time into their kids today. They certainly aren't in the inner cities where the families are largely broken and grandmothers are raising the kids. And bless their hearts, they do the best job they know how. But those kids are soon out in the streets, running around, being influenced more by peers than by family. The morally formative years, the experts tell us, are from one to eight or nine, with the younger years even more important. And yet we mock the traditional two-parent families. We laughed at Dan Quayle, but he was right and Murphy Brown was wrong.

Parents have to teach their kids responsible behavior in the earliest years or it's all catch-up thereafter. And then when the kids go to school they're told that there are no virtues, only values. I mean, Hitler had values; he didn't have virtues. Most so-called value-free education courses teach kids that they'll find their values themselves. And those kids are lost. I mean, their parents'll never get 'em back. Those are the kids that we're running into in prison.

The statistics are absolutely terrifying. There'll be a one-million increase in the fourteen- to seventeen-year-old population group in this country between now and 1998, and a twenty-five-percent increase in fourteen- to seventeen-year-olds by the year 2005. And the violent crime rate is going up; in the last eight years it doubled among kids in that age group. I mean, those are the kids with the dead eyes and the remorseless expressions. They would just as soon shoot you to get your shoes as say hello.

HUGH HEWITT: What you just said struck me. You just said, "their parents'll never get 'em back." Can God get them back?

CHARLES COLSON: Of course. And when I said "never get them back," that's hyperbole. Of course God can get them back. I work with people that most would consider beyond redemption. A story I tell in one book was of an inmate on death row in South Carolina. I was with him eleven days before he died. He had committed some awful crimes. And that man was just angelic. I mean, he was converted. He had a loving, tender heart, and he was leading other people on death row to Christ. Nobody's beyond redemption.

HUGH HEWITT: He was executed?

CHARLES COLSON: He was executed.

HUGH HEWITT: Ought he to have been executed?

CHARLES COLSON: Should he have been? In his case, I would say no. Not because he'd become a Christian, but because the crimes he committed were committed in a moment of passion when he was on drugs and there was a holdup. There are crimes for which the death penalty is warranted, yes. For many years I was opposed to the death penalty under any circumstances. I now think there are some cases where no other punishment fits. But in that case, no.

HUGH HEWITT: You see a lot of suffering. What does that do to Chuck Colson?

CHARLES COLSON: It's hard. There have been times when I've broken down and wept on my way out of a prison. I just did it in South America. I see human beings treated like subhumans, like animals. It's pretty hard to take. Sometimes somebody I've gotten to know and love is executed. Those are tough times. I pray for mercy. And I also pray that I'll be strong enough to do what God's called me to do.

HUGH HEWITT: Let me ask you about two more things. In your book *A Dangerous Grace* you go out of your way to quote a very famous passage from Augustine's *Confessions* about stealing a pear from a pear tree. And you write, "We [meaning Americans] sin not primarily because of outside influences or factors beyond our control, but simply because we choose to sin." Now if anything stands against the ethos of the day, that statement does.

CHARLES COLSON: Oh, sure. But it's absolutely true. People make wrong moral choices because they like them. We choose to do wrong. Augustine was really convicted because he stole a neighbor's pears, especially when he had pears on his own pear tree. It made him realize that he sinned because he really kind of enjoyed it. It wasn't because he needed it. He had no excuse. And that was one of the things that drove him to his own conversion.

We all do that. David took Bathsheba. When he could have had any other woman he wanted, he took Uriah's wife. That's human nature. It's the sin that is in us. Chesterton said that the doctrine of original sin is the only philosophy empirically validated by two thousand years of human history. It's true. I mean, that's just the way we are. And like it or not, we are sinful.

HUGH HEWITT: Chuck, you won the Templeton Prize in 1993. It's the world's richest award. It's given for progress in religion. And you won it. In the Templeton Prize address, the entire religious world focused on what you said. And on that occasion you denounced a number of things, one of them being the idea that man is good.

CHARLES COLSON: (laughs) I said that the greatest myth of the twentieth century is that man is good and getting better. Hegel was wrong when he said all we have to do is educate ourselves out of sin. The fact of the matter is that we have the most educated century in human history and also the bloodiest. We aren't good. We are sinners in need of the grace of God. If we really think we're good, then we get the supreme hubris of thinking that we can create the utopian society.

What we're watching in Washington right now is a debate between right-wing utopians and left-wing utopians. The left-wingers thought we could produce the perfect state and the Great Society. The right-wingers say we can create incentives to responsible behavior by re-engineering. They're all social engineers. They're all utopians. True conservatives just want to conserve the moral order and the tradition that is passed down from generation to generation. A false idea about the goodness of man leads to utopianism. And if we throw in the fact—as I did in the Templeton address—that we also live in a relativistic era in which we say there is no absolute truth, then whoever gets power decides what is good. And then we live in a radically individualistic era when we only care about ourselves and begin to destroy community.

Those things best describe the dilemma of the twentieth century, what I called the post-modernist impasse. We want to have everything our way. But as soon as we do, we have moral chaos. And we have to pay the consequences, and we don't like it.

> Hegel was wrong when he said all we have to do is educate ourselves out of sin. The fact of the matter is that we have the most educated century in human history and also the bloodiest. We aren't good. We are sinners in need of the grace of God.

So that's the dilemma. Earlier you asked why people are searching for God. They're searching for God because they have discovered the fraud of what they've been taught in the twentieth century: that they're good and getting better; that they can create their own society; that they can live with their own values; that they don't need God. They're paying the price for that today, and they're crying out inside and hurting.

HUGH HEWITT: You're a relatively young man, but you're getting older. Are you afraid of dying?

CHARLES COLSON: No, I'm not at all afraid of dying. There are many days when I think it'll be a very peaceful thing. The Apostle Paul said that "to live is Christ, and to die is gain." I think everybody fears the process of dying, though.

When I went in for cancer surgery, I had only one prayer. I was having major, radical surgery on my stomach. And I just prayed, "God, help me to be a good witness through all of this." I figured that if I died, I would cross the line and meet Christ, and I'd be fine. The only thing I could think of that night was, *How can people go through life and not know Jesus? How can they stand not being certain of their eternal destiny? How can they stand not being at peace with God?* No, I'm at peace with God. I'm ready to meet Him face-to-face when that time comes. All of us are cowards; we don't want to go through pain and suffering. But I can only pray as I did once before, that I'll be a good witness in that process.

HUGH HEWITT: And what do you mean you're ready to meet Christ "face-to-face"?

CHARLES COLSON: Well, I believe we will stand there utterly defenseless—that is, apart from the shed blood of Christ. I think that when we appear before God, the only thing we can appeal to is the fact that Christ died for us.

HUGH HEWITT: Chuck Colson, thank you for joining us.

CHARLES COLSON: Thank you.

A CONVERSATION WITH

HAROLD KUSHNER

Interviewed in Boston, Massachusetts, Harold Kushner has become acclaimed through his writings as "America's rabbi." Though he served as a pulpit rabbi for over thirty years, he feels he has been challenged by questions of faith for most of his life. It wasn't until his infant son was diagnosed with a fatal genetic disorder, however, that Kushner started to rethink the entire relationship between individuals and God. His first book, *When Bad Things Happen to Good People,* chronicles his test of faith and seeks to help others going through similar losses. The subsequent commercial success of the book brought about another test of faith. *When All You've Ever Wanted Isn't Enough,* published in 1985, details the clash between material success and the spiritual underdevelopment he experienced.

A CONVERSATION WITH
HAROLD KUSHNER

In the pulpit for over thirty years, Harold Kushner has been challenged by questions of faith for most of his life. But it was not until his infant son was diagnosed with a fatal genetic disorder that Kushner began to rethink the relationship between individuals and God. *How can God be so cruel to some,* Kushner thought, *and so good to others?* His first book, *When Bad Things Happen to Good People,* chronicles this test of faith and seeks to help others going through similar losses. The book recounts his efforts to reconcile his belief in the existence of a just and comforting God with the death of his only son at age fourteen.

The success of Kushner's book, selling over two million copies and dominating the *New York Times* best-seller list for almost a year, brought about another test of faith. *When All You've Ever Wanted Isn't Enough,* published in 1985, details the clashes between material success and spiritual under-development fostered by Kushner's own accomplishment.

He retired from his temple in 1990 to pursue a more ambitious writing and lecturing schedule. Rabbi Kushner maintains a "Rabbi Emeritus" position and frequently delivers sermons not only to his own congregation, but around the country. Immensely popular with people from all walks of live, Kushner's very public struggle with faith has redefined how Americans think of God and spirituality.

HUGH HEWITT: Rabbi Harold Kushner, thank you for joining us.

HAROLD KUSHNER: My pleasure to be here, Hugh.

HUGH HEWITT: Let's begin by talking about God. Who is this God who made a universe that contains new diseases, the Holocaust, random massacres that occur at regular intervals? Who is this God who allows young children to die, allows the proverbial Job to suffer?

HAROLD KUSHNER: Who is God? I don't know. As a number of theologians have said, He would be a pretty puny god if I could understand Him. My goal is not so much to understand God as to encounter God, to be helped by God. There are puzzles that come up. When we had to deal with the fact that our son was dying, it was not enough for me to believe in an abstract God. I had to know which side God was on; and so I wrestled with the question of why God permits evil, disease, crime, things like that. I could not shrug my shoulders the way some theologians do. I had to come to the conclusion that God was as outraged by the suffering as I am because otherwise I would be more moral than God.

But to understand God? No, I don't even try that. I know intellectually God is not a person who lives in the sky. He's not a man with a long beard or something like that. I know intellectually God doesn't have eyes, ears, mouth, hands, sexual organs; but my three-dimensional brain doesn't know how to conceive of God except to think about Him as a kind of a person. And so I'm stuck with that.

HUGH HEWITT: But I want to go back to the first question again because I think that's the reason a lot of people watch this particular show. Who is this God, and why would He make the world this way?

HAROLD KUSHNER: Your question, "Who is God?" is the wrong question. The real question, Hugh, I think is What does God do to make my life matter? What can God do to make my life bearable? It's not so much what God is as what God does.

There is a passage in the Bible, in the Book of Exodus; I think it's chapter 33, right after the incident with the golden calf. Moses says to God, "If I'm going to represent You for this people, I have to know more about who You are. Let me see Your face." And God says, "Nobody can see My face while alive. But hide in this cleft in the rock. I will pass by, and you will see My back." Now if you take that literally, it's an astonishing statement. What I take it to mean is that you cannot perceive God directly; you *can* see God's aftereffects.

In the same way that you can't see electricity, you *can* see what electricity turns on. You can't see God. You can't comprehend God. You can't define God. You *can* see what God turns on. You can see the fingerprints of God all through life. You can see weak people being made strong. You can see cowardly people being made brave. You can see damaged people replenish themselves. You can see the world evolving as an incredibly complex, beautiful place. You understand that the mind of God is behind all of those things.

HUGH HEWITT: But if you look at all of those things and see the back of God, you see the effects of the electricity, you still have to wonder, *Who is it? What are His properties? Why does God organize the world the way He does?* You can't get away from those questions, can you?

HAROLD KUSHNER: Why does God organize the world the way He does? My Jewish tradition has said that you don't try to read God's mind. Jewish theology is not about the nature of God; it's about the will of God. Your question "Why does God organize the world the way He does?" translates to my mind as *How shall I respond to the presence of God and to God's world? What does God want from me?*

The world is the way that it is. To take the example that you brought up before, it is a world in which people are capable of immense cruelty to each other. There is war. There is crime. There is rape. There is fraud. There is murder. What does God want *me* to do about it? And what I learn is that God created the world with people free to choose good or evil so that there would be the possibility of people choosing good. I believe that the most precious thing in the sight of God is the good deed freely chosen. It's when I choose to be generous, to be brave, to be truthful, to be forgiving. And I don't have to do those things. Because I'm free to do the other thing; I'm free to be the opposite. When I choose to do good, the Talmud tells me that God looks down and says, "For that moment alone it was worth creating the world." God created the world the way it is, my tradition teaches me, so that human beings who are free to choose between good and evil will freely choose the good.

HUGH HEWITT: I understand that. I find it persuasive, in fact. But I know that there are people who are saying, "He's referring to tradition." Rabbi Kushner is falling back on great scholars, and they are great scholars. But he's not answering my question, "Who is this God?" Did He exist from the beginning of time, in your understanding?

HAROLD KUSHNER: Oh, He was there before time. I am moved and I am persuaded by the opening words of the Bible, "In the beginning God created the heavens and the earth," which means that God was there before the beginning. God stands outside of time.

By the way, that's the answer to a question that a lot of college sophomores get stuck on: Does God know the future? It's an impossible question. God stands outside of time, so past and present and future don't exist for God in the way they do for us. It's not that the future has already happened and God knows it like the movie director who knows how the movie turns out while we're sitting in the theater not knowing what's going to happen next. I don't believe that. Does God know the future? Only in the sense that the future is not somewhere down the road for God; it's all simultaneous.

> I've got to believe that I'm a participant in writing the script of my life, and so to that extent the future hasn't been determined yet. But God is standing outside of time. God is the creator of time. God already possesses the future in a sense that none of us can.

I explain this to people by saying, "Imagine you're looking at the comics in the Sunday paper. You can see all seven panels at once. But the characters in the comic strip don't know in panel three what's going to happen in panels five, six, and seven. The comic strip characters have to get there. God is standing outside of time the way you're standing outside the two-dimensional world of comics."

God is not surprised by the future; we're surprised. But the future doesn't exist until we choose how to respond. I cannot accept the notion that the script of my life has already been written. I cannot accept the notion that there is a certain day when I am destined to dieand if that day is twenty years off I don't have to wear my seat belt, I can smoke, I don't have to exercise, I don't have to wear the right clothing on a cold day. No, I don't buy that. I've got to believe that I'm a participant in writing the script of my life, and so to that extent the future hasn't been determined yet. But God is standing outside of time. God is the creator of time. God already possesses the future in a sense that none of us can.

HUGH HEWITT: Do you know that God exists, or do you simply believe that He exists?

HAROLD KUSHNER: In a sense, I think belief is more solid than knowing. Belief is the way I understand the data of the world. I can't persuade someone who is an atheist to believe in God. All I can do is point to the evidence. And when I look at what happens in the world, when I am constantly seeing ordinary people doing extraordinary things, when I am blown away by the resiliency of the human spirit, when I see what people endure and get over, when I see the heights that people are capable of rising to, my hypothesis is that there is a God that makes this possible. I think this explains the data more plausibly than the hypothesis of the atheist.

I can't persuade anybody. If God were provable it would have been done a long time ago by somebody a lot smarter than I am. If God were provable, it would have been settled. No, I think it is a matter of seeing the same facts and choosing how you interpret them. It's not Which is the better argument? but two much more important questions: How does my life change if I assume there is a God and base my life decisions on it? How does my life change if I assume there is no God and base my life decisions on it?

I remember what Ivan Karamazov says in the Dostoevsky novel *The Brothers Karamazov:* "If there is no God, everything is permitted." By affirming the hypothesis that there is a God, I affirm that certain things are right and certain things are wrong. Take away the hypothesis that there is a God who not only exists but who cares about what kind of people we are, and except for the fact that I might get arrested, why shouldn't I do wrong? Why shouldn't I kill and steal and commit adultery? There would be no reason not to. Then the weak could fall victim to the strong and there would be nobody to stop it.

HUGH HEWITT: There are many evidences of God, but I think there are as many evidences on the other side. In *When Bad Things Happen to Good People,* your first book, by which most people will have come to know you, you wrote that anyone who has seen the Holocaust or the My Lai massacre cannot utter the words from Isaiah "Tell the righteous all will be well with them" because you yourself realize that not all is well with the righteous. So the evidence gets pretty darn equal pretty quick.

HAROLD KUSHNER: Hugh, you're talking to a man who saw his fourteen-year-old son die from a genetic disease. You don't have to convince me that this is not the best of all possible worlds. I cannot believe in the existence of a God who is kind of a Santa Claus figure, who knows who has been naughty and who has been nice, and gives you presents if you're good and gives you a lump of coal if you're bad.

No, that god clearly does not exist. And anybody who tries to affirm the existence of that kind of god inevitably paints himself into such a corner that he ends up looking fairly foolish. You end up saying bad is really good, there is a reason for the Holocaust, there is a reason for the child to be born retarded. No, I totally reject that. I believe in a God who does not send the tragedy but who sends the incredible grace to deal with the tragedy, to survive it. Anybody who has stood as I have at the bedside of a dying child walks away thinking, *May I be worthy of that child.* People have gone through the most horrible life experiences—victims of crime, victims of fraud, and victims of accident—and managed to pull their lives together again. They haven't given up on life. I cannot explain how they are capable of doing that solely on the basis of inner resources. Nobody has that much strength. Nobody has that much courage. Nobody has that much love . . . unless there really is a God who, when we use up all our strength, replenishes it.

HUGH HEWITT: And is this the God who created everything?

HAROLD KUSHNER: I'll go along with that, sure.

HUGH HEWITT: And He could have ordered the world as He wanted it ordered?

HAROLD KUSHNER: I'd say that.

HUGH HEWITT: Then why did He order it so it was necessary to develop the theology of tragedy? "Theology of tragedy" is your terminology, and it is persuasive. But why would the Orderer make such an order that would allow this to happen?

HAROLD KUSHNER: Hugh, a medieval Spanish king is supposed to have said, "Had I been present at the Creation, I could have told God how to make a better world." And that has occurred to me from time to time, though not so much about tragedy. Had God asked me, I could have suggested that health be as contagious as sickness. I could have suggested that the egos of young children not be as fragile as they are; then children would not be damaged by one terrible life experience when they are very young.

But in terms of tragedy, I don't know. I can believe that goodness would not be possible without the possibility of evil. I can believe that if we were forced, if we were programmed, if we were hard-wired always to do the right thing, it would be neat, it would be nice, it would be convenient. But it wouldn't be good, because it wouldn't be a choice. That I can understand.

I'm not sure I understand disease. I'm not sure I understand genetic accidents. I'm not sure I understand the vulnerability. One can explain to me scientifically that if our bones were so strong that if we fell down they wouldn't break, they would also be too heavy for us to walk. And biologically that's satisfying, but there is a part of me that says, *You know, if I were God, I could have come up with a better solution.* So I'm stumped by that. I can't read God's mind. All I can deal with is with the cards I'm dealt.

This is a world where human beings are vulnerable to crime, illness, injury. This is a world where people can as easily choose to be mean and vicious as they can choose to be good. In fact, sometimes it's easier to choose to be mean. There seems to a kind of moral law of gravity that pulls us down—that makes it easier to lie than to tell the truth when the truth is embarrassing, that makes it easier to sleep late than to get up early, that makes it easier to be selfish than to be generous.

If I were creating the world, I might have done it differently. I might have looked at the results and thought, *You know that was a mistake; it should have been the way God had it on the blueprint originally.* But I'm not involved in shaping the world. I'm only involved in dealing with it as I find it. I don't know why God made the world the way He did. I'm not prepared to say this is the best of all possible worlds. But this is the world we have. And I try to live in it.

HUGH HEWITT: Rabbi, you were prepared to write a diminishment of God by declaring He is not all-powerful.

HAROLD KUSHNER: Hugh, I will challenge the word *diminishment.* I don't think we add to God's glory when we say He wanted the plane to crash. . . . He wanted the child to be born deformed. . . . He wanted the young mother to come down with multiple sclerosis. What kind of God wants cancer? What kind of God wants Alzheimer's disease? What kind of God wants all of these terrible things that afflict people? I think I am *enhancing* God's greatness when I say these things happen for reasons independent of the will of God.

People diminish God when they say He is in favor of children being born retarded. They diminish God when they say He wills the Lou Gehrig's disease that strikes down a young wife and mother. Maybe in an earlier age when people lived in a world of all-powerful kings and czars—when the king had power of life and death and made the laws—maybe then theologians had to insist that God was at least as all-powerful as the human king. But in the twentieth century, why do we think that we do God a favor when we insist on holding Him responsible for the immoral, unfair, outrageous things that happen all the time?

I think I am limiting God, but I don't think I am diminishing Him. I think I am freeing Him from responsibilities that I cannot believe God wants to be saddled with.

HUGH HEWITT: "Where were you when I laid the earth's foundation? Tell Me, if you understand." That's what you're wrestling with. That's the answer God gives to Job. And I found it, of course, in your writings. Doesn't that alarm you a little bit?

HAROLD KUSHNER: No, it doesn't alarm me; it *challenges* me. But it's the wrong answer to the question. I can't understand God's answer to Job, out of the whirlwind in the biblical Book of Job. Because, you see, Job has been saying for thirty-five chapters that God is a bully. God is powerful but not decent. Then God

comes out and says, "You call Me a bully? I'll show you what I do to people who call Me a bully." How does God answer Job's challenge? By saying how powerful He is.

Now I know all the interpretations of Job. It is not morally satisfying to say God's answer to Job is that the universe is not geared to human needs, God has a wider canvass than that. I look to the Book of Job for a morally satisfying answer. The only one I can find—and I think this may be what the author had in mind although it's not the answer that I come up with—is that Job is gratified. Job is silenced by the *contact* with God, not by the *content* of what God says; that is, God's answer is irrelevant. God's answer is a

> I think one of the things the voice out of the whirlwind says is that it is a full-time job for God to try and control chaos. If God does control it, He does it over the course of time; He doesn't do it by snapping His fingers.

response to Job. You see what I'm saying? Just to know there's somebody in charge and that somebody says, "Don't worry, I know what I'm doing," answered Job. It doesn't answer me. It does not work for me. I think it may have been the answer of the author of Job.

HUGH HEWITT: Well, that's very attractive. But that's not what the whirlwind says. I mean, the whirlwind does say to us, "Yes, I am all-powerful."

HAROLD KUSHNER: Yes and no, Hugh. The voice out of the whirlwind also talks about the challenge of God to capture and tame Leviathan, which I take as a symbol for all the chaos in the world—everything that doesn't work out right, that doesn't play by the rules. It's arbitrariness. This person gets a disease and that one does not. The serial killer fastens on this victim and not on someone else.

I think one of the things the voice out of the whirlwind says is that it is a full-time job for God to try and control chaos. If God does control it, He does it over the course of time; He doesn't do it by snapping His fingers. And the implicit answer to Job is, "If you think it's so easy to run a totally fair world, *you* do it. And then you'll find out what a job it is."

HUGH HEWITT: During that long illness of your son, who died when he was fourteen, or since then, have you ever come up to the cusp of doubt?

HAROLD KUSHNER: I did right after the doctors told us what his life would be like. I went through a very dark night of faith. It was just about his third birthday in November. Outside it was a cold, dark time; internally it was a cold, dark time for me. For about two months after that I did not know if I could continue as a believer, as a religious man.

I mean, Hugh, I thought I had a deal with God. I thought I had a contract with God. I would be good, righteous, pious, obedient. I would work night and day to help other people be like that. And both to reward me and to set me up as a model to be emulated, God would protect and reward my family. Up until that day, it had worked. I was healthy. I was happily married. I had a good job. I was blessed in many ways.

The day we found out about Aaron's incurable sickness, I thought God had defaulted on His half of the contract. I didn't know if I could continue as a rabbi, where every Sabbath morning I officiated a service where somebody else's little boy would be celebrated for growing up and knowing that my son would never grow up. But I didn't want to give up believing in God. My faith had been very important to me. Yet I didn't want to worship a God who would do this to my son.

The answer for me was to separate God from the disease. To see the disease as a genetic accident that God did not want to happen. To recognize God as the source of the incredible strength and grace for our son, who had to live with physical and psychological pain every day for eleven years. That God was the source of the ability my wife and I found in ourselves to raise him, to love him, to comfort him, to rejoice in him, and ultimately to lose him and mourn for him. We could not have done that on the basis of our own resources. We could not have done that without God.

I have known many families who have had to deal with the tragedy of a sick child, a mentally ill child, a parent with Alzheimer's disease, a wife with a debilitating illness. I have seen them cope with this, and I don't understand how they were capable of it . . . except to believe that God, who did not send them the problem, sent them the strength, the grace, the love to cope with the problem.

HUGH HEWITT: Did Aaron think much about God during his years of illness?

HAROLD KUSHNER: There was a time, maybe when he was twelve, when this was a big issue for him. He went to a Jewish parochial school, a religious school, and he somehow picked up the idea that God rewards the good and punishes the wicked. And he went through a stretch where he thought if he would be really good, God would cure him and make him whole. And he was very hurt when no matter how good he tried to be, that didn't happen. Very frankly, Hugh, I hope there is a special place in hell for people who tell little children that if they would only be good enough, their sickness would be cured. It is a cruel thing to do to people.

HUGH HEWITT: During that illness, and since you became a rabbi to almost the entire country in terms of dealing with suffering, people have told you one tragic story after another. Has your faith buckled under that?

HAROLD KUSHNER: On the contrary, no. Somebody asked me just recently if I were to write *When Bad Things Happen to Good People* today, would I write it differently? The only difference would be that people have told me more incredibly moving stories about what happened to them, stories that I would incorporate in the book. How religion hurt them or how religion helped them.

> Why is the world so constructed that people who lie and cheat and steal and take advantage of your good nature get to the head of the line? My answer is that they don't get away with it. My answer is that you pay for everything you take in this world, in one currency or another.

No, the experience of these fifteen years has reassured me that my ideas work, that they are valid, that they make sense. Some people are not helped by my theology. After a lecture, a woman came up to me and said that she and her husband could handle the tragedy of their retarded child only because they believed God had selected them to parent the child because they were qualified to do it right. She said, "If I thought it was only genetics, I'd go to pieces." So I told her, "Don't read my book; throw it out."

A person who has a really deep need to believe that God is pulling all the strings should not read my book. But I've found that my book helps everybody else—people who want to believe in God but can't understand why God is cruel, why God doesn't hear their prayers. I would write the same book today.

HUGH HEWITT: You counsel people to redeem tragedies by imposing meaning on them. Well, wasn't the woman that you just referenced an example of redeeming by imposing meaning?

HAROLD KUSHNER: Sure. That's why I told her not to read my book. But her explanation wouldn't work for me. I tried to say to myself, *Maybe God is imposing this challenge on us because we are so strong in our religious faith that we could handle it and be an example for others.* What I heard myself saying in response was *If that's the case, I wish I was less religious.* And, *Let God make an example of some other family and give us a healthy child.* No, when I tried that on myself, my response was pain, grief, anger, outrage. Didn't work for me. If it works for some other people, I'd be the last person in the world to take away the religious structure that helps them understand what is going on in their lives.

HUGH HEWITT: Rabbi, let's turn the coin now to when good things happen to bad people. Does that side of the injustice coin give you trouble?

HAROLD KUSHNER: Why do bad people get away with murder? Why is the world so constructed that people who lie and cheat and steal and take advantage of your good nature get to the head of the line? My answer is that they don't get away with it. My answer is that you pay for everything you take in this world, in one currency or another. The punishment for the mean, selfish, unscrupulous, deceitful person may not be that he is arrested and exposed and sent to prison. It may be that the only punishment is that he will never know what it feels like to be a good person. That's a really severe punishment.

Without a doubt, the average person is going to respond, "If there is a wonderful movie I've never heard of, do I feel deprived if I don't see it?" But that's not what I'm talking about. A blind person doesn't know what he's missing. But anybody who has seen a sunset, anybody who has seen the first flowers come up in the spring after a cruel winter, will have to feel sorry for someone who will live his whole life and never see that. In the same way, a mean, selfish person doesn't know what he's missing. But if you have had the experience of being kind, of being generous, of forgiving or being forgiven, if you have had the experience of loving and being loved, you will never envy a person who has gone through life and made a lot of money but missed out on all those experiences. Good things happen to bad people. But the really *good* things? Those people never get to experience them at all.

HUGH HEWITT: You'll never envy them? You're confident of that?

HAROLD KUSHNER: I'm confident of that. Look, if you had to choose between being a rich person who had never known what it feels like to love or a loving person who never knew what it feels like to be rich, is there a second's hesitation in your mind which you would rather be?

HUGH HEWITT: No, but I think there is probably more than a second's hesitation in the minds of many hundreds of thousands of people who are watching. They're probably saying, "That sounds good, Rabbi, but I'd rather have the eight million bucks and a house on the coast and a good car as opposed to being a wonderful person who is in service all the time and no one ever notices."

HAROLD KUSHNER: Well, Hugh, that's because all your viewers watch public television. But what about all the viewers who watch *Dallas*? And *Dynasty*? And all these soap operas about rich people whose lives are miserable. Don't they get the message? What about people who read about Howard Hughes? He ended up totally lonely, friendless, abandoned, and crazy. All his money didn't help him.

No, you don't envy people like that. It might be nice to speculate, because in the back of our minds we say, *Well, I would like to have all that money but I wouldn't really become so corrupt to get it.* But if it means becoming so unscrupulous that you will do anything to become financially successful, and it costs you the sense of being a good husband or wife, being a good parent, being a good neighbor, who is going to pay that price? Some people are going to pay the price, and I tell you they will live to regret it. They will look back and think, *Darn it, it wasn't worth it. What I gave up was more valuable than what I gained.* And even if they don't, everybody on the other side—everybody who has known the satisfactions of generosity, of courage, of love, of helpfulness—is going to think, *My treasure is more valuable than theirs.*

HUGH HEWITT: Rabbi Kushner, people know you because of your book. But if they haven't read it, they may not know why you came to write it. Tell us that story.

HAROLD KUSHNER: My wife and I had a son named Aaron, who, when he was about eight months old, stopped growing and thriving the way that charts said a newborn was supposed to. And when he was three years old, he was diagnosed with an extremely rare disease called *progeria,* the rapid-aging syndrome. It essentially meant that the life-process was speeded up. He started growing old when he was still a little boy. He never got beyond the size of a three-year-old. He lost all his hair, lost all his subcutaneous fat. When he was still very young he developed hardening of the arteries, arthritis in his joints, and ultimately congestive heart failure. He died of a heart attack—essentially he died of the symptoms of old age—the day after his fourteenth birthday. It was one of those events that cleaves your life right down the middle and everything is calculated before and after.

HUGH HEWITT: How old were you at the time?

HAROLD KUSHNER: In 1966, when the doctors told us about his illness, I was thirty-one. And I was forty-two when he died.

HUGH HEWITT: That kind of a tragedy can harden a lot of people. I'm sure you've seen that. What stopped you from hardening? Who comforted you?

HAROLD KUSHNER: I guess Aaron did. He was just such a wonderful, fun-loving, bright, happy child. Somehow, for the first couple of years of his life, before we realized how sick he was, we were able to love him unreservedly. And even after that we were able to love him unreservedly. And that gave him the foundation to love himself and to believe in himself.

I've found that this tends to be the key to people with solid self-esteem, people who believe that they are essentially good and lovable. Even if something really terrible happens to them, they get up, dust themselves off, and they keep on going. There were times when Aaron felt very sorry for himself, but most of the time I think he felt sorry for people who were not as bright, as sharp, as filled with friends as his life was.

HUGH HEWITT: Where is Aaron now?

HAROLD KUSHNER: Dead.

HUGH HEWITT: And his soul?

HAROLD KUSHNER: Hugh, I believe that when a person dies, the body is buried and returns to life. The soul is a word that I use for everything about us that is not physical; that is, our soul comprises our personality, our values, our memories, our sense of humor, our interrelationships. The soul is everything that's not physical, because it's not physical, cannot die. So you see, to say that the soul lives on when the person dies is not a religious statement; it's an irrefutable scientific fact. Because it's not physical, it can't die the way an idea can't die, the way a joke can't die.

But you see, my three-dimensional mind cannot understand what it means for a noncorporeal entity to exist without a body to incarnate it. I know that Aaron's soul lives on. I feel him present when I think about him, when I do things I used to do with him, when someone reminds me of having met him when they were in school together. I feel his non-physical reality, his soul, his personality, his sense of humor. I feel them with me. It's only his physical body that's been taken away. And I suspect

> I know that Aaron's soul lives on. I feel him present when I think about him, when I do things I used to do with him, when someone reminds me of having met him when they were in school together. I feel his non-physical reality, his soul, his personality, his sense of humor. I feel them with me.

that when I die and my body is returned to the earth, the noncorporeal, the nonphysical part of me will continue to inhabit this earth. And I will continue to be present for people who knew me, people who met me, and people who were helped by me.

HUGH HEWITT: When the memory of anyone vanishes, though, does that mean the soul has also vanished from the earth?

HAROLD KUSHNER: You mean when the last person who ever knew me dies and when the last copy of my books is taken off the library shelf?

HUGH HEWITT: It's a long time.

HAROLD KUSHNER: I don't know. I'm inclined to say the soul is still there. People may not be connecting with it, sort of like a TV show that's out over the airwaves even if no one is tuned in at the particular moment. But, I just don't know. I don't understand enough about noncorporeal entities. I mean, what does Aaron's soul look like? I can't even understand the question, let alone the answer. When my nonphysical soul survives the death of my body, without eyes and optic nerves will it be able to recognize Aaron's noncorporeal soul or the nonphysical souls of my parents who are deceased? I don't understand what that means. And so I really don't spend a lot of time worrying about it.

HUGH HEWITT: This is what's so interesting about your theology, Rabbi Kushner. God would be too harsh if He controlled everything and brought disease, not just to your family but to the world. But it's too easy to believe in heaven; it's too comfortable for you. Do you see what I'm getting at?

HAROLD KUSHNER: Oh, sure. I have no idea if there really is a paradise. A lot of it sounds like wishful thinking. A lot of it, I think, is based on the fact that we, in our three-dimensional physical existence can only understand living in our physical terms—eating and drinking and sleeping and hearing music and touching things. Maybe not quite as far as some of the caricatures of the Islamic paradise where every man will have three dozen women to satisfy him and nobody quite asks if these women are in heaven or in hell. Heaven is thought of as a physical place because we think in physical terms.

The best answer I know is the one that the medieval Jewish philosopher Maimonides gave—that the reward for the righteous is that when they die, their souls spend eternity in the presence of God. And the punishment for the wicked is not fire and brimstone and little red figures and pitchforks; the punishment for the wicked is that they don't get the reward of the righteous. Their souls don't spend eternity in the presence of God. I don't know what it means to spend eternity in a noncorporeal way in the presence of God. I suspect it means no eating, no drinking, no going to the bathroom, no sex, no sleeping, but just being aware of God, being close to God. And you know, that sounds pretty good.

HUGH HEWITT: Is it a question worth pondering?

HAROLD KUSHNER: Only when there's nothing else on my mind.

HUGH HEWITT: So, it's just not that important to you?

HAROLD KUSHNER: I think there's a very strong Jewish tendency to take this world with immense seriousness and postpone any consideration of a world to come, because we in our physical form cannot comprehend what that means. The danger of believing too strongly in heaven is that you'll forget to take this world seriously. You will shrug off the death of ten million people in Africa, because you'll think, *Well, this world is only a waiting room for the real kingdom of the future.* You will ignore the fact that the rich prey on the poor, that a lot of people never get a fair chance in life because you believe there's another reality where the last shall be first.

For me, I hear the voices of the biblical prophets of Isaiah and Amos saying, "Be outraged by the sufferings of the poor, by the oppression of the marginal in society. Don't give them pie in the sky. Don't ignore their suffering." My creed is that God so loved this world that He commanded us to take it with immense seriousness and not to shrug off the pain and the injustice we see in it in favor of some world to come.

HUGH HEWITT: But is there a judgment? Whether it is from Torah or Talmud, there is a judgment, is there not?

HAROLD KUSHNER: Let me tell you a story.

HUGH HEWITT: Please.

HAROLD KUSHNER: I saw it many years ago on television. A story of a man who dies and wakes up a moment later at the end of a long line. At the front of the line he sees two doors—one marked heaven and one marked hell. And there's an usher, and the usher says, "Move along, keep the line moving. Choose either door, heaven or hell, and walk in."

The man says to the usher, "What happened to the Last Judgment? Where are my deeds weighed and measured? Where am I told if I am a good person or a bad person?" The usher says, "You know, I don't know where that story ever got started. We don't do that here. We've never done it. We don't have the staff to do that here. I mean, look, ten thousand people arrive every minute. I'm supposed to sit down with every one and go over his whole life? We'd never get anywhere. Now, choose either door. Choose heaven or hell, and go in. I don't want to see you again."

And in the television sketch the man walks through the door marked hell. As I understand that, he makes that choice not because he thinks he's a bad person who wants to be punished, but because he believes he's a human being who wants to be judged. I think there is a human, fundamental need to be taken seriously as a moral agent. We need to believe that the universe cares if we are good or bad, if we are truthful or deceitful, if we are faithful or betraying our vows.

You know what it's like, Hugh? Can you remember when you were in college and you stayed up all Sunday night trying to finish a paper because you really wanted to be good? And you handed it in at ten o'clock Monday morning and you got it back at ten o'clock Wednesday morning with a little pencil check next to your name and nothing else on the paper? Clearly the professor never bothered to read it; he just gave you credit for doing it. How did you feel? You felt cheated. Why should you knock yourself out if nobody cares?

The ultimate challenge to a human being, I think, is that question: Why should we go to the trouble of being good if nobody cares? And that's why I must believe, not only that God exists; and not only that God replenishes the love, strength, and courage of human beings; but that God cares how we live. God cares how I earn and spend my money. God cares who I sleep with. God cares what kind of language I use. Because unless I believe that God cares, I don't feel that I am being taken seriously as a moral agent. That's where the need to believe in a moral agent, I think, comes from.

HUGH HEWITT: But you haven't said whether you, Rabbi Kushner, believe that God judges—that it's not the usher saying, "Pick your door."

HAROLD KUSHNER: Yes, I believe that God judges. The whole ethos of the Jewish tradition is based on the fact that we can invest every moment of our lives not only in our worship hours, but we can invest religious significance in the clothes we wear, the money we spend, the sexual behavior we elect, the food we eat.

As a traditional Jew, for example, I observe the dietary laws. I don't eat pork or ham or shell fish or any of those things. Not because I think they're intrinsically evil and not because I think they're unhealthy. It is a way of sanctifying breakfast, lunch, and supper. By introducing categories of permitted and forbidden. By taking something that I share with the animals, the need to eat on a regular basis, and elevating it above the animal level, turning it into a religious statement.

There may be something arbitrary about that, as there's something arbitrary about observing Saturday rather than Sunday or Friday as a day of rest. But for me, coming out of the Jewish tradition, it's a way of saying that this is how I eat as a human being, as a religious human being and not simply as a creature that requires nutrition.

HUGH HEWITT: We all have a need to be judged. We also have a need to be forgiven. I think you once said that we have a need for radical forgiveness. Does God do that as well?

HAROLD KUSHNER: I believe so. To say that God forgives is not a statement about God, about God's emotional state. We have no insights into God's emotional state. As I understand the statement that God forgives—the statement my religion and all religions make—is to say that something miraculous happens and I feel cleansed of the stain of having done something wrong.

I'm ashamed. I'm embarrassed. I feel guilty. And something miraculous happens, and a voice inside my head says, "Yes, but that's not the real you. The real you is sometimes weak, but often strong. Sometimes selfish, but often generous. Sometimes cowardly, but often brave. Emphasize the real you."

I can't imagine where that inner dialog comes from; it's not me talking to myself, because when I try to say it to myself I don't take it seriously. But this feeling comes over me that I don't have to be burdened by the stain of the past. I can change the way I behave. And the next time when I'm in that situation and find myself tempted to do the same thing, I know I can respond differently. This is what it means to say God forgives. It's not God's emotion; it's our own self-perception.

HUGH HEWITT: Do we have ample opportunities to forgive, and do you encourage people to do that?

HAROLD KUSHNER: When I was a congregational rabbi, I would frequently have this conversation with a single mother in my community. She'd come in and she'd say, "You know, ever since that no-good ex-husband of mine left, I've had to hold down two jobs to pay the bills. I've had to tell my kids we don't have money for new clothes, we don't have money to go to the movies. And my ex-husband is living it up with his new wife in a new state. How dare you ask me to forgive him?" And my answer to her would be, "I'm not asking you to forgive your husband because what he did was acceptable; it probably wasn't acceptable. It was a very mean, selfish, inconsiderate thing to do. I'm asking you to forgive him because he doesn't deserve the power to live in your head the way you're letting him live in your head."

HUGH HEWITT: It's self-interest.

HAROLD KUSHNER: That's exactly what it is. She needed to get him out of her emotional life the way he's out of her physical life. Forgiving him wouldn't mean giving him a clean bill. Forgiving would have meant that she was transcending bitterness, that she was leaving the role of victim. It would be for her own good to put down this burden of bitterness and resentment. That's what forgiveness means.

Should the Jews forgive the Nazis? If you mean that would mean saying to the Nazis, "What you did to innocent men, women, and children was understandable, not that terrible," God forbid, no. Absolutely not. If it means Jews should stop seeing themselves as victims of the world's cruelty and be able to see themselves as authors of history rather than objects of history, if they should get over bitterness, get over suspicion of gentiles, if that's what you mean by forgiveness, then yes, I'm in favor of it.

HUGH HEWITT: Do you believe, Rabbi, that a Messiah is coming?

HAROLD KUSHNER: I don't know what one means by that. Do I believe that a person is coming who's going to change everything? No, I have a lot of trouble believing that. Once upon a time, I can understand, people thought that all you needed to change the world would be one really good king. And you know, of course, that's what the word *messiah* means, "one anointed to be king."

Back in biblical days, back in the days of the prophet Isaiah, people thought that if we could just get rid of that crook who's on the throne now and get a really honest king, everything would be fine. You catch that today. Every now and then people fantasize, *If we elected another person president, all our problems would disappear.* And you know what happens? We elect a different president but all our problems are still there.

So I no longer believe that one person, however marvelous, has the power to make everything fine. I'll give you an example. The word *sovereign* used to refer to a person; now sovereign refers to the collective will

> The Jewish belief in the Messiah says that anything that can go right, ultimately will. Wait long enough, work on the world, do the right thing, and sooner or later this world will become the kind of world God originally wanted it to be.

of the people. I understand the word *messiah* to have gone through a very similar kind of evolution. Messiah used to be a person. The world is so complicated now that a person, no matter how marvelous, can't change everything.

I see Messiah as being the collective will of the people to bring about the Messianic age. For me, the belief in Messiah is not expectation of a gifted, supernatural person. It's sort of the Jewish equivalent of Murphy's Law. Murphy's Law says that anything that can go wrong, will. The Jewish belief in the Messiah says that anything that can go right, ultimately will. Wait long enough, work on the world, do the right thing, and sooner or later this world will become the kind of world God originally wanted it to be. For me, that's what the Messianic world means.

HUGH HEWITT: My next-door neighbors in California are members of Chabad. Chabad looks with great expectation for the return of the Messiah. Are they wrong?

HAROLD KUSHNER: Are they factually wrong? So far, yes.

HUGH HEWITT: Well, that's true. So far.

HAROLD KUSHNER: I think Chabad—the followers of the Lubavich branch of Hasidim—really dug themselves a pit in recent history with the belief that Rabbi Schneerson, the Rebbe, was the Messiah. I worry very much about the Chabad movement, because they will have to come to terms with the fact that their faith was so drastically misplaced. It could be emotionally very tragic for them. They may end up denying reality. They may end up wondering about the accuracy of their faith.

I think that because they wanted it so badly, they persuaded themselves that it was true. It's a phenomenon we've seen a lot of times. A teenage girl who falls in love persuades herself that the person she's in love with has a lot more to him than reality would attest. But if the Messiah does show up one day, I'll have to admit that the Chabad was right. If the Messiah turns out to be the Second Coming of Jesus, I'll have to admit that the Christians are right. Smart money's against it.

HUGH HEWITT: And God wouldn't mind if you were wrong in this instance? Am I getting that right? From all of our conversation, your books, God really doesn't care that much about the theology.

HAROLD KUSHNER: I think God doesn't care about theology. I think God cares about religion. Theology is talking about God; religion is experiencing God.

A couple of summers ago, I was invited to go to Argentina to speak in synagogues there. A woman asked me a question. She said, "How do I get my eleven-year-old son to believe in God?" I said, "It's the wrong question. Don't even discuss belief in God with an eleven-year-old. This is the question you should be asking: 'How do I get my eleven-year-old son to experience God? How do I get my eleven-year-old son to recognize that he has just met God?'"

When you go out on a sunny day and the world looks so beautiful, you have met God. When you go out on the first day of the snowfall in winter (those of us in the Northeast experience snow in winter), that's to encounter God. When you've been sick and one day you get up and you feel good, you've experienced God. When something used to be hard for you and you grow and learn how to do it, whether it's a school child learning long division or an adult learning how to operate a computer, that sense that you have grown in competence is an experience of God. When you fall and skin your knee and put a Band-Aid on it and your body heals itself, that's an experience of God. When you've done something that you're ashamed of and you find that your family forgives you, and you've learned that love is not tentative, love is permanent, you've experienced God.

It's not belief. It's not theology. It's not the nature of God. It's not Is God eminent or transcendent? or any of those things. I have met God in my life. Sometimes when I lecture, I do a very interesting experiment. I tell the audience, "There is one chapter of the Bible that all of you know by heart." Do you know which one I'm referring to?

HUGH HEWITT: The Twenty-third Psalm?

HAROLD KUSHNER: The Twenty-third Psalm, absolutely.

HAROLD KUSHNER: I say, "Take this distinction between theology and religion. Theology is talking about God; religion is meeting God. When does the author of the Twenty-third Psalm give us theology, and when does he give us religion?" Remember?

HUGH HEWITT: He gives us theology until the last line.

HAROLD KUSHNER: "The LORD is my shepherd, I shall not want. He makes me to lie down in green pastures, He leads me beside still waters, He restores my soul." That's all theology, talking about God. "Though I walk through the valley of the shadow of death, I will fear no evil, for You are with me." When all of a sudden life becomes problematic, that's when God becomes real, Hugh.

The cliché is that people lose faith in God when bad things happen to them. Just as often, that's when they discover faith in God. That's when they put religion in place of theology. Instead of abstract belief, instead of affirmations about God, statements about God, ideas about God, they experience God. I could not have gotten through this on my own. That's what the end of the Twenty-third Psalm says. The only way I can handle all the pain and all the fear in this world is that I feel that God is with me.

God holds the hand of the fearful is not an abstract statement; it's a personal testimony: I was terrified, and I felt God take my hand, and I felt better. People in hospitals ask me if they should pray, and I say, "Absolutely. Of course. Pray. Pray for a miracle. Pray for a cure. Pray that the surgeon's work comes out right. But also pray for something else. When it's late at night and all your relatives have gone away and you can't sleep and you're scared, pray—not *for* something, but to invite God to be in that dark, empty hospital room with you. Just to be with you. Not to make the tumor go away and not to feel better and not to make your broken bone knit any faster, but just to be there."

Years ago, I read about a fascinating experiment done at the University of Wisconsin, where there is a very sophisticated Pain Institute. A graduate student hired several dozen undergraduates to time how long they could keep a bare foot in a bucket of ice water. I mean, from this you get a Ph.D. What she learned, and I've never forgotten this, was that if there was somebody else in the room, you could keep you foot in the bucket twice as long. That is, the presence of another caring person doubles the amount of pain you can endure.

> Yes, the Bible is true. But it's not true in the way that the daily newspaper is true. There are a couple of ways of being true. Something can be true because it really happened. But something can be true the way a really great novel is true, the way a play is true.

The first implication, for me as a clergyman, for me as a neighbor, is that if I know somebody's going through a hard time, all I have to do is be there. All I have to do is tell that person I care about her and I'll double the amount of pain she can endure. And the second implication I get is that when the person is all by herself, and all her friends aren't there any longer, she should invite God to be present with her. Not to change anything, not to make anything better or easier, just to be there. So she'll know she's not alone. So she knows God has not rejected her. And she can handle a lot more pain and discomfort.

HUGH HEWITT: In your very complex writing about the Book of Job, you did have a few kind words for Job's friends—that they came and that they listened. They said the wrong things, but they came and they listened.

HAROLD KUSHNER: Best thing they did was come. Because I know how hard it is to visit a friend who's suffering. We want to help, but because we generally love the guy, it hurts us to see him in pain. So you see, Hugh, one of the things we do is try to hurry people through the grieving process. "You ought to be over it already. Put it behind you. It's been six months; get back to being yourself. Go on with your life." It's a little bit like saying to a friend who's pregnant in June, "I wish you'd have the baby in six months and not have to go through a hot summer." It's not what they need.

The best thing Job's friends do is to get over their squeamishness and show up. And they sit quietly for several days. Only they get so antsy sitting quietly, and they feel this need to say something, and of course they say the wrong thing. And that's where they spoil the whole effort. Had they just sat there and held Job's hands and said, "Hey, we feel bad for you, pal," that would have cured him. When they start saying "You must have done something to deserve this," when they start saying "Years from now you'll see this is the best thing that could have happened to you," which is really not a nice thing to say to someone whose children have just died, that's when they spoil it.

HUGH HEWITT: Let me ask you about Scripture generally. You love the Psalms. You've spent so much time with the Book of Job, you're conversant, and you write about all of it. Is it true?

HAROLD KUSHNER: Yes, the Bible is true. But it's not true in the way that the daily newspaper is true. There are a couple of ways of being true. Something can be true because it really happened. But something can be true the way a really great novel is true, the way a play is true. Not because it's accurate in terms of saying what happened, but because it says something valid about the human soul. Stories that never happened—fables, fairy tales—are true because they give us insight into the human soul. In that sense the Bible is truer than the daily paper, because the stuff in the daily paper really happened but it's irrelevant.

HUGH HEWITT: But help me out here with a little specificity, Rabbi. Was there an Abraham? Was there an Isaac? Was there a Jacob?

HAROLD KUSHNER: Doesn't matter. Functionally there was.

HUGH HEWITT: Well, wait a minute. It does matter. It matters to a lot of people. It matters a lot. You and I both know it matters. It may be difficult. It may be a complicated answer. But it matters.

HAROLD KUSHNER: No it doesn't, Hugh. It doesn't matter, because ultimately it's an unanswerable question. I mean, what would you need? Would you need a credit card slip with Abraham's signature on it?

Functionally, these people have shaped our history. We are who we are, as Jews and as Christians, because the stories of men named Abraham and Jacob and Moses have come down to us. They have shaped us. It's as irrelevant as the question of whether George Washington really chopped down that cherry tree and took the blame for it. I don't care if it happened or not. Our sense of what it means to be an American is shaped by stories of Washington and Franklin and Jefferson and Abraham Lincoln, whether they're true or not. Our story of what it means to be a human being has been shaped by the story of Adam and Eve. Now look, I do not believe that the human race started with two full-grown Hebrew-speaking adults and a talking snake. I think this is a story about what it means to be human.

HUGH HEWITT: Did Moses meet God on Mount Sinai?

HAROLD KUSHNER: Probably, because there are some parts of the Bible which are so self-evidently true that there's no disputing them.

HUGH HEWITT: That's what I'm looking for. Is that one of them?

HAROLD KUSHNER: I would say yes.

HUGH HEWITT: Now why? How do you get into the text so that you can make that judgment, which is perfectly logical to me: Adam and Eve and a serpent, no; Moses, yes.

HAROLD KUSHNER: Okay, at the other extreme, the stories of the kings of Israel. Yeah, I'm absolutely convinced that kings by those names really ruled, for that many years. Even the names that only a Bible specialist knows about. Yeah, that's true. Something seems to have happened at Mount Sinai. Something seems to have happened at the Red Sea. You start out at the beginning of the story with Hebrew slaves and at the end of the story with a people who are committed to a distinctive way of life. Something happened going from point A to point B. Moses on Mount Sinai is as plausible as anything else. Did he really spend forty days without eating or drinking? Very possibly not. Did a voice actually speak these words to him? As in the Cecil B. DeMille movie, did a bolt of lightning actually write these Hebrew letters on stone? Very possibly not. Something happened at Mount Sinai which had to do with Moses leading the people to commit themselves to a distinctive way of life. Because otherwise, how do you get from point A to point B? How does a band of slaves change into a nation committed to a distinctive lifestyle unless there was some sort of confrontation?

HUGH HEWITT: Rabbi, between point A and point B, what happened at Sinai, to the best of what you understand and make of it?

HAROLD KUSHNER: You mean, had I been there with a portable tape recorder, what would I have recorded? There are some very interesting Jewish traditions about that. Some of the sages say God spoke the Ten Commandments from the beginning to the end, and Moses stayed up for forty days to get all the other laws. Some say that God only spoke the first two Commandments, which are in the first person: "I am the Lord. You shall have no other Gods before Me." And the ones which talk about God in the third person, Moses spoke on God's behalf.

And then there's a very interesting comment by one of the nineteenth-century Hasidic masters that God only spoke the first letter of the first word, which in Hebrew is a silent letter; that is, God didn't say anything, but simply coming into His presence was an education. The way, for example, you come into the presence of a severely handicapped person who's coping with his disability. You learn a lesson about coping with disabilities without his having to teach you. There are certain people—you know this—in whose company you simply can't tell an off-color joke. There are certain people you simply cannot bring yourself to lie to—not because they say, "Don't do that; I'd be embarrassed," or "That's not nice," but just because of the kind of aura they exude.

My guess is something like that happened at Sinai. The Israelite people, newly freed from slavery, found themselves so really and intensely in the presence of God that they were changed by the encounter. They understood something the way, for example, a father looking down at his newborn son will understand some things about responsibility and immortality and obligation. The child doesn't have to say, "You're going to have to do the following for me, and I'll do this for you." The father understands it from the encounter.

HUGH HEWITT: Can Americans in 1996 have that same sort of experience?

HAROLD KUSHNER: Oh, I think so. I think all individuals can have this. You come to a point in your life when all of a sudden you understand something. I think, for example, of the scriptural story of Jacob in Genesis, coming back from the land of Haram, being prepared to meet his brother Esau, who he hasn't seen for twenty years. Esau's last words to him had been "The next time I see you, I'm going to kill you." Jacob is scared. And Jacob prays. And something happens to Jacob that night, when he suddenly realizes he has spent his whole life to this point, every time he's in a tight situation, lying and running away. And he understands he doesn't want to be like that anymore. He doesn't want to be somebody who responds to a crisis by lying and running. Something happens to him, and it's described in the Bible as his wrestling with an angel and being injured in the process and getting a blessing. I take that as a symbolic story. Jacob manages to shed his old skin as Jacob the trickster, the supplanter, and emerges as a brand-new person.

I think people have experiences like that. I think people come to a moment of crisis in their lives when they suddenly say, "I'm about to decide what type of person I want to be." Some people do this in public. A politician has to decide if he's going to run for office or how he will respond to something that happens in office. Businessmen do it when they have to make a crucial decision. Husbands and wives do it when they have to decide whether they're going to stay in a marriage or leave. Yes, people face a moment when they have to say, "I'm about to make a decision which will determine what kind of person I am."

I think you make that decision with the feeling that you're in the presence of God. And if you know what's right, and you're not sure you're strong enough to do what's right, that's when you invite God into your life. Not to tell you what you have to do; you know what you have to do. But to be with you, to be supportive, to give you the strength so that you can do what you know is right.

HUGH HEWITT: How do you hold onto that feeling? I think you call it "standing before God at the base of Mount Sinai." How do you hold onto that feeling in everyday life even if you believe that you're just weary of everyday life?

HAROLD KUSHNER: If you're weary of everyday life, one of the things religion does for you is replenish your strength. I think there are basically two ways—sacred time and sacred space. You could go to a church or a synagogue, but a place that has special meaning for you. A Jew might go to Jerusalem. Or a person might go to a place where he has had certain experiences of strengthening, religious experiences in his past. It could be a lakeside cottage where you grew up as a little boy or a little girl. Either you go to a place that has special meaning for you and you draw strength from that, or you do things which replenish your soul: a discipline of worship, a sense of reading the Psalms. When I'm emotionally drained, when I just feel like I've given away everything and I haven't been replenished, I'll sit and I'll read a good book, I'll put on music. And it restores my soul.

HUGH HEWITT: Some of our viewers have never been inside a church, but they're interested now. They've heard you or they've heard something they're interested in. What ought they to do?

HAROLD KUSHNER: Ask around among their friends, "Which church should I visit for a solid, affirming religious experience, and which one would be a waste of time?" Then ask themselves where they really felt as though they met God through the presence of a congregation.

The funny thing is, Hugh, human beings are social creatures. We are affected by the presence of people around us. You see the ball game better at home on television, but you experience the ball game better if you go out to the stadium. It's a hard thing to find God by yourself. If you can go to a church, synagogue, or mosque where the people around you have the sense of encountering God, you'll be caught up in that. If you go to a church, synagogue, or mosque where the ratio of tourists to natives is so out of whack that most people don't know what they're doing there, it's going to be very hard for you to experience God.

So if you're looking for an affirming religious experience, ask among your friends: "What service can I go to that's going to work? What place, what religious leader? What books can I read? What kind of meditative experience can I undergo so that I can feel that I am inviting God into my life?"

I think people are different. Some people, and I'm one, are comfortable finding God in a crowd, in a congregation. Other people have a much easier time finding God in a solo meditative experience—just going off in a dark room by themselves and trying to concentrate on that. I've never been able to do that, but I know a lot of people who do.

HUGH HEWITT: I'm given pause by the story in one of your books of the young woman who'd returned to her home after a rather desolate life of drugs and abuse, took a long shower, washed her hair, and said, "Let's go to the synagogue." She went to the synagogue and had an extraordinarily bad time.

HAROLD KUSHNER: Yes, there's an opulent bar mitzvah ceremony going on. And all the relatives are there, looking at their watches and waiting for lunch. The sermon is about the need to be vigilant against the rise of anti-Semitism. And there's nothing religious about it. The name of God is never mentioned in the entire sermon. And this is what she was hungry for. By the way, and I don't believe I told the end of the story in the book, she joined an evangelical group, a Christian group, for about six months. Found God there. And having found God, she left and went back to the synagogue.

HUGH HEWITT: Too often churches don't help people find God. You have heard a thousand times, "I don't need the church. Church is full of people who are showing off. Church is full of terrible people. Church is full of people that I know too well."

HAROLD KUSHNER: My answer is that a church or synagogue that only admits saints is like a hospital that only admits healthy people—a lot easier to run, but that's not what we're in business for. Listen, I have presided at I don't know how many hundreds of services that did not work. Services where a person coming to look for God would have gone home disappointed, like that twenty-two-year-old girl trying to find her way back from a life of what she thought was sin and turpitude. And I've presided

> The funny thing is, Hugh, human beings are social creatures. We are affected by the presence of people around us. You see the ball game better at home on television, but you experience the ball game better if you go out to the stadium. It's a hard thing to find God by yourself.

over a lot of services where I really felt that God was present. I never know in advance which is going to be which; I guess God doesn't show up on schedule. Sometimes everything comes together and I invoke the presence of God. And sometimes it falls flat. But there are times when something absolutely magical happens.

To these people who say they don't need the church, I say yes, Mozart didn't need piano lessons. If you're a spiritual genius you can find God without the tradition. If you're like most of us, you need the structure, you need the special place. You need the mood, the music, the presence of other people questing. It's a lot easier to do that than to do it on your own.

HUGH HEWITT: But these are modern times, Rabbi. These prayers that are said in your tradition and in mine are thousands of years old. And the songs that are sung are hundreds of years old. And the sermons are being recycled for the fortieth or fiftieth time. In modern America we don't need this. We're up-to-date.

HAROLD KUSHNER: Let me tell you a story, Hugh. Several years ago, a group of my colleagues and I were involved in writing some new prayers. We felt that the old prayers were a little stale and we'd write something contemporary. So we put out a little pamphlet and distributed it to our congregations. The first year it was very exciting. "Oh, wow! New, relevant prayers! Modern language!" The second year, "Oh, isn't that nice. Here come Rabbi Kushner's prayers again." The third year they had grown old.

Prayers thousands of years old retain their power to move because only the best ones have survived. And prayers three years old written by people like us have gone stale. The fact of the matter is that the twentieth century is a wonderful time for programming computers and a terrible time to write poetry. Because you have a society that understands and appreciates computers and doesn't understand and appreciate poetry. And prayers are poetry. A lot of people don't understand that.

HUGH HEWITT: Rabbi, you've also said prayer is a right-brain phenomenon.

HAROLD KUSHNER: Let me talk about that. I assume a sophisticated audience like

> Prayer is not talking with God. Prayer is joining other people in the liturgy so that as a result of this aesthetic event, as a result of this poetry, this verbal music, we invoke the presence of God.

ours is aware of the work that's been done on the mechanism of the brain—that the left half of the brain controls linear, intellectual, rational processes and the right half controls aesthetic, emotional responses. I am absolutely convinced that even though prayers use words, prayers are a right-brain aesthetic activity rather than a left-brain intellectual one. Prayer is not so much the meaning of the words. A friend of mine says the purpose of the words is to keep your left brain busy so the right brain can soar without embarrassment.

Asking what a prayer means is like asking what a flower means. What does a symphony mean? It doesn't "mean." It sort of rolls over you. It has an emotional impact on you. I was making that point to a young adult group here in Boston, and a young woman raised her hand and said, "Rabbi Kushner, I can prove to you that you're right." She said, "I'm a speech therapist. My job is to work with stroke patients who have lost the power of speech because of cerebral-vascular accident. I have a client who had a stroke. He cannot speak. He can't say hello, he can't tell you his name. But he can recite the entire Hebrew service by heart, because that's located in a different part of the brain than the powers of speech are." Prayer is not talking with God. Prayer is joining other people in the liturgy so that as a result of this aesthetic event, as a result of this poetry, this verbal music, we invoke the presence of God.

HUGH HEWITT: If you're right and you've concluded that God is not a vending machine for asking and receiving, what's the point of prayer?

HAROLD KUSHNER: Hugh, are you familiar with Garth Brooks's country music song "Unanswered Prayers"?

HUGH HEWITT: No, I'm not.

HAROLD KUSHNER: One of my favorites.

HUGH HEWITT: Go ahead. Tell me about it.

HAROLD KUSHNER: It's a story of a man in his mid-forties who sees this woman at a public event. She looks vaguely familiar. Then he realizes who she is. This is the girl he had a massive crush on in seventh grade. Every night he would go to sleep praying to God to make her love him the way he loved her. And he couldn't understand why God didn't answer the sincere prayer of this lovesick thirteen-year-old boy. Thirty years later, seeing who he's grown up to be, seeing who she's grown up to be, he concludes that some of God's greatest gifts are unanswered prayers. I like the song; I don't like the theology.

I've got real problems with the theology that says prayer means bringing our requests to God and God either says yes or He says no. I have colleagues who say God answers all prayers, but sometimes the answer is no. I think what we've done is confused God with Santa Claus. It's Santa Claus you bring your list to, and either he gives you what you want or he doesn't. That's not God. Prayer is not asking. Prayer is not pleading.

HUGH HEWITT: That's true. But the Psalmist predates Santa Claus by a lot of centuries, and he asks, "Wherefore art Thou, my God?"

HAROLD KUSHNER: Oh, that's not a request; that's a *cry!* That's a cry of pain. That's an outburst of the human soul that says, "Where is God now, and why is He letting these things happen, and why isn't He helping me?" That's not saying, "God, please bless my parents, my wife, my kids, my dog, my neighbors," and so on.

HUGH HEWITT: It's not saying, "Help me?"

HAROLD KUSHNER: No, it's not saying, "Help me." It's saying, "Why am I going through this?" in the same way that "Why me?" is not really a question but a cry of pain. "God, help me!" is not really a request but a cry of pain.

Personal story: I was in the 1989 San Francisco earthquake just before the World Series there. I was standing outside a restaurant at ten minutes after five, when the quake hit. I ran inside, ducked under a table. The whole thing took maybe fifteen seconds. When it was over, my first response was, *Thank God, I'm all right.* And my second response was, *Wait a minute; what do I mean by that? Do I really believe that God chose to spare me and to let all those other suckers on the freeway die? No, I don't believe that.* What I concluded was that "Thank God, I'm all right" was not a statement about thanks and gratitude to God; it was a spontaneous outburst of gratitude. I'm very lucky.

> If you could ask God why He created people, I'd be very interested in His answer. The answer my tradition gives me is that God created people so we would be nice to each other. God created people so that we would create the one thing in the world that God could not create by Himself, and that is the choice of goodness.

In the same way, a person who is in a very severe automobile accident and ends up in the hospital with a broken leg and a couple of facial lacerations says to me, "God was riding with me." I don't take that as a theological statement. If I did, then what would that say about the young man a week before who was killed in a similar accident? No, I take "God was riding with me" as a spontaneous ejaculation of gratitude. He means something good happened to him that he could not have arranged for on his own.

"God, help me!" is not a request to God; it's a cry of need. "I am hurting! I am desperate!" Prayer is not bringing our wish list to God. Prayer is simply coming into the presence of God and being changed by that. The greatest religious document ever written that nobody has ever heard of is the Seventy-third Psalm. I would challenge any of our listeners out there who are not professional professors of theology to identify the Seventy-third Psalm.

HUGH HEWITT: I can't.

HAROLD KUSHNER: No, I couldn't either until I ran across it. It is an absolute masterpiece. As soon as the program is over, all you viewers go home, get out your Bibles, and read Psalm 73. Psalm 73 is the story of a man who says: "I look at the world and all the terrible unfair things that happen, and I'm about ready to give up. I'm about ready to conclude that this is a sick world. It's not God's world. What answered me was to go into the temple and to have God take me by the hand. God doesn't answer my questions. God doesn't make the world better. Simply being in the presence of God makes it possible for me to live in a messy, unfair world." That is one of the most profound religious documents ever written by human hands. The purpose of praying to God when you're in dire straits is not to make the problem go away. It's to make it possible for you to live in a pain-filled world because God is holding your hand.

HUGH HEWITT: Then the question of questions is *Why are we here?* Rabbi, *why* were we created so we have to ask for help?

HAROLD KUSHNER: Hugh, I'm afraid you're putting that question to the wrong party. Maybe you could get an exclusive interview with God.

HUGH HEWITT: We've tried to book that, but it hasn't worked out.

HAROLD KUSHNER: If you could ask God why He created people, I'd be very interested in His answer. The answer my tradition gives me is that God created people so we would be nice to each other. God created people so that we would create the one thing in the world that God could not create by Himself, and that is the choice of goodness. It's the one thing lacking in God's world. Archibald MacLeish once gave a sermon about what he was trying to say in his play *J.B.*, his modern version of the Book of Job. He said that God can control everything except human love. And the only way God can be loved is to turn people loose in the world with the choice of loving Him or rejecting Him.

HUGH HEWITT: But you know God left wide margins between good and evil. He could have narrowed it down so that free choice could have been between being good and being bland, as opposed to being good and being really evil.

HAROLD KUSHNER: Again, you'd have to ask Him why He didn't or why He's not clearer. When you realize what a long, slow, painful process it has been to figure out what God wants from us. . . . Only one hundred and fifty years ago religious people were arguing, both sides quoting the Bible, whether or not the enslavement of the black race was legitimate or not, whether or not blacks were real human beings. Can you understand that? That in these last years of the nineteenth century people actually differed about that? That one hundred years ago people argued about whether or not women were capable of voting? That within our lifetime cities in the United States were segregated by race, with separate water fountains and separate rest rooms and separate schools and separate transportation? Why has it taken us so long to figure out what's right and what's wrong? I wish God had made it easier. But again, it's one of those things; had I been present at creation, I could have made it a lot easier for God.

HUGH HEWITT: You believe in progress, then?

HAROLD KUSHNER: I do.

HUGH HEWITT: Rabbi, we can look to central Europe, to Africa. We can look back just fifty years to the concentration camps. We can look everywhere, and there's no good case for progress.

HAROLD KUSHNER: Oh, I think there is a case for progress. I wish it were more one-sided. I wish it were stronger. Yet it is a fact that certain things which used to be taken for granted are no longer acceptable.

Yes, the story of ethnic cleansing in Bosnia was absolutely horrible. And the story of ethnic cleansing in Africa was absolutely horrible. But when the same stuff went on one or two hundred years ago, nobody thought this was horrible. They thought, *This is the way the world runs.* Read a Dickens novel or a Hardy novel about life in England in the nineteenth century and children die in every chapter. It was assumed you had to have seven or eight children so that two or three would live to adulthood. A hundred years ago you could not assume that children would grow up.

Today we assume that a child who is born will live to maturity. Now if a child should die, it is a searing, life-altering event. It's the sort of thing that people in the age of Dickens or Hardy would take in stride.

HUGH HEWITT: Let me change subjects here, Rabbi. Have you ever been attracted to the Jewish tradition of mysticism?

HAROLD KUSHNER: Not really. My parents were both born and raised in Lithuania and by Jewish tradition, Jews who came out of Lithuania were arch-rationalists. They looked with scorn on the Russian, Polish, and Hungarian Jews who would go into this mysticism. And whether it's genetic or cultural, I have developed this arch-rationalist approach. When I was younger, I would dismiss mysticism. As I get older and more mature, I'm less likely to dismiss it. I just feel that it's not my native language of faith. I can

appreciate it. I think there are insights that the mystics can reach that the rationalists cannot even approach. And in a sense I envy people who have that; it's just not me.

HUGH HEWITT: Last year I had a chance to have a conversation with the great Talmud scholar Adin Steinsaltz. And I asked him what was wrong with America. Rabbi Steinsaltz said, "What America wants is a good five-cent religion." His comment was about cheap mysticism, you know, crystals and things like that. Are you alarmed by that desire for a sort of cheap religion and cheap mysticism and cheap awareness?

HAROLD KUSHNER: Yes, I am. I refer to it in one of my books as "junk-food religion"—that is, something that's undemanding. Very comfortable going down, but ultimately not nourishing. I'm very concerned about what I perceive as New Age theology, which is largely about how to take advantage of God without what I find to be the unique dimension of the Judeo-Christian Scriptures—the fact that God makes moral demands on us.

I think too many people are looking for a religion that pats them on the head and holds their hand and doesn't make demands. I think people who liked my first book because it's comforting and then reject my later books because I talk about the demands that God makes are looking for cheap religion, a religion which only gives and doesn't require. And yet if you think about it, I believe there is something fundamental in the human soul that wants to be demanded of, that wants to be taken seriously as a moral agent. I think we want to have a God who takes us seriously.

HUGH HEWITT: Where do we get this list of demands?

HAROLD KUSHNER: For me, the biblical Scriptures are human beings writing down what they have come to understand as the will of God: how you live, how you treat each other, how you treat yourself, how you learn to control your impulses instead of being controlled by them. For me the Scriptures are sacred because they represent what some of the wisest souls in human history have understood as the will of God.

HUGH HEWITT: Then let's talk about the atheist out there who can argue and produce evidence of a life well lived, of enormous charity and of great compassion, but who doesn't believe, doesn't want any part of it, and thinks it's all sort of folk-culture that we've long abandoned. What do you say to this individual?

HAROLD KUSHNER: Hugh, I don't have a real strong motivation to convert the atheist. If God can tolerate him, I can put up with him. Certainly I cannot claim with a straight face that the difference between me and the atheist is that I am an honest, moral person and he's not. There are some people who use their atheism as an excuse for doing terrible things. There are some people who use their religion as an excuse for doing terrible things. The real difference between me and the atheist comes when we have both knocked ourselves out for the causes we believe in, when we have both spent ourselves working for world peace and religion and coming together, when we have both wearied ourselves holding the hands of the fearful and drying the tears of the grieving, when we are out of strength and out of love. Then if the atheist can only look down deep inside himself for more, he's going to reach bottom. There will be no more strength inside him.

I have a God who is not a figment of my imagination, who is real, who is outside me. He's a God to whom I can turn to replenish my strength so I can keep on giving. Because, you see, it's not my strength and it's not my love I'm sharing with these people; it is God's strength and God's love that is flowing through me. And whenever I give it away, I can be confident there is more where that comes from. The difference between me and the atheist is not what we believe is good. It's how long we can keep on doing it without emptying ourselves in the process.

HUGH HEWITT: But the atheist is not engaging in what Pascal would call "the great gamble."

HAROLD KUSHNER: No, and neither am I. For the less-sophisticated viewers out there, Pascal's gamble is that if there is a God and I believe in Him, I win. If there is no God and I believe in Him, what do I lose? If there is a God and I reject Him, He's going to be very teed-off at me. And therefore it is prudent to believe in God.

The flaw in Pascal's gamble is this: What if there is a God and one of the things He hates most is people believing in Him on a calculating basis rather than on the basis of love? There's a passage at the end of the

Book of Leviticus that some Jewish commentators see as God saying, in effect: "If you play it cool with Me, if you follow My ways because you've calculated it's in your interest, then I'm going to be very disappointed in you. But if you follow My ways warmly, out of love, out of enthusiasm, then I will cherish and reward you." And I think that's the flaw in Pascal's wager.

HUGH HEWITT: Rabbi, when did you first become aware of God?

HAROLD KUSHNER: Oh, it's like asking a fish when he first became aware of water. I grew up in a religious home—not Orthodox, but serious. We went to synagogue. We observed the Sabbath. We were very much immersed in Jewish culture, and God sort of came along with that.

I think, by the way, that Judaism is structurally different from Christianity. Judaism starts with a community, and you find God by means of a community. I think in Christianity you find the community by means of God.

So it wasn't that I made a faith decision and found other like-minded people. It's that I grew up in a community of people who took the existence of God, the demands of God, the customs and the values of the Jewish tradition with utmost seriousness. This was the milieu in which I grew up.

HUGH HEWITT: When did you decide that you were going to be a rabbi?

HAROLD KUSHNER: Not until my junior year in college. Why did I decide? Do we ever really understand why we make the major life-decisions in our lives? Who we marry, what kind of people we'll be, what we do for a living? It was for a lot of reasons. Partly it was because I admired my rabbi a lot, and I wanted to be like him. Partly because I saw a lot of people admiring him, and I wanted to be admired like that. And partly, I have a theory that men with strong fathers will do for a living what their fathers did as a hobby, or they will do as a sideline what their fathers did professionally. It's a way of following in your father's footsteps without having to compete with him.

My father was a businessman who was very active in our synagogue. I knew at a very young age that I had absolutely no head for business. I knew I was going to disappoint my father when I told him I had no interest in going into the company he had started and built up. But you see, by becoming a rabbi I could say to him, "I'm not rejecting your values. I am choosing to commit my life to some of the things you've taught me to believe in, even if not all of them."

> My religion tells me that every time I do something good and nobody applauds me, nobody thanks me, nobody gives me a medal, *somebody* finds out. The world is different because I chose to be honest, brave, helpful.

HUGH HEWITT: And was he happy with that choice?

HAROLD KUSHNER: Yes and no. I think to the end of his days, he never quite believed that one could make one's living as a rabbi, and he kept expecting me to do something else as a sideline. I found it gratifying that before he died he saw me become a best-selling author. That brought him some peace of mind.

HUGH HEWITT: Rabbi, in one of your writings you concluded that your grandfather in Lithuania, a house painter, had redeemed his life from anonymity and ordinariness by rigorous observance of the law. Explain that for me.

HAROLD KUSHNER: I think there's a fundamental human need for significance. In the same way that there's a need to eat, to sleep, to exercise, there is a need to make a difference to the world. My thirty years as a clergyman have taught me that people are not afraid of dying; people are afraid of not having lived. They can handle the idea they can't live forever. What they cannot handle is the notion that they will have lived and died and not made a difference to the world.

One of the things that religion gives us is the assurance that by being good, decent people we've made a difference to the world. There's this wonderful line by Oscar Wilde, "The nicest feeling in the world is to do a good deed anonymously and have somebody find out." My religion tells me that every time I do something good and nobody applauds me, nobody thanks me, nobody gives me a medal, *somebody* finds out. The world is different because I chose to be honest, brave, helpful. When my grandfather lived a religious life, despite the fact that he was a poor house painter who lived in very limited means, he knew that he was giving God pleasure. He knew that he was redeeming the world, making the world worthwhile, by being a good, kind, honest, observant person. That's what religion does; it redeems our life from insignificance. And that's something we desperately need.

HUGH HEWITT: But the rules. So many rules. You quote Hillel as giving this advice to a seeker who wanted to know what Judaism means: "Don't do bad things to others that you don't want done to yourself. All the rest is commentary. That's it. Now go study the commentary." Why all the commentary? The Golden Rule is a fairly simple thing.

HAROLD KUSHNER: No, it's not. It's a very complicated thing. Being human is very complicated. You say that the essence of being human is not doing to other people what you wouldn't want done to yourself. But what if there's something you don't mind, but it drives my wife crazy? Does that give you permission to do it to her? What if there's something that I don't really care about, but it's important to somebody else? What if there's something that I can't imagine happening to me, but if it happens to somebody else it ruins their life? What is my obligation to try and not do that?

It's a very simple thing to say, "Be a faithful husband and a good parent." But carrying that out day after day is complicated beyond belief—to the point where no matter how much you really want to, and no matter how good a person you are, you're going to make mistakes. You will disappoint your wife. You will disappoint your kids. You will want to be a good parent, but you'll come home from the office some days so tired that you're going to be cranky with them and they'll think it's their fault. You're going to read all the books about how to be a good mate, and you're going to be so hurt and angry by something your mate did that you're going to respond in the wrong way. It is so complicated to be a real human being, to do the right thing, that we need all the advice we can get. I think a lot of people, coming out of the traditions of Judaism and Christianity, are fixed at a fairly childish understanding of religion. They see it as a lot of rules you have to do to please God, and God grades you on a report card. I would like to think we are sophisticated enough to outgrow that very childish understanding of religion. The word *Torah*, for example, does not mean "law." *Torah* means "showing the way"; it means "teaching." This is guidance. What does it mean to respect another person's property? What does it mean to respect another person's feelings? To what degree can I criticize another person's behavior because I think it's wrong without offending him as a person? To what degree can I insist on my own prerogatives without short-changing others? These are immensely complicated questions.

HUGH HEWITT: Why is there so much emphasis on ritual? It's not just in Judaism; it's the same with every one of the people that we've spoken to on this show? You yourself are a big fan of Friday night service, of lighting the candles, of rigorous observance of the Sabbath. Why ritual?

HAROLD KUSHNER: Because it's magic. Because it's something that provokes very deep, very profound feelings. It's not just lighting the Sabbath candles. There's a difference between lighting the Sabbath candles and lighting a birthday candle or lighting a candle when a hurricane strikes and the power has gone out. To say "Praised are You, O Lord, our God, who has commanded us to do this to bring holiness into our lives by this way," is to say God is present. It's to perform a deed which invokes the presence of God.

You feel you are in the presence of God. That's a tremendous thing. To say a prayer over the food I eat means that God is present at my table. To feel an obligation to give charity means God is watching as I write checks. It's a very brave thing to live in the presence of God. There are things I would not do that I might otherwise do. There are things that I feel obliged to do because I know that God is with me and it's more comfortable, it's easier for me to do them. This is what ritual does. Special things, special ways, special language, give you a very special feeling.

HUGH HEWITT: I know you're at work on a book that asks, How good do we have to be? Well, how good *do* we have to be?

HAROLD KUSHNER: We don't have to be perfect; we have to be good enough. I think one of the most pernicious, one of the most harmful ideas that people have is that God wants us to be perfect. In one way it's been both amusing and exasperating for me to hear Protestants, Catholics, and Jews compete with each other as to whose religious education was more guilt-producing.

We read the story of Adam and Eve in the Garden of Eden, and we come away with a lesson that they made one mistake and were punished forever. And we think to ourselves, *Wow! If God did that to people who did one thing wrong, what's He going to do to me for all of the dozens of things I've done wrong?* We feel terribly guilty because we aren't perfect. We can't forgive our parents that they made mistakes when they were raising us. We're deeply disappointed in our children; after all we've done for them, they still didn't turn out perfect. We want our spouses to be perfect, and we feel betrayed when they're not.

If we could get over this myth that God wants perfection, we could be a lot happier. I think what God wants from us is not perfection, but integrity. I think God understands that being a good human being is so immensely complicated nobody can get it right. It's like expecting a ball player to bat a thousand and get a hit every time he's up. Nobody is that good.

HUGH HEWITT: We're back to the first question, Rabbi. Why *did* He set it up this way?

HAROLD KUSHNER: Because there wouldn't be any point in being good if it were automatic. That's not an achievement. That's like putting together a three-piece jigsaw puzzle that nobody could get wrong. Only if it's a challenge is the achievement of goodness something that really matters to the world.

HUGH HEWITT: I could understand why it would matter to the world, but why would it matter to God?

HAROLD KUSHNER: Because that's the one thing God could not produce by Himself—the free choice of goodness. This is the one thing we can do for God that God can't do for Himself. We can choose to be good instead of having to be good. When we do that, and if we do it much of the time, I've got to believe this is so pleasing to God that He has no complaints that we can't do it all of the time.

HUGH HEWITT: You are taken with the metaphor of fire for God. Why?

HAROLD KUSHNER: One day I was having a conversation with a Protestant theologian, David Griffin. He'd read my book and liked it. And he said, "Sometimes I think God is all-powerful. But God doesn't have the power to control; God has the power to enable. God can do anything working through us. God can put an end to cancer, but not by saying, 'Okay that's it, no more malignant tumors.' God will put an end to cancer by motivating people to spend their days and nights trying to find a cure for it. God will put an end to war when people decide not to kill each other over trivial reasons."

And I said to him, "David that's great. That's a wonderful insight. Now I understand why the Bible and so many other religions picture God as fire—the burning bush, the volcano at Mt. Sinai, things like that." Fire is not an object, fire is a process. Fire is the process of liberating the energy which is hidden inside a log of wood or a lump of coal. And I think that's the way we experience God.

I'm not going to make the mistake of saying that's what God is. God is not a person who lives in the sky. God is that astonishing process of liberating the power for goodness which is latent inside every one of us. We have the capacity to be good. We have the capacity to be generous. We have the capacity to be brave. And God comes, and just like the fire that turns the log into heat He liberates that potential capacity within us so we can actually live it out.

> We have the capacity to be good. We have the capacity to be strong. We have the capacity to be generous. We have the capacity to be brave. And God comes, and just like the fire that turns the log into heat He liberates that potential capacity within us so we can actually live it out.

HUGH HEWITT: Rabbi, a lot of people have been motivated to watch this program specifically because of your book *When Bad Things Happen to Good People* and because of your experience, watching the death of a child at a young age. So as we come to the conclusion of our conversation, I want to make sure I pose the question one more time. How do you find comfort when you're grieving?

HAROLD KUSHNER: Ten weeks after the bomb went off in the Federal Building in Oklahoma City, I was invited to Oklahoma City by the Jewish community there and by the governor of Oklahoma,

Governor Keating. He asked me to meet with families who had lost loved ones in the bombing, to try and bring them some comfort.

I asked them, "How do you cope? How do you manage to go on living?" And you know something? They all gave me the same answer. College graduates and high school drop-outs. Older people and younger people. Religious and agnostic. They all gave me the same answer. Know what the magic word was? *Community.* They all said that when friends, neighbors, total strangers from all over America, came and told them they cared about them, they knew they were not alone.

How do we cope? When life has been cruel to you and God comes to you incarnated in the presence of good, caring people, you are taught to believe in a loving God, not a punishing God. My one favorite sentence in my book about bad things happening to good people is a sentence I didn't write. It's a sentence I quote from a nineteenth-century Hasidic rabbi: "Human beings are God's language." You cry out to God and God doesn't send you theology, God doesn't send you explanations; God sends you people. He sends doctors and nurses to sit with you and try to make you whole. He sends friends and neighbors to come hold your hand and dry your tears. It doesn't change the physical realities; it changes what goes on inside of you.

You see, Hugh, when something bad happens to us, a part of our mind says, *Maybe I deserve this.* Cause and effect. Our effort to make sense of the world may be innate. It may be the product of religious training, people like Job's friends who come and say there must be a good reason why this happened. And so part of our mind says, *What did I do that this happened to me?* When people get over their squeamishness, and they come and sit with us, and they hold our hands, and they're smart enough not to give us theological explanations but just keep quiet and keep us company, we are reassured we are good people and that we don't deserve this sort of thing.

HUGH HEWITT: Are there people who refuse to be comforted?

HAROLD KUSHNER: Yes, there are. Many years ago, at a lecture about bad things happening to good people, somebody asked me a question, "Why does God send strength and consolation to some people and not to others?" And I answered, "Maybe God's strength and comfort are like the radio waves in the air. They're always there, but unless you turn your radio on you're not going to hear them."

Somebody came up to me afterward and said, "You know, Rabbi Kushner, I didn't like your answer. You did the same thing you criticize other people for doing. You blamed the victim. You said that if you were not open to God's comfort, it's your own fault; you didn't have your receiver on." I said, "You're right. I'm never going to give that answer again."

I don't know why some people are more amenable to being consoled than others. I know I have met some people who are afraid to get over their loss. They say, "I've physically lost my husband, my loved one, my child. If I ever got over grieving, I would lose them emotionally as well. I don't want to get better."

I've met people who found that when they were suffering, people felt sorry for them, people went out of their way to help them, people did things for them. And they didn't want to get normal again because then everybody would stop feeling sorry for them.

I've found people who were just so angry at God that it created a wall between them and the healing resources that God represents. And I say to these people, "Listen, you're angry at God. That's fine. So shout! Scream! Curse! Do whatever you need to do. The God I believe in is not so fragile that you're going to harm Him by shouting at Him. Nor is He so petty that He's going to zap you a second time because you've offended Him. Get the anger out of your system. And when you've done it, don't let it be a barrier between you and God's healing." And sometimes people have articulated their anger. I have given them permission to be angry. And when they were done, they were able to go back and open their souls to God again, seeing that they had not totally breached the relationship with Him by screaming and cursing.

HUGH HEWITT: Probably the most compelling line for me in Scripture, in terms of being descriptive, is "And Pharaoh hardened his heart." Do you run into people who consciously harden their hearts?

HAROLD KUSHNER: Yes, I run into people who are afraid of feeling pain, of grieving. I run into people who are so uncomfortable handling other people's pain that they cannot reach out to somebody they really care about. I get letters from women who tell me that when they got seriously ill or found out they had a very sick child, their husbands left. Not because the husband didn't care, but because the husband hurt so much to see somebody he loved in pain, he couldn't handle it and he had to run away so he wouldn't see it. Yes, there are people who harden their hearts because they don't believe they are strong enough to handle pain.

I think we need to teach these people about the resiliency of the human soul. I think we have to provide them with role models—the survivors of the Holocaust, victims of crimes, survivors of accidents, people who managed to put their lives together again and went on. And we have to say to them, "Don't be afraid of pain. A broken heart is like a broken leg; it hurts desperately, but ultimately it heals. And one day the pain will go away and you will still be there."

We have to make people brave enough to take off the armor and make themselves vulnerable to feeling. I deal with young people who are afraid to give themselves totally to a relationship because of what they saw in their parents' marriage or in their friends' marriage. They saw how much it hurt when love turned sour, and they're afraid to make themselves vulnerable to love for fear it will hurt them. And I want to soften their hearts. I want to teach them to stop anesthetizing themselves against feeling pain. Because when you do that, it works. You don't feel any pain, but you don't feel any joy either. And you don't feel any love, and you don't feel any happiness. You go through life numb. And I try and teach these people, "Don't be afraid that life will hurt." I can cut my hair and my fingernails, and I

> If God is there to assure us, not so much of the happy ending but of our capacity to survive and come to terms with whatever ending comes along, then we don't have to be afraid. We can take off the armor and make ourselves vulnerable to the world.

don't feel any pain because those are dead cells. But if I cut into my living flesh, it hurts me desperately. And that's how I know I'm alive. I say to these people, "Don't be so afraid of pain. Take off the armor. Let the anesthetic wear off. Be brave enough, be confident enough to believe that you can handle the pain and you'll see all the good things that come along with that."

HUGH HEWITT: What role does God play in the softening of the heart?

HAROLD KUSHNER: If we had to do it ourselves, I think we'd be afraid to do it. If we know that God is with us, if we know that it's the right thing in God's sight, that He gives us the courage to get over pain, that He sends the courage to the broken heart, then I think we're willing to do it. If God is there to assure us, not so much of the happy ending but of our capacity to survive and come to terms with whatever ending comes along, then we don't have to be afraid. We can take off the armor and make ourselves vulnerable to the world because we know that when it hurts, God will take away some of the pain and make the hurt go away.

HUGH HEWITT: Rabbi Harold Kushner, thank you for joining us.

A CONVERSATION WITH
ROBERTA HESTENES

Visited at the campus of Eastern College near Philadelphia, Pennsylvania, Roberta Hestenes has lead a life of "firsts." The first daughter of her parents, she is the first in her family to become born-again and the first to become a minister. She is the first woman to chair World Vision, the largest Christian relief organization in the world. She is also the first female Presbyterian president of the American Baptist affiliated Eastern College, and the first woman president in the Christian College Coalition, an association of seventy-seven Christian colleges nationwide. At Eastern, Hestenes has pushed the school in new directions, reaching out to Christians in South America, Europe, Africa, and Asia.

A CONVERSATION WITH
ROBERTA HESTENES

Visited at the campus of Eastern College near Philadelphia, Pennsylvania, Roberta Hestenes has lead a life of "firsts." The first daughter of her parents, she is the first in her family to become born-again and the first to become a minister. She is the first woman to chair World Vision, the largest Christian relief organization in the world. She is also the first female Presbyterian president of the American Baptist affiliated Eastern College, and the first woman president in the Christian College Coalition, an association of seventy-seven Christian colleges nationwide. At Eastern, Hestenes has pushed the school in new directions, reaching out to Christians in South America, Europe, Africa, and Asia.

A CONVERSATION WITH
Dr. Roberta Hestenes

Roberta Hestenes is no stranger to "firsts." She was the first in her family to be born again. She was the first to enter the ministry. She was also the first woman to serve on the board and later the first woman to chair World Vision, the largest Christian relief organization in the world. She is the first woman Presbyterian president of the American Baptist-affiliated Eastern College near Philadelphia, Pennsylvania. In fact, she is the first woman president in the Christian College Coalition, an association of seventy-seven Christian colleges nationwide.

HUGH HEWITT: Dr. Roberta Hestenes, thank you for joining us.

ROBERTA HESTENES: Thank you for asking.

HUGH HEWITT: Who is Jesus Christ?

ROBERTA HESTENES: First of all, He is my own Lord and Savior. But more importantly, He is God who came in the flesh to be with us and to share our life and to show us what God is like. And then He died and was resurrected and exists with God eternally. And He is the center of the Christian faith. He's the center of my own life. He is the most important figure in human history, I believe. And millions of others believe, I think, that Jesus is what it's all about.

HUGH HEWITT: People speak about knowing Jesus Christ. What's that mean?

ROBERTA HESTENES: Well, I suspect in our journeys of faith that there are different experiences for people. People come at this in such different ways, but let me tell you my story. My family wasn't Christian. In fact, my parents were upset about the Christian faith to such an extent that they didn't allow us to go to church. And so I grew up hungry for something, not knowing what I was searching for, but knowing that there was a vacuum inside. There was a hunger there.

I started going to church on my own in high school. And then I went off to college, and I said, "I'm going to get this stuff settled one way or another." But nothing happened. I tried to read the Bible, but I couldn't make sense out of it. And so I just went along until one day a faculty person said to me, "I have a very important question to ask you."

HUGH HEWITT: What's that?

ROBERTA HESTENES: "Do you know Jesus?" And I knew intuitively that there was only one thing that I could do with that question, which was lie. I didn't have a clue what he was talking about. And so I said, "Well, yes. Of course." And the inner dialogue was almost as if *I'm an American, aren't I?* but he began to talk about an experience he had had with Christ, one that had moved from a theoretical, abstract knowledge to a personal relationship with God through Christ.

And I can remember that day—the emotions and the feelings and the questions. And I didn't have a Bible. I was very poor. (I was on a full scholarship.) And I had just a little bit of money that I had saved laboriously. And I went to a bookstore and I said, "Do you sell Bibles?" And I bought a Bible that day and started to read it.

And that afternoon I was with this faculty friend in a home. And they were talking about knowing Christ, knowing God in a personal way. As they talked, I remember praying, "God, if You really can be personal, and if You want to or You're willing to know a person like me, then here I am." That night I went back to my dorm, and when I woke up the next morning I knew something tremendous had happened inside of me. I knew that God was real, that God was close, and that I was different.

HUGH HEWITT: What happened?

ROBERTA HESTENES: I didn't have the language at the time; the language I would use now is that I was born again. The relationship had moved from a kind of knowing. What does it mean to know God? One person has said that faith is a kind of meeting. And I think I met God. I'd heard about Him before, but now we'd been introduced.

HUGH HEWITT: Does that conversion experience have a physical sensation to it? What is it all about? People who have not had it are curious.

ROBERTA HESTENES: Well, I think this is so. How do you take the deepest realities and put them into words? It's very hard to do. But for me, there was a sense of being grasped. It wasn't a sense of my talking myself into something. It wasn't a sense of stepping out into the unknown. It was a sense of saying, "I'm here if You are," and then finding that God was there. So I didn't hear voices. I didn't have an ecstatic experience. But there has been a reality from that time to this that I don't adequately know how to put into words. I can say that it is a sense of God with me through Jesus that was and has been very real. And things changed in my life. I think one of the evidences of faith is not just what you feel or what you think, but the fact that your life changes. And my life began to change.

HUGH HEWITT: When I talk about knowing someone in the here and now, like knowing a good friend, I can tell you a lot about that friend. I can tell you his or her habits, where that person lives. When you speak about Jesus, can you speak about knowing Jesus in the same kinds of phrases that you might use to describe how you know your husband or how you know your children?

ROBERTA HESTENES: In some ways even more. I think that there is always a mystery about knowing the human person. And in some ways there is a greater mystery about God. I don't think that we know God in the sense that we put God in a box and have it all nailed down. There's mystery and wonder and awe and all of that, but the most important thing to know about people is if they are trustworthy. What are they like really? Are they caring? Are they at some level for me or against me? In any relationship, I think you ask yourself, "Is this person just all for himself, or does he really care about who I am?" And I think that I can say, with millions of Christians around the world and down through the centuries, that God as we know Him in Jesus is a caring, trustworthy, loving, reliable, worthy, honorable person.

> In any relationship, I think you ask yourself, "Is this person just all for himself, or does he really care about who I am?" And I think that I can say, with millions of Christians around the world and down through the centuries, that God as we know Him in Jesus is a caring, trustworthy, loving, reliable, worthy, honorable person.

HUGH HEWITT: So Jesus knows Roberta Hestenes?

ROBERTA HESTENES: Better than I know myself.

HUGH HEWITT: You are firmly convinced of that? Of the billions of people on this planet who have come before you and after you, He knows you?

ROBERTA HESTENES: Oh, yes. And that belief comes partly out of my own understanding of the Scripture, because one of the ways we know Jesus is through the Scripture. Through Scripture we know that God is the Creator. And just as I have an understanding of what I create, God has complete understanding of me, for I am His creation.

HUGH HEWITT: But let me ask you a troubling question about God. You grew up in a family without God. Why would God allow that to happen? Why would He allow you to go eighteen or twenty years without that embrace, that grasping that you referenced?

ROBERTA HESTENES: That's an interesting question. Let me put it in a different framework. My father was hostile when I became a Christian because he thought of Christians as hypocrites, people who said one thing and lived another thing. And he said to me, "It's too bad we didn't bring you up in the church.

Because if we had brought you up in the church, then you would never have become the kind of believer that you are now."

He believed that if he had brought me up inside the church, I would have been vaccinated against the real thing. And I think that sometimes people are so used to their own faith tradition that they are in fact inoculated against the real thing. And so I think that God was quite gracious to me. I think that people have different spiritual journeys, and God reaches to them in different ways. But for me, I knew I had a real conversion experience.

HUGH HEWITT: Why were your parents so hostile to God and religion?

ROBERTA HESTENES: Well, I think at root it was because my father had been raised in the Catholic tradition, my mother had been raised in the Baptist tradition, and it was at a time when it was assumed that both could not be Christian. If one was, the other wasn't. When my parents decided to marry, their families excommunicated them. Both families told them the marriage was wrong and unforgivable. And so they responded to that conflict by saying, in effect, "A pox on both of your houses. We won't have anything to do with any kind of religion. We won't let our children be contaminated by your hatred and distrust and conflict." They thought that they were doing the right thing to protect us from that.

My father died quite soon after my conversion, but when my mother came to the end of her life, she was a convinced and committed Christian. At one point Mother said that they hadn't realized that we all have a hunger and that faith is designed to help fill that hunger, and so they had left that hunger in our lives. And it was the same vacuum that was in their own lives. They had gotten rid of religion, but they hadn't gotten rid of our need and search for God.

HUGH HEWITT: What happens to the new convert? What happened to you in college immediately after this experience?

ROBERTA HESTENES: Well I suspect different things happen to different people. I had the wonderful fortune of coming to faith in a small community of loving, caring people. My family had been dysfunctional. My father was an alcoholic. There had been pain and struggle in my family, and I really didn't believe that love was possible. I thought people used each other. I was quite a cynic at the age of eighteen. I thought that if people had to be used or climbed on to get ahead, that was only to be expected. I was taught that.

But I came to faith in a caring community. I was informally adopted into a family, and they were wonderful people. I sat in on a lot of small-group Bible studies and learned the Bible. We formed a little Christian fellowship on the campus and started to do outreach Bible studies. We'd invite people in the dorm to these studies even though none of us knew much of anything, and we opened the Gospels and read about Jesus. And an astonishing thing happened; people would come to faith, over and over and over again.

Others would make fun of us, saying, "Isn't it very medieval to actually believe in God through Christ?" And we were discovering that it made sense out of life. Reading Plato's works made more sense when I read them from a Christian perspective. The same thing happened when I read Augustine, when I read the founding fathers, when I read history and science. All of that made more sense as a result of having a firm place to stand, rooted in a relationship with God through Christ.

HUGH HEWITT: When, as you put it, Christ grasps you, are you suddenly without sin? Do you become a perfect person? What happens?

ROBERTA HESTENES: Isn't that the fallacy? So often? Because it is so far from the truth! When I went home and told my family what had happened, there was a fair amount of scoffing and cynicism. And I was not wise in the way in which I shared my faith. I was so excited about it that I wasn't appropriately humble as I told my story. I wanted them to make the same discovery that I had . . . immediately.

My sister had my number, because she assumed that Christians claimed to be perfect. But to confess to be a Christian is not making any such claim at all. It's really an acknowledgment that I am a person who needs God. I am a person who is helped by God. I am a person who has been met by God. But being a Christian doesn't instantly turn us into something other that what we've been. Well, my sister said, "Okay, now that you're perfect I expect you to do the dishes every night." And I actually bought that for about a week—one of the stupidest things that I ever bought! And then I realized that being a Christian doesn't mean that I think that I am perfect, and God certainly knows that I am not perfect, and I at the beginning of a journey. And I think that when we become Christians, we are more sensitive to our faults than ever before.

HUGH HEWITT: Beginning of a journey to where?

ROBERTA HESTENES: Well ultimately it is a journey that leads to heaven, that leads to eternal life with God. I think that it is a journey in which you never know what is around the next corner.

HUGH HEWITT: Let's pause here for a second. What does "eternal life with God" mean to you?

ROBERTA HESTENES: Well, eternal life with God is something that doesn't disappear; it lasts. The Bible talks about this eternal life, and it also talks about abundant life. Abundant life is life the way that God meant it to be—full of love, joy, peace, patience, goodness, kindness, self-control.

I think of the Apostle Paul's life when he was at the end of his journey. He was in prison, and he was soon going to be executed by the Romans for his faith. He said, not that he had attained anything or had already been made perfect: "I press on to take hold of that for which Christ Jesus took hold of me. . . . Forgetting what is behind and straining toward what is ahead, I press on toward the goal to win the prize for which God has called me heavenward in Christ Jesus." So I think that eternal and abundant life is a journey in character. I think that life is a laboratory for learning how to love. It is not that we come into it knowing how to do that. But if we are fortunate, we start with love as a young child. But so many don't even start with that. The journey is about learning. It's about hoping. It's about trusting.

HUGH HEWITT: When you talk about eternity, you're talking about a very long time. Do you imagine that you're here as Roberta Hestenes for a very long time?

ROBERTA HESTENES: *For a very long time.* You have to unpack a phrase like that. Are you asking me if I believe that God's life in me means that I will survive death, that there is something beyond death, that death is not the end, that the grave is not the final word? Yes, I believe that. Do I know what life beyond death is like? No. Scripture uses pictures. It uses metaphors. Jesus has one very wonderful sentence about heaven: "In my Father's house are many rooms; if it were not so, I would have told you. I am going there to prepare a place for you." So the sense that life goes on is really about being with God, and as a Christian I do not believe that this person or any person who has faith in God through Christ is extinguished at death. Death does not have the final victory.

HUGH HEWITT: Are you confident?

ROBERTA HESTENES: I am, I am. Through God's goodness I have missed death at least twice. I'm confident for two reasons. The first is the historical reality of the Jesus who was crucified and resurrected. That is what Easter is about. We sing and we pray and we confess that because He was raised, we shall be raised. Because He lives, we live. And second, my confidence is rooted in God's promises.

I have had cancer. And through it I discovered that faith is a gift. I don't think that faith is something that we pump up inside ourselves or that we talk ourselves into. I think that faith is a response to evidence. Faith is trusting Him in a situation in which it is responsible to trust. It's not a stab in the dark; it's not a leap over a chasm. A scholar I once knew said that faith is the resting of the mind on the sufficiency of the evidence. I think that it is even more than that. It is a sense of God holding me.

The night before the cancer operation, the anesthesiologist brought me sheets of paper that told me about twelve different ways that I could die by the next day. It concentrates the mind wonderfully, looking at that. And the doctor had to say, because of legal reasons, "We hope, but we cannot guarantee." And I was face to face with the reality that maybe tomorrow would be my last day on earth. And I was grateful. I know of no other word to use. In fact, later, when I started to write down the feelings I was experiencing, my first journal entry was entitled "Gratitude." I was grateful because I had the sense of God holding me.

HUGH HEWITT: That night?

ROBERTA HESTENES: That night. And of not being alone. I was nervous. I don't mean that I had no anxiety. I can get as frightened and nervous and anxious as anybody. But I had this sense of "I am not alone. I am being cared for. At the heart of the universe is love."

HUGH HEWITT: Let's pause here for a moment on that night. It was a dark night of the soul. Besides feeling grateful, were you angry? You must have been very young at that time. And you had a career ahead of you. What was your reaction? Did you see God as an unjust God in an uncaring world?

ROBERTA HESTENES: Career wasn't an issue at all. But I had three children, and my children were still home. So the question that I had was, "Lord, are You positive that this isn't the wrong time for me to die?" So I did all that bargaining that people do in this kind of situation.

But angry? No. At one level, what good would it do to shake your fist in the face of an uncaring universe? It's only if you believe that there is a God that it makes any sense to get angry. And there are times when I have been mad at God. There have been times when I have said, "I don't think that this universe is being run the way I think it ought to be run." I have stood in famine camps, in places in Africa that have absolutely torn and broken my heart. And the question that comes is "Why?" And so those struggles, those questions *Isn't there a better way?* and *Isn't there another way?* are real.

> I don't think that faith is something that we pump up inside ourselves or that we talk ourselves into. I think that faith is a response to evidence. Faith is trusting Him in a situation in which it is responsible to trust. It's not a stab in the dark; it's not a leap over a chasm.

HUGH HEWITT: We'll come back to the why. I want to spend a lot of time on the why, as a matter of fact. But before we leave the hospital room, what do you pray in a situation like that, when your mind is "wonderfully focused," as Samuel Johnson used to say?

ROBERTA HESTENES: I have been there twice. There was the cancer, and just six weeks ago I had a heart attack. My heart actually stopped in the operating room, while I was conscious, and I heard the surgeon say, "Uh-oh." Because of the procedure, they hadn't wanted to put me totally under with anesthesia, so I was a bit in a twilight zone but still very conscious of what was going on. And I think at that moment I prayed a prayer much like the prayer of Jesus when He was in Gethsemane.

When Jesus was in the Garden of Gethsemane, He struggled with what was to come. And I think I struggled. But ultimately His prayer was, "Father, if You are willing, take this cup from me; yet not my will, but Yours be done." For me the issue was, *Do I trust the goodness of God enough so that I can relax and let myself experience what will be?* I'm a coward. I would much rather not, thank you. But in that moment, I prayed, "Lord, I'd rather wake up in the morning. I'd rather raise my children. But I trust You to be good." And that had not come easily for me. No, that had not come easily.

HUGH HEWITT: If you don't mind, I'd like to hear some more about your recent heart attack, because it does bring a glimpse of what we are all going to look at someday, which is mortality. How does Jesus figure into that conversation, to you, a dedicated evangelical Christian? Are you having a conversation with Him in the emergency room or the ward or wherever?

ROBERTA HESTENES: There's a famous saying: "Work as if everything depended on you, and then pray as if everything depended on God." And so you do what you should do. You take your medical treatment, the advice that your doctors have given you. But it's wonderful to be able to pray. And you can pray in an operating room.

I'll tell you one story. When I had cancer, I had to have radiation. Every day for a period of about three months I had radiation treatment, and it's a frightening experience. At least for me, it was. They strapped me down to this table, and I had these enormous machines over me. And then they got it all ready, and the technicians ran like mad to get out of the room. (If it was so safe, why were they running so fast?) And then the technician in the next room pushes a button that starts this treatment which lasts some period of time.

To handle all that, I prayed. And I couldn't hear anything from the next room, so I thought the room was soundproof. So I sang. For me, gospel hymns and renewal choruses and hymns of the church are wonderful faith builders. So I was singing these hymns. Three months went by. It was my last day of treatment. I got off the table, walked out, went around to shake hands with all of the people who had overseen my treatment for these three months . . . and they told me how much they had enjoyed my hymn singing! It had been broadcast in the hospital, and they'd all heard it. I nearly died of embarrassment! If I had known they could hear, I never would have done it. But singing had given me strength to pray and worship, and it was wonderful to have that kind of resource in that kind of circumstance.

HUGH HEWITT: You're obviously confident of your faith, particularly in light of your history. Why doesn't everybody have faith? If it is such an obviously good thing, such a necessary ingredient in people's lives when they're facing difficult nights in hospitals or experiencing any kind of a setback, why doesn't everyone get faith?

ROBERTA HESTENES: There are many different reasons. Who knows all of the mystery of that?

I think sometimes it's because people simply do not know that God is seeking them. It's not really a question of us seeking God. I believe that God searches for us. Back in the Garden of Eden, when Adam was trying to hide from Him, God called, "Where are you?" And I believe that God not only seeks us, but really wants us. And maybe for some people, no one has ever told them that, or no one credible has ever shared that with them. Or, perhaps their experiences have turned them off.

But I do think that in many ways our culture is so noisy that we become anesthetized. And we numb ourselves. We're watching television all the time, or the stereo is on. We keep our lives so busy and so full that we cannot hear the still, quiet voice of God.

You remember the Old Testament story about Elijah, who was afraid for his life. He was a very courageous man. But after a victory, he suffered a great depression. And he fled, felt "poor me," and was very depressed. And the Scripture tells us that there was an earthquake, there was wind, there was fire, and God was in none of those. But He spoke in a still, small voice. And I think that sometimes we need to find some quiet, we need to take some time to hear God's voice.

HUGH HEWITT: The problem with faith, though, is that if God's love for every individual is as a parent's toward a child, why doesn't God just zap everyone with faith?

ROBERTA HESTENES: I don't know. It's something that I think any thoughtful person struggles with—the problem of evil. How can suffering be allowed if God is good? How can there be so much pain in the world?

I'll use your parent illustration as an example. I have three kids. I want my children to be able to make good choices. In order for that to happen, I have to give them freedom. If I totally control every aspect of their life, there isn't any way they learn to make good choices; I make the choices, but they do not. I value freedom for them. And for whatever reason, God in His mystery values freedom and He has given it to human beings. And in that freedom, then, we have the potential for good and for evil.

HUGH HEWITT: Dr. Hestenes, that works for a lot of people. But I have read of your travels in Rumania, and there you saw sixty babies who had been confined to their cribs all day long, day after day, week after week, month after month, year after year, until they were crippled and could not move. Where's the freedom there?

ROBERTA HESTENES: I have never forgotten and will never forget walking into an orphanage ward in Rumania where every child had AIDS. They had used a needle to infect these children. And my cry, which was deep and still goes on, was not *Why does God do that?* My cry was *Why have humans used their freedom in such a horrible way—to wreak this kind of destruction on innocent children?*

It's what we've done with our freedom, as near as I can understand it. And I'm not saying that I really do understand it, because I think that there is mystery here and struggle. But as long as we have freedom, it can be used that way, for evil. And the sad thing in Rumania is not that that happened in the past, but that that is still going on today. That government has still not done what it should be doing in order to change conditions in those hospitals. And so there are not only orphans from the past who shouldn't be there. They're still infecting orphan babies. And I am infuriated by the evil that is there. But I don't blame that evil on God; I blame it on human beings.

HUGH HEWITT: But God is the Creator. I'll press you on this a little bit. By definition, God is God and He can do whatever He wants to do. He could stop evil.

ROBERTA HESTENES: On one level that definition is a word game. Because God cannot do that which is inconsistent with God's character. And I'm not saying that people do not have sincere struggles; they do. And there have been times in my own life when I have really struggled with the issues of darkness and evil and suffering. But I have, in a sense, fought my way through. And that doesn't mean that I won't plunge right in and struggle with it tomorrow.

HUGH HEWITT: Tell me about those times.

ROBERTA HESTENES: It's not that these issues are settled. I was standing in a famine camp in Ethiopia for the first time. And the shrouded bodies of babies were piled up shoulder height; they were just the babies who had died that day. And I was handed a child who looked to me to be about a year old, and I was told that the child was five but so severely malnourished that he would probably die. And we did, as Christians, go in there and save hundreds of thousands of lives because people cared.

On one level the question is, Why is there *goodness?* When you look at the world, it's a real question. Can you explain that? People tend to take goodness for granted. But if the world is self-created, or if we're all here just

> Faith is a personal meeting with God in reality—in our brokenness, in the struggles that every one of us goes through, and in the midst of the evil that is out there.

by some accidental happening, explain the goodness that we see, the love and care that are so real even if they're alongside evil.

As I walked in that camp, the mothers cried out to me—as mother to mother. And I noticed that every woman in that camp wore a cross around her neck. They were Christians. That country had been Christian from the earliest centuries. There are people who sometimes naively say that faith exempts us from participation in suffering, that faith is some kind of easy trip we make, that if we just accept Jesus we will be wealthy or successful or prosperous or things will be easy. But that's not what faith is about. Faith is a personal meeting with God in reality—in our brokenness, in the struggles that every one of us goes through, and in the midst of the evil that is out there.

But that reality also includes the beauty and the love and the other good things. And we could talk as long about the places where I've seen caring—where at the human level there was nothing in it for the people who cared. They gave themselves simply because they believed it was right. And that love was at the heart of the universe, and they were participating in that love. And I would have to say that so far in my journey, I have seen more of that good than I have of the other.

HUGH HEWITT: Let's spend a little time on joy and what that means. People talk about Christian joy all the time. It would be hard to walk past even the most secular of bookstores and not see some title devoted to joy. What's that supposed to be about?

ROBERTA HESTENES: I'm not sure. Because it isn't superficial happiness. It isn't that becoming a Christian is a shortcut through life. I'm not even sure that I'd buy the old formula that joy is Jesus first, others second, yourself last, because I'm not sure that you are last. It's more of a dance. And there's music. An old poem talks about the music of the spheres. And faith is like being invited to the dance.

I don't know how it was for you, but I hated it when it came to choosing sides in baseball. I was always worried that no one would ever choose me. And in the dances that we used to hold, I hated the anxiety of not knowing if I would be chosen for a partner. I think it's different today because the girls can ask the boys and not just wait for the boys to ask them.

But knowing that God has invited you and me and everyone to the dance of life, that's joy. Knowing that you're not alone. That's joy. And there are those moments. They're not the everyday moments, but there are those moments when I am with a group of Christians and I'm laughing and singing. Or I'm working on something that matters, and I'm making a difference in a world where everyone complains. At least I'm counting for something good. That's joy.

HUGH HEWITT: How did this happen? It didn't sound like you had a very happy home when you were growing up. It doesn't sound like you had a lot of confidence. I mean, you're president of a college, the past chair of World Vision. This is *success writ large* in the American way of thinking about success. What happened to you?

ROBERTA HESTENES: Well, my own belief is that God put His hand on my life, and He opened doors for me. I've been a part of a community. I think one of the most important parts of Christian faith is not simply the relationship you have as an individual person with God, though that's real. But the relationship you have with a community of people. And to discover that you're not alone on this journey, that there are lots of other people. And I've had the privilege of traveling all over the world; I can go into any country on the face of the planet. I've been in Nepal. Pick a place. I've been there. And there are Christians there. There's a church there. That's a wonderful thing. And I don't think I'm that extraordinary. I think you could scratch millions of people and find that they have not had the same journey as I have, but they have had the experience of God touching their lives and changing them.

> So what do I believe? I believe it is God's desire that everyone would be saved, that everyone would know the love of God. But I think that God has given us such freedom that we actually can say no to Him and He respects even our no.

HUGH HEWITT: Well, do you have the sense of being on a map that's already marked?

ROBERTA HESTENES: No. In fact, one of my favorite phrases comes from one of my heroes, who is in World Vision: "Now it's time to march *off* the map." And the old maps in the Middle Ages used to say, out there in the middle, "There be dragons." And to me, part of life is about marching off the map, right into the area where there are dragons.

HUGH HEWITT: Doing the St. George thing.

ROBERTA HESTENES: And finding out that dragons can be conquered . . . that love can take you right to the end of the earth.

HUGH HEWITT: In just a second I want to go to practicalities of living the faith-filled life. But first I want to do a difficult thing with theology. In Christian theology there is a very large school, not exclusive, that teaches, "If you don't go in, you never get to get in." I think of the fourteenth chapter of Luke and the people who turned down the master's supper invitation. They don't get to come back in, and there is an implicit condemnation of people who turn away from God. Do you believe in eternal damnation? Do you see what Jonathan Edwards saw, sinners in the hands of an angry God?

ROBERTA HESTENES: It's important to know that during the Great Awakening and the revivals, Jonathan Edwards preached months-long sermons on First Corinthians, chapter 13.

HUGH HEWITT: Which is?

ROBERTA HESTENES: Which is on love. It's the great New Testament chapter about love. And love brought about the Great Awakening. The sermon on "sinners in the hand of an angry God" gets all the press. But it actually was a long series of sermons on love that helped—along with the others—to spark the Great Awakening and change American history. John 3:17 says that Jesus did not come into the world to condemn the world. First Timothy says, "God wants all men to be saved and to come to a knowledge of the truth."

So what do I believe? I believe it is God's desire that everyone would be saved, that everyone would know the love of God. But I think that God has given us such freedom that we actually can say no to Him and He respects even our no. He takes us so seriously that He respects our no. So if a Hitler says no to God, I do not have the kind of faith that believes there is no judgment, no justice, no reckoning. Because I do believe that God is holy.

Now if you ask the harder question, What about people who have never heard, who've never known? I'd have to say that I do not know that answer. And I'm very grateful to God that I don't have to. I'm not God. It's not my decision. I place my confidence in the God revealed in the Scriptures. And He is loving and just, and somehow those two things come together.

HUGH HEWITT: Let me ask you about the particular approach of a woman to faith; you've written about that extensively. And isn't it true that the classical way for a Christian woman to follow Christ in ministry is to find and marry a Christian man who is committed to full-time Christian service? That's obviously not what's happened to you.

ROBERTA HESTENES: I did find a wonderful Christian man and married him. We've been married for thirty-six years now. He is a physiologist and biophysicist.

HUGH HEWITT: And you're the full-time Christian server.

ROBERTA HESTENES: I'm the one employed in Christian service.

HUGH HEWITT: Is Christian faith as easy for women as it is for men?

ROBERTA HESTENES: Some would say that it's easier for women. I think they would be wrong. I think that's too simplistic to say. Some would relegate the whole area of religion and faith to the female and talk about religion being for women and children.

In the nineteenth century there was a whole movement proposing that males belong out there in the tough public sphere, making a living, and women are the guardians of virtue and religious values and nurturing in the home. Implied in that was that faith came easier to women and men had to mess with the *real* world. I think faith is equally difficult and equally accessible for both . . . and that faith has to do with the real world.

Let me take a little side trip for a moment. To China. At the time of the Cultural Revolution, researchers outside China believed that in that whole country with a billion-plus population, there were no more than a hundred-thousand Christians. There had been forty years of Communism, Marxists trying to stamp out the Christian faith. Since the Cultural Revolution, when we could finally visit China, we've discovered that conservatively speaking there are between thirty and seventy million Chinese Christians.

There has been an enormous revival of Christians throughout China. There's an explosion of faith in China. When we looked carefully into the reason for that, we discovered what the Chinese call "meeting points," house churches. Like in the early church, Chinese Christians have met, without any official approval, in homes. We also discovered that by-and-large, between seventy-five and ninety percent of the house church leaders throughout rural China were women.

Why? Partly because these women were not highly regarded. (Female infanticide is still a problem in some places in the world.) The women moved into that opportunity and became leaders of the church throughout China. Some of the men, who were visible leaders, were jailed and martyred. But these

women, because they were women, were not persecuted in the same way; they simply weren't taken seriously. And so they had some freedom. Historical circumstance has something to do with the number of women in the faith, the number of men. The culture around makes a difference. Those kinds of things. To put it bluntly, I don't think women are more spiritual than men. And I don't think men are more spiritual than women. I think that they are partners in the journey.

HUGH HEWITT: Roberta, when you first converted, did you have an immediate sense of what you wanted to do with your life?

ROBERTA HESTENES: Oh, no. But, early on, I had a sense that I wanted to do something in missions, serving overseas. And at an invitation, I actually went forward to an altar and prayed. And I had this sense of *What presumption.*

HUGH HEWITT: Why presumption?

ROBERTA HESTENES: Oh, just that God must have better people to go and do all of the things that needed to be done. I really thought that I would be a housewife and that I would support my husband while he was a missionary or a pastor or whatever. I thought he'd probably be a missionary so that we would do something in a Third World country. And then the door to each chapter in my life opened because someone invited me to do something that I had never thought of doing before. So I encourage young people to plan for their lives, to think about their careers and what they need to do; but the reality of my own life is that it unfolded without my intentionally setting out to do it a particular way.

HUGH HEWITT: Well you've traveled the world. Has that given you the sense of being in missions?

ROBERTA HESTENES: Sixteen years ago, when I was asked to become involved with World Vision International, it was as if the old call that I had experienced was being fulfilled. World Vision is a relief and development agency that works in a hundred countries around the world. And it cares for over a million children. So it works in relief situations where there's war, disaster, or famine. And it works with the very poor, doing community development to help people create jobs and develop better agriculture, better education, better care for their children. And so that is what has taken me into a lot of places in the world.

HUGH HEWITT: So many of those situations of war and famine and injustice rise out of religious disagreements, not exclusively, but many of them.

ROBERTA HESTENES: In my years with World Vision those situations have been a small minority. They are real. Often, though, religion is used as the reason when the real reason is not about religion; it's about culture, it's about ethnicity, it's about history. It's not really the people of serious faith who are in conflict. But the press will use religious language to distinguish the participants. Most of what I have seen has been economic, has been the result of physical disaster, has been the result of impoverishment that left people on the edge so that when a physical disaster happened they were no longer able to cope or manage. So religion has not actually been a major factor in most of the conflicts.

HUGH HEWITT: In history, it surely has been. Think of Cromwell's Roundheads against the Cavaliers. Doctrine has slain a thousand believers in one form or another. Is that impossible for you to understand? Is that something religious people had to grow out of, or is it just the necessary result of being too dedicated a believer?

ROBERTA HESTENES: Well, one, we cannot say that it is the only history because it happens. Two, my own belief is that you are not looking at genuine religion or genuine faith when you see people slaying each other in the name of whatever god they choose to use to do that. For a follower of Jesus, it's quite difficult to justify some of the things that have been done in the name of Jesus. So I think that any time adherents of any religious faith do that which is wrong, destructive, damaging, in their own self-interest, that is not a failure of the religion as some people have said. Jesus can't be blamed for some of that stuff, because no one is seriously following Jesus when they are engaged in that behavior. So I don't think that it is too much belief; it is the wrong kind of belief. It's misguided belief.

HUGH HEWITT: You yourself are a Presbyterian. Presbyterianism is an outgrowth of John Calvin's teaching, and he was not the world's least-severe person in his faith.

ROBERTA HESTENES: He was serious. I don't know that *severe* is a fair word.

HUGH HEWITT: Well, people died in his time because of a failure to commit to a particular doctrine. Does that make you at all uncomfortable with the Presbyterian tradition?

ROBERTA HESTENES: Well first, let's do our history. Only one person died—

HUGH HEWITT: Who was that person?

ROBERTA HESTENES: Servetus. In Geneva. And I wish that he hadn't died.

Second, there were religious wars in the next century; they were following the Reformation and later. I think people often take the Crusades, the religious wars, and they put them all together as if that was the total reality. But they're looking at a fairly small slice of history.

The danger in American Christianity today, by and large, is not that we are too severe with our faith, but that we've watered it down so that it is hard to distinguish our faith from the secular culture around us. And my own belief is that the danger in American faith is not hellfire-and-brimstone preaching. When I hear people talking about being in reaction to hellfire and brimstone, I say, "When was the last time you really heard a sermon or a message of that type?" In the last decade, American Christians have so emphasized the love of God that we have sometimes forgotten the holiness of God. I think the Scripture shows us both faces, so to speak, of God.

HUGH HEWITT: Why, among the vast menu of Christian choices, did you pick Presbyterianism?

ROBERTA HESTENES: First, I am a Christian. That is my most important identity. I did not start out as a Presbyterian. I am a Presbyterian Christian because I have come to the conviction that the reformed tradition within Christianity is a careful attention to Scripture, the Bible, as the foundation that the Reformation was about. We believe *Sola Scriptura*, understanding the Bible as the truthful, authoritative foundation for our faith.

Presbyterianism is a Protestant communion which takes thinking seriously. So it is a place where you live the faith and think the faith. As a Presbyterian, you struggle as you confess. And I have found that it is easy to fall off the log on experience so that faith becomes just feeling. And it's also easy to trip on thought so that faith becomes dry and abstract. For me, the Presbyterian reformed tradition is a good combination of experience and reason. Calvin talked about the Word and the

> The danger in American Christianity today, by and large, is not that we are too severe with our faith, but that we've watered it down so that it is hard to distinguish our faith from the secular culture around us.... In the last decade, American Christians have so emphasized the love of God that we have sometimes forgotten the holiness of God.

Spirit. The Word is the Scriptures pointing to Jesus, the Living Word of God. And the Spirit is the Holy Spirit, who is active and alive in our lives and in history. We need both Word and Spirit. That's good Presbyterian two-handed faith.

HUGH HEWITT: Well, let's talk about the struggle. We've talked about looking at evil and perhaps being despondent, thinking of the children and the famine camps. But, the Presbyterian faith being an engaging faith, have you run into intellectual doubt about this whole construction?

ROBERTA HESTENES: Oh, of course. Pick a decade and there's a major intellectual battle going on.

HUGH HEWITT: Let's take the 1980's.

ROBERTA HESTENES: (laughing) Let's not.

HUGH HEWITT: (laughing) And say we did.

ROBERTA HESTENES: In the kaleidoscope, the mosaic of American Christianity, Presbyterianism would be understood as a pluralistic denomination, meaning that within the denomination the people are pluralistic. The same would be true for Methodists and American Baptists and Episcopalians and to some extent Lutherans; it would be the same for many of these large denominations. Some people within them are more conservative, and some are less conservative. So now the big conflicts in American Christianity are not between denominations, with the ecumenical movement, etcetera. They're within denominations.

HUGH HEWITT: I was wondering if Roberta Hestenes ever put down the Bible and said, "Oh, boy. Maybe this is just a beautiful book written by very talented authors, with a great marketing system behind it."

ROBERTA HESTENES: There probably are people who have had that struggle in their journey. And I am not disrespectful of the fact that there are people who struggle that way. But that hasn't been my journey.

HUGH HEWITT: You have no doubt at all? Maybe Jesus didn't really rise from the dead. Maybe He's just a good guy, a wise teacher.

ROBERTA HESTENES: There's a saying that birds will come around to feed, but you don't have to let them build a nest in your head. (laughs) So that kind of doubt is part of the faith process. Questions come. I mean, I'm fairly highly educated. I've done a lot of work. I've functioned as a theological professor. I've wrestled with all different kinds of issues. I guess doubt is a partner of faith, an accompaniment to faith. But in the sense of bag it? No.

HUGH HEWITT: Can you explain "bag it"?

ROBERTA HESTENES: Well, give it up. Believe I've committed my life to something that wasn't worth committing my life to. I have a friend who has said that even if it turned out not to be true, he'd rather have been a Christian than anything else. I believe Christianity is true. But I also believe that living as a Christian is the best way to live in the world. So when the doubts come, I wrestle with them. I try to think them through. I study. But they don't build a nest in my head.

HUGH HEWITT: Whenever I have talked about religion with nonbelievers or disbelievers (and I draw a distinction between them), I run into the objection that the narrow gate is a put-off to people. The claim to exclusivity to eternal life or salvation, or whatever tradition calls it, is negative to many people. Is there a narrow gate? In your view, do you have to believe certain things to have eternal life?

ROBERTA HESTENES: Jesus used the phrase, "the narrow gate." It's not a phrase that someone made up. He talked about the broad road that leads to destruction and the narrow road that leads to salvation. And research polls show that it's more off-putting, in fact, to not know what you believe.

We live in a relativistic and highly tolerant age. But I'm grateful, for instance, for a doctor who told me that I had a tumor and then told me what to do about the tumor. It wasn't good news in the short run, but it made a cure possible. Because then I could act on the facts. And Christianity has bad news in it. It says to people, "Hey, it's possible to go the wrong way. It's possible to screw up your life. It's possible to make decisions that lead to destruction. It's possible to live in such a way that relationships around you are contaminated. It's possible to live so selfishly that you not only hurt yourself, but you make the world a worse place." That's bad news when I have to face that. But that turns into good news when I discover that God has provided a way to put the wrong right, that there is a cure.

HUGH HEWITT: Let me put the hard question. You're very ecumenical in your efforts outside of your presidency even in World Vision. You've dialogued with a lot of different traditions. Do you believe people who are not Christian can be at complete peace in a way that a Christian would be after death?

ROBERTA HESTENES: Let me rephrase that question. After death, who knows? This side of death, of course. I meet sincere adherents of many traditions, and I don't think Christians have a monopoly on a certain kind of emotional experience. I think you can be a sincere, peaceful adherent believer.

HUGH HEWITT: But do Christians have a monopoly on salvation?

ROBERTA HESTENES: I think that what Scripture says is that Jesus says, "I am the way, the truth, and the life." I believe that. Yes, I believe that.

HUGH HEWITT: What does that mean for someone watching who isn't a Christian?

ROBERTA HESTENES: Well, it's a struggle to work it out, to be honest. And it's one of those areas where I have struggled a good bit.

In the Book of Romans, the Apostle Paul talks about people who have never heard the Jewish law and yet God had put a conscience within them and they were a law unto themselves. And there's more than a suggestion in that Romans language that God is absolutely fair and does not hold people accountable for that which they do not know and are unable to respond to. However, Paul says in Romans, chapter 3, that "all have sinned and fall short of the glory of God." Then he says in chapter 6 that "the gift of God is eternal life in Jesus Christ our Lord." I have to leave it there. I do believe Jesus is the way.

HUGH HEWITT: Roberta, you're the president of Eastern College. Let's say you're walking across campus and a freshman comes up to you and says, "I'm glad to be here because I love this college, but I spiritually don't believe in anything. But I'm curious. What ought I to do?" What ought that student to do?

ROBERTA HESTENES: Ah. It happens. And I'm always glad when that happens. I would tell that student to explore. I'd say, "Buy a Bible. Buy it in contemporary English so that the words themselves make sense to you. Start with the Gospel of Mark. And as you read about Jesus, consider praying this prayer: 'God, if You exist, show Yourself to me.' Read. And pray. And be open. And see what happens."

HUGH HEWITT: And how long does that take, that process?

ROBERTA HESTENES: Well, I recommend a thirty-day experiment. If you read half a chapter in Mark, which takes five minutes, in thirty days you will have read all the way through—from the beginning of Jesus' ministry to the crucifixion to the empty tomb and to the witnesses of Jesus' resurrection. And you could spend ten minutes a day working your way through that.

But I usually recommend something in addition, that you join a small group of people. They don't have to be believers, but it's nice if one or two of them are. Open Mark or another Gospel and start looking at this together. Read it, and say, "What do you think this is saying? What's the story here? What are the problems you have with

> I think Christians are called to be witnesses to the hope that's in them. To tell the truth. To share the story. To not keep silent. To name the name of Jesus when it's appropriate in a way that respects the other person's dignity, in a way that takes the person seriously. And then conversion is up to God and that person.

it? What are the doubts? What are the questions? What are the issues that come for you?" And my only belief (I've seen this over and over and over again) is that when you open the Scriptures with a receptive heart and you're open to what God wants to show you, very often, to use a phrase from a famous Christian, C. S. Lewis, you are "surprised by joy."

HUGH HEWITT: Is it your belief that anyone who does that particular discipline will in fact be converted?

ROBERTA HESTENES: There are no mechanics to conversion. This is relational. This isn't about a formula. I mean, often the counsel will include a prayer such as "Lord, I confess that I am a sinner and that I am in need of Your forgiveness, of Your love, of Your grace. Help me, a sinner." But I don't think there's anything mechanical. I think sometimes people are on a spiritual journey for a long time.

HUGH HEWITT: Do you count the conversions you've been instrumental in as achievements?

ROBERTA HESTENES: No, I surely don't. When I was a young Christian, there was a temptation with some people (I think I was part of it) to think of people coming to faith as if they were notches. I don't believe that anymore. I think Christians are called to be witnesses to the hope that's in them. To tell the truth. To share the story. To not keep silent. To name the name of Jesus when it's appropriate in a way that respects the other person's dignity, in a way that takes the person seriously. And then conversion is up to God and that person. And I think the person has real freedom to say yes or no. And I think God works when people are open. I do think that God is more than willing and does most of the work. The experience of conversion is, "Ah, I found God," but the reality of it is that God has embraced me.

HUGH HEWITT: You've written a lot about Christian reconciliation and Christian healing, particularly of old scars, old wounds, old hurts. How does that work?

ROBERTA HESTENES: I'm not aware about having written about that. May I be concrete?

HUGH HEWITT: Yes.

ROBERTA HESTENES: Two factions in Rwanda have turned on each other. And with machetes and knives and other weapons killed each other. Now, you can come into a situation like that and you can mourn. And you can look at the horror of it. It's genuinely horrible. The death. The destruction. The hatred. The evil. The incitement to evil in the name of ethnicity or "my group versus your group." No matter who starts it, who keeps it going, you can look at the horror and say, "How will this horror end?" If it's an eye for an eye, then we'll all be blind.

At some point, the process of the journey of reconciliation has to start. And so in Rwanda, Christians, Hutus, Tutsis, are coming together. And they are confessing to each other. They are owning the enormity of the horror. This is not easy, simplistic. I can say it in a sentence, but the reality of it is much more difficult. And they're asking for forgiveness and receiving that forgiveness from God. And receiving that forgiveness from each other.

HUGH HEWITT: Will God forgive that?

ROBERTA HESTENES: Yes. Where there is sincere repentance and the willingness to turn a new direction. *Repentance* means "to change direction." There is no cheap grace or easy forgiveness that says anyone can go right on slaughtering, murdering, killing, maiming, and there's forgiveness. No, not at all. God is holy. God is just. But where there is repentance and the desire to go another direction, yes; then there is forgiveness.

On the cross Jesus said, "Father, forgive them, for they do not know what they are doing." But without forgiveness, without genuine reconciliation, there is no hope. So either the anger, the hatred, the war, keeps going on or a new dynamic comes into play. And I, with many Christians in Rwanda, believe that hope is based on the reality of what God has done in Christ on the cross . . . on the forgiveness that God gives to wipe the slate clean, which sounds incredible. And yet where there is repentance and forgiveness, there *is* reconciliation. There is a possibility of a new beginning. And I think that forgiveness is the hope of the world . . . that kind of spirit which overcomes the hatred that will destroy us all if we give space to it in our hearts.

HUGH HEWITT: Dr. Hestenes, when people lose faith, and that happens a lot, what's the principle reason?

ROBERTA HESTENES: I think people sometimes lose faith when the experience of suffering is so great that they can't make any sense out of it. So a lot of people have a struggle, a dark night, and they don't seem to come out of it. They're not done yet. I think if faith was actually there at one time, then many, many times they will find a way home.

I think others lose faith because it interfers with a way of life that they really want to live, with a moral decision that they want to make. And then they find a way to justify what it was that they wanted to do anyway. I think more often than not those are people who didn't find faith in the first place.

Occasionally people lose faith because they've had a terrible experience in the church. They've been cheated. My father, for example was not a Christian. He had a Christian partner who cheated him, and so my father's conclusion about Christianity was a direct reflection of a Christian who behaved very poorly toward him.

So there are a lot of reasons why people have struggles in their journeys.

HUGH HEWITT: Roberta, there are some who would love to believe but just can't. What can you tell them?

ROBERTA HESTENES: Let me put the issue a little differently. I know people who would like to believe. They say to me: "I hear you. I'm glad for you. But it hasn't happened to me." I have occasionally talked to someone who said, in effect, "I prayed, and I'm the same person I was. I was hoping I'd be different. I was hoping lightning would strike. I was hoping I would feel something inside that would change me. And here I am, the same me." In one sense that happened to me when I was first baptized and I went home and my father looked and said, "You look just the same to me." And I realized that he was expecting that all of a sudden I was going to look different, or be different, or glow from within, or something.

And I think of the first disciples. I really believe that God respects and honors each person's journey. And Jesus didn't say to the early disciples, "Believe in Me." That wasn't the invitation. Jesus invited, "Come, follow Me." And when Peter who was a fisherman, and the brothers James and John, and the tax collector with his lousy reputation, and the others heard that invitation, did they know everything there was to know? Did they have wonderful feelings? I don't think so.

In fact, the evidence suggests that they were confused and bewildered and uncertain. And at one point it says that Jesus had set His face to go to Jerusalem, and Thomas knew that waiting in Jerusalem were hostile people who were not going to be helpful but were going to be a real problem. And Thomas, with as much faith as he has at that moment, says, "Well, let us go and die." The faith that was required was simply to walk with Jesus a while. And as that happened, reality began to change. But with the disciples you didn't see it for three years. Even at the cross you didn't see it. You didn't see it until after the resurrection, and even then it took time. As the awareness grew, as the reality broke in on them, these cringing, fearful people discovered that they had good news—something that could be shared with other people.

So I think the invitation is not to buy a package, to come and have your emotional life transformed, to come and have all your questions and your doubts answered. I think Jesus' invitation is, "Walk with Me awhile. Follow Me." And when we do that, in time I believe that gets honored.

HUGH HEWITT: Did your father die a nonbeliever?

ROBERTA HESTENES: Yes, as near as I know. No one knows, humanly speaking.

HUGH HEWITT: Of course, no one can ever know any other individual. Your mother died a believer?

ROBERTA HESTENES: Yes.

HUGH HEWITT: But there wasn't enough time for your father to see your conversion take effect. Is that a way of looking at what happened?

ROBERTA HESTENES: *There wasn't enough time* is one way of looking at it. Another is *Who knows* what goes on inside someone's heart? We don't. Only God does. I've fought with God a long time about that. You talk about dark night of the soul. That was one of the times when I really struggled and there were no good feelings. I wanted my father to know the joy that I knew. And he didn't.

HUGH HEWITT: So you loved him very much even though it sounds like he was harsh?

ROBERTA HESTENES: I cared very deeply. I mean, there were problems, but there was also love and caring and provision and lots of good things. One of the things about being an alcoholic, or being in an alcoholic family, is that you have highs as well as lows. So both highs and lows were true, and I cared about him very deeply. And I really did long for him to know something of what I had discovered. And perhaps he did. Perhaps he didn't. I have no way of knowing.

HUGH HEWITT: Let's turn our attention to the church in America. You wrote that "there are two great mantras in America that are spoken over and over again. They are 'It's not my fault' and 'It's not my job.'" Does it make any sense at all to hope for an awakening in the United States, or for an effective church in the United States, when you're running into mantras such as those?

ROBERTA HESTENES: I believe the church is more effective than people know. One of the great untold stories is the way in which people of faith are making a difference. They're in communities small and large all over this country. If we pulled all of the Christians out of every volunteer organization—out of every school district, off of every school board, out of the Red Cross, the YMCA, the YWCA—as well as out of their own church-directed activities, I think we'd be astonished. There are millions of people out there holding the civic society together, and they are people of faith. And they are involved in small and large ways because that faith moves them toward that type of involvement.

We're so used to what the church does. We take it for granted that there will be a food kitchen. That there will be shelters. That there will be programs with caring. That there will be education. That the children will be taught values in a place where values can be named and taught, and that is the church.

Could the church be more effective? Yes. Is an awakening or a renewal of the church necessary and important? Yes, I think the church needs renewal. I think the church has often compromised with the culture and looks too much like the culture. I do not mean that the church should attempt to dominate the culture. But the church needs real courage to live out its faith right in the middle of this increasingly secular, materialistic, hedonistic society. And awakening is one of the ways in which the church is rekindled.

> I think the church has often compromised with the culture and looks too much like the culture. I do not mean that the church should attempt to dominate the culture. But the church needs real courage to live out its faith right in the middle of this increasingly secular, materialistic, hedonistic society.

Actually, there are a lot of signs of renewal in the country. We may be on the eve of something like this. As Charles Dickens said about his day, "It's the best of times; it's the worst of times." The church has wonderful signs of life and lots of signs of deadness. And we always want more life and less deadness. And that's what we pray and work for.

HUGH HEWITT: How does God speak to people?

ROBERTA HESTENES: By the polls that have been taken, by what people report, people's experiences differ. For some people God speaks through the experience of music and art, in those kinds of encounters. For others He speaks through nature. I was in Wyoming recently, and I walked out and looked at the stars . . . with no smog. And I saw the incredible nature that is there. For some people that's an experience of God. Other people look at nature and see cold masses of material.

HUGH HEWITT: Some people hear God; that is, they say they hear the audible voice of God. Do you believe that? Does God speak audibly to people?

ROBERTA HESTENES: I don't want to joke about something that serious, but on what ward were they? I have never known anyone who has claimed to hear audible voices—other than having an occasional experience when in a major crisis and they heard a word or had an experience that went beyond the normal. But when most Christians say that they have heard God, they mean something like this: "I have read the Bible, which is the Word of God, and it has 'spoken to my condition,'" to use a Quaker phrase. They'll say, "I have prayed, and I have felt the presence of God." That means they've had a sense of being accompanied, of not being alone. "I have worshiped and been in the community of faith, and I had a sense of God's reality in the midst of that community." Or, "I have held my newborn baby, and I said 'thank You' to God because something in me wanted to thank Him for the beauty and the miracle of this new baby." So I think the voice of God is different for different people.

HUGH HEWITT: Roberta Hestenes, thank you for joining us.

ROBERTA HESTENES: Thank you.

SEARCHING FOR GOD IN AMERICA

A CONVERSATION WITH
SEYYED HOSSEIN NASR

One of the foremost Islamic scholars in the world, Seyyed Hossein Nasr has devoted himself to helping the West understand his religion. From his earliest days in Iran to his present position as University Professor of Islamic Studies at George Washington University, Seyyed Hossein Nasr has remained unswerving in his devotion to faith. Although he began his academic career in the sciences, studying physics at M.I.T., Nasr's interest in religion caused him to change fields and the course of his life. He has written extensively about philosophy, expressing his conviction that Eastern thinkers should be given predominance over those in the West. In his book, *The Need for a Sacred Science*, he professes that science is marred by its lack of a spiritual base. Seyyed Hossein Nasr was interviewed near the campus of George Washington University in Washington, D.C.

A CONVERSATION WITH
SEYYED HOSSEIN NASR

From his earliest days in Iran to his present position as University Professor of Islamic Studies at George Washington University, **Seyyed Hossein Nasr** has remained unswerving in his devotion to faith. Born in Tehran, Iran, in 1933, Nasr was the product of a family fiercely committed to education, so much so that they sent their son to the United States to study at the young age of thirteen. Nasr received his degrees from M.I.T. and Harvard, and he returned to Iran, where he rose to become president of the Imperial Academy of Philosophy. Following the Iranian Revolution, Dr. Nasr took up residence in the United States, where his scholarly output is astonishing. Dr. Nasr has set for himself a goal of explaining Islam to the West, an objective he has achieved in nearly two dozen books and hundreds of articles in recent years. Although he began his academic career in the sciences, studying physics at M.I.T., Nasr's interest in religion caused him to change fields—and thus change the course of his life. Having begun a Ph.D. in geology and geophysics at Harvard, Nasr soon switched to history and philosophy. Feeling the tug of his father's teachings about the importance of

HUGH HEWITT: Dr. Nasr, thank you for joining us.

SEYYED HOSSEIN NASR: Thank you.

HUGH HEWITT: Many media organizations, many people in general, have noticed an increased interest in spirituality in the West. Have you noticed this?

SEYYED HOSSEIN NASR: Yes, I have. In fact, since my student days when I was in the United States, in the fifties, there's certainly a big, very big difference in the intensity of interest and diversity of interest, both.

HUGH HEWITT: Does it extend to Islam as well as mainstream Christianity and Judaism?

SEYYED HOSSEIN NASR: You mean, interest on the part of Americans in Islam? Or, within the Islam community in the spirituality?

HUGH HEWITT: Both.

SEYYED HOSSEIN NASR: As far as the first is concerned, yes. Interest of Americans in general in non-Western religions, including Islam, of course, has increased a great deal during the last few decades, and also in the aspect of spirituality in Islam, which is usually associated with Sufism.

There's been a very great deal of interest, which has increased from almost year-to-year since, I would say, the 1950's. As for the Islamic world itself, within the Islamic world one also sees very great draws of interest in the spiritual dimension of Islam, in almost every country.

HUGH HEWITT: You've written that Sufism as understood in the United States, is sometimes not the traditional understanding of Sufism in the Islam world. Can you explain that?

SEYYED HOSSEIN NASR: Yes. It's really very unfortunate, because Sufism is the inner dimension of the Islamic revelation. It is not something that is extra, or that is outside of Islam, or which could be practiced seriously without paying attention to, or without practicing the Islam religion itself. But, there are many people here in this country who are looking for a rapid way of realizing spiritual truths, or having a spiritual life, and who want to circumvent the usual disciplines that have been connected with a spiritual path. And therefore they try to approach Sufism without any interest in Islam, and that is not going to get very far.

HUGH HEWITT: Are there no shortcuts, then?

SEYYED HOSSEIN NASR: No. There are no shortcuts unless God wills it.

HUGH HEWITT: Why is that, Dr. Nasr? Why is it that there are no shortcuts? Why has God set it up that way?

SEYYED HOSSEIN NASR: Well, the answer to that is: What are we doing in this world? From the religious point of view, we are in this world in order to find what we had really never lost—that is, God. And therefore the search for God is not only a part of our life, it is the ultimate goal of human life. And depending on who we are—our tradition, he began to read Eastern philosophy and eventually turned away from a westernized practice of Islam. After finishing his studies at Harvard and even teaching there for a period, Nasr returned to Iran, feeling that his education, though remarkably extensive, was incomplete. He needed to learn the spirituality of his people; he thirsted for a deeper knowledge of Islam. For ten years he studied the Islamic faith under the tutelage of the country's leading religious authorities where, he writes, he "was taught many things not contained in books." Nasr explains that his true education began after his return to Iran, where "Islamic wisdom became a most intense living reality," in contrast to Western scientific thought which never came to life for him in the same way. He goes on to write that he was "set upon the intellectual path that I have followed ever since." In his study of Islam, Nasr has combined his Western teaching with an Eastern bent. He has written extensively about philosophy, expressing his conviction that Eastern thinkers should be given predominance over those in the West. He believes that the enduring questions of our time cannot be answered through rationalistic philosophy, but only through a more numinous quest, through learning to lead a life in which analytical thought and spiritual contemplation are combined.

inner nature, the various forces within us, the various elements within our soul, and our mind, and our spirit—that search can be shorter or longer. But it cannot be shortened if we compare it to what we are, ourselves, and how long it would take in order for us to reach the goal. This should be compared, actually, not to a mechanical model—which oftentimes people are imbued with—but with the organic world. A tree has a certain cycle during which it grows. If you feed it more, if you give it more sun, you can accelerate it a little bit. But if you have negative elements, it slows down. You cannot change the rapidity with which a tree grows, at will.

HUGH HEWITT: So, different souls have different spiritual growth cycles?

SEYYED HOSSEIN NASR: That's right.

HUGH HEWITT: And they have to be respected?

SEYYED HOSSEIN NASR: Oh, yes. Definitely. Definitely.

HUGH HEWITT: Let's return to Islam before we come back to Sufism. In the West, and particularly in the United States, the understanding of Islam is often thimble-sized. What are the biggest misunderstandings about Islam that you run into in the United States?

SEYYED HOSSEIN NASR: There are several which, unfortunately, are accentuated—not by accident, but by ill will, which is very, very sad. The first is that Islam is a religion that is spread by the sword, and therefore there is the association of Islam with war. Now this, of course, is not true. But it has a certain element that has to be studied; that is, the first spread of Islam outside of Arabia was through the Arab armies. Christianity, on the other hand, spread within the Roman Empire and caused the crumbling from within itself, you might say. But once Christianity became the religion of the West, it certainly fought as many wars as Islam or Hinduism or any other religion. And the Crusades were not begun by Muslims; they were begun by the Cluny monks, in the eleventh century, in France. But nevertheless, the idea that Christianity is the religion of peace and Islam is the religion of war has remained in the minds of many Westerners.

The second point, which is very important, is that oftentimes today—in the United States even more than in Europe—whatever social experimentation is going on is taken to be the norm without people even having come to conclusions. Relation between men and women; marriage; single-parent family or two parents in a family; or what you do with children; and so forth, and so on. And whatever civilization does not conform with what happens to be acceptable in American today is repudiated, is rejected as not understanding what is going on, or being backward. Now, among the non-Western civilizations, Islam is the one that clings most firmly to its traditional structures in society. And therefore, many people in America are put off by the fact that "it's not like what we are." The best example is the question of women. For example, many people judge the Islamic world by the role of women. But the role of women in 1896—a hundred years ago—in Washington or Boston was very different from 1996. And in 2096, it is going to be very different from 1996. Why is it that you have to judge another civilization, another religion, according to whatever a particular decade happens to think of what's going on? There are a lot of very major experiments going on today in the West, sociologically, in society. And oftentimes—without those having come to conclusions which could be accepted and lived by—there are results, the as-yet-untold results. And phony results are applied to other civilizations. And Islam stands, most of all, in the way.

Nasr has also deeply examined the relationship of science and faith, particularly in his book *The Need for a Sacred Science*, in which he elucidates the idea that science is marred by its lack of a spiritual base. Nasr maintains that present-day science suffers from a lack of connection to nature and humanity. This disconnection from reality comprises much of the reason behind Nasr's abandonment of a scientific career.

Nasr's own spiritual quest has led him to a deep study of Sufism, which he feels is the heart of Islam. He writes that his greatest joy has been in attempting to "become transparent before the ray of Truth which shines whenever or wherever the veil is lifted. . . ." This idea of accessing an essential Truth is a Sufi one—the idea that one cannot form one's own truth, but must try to experience an absolute Truth, an eternal wisdom that lives only in the holiest of men.

Today Nasr lives and works in Washington, D.C., teaching at George Washington University. He continues to write and teach about Islam, using the power of the word to express his strong feelings about Islam, attempting to help others to see the importance of tradition, the values of those who have gone before.

And finally, there is a very major political and economic reason. The political reason is the fact that there's a piece of land which Muslims and Jews believe they own. That is the Palestinian-Israeli contention over the sacred land around Jerusalem . . . which does not exist for Hinduism and Buddhism and other religions. And the fact that a very great tragedy took place in Europe against the Jews (and not in the Islamic world or other places) has brought this almost-blindness on behalf of Western societies to the interests of anybody other than the Jewish community, which does not want to suffer again as it did in Germany in the 1930's and 1940's.

HUGH HEWITT: Dr. Nasr, I want to pause on two of the points you brought up. One is the subject of women in Islam. The other is the subject of the Western fear of Islam that is sometimes palpable in the United States. First, what does Islam think about women and spirituality?

SEYYED HOSSEIN NASR: Well, this is two different questions. First of all, what Islam thinks and what goes on in Islamic society are not necessarily identical. In the same way, if a Muslim in Egypt would say, "What does Christianity think about killing people, and what is going on in Washington?" you could not identify the two together, obviously. So, let's understand that first of all.

Now, as far as Islam is concerned, Islam first of all believes that men and women are equal before God in the responsibilities that they have for their lives in this world and the possibility, in fact, of reaching God. That is the highest possibility that exists in the whole of the universe, to reach back to the source and origin of the universe. Therefore, spiritually speaking the road is open for both of them in the same way. On the social level, although the religious duties are equal for men and women, the social and economic duties are oftentimes presented in a complementary manner rather than in equality. That is considered to be most important. That is, men and women are to, in a sense, complement each other in their responsibilities, in the bringing up of children, in the economic life. And as far as the

> . . . the search for God is not only a part of our life, it is the ultimate goal of human life. And depending on who we are—our inner nature, the various forces within us, the various elements within our soul, and our mind, and our spirit—that search can be shorter or longer.

participation of women in domains of life other than that of family concerns, that has not been the same throughout Islamic history. It changes from time to time.

For example, at the time of the Prophet himself, Arab Bedouin women had a lot more say politically than in later centuries, because social customs came into play. And people oftentimes forget. For example, they think that only Muslim women put on scarves; nobody remembers that there's never been a painting or icon of the Virgin Mary without her hair being covered. They don't remember that in Georgia or Armenia, which are Christian countries now that they're out of the Soviet Union, we never find that traditional Georgian women do not have their hair covered. These are social customs which were added to the Islamic injunction of modesty and preserving one's what is called *ornament* in the Koran from the eyes of those who are not of one's immediate family—one's husband and father, and so forth.

HUGH HEWITT: And do women follow the same spiritual path that men follow in the interior life?

SEYYED HOSSEIN NASR: That's right. That aspect of Islam, of course, is not manifested externally. But all of the principles which have to do with meditation, with invocation, with silence, with inner fasting, with all of the spiritual disciplines which exist in Sufism, are the same for men and women. Of course there are differences, but that's not a difference in gender; it's a difference between every human being, because no two human beings are the same, whether male or female, when they go to a spiritual teacher. He will not say, "All right, now, everybody take this aspirin." Everything has to be tailored to the particular individual, and there are differences among various women as there are differences among various men. But by-and-large, the same discipline applies to both men and women.

HUGH HEWITT: Dr. Nasr, your scholarship is immense, and it's very respected around the world. In reading the massive amount that you've written, I came to the conclusion that a Westerner could never become truly Islamic, because there's so much tradition that you almost have to be born into and breathe. Is that true, or am I cutting off the potential of Islam in the West?

SEYYED HOSSEIN NASR: In fact, you're not correct at all in this matter. My function is to try to present the whole of Islam tradition in a contemporary language, primarily for the West but also to the Islamic world itself, to the younger generations. I talk about Islamic philosophy, theology, metaphysics, science, poetry, art. And one does not have to embrace all of those in order to be a Muslim. In the same way, if a simple villager in the Congo becomes Christian through an encounter with a Catholic or Protestant missionary, he doesn't have to read St. Thomas Aquinas and St. Bonaventure, and know Bach's *B-Minor Mass* and Vermeer's painting, and so forth and so on. That is not the case. Civilization grows out of each religion; that is, the religion is the center and origin of a whole civilization, and no one will have to know all of that civilization in order to accept that religion.

HUGH HEWITT: What is the essence of Islam, Dr. Nasr?

SEYYED HOSSEIN NASR: No religion in the world is as simple as Islam to understand and to embrace. Because the essence of Islamic revelation is to accept the unity of God; that is, there is no divinity but God. And then to accept the messengership of the Prophet of Islam, Muhammad; that is, Muhammad is the messenger of God, who also confirms the prophecy of all the prophets before the Prophet of Islam. Once you do that, you're already a Muslim. It is very simple.

HUGH HEWITT: And, what is the essence of Sufism within Islam?

SEYYED HOSSEIN NASR: Sufism is also, in its essence, very simple. It's to actually realize that unity. To talk of unity is one thing. But to live in unity in such a way that our actions, our thoughts, our emotions, all conform to a divine center, that's a very difficult art to achieve.

HUGH HEWITT: What is the intellectual commitment of Islam versus the spiritual transformation of Sufism?

SEYYED HOSSEIN NASR: Well, that opposition is not correct. Because even for those who do not practice Sufism, to accept Islam is not only intellectual, but it's a question of faith. It's to have faith in the oneness of God, not only to understand it philosophically.

HUGH HEWITT: How does someone who is already within Islam and who is a believer in Allah make that leap to Sufism?

SEYYED HOSSEIN NASR: When a person is a Muslim, he or she practices Islamic law. Islam (much more like Judaism and less like Christianity on this particular point) emphasizes *doing* more than *theology*.

You say your five daily prayers. You fast. The month of Ramadan is just beginning now, and you try once in your life to make the pilgrimage to Mecca. You try to give alms to the poor. You do not lie. You follow the Ten Commandments. You do not commit adultery. Do this, and do that—like every religion, especially the sister religions of Judaism and Christianity. Those principles are very similar.

Now, what does the *Sufi* do? A Sufi wants to realize God here and now. He does not only want to live according to the will of God that everybody does in a kind of passive way. He wants to live according to the will of God at every moment of life. He wants to remember God at all times. And therefore he wants to go from the element of outwardness to that of inwardness. Sufism is, in a sense, inwardness within Islam. It is mysticism in the original sense of that term,

> Civilization grows out of each religion; that is, the religion is the center and origin of a whole civilization, and no one will have to know all of that civilization in order to accept that religion.

having to do with the divine mysteries. The very word *mystery,* from *mysterium* in Latin, originally comes from the Greek, meaning "to keep your mouth shut, to be silent." It is to go from the world of noise to that of silence. And therefore a transformation has to come about, because we are all scattered. Whether we are religious people or irreligious people, our mind is scattered. We cannot concentrate on anything for five minutes, not even for fifty seconds. It's to be able to concentrate, to bring the mind to its center. Because the word *concentrate* already implies a center. *Con-cen-trate.* The very word reveals its implication, to be centered. To concentrate is to be centered. And so, to find one's center, which is at the center of one's heart, and then to live from that center is the art of being a Sufi.

HUGH HEWITT: There's a commonality in silence. In the course of conducting this series, I've talked to Thomas Keating, a Trappist monk. I've talked to the Dalai Lama. Everyone I've talked to has emphasized silence. Everyone has emphasized focus, centering. Is this a common strain among mystical traditions and the various religious traditions?

SEYYED HOSSEIN NASR: Yes, it is. There is no doubt that there are elements which are different in various mysticisms. But at the heart of all mysticism on the highest level, there is the realization of the center. And in the center there is always silence. If noise symbolizes manifestation, silence symbolizes the unmanifested. There is that reality which is as yet unmanifested. And therefore, in fact, a great and saintly person always lives from a center of silence.

HUGH HEWITT: How long does it take to develop that capacity, Dr. Nasr? Do you have it?

SEYYED HOSSEIN NASR: I do not feel very comfortable talking about personal elements. Let me say that for over forty years I've been searching for it, and I try to live in that center.

HUGH HEWITT: What does it mean to live in the center?

SEYYED HOSSEIN NASR: I will explain that in Western theological language because it is the primary language of this part of the world and because America is the inheritor of European civilization, which is predominantly Christian. To live in the center is actually to live with the remembrance and presence of God at all times. It is to remember God at all times. The easiest thing to becoming a saint is (and it's the easiest thing to become a saint) that all you have to do is to remember God. But it's also the most difficult thing in the world, because you always live in the state of forgetfulness.

HUGH HEWITT: How does one develop a discipline? Traffic is hectic, jobs are demanding, the speaking schedule is ever-present, the books have to get out, the television show has to be done. How does one constantly remember God?

SEYYED HOSSEIN NASR: That has to do with the degree to which, in fact, we are in contact with the inner human being. That is, you are not only an outer man. Here I'm using the word *man* in place of *human being,* not as male versus female. You are not only the outer man; there's also an inner man. The inner man is always in God's presence. But oftentimes in our lives we have lost contact and continue to lose contact with that inner man. And the role we have in this life is to recreate that contact—that is, to live inwardly with God. And once you live inwardly with God, the external activities begin to carry the aroma of that inner life, of that inner God that we carry within ourselves. And no matter what you do externally, that does not distract us from the remembrance of God.

HUGH HEWITT: Before I go too far and forget, I do want to return to the Western misconception of Islam. As I was reading some of your work, you quoted the Sufi poet Rumi, who put into the mouth of Ali the words, "I am the lion of God, I am not the lion of passion." Perhaps that is the image that we in the West have of Islam—of the lion. A great deal of fear in the West may arise from that image. Is that true, but yet not to be a source of fear for the West?

SEYYED HOSSEIN NASR: Of course the lion is a solar animal, and therefore it symbolizes the divine presence in the world. And Ali—who was the son-in-law of the Prophet, the Fourth Caliph of Sunni Islam—was given the title the Lion of God. And Rumi alludes to that. In fact, this was such a profound title that when Islam came to Spain, Spanish mystics began to give this title to Christ. And the title's survived right into the twentieth century. In his very famous poem "The Christ of Velasquez," the famous Spanish poet Miguel de Unamuno writes that Christ is the lion of God. There are no lions in Spain, but that is a very powerful image. The lion is not only symbolically a ferocious animal, but it's the animal that protects. That is, the symbolic king of the jungle is actually the protector—giving, creating order, preserving God's order on earth. And, you might say, one should not be afraid of it unless one breaks the law of the jungle. Even this film that you have recently made in America, *Lion King*, has this aspect of the good lion as the preserver of law and order.

> The West is afraid of something very profound. I don't mean everybody in the West is afraid, because Christianity is still a living element in the West. But secular Western society, which has come to the fore, wants to live in secularism and not be challenged by any power.

At one time in its history, the West did fear Islam because Islam had taken over the Mediterranean Sea and converted it into what one Belgian historian called an Arab lake. And so Christianity felt physically threatened. The second time Christianity felt threatened was after the seventeenth century, when the Ottomans took over Eastern Europe.

HUGH HEWITT: Up to the gates of Vienna.

SEYYED HOSSEIN NASR: Actually, their army was in the hills of Vienna overlooking the city. But that fear is absurd now . . . if you realize the fact that there's no comparison to the military power that the West exercises.

HUGH HEWITT: Military power is not always the key to expansion.

SEYYED HOSSEIN NASR: Let me come to that.

The fear that, let's say, a bishop might have had in Salonika in 800 or in Paris in the year 900, that kind of fear is not rational. The Iraqi War proved it so well. It drummed up the passion of the fourth-greatest army in the world, and everybody thought they were going to meet the Wehrmacht. And after seventy-two hours, a hundred thousand Iraqi soldiers killed a hundred American soldiers and it was finished. It was one of the biggest fiascos in human history, as far as two sides fighting a war with equal power is concerned.

Nevertheless, you point out something very important. A threat comes not only from military or economic power, but also from spiritual power. Now, the West is innately afraid of the Islamic world—not because, let's say, it feels that Egypt is going to send an army and capture Italy. The West is afraid of something very profound. I don't mean everybody in the West is afraid, because Christianity is still a living element in the West. But secular Western society, which has come to the fore, wants to live in secularism and not be challenged by any power. Separation of church and state in America is only a very minor aspect of this secularism. The fact is that religion has been marginalized in human society; it's for Sunday morning, but the laws on Wall Street have nothing to do with Christ. The few moral laws that remain from the founders of the American Revolution have been challenged during the last decade, and that's why there's such turmoil over the question of abortion, and so forth, which is tearing American society apart.

Europe—which is even more secularized than America—does not want to be challenged by any other world view, even one that would be viable and at the same time not secular.

So in the West the sacred has been evicted or destroyed. And into this vacuum might flow the spiritual value of Islam, where the sacred has not been evicted and destroyed. That is why the West doesn't feel such a challenge from China and India and Japan, the other three great civilizations of Asia. Japan is trying to be more American than America. We do not know what will happen in the future, but for the moment India's spirituality is inside, although the government tries to play the role of a great secular democracy. And of course, China is Marxist.

HUGH HEWITT: Well, Dr. Nasr, you've looked back over many centuries. Now let's look ahead a century. What will be Islam's role in the world at the end of the next hundred years?

SEYYED HOSSEIN NASR: I think Islam's role in the world is precisely to uphold the primacy of the sacred. And it will do so until the end of history itself. Islam is not going to follow the same trajectory of the West: from a Christian Middle Ages to a somewhat-less-Christian Renaissance to the Age of Enlightenment to the rise of secularism and finally to evolutionism and twentieth-century out-and-out secularism. This is not going to happen in the Islamic world. And so, what you're going to have in the future is not the West versus the Islamic world, which everybody's trying to talk about today. It will really be the secularized West against its own Christian and Jewish elements and the Islamic world.

HUGH HEWITT: Dr. Nasr, you've written extensively on modernity and hyper-rationalism's assault, secularism's assault on the sacred. What makes you think Islam has the ability to withstand what Christianity and Judaism have only imperfectly defended themselves against?

SEYYED HOSSEIN NASR: Part of the answer to that question is very complicated metaphysically and, really, very difficult to discuss on a public program like this. But one of the most important advantages of Islam is that it can learn from the lessons of Christianity and Judaism in the West. When Christianity was playing with fire, there was no prior example. But Islam is seeing what has happened to Christianity. In the late nineteenth century, a large number of Muslim thinkers thought to follow Christianity and the West blindly. In fact, the Western approach to living and to reality was much more popular a century ago in the Islamic world than it is today. So, this is one very important factor.

The second important factor is that Christianity is, essentially, a religion of love. So once a religious knowledge of reality was challenged by modern science and modern philosophy, Christianity simply withdrew (after the trial of Galileo, especially), saying, "Mine is the religion of love; it's a question of conscience. Whatever the world is made of, whatever the nature of the physical world of the universe is, that is not my concern." Islam has a message of knowledge, and it cannot remain impervious to challenges which are of an intellectual kind.

And finally, the third and most important element is that the secular modern world is falling apart, and it's falling apart very rapidly. Therefore it's not like it was in the nineteenth century, when the British and French empires were sitting very solidly with a world view that everyone thought was the wave of the future.

> The phenomenon of post-modernism in the West questions not only religion in the West, but modernity itself. Combined with the doubt and suspicion brought about by the application of modern technology, that phenomenon takes the pressure off of the Islamic world and, in fact, off other non-Western civilizations.

Karl Marx wrote that it was the deterministic flow of history. Nobody takes that seriously anymore. The phenomenon of post-modernism in the West questions not only religion in the West, but modernity itself. Combined with the doubt and suspicion brought about by the application of modern technology, that phenomenon takes the pressure off of the Islamic world and, in fact, off other non-Western civilizations. With unbelievable social dislocations, which are getting more and more severe every year, we in America are destroying the very environment which feeds us. Of course there is another side to this—that modern means of communication, and so forth, make the encroachment of those civilizations much more easy.

HUGH HEWITT: It's not as though modernity is falling back; it's reaching into every civilization.

SEYYED HOSSEIN NASR: While it is dying at home, it is reaching into every civilization. It's very interesting, the question of the race: "Who's going to win?"

HUGH HEWITT: Dr. Nasr, I'd like to cover some of the basic belief points of Islam. For the benefit of an audience that doesn't understand much beyond "There is one God, He is Allah, and Muhammad is His Prophet," what does Islam say about why man is here to begin with?

SEYYED HOSSEIN NASR: As the Koran says, man is here in order to have his faith in God tested. In a sense, we are here so that we will remember what we were before we came here.

HUGH HEWITT: What were we before we came here?

SEYYED HOSSEIN NASR: We were as God created us, in perfection. That is symbolized by the creation of Adam—a state in which we were always present before God, always remembering God, and active as if we were God's mirror, which reflected God's names and qualities.

HUGH HEWITT: Why did God exile man? Or, do I have that quite wrong?

SEYYED HOSSEIN NASR: Exile in Islam and Christianity are not exactly the same thing, because Islam does not accept original sin. Nevertheless, there is this fall of man from the state of perfection. And the reason for that fall is, in fact, the mystery of creation itself: *Why* did God create? Islam explains that in a very beautiful saying, in which God speaks in the first person through the mouth of the Prophet. These are called sacred sayings, distinct from the Koran. The saying is: "I was the hidden treasure. I wanted to be known. Therefore I created the world so that I would be known." The creation of the world, and the placing of man in it, was because God wanted to manifest the hidden treasure externally. And created beings, being externalized, would reflect that hidden treasure, that inner reality, and by knowing it bring things back to that inner realism.

> . . . Islam, like Christianity, believes in the immortality of the soul. You cannot get rid of the responsibility of the earth so easily as to die and have everything disappear. We have a substance within us which is born for immortality and which does not perish with death.

HUGH HEWITT: So, then, is a perfection not perfection unless it is understood by an external force to be perfection?

SEYYED HOSSEIN NASR: No, perfection is perfection in itself. God is both infinite and absolute. But in order to be perfect and complete, He also had to externalize himself. If God had not externalized Himself, not all of the possibilities would have been there. God would not have been infinite, because the infinite reality is a reality which includes all possibilities, including the possibility of externalization and its own negation.

HUGH HEWITT: But if man mirrors Allah, why is man such a badly fractured mirror?

SEYYED HOSSEIN NASR: Because God wants man to return to Him through his free will. Because God loves man, and love always implies freedom of will. If you coerce a woman to love you, that is not love. And with love comes freedom. God gives something of His own freedom to us. We are free, therefore, also to negate God. And with the freedom comes this tremendous responsibility that characterizes the human state. Man can experience the grandeur of becoming godlike and returning to God or play a role of god on earth and destroy everything.

HUGH HEWITT: Dr. Nasr, why would God create such suffering? And among innocent people? Not necessarily among men who disregard God, but among innocent children who are born handicapped?

SEYYED HOSSEIN NASR: Well, the problem of pain must be understood in the context of the totality of our reality, and not only our earthly reality. If you only look upon those years of life on earth—from the time that we are born until the time we die—many events occur which we cannot explain logically, either on the basis of divine justice or on the basis of divine mercy. But that's because we are only looking at a part of a very, very long curve of existence, from the point in which we leave God until we return to Him. All of these elements of suffering must be understood in the light of that.

Secondly, we always look at the negative aspect of suffering. We rarely look at the aspect of suffering as a necessity for growth.

HUGH HEWITT: Can that be applicable to a child born without full capacity?

SEYYED HOSSEIN NASR: To say that is to look at suffering in a way which is not metaphysically correct. That is to expect of God's creation a perfection which belongs to God alone. The question How can a perfect God create a world which is not perfect? is absurd. Because when you say create a *world,* that means a reality other than God. And any reality other than God cannot share in God's perfection. And that's why even Christ says, "Do not say that I am good. Only the one, My Father in heaven, is good."

HUGH HEWITT: But people can aspire.

SEYYED HOSSEIN NASR: People can aspire. But being in this world means we are already in the world of imperfection. And therefore a child born blind, or someone lame, or someone dying at the peak of his or her life, they are really parts of the imperfection of this world. We feel that a great deal of injustice has been done to the subject of individual suffering. We have no right to judge that, because we do not know the whole history.

HUGH HEWITT: How does Islam counsel the person who's suffering, who's very ill, who's facing death?

SEYYED HOSSEIN NASR: First of all, rely upon the will of God. Muslims face death fairly easily. One of the leading French generals of the French army in North Africa had captured Morocco. He wrote back to the President of France (or was it Napoleon III, I've forgotten) in the nineteenth century, saying that what astounded him most was how the Muslim soldiers died so easily in the field. And that came from their sense of confidence in God and in God's will.

That is, God wants us to do His will. And if there's one moment in life when we really do God's will, it is when we die . . . because that is not in our will. At all other times, we will to do this or to do that, and we're not sure that we're doing God's will. So we say in the Lord's Prayer, "Thy will be done on earth as it is in heaven," but we *hope* His will will be done. We're not sure. But there is one act in life which is definitely God's will, and that's dying.

HUGH HEWITT: That's one of the things that's very scary for the West, isn't it?

SEYYED HOSSEIN NASR: It should not be. If the West goes back to its own deeper Christian heritage, the attitudes there are very, very similar.

HUGH HEWITT: Tell me what happens to the soul after death.

SEYYED HOSSEIN NASR: Islamic eschatology is very similar to the Christian—not in details, but in the grand design. As far as macro-eschatology is concerned, Muslims like Christians believe that it's Christ who comes back at the end of history, not the Prophet of Islam. We believe in the same coming of Christ. Many Christians do not know that. In fact, we believe that the descent of Christ upon the Mount of Olives will mark the end of human history. After that, terrestrial reality will be leveled, and everyone will be resurrected and judged by the supreme Judge. And so, these macro elements of Islamic eschatology are very similar to the Christian.

There is a great deal of similarity in the micro aspect of Islamic eschatology—as it involves the microcosm, you and me. First of all, Islam, like Christianity, believes in the immortality of the soul. You cannot get rid of the responsibility of the earth so easily as to die and have everything disappear. We have a substance within us which is born for immortality and which does not perish with death. Secondly, we are responsible for our actions in this world. In the deepest sense, we weave a body of resurrection through our own actions in this world.

HUGH HEWITT: Expand on weaving the body of resurrection.

SEYYED HOSSEIN NASR: Well, every time we act, it is as if we are weaving a dress. We're forming a body of resurrection. And therefore if we live well in this world, we'll also die well and go to a paradisiacal state. As the famous Latin adage goes, "He who lives well, dies well." And if we do not live well, we will go into an infernal state. And Islam, in contrast to Protestantism but in agreement with Catholicism, has the purgatorial states.

HUGH HEWITT: Let me ask you to pause on living well and dying well. Does Allah forgive one for past transgressions, as God does in Christianity?

SEYYED HOSSEIN NASR: Yes. The Koran (which for us is the word of God and is by Christ Himself) says, "Never lose hope in the mercy of God." And Islam believes that God will forgive every possible sin, except the sin of taking a partner unto God.

HUGH HEWITT: Meaning having a second god.

SEYYED HOSSEIN NASR: Yes. As the Jewish Decalogue also emphasizes so much. Because once you do that, you have cut yourself off from God anyway, and so His mercy does not apply to you. But one can ask God for forgiveness for all other transgressions—even the great transgressions such as murder, and theft, and adultery, and so forth. And God can forgive.

HUGH HEWITT: But there is damnation. There is hell. What is that as presented in the Koran?

SEYYED HOSSEIN NASR: The Koran is very dramatic about these great possibilities of heaven and hell, which stand before the human soul. And like Christianity (again, the eschatology of these two religions are very similar), the purpose of this black-and-white presentation is to present to human beings a plan for the future of life so as to avoid living in an evil fashion. Eschatology is a very complicated matter. And in Islamic philosophy, and in Sufism, there are very elaborate discussions of eschatology.

HUGH HEWITT: Have you noticed that in the West, hell and heaven have been vastly downplayed? People don't want to talk about hell.

SEYYED HOSSEIN NASR: Yes. And from the religious point of view, that is the greatest tragedy possible. Because once there is no hell, there is no heaven. One of the Christian saints said that the greatest interest of the devil is to have himself be negated by man. Because once you negate the devil, you also negate God.

HUGH HEWITT: Is there a Satan in the world of Islam?

SEYYED HOSSEIN NASR: Very much so. Satan is the personification of the force of evil in the cosmos.

HUGH HEWITT: Well, where does Satan come from? What's his role?

SEYYED HOSSEIN NASR: Where Satan comes from is not identical in Christianity and Islam, but there again we find similarities. As far as Islam is concerned, Satan was an angel who occupied a very high level in the hierarchy of angels. And when God created man, and breathed his spirit unto him, God asked all the angels to prostrate before Adam. And all prostrated except Satan, who said to God: "You have made Adam of clay, and you have made me of fire. Fire is a more noble element than clay. Therefore why should I bow before Adam?" And God then cast him aside for disobedience and said: "You're damned for having disobeyed My commands. But I give you the power, until the end of the world, to try to dominate the children of Adam."

Now, why did this event take place? What does this mean in-depth? It is the following: First of all, the first being who used rational and syllogistic thinking in order to judge a religious matter was Satan. He was the first rationalist, you might say, and therefore a kind of condemnation of simple human reasoning before the grandeur of the divine reality. But more profoundly than that, you cannot have a world without evil, because only God is good and all that is other than God cannot be completely good. That removal from the source of goodness is the origin of evil. It's like the light. If God is pure light, as soon as you move away from that light you already have an element of darkness. Now, that darkness is nothing but the lack of light. But on the level of lesser light, that darkness is real.

HUGH HEWITT: In Islamic eschatology, Dr. Nasr, what happens to Christians and Jews and Buddhists and Hindus?

SEYYED HOSSEIN NASR: That's a very profound question, and it is debated to this very day among Muslims. Let's be clear. The Koran is very clear about having sent religion to all peoples of the world. There's no sacred scripture which is as explicit about the universality of revelation. But the Koran says, "Verily, to every people we have sent a messenger." Sometimes the Koran talks about the Prophet of Islam and the sacred text of Islam; nevertheless, it talks about the other prophets too. And one verse says, "We do not make a distinction among our prophets to that extent."

After the Koran's revelations, the question came up, Who was saved? and What about the other people? And a debate took place. From the point of Islamic law, it is incumbent upon all Muslims to protect the life, the property, and even the religious laws of the people of the Book. Which meant, first of all, Jews and Christians. Later on, there were Zoroastrians, when Islam went to Persia. And when it went to India, for many of the religious scholars it includes even Hindus. The secret why throughout history there were no Holocausts in the Islamic world, no 1492's in the Islamic world, no Inquisitions in the Islamic world, is that Islam forces its followers to respect the Christians and Jews.

It's against Islamic law to do what the Serbs just did last year, and still, just until a few months ago, in Bosnia. You don't have to go back to the fifteenth century in Spain. You can come to our own century, five hundred years later. This would be inconceivable in Islam. I mean, Syria is supposed to be a very rough government. And in Iraq, which has been demonized, what happened to all the Christians there? Nothing.

HUGH HEWITT: But having protected them in this world, what will happen to them in the next?

SEYYED HOSSEIN NASR: Some Muslims say, "Islam has come, and the Christians and Jews and other people of the Book did not accept Islam. Therefore they will not be saved. They will go to hell." Other Muslims say, "No, this is not at all the case." Some say, "We should leave it in God's hands." And some say, "No, whoever follows his or her religion correctly will go to heaven. They can be saved." And I am of the view of the third group. Almost all Sufis believe in this. And the argument which no one can answer (I debated it just a few months ago in Pakistan with some of the great scholars) is that if all Christians and Jews were to be condemned, why should Muslims be asked by God to protect their life, their property, and their laws? Why should God protect people to go to hell?

> The transcendent unity of religions is like the top of Mount Everest. All of the paths that you use to climb up that mountain reach that top. But we're not at the top yet. We are at the bottom of the mountain.

So, I believe that this idea that people are damned is a kind of esoteric idea within a religious community. It exists within every religion—Christianity, Judaism, Islam, even Buddhism, Hinduism, and Confucianism. Once you're outside of the religious community, in a sense, you don't participate in the act of salvation. But I think for the solid metaphysicians, theologians, and especially the Sufis, it's always been this other view—that is, the transcending unity of religions. God has sent messengers to other peoples as their means of salvation, as long as they have not lost the sense of divine unity.

HUGH HEWITT: You write a lot about the transcendent unity of all religions, but at the same time you are adamant that all religions maintain their traditions with great specificity and particularity. Now, how can great transcendent unity be combined with this call to defend tradition?

SEYYED HOSSEIN NASR: In fact, one is absolutely a necessary complement of the other. Let me give you an example. The transcendent unity of religions is like the top of Mount Everest. All of the paths that you use to climb up that mountain reach that top. But we're not at the top yet. We are at the bottom of the mountain. The specificity of every single path leading to that mountain top is extremely important. If you are climbing one of these big mountains, the path before you is extremely important. If you are two feet to one side of that path, you'll fall down and break your neck. It's true that at the end, these paths lead to the same summit. But the fact that they're different at the start of different parts of the valley, that they require different kinds of turning left and right, and different disciplines, that's also extremely precious and important.

HUGH HEWITT: Do you recommend that people change paths in mid-course?

SEYYED HOSSEIN NASR: Only if there is a necessity. The going from one religion to another is always a possibility, especially when a religion has lost its spiritual or esoteric dimension. And there are people who seek certain things which they no longer find in that religion. This has been shown throughout history. But just to do it ad hoc, for no reason at all, I would not recommend at all.

HUGH HEWITT: In some of your writings you point out false spiritualism in the United States. Is that a result of just putting on one religion after another?

SEYYED HOSSEIN NASR: It's the result of several things. It's, first of all, the result of trying to eat a walnut without the shell—that is, trying to reject the formal in the name of the formless and without first possessing the form. What has attracted Americans, especially to Zen Buddhism, is the iconoclasm . . . burning the Buddhist scrolls and tearing down the Buddha image and so forth. This appeals to a lot of people from a Christian or Jewish setting, who are coming out of an unhappy religious experience in childhood or something like that. And they say, "Oh, finally I can throw all of these things away and just concentrate on illumination," which is totally absurd. Absolutely absurd. Because you cannot reach the formless except through form. The main reason for this wishy-washy spiritualism which doesn't get anywhere, except to make some people rich, is that rejection of the forms which God has revealed Himself.

HUGH HEWITT: You cannot reach the formless without the form. Will you expand on that a little bit?

SEYYED HOSSEIN NASR: Yes. You have, for example, these great sages of Islam and Hinduism, who have oftentimes spoken much more openly about the formless, about the one that transcends all forms. And you can hear them speaking: "My heart is open to every religion. It's the temple, and a mosque, and a synagogue. And let the gazelle roam in it." And "Mine is the religion of love." They've all spoken about this—the Persian and Arab mystics; and Sufis; and in India, Hindu seers like Rama Krishna. But how did they get there, to be able to say such a thing? They lived for years and years as devout Hindus or Muslims, and they never ceased to be devout Hindus or Muslims until they died.

> The great mystery of religious forms is that they're not closed forms, like man-made forms. They open inwardly to the infinite. But the religious forms are extremely important, because they're the only doors that we have to the infinite.

We forget that. We forget that someone like Rumi never missed a prayer for every year of his life since he was a teenager until he died. Or in Arabic, the same way. And we want to repeat the utterances which they make after having traversed the whole path and reached the top of the mountain, without having done the mountain climbing.

In Christianity, sacred form is the rite that is given by Christ. It's the Eucharist. Eucharist was taken by all traditional Christians over the centuries. But in the thirteenth century, the great German mystic Meister Eckart said, "I swam in the ocean of divinity until I went beyond the Trinity." And he was castigated by the church for having said that. He said he swam in the ocean of divinity, having gone beyond the Father, the Son, and the Holy Ghost, and beyond the Christian Trinity, in the ocean of divine Godhead. Now, he went to mass every day. So the form was always there. It was the inner reality which the form led to, which is beyond form itself.

The great mystery of religious forms is that they're not closed forms, like man-made forms. They open inwardly to the infinite. But the religious forms are extremely important, because they're the only doors that we have to the infinite. So once we reject them and try to go for the walnut without the shell, we can never have access to it. And we usually have to satisfy ourselves with the psychologization of the spiritual.

HUGH HEWITT: I read your essay on the psychologization of the spiritual, but you might want to explain it for our audience.

SEYYED HOSSEIN NASR: There's a very major difference between the spirit and the psyche; we have both within us. Our body and our psyche are interrelated. When we are happy, we don't have a headache; when we are not, we have a headache. So they interact, but they're not the same thing, obviously. You're asleep in your bed, and some part of you, which is your psyche, is roaming around in California or Indonesia, someplace.

Now the spirit is like that, also. There is within us not only the psyche, but the spirit. And all authentic religion, all symbolism, all sacred art—although it has an influence upon the world of the psyche—really comes from the world of the spirit. And when one rejects that, one transforms the spiritual into the psychological. But this theory, of course, doesn't allow itself to have this transformation come about, so it's we who are making a mistake; that is, we are swimming in the labyrinth of the psyche, thinking that we are bathing in the sun of the spirit. And so, we swim and swim and never get anywhere.

And there is a second element that is added to this psychologization, and that is a kind of shallow eclecticism. As if it was a smorgasbord, a man says: "Well, I love this aspect of this religion; I'll take that. And I like this aspect of another religion." If he says that, it means he's God, that he was doing it. That "I" is the ultimate judge. And so he would not be submitting himself to anything. It's his ego that is his god, ultimately.

HUGH HEWITT: Has traditional Islam withstood this eclecticism as well as, or as poorly as, Christianity in the West?

SEYYED HOSSEIN NASR: It's stood it somewhat better than Christianity. As far as eclecticism is concerned, Christianity began to buckle under in the twentieth century. It really began in the late nineteenth century, with the Theosophical Society and some occultist groups in England and France. It was really in the twentieth century—especially the 1940's in New Mexico, California, and places like that—that so many young people got involved with this New Age so-called spirituality, where you do nothing hard.

HUGH HEWITT: What do you make of New Age?

SEYYED HOSSEIN NASR: I think a lot of them are well-intentioned people looking in the wrong place for the right thing.

HUGH HEWITT: Dr. Nasr, you've seemed to have an intellectual preference for Roman Catholicism over Protestant theology. I'm wondering why?

SEYYED HOSSEIN NASR: Not all Protestant theology. I do consider the Roman Catholic theology richer than Protestant theology. But I also have a lot of respect for traditional Protestant theology—Lutheran theology and the like. But a lot of Protestant theology doesn't stand firm anywhere. Every few years it changes positions on the basis of what happens to be fashionable at the time.

HUGH HEWITT: But Islam does not do that.

SEYYED HOSSEIN NASR: Has not done it until now.

HUGH HEWITT: Are there people trying to do that?

SEYYED HOSSEIN NASR: That's right.

HUGH HEWITT: And where are they coming from? And who are they?

SEYYED HOSSEIN NASR: They are almost all people influenced by the West. They have studied in the West. And then, as soon as they speak, they become the great heroes of the West. It's not only that it aggrandizes someone like Salman Rushdie—who is a gifted writer, cursing the Islamic religion. They don't care whether it breaks down the sacred history of the tradition or not. Since the nineteenth century people have tried to become the Martin Luthers of Islam, you might say, and bring about a kind of Protestant reform of Islam. They're always considered to be that wave of the future. Now, Luther and Lutheranism is a very special phenomenon within Christianity. It came at a particular time, for very special reasons. I do not believe that that is going to happen in the Islamic world.

HUGH HEWITT: Why is the West so desperate to destroy faith?

SEYYED HOSSEIN NASR: That has a lot to do with your question, "Why is it that we deny evil and the devil?" The devil being everywhere, it's in his interest to be denied. And so we live in a world in which faith has been removed for most people. And people who have lost their faith are not happy to lose their own faith; they want others to lose faith as well. They have a kind of missionary zeal. The psyche, the soul, seeks very deeply to have people participate and share in its fall, which then it can convert into a new birth or whatever language it wants to use. That's the deep reason.

HUGH HEWITT: Dr. Nasr, in the assault on faith in the West, that you've written about, science seems to be in the lead guard. Why has that happened?

SEYYED HOSSEIN NASR: The reason that has happened is that science is now accepted as the only legitimate form of knowledge in the mainstream of Western society. Of course by science I mean modern Western science, which developed after the scientific revolution in the seventeenth century. And this science, by definition, is divorced from the world of the sacred. In fact, the term *sacred* has no meaning in the context of physics or chemistry or biology or astronomy. And since this is the only legitimate science, the only legitimate form of knowledge accepted in the West, it's spread and its acceptance eliminates the presence of the sacred in the world.

HUGH HEWITT: Is Islam trying to preserve a sacred science?

SEYYED HOSSEIN NASR: After a century when the Muslims thought that Western science was simply the continuation of Islamic science, science became the subject of debate. It was in the fifties when I first began to write about Islamic science being an alternative way of looking at the world of nature. A great deal of debate is going on right now. One of the crucial questions within the Islamic world is how Islam can develop and adapt itself to modern science . . . adopt Western science for itself without the secularization destroying Islam itself?

HUGH HEWITT: Dr. Nasr, I'd like to turn to Sufism for just a moment. The great Sufi poet Rumi wrote, "Do not seek water, but seek thirst." Can you explain that for us?

SEYYED HOSSEIN NASR: That's a very profound verse, because God is always there and His mercy is always available. He is not veiled from us. It is we who are veiled from Him, and therefore the first step in the spiritual path is to create thirst within ourself. Once we are thirsty, we'll go after the water. The trouble is that most people have no thirst for the spiritual life, and that is why they don't seek. Christ says, "Seek, and ye shall find." The important thing is to have the gift given to us by God to seek—that is, to have that thirst.

HUGH HEWITT: How do you counsel people to develop that thirst?

SEYYED HOSSEIN NASR: You cannot counsel to develop that thirst. You can direct. In fact, many of the defeats, dissatisfactions in life, and despair that people have show that they are, in fact, aiming all their energy in the wrong direction. They should be thirsting for the real water.

HUGH HEWITT: One of the essays that you wrote on Sufism suggests there are as many as forty different stations along the road that begins with intention and conversion and ends with purification of all desire. That seems like an awful lot of work, Dr. Nasr.

SEYYED HOSSEIN NASR: It is a "pilgrim's progress." A person might traverse all forty of these stations in forty days and become a great saint. Another person might take forty years. These are ways of discussing the various transformations which the soul undergoes. It's very much like Pilgrim's progress in the classical book that you know about. Or, like the ladder of perfection that so many Christian saints have written about. These rungs of the ladder, each represents one of these stations, one of the steps that the soul takes.

HUGH HEWITT: One of the distinct contrasts between Sufism and the Christian method is the absolute necessity in Sufism of a disciple to seek out and submit to a Master. In Christianity there is the Ignatian tradition and others, but this disciple-Master relationship is not so predominant.

SEYYED HOSSEIN NASR: That's right. You cannot have authentic Sufism without a Master. Because you need the spiritual teacher. (In Christianity, Christ plays that directly for certain mystics.) Because the whole of Sufism is based on methods of meditation, location and concentration. These are impossible to do without the guidance of somebody else who's already done it. Like mountain climbing. You cannot do mountain climbing without a guide who's already climbed the mountain.

> Once we are thirsty, we'll go after the water. The trouble is that most people have no thirst for the spiritual life, and that is why they don't seek. Christ says, "Seek, and ye shall find." The important thing is to have the gift given to us by God to seek—that is, to have that thirst.

HUGH HEWITT: How do you discern that you have the right Master?

SEYYED HOSSEIN NASR: Even Rumi, seven hundred years ago, said, "Do not extend your hand to everyone who considers himself to be a Master." That depends on who you are; that is, there must be a sense of discernment within ourselves. And God protects us. We have to ask His help to protect us from discerning a false Master for a true one, and vice versa. And that is one of the great trials of life.

HUGH HEWITT: I read your only autobiographical essay, and you're very Spartan when it comes to autobiographical essay, Dr. Nasr. But it seems that at the age of thirteen you came from Iran after a family tragedy or some great dilemma. What was that?

SEYYED HOSSEIN NASR: My father was about to die. He had a very bad accident. I was very close to him. He was my first teacher. Also first spiritual teacher. He was, himself, both a Sufi and a physician. And one of the founders of education in Iran. And my mother also came from a very important religious family. They both gave me a very important education religiously and also in the Sufi, although I was a young boy. But he was about to die, and I was so close to him, my family didn't want me to be near him. So they sent me to my uncle, who was then our consul in New York. And so I came to America.

HUGH HEWITT: Wasn't that a shattering experience?

SEYYED HOSSEIN NASR: Absolutely shattering.

HUGH HEWITT: Did it destroy your belief in Islam at that time?

SEYYED HOSSEIN NASR: No. It never destroyed my belief in either Islam or God. But it led, three or four years later, to a kind of philosophical doubt, which I had by age sixteen or so. I was very precocious in the fields of mathematics and science; that's why I first went to M.I.T. And also, I was reading books in philosophy when I was sixteen, seventeen years old. And so it caused philosophical doubts in me for awhile. But that was settled by the time I was eighteen years old. I had regained, you might say, certitude in the world of faith. Not only from my childhood upbringing, but intellectually.

HUGH HEWITT: But the atmosphere in Cambridge has never been particularly receptive to faith.

SEYYED HOSSEIN NASR: That's right.

HUGH HEWITT: As an undergraduate at M.I.T. and as a doctoral student at Harvard, did anyone attempt to disabuse you of these quaint, traditional notions of God, etcetera?

SEYYED HOSSEIN NASR: Of course. The whole of the ambience. I was not only a physics major, but I was reading a great deal of works on philosophy, taking courses in philosophy. I really was turning away from science to study philosophy and metaphysics. In a lecture, the famous English philosopher Bertrand Russell—himself a skeptic, of course—said that modern physics will not allow one to learn the nature of reality, even physical reality. And the nature of reality was what I was really searching for. And so I decided to change my field from science to philosophy and the history of science. But I encountered many, many people—professors, students—who were skeptical. Nevertheless, I was given by God a powerful intellectual vision—not only sentimental attachment through faith to religion, but also an intellectual one. And that saw me through.

HUGH HEWITT: But wasn't it dangerous for you to dip into other traditions? You dipped into Hinduism.

SEYYED HOSSEIN NASR: Very much so. But I dipped not in the ordinary way, but through the writings of the traditional school. All spoke about the transcendent unity of religions, about the truth which transcends forms, and were extremely respectful of the sacred forms of each tradition. And therefore, my point is (with Hinduism and, later on, with with Zen Buddhism and the like) that dipping into these things was actually a kind of confirmation of the world view which I had already espoused at that time.

HUGH HEWITT: But would you recommend it to someone who was less versed in their own tradition? Isn't that going in harm's way?

SEYYED HOSSEIN NASR: I would never give advice to anyone on these matters until I were to meet with that person individually. For every person, there is a separate prescription to be given.

HUGH HEWITT: After your education in the United States was complete, you returned to Iran and became, before the revolution, the president of the Imperial Academy of Philosophy. Obviously you were honored in your own country. Did the revolution constitute any kind of assault on your faith?

SEYYED HOSSEIN NASR: It was, perhaps, the greatest test upon my faith. First of all, my life was physically in danger for some time. But what was really remarkable (you read about it in books, but it doesn't usually happen in human life) was that within a period of three days—from having six drivers and a general saluting me in the Teheran airport—I became a destitute person walking the streets of London with no money, no status, no passport, just a family on my hands. And I had to start all of life from zero at the age of forty-five.

HUGH HEWITT: Did you despair?

SEYYED HOSSEIN NASR: No, absolutely not. In fact, if I hadn't had children who were just about ready to go to college, I would have retired from the world. I would have gone to a faraway place and spent the rest of my life in contemplation, and nobody would have heard of me again. But I felt I had a duty and responsibility, and so I did not despair.

HUGH HEWITT: What was your prayer to Allah at that time?

SEYYED HOSSEIN NASR: To accept his will.

HUGH HEWITT: And was that a comfort in such a stressful time?

SEYYED HOSSEIN NASR: Absolutely. I was at peace with myself. I mean that. Half of my friends died within a period of the next few months. My house disappeared. My property was plundered. But I lived in unbelievable peace and serenity.

HUGH HEWITT: Now, how could that have been a part of Allah's will for you or for the world? Is that something that you've spent time wondering?

SEYYED HOSSEIN NASR: Seventeen years later, I certainly realize that had this not occurred, the very humble service that I render in this country—of training students, of giving lectures, of writing for the Western world—would not have taken place. I would have never left Iran under any condition.

HUGH HEWITT: Dr. Nasr, one of the things I find fascinating is that after the revolution, you came to Utah to live among the Latter-day Saints.

SEYYED HOSSEIN NASR: That was not a choice on my part. The president of the University of Utah at that time (who later on became president of the University of California), David Gardner, was a good friend of mine. When I was president of the university in Iran, I was his host. And I'd written to friends, desperate to find a place to teach. And he was the only one who responded. He invited me to come to the University of Utah. And that's why I went there.

I would have preferred, in fact, not to go there if possible. But he and the faculty there were very hospitable and very kind, and I shall never forget their kindness. And I did not have too much contact with the Mormons, with the Latter-day Saints thinkers there. I was teaching in the university.

Interestingly enough, I think Mormonism has certain elements within itself which are similar to Islam—for example, the dividing of the priestly function among men. There is not one priestly class, as in Catholicism, or pastors as in Protestantism. There's a great deal of emphasis upon the ethical norms of society and the family. These elements are similar. Of course other elements are not similar at all.

But to be transplanted from Teheran to London to Utah, all within a period of two months, was really quite an experience for me.

HUGH HEWITT: In all these trials, Doctor—whether it was the early death of your father, the philosophical trials of education in Cambridge, the revolution, the exile, or the financial destitution—did you ever rage against God?

SEYYED HOSSEIN NASR: No. You see, it's the question of my attitude toward God. If one is close enough to God, the beauty and the love and the glow of the presence is such that nothing else really matters very much. I've never lost my sense of serenity and peace with God under all of these conditions.

HUGH HEWITT: As we come to the conclusion, I want to ask you about the essay that I found the most interesting for me. It's on spiritual chivalry. What is that?

SEYYED HOSSEIN NASR: This is called *fatuwa*. It is very difficult to translate, really, but I've translated it as spiritual chivalry. It is an attitude of the soul and character which is giving of itself, is generous, is noble. A soul that is hard with itself, but generous with others. That is willing to forego its own comforts for others. And which acts, sort of, as God's knight. K-n-i-g-h-t. I don't mean night, in that other sense. God's knight, God's *chevalier*, and therefore the word *chivalry*.

And this chivalry is very important to Sufism. It's also very important in Islamic spirituality in general. Ali was the personification of it in Islamic tradition and is, to this day, for both Sunnis and Shi'ites. And perhaps through contact with Islamic sources, the Order of the Knights appeared in the Christian form in the Middle Ages, but without any precedence. Spiritual chivalry has nothing whatsoever to do with the Roman Empire. It's something which the modern world has lost.

HUGH HEWITT: Well, you wrote (and I paraphrase) that Abraham was the initiator. He passed the concept of spiritual chilvalry to Isaac, Isaac to Jacob, Jacob to Joseph. From there to Christianity. And from Christianity through the Prophets to Ali. So this is a unifying force among all the great religions?

SEYYED HOSSEIN NASR: Exactly. It's a line that connects prophecy itself, which comes from Abraham, the father—monotheism through Moses and Christ to the Prophet of Islam. It's an attitude. It's a kind of spiritual attitude toward the world that had to do, also, with initiation . . . with a kind of mystical attachment that goes back to Abraham.

HUGH HEWITT: There is within Islam, as there is within Protestant theology, a fundamentalist movement which is understood by the media to be backward-looking, or very severe, very hard. Does spiritual chivalry exist within that movement in Islam?

SEYYED HOSSEIN NASR: Even within that movement. First of all, the term *Islam fundamentalism* is a very unfortunate appellation which came in 1979. Before that, fundamentalism was associated with a Christian-Protestant phenomenon in America, not even in Europe. And it meant people who took the

Bible literally, and they did not like many of the things that were going on in American civil society, and so forth and so on. Islam fundamentalism was something very different. Oftentimes it meant the political use of Islam for certain goals which, in fact, Protestants in America did not have at all. The word *fundamentalism* was demonized, too, so it was the kind of word used for whatever people didn't like. And it covered too big a spectrum; it had so many different things in it that it didn't really mean anything.

What do we mean by Islamic fundamentalism? The fundamental element is that religion is permanent, immutable, and it's real. This is essential, and it's something that so-called Islamic fundamentalism and Christian fundamentalism share. That is, God's laws and God's commands must determine how we live—not that how we live must determine what God's commands are.

There is now much virulent opposition to what is called Islamic fundamentalism. And some of it is politically radical. The main question (which really is fundamental to the future) is What determines our attitude toward the spiritual, toward religion, toward God? For some people, the times (whatever they call the times) determine the interpretation of God and God's laws. For others, God and His laws must determine the times. This is the deepest chasm. It separates two different ways of looking at life and looking at the world.

And that's why I've said that there are many people in the West who, deep-down, are much closer to the Islamic world than they are to what you call the West. So often today people say: "Oh, but this is 1995. Why do we have to do things the way they were done a thousand or two thousand years ago?" Now, what is so special about 1995? It will soon be like 1985, which is already prehistory for some young people. And so this struggle is a very important one that is not going to go away. And in this sense, Christian fundamentalism and Islamic fundamentalism have much in common.

HUGH HEWITT: Let me ask you about the general search for God. And I know you don't want to make recommendations to people unless you've met them on an individual level, but our audience won't have that opportunity. What do you recommend to people who are interested in the sacred? What ought they to do?

SEYYED HOSSEIN NASR: If they are already within a religion, they should, first of all, deepen their study of that religion. Learn its tradition before the advent of modernism, before the narrowing-down of the expanse of the view of religion by all the forces that have oppressed it in the last few centuries. Try to go deeper into that.

For those who are outside of all religion but nevertheless have a need for the discovery of the sacred, I recommend they try to study the various sacred traditions. The historical religions. By that I mean religions like Christianity, Judaism, Islam, Hinduism, Buddhism, Confucianism, Taoism, and the like. Not things invented by someone living somewhere and collecting money from his disciples. I mean authentic religions that have proven themselves over the millennia, and over the centuries. To study those with an open heart and open mind, and to see what is more conducive to their inner nature. And, on another level, to try

> The fundamental element is that religion is permanent, immutable, and it's real. This is essential, and it's something that so-called Islamic fundamentalism and Christian fundamentalism share. That is, God's laws and God's commands must determine how we live—not that how we live must determine what God's commands are.

to approach the sacred as much as possible through the two great sacred arts which we have in this world. One is the world of nature, which is God's creation, which we are destroying so rapidly. And one is the sacred art of the great religions. Various religions of the world—where, without theology and philosophy and the need to learn languages, one is confronted with the deepest message of those religious universes.

HUGH HEWITT: Dr. Nasr, in your writings on the contemplative life you strike those two themes—be a contemplative in nature and be a contemplative before great art.

SEYYED HOSSEIN NASR: That's right. Those are very deeply interrelated, and they're really a kind of mercy from God in a world such as ours, where ugliness is everywhere. I mean, it's so difficult to find beauty. To be fed by that. That is not a luxury. That is something which feeds the soul at its deepest level.

HUGH HEWITT: So the path to God begins, for some at least, with objects of beauty both natural and man-made?

SEYYED HOSSEIN NASR: With an examination of ourselves, of how we respond to those objects of beauty. You must seek those objects of beauty which, in fact, cause a response within us, because different human beings are made in different ways. Let's say, for example, that a person who is very musically inclined searches within the Western musical tradition. If the soul opens up to it, that person will be spiritually fed by Gregorian chant or some Bach choral work such as the *B-Minor Mass,* the great masterpieces which are really sacred music of a high level. If a person, in fact, is not sonorous and musical, but is visual, then that person could go after the view of icons or Islamic calligraphy or Hindu statuary or whatever it is that one has access to.

HUGH HEWITT: What do you make of the great proliferation of the works of Rumi? All of a sudden, this ancient poet is everywhere on Western bookshelves.

SEYYED HOSSEIN NASR: That's the proof (if there need be proof) that the spirit does not die. In the middle of this desert the thirst of people for literature which has a spiritual message must be very, very great. Otherwise Rumi would not be such a popular poet—even here, where language itself is being desecrated, where the Bible is being turned into base English, where all the beautiful literature of the English language is being torn apart for all kinds of political correctness.

HUGH HEWITT: Let us conclude with that which will conclude all time. In the West and in some circles of Christianity, there's a great deal of thought and effort given over to predicting the world's end. And as the millennium approaches, people get very nervous in some circles. Does Islam give much time over to worrying about the end days and when it will occur?

SEYYED HOSSEIN NASR: Certainly there are people who have worried about it or do worry about it. And there are people within the Islamic world who are expecting the coming of Mahdi—that is, the figure who will presage the coming of Christ very soon. There is no doubt about that.

HUGH HEWITT: Does the end times portend revolution and war and great upheaval?

SEYYED HOSSEIN NASR: Muslims believe that a person will come whose name is Mahdi. And he will bring justice to the world where justice has been destroyed. He will remove oppression where oppression has taken over. And he will rule and bring back peace upon the earth for some years, nobody knows how many. Some people say seven, some people say forty. And at the end of that time, Christ will appear in the world.

So the Islamic expectations combine Mahdi and Christ. Now, this having been said, however, many people have recourse to the saying of the Prophet of Islam. When someone asked the Prophet, "When will the last hour come?" the Prophet said, "Whoever predicts the last hour is a liar, because that rests only in the knowledge of God." And so the idea of meditating upon or thinking about when the last day will come (as some television broadcasters do) is a kind of pettiness before God, from the Islamic point of view.

> One has to be a realist. And I believe that, ultimately, truth shall always triumph. I always believe in the famous Medieval Latin adage *Vincit omnia veritas.* And since faith is on the side of the truth, the truth shall always triumph.

HUGH HEWITT: We haven't talked much about the Koran and its place in Islam and in your own spiritual life, Doctor.

SEYYED HOSSEIN NASR: The Koran is a central, sacred reality of Islam. It is, for Muslims, the verbatim word of God and it corresponds to Christ. It is sacred in the same way that Christ in Christianity is sacred. Everything about Him is sacred—His body, even His robe, His voice, His Word, and His Spirit. In that way, everything about the Koran is sacred for Muslims. There is the physical Koran that they carry. The calligraphy which writes the word. Of course the sonorous aspect is significant—the chanting of the Koran—because the Koran was first revealed through sound. The Prophet heard it. And then, of course, the content and the ideas and the teachings. And I can hardly overemphasize the significance of the Koran in the everyday life of Muslims.

HUGH HEWITT: And is it read on a daily basis?

SEYYED HOSSEIN NASR: Yes. You asked me about it personally. First of all, when you say your daily prayers. Every day you repeat certain verses of the Koran. And there are those who, in fact, know the whole of the Koran by heart and who chant it all the time. And, when you go in the Islamic world, you always hear the Koran wherever you go.

HUGH HEWITT: Dr. Nasr, my last question is this: As you consider this fight between faith and secularism, are you an optimist or a pessimist?

SEYYED HOSSEIN NASR: I think optimism and pessimism are both sentimental attitudes. One has to be a realist. And I believe that, ultimately, truth shall always triumph. I always believe in the famous medieval Latin adage *Vincit omnia veritas*. And since faith is on the side of the truth, the truth shall always triumph.

HUGH HEWITT: Dr. Nasr, thank you for speaking with us.

SEYYED HOSSEIN NASR: You're quite welcome.

A CONVERSATION WITH
REVEREND CECIL MURRAY

The Reverend Cecil "Chip" Murray became the spiritual leader for a burning Los Angeles during the 1992 riots. For almost two decades, Reverend Murray, senior pastor of Los Angeles's First African Methodist Episcopalian Church, has striven to create a model of social outreach based on the Christian gospel. From his first days in 1977, through a long-lasting economic depression, increasing racial division and riots, Reverend Murray has steered his congregation from a paltry three hundred members to its current roll of seven thousand-plus. All the while, he has remained committed to teaching God's magnificence and using the power of Christianity to aid and strengthen a community under siege. Reverend Murray is visited at the Rare Book Room in the Los Angeles Public Library.

A CONVERSATION WITH
REVEREND CECIL MURRAY

The Reverend Cecil "Chip" Murray became the spiritual leader for a burning Los Angeles during the 1992 riots. For almost
two decades, Reverend Murray, senior pastor of Los Angeles's First African Methodist Episcopalian Church, has striven to create a model of
social outreach based on the Christian gospel. From his first days in 1977, through a long-lasting economic depression, increasing racial
division and riots, Reverend Murray has steered his congregation from a paltry three hundred members to its current roll of
seven thousand-plus. All the while, he has remained committed to teaching God's magnificence and using the power of Christianity to aid
and strengthen a community under siege. Reverend Murray is visited at the Rare Book Room in the Los Angeles Public Library.

A CONVERSATION WITH
REVEREND CECIL MURRAY

As the senior pastor of south central Los Angeles's First African Methodist Episcopalian Church for almost two decades, the **Reverend Cecil "Chip" Murray**'s watch has not been a peaceful one. Reverend Murray has striven to create a model of social outreach based on the Christian gospel. From his first days in 1977, through a long-lasting economic depression in South L.A., continuing amid increasing racial division and 1992's civil unrest—when First A.M.E. became the trauma center for a burning Los Angeles, Reverend Murray has steered his congregation to its now central role in the life of Los Angeles.

Another event that to this day bears an impact on Reverend Murray comes from his distinguished career as a pilot in the U.S. Air Force. A former captain, Murray spent a decade in the service, first as a jet radar intercept officer in the Air Defense Command and later as a navigator in the Air Transport Service. In his seventh year, tragedy struck. During takeoff from the Oxnard Air Force Base, the nose tank of his jet exploded and engulfed the plane in flames. The pilot made it out of the cockpit only to catch fire from the engines.

HUGH HEWITT: Pastor Cecil Murray, thank you for joining us.

CECIL MURRAY: Thank you, Hugh, for having me.

HUGH HEWITT: Our great pleasure. I would like to begin when you were in the Air Force. You had roughly ten years in the service. You were a captain and decorated for valor. Then you retired and went off to the School of Theology at Claremont. Why did you do that?

CECIL MURRAY: Well I didn't retire; I took an early out after ten years. I had always felt the call of God. But I resisted it because I didn't like the image of the preacher—particularly, at that time, the black preacher. I thought he was too heaven bound, not enough earthly concern. So I shied away from it. And in the trauma of a jet accident at Oxnard Air Force Base, I was called to sit down and visit with myself. I had the extra blessing that my wife said, "We don't have to stay. We can go, if you wish." So I turned in my resignation. I was a regular officer. And they accepted it. I was released and started training at Claremont. I had a job. She had a job. I had a scholarship, I had the G.I. Bill. I was able to go through and complete my training. I never looked back. But thank God for the world travel, thank God for the world exposure. It really helps equip one for ministry.

HUGH HEWITT: Let's unpack a couple of things about what you just said. You had been resisting a call, I want to get into that. But first tell me about the trauma of the crash.

CECIL MURRAY: We were in a two-seated jet fighter, the F-89 Scorpion. The pilot was William Berbich, a South Carolinian white young adult male. I was the backseat jet radar intercept officer. We were scrambling off on a routine mission. We did not negotiate the takeoff. Had to abort. The nose tank erupted. The plane was engulfed in flames.

He was able to get out. I was trapped because the automatic handle that's supposed to blow the cockpit covering did not work properly; it must have been damaged in the crash. So there I was. I was so pleased when I saw him get out. Then I looked around. And there was only the tiniest opening down at the bottom of the canopy covering and the plane itself. I remember, Hugh, "Lord, help!" I took off my helmet. I took off my parachute. I took off my Mae West life vest jacket. I unbuttoned. I put my head through the hole, climbed out, pulled the rest of my body out through the smallest of openings. Then I was able to get out on the wing of the plane.

I saw him running. He was a human torch. And I jumped off to the ground. He says, "Chip! Help!" I caught him, rolled him over, rolled him over, rolled him over. The flames were extinguished, but he ultimately died. He was a beautiful, beautiful human being. And several things came out of the smoke of that plane. One was a determination to make my life count for something. And two, now I live for two instead of one. And three, it is impossible for us not to live as a multi-ethnic village. White male,

Murray ran into the fire and rescued the pilot, but not before the man suffered burns on ninety percent of his body. At the hospital the dying pilot sent for Murray—"just to thank me, just to tell me he loved me," Murray recalls. "And he was this young white southern guy from South Carolina, where racism was—and still is—rife." The man's gesture gave the future reverend hope—that there is a goodness to human nature that supercedes racism. To this day that event propels Murray to work for white and black reconciliation and the ideals of all-encompassing compassion and love.
In 1961, Murray left the service and went to earn his doctorate in theology from Claremont Graduate School in Pomona, California. After ordination in the mid-1960's, he preached in a small church in Pomona, then moved on to Kansas City, Seattle, and then to First A.M.E. in Los Angeles. Today the church's membership numbers more than seven thousand.

South Carolina. Black male, Florida. In a cause bigger than themselves. One dies, the other now lives for two. I was focused from that point on. I was focused.

HUGH HEWITT: What's God got to do with Mr. Berbich dying and you living?

CECIL MURRAY: I think the bigger question is What's *God* got to do with me living? Because I don't think that God would choose me over any other person. Circumstances combined so that he died. I might have died. It's like these two brothers who were standing in the middle of the field, and lightning struck in a sudden storm. One brother was killed. The other, Martin Luther, lived. So I wouldn't ask, "Why did God kill the other brother?" I would ask Martin Luther, "What are you going to do with your life for God now that you've been spared?" I think we are killed. We die through causes that can be explained. We live for causes that cannot be explained. So we make the best of that life.

HUGH HEWITT: Let me ask you about the first comment you made—resisting God's call for what sounds like a long time. What's that mean? Resisting God's call?

CECIL MURRAY: I think one feels an inner yearning. Just as you are very happy in your field, there is something in the chemistry of you, in the alchemy of you, that gives you a ministry immediately. I had this ministry from the earliest. When I was three I said, "I want to be a minister." When I finished high school, the yearbook said, "He is now pastor in his church in San Francisco." They got the wrong city but the right state.

And yet, when I looked at preachers in the city, I saw a few great ones working for their people, but I was too judgmental. The youth are judgmental. I thought the preacher lived too high. I thought he was a little too egocentric. I thought that he was sheltering the system of discrimination instead of fighting against its walls. I thought the church was geared to the elderly instead of the youth *and* the elderly. I later learned that you don't change things from the outside; you change things from the inside. And if you know so much, then get in and help make a difference. I was wrong, and I take my hat off to those ministers—many of whom were making twenty-five dollars a week, fifty, seventy-five dollars a week. Their children staying in parsonages that leaked, and all.

I still don't like the image of the typical minister. But again, that is judgmental. I wish we were radical, with a radical gospel, and that does not mean negatively radical. That means having a program that dares to believe that we can make a difference in this world and in this society. Don't be busy about personal religion alone. But not only personal religion, but social religion, or public religion. We have to change systems as well as people. So we'll have prayer meetings on Wednesday night and worship on Sunday; sending people out feeling good is only fifty percent of it. What do you do with the church beyond the walls? I wish we were that radical ministry.

HUGH HEWITT: One of the things I read that struck me, in interviews that you've done in the past, was this quote: "We hang too much on this business of saving souls." What did you mean?

CECIL MURRAY: I think that it tends to be a score sheet. Bring him to Jesus! Fine, that ought to be a given, that ought to be a given. If the church is anything at all, we ought to be a magnet pulling people in. Now the challenge is what to do with that rejuvenated person. Our homeless ministry—we can't just go feed homeless people alone, give toys to their children, sing for them, take clothing to them. That isn't enough. Can't we find a way to use those who have freed their minds to help free other homeless? They know the secret better than we know the secret. I think that saving souls is something that a religious movement ought to take for granted. We will always get converts, we will always get accessions. God sends us twenty-three new accessions a Sunday. But if we are blessed, we can take three or four of those twenty-three and radicalize them so that they go beyond the pews, beyond the walls, to help us change systems.

HUGH HEWITT: Reading about your life, it was not easy. You had a number of setbacks early on. Your mom died when you were very young.

CECIL MURRAY: Yes, I was three.

HUGH HEWITT: Your father was ill.

CECIL MURRAY: My father died of alcoholism, but he was a beautiful human being.

HUGH HEWITT: But these are tough things. Was your faith ever shaken?

CECIL MURRAY: Oh, goodness no. I think people die even as a child because of causes. People become alcoholic because of causes. And rather than bemoan the causes, we are called upon to change the causes. Then we look at the pluses. The natural mother dies, so God sends a stepmother. She died a few years ago, three years ago. What a jewel of a woman to take on three children—and to love them. And we were with my natural mother's folk in South Carolina at the time, tattered and torn, wasted. When she rolled down that road with her new husband and looked at the three of us, she got out of the car and hugged us. And wept. I don't know whether she was weeping from joy or remorse, but she was there for us. So there were blessings. I think religion that's real religion knows that God compensates. You lose a right leg, there's a left leg. Right kidney goes, there's a left kidney that grows. Born in poverty, it can make you strong against the odds, it can make you as strong as the odds. God compensates.

HUGH HEWITT: But some people meet suffering and pain, and they do grow stronger. Some people collapse. I'm sure you've seen that a lot more than I have.

CECIL MURRAY: Oh, golly yes, Hugh. But that's where those who have are called upon to help those who do not have. If God has enabled me to get an education, I owe it to my brothers and sisters who have not been able to. If God feeds me, I owe bread to someone else. There is no option. I cannot ask, "Why aren't you achieving?" I already know why they're not achieving. Because at a certain juncture in their life they went that way. I may have gone that way. Now why did I go that way? Somebody whispered in my ear something good. Somebody failed to whisper in his ears or her ears something good. So let me do the whispering.

HUGH HEWITT: You ran into hatred at a fairly young age. You took some body blows, some beatings, for that as a result.

CECIL MURRAY: Yeah, I think of Southern racism in its overt stages and Northern racism in its covert stages. White America needs to back up and look at how a soul gets damaged. We learn fifty percent of our intelligence in the first four years of our lives. We are fairly well shaped by fifteen or age eighteen, or age twenty. To encounter the pain—especially if you are a caring, sensitive person—and to rise above the pain, you need God. Now what about those who encounter the pain and

> I think religion that's real religion knows that God compensates. You lose a right leg, there's a left leg. Right kidney goes, there's a left kidney that grows. Born in poverty, it can make you strong against the odds, it can make you as strong as the odds. God compensates.

it devastates them? I don't think they are totally to blame. They cannot claim they're victims, of course, because we make decisions in life. But you cannot ask people to be superhuman. And when those who, for some reason, do rise above through superhuman effort, you give them medals. But you don't down or bemoan those who don't quite rise.

You should have average circumstances to produce an average person. You should have an open door for those who will to walk through. Now if you open the door for your son and slam it for my son, then you wonder why my son becomes distorted; that's not even intelligent. We will all have blows. The racism

of the Deep South and the Far North and the Far West are still having repercussions on people—black, white, brown, yellow, all of us. American Indians and all. But in the twenty-first century, where we are, it would seem we would be a little more impatient with it. I could have been devastated when the Klan rode through our neighborhood. I could have been devastated. When there was food during the Depression (they called it the barn on the edge of town), the white gangs wouldn't let black people get to the food. So they could not eat. So they had to form groups of fifty, sixty, to get to the barn. And the gang's led by the son of the chief of police. These are things that hurt you. I passed by the white library, and I never knew what it was to go inside. And the officers of the white church stood and did not let black people into a church. You walked down the sidewalk and if there was no room for you and white people, you stepped off the sidewalk. You paid the same fare and sat in the back seat.

HUGH HEWITT: But what did that do to a Jesus who's supposed to be beyond color? I mean, you're raised in a religious family and you run into this hatred. You not only did not get the food, but you were beaten.

CECIL MURRAY: You know, in life you have choices. And America must return to that understanding about choices. You have at least three levels, maybe more. You can be an eagle, a high-altitude bird. Or you can be a buzzard, a mid-altitude bird. Or you can be a turkey, a no-altitude bird, a chicken.

Far too many people who are gifted, who can fly higher, are walking around in the henhouse, in the barnyard. And they're looking up, throwing spitballs at people who are eagles. Now, you got a lot of turkeys with good bank accounts. You have a lot of turkeys with a two-car garage. You have a lot of buzzards who don't kill—they don't have the capacity to kill—but they're just hovering around, waiting on somebody to die, waiting on somebody to be hurt.

Eagles take the high ground. We are called upon to take the high ground. And no matter if you were once a buzzard, you can still zoom up. If you're a turkey, you can still change. So I think when we make the right decision, that determines how we show up in history. The problem is, you can't take an absolute zero and say, "Become hero." You got to take that zero, scrub him up, scrub her up, show them some options. Mentor, hand hold, walk with him. Then, at the proper stage say, "Now, here are your choices: eagle, buzzard, turkey. Which?" If they choose to be a buzzard, all right, we got lots of buzzards in the world. If they choose to be a turkey, lots of turkeys. But at least you've been fair enough to give them options and to give them the capacity to make the right decision.

HUGH HEWITT: I think Lincoln said that during the Civil War, the South and the North called upon the same God to aid them in the same war. It made no sense at all to him. Do you suppose it ever crept into his head that this can't be true if the white church is busy oppressing the black church?

CECIL MURRAY: But we serve different Jesuses. And just because what comes against Jesus is negative, that doesn't make Jesus negative. We didn't throw out the country because George Washington owned slaves. We didn't throw out the country or the Declaration of Independence because Thomas Jefferson, a great draftsperson, owned slaves. Lincoln had to come to see that if slavery is not wrong, nothing is wrong. We don't throw out religion because of those who misuse it. We don't throw out Jesus. Now, in the sixties and seventies we began to wonder about this white, blue-eyed, blond-headed Jesus.

HUGH HEWITT: This Nordic Jesus.

CECIL MURRAY: This Nordic Jesus. At least He should look Semitic. But then as we explore a little longer and a little deeper, we say, "Oh-ho, He looked like *us*." So when He was under fire, being chased by Herod, according to the early stories, they don't take Him to London. They don't take him to Paris to hide Him. They don't take Him to Norway to hide him. They take Him to Egypt. You can hide chocolate in the midst of chocolate, but you can't hide vanilla in the midst of chocolate.

We looked at His lineage. Solomon boasts, "I am black but comely." We look at David and Bathsheba. Bathsheba looked like me. And out of that tribe come legitimate ones. Moses marries Zipporah, a Cushite woman, a black woman. His father-in-law, Jethro, teaches him about Yahweh, teaches him about the sacred mountain. This Cushite was the son of Abraham by Tehrah, his third wife. And you go on and on. The earliest Israelites were black. Now all of this, of course you can argue against it. But there are as many arguments for it as there are against it. And there are many Old Testament Jews who will say, "Yes, it's possible the earliest Israelites were black."

As you begin to get that understanding, you see this Nordic Jesus who oppresses you and puts you down, and is in your stained-glass windows, and is in your mind. (If you're white, you're right; if you're yellow, you're mellow; if you're brown, stick around; but if you're black, get back—three hundred years of "Get Back!") Then you look and see God is white? That does something to your mind. Then John 8:32 says, "You shall know the truth, and the truth shall set you free." Black people have been denied that truth. The black church must educate black people and white people and yellow people and red people.

HUGH HEWITT: Is there just one Jesus, regardless of color? Are the people worshiping Him?

CECIL MURRAY: I think a deeper question is, "Are we called upon to be color-blind? Are we called upon to be color-rich?" I look at you; I see. You look at me; you see. Now the question of a civilized person is, "So what?" I want to know what you know. You want to know what I know. Yes, my lips are generous. Yes, your lips are linear. Yes, my hair goes up and yours goes down, whatever is left of it. What can I gain from your culture? What can you gain from mine? I don't want to be color-blind. If I wanted to be color-blind, which I wanted for three centuries, I'm sure. You're not allowed to be color-blind in this world culture. We have a hundred fifty nationalities in Los Angeles. We are not going to be color-blind. But if we are color-rich, if we draw from each his or her best, then we can have right here on this earth a prototype of what can be in the twenty-first century. Because the world is becoming a global world. And our God must look at us through many prisms.

HUGH HEWITT: Let's stay awhile on matters of theology. In the African Methodist Episcopal tradition, what standing has Scripture? You've quoted it generously thus far.

CECIL MURRAY: Scripture has the same legitimate standing as for all Protestants or Catholics. Scripture alone is the basis. We cannot *eisegete*, read into Scripture. We must *exegete*, read out of the Scripture. Indeed, it is because of the Scripture that we began to yearn to be free. Massah would not let us have training, and a white man who trained a black man to read was jailed for breaking the law. We were not allowed to have learning. But they made the mistake of thinking that religion would keep us in bondage. He let us go off in the woods to pray and shout and preach. And that preacher, having read about Moses and Israel and Egypt, preached a gospel of liberation. And the songs we sang, "Go down Moses, tell old Pharaoh to let my people go!" and "Steal away to Jesus," were the signal for the Underground Railway with Harriet Tubman and all. So the same religion that was thought would entrap us in self-hatred and slavery, that religion freed us. So the Word of God is the salvation of all people, but particularly of the people who have been in slavery. The Word is all we have.

> We have a hundred fifty nationalities in Los Angeles. We are not going to be color-blind. But if we are color-rich, if we draw from each his or her best, then we can have right here on this earth a prototype of what can be in the twenty-first century.

HUGH HEWITT: I understand you teach the Bible. Still—after all these years in the pulpit—you still teach the Bible. Is it still a joy for you to do?

CECIL MURRAY: It is because it liberates the teacher and the taught. On Tuesday nights we have perhaps some three hundred at the church. I had the pleasure of being adjunct professor for several seminaries wherever I was stationed as a pastor. But to learn of the Word of God! There are supplemental things. We must mentor. We must do job searches. We must do micro-loans (several companies have enabled us to do loans). We have forty task-forces in the church. But the chief thing is to teach the Word. Because when you know God, God is expansive. And God is inclusive, not exclusive. And God keeps saying, "I don't love you any more than I love you over there. I love you both equally. I want you both to make something of yourselves. And when you need a little help, here I am. Just hold your hand up and I'll take your hand." That's what you encounter in the Word, something you can encounter no other place, no other place.

HUGH HEWITT: You preached at a funeral before coming here today. You preach at a lot of funerals, and way too many of them involve young people. Does that lead you to despair?

CECIL MURRAY: I think the only thing that prevents despair is God. And realizing you're an instrument and you're not final. You're an instrument. We average 2.3 funerals a week. Now, the endangered species among young black men is among the ages twenty through thirty. The Sentencing Commission out of D.C. reveals that one out of three is in prison, on probation, or on parole.

Now before whites feel totally threatened by that, they need to understand the victims. Secondly, this is less than one generation old. It came out of the seventies. The dissolution of the family came out of the seventies and the eighties. Drugs being poured into black communities with intent, it came out of the eighties and the nineties. Weapons being poured into the black community for profits. So now you've got weapons, drugs, a depressed economy, a depressed mentality, a depressed family, and you've got the ingredients for destroying a whole level of young males.

We can stop it. But to have the funeral and to see the young men marching by—maybe several hundred, and you read their faces—it makes you want to weep. You ought to be happy at twenty. You ought to feel immortal. And the jargon is, "Well I'm not going to make it till twenty-one, anyway." You say, "Okay, that's rhetoric." But that's the wrong rhetoric for a twenty-year-old. This is not a front-line soldier in Vietnam who's trying to protect himself psychologically, "If I prepare to die, then I won't be afraid of death." He's doing the same thing on the streets, but it's not for a good cause.

HUGH HEWITT: What's a preacher supposed to do in a situation like that?

CECIL MURRAY: A preacher is supposed to go to the inner city. To stand in the projects. To stand before corporations and try to solicit jobs. To make the members of the church write to Washington, to politicians, saying, "You've got to get a Marshall Plan for the inner city." To sensitize blacks and whites and all to the fact that we are tied together. You can't just act as if it's a black problem or a Latino problem. We're going to have to do something about those young men. If they were given a chance, seventy percent, eighty percent would probably go plus. Five, ten, fifteen would go minus. Now, my goodness, thirty-three percent is going minus!

HUGH HEWITT: Do you get help from your colleagues in white churches—the help that you need or you expect or that you believe is commanded by Scripture?

CECIL MURRAY: White ministers have great challenges. And when you see them rise to the challenge of a prophetic ministry, you have to say, "Wow!" I don't think you can necessarily down the white minister who is not prophetic. He says, "I'm a priest, not a prophet. I hold what we've got. My members might downsize if I get too socially concerned. My members reflect society, so I will get their souls washed so that they'll go out and perhaps wash other souls." You say, "All right, but I think that you have a choice in ministry. You may be prophetic, or you may be pathetic. Here you are with the power of God. God gives you the power, the dynamite to turn the world upside down, and you're using it to blow your nose."

Now, it isn't whites alone. Black ministers. And we cannot point the finger too much, because they're there pointing right back at me every time I point the finger. I'm talking about the challenge that faces all of us to radicalize our ministry and have enough intelligence not to scare our congregations away because they have problems. Then they come to church. "Oh my goodness, we're going to have to face it again." You have to use the wisdom God has given. And then it isn't the sermon alone. It's the instrumentality of groups and calling people together and having ministries in the church that are going to make a change. Ours is not a failure of know-how. Ours is a failure of will.

HUGH HEWITT: It was Christians in this country who originally led abolition. It was Harriet Beecher Stowe coming from that family of ministers—minister after minister after minister—who went out and rallied and wrote the great book that turns so many heads. Is religion failing the inner city?

CECIL MURRAY: That was so beautiful because if you'd said is religion failing, I would not have had an answer. Is religion failing the inner city? I would say, in large part, yes. There are pockets of care packages—churches and mosques and synagogues and temples that are care packages. But by and large, churches and Christians do the same thing that whites do on the Harbor Freeway. They keep going till they reach the end, neither looking right nor left to see what's happening and not seeing who's dying in the ditch.

We need radical religion. And radical doesn't mean violent; radical just means militant. And the church is called on to be militant. The temple, the mosque, these are called upon to be militant. The church militant becomes the church triumphant. Why aren't we pushing corporate America to have more training programs? Why aren't we taking these military bases that are now downsized or shut down and using them? Why don't we take that mass volunteerism and train and re-train? Why are we living with a hundred thirty thousand homeless in the county and thirty-five thousand homeless in the city? Why are twelve million children going to bed hungry every night in America? Why in New York, South Dakota, and California is there an eighteen percent increase in chronic hunger among children? Why aren't we doing something about it?

We first have to ask the questions. The questions lead us to the answers. But it's easier to run to suburbia. It's easier to have your sixty-minute worship on Sunday morning with your well-read, well-documented sermon with your well-bred, well-documented pastor. Shake hands at the door. "I'll see you next week. Don't bring any social programs into this church, and *do not* bring those homeless people because they offend our noses."

HUGH HEWITT: Pastor Murray, I'm sure at least a few tens of thousands of people have just heard that and they're saying, "That's not the gospel. That's politics. I thought this show was about the gospel." Is that the gospel that you're talking? Or is that politics?

CECIL MURRAY: *Politics* comes from the Latin word *polis*. It means "people." You cannot minister to people without ministering to the systems that control them. The economics that propel them. The emotions that afflict them. The schools that somehow either educate or mis-educate them. A person must be taken holistically. If we could take one segment of the religious garden, the Jesus segment, He makes it very clear: "I send you out to feed the hungry, house the homeless, clothe the

> We need radical religion. And radical doesn't mean violent; radical just means militant. And the church is called on to be militant. The temple, the mosque, these are called upon to be militant. The church militant becomes the church triumphant.

naked, to lift the fallen, to heal the wounded, to raise the dead." He didn't say, "I send you out to get a good sermon and go home feeling good about yourself." That's egocentric religion. That's personal salvation. I send you out for *social* salvation.

It's a copout to say a vitally involved congregation is political. What you're really saying is, "Don't bother me with that stuff. I want to park in the church lot. I want to go in. I want to meet people who are just like me. I want to feel good, come out, get in my car, and go home." Now, to feel good and to do good are two parts of religion. You cannot do one without the other. Just like the so-called social gospel is no good without the gospel grounded in the Word of God. But the Word of God just as the Word of God is no good. The Word must become flesh. Then you have it legitimately. You cannot live in a community without involving yourself in the totality of the community.

HUGH HEWITT: Let's stay in the Jesus segment of the religious garden, to use your phrase. Is He the Son of God?

CECIL MURRAY: For Christians, not only is Jesus the Son of God, but Christianity says Jesus is *the way.* Buddhism means the enlightened way. Islam means the way. Judaism, the way. Taoism, the way. Jesus Christ is the Son of God in the regard that if I see what God looks like, God would look like Jesus. And what is that? A love that goes all of the way out of the way to help somebody who has lost the way. God is love. Jesus is love. And it is sacrificial love . . . and dying for me. So that this carpenter is the very embodiment of the invisible, indivisible God. If I could see what God looks like, He would look like Jesus. Jesus is the Son of God. It took us three hundred years to come to that formula. We still haven't finalized it. To say that God is on Mars and He sends down His Son, His Heir, to earth, and then He goes back to Mars, and He's coming back again one of these days, and everybody who's got his soul washed is going to Mars with Him, that is so childish and so useless and so unintelligent.

HUGH HEWITT: Then what does it mean when He calls himself the Narrow Gate?

CECIL MURRAY: He's talking to people who are His followers. I am the way. I am the only the way for you. But to force Him on others . . . The roots of religion bring up many branches. And *religion* comes from the Latin word *religare* that means "to tie, to bind." I have no right to offend my Buddhist brother or sister. I have no right to offend my Jewish brother or sister, my Islamic brother or sister, my Hindu brother or sister. There are many ways to the top of the mountain. Jesus says, "Follow Me. I am the way. I am the door." But is there only one door to the house of God? Is God that poor at home design that He would not have many doors facing many directions? There were twelve gates to Jerusalem. And there were many doors to the Temple. So I do not want to lock anybody in. "Here is the way for me. May I explain it to you? Would you like it? Good. Let's go together."

> There are many ways to the top of the mountain. Jesus says, "Follow Me. I am the way. I am the door." But is there only one door to the house of God? Is God that poor at home design that He would not have many doors facing many directions?

Now, Hugh, I think our salvation is not being of one philosophy, but being of one program. We covenant with Jewish Temple Isaiah. We covenant with several Korean temples. We covenant with Suni Muslims and the Nation of Islam. We do programs. We covenant with several Korean churches. We are not going to have the same theology, thank God! We're not going to have the same philosophy, thank God! But there are four housing projects that need us. Let's work on that, and that will keep us from working on each other. What you call God is your business. What I call God is my business. All I know is we can do God's business far better by helping the needy than by trying to convert each other.

HUGH HEWITT: What happens to the person, in any of those religions, but specifically in the African Methodist Episcopal church, when they die? What happens to that soul?

CECIL MURRAY: The Bible gives us several options. One is conditional immortality. The good folks go to heaven. The bad folks go to hell. Another is that you are extinguished. You die. You're dead. You're done. That's it. Hope you enjoyed it. Another is that everything is reclaimed. Several levels, you go to 'em. When you reach the seventh level, you get the beatific vision of heaven. I believe (and I'd quit the ministry this moment if I did not believe it) that the spirit of a human being is the most crucial, the most beautiful thing in the world. That spirit lives on. This tent is vacated. That essential life goes on to existence of another kind. We describe it in many euphoric terms and all. But we do know that there have been genuine scientists who've had out-of-body experiences. "I have stood and seen my corporeal tent, and here I am floating above it." So we can no longer laugh at that. The spirit is what America is rediscovering now. America is discovering that materialism is not enough. Me-too-ism is not enough. Cynicism, pessimism, is not enough. So that spirit, when the body dies, lives on. Now whether or not there's a burning hell and all, we'll see.

HUGH HEWITT: America is rediscovering this? Are you talking about a renewal, a revival of sorts?

CECIL MURRAY: America is discovering it through her pain. America went for materialism. You remember the classic story of this young man lying on the sidewalk. He's had this terrible car accident and he keeps moaning, "Ooooh, my BMW! Oh, my BMW!" And the medic says, "Man, you're here moaning about your BMW. We can't even find your left arm!" "My left arm? Ooooh, my Rolex watch! Ooooh, my!" Materialism doesn't please. What you ride, what you wear, what you eat, it's a phase. You got to grow up sometime. That doesn't do it. Me-too-ism. What's everybody eat? What's everybody drinking? What race is everybody hating this month? What slang are we using to put women down? Or to put browns down? Me-too-ism.

HUGH HEWITT: But I don't see this revival. I wish I could see it.

CECIL MURRAY: I don't mean it's a revival. Do you see the insanity in America?

HUGH HEWITT: Oh, I agree with you.

CECIL MURRAY: Thank you. That is a pure sign. People are going crazy. And those that aren't going have already arrived. We are going to have to rediscover and reinvent ourselves spiritually. Escapism, that's an example.

HUGH HEWITT: Is it necessarily God's plan for that to happen, Rev. Murray?

CECIL MURRAY: I don't think God causes the negative. I think that God says, "When you're sick of being sick, here I am. I told you what it takes to have your garden, but you want to live east of Eden. You don't want to live in Eden. You want to be your own god. Now where did it lead you? Even with your wars, you win the wars and then you lose them because the people you defeated are richer, wealthier, steadier, than you are. When are you going to stop hurting each other? When you're ready, here's a way, here's a formula." That's all God can do. "I stand at the door and knock. I can't knock your head off. I give you a certain amount of freedom to make a decision. Your bad decisions are killing you. Look at you. Drugs. The divorce rate is fifty percent in America, sixty percent according to some figures. Children have very little respect for their elders, who won't respect themselves."

HUGH HEWITT: But do you see a turning point? Do you see a reason to be optimistic?

CECIL MURRAY: Oh yes! Because we have hit the floor. If we haven't, we will in a few years. And you can't fall off the floor, so you got to go up. Sure can't fall off the floor.

HUGH HEWITT: Pastor Murray, you went off to Claremont School of Theology after ten years of a great career in the Air Force, where everything you wanted was coming your way. After that bad jet accident you put yourself through school. And you had no money. You had a job, but not a great one. Did you sense that there was a plan for your life?

CECIL MURRAY: Do you know? I don't think there's a human being on earth who doesn't know two things: one, when he's going to die. Because I think God prepares you whether it's five seconds or five minutes. Two, what God has for you in your life. Now, if you can somehow remove the distortion of fear and ego, you and God can talk together.

"But Lord, I could retire in ten years. Live comfortably. Not bad for a little swamp alligator from Florida."

"What? Your bread? Is that all that's important to you? Your car? Your home? Your retirement? Is that really all you're about? You think about that. I've got something else for you to do. You may not have the money, but I'll take care of you. Do you believe it? If you believe it, why do you look back?"

HUGH HEWITT: What's the hardest thing God's asked you to do?

CECIL MURRAY: Man, that's good. I don't even know, because who am I" If God asked you do it, God gives you the power to do it.

HUGH HEWITT: You've been in pulpits in Pomona, Kansas City, Seattle. Is God leading you from pulpit to pulpit? Was there a plan for Cecil Murray to end up at First A.M.E. in time to build a church? In time to be the center of the city when the city goes to hell in a handbasket in April of 1992?

CECIL MURRAY: I think you're given two hands. One is in God's. And one is on the task. Sometimes we take the one out of God's hand and sing like Frank Sinatra, "I did it my way," instead of "I did it God's way." Or, we take our hand off the task and put it in God's hand. And then I hear, "God has a Holy Joe, Holy Jane. Heavenly good, but no earthly good."

You can't fail if you go out into the darkness, put your hand in God's hand, and walk on. That's the light. So I don't even look at failure or success, because success implies failure and failure implies success. Blacks say it every Sunday and in every pulpit: "Just to know I've done my best as I go to take my rest. Let my name be with the blessed. Oh Lord, today." That's all you can do.

HUGH HEWITT: Well then, how do people put their hand in the hand of God?

CECIL MURRAY: When it's hot, you take off your coat. How you take off your coat? When you're over-heated, you dress down. How do you take off your*self*? You will it. First off all, it's easy to do because you're sick of yourself. The typical one of us doesn't have the amount of self-love we want. We are sick of our-selves. The typical one of us is always tripping, ego-tripping. it's like your shoestrings are loose, and you're trippin', trippin'. You need to reach down and tie up the loose ends. *What am I here for? Health? Income? Career? Sex? Family? Religion?* You have to make decisions in these categories. And once you make deci-sions, you're so busy working on that you don't have time to work on this. We need to be forward-oriented.

But you count the times the typical one of us says "I" in a conversation: "I, I, I, I, me, me, me." Makes us sound like opera singers. Very seldom say "we," very seldom talking of anything bigger than ourselves. And then we go home. And we either get drunk or we get on the phone and gossip and run somebody down or we get physical with our mates or with our children or with ourselves. Because we've broken the eleventh commandment. You know what the eleventh commandment is, Hugh? "Thou shalt not bore people." People get sick of us being preoccupied with us. That's why racism hurts so bad. People get sick of the same little old tight-natured people. They yearn for a bigger world, and they're trapped in this small world.

HUGH HEWITT: So what should they do?

CECIL MURRAY: Make a decision. Make a decision.

"Look, Lord, what did You put me here for? Is this it?"

"Well, no. I had something bigger for you."

"Then, when are You going to show it to me?"

"When are you going to see it? Okay, I'll tell you what: I'm going to give you a discipline. Every morning when you roll out of bed (not fifteen minutes, fifteen seconds), get on your knees by the side of your bed. Pray, 'Lord, what do You have for me?' Every night before you go to bed (and I don't care how tired you are, how drunk you are, how mad you are), spend fifteen seconds on your knees to pray, 'Lord, what do You have for me?' Then I'll reveal My will. And no flashing lightning in the sky, no thunder rolling. I got more to do than flash lightning for you when the streetlight goes out. I will reveal My will in the normal events following your prayer. A phone call, something you read, a conversation, a sermon preached, a message on television, something that will cause your spine to tingle."

But the important thing is not to define the answer, but to refine the question, "What am I living for?"

HUGH HEWITT: In your daily work at First A.M.E. Church, you begin and end every meeting with prayer. Why do you do that?

CECIL MURRAY: I think prayer envelopes us. "God, please, there are three of us. Will You come in and make us four?" It's God's house. It's God's event. It's God's circle. Secondly, we ask God to eventuate an understanding in the meeting so we don't start ego-tripping, so we don't start acting negative, so we don't start problem-analyzing instead of problem-solving. And thirdly, we bring ourselves to God, invoking our own awareness that God is already present. And then if we do some good in the meeting, praise be to God. If we don't do any good in the meeting, then we've obviously gotten in God's way because God can't fail.

We pray whether we pray consciously or not. If you don't believe it, you let that wino get into trouble. Lord, have mercy! You let that Las Vegas sophisticate get into trouble. Lord, have mercy! You let that entrepreneur go from millionaire to hundredaire. Lord, have mercy! I guess disaster is God's way of getting our attention. God doesn't cause it, but we can't listen when we're not needy.

> When we get needy, then we listen to a voice that helps us supply that need. But as long as I'm singing "I did it my way!" instead of "I did it God's way!" and as long as I am preoccupied with this pusillanimous little individual, God just stands at the door and knocks. The latch is on the inside.

When we get needy, then we listen to a voice that helps us supply that need. But as long as I'm singing "I did it my way!" instead of "I did it God's way!" and as long as I am preoccupied with this pusillanimous little individual, God just stands at the door and knocks. The latch is on the inside.

HUGH HEWITT: Pastor Murray, I want to talk to you about old Nick. I want to talk to you about evil in the world. Your church has been threatened with bombs. You've had gang members threaten you. You've walked up to vans where people have committed murder. You've seen evil. Is that something that can be turned around, or is that just going to be a part of every day of every month of every year that the globe keeps turning?

CECIL MURRAY: I suppose we'll always have the negative with the system. But it's the proportions, it's the ethos. It's in the very atmosphere. Children no longer insult each other. Children no longer throw things at each other. Children no longer fistfight. They shoot. And until we muster some large-scale righteous indignation; until every church accepts responsibility for its immediate community and its area school; until every mosque, every synagogue, begins to say, "This cloverleaf is mine," and we come together and we work on it, then I don't think it's going to go away. We don't have enough money to throw at the problem. We don't have enough will for the government to come and do a massive program. It will be the religious community taking over its local community, saying to mothers with children, "Come; we have programs. Hungry and homeless, come; we will feed you. Unemployed, come; we will help recycle your skills."

HUGH HEWITT: They have to come, but does the church have to go find these people first?

CECIL MURRAY: I remember one preacher. He wasn't highly schooled, but fifty years ago he preached this sermon: "Come. Tarry. Go." And that is the imperative of God: "Come. tarry. Go." We are sent out to each other. We have no option.

HUGH HEWITT: How do you get that going in your own church?

CECIL MURRAY: Programmatically. I think people want to have flowery beds of ease and be carried to the sky. Now we're no great model; but as you ask, we have task forces in our church. Substance abuse. Youth. Pan-Africanism. Gangs. Bone marrow.

HUGH HEWITT: Let's stop there. What do you do about gangs?

CECIL MURRAY: Well, we go to them. We assign them mentors. We meet with them periodically, monthly at least. We promise jobs for those who are willing to go through the period of preparation. We hand-hold them on the jobs. We will visit with the parents, whatever is required. It's like substance abuse. We treated three hundred fifty substance-abused families last year. We do whatever it takes. And it chiefly takes that twelve-step program and some hand-holding and some job-finding and some consciousness-lifting. "You are more than a pusher of a shopping basket. You are the oldest people on earth. Come on." Some come.

HUGH HEWITT: Are you without fear? Are your people in the church without fear? These people threatened to blow up your church a year and a half ago; the FBI got it just before it happened.

CECIL MURRAY: I guess fear is constantly to be defiant because you can only tremble so long. And then your fear must turn to something else. It can either turn to depression or it can turn to anger or it can turn to resolution. You tremble, you tremble, and then the body says, "I'm sick of this. Make a decision." So you say, "Okay, let's go with it. Let's rise above it. Let's fly higher and back."

And that's what a core group has done because we couldn't spread the word too much; that would've created hysteria. But with the threatened bombings and threatened mayhem, we had to decide. And so we said, "All right, if what we see is unusual, we will call attention to it. But under no circumstances will we be a bad commercial for Christ." You're not a commercial for Christ when things are all right. It's when things are all wrong that your commercial for Christ is in the intensive care unit. Then you witness to your doctors and the nurses and the visitors when you say, "Why, God, are You doing this to me?" Bad commercial. Anybody can be all right when things are all right. It's when things are all wrong and the joy of life is that things are not constantly all wrong.

> Perfect love doesn't eliminate fear, it casts it out. The fear comes with the mentality. The fear comes with the flesh and blood. But you can only tremble so long. Then you have to make a decision how you want to show up before the throne of grace.

HUGH HEWITT: A mutual friend told me of a time, after a drive-by shooting, when you were out walking the streets with some of the men of your church and you spotted the shooter. And you went up and talked to that person. At that point were you thinking that God needed Cecil Murray to walk up and talk to that person?

CECIL MURRAY: I guess if not me, then who? If not now, when? If not this, what? I was out with about seventy-five men patrolling the community. I've done it now for about ten years. We say to pushers, "Not here." To strawberries (ladies of the street), "not here." We try to offer positive things—food, clothes.

Then bang, bang, bang, shots, shots, shots. We hit the deck, hit the street. Two police persons were walking with us, because the policemen in the church were walking with us. At that time Mayor Bradley had endorsed the program. So the southwest division—our division—had people, and they said to us, "It's dangerous. You're civilians. Go back." The men huddled, and we said, "Now we understand that some of you have families, and some of you will not want to go on. We are going to have a word of prayer. Leave while we pray. After our prayers, those who remain will go on."

They prayed. The leader of the prayer was a young man I had never heard pray before, a beautiful man. And we prayed. Amen-rah! Not one person had left. Then as we moved on, the seventy-five became a hundred, a hundred twenty-five, because neighbors who had been watching all of this came and joined. Down-and-outers came and joined. Homeless people came and joined. People just on the side came and joined. So that by the time we had made our circuit for the two hours and came back to the parking lot, and they came back singing "I'm on the Battlefield for My Lord."

We were never the same after that. It was a born-again experience. I guess Paul was right. It was a conversion experience. Perfect love doesn't eliminate fear, it casts it out. The fear comes with the mentality. The fear comes with the flesh and blood. But you can only tremble so long. Then you have to make a decision how you want to show up before the throne of grace.

HUGH HEWITT: You just mentioned that they came back singing. Let's turn to a different subject—music. You're a music junkie, if I can use that term. What is the connection between God and music, men and women?

CECIL MURRAY: "Without a song, the day would never end. Without a song, the road would never bend. Without a song a man ain't got a friend." Hugh, never trust anybody that tells you they can't sing. Only the small birds sing in nature—the robin, the sparrow, the wren. The eagle and hawk don't sing, and that's the problem. Without music, rhythm, you have no soul because you can only express technical feelings verbally. A poem occasionally comes out. But a poem is a song, like the Old Testament Psalms; they're the *songs* of the Old Testament. When you are depressed, sing a sad song. When you're angry, sing an angry song. When you're happy, sing a happy song. You say it's catharsis? Yes, but it's also instruction. That song is teaching you. There ought to be a song that goes with fear. There ought to be a song that goes with pain. There ought to be a song that goes with sickness. My generation had songs for all occasions, and you would know a person by his or her song more than by his or her name. One of the favorite songs was "Jesus, Keep Me Near the Cross," when they were hurting badly. You could just feel the tears when they sang, "Jesus, keep me near the cross." But the problem is we want to be near the cross but we don't want to be on it. So when we get on the cross, we don't have a song.

HUGH HEWITT: Five choirs at First A.M.E.? Why five?

CECIL MURRAY: Six, really.

HUGH HEWITT: Okay, six!

CECIL MURRAY: The men's choir sings every fifth Sunday. Because black culture is storytelling culture. Black culture has a story to tell. If you're preaching, well, that's a pulpit story. But if you're singing, that's an eternal story. The only original American contribution to the world of music and art is black music. Spirituals, minstrelsy, ragtime, blues, jazz, swing, gospel tunes even hip hop. Everything else we imported from Europe and Scandinavia and other parts of the world.

The music that was born on American soil is the music that was torn out of the breast of the little black bird in slavery. It was a means of communication. It was a means of excitation, to get the masses together. It was a means of fighting off humiliation. The work song was a means of getting the rhythm of the work, because when you are doing something again and again you begin to develop a little rhythm with it. And to keep from getting assembly line psychosis, you better sing a song. And it's true it takes a happy man to sing a happy song. It takes a happy man to sing a happy song. And it's true that it takes a happy woman to finish a happy song. So you can identify a person in two ways—by his or her nickname and by his or her song.

But the songs that are genuine are the songs that are torn out of you. Beethoven hears four knocks in the night—boom, boom, boom, boom. They are repeated. It's a bleak night, and the only sounds are those four knocks. He goes on to compose a great symphony. And then when you hear that Beethoven had a Moorish mother, that Beethoven was black, wow! You begin to see why there was so much pathos in his music. So I think the song is given to you to preserve your sanity, to preserve your story and to help others who will sooner or later find themselves in that same shape.

HUGH HEWITT: Music is such a powerful thing that it has carried young people to the wrong side, but it can also work inside of a church. Is music one way that you are reaching out to youth, to get them in or get them churched or bring the gospel to them?

CECIL MURRAY: Boy, you are so right. We have twenty-seven youth task forces under the Youth Task Force, one of forty. Reverend Mary Minor Reed is our minister of youth, and she does so well. But we realize the door to the other twenty-seven youth ministries is music. Get them interested in the choir and then we can feed them to the other ministries. Their health is pretty well gauged by their dedication to the choir.

HUGH HEWITT: The African Methodist Episcopal Church is a denomination as old as the republic.

CECIL MURRAY: Yes, it's the oldest black denomination in North America.

HUGH HEWITT: Where does it fit in the theological spectrum? Why this church, why this denomination?

CECIL MURRAY: You know mainstream Methodism, which is now the United Methodist Church. The African Methodist Episcopal Church came out of the then Methodist Episcopal Church in 1787. It was the Methodist Episcopal Church, and blacks were called Africans. And when Richard Allen led the walkout of St. George's Methodist Episcopal Church in Philadelphia protesting segregation, they took the designation African Methodist Episcopal Church. So in polity and practice we are pretty similar, in our beliefs we are pretty similar. The church adopted as its motto "God Our Father, Christ Our Redeemer,

Man Our Brother, Woman Our Sister." It is extremely inclusive. Non-blacks are always welcome. It is socially concerned, beyond regular church work, because in its infancy the yellow plague broke out in Philadelphia and the people of that particular church were the only ones who were willing to work with the dead and the dying. That was when they gained prominence.

The churches built later were stops on the underground railroad leading to Canada and the North. A.M.E. adopted a program of social concerns. It founded the first black hospital in Kansas City, the first black corporation, the first black newspaper, eleven black colleges (the first black colleges). So it kind of goes with the territory that we are to be concerned beyond ourselves, we are to be concerned with all people, and we are to work hard to make a change.

HUGH HEWITT: Is it a good thing that there is a black church in America, or does it allow the white church in America to say, "Not our problem, not our ministry, not today"?

CECIL MURRAY: I dream your dream that one day the distinctions will not be necessary. That dream threatens to become a nightmare, because the religious right is now pulling us back into conservatism and the polarization is setting in among races in America mentally. But again that may be the storm before the calm. It may be our wakeup call to see a black church, a white church, every Asian church, so on and on and on.

I guess if we lived in the best of all possible worlds we would not see hyphenated churches, but we are talking about the ought-brokenness and the is-brokenness. We are in a racist economy, a racist society. So we must work within our own purview to help each be less threatening to the other. "Hey, let's do an agenda together, and let's stay on the agenda and off of each other." But we draw the lines racially, and that hurts religion. You can fight over anything else in religion except the ethnicity, and that's when religion gets deadly. The last thirty-two hundred years we've had less than three hundred years of peace. And ninety-five percent of those wars were some way connected to religious disagreement, or at least everybody thought, "I've got the Lord on my side because I'm on the right side of the Lord." And when you start fighting for the Lord, you've got something dangerous. You have a fool looking for a cliff. The Lord doesn't need us to fight for the Lord. The Lord needs us to fight to eliminate the problems. Let the Lord be the Lord.

It's like shouting in some religious language. Why would any fair-minded person disagree with women who want to take the chauvinism out of the Bible? The Bible was written making God *He* and making all the heroes *he*, and everybody's a *he*. Moses was a man, Jesus was a Man. But the Spirit of God—God herself? himself? itself? We have to look at these and stop just relying on what Granddaddy handed me down. Because if Grandmama and Granddaddy were so wise, why are we in so much trouble now? We have to reinvent ourselves, and religion is constantly renewing. The Bible is an opened revelation. It didn't end at the Book of Revelation; it is an open-ended revelation. We are in a new world. You cannot dominate women. You cannot take children by the heels and dash their heads against the stone because they come from an alien culture. You cannot ask, "Who gives this woman to this man?" as if a woman were the chattel of her father. This is a different date, and God will lead us if we will follow. Now that doesn't mean throwing the values of yesterday away. I don't think any intelligent person would think that. But every morning when we awaken, we ask a new set of questions.

HUGH HEWITT: You mentioned the Book of Revelation. I just want to ask as we're approaching the millennium, is it of any significance for you?

CECIL MURRAY: No, because the Millennium was when that man drove his family down that alley and had to make a U-turn and the gangs fired and killed his daughter. The Millennium is that in Los Angeles a thousand persons will have weeping mothers from the killings this year. The Millennium is that you can walk down any avenue and see people pushing shopping carts, blanks stares in their eyes, because we cannot treat people with mental illness and fifty percent of the homeless are mentally ill. The Millennium is that in the projects, children are afraid to go outdoors and every time a car backfires, they hit the floor. The Millennium is that privileged people have run to suburbia and have discovered to their detriment that everywhere you go, you take yourself. The Millennium is now. I don't think it is God that is destroying us, I think we are destroying ourselves. I think God wants to save us, but God can't do anymore with us than we can do with ourselves.

HUGH HEWITT: Please be frank with what you think about this, Pastor. What does the gospel say to that suburbanite? Because that's me, an affluent white suburbanite, and that's most of the people in our audience. What do you think the gospel says to us about that catalogue of Millennium-like evil you just rattled off?

CECIL MURRAY: I think the radical demand for love is for love to extemporize itself. Keep your home, keep your 2.3 children, keep your wall-to-wall carpeting, your retirement plans. But for God's sake, literally give a tithe of your time and your talent to someone who is less well-positioned. It's not asking too much. "Well I got mine, why can't they get theirs?" You got yours because the calculation of circumstances favored you in certain ways. You worked very hard. You worked very hard. You've done real well. That's not taking anything away from you.

By all means, religion is not a minus. Religion is a plus. The cross of Christ is a plus sign. You take a negative and you make it a positive. So as Christians, let's give something back. Let's stop acting as if we were born Daddy Warbucks. Because Great-granddaddy in this country—white, black, or anything else—was pretty much a farmer. And instead of running away from problems, let's stabilize and solve the problems.

HUGH HEWITT: Pastor Murray, that I understand. That's the same gospel I read. But does it require a particular politics? When you look at conservatives (and I'm one of them, Pastor, you know that; we've known each other for a number of years), do you just think that we are out of our minds? Or do you think that we just might be coming to a different conclusion from a different set of facts? Does the gospel allow me to be a conservative and you not to be?

CECIL MURRAY: The gospel tells us that we become our thoughts. We have had too many negative thoughts about each other. And communications got radicalized forty years ago, just as transportation with jet travel and all, so now everybody in the world can see how everybody else is living. Now to this stranger, this white, here comes this black—he's a pimp, she's a prostitute; they are killers.

Then you say, "Please explain it to me. I'm one of three born to poor folks and I made it. And so they can make it." Now you didn't ask me; you're telling me. So you're making speeches again. Why didn't you ask what made the difference? Because in my high school class ninety-three percent went on to college, and of that eighty-seven percent finished college. Now we can't say "I made it!" Every ten seconds a black child drops out of school. There are more black men in prison than in college. There are more black women in college than black men.

We keep on looking. Then we come up with some answers, and we move on these answers rather than assuming that we've either got to go into denial of the problem or we have to have a scapegoat. If my thoughts are that whites are demonic, then my thoughts extemporize themselves. And I'm wrong. If I think I am demonic, then I tend to act that way.

HUGH HEWITT: Cecil Murray, what *did* make the difference with you?

CECIL MURRAY: Oh, we had extended family in my childhood. As we walked down the street (seven blocks to school) we'd say, "Hello, Mrs. Smith. How are you, Mrs. Young? Hello, Mrs. Brown." And if we missed speaking to one person, bad news beat us home. The drums would tell you. Everybody was your mother, everybody was your father.

Second, the family was solid. Now we can bemoan the fact that the family is not solid. But that's the ought-brokenness and the is-brokenness of the family in America. So we're gonna have to have a mass mentoring program for the fifty or a hundred years until we can get the family back together again.

Third, there was a different pace of living. Everybody walked. Now everybody drives. Now there's kids fifteen years old zooming down the street.

HUGH HEWITT: Where was God in this calculus?

CECIL MURRAY: God was right there because it was a God-centered community. Paine Chapel A.M.E. Church. Tabernacle Baptist Church. The Seventh Day Adventist Church? "Wow! What's that?" The Pentecostal Church, and everybody jumpin' and jumpin' and everybody belonged.

Now there are a hundred options for anybody. The church is just one of them. So the church has to radicalize itself; it has to reinvent itself. We cannot have the lifestyle and the philosophy of yesterday and all the conveniences of today. That is unfair. Along with urban centers, megalopolis, goes crime, goes discrimination. And so we have modern problems. But this is what God gave us brains for. And denial is not a solution. We have to keep reminding ourselves that denial is a river in Egypt.

> Now there are a hundred options for anybody. The church is just one of them. So the church has to radicalize itself; it has to reinvent itself. We cannot have the lifestyle and the philosophy of yesterday and all the conveniences of today. That is unfair.

HUGH HEWITT: Pastor Murray, do you have any advice for the spiritually restless?

CECIL MURRAY: Augustine said, "Thou hast made us for Thyself, and our souls are restless until they rest in Thee." Religion involves an inner yearning and an outer calling. I have an intrinsic yearning and an extrinsic calling. And the ball is in my court. Moses, yes. Abraham, yes. Jesus, yes. Gotama Buddha, yes. Muhammad, yes. Lao Tse, yes. And they went on to found great religious systems. But how many have said, "No"?

There's an inner yearning in me defined "at-one-ment" with God. It's a yearning for at-one-ment with the people around me and with myself. And I can't find at-one-ment with you unless I find at-one-ment with myself. So I think we don't have to invent our religious feelings. They're given to us. They're as instinctual as the drive for food, the drive for satisfaction, the drive for recognition, the drive for sex. These are innate yearnings. I want to be more than this tent. I want to be more than my appetites. Too many of us stay in the cocoon and we never ever get to see the butterfly.

HUGH HEWITT: You told us about the jet crash and your decision to give up the retirement, give up the career, give up the house and car. Go off and become a preacher. But you picked a particular kind of ministry. It's an urban ministry. It's a social gospel as well as an evangelical gospel. Where did that sense of mission come from?

CECIL MURRAY: It was given because there is no other kind for me. I am a black man who has experienced firsthand what it has meant to be black in America. The negative and the positive. I have been able to endure and to transcend. There is no choice for me but to go back and to give. And to make very certain I never hurt God. Because some will believe in me. And if I let them down, then I've let God down. To never hurt the vision of God. And to never associate it with any vision of mine. I see that God has vision. So I guess the central thing is to believe with all your heart, your mind, and your soul that you're called to make a difference. Now St. Jerome worked among wealthy people. Totally legitimate. Because if you can convert the wealthy, they can open up some jobs, they can open up some plans in Congress. But it just happened that in this particular case I was called to work with the disinherited.

HUGH HEWITT: You've said to me that sensitivity often comes from trauma. Is your sensitivity from the trauma of others or from a personal trauma?

CECIL MURRAY: All of us should be sensitized for God. I remember when the kitchen stove caught on fire. I may have been in second grade. We had kerosene stoves at the time, and it was burning. My sister was running for sand out in the backyard. And my brother was running for water. I was on my knees praying! Now, I was wrong, because that wasn't praying time; that was working time.

But I think religious consciousness is present in all of us in various manifestations. Getting the sand, God led her to get the sand. The water, God led him to believe that the house didn't have to burn down. But me on my knees, I was probably the least worthy belief system. But it does show that there's a religious consciousness. And with time perhaps I came to be a little more discerning.

But God is there. You have to learn how to get out of the way so God can come in.

HUGH HEWITT: But I want to ask you about two instances of shaking your fist at God. I'm not saying that you did; I'm just thinking that the temptation must have been there. I read the poignant story of the last time you saw your father. At that time the disease of alcoholism was far advanced. I mean, did you want to just shake your fist at God and say, "This isn't fair. This is a good man"?

CECIL MURRAY: I wanted to shake my fist at white people.

If I am in error about God, I stand to be corrected. I don't think God creates the negatives in our lives. I think God creates the positives out of the negatives. Society, we, bad decisions, whatever, create the negatives. My father was a man utterly sensitive to fairness. He was the principal of the school, and of course that's not like the modern principal. Having a black school in the Deep South in the sixties, fifties, forties, meant you had to be everything. You had to design curriculum. You had to motivate. You had to patrol the campus. You had to keep the street boys from intimidating the campus boys. And you had to do it on a salary that was just a token. You had to accommodate yourself somehow to the white system. The white schools look like junior colleges. And we went from first grade to twelfth grade right in the same building.

So the sensitivity and fighting the discrimination, I think, ultimately drove him within himself. Then he tried to drown that pain with alcohol. It's just a lay diagnosis. I've often wondered what would have happened if he had not had the normal problems *plus*. It's the *plus* that destroys people. We can all take problems up to a point. It's the *plus*. And racism constantly puts the *plus* on the backs of black men. He kept his best foot forward in front of us. He made us stand up and recite the classics and everything. He tried to give us a sense of self and of worth. And when he would be drunk, he would straighten himself up and try to walk straight. But we never were judgmental about him. Because I think the whole society says that life has pluses and minuses. Don't expect life without minuses. Thus a husband and wife would argue on Saturday nights; you can't have a relationship without arguments. You can't have life without death. You can't have a job without at times being overlooked. But on the other hand, you can't have *de*motion without a *pro*motion opening up. You can't have death without life. You can't have hard work without eventual profits.

HUGH HEWITT: So, no anger at God? No "Why did this have to be?"

CECIL MURRAY: I don't think you will find but a handful of blacks who will shake their fist at God. Camus said, "I rebel; therefore I exist." I think there's great truth in that. Of course he was talking about rebelling against God, and he had a lot to say. But I don't hear much talk. I only hear some self-pity. "Why is God putting this on me?" And I can't argue, because they need to be consoled and I can say later, "God didn't put this on you. A drive-by shooting did it for your son," or, "Prostate cancer took your husband."

HUGH HEWITT: What about during the riots of Los Angeles? April of 1992. Those were hard nights for the community and your church. Did you despair? Was that the temptation? Because everything was being destroyed. Stuff you'd worked on for fifteen years was going up in flames, and the community was being broken in a way that takes decades to repair.

CECIL MURRAY: I'll give you an example, Hugh. We gave out fifteen hundred turkeys at the church on Thanksgiving four years ago. Next morning, a man came: "I want a turkey." It was a brother. "Sorry, so sorry. We don't have any. We gave them all—" "I want a turkey!" "Okay, all right."

But as I went to see where we could drum up enough money from the staff to get a turkey, one of the officers told him, "No, go away. You should have been here yesterday. No turkey." The brother set the church on fire. Eighteen thousand dollars' worth of damage. You can get bitter over one little crazy-in-the-head brother. Now, does that make you go overboard and start overreacting? Nah, once in awhile the church gets burned. Once in awhile your world falls. Once in awhile somebody says something that cuts you to the quick. You can't generalize from the small negative to the large negative. You can only keep the small negative small.

So I think too many of us are caught up in the Garden of Eden mentality. We really think we were promised a rose garden, and we weren't. The only way to keep the garden from going to the weeds is to work on it. And there'll be other problems, but you won't have the same problems. The problem in America is that we've had the same cotton-pickin' problem for three hundred years, and we're sick of it! It is time we eliminated the problem of racism and discrimination. Because we've got to live together.

HUGH HEWITT: Let's turn to something that doesn't know race to illness. You've counseled a lot of people, I'm sure, who have been deathly sick before their time. Can God heal those people?

CECIL MURRAY: I think the occasions when God sets aside the doctor's prescription are rare, because modern doctors and nurses really are healers. And if they say, "The time is limited—a week, two weeks, two months," it's probably going to be that way. I don't think the outcome is the great concern of religion.

I think above the line is where we fit in. "What's your doctor said to you?" "I don't have long." "What's God said to you?" "Oh, I don't know." All right. Get the oil and put your hand on that's person's forehead and ask God for healing. Suppose the person doesn't get healed. What person? The body or the spirit? God says, "Come to Me as children." Children say, "Mom, Dad, I'm hungry. May I have some bread?" And the parent says, "Yes," or perhaps "No, because dinner's about ready." And we are to come as children. And all the sophistication of the world is not there in children. You ask God for what you want. You leave it to God. Death is not the ultimate enemy. I bury 2.3 people a week. And I'd be willing to gamble that sixty percent of the people I bury have never really lived. Seventy percent of the people on the sidewalk are walking dead. Death is not our worst enemy. Our worst enemy is to die never really having lived . . . or to live only for ourselves.

> . . . I think too many of us are caught up in the Garden of Eden mentality. We really think we were promised a rose garden, and we weren't. The only way to keep the garden from going to the weeds is to work on it.

HUGH HEWITT: Then what does someone pray for when they're grieving?

CECIL MURRAY: For strength. For strength. Thirty-four years the couple had been married that we buried today. Three weeks ago, sixty-one years married. "Dear daughter, what are you and God talking about?" "Oh, I'm just asking God to help me make it through the night." Because that's all you can do. We have words, of course. And we have rituals, of course. But the truth of the matter is when the darkness appears, you cannot control the darkness. When you've done the very best you can, then your only trick is to make it through the night. Despair comes when you don't think morning will come. Despair comes when you think darkness is eternal. That's when you go crazy.

HUGH HEWITT: Open-ended question, Pastor Murray. Do you see any miracles?

CECIL MURRAY: Oh yeah, yeah, yeah, yeah, yeah.

But Hugh, you know what most people confuse with miracles? Magic. And there's a difference between magic and miracles. "Lord, I sure need some money. Flesh it. And would You help me catch the lottery?" No lottery, no catch. "Lord, I need some money! Would You help me catch the lottery?" Still no luck. "I thought You were my friend! I thought You were so great! Why couldn't You help me catch the lottery?" Voice from heaven: "At least you could buy a ticket!"

We think God is a magician, instead of seeing that God is a miracle worker. Now, magic: abracadabra. Miracle: process. I want to be a doctor. High school, college, medical school, scholarship, job (or jobs), work ethic, fifteen hours a day, credentialed. Process. Now, where does God come in? The job? The scholarship? The professor who will say, "Hey, come here. I'm going to take you under my arm. I'm the world's foremost expert on internal medicine. I'm going to help you." That's where God comes in. The wind that held back the sea of reeds, a shallow portion of the Red Sea. It's happened three or four times in history since then. The miracle isn't the sirocco wind that causes the water in this shallow area to stand up on one side. The miracle is in the timing. God's miracle is in the timing. But does God work through normal processes? It took wind to do it. It didn't just go "abracadabra." Suppose, just suppose that with all of your viewers at this very moment, God is using you to communicate. Because Jesus said, "Greater things than I've done, you shall do." Because He didn't have television. He didn't have jet travel. He didn't have your college credentials. He didn't have all of these wires and these entries into people's homes.

But He did pretty good.

HUGH HEWITT: Pastor Murray, let's close our conversation with the most difficult issue in America. What does the gospel tell people to do about this problem which is just tearing the country up?

CECIL MURRAY: Truly I perceive that God is no respecter of persons. Truly I perceive that all are one. Modern humankind—twenty thousand years ago, sub-Sahara Africa, we start there. Then we move up north: the Horn of Africa and around, and some go over into the Iberian Peninsula. Some go to China. Lord have mercy, a hundred seventeen million years ago some pre-modern man was in Africa. A hundred five million years ago a man was in Ethiopia. A hundred two million years ago in China. Ninety millions of years ago in Europe. And so by the time the Europeans flourished, come down the trees, the Africans had already been down twenty-seven million years ago. We all come from one. If you take a black person with nappy hair and move him to the North Pole and let him stay there for twelve thousand years, the skin will lighten, the hair will come down, the nose will narrow to serve as a venturi tube to heat up the cold air before it goes down to the lungs. Take him back down to the hot tropics, the nose will flair. We are one. A simple exercise will help the typical American. The next time, white, you see black, see that black as white. The next time, black, you see white, see that white as black. And you begin to understand under the skin, all people are kin. We got to come there. And it's true: Martin wasn't the first to say it, but he really emphasized it: we shall live together as family, brothers, sisters, or we shall perish separately as fools.

> A simple exercise will help the typical American. The next time, white, you see black, see that black as white. The next time, black, you see white, see that white as black. And you begin to understand under the skin, all people are kin.

HUGH HEWITT: Pastor Cecil Murray, thank you for joining us.

CECIL MURRAY: Thank you, Hugh. Thank you.

A CONVERSATION WITH
ELDER NEAL MAXWELL

Born in 1926, in a suburb of Salt Lake City, Neal A. Maxwell was raised in the Church of Jesus Christ of Latter-day Saints (Mormons). It was a faith that was only to grow stronger with the passage of time, as Maxwell now serves as a member of the Quorum of Twelve Apostles, the Church's highest governing body. The author of seventeen books on faith, he is best known among peers for his outstanding writing and oratory skills. In recent years, the Mormon Church—a religion based on the essential tenet that the resurrected Jesus Christ appeared to the ancient peoples of the Americas—has gone through a series of growing pains. As a member of the Quorum of Twelve, Maxwell has stood at the center of these conflicts, maintaining the Church's purity of vision and helping to keep it true to the beliefs of its founders. Neal A. Maxwell is interviewed at the historic Beehive House, Brigham Young's original home in Salt Lake City.

A CONVERSATION WITH
ELDER NEAL MAXWELL

With over eight million members worldwide, the Church of Jesus Christ of Latter-day Saints is one of the fastest-growing religions in the world. Indeed, if the Church's phenomenal growth continues, it could emerge as one of the world's largest denominations by the end of the next century.

The Mormons are governed by a well-known hierarchy, which includes a three-member First Presidency and the Quorum of Twelve Apostles. **Elder Maxwell** was ordained an Apostle in July of 1981, at age fifty-five. The calling of the Apostles is to serve as special witnesses of Jesus Christ. In addition to their church-wide policy-making responsibility, each member of the Twelve Apostles is given special responsibility for a geographical division of the globe. Elder Neil Maxwell assumes responsibility for the North America West area in 1995. Neil Maxwell is married to Colleen Hinckley Maxwell. They have four children and twenty-two grandchildren.

HUGH HEWITT: Elder Neal Maxwell, thank you for joining us.

NEAL MAXWELL: I appreciate being with you, Hugh.

HUGH HEWITT: After three days in Salt Lake City, preparing for this interview and walking around Temple Square, it seems to me that it all comes down, the Church of Jesus Christ of Latter-day Saints, to the Book of Mormon and whether someone believes in it. How do you personally know it to be true?

NEAL MAXWELL: In three ways. One would be the witness of the Spirit, which is the most powerful. The other would be the searching of its pages in terms of its antiquity and the marvelous doctrines which were far beyond the capacity of Joseph Smith or anyone else to produce. And the third way would be the manner in which it lines up so beautifully and correlates so beautifully with what else we have in Holy Writ. It is rich and it is ancient, but the witness of the Spirit is there. Yet the Book of Mormon will always remain in the realm of faith. It has a bodyguard of scholars who now surround it and protect it from the frail attacks often made on it. But even so, it's the witness of the Spirit and the intrinsic evidence within the Book itself. It's drenched with that kind of evidence.

HUGH HEWITT: Talk to me about the witness of the Spirit. What is that?

NEAL MAXWELL: The witness of the Spirit would be God's telling us in mind and in heart what He wishes to tell us. And sometimes that would come in phrases or sentences, but it's affirmation of the truthfulness of something. As in the case of Jesus' Atonement, we don't have many secular records about Jesus' ministry. Tacitus and a couple of others wrote more sentences about Jesus. But the witness of the New Testament plus the Book of Mormon and other things by the Spirit affirm that He lived and that He died and that He lives now.

HUGH HEWITT: In one respect, I as a Presbyterian, you as a Mormon, both believe extraordinary things.

NEAL MAXWELL: Yes.

HUGH HEWITT: But mine are so far removed from present day that Rex Lee, former Solicitor General of the United States, in his book poses the hypothetical question which I'll pose to you: How could anyone believe that these sorts of things happened in modern times?

NEAL MAXWELL: Because of the secular mind. We're heavily sedated by secularism and we have to throw off that sedation. As Paul says, the natural man regards these things as foolishness. (See 1 Corinthians 2:14.) But the Spirit is the key and it's the Spirit that can talk to the heart and mind and affirm the reality of these things, whether it's two thousand years ago or four thousand years ago. The Spirit cuts across cultures, cuts across languages—all of those things with the laser light precision that only the Spirit can give us.

HUGH HEWITT: When did you first feel that witness of the Spirit in your life?

NEAL MAXWELL: Probably around the time my sister was ill. It had nothing to do with the Book of Mormon, but it did in a related sense. She lay dying of whooping cough, six weeks old. Antibiotics were not available. I watched my father, after the manner of the New Testament, bless her by the power of the priesthood, and I saw her begin to breathe again. I knew then the power of the priesthood was real. She's a mother of seven and a nurse today, and so on. But at that moment I had experienced seeing the Spirit operate. Now, only later did I read the Book of Mormon. It came along later. But I began to feel a transcendent relationship with God encouraging these things which did not depend upon the pedestrian ways of knowing that to most people are all they have.

HUGH HEWITT: How old were you when you witnessed your sister's healing?

NEAL MAXWELL: I'd have been about fourteen. I was a grease monkey at a Greyhound Bus Depot. I came home at three in the morning, saw the lights on. I knew she was ill and said to myself, "This is big trouble." And when I got inside, she was in lying on the round dining room table and had stopped breathing. And then, the ordinance we utilize with the priesthood in the Church occurred, and she began to breathe again.

HUGH HEWITT: And you hadn't read the Book of Mormon at that point?

NEAL MAXWELL: No. No, I hadn't. My grandchildren are doing much better at their ages. They've read the Book of Mormon. But at that point though, it was in our home, at fourteen I hadn't really delved into its pages. Later my intellectual testimony came to me as I consumed it and so many other writings. But experientially and involving the Spirit, this other occurred first as I began to be familiar with these things.

HUGH HEWITT: So much of the Mormon practice concerns itself with the family.

NEAL MAXWELL: It does.

HUGH HEWITT: And the passing on of the belief system through families. Did that go on in your home when you were small?

NEAL MAXWELL: It did. The faith was inherited in a sense, so then I needed to examine and validate it. But I remember my parents giving vocal prayers. One night when I was coming home from a date—they didn't know I was standing and waiting courteously for them to finish—and I heard them pleading for me by name and for my sisters. They were a praying family. My father was what we call a ward clerk. On fast day he would count the tithing from the people and stack up the coins. Nobody had checks in those days, or big bills. He cared for those sacred funds, and again I could see that this principle was special to him as he used that same round dining room table. So I saw prayer, I saw the power of healing occur. I saw my parents thrilled with the Scriptures. So it was a pervasive thing in our home. We were poor but rich in the things of the Spirit.

HUGH HEWITT: Did you ever imagine in your early life that you would be called to a leadership position in this Church of nine million living members?

NEAL MAXWELL: No, not at all. Not at all. In fact, early in life my level of self-esteem was quite low. I raised pigs. I had a severe case of acne. I didn't grow when I should have and did not make the basketball team. Things looked difficult. It was then, it seems to me Hugh, that the Lord was nudging me away from basketball—maybe the acne gave me greater empathy for people—but He was doing things with me that I wasn't conscious of. And certainly there was no thought of any kind of high Church position at that point.

HUGH HEWITT: Does the Lord work that way? By inflicting small or large pains on our lives so that fruit would come later?

NEAL MAXWELL: I think He does. He gives us shaping tutorials—not only early in life but all through life. And for me that has happened enough times that I can acknowledge divine design and turn around and look at the montage and see pattern and purpose. But when you're in the middle of them, that's where faith comes in.

HUGH HEWITT: I'm sure you've heard the objection: "That sounds like a rather sadistic God, to force people to suffer. To what end?"

NEAL MAXWELL: He says in one of our Scriptures, "All these things shall give the experience and shall be for thy good." It's tutorial from a loving God who wants us to be stretched, to become more like His Son Jesus. And you can't learn patience without the clinical experiences. That's one of my challenges. When I first realized years ago that I had to be more patient—I was so immature—I thought, *All right, Heavenly Father, if I've got to be more patient, let's get it over with right now!* Instead, I have to pass through the clinical experiences. As difficult a passage as it is, it's what's really going on. And there really is no other way, but He gives us the kind of customized challenges that we need.

HUGH HEWITT: Any experiences of doubt?

NEAL MAXWELL: Oh, I think doubt in the sense that I would wonder at times how God would be able to achieve His purposes out of a situation that appeared so bleak and difficult to me. We have another scripture, Hugh, that says, I do not know the meaning of all things, but I know that God loves His children. There are ever so many times that we don't know the meaning of things: what's happening to us, or around us. But, we know He loves us. And that love is felt. It reassures us even when we can't give glib responses as to why something is happening.

HUGH HEWITT: I think you quoted Nephi just now.

NEAL MAXWELL: I did.

HUGH HEWITT: So my question is . . . "I do not know the meaning of all things." It's in a lot of Mormon literature. I'm not well read in the Book of Mormon. But I always ask myself then, *Well, why not? Why not let us know all things?*

NEAL MAXWELL: First of all, I don't think we're intellectually able to understand all things from the beginning to the end the same way that God does. Secondly, we're to pass through this life and overcome by faith. That means, yes, we're to acquire knowledge, and we validate certain doctrines, but He wants us to develop faith because it's an everlasting quality that we will need. So He tries and develops our faith and our patience. He doesn't try our ability to make money or achieve political power. He tries our faith and patience. All the trappings we have here, we leave behind when we go through the veil of death. But faith and patience, mercy, empathy—these are portable. They go with us.

HUGH HEWITT: But what do the Scriptures reveal about the "why" of developing faith? I assume God the Almighty could have made us any way He wanted to make us. Why this way?

NEAL MAXWELL: I think He wants us to become like Him, and there's no way we can have greater empathy and patience and long-suffering except we go through the clinical experiences. I don't know how one could have empathy in the abstract. To stand as we did around the grave of our first grandchild who died at birth helped me to be a more compassionate person. And maybe the acne gave me a little more empathy—not enough mind you, but a little more than I'd have had. All the experiences become relevant if we are to become more like Jesus. In fact He says that, Hugh. He says, "Take My yoke upon you and learn of Me." And for us to take His yoke upon us means we, in our small way, experience some of the things He experienced, and thereby we learn of Him. I don't know how you do all that in the abstract.

> There are ever so many times that we don't know the meaning of things: what's happening to us, or around us. But, we know He loves us. And that love is felt. It reassures us even when we can't give glib reponses as to why something is happening.

HUGH HEWITT: You've mentioned the acne of your youth a couple of times. Was that a searingly painful problem at that age?

NEAL MAXWELL: It was for me socially, and it combined with the fact that I raised pigs. So I'm still somewhat scarred from it. Being excluded or being left out matters so greatly when we're young. I had a lot of wonderful friends, but I sensed that I wasn't always in the inner circle of things.

HUGH HEWITT: Did you ever feel . . . I know you've seen the healing of your sister, and I assume other miracles which I'll come back to. But did you ever feel the hand of God at any particular moment?

NEAL MAXWELL: Oh, I see it in what you'd call "micro-ways" all the time. The intertwining of our lives, the experiences through which we pass. But one answer would be the island of Okinawa, fifty years ago, in the middle of battle, being eighteen years of age. The Japanese had tried to find our mortar position, unsuccessfully. All of us, I'm sure, were praying, not just I. But the Japanese artillery finally found the range with one shell, and they should have fired for effect. But I, and I'm sure others, pled with Him to stop the shelling. No more shells fell. I made a commitment right then to try to serve Him for the rest of my life. So while the blessing was a collective blessing, I made an individual promise to Him. Obviously, better men than I died on Okinawa, but I've tried to keep that promise.

HUGH HEWITT: That's not quite the fox-hole conversion that we've heard about, because you were already a believer when you were in it.

NEAL MAXWELL: Already a believer.

HUGH HEWITT: But was it a bargain with God?

NEAL MAXWELL: It was my naive pledge in which I thought I could pay Him back. Now I'm in worse shape than ever—I owe Him so much more! But in my ignorance I thought that if I served Him, maybe I could pay Him back. By the way, it was in that same and another fox-hole. Having been ordained a priest in the Church, though a young man, I blessed my sacrament on what I thought had been Sundays, as best I could tell, because I'd been trained at home that you have sacrament on Sunday. So I would get a C-ration biscuit and some canteen water and bless them and have my sacrament. No big deal for me; that's how I'd been trained. But the training matters in the sense that I understood about prayer and made my selfish plea to God, and I'm now trying to keep the promise I made.

> There will be the great winding up scene where Jesus will come again not to the meekness of the manger, but in majesty and power. And it will come in a time of great tribulation, including in Jerusalem. And so all of His purposes will be achieved.

HUGH HEWITT: Okinawa was one of the bloodiest battles of World War II.

NEAL MAXWELL: About two hundred twenty thousand people died.

HUGH HEWITT: Did that call into question the justice of a God that would allow that sort of thing to happen?

NEAL MAXWELL: I'm sure at that time I couldn't have processed that question very well, but in retrospect it seems to me that God leaves us free. He is deeply committed to our moral agency and to letting people make mistakes if they choose to. And war is the reflection of how institutions fail and of the corruption of individuals. And yet, God leaves us mortals free to make decisions. Sometimes God intervenes as in the Noachian flood, or in Sodom and Gomorrah, but not always. And so needless and terrible tragedies occur because of leaders' and people's misuse of their freedom.

HUGH HEWITT: The Latter-day Saints are now busy in Japan. Is there some irony in that?

NEAL MAXWELL: There was great irony in my going back to Okinawa this June, after fifty years, and ordaining what we call a patriarch in the Church. It was a man who survived at the age of eight the onslaught of that terrible battle and saw his father and his brother killed in the battle of Shuri, in which our outfit was somewhat involved. And to place my hands on his head and ordain him a patriarch in the Church was especially meaningful. Of course, he and I didn't know each other then, but in 1945 I had with me a tattered carbon copy of my own patriarchal blessing that I took with me to war; it said I would survive. I believed in it. Hence to be able to ordain him a patriarch, another survivor of the Battle of Okinawa, was one of those positive ironies that life is filled with, as well as negative ironies.

HUGH HEWITT: Is God acting through history to a conclusion?

NEAL MAXWELL: Yes, all His purposes will be achieved. There will be the great winding up scene where Jesus will come again not to the meekness of the manger, but in majesty and power. And it will come in a time of great tribulation, including in Jerusalem. And so all of His purposes will be achieved. Meanwhile, each of us goes through the mortal experience, hopefully learning in such a way that we can become more like Him and His Son Jesus.

HUGH HEWITT: Do the Saints spend much time, as some denominations do, worrying about exactly when the Second Coming will be?

NEAL MAXWELL: No, because we're told that the angels up in heaven don't know, and they're a reasonably informed group. So if they don't know, then there's no real point in our trying to be too calendric about that. But, Jesus does tell us to notice the leaves on the fig tree; and once they sprout, they don't retract. So while we're chiliastic, we're not preoccupied with the Second Coming. But neither should we be surprised if some of the events converge in our time.

HUGH HEWITT: Let me turn now to some of the theology or the doctrine of the Latter-day Saints, and I'll quote Rex Lee. It's a wonderful book, *What Mormons Believe*.

NEAL MAXWELL: Yes, he's a wonderful man.

HUGH HEWITT: At one point he writes, "The Church of Jesus Christ of the Latter-day Saints is not just another church, it is the kingdom of God." Unpack that for me.

NEAL MAXWELL: To ears that are not prepared to understand us, it will sound very bold. We believe that the church that existed anciently with apostles and prophets was restored in 1830. Further, that we carry the keys to the priesthood and the Kingdom's major doctrines, such as the Atonement, forward into the world. So, it isn't in our view simply another church, it really does represent a restoration. We know that sounds strange to people. We try not to forget that we need to be very meek and humble in the midst of that bestowal. But Rex is right in what he said. For instance, Hugh, in the Bible you will not read the phrase, "plan of salvation." Obviously implicit in the Scriptures is that God has a plan. In the Restoration Scriptures it's mentioned many times that we're sent here by God to be proved and tested after which will come the Resurrection and the Judgment. We, therefore, have a context, a framework for our faith that is really quite unique.

HUGH HEWITT: Restoration of what?

NEAL MAXWELL: All that God ever bestowed upon man in terms of doctrines and ordinances. We don't believe, for instance, that Christianity began with Christ in the meridian of time. We roll it back to the time of Adam when the gospel was there and Jesus, as Jehovah, helped to tutor Adam. Then various apostasies occurred. Then Jesus' ministry occurred with an apostasy after that. Hence the Restoration in the nineteenth century.

HUGH HEWITT: What was the apostasy after Jesus? That's where I lose the thread.

NEAL MAXWELL: The loss of the Apostles. The fragmentation of some of the key doctrines. The loss of priesthood power and the ordinances of the holy temple. The loss of revelation to an institution. Thus we come along and say we have additional Scriptures including the Book of Mormon, which you have sitting on your lap. It has as its subtitle, "Another Testament of Jesus." So we see all this as Christocentric and as restorative. And, again, we try to be meek and humble in view of the boldness of these assertions.

HUGH HEWITT: The Apostle Paul . . . In all of your books, Elder Maxwell, you quote freely from Paul and indeed from all of Scripture.

NEAL MAXWELL: Paul was so very literate.

HUGH HEWITT: Were they part of the restored Church—the falling out occurred afterward—or an incomplete church?

NEAL MAXWELL: Paul had the fullness when he was there, but he warned that the Second Coming would not occur except that there occur a great falling away first. (See 2 Thessalonians 2:3.) And much of

Paul's writing concerns the apostasy that was happening in his time. He saw the ending, we think, of the meridian church and looked forward to a restitution of all things. So it's there in his writings. In fact, I gave a long sermon on the apostasy once and quoted liberally from Paul. He was quite concerned, deeply concerned, about what was happening in the fragmentation of the faith while he was still alive.

HUGH HEWITT: The implication can be unsettling, particularly for an evangelical Presbyterian like me. But luckily we don't live in an age where we go to war over these things.

NEAL MAXWELL: Exactly.

HUGH HEWITT: What does it imply for my theology that yours is restored and mine is not?

NEAL MAXWELL: Keep everything that you've got that's good and true, which is much. Let us add to what you already have—what we consider to be the fullness of the faith, including much more information about Jesus. All this would give you more understanding of the plans and purposes of life. So we would salute you for all the faith you have and then ask if you would consider letting us share with you what we have by way of abundance in the Restoration.

HUGH HEWITT: When I visited the Temple Square Visitor Center—a wonderful facility—a Sister Hougue from Switzerland took me through. And it's a nice explanation of Mormon doctrine and Mormon teaching. But she said it was all summarized in the three words, "Read, ponder and pray." Is it the belief of the Church that anyone who will read the Book of Mormon, ponder it, and pray as to whether or not it's true, it will be revealed that it is true?

NEAL MAXWELL: We believe that, we teach that, and we say that. And, in fact, the Book of Mormon itself says that when you receive these things, ask God if they are true. So we believe in a process of self-verification. People with an open mind can read the Book and verify it for themselves. Of course that's now happened in millions of cases. So yes, we do think self-validation happens and that's the strength of the Church. Individuals don't have to depend upon my testimony; they can have one of their own, each member.

HUGH HEWITT: Nine million souls alive and growing. Fifty plus temples?

NEAL MAXWELL: Forty-eight.

HUGH HEWITT: Forty-eight.

NEAL MAXWELL: More to come.

HUGH HEWITT: What's your vision for the Church at the end of time? Do you have an idea of what it ought to look like or what it will look like?

NEAL MAXWELL: Well, demographically, we're probably going to be a Church of forty or fifty million in another several decades. But, the Book of Mormon tells us the real demography, namely, that while we'll be scattered all around the face of the earth, our dominions will be comparatively small. We are never going to be, by the world's standards, massive. And therefore, we see that as consistent with the words of Jesus, that "straight and narrow is the way and few there be that find it." There is a great theological safety net, however, Hugh, placed under all of this in our theology: Any who have not heard about the Restoration in their lifetime will receive a chance to hear about it in the spirit world, in paradise, before the Final Judgment. But demographically, we're minuscule and won't ever be massive.

HUGH HEWITT: Well now I have heard. You know, if I were not to convert, do I get the safety net?

NEAL MAXWELL: You've got the safety net, unless you've really heard it and rejected it. Which you haven't.

HUGH HEWITT: Explain that for me.

NEAL MAXWELL: Sometimes in our naiveté, as I did as a missionary, I would knock on people's doors in eastern Canada and be rejected thinking, *They had their chance.* They hadn't had a full chance at all. It has to be a true testing and evaluation with praying and pondering and enough time so that people can say, I believe it, or, I don't believe it. And most people never get that chance in this life.

HUGH HEWITT: Picking up on your missionary work in eastern Canada. How long were you there—

NEAL MAXWELL: Two years.

HUGH HEWITT: Two years? Why does the Church send so many young people off to do missions?

NEAL MAXWELL: Because of this major responsibility we feel to tell people about the Restoration. I went to a town with a wonderful Baptist minister in rural Ontario. And he went on the radio and told people, "Don't open your doors to those two boys." And they didn't. We went about six weeks before we were invited in. We go out because we're saying, "We love the Bible too, but we've got another witness for Jesus Christ and we'd like to share it with you: the Book of Mormon." That's why we go. Incidentally, it's very good training for young men and young women to have that experience, and it was for me. I'd been a first sergeant in the infantry and I needed to be more meek and more humbled. And I was humble.

> When Jesus said in the New Testament, "I have other sheep not of this fold," He was referencing the people here in the Americas. When He came here, He then referenced His visit to the lost tribes. So it's an open-ended canon of Scripture, which is rather unusual.

HUGH HEWITT: I think it was your son Cory who said, "When it's necessary to bring Dad down a peg, we remind him that he had to excommunicate more people than he converted."

NEAL MAXWELL: I did. I went back after the war and there were some of our number who had fallen away and we held several Church disciplinary councils since they didn't want to belong anymore, and we accommodated them. Thus I was not the most productive missionary, because I entered upon the scene after World War II and things were a little bit in disarray in one location.

HUGH HEWITT: What does it mean to excommunicate someone now?

NEAL MAXWELL: Most of the time, Hugh, when people are excommunicated, they've already left the church themselves. So they've ceased believing, or ceased believing in the Church institutional, lost their testimony, or in some cases, misbehaved in some gross way. Then, the only thing we have, and the only thing we should have, is ecclesiastical power to withdraw the fellowship of the Church, while hoping they will come back in some time. And of course many do. But not enough.

HUGH HEWITT: Elder Maxwell, from the very first conversation I have had in preparation for this series with a member of the Latter-day Saints, everyone has stressed to me that it is a Church of continuing revelation. Would you explain what that means?

NEAL MAXWELL: In the body of doctrine and in the Scriptures, our canon is open ended. We have the Book of Mormon, the Doctrine and Covenants, and Pearl of Great Price—so it is an expanding array of Scriptures. That's the corporate or institutional part of my response to your inquiry. The other part is more operational and personal, the part where people seek and receive on occasion guidance for their personal lives. This part comes to us individually. While the other part is the additional volumes of Scripture. We believe that there is another book to come forth, a record of the ten lost tribes of Israel. When Jesus said in the New Testament, "I have other sheep not of this fold," He was referencing the people here in the Americas. When He came here, He then referenced His visit to the lost tribes. So it's an open-ended canon of Scripture, which is rather unusual.

HUGH HEWITT: Is there any idea where that lost tribes book will come forth from?

NEAL MAXWELL: No, we have no idea whatsoever.

HUGH HEWITT: On the question of revelation, have you experienced it?

NEAL MAXWELL: Yes, I have. Often it comes in words or phrases such as when I am trying to select a state president to preside over a body of several thousand Saints. I may have a strong personal preference after I have interviewed thirty men but often the Spirit will say it should be so and so. I have also experienced it often in what might be very mild forms where it is time to go see someone in the hospital—only to get there a few moments before some major procedure is to happen and so on. I call that tactical revelation, but it's just as real as if it were theological.

HUGH HEWITT: Does it ever amount to the audible voice of God?

NEAL MAXWELL: The voice in the mind is there. I was about to pray a few days ago for an afflicted sister who was dying of cancer and about to leave four children. As I was about to pray the Spirit said, "That will not be necessary." I received a phone call about an hour later from Spokane saying that she had just died. Now for me, revelation doesn't have to be spectacular or global. It's the personalness of revelation that matters the most.

HUGH HEWITT: In your role as a steward of the Church, as one of the twelve Apostles who along with the three members of the First Presidency guide this massive Church, are there moments collectively or individually when there is a very obvious revelation?

NEAL MAXWELL: Yes, I have been present on four or five occasions in the upper room of the temple where that has happened. It's a very sacred special thing. Most of the time we give our views out of our own backgrounds and talents as we have to make a decision. But there are times when the President of the Church will be impressed to cut across that process in terms of announcing to us that something needs to be done. And we can't always explain the process but soon see the wisdom.

HUGH HEWITT: Can you describe it? I mean, what is that process like?

NEAL MAXWELL: It's the voice of the Spirit. It's the voice in the mind. It is the Lord speaking to us in such a way that when men may have had different opinions on something, then comes the prophetic intervention. There is a calmness and a serenity, and we vote to sustain that action, feeling the peace in our hearts even though a few moments before we might have felt differently about a matter. Now Paul says—and Hugh, this must be emphasized—that to the natural man, these things are foolishness, but the things of the Spirit are understood by the spirit. It's a lifelong experience—at least it has been for me, getting familiar with the Spirit and the nuances of it and trying to live in such a way that the Lord can speak to me more often; for instance, to be prompted to write a letter to a young man who was about to leave the missionary training center. He was discouraged and couldn't learn the language. The Spirit said, "Write the letter now." The letter apparently arrived when his bags were packed and he was leaving. So that's another example of tactical revelation. He stayed and then, went ahead with his mission. Thus I have to be careful so that I don't get so busy with paper that I neglect the Spirit.

HUGH HEWITT: About the Church's beliefs in common with the rest of Protestant Christianity: Jesus Christ is the Savior?

NEAL MAXWELL: Yes.

HUGH HEWITT: Jesus Christ atones for sins?

NEAL MAXWELL: Yes.

HUGH HEWITT: Where do—and I'll let you answer—where do Mormon theology and Protestant theology agree? And where do they disagree?

NEAL MAXWELL: We rejoice in sharing, as we do, what you've just described. It again is a matter of richness. For instance, for us in the Atonement of Jesus we understand that not only did He bear our sins to atone for them—what I call the "awful arithmetic of the Atonement"—but we're advised by Restoration Scriptures that He also took upon Him our sicknesses that He might understand what we go through when we have pain and grief. Mormon Scriptures say Jesus descended below all things in order to comprehend all things. So He has this resplendent empathy because He understood personally and perfectly the sicknesses and pains through which we pass. Not only was there the awful arithmetic of the Atonement, but there was the terrible, incredible aloneness that He endured when the Father withdrew His Spirit and left Jesus alone in Gethsemane and Calvary when we get the great forsakenness cry: "My God, My God, why hast Thou forsaken Me?" There is no answer to Jesus' why, yet He was submissive, He went forward with the Atonement and completed it so that there might be a Universal Resurrection. It is this enrichment and the sense of His being our Personal Savior that is so remarkable. One other thing: He created the worlds and some undisclosed part of the universe under the direction of the Father. Some want to regard Jesus as a great moral teacher. He is the greatest moral teacher. But He is so much more than that. He is the Lord of the universe. He is the executor of the Great Atonement. Hence each of us is an innkeeper, and we decide if there is room for Jesus. Christ is the Light of the World, and we so see Him, but then we also see everything else by His light.

HUGH HEWITT: Much of what you've said I can understand and consent to and agree with. Where do we disagree?

NEAL MAXWELL: I don't know regards the Atonement that there is great disagreement, because He is either the Redeemer or He's not. And if He is, and He is, then we have great compatibility around the thing that matters most. It's the central act of all human history. Everything else is ancillary compared to the Atonement.

HUGH HEWITT: The Nicene Creed begins, "We believe in God the Father, the Almighty, Maker of heaven and earth, and in Jesus Christ His only begotten Son"—sort of the great common bond of Christianity. Can Mormons consent to that as well, or is there a difference?

NEAL MAXWELL: On the Atonement, with God the Father as the One who had His Son redeem mankind, there would be great compatibility.

HUGH HEWITT: Well then, what happens to all of us, believers, Christians, non-believers, everyone, after we die?

NEAL MAXWELL: Everybody is to be resurrected. There is a Universal Resurrection because of Jesus' Atonement. Down at the battle monument at Corregidor, Hugh, there is this phrase about how, for those who have fallen, the day would come when they would hear "the low, clear reveille of God." All will be given the blessing of the Resurrection, but as Jesus said, "In My Father's house are many mansions." So we believe in a graded salvation depending on our performance here. A sweet Christian

> Some want to regard Jesus as a great moral teacher. He is the greatest moral teacher. But He is so much more than that. He is the Lord of the universe. He is the executor of the Great Atonement. Hence each of us is an innkeeper, and we decide if there is room for Jesus.

lady who has never asked for much, who has been a high performer in life though a low demander, has a greater reward than somebody who has not been careful about spiritual things. But everybody will be resurrected. The Resurrection will be universal.

HUGH HEWITT: I have been much taken by the discussion of the many mansioned room because even the Catholic three tiers of hell, purgatory, and heaven is much less complex than Mormon theology when it comes to the afterlife. Can you expand for our audience, which I'm sure shares this curiosity with me, as to what the Latter-day Saints believe?

NEAL MAXWELL: In the terrestrial world these are those who misbehave badly and yet it is still a kingdom of glory, showing the generosity of God. The Terrestrial Kingdom is for the honorable people of the earth and for those who have not been valiant in their testimony of Jesus, decent, good people. The

Celestial Kingdom, which Paul calls the glory of the sun, is for those who have received Jesus fully, received all of His ordinances and have tried to become more and more like Him and who have had a very, very serious discipleship throughout their lives. These have endured well to the end. Within that degree of glory is the upper realm of the Celestial Kingdom, and that is related to having been faithful to what we call our sacred temple ordinances where we are asked to be much more committed and consecrated to Him. In that sense the gradations are more abundant than in other faiths.

HUGH HEWITT: Baptism for the dead. Does that free someone to become a member of the Celestial Kingdom as opposed to the Terrestrial Kingdom?

NEAL MAXWELL: If they accept the gospel beyond the veil of death, then they will be entitled to all the blessings just as if they had accepted it here. That's the safety net that undergirds the massive human family—what, seventy billion of us so far? And we have reached but a small portion of those in terms of preaching the gospel here. So the mercy of God is seen in that all will have had the opportunity; they who accept the gospel in paradise will have all the same blessings just as if they received the gospel in mortality.

HUGH HEWITT: Let me turn to quote you back to yourself from your book, *Lord Increase Our Faith*— I think it is your most recent one or at least at the time of this interview. "How large is the Lord's work? There are now nearly nine million members of the Church living on the earth. However, there are several million members beyond the veil. It is likewise expansive to learn that God's work is not confined to this planet." In a letter to one of your grandchildren you hit on the same point. What does that mean?

NEAL MAXWELL: God created a multiplicity of worlds besides this one. God isn't the God of just one planet. In fact the New Testament says the worlds were created by Jesus, plural. Our theology, again in its richness, would say there are worlds without number. We don't know how many have people on them, we don't know where these planets are. But there are other people on other planets unknown to us. Our Scriptures say that God told Moses only about this planet. I guess he

> Our Scriptures say that God told Moses only about this planet. I guess he didn't have a high enough security clearance to be given all that other data! But we're not worshiping a one-planet God. How vast in space His dominions are we do not know, but we are not alone in the universe.

didn't have a high enough security clearance to be given all that other data! But we're not worshiping a one-planet God. How vast in space His dominions are we do not know, but we are not alone in the universe. And that again gives us a different sense of Jesus as the Creator, versus His being only a moral teacher or one of the minor prophets.

HUGH HEWITT: In all of the artwork surrounding Temple Square and in the initiation of visitors there is a lot of emphasis put on the cosmos and its expansiveness. Why?

NEAL MAXWELL: I guess it's because we're told so much about it. The Prophet Joseph Smith was told that God had created worlds without number. They are not numbered unto man, but they are numbered unto God, and that the inhabitants thereof are begotten sons and daughters unto Him. We're thus advised enough to excite and fire the imagination about space and what is out there, even though we can't give you any detail. It's embedded deeply in our theology. There is a phrase in our theology in which the Lord says, "My course is one eternal round," which suggests to me a repetitiveness in the execution of His plan of salvation that goes beyond this planet. We don't have the data, but the implications are clear.

HUGH HEWITT: So that somewhere else someone is at a different point in the time line of history?

NEAL MAXWELL: Yes, the process would be the same. One of the great clarion and crisp assertions in the modern Restoration Scriptures is that God describes what He is doing: "This is My work and My glory to bring to pass the immortality and eternal life of man." That's what's really going on.

HUGH HEWITT: The idea that also emerged from a number of your books is that Jesus volunteered in some sense to be the great atoner. What is the concept there? That's different from my concept.

NEAL MAXWELL: The concept. Again, it's the plan of salvation where, in the pre-mortal world, you and I existed as individuals, the Father described a need for a Redeemer on this planet who would atone for us and Jesus stepped forward and meekly said, "Here am I. Send Me." I've often said, "Never has anyone offered to do so much for so many with so few words as when Jesus said, 'Here am I. Send Me.'" He was then anointed to become the Messiah and the Redeemer of this planet and volunteered to take that on with so few words. And then occurred the birth at Bethlehem and, of course, Gethsemane and Calvary are the completion of that commitment on His part to redeem mankind for the Atonement.

HUGH HEWITT: Elder Maxwell, then do men and women aspire to be *like* Christ or be *equal* to Christ?

NEAL MAXWELL: To be *like* Him. He says in our Scriptures, "What manner of men and women ought you to be? I say unto you even as I am." And that means developing the attributes of love and mercy and empathy and submissiveness. He will always be our Savior. We can never be equal to Him, but we can become more like Him in those attributes. And that is where the clinical experiences come in. And that's why it is so important that we be willing to submit, because there is no way I can be more patient without the experiences that we're talking about. And we can't go home to Him unless we are more like Him. The Prophet Mormon, who is one of the last writers in the Book of Mormon, speaks of how Jesus waits for us with open arms. At that transcending moment at the entrance to His kingdom we can be clasped in the arms of Jesus. We can't have that transcendent experience except if we become more like Him. This is the journey of discipleship. It's worth all the tests and the trials and the inexplicable things through which we must pass.

HUGH HEWITT: How much time do you spend meditating on this or praying about this or considering your understanding of God?

NEAL MAXWELL: The interplay would be Scripture study, meditation, and prayer, and they go in different combinations. If I'm going to go bless the sick and somebody is dying of cancer, then I want to be able to say to that person what I am supposed to say. So some of it is operational, and some of it is pushing back one's chair and thinking about human suffering and how does one handle it, because it's so massive. And the presence of evil in the world which is so massive, too, except we begin to integrate into our thinking God's plan of salvation, knowing that He has made ample provision to see that His purposes are fulfilled. I do a lot of thinking about that and, of course, a lot of talking about it—probably too much talking. My investment in the Scriptures has been so intense in recent years, but I have never come out of that well of living water without a drink yet. The Scriptures are there, and I need always to be ready to discover them and their sudden blossoming into beauty and reality, such as a verse that's been there all the time, and I finally discovered it, because now I am ready.

HUGH HEWITT: You must have encountered people who I think the Old Testament phrase would be "hardened hearts." How do you persuade or tempt people with hardened hearts in Scripture or revelation?

NEAL MAXWELL: I don't know that you can do much, Hugh. I think it's a matter of loving and appreciating people whether they are doubters or agnostics. They are all the children of Heavenly Father. That's one of the great things that the plan of salvation tells us: who we and they are. They don't know who they are, but I do; and I must learn to love them, even if I disagree with them or they disagree with me. Even if they are critical of me, because they are my brothers and sisters. So I've got a transcendental relationship with them that goes beyond the tactical moments down here on earth as we may be colliding over some issue.

HUGH HEWITT: Well, you know, I've heard an awful lot of preachers in a lot of places, Elder Maxwell, talk about loving enemies. Does anybody really love their enemies?

NEAL MAXWELL: Well, Jesus did. He's the perfect example. I think some of the rest of us begin to approach it. It is one of the hardest things to do. Brigham Young said, in effect, near the end of his ministry, of loving his enemies, "You know it is hard to love someone who is trying to kill you, but I am trying and I am making some progress." The act of loving one's enemies and submissiveness are the greatest and the crowning things in discipleship. It shouldn't surprise us that they don't come early in one's discipleship. Instead they come near the end of the trail, when we are less selfish and less caught up with ego, so I don't think we should expect to arrive there quickly.

HUGH HEWITT: Well, you've anticipated my question about Church history, but I don't want to go over it yet. I want to come back to Church history and the history of the persecution of the Mormons. I'd like to tarry a little bit on this idea of compassion for your enemies and another quality you've written a lot about. You've written extensively about meekness and why it is important. Would you explain both what it is and why it is so important?

NEAL MAXWELL: Meekness has been a challenge for me. Not much can happen to us spiritually unless we're meek, unless we're pliable and teachable. If the ego is so intrusive, then not much can happen. So when one sees meekness in a George Washington, it's very, very impressive. When one sees the lack of meekness, you know there's going to be trouble. Much as I admire Winston Churchill, I would not describe him as meek. I admire it so much in those who have it. I think General George Marshall had it, to pick an Eisenhower who was way down in the ranks and bring him in to a position that later gave him the very Supreme Command that Marshall himself wanted. But FDR said, "I need you here," and Marshall said, "Mr. President, if that's where you need me, I'll stay." I love to see that meekness, because it facilitates all other virtues. If we are not meek, then it is going to be hard to love our enemies.

HUGH HEWITT: It must be a constant struggle for an Apostle of the Church, for whom hundreds if not thousands of people stand ready to do exactly what you want them to do.

NEAL MAXWELL: Adulation can be our ruination. We have to be very careful with it and, in a sense, not to inhale. To be meek—and that's again why the virtue is so important—is to realize that people sustain us because of the office we hold, in spite of our imperfections. We're struggling to be better disciples as are the members of the Church, and the fact that they love us and listen to us and follow us is wonderful, but I am under no illusions about how much of my developmental journey is left.

HUGH HEWITT: How do you, Neal Maxwell, cultivate you?

NEAL MAXWELL: I find it most useful to be serving people and to see, as I have done so many times lately, people who are full of faith in the midst of their life crises. I draw strength from them. I may give them some, but I draw strength from them. It helps to be out, as it were, among those who are wounded by life and to see a prodigal come home. This helps me with my weaknesses, because I see the long-suffering of God for them and see how much I still depend upon it for me.

HUGH HEWITT: At last year's General Assembly you gave a set of remarks which I had the opportunity to view, which cannot only be described as guardedly pessimistic; they were out-and-out pessimistic. You cited statistics of the number of children who wake up in homes without fathers, you talked about the incapacity named *evil*, per se. From small things as the coarsening of speech to large things like the level of violence. Why so bleak when you have the Restoration gospel in your hand?

NEAL MAXWELL: We need to know the context in which we function. It is not going to be a picnic. The context in which we function is one in which evil is aggressive and in which there is a kind of arrogant irreligion in the world. We still have to be meek, but we must recognize the enemy's order of battle, so to speak. But I am optimistic about the outcomes. However, the human family without the gospel or without strong families is not going to go very far. Unless we can fix families, you can't fix anything else. Most of the problems that are most vexing are things government really can't fix. They have to be fixed at a different level. That's the urgency of our message. I'd rather have ten commandments than ten thousand regulations, federal regulations. The government doesn't mean to be inept; it just finds a way to do that all the time. And unless we rebuild marriages and families, then we really are straightening deck chairs on the Titanic.

HUGH HEWITT: Is the Church of Jesus Christ of Latter-day Saints too insular, or is it sufficiently in the world that you looked out from that podium in that tabernacle and saw it to be in such bad shape?

NEAL MAXWELL: It's a good question. In February of 1996, the lines will cross for the first time; we will have more members of the Church outside the United States and Canada than inside. Thus we are in thousands of congregations in a hundred and fifty nations. Whatever insularity may have been there as a function of our past is rapidly being addressed because we're in the world. I myself have recently formed a stake in Singapore and in Bangkok, Thailand.

> Unless we can fix families, you can't fix anything else. Most of the problems that are most vexing are things government really can't fix. They have to be fixed at a different level. That's the urgency of our message.

We learn from these members in the world, and we become less provincial. Now one of our challenges is to make sure that it is the gospel that we share, not American management style such as when we go to Bangkok. We've got to distinguish between what is American and what is Christian. Sometimes there are happy coincidences, but not always.

HUGH HEWITT: People know the Mormon Church—when they don't know much about the Mormon Church—by a couple of things. One is the emphasis on family. One is the commitment with which tithing is pursued. Are you proud of these distinctive marks?

NEAL MAXWELL: I am, in the sense that at least it shows we know what matters, such as in terms of the institution of the family. We're not off on some tangential pathway that really isn't relevant. We shouldn't be proud in the sense that we feel any preeminence, but I'm grateful that we are focused on something so fundamental as the family. Sacrifice is so bound up with discipleship—tithing is a law of sacrifice. People think of the Church as being wealthy, when in fact we tend to spend what we take in and that includes the widow's mite. To watch people pay that tithe when they have so little, which is the case with most of our members overseas, is a marvelous thing. To see it in the Philippines where the people are poor, and to see it in India, fills me with gratitude that we are committed enough to ask our people to sacrifice—and to make some demands of them.

HUGH HEWITT: It's a uniquely American church, as we'll discuss shortly. Does it have a rough edge for other cultures? Is it just too American for other cultures? Obviously it's not—you're building temples, you have congregations across the globe.

NEAL MAXWELL: You know, I used to worry about it. Again, back to Book of Mormon. One prophet said, "In every nation Heavenly Father has placed people who can teach and lead their own people." And we're validating that all the time. They handle the cultural things pretty well. If we at headquarters are a little insensitive, unintentionally, they know how to handle that so that the family and tithing and temples go forward. So the rough edge, if it is there, would be unintended and probably quickly abated by the way the leaders transculturize the whole thing.

HUGH HEWITT: Why are temples so important?

NEAL MAXWELL: Because within them we receive the crowning ordinances. The sealing of a marriage for time and for all eternity and the sealing of children to parents for time and eternity are accomplished only in temples. We believe the family can be a forever institution, and that's why temples administer these crowning ordinances. Again, these distinguish us from the world, because we're married not simply till death do us part but for time and for all eternity. Our task is to be faithful to those ordinances and covenants, and not all of us are.

HUGH HEWITT: Elder Maxwell, you've written repeatedly that people need to be valiant for the truth. What's that mean?

NEAL MAXWELL: At one level, Hugh, it means that we would honor Jesus enough to be able to partake of our own bitter cups without becoming bitter. It would mean that we would honor Him enough that if we've participated in a relationship that needs to be mended, we'll take the initiative and not hold back. In a broader way, it means not throwing in with the world, not being captivated by the world and all that it has to offer. We can be neighborly but distinctive not only in how we believe, but how we behave. The latter, of course, is harder to do.

HUGH HEWITT: What's it mean vis-à-vis people who are not members of the Saints? I know we're on television; I know it's hard not to be self-conscious of that. But what, as an Apostle, do you need to tell a Presbyterian like me to be valiant for the truth?

NEAL MAXWELL: For you, in the context of your theology, it includes to make sure that you talk about the Atonement of Jesus. And that your children and loved ones know how you feel about Him. Thus religion isn't something that's off to the side or is an occasional thing—I'm sure it's not with you. But for a lot of people, religion is something that has to do with christenings and marriages and funerals. Hence to fly the flag, so to speak—whether one is a Presbyterian or a Mormon—means to convey to our children, as best we can, how much this all means to us. Again, one can do that without being confrontive, but I worry about people for whom religion is such an occasional thing that you can hardly know that it's operative in their lives. Commitment doesn't mean you have to be flamboyant.

HUGH HEWITT: But I expected that you would tell me *I* ought to, and by extension our television viewers, that *they* ought to investigate seriously consider joining the Mormon Church because it is the Kingdom of God on Earth.

NEAL MAXWELL: I'd be delighted if you were to do that and would assist you, but our friendship isn't conditioned upon your doing that.

HUGH HEWITT: But how urgent is that missionary zeal in the Church?

NEAL MAXWELL: Oh, it's quite urgent. It's quite urgent. And we have forty-nine thousand missionaries out now. One of them will soon be a grandson of mine—don't know where he'll be going to. It's quite urgent, but we can be infused with a feeling of urgency without being oppressive and without being offensive. Generally, we do best when people are, again in the words of the Book of Mormon, "in a preparation to hear the Word." That's when we're most effective. Meanwhile, I think our friendships are to be conducted in a way that would befit a Presbyterian and a Mormon. Let it be that kind of spiritual conviviality.

HUGH HEWITT: Let's turn to Church history. And I've got to compliment the Church on the way it is arranged at Temple Square, both in the films and in the beauty of the Square. It is a difficult history. The early history is a crisis followed by a disaster followed by crisis followed by killings and murders. And I came to the conclusion there were three reasons. Either it's polygamy, or blasphemy, or anti-slavery, or all three. Why is it that the Saints were so persecuted for so long?

NEAL MAXWELL: It is a composite of what you describe. The distinctiveness of the theology would account for a good part of it. Yes, people worried about whether Church members would have too much political power in Missouri and Illinois. It's more the distinctiveness of the theology which irritates people. And I suppose we at times contributed to that unwittingly, since Jesus said, "By their fruits you shall know them"; we need to be more fruitful, some of us. Even so, others need to be less critical. Unwittingly at times, some of us have been a little too bombastic or single-minded, when we might have been better neighbors. Having said all of that, it is in the very nature of the theology that it's going to irritate some people, because of the seeming exclusivity that surrounds it and to which they react differently.

HUGH HEWITT: Is it "*seeming* exclusivity," or is it *real* exclusivity?

NEAL MAXWELL: Oh, it's *real* in the sense of the reality of the "straight and narrow path and few there be that find it." But the "seeming" is applicable when we are not as diplomatic as we ought to be or are not as participative as we ought to be in the hopes and dreams of other people, because we get so busy with life in the Church. So, unwittingly we may contribute to that feeling. But, as you point out, after all the traumas and we came west to a place nobody else wanted, the enemies of the Church were not long in following us up and attempting to make life a little miserable. Brigham Young got pretty philosophical about opposition. We're meeting in his house, of course, for this interview. He was hauled in front of a territorial judge near the end of his life. Some of the Church members said, "You don't have to put up with that." Brigham said, in effect, "Don't worry about it." There was tranquillity in him and less excitation over what, if it had occurred earlier in his life, might have caused him to be very agitated. In fact, Brigham said near the end of his life: "I can now hear the stories of our persecution and they don't make me agitated as they used to."

> The big challenge for Christians is secularism and the arrogant irreligion in the world. In America we're not supposed to have an established church but we're supposed to permit the free exercise of religion under the First Amendment. I hope irreligion doesn't become the state religion by default.

HUGH HEWITT: You wrote a book reflecting on Joseph Smith's letters from Liberty Jail, where he's writing from Liberty Jail. What does Joseph Smith mean to you?

NEAL MAXWELL: He is the Restoration Prophet. He is the person through whom the Lord poured the translations and the revelations of those last days and to whom the keys were restored. Restoration theology is not passive; it is very bold. For us to claim—as we do—that Elijah came back and restored the sealing power to Joseph that is now used in the holy temples is a very bold assertion. All of that happened through the Prophet Joseph Smith, compressed in a time frame of but a few years. So he is absolutely remarkable. But he said near the end of his life, in Nauvoo, "I never told you I was perfect, but there is no error in the revelations which I have taught you."

HUGH HEWITT: Is there some modern skepticism about Joseph Smith because of the number of false prophets that populate the world today?

NEAL MAXWELL: Oh I expect there is. The whole notion of having a modern prophet is rejected by many. The whole notion of having additional Scriptures is rejected by some who think the Bible is all there is. So we start off on a foundation that is unusual to begin with. This is complicated further by others who come and go with their claims, thus keeping some from examining the substance of Joseph's ministry which bears up well under any scrutiny. I don't know that anyone has had the scrutiny in the religious world in modern times that Joseph had.

HUGH HEWITT: Do you, are you troubled by . . . ? Well, let me introduce this by telling you what happened: I told a number of my friends that I was coming over to visit you and chat in connection with this show, and my evangelical friends—a few of them—came forward with book after book.

NEAL MAXWELL: Anti-Mormon literature.

HUGH HEWITT: You bet! "I've got a basketful of it back at the house. Why that level of hostility?

NEAL MAXWELL: Part of it, to give them the benefit of the doubt, occurs because they don't think we're Christians. They use definition as a way of creating exclusion. So our not being Christians, in their eyes, bothers some of them. This creates a plethora of anti-Mormon literature. Interestingly enough, the names Jesus and Christ appear in the formal names of the Church. The Book of Mormon is "another testament of Jesus Christ." We see Him as the Light of the World. But we can't persuade people against their will, and so they create a lot of literature. Some people actually have a business interest in anti-Mormon literature. But, again, for me, all that's not consequential.

HUGH HEWITT: You don't get angry?

NEAL MAXWELL: No, no. Years ago it used to irritate me. Now it amuses me. The big challenge for Christians is secularism and the arrogant irreligion in the world. In America we're not supposed to have an established church but we're supposed to permit the free exercise of religion under the First Amendment. I hope irreligion doesn't become the state religion by default. That's the real challenge, not the fact that one church may irritate another church. We'll just have to bear up under that. We have borne up all the time, and it's not in my judgment consequential. Meanwhile we need to continue to bring forth the fruit that will be the evidence that we really are Christians.

HUGH HEWITT: Does the Book of Mormon incite any kind of persecution around the globe the way that it incited persecution in the early days?

NEAL MAXWELL: Not around the globe. I've traveled a lot in recent years, and it is interesting to see the Book of Mormon take hold in a non-Christian culture where people have to come directly to Christianity and into the Church. Whereas here, as we proselytize in America, someone may have been a Catholic, a Baptist, a Presbyterian. That's not so in some of the Asian countries. They have to decide if it is a prophetic book. For some of them, that's quite easy to do; they have a tradition of prophets. So the fact that there might be a modern prophet doesn't "throw them" the way we find at times in Western culture.

HUGH HEWITT: The theology of continuing revelation where the President of the Church is also the Prophet of the Church, right now President Hinckley.

NEAL MAXWELL: Yes.

HUGH HEWITT: Isn't it a dangerous concept, the theology's constantly unfolding, that new revelations would come along? Isn't that an awful lot to vest in one individual?

NEAL MAXWELL: It is, but most of all, he has the meekness and the humility that go with that calling. He has two wonderful counselors, and he's got twelve Apostles to rely upon. Thus these things are not done in a corner. When there is to be a declaration, then it's handled in such a way that there is participation by those who are formally sustained as prophets, seers and revelators. So there's a constitutional protection, a procedural protection. Yet we like to have the Prophet be free, as he is, to be declarative so that we take full advantage of what the Spirit says to him. Brigham Young knew, for instance, that we were supposed to be in this valley; he'd seen it before he got here. Well, you don't want to have to process a vision through a committee.

HUGH HEWITT: Did he literally see it?

NEAL MAXWELL: He so said on several occasions that he had seen it in vision. Furthermore, one of his compatriots, Wilford Woodruff, later President of the Church, knew that the temple would be built out of granite years before they ever built it. Brigham Young began building it with a different kind of stone. Wilford Woodruff let that be, and finally they came around to putting the temple up in granite. We often get insights ahead of time, and, therefore, one would not want to impede that marvelous process. John Taylor, another President, said in England, he knew the Saints would soon be asked to leave England and gather to America. But it wasn't time yet, so he had to hold back. So prophets sometimes hold back until the Lord tells them the time is right. But I don't worry about any misuse of power. Embedded again in our theology is the fact that the Lord would never let the President of the Church lead the Church astray. And we rely upon that. But there are these other safeguards I've mentioned.

HUGH HEWITT: I want to go back for a minute to the most difficult concept in the theology for me and where it's really distinctive from my upbringing, my teaching, which is this idea of the pre-born state.

NEAL MAXWELL: Yes.

HUGH HEWITT: At one point in your writings you suggest that the handicapped may in fact choose to be handicapped in their pre-born state.

NEAL MAXWELL: One of the early leaders said that.

HUGH HEWITT: Well, explain that.

NEAL MAXWELL: We don't know that as settled Church doctrine. But it is true that in the pre-mortal estate things would have been explained to us in a way that we cannot comprehend now. Then there was, as we say in the Church, a kind of veil drawn over memories of the pre-mortal world, and we're operating now by faith. Illustratively, here comes a new grandchild without a left hand into our family. We regard her as a special spirit.

HUGH HEWITT: Your family?

NEAL MAXWELL: Into my own family. Instead of being dismayed by that—and we know there are lots of surgeries and problems that lie ahead—we trust the Lord. Thus, the Nephi quote again: "I don't know the meaning of all these things," but I know God loves His children. We regard God as omniscient. He knows about all these things, He has made ample provision to help us, individually, through whatever our circumstances may be. As to what role we had in choosing, I don't know. But we were likely well-informed ahead of time as to what to expect when we came here. Of course, Jeremiah was told by the Lord, "Before I formed thee in the belly, I ordained thee a prophet unto the nations." So the pre-mortal existence is part of the plan of salvation, and it makes a tremendous difference in the perspective we have with regard to this life.

> . . . Jeremiah was told by the Lord, "Before I formed thee in the belly, I ordained thee a prophet unto the nations." So the pre-mortal existence is part of the plan of salvation, and it makes a tremendous difference in the perspective we have with regard to this life.

HUGH HEWITT: I have seen the film of you teaching your extended family, all those grandchildren—and there are a lot of them. And when you told me when we sat down that your new granddaughter had been born without a hand, I thought to myself, *Now, there was an occasion for someone to get angry with God.* That never crossed your mind?

NEAL MAXWELL: No, no. In fact when the little girl's parents came over four months before her birth, to tell us that they'd done the ultrasounds, my first response was, "That means we've got a special spirit coming." This is how we feel about Anna-Josephine. I can't comprehend all that it will mean, but there's no anger. It's a cause for submissiveness. She is, she's already lighting up the landscape. And as one watches her siblings hold her, it isn't just Anna-Josephine who's going to learn. The siblings are getting an experience in love. Heavenly Father gets multiple use out of single situations. He's always teaching—if we're ready to learn. In all these things, there's no occasion for bitterness. Puzzlement, yes. What did Paul say? We're perplexed but not in despair.

HUGH HEWITT: Did it make you more compassionate for people who grow angry with God?

NEAL MAXWELL: I have compassion or empathy for people who get angry with God, because it seems to them that they've had a poor circumstance in which to live. I have admiration for those without certain blessings, as with the man from India, when I was with him out in the midst of the poverty. He was one of our priesthood leaders there. I said, "How do you handle all of this suffering and poverty?" He said, "Brother Maxwell, everybody has a cross to bear. In India, we are poor economically, but we are rich in our families. In America, you're rich economically, but your families are poor; they are in trouble." Now to have him process the massive suffering and deprivation in India in the context of faith was a great strength to me. I've said so many times, "I draw strength from people." I hope I give a little bit, but I draw strength from them.

HUGH HEWITT: In one of your books you wrote about the need to cultivate spiritual memories.

NEAL MAXWELL: Yes.

HUGH HEWITT: What did that mean?

NEAL MAXWELL: It means to make sure that enriching memories are not lost to the family and posterity. My wife and I, as grandparents, share those memories with our children and grandchildren, so that the family institutional memory is not lost in the generations but, rather, is preserved. Hence my father's experience as a convert to the Church is preserved. My great-grandfather and mother's experience coming across the plains is preserved. This is really, in a sense, as much a part of family history as names on a page. It takes work. My wife really deserves so much credit for preserving it. She has done an individual history and genealogical book for all twenty-two of our grandchildren with not just names but, in the back of the book, the spiritual experiences. I will give a speech Wednesday night that will be somewhat autobiographical. We will preserve that for all of them. It's going to have in it a report card when I got a D+ in English that I didn't deserve fully from a teacher who loved me enough to discipline me and beckon me to be more interested in the world of words. Now my grandchildren will have a copy of that report card. They're doing much better than I, by the way, but they need to know that it was a defining experience for their grandfather. This, too, is part of spiritual memory.

HUGH HEWITT: Are you driven? Are all LDS people, but especially you, Neal Maxwell, driven to discover their ancestors, to bring them into the full community of what I guess is the celestial state to be?

NEAL MAXWELL: We call that the Spirit of Elijah in which there is an Alex Hailey Roots phenomenon going on in the Church. Yes, we do have this keen interest in discovering them and bringing them forward so the temple ordinances can be done. But, as I said earlier, it is not just the ordinances; I genuinely want to know more about them. I'm interested to know my grandfather saw a bag of money fall off a stagecoach once. He was in the midst of poverty, but—and nobody saw him—he picked it up and returned it to the person on the stagecoach. I want my youngsters to know about that episode.

HUGH HEWITT: Is that one of the spiritual memories, then?

NEAL MAXWELL: Yes. Or, my father as wardclerk, at that round dining room table stacking up the tithing dimes and quarters and dollars, when we were so poor. I knew he knew these were sacred funds. Besides, everybody else was poor along with us, but we didn't know we were poor.

HUGH HEWITT: Well let's talk about wealth for a second. The Mormon Church has a very good reputation—not just for tithing but for having successful people associated with it. Joel Kotkin wrote the new book, *Tribes,* in which he identifies the Mormons as a leading economic engine. Joel's a friend of mine. With that great wealth, what's the responsibility of that great wealth?

NEAL MAXWELL: To do good with it. The Book of Mormon says it's all right if we seek it first, in order to do good. So the test, once again: Are wealthy persons being meek enough that they won't forget other people less well situated? This includes not just of what we give the Church, but what we do in private, quiet charity and charitable acts to people. Meek people won't forget poor people. But if we're not meek, once again, that's the virtue that drives so many other things. Then wealth will canker. Even if we don't misbehave, we get desensitized by it. Again, being out among the poor, the fast offering we have, the hundreds of humanitarian service projects we have, are various stimuli to remind us who we are and who those other people out there are.

HUGH HEWITT: One of the great common parables is the rich young man who comes to Jesus and says, "What do I have to do to be saved? I have kept all the commandments." He says, "Give it all away!" Why is it that—not just in the LDS, but in all Christian churches and all great religions, sort of—the vow of poverty is not more evident?

NEAL MAXWELL: I would regard that commandment of Jesus to that rich young man, in which He said, "One thing thou lackest," as customized. I wish I lacked just one thing. In his case, because he had much goods, it meant too much to him. You could have one wealthy person who would sit down tomorrow and write out a check for everything he owns and give it to the Church. No challenge for that person, but something else might be for him. This is where the customized challenges come in. I don't think a vow of poverty needs to be universal. I think loving our neighbor does. And then how we carry out that second commandment becomes an individual thing.

HUGH HEWITT: The customized challenge. God knows each individual well enough to customize a challenge for each individual. Persuade me of that, Neal Maxwell.

NEAL MAXWELL: I'm not sure I can persuade. I can only give you my autobiographical data. Patience for me has been a challenge. It seems I have repetitions of a course I thought I'd already been through but along came new clinical experiences to help me become more patient. For someone else who's quite patient this might not be a challenge. But instead in his case, he's not sweetly bold enough to do missionary work. God gives us what we need to bring us along, and it varies from person to person. Paul, for instance, didn't lack diligence. He was a zealot in persecuting Christians. What did he need? He needed charity. That's one of the reasons later on we get the thirteenth chapter of First Corinthians with its sublime words about charity!

HUGH HEWITT: But that's almost a warning because I want to test your patience again. You've been very diplomatic in discussing the differences in that which binds all Christianity and LDS together. But I think our audience is genuinely curious as to what is distinctive between the two religions or the different denominations within the One World Religion. What is the most distinctive thing that the Restoration Church claims that the rest of Christianity would not recognize?

NEAL MAXWELL: It would be the prophetic and apostolic keys with the channel of revelation open to modern man along with the return of all the ordinances necessary for salvation in their fullness and their completeness.

HUGH HEWITT: What is an ordinance?

NEAL MAXWELL: An ordinance is a baptism. An ordinance is a sealing in the temple to be married for time and for all of eternity. Those ordinances are part of what came back. I'd have to add quickly the Restoration Scriptures. The Bible is just precious beyond my capacity to describe its value, but it needs support. To have another book alongside it that witnesses that Jesus is the Christ is also an incredibly important thing in an age that's described by some as post-Christian. In modernity Jesus is diminished, yet here we come along with an enhanced Jesus and an enhanced understanding of who He is. We don't just have admiration for Jesus; we have adoration.

> Jesus let Himself be baptized—another ordinance, not for the remission of sins (He was sinless), but to show forth His obedience to God. Every one of the ordinances is required. They're nonnegotiable. They're not something we can parley over.

HUGH HEWITT: Let me pick up on one, personalize it again. My wife and I were married by both a Catholic priest and a Presbyterian; we got a double dose of marriage. But we're not ordained in a temple. So what is my relationship, in your understanding, to my wife in the next life?

NEAL MAXWELL: Well, I assume that such a marriage ends in death, and whatever degree of glory you would earn you would be given, but you would be separate and single, unless you had received the sealing ordinances for yourself and for your children. In that case you would be an eternal family. But not unless you do.

HUGH HEWITT: That's very bracing. What does that mean, "separate and single"? As opposed to? This must have been given a lot of consideration by Church theologians.

NEAL MAXWELL: Oh, yes. It means unwed, unmarried, and with no special relationship to your posterity. Perhaps that's why this sublime ordinance of sealing irritates people, because it seems so bold. Jesus let Himself be baptized—another ordinance, not for the remission of sins (He was sinless), but to show forth His obedience to God. Every one of the ordinances is required. They're nonnegotiable.

They're not something we can parley over. They're required. Whether it's baptism or the sealing ordinance, there are no exceptions.

HUGH HEWITT: A last question on that. For those like me, without a sealed marriage, does that mean they would not know their wife or their children at all?

NEAL MAXWELL: Oh, no, I'm sure you would know them, but there would probably be a difference in the sense of ultimately belonging to a family in perpetuity versus being part of a generalized group. That would be just one example. We really believe that everybody will have a chance to hear about these ordinances either here or in the spirit world before the Judgment and Resurrection. I would guess, generally, that the receptivity there will be much higher than it is here. The clutter that goes with the secular scene—the vaunting ambition and all of the things that consume us here—will fall away. People there will have a chance to hear the gospel. I do not know how many will accept it. But my own judgment is that there will be a higher acceptance level than here.

HUGH HEWITT: I can't remember if I read it in Rex Lee's book or in one of yours that the Millennium that follows Christ's return is also the time when the work of the Restoration Church flourishes. Have I got that right?

NEAL MAXWELL: Yes it does. Even so, Brigham Young taught us that not everyone's going to be a member of the Church in the Millennium. Most won't be. But religious freedom will be more pervasive than now. And we will not have some of the distractions we have now. So I think the world will flourish in the Millennium. It will be a time of very intense temple work, by the way.

HUGH HEWITT: The most comfortable response from non-believers is that I'm betting on, I'm banking on a God who's all-merciful. And as a result, no matter what I do, or how I do it, in the next life, if He's there, He's going to let me off because He's like a Father.

NEAL MAXWELL: He is a generous God, but He's not only perfect in His mercy, He's also perfect in His justice. This means that we will not receive unearned blessings, for embedded in our theology is the reality that we receive blessings based upon our obedience to the principles upon which they are predicated. No one will harvest a blessing which they have not planted. But, yes, He'll be a generous God. And the Terrestrial Kingdom, which is the lower of the three, is nevertheless a Kingdom of Glory. So God is a generous God, but, once again, except a man become as a little child, he cannot enter the Kingdom of Heaven. There's no footnote at the bottom of that page that says, "Of course we'll consider the following exceptions."

HUGH HEWITT: Is it your understanding that the members of the Terrestrial Kingdom will be aware of the Celestial Kingdom?

NEAL MAXWELL: Oh, yes.

HUGH HEWITT: That puts quite a burden on them, doesn't it?

NEAL MAXWELL: Well, it does, except everyone will feel that they have received far more than they were entitled to. So if some things are withheld, it is determined by a generous God who presides over and loves all of His children in all of His kingdoms.

HUGH HEWITT: Elder Maxwell, you're an Apostle of the Mormon Church. That is, as I understand the theology, the descent of authority directly from Peter, James, and John. Isn't that an awful burden?

NEAL MAXWELL: It is. It's a calling in which one would never feel adequate. I don't. When I was called, I felt inadequate. I still feel inadequate. The saving grace in all of that is that I didn't call myself. The Lord called me, so I have reason to believe He'll try to help me with my inadequacies, and He does, painful as the process may be. But it is overwhelming. One cannot be in an Islamic country and not be conscious of the tremendous challenge it is to bear a witness of Jesus' name in a nation where there may be hostility towards Jesus, per se.

HUGH HEWITT: Do you call upon your predecessors as Apostles—I mean the ancient ones as saints in heaven—to assist you in your work?

NEAL MAXWELL: No, we do not pray to them. We regard them and their works as instructive and inspiring to us, but we would make no petitions to them, per se. There is embedded in the Church a sense that the councils that have gone before, who have preceded us, are obviously still keenly interested in their work here. But our petitions are to Heavenly Father in the name of Christ, and we would look to the living Prophet for his particular guidance.

HUGH HEWITT: Well, if I'm not mistaken, we're doing this interview two days before your forty-fifth wedding anniversary.

NEAL MAXWELL: Correct.

HUGH HEWITT: Congratulations.

NEAL MAXWELL: Thank you very much. I married up, spiritually.

HUGH HEWITT: Well, I'm wondering, though, about a line that President Hinckley said at his installation: He and his wife were "discovering the golden years that are lined with lead."

NEAL MAXWELL: Yes!

HUGH HEWITT: Isn't there a time when you just want to stop doing this, to play tennis, enjoy those twenty-two odd grandchildren, and just say, "Enough of this Apostleship"?

NEAL MAXWELL: That's a tender question. I love those grandchildren, and we'll all be together two nights from now. No, the zest to do the work remains. I am more physically tired; the aging process obviously is taking its toll. But the Scriptures say that we will be blessed with the renewing of our bodies. I see that happen all the time in coping with jet lag. We hop off an airplane, and we're supposed to go before an audience and inspire and lift them, and we try to do that. But I do notice the aging process, and our work is really never done. We work all week and then weekends, too, we're out with the people. We're supposed to have Mondays off, but only rarely does that happen. In a sense, it doesn't matter. With my wife's great help we maximize the time with those grandchildren. We have a periodic little family study session with those who are older, and they bring their Scriptures. So we do all we can when we're with them. But they know that I have an Apostolic calling and that means that sometimes I miss out on an ordination or a blessing for one of them because I'm somewhere overseas.

HUGH HEWITT: The expectations that must greet you, especially when an Apostle of this Church enters a hospital, must be an awful burden.

NEAL MAXWELL: Oh, yes.

HUGH HEWITT: My kind of sense would be that everyone's expecting a healing when Neal Maxwell or one of your eleven colleagues or a member of the First Presidency shows up. Is that in fact the case?

NEAL MAXWELL: You go to bless a particular person, but you don't get out of an intensive care unit without doing some other blessings. I try, when I can, Hugh, to talk a little before giving the blessing to see where people are at in terms of their faith. Some are ready to let go and would like a blessing of release with as much freedom from pain as possible. Others desperately want to be healed. I try to talk with them and then under the inspiration of heaven, to bless. Frankly there are times when there have been dramatic healings, and there have been times when I myself have been disappointed to see that somebody was not healed. One has various experiences as we're the agents of the Lord in this regard. While the expectations are high, there is in people whose faith is reasonably well developed a kind of submissiveness. This means, after the blessing, they will pat your hand and thank you for the blessing and say, "I'm ready now for whatever the Lord wants." This lifts me even though I have come to lift them.

HUGH HEWITT: Upon entering into the Apostolic calling, did you feel suddenly equipped with that which you had not had before—perhaps a special power of discernment?

NEAL MAXWELL: The mantle makes a difference in the sense that one can be more declarative at times in a sermon, but the sense of inadequacy is there. I don't think it will ever leave. There are blessings that come to us as you implied in your question, such as having the Scriptures opened up to me much more than before. I feel the weight of the calling in an emancipatory way in that I really know I must truly strive to become more like Jesus. My ultimate witness has to be the eloquence of example. While this becomes a much more serious thing, it is emancipatory in that it frees me from a lot of other concerns. But the inadequacy is there, and I expect it will never quite leave.

HUGH HEWITT: Is there from your experience as an Apostle beforehand a sense of a missed opportunity? Is anything bothering you after all these years, that you missed an opportunity with someone?

NEAL MAXWELL: No if you had asked me that—

HUGH HEWITT:—that you didn't do the work of the Church?

NEAL MAXWELL: You know I once had the possibility of a political career, but the fire in the belly had gone out long before the call to become a Church leader came. So there's nothing I'm looking back over my shoulder at wishing I had done. There's a perspective that comes with the sunset years that's very, very precious. The honors of men, even if appreciatively bestowed, don't mean much. As to the political scene, I think of the line, "Princes come and princes go, an hour of pomp, an hour of show." There is a perspective that settles in. Wife and family loom larger. Most particularly, I think Jesus looms larger and larger as I ponder the eloquence of His example. This tends to fasten one's gaze on those eternal things in ways which would have been most unusual for me in the 1960's, when I taught political science.

> I think Jesus looms larger and larger as I ponder the eloquence of His example. This tends to fasten one's gaze on those eternal things in ways which would have been most unusual for me in the 1960's, when I taught political science.

HUGH HEWITT: We've talked a lot about theology, and certainly the bookstores are awash in books on angels and heaven and it's very much the rage right now. Let's talk a little bit about the enemy, adversary, whom you refer to frequently in your books. Do you believe that Satan is real?

NEAL MAXWELL: Yes, he's a real person. We regard him as does the New Testament, as one who was with us in the pre-mortal state but who fell. A brilliant son of the morning, he is very clever—not wise, but very, very clever. He is very, very real, but he is not permitted to abrogate our agency. He can customize the temptations and is aggressive. I've said of him before that he is an incurable insomniac.

HUGH HEWITT: And do you feel that the Apostles, the leadership of the Church, would be a special target for him?

NEAL MAXWELL: Yes. We must be very, very careful. Adulation can be our ruination. I think we must be careful, too, that our imperfections not be transmitted to the people. Our shortcomings should not come to bear upon the institution in a way that would be regrettable. If I have any hobbies, or any particular administrative passions, these should not be in Church administration. I have to be very careful about that. This is why in the collegial relationships we have a chance to work with one another, and one gets to see if his ideas will have a life of their own. If not, maybe you'd better let them go.

HUGH HEWITT: These men that you share this duty with, have any of them come to their positions after a great struggle? Because I'm sure a lot of people in our audience are watching and saying or reading and concluding, "Too easy for me." This man was just born into the Mormon family, raised in the Mormon Church, did the Mormon mission, rose in the Mormon administration. This is just the darndest easiest thing I've ever heard. He don't know what struggle is."

NEAL MAXWELL: Well, the struggle comes in quiet as well as spectacular ways. We all know struggle in the acceptance of the call, because it asks for total commitment. It's not a five-day-a-week thing. And we feel inadequate—I do. But as I look over the men with whom I sit—David Haight has had two massive heart attacks, and has come through marvelously. I look around the circle at men whose wives have died. My generalization would be that there are no immunities from adversities, only variations. Some of the variations are small and subtle, but they are there, and they are very real. So no one comes to this calling untested, even though there may not be public, spectacular things such as in Paul's case, to report. These men are not strangers to suffering.

HUGH HEWITT: Let me talk to you about sin. Catholics have individual confession, Presbyterians and Protestants generally, general confession. What do Mormons do about sin?

NEAL MAXWELL: In some cases it is a matter of our personal petition to Heavenly Father for forgiveness. In other cases there would be a requirement to approach one's bishop and, if necessary, to experience Church discipline. Church discipline is very, very redemptive. Excommunication is not outer darkness. But, indeed, we have both a personal and an institutional way of dealing with sins depending upon their nature. There's a phrase in the Book of Mormon, "faith unto repentance." It takes faith to repent, *repentance* being, in the Greek, "to change one's mind," one's view of life and people and God and the universe. It takes faith to change, and the challenge is, for instance, if one has spoken harshly to another and needs to set that right, then Jesus says, "Go to him privately and get it done." Well, the Church doesn't need to be involved in that as an institution. If one, on the other hand, occupied a position of trust and misbehaved, then there would be an institutional dimension to discipline. So it's personal or institutional depending on the nature of the challenge.

HUGH HEWITT: As we come to the conclusion of this, and thank you for your patience, . . .

NEAL MAXWELL: You have been very genuine in your desire for conversation.

HUGH HEWITT: Let's talk about the joy of your beliefs and of belief generally, because we've been focusing on a lot of the theology and a lot of the discipline, etcetera.

NEAL MAXWELL: Yes.

HUGH HEWITT: Where is the joy in this rigorous living?

NEAL MAXWELL: Seeing a prodigal return. To be a small part of seeing that happen is a marvelous thing. To see someone, in the words of Scripture, who comes to himself and resolves that "I will go to my Father" is a marvelous journey for someone to make. The joy comes in seeing someone who has been crusty and difficult to deal with become more meek, or to see a family really come to love and appreciate each other. Those are the real miracles. The multitude were fed five thousand loaves and fishes, yet they were hungry again the next day. But Jesus is the Bread of Life, and if we partake thereof then we will never be hungry again. The most lasting miracles are the miracles of transformation in people's lives. These give one much joy, and while we can't cause these to happen, the Lord lets us, at times, be instruments in that process. This brings great joy.

> We're told that all flesh will see Him together. And everyone will acknowledge Him. How the Lord will handle that optically on this sphere, I don't know. But it's dramatic beyond our capacity to comprehend.

HUGH HEWITT: As you look forward to the Second Coming, as the Church looks forward to the Second Coming, is that going to be an event of tribulation or an event of joy? I think your theology has that Jesus will return dressed in red for some reason.

NEAL MAXWELL: Yes. He will come in reminding red attire. The Bible mentions this as well. Tribulation, followed by much joy. We're told that all flesh will see Him together. And everyone will acknowledge Him. How the Lord will handle that optically on this sphere, I don't know. But it's dramatic beyond our capacity to comprehend. Stars will fall from their places in the heavens. Yet it will not be that spectacular solar display that touches us, Hugh. It will be Jesus coming and His voice being heard to say, "I have trodden the wine press alone and none was with Me"—a reference to the profound atoning aloneness that He knew. We will then praise Him, and the Scriptures say we will praise Him forever and ever. Ultimate, consummate joy. But there will be much tribulation ahead of that time. Yet we do not focus upon it unduly, nor are we preoccupied with it. But the joy that will come will indeed be transcending. Frankly, that is worth enduring a lot, to get there.

HUGH HEWITT: And do you, Neal Maxwell, fear death?

NEAL MAXWELL: No, not really. I have a sense of still wanting to get things done. I wonder, "if I die tomorrow," about this or that grandchild, but there is nevertheless a sense of anticipation. As you get older, you get enough people on the other side of the veil that all your loved ones are not here. I would hope that I would be as brave as my father and mother were when they died, full of faith. As Dad drew near to her, she was speaking in mere whispers and she said, "Clarence, I love you." He couldn't hear her, so we had to tell him what she had said. It was a very tender moment. And then Dad, being an ardent genealogist with no fear of death for her or himself, said, "Now Emma, I've been working on this particular line. When you get there you've got to get me some help." In a few moments she was gone. When my father was nearing his time two years ago, he showed the same kind of faith. He'd written out his obituary. I said, "Dad where is it? You're getting close." He said, "I think it's in my Bible." We went to get it, but it was not there. He said, "Well, then I'll have to do another one, and it will be the inspired version." I said to him, "How hard is dying?" He said, "Harder than I thought, harder than I thought." But he never complained. Near the end, when he was coughing quite a bit, one of his returned missionary granddaughters came in. She said, "Grandpa, can I help you cough?" And he said, knowing that she had been on a mission to Korea, "What language will you cough in?" She said, "In Korean, of course." And he said, "I can only cough in English." And then a short while later, he was gone. You cannot be reared in that kind of home without having some anticipation, not foreboding. Meanwhile my challenge is to be more patient and to be more loving and to be more like Jesus. That's the ultimate witness I can bear of Him. And I gladly seek to do that.

HUGH HEWITT: Neal Maxwell, thank you for sharing your time with us.

NEAL MAXWELL: Thank you, Hugh, very much.

SEARCHING FOR GOD IN AMERICA

A CONVERSATION WITH
FATHER THOMAS KEATING

As the leader of the internationally known Contemplative Prayer movement, Thomas Keating has been at the forefront of a worldwide revival in the power of prayer. At twenty he entered a Trappist monastery in Rhode Island, drawn by the idea of a permeating spirit found everywhere. Inspired by the writings of Thomas Merton, he became fascinated by the ways in which the traditions of Catholicism and Buddhism seemed to overlap. At the backbone of Keating's spirituality lies an ancient Christian method of prayer that "centers" one's spirit within the holiness of God. The organization Keating helped to found, Contemplative Outreach, is dedicated to furthering centering prayer in the modern religious landscape. Father Keating is interviewed at St. Benedict's Monastery in the mountains outside of Snowmass, Colorado.

A CONVERSATION WITH
FATHER THOMAS KEATING

Father Thomas Keating, who presently resides at St. Benedict's monastery in Colorado, has been a Trappist monk since the age of twenty. He founded the centering prayer movement, which is officially called Contemplative Outreach, Ltd., in 1978, in an effort to help people become closer to God through meditative prayer. The movement has nearly fifty thousand followers. A graduate of Fordham University, he has written numerous books about the need to incorporate contemplative prayer into the busy modern lifestyle, including *Intimacy with God* and *Open Mind, Open Heart.* Although he is ostensibly retired, he continues to lead seminars and write as well as maintain a rigorous personal regimen of prayer and spiritual searching.

HUGH HEWITT: Father Thomas Keating, thank you for joining us.

THOMAS KEATING: Thank you.

HUGH HEWITT: You have been a monk fifty-three years, the last fourteen of them here at St. Benedict's in the Colorado Rockies. After all that time and all that prayer, what is it that you would have people know most about God?

THOMAS KEATING: That He is extremely accessible. And is always with us. Perhaps the simplest thing is that He can't *not* be with us. As the source of existence, He must be present where anything else exists. So that if you have any doubts about it, you just have to say, "Am *I* here?" If the answer is yes, then God must be here, too. It's that simple.

HUGH HEWITT: If He's extremely accessible, why did you pick the life of a monk to access Him?

THOMAS KEATING: Because I wasn't too accessible to Him; that was the problem. And I think that's a problem many people feel. You have a hunger for God, or at least an interest, but there're so many other options that are closer at hand and in front of the five senses that unless something is done to sort of focus on this deeper hunger, then we forget and we lose it. So when I realized I wanted God and nothing more than that, I looked around for the best way to do it. And in those days, a monastery was one very good way of focusing on that search.

HUGH HEWITT: You have recently completed a five-month period of silence. Why did you do that?

THOMAS KEATING: Well, I had several motives. One, since I came back to Colorado for the second time, I started a movement called Contemplative Outreach. It was designed to share the essence of monastic prayer with people outside the monastery, because it's basically very simple. And when I gave brief lectures or retreats about this, the response was way beyond what I had expected. I had originally thought maybe only priests or religious would be interested, maybe an occasional minister. But it turned out that laypersons were the most interested. And so I've been extremely active in trying to develop the components of it, a support system for it, and writing books to support people who can't come to retreats. So it has become a fairly absorbing ministry for me.

Then, three years ago I got sick with viral pneumonia and, in fact, never really fully recovered. And I had a fibrillation of the heart after that. This has made it difficult for me to function on any kind of administrative level. So I thought I would go into solitude and pray to see what my role in the movement should be at this time—whether I should turn it over to others, whether it was ready to get along without me, whether I was in the way, whether I was too weak to handle it, all the difficulties that arise in any growing kind of organism. That's why I went. I think it clarified that for me.

HUGH HEWITT: Most people who face a choice like that convene a committee. When they've been sick, and they have a big organization that's growing, they talk to everybody, the vice presidents and the CEOs. But you went into solitude for five months. What does solitude offer that the suggestions and the counsel of your colleagues in Contemplative Outreach didn't?

THOMAS KEATING: Well, they can't arrange my conscience for me. They can give me advice, which I've taken. And we talked about it. And they would like me to stay on a little longer. I'm a little like a car on a half a tank of gas going on a long journey. I hope to hit an oasis every now and then. So I have to figure out what the hazards are, what the benefits are, and if I really am more help than hindrance. And because we're a young organization, only barely twelve years old, I came to the conclusion that it's not yet time for me to resign and to become a kind of honorary member and write things from a safe distance. I wish I could do more, but I decided that I would have to do what I could, because in my view the organism isn't quite ready to be launched on its own momentum. There are a lot of unfinished areas in our structure.

HUGH HEWITT: How does the practice of silence bring you that kind of discernment?

THOMAS KEATING: When you're in the midst of activities, even the most devout and the most generous, what happens to you is that you sometimes get insights, perhaps during a liturgy or during one's prayer or in the events of the day, the people you meet. And you have an insight that tells you that this is something you really should reflect on or you're about to learn something. And then along comes a whole slew of unexpected duties that you just have to do, and you lose it. You lose the edge. And when you finally get around to getting back to that particular light, it's kind of vague.

So the great advantage of solitude that I found is that when one really quiets the mind and stops reflecting a lot and analyzing and hearing about all the problems in the organization, then the dust kind of settles and I get an insight that I can pursue to the end. It becomes crystal clear. I don't recommend solitude to everybody. That was the longest retreat I ever had in solitude.

HUGH HEWITT: Have you gone into silence at other periods in your monastic life about other issues?

THOMAS KEATING: Yes, and just about the ordinary issues of life in the monastery. We all take a yearly retreat. And with the work I had, I tried to take two or three weeks twice a year, up until the time I got sick. And that seemed to do the job. But remember that this ministry has been built on about thirty-five years of monastic life and practice and prayer, and so it's not something I would recommend people to start out with, because there are some difficulties with solitude. It can be very lonesome. You can be face to face with your interior demons.

> …the great advantage of solitude that I found is that when one really quiets the mind and stops reflecting a lot and analyzing and hearing about all the problems in the organization, then the dust kind of settles and I get an insight that I can pursue to the end. It becomes crystal clear.

HUGH HEWITT: "With your interior demons" meaning what?

THOMAS KEATING: Meaning that in solitude, the same thing happens as in contemplative prayer. You stop doing so much thinking. Thinking seems to be the kind of manhole cover that keeps whatever is in the unconscious from rising into consciousness. And we really need to know what's in the unconscious to know ourselves, especially on the spiritual journey, especially in a role of leadership.

And so when you take off that manhole, by stopping thinking, or at least by not pursuing thoughts too much, then the contents of the unconscious begin to come into consciousness, such as the emotional programs for happiness in early childhood. These were established for security needs, control needs, issues of affection and esteem. All these things were put together in early childhood in order to survive, and they were appropriate at that period. But because we did not know God then, we didn't have the experience of God, we identified happiness with one or another of those basic instinctual needs. And so we arrived at self-consciousness without the experience of God and yet with this sense of hunger for happiness that we now identify with the basic childhood drives for security, control, affection, and esteem.

And those basic instinctual needs move the world. Just take a look at any advertising; it appeals to one of those instincts. The instincts are what John in his Epistle called "worldliness." And they can follow you into the monastery. Because wherever you go, your unconscious goes too . . . until you work with it. Those who go through deep psychotherapy have a good start on this project. The Divine Spirit is a kind of divine psychotherapist, if you're willing, who seems to go deeper and digs through the whole of your personal history and brings out where you were motivated by selfishness.

HUGH HEWITT: After fifty-three years, hasn't all that been done for you?

THOMAS KEATING: This is the fascinating thing about the spiritual journey. I don't consider it as ever ending. I think it's a series of new beginnings, new breakthroughs. But you go to a new level of understanding, perhaps, and of self-knowledge. And you enjoy for a few moments—or perhaps for a few weeks or a few months, maybe in some cases a few years—a certain plateau where you work that insight into all your relationships with God, yourself, other people. And then, all of a sudden the Spirit says, "Now let's take a look at something deeper. Let's look at something even earlier in your life that you don't realize is secretly influencing some of your decisions as you function."

And so I compare the spiritual journey to a spiral staircase on which you're descending, with periods of transition. It's painful. Then you hit a plateau and you get the benefits of having that new insight, that new freedom from the false self system and the emotional programs for happiness that just won't work. And so you get detached from your security demands, your control needs, your esteem needs. When one sits down in meditation, one identifies oneself as sitting at the foot of the cross and identifying with Jesus on the cross—in fact, as being on the cross with Christ. This is the attitude that one brings to the prayer, so that one is open to the pain and suffering that one has in oneself. And at the same time, one takes in all the suffering of the world and unites that with Christ, because that's really what He did on the cross. And so one's own suffering becomes redeeming. One's concern for the suffering of others goes beyond just a casual sympathy or pity; it becomes real compassion, which is also one of the great principles of the Buddhist religion.

HUGH HEWITT: Isn't that exhausting, to vision yourself on the cross with Christ and to suffer that pain? Is that something you do on a daily basis?

THOMAS KEATING: You do it implicitly, as soon as you sit down in meditation. You are automatically entering into what in Christian tradition is called *the path of mystery*, which is the Passion, death and Resurrection of Christ. Just as He took all the suffering of the world into Himself and redeemed it, so we, in order to become like Christ or identified with Him at the deepest level of His spirituality, have to be willing to allow all the suffering of the world to enter ourselves, without making an issue of particular points.

It's an intention. It's sometimes accompanied by the breathing. It would be an exercise you do before you enter deeply into the prayer. You breathe in, so to speak, all the misery, especially the sufferings of your enemies and those who oppose you. And you take all that suffering on yourself—not as though you could handle it, but in order to unite it with Christ. And then you breathe out this loving heart of Christ, so to speak, which is the Holy Spirit. As you exhale, you breathe out compassion, understanding and forgiveness. That's your intention.

Now that doesn't mean you're going to succeed right away, but as a daily practice, a daily way of identifying yourself with the mystery of Christ's Passion, death and Resurrection, you begin to understand how your own unloading of your own unconscious begins to have a redeeming effect. And so the undigested emotional problems from early childhood begin to arise. And they're seen now, not as disasters that cause one to run to a psychiatrist (though that could be helpful, too), but as issues for the Spirit as your psychiatrist, so to speak. He invites you to deeper penetration, to look at your deepest motivation.

I think we can say, in Christianity, that motivation is everything. You just listen to the way that Jesus talks to His disciples. He's always asking them, "Well, why did you do this?" or, "Why do you identify with society the way you do? Why do you think social structures have to be this way?" And it's that Why? Why? Why? that gets deeper, more penetrating, and eventually brings us to the bottom (which I think is bottomless in this life) of our capacity to surrender to God the last vestiges of our demands for security, for control, for power, and for affection and esteem. And that is the freedom of the children of God, where one doesn't need the symbols of those emotional needs that the culture provides.

HUGH HEWITT: As you go deeper and deeper into your silence or into your monastic practice or into your centering prayer, do you ever run into doubt there—that perhaps it's a very nice story, Jesus and the Bible, but it's a story?

THOMAS KEATING: Doubt is very valuable, because one of the other things that needs to be dealt with in the unloading of our unconscious is the unquestioning assumption. From about the age of four to eight, we accepted values from the culture—our parents, our school, our peer groups, and now the television values (or non-values, as you care to see them). And so a certain amount of de-roling has to go on; that is to say, we identify with our role as a parent, as a teacher, as whatever our profession is. It's precisely in being detached from what you're doing that enables you to do it well. Because then you're doing it as a service of God and your neighbor, not as a personal need. Even in ministry, if it's a personal need, it's not going to go very far. It's when ministry is a pure gift that it has the power of the Spirit behind it, because then God sends *you* rather than your unconscious drives for applause or for success or for security or control, as the case may be.

HUGH HEWITT: Now I'm confused, Father Keating. I asked you whether or not you've encountered doubt about God's existence and Jesus' divinity, but you answered me in terms of psychology. Is God an invention of our psyche?

THOMAS KEATING: I'm giving you a little background before I get to the question, because I don't think you grasp what I'm trying to say. Another half a minute here. When the child begins to socialize, about four to eight, then it becomes much more complex, because it runs into other egos that are developing. And according to the developmental psychologists, whom I'm following here, there's a stage of increased self-awareness, self-consciousness, until one comes to a certain self-reflective fullness that we call the age of reason.

Now, if one comes to that place with this baggage of ideas about God that were communicated from four to eight in a way that was over-strict or in a way that presented God as a monster because of His demands, then this colors one's attitude toward God even as a grownup . . . unless, at some point, there's a conversation with somebody who straightens one out. And so, when you enter the spiritual journey at a deep level, there is some residue of wrong ideas of God that God put up with because He's as happy with the prayers of a child as those of a great mystic. They are all sincere.

But the movement of our Christian maturity is toward recognizing in God someone who transcends all our ideas and concepts of what God is. Our old ideas seem to die, and because we identify them with God, God dies. But God does *not* die; only our idea of God dies. And it should die, at a certain point, because now we're capable through faith of relating to God in a more spiritual way, in a more human way. I could give you an example of that.

HUGH HEWITT: Please.

THOMAS KEATING: I had great consolations and great friendship with Christ in the beginning of my conversion. And that's why I looked around for what seemed to be the best environment to pursue it. And I felt called to the contemplative life that I saw was laid out in the fathers of the church that I happened to

read at the Sterling Library at Yale University when I was there. I was so interested in the fathers and their interpretation of Scripture, and I saw that this was not the way that I had been taught the Catholic religion. This was the kind of religion that I was interested in—one which was sapiential and experiential, one which looked at the Scriptures not only for their literal meaning, but for the spiritual sense or the symbolic sense.

And, of course, I was interested in the typological sense, which describes how grace works in people . . . and not only in Jesus' time, the way He related with Peter and the other apostles, but right now. That same Christ is present in His Spirit today, relating to us as teacher, as the master. He is trying to free us from those false self-system projects that can't work and of our over-identification with the cultural or national or even religious prejudices and biases that we picked up in early childhood and never question. All the parables are questioning

> That same Christ is present in His Spirit today, relating to us as teacher, as the master. He is trying to free us from those false self-system projects that can't work and of our over-identification with the cultural or national or even religious prejudices and biases that we picked up in early childhood and never question.

the social structure of Jesus' time, including the religious structure. So Jesus is after honesty. He's after us, who we are without all this baggage that was impressed upon us in early childhood by other people.

And so doubts are very precious to us. They're frequent at a certain period in our spiritual evolution so that God can invite us to look at some of our attitudes toward Him and hear Him say, "That was childish. Put that away. What you think I am is the last thing that I am. Give Me a chance." This can be experienced as a kind of partial atheism. It's not atheism. It's just the loss of the god who never existed anyway, the one that we created in our imagination.

HUGH HEWITT: Have you ever questioned whether or not Jesus was God?

THOMAS KEATING: Well I had doubts about the faith when I was an undergraduate at Yale. But during that time I had also a very deep conversion to Christ and read a great deal, and obviously I wouldn't have entered a monastery for any other reason. I didn't tell you my story, however.

HUGH HEWITT: Well, Father Keating, let's go back to 1943, when you decided to become a monk. What happened?

THOMAS KEATING: I became one. I was riding on a bus, actually, on Lexington Avenue in New York, when I felt challenged to choose a life that was the most conducive to contemplative prayer. That was the ideal I had picked up from the fathers of the church whose works I read at Yale. And, sure enough, I did enter the monastery, with a good deal of distress from the family. In those days it was a complete break with your friends and relatives and your ordinary life up till then.

HUGH HEWITT: What happened on the bus?

THOMAS KEATING: I just felt challenged, inwardly (not inner voices, but my conscience) to think, *If you're interested in the contemplative life, well, here are the Trappists. You've seen it, and you know what they're like. Make up your mind.* I wasn't able to enter for a whole year because of parental refusal. I was only, what, nineteen? I changed then from Yale to Fordham University, to await being drafted. I didn't want to be a diocesan priest; it wasn't my attraction.

The family was very opposed to my being a Trappist, so I just waited to see what would happen. And by God's grace, I left myself very completely in God's hands. Any day I could have been called up. We had a house in Long Island, and when I was home for vacation I used to walk to daily Mass. And a dear old housekeeper used to see this young man walking to and from daily Mass. In those days there weren't too many doing that. And she thought I should be in the seminary. So she talked to the pastor, I guess. And then one day she accosted me and said, "Why don't you see the Monsignor? He's really very fatherly." She was trying to encourage me, you know, and so I said, "Well, I have nothing to lose."

So I went to see him. And he was indeed very fatherly, this pastor, a really holy man. He said, "Let me send you to the bishop for a deferment so that you can be in the seminary and get a 4D," because the military was interested in having chaplains. That kind of deferment was an honorable one in those days. So I went to see the bishop, and he agreed to have me. And then I went back to see the Monsignor. But I felt a little uneasy because my friends were going to war and were being killed and so on, and I didn't really intend to become a diocesan priest. So getting a deferment seemed to me a little bit devious. I explained that to him, and he said to me, just casually, "This war is not meant for you." And for some reason, those words brought peace to my heart and I figured I'd just see what happens.

Twenty years later I understood what those words meant. I guess, in Scripture, they are called the "words of wisdom," which is a casual word that someone says (it might even be a joke) that goes to your heart and you know that God has spoken to you through this means. So I went into the monastery at twenty. In those days we could only speak to the abbot and the novice master. So it was a very intense hermetical life, lived in solitude, but I was never alone.

HUGH HEWITT: Twenty years later, what *did* those words mean to you?

THOMAS KEATING: Well, twenty years later, I had become abbot of this monastery, and it was just after Vatican Council II, when all the religious orders were invited to review their rules in the light of the gospel and their founders. Everything seemed to be up for grabs, and the more conservative group in the monastery didn't want any change. They had staked their life on this kind of life and its strictness. Others were coming from a more contemporary attitude and wanted change, wanted the monastery to become more humane in the sense of a better place in which to develop one's human qualities and not just one's spirituality.

> Roman Catholics and others believe, and Christ has said, that wherever two or three are gathered He's really present in some transcendent way in the Eucharist. So I kind of experienced that gift.

On this occasion I was in Rome with some other abbots who were similarly afflicted, and we were talking about these problems. One afternoon we took a ride to Anzio Beach and visited the American cemetery there. And as I walked down the lane and saw the crosses one after another, and the Stars of David, I realized they all were from the time that I entered the monastery. Now, my intention on entering the monastery was to offer that difficult life and its sacrifices in prayer for those who were in the war, especially those my age, and especially those in Africa who were being killed. On no merit of my own, I had somehow been picked out of that war in order to be put into this other kind of lifestyle, which was specially designed to pray for those in need. So I was offering everything I was doing, which was fairly rigorous, for those people.

And when I saw those names, all of a sudden I was enveloped with the sense of coming home. As if the people who were buried there were my friends. I didn't hear any words, of course, but it was as if they were saying to one another, "Here's the guy who was praying for us while we were going up the Poe Valley and being blown to pieces. Now it looks to us as though maybe he'll need some help." And it was at that moment that the words of the priest came back to me: "This war—*this* war—is not meant for you." And I felt that these young men, who perhaps I had helped through my prayers, would now help me in the spiritual war that I was in at the monastery.

HUGH HEWITT: The reformation of the monastery.

THOMAS KEATING: Renewal of the monastery was requiring incredible trials and difficulties. And so this experience gave me the courage to keep going when the going was extremely tough. No matter what decision was made—and everybody looked to me, as abbot, to decide—half the people would be displeased.

HUGH HEWITT: Let me go back to your early days, before you entered the monastery. In one of your books, *Intimacy with God*, you recount an Easter Sunday experience. You had sneaked away from your parents' house and gone down to the monastery. And, you wrote, "As the celebrant raised the Host, in the course of the Mass, all of a sudden, without knowing what happened, I was completely identified with Christ present in the Host. That insight penetrated the whole of my being and lingered in various degrees of intensity for three days." What does it mean to be completely identified with Christ present in the Host?

THOMAS KEATING: I don't know, except that I just knew that He was there and that I was united to Him in that Eucharistic event. And actually, that's what happens in any worship service. Roman Catholics and others believe, and Christ has said, that wherever two or three are gathered He's really present in some transcendent way in the Eucharist. So I kind of experienced that gift. Thomas Merton seems to have had the same experience before he entered the monastery, as he records, when he was in one of the Caribbean Islands.

HUGH HEWITT: Are these rare occurrences?

THOMAS KEATING: It's not an unusual experience, but I think you have to be very open to this sort of thing. It happens when you're searching with great enthusiasm, when you're reading and praying a lot, when you're making sacrifices in order to come closer to Christ. Temporarily at least, you open up to some of the potentialities for union with Christ that the gospel holds out to us. You're not suddenly cured of your false self system and the emotional programs for happiness that I spoke about earlier. You're given a gift; it's like a Christmas gift. I mean, the family doesn't give you a gift every day.

HUGH HEWITT: Will God give anyone who asks that kind of a gift?

THOMAS KEATING: He gives you whatever you need. And that kind of gift is certainly not a sign that you're better than anyone else. It may be a sign that you're weaker than others and need some encouragement, like a little stroke to keep going in the journey. And since the journey I was on was kind of tough and I had lots of oppositions, maybe He thought that in my weakness I needed a little kiss to get me through a few days. It all dissolved after three days, and then I was back in daily life with this memory. And while that keeps you going, it doesn't make life any easier.

HUGH HEWITT: In your half century in the monastery, how often does one have one of these spiritual mountain-top experiences?

THOMAS KEATING: I would say it was rare. I mean, let's count them up (laughs). Okay, there was that one. That was before I even entered. And there were moments of deep prayer throughout my novitiate. And the day I was ordained there was a deep sense of union with Christ, but much more quiet and much more indescribable; it was just a sense of union. And that's all.

I'd like to spend one more second on what happened at Anzio Beach, because it permanently changed my idea of prayer. Some experiences are just encouragement, are just consolations. They can be spiritual junk food, really, keeping you going a few days but not permanently. Other experiences are very profound, and they're life-transforming. And they may not be as sensational, but they're usually not as sensible as they are in the beginning. They don't begin in the feelings; they begin in some deeper place, within some insight. What struck me as so universal about Anzio was that through the monastic discipline—and it occurs also in some of the Eastern religions—you really reach people through a ministry of prayer and sacrifice, through the power of your will and intention, and your fidelity to your particular way of life.

And I realized that we are, all of us, united at a deeper level than appears to us. I mean, as you deepen the contemplative prayer, you sense that the same Christ—or the divine energy—that is moving in you is in somebody else. And you relate to this. And you know that you can help them and that they can help you, and there are no barriers. In other words, the more the contemplative life expands, the more barriers and emotional blocks that separate us from other people come down.

HUGH HEWITT: But I had always thought that prayer was sort of a telegraphing up of wishes, desires, intentions, and needs. And then, if the God was so disposed, He'd telegraph them back down.

THOMAS KEATING: Well, that is a little primitive, if I may say so. You're entitled to your own opinion, but I think that prayer is a lot more than that. It's a relationship with God. And to live, the relationship has to grow. And so there are levels of this relationship with God, just as there are in a human relationship. You go from acquaintanceship and a certain awkwardness to a certain friendliness in which you feel at ease with the other person. And then there's usually a crisis of trust, that forces you to decide whether or not to commit yourself to a friendship or even a permanent relationship like marriage. Then you have a whole new life opening in which your relationship continues to grow, if it's healthy, into deeper levels of union and a spiritual friendship.

This is a model that works in our relationship with God. The more this union develops, the more our concern for what God is interested in supercedes our particular concerns, our selfish concerns, the more our concerns are His, and His concern is that people love each other. I mean, I don't think He gives much of a hoot about social structures and things like that except insofar as they promote an environment in which people can grow in the knowledge of God, which is experiential. The two instances of a closer union with God that I related to you were experiential. And these are the things that enable us to know God more as He really is. Yet, whatever we know of Him, there's always more. To come closer requires both purification of our innermost being and liberation from our false ideas of God and our selfish programs for happiness.

HUGH HEWITT: Why doesn't God make it a whole lot easier than it appears to be? Why doesn't He just simply allow for that well-developed relationship? Why doesn't He blow away the psychological baggage that takes so long to do?

THOMAS KEATING: At least in my view, the problem is in *us*. In other words, what is missing in a child's development is the experience of God's presence, which is true happiness. We're geared for happiness. It's a desire we can't prevent or help, and we don't know what true happiness is because of the fall. And so we seek happiness in childish programs based on instinctual needs. In turn, these needs gradually become energy centers around which our universe and other people circulate like planets around the sun. So we're dominated by other things. And so God can't get through.

HUGH HEWITT: If He wants to, God can get through anything, can't He?

THOMAS KEATING: Yes, but He has a certain way that seems good to Him, and that way is normal development. After we recognize our need for God and dependence on God, normal development enables us to come to the knowledge of God. If I may dare to say so, Adam was created fresh—he didn't have any problems. And as a result of not having gone through the humiliating experiences of dismantling his false self, he had difficulty coming to the knowledge of God. So God isn't going to make that mistake again, if I may be so bold.

HUGH HEWITT: There is one question that people who talked to me about doing this series repeatedly asked: "Why does God manipulate us?" Father Keating, why does God enjoy seeing people on this earth trying to figure out how to get in touch with Him?

THOMAS KEATING: Well, it increases their desire for God, for one thing. If God is just another store at the mall, so to speak, you don't appreciate what you're getting.

Perhaps it would help if I shared one more incident that deepened my understanding of God, that moved me beyond the level of even the monastic observances that had been sustaining me. Anything that we depend upon to go to God is itself a hindrance to God. Even the desire for God can become a hindrance because the purity of God (what He has to communicate to us, which is the divine life) cannot coexist with our selfish programs for happiness and our

> To find this true happiness we have to be motivated out of our self-centeredness. And not only when we're cooperating with Him, but through the trials and difficulties of life, it takes God a lot of time to get the message across that maybe our programs for happiness are not so hot.

unforgiving natures and our biases and our prejudices. These are barriers that we freely put up as a result of coming to full reflective self-consciousness without knowing that true happiness is in God. He is the true independence. He is the true love.

To find this true happiness we have to be motivated out of our self-centeredness. And not only when we're cooperating with Him, but through the trials and difficulties of life, it takes God a lot of time to get the message across that maybe our programs for happiness are not so hot. We may have to find ourselves in tragedy, in a terrible divorce, in a rehab center, before we begin to wonder whether our programs for happiness around power and affection, esteem and security, were really the right ones.

In other words, midlife crisis is probably a natural dark night in which people question the values out of which they have lived their lives. Many people find that a very difficult period. And they settle for getting a divorce and starting out on a second career in which they bring all the problems they had in the first marriage and in the first part of life into the second one, to no avail.

It's contemplative prayer that takes the manhole off the unconscious where the real motivation is. We may think we're motivated for many good deeds, but we experience jealousy and anger and the other capital sins when we're frustrated. And we wonder what went wrong. I myself experience those tendencies, as I wrote about in one book during a time of deep purification. At that point I was attached to prayer itself as a security blanket.

So we bring some very real psychological paraphernalia to the spiritual journey. God could miraculously take it away. But out of respect for our freedom and His own divine plan, He allows things to evolve. The ordinary course of daily life tests our attitudes toward God and challenges them, if we are praying, and He gives us the grace to change.

If He had just dropped on us the whole of the spiritual journey as a sheer gift, He would have negated the potential to choose Him freely, which is what divine love has done in our regard. This is a mystery that you can't really convince people of unless they pray. It will become quite clear, if one prays on a regular basis, because then God can speak to us in the silence of our heart and not get shut out by our thoughts and our pre-packaged values and our presuppositions.

HUGH HEWITT: If people refuse to pray, if they refuse to exercise the freedom to engage in this search, do they end up in hell?

THOMAS KEATING: Well, I haven't been to the next life, so I don't consider myself capable of answering your question. I think I'll also just say that Roner says we must believe in hell, as Christians, but we don't have to believe that anybody is there. That's quite a difference. So hell is perhaps a threat that a loving God makes to people who are so dense that you can't get through to them unless you hit them over the head with a two-by-four. And so it's actually an exercise of divine love.

HUGH HEWITT: Well, square this for me, Father. I have read of your great devotion to Our Lady, to the Virgin Mary, which may not be very accessible to non-Catholics (so you may have to expand on why that is), but do you believe, for example, that Mary came to Fatima and showed the children a vision of hell?

THOMAS KEATING: I don't feel required to believe that. I think that all kinds of visions are subject to interpretation. And remember that a child's mind has already been preconditioned by the catechism and whatever the local priests taught. And for centuries, hell was a very popular teaching. It's since fallen into desuetude—maybe too much, I don't know. But I think Fatima has many beautiful things in it, and I think it's meant to encourage us in a period of great distress like this century, to reinforce the truth that God loves us. But the particular details, I think, are subject to the psyches of the particular seers. Everything is culturally conditioned. Jesus Himself is culturally conditioned.

HUGH HEWITT: If everything is culturally conditioned, isn't the great edifice of the Roman Catholic Church shaky?

THOMAS KEATING: It should be shaky about what is culturally conditioned, but not about the essence of the Christian message. Vatican II initiated the demythologizing of some of the cultural trappings of an organization that has survived for two thousand years. We have that work ahead of us. Just look at some of the ritual that Vatican II set aside, that I believe came from the Roman Empire and from a monarchical, not gospel-orientated, structure. So we are invited to rethink a lot of the attitudes. And I think all religions have to update. They need to accept the fact that psychology exists and to integrate the new sciences or at least have dialogue with them, to see where they coincide and where they differ. And this is going to be the work of a couple of centuries, I think.

HUGH HEWITT: In your prayers, do you believe in Mary as an agent of divine grace?

THOMAS KEATING: Apparently I was an agent of divine grace and God to those guys in Anzio, if my experience was genuine. And I would say if I could do it, certainly the mother of Jesus ought to be able to do it, in a big way. I think she's really a symbol of the perfect response to the gospel and to Christ, which is total self-surrender and total selflessness. She's an inspiration to those who are seeking the contemplative life precisely for that reason.

In John's Gospel, when she says, "They have no wine," she's talking about people who say, "Why doesn't God fix us up easily?" She sees a young couple embarrassed by the fact that all the guests are there and the wine has run out. So she says to her Son, "Why don't You do something about it?" And He says, "Well, what's that to us?" In other words, maybe that reflects the divine feeling. But precisely because of His love for her and because He saw that He could change this into a salvific and symbolic event, He went ahead and produced enough wine for an army.

I mean, there's a depth of levels of relating, which is part of this idea of prayer as relationship. And each time you reach a new level, you get a whole new view of the gospel. And you have to reinterpret it in terms of your new experience of God. That's because grace, which is God's gift to us, is working in us now just as much as in the Old Testament, just as much as in Christ. In the Christian community, Christ is living, not dead. He's living in His glorified body, and He's made present by Christians coming together in love.

> In the Christian community, Christ is living, not dead. He's living in His glorified body, and He's made present by Christians coming together in love. *This is a process.* Apparently God likes this process, because the process speaks to us exactly where we are....

This is a process. Apparently God likes this process, because the process speaks to us exactly where we are, which is under the influence of the false self-system, and invites us to grow out of our childhood into the mature life of a Christian and a grownup human being. And thus we are called to cooperate in our own redemption and in the redemption of others. That's the way He likes it, I would say, from what I've seen.

HUGH HEWITT: Father Keating, I'm wondering if our viewers aren't having the same reaction as I am to some of your answers. I spent twelve years in parochial education, with the sisters of Notre Dame teaching the *Baltimore Catechism,* learning about limbo and purgatory and the states of graces and the venial and mortal sins, but you seem to be saying that that's all sort of a parable for living. Maybe hell exists; maybe it doesn't. What do Catholics hold on to when that kind of a consideration enters into their life? Maybe as a mature monk that's something you can cope with, but what do Catholics hold on to then?

THOMAS KEATING: The basic teaching of Christianity, and of the Catholic church in particular, is that Jesus suffered, died, and rose again. And that we are called to participate in that movement, which is a living symbol of what the ultimate reality is, whom we call God in the Christian religion. And that within the oneness of the ultimate reality is a community of relationships. And that Jesus Christ has manifested this in the most integrated and comprehensive way. The essence of God is universal compassion, unconditional love. Now that's the heart of Christianity and those are the doctrines, along with the firm belief that the divine indwelling takes place within us, through baptism or the desire for baptism, the equivalent of baptism. These are the doctrines and dogmas that are life-giving and which form the basis for a true contemplative life. The other doctrines have their importance, but I'm interested in those that chiefly support the spiritual life of contemplative prayer. The others, then, fall into place according to their relative value to those central mysteries: the Trinity, the Incarnation.

Meanwhile, a lot of other people have thought about this and given their ideas. And some of them were biased, some of them were cultured, some of them were stupid, some of them were (laughs) brilliant. We have a tradition in which there are a number of different theologies, and the Reformation multiplied that again a few hundred times. So I don't wish to be in a position of judging what has occurred to doctrines over the course of history of the Catholic church. All I know is that prior to the second Vatican Council the Roman Catholic Church had been in a very defensive position because of the challenges of the Reformers. And it had allowed the contemplative dimension of the gospel, which had been prominent in the Middle Ages, at least in monasteries, to fall into the background. It made the Catholic church look like a legalistic corporation, with laws that had no life to them.

Now rules and laws have a certain value to an ongoing organization. But they don't communicate the experience. This is only communicated through prayer and the sacraments. So there was an undue emphasis on the externals of the Catholic religion that the second Vatican Council and the fathers there tried to shift by returning to a biblical theology and encouraging people to read the better of the fathers of the church again. So we're in a period of renewal in the Catholic community, which I think has affected some of the other denominations as well.

HUGH HEWITT: Father, you've written that if one understands the four verses found in Luke, chapter 21, about the widow's mite, one also understands Jesus Christ. Why is that?

THOMAS KEATING: The widow represents the total gift of oneself to God.

A poor widow—she had no financial support—came into the temple and dropped into the poor box the only two coins she had, which would amount to less than a penny. The other temple benefactors were dropping in larger donations, which made a big clang. But of course, hers didn't make much of a clang. And then she went off on her way. Well, Jesus was thrilled, apparently, by this woman. And He called His disciples together and said, "Look, this widow, poor as she is, has given more than all the others, because she gave out of her want, while all the others have given out of their abundance."

HUGH HEWITT: Why is that the essence of Jesus?

THOMAS KEATING: Because it's His message. Because that's what we're supposed to do. We're supposed to give our whole being to God. And if we know who we really are, that amounts to half of nothing. It's just two bits.

It's not how grandiose your gift is, but the motive of your gift that counts. She must have had incredible trust in God that He would take care of her no matter what happened. And so she wanted to give the little she had, which was all she had, to God. And this is what contemplatives do. Not right away, but in the process of this deepening relationship.

This brings me to the story you were interested in, which was perhaps the most decisive experience of God in my monastic life. I was still abbot, and I just had an operation, a minor one. I was recovering in the infirmary, and we were still in this heavy dialogue in which the community was trying to decide, you know, "Shall we do this experiment? Shall we do that?" And really, there were more changes in the Trappists' lifestyle in those days, in two or three years, than in the previous fifteen hundred. People were dialoguing who didn't know how to dialogue, because we had kept silence all those years. So people would monologue, and people would have hidden agendas. And we lacked all those skills, so we had to try to get them through professionals. Meanwhile, community life was tense. And it was made more tense by many people leaving. And so I had the feeling of total failure as abbot, as well as the grief in losing people, many of whom were outstanding.

They felt, for the first time, free to question their original commitment. They had read the *Baltimore Catechism,* too, and they had interiorized a spirituality that was external and which they tried to fulfill. Now as they saw that it had to be interior, they questioned whether this was the right place for them, and perhaps rightly so. The whole emphasis in pre-Vatican II was on God out there someplace, which is an inheritance from some of the early fathers, and which is not scriptural. The Eastern fathers are much more interior, and they speak of the divinization of the human spirit as part of the divine transformation process of the gospel.

Well, anyway, I was thinking about my whole life. And because of the dark night I was in, there was this emergence from the unconscious of my mixed motivation. And I was questioning some of the decisions

I had made. In other words, I was feeling like the poor widow who didn't have two cents to offer the Lord and I was being invited to accept myself as I was. All that I had hoped to do for God in the way of renewing the contemplative life in this monastery had crumbled. Whether the monastery would even survive was at question at some point, as people were leaving and there weren't enough people to do the work, and we had all kinds of problems.

Well, with that battering from without and the blurring from within, the confrontation with my own weakness and residue of my emotional programs for happiness, my desire for control and the frustration of not being respected anymore as an authority, the questioning was enormous.

Well, I just happened to take a little walk in the twilight. And as I stepped out on the tarmac, I just noticed that there was a full moon, the harvest moon; it was in October, 1970. And suddenly I was engulfed in this marvelous presence, which was so tender, which was majestic, and yet was so humble. So immense, and yet so . . . so respectful of my freedom. And I realized that God knew everything about me and still loved me. That He had brought everything to this moment when I could truly give myself to Him from the bottom of my heart, with all my weakness and limitations, turn it over completely to Him. And I was filled with this sense of incredible freedom, this sense of joy and gratitude. And I even sensed a certain amusement (laughs), if I could dare to use the word on God's part, at my amazement. I felt that He was enjoying this encounter, too. And all of a sudden He, God, made me understand that He had created the moon just for me. So that I could celebrate this moment when He revealed His love to me. I couldn't believe that. I'm not that kind of person.

Anyway, I started walking down the path, and a tree suddenly became translucent. And my whole life, with everything in it, went by in just a flash, and all I knew was that everything was okay. God knew everything about it and still loved me. Then the whole countryside became kind of luminous, and I wandered out into a hay field and started jumping up and down. I couldn't contain the joy. I could feel God's presence in the hay and in the hills all around. I realized how He penetrates the whole of everything that exists. It lasted about an hour or two. And then as I came home, I realized that it would take me years to understand what had happened, and that's true. It has taken years. But obviously that started a whole new life for me. That joy and that presence faded into ordinary life, as all these experiences do, and I am still confronted with my own great weaknesses and failures. And yet I now have a trust in God that does not waver, no matter what happens.

HUGH HEWITT: How do you know that that was real, that that was God?

THOMAS KEATING: Well, you just know it. You have a way of telling that its effects are in your life, your daily life. From then on, I could sense and respect the presence of God in others. Since He could love me, I could love everybody else. And I could sense His presence in nature; He is present in everything that exists. The trans-luminous character of the divine presence—who Christ really is, the glorified Christ—is so much more than all appearances, even rituals, even sacraments. These are to bring us to the experience of union with God, and yet that union is always the beginning of a new life that starts from there and has a whole new set of relationships. Whenever you move to a new level of faith and love, then your relationships with God and yourself and other people have to change. And it takes years to work that experience into every aspect of daily life. And then you may hit another purification experience that sends you on to another level.

HUGH HEWITT: Hundreds of thousands of people have just heard you talk about walking out into the moonlight and seeing a translucent tree and a translucent countryside. Can each individual who's watching this show have that kind of experience?

THOMAS KEATING: Why not? Who am I? I mean, I'm nobody. I had all kinds of faults and sins. We don't realize how much God is only interested in loving us and persuading us to love each other. And by love here, I don't mean the sentiment, but I mean love as a choice, as the spiritual will, choosing to show mercy, to show compassion, to forgive. It's that experience of being so profoundly forgiven that enables one to forgive anything. And to realize that all the suffering in the world, as terrible as it is, is somehow contained in God and is not the end of the story. So it enables one to deal with enormous tragedy.

A few years ago I was privileged to be at a conference of contemplatives from all the great world religions. And they had a panel of people who had been in the most barbaric situations of our century, which probably takes the prize for barbarism. There was someone from the Holocaust, someone from Cambodia, someone from Palestine. And one after the other, they told their stories. But the one who impressed me the most was a Jewish lady who had been a girl in the Holocaust. Her family had all been destroyed, but somehow she had survived. She was now working for a humanitarian group that she had founded to try to make sure that something like the Holocaust didn't happen again. She said, just casually, "When I saw the children thrown into the flames, I became an atheist. But you know, I could never engage in this humanitarian activity unless I realized that if the circumstances were a little different, I could have done the same thing the Nazis did to us." When I heard that, I thought, T*his woman thinks she's an atheist, but she's very close to the real God.* The god that died in the Holocaust was her childhood image of Him.

But the insight into the total dependence that we have on God is one of the great graces of purification in the depths of the soul that John of the Cross calls the dark night. That is the heart of contemplative prayer, and not the experiences that I described. They're just casual events that may be meant to encourage you or put you on a certain level so that you can endure and benefit from the real heart of the contemplative dimension of the gospel, which is nothing less than the radical purification of our unconscious and the transformation of our inmost being into the life of God. In other words, grace is the life of the

> …perhaps the reason there is suffering is because God suffers. At least all suffering is contained in Him. It's an insight you find in the great Hindu religions. There is something about God that only experience can penetrate. You can't rationalize it. Infinite love has a place for suffering.

Trinity offered to us and going on inside of us. And when I interpreted God as making me understand that He made the moon for me, He was seeing His Son in me. I had merged into Jesus in some way, just as He sees Christ in every other human being who is open to the mystery of oneness, to the mystery of love.

HUGH HEWITT: I can understand your explanation of why the process is set up this way. Otherwise we wouldn't appreciate it so much. But then why is there so much suffering, why so much evil?

THOMAS KEATING: This is a mystery. There's something about suffering that tells us who God is in a way that nothing else can do. And this is an imperfect universe. Just on the basis of sheer physics, the Big Bang went awry at some point, and these galaxies were formed. If it was perfect, then we wouldn't be here. Tragedy and great suffering are part of God's plan in which He reveals who God is. If we can see it, we have the wisdom to penetrate the impossible situation—which is not to offer people platitudes, because there's no human explanation or rational explanation for suffering.

But perhaps the reason there is suffering is because God suffers. At least all suffering is contained in Him. It's an insight you find in the great Hindu religions. There is something about God that only experience can penetrate. You can't rationalize it. Infinite love has a place for suffering. And in that suffering, one understands something about God if one can accept it and let it happen. That's part of total self-surrender, which takes so many years to really make. That experience I described on the blacktop was thirty years after I began the spiritual journey. So I hadn't really given myself completely to God until that moment. I had given Him all kinds of other stuff, and He said, "To hell with this stuff (laughs); I don't care what you do. You can be abbot of twenty monasteries. You can be bishop. You can go on ministering, but I'm interested in you—in the whole of you, just as you are, with all your personality defects, the temperamental mess you've been in, and your personal sins, by which I've taught you something, too, once you're sorry for them."

HUGH HEWITT: I can almost hear our viewers say, "Okay, there's a Trappist monk. If it took him thirty years to reach that level of spirituality, of revelation, I'll never get there. I'm just going to wait, and when I die, hopefully I'll get to heaven."

THOMAS KEATING: Well, I think that spiritual growth can actually happen faster with lay people. They should put aside a period for just being with God. And this doesn't mean grandiose thoughts. Here's a guy, let us say, working family. Blue-collar guy. He comes home at the end of the day. If he just sits down in a corner after he's greeted the family and all, and just says, "God, I'm dead tired, I can't think of a thing. I can't read the Holy Book; I have no attraction to it. It's been a hell of a day. I'll just sit here with You and try to love You. Help me." The best prayer in the world is only two words, *Help me,* when it comes from the bottom of your heart. And you don't have to do anything. God is so accessible, you don't have to say anything more.

Other things will be helpful, too. And as the relationship deepens, you will want to know more and more about this wonderful person. That happens automatically once you establish a basic faith in the fact that God is within you, is closer than breathing, closer than consciousness itself. You can't get away from Him even if you wanted to. And it's only your thought that you're not united to Him that is standing in the way. So if you stop thinking and intentionally give yourself to God, you're starting a journey that the Spirit will gradually unfold, both by awakening you to some of the wonderful aspects of God and by awakening you to some of the humiliating aspects of your own motivation.

HUGH HEWITT: Father Keating, do you expect that when you die you're going to see those people from Anzio, that you're going to be in communion with the brothers and the priests that you've been in monastery life for fifty years? What do you expect?

THOMAS KEATING: These are questions that don't interest me. Because I want to be in God, okay? And when you're in God, you'll be with everybody else in the right place, and everything will be in the right time and place. You'll know everybody you love but in a different way, and I don't know what that is. I mean, it's so transcendent and we're so limited by what the brain can figure out in this life that to me it seems fruitless to raise those questions.

HUGH HEWITT: Why is the culture so obsessed with the angels and the visions of heaven and this New Age spirituality, then?

THOMAS KEATING: There's a hunger for spirituality because there's a lack of meaning in modern society that has been created by the two world wars and a few accessory wars and a loss of the structures that used to hold a simpler blind faith together. So people are called to a maturity they are not capable of. But they feel that hunger, and they desperately need the help of people like monastics who have some experience of the journey. With a little time and training, it's all there in the tradition. There are plenty of things to read if one has time to read. And one needs to realize that faith, hope, and charity is a process that keeps unfolding. And God will provide you with the tools you need at each stage of the journey, if you trust Him. The real problem is a lack of trust in God, because we don't see Him and we can't feel Him and we want the security of certitude. It's precisely giving up certitude about God that is the path to knowing the unknowable, or the unknown God.

HUGH HEWITT: Father Keating, does the silence of monastic life always work to make your interior life better?

THOMAS KEATING: Not always, because some people leave. But if it's well-balanced with opportunities for community exchanges, I think that silence is extremely valuable in providing an environment for prayer. In our effort to make monastic prayer available to people in the world, we have suggested a twice-daily period of silence, insofar as that's possible to find in the world. There may be no place to find it except in the bathtub, I don't know.

HUGH HEWITT: What did Vatican Council II do for your life as a monk?

THOMAS KEATING: After Vatican Council II there was a request from the authorities for every religious order, including the monastic orders, to rethink or to review their lifestyle in the light of the gospel and of the spirit of the founder. And also to bring it up-to-date with modern conditions. So this opened the door to an immense, reflective self-examination of both individual monks and of the order as a whole. The period of experimentation lasted (perhaps it isn't over yet) fifteen or twenty years, and each monastery could choose the experiments. Some chose to keep strict silence, and others chose to moderate that to just times and places.

HUGH HEWITT: What is the life here at St. Benedict's like—the average day for the average monk?

THOMAS KEATING: It's wonderful (laughs). It starts out about three-thirty with vigils. And then at four-thirty there's a period of extended meditation for an hour or a half hour, as they choose. There is time for spiritual reading, and then the liturgy is at seven-thirty. They work three or four hours, and lunch is at twelve-thirty. There's a brief prayer service in common after lunch, and then vespers is at seven in the evening. In the winter some afternoons are free for more study and prayer, but in the summer there's so much work that everybody is lucky to get in time for vespers, which is seven o'clock.

HUGH HEWITT: Was there a particular season in your life as a monk that can you look back to and say was when you really understood the monastic life?

THOMAS KEATING: No. The longer I live, the less I understand about the monastic life. Because other questions come in as you grow older. I believe in the essence of monastic life, but I think it's a vocation for very few people. But I think that what monks are trying to do should be done by everybody, according to their state of life, because this really is the basis of a deep life of prayer.

HUGH HEWITT: When I was in conversation with the Dalai Lama, he told me that he envisioned his death every day as a means of removing the fear from it. Are you afraid of dying?

THOMAS KEATING: Well, there's a natural fear of dying, but I've had about five or six close calls. So I mean, you get used to it after awhile. And since I've had this illness, every now and then I think, "Well, this is the end." So I'm getting a little better at it. All I do is turn myself and the illness (or the accident, or whatever it is) over to God.

HUGH HEWITT: What do you mean when you say "turn it over to God"?

THOMAS KEATING: With your will. The will is what does things. We have a too-narrow view of intentionality and the power of the will. Just think what happens when you say "I do" when you get married. I mean, your whole life is changed (laughs), and yet you didn't do any great work. I mean, "I do" is only two words, but they contain a whole wealth of meaning. And so when we say to God, "I am here," or "I love You," or "I'm Your servant," or "I turn my life over to You," if you mean it, it happens. It's as simple as that.

HUGH HEWITT: What happens?

THOMAS KEATING: God accepts your gift and takes over your life. And this can be incredibly intimate. He can direct your *life;* that's one level. He can also direct *you,* in which case the Spirit can suggest in great detail what He wants you to do on a day-to-day basis—when to eat and when to get up, who not to talk to and who to talk to.

HUGH HEWITT: I've heard people say, "Turn your life and your will over to God, and He will direct you." But how? People don't hear audible voices.

THOMAS KEATING: No, but you have to be alert and awake. And you have work at this thing every day. In other words, daily life has to become your daily practice. In the centering prayer practice, it's not just a method of prayer; I mean, there are lots of those. It's a whole way of life. It consists of doing the prayer twice a day for half an hour or so, as best you can, and then daily working out the effects of that silence, that surrender to God, and that taking of the whole world's sufferings as well as its joys into you and bringing it to the cross, to the interior cross. Because it's we who are sharing in Christ's crucifixion now, and Christ is living His crucified life and His life of grace in us each day. So contemplative prayer—which is really a heightened degree of faith—perceives that the events of the day are not just events. Work is not just for profit or to feed the family. Work becomes an expression of your ministry, of your service of God, so that you bring Christ and your experience of God into the marketplace. Not by proselytizing, but by just being you. By the way you treat other people and by the great Christian virtues of forgiveness and compassion.

HUGH HEWITT: One of the things that you wrote in the book *Crisis of Faith* was surprising to me. You said, "If God loves you very, very much, do not expect that He is going to be on the job the moment you have need of Him. He feigns disinterest." What is that?

THOMAS KEATING: Well, you see that in the Gospels of Matthew and Mark. Look at the Canaanite woman in Matthew, chapter 15. She came looking for help that a lot of other people had gotten, and Christ ignored her. In fact, He insulted her.

Her daughter has a demon or is sick or something, and He doesn't even answer her when she asks for help. Then she asks the apostles for help, and He pays no attention to them. She gets down on her hands and knees and prays for help, and He still ignores her. And then when she stays there, He says He can't give the bread meant for the children to the dogs. If that isn't an insult, I don't know what is. In other words, just because you're seeking God doesn't mean that you're going to get the red-carpet treatment. You may get an occasional breakthrough that is encouraging, but most of life is very down-to-earth, very much a case of everyday routines. And it's your attitude to daily life that counts.

Now in that little dialogue, Christ brought her from a fairly low level of faith to the very heights of faith. So she was inspired to say, and I paraphrase, "I know the children are entitled to the food at the table, but here I am a dog, as You said. How about dropping a few crumbs from the table? That's all I'm interested in." When she said that, He had brought her to total self-surrender. And so He said to her, "My good woman, you can have anything you want. Anything." Because all she had was Christ's, and all He had was hers.

> Work becomes an expression of your ministry, of your service of God, so that you bring Christ and your experience of God into the marketplace. Not by proselytizing, but by just being you. By the way you treat other people and by the great Christian virtues of forgiveness and compassion.

That level of faith was inspired by silence on God's part. It's the sense of of rejection we all go through. Sometimes it's the inner sense that God has abandoned us because of our sins. And sometimes He seems to insult us and appears not to be interested in us anymore. This is what John of the Cross poetically calls "the dark night." It's precisely this moving off of Christ's sensible presence, this losing of the usual rituals that supported us in the beginning. We hadn't realized we were attached to them for our own sake, not for God's sake. God has this enormous enthusiasm and desire to bring us to a more and more complete participation in the divine life. And so God has to temper us gradually. He gives us encouragement and then withdraws it, leaving us high and dry. I might feel that God has abandoned me and I should have never entered this monastery, and so on. It's just baloney. It's just the self looking for security.

HUGH HEWITT: Is it baloney to feel abandoned in a monastery after you've been doing it for twenty or thirty years?

THOMAS KEATING: Yes, because one should know after that many years that God is just as present by His absence as He is by a felt presence. And anything we feel of God is just our interpretation. God is God, and He's present everywhere, and He's always on the job, and He's always pouring His love into us. And so it's just our psychological interpretation of our experience of the spiritual journey that makes God look like a jerk, you might say. The problem is all in *us*, because we're projecting our human feelings, our unconscious desire, onto Him.

HUGH HEWITT: But can you end the dark night of the soul like that?

THOMAS KEATING: He'll end it when it's time, when we've learned our lesson.

HUGH HEWITT: How long can it go on?

THOMAS KEATING: For as long as we live.

HUGH HEWITT: Don't some people despair?

THOMAS KEATING: Not if they're in the dark night. Because the character of that is to feel ever more in this interior freedom. And though their journey is full of much absence and it's so down-to-earth and dry, there's an interior reassurance that it's producing good fruit. And what is the chief good fruit? Humility. You stop judging other people. You realize that you're as bad off as they are if your real self was known. You begin to make less demands of a selfish kind on yourself and other people. You put up with trials. You accept suffering from God. In other words, you're much more flexible and free to be at God's disposal than when you started out.

And without those interior trials, it just doesn't happen. We blissfully think we've served God, we contribute to the church, blah, blah, blah. Well, fine. That's good as far as it goes. But this is not the spiritual journey. The spiritual journey deals with the transformation of our inmost being, not just putting a nice vestment on.

HUGH HEWITT: Let me go back to the early 1940's. You've taken Aquinas off a shelf of the Yale library and you've been convicted to enter the monastic life. Well, it's fifty-three years later.

THOMAS KEATING: Not convicted, but *convinced*.

HUGH HEWITT: Is what you imagined then what it in fact turned out to be?

THOMAS KEATING: Absolutely not. You can't imagine what the spiritual journey has in store for you when you begin. The general rule I give is "Whatever you expect will not happen." Because as soon as you start expecting, you're taking control of the spiritual life, which is going in the opposite direction. The true spiritual life begins at the narrow gate, if you want to talk about that. And it's the totality of the widow's gift. The poor widow in the temple gave all she had over to God and let Him take control of her life, even to the point of providing daily bread when she had nothing.

HUGH HEWITT: Exactly what is Jesus Christ referring to in Matthew 7, where it's recorded that He says, "Enter by the narrow gate"?

THOMAS KEATING: Lots of authorities have worked on that text, of course. But the narrow gate suggests the entrance to the corral that the shepherds took their sheep into for the night to protect them from the wolves. The narrow gate enabled the shepherd to identify his own sheep, going in or going out. If they went through in a bunch, it would be hard to tell. So the passage probably means that entering the narrow gate is to develop a personal union with Christ as our Shepherd. And this means that we go into the corral and enjoy the safety of His protection, and we also go out and run the risks of the countryside during the day. But we trust in our Shepherd. Jesus made a lot of that. "I am the Good Shepherd; I know My own and My own know Me." That was really the essence of the experience I had on the tarmac. I knew once and for all that Christ knew me, and that it was okay.

HUGH HEWITT: When people who are not of the Christian faith ask you about the narrow gate, what can you tell them about their spiritual life and their reward beyond? You must have been asked about that a thousand times.

> God has this enormous enthusiasm and desire to bring us to a more and more complete participation in the divine life. And so God has to temper us gradually. He gives us encouragement and then withdraws it, leaving us high and dry.

THOMAS KEATING: Well, I'm very interested in and have participated in interfaith dialogues since the early seventies. We even have a dialogue group of various world religions, and spiritual teachers meet here once a year. We've done that for nearly ten years. And I belong to an interfaith peace council, so I know all these people, and I know that they have as much or more grace than I have. So of course God is working in them; of course grace is working in them.

And Vatican II has made a hundred-and-eighty-degree shift in the previous teaching of the Roman Catholic Church that looked upon Eastern religions as demonic. Now dialogue is encouraged at every level, from His Holiness, Pope John Paul II, on down. Each of the great revelations of God have been given separately, so that now, for the first time in history, they're coming together at a deep level, in a way that was never possible before. So the new theological questions come up, and no real theology for interfaith dialogue has yet been developed that I know of. All I know is that I have been greatly enriched by my dialogue with Eastern masters and gurus, and we have developed wonderful friendships in the group that meets here for the interreligious conference.

HUGH HEWITT: Are you tempted to evangelize?

THOMAS KEATING: Absolutely not. All religions, all the great revelations are unique. And perhaps we don't know what God's purpose was in keeping them apart until now, but they may be complementary. Certainly meeting the Eastern gurus and masters has challenged me personally, as an abbot, to develop a method of contemplative prayer. It's as though they arrived on the scene and said, "Here's our method. Where's yours?" and the Christians didn't have an answer to that; there wasn't one comparable to theirs. And so we've developed centering prayer, a method which crystallizes the essence of monastic prayer, precisely because this seems to be the way people expect to hear about prayer today.

HUGH HEWITT: You warn in your books, Father Keating, about the possibility of having too great of an attachment to mysticism, to the gifts of the Spirit. What's the danger of speaking in tongues and of prophesying and all that?

THOMAS KEATING: Well, it could be an ego trip. Until the interior is completely purified, the same programs for happiness that are used to seek satisfaction in becoming a secular CEO are used in ecclesiastical climbing. Of if they're men of prayer, they're interested in experiences that are less than God. Any experience of God is not God. As you reflect on it, it becomes a photograph and you lose the experience in some degree. God's gift of Himself is always in the present moment. And when the present moment is over, if you try to hang on to it, you're out-of-date. God has already moved on to the next moment and is saying, "Where are you?" So the gifts of God must be respected and treasured, but as John of the Cross teaches, if you get attached to them, they slow down or stop your journey. The same problem emerges in Buddhism—settling for a certain level of spirituality. It's like getting off at the eighty-sixth floor of the Empire State Building instead of going to the hundred-and-tenth floor.

HUGH HEWITT: If not in this life, then the next, does one ever get to the top of the skyscraper?

THOMAS KEATING: I doubt if it's possible. There is some speculation about the ultimate experience of God and if it is the same in all religions. That's an academic question that doesn't concern too many people. I wish there were enough people approaching it so that there could be a great discussion.

HUGH HEWITT: Father Keating, please summarize what centering prayer is and why people ought to at least consider trying it.

THOMAS KEATING: A centering prayer is just one method of accessing the contemplative gifts of the Spirit. The purpose of a method is to reduce the obstacles. Earlier you brought up the question of why God doesn't help us—do this and do that—to avoid a lot of needless suffering. Well, He does help. He also expects *us* to do something sometimes. He wants to draw us into this free gift of self that the Canaanite woman and the poor widow represent. And He wants us to have the experience of living in the Trinitarian life, even in our humdrum activities.

So different practices have been developed in different spiritualities. But in our dialogues, we have discovered that these practices are similar in all the great traditions. Like mindfulness in daily life. Paying attention to what you're doing. Having a spiritual guide. Chanting. Sacred dance. Spiritual reading. All the great spiritual traditions of the world have these things, or at least most of them.

In comparison, centering prayer is a very simple method. We open ourselves to God and consent to His presence and action within us. We don't conceive of God as static, but as actually working with us, both with our prayer and with the obstacles to our prayer. As a result, our prayer can be taken over more and more by the gifts of wisdom and understanding, which are the contemplative gifts of the Spirit. And by doing practicing this on a day-to-day basis, we even help our human nature by creating an oasis of silence and peace in an otherwise hectic and noisy life.

In order to have this moment to be with God and to be open with God and to maintain the intention to surrender to God like the woman in the Gospel, we use some sacred symbol such as a word that symbolizes our consent. Or we use breathing, which symbolizes the reception of the Spirit and the exhaling of love into the world. Or we imagine ourselves—in a nonvisual kind of visible analogy—in the arms of God, or embraced by God, or under God's loving gaze. And we return to that when other thoughts inevitably come down the stream of consciousness.

So it's not a question of having no thoughts, but of disregarding all the thoughts. And as that happens, the habit of being dominated by our thoughts and external events begins to let go. Our spiritual nature, which is free to choose, begins to experience the peace and inner freedom and sometimes the consolation that belongs to our spiritual nature. And that helps our motivation to keep going.

We still have to bring the fruits of that into daily life, however. And we can use any number of methods. But perhaps the best one of these is to have a little word such as the Jesus prayer to keep saying in spare moments. And when our affective emotions go off as a result of some event, which is a sure sign that we have some attachment to one of those basic energy centers in the unconscious, we need to deliberately let go of the obstacles to maintaining peace and calm, which is the atmosphere in which God and His Holy Spirit work the most.

HUGH HEWITT: Father Keating, we have not talked about the agency of Christ as forgiveness for sins, as the perfect sacrifice. Does asking for forgiveness have any place in centering prayer?

THOMAS KEATING: Oh, absolutely. That is presupposed. By consenting to God's presence, obviously one is consenting to the redemption of Christ and His salvation and implicitly asking for forgiveness.

> It is one of our dearest wishes that through the practice of centering prayer an enormous amount of creative energy will be released to take responsibility for this world, its economy and its ecology, and to help the poor and needy.

HUGH HEWITT: Father Keating, after fifty years in the monastery, what is your perspective of the world? Is the world getting better, or is it getting worse? Are you alarmed as we approach the second millennium?

THOMAS KEATING: I think an awful lot has to be done. It is one of our dearest wishes that through the practice of centering prayer an enormous amount of creative energy will be released to take responsibility for this world, its economy and its ecology, and to help the poor and needy. We have to let go of some of the intensity of the drive for happiness in selfish projects of security and power and affection and esteem. And this is already happening. Some of our members are doing wonderful work in social action. But it's precisely when our selfishness is reduced that we can energetically begin to put the gospel precepts of social concern and justice and hospitality into practice.

HUGH HEWITT: Father Thomas Keating, thank you for joining us.

THOMAS KEATING: It was great to meet you, and thank you. Blessings.

SEARCHING FOR GOD IN AMERICA

A CONVERSATION WITH
HIS HOLINESS THE
XIV DALAI LAMA OF TIBET

Recognized for his uncompromising stands on universal human rights and his position as leader-in-exile of Chinese-occupied Tibet,
His Holiness the XIV Dalai Lama of Tibet heads one of the largest schools of Buddhism and one of the most rapidly growing Eastern religions
in the United States. As the incarnation of the Buddha of Compassion, the Dalai Lama represents the paragon of the Tibetan Buddhist way.
In fact, millions of people around the world believe him to be a Living Buddha. On winning the Nobel Peace Prize in 1989 for his dedication to
liberating Tibet, he said, "The prize reaffirms our conviction that with truth, courage and determination as our weapons, Tibet will be liberated.
Our struggle must remain nonviolent and free of hatred." The Dalai Lama was interviewed while visiting the Tibetan community
in Atlanta, Georgia, during his fourteenth visit to North America.

A CONVERSATION WITH
HIS HOLINESS THE XIV DALAI LAMA OF TIBET

He was born in 1935, in a small village in northeastern Tibet, and recognized at the age of two as the fourteenth reincarnation of the **Dalai Lama**. His Holiness was still in his teens when he assumed full political responsibility as Tibetan head-of-state. Completing his Doctorate of Buddhist Philosophy the same year as the Chinese invasion of Tibet, he and eighty thousand of the world's one hundred twenty-five thousand Tibetan refugees worldwide sought safety in northern India. From his base in Dharamsala, India, the Dalai Lama currently heads up efforts to maintain Tibetan culture while working for an end to the forty-year Chinese occupation. The Dalai Lama was awarded the Nobel Peace Prize in 1989. With an estimated 311 million adherents worldwide, Buddhism breaks down into three major groupings. Mahayana Buddhism, of which Tibetan Buddhism is a part, claims upward of fifty percent of all Buddhists. Theravada Buddhism, prevalent in Southeast Asia and the

HUGH HEWITT: Your Holiness, welcome to the United States. There are six million Buddhists in the United States, Your Holiness, and over half a million of them are recent converts. Many of us in the West do not understand Buddhism. For those of us who do not, what is most important for us to understand?

THE DALAI LAMA: Usually I describe the basic teaching of Buddhism like this: From the theoretical, material side, Buddhist theory is the view of interdependency; existence very much depends on other factors. Things are related to one another. That is the Buddhist view.

Because of that, one's own future very much depends on other factors. So in order to achieve one's own happiness, one's own good future, you have to take care of all these factors. This is implicit in the practice of nonviolence. If you hurt or harm another, then ultimately you will suffer. If you help another, if you give another happiness or satisfaction, then ultimately you will get the benefit. On that basis, then, the daily practice of the Buddhists is nonviolence.

Of nonviolence there can be two levels. The first, to refrain from harming others. The second, not only to refrain from harming, but to serve others. So that is the practice of nonviolence.

HUGH HEWITT: In your book you wrote that the intense competitiveness of life in the West breeds fear and a deep sense of insecurity. Did that lead to this increase in Buddhism in the United States, this fear and this sense of insecurity?

THE DALAI LAMA: I don't know. Basically I feel that in humanity there is a different blend of dispositions which is quite, quite natural. Now, for example, Tibet has historically been a Buddhist country and the majority of Tibetans are Buddhist. At the same time, among Tibetans there are Muslims; that has been so for at least the last four or five centuries. And also since this century there are some Christians over there—a very small number, but some. So you see, when the information of other religious traditions reaches your place, then to some people the new religious tradition may be effective or they may find it suitable.

And then, some people describe Buddhism as a science of mind rather than a religion. Some people feel a little bit uncomfortable with faith. Some people might feel that it is too simple. And some people prefer some kind of training of mind. So that also is one factor.

My position is that generally speaking, it is better to follow one's own traditional religion.

HUGH HEWITT: As a practicing Christian, I was fascinated by your relationship with Thomas Merton, the Trappist monk. And in your autobiography you commented

Pacific Islands, comprises an additional thirty-eight percent, and Tantrayana, or Japanese Buddhism, makes up six percent of Buddhists worldwide. Though Buddhism is not a major religion in the United States (only 0.4 percent of the U.S. population), with high-profile adherents including Richard Gere and other Hollywood celebrities, Tibetan Buddhism with its teachings of tolerance and compassion has a strong foothold in American culture. More and more Americans are turning to Buddhism for its messages of worldwide personal interconnectedness in a time when communities are becoming more and more fragmented.

that Catholicism and Buddhism have quite a lot in common. What is that common ground?

THE DALAI LAMA: I could see in his face something very close to me. When we looked in each other's eyes, there was some kind of very positive expression.

Anyway, I do believe the various major world religions—in spite of different philosophy, different traditions—have great potential to give humanity peace of mind, tranquility. This especially I learned from the late Thomas Merton. And from him I learned the great potential of Christianity to produce compassion, inner peace. So then, later, I considered him to be a strong bridge between Christianity, especially Catholicism, and Tibetan Buddhism. That was also as a result of meeting some of the other major Christian practitioners. I met some in Europe and different parts of the world and also in India, where I consulted Mother Teresa. You see, it shows the potential of a decent Christian.

HUGH HEWITT: Is it always in the eyes of a believer, Your Holiness, that you can sense one's faith or inner life? Can you tell from another person's eyes if they have an inner space that is rich and developed?

THE DALAI LAMA: I don't know how to explain. Some kind of spiritual vibration is there.

I remember a similar experience with one Spanish Catholic monk in Barcelona. There is one old monastery in Monsarrat. Behind that monastery there is a small mountain. That monk spent a few years on that mountain without a hot meal, just tea, I was told. And when I was there he came to see me, and I asked him, "What kind of practice were you doing in those years on the mountain?" His English was very poor, I think even worse than mine, and through his broken English he told me, "Love." And in his eyes there was some kind of peace, some kind of gentleness.

HUGH HEWITT: Where does that love and gentleness come from?

THE DALAI LAMA: Once you develop some kind of genuine peace within yourself, then you see your attitude toward others becomes similarly more gentle, more calm, more friendly, more peaceful.

How to develop inner peace? I believe compassion, loving-kindness. These are the basic factors of peace of mind. Because once these things develop, some kind of what I call inner door automatically opens. So then you find it easier to communicate to everyone, including birds, animals.

HUGH HEWITT: Your Holiness, is there a God as we understand one in the West? In Buddhist practice, is there a Creator, an Orderer, to whom all things are accountable?

THE DALAI LAMA: In Buddhist practice, no. But much depends on how you interpret the meaning of God.

God is an ultimate truth. Also I think we can say, an ultimate energy. Buddhists do accept their ultimate nature and that everything comes from that reality. I think that God, in a sense, is infinite love. Perhaps there is a common interpretation with Buddhism.

And then God as a being, a creator, something absolute . . . Usually Buddhists say clearly, everything depends on one's own mind. So in that context, one's own mind is creator. You see, the positive mind creates better life, ultimately Nirvana or salvation or liberation. If the mind becomes negative, then all sorts of pains and sorrows will come. Ultimately, a better life, a happy life or negative life, is due to one's own mind.

HUGH HEWITT: Nirvana is much in your teachings, and of course as a Christian I immediately relate it to heaven. Do you understand the concepts of Nirvana and heaven as parallel or the same? Or are they completely different ideas?

THE DALAI LAMA: I think there are some differences. Nirvana is not a place where everything is positive, with no word of pain. Not that kind. You see, in one's own mind, through training, all the negative emotion is eliminated. Then the state of mind we call Nirvana comes.

More precisely, according to some Buddhist schools of thought, the real nature of salvation is the ultimate reality of mind purified through training. That ultimate reality we call Nirvana or *moksha*, "salvation." Here, ultimate reality means emptiness, the absence of independent existence. So everything is nature, including the mind.

So the ultimate nature of the mind is emptiness. Through training one is purified. Then the ultimate reality of that particular mind we call Nirvana.

HUGH HEWITT: Many people know the story of the attendant dressed as a Lama who came to your parents' home and recognized you as the next reincarnation of the thirteenth Dalai Lama, and then by the age of six you were in the monastery and training for many, many years to achieve emptiness of mind. Can that emptiness of mind be accessible to anyone who hasn't undergone that type of training?

THE DALAI LAMA: Of course. First study so that some kind of understanding can develop. Then practice meditation, which helps the single-pointedness of mind. These combine. Then you get a deeper awareness of feeling or experience of emptiness. It's not easy.

HUGH HEWITT: When you were a little boy, you wrote about looking out the palace windows at the children in the streets below. There were no children in your palace, only adult monks feeding you. You wrote about the excruciating loneliness of those years. Did that loneliness teach you something about life, or is that just too personal to communicate?

THE DALAI LAMA: That I don't know.

HUGH HEWITT: Let me ask you about the suffering that went with exile. You were still a young man when you were forced to travel seventeen days to flee the occupying communists. At one point you were three hundred yards away from the Chinese guards. Were you trained to keep the fear away? Did you remain calm at that point?

THE DALAI LAMA: There was some fear at that time, of course. Fear is a part of our mind, part of our life.

But here, you see, due to fear there is some kind of turbulence of mind. Now that I think you can deduce. And also, there are different kinds of fear. One kind of fear is actually mind protection, or mental creation, due to some kind of negative experience; for example, strong hatred or anger develops. During that moment when you look around, everything seems negative. Even from early morning, due to the previous night's nightmares, your mood is not good. Then during that day, everything seems not so good. (By the contrary, if your mood is good, then in everything appears something positive.) So here, due to something wrong inside, a lot of mental distress or some uncomfortable insight, mentally you create negative things and a sense of insecurity and fear come. That we can deduce. Once we develop the proper mental attitude, that kind of fear suddenly can be reduced.

But then say you see a mad dog approach, and you fear. That kind of fear I think is necessary and useful. And you have to run. Without fear I think you might get a biting (laughs).

HUGH HEWITT: Did the training in your early years help you at all? You had to cope with enormous responsibility. When you were enthroned, at sixteen years of age, you were made not only spiritual but temporal ruler. Did the practice of Buddhism equip you to deal with that?

THE DALAI LAMA: I think so. The teaching of impermanence. The teaching of the suffering nature. And also the teaching of the Buddha nature. You see, there is great potential to become Buddha. Every sentient being, including myself, has great potential. Buddha seed, you know. One can be Buddha. So every negative, suffering, is firstly impermanent, secondly can be reduced or eliminated. And there is always the possibility of enlightenment.

Then the teaching of all sentient beings. All human beings, even other species of animals, all are considered one's closest relatives. Usually we describe this as other sentient beings.

You see, with training according to these teachings, one's own attitude—including toward your own enemy, toward your own suffering, toward problems—is much changed. Of course we do realize the enemy is the enemy. Individuals or groups of people who create trouble for you we call enemy. But overall these are similar sentient beings—brothers, sisters. And also the being itself is not necessarily negative but for the time being, a short period, because of negative mind or negative emotion such as greed, such as hatred, such as anger, such as jealousy, the person's attitude becomes negative.

But this does not mean the negative must remain there; a person can change. Negative emotion brings negative action, but this is very temporary. Like a wave it comes and goes, comes and goes. So I think the Buddhist training broadens your outlook and your attitude toward others, toward problems. This, according to my own little experience, is very helpful when you're passing through a difficult period.

HUGH HEWITT: You have written that death is like changing an old set of clothes and that you visualize death every day.

THE DALAI LAMA: Right.

HUGH HEWITT: Why?

THE DALAI LAMA: (laughs) Because it is part of my practice. Actually, of the Buddhist practice there are a lot of explanations. Now that's a little bit complicated. But on the practical level, through meditation, if you familiarize these things, then your mind is well equipped for death or all different kinds of suffering. So when these things actually happen, you feel, "Oh, it is normal." And so you cannot disturb your inner peace.

HUGH HEWITT: What happens to people when they die?

THE DALAI LAMA: The answer will be different according to different philosophies. According to Buddhism, after death your being is still there. That means you split from the body; the body ceases, but the being is still there. And so the activity of rebirth is to come. According to some Buddhist schools of thought, there is no beginning but there is an end. According to higher Buddhist doctrine, there is no end; the being continues. At the Buddha stage—the Buddha stage is a fully enlightened one—the individual identity is still there.

HUGH HEWITT: Your Holiness, in your autobiography you wrote about your many great teachers. And one of them also became a close friend. What was the most important thing that he imparted to you as teacher and friend?

THE DALAI LAMA: Of course, many teachings I received from those teachers. Then also, certain blessing or subtle energy can be received at the time of initiation. These initiations and blessings or subtle energy you see continue through the lineage from Siddhartha the Buddha himself. And the late Ling Rinpoche, who gave me the highest ordained monk vow, he I consider the most important of my teachers. He took special care about my teaching when I was a young lazy student.

HUGH HEWITT: Didn't he scare you?

THE DALAI LAMA: Oh yes, at the beginning I was really scared of him (laughs)! When I heard the noise of his shoes—tock, tock, tock, tock—I'd become a little bit nervous.

HUGH HEWITT: Your Holiness, when you were a very young man you went to Beijing to plead for your country, and you sat with Mao many times. In one of those conversations, I think it was the last, he said, "Your Holiness, religion is poison." And according to your book, you thought to yourself, "Ah, you are a destroyer of the Dharma." Was that a sudden awareness on your part, or had you always hoped that Tibet and China could coexist?

THE DALAI LAMA: In Tibet there was quite a clear awareness that what happened in Mongolia was the communist destruction of Dharma. At other meetings, Chairman Mao gave me some new hope, a different picture about communists. And I developed great enthusiasm: "Oh, we can work together." And many Tibetans are really concerned about Tibetan material progress or development, so they share a similar feeling. Then at that meeting he expressed that Dharma is poison. Just a few months before I had developed some different opinion toward the Chinese Communist Party. Now I find some kind of contradiction and confusion. One way I feel he was great as a revolutionary, as a great leader. On the other hand, there were a lot of different stories. But I don't know; it's difficult.

HUGH HEWITT: Do you believe he has been reincarnated, Your Holiness?

THE DALAI LAMA: Yes, I believe.

HUGH HEWITT: Any ideas in what form Mao might have come back?

> According to Buddhism, after death your being is still there. That means you split from the body; the body ceases, but the being is still there. And so the activity of rebirth is to come.

THE DALAI LAMA: Oh yes, certainly. As a Buddhist, you see, we believe in different worlds. I mean there's a visible world, an invisible world. And also sometimes we as a part of the visible world, sometimes we interfere in the invisible world. So according to some information, Chairman Mao had previous positive karma—positive action, virtuous action. Due to that he had powerful karmic force, which has the potential to produce two human births. So now I think he already took energy as a human body. But this is very mysterious, very difficult to say for definite.

HUGH HEWITT: Let me talk to you about the karmic force of the Tibetan people. The suffering has been intense. Six thousand monasteries, most of them destroyed. Tens of thousands of monks executed. More than a million people dead as a result of the Chinese invasion of Tibet. And you practice compassion. Aren't you almost reduced to despair when you contemplate what has happened in Tibet?

THE DALAI LAMA: No, no. You know, the genuine compassion which we practice, which we are trying to practice, that compassion is not based on the attitude of others. If one helps me, is very kind to me, so therefore I take care about him or about her, that kind of sense of concern is very biased. Such a sense of concern cannot go toward your enemy.

But the compassion which I emphasize the importance of, that compassion is not on that basis. Others just like myself want happiness, do not want suffering, have the right to overcome suffering. Yet sometimes the suffering is there. So you develop some kind of concern that is genuine compassion. This is unbiased. This compassion goes toward all sentient beings, including your enemy.

In our case, the Tibetans, there's the victims' side. And then there is the other side—the people who created the problem, the suffering. Now from the Buddhist viewpoint, the victims' viewpoint, it removed their previous negative karma. So they have no more consequences. The other side, who created the sufferings on another, they just begin new negative karmic forces. Therefore they have to face long-term negative consequences. So there is more reason to feel compassion toward people who create suffering on others than toward victims.

HUGH HEWITT: Did negative karma of the Tibetan people as a whole force this tragedy on them? Or was it ordained, almost, to drive Tibetan Buddhism out of the mountains and into the rest of the world? Have you pondered on that?

THE DALAI LAMA: For every event, there are many different aspects, many different consequences. This is true for the tragic Tibetan experience. For example, the tragedy brings more interest from the outside world toward Tibet culture, Tibetan spirituality, these things.

When one tragic event happens, I try to look from a different angle. That is one method to reduce mental burden. Now look at our own experience. If we think only about the negative side, then we see more sadness. At the same time, try to look from different angles. Yes, it is bad, but there are other positive sides there. This reduces the mental frustration.

So for every experience of pain and trouble at family level or individual level or community level, I think it is useful to look from different angles. When we look only from one aspect, when it's negative, the feeling of sadness increases, then eventually frustration or desperation comes.

Then if something positive happens, if you look only at the positive things, then you see so much excitement, you get so excited that you may burst! Well, I think that in order to maintain more calm, more balance, it is useful to look from various aspects so that the external development may not affect your peace of mind. For our minds to be up and down too much, even for the physical health, it is not too good. It is, I think, useful to be more steady.

> In order to live happily, harmlessly, peacefully, friendly right from the beginning, while we are still carrying on freedom's struggle, it is extremely necessary to follow strictly nonviolence. And when our goal, some kind of freedom, is achieved, it will not affect our genuine friendship.

HUGH HEWITT: Many of your people in Tibet have talked about turning to violence toward the occupying Communists. If it was possible to achieve freedom for Tibet through violence, would you recommend it?

THE DALAI LAMA: No. Theoretically speaking, the method is not so important. Motivation is important, and then the goal. If the motivation is positive, compassionate, and the goal is a benefit for a large community, then, theoretically speaking, some kind of violence can be okay. But on a practical level, violence is very dangerous, very risky. Although your goal is clear, your motivation may be positive but still not very sure. That violent method may bring a satisfactory result or more negative consequences. The violent method is very strong, side effects immense, so it's always better to avoid.

The Korean War, or perhaps in some extent the Second World War, according to the historical event, yes, there was some reason to justify violence. But judging whether this violence will produce a positive result and will not produce a side effect is very difficult. So it's better to avoid right from the beginning.

And especially in our case, whether we like it or not, we Tibetans and Chinese have to live as neighbors, side by side. In order to live happily, harmlessly, peacefully, friendly right from the beginning, while we are still carrying on freedom's struggle, it is extremely necessary to follow strictly nonviolence. And when our goal, some kind of freedom, is achieved, it will not affect our genuine friendship.

As a sort of effort based on nonviolence, already some of the Chinese intellectuals, writers and thinkers—although it's a small number, but already it's not only outside, but even inside China—are already beginning to show their sympathy, their spirit of solidarity and their concern about Tibet. Now this I think is a very very positive development. So on the Tibet issue, I am always telling people nonviolence is the only way. It is practical for both temporary benefit and long-term benefit. This is my belief.

HUGH HEWITT: It must be very difficult to control your anger, even hatred, of the occupiers when you make a practice of meeting every refugee who comes to your exile capital in India. I've read some of the tales you've been told—of twenty years of imprisonment and torture and horrific circumstances. Do you ever lose control of that anger and that hatred?

THE DALAI LAMA: Anger sometimes comes, with tears sometimes. But I listen to really some shocking stories. Some sad stories then; sometimes they themselves are crying. And I also, sometimes some tears in my eyes. Sometimes really a sort of agitation, anger, sometimes comes. But that negative feeling, the ill feeling, that almost none.

In my daily prayer, in my daily analytical meditation, I always practice a taking and giving. Taking from others the suffering and pains, and particularly those of people who create the suffering and hurt, harms. I visualize these people and deliberately take their negative action, their negative motivation, and give to them all my positive feelings such as compassion or love. That practice is very useful, very helpful. Then when some negative instances happen, although there is some anger, some disturbances happen, they do not remain long.

HUGH HEWITT: Your Holiness, we have tens of thousands of people watching this show because we've told people we're out searching for God in America, that we're looking for spirituality. As a result, sick people, poor people, those who are in a great deal of pain and despair, are going to look to you for inspiration and hope. What do you tell people like that? What should they do?

THE DALAI LAMA: We have to categorize by religious belief—for example, Christians or Muslims or followers of Judaism as they look for God. If the negative experience appears, you see, with the Creator, the All-Merciful, the Almighty, there must be some mysterious reasons for negative experience which we ordinarily cannot see. So think on these lines, although it is something uncomfortable, but there must be some meaning. I think that way is useful to reduce mental disturbance.

For a practitioner of Jainism or a practitioner of Buddhism, of course, all negative experiences happen due to one's own past negative action. Then actually the blame should go toward oneself rather than another. And sometimes the pains of suffering are useful to develop some positive attitude. Because of your own pain experience, you can easily understand another's pain. That can be very useful. That can be a basis of the development of compassion. And also sometimes the pain happens because of the negative action. So this is helpful to prevent the future commitment of negative action.

So this is the way to look at pains and trouble and suffering which is not negative, these sufferings which nobody wants, and which we have a right to overcome. And actually something happens. Instead of crying or shouting, try to look from another angle. At least mentally there's less disturbance. That's one way. Then for nonbelievers, I think perhaps of illness and death, it would be useful to become more aware. You see, this is a part of our life. And also, if something happens, that is something unfortunate not only for that particular person but there are millions of people who have the same suffering, the same kind of experiences. So, you see, to remember there is not only me, but there are many others, mentally it helps.

HUGH HEWITT: You wrote yourself that all religions can exploit, and they can do harm. In the West, we have lots of stories of religions exploiting and doing harm, even ending up killing people. Should nonbelievers use that as an excuse to stay away from a spiritual path? Or how do they go about finding the right spiritual path?

THE DALAI LAMA: We are entering the twenty-first century. Generally speaking, on this planet there is a lot of material progress on the basis of scientific technology. Yet those societies or communities with the best facility of material comfort still have some form of problems, some form of mental unrest or mental disturbance. Always there. And in some cases there is more divorce, more unhealthy situations. This shows after all we are human beings not made by machines. All our needs, all our requirements cannot be provided by machines alone. Or by money alone.

So we need some kind of spirituality, not necessarily religious faith. And therefore today I think the various major religious traditions still have an important role among humanity. Yes, useful.

However, I feel in the name of religion some bad things happened in the past and happen even today. Look at Bosnia, even in Africa. So as a result, in people all the negative emotions are intact here (holds his heart), fully; they're ready to act. But religion remains here (motions to his lips). A few prayers, that's all. Not deep enough inside (points to his heart). So the inner transformation has not yet taken place. Then when negative emotion develops, they use the name of religion. So that's, I feel, one factor.

Another factor is lack of understanding, level of awareness, of the other religious traditions. Just belief in one religion, one truth. That sort of limited attitude, I think, also causes unfortunate events. But I think the value of religious traditions is still there.

Now, we can reduce or eliminate conflict in the name of religion among the religious traditions. In spite of different philosophy, different traditions all teach, "Be good human beings." All carry the same message: love, compassion, spiritual forgiveness. All teachers carry the same message. There is common ground. We can work on this common ground, we can develop mutual understanding, mutual respect, mutual learning. Already among the various religious traditions some kind of idea of pluralism is coming. I think that is a healthy sign.

Then as I mentioned before, we need some kind of spirituality, but not necessarily religious faith. This means basic human good quality such as human affection for one another. You see, from birth, we have that. Molecules of our body go very well with peace of mind. And peace of mind comes, as I said before, with compassion, gives us inner strength. As a result, peace of mind will develop.

So therefore, to the nonbeliever or ordinary people who have no special interest toward religion: Yes, okay, live as a nonbeliever, but be a kind person, warm-hearted person. The good quality of human beings I call another kind of spirituality that we really need.

Your previous question was about people who had a lot of tragic experiences and yet have no particular religious faith. I tell people there is certain mental, how you say, technical thinking. Something happened already, maybe some tragic thing is now final. Think about it. If there is a way to overcome, then there's no use to worry, because there's no way to overcome. I think a sort of optimistic attitude is very useful. Being a human being we have this marvelous human brain and human heart, good heart. So, combine these two.

> I think China, this most populated nation and huge country—long history, deep culture—I think eventually will become more prosperous, with freedom, with liberty. So you see with that, the Tibetan issue is easily transformed. After all, we are not against China.

Generally speaking, we have the potential to overcome suffering, to overcome problems with self-confidence. "Oh, yes, something happened. Okay." "In the future I will try to avoid it, or I have the potential to overcome this suffering." So you see, they should not lose confidence and hope. That I feel is very important. Right from the beginning, try to keep optimistic attitude. If right from the beginning you lose hope and remain pessimistic, that's the real source of failure.

HUGH HEWITT: Your Holiness, when you meditate do you meditate on returning to Lhasa?

THE DALAI LAMA: Oh yes.

HUGH HEWITT: Will that happen?

THE DALAI LAMA: All Tibetans who live outside Tibet believe and hope that in few years' time we can return to Tibet.

HUGH HEWITT: Will that come about because you've changed the hearts of the Chinese rulers?

THE DALAI LAMA: I think recent world events include big changes. Now I think the world as a whole is making some kind of transformation. Including China. Look at the Tiananmen Square event. I think it clearly shows the people of China, particularly students, really want more liberty, more freedom. So it's only a question of time.

I think China, this most populated nation and huge country—long history, deep culture—I think eventually will become more prosperous, with freedom, with liberty. So you see with that, the Tibetan issue is easily transformed. After all, we are not against China. We respect China. And I believe that through negotiation a mutually agreeable solution we definitely will find.

HUGH HEWITT: And you're willing to go to Beijing without precondition?

THE DALAI LAMA: Yes, for negotiation. I'm ready to go anywhere, anytime, without any precondition.

HUGH HEWITT: Let me close our conversation, Your Holiness, by asking you about Lhasa and what you remember about it and how you used those years in the temple and that year of upbringing with the monks and your friends. How did that help you? How do you use memory in your spiritual life?

THE DALAI LAMA: I mentioned earlier training of mind and memory. Sometimes I get some kind of little regret of the best time, the best period of my study. I think I wasted some (laughs), at least a few hours every day.

HUGH HEWITT: Well, Your Holiness, I thank you very much for spending this time with us.

THE DALAI LAMA: Thank you.

SELECTIONS FROM AMERICA'S SPIRITUAL TREASURY

SEARCHING FOR GOD IN AMERICA

THE MAYFLOWER COMPACT

1620

IN THE NAME OF GOD, AMEN.

We whose names are underwritten, the loyal subjects of our dread Sovereign Lord King James, by the Grace of God of Great Britain, France, and Ireland King, Defender of the Faith, etc.

I begin with the **Compact** because the country begins with the Compact. Of course Native Americans populated the New World before the settlers. And the Spanish had established settlements in Florida and New Mexico, and the English had already landed to the south in Virginia. But it was the Puritans who foreshadowed both self-government and religious fervor, their twin passions that would make America great.

Having undertaken, for the Glory of God and advancement of the Christian Faith and Honour of our King and Country, a Voyage to plant the First Colony in the Northern Parts of Virginia, do by these presents solemnly and mutually in the presence of God and one of another, Covenant and Combine ourselves together into a Civil Body Politic, for our better ordering and preservation and furtherance of the ends aforesaid; and by virtue hereof to enact, constitute and frame such just and equal Laws, Ordinances, Acts, Constitutions and Offices, from time to time, as shall be thought most meet and convenient for the general good of the Colony, unto which we promise all due submission and obedience. In witness whereof we have hereunder subscribed our names at Cape Cod, the 11th of November, in the year of the reign of our Sovereign Lord King James, of England, France and Ireland the eighteenth, and of Scotland the fifty-fourth. Anno Domini 1620.

JOHN WINTHROP
1588 - 1649

JOHN WINTHROP'S CHRISTIAN EXPERIENCE

In my youth I was very lewdly disposed, inclining unto and attempting (so far as my yeares enabled mee) all kind of wickednesse, except swearing and scorning religion, which I had no temptation unto in regard of my education. About ten years of age, I had some notions of God, for in some great frighting or danger, I have prayed unto God, and have found manifest answer; the remembrance whereof many yeares after made mee think that God did love mee, but it made mee no whit the better:

After I was 12. yeares old, I began to have some more savour of Religion, and I thought I had more understanding in Divinity then many of my yeares; for in reading of some good books I conceived, that I did know divers of those points before, though I knew not how I should come by such knowledge (but since I perceived it was out of some logicall principles, whereby out of some things I could conclude others) yet I was still very wild, and dissolute, and as years came on my lusts grew stronger, but yet under some restraint of my naturall reason; whereby I had the command of my self that I could turne into any form. I would as occasion required write letters etc. of meer vanity; and if occasion were I could write others of savory and godly counsell.

About 14 years of age, being in Cambridge I fell into a lingring feaver, which took away the comfort of my life. For being there neglected, and despised, I went up and down mourning with myself;

Considered the perfect earthly ruler by Puritan thinker Cotton Mather, **John Winthrop** is remembered best for his stewardship of the Massachusetts Bay Colony. Governor of the colony for nearly twenty years, Winthrop helped steer the fledging community to success with nothing but gut instinct and a lively Christian faith to guide him. Born in Groton, England, in 1588, the governor emigrated to the Colonies in 1630, with seven hundred other passengers, seeking religious and political freedom from the oppressive environment of the England of Charles I. So began "The Company of Massachusetts Bay in New England," and so began our history. In the following, excerpted from Winthrop's personal writing, he tells the story of his youth and passionate conversion to Christianity. Although the language is archaic and some of the biblical references obscure, modern-day readers are certain to find some common ground with this early American's dedication to the salvation of his spirit.

and being deprived of my youthfull joyes, I betook my self to God whom I did believe to bee very good and mercifull, and would welcome any that would come to him, especially such a yongue soule, and so well qualifyed as I took my self to bee; so as I took pleasure in drawing neer to him. But how my heart was affected with my sins, or what thoughts I had of Christ I remember not. But I was willing to love God, and therefore I thought hee loved mee. But so soon as I recovered my perfect health, and met with somewhat els to take pleasure in, I forgot my former acquaintance with God, and fell to former lusts, and grew worse then before. Yet some good moodes I had now, and then, and sad checks of my naturall Conscience, by which the Lord preserved mee from some foule sins, which otherwise I had fallen into. But my lusts were so masterly as no good could fasten upon mee, otherwise then to hold mee to some task of ordinary dutyes for I cared for nothing but how to satisfy my voluptuous heart.

About 18 yeares of age (being a man in stature, and in understanding as my parents conceived mee) I married into a family under Mr. Culverwell his ministry in Essex; and living there sometimes I first found the ministry of the word to come to my heart with power (for in all before I found onely light) and after that I found the like in the ministry of many others. So as there began to bee some change which I perceived in my self, and others took notice of. Now I began to come under strong excersises of Conscience: (yet by fits only) I could no longer dally with Religion. God put my soule to sad tasks sometimes, which yet the flesh would shake off, and outweare still. I had withall many sweet invitations which I would willingly have intertained, but the flesh would not give up her interest. The mercifull Lord would not thus bee answered, but notwithstanding all my stubbornesse, and unkind rejections of mercy, hee left mee not till hee had overcome my heart to give up itself to him, and to bid farewell to all the world, and untill my heart could answer, Lord what wilt thou have mee to doe?

Now came I to some peace and comfort in God and in his wayes, my cheif delight was therein, I loved a Christian, and the very ground hee went upon. I honoured a faythful minister in my heart and could have kissed his feet: Now I grew full of zeal (which outranne my knowledge and carried mee sometimes beyond my calling) and very liberall to any good work. I had an unsatiable thirst after the word of God and could not misse a good sermon, though many miles off, especially of such as did search deep into the conscience. I had also a great striveing in my heart to draw others to God. It pittyed my heart to see men so little to regard their soules, and to despise that happines which I knew to bee better then all the world besides, which stirred mee up to take any opportunity to draw men to God, and by successe in my endeavors I took much encouragement hereunto. But those affections were not constant but very unsetled. By these occasions I grew to bee of some note for religion (which did not a little puffe mee up) and divers would come to mee for advice in cases of conscience; and if I heard of any that were in trouble of mind I usually went to comfort them; so that upon the bent of my spirit this way and the successe I found of my endeavors, I gave up my selfe to the study of Divinity, and intended to enter into the ministry, if my freinds had not diverted mee.

But as I grew into employment and credit thereby; so I grew also in pride of my guifts, and under temptations which sett mee on work to look to my evidence more narrowly then I had done before (for the great change which God had wrought in mee, and the generall approbation of good ministers and other Christians, kept mee from makeing any great question of my good estate, though my secrett corruptions, and some tremblings of heart (which was greatest when I was among the most Godly persons) put me to some plunges; but especially when I perceived a great decay in my zeale and love, etc.) And hearing sometimes of better assurance by the seale of the spirit, which I also knew by the word of God, but could not, nor durst say that ever I had it; and finding by reading of Mr. Perkins and other books that a reprobate might (in appearance) attaine to as much as I had done: finding withall much hollownes and vaine glory in my heart, I began to grow very sad, and knew not what to doe, I was ashamed to open my case to any minister that knew mee; I feared it would shame my self and religion also, that such an eminent professour as I was accounted, should discover such corruptions as I found in my selfe, and had in all this time attained no better evidence of salvation; and I should prove a hypocrite it was too late to begin anew: I should never repent in truth having repented, so oft as I had done. It was like hell to mee to think of that in Hebr: 6. Yet I should sometimes propound questions afarre off to such of the most Godly ministers as I mett, which gave mee ease for the present, but my heart could not find where to rest; but I grew very sad, and melancholy; and now to hear others applaud mee was a dart through my liver; for still I feared I was not sound at the root, and sometimes I had thoughts of breaking from my profession, and proclaiming myself an Hipocrite. But those troubles came not all at once but by fits, for sometimes I should find refreshing in prayer, and sometimes in the love that I had had to the Saints: which though it were but poor comfort (for I durst not say before the Lord that I did love them in truth) yet the Lord upheld mee, and many times outward occasions put these feares out of my thoughts. And though I had knowne long before the Doctrine of free Justification by Christ and had often urged it upon my owne soul and others, yet I could not close with Christ to my satisfaction. I have many times striven to lay hold upon Christ in some promise and have brought forth all the arguments that I had for my part in it. But insteed of finding it to bee mine, I have lost sometimes the fayth of the very general truth of the promise, sometimes after much strieving by prayer for fayth in Christ, I have thought I had received some power to apply Christ unto my soule: but it was so doubtfull as I could have little comfort in it, and it soon vanished.

Upon these and the like troubles, when I could by no meanes attaine sure and setled peace; and that which I did get was still broken off upon every infirmity; I concluded there was no way to help it, but by walking more close with God and more strict observation of all dutyes; and hereby though I put myself to many a needlesse task, and deprived my self of many lawfull comforts, yet my peace would fayle upon every small occasion, and I was held long under great bondage to the Law (sinne, and humble myself; and sinne, and to humiliation again, and so day after day) yet neither got strength to my Sanctification nor betterd my Evidence, but was brought to such bondage, as I durst not use any recreation, nor meddle with any worldly businesse etc.: for feare of breaking my peace (which even such as it was, was very preteous to mee) but this would not hold neither, for then I grew very melancholy and mine own thoughts wearied mee, and wasted my spirits.

While I wandred up and downe in this sad and doubtful estate (wherein yet I had many intermissions, for the flesh would often shake off this yoake of the law, but was still forced to come under it again) wherein my greatest troubles were not the sense of Gods wrath or fear of damnation, but want of assurance of salvation, and want of strength against my corruptions; I knew that my greatest want was fayth in Christ, and faine would I have been united to Christ but I thought I was not holy enough. I had many times comfortable thoughts about him in the word prayer, and meditation, but they gave mee no satisfaction but brought mee lower in mine own eyes, and held mee still to a constant use of all meanes, in hope of better thinges to come. Sometimes I was very confident that hee had given mee a hungring and thirsting soule after Christ and therefore would surely satisfy mee in his good time. Sometimes againe I was ready to entertaine secret murmurings that all my paines and prayers etc. should prevayle no more: but such thoughts were soon rebuked: I found my heart still willing to justify God. Yea I was perswaded I should love him though hee should cast mee off.

Being in this condition it pleased the Lord in my family excercise to manifest unto mee the difference between the Covenant of grace, and the Covenant of workes (but I took the foundation of that of workes to have been with man in innocency, and onely held forth in the law of Moses to drive us to Christ). This Covenant of grace began to take great impression in mee and I thought I had now enough: To have Christ freely, and to bee justifyed freely was very sweet to mee; and upon sound warrant (as I conceived) but I could not say with any confidence, it had been sealed to mee, but I rather took occasion to bee more remisse in my spirituall watch, and so more loose in my conversation.

I was now about 30 yeares of age, and now was the time come that the Lord would reveale Christ unto mee whom I had long desired, but not so earnestly as since I came to see more clearly into the covenant of free grace. First therefore hee laid a sore affliction upon mee wherein hee laid mee lower in myne owne eyes then at any time before, and showed mee the emptines of all my guifts, and parts; left mee neither power nor will, so as I became as a weaned child. I could now no more look at what I had been or what I had done nor bee discontented for want of strength or assurance mine eyes were onely upon his free mercy in Jesus Christ. I knew I was worthy of nothing for I knew I could doe nothing for him or for my selfe. I could only mourn, and weep to think of free mercy to such a vile wretch as I was. Though I had no power to apply it yet I felt comfort in it. I did not long continue in this estate, but the good spirit of the Lord breathed upon my soule, and said I should live. Then every promise I thought upon held forth Christ unto mee saying I am thy salvation. Now could my soule close with Christ, and rest there with sweet content, so ravished with his love, as I desired nothing nor feared anything, but was filled with joy unspeakable, and glorious and with a spirit of Adoption. Not that I could pray with more fervency or more enlargement of heart than sometimes before, but I could now cry my father with more confidence. Mee thought this condition and that frame of heart which I had after, was in respect of the former like the reigne of Solomon, free, peaceable, prosperous and glorious, the other more like that of Ahaz, full of troubles, feares and abasements. And the more I grew thus acquainted with the spirit of God the more were my corruptions mortifyed, and the new man quickened: the world, the flesh and Satan were for a time silent, I heard not of them: but they would not leave mee so. This Estate lasted a good time (divers months), but not alwayes alike, but if my comfort, and joy slackened a while, yet my peace continued, and it would returne with advantage. I was now growne familiar with the Lord Jesus Christ, hee would oft tell mee he loved mee, I did not doubt to believe him; If I went abroad hee went with mee, when I returned hee came home with mee. I talked with him upon the way, hee lay down with mee and usually I did awake with him. Now I could goe into any company and not loose him: and so sweet was his love to mee as I desired nothing but him in heaven or earth.

This Estate would not hold neither did it decline suddainly but by degrees. And though I found much spirituall strength in it, yet I could not discerne but my hunger after the word of God, and my love to the Saints had been as great (if not more) in former times. One reason might bee this, I found that the many blemishes and much hollow heartednesse which I discerned in many professors, had weakned the esteem of a Christian in my heart. And for my comfort in Christ, as worldly imployments, and the love of temporall things did steal away my heart from him so would his sweet countenance bee withdrawne from mee. But in such a condition hee would not long leave mee, but would still recall mee by some word or affliction or in prayer or meditation, and I should then bee as a man awakened out of a dreame or as if I had been another man. And then my care was (not so much to get pardon for that was sometimes sealed to mee while I was purposing to goe seek it, and yet sometimes I could not obtaine it without seeking and wayteing also but) to mourn for my ingratitude towards my God, and his free, and rich mercy. The

consideration whereof would break my heart more, and wring more teares from myne eyes, then ever the fear of Damnation or any affliction had done; so as many times and to this very day a thought of Christ Jesus, and free grace bestowed on mee melts my heart that I cannot refraine.

Since this time I have gone under continuall conflicts between the flesh and the spirit, and sometimes with Satan himself (which I have more discerned of late then I did formerly) many falls I have had, and have lyen long under some, yet never quite forsaken of the Lord. But still when I have been put to it by any suddaine danger or fearefull temptation, the good spirit of the Lord hath not fayled to beare witnesse to mee, giveing mee comfort, and courage in the very pinch, when of my self I have been very fearefull, and dismayed. My usuall falls have been through dead heartedness, and presumptuousnesse, by which Satan hath taken advantage to wind mee into other sinnes. When the flesh prevayles the spirit withdrawes, and is sometimes so greived as hee seemes not to acknowledge his owne work. Yet in my worst times hee hath been pleased to stirre, when hee would not speak, and would yet support mee that my fayth hath not fayled utterly.

The Doctrine of free justification lately taught here, took mee in as drowsy a condition, as I had been in (to my remembrance) these twenty yeares, and brought me as low (in my owne apprehension) as if the whole work had been to begin anew. But when the voice of peace came, I knew it to bee the same that I had been acquainted with before, though it did not speak so loud nor in that measure of joy that I had felt sometimes. Onely this I found that I had defiled the white garments of the Lord Jesus. That of Justification in undervalueing the riches of the Lord Jesus Christ and his free grace, and setting up Idolls in myne own heart, some of them made of his sylver, and of his gold, and that other garment of Sanctification by many foule spotts which Gods people might take notice of and yet the inward spotts were fouler than those.

The Lord Jesus who (of his owne free grace) hath washed my soule in the blood of the everlasting Covenant, wash away all those spotts also in his good time. Amen even so doe Lord Jesus.

— JOHN WINTHROP.

The 12th of the 11th month, 1636.
in the 49th year of my age just compleat.

ANNE BRADSTREET
1612 - 1672

Anne Bradstreet was the author of our nation's first published book of poems. Born in England in 1612, Bradstreet emigrated to the New World as part of John Winthrop's party of colonists. At first unhappy and homesick, Bradstreet consoled herself with faith, writing that after she "was convinced it was the way of God," she accepted her new life and became a practicing Puritan. Faith, as it is for so many, was a comfort to Bradstreet in times of need, as is made apparent in the following poem, "Here Follows Some Verses upon the Burning of Our House, July 10th, 1666." In the poem, the poet consoles herself with the knowledge that the "treasure lies above," that God's presence is our most prized possession, not candlesticks or tabletops.

THE
TENTH MUSE
Lately sprung up in AMERICA.
OR
Severall Poems, compiled
with great variety of VVit
and Learning, full of delight.
Wherein especially is contained a compleat discourse and description of
The Four {Elements,
Constitutions,
Ages of Man,
Seasons of the Year.
Together with an Exact Epitomie of
the Four Monarchies, viz.
The {Assyrian,
Persian,
Grecian,
Roman.
Also a Dialogue between Old England and
New, concerning the late troubles.
With divers other pleasant and serious Poems.
By a Gentlewoman in those parts.
Printed at London for Stephen Bowtell at the figne of the
Bible in Popes Head-Alley. 1650.

In silent night when rest I took
For sorrow near I did not look
I wakened was with thund'ring noise
And piteous shrieks of dreadful voice.
That fearful sound of "Fire!" and "Fire!"
Let no man know is my desire.
I, starting up, the light did spy,
And to my God my heart did cry
To strengthen me in my distress
And not to leave me succorless.
Then, coming out, beheld a space
The flame consume my dwelling place.
And when I could no longer look,
I blest His name that gave and took,
That laid my goods now in the dust.
Yea, so it was, and so 'twas just.
It was His own, it was not mine,
Far be it that I should repine;
He might of all justly bereft
But yet sufficient for us left.
When by the ruins oft I past
My sorrowing eyes aside did cast,
And here and there the places spy
Where oft I sat and long did lie:
Here stood that trunk, and there that chest,
There lay that store I counted best.
My pleasant things in ashes lie,
And them behold no more shall I.
Under thy roof no guest shall sit,

Nor at thy table eat a bit.
No pleasant tale shall e'er be told,
Nor things recounted done of old
No candle e'er shall shine in thee,
Nor bridegroom's voice e'er heard shall be.
In silence ever shall thou lie,
Adieu, Adieu, all's vanity.
Then straight I 'gin my heart to chide,
And did thy wealth on earth abide?
Didst fix thy hope on mold'ring dust?
The arm of flesh didst make thy trust?
Raise up thy thoughts above the sky
That dunghill mists away may fly.
Thou hast an house on high erect,
Framed by that mighty Architect,
With glory richly furnished,
Stands permanent though this be fled.
It's purchaséd and paid for too
By Him who hath enough to do.
A price so vast as is unknown
Yet by His gift is made thine own;
There's wealth enough, I need no more,
Farewell, my pelf, farewell my store.
The world no longer let me love,
My hope and treasure lies above.

MARY ROWLANDSON
1635 - 1678

The morning being come, they prepared to go on their way. One of the Indians got up on a horse and they set me up behind him, with my poor sick babe in my lap. A very wearisome and tedious day I had of it, what with my own wound, and my child being so exceedingly sick, and in a lamentable condition with her wound. It may be easily judged what a poor, feeble condition we were in, there being not the least of crumb of refreshing that came within either of our mouths from Wednesday night to Saturday night, except only a little cold water. This day in the afternoon, about an hour by sun, we came to the place where they intended, viz., an Indian town called Wenimesset, northward of Quabaug. When we were come, oh the number of pagans (now merciless enemies) that there came about

While her tale may be unfamiliar to modern readers, it certainly was not to Puritan **Mary Rowlandson**'s contemporaries. Captivity narratives, as they were known, were popular reading among the colonists, and Mrs. Rowlandson's was among the best of them. Captured by a Native American tribe during a raid on her Massachusetts village, the author spent several weeks as a virtual slave to one of the wives. In reading this text drawn from the *The Capture and Restoration of Mrs. Mary Rowlandson*, one quickly sees that her experiences deepened and strengthened her faith.

me, that I may say as David, Psalm 27:13. "I had fainted, unless I had believed," etc.

The next day was the Sabbath. I then remembered how careless I had been of God's holy time, how many Sabbaths I had lost and mispent, and how evily I had walked in God's sight, which lay so close unto my spirit that it was easie for me to see how righteous it was with God to cut off assault and burn Medfield. In this time of the absence of his master, his dame brought him to see me. I took this to be some gracious answer to my earnest and unfeigned desire. The next day, viz. to this, the Indians returned from Medfield. All the company, and those that belonged to the other small company, came through the town that now we were at, but before they came to us, oh! the outrageous roaring and hooping that there was. They began their din about a mile before they came to us. By their noise and hooping they signified how many they had destroyed (which was at that time twenty-three.) Those that were with us at home, were gathered together as soon as they heard the hooping, and every time that the other went over their number, these at home gave a shout, that the very earth rang again. And thus they continued till those that had been upon the expedition were come up to the Saggamores' wigwam. And then, oh, the hideous insulting and triumphing that there was over some Englishmen's scalps that they had taken (as their manner is) and brought with them.

I cannot but take notice of the wonderfull mercy of God to me in those afflictions, in sending me a Bible. One of the Indians that came from Medfield fight, had brought some plunder, came to me and asked me if I would have a Bible. He had got one in his basket. I was glad of it, and asked him whether he thought the Indians would let me read. He answered, yes, so I took the Bible, and in that melancholy time, it came into my mind to read first the 28th Chapter of Deuteronomy, which I did, and when I had read it, my dark heart wrought on this manner, that there was no mercy for me, that the blessings were gone and the curses came in their room, and that I had lost my opportunity. But the

Lord helped me still to go on reading till I came to Chapter 30, the seven first verses, where I found, there was mercy promised again, if we would return to Him by repentance, and though we were scattered from one end of the earth to the other, yet the Lord would gather us together, and turn all those curses upon our enemies. I do not desire to live to forget this scripture, and what comfort it was to me.

Now the Indians began to talk of removing from this place, some one way, and some another. There were now, besides myself, nine English captives in this place, all of them children, except one woman. I got an opportunity to go and take my leave of them, they being to go one way, and I another. I asked them whether they were earnest with God for deliverance; they told me they did as they were able, and it was some comfort to me that the Lord stirred up children to look to Him. The woman, viz. Goodwife Joslin told me, she shou'd never see me again, and that she could find in her heart to run away. I wisht her not to run away by any means, for we were near thirty miles from any English town, and she very big with child, and had but one week to reckon, and another child in her arms, two years old. And bad rivers there were to go over, & we were feeble with our poor & coarse entertainment. I had my Bible with me; I pulled it out, and asked her whether she would read. We opened the Bible and lighted on Psalm 27, in which Psalm we especially took notice of that verse, viz. "Wait on the Lord, be of good courage, and He shall strengthen thine heart. Wait, I say, on the Lord." . . .

In my travels an Indian came to me and told me, if I were willing, he and his squaw would run away and go home along with me. I told him no. I was not willing to run away, but desired to wait God's time, that I might go home quietly, and without fear. And now God hath granted me my desire.

O the wonderfull power of God that I have seen, and the experience that I have had! I have been in the midst of those roaring lyons, and salvage bears, that feared neither God, nor man, nor the devil, by night and day, alone and in company, sleeping all sorts together. And yet not one of them ever offered me the least abuse of unchastity to me, in word or action. Though some are ready to say I speak this for my own credit, I speak it in the presence of God, and to His glory. God's power is as great now, and as sufficient to save, as when He preserved Daniel in the lyons den, or the three children in the firey furnace. I may well say as His Psalm 107:12, "Oh give thanks unto the Lord for He is good, for His mercy endureth for ever. Let the redeemed of the Lord say so, whom He hath redeemed from the hand of the enemy," especially that I should have come away in the midst of so many hundreds of enemies quietly and peacefully, and not a dog moving his tongue.

So I took my leave of them, and in coming along my heart melted into tears, more than all the while I was with them, and I was almost swallowed up with the thoughts that ever I should go home again. About the sun going down, Mr. Hoar and myself and the two Indians came to Lancaster, and a solemn sight it was to me. There had I lived many comfortable years amongst my relations and neighbours, and now not one Christian was to be seen, nor one house left standing. We went on to a farm-house that was yet standing, where we lay all night, and a comfortable lodging we had, though there was nothing but straw to ly on. The Lord preserved us in safety that night, and raised us up again in the morning, and carried us along, that before noon we came to Concord. Now I was full of joy, and yet not without sorrow: joy to see such a lovely sight, so many Christians together, and some of my neighbours. There I met with my brother, and my brother in law, who asked me if I knew where his wife was. Poor heart! He had helped to bury her, and knew it not. She being shot down by the house was partly burnt, so that those who were at Boston at the desolation of the town and came back afterward and buried the dead did not know her. Yet I was not without sorrow, to think how many were looking and longing, and my own children among the rest, to enjoy that deliverance that I had now received. And I did not know whither ever I should see them again.

Being recruited with food and raiment, we went to Boston that day, where I met with my dear husband, but the thoughts of our dear children, one being dead, and the other we could not tell where, abated our comfort each to other. I was not before so much hem'd in with the merciless and cruel heathen, but now as much with pitiful, tenderhearted, and compassionate Christians. In that poor and distressed and beggarly condition I was received in, I was kindly entertained in several houses. So much love I received from several (some of whom I knew, and others I knew not) that I am not capable to declare it. But the Lord knows them all by name. The Lord reward them seven fold into their bosoms of His spirituals for their temporals. The twenty pounds, the price of my redemption, was raised by some Boston gentlemen, and Mr. Usher, whose bounty and religious charity, I would not forget to make mention of. . . .

Our family being now gathered together (those of us that were living), the South Church in Boston hired a house for us. Then we removed from Mr. Shepard's, those cordial friends, and went to Boston, where we continued about three quarters of a year. Still the Lord went along with us, and provided graciously for us. I thought it somewhat strange to set up house-keeping with bare walls, but as Solomon says, money answers all things, and that we had through the benevolence of Christian friends, some in this town, and some in that, and others, and some from England, that in a little time we might look, and see the house furnished with love. The Lord hath been exceeding good to us in our low estate, in that when we had neither house nor home, nor other necessaries, the Lord so moved the hearts of these and those towards us that we wanted neither food, nor raiment for ourselves or ours, Proverbs 18:24, "There is a friend which sticketh closer than a brother." And how many such friends have we found, and are now living amongst? And truly such a friend have we found him to be unto us, in whose house we lived, viz., Mr. James Whitcomb, a friend unto us near hand, and afar off.

I can remember the time, when I used to sleep quietly without workings in my thoughts, whole nights together, but now it is other wayes with me. When all are fast about me, and no eye open, but His who ever waketh, my thoughts are upon things past, upon the awfull dispensation of the Lord towards us, upon His wonderfull power and might, in carrying us through so many difficulties, in returning us to safety, and suffering none to hurt us. I remember in the night season, how the other day I was in the midst of thousands of enemies, & nothing but death before me. It was then hard work to perswade my self, that ever I should be satisfied with bread again. But now we are fed with the finest of the wheat, and, as I may say, with honey out of the rock. In stead of the husk, we have the fatted calf. The thoughts of these things in the particulars of them, and of the love and goodness of God towards us, makes it true of me, what David said to himself, Psalm 6:5, "I watered my couch with my tears." Oh! the wonderfull power of God that mine eyes have seen, affording matter enough for my thoughts to run in, that when others are sleeping mine eyes are weeping. I have seen the extreme vanity of this world: one hour I have been in health, and wealth, wanting nothing, but the next hour in sickness, and wounds, and death, having nothing but sorrow and affliction.

Before I knew what affliction meant, I was ready sometimes to wish for it. When I lived in prosperity;, having the comforts of the world about me, my relations by me, my heart cheerfull, and taking little care for anything, and yet seeing many, whom I preferred before myself, under many tryals and afflictions, in sickness, weakness, poverty, losses, crosses, and cares of the world, I should be sometimes jealous least I should have my portion in this life. And that scripture would come to my mind, Hebrews 12:6, "For whom the Lord loveth He chasteneth, and scourgeth every son whom He receiveth." But now I see the Lord had His time to scourge and chasten me. The portion of some is to have their affliction by drops, now one drop and then another, but the dregs of the cup, the wine of astonishment, like a sweeping rain that leaveth no food, did the Lord prepare to be my portion. Affliction I wanted, and affliction I had, full measure (I thought) pressed down and running over. Yet I see, when God calls a person to anything, and through never so many difficulties, yet He is fully able to carry them through and make them see, and say they have been gainers thereby. And I hope I can say in some measure, as David did, it is good for me that I have been afflicted. The Lord hath shewed me the vanity of these outward things. That they are the vanity of vanities, and vexation of spirit, that they are but a shadow, a blast, a bubble, and things of no continuance. That we must rely on God Himself, and our whole dependence must be upon Him. If trouble from smaller matters begin to arise in me, I have something at hand to check my self with, and say, "Why am I troubled?" It was but the other day that if I had had the world, I would have given it for my freedom, or to have been a servant to a Christian. I have learned to look beyond present and smaller troubles, and to be quieted under them, as Moses said, Exodus 14:13, "Stand still and see the salvation of the Lord."

FINIS.

JONATHAN EDWARDS
1703 - 1758

I had a variety of concerns and exercises about my soul from my childhood; but had two more remarkable seasons of awakening, before I met with that change by which I was brought to those new dispositions, and that new sense of things, that I have since had. The first time was when I was a boy, some years before I went to college, at a time of remarkable awakening in my father's congregation. I was then very much affected for many months, and concerned about the things of religion, and my soul's salvation; and was abundant in duties. I used to pray five times a day in secret, and to spend much time in religious talk with other boys, and used to meet with them to pray together. I experienced I know not what kind of delight in religion. My mind was much engaged in it, and had much self-righteous pleasure; and it was my delight to abound in religious duties. I with some of my schoolmates joined together, and built a booth in a swamp, in a very retired spot, for a place of prayer. And besides, I had particular secret places of my own in the woods, where I used to retire by myself; and was from time to time much affected. My affections seemed to be lively and easily moved, and I seemed to be in my element when engaged in religious duties. And I am ready to think, many are deceived with such affections, and such a kind of delight as I then had in religion, and mistake it for grace.

But in process of time, my convictions and affections wore off; and I entirely lost all those affections and delights and left off secret prayer, at least as to any constant performance of it; and returned like a dog to his vomit, and went on in the ways of sin. Indeed I was at times very uneasy, especially towards the latter part of my time at college; when it pleased God, to seize me with the pleurisy; in which he brought me nigh to the grave, and shook me over the pit of hell. And yet, it was not long after my recovery, before I fell again into my old ways of sin. But God would not suffer me to go on with my quietness; I had great and violent inward struggles, till, after many conflicts, with wicked inclinations, repeated resolutions,

A central figure in the first Great Awakening, a revival movement that swept the Colonies with religious fervor and sought to convert all whom it passed, **Jonathan Edwards** was an extraordinarily disciplined man. He experienced an urgent desire to "perfect" himself, and it was this urge that propelled his exuberant preaching and tireless intellectual pursuits. Born in East Windsor, Connecticut, he was the product of a family of famous clergymen. Edwards's own name soon became better known than those of his forebears, as he took to the pulpit and began energetically to convert the masses. Although we remember him best for this energetic preaching style that produced bristling hell-fire and brimstone sermons such as "Sinners in the Hands of an Angry God," it was a warmer, more generous philosophy— called the "Gospel of Love" by my interview subject Roberta Hestenes—that formed a cornerstone of his teachings. The meditative and thoughtful passages that follow, culled from Edwards's *Personal Narrative* and his dissertations "Concerning the End for Which God Created the World" and "The Nature of True Faith," perhaps reveal a more loving and kinder side of this great man of God.

and bonds that I laid myself under by a kind of vows to God, I was brought wholly to break off all former wicked ways, and all ways of known outward sin; and to apply myself to seek salvation, and practice many religious duties; but without that kind of affection and delight which I had formerly experienced. My concern now wrought more by inward struggles and conflicts, and self-reflections. I made seeking my salvation the main business of my life. But yet, it seems to me, I sought after a miserable manner; which has made me sometimes since to question, whether ever it issued in that which was saving; being ready to doubt, whether such miserable seeking ever succeeded. I was indeed brought to seek salvation in a manner that I never was before; I felt a spirit to part with all things in the world, for an interest in Christ.—My concern continued and prevailed, with many exercising thoughts and inward struggles; but yet it never seemed to be proper to express that concern by the name of terror.

From my childhood up, my mind had been full of objections against the doctrine of God's sovereignty, in choosing whom he would to eternal life, and rejecting whom he pleased; leaving them eternally to perish, and be everlastingly tormented in hell. It used to appear like a horrible doctrine to me. But I remember the time very well, when I seemed to be convinced, and fully satisfied, as to this sovereignty of God, and his justice in thus eternally disposing of men, according to his sovereign pleasure. But never could give an account, how, or by what means, I was thus convinced, not in the least imagining at the time, nor a long time after, that there was any extraordinary influence of God's Spirit in it; but only that now I saw further, and my reason apprehended the justice and reasonableness of it. However, my mind rested in it; and it put an end to all those cavils and objections. And there has been a wonderful alteration in my mind, with respect to the doctrine of God's sovereignty, from that day to this; so that I scarce ever have found so much as the rising of an objection against it, in the most absolute sense, in God's shewing mercy to whom he will shew mercy, and hardening whom he will. God's absolute sovereignty and justice, with respect to salvation and damnation, is what my mind seems to rest assured of, as much as of any thing that I see with my eyes; at least it is so at times. But I have often, since that first conviction, had quite another kind of sense of God's sovereignty than I had then. I have often since had not only a conviction, but a delightful conviction. The doctrine has appeared exceeding pleasant, bright, and sweet.

Absolute sovereignty is what I love to ascribe to God. But my first conviction was not so.

The first instance that I remember of that sort of inward, sweet delight in God and divine things that I have lived much in since, was on reading those words, 1 Tim. i: 17. *Now unto the King eternal, immortal, invisible, the only wise God, be honor and glory forever and ever, Amen.* As I read the words, there came into my soul, and was as it were diffused through it, a sense of the glory of the Divine Being; a new sense, quite different from any thing I ever experienced before. Never any words of scripture seemed to me as these words did. I thought within myself, how excellent a being that was, and how happy I should be, if I might enjoy that God, and be wrapt up in heaven, and be as it were swallowed up in him forever! I kept saying, and as it were singing over these words of scripture to myself; and went to pray to God that I might enjoy him, and prayed in a manner quite different from what I used to do; with a new sort of affection. But it never came into my thought, that there was any thing spiritual, or of a saving nature in this.

From about that time, I began to have a new kind of apprehensions and ideas of Christ, and the work of redemption, and the glorious way of salvation by him. An inward, sweet sense of these things, at times, came into my heart; and my soul was led away in pleasant views and contemplations of them. And my mind was greatly engaged to spend my time in reading and meditating on Christ, on the beauty and excellency of his person, and the lovely way of salvation by free grace in him. I found no books so delightful to me, as those that treated of these subjects. Those words, Cant. ii: 1, used to be abundantly with me. *I am the Rose of Sharon, and the Lily of the valleys.* The words seemed to me, sweetly to represent the loveliness and beauty of Jesus Christ. The whole book of Canticles used to be pleasant to me, and I used to be much in reading it, about that time; and found, from time to time, an inward sweetness, that would carry me away, in my contemplations. This I know not how to express otherwise, than by a calm, sweet abstraction of soul from all the concerns of this world; and sometimes a kind of vision, or fixed ideas and imaginations, of being alone in the mountains, or some solitary wilderness, far from all mankind, sweetly conversing with Christ, and wrapt and swallowed up in God. The sense I had of divine things, would often of a sudden kindle up, as it were, a sweet burning in my heart; an ardor of soul, that I know not how to express.

Not long after I began to experience these things, I gave an account to my father of some things that had passed in my mind. I was pretty much affected by the discourse we had together; and when the discourse was ended, I walked abroad alone, in a solitary place in my father's pasture for contemplation. And as I was walking there and looking up on the sky and clouds, there came into my mind so sweet a sense of the glorious *majesty* and *grace* of God, that I know not how to express. I seemed to see them both in a sweet conjunction; majesty and meekness joined together; it was a gentle, and holy majesty; and also a majestic meekness; a high, great, and holy gentleness.

After this my sense of divine things gradually increased, and became more and more lively, and had more of that inward sweetness. The appearance of every thing was altered; there seemed to be, as it were, a calm, sweet cast, or appearance of divine glory, in almost every thing. God's excellency, his wisdom, his purity and love, seemed to appear in every thing; in the sun, moon, and stars; in the clouds, and blue sky; in the grass, flowers, trees; in the water, and all nature; which used greatly to fix my mind. I often used to sit and view the moon for continuance; and in the day, spent much time in viewing the clouds and sky, to behold the sweet glory of God in these things; in the mean time, singing forth, with a low voice, my contemplations of the Creator and Redeemer. And scarce any thing, among all the works of nature, was so delightful to me as thunder and lightning; formerly, nothing had been so terrible to me. Before, I used to be uncommonly terrified with thunder, and to be struck with terror when I saw a thunder storm rising; but now, on the contrary, it rejoiced me. I felt God, so to speak, at the first appearance of a thunder storm; and used to take the opportunity, at such times, to fix myself in order to view the clouds, and see the lightnings play, and hear the majestic and awful voice of God's thunder, which oftentimes was exceedingly entertaining, leading me to sweet contemplations of my great and glorious God. While thus engaged, it always seemed natural to me to sing, or chant for my meditations; or, to speak my thoughts in soliloquies with a singing voice.

I felt then great satisfaction, as to my good state; but that did not content me. I had vehement longings of soul after God and Christ, and after more holiness, wherewith my heart seemed to be full, and ready to break; which often brought to my mind the words of the Psalmist, Psal. cxix. 28: *My soul breaketh for the longing it hath.* I often felt a mourning and lamenting in my heart, that I had not turned to God sooner, that I might have had more time to grow in grace. My mind was greatly fixed on divine things; almost perpetually in the contemplation of them. I spent most of my time in thinking of divine things, year after year; often walking alone in the woods, and solitary places, for meditation, soliloquy, and prayer, and converse with God; and it was always my manner, at such times, to sing forth my contemplations. I was almost constantly in ejaculatory prayer, wherever I was. Prayer seemed to be natural to me, as the breath by which the inward burnings of my heart had vent. The delights which I now felt in the things of religion, were of an exceedingly different kind from those before mentioned, that I had when a boy; and what I then had no more notion of, than one born blind has of pleasant and beautiful colors. They were of a more inward, pure, soul-animating and refreshing nature. Those former delights never reached the heart; and did not arise from any sight of the divine excellency of the things of God; or any taste of the soul-satisfying and life-giving good there is in them.

My sense of divine things seemed gradually to increase, until I went to preach at New York, which was about a year and a half after they began; and while I was there, I felt them, very sensibly, in a higher degree than I had done before. My longings after God and holiness, were much increased. Pure and humble, holy and heavenly Christianity, appeared exceedingly amiable to me. I felt a burning desire to be in every thing a complete Christian; and conform to the blessed image of Christ; and that I might live, in all things, according to the pure and blessed rules of the gospel. I had an eager thirsting after progress in these things; which put me upon pursuing and pressing after them. It was my continual strife day and night, and constant inquiry, how I should *be* more holy, and *live* more holily, and more becoming a child of God, and a disciple of Christ. I now sought an increase of grace and holiness, and a holy life, with much more earnestness, than ever I sought grace before I had it. I used to be continually examining myself, and studying and contriving for likely ways and means, how I should live holily, with far greater diligence and earnestness, than ever I pursued any thing in my life; but yet with too great a dependance on my own strength; which afterwards proved a great damage to me. My experience had not then taught me, as it has done since my extreme feebleness and impotence, every manner of way; and the bottomless depths of secret corruption and deceit there was in my heart.

However, I went on with my eager pursuit after more holiness, and conformity to Christ.

The heaven I desired was a heaven of holiness; to be with God, and to spend my eternity in divine love, and holy communication with Christ. My mind was very much taken up with contemplations on heaven, and the enjoyments there; and living there in perfect holiness, humility and love. And it used at that time to appear a great part of the happiness of heaven, that there the saints could express their love to Christ. It appeared to me a great clog and burden, that what I felt within, I could not express as I desired. The inward ardor of my soul, seemed to be hindered and pent up, and could not freely flame out as it would. I used often to think, how in the heaven this principle should freely and fully vent and express itself. Heaven appeared exceedingly delightful, as a world of love; and that all happiness consisted in living in pure, humble, heavenly, divine love.

I remember the thoughts I used then to have of holiness; and said sometimes to myself, "I do certainly know that I love holiness, such as the gospel prescribes." It appeared to me, that there was nothing in it but what was ravishingly lovely; the highest beauty and amiableness—a *divine* beauty; far purer than any thing here upon earth; and that every thing else was like mire and defilement, in comparison of it.

Holiness, as I then wrote down some of my contemplations on it, appeared to me to be of a sweet, pleasant, charming, serene, calm nature; which brought an inexpressible purity, brightness, peacefulness and ravishment to the soul. In other words, that it made the soul like a field or garden of God, with all manner of pleasant flowers; all pleasant, delightful, and undisturbed; enjoying a sweet calm, and the gently vivifying beams of the sun. The soul of a true Christian, as I then wrote my meditations, appeared like such a little white flower as we see in the spring of the year; low and humble on the ground, opening its bosom to receive the pleasant beams of the sun's glory; rejoicing as it were in a calm rapture; diffusing around a sweet fragrancy; standing peacefully and lovingly, in the midst of other flowers round about; all in like manner opening their bosoms, to drink in the light of the sun. There was no part of creature holiness, that I had so great a sense of its loveliness, as humility, brokenness of heart and poverty of spirit; and there was nothing that I so earnestly longed for. My heart panted after this, to lie low before God, as in the dust; that I might be nothing, and that God might be ALL, that I might become as a little child.

While at New York, I was sometimes much affected with reflections on my past life, considering how late it was before I began to be truly religious; and how wickedly I had lived till then; and once so as to weep abundantly, and for a considerable time together.

On *January* 12, 1723, I made a solemn dedication of myself to God, and wrote it down; giving up myself, and all that I had to God; to be for the future in no respect my own; to act as one that had no right to himself, in any respect. And solemnly vowed to take God for my whole portion and felicity; looking on nothing else as any part of my happiness, nor acting as if it were; and his law for the constant rule of my obedience; engaging to fight with all my might, against the world, the flesh and the devil, to the end of my life. But I have reason to be infinitely humbled, when I consider how much I have failed of answering my obligation.

I had then abundance of sweet religious conversation in the family where I lived, with Mr. John Smith and his pious mother. My heart was knit in affection to those in whom were appearances of true piety; and I could bear the thoughts of no other companions, but such as were holy, and the disciples of the blessed Jesus. I had great longings for the advancement of Christ's kingdom in the world; and my secret prayer used to be, in great part, taken up in praying for it. If I heard the least hint of any thing that happened, in any part of the world, that appeared, in some respect or other, to have a favorable aspect on the interest of Christ's kingdom, my soul eagerly catched at it; and it would much animate and refresh me. I used to be eager to read public news letters, mainly for that end; to see if I could not find some news favorable to the interest of religion in the world.

I very frequently used to retire into a solitary place, on the banks of Hudson's river, at some distance from the city, for contemplation on divine things, and secret converse with God; and had many sweet hours there. Sometimes Mr. Smith and I walked there together, to converse on the things of God; and our conversation used to turn much on the advancement of Christ's kingdom in the world, and the glorious things that God would accomplish for his church in the latter days. I had then, and at other times the greatest delight in the holy scriptures, of any book whatsoever. Oftentimes in reading it, every word seemed to touch my heart. I felt a harmony between something in my heart, and those sweet and powerful words. I seemed often to see so much light exhibited by every sentence, and such a refreshing food communicated, that I could not get along in reading; often dwelling long on one sentence, to see the wonders contained in it; and yet almost every sentence seemed to be full of wonders.

I came away from New York in the month of April, 1723, and had a most bitter parting with Madam Smith and her son. My heart seemed to sink within me at leaving the family and city, where I had enjoyed so many sweet and pleasant days. I went from New York to Weathersfield, by water, and as I sailed away, I kept sight of the city as long as I could. However, that night, after this sorrowful parting, I was greatly comforted in God at Westchester, where we went ashore to lodge; and had a pleasant time of it all the voyage to Saybrook. It was sweet to me to think of meeting dear Christians in heaven, where we should never part more. At Saybrook we went ashore to lodge, on Saturday, and there kept the Sabbath; where I had a sweet and refreshing season, walking alone in the fields.

After I came home to Windsor, I remained much in a like frame of mind, as when at New York; only sometimes I felt my heart ready to sink with the thoughts of my friends at New York. My support was in contemplations on the heavenly state; as I find in my Diary of May 1, 1723. It was a comfort to think of that state, where there is fulness of joy; where reigns heavenly, calm, and delightful love, without alloy; where there are continually the dearest expressions of this love; where is the enjoyment of the persons loved, without ever parting; where those persons who appear so lovely in this world, will really be inexpressibly more lovely and full of love to us. And how sweetly will the mutual lovers join together to sing the praises of God and the Lamb! How will it fill us with joy to think, that this enjoyment, these sweet exercises will never cease, but will last to all eternity! I continued much in the same frame, in the general, as when at New York, till I went to New Haven as tutor to the college; particularly once at Bolton, on a journey from Boston, while walking out alone in the fields. After I went to New Haven I sunk in religion; my mind being diverted from my eager pursuits after holiness, by some affairs that greatly perplexed and distracted my thoughts.

In September, 1725, I was taken ill at New Haven, and while endeavoring to go home to Windsor, was so ill at the North Village, that I could go no further; where I lay sick for about a quarter of a year. In this sickness God was pleased to visit me again with the sweet influences of his Spirit. My mind was greatly engaged there in divine, pleasant contemplations, and longings of soul.

I observed that those who watched with me, would often be looking out wishfully for the morning; which brought to my mind those words of the Psalmist, and which my soul with delight made its own language, *My soul waiteth for the Lord, more than they that watch for the morning, I say, more than they that watch for the morning;* and when the light of day came in at the windows, it refreshed my soul from one morning to another. It seemed to be some image of the light of God's glory.

I remember, about that time, I used greatly to long for the conversion of some that I was concerned with; I could gladly honor them, and with delight be a servant to them, and lie at their feet, if they were but truly holy. But some time after this, I was again greatly diverted in my mind with some temporal concerns that exceedingly took up my thoughts, greatly to the wounding of my soul; and went on through various exercises, that it would be tedious to relate, which gave me much more experience of my own heart, than ever I had before.

Since I came to this town, I have often had sweet complacency in God, in views of his glorious perfections and the excellency of Jesus Christ. God has appeared to me a glorious and lovely being, chiefly on the account of his holiness. The holiness of God has always appeared to me the most lovely of all his attributes. The doctrines of God's absolute sovereignty, and free grace, in shewing mercy to whom he would shew mercy; and man's absolute dependance on the operations of God's Holy Spirit, have very often appeared to me as sweet and glorious doctrines. These doctrines have been much my delight. God's sovereignty has ever appeared to me, a great part of his glory. It has often been my delight to approach God, and adore him as a sovereign God, and ask sovereign mercy of him.

I have loved the doctrines of the gospel; they have been to my soul like green pastures. The gospel has seemed to me the richest treasure; the treasure that I have most desired, and longed that it might dwell richly in me. The way of salvation by Christ has appeared, in a general way, glorious and excellent, most pleasant and most beautiful. It has often seemed to me, that it would in a great measure spoil heaven, to receive it in any other way. That text has often been affecting and delightful to me. Isa. xxxii: 2. *A man shall be an hiding place from the wind, and a covert from the tempest,* &c.

It has often appeared to me delightful, to be united to Christ; to have him for my head, and to be a member of his body; also to have Christ for my teacher and prophet. I very often think with sweetness, and longings, and paintings of soul, of being a little child, taking hold of Christ, to be led by him through the wilderness of this world. That test, Matth. xviii: 3, has often been sweet to me, *except ye be converted and become as little children,* &c. I love to think of coming to Christ, to receive salvation of him, poor in spirit, and quite empty of self, humbly exalting him alone; cut off entirely from my own root, in order to grow into, and out of Christ; to have God in Christ to be all in all; and to live by faith on the Son of God, a life of humble unfeigned confidence in him. That scripture has often been sweet to me, Psal. cxv: 1. *Not unto us, O Lord, not unto us, but to thy name give glory, for thy mercy and for the truth's sake.* And those words of Christ, Luke x: 21. *In that hour Jesus rejoiced in spirit, and said, I thank thee, O Father, Lord of heaven and earth, that thou hast hid these things from the wise and prudent, and hast revealed them unto babes; even so, Father, for so it seemed good in thy sight.* That sovereignty of God which Christ rejoiced in, seemed to me worthy of such joy; and that rejoicing seemed to show the excellency of Christ, and of what spirit he was.

Sometimes, only mentioning a single word caused my heart to burn within me; or only seeing the name of Christ, or the name of some attribute of God. And God has appeared glorious to me, on account of the Trinity. It has made me have exalting thoughts of God, that he subsists in three persons; Father, Son and Holy Ghost. The sweetest joys and delights I have experienced, have not been those that have arisen from a hope of my own good estate; but in a direct view of the glorious things of the gospel. When I enjoy this sweetness, it seems to carry me above the thoughts of my own estate; it seems at such times a loss that I cannot bear, to take off my eye from the glorious pleasant object I behold without me, to turn my eye in upon myself, and my own good estate.

My heart has been much on the advancement of Christ's kingdom in the world. The histories of the past advancement of Christ's kingdom have been sweet to me. When I have read histories of past ages, the pleasantest thing in all my reading has been, to read of the kingdom of Christ being promoted. And when I have expected, in my reading, to come to any such thing, I have rejoiced in the prospect, all the way as I read. And my mind has been much entertained and delighted with the scripture promises and prophecies, which relate to the future glorious advancement of Christ's kingdom upon earth.

I have sometimes had a sense of the excellent fulness of Christ, and his meetness and suitableness as a Saviour, whereby he has appeared to me, far above all, the chief of ten thousands. His blood and atonement have appeared sweet, and his righteousness sweet: which was always accompanied with ardency of spirit; and inward strugglings and breathings, and groanings that cannot be uttered, to be emptied of myself, and swallowed up in Christ.

Once as I rode out into the woods for my health, in 1737, having alighted from my horse in a retired place, as my manner commonly has been, to walk for divine contemplation and prayer, I had a view that for me was extraordinary, of the glory of the Son of God, as Mediator between God and man, and his wonderful, great, full, pure and sweet grace and love, and meek and gentle condescension. This grace that appeared so calm and sweet, appeared also great above the heavens. The person of Christ appeared ineffably excellent with an excellency great enough to swallow up all thought and conception—which continued as near as I can judge, about an hour; which kept me the greater part of the time in a flood of tears, and weeping aloud. I felt an ardency of soul to be, what I know not otherwise how to express, emptied and annihilated; to lie in the dust, and to be full of Christ alone; to love him with a holy and pure love; to trust in him; to live upon him; to serve and follow him; and to be perfectly sanctified and made pure, with a divine and heavenly purity. I have, several other times, had views very much of the same nature, and which have had the same effects.

I have many times had a sense of the glory of the third person in the Trinity, in his office of Sanctifier; in his holy operations, communicating divine light and life to the soul. God, in the communications of his Holy Spirit, has appeared as an infinite fountain of divine glory and sweetness; being full, and sufficient to fill and satisfy the soul; pouring forth itself in sweet communications; like the sun in its glory, sweetly and pleasantly diffusing light and life. And I have sometimes had an affecting sense of the excellency of the word of God, as a word of life; as the light of life; a sweet, excellent, lifegiving word; accompanied with a thirsting after that word, that it might dwell richly in my heart.

Often, since I lived in this town, I have had very affecting views of my own sinfulness and vileness; very frequently to such a degree as to hold me in a kind of loud weeping, sometimes for a considerable time together; so that I have often been forced to shut myself up. I have had a vastly greater sense of my own wickedness, and the badness of my own heart, than ever I had before my conversion. It has often appeared to me, that if God should mark iniquity against me, I should appear the very worst of all mankind; of all that have been, since the beginning of the world to this time; and that I should have by far the lowest place in hell. When others, that have come to talk with me about their soul concerns, have expressed the sense they have had of their own wickedness, by saying that it seemed to them, that they were as bad as the devil himself; I thought their expression seemed exceedingly faint and feeble, to represent my wickedness.

My wickedness, as I am in myself, has long appeared to me perfectly ineffable, and swallowing up all thought and imagination; like an infinite deluge, or mountains over my head. I know not how to express better what my sins appear to me to be, than by heaping infinite upon infinite, and multiplying infinite by infinite. Very often, for these many years, these expressions are in my mind, and in my mouth, "Infinite upon infinite— Infinite upon infinite!" When I look into my heart, and take a view of my wickedness, it looks like an abyss infinitely deeper than hell. And it appears to me, that were it not for free grace, exalted and raised up to the infinite height of all the fulness and glory of the great Jehovah, and the arm of his power and grace stretched forth in all the majesty of his power, and in all the glory of his sovereignty, I should appear sunk down in my sins below hell itself; far beyond the sight of every thing, but the eye of sovereign grace, that can pierce even down to such a depth. And yet, it seems to me, that my conviction of sin is exceedingly small, and faint; it is enough to amaze me, that I have no more sense of my sin. I know certainly, that I have very little sense of my sinfulness. When I have had turns of weeping and crying for my sins, I thought I knew at the time, that my repentance was nothing to my sin.

I have greatly longed of late, for a broken heart, and to lie low before God; and, when I ask for humility, I cannot bear the thoughts of being no more humble than other Christians. It seems to me, that though their degrees of humility may be suitable for them, yet it would be a vile self-exaltation to me, not to be lowest in humility of all mankind. Others speak of their longing to be "humbled to the dust"; that may be a proper expression for them, but I always think of myself, that I ought, and it is an expression that has long been natural for me to use in prayer, "to lie infinitely low before God." And it is affecting to think, how ignorant I was, when a young Christian, of the bottomless, infinite depths of wickedness, pride, hypocrisy and deceit, left in my heart.

I have a much greater sense of my universal, exceeding dependance on God's grace and strength, and mere good pleasure, of late, than I used formerly to have; and have experienced more of an abhorrence of my own righteousness. The very thought of any joy arising in me, on any consideration of my own amiableness, performances, or experiences, or any goodness of heart or life, is nauseous and detestable to me. And yet I am greatly afflicted with a proud and self-righteous spirit, much more sensibly than I used to be formerly. I see that serpent rising and putting forth its head continually, every where, all around me.

Though it seems to me, that, in some respects, I was a far better Christian, for two or three years after my first conversion, than I am now; and lived in a more constant delight and pleasure; yet, of late years, I have had a more full and constant sense of the absolutely sovereignty of God, and a delight in that sovereignty; and have had more of a sense of the glory of Christ, as a Mediator revealed in the gospel. On one Saturday night, in particular, I had such a discovery of the excellency of the gospel above all other doctrines, that I could not but say to myself, "This is my chosen light, my chosen doctrine;" and of Christ, "This is my chosen Prophet." It appeared sweet, beyond all expression, to follow Christ, and to be taught, and enlightened, and instructed by him; to learn of him, and live to him. Another Saturday night (*January, 1739*) I had such a sense, how sweet and blessed a thing it was to walk in the way of duty; to do that which was right and meet to be done, and agreeable to the holy mind of God; that it caused me to break forth into a kind of loud weeping, which held me some time, so that I was forced to shut myself up, and fasten the doors. I could not but, as it were, cry out, "How happy are they which do that which is right in the sight of God! They are blessed indeed, they are the happy ones!" I had, at the same time, a very affecting sense, how meet and suitable it was that God should govern the world, and order all things according to his own pleasure; and I rejoiced in it, that God reigned, and that his will was done.

JUNIPERO SERRA
1713 - 1784

To Father Fray Francisco Serra:

This is my letter of farewell. We are all packed. In four days the *Villasota* will have weighed anchor and we shall have left Cadiz.

My dear, dear friend, words cannot express what I am feeling at this hour of separation. I know that my parents are in mortal grief; at this moment I commend them to you once more, and tell you again that it is you upon whom I rely for their comforting. Ah, if it were only possible for me to make them share my own immeasurable happiness, they themselves would urge me on! Could they dream, indeed, of a nobler vocation for their son than that of apostolic missionary?

A Franciscan missionary, **Junipero Serra** was born in Majorca in 1713. Famous for his missionary work in the New World, Father Serra covered long distances on foot, converting and teaching as he traveled. He founded the first mission in California in 1769. The following excerpt, a letter written to his family on the eve of his initial departure for the Americas, finds him expressing his urgent need to convert and preach, despite his sadness at leaving all that is familiar and beloved at home.

Advanced in age as they are, and with their days numbered, the life that remains to them on this earth is only a moment in relation to eternity. Brief, alas, would have been the consolation which my presence would have given them. Would it be reasonable, and in conformity with the will of God, to cling henceforth to that? It is better to renounce seeing each other again in this world, so that we may deserve to be united forever in heaven.

Tell them, make them realize, that I suffer deeply in no longer being near them, as I once was, to solace their old age. But they know that what is essential must come before all else; and what is essential is for us to carry out the divine will. God alone, indeed, is responsible for my going away; it is His love alone which has snatched me beyond reach of their tenderness. May this same love so inspire them that they may generously accept our separation! Their confessor will say this to them again; may they listen well to his counsel: they will derive from it that holy patience, that resignation to the divine will, which will restore their souls' serenity; and they will feel that the Lord has never called down such a blessing upon their home. By grace of repeating to themselves, as I repeat to them, that it is Our Lord and no one else who is the author of their ordeal, they will come to find, at last, that His yoke is easy, and their tribulation will be transformed into a calm happiness.

Since nothing in this world is worthy of our finding affliction in its loss, is it not better to concentrate our endeavors on fulfilling God's will and preparing ourselves for a good death? With a righteous death, everything is saved; without a death in righteousness, all is lost.

May they come to esteem themselves happy, these dear parents of mine, in having a son who, unworthy and a sinner as he is, prays at the altar for them every morning, with all his heart, imploring that God will give them the necessities of life, patience in trials, resignation to His holy will, the grace to live in peace and friendship with those about them, and, when at last God's summons comes, the grace of a sanctified death! In thinking of me—my beloved parents, and also my little sister Juanita and my brother-in-law Miguel—may they devote themselves wholly to beseeching God that I may become a good priest and a good friar. . . .

You remember, my dear Father, what you said to me some fifteen years ago, when, having received extreme unction, you believed yourself close to appearing before God? . . . I recall your words as if they had fallen this very moment from your lips; and with them I recall the promise I made to you, as you asked me, then: "Always to be a good son of St. Francis." Very well, then! It is to carry out your will, which is also the will of God, that I am now on the way to Mexico.

My dear Mother, as for you, I know that this is what you too have always asked of God for me, in your prayers. He has answered them already, in setting me upon the path on which I have entered. Be happy then, beloved Mother; and when you suffer say again, with your son, "Blessed be God! May His holy will be done!". . .

May she [Serra's sister Juanita], and her husband with her, show patience, respect, and compassion toward them; may they two live together as a good husband and wife who love each other; may they bring up their three children well; may the entire family continue in the practice of piety, going regularly to church, keeping close to the sacraments, assiduously making the Stations of the Cross.

And now we are parting, promising, as we do so, to pray for one another a very great deal. God will be the close protector of us all; He will give us His grace in this life and His glory in the life to come. Farewell then, my cherished Father! farewell, my fond Mother! farewell, little sister Juanita! farewell, Miguel, my dear brother-in-law! You will be able, each and all of you, to count upon the deep feeling in the heart of the one who is going away. Farewell! Farewell!

Farewell to you, Father Serra, my very dear colleague [and cousin, Fray]! Henceforth my letters will be of necessity less frequent; but you love my parents and they love you. That is why I commend them to you again, to you first of all; I commend them also to the loving-kindness of the Father Guardian, the Father Vicar,

and the Father Master of Novices. If the last-named two could be present at the reading of this letter, I am sure that this would give pleasure to my parents and would add to their solace. . . .

Your affectionate friend in Our Lord,
Fray Junípero Serra, very unworthy priest.

GEORGE WHITEFIELD
1714 - 1770

A leader in the Great Awakening, **George Whitefield** emigrated to America from England, where he was born in 1714. A Methodist preacher, Whitefield traveled through the Colonies on horseback, preaching to whoever would listen and converting whenever possible. Ours is a history full of passionate evangelists, and Whitefield was no exception. He launched a trend for huge outdoor revivals that attracted hundreds. This excerpt is from his journals and relates the story of his conversion from a misguided and decadent student to a deeply convinced and committed Christian.

ALTHOUGH the following Account of what God has done for my soul, will undoubtedly be differently judged of by different people; yet, since I believe a single eye to God's glory moves me to write, and I find myself much pressed in spirit to publish it at this time, I am not in the least solicitous about the reception it will meet with in the world.

The benefit I have received from reading the Lives of others, the examples we have in Scripture of the sacred authors composing their own histories, and more especially the assistance I have had from the Holy Spirit, in bringing many things to my remembrance, which otherwise I would have forgotten, seemed to me reasons sufficient to justify my conduct in the sight of God and good men.

Further, as God has been pleased of late to call me to a public work, I thought His children would be glad to know how I was trained up for it. And though some may think this had been as well deferred till after my death, or written by some other person, yet I thought it might be more beneficial, and be better credited, if written with my own hand, and published whilst I was yet alive.

In the accounts of good men which I have read, I have observed that the writers of them have been partial. They have given us the bright, but not the dark side of their character. This, I think, proceeded from a kind of pious fraud, lest mentioning persons' faults should encourage others in sin. It cannot, I am sure, proceed from the wisdom which cometh from above. The sacred writers give an account of their failings as well as their virtues. Peter is not ashamed to confess that with oaths and curses he thrice denied his Master; nor do the Evangelists make any scruple of telling us, that out of Mary Magdalene Jesus Christ cast seven devils. . . .

My very infant years must necessarily not be mentioned; yet I can remember such early stirrings of corruption in my heart, as abundantly convinces me that I was conceived and born in sin; that in me dwelleth no good thing by nature, and that if God had not freely prevented me by His grace, I must have been for ever banished from His Divine presence. . . .

It would be endless to recount the sins and offences of my younger days. They are more in number than the hairs of my head. My heart would fail me at the remembrance of them, was I not assured that my Redeemer liveth, ever to make intercession for me. However the young man in the Gospel might boast how he had kept the commandments from his youth, with shame and confusion of face I confess that I have broken them all from my youth. Whatever foreseen fitness for salvation others may talk of and glory in, I disclaim any such thing. If I trace myself from my cradle to my manhood, I can see nothing in me but a fitness to be damned. [I speak the truth in Christ, I lie not.] If the Almighty had not prevented me by His grace, and wrought most powerfully upon my soul, quickening me by His free Spirit when dead in trespasses and sins, I had now either been sitting in darkness, and in the shadow of death, or condemned, as the due reward of my crimes, to be for ever lifting up my eyes in torments.

But such was the free grace of God to me, that though corruption worked so strongly in my soul, and produced such early and bitter fruits, yet I can recollect very early movings of the blessed Spirit upon my heart, sufficient to satisfy me that God loved me with an everlasting love, and separated me even from my mother's womb, for the work to which He afterwards was pleased to call me.

I had some early convictions of sin; and once, I remember when some persons (as they frequently did) made it their business to tease me, I immediately retired to my room, and kneeling down, with many tears, prayed over that Psalm wherein David so often repeats these words—"*But in the Name of the Lord will I destroy them.*" I was always fond of being a clergyman and used frequently to imitate the ministers reading prayers, etc. Part of the money I used to steal from my parent I gave to the poor, and some books I privately took from others, for which I have since restored four-fold, I remember were books of devotion. . . .

[But He Who was with David when he was following the sheep big with young, was with me even here. For] notwithstanding I was thus employed in a common inn, and had sometimes the care of the whole house upon my hands, yet I composed two or three sermons, and dedicated one of them in particular to my elder brother. One time, I remember, I was much pressed to self-examination, and found myself very unwilling to look into my heart. Frequently I read the Bible when sitting up at night. Seeing the boys go by to school has often cut me to the heart. And a dear youth, now with God, would often come entreating me, when serving at the bar, to go to Oxford. My general answer was, "I wish I could."

After I had continued about a year in this servile employment, my mother was obliged to leave the inn. My brother who had been bred up for the business, married; whereupon all was made over to him; and I, being accustomed to the house, it was agreed that I should continue there as an assistant. [But God's thoughts were not as our thoughts. By His good Providence] I went to see my elder brother then settled in Bristol.

Here God was pleased to give me great foretastes of His love, and fill me with such unspeakable raptures, particularly once in St. John's Church, that I was carried out beyond myself. I felt great hungerings and thirstings after the blessed Sacrament, and wrote many letters to my mother, telling her I would never go into the public employment again. Thomas à Kempis was my great delight. . . . But in the midst of these illuminations something surely whispered, *"This will not last."*

And, indeed, so it happened. For—oh that I could write it in tears of blood!—when I left Bristol, as I did in about two months, and returned to Gloucester, I changed my devotion with my place. Alas! all my fervour went off: I had no inclination to go to Church, or draw nigh unto God. In short, my heart, though I had so lately tasted of His love, was far from Him.

However, I had so much religion left, as to persist in my resolution not to live in the inn; and therefore my mother gave me leave, though she had but a little income, to have a bed upon the ground, and live at her house, till Providence should point out a place for me.

Having now, as I thought, nothing to do, it was a proper season for Satan to tempt me. Much of my time I spent in reading plays, and in sauntering from place to place. I was careful to adorn my body, but took little pains to deck and beautify my soul. Evil communications with my old schoolfellows soon corrupted my good manners. By seeing their evil practices, the sense of the Divine Presence I had vouchsafed unto me insensibly wore off my mind, and I at length fell into abominable secret sin, the dismal effects of which I have felt, and groaned under ever since.

[But God, whose gifts and callings are without repentance, would let nothing pluck me out of His hands, though I was continually doing despite to the Spirit of Grace. He saw me with pity and compassion, when lying in my blood. He passed by me; He said unto me, *Live*, and even gave me some foresight of His providing for me.

One morning, as I was reading a play to my sister, said I, "Sister, God intends something for me which we know not of. As I have been diligent in business, I believe many would gladly have me for an apprentice, but every way seems to be barred up, so that I think God will provide for me some way or other that we cannot apprehend." . . .

But, oh stupendous love! God even here stopped me, when running on in a full career to hell. For, just as I was upon the brink of ruin, He gave me such a distaste of their principles and practices, that I discovered them to my master, who soon put a stop to their proceedings.

Being thus delivered out of the snare of the Devil, I began to be more and more serious, and felt God at different times working powerfully and convincingly upon my soul. One day in particular, as I was coming downstairs, and overheard my friends speaking well of me, God so deeply convicted me of hypocrisy, that though I had formed frequent but ineffectual resolutions before, yet I had then power given me over my secret and darling sin. Notwithstanding, some time after being overtaken in liquor, as I have been twice or thrice in my lifetime, Satan gained his usual advantage over me again,—an experimental proof to my poor soul, how that wicked one makes use of men as machines, working them up to just what he pleases, [when by intemperance they have chased away the Spirit of God from them.] . . .

Near this time I dreamed that I was to see God on Mount Sinai, but was afraid to meet Him. This made a great impression upon me; and a gentlewoman to whom I told it, said, "George, this is a call from God."

At my first setting out, in compassion to my weakness, I grew in favour both with God and man, and used to be much lifted up with sensible devotion, especially at the blessed Sacrament. But when religion began to take root in my heart, and I was fully convinced my soul must totally be renewed ere it could see God, I was visited with outward and inward trials.

The first thing I was called to give up for God was what the world calls my fair reputation. I had no sooner received the sacrament publicly on a week-day at St. Mary's, but I was set up as a mark for all the polite students that knew me to shoot at. [By this they knew that I was commenced Methodist; for though there is a sacrament at the beginning of every term, at which all, especially the seniors, are by statute, obliged to be present, yet so dreadfully has that once faithful city played the harlot, that very few Masters, and no undergraduates but the Methodists, attended upon it. . . .

From my first awakenings to the Divine life, I felt a particular hungering and thirsting after the humility of Jesus Christ. Night and day I prayed to be a partaker of that grace, imagining that the habit of humility would be instantaneously infused into my soul. But as Gideon taught the men of Succoth with thorns, so God, if I am yet in any measure blessed with true poverty of spirit, taught it me by the exercise of strong temptations. . . .

God only knows how many nights I have lain upon my bed groaning under the weight I felt, [and bidding Satan depart from me in the Name of Jesus.] Whole days and weeks have I spent in lying prostrate on the ground, [and begging for freedom from those proud hellish thoughts that used to crowd in upon and distract my soul. But God made Satan drive out Satan; for these thoughts and suggestions created such a self-abhorrence within me, that I never ceased wrestling with God, till He blessed me with a victory over them. Self-love, self-will, pride and envy, so buffeted me in their turns, that I was resolved either to die or conquer. I wanted to see sin as it was, but feared, at the same time, lest the sight of it should terrify me to death. . . .

His main drift was to lead me into a state of quietism, (he generally ploughed with God's heifer); and when the Holy Spirit put into my heart good thoughts or convictions, he always drove them to extremes. For instance, having out of pride, put down in my diary what I gave away, Satan tempted me to lay my diary quite aside. When Castaniza advised to talk but little, Satan said I must not talk at all. So that I, who used to be the most forward in exhorting my companions, have sat whole nights almost without speaking at all. Again, when Castaniza advised to endeavour after a silent recollection and waiting upon God, Satan told me I must leave off all forms, and not use my voice in prayer at all. The time would fail me to recount all the instances of this kind in which he had deceived me. But when matters came to an extreme, God always showed me my error, and by His Spirit, pointed out a way for me to escape.

The Devil also sadly imposed upon me in the matter of my college exercises. Whenever I endeavoured to compose my theme, I had no power to write a word, nor so much as tell my Christian friends of my inability to do it. Saturday being come, which is the day the students give up their compositions, it was suggested to me that I must go down into the Hall, and confess I could not make a theme, and so publicly suffer, as if it were for my Master's sake. When the bell rung to call us, I went to open the door to go down stairs, but feeling something give me a violent inward check, I entered my study, and continued instant in prayer, waiting the event. For this my tutor fined me half-a-crown. The next week Satan served me in like manner again; but now having got more strength, and perceiving no inward check, I went into the Hall. My name being called, I stood up, and told my tutor I could not make a theme. I think he fined me a second time; but, imagining that I would not willingly neglect my exercise, he afterwards called me into the Common Room, and kindly enquired whether any misfortune had befallen me, or what was the reason I could not make a theme. I burst into tears, and assured him that it was not out of contempt of authority, but that I could not act otherwise. Then, at length he said, he believed I could not; and when he left me, told a friend, as he very well might, that he took me to be really mad. This friend hearing from my tutor what had happened, came to me, urging the command of Scripture, to be subject to the higher powers. I answered, "Yes; but I had a new revelation." Lord, what is man?

As I daily got strength, by continued, though almost silent, prayer, in my study, my temptations grew stronger also, particularly for two or three days before deliverance came. . . .

To proceed—I had now taken up my externals again [and though Satan for some weeks had been biting my heel, God was pleased to show me that I should soon bruise his head.] A few days after, as I was walking along, I met with a poor woman, whose husband was then in Bocardo, or Oxford Town-Gaol, [which I constantly visited.] Seeing her much discomposed, I enquired the cause. She told me, not being able to bear the crying of her children, ready to perish for hunger, and having nothing to relieve them, she had been to drown herself, but was mercifully prevented, and said she was coming to my room to inform me of it. I gave her some immediate relief, and desired her to meet me at the prison with her husband in the afternoon. She came, and there God visited them both by His free grace. She was powerfully quickened from above; and when I had done reading, he also came to me like the trembling gaoler, and, grasping my hand, cried out, "I am upon the brink of hell!" From this time forward, both of them grew in grace. God, by His providence, soon delivered him from his confinement. Though notorious offenders against God and one another before, yet now they became helpmeet for each other in the great work of their salvation. They are both now living, and, I trust, will be my joy and crown of rejoicing in the great day of our Lord Jesus.

Soon after this, [the holy season of] Lent came on, which our friends kept very strictly, eating no flesh during the six weeks, except on Saturdays also, and ate nothing on the other days, except on Sunday, but sage-tea without sugar, and coarse bread. I constantly walked out in the cold mornings till part of one of my hands was quite black. This, with my continued abstinence, and inward conflicts, at length so emaciated my body, that, at Passion-week, finding I could scarce creep upstairs, I was obliged to inform my kind tutor of my condition, who immediately sent for a physician to me.

This caused no small triumph amongst the collegians, who began to cry out, "What is his fasting come to now?" [But I rejoiced in this reproach, knowing that, though I had been imprudent, and lost much of my flesh, yet, I had nevertheless increased in the Spirit.]

[This fit of sickness continued upon me for seven weeks, and a glorious visitation it was. The blessed Spirit was all this time purifying my soul. All my former gross and notorious, and even my heart sins also, were now set home upon me, of which I wrote down some remembrance immediately, and confessed them before God morning and evening. Though weak, I often spent two hours in my evening retirements, and

prayed over my Greek Testament and Bishop Hall's most excellent *Contemplations*, every hour that my health would permit.] About the end of the seven weeks,[1] [and after I had been groaning under an unspeakable pressure both of body and mind for above a twelvemonth, God was pleased to see me free in the following manner. One day, perceiving an uncommon drought and a disagreeable clamminess in my mouth and using things to allay my thirst, but in vain, it was suggested to me, that when Jesus Christ cried out, "I thirst," His sufferings were near at an end. Upon which I cast myself down on the bed, crying out, "I thirst! I thirst!" Soon after this, I found and felt in myself that I was delivered from the burden that so heavily oppressed me. The spirit of mourning was taken from me, and I knew what it was truly to rejoice in God my Saviour; and, for some time, could not avoid singing psalms wherever I was; but my joy gradually became more settled, and, blessed be God, has abode and increased in my soul, saving a few casual intermissions, ever since.

Thus were the days of my mourning ended. After a long night of desertion and temptation, the Star, which I had seen at a distance before, began to appear again, and the Day Star arose in my heart. Now did the Spirit of God take possession of my soul, and, as I humbly hope, seal me unto the day of redemption.]

JOHN WOOLMAN
1720 - 1772

CHAPTER I

*His Birth and Parentage, with some
Account of the Operations of divine Grace on
his Mind in his Youth—His first Appearance
in the Ministry—And his Considerations,
while young, on the keeping of Slaves*

I HAVE often felt a Motion of Love to leave some Hints in Writing of my Experience of the Goodness of God; and now, in the thirty-sixth Year of my Age, I begin this Work.

---

[1] "After having undergone innumerable buffetings of Satan, and many months inexpressible trials by night and day under the spirit of bondage, God was pleased at length to remove the heavy load, to enable me to lay hold on His dear Son by a living faith, and, by giving me the spirit of adoption, to seal me, as I humbly hope, even to the day of everlasting redemption. But oh! with what joy—joy unspeakable—even joy that was full of, and big with glory, was my soul filled, when the weight of sin went off, and an abiding sense of the pardoning love of God, and a full assurance of faith broke in upon my disconsolate soul! Surely it was the day of my espousals,—a day to be had in everlasting remembrance. At first my joys were like a spring tide, and, as it were, overflowed the banks. Go where I would, I could not avoid singing of psalms aloud; afterwards it became more settled—and, blessed be God, saving a few casual intervals, has abode and increased in my soul ever since. But to proceed."—Edit. 1756.

I was born in *Northampton*, in *Burlington* County, *West-Jersey*, in the Year 1720; and before I was seven Years old I began to be acquainted with the Operations of divine Love. Through the Care of my Parents, I was taught to read nearly as soon as I was capable of it; and, as I went from School one seventh Day, I remember, while my Companions went to play by the Way, I went forward out of Sight, and, sitting down, I read the 22d Chapter of the *Revelations:* "He shewed me a pure River of Water of Life, clear as Chrystal, proceeding out of the Throne of God and of the Lamb, *etc.*" and, in reading it, my Mind was drawn to seek after the pure Habitation, which, I then believed, God had prepared for his Servants. The Place where I sat, and the Sweetness that attended my Mind, remain fresh in my Memory.

A Quaker minister, **John Woolman** was responsible for the first resolution opposing slavery in this country. Indeed, he campaigned tirelessly for abolition long in advance of the abolition movement's gathering of political strength. As he worked as a traveling preacher, Woolman began to set his thoughts down at the age of thirty-six. The result was his journal, a thoughtful and detailed meditation on life in Colonial America, which also illustrates Woolman's strong ideals rooted in a quiet yet unswerving faith in God.

This, and the like gracious Visitations, had that Effect upon me, that when Boys used ill Language it troubled me; and, through the continued Mercies of God, I was preserved from it.

The pious Instructions of my Parents were often fresh in my Mind when I happened to be among wicked Children, and were of Use to me. My Parents, having a large Family of Children, used frequently, on first Days after Meeting, to put us to read in the holy Scriptures, or some religious Books, one after another, the rest sitting by without much Conversation; which, I have since often thought, was a good Practice. From what I had read and heard, I believed there had been, in past Ages, People who walked in Uprightness before God, in a Degree exceeding any that I knew, or heard of, now living: And the Apprehension of there being less Steadiness and Firmness, amongst People in this Age than in past Ages, often troubled me while I was a Child.

A Thing remarkable in my Childhood was, that once, going to a Neighbour's House, I saw, on the Way, a *Robin* sitting on her Nest, and as I came near she went off, but, having young ones, flew about, and with many Cries expressed her Concern for them; I stood and threw Stones at her, till, one striking her, she fell down dead:

At first I was pleased with the Exploit, but after a few Minutes was seized with Horror, as having, in a sportive Way, killed an innocent Creature while she was careful for her Young: I beheld her lying dead, and thought these young ones, for which she was so careful, must now perish for want of their Dam to nourish them; and, after some painful Considerations on the Subject, I climbed up the Tree, took all the young Birds, and killed them; supposing that better than to leave them to pine away and die miserably: And believed, in this Case, that Scripture-proverb was fulfilled, "The tender Mercies of the Wicked are cruel." I then went on my Errand, but, for some Hours, could think of little else but the Cruelties I had committed, and was much troubled. Thus he, whose tender Mercies are over all his Works, hath placed a Principle in the human Mind, which incites to exercise Goodness towards every living Creature; and this being singly attended to, People become tender hearted and sympathising; but being frequently and totally rejected, the Mind becomes shut up in a contrary Disposition.

About the twelfth Year of my Age, my Father being abroad, my Mother reproved me for some Misconduct, to which I made an undutiful Reply; and, the next first Day, as I was with my Father returning from Meeting, he told me he understood I had behaved amiss to my Mother, and advised me to be more careful in future. I knew myself blameable, and in Shame and Confusion remained silent. Being thus awakened to a Sense of my Wickedness, I felt Remorse in my Mind, and, getting home, I retired and prayed to the Lord to forgive me; and do not remember that I ever, after that, spoke unhandsomely to either of my Parents, however foolish in some other Things.

Having attained the Age of sixteen Years, I began to love wanton Company; and though I was preserved from prophane Language, or scandalous Conduct, still I perceived a Plant in me which produced much wild Grapes; yet my merciful Father forsook me not utterly, but, at Times, through his Grace, I was brought seriously to consider my Ways; and the Sight of my Backslidings affected me with Sorrow; but, for want of rightly attending to the Reproofs of Instruction, Vanity was added to Vanity, and Repentance to Repentance: Upon the whole, my Mind was more and more alienated from the Truth, and I hastened toward Destruction. While I meditate on the Gulph towards which I travelled, and reflect on my youthful Disobedience, for these Things I weep, mine Eyes run down with Water.

Advancing in Age, the Number of my Acquaintances increased, and thereby my Way grew more difficult; though I had found Comfort in reading the holy Scriptures, and thinking on heavenly Things, I was now estranged therefrom: I knew I was going from the Flock of Christ, and had no Resolution to return; hence serious Reflections were uneasy to me, and youthful Vanities and Diversions my greatest Pleasure. Running in this Road I found many like myself; and we associated in that which is the reverse of true Friendship.

But in this swift Race it pleased God to visit me with Sickness, so that I doubted of recovering; and then did Darkness, Horror, and Amazement, with full Force, seize me, even when my Pain and Distress of Body was very great. I thought it would have been better for me never to have had a Being, than to see the Day which I now saw. I was filled with Confusion; and in great Affliction, both of Mind and Body, I lay and bewailed myself. I had not Confidence to lift up my Cries to God, whom I had thus offended; but, in a deep Sense of my great Folly, I was humbled before him; and, at length, that Word which is as a Fire and a Hammer, broke and dissolved my rebellious Heart, and then my Cries were put up in Contrition; and in the multitude of his Mercies I found inward Relief, and felt a close Engagement, that, if he was pleased to restore my Health, I might walk humbly before him.

After my Recovery, this Exercise remained with me a considerable Time; but, by Degrees, giving Way to youthful Vanities, they gained Strength, and, getting with wanton young People, I lost Ground. The Lord had been very gracious, and spoke Peace to me in the Time of my Distress; and I now most ungratefully turned again to Folly; on which Account, at Times, I felt sharp Reproof. I was not so hardy as to commit Things scandalous; but to exceed in Vanity, and promote Mirth, was my chief Study. Still I retained a Love for pious People, and their Company brought an Awe upon me. My dear Parents, several Times, admonished me in the Fear of the Lord, and their Admonition entered into my Heart, and had a good Effect for a Season; but, not getting deep enough to pray rightly, the Tempter, when he came, found Entrance. I remember once, having spent a Part of the Day in Wantonness, as I went to Bed at Night, there lay in a Window, near my Bed, a Bible, which I opened, and first cast my Eye on this Text, "We lie down in our Shame, and our Confusion covers us:" This I knew to be my Case; and, meeting with so unexpected a Reproof, I was somewhat affected with it, and went to Bed under Remorse of Conscience; which I soon cast off again.

Thus Time passed on: My Heart was replenished with Mirth and Wantonness, and pleasing Scenes of Vanity were presented to my Imagination, till I attained the Age of eighteen Years; near which Time I felt the Judgments of God, in my Soul, like a consuming Fire; and, looking over my past Life, the Prospect was moving.—I was often sad, and longed to be delivered from those Vanities; then again, my Heart was strongly inclined to them, and there was in me a sore Conflict: At Times I turned to Folly, and then again, Sorrow and Confusion took hold of me. In a while, I was resolved totally to leave off some of my Vanities; but there was a secret Reserve, in my Heart, of the more refined Part of them, and I was not low enough to find true Peace. Thus, for some Months, I had great Troubles; there remaining in me an unsubjected Will, which rendered my Labours fruitless, till at length, through the merciful Continuance of heavenly Visitations, I was made to bow down in Spirit before the Lord. I remember one Evening I had spent some Time in reading a pious Author; and walking out alone, I humbly prayed to the Lord for his Help, that I might be delivered from all those Vanities which so ensnared me. Thus, being brought low, he helped me; and, as I learned to bear the Cross, I felt Refreshment to come from his Presence; but, not keeping in that Strength which gave Victory, I lost Ground again; the Sense of which greatly affected me; and I sought Desarts and lonely Places, and there, with Tears, did confess my Sins to God, and humbly craved Help of him. And I may say with Reverence, he was near to me in my Troubles, and in those Times of Humiliation opened my Ear to Discipline. I was now led to look seriously at the Means by which I was drawn from the pure Truth, and learned this, that, if I would live in the Life which the faithful Servants of God lived in, I must not go into Company as heretofore in my own Will; but all the Cravings of Sense must be governed by a divine Principle. In Times of Sorrow and Abasement these Instructions were sealed upon me, and I felt the Power of Christ prevail over selfish Desires, so that I was preserved in a good degree of Steadiness; and, being young, and believing at that Time that a single Life was best for me, I was strengthened to keep from such Company as had often been a Snare to me.

I kept steadily to Meetings; spent First-day Afternoons chiefly in reading the Scriptures and other good Books; and was early convinced in Mind, that true Religion consisted in an inward Life, wherein the Heart doth love and reverence God the Creator, and learns to exercise true Justice and Goodness, not only toward all Men, but also toward the brute Creatures.—That as the Mind was moved, by an inward Principle, to love God as an indivisible incomprehensible Being, by the same Principle it was moved to love him in all his Manifestations in the visible World.—That, as by his Breath the Flame of Life was kindled in all animal sensible Creatures, to say we love God, and, at the same Time exercise Cruelty toward the least Creature, is a Contradiction in itself.

I found no Narrowness respecting Sects and Opinions; but believed, that sincere upright-hearted People, in every Society, who truly love God, were accepted of him.

As I lived under the Cross, and simply followed the Openings of Truth, my Mind, from Day to Day, was more enlightened; my former Acquaintance were left to judge of me as they would, for I found it safest for me to live in private, and keep these Things sealed up in my own Breast. While I silently ponder on that Change wrought in me, I find no Language equal to it, nor any Means to convey to another a clear Idea of it. I looked on the Works of God in this visible Creation, and an Awfulness covered me; my Heart was tender and often contrite, and universal Love to my Fellow-creatures increased in me: This will be understood by such as have trodden the same Path. Some Glances of real Beauty may be seen in their Faces, who dwell in true Meekness. There is a Harmony in the Sound of that Voice to which divine Love gives Utterance, and some Appearance of right Order in their Temper and Conduct, whose Passions are regulated; yet all these do not fully shew forth that inward Life to such as have not felt it: But this white Stone and new Name is known rightly to such only as have it.

Though I had been thus strengthened to bear the Cross, I still found myself in great Danger, having many Weaknesses attending me, and strong Temptations to wrestle with; in the feeling whereof I frequently withdrew into private Places, and often with Tears besought the Lord to help me, whose gracious Ear was open to my Cry.

All this Time I lived with my Parents, and wrought on the Plantation; and, having had Schooling pretty well for a Planter, I used to improve it in Winter Evenings, and other leisure Times; and, being now in the twenty-first Year of my Age, a Man, in much Business at shop-keeping and baking, asked me, if I would hire with him to tend Shop and keep Books. I acquainted my Father with the Proposal; and, after some Deliberation, it was agreed for me to go.

At Home I had lived retired; and now, having a Prospect of being much in the Way of Company, I felt frequent and fervent Cries in my Heart to God, the Father of Mercies, that he would preserve me from all Corruption; that in this more publick Employment, I might serve him, my gracious Redeemer, in that Humility and Self-denial, with which I had been, in a small Degree, exercised in a more private Life. The Man, who employed me, furnished a Shop in *Mount-Holly*, about five Miles from my Father's House, and six from his own; and there I lived alone, and tended his Shop. Shortly after my Settlement here I was visited by several young People, my former Acquaintance, who knew not but Vanities would be as agreeable to me now as ever; and, at these Times, I cried to the Lord in secret, for Wisdom and Strength; for I felt myself encompassed with Difficulties, and had fresh Occasion to bewail the Follies of Time past, in contracting a Familiarity with libertine People; and, as I had now left my Father's House outwardly, I found my heavenly Father to be merciful to me beyond what I can express.

By Day I was much amongst People, and had many Trials to go through; but, in the Evenings, I was mostly alone, and may with Thankfulness acknowledge, that, in those Times, the Spirit of Supplication was often poured upon me; under which I was frequently exercised, and felt my Strength renewed.

In a few Months after I came here, my Master bought several *Scotchmen*, Servants, from on-board a Vessel, and brought them to *Mount-Holly* to sell; one of which was taken sick, and died.

In the latter Part of his Sickness, he, being delirious, used to curse and swear most sorrowfully; and, the next Night after his Burial, I was left to sleep alone in the same Chamber where he died; I perceived in me a Timorousness; I knew, however, I had not injured the Man, but assisted in taking Care of him according to my Capacity; and was not free to ask any one, on that Occasion, to sleep with me: Nature was feeble; but every Trial was a fresh Incitement to give myself up wholly to the Service of God, for I found no Helper like him in Times of Trouble.

After a While, my former Acquaintance gave over expecting me as one of their Company; and I began to be known to some whose Conversation was helpful to me: And now, as I had experienced the Love of

God, through Jesus Christ, to redeem me from many Pollutions, and to be a Succour to me through a Sea of Conflicts, with which no Person was fully acquainted; and as my Heart was often enlarged in this heavenly Principle, I felt a tender Compassion for the Youth, who remained entangled in Snares, like those which had entangled me from one Time to another: This Love and Tenderness increased; and my Mind was more strongly engaged for the Good of my Fellow-creatures. I went to Meetings in an awful Frame of Mind, and endeavoured to be inwardly acquainted with the Language of the true Shepherd; and, one Day, being under a strong Exercise of Spirit, I stood up, and said some Words in a Meeting; but, not keeping close to the divine Opening, I said more than was required of me; and being soon sensible of my Error, I was afflicted in Mind some Weeks, without any Light or Comfort, even to that Degree that I could not take Satisfaction in any Thing: I remembered God, and was troubled, and, in the Depth of my Distress, he had Pity upon me, and sent the Comforter: I then felt Forgiveness for my Offence, and my Mind became calm and quiet, being truly thankful to my gracious Redeemer for his Mercies; and, after this, feeling the Spring of divine Love opened, and a Concern to speak, I said a few Words in a Meeting, in which I found Peace; this, I believe, was about six Weeks from the first Time: And, as I was thus humbled and disciplined under the Cross, my Understanding because more strengthened to distinguish the pure Spirit which inwardly moves upon the Heart, and taught me to wait in Silence sometimes many Weeks together, until I felt that rise which prepares the Creature.

From an inward purifying, and stedfast abiding under it, springs a lively operative Desire for the Good of others: All the Faithful are not called to the public Ministry; but whoever are, are called to minister of that which they have tasted and handled spiritually. The outward Modes of Worship are various; but, wherever any are true Ministers of Jesus Christ, it is from the Operation of his Spirit upon their Hearts, first purifying them, and thus giving them a just Sense of the Conditions of others.

This Truth was clearly fixed in my Mind; and I was taught to watch the pure Opening, and to take Heed, lest, while I was standing to speak, my own Will should get uppermost, and cause me to utter Words from worldly Wisdom, and depart from the Channel of the true Gospel-Ministry.

In the Management of my outward Affairs, I may say, with Thankfulness, I found Truth to be my Support; and I was respected in my Master's Family, who came to live in *Mount-Holly* within two Years after my going there.

About the twenty-third Year of my Age, I had many fresh and heavenly Openings, in respect to the Care and Providence of the Almighty over his Creatures in general, and over Man as the most noble amongst those which are visible. And being clearly convinced in my Judgment, that to place my whole Trust in God was best for me, I felt renewed Engagements, that in all Things I might act on an inward Principle of Virtue, and pursue worldly Business no farther, than as Truth opened my Way therein.

About the Time called *Christmas*, I observed many People from the Country, and Dwellers in Town, who, resorting to Public-Houses, spent their Time in drinking and vain Sports, tending to corrupt one another; on which Account I was much troubled. At one House, in particular, there was much Disorder; and I believed it was a Duty incumbent on me to go and speak to the Master of that House. I considered I was young, and that several elderly Friends in town had Opportunity to see these Things; but though I would gladly have been excused, yet I could not feel my Mind clear.

The Exercise was heavy; and as I was reading what the Almighty said to *Ezekiel*, respecting his Duty as a Watchman, the Matter was set home more clearly; and then, with Prayers and Tears, I besought the Lord for his Assistance, who, in Loving-kindness, gave me a resigned Heart: Then, at a suitable Opportunity, I went to the Public-house, and, seeing the Man amongst much Company, I went to him, and told him, I wanted to speak with him; so we went aside, and there, in the Fear of the Almighty, I expressed to him what rested on my Mind; which he took kindly, and afterward shewed more Regard to me than before. In a few Years afterwards he died, middle-aged; and I often thought that, had I neglected my Duty in this Case, it would have given me great Trouble; and I was humbly thankful to my gracious Father, who had supported me herein.

My Employer having a Negro Woman, sold her, and desired me to write a Bill of Sale, the Man being waiting who bought her: The Thing was sudden; and, though the Thoughts of writing an Instrument of Slavery for one of my Fellow-creatures felt uneasy, yet I remembered I was hired by the Year, that it was my Master who directed me to do it, and that it was an elderly Man, a Member of our Society, who bought her; so, through Weakness, I gave way, and wrote; but, at the executing it, I was so afflicted in my Mind, that I said, before my Master and the Friend, that I believed Slave-keeping to be a Practice inconsistent with the *Christian* Religion: This in some Degree abated my Uneasiness; yet, as often as I reflected seriously upon it, I thought I should have been clearer, if I had desired to have been excused from it, as a Thing against my Conscience; for such it was. And, some Time after this, a young Man, of our Society, spoke to me to write a Conveyance of a Slave to him, he having lately taken a Negro into his House: I told him I was not easy to write it; for, though many of our Meeting and in other Places kept Slaves, I still believed the Practice was not right, and desired to be excused from the writing. I spoke to him in Good-will; and he told me that keeping Slaves was not altogether agreeable to his Mind; but that the Slave being a Gift to his Wife, he had accepted of her.

CHAPTER IV

. . . About this Time I wrote an Epistle to Friends in the Back-settlements of *North Carolina*, as follows:

To Friends at their Monthly-meeting at *New-Garden* and *Cane-Creek*, in *North Carolina*.

Dear Friends,—It having pleased the Lord to draw me forth on a Visit to some Parts of *Virginia* and *Carolina*, you have often been in my Mind; and though my Way is not clear to come in Person to visit you, yet I feel it in my Heart to communicate a few Things, as they arise in the Love of Truth. First, my dear Friends, dwell in Humility, and take Heed that no Views of outward Gain get too deep hold of you, that so your Eyes being single to the Lord, you may be preserved in the Way of Safety. Where People let loose their Minds after the Love of outward Things, and are more engaged in pursuing the Profits, and seeking the Friendships, of this World, than to be inwardly acquainted with the Way of true Peace; such walk in a vain Shadow, while the true Comfort of Life is wanting: Their Examples are often hurtful to others; and their Treasures, thus collected, do many Times prove dangerous Snares to their Children.

But where People are sincerely devoted to follow Christ, and dwell under the Influence of his holy Spirit, their Stability and Firmness, through a divine Blessing, is at Times like Dew on the tender Plants round about them, and the Weightiness of their Spirits secretly works on the Minds of others; and in this Condition, through the spreading Influence of divine Love, they feel a Care over the Flock; and Way is opened for maintaining good Order in the Society: And though we meet with Opposition from another Spirit, yet, as there is a dwelling in Meekness, feeling our Spirits subject, and moving only in the gentle peaceable Wisdom, the inward Reward of Quietness will be greater than all our Difficulties. Where the pure Life is kept to, and Meetings of Discipline are held in the Authority of it, we find by Experience that they are comfortable, and tend to the Health of the Body.

While I write, the Youth come fresh in my Way:— Dear young People, choose God for your Portion; love his Truth, and be not ashamed of it: Choose for your Company such as serve him in Uprightness; and shun, as most dangerous, the Conversation of those whose Lives are of an ill Savour; for, by frequenting such Company, some hopeful young People have come to great Loss, and have been drawn from less Evils to greater, to their utter Ruin. In the Bloom of Youth no Ornament is so lovely as that of Virtue, nor any Enjoyments equal to those which we partake of, in fully resigning ourselves to the divine Will: These Enjoyments add Sweetness to all other Comforts, and give true Satisfaction in Company and Conversation, where People are mutually acquainted with it; and, as your Minds are thus seasoned with the Truth, you will find Strength to abide stedfast to the Testimony of it, and be prepared for Services in the Church.

And now, dear Friends and Brethren, as you are improving a Wilderness, and may be numbered amongst the first Planters in one Part of a Province, I beseech you, in the Love of Jesus Christ, to wisely consider the Force of your Examples, and think how much your Successors may be thereby affected: It is a Help in a Country, yea, and a great Favour and a Blessing, when Customs, first settled, are agreeable to sound Wisdom; so, when they are otherwise, the Effect of them is grievous; and Children feel themselves encompassed with Difficulties prepared for them by their Predecessors.

As moderate Care and Exercise, under the Direction of true Wisdom, are useful both to Mind and Body; so by this Means in general, the real Wants of Life are easily supplied: Our gracious Father having so proportioned one to the other, that keeping in the true Medium we may pass on quietly. Where Slaves are purchased to do our Labour, numerous Difficulties attend it. To rational Creatures Bondage is uneasy, and frequently occasions Sourness and Discontent in them; which affects the Family, and such as claim the Mastery over them: And thus People and their Children are many Times encompassed with Vexations, which arise from their applying to wrong Methods to get a Living.

I have been informed that there is a large Number of Friends in your Parts, who have no Slaves; and in tender and most affectionate Love, I beseech you to keep clear from purchasing any. Look, my dear Friends, to divine Providence; and follow in Simplicity that Exercise of Body, that Plainness and Frugality, which true Wisdom leads to; so will you be preserved from those Dangers which attend such as are aiming at outward Ease and Greatness.

Treasures, though small, attained on a true Principle of Virtue, are sweet in the Possession, and, while we walk in the Light of the Lord, there is true Comfort and Satisfaction. Here, neither the Murmurs of an oppressed People, nor an uneasy Conscience, nor anxious Thoughts about the Events of Things, hinder the Enjoyment of it.

When we look toward the End of Life, and think on the Division of our Substance among our Successors; if we know that it was collected in the Fear of the Lord, in Honesty, in Equity, and in Uprightness of Heart before him, we may consider it as his Gift to us; and with a single Eye to his Blessing, bestow it on those we leave behind us. Such is the Happiness of the plain Ways of true Virtue. "The Work of Righteousness shall be Peace; and the Effect of Righteousness, Quietness and Assurance for ever." Isa. xxxii 17.

Dwell here, my dear Friends; and then, in remote and solitary Desarts, you may find true Peace and Satisfaction. If the Lord be our God, in Truth and Reality, there is Safety for us; for he is a Stronghold in the Day of Trouble, and knoweth them that trust in him.

ISLE OF WIGHT COUNTY, IN VIRGINIA,
29th of the 5th Month, 1757

MOTHER ANN LEE
1736 - 1784

God, in His all wise providence, had laid the foundation of man's redemption in Judea, among the Jews, who were called his Chosen People. It was there the *First Born* in the *New Creation*, who was to be the Saviour of the world, was first revealed. There he fulfilled his ministry in his earthly tabernacle, and drank the full cup of his sufferings on earth; and from thence he ascended to His Father, that the way might be prepared for his Second Coming, in the female part of his manhood, for the travel of souls in the regeneration. And when the time was fully come, according to the appointment of God, Christ was again revealed, not in Judea, to the Jews, nor in the person of a male; but in England, to a Gentile nation, and in the person of a female.

This extraordinary female, whom, her followers believe God had chosen, and in whom Christ did visibly make his second appearance, was Ann Lee. She was born in the year 1736, in the town of Manchester, in England. Her father's name was John Lee; by trade a blacksmith; she had five brothers, viz.—Joseph, James, Daniel, William and George, and two sisters, Mary and Nancy. Her father, though poor, was respectable in character, moral in principle, honest and punctual in his dealings, and industrious in business. Her mother was counted a strictly religious, and very pious woman.

3. Their children, as was then common with poor people, in manufacturing towns, were taught to work, instead of being sent to school. By this means Ann acquired a habit of industry, but was very illiterate, so that she could neither read, nor write. She was employed, during her childhood and youth in a cotton factory, in preparing cotton for the looms, and in cutting velvet. It has been said that she was also employed as a cutter of hatter's fur, but this was probably afterward.

4. From her childhood she was the subject of religious impressions and divine manifestations. She had great light and conviction concerning the sinfulness and depravity of human nature, and especially concerning the lusts of the flesh, which she often made known to her parents, entreating them for that counsel and protection by which she might be kept from sin.

5. It is remarkable, that, in early youth, she had a great abhorrence of the fleshly cohabitation of the sexes, and so great was her sense of its impurity, that she often admonished her mother against it, which, coming to her father's ears, he threatened, and actually

Mother Ann sounds way out there—a cult leader. The psychologists would have a field day with her. America has produced thousands and thousands of very charismatic religious leaders. Mother Ann's theology was odd—she believed herself to be the second coming of Christ. And the utopian community she pioneered was doomed, given her instructions to avoid sex. The lure of faith is so strong that mixed with charismatic men and women it can and still does lead to extraordinary excess. Thus do the often-maligned traditions of mainstream religion gain in my esteem. The old churches may be rigid. They may evolve slowly. They may be "out-of-touch" with post-modern America. But they are the guardrails of faith, channeling the power of received truth so that believers do not miss a turn. False prophets have marked all religions in all ages. The endurance of tradition seems to me to be a good sign of truth.

attempted to whip her; upon which she threw herself into her mother's arms, and clung around her to escape his strokes. In this we may see an early and significant manifestation of the testimony she was destined to bear, and the sufferings she was destined to pass through in consequence of her testimony.

6. But not having then attained to that knowledge of God which she so early desired, nor having any one to strengthen and assist her in withstanding the powerful examples and practices of a lost world, and the ensnaring temptations of a fallen nature, she grew up in the same fallen nature, and was married to Abraham Stanley, who was a blacksmith by trade, and lived with her, at her father's house, while she remained in England;—by him she had four children, who all died in infancy.

7. During this period of her cohabitation with her husband she fell under great exercise of mind, and, for a season passed through excessive tribulation and sufferings of soul; without any mortal guide to instruct and lead her in the way of truth, till she became acquainted with James and Jane Wardley. She became a subject of the work of God under their ministration, and united herself to that society in the month of September, 1758, being then about twenty-two years of age.

8. As these people had been favored with a greater degree of divine light, and a more clear and pointed testimony against sin than had hitherto been made manifest, Ann readily embraced their testimony. And, as their light had led them to the open confession of every known sin, and to the taking up of a full and final cross against all evil in their knowledge, they were thereby endowed with great power of God over sin, by which means Ann found a good degree of that protection which she had so long desired, and so earnestly sought after. And, by her faithful obedience to the instruction of her Leaders, she attained to the full knowledge and experience in spiritual things which they had found.

9. But Ann was destined to still deeper sufferings, in order to prepare her for a far greater work, and therefore could not rest satisfied with what she had already attained. In watchings, fastings, tears and incessant cries to God, she labored, day and night, for deliverance from the very nature of sin. And under the most severe tribulation of mind, and the most violent temptations and buffetings of the enemy, she was often in such extreme agony of soul as caused the blood to perspire through the pores of her skin. Well might her sufferings and trials be compared to those of the Lord Jesus, when he was in the wilderness, tempted of the devil.

10. As she was ordained of God, as her followers believe, to be the first Mother of all souls in the regeneration, she had, not only to labor and travel for her own redemption, through scenes of tribulation, and to set the example of righteousness, and mark out the line of self-denial and the cross for her followers, but also to see and feel the full depth of man's loss, and the pain and judgment which every description of lost souls were under.

11. Hence she was destined to pass through inexpressible sufferings for their redemption. Sometimes for whole nights together, her cries, screeches and groans were such as to fill every soul around her with fear and trembling, and could be compared to nothing but the horrors and agonies of souls under sufferings for the violation of the laws of God, whose awful states were laid upon her, and whose various agonies she was, by turns, made to feel.

12. By such deep mortification and sufferings, her flesh wasted away till she became like a mere skeleton. Elder John Hocknell, who had been a member of the society under James and Jane Wardley, and was well acquainted with Mother Ann through all her sufferings, testified that he had known her to be under such power and operations of God, attended with such severe sufferings, for six weeks together, that her earthly tabernacle was so reduced that she was as weak as an infant; and was fed and supported by others, but utterly incapable of helping herself; though naturally of a sound and strong constitution, and invincible fortitude of mind.

13. Though Ann was wrought upon in this manner, more or less, for the space of nine years, yet she had intervals of releasement, and was, at times, filled with visions and revelations of God. By this means the way of God, and the nature of His work, gradually opened upon her mind, with increasing light and understanding. At length, about the year 1770, after a scene of deep tribulation, and the most excessive sufferings and cries to God, she received a full revelation of the root and foundation of human depravity, and of the very transgression of the first man and woman in the garden of Eden. Then, she clearly saw whence and wherein all mankind were lost and separated from God, and the only possible way of recovery.

14. By the immediate revelation of God, she henceforth bore an open testimony against the lustful gratifications of the flesh, as the source and foundation of

human corruption. Her testimony was delivered with such power of God and accompanied with the word of prophecy in such a marvelous and searching manner, that it entered into the very secrets of the heart; by which means the most hidden abominations were brought to light! She testified in the most plain and pointed manner, that no soul could follow Christ in the regeneration, while living in the works of natural generation, and wallowing in their lusts.

15. The light and power of God revealed in Ann, and through her revealed to those who received her testimony, had such sensible effect in giving them power over all sin, and filling them with visions, revelations, and gifts of God, that she was received and acknowledged as the first spiritual Mother in Christ, and the second heir of the *Covenant of Life* in the *New Creation*. Hence she received the title of Mother; and hence those who received and obeyed her testimony found a great increase in the power and gifts of God; while those who rejected it lost all their former light and power, and fell back into a state of darkness, and into the common course of the world.

16. The piercing and heart searching power of Mother's testimony against sin, together with the powerful operations of the spirit of God which prevailed in the meetings of her little family through her ministration, stirred up the rage and enmity of professor and profane, of almost every class and description, to such a degree, that, by formal opposition and tumultuous mobs, open persecution and secret malice, her very life and existence seemed in continual jeopardy. She was often shamefully and cruelly abused, and a number of times imprisoned. But, her testimony continued to grow and increase in the hearts of Believers in England, till, by the special revelation of God, she embarked for America.

17. On the 19th of May, 1774, she sailed from Liverpool, in company with her husband (who then professed the same faith), her brother,—William Lee, James Whittaker, John Hocknell, Richard Hocknell,—son of John Hocknell, James Shepherd, Mary Partington, and Nancy Lee—a niece of Mother Ann. After enduring the storms and dangers of the sea, in an old leaky vessel, in which they came very near being shipwrecked, they all arrived safely in New York, on the 6th of August following.

18. After their arrival in New York, Mother Ann obtained lodgings at the house of one "Smith" in Queen street, by whom Abraham—her husband, was employed as a journeyman, in the blacksmith business. Mother employed herself in washing and ironing, for her living, and, by her meekness, humility and amiable deportment, she gained the love and esteem of the woman of the house, by whom she was treated with great kindness. From this woman Mother afterward received offers, which, considered in a temporal view, were both honorable and advantageous, but which she declined, as being incompatible with the gift and calling of God to her; and chose rather to endure poverty and sufferings, than to turn aside from her duty to God, for the sake of any temporal advantages.

19. John Hocknell, soon after their arrival, went up the river, and purchased a place at Niskayuna, near Albany, for their future residence. He then returned to New York, and soon after, sailed for England, in order to settle his affairs, and bring out his family. The remainder of the company were scattered, seeking their livelihood, by their hand labor, wherever they could find employment. Most of them went up the river, and remained in, and about Albany. William Lee, being a blacksmith by trade, was employed in that business at Albany, by one Fairchild. James Whittaker was, by occupation, a weaver, and found employment in that business.

20. During John Hocknell's absence to England, Mother Ann went several times up the river, and visited the Believers in and about Albany, and was occasionally visited by some of them, but still continued her residence in New York. On the 25th of December, 1775, John, and his family, arrived at Philadelphia, and proceeded to New York by land, where they found Mother Ann, and soon after moved up to Niskayuna,—now Watervliet. In the spring following, Mother left New York, and came up the river, and joined the rest of the society.

———

1. Mother Ann and the Elders, in the course of their labors with the Believers, occasionally related some of their own experience and sufferings in the early seasons of their faith. Mother's experience in particular as it evinced her indefatigable zeal, and invincible fortitude of soul, was not only very interesting but very instructive to those who had but just set out in the same faith, and had a great effect in inciting them to zeal and faithfulness in the way of God.

2. Soon after the gospel opened at Watervliet in 1780, in the presence of a number of the young Believers, Mother related some of her experience as follows: "I love the day when I first received the gospel; I call it my birthday. I cried to God three days

and nights without intermission, that He would give me true desires."

3. "I was sometimes under such sufferings and tribulation that I could not rest in my bed anights; but had to get up and walk the floor. I feared to go to sleep, lest I should awaken to find myself suffering the just consequences of violation of God's laws. When I felt my eyes closing with sleep I used to pull them open with my fingers, and say within myself, I had better open my eyes here than in hell."

4. "I labored to feel a sense of the sufferings and torments of hell, that I might keep my soul continually awake to God. I felt such a sense of my sins that I was willing to confess them before the whole world. I confessed my sins to my Elders, one by one, and repented of them in the same manner. When my Elders reproved me, I felt determined not to be reproved twice for one thing, but to labor to overcome the evil for myself."

5. "I had not been in the Church more than six months before it was made known to me, by the revelation of God, that He would support me through all my trials, and establish me an Elder in the Church. The man to whom I was married, was very kind, according to nature; he would have been willing to pass through a flaming fire for my sake, if I would but live in the flesh with him, which I refused to do." *Hannah Cogswell.*

6. Just before Mother Ann was imprisoned in Albany, many of the Believers being assembled together at Watervliet, were under considerable tribulation, because it was expected that Mother and the Elders would soon be driven away from that place by the wicked. Mother came into the room, and, with tears running from her eyes, said, "The wicked are plotting against us; they mean to drive us away from this place, and it is unknown to me whether I shall ever see you again in this world."

7. When I set out to serve God, I served Him day and night, and cried to God, day and night, for deliverance from all sin. I did not receive a gift of God and then go away and think it was sufficient, without traveling any further; but I stood faithful, day and night, warring against all sin, and crying to God for deliverance from the very nature of sin. And can you expect to find power over sin without the same labor and travel of soul?" The people were all filled with the gift of God from Mother, and were sent away with a blessing.

Mehetable Farrington.

8. At Harvard, in 1781, in conversation with Sarah Barker, of New Lebanon, Mother Ann said, "Soon after I sat out in the way of God, I labored anights, in the works of God. Sometimes I labored all night crying to God for my own redemption. Sometimes I went to bed and slept, but, in the morning I could not feel that sense of the work of God that I did before I slept."

9. This brought me into great tribulation, then I cried to God, and promised Him that if He would give me the same sense I had before I slept, I would labor all night. This I did many nights, and, in the day time I put my hands to work, and my heart to God; and when I felt weary, and need of rest, I labored for the power of God, and the refreshing operations of the power of God would release me, so that I would feel able to go again to my work.

10. "Many times when I was about my work I felt great gifts of sorrow; and I used to work as long as I could keep it concealed, and then run to get out of sight, lest some one should pity me with that pity which God did not."

11. Soon after the gospel began to open at New Lebanon, Hannah Goodrich, with her husband—Nathan Goodrich, went to Niskayuna, received faith and confessed their sins; after which Mother related to them some of her experience, as follows: "When I set out to obey the gospel, I cried to God to bring my sins to remembrance; and I confessed them, one by one, as I committed them; and I denied myself of every gratification of a carnal nature; of every thing which my appetite craved, and ate and drank that which was mean and poor, that my soul might hunger for nothing but God."

12. "I often rose from my bed in the night, and walked the floor in my stocking-feet, for fear of waking up the people. I did not let my husband know my troubles, lest I should stir up his affections; and I was careful not to lay any temptations before him. I also prayed to God, that no man might suffer in hell on my account."

13. "Thus I labored in strong cries and groans to God, day and night, till my flesh wasted away and I became like a skeleton, and a kind of down came upon my skin, and my soul broke forth to God, which I realized with the greatest precision. Then I felt unspeakable joy in God, and my flesh came upon me like the flesh of an infant." *Hannah Goodrich.*

14. At Enfield, to Mary Tiffany and others, Mother Ann related some of her experience as follows: "After I opened my mind, and set out in my travel, I received great power of God, and in my travel, it was revealed to me what the loss of man was,—that it was the lusts of the flesh."

15. "My husband was opposed to me, and went and complained of me to the Church; the Church opposed my testimony and tried to persuade me to give it up; but I had to stand the test against my husband, my relations, and the Church; and I soon received such power of God that my bed would rock under me; and my husband was glad to leave it."

16. "In my travel and tribulation my sufferings were so great that my flesh consumed upon my bones, and bloody sweat pressed through the pores of my skin, and I became as helpless as an infant. And when I was brought through, and born into the spiritual kingdom, I was like an infant just born into the world; they see colors and objects, but they know not what they see; and so it was with me, when I was born into the spiritual world; but, before I was twenty-four hours old, I saw, and knew what I saw.   *Mary Tiffany.*

17. When Nathan Tiffany, (then a young Believer) first went to see Mother Ann, she spoke to him concerning her manner of travel in the first of her faith. She said, "I traveled in such tribulation, wringing my hands and crying to God, that the blood gushed out from under my nails, and with tears flowing down my cheeks until the skin cleaved off; and you are not going to find redemption any cheaper than I, according to your place."
Nathan Tiffany.

18. The first time that Daniel Wood went to see Mother Ann, soon after she was released from prison, he related to her the conviction he had been under for fifteen years past, respecting the flesh, that the works thereof were evil; but confessed that he had not fully lived up to his faith; Mother replied, "You could not live up to that faith, because you had not confessed your sins."

19. She then related some of her own experience, as follows: "Some time after I set out to live up to the light of God manifested to me, through James and Jane Wardley, I fell under heavy trials and tribulation on account of lodging with my husband; and as I looked to them for help and counsel, I opened my trials to Jane." She said, "James and I lodge together; but we do not touch each other any more than two babes. You may return home and do likewise."

20. "In obedience to Jane, I went to bed with my husband; but could not sleep seemingly any more than if I had been in a bed of embers. I quitted the bed in great tribulation and continued laboring, and crying to God for the space of twelve days and nights, to know

how the creation was fallen, and how the restoration should take place."

21. "While I was in this labor, I saw the Lord Jesus in his kingdom and glory. He revealed to me the depth of man's loss, what it was, and the way of redemption. Then I was made able to bear an open testimony against that sin which is the root of all evil; and I felt the power of God flow into my soul like a fountain of living water. From that day to this, I have taken up a full cross against the doleful works of the flesh."
Daniel Wood.

BENJAMIN FRANKLIN
1706 - 1790

Imagining it may be equally agreeable to you to know the circumstances of my life, many of which you are yet unacquainted with, and expecting the enjoyment of a week's uninterrupted leisure in my present country retirement, I sit down to write them for you. To which I have besides some other inducements. Having emerged from the poverty and obscurity in which I was born and bred to a state of affluence and some degree of reputation in the world, and having gone so far through life with a considerable share of felicity, the conducing means I made use of, which with the blessing of God so well succeeded, my posterity may like to know, as they may find some of them suitable to their own situations, and therefore fit to be imitated. . . .

American history's most practical man pauses, briefly, to note and thank God.

And now I speak of thanking God, I desire with all humility to acknowledge that I owe the mentioned happiness of my past life to his kind providence, which lead me to the means I used and gave them success. My belief of this induces me to *hope*, though I must not *presume*, that the same goodness will still be exercised toward me, in continuing that happiness, or enabling me to bear a fatal reverse, which I may experience as others have done; the complexion of my future fortune being known to Him only in whose power it is to bless to us even our afflictions.

GEORGE WASHINGTON

1732 - 1799

O f all the dispositions and habits which lead to political prosperity, Religion and morality are indispensable supports. In vain would that man claim the tribute of Patriotism, who should labour to subvert these great Pillars of human happiness, these firmest props of the duties of Men and citizens. The mere Politician, equally with the pious man ought to respect and to cherish them. A volume could not trace all their connections with private and public felicity. Let it simply be asked where is the security for property, for reputation, for life, if the sense of religious obligation *desert* the oaths, which are the instruments of investigation in Courts of Justice? And let us with caution indulge the supposition, that morality can be maintained without religion. Whatever may be conceded to the influence of refined education on minds of peculiar structure, reason and experience both forbid us to expect that National morality can prevail in exclusion of religious principle.

With the exclusion of religious principle from public life, we can judge the accuracy of **Washington**'s backhanded predictions. Has national morality prevailed?

FRANCIS ASBURY

1745 - 1816

Most dear and tender friends:

W hose I am, and whom under God I desire to serve; to build you up in holiness and comfort hath been through grace my great ambition. This is that which I laboured for; this is that which I suffer for: and in short, the end of all my applications to you, and to GOD for you. How do your souls prosper? Are they in a thriving case? What progress do you make in sanctification? Both the house of *Saul* grow weaker and weaker, and the house of *David* stronger and stronger? Beloved, I am jealous of

Born near Hampstead Bridge in England, **Francis Asbury** strove to spread Methodism across early America. One of the first bishops of the Methodist church, Asbury was a traveling clergyman,

you with a godly jealousy, lest any of you should lose ground in these declining times: and therefore cannot but be often calling upon you to look to your standing, and to watch and hold fast, that no man take your crown. Ah! how surely shall you reap in the end, if you faint not! Take heed therefore that you lose not the things you have wrought, but as you have begun well, so go on in the strength of Christ, and give diligence to the full assurance of hope to the end.

Do you need motives? 1. *How much are you behind hand?* Oh, the fair advantages that we have lost! What time, what sabbaths, sermons, sacraments, are upon the matter lost! How much work have we yet to do! Are you sure of heaven yet? Are you fit to die yet? Surely they that are under so many great wants, had need to set upon some more thriving courses.

Secondly, *Consider what others have gained, whilst we, it may be, sit down by the loss:* Have we not met many vessels richly laden, while our souls are empty? Oh, the golden prizes that some have won! While we have folded the hands to sleep, have not many of our own standing in religion, left us far behind them?

Thirdly, *Consider you will all find little enough when you come to die:* The wife among the virgins has no oil to spare at the coming of the bridegroom; temptation and death will put all your graces to it. How much ado have many had at last to put into this harbour! *David* cried for respite till he had recovered a little more strength.

Fourthly, *Consider how short your time for gathering in probably is?* The Israelites gathered twice so much manna against the sabbath as they did at other times, because at that time there was no manna fell. Brethren, you know not how long you have to lay in for. Do you ask for marks, how you may know your souls to be in a thriving case?

First, If your appetites be more strong. Do you thirst after GOD and grace, more than heretofore? Do your cares for and desires after the world abate? And do you hunger and thirst after righteousness? Whereas you were wont to come with an ill-will to holy duties, do you now come to them as hungry stomach to its meat?

Secondly, If your pulses beat more even. Are you still off and on, hot and cold? Or is there a more even spun

preaching his way across nearly three hundred thousand miles before his death. The following displays a bit of Asbury's strict observance of religion—a regimen which he himself followed, even though it caused his death in 1816 while serving as a missionary.

thread of holiness through your whole course? Do you make good the ground from which you were formerly beaten off?

Thirdly, If you do look more to the carrying on together the duties of both tables. Do you not only look to the keeping of your own vineyards, but do you lay out yourselves for the good of others? and are ye filled with zealous desires for their conversion and salvation? Do you manage your talk and your trade, by the rules of religion?

Do you eat and sleep by rule? Doth religion form and mould, and direct your carriage towards husbands, wives, parents, children, masters, servants? Do you grow more universally conscientious? Is piety more diffusive than ever with you? Doth it come more abroad with you, out of your closets, into your houses, your shops, your fields? Doth it journey with you, and buy and sell for you? Hath it the casting voice in all you do?

Fourthly, If the duties of religion be more delightful to you. Do you take more delight in the word than ever? Are you more in love with secret prayer, and more abundant in it? Cannot you be content with your ordinary seasons, but are ever and anon making extraordinary visits to heaven? And upon all occasions turning aside to talk with God in some short ejaculations? Are you often darting up your soul heavenwards? Is it meat and drink for you to do the will of GOD? Do you come off more freely with GOD, and answer his calls with more readiness of mind?

Fifthly, If you are more abundant in those duties which are most displeasing to the flesh. Are you more earnest in mortification? Are you more strict and severe than ever in the duty of daily self-examination, and holy meditation? Do you hold the reins harder upon the flesh than ever? Do you keep a stricter watch upon your appetites? Do you set a stronger guard upon your tongues? Have you a more jealous eye upon your hearts?

Sixthly, If you grow more vile in your own eyes. Do you grow more out of love with men's esteem, and set less by it? Are you not marvellous tender of being slighted? Can you rejoice to see others preferred before you? Can you heartily value and love them that think meanly of you?

Seventhly, If you grow more quick of sense, more sensible of divine influences, or withdrawings. Are you more afraid of sin than ever? Are your sins a greater pain to you than heretofore? Are your very infirmities your great afflictions? and the daily working of corruption a continued grief of mind to you?

I must conclude abruptly, commending you to GOD, and can only tell you that I am

Yours in the Lord Jesus,
F. A.
The Arminian Magazine, *II*
(Philadelphia, 1790), 251-54

JOHN ADAMS
1735 - 1826

The human Understanding is a revelation from its Maker which can never be disputed or doubted. There can be no Scepticism, Pyrrhonism or Incredulity or Infidelity here. No Prophecies, no Miracles are necessary to prove this celestial communication. This revelation has made it certain that two and one make three; and that one is not three; nor can three be one. We can never be so certain of any Prophecy, or the fulfillment of any Prophecy; or of any miracle, or the design of any miracle as We are, from the revelation of nature i.e. natures God that two and two are equal to four. Miracles or Prophecies might frighten Us out of our Witts; might scare us to death; might induce Us to lie; to say that We believe that 2 and 2 make 5. But We should not believe it. We should know the contrary.

Adams, the patrician President who ought to have been comfortable with Calvin's God, is fighting for Jefferson's God—perhaps because Jefferson is too busy fashioning a deity who will not much care what folks do with their lives. Adams is arguing for an expansive, mercy-filled God, tender toward all His people. A very appealing God.

Had you and I been forty days with Moses on Mount Sinai and admitted to behold, the divine Shekinah, and there told that one was three and three, one: We might not have had courage to deny it, but We could not have believed it. The thunders and Lightenings and Earthqu[ak]es and the transcendant Splendors and Glories, might have overwhelmed Us with terror and Amazement: but We could not have believed the doctrine. We should be more likely to say in our hearts, whatever We might say with our Lips, This is Chance. There is no God! No Truth. This is all delusion, fiction and a lie: or it is all Chance. But what is Chance? It is motion; it is Action; it is Event; it is Phenomenon, without Cause. Chance is no cause att all. It is nothing. And Nothing has produced all this

Pomp and Splendor; and Nothing may produce Our eternal damnation in the flames of Hell fire and Brimstone for what We know, as well as this tremendous Exhibition of Terror and Falshood.

God has infinite Wisdom, goodness and power. He created the Universe. His duration is eternal, a parte Ante, and a parte post. His presence is as extensive as Space. What is Space? an infinite, spherical Vaccuum. He created this Speck of Dirt and the human Species for his glory: and with the deliberate design of making, nine tenths of our Species miserable forever, for his glory. This is the doctrine of Christian Theologians in general: ten to one.

Now, my Friend, can Prophecies, or miracles convince You, or Me, that infinite Benevolence, Wisdom and Power, created and preserves, for a time, innumerable millions to make them miserable, forever; for his own Glory? Wretch! What is his Glory? Is he ambitious? does he want promotion? Is he vain? tickled with Adulation? Exulting and tryumphing in his Power and the Sweetness of his Vengeance? Pardon me, my Maker, for these Aweful Questions. My Answer to them is always ready: I believe no such Things. My Adoration of the Author of the Universe is too profound and too sincere. The Love of God and his Creation; delight, Joy, Tryumph, Exultation in my own existence, 'tho but an Atom, a Molecule Organique, in the Universe; are my religion. Howl, Snarl, bite, Ye Calvinistick! Ye Athanasian Divines, if You will. Ye will say, I am no Christian: I say Ye are no Christians: and there the Account is ballanced. Yet I believe all the honest men among you, are Christian in my Sense of the Word.

THOMAS JEFFERSON
1743 - 1826

To Peter Carr, with Enclosure

DEAR PETER   Paris Aug. 10. 1787.

I have received your two letters of Decemb. 30. and April 18. and am very happy to find by them, as well as by letters from Mr. Wythe, that you have been so fortunate as to attract his notice and good will: I am sure you will find this to have been one of the most fortunate events of your life, as I have ever been sensible it was of mine. I inclose you a sketch of the sciences to which I would wish you to apply in such order as Mr. Wythe shall advise: I mention also the books in them worth your reading, which submit to his correction. Many of these are among your father's books, which you should have brought to you. As I do not recollect those of them not in his library, you must write to me for them, making out a catalogue of such as you think you shall have occasion for in 18 months from the date of your letter, and consulting Mr. Wythe on the subject. To this sketch I will add a few particular observations.

1. Italian. I fear the learning this language will confound your French and Spanish. Being all of them degenerated dialects of the Latin, they are apt to mix in conversation. I have never seen a person speaking the three languages who did not mix them. It is a delightful language, but late events having rendered the Spanish more useful, lay it aside to prosecute that.

2. Spanish. Bestow great attention on this, and endeavor to acquire an accurate knowledge of it. Our future connections with Spain and Spanish America will render that language a valuable acquisition. The antient history of a great part of America too is written in that language. I send you a dictionary.

3. Moral Philosophy. I think it lost time to attend lectures in this branch. He who made us would have been a pitiful bungler if he had made the rules of our moral conduct a matter of science. For one man of science, there are thousands who are not. What would have become of them? Man was destined for society. His morality therefore was to be formed to this object. He was endowed with a sense of right and wrong merely relative to this. This sense is as much a part of his nature as the sense of hearing, seeing, feeling; it is the true foundation of morality, and not the το χαλον truth, &c., as fanciful writers have imagined. The moral sense, or conscience, is as much a part of man as his leg or arm. It is given to all human beings in a stronger or weaker degree, as force of members is given them in

Jefferson, the skeptic. Has anyone done more harm to the possibility of belief in America than Jefferson? Even intellectuals who have not read his works put on Jefferson like an off-the-rack suit. But I wonder about his skepticism. Could he, a slaveholder aware of slavery's immorality, have allowed himself belief in a God who demands personal accountability to set law? Certainly many slaveholders persuaded themselves that the "peculiar institution" was ordained by God. Jefferson knew, however, that slavery was unjust. With that knowledge, could he allow himself belief in a just, judging, and perhaps avenging God? I believe Jefferson's skepticism was armor against the consideration of a Judgment Day on which slavery would matter.

a greater or less degree. It may be strengthened by exercise, as may any particular limb of the body. This sense is submitted indeed in some degree to the guidance of reason; but it is a small stock which is required for this: even a less one than what we call Common sense. State a moral case to a ploughman and a professor. The former will decide it as well, and often better than the latter, because he has not been led astray by artificial rules. In this branch therefore read good books because they will encourage as well as direct your feelings. The writings of Sterne particularly form the best course of morality that ever was written. Besides these read the books mentioned in the inclosed paper; and above all things lose no occasion of exercising your dispositions to be grateful, to be generous, to be charitable, to be humane, to be true, just, firm, orderly, couragious &c. Consider every act of this kind as an exercise which will strengthen your moral faculties, and increase your worth.

4. Religion. Your reason is now mature enough to receive this object. In the first place divest yourself of all bias in favour of novelty and singularity of opinion. Indulge them in any other subject rather than that of religion. It is too important, and the consequences of error may be too serious. On the other hand shake off all the fears and servile prejudices under which weak minds are servilely crouched. Fix reason firmly in her seat, and call to her tribunal every fact, every opinion. Question with boldness even the existence of a god; because, if there be one, he must more approve the homage of reason, than that of blindfolded fear. You will naturally examine first the religion of your own country. Read the bible then, as you would read Livy or Tacitus. The facts which are within the ordinary course of nature you will believe on the authority of the writer, as you do those of the same kind in Livy and Tacitus. The testimony of the writer weighs in their favor in one scale, and their not being against the laws of nature does not weigh against them. But those facts in the bible which contradict the laws of nature, must be examined with more care, and under a variety of faces. Here you must recur to the pretensions of the writer to inspiration from god. Examine upon what evidence his pretensions are founded, and whether that evidence is so strong as that it's falshood would be more improbable than a change of laws of nature in the case he relates. For example in the book of Joshua we are told the sun stood still several hours. Were we to read that fact in Livy or Tacitus we should class it with their showers of blood, speaking of statues, beasts &c., but it is said that the writer of that book was inspired. Examine therefore candidly what evidence there is of his having been inspired. The pretension is entitled to your enquiry, because millions believe it. On the other hand you are Astronomer enough to know how contrary it is to the law of nature that a body revolving on it's axis, as the earth does, should have stopped, should not by that sudden stoppage have prostrated animals, trees, buildings, and should after a certain time have resumed it's revolution, and that without a second general prostration. Is this arrest of the earth's motion, or the evidence which affirms it, most within the law of probabilities? You will next read the new testament. It is the history of a personage called Jesus. Keep in your eye the opposite pretensions. 1. Of those who say he was begotten by god, born of a virgin, suspended and reversed the laws of nature at will, and ascended bodily into heaven: and 2. of those why say he was a man, of illegitimate birth, of a benevolent heart, enthusiastic mind, who set out without pretensions to divinity, ended in believing them, and was punished capitally for sedition by being gibbeted according to the Roman law which punished the first commission of that offence by whipping, and the second by exile or death *in furcâ*. See this law in the Digest Lib. 48. tit. 19 § 28. 3. and Lipsius Lib. 2. de cruce. cap. 2. These questions are examined in the books I have mentioned under the head of religion, and several others. They will assist you in your enquiries, but keep your reason firmly on the watch in reading them all. Do not be frightened from this enquiry by any fear of it's consequences. If it ends in a belief that there is no god, you will find incitements to virtue in the comfort and pleasantness you feel in it's exercise, and the love of others which it will procure you. If you find reason to believe there is a god, a consciousness that you are acting under his eye, and that he approves you, will be a vast additional incitement. If that there be a future state, the hope of a happy existence in that increases the appetite to deserve it; if that Jesus was also a god, you will be comforted by a belief of his aid and love. In fine, I repeat that you must lay aside all prejudice on both sides, and neither believe nor reject any thing because any other person, or description of persons have rejected or believed it. Your own reason is the only oracle given you by heaven, and you are answerable not for the rightness but uprightness of the decision. —I forgot to observe when speaking of the New testament that you should read all the histories of Christ, as well of those whom a council

of ecclesiastics have decided for us to be Pseudo-evangelists, as those they named Evangelists, because these Pseudo-evangelists pretended to inspiration as much as the others, and you are to judge their pretensions by your own reason, and not by the reason of those ecclesiastics. Most of these are lost. There are some however still extant, collected by Fabricius which I will endeavor to get and send you.

5. Travelling. This makes men wiser, but less happy. When men of sober age travel, they gather knowledge which they may apply usefully for their country, but they are subject ever after to recollections mixed with regret, their affections are weakened by being extended over more objects, and they learn new habits which cannot be gratified when they return home. Young men who travel are exposed to all these inconveniences in a higher degree, to others still more serious, and do not acquire that wisdom for which a previous foundation is requisite by repeated and just observations at home. The glare of pomp and pleasure is analogous to the motion of their blood, it absorbs all their affection and attention, they are torn from it as from the only good in this world, and return to their home as to place of exile and condemnation. Their eyes are for ever turned back to the object they have lost, and it's recollection poisons the residue of their lives. Their first and most delicate passions are hackneyed on unworthy objects here, and they carry home only the dregs, insufficient to make themselves or any body else happy. Add to this that a habit of idleness, an inability to apply themselves to business is acquired and renders them useless to themselves and their country. These observations are founded in experience. There is no place where your pursuit of knowledge will be so little obstructed by foreign objects as in your own country, nor any wherein the virtues of the heart will be less exposed to be weakened. Be good, be learned, and be industrious, and you will not want the aid of travelling to render you precious to your country, dear to your friends, happy within yourself. I repeat my advice to take a great deal of exercise, and on foot. Health is the first requisite after morality. Write to me often and be assured of the interest I take in your success, as well as of the warmth of those sentiments of attachment with which I am, dear Peter, your affectionate friend,

TH: JEFFERSON

P.S. Let me know your age in your next letter. Your cousins here are well and desire to be remembered to you.

JOSEPH SMITH
1805 - 1844

I was born in the year of our Lord one thousand eight hundred and five, on the twenty-third day of December, in the town of Sharon, Windsor county, state of Vermont. My father, Joseph Smith, Senior, left the state of Vermont, and moved to Palmyra, Ontario (now Wayne) county, in the state of New York, when I was in my tenth year, or thereabouts. In about four years after my father's arrival in Palmyra he moved with his family into Manchester, in the same county of Ontario.

Some time in the second year after our removal to Manchester, there was in the place where we lived an unusual excitement on the subject of religion. It commenced with the Methodists, but soon became general among all the sects in that region. Indeed, the whole district seemed affected by it, and great multitudes united themselves to the different religious parties, which created no small stir and division amongst the people, some crying, "Lo, here!" and others "Lo, there!" Some were contending for the Methodist faith, some for the Presbyterian, and some for the Baptist.

For notwithstanding the great love which the converts to these different faiths expressed at the time of their conversion, and the great zeal manifested by the respective clergy, who were active in getting up and promoting this extraordinary scene of religious feeling, in order to have everybody converted, as they were pleased to call it, let them join what sect they pleased—yet when the converts began to file off, some to one party and some to another, it was seen that the seemingly good feelings of both the priests and the converts were more pretended than real; for a scene of great confusion and bad feeling ensued; priest contending against priest, and convert against convert; so that all their good feelings one for another, if

When he was a mere teenager, the founder of that uniquely American faith, the Church of Jesus Christ of Latter-day Saints, received the revelations that led him to form a new religion. **Joseph Smith** claimed that the angel Moroni appeared to him in a vision and led him to golden tablets, whose hieroglyphic inscriptions he translated and later published as The Book of Mormon. Characterized by the belief that the resurrected Jesus Christ had come to the Americas, the new faith quickly grew after 1830, despite being beleaguered by prejudice and anti-Mormon harassment. The first church building was constructed in Kirtland, Ohio, and the Mormons worshiped there until harassment forced them to relocate, first to Missouri and then to Illinois. There they founded the city of Nauvoo, with Joseph Smith at the city's helm. Religious persecution again appeared, and Smith was eventually murdered,

with his brother, in a mob melee in June 1844. The man, considered by Mormons to be one of God's prophets, set his experiences down on paper. Here Smith tells of his visions and revelatory experiences.

they ever had any, were entirely lost in a strife of words and a contest about opinions.

I was at this time in my fifteenth year. My father's family was prose-lyted to the Presbyterian faith, and four of them joined that church, namely—my mother, Lucy; my brothers Hyrum and Samuel Har-rison; and my sister Sophronia.

During this time of great excite-ment, my mind was called up to serious reflection and great uneasi-ness; but, though my feelings were deep and often poignant, still I kept myself aloof from all these parties, though I attended their several meetings as often as occasion would permit. In process of time my mind became somewhat partial to the Methodist sect, and I felt some desire to be united with them; but so great were the confusion and strife among the different denominations, that it was impossible for a person young as I was, and so unacquainted with men and things, to come to any certain conclusion who was right and who was wrong.

My mind at times was greatly excited, the cry and tumult were so great and incessant.

In the midst of this war of words and tumult of opinions, I often said to myself, What is to be done? Who of all these parties are right; or, are they all wrong together? If any one of them be right, which is it, and how shall I know it?

While I was laboring under the extreme difficulties caused by the contests of these parties of religionists, I was one day reading the Epistle of James, first chapter and fifth verse, which reads: *If any of you lack wisdom, let him ask of God, that giveth to all men liberally, and upbraideth not; and it shall be given him.*

Never did any passage of scripture come with more power to the heart of man than this did at this time to mine. It seemed to enter with great force into every feeling of my heart. I reflected on it again and again, knowing that if any person needed wisdom from God, I did; for how to act I did not know, and unless I could get more wisdom than I then had, I would never know; for the teachers of religion of the different sects under-stood the same passage of scripture so differently as to destroy all confidence in settling the question by an appeal to the Bible.

HIS FIRST VISION

At length I came to the conclusion that I must either remain in darkness and confusion, or else I must do as James directs, that is, ask of God. I at length came to the determination to "ask of God," concluding that if He gave wisdom to them that lacked wisdom, and would give liberally, and not upbraid, I might venture.

So, in accordance with this, my determination to ask of God, I retired to the woods to make the attempt. It was on the morning of a beautiful, clear day, early in the spring of eighteen hundred and twenty. It was the first time in my life that I had made such an attempt, for amidst all my anxieties I had never as yet made the attempt to pray vocally.

After I had retired to the place where I had previ-ously designed to go, having looked around me, and finding myself alone, I kneeled down and began to offer up the desires of my heart to God. I had scarcely done so, when immediately I was seized upon by some power which entirely overcame me, and had such an astonishing influence over me as to bind my tongue so that I could not speak. Thick darkness gathered around me, and it seemed to me for a time as if I were doomed to sudden destruction.

But, exerting all my powers to call upon God to deliver me out of the power of this enemy which had seized upon me, and at the very moment when I was ready to sink into despair and abandon myself to destruction—not to an imaginary ruin, but to the power of some actual being from the unseen world, who had such marvelous power as I had never before felt in any being—just at this moment of great alarm, I saw a pillar of light exactly over my head, above the brightness of the sun, which descended gradually until it fell upon me.

It no sooner appeared than I found myself delivered from the enemy which held me bound. When the light rested upon me I saw two Personages, whose bright-ness and glory defy all description, standing above me in the air. One of them spake unto me, calling me by name, and said—pointing to the other—This is My Beloved Son. Hear Him!

My object in going to inquire of the Lord was to know which of all the sects was right, that I might know which to join. No sooner, therefore, did I get pos-session of myself, so as to be able to speak, than I asked the Personages who stood above me in the light, which of all the sects was right—and which I should join.

I was answered that I must join none of them, for they were all wrong, and the Personage who addressed me said that all their creeds were an abomination in His sight; that those professors were all corrupt; that "they draw near to me with their lips, but their hearts are far from me; they teach for doctrines the commandments of men: having a form of godliness, but they deny the power thereof."

He again forbade me to join any of them; and many other things did he say unto me, which I cannot write at this time. When I came to myself again, I found myself lying on my back, looking up into heaven.

Some few days after I had this vision, I happened to be in company with one of the Methodist preachers, who was very active in the beforementioned religious excitement; and, conversing with him on the subject of religion, I took occasion to give him an account of the vision which I had had. I was greatly surprised at his behavior; he treated my communication not only lightly, but with great contempt, saying, it was all of the devil, that there were no such things as visions or revelations in these days; that all such things had ceased with the apostles, and that there would never be any more of them.

I soon found, however, that my telling the story had excited a great deal of prejudice against me among professors of religion, and was the cause of great persecution, which continued to increase; and though I was an obscure boy, only between fourteen and fifteen years of age, and my circumstances in life such as to make a boy of no consequence of the world, yet men of high standing would take notice sufficient to excite the public mind against me, and create a bitter persecution; and this was common among all the sects—all united to persecute me.

It caused me serious reflection then, and often has since, how very strange it was that an obscure boy, of a little over fourteen years of age, and one, too, who was doomed to the necessity of obtaining a scanty maintenance by his daily labor, should be thought a character of sufficient importance to attract the attention of the great ones of the most popular sects of the day, and in a manner to create in them a spirit of the most bitter persecution and reviling. But strange or not, so it was, and it was often the cause of great sorrow to myself.

However, it was nevertheless a fact that I had beheld a vision. I have thought since, that I felt much like Paul, when he made his defense before King Agrippa, and related the account of the vision he had when he saw a light, and heard a voice; but still there were but few who believed him; some said he was dishonest, others said he was mad; and he was ridiculed and reviled. But all this did not destroy the reality of his vision. He had seen a vision, he knew he had, and all the persecution under heaven could not make it otherwise; and though they should persecute him unto death, yet he knew, and would know to his latest breath, that he had both seen a light and heard a voice speaking unto him, and all the world could not make him think or believe otherwise.

So it was with me. I had actually seen a light, and in the midst of that light I saw two Personages, and they did in reality speak to me; and though I was hated and persecuted for saying that I had seen a vision, yet it was true; and while they were persecuting me, reviling me, and speaking all manner of evil against me falsely for so saying, I was led to say in my heart: Why persecute me for telling the truth? I have actually seen a vision; and who am I that I can withstand God, or why does the world think to make me deny what I have actually seen? For I had seen a vision; I knew it, and I knew that God knew it, and I could not deny it, neither dared I do it; at least I knew that by so doing I would offend God, and come under condemnation.

I had now got my mind satisfied so far as the sectarian world was concerned—that it was not my duty to join with any of them, but to continue as I was until further directed. I had found the testimony of James to be true—that a man who lacked wisdom might ask of God, and obtain, and not be upbraided.

MORONI'S VISIT

I continued to pursue my common vocations in life until the twenty-first of September, one thousand eight hundred and twenty-three, all the time suffering severe persecution at the hands of all classes of men, both religious and irreligious, because I continued to affirm that I had seen a vision.

During the space of time which intervened between the time I had the vision and the year eighteen hundred and twenty-three—having been forbidden to join any of the religious sects of the day, and being of very tender years, and persecuted by those who ought to have been my friends and to have treated me kindly, and if they supposed me to be deluded to have endeavored in a proper and affectionate manner to have reclaimed me—I was left to all kinds of temptations; and, mingling with all kinds of society, I frequently fell into many foolish errors, and displayed the weakness of youth, and the foibles of human nature; which, I am sorry to say, led me into divers temptations, offensive in the sight of God. In making this confession, no one need

suppose me guilty of any great or malignant sins. A disposition to commit such was never in my nature.

In consequence of these things, I often felt condemned for my weakness and imperfections; when, on
the evening of the above-mentioned twenty-first of
September, after I had retired to my bed for the night,
I betook myself to prayer and supplication to Almighty
God for forgiveness of all my sins and follies, and also for
a manifestation to me, that I might know of my state
and standing before him; for I had full confidence in
obtaining a divine manifestation, as I previously had one.

While I was thus in the act of calling upon God,
I discovered a light appearing in my room, which continued to increase until the room was lighter than at
noonday, when immediately a personage appeared at my
bedside, standing in the air, for his feet did not touch
the floor.

He had on a loose robe of most exquisite whiteness.
It was a whiteness beyond anything earthly I had ever
seen; nor do I believe that any earthly thing could be
made to appear so exceedingly white and brilliant. His
hands were naked, and his arms also, a little above the
wrists; so, also, were his feet naked, as were his legs,
a little above the ankles. His head and neck were also bare.
I could discover that he had no other clothing on but this
robe, as it was open, so that I could see into his bosom.

Not only was his robe exceedingly white, but his
whole person was glorious beyond description, and his
countenance truly like lightning. The room was exceedingly light, but not so very bright as immediately around
his person. When I first looked upon him, I was afraid;
but the fear soon left me.

He called me by name, and said unto me that he was
a messenger sent from the presence of God to me, and
that his name was Moroni; that God had a work for me
to do; and that my name should be had for good and
evil among all nations, kindreds, and tongues, or that it
should be good and evil spoken of among all people.

He said there was a book deposited, written upon
gold plates, giving an account of the former inhabitants
of this continent, and the source from whence they
sprang. He also said that the fulness of the everlasting
Gospel was contained in it, as delivered by the Savior to
the ancient inhabitants.

Also, that there were two stones in silver bows—and
these stones, fastened to a breastplate, constituted what
is called the Urim and Thummim—deposited with the
plates; and the possession and use of these stones were
what constituted "seers" in ancient or former times; and

that God had prepared them for the purpose of translating the book.

After telling me these things, he commenced quoting
the prophecies of the Old Testament. He first quoted
part of the third chapter of Malachi; and he quoted also
the fourth or last chapter of the same prophecy, though
with a little variation from the way it reads in our
Bibles. Instead of quoting the first verse as it reads in
our books, he quoted it thus:

*For behold, the day cometh that shall burn as an
oven, and all the proud, yea, and all that do wickedly
shall burn as stubble; for they that come shall burn them,
saith the Lord of Hosts, that it shall leave them neither
root nor branch.*

And again, he quoted the fifth verse thus: *Behold,
I will reveal unto you the Priesthood, by the hand of Elijah
the prophet, before the coming of the great and dreadful
day of the Lord.*

He also quoted the next verse differently: *And he
shall plant in the hearts of the children the promises
made to the fathers, and the hearts of the children shall
turn to their fathers. If it were not so, the whole earth
would be utterly wasted at his coming.*

In addition to these, he quoted the eleventh chapter
of Isaiah, saying that it was about to be fulfilled. He
quoted also the third chapter of Acts, twenty-second
and twenty-third verses, precisely as they stand in our
New Testament. He said that that prophet was Christ;
but the day had not yet come when "they who would
not hear his voice should be cut off from among the
people," but soon would come.

He also quoted the second chapter of Joel, from the
twenty-eighth verse to the last. He also said that this was
not yet fulfilled, but was soon to be. And he further stated
that the fulness of the Gentiles was soon to come in. He
quoted many other passages of scripture, and he offered
many explanations which cannot be mentioned here.

Again, he told me, that when I got those plates of
which he had spoken—for the time that they should be
obtained was not yet fulfilled—I should not show them
to any person; neither the breastplate with the Urim and
Thummim; only to those to whom I should be commanded to show them; if I did I should be destroyed.
While he was conversing with me about the plates, the
vision was open to my mind that I could see the place
where the plates were deposited, and that so clearly and
distinctly that I knew the place again when I visited it.

After this communication, I saw the light in the room
begin to gather immediately around the person of him

who had been speaking to me, and it continued to do so until the room was again left dark, except just around him; when, instantly I saw, as it were, a conduit open right up into heaven, and he ascended till he entirely disappeared, and the room was left as it had been before this heavenly light had made its appearance.

I lay musing on the singularity of the scene, and marveling greatly at what had been told to me by this extraordinary messenger; when, in the midst of my meditation, I suddenly discovered that my room was again beginning to get lighted, and in an instant, as it were, the same heavenly messenger was again by my bedside.

He commenced, and again related the very same things which he had done at his first visit, without the least variation; which having done, he informed me of great judgments which were coming upon the earth, with great desolations by famine, sword, and pestilence; and that these grievous judgments would come on earth in this generation. Having related these things, he again ascended as he had done before.

By this time, so deep were the impressions made on my mind, that sleep had fled from my eyes, and I lay overwhelmed in astonishment at what I had both seen and heard. But what was my surprise when again I beheld the same messenger at my bedside, and heard him rehearse or repeat over again to me the same things as before; and added a caution to me, telling me that Satan would try to tempt me (in consequence of the indigent circumstances of my father's family), to get the plates for the purpose of getting rich. This he forbade me, saying that I must have no other object in view in getting the plates but to glorify God, and must not be influenced by any other motive than that of building his kingdom; otherwise I could not get them.

After this third visit, he again ascended into heaven as before, and I was again left to ponder on the strangeness of what I had just experienced; when almost immediately after the heavenly messenger had ascended from me for the third time, the cock crowed, and I found that day was approaching, so that our interviews must have occupied the whole of that night.

I shortly after arose from my bed, and, as usual, went to the necessary labors of the day; but, in attempting to work as at other times, I found my strength so exhausted as to render me entirely unable. My father, who was laboring along with me, discovered something to be wrong with me, and told me to go home. I started with the intention of going to the house; but, in attempting to cross the fence out of the field where we were, my strength entirely failed me, and I fell helpless on the ground, and for a time was quite unconscious of anything.

The first thing that I can recollect was a voice speaking unto me, calling me by name. I looked up, and beheld the same messenger standing over my head, surrounded by light as before. He then again related unto me all that he had related to me the previous night, and commanded me to go to my father and tell him of the vision and commandments which I had received.

I obeyed; I returned to my father in the field, and rehearsed the whole matter to him. He replied to me that it was of God, and told me to go and do as commanded by the messenger. I left the field, and went to the place where the messenger had told me the plates were deposited; and owing to the distinctness of the vision which I had had concerning it, I knew the place the instant that I arrived there.

THE SACRED RECORD

Convenient to the village of Manchester, Ontario County, New York, stands a hill of considerable size, and the most elevated of any in the neighborhood. On the west side of this hill, not far from the top, under a stone of considerable size, lay the plates, deposited in a stone box. This stone was thick and rounding in the middle on the upper side, and thinner towards the edges, so that the middle part of it was visible above the ground, but the edge all around was covered with earth.

Having removed the earth, I obtained a lever, which I got fixed under the edge of the stone, and with a little exertion raised it up. I looked in, and there indeed did I behold the plates, the Urim and Thummim, and the breastplate, as stated by the messenger. The box in which they lay was formed by laying stones together in some kind of cement. In the bottom of the box were laid two stones crossways of the box, and on these stones lay the plates and the other things with them.

I made an attempt to take them out, but was forbidden by the messenger, and was again informed that the time for bringing them forth had not yet arrived, neither would it, until four years from that time; but he told me that I should come to that place precisely in one year from that time, and that he would there meet with me, and that I should continue to do so until the time should come for obtaining the plates.

Accordingly, as I had been commanded, I went at the end of each year, and at each time I found the same messenger there, and received instruction and intelligence from him at each of our interviews, respecting what the Lord was going to do, and how and in what manner his kingdom was to be conducted in the last days.

As my father's worldly circumstances were very limited, we were under the necessity of laboring with our hands, hiring out by day's work and otherwise, as we could get opportunity. Sometimes we were at home, and sometimes abroad, and by continuous labor were enabled to get a comfortable maintenance.

. . . In the month of October 1825, I hired with an old gentleman by the name of Josiah Stoal, who lived in Chenango county, State of New York.

During the time that I was thus employed, I was put to board with a Mr. Isaac Hale, of [Harmony, Susquehanna County, Pennsylvania]; it was there I first saw my wife (his daughter), Emma Hale. On the 18th of January 1827, we were married, while I was yet employed in the service of Mr. Stoal.

Immediately after my marriage, I left Mr. Stoal's, and went to my father's, and farmed with him that season.

At length the time arrived for obtaining the plates, the Urim and Thummim, and the breastplate. On the twenty-second day of September, one thousand eight hundred and twenty-seven, having gone as usual at the end of another year to the place where they were deposited, the same heavenly messenger delivered them up to me with this charge: that I should be responsible for them; that if I should let them go carelessly, or through any neglect of mine, I should be cut off; but that if I would use all my endeavors to preserve them, until he, the messenger, should call for them, they should be protected.

I soon found out the reason why I have received such strict charges to keep them safe, and why it was that the messenger had said that when I had done what was required at my hand, he would call for them. For no sooner was it known that I had them, than the most strenuous exertions were used to get them from me. Every stratagem that could be invented was resorted to for that purpose. The persecution became more bitter and severe than before, and multitudes were on the alert continually to get them from me if possible. But by the wisdom of God, they remained safe in my hands, until I had accomplished by them what was required at my hand. When, according to arrangements, the messenger called for them, I delivered them up to him; and he has them in his charge until this day, being the second day of May, one thousand eight hundred and thirty-eight.

The excitement, however, still continued, and rumor with her thousand tongues was all the time employed in circulating falsehoods about my father's family, and about myself. If I were to relate a thousandth part of them, it would fill up volumes. The persecution, however, became so intolerable that I was under the necessity of leaving Manchester, and going with my wife to Susquehanna county in the state of Pennsylvania. While preparing to start—being very poor, and the persecution so heavy upon us that there was no probability that we would ever be otherwise—in the midst of our afflictions we found a friend in a gentleman by the name of Martin Harris, who came to us and gave me fifty dollars to assist us on our journey. Mr. Harris was a resident of Palmyra township, Wayne county, in the state of New York, and a farmer of respectability.

By this timely aid was I enabled to reach the place of my destination in Pennsylvania; and immediately after my arrival there I commenced copying the characters off the plates. I copied a considerable number of them, and by means of the Urim and Thummim I translated some of them, which I did between the time I arrived at the house of my wife's father, in the month of December, and the February following.

Sometime in this month of February, the aforementioned Mr. Martin Harris came to our place, got the characters which I had drawn off the plates, and started with them to the city of New York. For what took place relative to him and the characters, I refer to his own account of the circumstances, as he related them to me after his return, which was as follows:

"I went to the city of New York, and presented the characters which had been translated, with the translation thereof, to Professor Charles Anthon, a gentleman celebrated to his literary attainments. Professor Anthon stated that the translation was correct, more so than any he had before seen translated from Egyptian. I then showed him those which were not yet translated, and he said that they were Egyptian, Chaldaic, Assyriac, and Arabic; and he said they were true characters. He gave me a certificate, certifying to the people of Palmyra that they were true characters, and that the translation of such of them as had been translated was also correct. I took the certificate and put it into my pocket, and was just leaving the house, when Mr. Anthon called me back, and asked me how the young man found out that there were gold plates in the place where he found them. I answered that an angel of God had revealed it unto him.

"He then said to me, 'Let me see that certificate.' I accordingly took it out of my pocket and gave it to him, when he took it and tore it to pieces, saying that there was no such thing now as ministering of angels, and that if I would bring the plates to him he would translate them. I informed him that part of the plates were sealed, and that I was forbidden to bring them. He replied, 'I cannot read a sealed book.' I left him and went to Dr. Mitchell, who sanctioned what Professor Anthon had said respecting both the characters and the translation."

On the 5th day of April 1829, Oliver Cowdery came to my house, until which time I had never seen him. He stated to me that having been teaching school in the neighborhood where my father resided, and my father being one of those who sent to the school, he went to board for a season at his house, and while there the family related to him the circumstances of my having received the plates, and accordingly he had come to make inquiries of me.

Two days after the arrival of Mr. Cowdery (being the 7th of April) I commenced to translate the Book of Mormon, and he began to write for me.

PRIESTHOOD RESTORED

We still continued the work of translation, when, in the ensuing month (May 1829), we on a certain day went into the woods to pray and inquire of the Lord respecting baptism for the remission of sins, that we found mentioned in the translation of the plates. While we were thus employed, praying and calling upon the Lord, a messenger from heaven descended in a cloud of light, and having laid his hands upon us, he ordained us, saying:

Upon you my fellow servants, in the name of Messiah, I confer the Priesthood of Aaron, which holds the keys of the ministering of angels, and of the gospel of repentance, and of baptism by immersion for the remission of sins; and this shall never be taken again from the earth until the sons of Levi do offer again an offering unto the Lord in righteousness.

He said this Aaronic Priesthood had not the power of laying on hands for the gift of the Holy Ghost, but that this should be conferred on us hereafter; and he commanded us to go and be baptized, and gave us directions that I should baptize Oliver Cowdery, and that afterwards he should baptize me.

Accordingly we went and were baptized. I baptized him first, and afterwards he baptized me—after which I laid my hands upon his head and ordained him to the Aaronic Priesthood, and afterwards he laid my hands on me and ordained me to the same Priesthood—for so we were commanded.

The messenger who visited us on this occasion and conferred this Priesthood upon us, said that his name was John, the same that is called John the Baptist in the New Testament, and that he acted under the direction of Peter, James and John, who held the keys of the Priesthood of Melchizedek, which Priesthood, he said, would in due time be conferred on us, and that I should be called the first Elder of the Church, and he (Oliver Cowdery) the second. It was on the fifteenth day of May 1829, that we were ordained under the hand of this messenger, and baptized.

Immediately on our coming up out of the water after we had been baptized, we experienced great and glorious blessings from our Heavenly Father. No sooner had I baptized Oliver Cowdery, than the Holy Ghost fell upon him, and he stood up and prophesied many things which should shortly come to pass. And again, so soon as I had been baptized by him, I also had the spirit of prophecy, when, standing up, I prophesied concerning the rise of this Church, and many other things connected with the Church, and this generation of the children of men. We were filled with the Holy Ghost, and rejoiced in the God of our salvation.

Our minds being now enlightened, we began to have the scriptures laid open to our understandings, and the true meaning and intention of their more mysterious passages revealed unto us in a manner which we never could attain to previously, nor ever before had thought of. In the meantime we were forced to keep secret the circumstances of having received the Priesthood and our having been baptized, owing to a spirit of persecution which had already manifested itself in the neighborhood.

We had been threatened with being mobbed, from time to time, and this, too, by professors of religion. And their intentions of mobbing us were only counteracted by the influence of my wife's father's family (under Divine providence), who had become very friendly to me, and who were opposed to mobs, and were willing that I should be allowed to continue the work of translation without interruption; and therefore offered and promised us protection from all unlawful proceedings, as far as in them lay. (Joseph Smith—History 1:3-75.)

WITNESSES

In the course of the work of translation, we ascertained that three special witnesses were to be provided by the Lord, to whom He would grant that they should see the plates from which the Book of Mormon should be translated; and that these witnesses should bear record of the same, as will be found recorded, in the Book of Mormon, Ether 5:2-4 and 2 Nephi 27:12. Almost immediately after we had made this discovery, it occurred to Oliver Cowdery, David Whitmer, and Martin Harris that they would have me inquire of the Lord to know if they might not obtain of Him the privilege to be these three special witnesses. [Inquiry was made of the Lord and it was revealed that these three should be the special witnesses.]

Not many days after, Martin Harris, David Whitmer, Oliver Cowdery and myself agreed to retire into the woods and try to obtain, by fervent and humble prayer, the fulfillment of the promises given—that they should have a view of the plates. We accordingly made choice of a piece of woods convenient to Mr. Whitmer's house, to which we retired, and having knelt down, we began to pray in much faith to Almighty God to bestow upon us a realization of these promises.

According to previous arrangement, I commenced by vocal prayer to our Heavenly Father, and was followed by each of the others in succession. We did not at the first trial, however, obtain any answer or manifestation of divine favor in our behalf. We again observed the same order of prayer, each calling on and praying fervently to God in rotation, but with the same result as before.

Upon this, our second failure, Martin Harris proposed that he should withdraw himself from us, believing, as he expressed himself, that his presence was the cause of our not obtaining what we wished for. He accordingly withdrew from us, and we knelt down again, and had not been many minutes engaged in prayer, when presently we beheld a light above us in the air, of exceeding brightness; and behold, an angel stood before us. In his hands he held the plates. He turned over the leaves one by one, so that we could see them, and discern the engravings thereon distinctly. He then addressed himself to David Whitmer, and said, "David, blessed is the Lord, and he that keeps his commandments"; when, immediately afterwards, we heard a voice from out of the bright light above us, saying, "These plates have been revealed by the power of God, and they have been translated by the power of God. The translation of them which you have seen is correct, and I command you to bear a record of what you now see and hear."

I now left David and Oliver and went in pursuit of Martin Harris, whom I found at a considerable distance fervently engaged in prayer. He soon told me, however, that he had not yet prevailed with the Lord, and earnestly requested me to join him in prayer, that he also might realize the same blessings which we had just received. We accordingly joined in prayer, and ultimately obtained our desires, for before we had yet finished, the same vision was opened to our view, at least it was again open to me, and I once more beheld and heard the same things; whilst at the same moment, Martin Harris cried out, apparently in an ecstasy of joy. "Tis enough, 'tis enough! mine eyes have beheld; mine eyes have beheld"; and jumping up, he shouted, "Hosanna," blessing God, and otherwise rejoicing exceedingly.

Having thus, through the mercy of God, obtained these glorious manifestations, it now remained for these three individuals to fulfill the commandment which they had received, viz., to bear record of these things; in order to accomplish which, they drew up and subscribed the following document:

THE TESTIMONY OF THREE WITNESSES

"Be it known unto all nations, kindreds, tongues, and people, unto whom this work shall come: That we, through the grace of God the Father, and our Lord Jesus Christ, have seen the plates which contain this record, which is a record of the people of Nephi, and also of the Lamanites, their brethren, and also of the people of Jared, who came from the tower of which hath been spoken. And we also know that they have been translated by the gift and power of God, for his voice hath declared it unto us; wherefore we know of a surety that the work is true. And we also testify that we have seen the engravings which are upon the plates; and they have been shown unto us by the power of God, and not of man. And we declare with words of soberness, that an angel of God came down from heaven, and he brought and laid before our eyes, that we beheld and saw the plates, and the engravings thereon; and we know that it is by the grace of God the Father, and our Lord Jesus Christ, that we beheld and bear record that these things are true. And it is marvelous in our eyes. Nevertheless, the voice of the Lord commanded us that we should bear record of it; wherefore, to be obedient unto the commandments of God, we bear testimony of these things. And we know that if we are faithful in Christ, we shall rid our garments of the blood of all men, and be found spotless before the judgment seat of Christ, and shall dwell with him eternally in the heavens. And the honor be to the

Father, and to the Son, and the Holy Ghost, which is one God. Amen."

Oliver Cowdery
David Whitmer
Martin Harris

Soon after these things had transpired, the following additional testimony was obtained.

THE TESTIMONY OF EIGHT WITNESSES

"Be it known unto all nations, kindreds, tongues, and people, unto whom this work shall come: That Joseph Smith, Jun., the translator of this work, has shown unto us the plates of which hath been spoken, which have the appearance of gold; and as many of the leaves as the said Smith has translated we did handle with our hands; and we also saw the engraving thereon, all of which has the appearance of ancient work, and of curious workmanship. And this we bear record with words of soberness, that the said Smith has shown unto us, for we have seen and hefted, and know of a surety that the said Smith has got the plates of which we have spoken. And we give our names unto the world, to witness unto the world, that which we have seen. And we lie not, God bearing witness of it."

Christian Whitmer	Hiram Page
Jacob Whitmer	Joseph Smith, Sen.
Peter Whitmer, Jun.	Hyrum Smith
John Whitmer	Samuel H. Smith

We now became anxious to have that promise realized to us, which the angel that conferred upon us the Aaronic Priesthood had given us, viz., that provided we continued faithful, we should also have the Melchizedek Priesthood, which holds the authority of the laying on of hands for the gift of the Holy Ghost.

(The Prophet declared that the Melchizedek Priesthood was thereafter received under the hands of Peter, James, and John, at a place along the banks of the Susquehanna River, between Harmony, Susquehanna County, Pennsylvania, and Colesville, Broome County, New York.)

THE CHURCH ESTABLISHED

Whilst the Book of Mormon was in the hands of the printer, we still continued to bear testimony and give information, as far as we had opportunity; and also made known to our brethren that we had received a commandment to organize the Church; and accordingly we met together for that purpose, at the house of Mr. Peter Whitmer, Sen., (being six in number) on Tuesday, the sixth day of April, A.D., one thousand eight hundred and thirty. Having opened the meeting by solemn prayer to our Heavenly Father, we proceeded, according to previous commandment, to call on our brethren to know whether they accepted us as their teachers in the things of the Kingdom of God, and whether they were satisfied that we should proceed and be organized as a church according to said commandment which we had received. To these several propositions they consented by a unanimous vote. I then laid my hands upon Oliver Cowdery, and ordained him an Elder of the "Church of Jesus Christ of Latter-day Saints"; after which he ordained me also to the office of an Elder of said Church. We then took bread, blessed it, and brake it with them; also wine, blessed it, and drank it with them. We then laid our hands on each individual member of the Church present, that they might receive the gift of the Holy Ghost, and be confirmed members of the Church of Christ. The Holy Ghost was poured out upon us to a very great degree—some prophesied, whilst we all praised the Lord, and rejoiced exceedingly.

We now proceeded to call out and ordain some others of the brethren to different offices of the Priesthood, according as the Spirit manifested unto us; and after a happy time spent in witnessing and feeling for ourselves the power and blessings of the Holy Ghost, through the grace of God bestowed upon us, we dismissed with the pleasing knowledge that we were now individually members of, and acknowledged of God, "The Church of Jesus Christ," organized in accordance with commandments and revelations given by Him to ourselves in these last days, as well as according to the order of the Church as recorded in the New Testament.

This is the simple, direct testimony of Joseph Smith, giving some of those events that led to the founding of The Church of Jesus Christ of Latter-day Saints.

Shortly after the establishment of the Church, he with his followers moved from New York to Kirtland, Ohio (near Cleveland). A beautiful temple was built, extensive missionary work was instituted, and the Church made substantial gains in membership. Among the missions opened was one in Missouri, and the body of the Church later moved to Missouri.

This was a time of religious intolerance. Antagonism was soon stirred up against the Latter-day Saints. Mobs dispossessed them. They were compelled to move, leaving behind their homes, well-cultivated farms, and their houses of worship.

They went to Illinois and in their distress were received kindly. At a desolate spot on the Mississippi

River they purchased a large tract of swamp land. They drained this swampy area and built what was at that time the largest city in Illinois—Nauvoo, "the beautiful." Missionary efforts, both in America and England, greatly increased their numbers, and they prospered for a season.

The peace of Nauvoo was short-lived. Again bitter religious intolerance led to persecution. Joseph Smith and his brother Hyrum were imprisoned under false charges in Carthage, Illinois. While awaiting trial under the guaranteed protection of the state, they were shot and killed June 27, 1844, by an armed mob with painted faces.

Brigham Young succeeded to the leadership of the Church. Under his direction the Latter-day Saints left Illinois and made their historic trek to the Rocky Mountains, where through struggle and faith they have become a mighty people.

Joseph Smith is today held in remembrance as a prophet of God by hundreds of thousands in many lands. The virtues and achievements of those who have accepted his testimony stand as a monument to his divine calling. The Church of Jesus Christ of Latter-day Saints has its foundation in the revelations he received, the sacred truths he taught, and the authority of the priesthood restored through him.

BRIGHAM YOUNG
1801 - 1877

It was revealed to me in the commencement of this Church, that the Church would spread, prosper, grow and extend, and that in proportion to the spread of the Gospel among the nations of the earth, so would the power of Satan rise.". . .

We talk about our trials and troubles here in this life: but suppose that you could see yourselves thousands and millions of years after you have proved faithful to your religion during the few short years in this time, and have obtained eternal salvation and a crown of glory in the presence of God; then look back upon your lives here, and see the losses, crosses, and disappointments, the sorrows . . . you would be constrained to exclaim, "But

The second president of the Church of Jesus Christ of Latter-day Saints, **Brigham Young** assumed leadership of the church and its members after the death of Joseph Smith. In 1846, fleeing religious persecution, Young led his flock in the great migration from Illinois to Utah on what is known

what of all that? Those things were but for a moment, and we are now here. We have been faithful during a few moments in our mortality, and now we enjoy eternal life and glory, with power to progress in all the boundless knowledge and through the countless stages of progression, enjoying the smiles and approbation of our Father and God, and of Jesus Christ our elder brother.". . .

Then instead of concluding that the Lord has drawn us into difficulties, and compelled us to do that which is unpleasant to our feelings, and to suffer sacrifice upon sacrifice to no purpose, we shall understand that He has designed all this to prepare us to dwell in His presence. . . . He has so ordained it, that by the natural mind we cannot see and understand the things of God, therefore we must then seek unto the Lord, and get His Spirit and the light thereof, to understand His will. And when He is calling us to pass through that which we call afflictions, trials, temptations, and difficulties, did we possess the light of the Spirit, we would consider this the greatest blessing that could be bestowed upon us. . . .

God never bestows upon His people, or upon an individual, superior blessings without a severe trial to prove them . . . to see whether they will keep their covenants with Him. . . . For this express purpose the Father withdrew His spirit from His Son, at the time he was to be crucified. Jesus had been with his Father, talked with Him, dwelt in His bosom, and knew all about heaven, about making the earth, about the transgression of man, and what would redeem the people, and that he was the character who was to redeem the sons of earth, and the earth itself from all sin that had come upon it. The light, knowledge, power, and glory with which he was clothed were far above, or exceeded that of all others who had been upon the earth after the fall, consequently at the very moment, at the hour when the crisis came for him to offer up his life, the Father withdrew Himself, withdrew His Spirit, and cast a veil over him. That is what made him sweat blood. If he had had the power of God upon him, he would not have sweat blood; but all was withdrawn from him, and a veil was cast over him, and he then plead with the Father not to forsake him.

as the Mormon Trail. Young was head of the Mormon church until his death in 1877, by which time the group had become deeply rooted in the Utah wilderness. They quickly developed into a series of sustainable settlements. These excerpts are from Young's *Journal of Discourses*.

HENRY DAVID THOREAU
1817 - 1862

It is not when I am going to meet him, but when I am just turning away and leaving him alone, that I discover that God is. I say, God. I am not sure that that is the name. You will know what I mean. . . .

I believe that what so saddens the reformer is not his sympathy with his fellows in distress, but, though he be the holiest son of God, is his private ail. Let this be righted, let the spring come to him, the morning rise over his couch, and he will forsake his generous companions without apology. My excuse for not lecturing against the use of tobacco is, that I never chewed it; that is a penalty which reformed tobacco-chewers have to pay; though there are things enough I have chewed, which I could lecture against. If you should ever be betrayed into any of these philanthropies, do not let your left hand know what your right hand does, for it is not worth knowing. Rescue the drowning and tie your shoe-strings. Take your time, and set about some free labor.

Born in Concord in 1817, **Henry David Thoreau** is remembered best for his authorship of *Walden*, from which we quote here. An amateur naturalist, Thoreau "went into the woods to live deliberately," unaffected by his fellow man, of whom he was not fond. Considered a transcendentalist, Thoreau, like his fellow writers, elevated nature to an almost divine place in his heart, certainly giving it greater credence than the traditional deity. A social reformer as well as a nature lover, he is remembered for his abolitionist activity and anti-war convictions.

Our manners have been corrupted by communication with the saints. Our hymn-books resound with a melodious cursing of God and enduring him forever. One would say that even the prophets and redeemers had rather consoled the fears than confirmed the hopes of man. There is nowhere recorded a simple and irrespressible satisfaction with the gift of life, any memorable praise of God. All health and success does me good, however far off and withdrawn it may appear; all disease and failure helps to make me sad and does me evil, however much sympathy it may have with me or I with it. If, then, we would indeed restore mankind by truly Indian, botanic, magnetic, or natural means, let us first be as simple and well as Nature ourselves, dispel the clouds which hang over our own brows, and take up a little life into our pores. Do not stay to be an overseer of the poor, but endeavor to become one of the worthies of the world.

I read in the Gulistan, or Flower Garden, of Sheik Sadi of Shiraz, that "They asked a wise man, saying; Of the many celebrated trees which the Most High God has created lofty and umbrageous, they call none azad, or free, excepting the cypress, which bears no fruit; what mystery is there in this? He replied; Each has its appropriate produce, and appointed season, during the continuance of which it is fresh and blooming, and during their absence dry and withered; to neither of which states is the cypress exposed, begin always flourishing; and of this nature are the azads, or religious independents.—Fix not thy heart on that which is transitory; for the Dijlah, or Tigris, will continue to flow through Bagdad after the race of caliphs is extinct: if thy hand has plenty, be liberal as the date tree; but if it affords nothing to give away, be an azad, or free man, like the cypress."

I went to the woods because I wished to live deliberately, to front only the essential facts of life, and see if I could not learn what it had to teach, and not, when I came to die, discover that I had not lived. I did not wish to live what was not life, living is so dear; nor did I wish to practise resignation, unless it was quite necessary. I wanted to live deep and suck out all the marrow of life, to live so sturdily and Spartan-like as to put to rout all that was not life, to cut a broad swath and shave close, to drive life into a corner, and reduce it to its lowest terms, and, if it proved to be mean, why then to get the whole and genuine meanness of it, and publish its meanness to the world; or if it were sublime, to know it by experience, and be able to give a true account of it in my next excursion. For most men, it appears to me, are in a strange uncertainty about it, whether it is of the devil or of God, and have *somewhat hastily* concluded that it is the chief end of man here to "glorify God and enjoy him forever."

JARENA LEE
1783 - 1850

ALL SINS SWEPT AWAY

I inquired of the head cook of the house respecting the rules of the Methodists, as I knew she belonged to that society, who told me what they were—on which account I replied that I should not be able to abide by such strict rules not even one year. However, I told her that I would go with her and hear what they had to say.

Born in New Jersey in 1783, **Jarena Lee** was one of the first female preachers in the African Methodist Episcopalian church. She began to preach after gaining hard-won permission from Richard Allen, the church's founder, who was reluctant
to permit women to take positions of church leadership. Lee was converted at the age of twenty-one and immediately experienced a desire to lead worship services. In this excerpt from her autobiography, *The Religious Experience of Mrs. Jarena Lee*, she tells of her

The man who was to speak in the afternoon of that day was the Reverend Richard Allen, since bishop of the African Episcopal Methodists in America. During the labors of this man that afternoon, I had come to the conclusion that this is the people to which my heart unites. And it so happened that, as soon as the service closed, he invited such as felt a desire to flee the wrath to come, to unite on trial with them—I embraced the opportunity.

Three weeks from that day, my soul was gloriously converted to God under preaching, at the very outset of the sermon. The text was barely pronounced, which was "I perceive thy heart is not right in the sight of God" [Acts 8:21], when there appeared to *my* view, in the center of the heart, *one* sin, and this was *malice*—against one particular individual who had strove deeply to injure me, which I resented.

At this discovery I said, "*Lord*, I forgive *every* creature."

That instant it appeared to me as if a garment, which had entirely enveloped my whole person even to my fingers' ends, split at the crown of my head and was stripped away from me, passing like a shadow from my sight—when the glory of God seemed to cover me in its stead. That moment, though hundreds were present, I did leap to my feet and declare that God, for Christ's sake, had pardoned the sins of my soul. Great was the ecstasy of my mind, for I felt that not only the sin of malice was pardoned, but all other sins were swept away together.

That day was the first when my heart had believed and my tongue had made confession unto salvation. The first words uttered, a part of that song which shall fill eternity with its sound, was "Glory to God!" For a few moments, I had power to exhort sinners and to tell of the wonders and of the goodness of him who had clothed me with *his* salvation.

RALPH WALDO EMERSON
1803 - 1862

Although he began his career as a minister, **Ralph Waldo Emerson**'s theology is hardly mainstream. Born in Boston in 1803, this great thinker helped to originate the principles of transcendentalism, an American philosophy that cherished individualism and rendered the natural as divine, while resisting traditional forms of religion. A close friend of Thoreau, Emerson lived and worked in the Northeast, making his living as a writer and lecturer. The passages contained in this book were drawn from *Nature*, a seminal text for followers of that movement.

The errors of traditional Christianity as it now exists, the popular faith of many millions, need to be removed to let men see the divine beauty of moral truth. I feel myself pledged, if health and opportunity be granted me, to demonstrate that all necessary truth is its own evidence; that no doctrine of God need appeal to a book; that Christianity is wrongly received by all such as take it for a system of doctrines,—its stress being upon moral truth; it is a rule of life, not a rule of faith.

REVEREND CHARLES G. FINNEY
1792 - 1875

On a Sabbath evening in the autumn of 1821, I made up my mind that I would settle the question of my soul's salvation at once, that if it were possible I would make my peace with God. But as I was very busy in the affairs of the office, I knew that without great firmness of purpose, I should never effectually attend to the subject. I therefore, then and there resolved, as far as possible, to avoid all business, and everything that would divert my attention, and to give myself wholly to the work of securing the salvation of my soul. I carried this resolution into execution as sternly and thoroughly as I could. I was, however, obliged to be a good deal in the office. But as the providence of God would have it, I was not much occupied either on Monday or Tuesday; and had opportunity to read my Bible and engage in prayer most of the time.

A lawyer turned revivalist, **Charles Finney** roamed the continent in search of converts. Born in 1792, he served as president of Oberlin College and was a member of the Presbyterian faith. As an evangelist, he was involved in social reform, lending his persuasive preaching to the causes of abolition and temperance. Finney meticulously detailed his conversion experience in his autobiography.

But I was very proud without knowing it. I had supposed that I had not much regard for the opinions of others, whether they thought this or that in regard to myself; and I had in fact been quite singular in attending prayer meetings, and in the degree of attention that I had paid to religion, while in Adams. In this respect I had been so singular as to lead the church at times to think that I must be an anxious inquirer. But I found, when I came to face the question, that I was very unwilling to have any one know that I was seeking the salvation of my soul. When I prayed I would only whisper my prayer, after having stopped the key-hole to the door, lest some one should discover that I was engaged in prayer. Before that time I had my Bible lying on the table with the law-books; and it never had occurred to me to be ashamed of being found reading it, any more than I should be ashamed of being found reading any of my other books.

But after I had addressed myself in earnest to the subject of my own salvation, I kept my Bible, as much as I could, out of sight. If I was reading it when anybody came in, I would throw my law-books upon it, to create the impression that I had not had it in my hand. Instead of being outspoken and willing to talk with anybody and everybody on the subject as before, I found myself unwilling to converse with anybody. I did not want to see my minister, because I did not want to let him know how I felt, and I had no confidence that he would understand my case, and give me the direction that I needed. For the same reasons I avoided conversation with the elders of the church, or with any of the Christian people. I was ashamed to let them know how I felt, on the one hand; and on the other, I was afraid they would misdirect me. I felt myself shut up to the Bible.

During Monday and Tuesday my convictions increased; but still it seemed as if my heart grew harder. I could not shed a tear; I could not pray. I had no opportunity to pray above my breath; and frequently I felt, that if I could be alone where I could use my voice and let myself out, I should find relief in prayer. I was shy, and avoided, as much as I could, speaking to anybody on any subject. I endeavored, however, to do this in a way that would excite no suspicion, in any mind, that I was seeking the salvation of my soul.

Tuesday night I had become very nervous; and in the night a strange feeling came over me as if I was about to die. I knew that if I did I should sink down to hell; but I quieted myself as best I could until morning.

At an early hour I started for the office. But just before I arrive at the office, something seemed to confront me with questions like these: indeed, it seemed as if the inquiry was within myself, as if an inward voice said to me, "What are you waiting for? Did you not promise to give your heart to God? And what are you trying to do? Are you endeavoring to work out a righteousness of your own?"

Just at this point the whole question of Gospel salvation opened to my mind in a manner most marvellous to me at the time. I think I then saw, as clearly as I ever have in my life, the reality and fulness of the atonement of Christ. I saw that his work was a finished work; and that instead of having, or needing, any righteousness of my own to recommend me to God, I had to submit myself to the righteousness of God through Christ. Gospel salvation seemed to me to be an offer of something to be accepted; and that it was full and complete; and that all that was necessary on my part, was to get my own consent to give up my sins, and accept Christ. Salvation, it seemed to me, instead of being a thing to be wrought out, by my own works, was a thing to be found entirely in the Lord Jesus Christ, who presented himself before me as my God and my Saviour.

Without being distinctly aware of it, I had stopped in the street right where the inward voice seemed to arrest me. How long I remained in that position I cannot say. But after this distinct revelation had stood for some little time before my mind, the question seemed to be put, "Will you accept it now, to-day?" I replied, "Yes; I will accept it to-day, or I will die in the attempt."

North of the village, and over a hill, lay a piece of woods, in which I was in the almost daily habit of walking, more or less, when it was pleasant weather. It was now October, and the time was past for my frequent walks there. Nevertheless, instead of going to the office, I turned and bent my course toward the woods, feeling that I must be alone, and away from all human eyes and ears, so that I could pour out my prayer to God.

But still my pride must show itself. As I went over the hill, it occurred to me that some one might see me and suppose that I was going away to pray. Yet probably there was not a person on earth that would have suspected such a thing, had he seen me going. But so great was my pride, and so much was I possessed with the fear of man, that I recollect that I skulked along under the fence, till I got so far out of sight that no one from the village could see me. I then penetrated into the woods, I should think, a quarter of a mile, went over on the other side of the hill, and found a place where some large trees had fallen across each other, leaving an open place between. There I saw I could make a kind of closet. I crept into this place and knelt down for prayer. As I turned to go up into the woods, I recollect to have said, "I will give my heart to God, or I never will come down from there." I recollect repeating this as I went up—"I will give my heart to God before I ever come down again."

But when I attempted to pray I found that my heart would not pray. I had supposed that if I could only be where I could speak aloud, without being overheard, I could pray freely. But lo! when I came to try, I was dumb; that is, I had nothing to say to God; or at least I could say but a few words, and those without heart. In attempting to pray I would hear a rustling in the leaves, as I thought, and would stop and look up to see if somebody were not coming. This I did several times.

Finally I found myself verging fast to despair. I said to myself, "I cannot pray. My heart is dead to God, and will not pray." I then reproached myself for having promised to give my heart to God before I left the woods. When I came to try, I found I could not give my heart to God. My inward soul hung back, and there was no going out of my heart to God. I began to feel deeply that it was too late; that it must be that I was given up of God and was past hope.

The thought was pressing me of the rashness of my promise, that I would give my heart to God that day or die in the attempt. It seemed to me as if that was binding upon my soul; and yet I was going to break my vow. A great sinking and discouragement came over me, and I felt almost too weak to stand upon my knees.

Just at this moment I again thought I heard some one approach me, and I opened my eyes to see whether it were so. But right there the revelation of my pride of heart as the great difficulty that stood in the way, was distinctly shown to me. An overwhelming sense of my wickedness in being ashamed to have a human being see me on my knees before God, took such powerful possession of me, that I cried at the top of my voice, and exclaimed that I would not leave that place if all the men on earth and all the devils in hell surrounded me. "What!" I said, "such a degraded sinner as I am, on my knees confessing my sins to the great and holy God; and ashamed to have any human being, and a sinner like myself, find me on my knees endeavoring to make my peace with my offended God!" The sin appeared awful, infinite. It broke me down before the Lord.

Just at that point this passage of Scripture seemed to drop into my mind with a flood of light: "Then shall ye go and pray unto me, and I will hearken unto you. Then shall ye seek me and find me, when ye shall search for me with all your heart." I instantly seized hold of this with my heart. I had intellectually believed the Bible before; but never had the truth been in my mind that faith was a voluntary trust instead of an intellectual state. I was as conscious as I was of my existence, of trusting at that moment in God's veracity. Somehow I knew that that was a passage of Scripture, though I do not think I had ever read it. I knew that it was God's word, and God's voice, as it were, that spoke to me. I cried to Him, "Lord, I take thee at thy word. Now thou knowest that I do search for thee with all my heart, and that I have come here to pray to thee; and thou hast promised to hear me."

That seemed to settle the question that I could then, that day, perform my vow. The Spirit seemed to lay stress upon that idea in the text, "When you search for me with all your heart." The question of when, that is of the present time, seemed to fall heavily into my heart. I told the Lord that I should take him at his Word; that he could not lie, and that therefore I was sure that he heard my prayer, and that he would be found of me.

He then gave me many other promises, both from the Old and the New Testament, especially some most precious promises respecting our Lord Jesus Christ. I never can, in words, make any human being understand how precious and true those promises appeared to me. I took them one after the other as infallible truth, the assertions of God who could not lie. They

did not seem so much to fall into my intellect as into my heart, to be put within the grasp of the voluntary powers of my mind; and I seized hold of them, appropriated them, and fastened upon them with the grasp of a drowning man.

I continued thus to pray, and to receive and appropriate promises for a long time, I know not how long. I prayed till my mind became so full that, before I was aware of it, I was on my feet and tripping up the ascent toward the road. The question of my being converted, had not so much as arisen to my thought; but as I went up, brushing through the leaves and bushes, I recollect saying with great emphasis, "If I am ever converted, I will preach the Gospel."

I soon reached the road that led to the village, and began to reflect upon what had passed; and I found that my mind had become most wonderfully quiet and peaceful. I said to myself, "What is this? I must have grieved the Holy Ghost entirely away. I have lost all my conviction. I have not a particle of concern about my soul; and it must be that the Spirit has left me." "Why!" thought I, "I never was so far from being concerned about my own salvation in my life."

Then I remembered what I had said to God while I was on my knees—that I had said I would take him at his word; and indeed I recollected a good many things that I had said, and concluded that it was no wonder that the Spirit had left me; that for such a sinner as I was to take hold of God's word in that way, was presumption if not blasphemy. I concluded that in my excitement I had grieved the Holy Spirit, and perhaps committed the unpardonable sin.

I walked quietly toward the village; and so perfectly quiet was my mind that it seemed as if all nature listened. It was on the 10th of October, and a very pleasant day. I had gone into the woods immediately after an early breakfast; and when I returned to the village I found it was dinner time. Yet I had been wholly unconscious of that time that had passed; it appeared to me that I had been gone from the village but a short time.

But how was I to account for the quiet of my mind? I tried to recall my convictions, to get back again the load of sin under which I had been laboring. But all sense of sin, all consciousness of present sin or guilt, had departed from me. I said to myself, "What is this, that I cannot arouse any sense of guilt in my soul, as great a sinner as I am?" I tried in vain to make myself anxious about my present state. I was so quiet and

peaceful that I tried to feel concerned about that, lest it should be a result of my having grieved the Spirit away. But take any view of it I would, I could not be anxious at all about my soul, and about my spiritual state. The repose of my mind was unspeakably great. I never can describe it in words. The thought of God was sweet to my mind, and the most profound spiritual tranquility had taken full possession of me. This was a great mystery; but it did not distress or perplex me.

I went to my dinner, and found I had no appetite to eat. I then went to the office, and found that Squire W— had gone to dinner. I took down my bass-viol, and, as I was accustomed to do, began to play and sing some pieces of sacred music. But as soon as I began to sing those sacred words, I began to weep. It seemed as if my heart was all liquid; and my feelings were in such a state that I could not hear my own voice in singing without causing my sensibility to overflow. I wondered at this, and tried to suppress my tears, but could not. After trying in vain to suppress my tears, I put up my instrument and stopped singing.

After dinner we were engaged in removing our books and furniture to another office. We were very busy in this, and had but little conversation all the afternoon. My mind, however, remained in that profoundly tranquil state. There was a great sweetness and tenderness in my thoughts and feelings. Everything appeared to be going right, and nothing seemed to ruffle or disturb me in the least.

Just before evening the thought took possession of my mind, that as soon as I was left alone in the new office, I would try to pray again—that I was not going to abandon the subject of religion and give it up, at any rate; and therefore, although I no longer had any concern about my soul, still I would continue to pray.

By evening we got the books and furniture adjusted; and I made up, in an open fire-place, a good fire, hoping to spend the evening alone. Just at dark Squire W—, seeing that everything was adjusted, bade me good-night and went to his home. I had accompanied him to the door; and as I closed the door and turned around, my heart seemed to be liquid within me. All my feelings seemed to rise and flow out; and the utterance of my heart was, "I want to pour my whole soul out to God." The rising of my soul was so great that I rushed into the room back of the front office, to pray.

There was no fire, and no light, in the room; nevertheless it appeared to me as if it were perfectly light. As I went in and shut the door after me, it seemed as if

I met the Lord Jesus Christ face to face. It did not occur to me then, nor did it for sometime afterward, that it was wholly a mental state. On the contrary it seemed to me that I saw him as I would see any other man. He said nothing, but looked at me in such a manner as to break me right down at his feet. I have always since regarded this as a most remarkable state of mind; for it seemed to me a reality, that he stood before me, and I fell down at his feet and poured out my soul to him. I wept aloud like a child, and made such confessions as I could with my choked utterance. It seemed to me that I bathed his feet with my tears; and yet I had no distinct impression that I touched him, that I recollect.

I must have continued in this state for a good while; but my mind was too much absorbed with the interview to recollect anything that I said. But I know, as soon as my mind became calm enough to break off from the interview, I returned to the front office, and found that the fire that I had made of large wood was nearly burned out. But as I turned and was about to take a seat by the fire, I received a mighty baptism of the Holy Ghost. Without any expectation of it, without ever having the thought in my mind that there was any such thing for me, without any recollection that I had ever heard the thing mentioned by any person in the world, the Holy Spirit descended upon me in a manner that seemed to go through me, body and soul. I could feel the impression, like a wave of electricity, going through and through me. Indeed it seemed to come in waves and waves of liquid love; for I could not express it in any other way. It seemed like the very breath of God. I can recollect distinctly that it seemed to fan me, like immense wings.

No words can express the wonderful love that was shed abroad in my heart. I wept aloud with joy and love; and I do not know but I should say, I literally bellowed out the unutterable gushings of my heart. These waves came over me, and over me, and over me, one after the other, until I recollect I cried out, "I shall die if these waves continue to pass over me." I said, "Lord, I cannot bear any more;" yet I had no fear of death.

How long I continued in this state, with this baptism continuing to roll over me and go through me, I do not know. But I know it was late in the evening when a member of my choir—for I was the leader of the choir—came into the office to see me. He was a member of the church. He found me in this state of loud weeping, and said to me, "Mr. Finney, what ails you?" I could make him no answer for some time.

He then said, "Are you in pain?" I gathered myself up as best I could, and replied, "No, but so happy that I cannot live."

He turned and left the office, and in a few minutes returned with one of the elders of the church, whose shop was nearly across the way from our office. This elder was a very serious man; and in my presence had been very watchful, and I had scarcely ever seen him laugh. When he came in, I was very much in the state in which I was when the young man went out to call him. He asked me how I felt, and I began to tell him. Instead of saying anything, he fell into a most spasmodic laughter. It seemed as if it was impossible for him to keep from laughing from the very bottom of his heart.

There was a young man in the neighborhood who was preparing for college, with whom I had been very intimate. Our minister, as I afterward learned, had repeatedly talked with him on the subject of religion, and warned him against being misled by me. He informed him that I was a very careless young man about religion; and he thought that if he associated much with me his mind would be diverted, and he would not be converted.

After I was converted, and this young man was converted, he told me that he had said to Mr. Gale several times, when he had admonished him about associating so much with me, that my conversations had often affected him more, religiously, than his preaching. I had, indeed, let out my feelings a good deal to this young man.

But just at the time when I was giving an account of my feelings to this elder of the church, and to the other member who was with him, this young man came into the office. I was sitting with my back toward the door, and barely observed that he came in. He listened with astonishment to what I was saying, and the first I knew he partly fell upon the floor, and cried out in the greatest agony of mind, "Do pray for me!" The elder of the church and the other member knelt down and began to pray for him; and when they had prayed, I prayed for him myself. Soon after this they all retired and left me alone.

The question then arose in my mind, "Why did Elder B— laugh so? Did he not think that I was under a delusion, or crazy?" This suggestion brought a kind of darkness over my mind; and I began to query with myself whether it was proper for me—such a sinner as I had been—to pray for that young man. A cloud seemed to shut in over me; I had no hold upon anything in which I could rest; and after a little while I retired to bed, not distressed in mind, but still at a loss to know what to make of my present state. Notwithstanding the baptism I had received, this temptation so obscured my view that I went to bed without feeling sure that my peace was made with God.

I soon fell asleep, but almost as soon awoke again on account of the great flow of the love of God that was in my heart. I was so filled with love that I could not sleep. Soon I fell asleep again, and awoke in the same manner. When I awoke, this temptation would return upon me, and the love that seemed to be in my heart would abate; but as soon as I was asleep, it was so warm within me that I would immediately awake. Thus I continued till, late at night, I obtained some sound repose.

When I awoke in the morning the sun had risen, and was pouring a clear light into my room. Words cannot express the impression that this sunlight made upon me. Instantly the baptism that I had received the night before returned upon me in the same manner. I arose upon my knees in the bed and wept aloud with joy, and remained for some time too much overwhelmed with the baptism of the Spirit to do anything but pour out my soul to God. It seemed as if this morning's baptism was accompanied with a gentle reproof, and the Spirit seemed to say to me, "Will you doubt?" "Will you doubt?" I cried, "No! I will not doubt; I cannot doubt." He then cleared the subject up so much to my mind that it was in fact impossible for me to doubt that the Spirit of God had taken possession of my soul.

In this state I was taught the doctrine of justification by faith, as a present experience. That doctrine had never taken any such possession of my mind, that I had ever viewed it distinctly as a fundamental doctrine of the Gospel. Indeed, I did not know at all what it meant in the proper sense. But I could now see and understand what was meant by the passage, "Being justified by faith, we have peace with God through our Lord Jesus Christ." I could see that the moment I believed, while up in the woods all sense of condemnation had entirely dropped out of my mind; and that from that moment I could not feel a sense of guilt or condemnation by any effort that I could make. My sense of guilt was gone; my sins were gone; and I do not think I felt any more sense of guilt than if I never had sinned.

This was just the revelation that I needed. I felt myself justified by faith; and, so far as I could see, I was in a state in which I did not sin. Instead of feeling that I was sinning all the time, my heart was so full of love that it overflowed. My cup ran over with blessing and with love; and I could not feel that I was sinning against God. Nor could I recover the least sense of guilt for my past sins. Of this experience I said nothing that I recollect, at the time, to anybody; that is, of this experience of justification.

Red Jacket
1750 - 1830

Friend and Brother! It was the will of the Great Spirit that we should meet together this day. He orders all things, and he has given us a fine day for our council. He has taken his garment from before the sun, and caused it to shine with brightness upon us. Our eyes are opened that we see clearly. Our ears are unstopped that we have been able to hear distinctly the words you have spoken. For all these favors we thank the Great Spirit, and him only. . . .

Brother! Continue to listen. You say that you are sent to instruct us how to worship the Great Spirit agreeably to his mind; and if we do not take hold of the religion which you white people teach, we shall be unhappy hereafter. You say that you are right and we are lost. How do we know this to be true? We understand that your religion is written in a book. If it was intended for us as well as for you, why has not the Great Spirit given it to us; and not only to us, but why did he not give to our forefathers the knowledge of that book, with the means of understanding it rightly? We only know what you tell us about it. How shall we know when to believe, being so often deceived by the white people?

Brother! You say there is but one way to worship and serve the Great Spirit. If there is but one religion, why do you white people differ so much about it? Why do not all agree, as you can all read the book?

The famous speech "We Never Argue About Religion" was given in 1828, as a reply by the Iroquois leader to a Boston Missionary Society representative who was seeking to do missionary work among the Iroquois in upstate New York.

Brother! We do not understand these things. We are told that your religion was given to your forefathers, and has been handed down from father to son. We also have a religion which was given to our forefathers, and has been handed down to us their children. We worship that way. It teacheth us to be thankful for all the favors we receive, to love each other, and to be united. We never quarrel about religion. . . .

ALEXIS DE TOCQUEVILLE
1805 - 1859

Every religion has some political opinion linked to it by affinity. The spirit of man, left to follow its bent, will regulate political society and the City of God in uniform fashion; it will, if I dare put it so, seek to *harmonize* earth with heaven.

Most of English America was peopled by men who, having shaken off the pope's authority, acknowledged no other religious supremacy; they therefore brought to the New World a Christianity which I can only describe as democratic and republican; this fact singularly favored the establishment of a temporal republic and democracy. From the start politics and religion agreed, and they have not since ceased to do so.

About fifty years ago Ireland began to pour a Catholic population into the United States. Also American Catholicism made converts. There are now in the United States more than a million Christians professing the truths of the Roman Church.

These Catholics are very loyal in the practice of their worship and full of zeal and ardor for their beliefs. Nevertheless, they form the most republican and democratic of all classes in the United States. At first glance this is astonishing, but reflection easily indicates the hidden causes therefore.

I think one is wrong in regarding the Catholic religion as a natural enemy of democracy. Rather, among the various Christian doctrines Catholicism seems one of those most favorable to equality of conditions. For Catholics religious society is composed of two elements: priest and people. The priest is raised above the faithful; all below him are equal.

In matters of dogma the Catholic faith places all intellects on the same level; the learned man and the ignorant, the genius and the common herd, must all subscribe to the same details of belief; rich and poor must follow the same observances, and it imposes the same austerities upon the strong and the weak; it makes no compromise with any mortal, but applying the same standard to every human being, it mingles all classes of society at the foot of the same altar, just as they are mingled in the sight of God.

Catholicism may dispose the faithful to obedience, but it does not prepare them for inequality. However, I would say that Protestantism in general orients men much less toward equality than toward independence.

Catholicism is like an absolute monarchy. The prince apart, conditions are more equal there than in republics.

It has often happened that a Catholic priest has left his sanctuary to become a power in society, taking his place in the social hierarchy; he has then sometimes used his religious influence to assure the duration of a political order of which he is part; then, too, one has found Catholic partisans of the aristocracy from religious motives.

But once priests are excluded or exclude themselves from the government, as happens in the United States, no men are more led by their beliefs than are Catholics to carry the idea of equality of conditions over into the political sphere.

So while the nature of their beliefs may not give the Catholics of the Unites States any strong impulsion toward democratic and republican opinions, they at least are not naturally contrary thereto, whereas their social position and small numbers constrain them to adopt them.

Most of the Catholics are poor, and unless all citizens govern, they will never attain to the government themselves. The Catholics are in a minority, and it is important for them that all rights should be respected so that they can be sure to enjoy their own in freedom. For these two reasons they are led, perhaps in spite of themselves, toward political doctrines which, maybe, they would adopt with less zeal were they rich and predominant.

The practiced eye of **Alexis de Tocqueville** did not miss much. "The religious atmosphere of the country was the first thing that struck me on arrival in the United States," he writes in the classic, *Democracy in America.* The Frenchman's journey through a young and very robust republic in 1831 and 1832 obliged him to deliver an extended observation on religion in the United States.

The Catholic clergy in the United States has made no effort to strive against this political tendency but rather seeks to justify it. American Catholic priests have divided the world of the mind into two parts; in one are revealed dogmas to which they submit without discussion; political truth finds its place in the other half, which they think God has left to man's free investigation. Thus American Catholics are both the most obedient of the faithful and the most independent citizens.

Therefore one can say that there is not a single religious doctrine in the United States hostile to democratic and republican institutions. All the clergy there speak the same language; opinions are in harmony with the laws, and there is, so to say, only one mental current.

While I was temporarily living in one of America's great cities, I was invited to attend a political meeting designed to aid the Poles by helping them to get arms and money.

I found two or three thousand people in a vast hall prepared for their reception. Soon a priest dressed in his ecclesiastical habit came forward onto the platform. The audience took off their hats and stood in silence while he spoke as follows:

"Almighty God! Lord of Hosts! Thou who didst strengthen the hearts and guide the arms of our fathers when they fought for the sacred rights of their national independence! Thou who didst make them triumph over a hateful oppression and didst grant to our people the blessings of peace and of liberty, look with favor, Lord, upon the other hemisphere; have pity upon a heroic people fighting now as we fought before for the defense of these same rights! Lord, who hast created all men in the same image, do not allow despotism to deform Thy work and maintain inequality upon the earth. Almighty God! Watch over the destinies of the Poles and make them worthy to be free; may Thy wisdom prevail in their councils and Thy strength in their arms; spread terror among their enemies; divide the powers that contrive their ruin; and do not allow that injustice which the world has witnessed for fifty years to be consummated in our time. Lord, who holdest in Thy strong hand the hearts of peoples and of men, raise up allies to the sacred cause of true right; arouse at last the French nation, that, forgetting the apathy in which its leaders lull, it may fight once more for the freedom of the world.

"O Lord! Turn not Thou Thy face from us, and grant that we may always be the most religious and the most free nation upon earth.

"God Almighty, hear our supplications this day, and save the Poles. We beseech Thee in the name of Thy beloved son, our Lord Jesus Christ, who died upon the cross for the salvation of all men. Amen."

The whole assembly answered reverently, "Amen."

I have just pointed out the direct action of religion on politics in the United States. Its indirect action seems to me much greater still, and it is just when it is not speaking of freedom at all that it best teaches the Americans the art of being free.

There is an innumerable multitude of sects in the United States. They are all different in the worship they offer to the Creator, but all agree concerning the duties of men to one another. Each sect worships God in its own fashion, but all preach the same morality in the name of God. Though it is very important for man as an individual that his religion should be true, that is not the case for society. Society has nothing to fear or hope from another life; what is most important for it is not that all citizens should profess the true religion but that they should profess religion. Moreover, all the sects in the Unites States belong to the great unity of Christendom, and Christian morality is everywhere the same.

One may suppose that a certain number of Americans, in the worship they offer to God, are following their habits rather than their convictions. Besides, in the United States the sovereign authority is religious, and consequently hypocrisy should be common. Nonetheless, America is still the place where the Christian religion has kept the greatest real power over men's souls; and nothing better demonstrates how useful and natural it is to man, since the country where it now has widest sway is both the most enlightened and the freest.

I have said that American priests proclaim themselves in general terms in favor of civil liberties without excepting even those who do not admit religious freedom; but none of them lend their support to any particular political system. They are at pains to keep out of affairs and not mix in the combinations of parties. One cannot therefore say that in the United States religion influences the laws or political opinions in detail, but it does direct mores, and by regulating domestic life it helps to regulate the state.

I do not doubt for an instant that the great severity of mores which one notices in the United States has its primary origin in beliefs. There religion is often powerless to restrain men in the midst of innumerable temptations which fortune offers. It cannot moderate their eagerness to enrich themselves, which everything contributes to arouse, but it reigns supreme in the souls of the women, and it is women who shape mores. Certainly of all countries in the world America is the one in which the marriage tie is most respected and where the highest and truest conception of conjugal happiness has been conceived.

In Europe almost all the disorders of society are born around the domestic hearth and not far from the nuptial bed. It is there that men come to feel scorn for natural ties and legitimate pleasures and develop a taste for disorder, restlessness of spirit, and instability of desires. Shaken by the tumultuous passions which have often troubled his own house, the European finds it hard to submit to the authority of the state's legislators. When the American returns from the turmoil of politics to the bosom of the family, he immediately finds a perfect picture of order and peace. There all his pleasures are simple and natural and his joys innocent and quiet, and as the regularity of life brings him happiness, he easily forms the habit of regulating his opinions as well as his tastes.

Whereas the European tries to escape his sorrows at home by troubling society, the American derives from his home that love of order which he carries over into affairs of state.

In the United States it is not only mores that are controlled by religion, but its sway extends even over reason.

Among the Anglo-Americans there are some who profess Christian dogma because they believe them and others who do so because they are afraid to look as though they did not believe in them. So Christianity reigns without obstacles, by universal consent; consequently, as I have said elsewhere, everything in the moral field is certain and fixed, although the world of politics seems given over to argument and experiment. So the human spirit never sees an unlimited field before itself; however bold it is, from time to time it feels that it must halt before insurmountable barriers. Before innovating, it is forced to accept certain primary assumptions and to submit its boldest conceptions to certain formalities which retard and check it.

The imagination of the Americans, therefore, even in its greatest aberrations, is circumspect and hesitant; it is embarrassed from the start and leaves its work unfinished. These habits of restraint are found again in political society and singularly favor the tranquillity of the people as well as the durability of the institutions they have adopted. Nature and circumstances have made the inhabitant of the United States a bold man, as is sufficiently attested by the enterprising spirit with which he seeks his fortune. If the spirit of the Americans were free of all impediment, one would soon find among them the boldest innovators and the most implacable logicians in the world. But American revolutionaries are obliged ostensibly to profess a certain respect for Christian morality and equity, and that does not allow them easily to break the laws when those are opposed to the executions of their designs; nor would they find it easy to surmount the scruples of their partisans even if they were able to get over their own. Up till now no one in the United States has dared to profess the maxim that everything is allowed in the interests of society, an impious maxim apparently invented in an age of freedom in order to legitimatize every future tyrant.

Thus, while the law allows the American people to do everything, there are things which religion prevents them from imagining and forbids them to dare.

Religion, which never intervenes directly in the government of American society, should therefore be considered as the first of their political institutions, for although it did not give them the taste for liberty, it singularly facilitates their use thereof.

The inhabitants of the United States themselves consider religious beliefs from this angle. I do not know if all Americans have faith in their religion—for who can read the secrets of the heart?—but I am sure that they think it necessary to the maintenance of republican institutions. That is not the view of one class or party among the citizens, but of the whole nation; it is found in all ranks.

In the United States, if a politician attacks a sect, that is no reason why the supporters of that very sect should not support him; but if he attacks all sects together, everyone shuns him, and he remains alone.

While I was in America, a witness called at assizes of the county of Chester (state of New York) declared that he did not believe in the existence of God and the immortality of the soul. The judge refused to allow him to be sworn in, on the ground that the witness had destroyed beforehand all possible confidence in his testimony.[1] Newspapers reported the fact without comment.

---

[1] This is how the New York *Spectator* of August 23, 1831, reported the matter: "The court of common pleas of Chester county (New York) a few days since, rejected a witness who declared his disbelief in the existence of God. The presiding judge remarked that he was not before aware that there was a man living who did not believe in the existence of God; that this belief constituted the sanction of all testimony in a court of justice; and that he knew of no cause in a Christian country, where a witness had been permitted to testify without such belief." [Tocqueville quotes this in English.]

For the Americans the ideas of Christianity and liberty are so completely mingled that it is almost impossible to get them to conceive of the one without the other; it is not a question with them of sterile beliefs bequeathed by the past and vegetating rather than living in the depths of the soul.

I have known Americans to form associations to send priests out into the new states of the West and establish schools and churches there; they fear that religion might be lost in the depths of the forest and that the people growing up there might be less fitted for freedom than those from whom they sprang. I have met rich New Englanders who left their native land in order to establish the fundamentals of Christianity and of liberty by the banks of the Missouri or on the prairies of Illinois. In this way, in the United States, patriotism continually adds fuel to the fires of religious zeal. You will be mistaken if you think that such men are guided only by thoughts of the future life; eternity is only one of the things that concern them. If you talk to these missionaries of Christian civilization you will be surprised to hear them so often speaking of the goods of this world and to meet a politician where you expected to find a priest. "There is a solidarity between all the American republics," they will tell you; "if the republics of the West were to fall into anarchy or to be mastered by a despot, the republican institutions now flourishing on the Atlantic coast would be in great danger; we therefore have an interest in seeing that the new states are religious so that they may allow us to remain free."

That is what the Americans think, but our pedants find it an obvious mistake; constantly they prove to me that all is fine in America except just that religious spirit which I admire; I am informed that on the other side of the ocean freedom and human happiness lack nothing but Spinoza's belief in the eternity of the world and Cabanis' contention that thought is a secretion of the brain. To that I have really no answer to give, except that those who talk like that have never been in America and have never seen either religious peoples or free ones. So I shall wait till they come back from a visit to America.

There are people in France who look on republican institutions as a temporary expedient for their own aggrandizement. They mentally measure the immense gap separating their vices and their poverty from power and wealth, and they would like to fill this abyss with ruins in an attempt to bridge it. Such people stand toward liberty much as the medieval *condottieri* stood toward the kings; they make war on their own account, no matter whose colors they wear: the republic, they calculate, will at least last long enough to lift them from their present degradation. It is not to such as they that I speak, but there are others who look forward to a republican form of government as a permanent and tranquil state and as the required aim to which ideas and mores are constantly steering modern societies. Such men sincerely wish to prepare mankind for liberty. When such as these attack religious beliefs, they obey the dictates of their passions, not their interests. Despotism may be able to do without faith, but freedom cannot. Religion is much more needed in the republic they advocate than in the monarchy they attack, and in democratic republics most of all. How could society escape destruction if, when political ties are relaxed, moral ties are not tightened? And what can be done with a people master of itself if it is not subject to God?

Eighteenth-century philosophers had a very simple explanation for the gradual weakening of beliefs. Religious zeal, they said, was bound to die down as enlightenment and freedom spread. It is tiresome that the facts do not fit this theory at all.

There are sections of the population in Europe where unbelief goes hand in hand with brutishness and ignorance, whereas in America the most free and enlightened people in the world zealously perform all the external duties of religion.

The religious atmosphere of the country was the first thing that struck me on arrival in the United States. The longer I stayed in the country, the more conscious I became of the important political consequences resulting from this novel situation.

In France I had seen the spirits of religion and of freedom almost always marching in opposite directions. In America I found them intimately linked together in joint reign over the same land.

My longing to understand the reason for this phenomenon increased daily.

To find this out, I questioned the faithful of all communions; I particularly sought the society of clergymen, who are the depositaries of the various creeds and have a personal interest in their survival. As a practicing Catholic I was particularly close to the Catholic priests, with some of whom I soon established a certain intimacy. I expressed my astonishment and revealed my doubts to each of them; I found that they all agreed with each other except about details; all thought that the main reason for the quiet sway of religion over their country was the complete separation of church and state. I have no hesitation in stating that throughout my stay in America I met nobody, lay or cleric, who did not agree about that.

This led me to examine more closely than before the position of American priests in political society. I was surprised to discover that they held no public appointments.[2] There was not a single one in the administration, and I found that they were not even represented in the assemblies.

In several states the law,[3] and in all the rest public opinion, excludes them from a career in politics.

When I finally came to inquire into the attitudes of the clergy themselves, I found that most of them seemed voluntarily to steer clear of power and to take a sort of professional pride in claiming that it was no concern of theirs.

I heard them pronouncing anathemas against ambition and bad faith, under whatsoever political opinions those were at pains to hide. But I learned from their discourses that men are not guilty in the sight of God because of these very opinions, provided they are sincere, and that it is no more a sin to makea mistake in some question of government than it is a sin to go wrong in building one's house or plowing one's field.

I saw that they were careful to keep clear of all parties, shunning contact with them with all the anxiety attendant upon personal interest.

These facts convinced me that I had been told the truth. I then wished to trace the facts down to their causes. I wondered how it could come about that by diminishing the apparent power of religion one increased its real strength, and I thought it not impossible to discover the reason.

The short space of sixty years can never shut in the whole of man's imagination; the incomplete joys of this world will never satisfy his heart. Alone among all created beings, man shows a natural disgust for existence and an immense longing to exist; he scorns life and fears annihilation. These different instincts constantly drive his soul toward contemplation of the next world, and it is religion that leads him thither. Religion, therefore, is only one particular form of hope, and it is as natural to the human heart as hope itself. It is by a sort of intellectual aberration, and in a way, by doing moral violence to their own nature, that men detach themselves from religious beliefs; an invincible inclination draws them back. Incredulity is an accident; faith is the only permanent state of mankind.

Considering religions from a purely human point of view, one can then say that all religions derive an element of strength which will never fail from man himself, because it is attached to one of the constituent principles of human nature.

I know that, apart from influence proper to itself, religion can at times rely on the artificial strength of laws and the support of the material powers that direct society. There have been religions intimately linked to earthly governments, dominating men's souls both by terror and by faith; but when a religion makes such an alliance, I am not afraid to say that it makes the same mistake as any man might; it sacrifices the future for the present, and by gaining a power to which it has no claim, it risks its legitimate authority.

When a religion seeks to found its sway only on the longing for immortality equally tormenting every human heart, it can aspire to universality; but when it comes to uniting itself with a government, it must adopt maxims which apply only to certain nations. Therefore, by allying itself with any political power, religion increases its strength over some but forfeits the hope of reigning over all.

As long as a religion relies only upon the sentiments which are the consolation of every affliction, it

---

[2]Unless the phrase is taken to cover their work in the schools. The greater part of education is entrusted to the clergy.

[3]See the Constitution of New York, Article VII, paragraph 4.

Idem of North Carolina, Article XXXI. [Tocqueville refers to the Constitution of 1776.]

Idem of Virginia.

Idem of South Carolina, Article I, section 23. [Constitution of 1790.]

Idem of Kentucky, Article II, section 26. [Tocqueville refers to the Constitution of 1799.]

Idem of Tennessee, Article VIII, section I. [Constitution of 1796.]

Idem of Louisiana, Article II, section 22.

The Article of the Constitution of New York is convinced thus:

"And whereas the ministers of the gospel are, by their profession, dedicated to the service of God and the cure of souls and ought not to be diverted from the great duties of their functions, therefore, no minister of the gospel or priest of any denomination whatever . . . be eligible to or capable of holding any civil or military office of place within this state." [Article VII, Section 4 of the Constitution of 1821.]

can draw the heart of mankind to itself. When it is mingled with the bitter passions of this world, it is sometimes constrained to defend allies who are such from interest rather than from love; and it has to repulse as adversaries men who still love religion, although they are fighting against religion's allies. Hence religion cannot share the material strength of the rulers without being burdened with some of the animosity roused against them.

Even those political powers that seem best established have no other guarantee of their permanence beyond the opinions of a generation, the interests of a century, or often the life of one man. A law can modify that social state which seems most fixed and assured, and everything changes with it.

Like our years upon earth, the powers of society are all more or less transitory; they follow one another quickly, like the various cares of life; and there has never been a government supported by some invariable disposition of the human heart or one founded upon some interest that is immortal.

So long as a religion derives its strength from sentiments, instincts, and passions, which are reborn in like fashion in all periods of history, it can brave the assaults of time, or at least it can only be destroyed by another religion. But when a religion chooses to rely on the interests of this world, it becomes almost as fragile as all earthly powers. Alone, it may hope for immortality; linked to ephemeral powers, it follows their fortunes and often falls together with the passions of a day sustaining them.

Hence any alliance with any political power whatsoever is bound to be burdensome for religion. It does not need their support in order to live, and in serving them it may die.

The danger I have just pointed out exists at all times but is not always equally obvious.

There are centuries when governments appear immortal and others when society's existence seems frailer than that of a man.

Some constitutions keep the citizens in a sort of lethargic slumber, while others force them into feverish agitation.

When governments seem so strong and laws so stable, men do not see the danger that religion may run by allying itself with power.

When governments are clearly feeble and laws changeable, the danger is obvious to all, but often then there is no longer time to avoid it. One must therefore learn to perceive it from afar.

When a nation adopts a democratic social state and communities show republican inclinations, it becomes increasingly dangerous for religion to ally itself with authority. For the time is coming when power will pass from hand to hand, political theories follow one another, and men, laws, and even constitutions vanish or alter daily, and that not for a limited time but continually. Agitation and instability are natural elements in democratic republics, just as immobility and somnolence are the rule in absolute monarchies.

If the Americans, who change the head of state every four years, elect new legislators every two years and replace provincial administrators every year, and if the Americans, who have handed over the world of politics to the experiments of innovators, had not placed religion beyond their reach, what could it hold on to in the ebb and flow of human opinions? Amid the struggle of parties, where would the respect due to it be? What would become of its immortality when everything around it was perishing?

The American clergy were the first to perceive this truth and to act in conformity with it. They saw that they would have to give up religious influence if they wanted to acquire political power, and they preferred to lose the support of authority rather than to share its vicissitudes.

In America religion is perhaps less powerful than it has been at certain times and among certain peoples, but its influence is more lasting. It restricts itself to its own resources, of which no one can deprive it; it functions in one sphere only, but it pervades it and dominates there without effort.

On every side in Europe we hear voices deploring the absence of beliefs and asking how religion can be given back some remnant of its former power.

I think we should first consider attentively what ought to be the *natural state* of man with regard to religion at the present day; then, knowing what we can hope and what we must fear, we can clearly see the aim to which our efforts should be directed.

Two great dangers threaten the existence of religion: schism and indifference.

In ages of fervor it sometimes happens that men abandon their religion, but they only escape from its yoke in order to submit to that of another. Faith changes its allegiance but does not die. Then the former religion rouses in all hearts ardent love or implacable hatred; some leave it in anger, others cling to it with renewed ardor: beliefs differ, but irreligion is unknown.

But this is not the case when a religious belief is silently undermined by doctrines which I shall call negative because they assert the falseness of one religion but do not establish the truth of any other.

Then vast revolutions take place in the human mind without the apparent cooperation of the passions of man and almost without his knowledge. One sees some men lose, as from forgetfulness, the object of their dearest hopes. Carried away by an imperceptible current against which they have not the courage to struggle but to which they yield with regret, they abandon the faith they love to follow the doubt that leads them to despair.

In such ages beliefs are forsaken through indifference rather than from hate; without being rejected, they fall away. The unbeliever, no longer thinking religion true, still considers it useful. Paying attention to the human side of religious beliefs, he recognizes their sway over mores and their influence over laws. He understands their power to lead men to live in peace and gently to prepare them for death. Therefore he regrets his faith after losing it, and deprived of a blessing whose value he fully appreciates, he fears to take it away from those who still have it.

On the other hand, he who still believes is not afraid openly to avow his faith. He looks on those who do not share his hopes as unfortunate rather than as hostile; he knows he can win their esteem without following their example; hence he is at war with no man; for him society is not an arena where religion has to fight a relentless battle against a thousand enemies, and he loves his contemporaries, while condemning their weaknesses and sorrowing over their mistakes.

With unbelievers hiding their incredulity and believers avowing their faith, a public opinion favorable to religion takes shape; religion is loved, supported, and honored, and only by looking into the depths of men's souls will one see what wounds it has suffered.

The mass of mankind, never left without religious feeling, sees no impediments to established beliefs. The instinctive sense of another life without difficulty leads them to the foot of the altar and opens their hearts to the precepts and consolations of faith.

Why does this picture not apply to us?

There are some among us who have ceased to believe in Christianity without adopting any other religion.

There are others in a permanent state of doubt who already pretend no longer to believe.

Yet others are still believing Christians but do not dare to say so.

Amid these tepid friends and ardent adversaries there are finally a very few faithful ready to brave all obstacles and scorn all dangers for their beliefs. These have triumphed over human weakness to rise above common opinion. Carried away by the very force of this effort, they no longer know precisely where to stop. Since they have seen in their country that the first use made of independence has been to attack religion, they dread their contemporaries and recoil in alarm from the freedom which they seek. Imagining unbelief to be something new, they comprise all that is new in one indiscriminate animosity. They are at war with their age and country and see each opinion professed as a necessary enemy of faith.

That should not now be the natural state of men with regard to religion.

Therefore with us there must be some accidental and particular cause preventing the human spirit from following its inclination and driving it beyond those limits within which it should naturally remain.

I am profoundly convinced that this accidental and particular cause is the close union of politics and religion.

Unbelievers in Europe attack Christians more as political than as religious enemies; they hate the faith as the opinion of a party much more than as a mistaken belief, and they reject the clergy less because they are the representatives of God than because they are the friends of authority.

European Christianity has allowed itself to be intimately united with the powers of this world. Now that these powers are falling, it is as if it were buried under their ruins. A living being has been tied to the dead; cut the bonds holding it and it will arise.

I do not know what is to be done to give back European Christianity the energy of youth. God alone could do that, but at least it depends on men to leave faith the use of all the strength it still retains.

PHOEBE PALMER
1807 - 1874

Have you not noticed that in all the homeward way of the believer, new and unthought of phases of experience present themselves: I do not mean that these are experiences of which a wherefore may not be found infered from the Scriptures. These are in fact the divine chart which alone describes the way by which the redeemed of the Lord return to Zion.

But I have had during the past summer months some new experiences which I am sure I could have known little about, if my course had not been onward and upward. There is untold significance in the passage, "Then shall ye know if ye follow on to know." And let me assure you that my soul has of late been following hard after God. O with what indiscribable longings have I been pressing after greater conformity to the image of the heavenly. That these breathings after God and soul communings with Him have been transforming, I do not doubt.

The peculiar experience of which I am about to speak occurred August 1840, was preceded by humiliations of soul that I can scarcely attempt to describe. I am sure I know what David meant when he exclaimed "I am a worm and no man." I knew, and *felt* that I was shielded by the atonement, and therefore there was no condemnation, but the *Word of the Lord* was intensified, in a manner that human language cannot portray. For days, and nights in succession it penetrated my soul, as if it would part it asunder "sharper than any two-edged sword, piercing even to the dividing of soul, and spirit, and of the joints and marrow, and as a discerner of the thoughts and intents of the heart." My naked soul seemed to be tending as in the more immediate presence of the All-seeing, to whom all things are naked and open. Such piercing views of my utter nothingness, and the intense spirituality of the *Word of God*, seemingly would have crushed me, but I pleaded that my spirit might not fail before Him. In a sense beyond any former experiences I could say

"I have heard of thee by the hearing of the ear; but now mine eye seeth thee, wherefore I abhor myself in dust and ashes."

Previous to this deep realization of the sharpness of the two-edged sword, my experience had generally been joyous. Though I had not been without oft repeated conflicts, conquest had so quickly succeeded each conflict, that the joy of victory was ever in my heart, and on my lips. For many days in succession all sensible, joyous experiences were withheld, and I was shut up to the exercise of "naked faith in a naked promise." The cruel tempter said, that the Lord whom I loved supremely, had forsaken me, that I had surely in some unknown way offended. But I kept hold of the promise, "If in any thing ye be otherwise minded, God will reveal even this to you." And as God in answer to special and importunate prayer did not reveal anything, I still held strongly the shield of faith, saying sooner will I die than doubt. Often amid this great trial of my faith, did the providences of God seem to contradict the promises. Yet knowing that the ways of God are all perfect, I knew that in the end He would bring order out of apparent confusion.

Day and night the fight of *faith* went on. With the veteran warrior David I could say, night after night "He holdeth my eyes waking." And during all this season of conflict, it did not seem expedient that I should open my mind to any earthly friend. Believing then, as I do now, that God had hidden purposes, in these trainings of grace, intended for my instruction as an individual, and therefore not to be understood by another.

One morning, after a night of wakefulness spent as in the more immediate presence of Him who searcheth the heart and trieth the reins, I took the Word of the Lord in my hand. Before opening it I said, "O thou who in an ancient time did'st speak through the urim and thummin, wilt Thou not now speak to me through the *Word*, cause me now to learn the lesson that Thou wouldst teach me by these extraordinary exercises. I would not ask signs but only desire to apprehend the design of these peculiarly trying, penetrating, soul-searching influences.

It is the Holy Spirit alone that incited the Word, that can reveal to the soul its hidden meaning. On opening the precious Word as it lay before me my eye rested on the words, "In that day, saith the Lord of hosts, will I take thee O Zerubbabel my servant saith the Lord, and will make thee as a signet; for I have chosen thee

Born in New York in 1807, **Phoebe Palmer** devoted her life to the Methodist faith, attempting to join the two terrains of inner spirit and outer world through a program of Christian social reform. Palmer, who married physician Walter C. Palmer at the age of nineteen, began her journey to faith by attending Christian gatherings in her sister's home. She soon began preaching in revivals, spreading the doctrine of "entire sanctification," which teaches that every aspect of our lives can be pure and this purity can be attained through love for Christ. Palmer was an active worker for social reform, overseeing the construction of a mission in an underprivileged district of New York—an institution which contained free housing, schoolrooms, a chapel, and bathing facilities. Palmer was a popular writer in her day, the author of a number of books about Methodist faith. In the following excerpt, culled from Palmer's letters and writings, the evangelist expounds on faith and conversion.

saith the Lord of hosts." If I could disclose to you the revelations of that hour, the peculiarity of some tests through which I have passed would not seem mysterious, but only as might have been anticipated from the forshowings of that memorable hour.

The curtain of the future seemed uplifted. Yes! The Spirit took of things to come and revealed them to me. Perceptions of the great blessedness of the work to which the Lord might call me in identification with the great fundamental truth of Christianity *"Holiness to the Lord,"* were granted, but with these glorious perceptions, a view was also given of the trials I should be called to endure, in connection with my open identification with truth. Yea, said the Spirit, "A sword shall pierce through thine own soul also; that the thoughts of many hearts may be revealed."

Since that hour I have experimentally apprehended the solemn significance of my holy calling as never before. Perhaps you have wondered that when an onset against the doctrine or profession of holiness has been attempted, by partisans, it is oftener than with any one else that the name of your friend has been victimized. But in all, how wondrously has truth triumphed! And this leads me to what I have been wishing to record to the praise of infinite grace,—. Thus far my trials have been triumphs. Every new conflict has furnished an occasion for a new victory.

And now in praise of the faithfulness of God I wish to say, that just the lesson that the Lord taught me in that eventful hour thirty four years ago when He said, "*I have chosen thee as a signet*," has been most graciously fulfilled.

While He revealed to me that I should have great trials, He also assured me that I should have great triumphs. So great and continuous have been the triumphs of truth in connection with the precious theme of Holiness, that my life has been one great Psalm of "Glory to God in the highest."

WALT WHITMAN
1819 - 1892

SONG OF MYSELF

Swiftly arose and spread around me
the peace and knowledge that pass
all the argument of the earth,
And I know that the hand of God
is the promise of my own,

Considered by many to be the father of American poetry, **Walt Whitman** was born in 1819, in New York. An innovator in poetic form, Whitman wrote in blank verse and thought no subject beneath his consideration. His poems were so iconoclastic that no publisher would publish them, forcing him to publish his first volume at his own expense. That first volume, *Leaves of Grass*, contained the lyric poem "Song of Myself" from which these excerpts are culled. "Song of Myself" is a joyful piece of work in which the speaker sings of himself without any reservation or repression. The result is a unique vision of one who loves the world unconditionally, and while he may not worship a traditional God, he is certainly not without a deeply felt spirituality.

And I know that the spirit of God
is the brother of my own,
And that all the men ever born are
also my brothers, and the women
my sisters and lovers,
And that a kelson of the creation is love,
And limitless are leaves stiff or
drooping in the fields,
And brown ants in the little wells
beneath them,
And mossy scabs of the worm fence,
heap'd stones, elder, mullein
and poke-weed. . . .

I do not despise you priests, all time,
the world over,
My faith is the greatest of faiths
and the least of faiths,
Enclosing worship ancient and modern
and all between ancient and modern,
Believing I shall come again upon
the earth after five thousand years,
Waiting responses from oracles,
honoring the gods, saluting the sun,
Making a fetich of the first rock or stump,
powowing with sticks in the circle of obis,
Helping the llama or brahmin
as he trims the lamps of the idols,
Dancing yet through the streets in
a phallic procession, rapt and
austere in the woods a gymnosophist,

Drinking mead from the skull-cup,
  to Shastas and Vedas admirant,
  minding the Koran,

Walking the teokallis, spotted with
  gore from the stone and knife,
  beating the serpent-skin drum,

Accepting the Gospels, accepting him
  that was crucified, knowing assuredly
  that he is divine,

To the mass kneeling or the puritan's prayer
  rising, or sitting patiently in a pew,

Ranting and frothing in my insane crisis,
  or waiting dead-like till my spirit
  arouses me,

Looking forth on pavement and land,
  or outside of pavement and land,

Belonging to the winders of
  the circuit of circuits.

One of that centripetal and centrifugal gang
  I turn and talk like a man leaving charges
  before a journey.

Down-hearted doubters dull and excluded,

Frivolous, sullen, moping, angry, affected,
  dishearten'd, atheistical,

I know every one of you, I know the sea of
  torment, doubt, despair and unbelief.

How the flukes splash!

How they contort rapid as lightning,
  with spasms and spouts of blood!

Be at peace bloody flukes of doubters
  and sullen mopers,

I take my place among you as much
  as among any,

The past is the push of you, me, all,
  precisely the same.

And what is yet untried and afterward
  is for you, me, all, precisely the same.

I do not know what is untried and afterward,

But I know it will in its turn prove sufficient,
  and cannot fail.

Each who passes is consider'd, each
  who stops is consider'd, not a single
  one can it fail.

It cannot fail the young man
  who died and was buried,

Nor the young woman who died
  and was put by his side,

Nor the little child that peep'd in at the door,
  and then drew back and was never seen again,

Nor the old man who has lived
  without purpose, and feels it with
  bitterness worse than gall,

Nor him in the poor house tubercled
  by rum and the bad disorder,

Nor the numberless slaughter'd and wreck'd,
  nor the brutish call'd the ordure of humanity,

Nor the sacs merely floating with
  open mouths for food to slip in,

Nor any thing in the earth, or down
  in the oldest graves of the earth,

Nor any thing in the myriads of spheres,
  nor the myriads of myriads that
  inhabit them,

Nor the present, nor the least wisp
  that is known. . . .

And I say to mankind, Be not curious
  about God,

For I am who am curious about each
  am not curious about God,

(No array of terms can say how much I am
  at peace about God and about death.)

I hear and behold God in every object,
  yet understand God not in the least,

Nor do I understand who there can
  be more wonderful than myself.

Why should I wish to see God better
  than this day?

I see something of God each hour of the
  twenty-four, and each moment then,

In the faces of men and women I see God,
  and in my own face in the glass,

I find letters from God dropt in the street,
  and every one is sign'd by God's name,

And I leave them where they are,
  for I know that wheresoe'er I go,

Others will punctually come
  for ever and ever.

JULIA WARD HOWE

1819 - 1910

I remember moments in which the enlargement of my horizon of thought and of faith became strongly sensible to me, in the quiet of my reading, in my own room. A certain essay in the "Wandsbecker Bote" of Matthias Claudius ends thus: "And is he not also the God of the Japanese?" Foolish as it may appear, it had never struck me before that the God whom I had been taught to worship was the God of any peoples outside the limits of Judaism and Christendom. The suggestion shocked me at first, but, later on, gave me much satisfaction. Another such moment I recall when, having carefully read "Paradise Lost" to the very end, I saw presented before me the picture of an eternal evil, of Satan and his ministers subjugated indeed by God, but not conquered, and able to maintain against Him an opposition as eternal as his goodness. This appeared to me impossible, and I threw away, once and forever, the thought of the terrible hell which till then had always formed part of my belief. In its place, I cherished the persuasion that the victory of goodness must consist in making everything good, and that Satan himself could have no shield strong enough to resist permanently the divine power of the divine spirit.

*If her name doesn't strike a chord for you, her famous song certainly will. This social reformer and suffragette is the author of "The Battle Hymn of the Republic," the anthem of the Union troops during the Civil War and a classic of our nation's musical repertoire. **Julia Ward Howe** is also remembered for another American tradition; she invented Mother's Day. Here she describes the inspiration, both patriotic and religious in origin, that led her to write that great American anthem.*

This was a great emancipation for me, and I soon welcomed with joy every evidence in literature which tended to show that religion has never been confined to the experience of a particular race or nation, but has shown itself at all times, and under every variety of form, as a seeking for the divine and a reverence for the things unseen.

So much for study! . . .

It would be impossible for me to say how many times I have been called upon to rehearse the circumstances under which I wrote the "Battle Hymn of the Republic." I have also had occasion more than once to state the simple story in writing. As this oft-told tale has no unimportant part in the story of my life, I will briefly add it to these records. I distinctly remember that a feeling of discouragement came over me as I drew near the city of Washington at the time already mentioned. I thought of the women of my acquaintance whose sons or husbands were fighting our great battle; the women themselves serving in the hospitals, or busying themselves with the work of the Sanitary Commission. My husband, as already said, was beyond the age of military service, my eldest son but a stripling; my youngest was a child of not more than two years. I could not leave my nursery to follow the march of our armies, neither had I the practical deftness which the preparing and packing of sanitary stores demanded. Something seemed to say to me, "You would be glad to serve, but you cannot help any one; you have nothing to give, and there is nothing for you to do." Yet, because of my sincere desire, a word was given me to say, which did strengthen the hearts of those who fought in the field and of those who languished in the prison.

We were invited, one day, to attend a review of troops at some distance from the town. While we were engaged in watching the manœuvres, a sudden movement of the enemy necessitated immediate action. The review was discontinued, and we saw a detachment of soldiers gallop to the assistance of a small body of our men who were in imminent danger of being surrounded and cut off from retreat. The regiments remaining on the field were ordered to march to their cantonments. We returned to the city very slowly, of necessity, for the troops nearly filled the road. My dear minister was in the carriage with me, as were several other friends. To beguile the rather tedious drive, we sang from time to time snatches of the army songs so popular at that time, concluding, I think with

"John Brown's body lies a-mouldering in the ground;

His soul is marching on."

The soldiers seemed to like this, and answered back, "Good for you!" Mr. Clarke said, "Mrs. Howe, why do you not write some good words for that stirring tune?" I replied that I had often wished to do this, but had not as yet found in my mind any leading toward it.

I went to bed that night as usual, and slept, according to my wont, quite soundly. I awoke in the gray of the morning twilight; and as I lay waiting for the dawn, the long lines of the desired poem began to twine themselves in my mind. Having thought out all the stanzas, I said to myself, "I must get up and write these verses down, lest I fall asleep again and forget them." So, with a sudden effort, I sprang out of bed, and found in the dimness an old stump of a pen which I remembered to have used the day before. I scrawled the verses almost without looking at the paper. I had learned to do this when, on previous occasions, attacks of versification had visited me in the night, and I feared to have recourse to a light lest I should wake the baby, who slept near me. I was always obliged to decipher my scrawl before another night should intervene, as it was only legible while the matter was fresh in my mind. At this time, having completed my writing, I returned to bed and fell asleep, saying to myself, "I like this better than most things that I have written."

The poem, which was soon after published in the "Atlantic Monthly," was somewhat praised on its appearance, but the vicissitudes of the war so engrossed public attention that small heed was taken of literary matters. I knew, and was content to know, that the poem soon found its way to the camps, as I heard from time to time of its being sung in chorus by the soldiers.

As the war went on, it came to pass that Chaplain McCabe, newly released from Libby Prison, gave a public lecture in Washington, and recounted some of his recent experiences. Among them was the following: He and the other Union prisoners occupied one large, comfortless room, in which the floor was their only bed. An official in charge of them told them, one evening, that the Union arms had just sustained a terrible defeat. While they sat together in great sorrow, the negro who waited upon them whispered to one man that the officer had given them false information, and that the Union soldiers had, on the contrary, achieved an important victory. At this good news they all rejoiced, and presently made the walls ring with my Battle Hymn, which they sang in chorus, Chaplain McCabe leading. The lecturer recited the poem with such effect that those present began to inquire, "Who wrote this Battle Hymn?" It now became one of the leading lyrics of the war. In view of its success, one of my good friends said, "Mrs. Howe ought to die now, for she has done the best that she will ever do." I was not of this opinion, feeling myself still "full of days' works," although I did not guess at the new experiences which then lay before me.

HERMAN MELVILLE
1819 - 1891

FROM *MOBY DICK*

Father Mapple rose, and in a mild voice of unassuming authority ordered the scattered people to condense. "Starboard gangway, there! side away to larboard—larboard gangway to starboard! Midships! midships!"

There was a low rumbling of heavy sea-boots among the benches, and a still slighter shuffling of women's shoes, and all was quiet again, and every eye on the preacher.

He paused a little; then kneeling in the pulpit's bows, folded his large brown hands across his chest, uplifted his closed eyes, and offered a prayer so deeply devout that he seemed kneeling and praying at the bottom of the sea.

This ended, in prolonged solemn tones, like the continual tolling of a bell in a ship that is foundering at sea in a fog—in such tones he commenced reading the following hymn; but changing his manner towards the concluding stanzas, burst forth with a pealing exultation and joy —

Most famous for *Moby Dick, or the Great White Whale,* **Herman Melville** earned experience for his great novel the hard way; he began his career not as a writer, but as a sailor aboard a whaling ship. Melville's time spent on the high seas provided background and inspiration for a great many of his works, including *Billy Budd* and *Typee.* It was only in the 1920's, decades after Melville's death, that his work began to receive acclaim. This excerpt is a rousing description of worship at sea, as the chaplain of the Pequod leads services for the crew members.

"The ribs and terrors in the whale,
Arched over me a dismal gloom,
While all God's sun-lit waves rolled by,
And lift me deepening down to doom.

"I saw the opening maw of hell,
With endless pains and sorrows there;
Which none but they that feel can tell —
Oh, I was plunging to despair.
"In black distress, I called my God,
When I could scarce believe him mine,
He bowed his ear to my complaints —
No more the whale did me confine.

"With speed he flew to my relief,
As on a radiant dolphin borne;
Awful, yet bright, as lightning shone
The face of my Deliverer God.

"My song for ever shall record
  That terrible, that joyful hour;
I give the glory to my God,
  His all the mercy and the power."

Nearly all joined in singing this hymn, which swelled high above the howling of the storm. A brief pause ensued; the preacher slowly turned over the leaves of the Bible, and at last, folding his hand down upon the proper page, said: "Beloved shipmates, clinch the last verse of the first chapter of Jonah—'And God had prepared a great fish to swallow up Jonah.'

"Shipmates, this book, containing only four chapters—four yarns—is one of the smallest strands in the mighty cable of the Scriptures. Yet what depths of the soul does Jonah's deep sealine sound! what a pregnant lesson to us is this prophet! What a noble thing is that canticle in the fish's belly! How billow-like and boisterously grand! We feel the floods surging over us; we sound with him to the kelpy bottom of the waters; seaweed and all the slime of the sea is about us! But *what* is this lesson that the book of Jonah teaches? Shipmates, it is a two-stranded lesson; a lesson to us all as sinful men, and a lesson to me as a pilot of the living God. As sinful men, it is a lesson to us all, because it is a story of the sin, hard-heartedness, suddenly awakened fears, the swift punishment, repentance, prayers, and finally the deliverance and joy of Jonah. As with all sinners among men, the sin of this son of Amittai was in his wilful disobedience of the command of God— never mind now what that command was, or how conveyed—which he found a hard command. But all the things that God would have us do are hard for us to do—remember that—and hence, he oftener commands us than endeavors to persuade. And if we obey God, we must disobey ourselves; and it is in this disobeying ourselves, wherein the hardness of obeying God consists.

"With this sin of disobedience in him, Jonah still further flouts at God, by seeking to flee from Him. He thinks that a ship made by men, will carry him into countries where God does not reign, but only the Captains of this earth. He skulks about the wharves of Joppa, and seeks a ship that's bound for Tarshish. There lurks, perhaps, a hitherto unheeded meaning here. By all accounts Tarshish could have been no other city than the modern Cadiz. That's the opinion of learned men. And where is Cadiz, shipmates? Cadiz is in Spain; as far by water, from Joppa, as Jonah could possibly have sailed in those ancient days, when the Atlantic was

an almost unknown sea. Because Joppa, the modern Jaffa, shipmates, is on the most easterly coast of the Mediterranean, the Syrian; and Tarshish or Cadiz more than two thousand miles to the westward from that, just outside the Straits of Gibraltar. See ye not then, shipmates, that Jonah sought to flee world-wide from God? Miserable man! Oh! most contemptible and worthy of all scorn; with slouched hat and guilty eye, skulking from his God; prowling among the shipping like a vile burglar hastening to cross the seas. So disordered, self-condemning is his look, that had there been policemen in those days, Jonah, on the mere suspicion of something wrong, had been arrested ere he touched a deck. How plainly he's a fugitive! no baggage, not a hat-box, valise, or carpetbag,—no friends accompany him to the wharf with their adieux. At last, after much dodging search, he finds the Tarshish ship receiving the last items of her cargo; and as he steps on board to see its Captain in the cabin, all the sailors for the moment desist from hoisting in the goods, to mark the stranger's evil eye. Jonah sees this; but in vain he tries to look all ease and confidence; in vain essays his wretched smile. Strong intuitions of the man assure of the mariners he can be no innocent. In their gamesome but still serious way, one whispers to the other—'Jack, he's robbed a widow;' or, 'Joe, do you mark him; he's a bigamist;' or 'Harry lad, I guess he's the adulterer that broke jail in old Gomorrah, or belike, one of the missing murderers from Sodom.' Another runs to read the bill that's stuck against the spile upon the wharf to which the ship is moored, offering five hundred gold coins for the apprehension of a parricide, and containing a description of his person. He reads, and looks from Jonah to the bill; while all his sympathetic shipmates now crowd round Jonah, prepared to lay their hands upon him. Frighted Jonah trembles, and summoning all his boldness to his face, only looks so much the more a coward. He will not confess himself suspected; but that itself is strong suspicion. So he makes the best of it; and when the sailors find him not to be the man that is advertised, they let him pass, and he descends into the cabin.

"'Who's there?' cries the Captain at his busy desk, hurriedly making out his papers for the Customs— 'Who's there?' Oh! how that harmless question mangles Jonah! For the instant he almost turns to flee again. But he rallies. 'I seek a passage in this ship to Tarshish; how soon sail ye, sir?' Thus far the busy Captain had not looked up to Jonah, though the man now stands before him; but no sooner does he hear that hollow voice, than he darts a scrutinizing glance. 'We sail with the next coming tide,' at last he slowly answered, still intently eyeing him. 'No sooner, sir?'—'Soon enough for any honest man that goes a passenger.' Ha! Jonah, that's another stab. But he swiftly calls away the Captain from that scent. 'I'll sail with ye,'—he says,—'the passage money, how much is that?—I'll pay now.' For it is particularly written, shipmates, as if it were a thing not to be overlooked in this history, 'that he paid the fare thereof' ere the craft did sail. And taken with the context, this is full of meaning.

"Now Jonah's Captain, shipmates, was one whose discernment detects crime in any, but whose cupidity exposes it only in the penniless. In this world, shipmates, sin that pays its way can travel freely, and without a passport; whereas Virtue, if a pauper, is stopped at all frontiers. So Jonah's Captain prepares to test the length of Jonah's purse, ere he judge him openly. He charges him thrice the usual sum; and it's assented to. Then the Captain knows that Jonah is a fugitive; but at the same time resolves to help a flight that paves its rear with gold. Yet when Jonah fairly takes out his purse, prudent suspicions still molest the Captain. He rings every coin to find a counterfeit. Not a forger, any way, he mutters; and Jonah is put down for his passage. 'Point out my state-room, Sir,' says Jonah now, 'I'm travel-weary; I need sleep.' 'Thou look'st like it,' says the Captain, 'there's thy room.' Jonah enters, and would lock the door, but the lock contains no key. Hearing him foolishly fumbling there, the Captain laughs lowly to himself, and mutters something about the doors of convicts' cells being never allowed to be locked within. All dressed and dusty as he is, Jonah throws himself into his berth, and finds the little state-room ceiling almost resting on his forehead. The air is close, and Jonah gasps. Then, in that contracted hole, sunk, too, beneath the ship's water-line, Jonah feels the heralding presentiment of that stifling hour, when the whale shall hold him in the smallest of his bowel's wards.

"Screwed at its axis against the side, a swinging lamp slightly oscillates in Jonah's room; and the ship, heeling over towards the wharf with the weight of the last bales received, the lamp, flame and all, though in slight motion, still maintains a permanent obliquity with reference to the room; though, in truth, infallibly straight itself, it but made obvious the false, lying levels among which it hung. The lamp alarms and frightens Jonah; as lying in his berth his tormented eyes roll around the place, and this thus far successful fugitive finds no refuge for his restless glance. But that contradiction in the lamp more and more appals him. The floor, the ceiling, and the side, are all awry. 'Oh! so my conscience hangs in me!' he groans, 'straight upward, so it burns; but the chambers of my soul are all in crookedness!'

"Like one who after a night of drunken revelry hies to his bed, still reeling, but with conscience yet pricking him, as the plungings of the Roman race-horse but so much the more strike his steel tags into him; as one who in that miserable plight still turns and turns in giddy anguish, praying God for annihilation until the fit be passed; and at last amid the whirl of woe he feels, a deep stupor steals over him, as over the man who bleeds to death, for conscience is the wound, and there's naught to staunch it; so, after sore wrestlings in his berth, Jonah's prodigy of ponderous misery drags him drowning down to sleep.

"And now the time of tide has come; the ship casts off her cables; and from the deserted wharf the uncheered ship for Tarshish, all careening, glides to sea. That ship, my friends, was the first of recorded smugglers! the contraband was Jonah. But the sea rebels; he will not bear the wicked burden. A dreadful storm comes on, the ship is like to break. But now when the boatswain calls all hands to lighten her; when boxes, bales, and jars are clattering overboard; when the wind is shrieking, and the men are yelling, and every plank thunders with trampling feet right over Jonah's head; in all this raging tumult, Jonah sleeps his hideous sleep. He sees no black sky and raging sea, feels not the reeling timbers, and little hears he or heeds he the far rush of the mighty whale, which even now with open mouth is cleaving the seas after him. Aye, shipmates, Jonah was gone down into the sides of the ship—a berth in the cabin as I have taken it, and was fast asleep. But the frightened master comes to him, and shrieks in his dead ear, 'What meanest thou, O sleeper! arise!' Startled from his lethargy by that direful cry, Jonah staggers to his feet, and stumbling to the deck, grasps a shroud, to look out upon the sea. But at that moment he is sprung upon by a panther billow leaping over the bulwarks. Wave after wave thus leaps into the ship, and finding no speedy vent runs roaring fore and aft, till the mariners come nigh to drowning while yet afloat. And ever, as the white moon shows her affrighted face from the steep gullies in the blackness overhead, aghast Jonah sees the rearing bowsprit pointing high upward, but soon beat downward again towards the tormented deep.

"Terrors upon terrors run shouting through his soul. In all his cringing attitudes, the God-fugitive is now too plainly known. The sailors mark him; more and more certain grow their suspicions of him, and at last, fully to test the truth, by referring the whole matter to high Heaven, they fall to casting lots, to see for whose cause this great tempest was upon them. The lot is Jonah's; that discovered, then how furiously they mob him with their questions. 'What is thine occupation? Whence comest thou? Thy country? What people?' But mark now, my shipmates, the behavior of poor Jonah. The eager mariners but ask him who he is, and where from; whereas, they not only receive an answer to those questions, but likewise another answer to a question not put by them, but the unsolicited answer is forced from Jonah by the hard hand of God that is upon him.

" 'I am a Hebrew,' he cries—and then—'I fear the Lord the God of Heaven who hath made the sea and the dry land!' Fear him, O Jonah? Aye, well mightest thou fear the Lord God *then*! Straightway, he now goes on to make a full confession; whereupon the mariners became more and more appalled, but still are pitiful. For when Jonah, not yet supplicating God for mercy, since he but too well knew the darkness of his deserts,— when wretched Jonah cries out to them to take him and cast him forth into the sea, for he knew that for *his* sake this great tempest was upon them; they mercifully turn from him, and seek by other means to save the ship. But all in vain; the indignant gale howls louder; then, with one hand raised invokingly to God, with the other they not unreluctantly lay hold of Jonah.

"And now behold Jonah taken up as an anchor and dropped into the sea; when instantly an oily calmness floats out from the east, and the sea is still, as Jonah carries down the gale with him, leaving smooth water behind. He goes down in the whirling heart of such a masterless commotion that he scarce heeds the moment when he drops seething into the yawning jaws awaiting him; and the whale shoots-to all his ivory teeth, like so many white bolts, upon his prison. Then Jonah prayed unto the Lord out of the fish's belly. But observe his prayer, and learn a weighty lesson. For sinful as he is, Jonah does not weep and wail for direct deliverance. He feels that his dreadful punishment is just. He leaves all his deliverance to God, contenting himself with this, that spite of all his pains and pangs, he will still look towards His holy temple. And here, shipmates, is true and faithful repentance; not clamorous for pardon, but grateful for punishment. And how pleasing to God was this conduct in Jonah, is shown

in the eventual deliverance of him from the sea and the whale. Shipmates, I do not place Jonah before you to be copied for his sin but I do place him before you as a model for repentance. Sin not; but if you do, take heed to repent of it like Jonah."

While he was speaking these words, the howling of the shrieking, slanting storm without seemed to add new power to the preacher, who, when describing Jonah's sea-storm, seemed tossed by a storm himself. His deep chest heaved as with a ground-swell; his tossed arms seemed the warring elements at work; and the thunders that rolled away from off his swarthy brow, and the light leaping from his eye, made all his simple hearers look on him with a quick fear that was strange to them.

There now came a lull in his look, as he silently turned over the leaves of the Book once more; and, at last, standing motionless, with closed eyes, for the moment, seemed communing with God and himself.

But again he leaned over towards the people, and bowing his head lowly, with an aspect of the deepest yet manliest humility, he spake these words:

"Shipmates, God has laid but one hand upon you; both his hands press upon me. I have read ye by what murky light may be mine the lesson that Jonah teaches to all sinners; and therefore to ye, and still more to me, for I am a greater sinner than ye. And now how gladly would I come down from this mast-head and sit on the hatches there where you sit, and listen as you listen, while some one of you reads *me* that other and more awful lesson which Jonah teaches to *me*, as a pilot of the living God. How being an anointed pilot-prophet, or speaker of true things, and bidden by the Lord to sound those unwelcome truths in the ears of a wicked Nineveh, Jonah, appalled at the hostility he should raise, fled from his mission, and sought to escape his duty and his God by taking ship at Joppa. But God is everywhere; Tarshish he never reached. As we have seen, God came upon him in the whale, and swallowed him down to living gulfs of doom, and with swift slantings tore him along 'into the midst of the seas,' where the eddying depths sucked him ten thousand fathoms down, and the weeds were wrapped about his head,' and all the watery world of woe bowled over him. Yet even then beyond the reach of any plummet—'out of the belly of hell'—when the whale grounded upon the ocean's utmost bones, even then, God heard the engulphed, repenting prophet when he cried. Then God spake unto the fish; and from the shuddering cold and blackness of the sea, the whale came breeching up towards the warm and pleasant sun, and all the delights of air and earth; and 'vomited out Jonah upon the dry land;' when the word of the Lord came a second time; and Jonah, bruised and beaten—his ears, like two sea-shells, still multitudinously murmuring of the ocean—Jonah did the Almighty's bidding. And what was that, shipmates? To preach the Truth to the face of Falsehood! That was it!

"This, shipmates, this is that other lesson; and woe to that pilot of the living God who slights it. Woe to him whom this world charms from Gospel duty! Woe to him who seeks to pour oil upon the waters when God has brewed them into a gale! Woe to him who seeks to please rather than to appal! Woe to him whose good name is more to him than goodness! Woe to him who, in this world, courts not dishonor! Woe to him who would not be true, even though to be false were salvation! Yea, woe to him who, as the great Pilot Paul has it, while preaching to others is himself a castaway!"

He drooped and fell away from himself for a moment; then lifting his face to them again, showed a deep joy in his eyes, as he cried out with a heavenly enthusiasm,—"But oh! shipmates! on the starboard hand of every woe, there is a sure delight; and higher the top of that delight, than the bottom of the woe is deep. Is not the maintruck higher than the kelson is low? Delight is to him—a far, far upward, and inward delight—who against the proud gods and commodores of this earth, ever stands forth his own inexorable self. Delight is to him whose strong arms yet support him, when the ship of this base treacherous world has gone down beneath him. Delight is to him, who gives no quarter in the truth, and kills, burns, and destroys all sin though he pluck it out from under the robes of Senators and Judges. Delight,—top-gallant delight is to him, who acknowledges no law or lord, but the Lord his God, and is only a patriot to heaven. Delight is to him, whom all the waves of the billows of the seas of the boisterous mob can never shake from this sure Keel of the Ages. And eternal delight and deliciousness will be his, who coming to lay him down, can say with his final breath—O Father!—chiefly known to me by Thy rod—mortal or immortal, here I die. I have striven to be Thine, more than to be this world's, or mine own. Yet this is nothing; I leave eternity to Thee; for what is man that he should live out the lifetime of his God?"

He said no more, but slowly waving a benediction, covered his face with his hands, and so remained kneeling, till all the people had departed, and he was left alone in the place.

HARRIET BEECHER STOWE
1811 - 1896

Brunswick, July 9, 1851.

FREDERICK DOUGLASS, ESQ.:

Sir,—You may perhaps have noticed in your editorial readings a series of articles that I am furnishing for the "Era" under the title of "Uncle Tom's Cabin, or Life among the Lowly."

In the course of my story the scene will fall upon a cotton plantation. I am very desirous, therefore, to gain information from one who has been an actual laborer on one, and it occurred to me that in the circle of your acquaintance there might be one who would be able to communicate to me some such information as I desire. I have before me an able paper written by a Southern planter, in which the details and *modus operandi* are given from his point of sight. I am anxious to have something more from another standpoint. I wish to be able to make a picture that shall be graphic and true to nature in its details. Such a person as Henry Bibb, if in the country, might give me just the kind of information I desire. You may possibly know of some other person. I will subjoin to this letter a list of questions, which in that case you will do me a favor by inclosing to the individual, with the request that he will at earliest convenience answer them.

For some few weeks past I have received your paper through the mail, and have read it with great interest, and desire to return my acknowledgments for it. It will be a pleasure to me at some time when less occupied to contribute something to its columns. I have noticed with regret your sentiments on two subjects,—the church and African colonization, . . . with the more regret because I think you have a considerable share of reason for your feelings

A writer and an abolitionist, **Harriet Beecher Stowe** is most famous for her anti-slavery novel *Uncle Tom's Cabin,* which is considered by many to have been a catalyst for the Civil War. The daughter of a Congregationalist minister and sister of evangelist Henry Ward Beecher, Stowe was a devoted Christian. Her faith helped to inspire and steady her, even as her overnight fame turned to infamy in the Southern states. In the following letter to Frederick Douglass, Stowe identifies in passionate terms the link between anti-slavery reform and Christianity.

on both these subjects; but I would willingly, if I could, modify your views on both points.

In the first place you say the church is "pro-slavery." There is a sense in which this may be true. The American church of all denominations, taken as a body, comprises the best and most conscientious people in the country. I do not say it comprises none but these, or that none such are found out of it, but only if a census were taken of the purest and most high-principled men and women of the country, the majority of them would be found to be professors of religion in some of the various Christian denominations. This fact has given to the church great weight in this country,—the general and predominant spirit of intelligence and probity and piety of its majority has given it that degree of weight that it has the power to decide the great moral questions of the day. Whatever it unitedly and decidedly sets itself against as moral evil it can put down. In this sense the church is responsible for the sin of slavery. Dr. Barnes has beautifully and briefly expressed this on the last page of his work on slavery, when he says: "Not all the force out of the church could sustain slavery an hour if it were not sustained in it." It then appears that the church has the power to put an end to this evil and does not do it. In this sense she may be said to be pro-slavery. But the church has the same power over intemperance, and Sabbath-breaking, and sin of all kinds. There is not a doubt that if the moral power of the church were brought up to the New Testament standpoint it is sufficient to put an end to all these as well as to slavery. But I would ask you, Would you consider it a fair representation of the Christian church in this country to say that it is pro-intemperance, pro-Sabbath-breaking, and pro everything that it might put down if it were in a higher state of moral feeling? If you should make a list of all the abolitionists of the country, I think that you would find a majority of them in the church,—certainly some of the most influential and efficient ones are ministers.

I am a minister's daughter, and a minister's wife, and I have had six brothers in the ministry (one is in heaven); I certainly ought to know something of the feelings of ministers on this subject. I was a child in 1820 when the Missouri question was agitated, and one of the strongest and deepest impressions on my mind was that made by my father's sermons and prayers, and the anguish of his soul for the poor slave at that time. I remember his preaching drawing tears down the hardest faces of the old farmers in his congregation.

I will remember his prayers morning and evening in the family for "poor, oppressed, bleeding Africa," that the time of her deliverance might come; prayers offered with strong crying and tears, and which indelibly impressed my heart and made me what I am from my very soul, the enemy of all slavery. Every brother I have has been in his sphere a leading anti-slavery man. One of them was to the last the bosom friend and counselor of Lovejoy. As for myself and husband, we have for the last seventeen years lived on the border of a slave State, and we have never shrunk from the fugitives, and we have helped them with all we had to give. I have received the children of liberated slaves into a family school, and taught them with my own children, and it has been the influence that we found in the church and by the altar that has made us do all this. Gather up all the sermons that have been published on this offensive and unchristian Fugitive Slave Law, and you will find that those against it are numerically more than those in its favor, and yet some of the strongest opponents have not published their sermons. Out of thirteen ministers who meet with my husband weekly for discussion of moral subjects, only three are found who will acknowledge or obey this law in any shape.

After all, my brother, the strength and hope of your oppressed race does lie in the church,—in hearts united to Him of whom it is said, "He shall spare the souls of the needy, and precious shall their blood be in his sight." Everything is against you, but Jesus Christ is for you, and He has not forgotten his church, misguided and erring though it be. I have looked all the field over with despairing eyes; I see no hope but in Him. This movement must and will become a purely religious one. The light will spread in churches, the tone of feeling will rise, Christians North and South will give up all connection with, and take up their testimony against, slavery, and thus the work will be done.

ROBERT E. LEE
1807 - 1870

I will commence this holy day by writing to you. My heart is filled with gratitude to Almighty God for His unspeakable mercies with which He has blessed us in this day, for those He has granted us from the beginning of life, and particularly for those He has vouchsafed us during the past year. What should have

On Christmas Day in 1862, **Robert E. Lee** wrote a letter to his wife that would underscore Lincoln's ironic summary of the Civil War in Lincoln's Second Inaugural: "Both invokes his aid against the other." Lee does not pray for God's guidance, but rather for God's guidance for his enemies.

become of us without His crowning help and protection? Oh, if our people would only recognise it and cease from vain self-boasting and adulation, how strong would be my belief in final success and happiness to our country! But what a cruel thing is war; to separate and destroy families and friends, and mar the purest joys and happiness God has granted us in this world; to fill our hearts with hatred instead of love for our neighbours, and to devastate the fair face of this beautiful world! I pray that, on this day when only peace and good-will are preached to mankind, better thoughts may fill the hearts of our enemies and turn them to peace.

ABRAHAM LINCOLN
1809 - 1865

A t this second appearing to take the oath of the presidential office, there is less occasion for an extended address than there was at the first. Then a statement, somewhat in detail, of a course to be pursued, seemed fitting and proper. Now at the expiration of four years, during which public declarations have been constantly

I have been schooled that an education in **Lincoln** is an education in American ideals. His Second Inaugural, arriving near the end of the great war and the great life, is suffused with the faith . . . and the insight that only the harshest suffering can birth.

called forth on every point and phase of the great contest which still absorbs the attention and engrosses the energies of the nation, little that is new could be presented. The progress of our arms, upon which all else chiefly depends, is as well known to the public as to myself; and it is, I trust, reasonably satisfactory and encouraging to all. With high hope for the future, no prediction in regard to it is ventured.

On the occasion corresponding to this four years ago, all thoughts were anxiously directed to an impending civil-war. All dreaded it—all sought to avert it. While the inaugural address was being

delivered from this place, devoted altogether to saving the Union without war, insurgent agents were in the city seeking to destroy it without war—seeking to dissolve the Union, and divide effects, by negotiation. Both parties deprecated war; but one of them would make war rather than let the nation survive; and the other would accept war rather than let it perish. And the war came.

One-eighth of the whole population were colored slaves, not distributed generally over the Union, but localized in the Southern part of it. These slaves constituted a peculiar and powerful interest. All knew that this interest was, somehow, the cause of the war. To strengthen, perpetuate, and extend this interest was the object for which the insurgents would rend the Union, even by war; while the government claimed no right to do more than to restrict the territorial enlargement of it.

Neither party expected for the war, the magnitude, or the duration, which it has already attained. Neither anticipated that the *cause* of the conflict might cease with, or even before, the conflict itself should cease. Each looked for an easier triumph, and a result less fundamental and astounding. Both read the same Bible, and pray to the same God; and each invokes His aid against the other. It may seem strange that any men should dare to ask a just God's assistance in wringing their bread from the sweat of other men's faces; but let us judge not that we be not judged. The prayers of both could not be answered; that of neither has been answered fully.

The Almighty has His own purposes. "Woe unto the world because of offences! for it must needs be that offences come; but woe to that man by whom the offence cometh! "If we shall suppose that American slavery is one of those offences which, in the providence of God, must needs come, but which, having continued through His appointed time, he now wills to remove, and that he gives to both North and South this terrible war, as the woe due to those by whom the offence came, shall we discern therein any departure from those divine attributes which the believers in a Living God always ascribe to him? Fondly do we hope—fervently do we pray—that this mighty scourge of war may speedily pass away. Yet, if God wills that it continue until all the wealth piled by the bond-man's two hundred and fifty years of unrequited toil shall be sunk, and until every drop of blood drawn with the lash shall be paid by another drawn with the sword, as was said three thousand years ago, so still it must be said, "The judgments of the Lord are true and righteous altogether."

With malice toward none; with charity for all; with firmness in the right, as God gives us to see the right, let us strive on to finish the work we are in; to bind up the nation's wounds; to care for him who shall have borne the battle, and for his widow, and his orphan—to do all which may achieve and cherish a just, and a lasting peace, among ourselves, and with all nations.

EMILY DICKINSON
1830 - 1886

Amherst, *Jan.* 29, 1850

Very Dear A.,—The folks have all gone away; they thought that they left me alone, and contrived things to amuse me should they stay long, and *I* be lonely. Lonely, indeed,—they didn't look, and they couldn't have seen if they had, who should bear me company. *Three* here, instead of *one,* wouldn't it scare them? A curious trio, part earthly and part spiritual two of us, the other, all heaven, and no earth. *God* is sitting here, looking into my very soul to see if I think right thoughts. Yet I am not afraid, for I try to be right and good; and He knows every one of my struggles. He looks very gloriously, and everything bright seems dull beside Him; and I don't dare to look directly at Him for fear I shall die. Then *you* are here, dressed in that quiet black gown and cap,—that funny little cap I used to laugh at you about,—and you don't appear to be thinking about anything in particular,—not in one of your *breaking-dish* moods, I take it. You seem aware that I'm writing you, and are amused, I should think, at any such friendly manifestation when you are already present. *Success,* however, even in making a fool of myself, isn't to be despised; so I shall persist in writing, and you may in laughing at me,—if you are fully aware of the value of time as regards your immortal spirit. I can't

The daughter of a Massachusetts minister, **Emily Dickinson,** whose extraordinary poetry was not published during her lifetime, lived the life of a virtual recluse, rarely venturing out and never marrying. Her relationship to faith was a complex one. We catch her as a teenager in this letter to friend Mrs. A. P. Strong, pondering the earthly presence of the Almighty. The questions she poses about God were to evolve into decidedly transcendental spiritual leanings in later life. But here we see her as a young woman, full of curiosity and a charming if vivid imagination.

say that I advise you to laugh; but if you are punished, and I warned you, that can be no business of mine. So I fold up my arms, and leave you to fate—may it deal very kindly with you! The trinity winds up with me, as you may have surmised, and I certainly wouldn't be at the fag-end but for civility to you. This self-sacrificing spirit will be the ruin of me!

I am occupied principally with a cold just now, and the dear creature *will* have so much attention that my time slips away amazingly. It has heard *so* much of New Englanders, of their kind attentions to strangers, that it's come all the way from the Alps to determine the truth of the tale. It says the half wasn't told it, and I begin to be afraid it wasn't. Only think—came all the way from that distant Switzerland to find what was the truth! Neither husband, protector, nor friend accompanied it, and so utter a state of loneliness gives friends if nothing else. You are dying of curiosity; let me arrange that pillow to make your exit easier. I stayed at home all Saturday afternoon, and treated some disagreeable people who insisted upon calling here as tolerably as I could; when evening shades began to fall, I turned upon my heel, and walked. Attracted by the gayety visible in the street, I still kept walking till a little creature pounced upon a thin shawl I wore, and commenced riding. I stopped, and begged the creature to alight, as I was to hoard them! They tell me those were poor early have different views of gold. I don't know how that is.

God is not so wary as we, else He would give us no friends, lest we forget Him! The charms of the heaven in the bush are superseded, I fear, by the heaven in the hand, occasionally.

Summer stopped since you were here. Nobody noticed her—that is, no men and women. Doubtless, the fields are rent by petite anguish, and "mourners go about" the woods. But this is not for us. Business enough indeed, our stately resurrection! A special courtesy, I judge, from what the clergy say! To the "natural man" bumblebees would seem an improvement, and a spicing of birds, but far be it from me to impugn such majestic tastes!

Our pastor says we are a "worm." How is that reconciled? "Vain, sinful worm" is possibly of another species.

Do you think we shall "see God"? Think of Abraham strolling with Him in genial promenade!

The men are mowing the second hay. The cocks are smaller than the first, and spicier. I would distil a cup, and bear to all my friends, drinking to her no more astir, by beck, or burn, or moor!

Good-night, Mr. Bowles. This is what they say who come back in the morning; also the closing paragraph on repealed lips. Confidence in daybreak modifies dusk.

Blessings for Mrs. Bowles, and kisses for the bairns' lips. We want to see you, Mr. Bowles, but spare you the rehearsal of "familiar truths."

Good-night,

Emily

LOUISA MAY ALCOTT
1832 - 1888

The author of *Little Women* began to write as a means to support herself and her struggling family, who were troubled by poverty in nineteenth-century Massachusetts. The daughter of a well-respected educator, **Alcott** grew up in a stimulating and intellectual environment that included such notables as Thoreau and Emerson. She worked as a nurse during the Civil War as well as on the battle grounds of the temperance and women's suffrage movements. She had an informal, rather pantheistic attitude toward faith, as is apparent in this journal entry in which she experiences the nearness of God during a walk in the woods.

I had an early run in the woods before the dew was off the grass. The moss was like velvet, and as I ran under the arches of yellow and red leaves, I sang for joy, my heart was so bright and the world so beautiful. I stopped at the end of the walk and saw the sunshine out over the wide "virginia meadows." It seemed like going through a dark life or grave into heaven beyond. A very strange and solemn feeling came over me as I stood there, with no sound but the rustle of the pines, no one near me, and the sun so glorious, as for me alone. It seemed as if I *felt* God as I never did before, and I prayed in my heart that I might keep that happy sense of nearness all my life.

MARK TWAIN
1835 - 1910

FIRST SELECTION

The day of rest comes but once a week, and sorry I am that it does not come oftener. Man is so constituted that he can stand more rest than this. I often think regretfully that it would have been so easy to have two Sundays in a week, and yet it was not so ordained. The omnipotent Creator could have made the world in three days just as easily as he made it in six, and this would have doubled the Sundays. Still it is not our place to criticise the wisdom of the Creator. When we feel a depraved inclination to question the judgment of Providence in stacking up double eagles in the coffers of Michael Reese and leaving better men to dig for a livelihood, we ought to stop and consider that we are not expected to help order things, and so drop the subject. If all-powerful Providence grew weary after six days' labor, such worms as we are might reasonably expect to break down in three, and so require two Sundays—but as I said before, it ill becomes us to hunt up flaws in matters which are so far out of our jurisdiction. I hold that no man can meddle with the exclusive affairs of Providence and offer suggestions for their improvement, without making himself in a manner conspicuous. Let us take things as we find them— though, I am free to confess, it goes against the grain to do it, sometimes.

What put me into this religious train of mind, was attending church at Dr. Wadsworth's this morning. I had not been to church before for many months, because I never could get a pew, and therefore had to sit in the gallery, among the sinners. I stopped that because my proper place was down among the elect, inasmuch as I was brought up Presbyterian, and consider myself a brevet member of Dr. Wadsworth's church. I always was a brevet. I was sprinkled in infancy, and look upon that as conferring the rank of Brevet Presbyterian. It affords none of the emoluments of the Regular Church—simply confers honorable rank upon the recipient and the right to be punished as a Presbyterian hereafter; that is, the substantial Presbyterian punishment of fire and brimstone instead of this heterodox hell of remorse of conscience of these blamed wildcat religions. The heaven and hell of the wildcat religions are vague and ill defined but there is nothing mixed about the Presbyterian heaven and hell. The Presbyterian hell is all about misery; the heaven all happiness—nothing to do. But when a man dies on a wildcat basis, he will never rightly know hereafter which department he is in—but he will think he is in hell anyhow, no matter which place he goes to; because in the good place they pro-gress, pro-gress, pro-gress—study, study, study, all the time—and if this

Hard not to thank the Lord for **Twain**. If God has a sense of humor (and I believe He does because I believe we are created in His image), then Twain got a free pass, and one which he surely enjoys displaying to Presbyterians arriving via conventional passage. Two of his essays follow— "Reflections on the Sabbath" and "Thoughts on God."

isn't hell I don't know what is; and in the bad place he will be worried by remorse of conscience. Their bad place is preferable, though, because eternity is long, and before a man got half through it he would forget what it was he had been so sorry about. Naturally he would then become cheerful again; but the party who went to heaven would go on progressing and progressing, and studying and studying until he would finally get discouraged and wish he were in hell, where he wouldn't require such a splendid education.

Dr. Wadsworth never fails to preach an able sermon; but every now and then, with an admirable assumption of not being aware of it, he will get off a firstrate joke and then frown severely at any one who is surprised into smiling at it. This is not fair. It is like throwing a bone to a dog and then arresting him with a look just as he is going to seize it. Several people there on Sunday suddenly laughed and as suddenly stopped again, when he gravely gave the Sunday school books a blast and spoke of "the good little boys in them who always went to Heaven, and the bad little boys who infallibly got drowned on Sunday," and then swept a savage frown around the house and blighted every smile in the congregation.

SECOND SELECTION

How often we are moved to admit the intelligence exhibited in both the designing and the execution of some of His works. Take the fly, for instance. The planning of the fly was an application of pure intelligence, morals not being concerned. Not one of us could have planned the fly, not one of us could have constructed him; and no one would have considered it wise to try, except under an assumed name. It is believed by some that the fly was introduced to meet a long-felt want. In the course of ages, for some reason or other, there have been millions of these persons, but out of this vast multitude there has not been one who has been willing to explain what the want was. At least satisfactorily. A few have explained that there was need of a creature to remove disease-breeding garbage; but these being then asked to explain what long-felt want the disease-breeding garbage was introduced to supply, they have not been willing to undertake the contract.

There is much inconsistency concerning the fly. In all the ages he has not had a friend, there has never been a person in the earth who could have been persuaded to intervene between him and extermination; yet billions of persons have excused the Hand that made him—and this without a blush. Would they have excused a Man in the same circumstances, a man positively known to have invented the fly? On the contrary. For the credit of the race let us believe it would have been all day with that man. Would these persons consider it just to reprobate in a child, with its undeveloped morals, a scandal which they would overlook in the Pope?

When we reflect that the fly was not invented for pastime, but in the way of business; that he was not flung off in a heedless moment and with no object in view but to pass the time, but was the fruit of long and pains-taking labor and calculation, and with a definite and far-reaching purpose in view; that his character and conduct were planned out with cold deliberation; that his career was foreseen and foreordered, and that there was no want which he could supply, we are hopelessly puzzled, we cannot understand the moral lapse that was able to render possible the conceiving and the consummation of this squalid and malevolent creature.

Let us try to think the unthinkable; let us try to imagine a Man of a sort willing to invent the fly; that is to say, a man destitute of feeling; a man willing to wantonly torture and harass and persecute myriads of creatures who had never done him any harm and could not if they wanted to, and—the majority of them—poor dumb things not even aware of his existence. In a word, let us try to imagine a man with so singular and so lumbering a code of morals as this: that it is fair and right to send afflictions upon the *just*—upon the unoffending as well as upon the offending, without discrimination.

If we can imagine such a man, that is the man that could invent the fly, and send him out on his mission and furnish him his orders: 'Depart into the uttermost corners of the earth, and diligently do your appointed work. Persecute the sick child; settle upon its eyes, its face, its hands, and gnaw and pester and sting; worry and fret and madden the worn and tried mother who watches by the child, and who humbly prays for mercy and relief with the pathetic faith of the deceived and the unteachable. Settle upon the soldier's festering wounds in field and hospital and drive him frantic while he also prays, and betweentimes curses, with none to listen but you, Fly, who get all the petting and all the protection, without even praying for it. Harry and persecute the forlorn and forsaken wretch who is perishing of the plague, and in his terror and despair praying; bite, sting, feed upon his ulcers, dabble your feet in his rotten blood, gum them thick with plague-germs— feet cunningly designed and perfected for this function ages ago in the beginning—carry this freight to a hundred tables, among the just and the unjust, the high and the low, and walk over the food and gaum it with filth and death. Visit all; allow no man peace till he get it in the grave; visit and afflict the hard-worked and unoffending horse, mule, ox, ass, pester the patient cow, and all the kindly animals that labor without fair reward here and perish without hope of it hereafter; spare no creature, wild or tame; but wheresoever you find one, make his life a misery, treat him as the innocent deserve; and so please Me and increase My glory Who made the fly.'

We hear much about His patience and forbearance and long-suffering; we hear nothing about our own, which much exceeds it. We hear much about His mercy and kindness and goodness—in words—the words of His Book and of His pulpit—and the meek multitude is content with this evidence, such as it is, seeking no further; but whoso searcheth after a concreted sample of it will in time acquire fatigue. There being no instances of it. For what are gilded as mercies are not in any recorded case more than mere common justices, and *due*—due without thanks or compliment. To rescue without personal risk a cripple from a burning house is not a mercy, it is a mere commonplace duty; anybody would do it that could. And not by proxy, either—delegating the work but confiscating the credit for it. If men neglected 'God's poor' and 'God's stricken and helpless ones' as He does, what would become of them? The answer is to be found in those dark lands where man follows His example and turns his indifferent back upon them: they get no help at all; they cry, and plead and pray in vain, they linger and suffer, and miserably die. If you will look at the matter rationally and without prejudice, the proper place to hunt for the *facts* of His mercy, is not where man does the mercies and He collects the praise, but in those regions where He has the field to Himself.

It is plain that there is one moral law for heaven and another for the earth. The pulpit assures us that wherever we see suffering and sorrow which we can relieve and do not do it, we sin, heavily. *There was never yet a case of suffering or sorrow which God could not relieve.* Does He sin, then? If He is the Source of Morals He does—certainly nothing can be plainer than that, you will admit. Surely the Source of law cannot violate law and stand unsmirched; surely the judge upon the bench cannot forbid crime and then revel in it himself unreproached. Nevertheless we have this curious spectacle: daily the trained parrot in the pulpit gravely delivers himself of these ironies, which he has acquired at second-hand and adopted without examination, to a trained congregation which accepts them without examination, and neither the speaker nor the hearer laughs at himself. It does seem as if we ought to be humble when we are at a bench-show, and not put on airs of intellectual superiority there.

early 1890s

Black Elk
1863 - 1950

BEING THE LIFE STORY OF A HOLY MAN OF THE OGLALA SIOUX
III
THE GREAT VISION

What happened after that until the summer I was nine years old is not a story. There were winters and summers, and they were good; for the Wasichus had made their iron road[1] along the Platte and traveled there. This had cut the bison herd in two, but those that stayed in our country with us were more than could be counted, and we wandered without trouble in our land.

Now and then the voices would come back when I was out alone, like someone calling me, but what they wanted me to do I did not know. This did not happen very often, and when it did not happen, I forgot about it; for I was growing taller and was riding horses now and could shoot prairie chickens and rabbits with my bow. The boys of my people began very young to learn the ways of men, and no one taught us; we just learned by doing what we saw, and we were warriors at a time when boys now are like girls.

It was the summer when I was nine years old, and our people were moving slowly towards the Rocky Mountains. We camped one evening in a valley beside a little

In this excerpt from *Black Elk Speaks*, **Black Elk** recounts the story of his first vision, which came to him at the age of nine. Black Elk, who was an Oglala Sioux holy man and a second cousin of Crazy Horse, gained a modicum of fame when his story was recounted and published by poet John Neihardt. The Sioux medicine man, who was born sometime in the mid-nineteenth century, lived through the great battles between whites and Native Americans, battles that marked the end of the frontier era.

---

[1] The Union Pacific Railway.

creek just before it ran into the Greasy Grass,[2] and there was a man by the name of Man Hip who liked me and asked me to eat with him in his tepee.

While I was eating, a voice came and said: "It is time; now they are calling you." The voice was so loud and clear that I believed it, and I thought I would just go where it wanted me to go. So I got right up and started. As I came out of the tepee, both my thighs began to hurt me, and suddenly it was like waking from a dream, and there wasn't any voice. So I went back into the tepee, but I didn't want to eat. Man Hip looked at me in a strange way and asked me what was wrong. I told him that my legs were hurting me.

The next morning the camp moved again, and I was riding with some boys. We stopped to get a drink from a creek, and when I got off my horse, my legs crumpled under me and I could not walk. So the boys helped me up and put me on my horse; and when we camped again that evening, I was sick. The next day the camp moved on to where the different bands of our people were coming together, and I rode in a pony drag, for I was very sick. Both my legs and both my arms were swollen badly and my face was all puffed up.

When we had camped again, I was lying in our tepee and my mother and father were sitting beside me. I could see out through the opening, and there two men were coming from the clouds, head-first like arrows slanting down, and I knew they were the same that I had seen before. Each now carried a long spear, and from the points of these a jagged lightning flashed. They came clear down to the ground this time and stood a little way off and looked at me and said: "Hurry! Come! Your Grandfathers are calling you!"

Then they turned and left the ground like arrows slanting upward from the bow. When I got up to follow, my legs did not hurt me any more and I was very light. I went outside the tepee, and yonder where the men with flaming spears were going, a little cloud was coming very fast. It came and stooped and took me and turned back to where it came from, flying fast. And when I looked down I could see my mother and my father yonder, and I felt sorry to be leaving them.

Then there was nothing but the air and the swiftness of the little cloud that bore me and those two men still leading up to where white clouds were piled like mountains on a wide blue plain, and in them thunder beings lived and leaped and flashed.

Now suddenly there was nothing but a world of cloud, and we three were there alone in the middle of a great white plain with snowy hills and mountains staring at us; and it was very still; but there were whispers.

Then the two men spoke together and they said: "Behold him, the being with four legs!"

I looked and saw a bay horse standing there, and he began to speak: "Behold me!" he said, "My life-history you shall see." Then he wheeled about to where the sun goes down, and said: "Behold them! Their history you shall know."

I looked, and there were twelve black horses yonder all abreast with necklaces of bison hoofs, and they were beautiful, but I was frightened, because their manes were lightning and there was thunder in their nostrils.

Then the bay horse wheeled to where the great white giant lives (the north) and said: "Behold!" And yonder there were twelve white horses all abreast. Their manes were flowing like a blizzard wind and from their noses came a roaring, and all about them white geese soared and circled.

Then the bay wheeled round to where the sun shines continually (the east) and bade me look; and there twelve sorrel horses, with necklaces of elk's teeth, stood abreast with eyes that glimmered like the day-break star and manes of morning light.

Then the bay wheeled once again to look upon the place where you are always facing (the south), and yonder stood twelve buckskins all abreast with horns upon their heads and manes that lived and grew like trees and grasses.

And when I had seen all these, the bay horse said: "Your Grandfathers are having a council. These shall take you; so have courage."

Then all the horses went into formation, four abreast—the blacks, the whites, the sorrels, and the buckskins—and stood behind the bay, who turned now to the west and neighed; and yonder suddenly the sky was terrible with a storm of plunging horses in all colors that shook the world with thunder, neighing back.

Now turning to the north the bay horse whinnied, and yonder all the sky roared with a mighty wind of running horses in all colors, neighing back.

And when he whinnied to the east, there too the sky was filled with glowing clouds of manes and tails of horses in all colors singing back. Then to the south he called, and it was crowded with many colored, happy horses, nickering.

---

2 The Little Big Horn River.

Then the bay horse spoke to me again and said: "See how your horses all come dancing!" I looked, and there were horses, horses everywhere—a whole skyful of horses dancing round me.

"Make haste!" the bay horse said; and we walked together side by side, while the blacks, the whites, the sorrels, and the buckskins followed, marching four by four.

I looked about me once again, and suddenly the dancing horses without number changed into animals of every kind and into all the fowls that are, and these fled back to the four quarters of the world from whence the horses came, and vanished.

Then as we walked, there was a heaped up cloud ahead that changed into a tepee, and a rainbow was the open door of it; and through the door I saw six old men sitting in a row.

The two men with the spears now stood beside me, one on either hand, and the horses took their places in their quarters, looking inward, four by four. And the oldest of the Grandfathers spoke with a kind voice and said: "Come right in and do not fear." And as he spoke, all the horses of the four quarters neighed to cheer me. So I went in and stood before the six, and they looked older than men can ever be—old like hills, like stars.

The oldest spoke again: "Your Grandfathers all over the world are having a council, and they have called you here to teach you." His voice was very kind, but I shook all over with fear now, for I knew that these were not old men, but the Powers of the World. And the first was the Power of the West; the second, of the North; the third, of the East; the fourth, of the South; the fifth, of the Sky; the sixth, of the Earth. I knew this, and was afraid, until the first Grandfather spoke again: "Behold them yonder where the sun goes down, the thunder beings! You shall see, and have from them my power; and they shall take you to the high and lonely center of the earth that you may see; even to the place where the sun continually shines, they shall take you there to understand."

And as he spoke of understanding, I looked up and saw the rainbow leap with flames of many colors over me.

Now there was a wooden cup in his hand and it was full of water and in the water was the sky.

"Take this," he said. "It is the power to make live, and it is yours."

Now he has a bow in his hands. "Take this," he said. "It is the power to destroy, and it is yours."

Then he pointed to himself and said: "Look close at him who is your spirit now, for you are his body and his name is Eagle Wing Stretches."

And saying this, he got up very tall and started running toward where the sun goes down; and suddenly he was a black horse that stopped and turned and looked at me, and the horse was very poor and sick; his ribs stood out.

Then the second Grandfather, he of the North, arose with a herb of power in his hand, and said: "Take this and hurry." I took and held it toward the black horse yonder. He fattened and was happy and came prancing to his place again and was the first Grandfather sitting there.

The second Grandfather, he of the North, spoke again: "Take courage, younger brother," he said; "on earth a nation you shall make live, for yours shall be the power of the white giant's wing, the cleansing wind." Then he got up very tall and started running toward the north; and when he turned toward me, it was a white goose wheeling. I looked about me now, and the horses in the west were thunders and the horses of the north were geese. And the second Grandfather sang two songs that were like this:

"They are appearing, may you behold!
They are appearing, may you behold!
The thunder nation is appearing, behold!

They are appearing, may you behold!
They are appearing, may you behold!
The white geese nation is appearing, behold!"

And now it was third Grandfather who spoke, he of where the sun shines continually. "Take courage, younger brother," he said, "for across the earth they shall take you!" Then he pointed to where the daybreak star was shining, and beneath the star two men were flying. "From them you shall have power," he said, "from them who have awakened all the beings of the earth with roots and legs and wings." And as he said this, he held in his hand a peace pipe which had a spotted eagle outstretched upon the stem; and this eagle seemed alive, for it was poised there, fluttering, and its eyes were looking at me. "With this pipe," the Grandfather said, "you shall walk upon the earth, and whatever sickens there you shall make well." Then he pointed to a man who was bright red all over, the color of good and of plenty, and as he pointed, the red man lay down and rolled and changed into a bison that got up and galloped toward the sorrel horses of the east, and they too turned to bison, fat and many.

And now the fourth Grandfather spoke, he of the place where you are always facing (the south), whence comes the power to grow. "Younger brother," he said, "with the powers of the four quarters you shall walk, a relative. Behold, the living center of a nation I shall give you, and with it many you shall save." And I saw that he was holding in his hand a bright red stick that was alive, and as I looked it sprouted at the top and sent forth branches, and on the branches many leaves came out and murmured and in the leaves the birds began to sing. And then for just a little while I thought I saw beneath it in the shade the circled villages of people and every living thing with roots or legs or wings, and all were happy. "It shall stand in the center of the nation's circle," said the Grandfather, "a cane to walk with and a people's heart; and by your powers you shall make it blossom."

Then when he had been still a little while to hear the birds sing, he spoke again: "Behold the earth!" So I looked down and saw it lying yonder like a hoop of peoples, and in the center bloomed the holy stick that was a tree, and where it stood there crossed two roads, a red one and a black. "From where the giant lives (the north) to where you always face (the south) the red road goes, the road of good," the Grandfather said, "and on it shall your nation walk. The black road goes from where the thunder beings live (the west) to where the sun continually shines (the east), a fearful road, a road of troubles and of war. On this also you shall walk, and from it you shall have the power to destroy a people's foes. In four ascents you shall walk the earth with power."

I think he meant that I should see four generations, counting me, and now I am seeing the third.

Then he rose very tall and started running toward the south, and was an elk; and as he stood among the buckskins yonder, they too were elks.

Now the fifth Grandfather spoke, the oldest of them all, the Spirit of the Sky. "My boy," he said, "I have sent for you and you have come. My power you shall see!" He stretched his arms and turned into a spotted eagle hovering. "Behold," he said, "all the wings of the air shall come to you, and they and the winds and the stars shall be like relatives. You shall go across the earth with my power." Then the eagle soared above my head and fluttered there; and suddenly the sky was full of friendly wings all coming toward me.

Now I knew the sixth Grandfather was about to speak, he who was the Spirit of the Earth, and I saw that he was very old, but more as men are old. His hair was long and white, his face was all in wrinkles and his eyes were deep and dim. I stared at him, for it seemed I knew him somehow; and as I stared, he slowly changed, for he was growing backwards into youth, and when he had become a boy, I knew that he was

myself with all the years that would be mine at last. When he was old again, he said: "My boy, have courage, for my power shall be yours, and you shall need it, for your nation on the earth will have great troubles. Come."

He rose and tottered out through the rainbow door, and as I followed I was riding on the bay horse who had talked to me at first and led me to that place.

Then the bay horse stopped and faced the black horses of the west, and a voice said: "They have given you the cup of water to make live the greening day, and also the bow and arrow to destroy." The bay neighed, and the twelve black horses came and stood behind me, four abreast.

The bay faced the sorrels of the east, and I saw that they had morning stars upon their foreheads and they were very bright. And the voice said: "They have given you the sacred pipe and the power that is peace, and the good red day." The bay neighed, and the twelve sorrels stood behind me, four abreast.

My horse now faced the buckskins of the south, and a voice said: "They have given you the sacred stick and you nation's hoop, and the yellow day; and in the center of the hoop you shall set the stick and make it grow into a shielding tree, and bloom." The bay neighed, and the twelve buckskins came and stood behind me, four abreast.

Then I knew that there were riders on all the horses there behind me, and a voice said: "Now you shall walk the black road with these; and as you walk, all the nations that have roots or legs or wings shall fear you."

So I started, riding toward the east down the fearful road, and behind me came the horsebacks four abreast—the blacks, the whites, the sorrels, and the buckskins—and far away above the fearful road the daybreak star was rising very dim.

I looked below me where the earth was silent in a sick green light, and saw the hills look up afraid and the grasses on the hills and all the animals; and everywhere about me were the cries of frightened birds and sounds of fleeing wings. I was the chief of all the heavens riding there, and when I looked behind me, all the twelve black horses reared and plunged and thundered and their manes and tails were whirling hail and their nostrils snorted lightning. And when I looked below again, I saw the slant hail falling and the long, sharp rain, and where we passed, the trees bowed low and all the hills were dim.

Now the earth was bright again as we rode. I could see the hills and valleys and the creeks and rivers passing under. We came above a place where three streams made a big one—a source of mighty waters[3]—and something terrible was there. Flames were rising from the waters and in the flames a blue man lived. The dust was floating all about him in the air, the grass was short and withered, the trees were wilting, two-legged and four-legged beings lay there thin and panting, and wings too weak to fly.

Then the black horse riders shouted "Hoka hey!" and charged down upon the blue man, but were driven back. And the white troop shouted, charging, and was beaten; then the red troop and the yellow.

And when each had failed, they all cried together: "Eagle Wing Stretches, hurry!" And all the world was filled with voices of all kinds that cheered me, so I charged. I had the cup of water in one hand and in the other was the bow that turned into a spear as the bay and I swooped down, and the spear's head was sharp lightning. It stabbed the blue man's heart, and as it struck I could hear the thunder rolling and many voices that cried "Un-hee!," meaning I had killed. The flames died. The trees and grasses were not withered any more and murmured happily together, and every living being cried in gladness with whatever voice it had. Then the four troops of horsemen charged down and struck the dead body of the blue man, counting coup; and suddenly it was only a harmless turtle.

You see, I had been riding with the storm clouds, and had come to earth as rain, and it was drouth that I had killed with the power that the Six Grandfathers gave me. So we were riding on the earth now down along the river flowing full from the source of waters, and soon I saw ahead the circled village of a people in the valley. And a Voice said: "Behold a nation; it is yours. Make haste, Eagle Wing Stretches!"

I entered the village, riding, with the four horse troops behind me—the blacks, the whites, the sorrels, and the buckskins; and the place was filled with moaning and with mourning for the dead. The wind was blowing from the south like fever, and when I looked around I saw that in nearly every tepee the women and the children and the men lay dying with the dead.

So I rode around the circle of the village, looking in upon the sick and dead, and I felt like crying as I rode. But when I looked behind me, all the women and the children and the men were getting up and coming forth with happy faces.

And a Voice said: "Behold, they have given you the center of the nation's hoop to make it live."

So I rode to the center of the village, with the horse troops in their quarters round about me, and there the people gathered. And the Voice said: "Give them now the flowering stick that they may flourish, and the sacred pipe that they may know the power that is peace, and the wing of the white giant that they may have endurance and face all winds with courage."

So I took the bright red stick and at the center of the nation's hoop I thrust it in the earth. As it touched the earth it leaped mightily in my hand and was a waga chun, the rustling tree,[4] very tall and full of leafy branches and of all birds singing. And beneath it all the animals were mingling with the people like relatives and making happy cries. The women raised their tremolo of joy, and the men shouted all together: "Here we shall raise our children and be as little chickens under the mother sheo's[5] wing."

Then I heard the white wind blowing gently through the tree and singing there, and from the east the sacred pipe came flying on its eagle wings, and stopped before me there beneath the tree, spreading deep peace around it.

Then the daybreak star was rising, and a Voice said: "It shall be a relative to them; and who shall see it, shall see much more, for thence comes wisdom; and those who do not see it shall be dark." And all the people raised their faces to the east, and the star's light fell upon them, and all the dogs barked loudly and the horses whinnied.

Then when the many little voices ceased, the great Voice said: "Behold the circle of the nation's hoop, for it is holy, being endless, and thus all powers shall be one power in the people without end. Now they shall break camp and go forth upon the red road, and your Grandfathers shall walk with them." So the people broke camp and took the good road with the white wing on their faces, and the order of their going was like this:

First, the black horse riders with the cup of water; and the white horse riders with the white wing and the sacred herb; and the sorrel riders with the holy pipe; and the buckskins with the flowering stick. And after these the little children and the youths and maidens followed in a band.

---

[3] Black Elk thinks this was the Three Forks of the Missouri.
[4] The cottonwood.
[5] Prairie hen.

Second, came the tribe's four chieftains, and their band was all young men and women.

Third, the nation's four advisers leading men and women neither young nor old.

Fourth, the old men hobbling with their canes and looking to the earth.

Fifth, old women hobbling with their canes and looking to the earth.

Sixth, myself all alone upon the bay with the bow and arrows that the First Grandfather gave me. But I was not the last; for when I looked behind me there were ghosts of people like a trailing fog as far as I could see—grandfathers of grandfathers and grandmothers of grandmothers without number. And over these a great Voice—the Voice that was the South—lived, and I could feel it silent.

And as we went the Voice behind me said: "Behold a good nation walking in a sacred manner in a good land!"

Then I looked up and saw that there were four ascents ahead, and these were generations I should know. Now we were on the first ascent, and all the land was green. And as the long line climbed, all the old men and women raised their hands, palms forward, to the far sky yonder and began to croon a song together, and the sky ahead was filled with clouds of baby faces.

When we came to the end of the first ascent we camped in the sacred circle as before, and in the center stood the holy tree, and still the land about us was all green.

Then we started on the second ascent, marching as before, and still the land was green, but it was getting steeper. And as I looked ahead, the people changed into elks and bison and all four-footed beings and even into fowls, all walking in a sacred manner on the good red road together. And I myself was a spotted eagle soaring over them. But just before we stopped to camp at the end of that ascent, all the marching animals grew restless and afraid that they were not what they had been, and began sending forth voices of trouble, calling to their chiefs. And when they camped at the end of that ascent, I looked down and saw that leaves were falling from the holy tree.

And the Voice said: "Behold your nation, and remember what your Six Grandfathers gave you, for thenceforth your people walk in difficulties."

Then the people broke camp again, and saw the black road before them towards where the sun goes down, and black clouds coming yonder; and they did not want to go but could not stay. And as they walked the third ascent, all the animals and fowls that were the people ran here and there, for each one seemed to have his own little vision that he followed and his own rules; and all over the universe I could hear the winds at war like wild beasts fighting.[6]

And when we reached the summit of the third ascent and camped, the nation's hoop was broken like a ring of smoke that spreads and scatters and the holy tree seemed dying and all its birds were gone. And when I looked ahead I saw that the fourth ascent would be terrible.

Then when the people were getting ready to begin the fourth ascent, the Voice spoke like some one weeping, and it said: "Look there upon your nation." And when I looked down, the people were all changed back to human, and they were thin, their faces sharp, for they were starving. Their ponies were only hide and bones, and the holy tree was gone.

And as I looked and wept, I saw that there stood on the north side of the starving camp a sacred man who was painted red all over his body, and he held a spear as he walked into the center of the people, and there he lay down and rolled. And when he got up, it was a fat bison standing there, and where the bison stood a sacred herb sprang up right where the tree had been in the center of the nation's hoop. The herb grew and bore four blossoms on a single stem while I was looking—a blue,[7] a white, a scarlet, and a yellow—and the bright rays of these flashed to the heavens.

I know now what this meant, that the bison were the gift of a good spirit and were our strength, but we should lose them, and from the same good spirit we must find another strength. For the people all seemed better when the herb had grown and bloomed, and the horses raised their tails and neighed and pranced around, and I could see a light breeze going from the north among the people like a ghost; and suddenly the flowering tree was there again at the center of the nation's hoop where the four-rayed herb had blossomed.

I was still the spotted eagle floating, and I could see that I was already in the fourth ascent and the people were camping yonder at the top of the third long rise. It was dark and terrible about me, for all the winds of the world were fighting. It was like rapid gun-fire and

---

[6] At this point Black Elk remarked: "I think we are near that place now, and I am afraid something very bad is going to happen all over the world." He cannot read and knows nothing of world affairs.

[7] Blue as well as black may be used to represent the power of the west.

like whirling smoke, and like women and children wailing and like horses screaming all over the world.

I could see my people yonder running about, setting the smoke-flap poles and fastening down their tepees against the wind, for the storm cloud was coming on them very fast and black, and there were frightened swallows without number fleeing before the cloud.

Then a song of power came to me and I sang it there in the midst of that terrible place where I was. It went like this:

A good nation I will make live.
This the nation above has said.
They have given me the power to make over.

And when I had sung this, a Voice said: "To the four quarters you shall run for help, and nothing shall be strong before you. Behold him!"

Now I was on my bay horse again, because the horse is of the earth, and it was there my power would be used. And as I obeyed the Voice and looked, there was a horse all skin and bones yonder in the west, a faded brownish black. And a Voice there said: "Take this and make him over; and it was the four-rayed herb that I was holding in my hand. So I rode above the poor horse in a circle, and as I did this I could hear the people yonder calling for spirit power, "A-hey! a-hey! a-hey! a-hey!" Then the poor horse neighed and rolled and got up, and he was a big, shiny, black stallion with dapples all over him and his mane about him like a cloud. He was the chief of all the horses; and when he snorted, it was a flash of lightning and his eyes were like the sunset star. He dashed to the west and neighed, and the west was filled with a dust of hoofs, and horses without number, shiny black, came plunging from the dust. Then he dashed toward the north and neighed, and to the east and to the south, and the dust clouds answered, giving forth their plunging horses without number—whites and sorrels and buckskins, fat, shiny, rejoicing in their fleetness and their strength. It was beautiful, but it was also terrible.

Then they all stopped short, rearing, and were standing in a great hoop about their black chief at the center, and were still. And as they stood, four virgins, more beautiful than women of the earth can be, came through the circle, dressed in scarlet, one from each of the four quarters, and stood about the great black stallion in their places; and one held the wooden cup of water, and one the white wing, and one the pipe, and one the nation's hoop. All the universe was silent, listening; and then the great black stallion raised his voice and sang. The song he sang was this:

"My horses, prancing they are coming.
My horses, neighing they are coming;
Prancing, they are coming.
All over the universe they come.
They will dance; may you behold them.
(4 times)
A horse nation, they will dance.
May you behold them."
(4 times)

His voice was not loud, but it went all over the universe and filled it. There was nothing that did not hear, and it was more beautiful than anything can be. It was so beautiful that nothing anywhere could keep from dancing. The virgins danced, and all the circled horses. The leaves on the trees, the grasses on the hills and in the valleys, the waters in the creeks and in the rivers and the lakes, the four-legged and the two-legged and the wings of the air—all danced together to the music of the stallion's song.

And when I looked down upon my people yonder, the cloud passed over, blessing them with friendly rain, and stood in the east with a flaming rainbow over it.

Then all the horses went singing back to their places beyond the summit of the fourth ascent, and all things sang along with them as they walked.

And a Voice said: "All over the universe they have finished a day of happiness." And looking down I saw that the whole wide circle of the day was beautiful and green, with all fruits growing and all things kind and happy.

Then a Voice said: "Behold this day, for it is yours to make. Now you shall stand upon the center of the earth to see, for there they are taking you."

I was still on my bay horse, and once more I felt the riders of the west, the north, the east, the south, behind me in formation, as before, and we were going east. I looked ahead and saw the mountains there with rocks and forests on them, and from the mountains flashed all colors upward to the heavens. Then I was standing on the highest mountain of them all, and round about beneath me was the whole hoop of the world.[8] And while I stood there I saw more than I can tell and I understood more than I saw; for I was seeing in a sacred manner

---

[8] Black Elk said the mountain he stood upon in his vision was Harney Peak in the Black Hills. "But anywhere is the center of the world," he added.

the shapes of all things in the spirit, and the shape of all shapes as they must live together like one being. And I saw that the sacred hoop of my people was one of many hoops that made one circle, wide as daylight and as starlight, and in the center grew one mighty flowering tree to shelter all the children of one mother and one father. And I saw that it was holy.

Then as I stood there, two men were coming from the east, head first like arrows flying, and between them rose the day-break star. They came and gave a herb to me and said: "With this on earth you shall undertake anything and do it." It was the day-break-star herb, the herb of understanding, and they told me to drop it on the earth. I saw it falling far, and when it struck the earth it rooted and grew and flowered, four blossoms on one stem, a blue, a white, a scarlet, and a yellow; and the rays from these streamed upward to the heavens so that all creatures saw it and in no place was there darkness.

Then the Voice said: "Your Six Grandfathers—now you shall go back to them."

I had not noticed how I was dressed until now, and I saw that I was painted red all over, and my joints were painted black, with white stripes between the joints. My bay had lightning stripes all over him, and his mane was cloud. And when I breathed, my breath was lightning.

Now two men were leading me, head first like arrows slanting upward—the two that brought me from the earth. And as I followed on the bay, they turned into four flocks of geese that flew in circles, one above each quarter, sending forth a sacred voice as they flew: Br-r-r-p, br-r-r-p, br-r-r-p, br-r-r-p!

Then I saw ahead the rainbow flaming above the tepee of the Six Grandfathers, built and roofed with cloud and sewed with thongs of lightning; and underneath it were all the wings of the air and under them the animals and men. All these were rejoicing, and thunder was like happy laughter.

As I rode in through the rainbow door, there were cheering voices from all over the universe, and I saw the Six Grandfathers sitting in a row, with their arms held toward me and their hands, palms out; and behind them in the cloud were faces thronging, without number, of the people yet to be.

"He has triumphed!" cried the six together, making thunder. And as I passed before them there, each gave again the gift that he had given me before—the cup of water and the bow and arrows, the power to make live and to destroy; the white wing of cleansing and the healing herb; the sacred pipe; the flowering stick. And

each one spoke in turn from west to south, explaining what he gave as he had done before, and as each one spoke he melted down into the earth and rose again; and as each did this, I felt nearer to the earth.

Then the oldest of them all said: "Grandson, all over the universe you have seen. Now you shall go back with power to the place from whence you came, and it shall happen yonder that hundreds shall be sacred, hundreds shall be flames! Behold!"

I looked below and saw my people there, and all were well and happy except one, and he was lying like the dead—and that one was myself. Then the oldest Grandfather sang, and his song was like this:

> "There is someone lying on earth
>   in a sacred manner.
> There is someone—on earth he lies.
> In a sacred manner I have made him to walk."

Now the tepee, built and roofed with cloud, began to sway back and forth as in a wind, and the flaming rainbow door was growing dimmer. I could hear voices of all kinds crying from outside: "Eagle Wing Stretches is coming forth! Behold him!"

When I went through the door, the face of the day of earth was appearing with the day-break star upon its forehead; and the sun leaped up and looked upon me, and I was going forth alone.

And as I walked alone, I heard the sun singing as it arose, and it sang like this:

> "With visible face I am appearing.
> In a sacred manner I appear.
> For the greening earth a pleasantness I make.
> The center of the nation's hoop
>   I have made pleasant.
> With visible face, behold me!
> The four-leggeds and two-leggeds,
>   I have made them to walk;
> The wings of the air, I have made them to fly.
> With visible face I appear.
> My day, I have made it holy."

When the singing stopped, I was feeling lost and very lonely. Then a Voice above me said: "Look back!" It was a spotted eagle that was hovering over me and spoke. I looked, and where the flaming rainbow tepee, built and roofed with cloud, had been, I saw only the tall rock mountain at the center of the world.

I was all alone on a broad plain now with my feet upon the earth, alone but for the spotted eagle guarding me. I could see my people's village far ahead, and

I walked very fast, for I was homesick now. Then I saw my own tepee, and inside I saw my mother and my father bending over a sick boy that was myself. And as I entered the tepee, some one was saying: "The boy is coming to; you had better give him some water."

Then I was sitting up; and I was sad because my mother and my father didn't seem to know I had been so far away.

ERNEST HOLMES
1887 - 1960

We believe in God, the Living Spirit Almighty; one, indestructible, absolute and self-existent Cause. This One manifests itself in and through all creation but is not absorbed by its creation. The manifest universe is the body of God; it is the logical and necessary outcome of the infinite self-knowingness of God. We believe in the incarnation of the Spirit in everyone and that all people are incarnations of the One Spirit. We believe in the eternality, the immortality, and the continuity of the individual soul, forever and ever expanding. We believe that Heaven is within us and that we experience it to the degree that we become conscious of it. We believe the ultimate goal of life to be a complete emancipation from all discord of every nature, and that this goal is sure to be attained by all. We believe in the unity of all life, and that the highest God and the innermost God is one God. We believe that God is personal to all who feel this Indwelling Presence. We believe in the direct revelation of Truth through the intuitive and spiritual nature of the individual, and that any person may become a revealer of Truth who lives in close contact with the indwelling God. We believe that the Universal Spirit, which is God, operates through a Universal Mind, which is the Law of God; and that we are surrounded by this Creative Mind which receives

The country is populated with countless offshoots of mainstream religion as well as independent sects that have developed original theologies for themselves. One group, the United Church of Religious Science, grew out of **Ernest Holmes**'s efforts to articulate his "Science of Mind" philosophy in the 1920's and 1930's. Holmes's ideas have spawned about two hundred congregations across the continent and abroad and a monthly magazine in continuous publication since 1927. His summary "What We Believe" was updated and reproduced in the October 1995 issue of *Science of Mind* magazine.

MARY BAKER EDDY
1821 - 1910

At the age of twelve I was admitted to the Congregational (Trinitarian) Church, my parents having been members of that body for a half-century. In connection with this event, some circumstances are noteworthy. Before this step was taken, the doctrine of unconditional election, or predestination, greatly troubled me; for I was unwilling to be saved, if my brothers and sisters were to be numbered among those who were doomed to perpetual banishment from God. So perturbed was I by the thoughts aroused by this erroneous doctrine, that the family doctor was summoned, and pronounced me stricken with fever.

My father's relentless theology emphasized belief in a final judgment-day, in the danger of endless punishment, and in a Jehovah merciless towards unbelievers; and of these things he now spoke, hoping to win me from dreaded heresy.

My mother, as she bathed my burning temples, bade me lean on God's love, which would give me rest, if I went to Him in prayer, as I was wont to do, seeking His guidance. I prayed; and a soft glow of ineffable joy came over me. The fever was gone, and I rose and dressed myself, in a normal condition of health. Mother saw this, and was glad. The physician marvelled; and the "horrible decree" of

Healed of a serious injury while reading Matthew 9:1-8, **Mary Baker Eddy** was convinced of God's power to miraculously cure the ailing. This conviction led her to found the Church of Christ, Scientist, a faith which discourages the use of modern medicine, advocating instead the use of spiritual healing in times of sickness. Eddy also founded one of the country's major newspapers, *The Christian Science Monitor*. Christian Science continues to thrive today, claiming followers all over the world. Eddy wrote of her revelations in her autobiography, *Retrospection and Introspection*, from which I quote here.

the direct impress of our thought and acts upon it. We believe in the healing of the sick through the power of this Mind. We believe in the control of conditions through the power of this Mind. We believe in the eternal Goodness, the eternal Loving-kindness, and the eternal Givingness of Life to all. We believe in our own soul, our own spirit, and our own destiny; for we understand that the life of all is God.

predestination—as John Calvin rightly called his own tenet—forever lost its power over me.

When the meeting was held for the examination of candidates for membership, I was of course present. The pastor was an old-school expounder of the strictest Presbyterian doctrines. He was apparently as eager to have unbelievers in these dogmas lost, as he was to have elect believers converted and rescued from perdition; for both salvation and condemnation depended, according to his views, upon the good pleasure of infinite Love. However, I was ready for his doleful questions, which I answered without a tremor, declaring that never could I unite with the church, if assent to this doctrine was essential thereto.

Distinctly do I recall what followed. I stoutly maintained that I was willing to trust God, and take my chance of spiritual safety with my brothers and sisters,—not one of whom had then made any profession of religion,—even if my creedal doubts left me outside the doors. The minister then wished me to tell him when I had experienced a change of heart; but tearfully I had to respond that I could not designate any precise time. Nevertheless he persisted in the assertion that I *had* been truly regenerated, and asked me to say how I felt when the new light dawned within me. I replied that I could only answer him in the words of the Psalmist: "Search me, O God, and know my heart: try me, and know my thoughts: and see if there be any wicked way in me, and lead me in the way everlasting."

This was so earnestly said, that even the oldest church-members wept. After the meeting was over they came and kissed me. To the astonishment of many, the good clergyman's heart also melted, and he received me into their communion, and my protest along with me. My connection with this religious body was retained till I founded a church of my own, built on the basis of Christian Science, "Jesus Christ himself being the chief corner-stone."

In confidence of faith, I could say in David's words, "I will go in the strength of the Lord God: I will make mention of Thy righteousness, even of Thine only. O God, Thou hast taught me from my youth: and hitherto have I declared Thy wondrous works." (Psalm lxxi. 16, 17.)

In the year 1878 I was called to preach in Boston at the Baptist Tabernacle of Rev. Daniel C. Eddy, D.D.,— by the pastor of this church. I accepted the invitation and commenced work.

The congregation so increased in number the pews were not sufficient to seat the audience and benches were used in the aisles. At the close of my engagement we parted in Christian fellowship, if not in full unity of doctrine.

Our last vestry meeting was made memorable by eloquent addresses from persons who feelingly testified to having been healed through my preaching. Among other diseases cured they specified cancers. The cases described had been treated and given over by physicians of the popular schools of medicine, but I had not heard of these cases till the persons who divulged their secret joy were healed. A prominent churchman agreeably informed the congregation that many others present had been healed under my preaching, but were too timid to testify in public.

One memorable Sunday afternoon, a soprano,—clear, strong, sympathetic,—floating up from the pews, caught my ear. When the meeting was over, two ladies pushing their way through the crowd reached the platform. With tears of joy flooding her eyes—for she was a mother—one of them said, "Did you hear my daughter sing? Why, she has not sung before since she left the choir and was in consumption! When she entered this church one hour ago she could not speak a loud word, and now, oh, thank God, she is healed!"

It was not an uncommon occurrence in my own church for the sick to be healed by my sermon. Many pale cripples went into the church leaning on crutches who went out carrying them on their shoulders. "And these signs shall follow them that believe."

The charter for The Mother Church in Boston was obtained June, 1879, and the same month the members, twenty-six in number, extended a call to Mary B. G. Eddy to become their pastor. She accepted the call, and was ordained A.D. 1881.

LUTHER STANDING BEAR
1868 - 1939

It was about the middle of the summer of 1879 that I saw the last great Sun Dance of the Sioux. The Brules were holding the dance about six miles southwest of Rosebud Agency, on the place where old Chief Two Strikes's band now have their allotments. As I started for Carlisle Indian School in the fall of 1879, I cannot say whether this was the last dance held or not.

Luther Standing Bear, the hereditary chief of the Oglala Sioux, wrote his autobiography in 1928. *My People, the Sioux* chronicles his life, from his early childhood on the reservation to his education at the Carlisle Indian School in Pennsylvania to his career in Hollywood, as an actor in Western films. "The Sun Dance" depicts an important rite of his tribe, a dance in which as many as forty braves participated, dancing to heal the ill or to bring on the buffalo.

I have read many descriptions of this dance, and I have been to different tribes which claimed they did the 'real thing,' but there is a great difference in their dances from the Sun Dance of the Sioux.

The Sun Dance started many years before Christopher Columbus drifted to these shores. We then knew that there was a God above us all. We called God 'Wakan Tanka,' or the 'Big Holy,' or sometimes 'Grandfather.' You call God Father. I bring this before you because I want you to know that this dance was our religious belief. According to our legend, the red man was to have this dance every summer, to fulfill our religious duty. It was a sacrificial dance.

During the winter if any member of the tribe became ill, perhaps a brother or a cousin would be brave enough to go to the medicine man and say, 'I will sacrifice my body to the Wakan Tanka, or Big Holy, for the one who is sick.' Or if the buffalo were beginning to get scarce, some one would sacrifice himself so that the tribe might have something to eat.

The medicine man would then take this brave up to the mountain alone, and announce to the Great Spirit that the young man was ready to be sacrificed. When the parents of this young man heard that he was to go through the Sun Dance, some of his brothers or cousins would sacrifice themselves with him as an honor.

If some young man of another band had the desire to go through the Sun Dance, some of his friends or relatives might offer to dance with him. Sometimes as many as thirty or forty braves went into the dance.

As soon as the women heard that there was to be a Sun Dance in their band, they began making all the things which were necessary for the ceremony. They placed beautiful porcupine-quill-work on the eagle-bone whistles which the men carried in their mouths during the dance, as well as beautiful head-dresses for the dancers. These were made from porcupine-quill-work. The dancer wore a piece of buckskin around the waist, hanging down like a skirt. This also had pretty quill-work decorations. Soon all the things were ready for the dance.

When the chiefs learned this dance was coming, they called a meeting and selected a place they thought as best suited to hold it. They then sent word to the other bands to get ready.

The main band would move to the place selected, and the other bands would come in one at a time, the boys and warriors mounted on ponies. They would all keep together until they were very near, when they would make an imitation charge on the camp, just as if it were an enemy camp.

After this 'attack' they would all go up to a hill nearby. Four men were then chosen who were to lead the parade. The warriors would now have a chance to show their beautiful war-ponies and good clothes. Then they would all parade into the village. Just about the time the parade was over, the rest of the camp would be moving in. The women would then be very busy erecting the tipis.

After the various bands had all arrived, there were some special tipis put up for those who were going to dance. These tipis were not erected in one place, but were sometimes considerably scattered. I have seen a camp of this sort which was a mile and a quarter in diameter. There were from four to six of these special tipis for the dancers. Everybody was allowed to go, and there was always plenty to eat in these tipis.

The first day all the people collected at the center of the camp and some scouts were selected to go out and look for the cottonwood pole which was to be used in the dance. After being chosen, these scouts retired to their tipis and dressed in their best clothes, mounted their war-ponies, and rode into the circle. Their parents gave away ponies and other pretty things as a token of respect that their sons had been chosen to act as scouts.

Among these scouts were one or two of the old-timers, who were to act as leaders. A fire was now built in the center of the circle, and the scouts rode their ponies around this fire three times, and, after the fourth time, they were off! They rode their ponies at full speed. All those on horseback rode as fast as they could and encircled the scouts as they went on.

The scouts would be gone about a half-hour. On their return they would come to the top of a hill and stop. The others in the camp would once more mount their ponies and ride out to meet the scouts. Then they would turn about and race back to the center of the circle, where they would wait for the scouts to ride in.

One of the old-timers would then relate how they had found a pole which was considered good enough to be used in the dance. Then everybody got ready to go to the place where the pole had been found.

All the various lodges of the tribe now gathered in the timber near the place where the pole was located. There was the White Horse, Bull, Fox, and Short Hair lodges. As each separate tribe had its form of ceremonies, each selected some of its people to go to the tree and 'chop it.' They did not really chop the tree, but just simply touched it. As they touched the tree, they gave away ponies or anything they wanted. They stayed here a long time, as they had plenty to eat all the time they were in the timber. If they knew a man who had plenty of ponies, they would select one of his children to come forward and touch the tree, and then he would give away a pony.

After all had finished their ceremonies, some one cut the tree down. There were about twenty men to carry this pole. They had long sticks which they put under it, and two men to a stick to carry it. Everybody was carrying something. Some carried forked branches, other limbs of the tree, etc. They had no one to order them around, but every one did his share toward this religious dance.

As the twenty men lifted the pole, they walked slowly toward the camp. The rest of the tribe trailed along behind. They stopped three times, and each time a medicine man howled like a wolf. The fourth time they stopped, all the men and boys raced their ponies as fast as they would go, trying to see who would be first to reach the center of the camp. Here they found the effigy of a man made from the limbs of trees. Each tried to be first to touch this. Here would be plenty of dust as these men and boys rode in to attack this wooden man. Sometimes two ponies would run together, and then some one was likely to be hurt.

At last the men came in with the pole. Then the lodges had some more ceremonies to be gone through with, while some of the men started to dig the hole in which to set the pole. Others would get busy arranging forked poles in a circle. This circle was to serve as our hall.

When the hole was ready, all the men from the different lodges got together to help erect the pole, which was sometimes sixty or seventy feet long. They tied two braided rawhide ropes about the middle of the pole, on which some brave was to hang. Other ropes were to be used to hoist the pole into place. These hoisting ropes were tied in such a way as to be easily removed, after the pole was in the right position. We had no stepladders nor any men with climbers on to go up and untie any ropes that might be left up when the pole was in place.

When all was ready, some of the men used forked poles, some held on to the ropes, and others got hold of the pole. It required about forty men to do this work properly. The pole must be raised and dropped in the hole at one operation, and with no second lifting. Some pushed, others pulled, while the men with the forked sticks lifted. As the pole dropped into the hole, everybody cheered.

There was a strong superstition regarding this pole. It was believed that if the pole dropped before it was set into the hole, all our wishes and hopes would be shattered. There would be great thunder-storms and high winds; our shade or council hall would be blown away, and there would be no Sun Dance. On top of this, it was believed that the whole tribe would have a run of bad luck.

Consequently, when this pole was being erected, every man used all his strength to ward off any accident or mishap. We were taught to believe that if all minds worked together, it helped a great deal. We were taught this by our parents, and we had strong faith in it.

The pole was always a cottonwood tree, as I have previously stated. No other tree would do. It was not always a straight tree, but there was always a branch which extended out from the main trunk. This would be about thirty or forty feet up. This branch would be cut off about four feet from the trunk. On the top of the pole, branches with leaves on would be left.

They made a bundle of branches from the tree which were wrapped in bark and tied together. This bundle was placed in the branch which had been cut off about four feet from the trunk. When this bundle was in place, it looked not unlike a huge cross, when viewed from a distance.

From this cross-piece hung something which resembled a buffalo and a man. These effigies were cut from rawhide and were tied up with a rawhide rope. They were suspended about ten feet down from the bundle of wood or the cross-piece. Both were painted black, the paint being made from burned cottonwood mixed with buffalo fat.

Sometimes there was a small bundle of sticks painted in a variety of colors. At the end of each, a small bag made of buckskin and filled with tobacco was hung. All this was suspended to the cross-piece. Under the pole were many little bags of tobacco, tied on little sticks, as a prayer offering to the spirit.

About ten feet to the west of this cross lay the skull of a buffalo on a bed made of sagebrush. The horns were attached to this skull and it was laid facing the east. Behind the skull, about two feet, were two forked sticks stuck in the ground, with another stick across them. Against this the pipe of peace rested, with the stem pointing toward the east.

The real meaning of having the effigy of the buffalo hanging from the cross was a prayer to the Wakan-Tanka, or Big Holy, for more 'pte,' or buffalo meat. The effigy of the man meant that in case of war we were to have victory over our enemies.

When the main big pole was all completed, the men bent their energies toward the dancing-hall, or shade, as it should rightfully be called. All the forked poles were placed in a double circle, about fifteen feet apart, with an opening left toward the east. Long sticks were laid from one forked pole to another in the inner circle as well as the outside circle. We used no nails in those days, and anything that was to be fastened must be bound with rawhide or tied with bark. In this case, we peeled off the bark of the willow trees and used that to fasten the poles together. Then the longest tipi poles would be brought in, and laid from the inner to the outer circle. The outside wall was made from entwined branches, and on top would be laid the largest tipi coverings, which made a fine shade. This 'shade' was about one hundred and fifty feet in diameter, with a depth of about fifteen feet. It was considered a great honor to have one's tipi covering chosen for this purpose.

After the shade was completed, if any one wanted to give a piece of buckskin, or some red or blue cloth, as an offering to the Great Spirit, he took a long stick and put a cross-piece on it, from which was suspended his offering. These pennants were hung all around the dance-shade. It quite resembled a great convention hall. Several beds of sagebrush were made for the dancers. Sometimes a big dance would precede the Sun Dance. This dance was known as 'owanka ona sto wacipi,' or 'smoothing the floor.' It was, in fact, a sort of 'house-warming' affair, and was for the braves and young men only. Each carried a weapon and wore his best clothes. The crowd came in from all the different bands in the camp, forming in lines like soldiers as they appeared. Sometimes there were as many as fifteen abreast.

Then an old chief came forward with a scalp-lock tied to a pole. He danced before the others, facing them. When he danced backward, the others danced forward, and *vice versa*. When the old chief led them toward the pole, those carrying guns shot at the buffalo and the effigy of the man, hanging from the pole.

While this dance was in progress, different medicine men were in the tipis with the young men who were to do the Sun Dance. From each tipi came six, eight, and sometimes ten from a band to dance. There was a leader, who carried a pipe of peace; the others followed one by one. They wore buffalo robes with the hair outside, and quite resembled a band of buffalo coming to a stream to drink.

After these Sun Dance candidates reached the shade from their tipis, they did not go in immediately, but marched around the outside three times. After the fourth time, they went in and took their places. Then the medicine man came forward and took charge of four or eight of the dancers. Four of them must be painted alike. They put on beautiful head-dresses richly ornamented with porcupine quills. Their wrists were wound around with sagebrush, and the eagle-bone whistles they used were likewise decorated.

This was a very solemn affair. These men were to dance for three or four days, without food or water. Some of their relatives cried; others sang to praise them and make them feel courageous.

The singers were now in their places. They used no tom-tom, but sat around a large buffalo hide which lay flat on the ground, using large sticks to beat upon the dried skin.

The braves started dancing as soon as the sun started to rise. They stood facing the sun with both hands raised above their heads, the eagle-bone whistles in their mouths, and they blew on these every time the singers hit the skin with their sticks. All day long they stood in one position, facing the sun, until it set.

The sunflower was used by the Sioux in this dance. They cut out a piece of rawhide the shape of a sun-flower, which they wore on a piece of braided buckskin suspended around the neck, with the flower resting on the breast. At that time I did not realize the significance of the sunflower, but now I know it is the only flower that follows the sun as it moves on its orbit, always facing it.

The dance would be kept up until one of the participants fainted, then he was laid out on one of the sagebrush beds. On the second day of the dance a young man who had started it would come into the shade. First he would walk all around the hall so that all could see him. Then he went straight to the pole. He was giving himself for a living sacrifice. Two medicine men would lift the young man and lay him down under the pole. An old man would then come forward with a very sharp-pointed knife. He would take hold of the breast of the young brave, pull the skin forward, and pierce it through with his knife. Then he would insert a wooden pin (made from the plum tree), through the slit and tie a strong buckskin thong to this pin.

From the pole two rawhide ropes were suspended. The candidate would now be lifted up and the buckskin string tied to the rawhide rope. The candidate was now hanging from his breasts, but the rope was long enough for him to remain on the ground. Although the blood would be running down from the knife incision, the candidate would smile, although every one knew he must be suffering intense pain.

At this point the friends or relatives of the young brave would sing and praise him for his courage. Then they would give away ponies or make other presents. The singers now began to sing and the young brave to dance. The other dancers were behind him, four in a line, and they accompanied his dancing. These dancers always stood in one spot while they danced, but the candidate danced and at the same time pulled at the rope, trying to tear out the wooden pin fastened through his breasts.

If he tried very hard and was unsuccessful, his friends and relatives possibly could not bear to see him suffer any longer; so they would give away a pony to some one who would help him tear loose. This party would stand behind the dancer and seize him around the waist, while the candidate at the same time would throw himself backward, both pulling with all their strength. If they could not yet tear the candidate loose, an old man with a sharp knife would cut the skin off, and the dancer would fall beneath the pole. Then he would be picked up and carried to a sagebrush bed. Occasionally a man with a very strong constitution, after tearing loose, would get off his bed and resume the dancing. I have often seen these braves with their own blood dried to their bodies, yet going on with the dance.

This brave candidate fasted three or four days; taking no food or water during that time, instead of the forty days the Saviour did. The candidate had his body pierced beneath the cross. I learned all about this religion in the natural way, but after learning how to read the white man's books I compared your religion with ours; but religion, with us Indians, is stronger.

Many things were done during this dance which were similar to what I have read about Christ. We had one living sacrifice, and he fasted three or four days instead of forty. This religious ceremony was not always held in the same place. We did not commercialize our belief. Our medicine men received no salary. Hell was unknown to us. We trusted one another, and our word was as good as the white man's gold of to-day. We were then true Christians.

After the dance was over, everybody moved away, going where he pleased. It was a free country then. But afterward, if we ever returned to that sacred spot where the pole was yet standing, with the cross-piece attached, we stood for a long time in reverent attitude, because it was a sacred place to us.

But things have changed, even among the white people. They tear down their churches and let playhouses be built on the spot. What can be your feeling of reverence when you think of the house of God, in which you worshiped, being used to make fun in?

As I have many times related in my story, I always wanted to be brave, but I do not think I could ever have finished one of these Sun Dances.

ELIZABETH CADY STANTON

1815 - 1902

From the inauguration of the movement for woman's emancipation the Bible has been used to hold her in the "divinely ordained sphere," prescribed in the Old and New Testaments.

The canon and civil law; church and state; priests and legislators; all political parties and religious denominations have alike taught that woman was made after man, of man, and for man, an inferior being, subject to man. Creeds, codes, Scriptures and statutes, are all based on this idea. The fashions, forms, ceremonies and customs of society, church ordinances and discipline all grow out of this idea. . . .

The Bible teaches that woman brought sin and death into the world, that she precipitated the fall of the race, that she was arraigned before the judgment seat of Heaven, tried, condemned and sentenced. Marriage for her was to be a condition of

In this preface to her work, *The Woman's Bible*, suffragette **Elizabeth Cady Stanton** attempts to explain that in her view, women have been kept down by institutionalized forces due to misinterpretation of the Creation story and a world of churches led by and organized for men. Stanton, her compatriots Lucretia Mott and Susan B. Anthony, were at the front lines of the women's suffrage movement. She advocates a faith that recognizes no disparity between the rights (and predilections for sinful behavior) between the sexes. Stanton, who delivered the famous "Address at Seneca Falls" in which she declared "all men and women are created equal," founded the National Woman Suffrage Association and helped to draft an initial woman suffrage amendment.

bondage, maternity a period of suffering and anguish, and in silence and subjection, she was to play the role of a dependent on man's bounty for all her material wants, and for all the information she might desire on the vital questions of the hour, she was commanded to ask her husband at home. Here is the Bible position of woman briefly summed up.

Those who have the divine insight to translate, transpose and transfigure this mournful object of pity into an exalted, dignified personage, worthy of our worship as the mother of the race, are to be congratulated as having a share of the occult mystic power of the eastern Mahatmas.

The plain English to the ordinary mind admits of no such liberal interpretation. The unvarnished texts speak for themselves. The canon law, church ordinances and Scriptures, are homogeneous, and all reflect the same spirit and sentiments.

These familiar texts are quoted by clergymen in their pulpits, by statesmen in the halls of legislation, by lawyers in the courts, and are echoed by the press of all civilized nations, and accepted by woman herself as "The Word of God." So perverted is the religious element in her nature, that with faith and works she is the chief support of the church and clergy; the very powers that make her emancipation impossible. When, in the early part of the Nineteenth Century, women began to protest against their civil and political degradation, they were referred to the Bible for an answer. When they protested against their unequal position in the church, they were referred to the Bible for an answer.

This led to a general and critical study of the Scriptures. Some, having made a fetish of these books and believing them to be the veritable "Word of God," with liberal translations, interpretations, allegories and symbols, glossed over the most objectionable features of the various books and clung to them as divinely inspired. Others, seeing the family resemblance between the Mosaic code, the canon law, and the old English common law, came to the conclusion that all alike emanated from the same source; wholly human in their origin and inspired by the natural love of domination in the historians. Others, bewildered with their doubts and fears, came to no conclusion. While their clergymen told them on the one hand, that they owed all the blessings and freedom they enjoyed to the Bible, on the other, they said it clearly marked out their circumscribed sphere of action: that the demands for political and civil rights were irreligious, dangerous to the stability of the home, the state and the church. Clerical appeals were circulated from time to time conjuring members of their churches to take no part in the anti-slavery or woman suffrage movements, as they were infidel in their tendencies, undermining the very foundations of society. No wonder the majority of women stood still, and with bowed heads, accepted the situation.

Listening to the varied opinions of women, I have long thought it would be interesting and profitable to get them clearly stated in book form . . . a large committee has been formed, and we hope to complete the work within a year.

Those who have undertaken the labor are desirous to have some Hebrew and Greek scholars, versed in Biblical criticism, to gild our pages with their learning. Several distinguished women have been urged to do so, but they are afraid that their high reputation and scholarly attainments might be compromised by taking part in an enterprise that for a time may prove very unpopular. Hence we may not be able to get help from that class.

Others fear that they might compromise their evangelical faith by affiliating with those of more liberal views, who do not regard the Bible as the "Word of God," but like any other book, to be judged by its merits. If the Bible teaches the equality of Woman, why does the church refuse to ordain women to preach the gospel, to fill the offices of deacons and elders, and to administer the Sacraments, or to admit them as delegates to the Synods, General Assemblies and Conferences of the different denominations? They have never yet invited a women to join one of their Revising Committees, nor tried to mitigate the sentence pronounced on her by changing one count in the indictment served on her in Paradise.

The large number of letters received, highly appreciative of the undertaking, is very encouraging to those who have inaugurated the movement, and indicate a growing self-respect and self-assertion in the women of this generation. But we have the usual array of objectors to meet and answer. One correspondent conjures us to suspend the work, as it is "ridiculous" for "women to attempt the revision of the Scriptures." I wonder if any man wrote to the late revising committee of Divines to stop their work on the ground that it was ridiculous for men to revise the Bible. Why is it more ridiculous for women to protest against her present status in the Old and New Testament, in the ordinances and discipline of the church, than in the statutes and constitution of the state? Why is it more ridiculous to arraign ecclesiastics for their false teaching and acts of injustice to women, than members of Congress and the House of Commons? Why is it more audacious to review Moses than Blackstone, the Jewish code of laws, than the English system of jurisprudence? Women have compelled their legislators in every state in this Union to so modify their statutes for women that the old common law is now almost a dead letter. Why not compel Bishops and Revising Committees to modify their creeds and dogmas? Forty years ago it seemed as ridiculous to timid, time-serving and retrograde folk for women to demand an expurgated edition of the laws, as it now does to demand an expurgated edition of the Liturgies and the Scriptures. Come, come, my conservative friend, wipe the dew off your spectacles, and see that the world is moving. Whatever your views may be as to the importance of the proposed work, your political and social degradation are but an outgrowth of your status in the Bible. . . .

Others say it is not *politic* to rouse religious opposition. This much-lauded policy is but another word for *cowardice.* How can woman's position be changed from that of a subordinate to an equal, without opposition, without the broadest discussion of all the questions involved in her present degradation? For so far-reaching and momentous a reform as her complete independence, an entire revolution in all existing institutions is inevitable.

Let us remember that all reforms are interdependent, and that whatever is done to establish one principle on a solid basis, strengthens all. Reformers who are always compromising, have not yet grasped the idea that truth is the only safe ground to stand upon. The object of an individual life is not to carry one fragmentary measure in human progress, but to utter the highest truth clearly seen in all directions, and thus to round out and perfect a well balanced character. . . .

Again there are some who write us that our work is a useless expenditure of force over a book that has lost its hold on the human mind. Most intelligent women, they say, regard it simply as the history of a rude people in a barbarous age, and have no more reverence for the Scriptures than any other work. So long as tens of thousands of Bibles are printed every year, and circulated over the whole habitable globe, and the masses in all English-speaking nations revere it as the word of God, it is vain to belittle its influence. The sentimental feelings we all have for those things we were educated to believe sacred, do not readily yield to pure reason. . . .

The only points in which I differ from all ecclesiastical teaching is that I do not believe that any man ever saw or talked with God, I do not believe that God inspired the Mosaic code, or told the historians what they say he did about woman, for all the religions on the face of the earth degrade her, and so long as woman accepts the position that they assign her, her emancipation is impossible. Whatever the Bible may be made to do in Hebrew or Greek, in plain English it does not exalt and dignify woman. . . .

There are some general principles in the holy books of all religions that teach love, charity, liberty, justice and equality for all the human family, there are many grand and beautiful passages, the golden rule has been echoed and re-echoed around the world. There are lofty examples of good and true men and women, all worthy our acceptance and imitation whose lustre cannot be dimmed by the false sentiments and vicious characters bound up in the same volume. The Bible cannot be accepted or rejected as a whole, its teachings are varied and its lessons differ widely from each other. In criticising the peccadilloes of Sarah, Rebecca and Rachel, we would not shadow the virtues of Deborah, Huldah and Vashti. In criticising the Mosaic code we would not question the wisdom of the golden rule and the fifth Commandment. . . .

The canon law, the Scriptures, the creeds and codes and church discipline of the leading religions bear the impress of fallible man, and not of our ideal great first cause, "the Spirit of all Good," that set the universe of matter and mind in motion, and by immutable law holds the land, the sea, the planets, revolving round the great centre of light and heat, each in its own elliptic, with millions of stars in harmony all singing together, the glory of creation forever and ever.

JANITIN

CIRCA 1800'S

I and two of my relatives went down from the Sierra of Neji to the beach of el Rosarito, to catch clams for eating and to carry to the Sierra as we were accustomed to do all the years; we did no harm to anyone on the road, and on the beach we thought of nothing more than catching and drying clams in order to carry them to our village.

Janitin, a member of the Kamia tribe, was forcibly brought to Catholicism, having been kidnapped and taken to the San Miguel Mission sometime in the 1820's.

While we were doing this, we saw two men on horseback coming rapidly towards us; my relatives were immediately afraid and they fled with all speed, hiding themselves in a very dense willow grove which then existed in the canyon of the Rancho del Rosarito.

As soon as I saw myself alone, I also became afraid of those men and ran to the forest in order to join my companions, but already it was too late, because in a moment they overtook me and lassoed and dragged me for a long distance, wounding me much with the branches over which they dragged me, pulling me lassoed as I was with their horses running; after this they roped me with my arms behind and carried me off to the Mission of San Miguel, making me travel almost at a run in order to keep up with their horses, and when I stopped a little to catch my wind, they lashed me with the lariats that they carried, making me understand by signs that I should hurry; after much traveling in this manner, they diminished the pace and lashed me in order that I would always travel at the pace of the horses.

When we arrived at the mission, they locked me in a room for a week; the father [a Dominican priest] made me go to his habitation and he talked to me by means of an interpreter, telling me that he would make me a Christian, and he told me many things that I did not understand, and Cunnur, the interpreter, told me that I should do as the father told me, because now I was not going to be set free, and it would go very bad with me if I did not consent in it. They gave me *atole de mayz* [corn gruel] to eat which I did not like because I was not accustomed to that food; but there was nothing else to eat.

One day they threw water on my head and gave me salt to eat, and with this the interpreter told me that now I was Christian and that I was called *Jesús*: I knew nothing of this, and I tolerated it all because in the end I was a poor Indian and did not have recourse but to conform myself and tolerate the things they did with me.

The following day after my baptism, they took me to work with the other Indians, and they put me to cleaning a *milpa* [cornfield] of maize; since I did not know how to manage the hoe that they gave me, after hoeing a little, I cut my foot and could not continue working with it, but I was put to pulling out the weeds by hand, and in this manner I did not finish the task that they gave me. In the afternoon they lashed me for not finishing the job, and the following day the same thing happened as on the previous day. Every day they lashed me unjustly because I did not finish what I did not know how to do, and thus I existed for many days until I found a way to escape; but I was tracked and they caught me like a fox; there they seized me by lasso as on the first occasion, and they carried me off to the mission torturing me on the road. After we arrived, the father passed along the corridor of the house, and he ordered that they fasten me to the stake and castigate me; they lashed me until I lost consciousness, and I did not regain consciousness for many hours afterwards. For several days I could not raise myself from the floor where they had laid me, and I still have on my shoulders the marks of the lashes which they gave me then.

FREDERICK DOUGLASS

1817 - 1895

Previously to my contemplation of the anti-slavery movement and its probable results, my mind had been seriously awakened to the subject of religion. I was not more than thirteen years old, when, in my loneliness and destitution, I longed for some one to whom I could go, as to a father and protector. The preaching of a white Methodist minister, named Hanson, was the means of causing me to feel that in God I had such a friend. He thought that all men, great and small, bond and free, were sinners in the sight of God; that they were by nature rebels against his government; and that they must repent of

Published in 1845, *Narrative of the Life of Frederick Douglass* caused its author to flee the country to avoid capture rather than to revel in his newfound fame. **Frederick Douglass**, born in 1817, came into this world a slave and left it as the most prominent black abolitionist

of his time, even lending advice to Abraham Lincoln on more than one occasion. Douglass explains in his autobiography that it was faith that enabled him to endure the privations of slavery and to remain hopeful that someday freedom would come.

their sins, and be reconciled to God through Christ. I cannot say that I had a very distinct notion of what was required of me, but one thing I did know well: that I was wretched and had no means of making myself otherwise. Though for weeks I was a poor, broken-hearted mourner traveling through doubts and fears, I finally found my burden lightened, and my heart relieved. I loved all mankind, slaveholders not excepted, though I abhorred slavery more than ever. I saw the world in a new light, and my great concern was to have everybody converted. My desire to learn increased, and especially did I want a thorough acquaintance with the contents of the Bible. I have gathered scattered pages of the Bible from the filthy street-gutters, and washed and dried them, that in moments of leisure I might get a word or two of wisdom from them.

While thus religiously seeking knowledge, I became acquainted with a good old colored man named Charles Lawson. This man not only prayed three times a day, but he prayed as he walked through the streets, at his work, on his dray—everywhere. His life was a life of prayer, and his words when he spoke to any one were about a better world. Uncle Lawson lived near Master Hugh's house, and becoming deeply attached to him, I went often with him to prayer-meeting and spent much of my leisure time on Sunday with him. The old man could read a little, and I was a great help to him in making out the hard words, for I was a better reader than he. I could teach him "the letter," but he could teach me "the spirit," and refreshing times we had together, in singing and praying. These meetings went on for a long time without the knowledge either of Master Hugh or my mistress. Both knew, however, that I had become religious, and seemed to respect my conscientious piety. My mistress was still a professor of religion, and belonged to class. Her leader was no less a person than Rev. Beverly Waugh, the presiding elder, and afterwards one of the bishops of the Methodist Episcopal Church.

In view of the cares and anxieties incident to the life she was leading, and especially in view of the separation from religious associations to which she was subjected, my mistress had, as I have before stated, become

lukewarm, and needed to be looked up by her leader. This often brought Mr. Waugh to our house, and gave me an opportunity to hear him exhort and pray. But my chief instructor in religious matters was Uncle Lawson. He was my spiritual father and I loved him intensely, and was at his house every chance I could get. This pleasure, however, was not long unquestioned. Master Hugh became averse to our intimacy, and threatened to whip me if I ever went there again. I now felt myself persecuted by a wicked man, and I *would* go. The good old man had told me that the Lord had great work for me to do, and I must prepare to do it; that he had been shown that I must preach the gospel. His words made a very deep impression upon me, and I verily felt that some such work was before me, though I could not see how I could ever engage in its performance. The good Lord would bring it to pass in his own good time, he said, and that I must go on reading and studying the Scriptures. This advice and these suggestions were not without their influence on my character and destiny. He fanned my already intense love of knowledge into a flame by assuring me that I was to be a useful man in the world. When I would say to him, "How can these things be? and what can I do?" his simple reply was, "Trust in the Lord." When I would tell him, "I am a slave, and a slave for life, how can I do anything?" he would quietly answer, "The *Lord* can make you free, my dear; all things are possible with Him; only have *faith* in God. 'Ask, and it shall be given you.' If you want liberty, ask the Lord for it in faith, and He will give it to you."

Thus assured and thus cheered on under the inspiration of hope, I worked and prayed with a light heart, believing that my life was under the guidance of a wisdom higher than my own. With all other blessings sought at the mercy seat, I always prayed that God would, of His great mercy, and in His own good time, deliver me from my bondage. . . .

IN THE unhappy state of mind described in the foregoing chapter, regretting my very existence because doomed to a life of bondage, and so goaded and wretched as to be even tempted at times to take my own life, I was most keenly sensitive to know any and everything possible that had any relation to the subject of slavery. I was all ears, all eyes, whenever the words slave or slavery dropped from the lips of any white person, and more and more frequently occasions occurred when these words became leading ones in high, social debate at our house. Very often I would overhear Master Hugh, or some of his company, speak with much warmth of the *abolitionists*. Who or what the *abolitionists* were, I was totally ignorant. I found, however, that whoever or whatever they might be, they were most cordially hated and abused by slaveholders of every grade. I very soon discovered too, that slavery was, in some sort, under consideration whenever the abolitionists were alluded to. This made the term a very interesting one to me. If a slave had made good his escape from slavery, it was generally alleged that he had been persuaded and assisted to do so by the abolitionists. If a slave killed his master, or struck down his overseer, or set fire his master's dwelling, or committed any violence or crime, out of the common way, it was certain to be said that such a crime was the legitimate fruits of the abolition movement. Hearing such charges often repeated, I, naturally enough, received the impression that abolition—whatever else it might be—was not unfriendly to the slave, nor very friendly to the slaveholder. I therefore set about finding out, if possible, who and what the abolitionists were, and why they were so obnoxious to the slaveholders. The dictionary offered me very little help. It taught me that abolition was "the act of abolishing," but it left me in ignorance at the very point where I most wanted information, and that was, as to the thing to be abolished.

A city newspaper—the Baltimore *American*—gave me the incendiary information denied me by the dictionary. In its columns I found that on a certain day a vast number of petitions and memorials had been presented to Congress, praying for the abolition of slavery in the District of Columbia, and for the abolition of the slave trade between the States of the Union. This was enough. The vindictive bitterness, the marked caution, the studied reserve, and the ambiguity practiced by our white folks when alluding to this subject, was now fully explained. Ever after that, when I heard the word abolition, I felt the matter one of a personal concern, and I drew near to listen whenever I could do so, without seeming too solicitous and prying. There was hope in those words. Ever and anon too, I could see some terrible denunciation of slavery in our papers—copied from abolition papers at the North—and the injustice of such denunciation commented on. These I read with avidity. I had a deep satisfaction in the thought that the rascality of slaveholders was not concealed from the eyes of the world, and that I was not alone in abhorring the cruelty and brutality of slavery. A still deeper train of thought was stirred. I saw that there was

fear as well as rage in the manner of speaking of the abolitionists, and from this I inferred that they must have some power in the country, and I felt that they might perhaps succeed in their designs. When I met with a slave to whom I deemed it safe to talk on the subject, I would impart to him so much of the mystery as I had been able to penetrate. Thus the light of this grand movement broke in upon my mind by degrees, and I must say that ignorant as I was of the philosophy of that movement, I believed in it from the first, and I believed in it, partly, because I saw that it alarmed the consciences of the slaveholders. The insurrection of Nat Turner had been quelled, but the alarm and terror which it occasioned had not subsided. The cholera was then on its way to this country, and I remember thinking that God was angry with the white people because of their slaveholding wickedness, and therefore his judgments were abroad in the land. Of course it was impossible for me not to hope much for the abolition movement when I saw it supported by the Almighty, and armed with death. . . .

I went one day on the wharf of Mr. Waters, and seeing two Irishmen unloading a scow of stone or ballast, I went on board unasked, and helped them. When we had finished the work one of the men came to me, aside, and asked me a number of questions, and among them if I were a slave? I told him I was a slave for life. The good Irishman gave a shrug, and seemed deeply affected. He said it was a pity so fine a little fellow as I should be a slave for life. They both had much to say about the matter, and expressed the deepest sympathy with me, and the most decided hatred of slavery. They went so far as to tell me that I ought to run away and go to the North, that I should find friends there, and that I should then be as free as anybody. I pretended not to be interested in what they said, for I feared they might be treacherous. White men were not unfrequently known to encourage slaves to escape, and then, to get the reward, they would kidnap them and return them to their masters. While I mainly inclined to the notion that these men were honest and meant me no ill, I feared it might be otherwise. I nevertheless remembered their words and their advice, and looked forward to an escape to the North as a possible means of gaining the liberty for which my heart panted. It was not my enslavement at the then present time which most affected me—the *being a slave for life* was the saddest thought. I was too young to think of running away immediately; besides, I wished to learn to write before going, as I might have occasion to write my own pass. I now not only had the hope of freedom, but a fore-shadowing of the means by which I might some day gain that inestimable boon. Meanwhile I resolved to add to my educational attainments the art of writing.

After this manner I began to learn to write. I was much in the shipyard—Master Hugh's, and that of Durgan & Bailey—and I observed that the carpenters, after hewing and getting ready a piece of timber to use, wrote on it the initials of the name of that part of the ship for which it was intended. When, for instance, a piece of timber was ready for the starboard side, it was marked with a capital "S." A piece for the larboard side was marked "L."; larboard forward was marked "L.F."; larboard aft was marked "L.A."; starboard aft, "S.A."; and starboard forward, "S.F." I soon learned these letters, and for what they were placed on the timbers.

My work now was to keep fire under the steambox, and to watch the shipyard while the carpenters had gone to dinner. This interval gave me a fine opportunity for copying the letters named. I soon astonished myself with the ease with which I made the letters, and the thought was soon present, "If I can make four letters I can make more." Having made these readily and easily, when I met boys about the Bethel church or on any of our playgrounds, I entered the lists with them in the art of writing, and would make the letters which I had been so fortunate as to learn, and ask them to beat that if they could. With playmates for my teachers, fences and pavements for my copybooks, and chalk for my pen and ink, I learned to write. I however adopted, after-ward, various methods for improving my hand. The most successful was copying the italics in *Webster's Spelling-Book* until I could make them all without looking on the book. By this time my little Master Tommy had grown to be a big boy, and had written over a number of copy books and brought them home. They had been shown to the neighbors, had elicited due praise, and had been laid carefully away. Spending parts of my time both at the shipyard and the house, I was often the lone keeper of the latter as of the former. When my mistress left me in charge of the house I had a grand time. I got Master Tommy's copy books and a pen and ink, and in the ample spaces between the lines I wrote other lines as nearly like his as possible. The process was a tedious one, and I ran the risk of getting a flogging for marking the highly prized copy books of the oldest son. In addition to these opportunities, sleeping as I did in the kitchen loft, a room seldom visited by any of the family, I contrived to get a flour-barrel up there and a chair, and upon the head of that barrel I have written, or endeavored to write, copying from the Bible and the Methodist hymn book, and other books which I had accumulated, till late at night, and when all the family were in bed and asleep. I was supported in my endeavors by renewed advice and by holy promises from the good father Lawson, with whom I continued to meet and pray and read the Scriptures. Although Master Hugh was aware of these meetings, I must say for his credit that he never executed his threats to whip me for having thus innocently employed my leisure time.

ANDREW CARNEGIE
1835 - 1919

A new horizon was opened up to me by this voyage. It quite changed my intellectual outlook. Spencer and Darwin were then high in the zenith, and I had become deeply interested in their work. I began to view the various phases of human life from the standpoint of the evolutionist. In China I read Confucius; in India, Buddha and the sacred books of the Hindoos; among the Parsees, in Bombay, I studied Zoroaster. The result of my journey was to bring a certain mental peace. Where there had been chaos there was now order. My mind was at rest. I had a philosophy at last. The words of Christ "The Kingdom of Heaven is within you," had a new meaning for me. Not in the past or in the future, but now and here is Heaven within us. All our duties lie in this world and in the present, and trying impatiently to peer into that which lies beyond is as vain as fruitless.

All the remnants of theology in which I had been born and bred, all the impressions that Swedenborg had made upon me, now ceased to influence me or to occupy my thoughts. I found that no nation had all the truth in the revelation it

Famous for his remarkable acts of philanthropy, millionaire **Andrew Carnegie** reveals in his autobiography that he had a firm foundation in Christian faith. Born in Dunfermline, Scotland, in 1835, Carnegie emigrated to the United States as a child and began working in a cotton factory almost immediately upon arrival. That inauspicious beginning eventually led to his career as a steel tycoon. Carnegie's personal worth was estimated at half a billion dollars at the time of his retirement. Among his many gifts were the over three million dollars he gave to various churches on behalf of peace in the world.

regards as divine, and no tribe is so low as to be left without some truth; that every people has had its great teacher; Buddha for one; Confucius for another; Zoroaster for a third; Christ for a fourth. The teachings of all these I found ethically akin so that I could say with Matthew Arnold, one I was so proud to call friend:

> *"Children of men! the unseen Power, whose eye*
> *For ever doth accompany mankind*
> *Hath looked on no religion scornfully*
> * That men did every find.*
>
> *Which has not taught weak wills*
> * how much they can?*
> *Which has not fall'n in the dry heart like rain?*
> *Which has not cried to sunk, self-weary man,*
> *'Thou must be born again."*

Among the conditions of life or the laws of nature, some of which seem to us faulty, some apparently unjust and merciless, there are many that amaze us by their beauty and sweetness. Love of home, regardless of its character or location, certainly is one of these. And what a pleasure it is to find that, instead of the Supreme Being confining revelation to one race or nation, every race has the message best adapted for it in its present stage of development. The Unknown Power has neglected none.

MUHAMMAD ALEXANDER RUSSEL WEBB
1846 - 1916

I have been requested to tell you why I, an American, born in a country which is nominally Christian, and reared under the drippings, or more properly perhaps the drivelling, of an orthodox Presbyterian pulpit, came to adopt the faith of Islam as my guide in life. I might reply promptly and truthfully that I adopted this religion because I found, after protracted study, that it was the best and only system adopted to the spiritual needs of humanity. And here let me say that I was not born as

An anomaly in his time, and perhaps in ours, **Webb** was a Presbyterian who converted to Islam. A journalist and essayist, Webb was appointed U.S. Consul to the Philippines in 1887, and it was there that he experienced his conversion. A man of letters, Webb expresses his reasons for conversion

some boys seem to be, with a fervently religious strain in my character. When I reached the age of 20, and became practically my own master, I was so tired of the restraint and dullness of the Church, that I wandered away from it and never returned to it. . . . Fortunately I was of an enquiring turn of mind—I wanted a reason for everything, and I found that neither laymen nor clergy could give me any rational explasm and monads, and yet not one of them could tell me what mysterious [sic] or that they were beyond my comprehension. About eleven years ago I became interested in the study of Oriental religions. . . . I saw Mill and Locke, Kant, Hegel, Fichte, Huxley, and many other more or less learned writers discoursing with a great show of wisdom concerning protoplasm and monads and yet not one of them could tell me what the soul was or what became of it after death. . . . I have spoken so much of myself in order to show you that my adoption of Islam was not the result of misguided sentiment, blind credulity, or sudden emotional impulse, but that it was born of earnest, honest, persistent, unprejudiced study and investigation and an intense desire to know the truth.

eloquently, if perhaps a bit defensively, in this excerpt from *Islam Our Choice*, explaining that he embraced Islam not for rash or impulsive reasons, but rather out of his deep admiration of its ideas and values.

The essence of the true faith of Islam is resignation to the will of God and its corner stone is prayer. It teaches universal fraternity, universal love, and universal benevolence, and requires purity of mind, purity of action, purity of speech and perfect physical cleanliness. It, beyond doubt, is the simplest and most elevating form of religion known to man.

WILLIAM JAMES
1842 - 1910

FIRST SELCTION
LECTURE IX
CONVERSION—

To be converted, to be regenerated, to receive grace, to experience religion, to gain an assurance, are so many phrases which denote the process, gradual or sudden, by which a self hitherto divided, and consciously wrong inferior and unhappy, becomes unified and consciously

One of the nation's first psychologists, **William James** has long been hailed for his perceptive and intelligent analysis of faith.

Born in New York and educated at Harvard, he wrote extensively on religion and religious philosophy, slowly coming to the conclusion that we reach truth through experience rather than through ready acceptance of absolute principles. James, who held professorships at Harvard in the fields of philosophy, physiology, and psychology, was not a believer himself, but that did not detract from his investigation of the vagaries of faith. By applying psychological methodology to an examination of religion, the author affected the scientific understanding of faith in an almost revolutionary way, as this excerpt from *The Varieties of Religious Experience* demonstrates.

right superior and happy, in consequence of its firmer hold upon religious realities. This at least is what conversion signifies in general terms, whether or not we believe that a direct divine operation is needed to bring such a moral change about.

Before entering upon a minuter study of the process, let me enliven our understanding of the definition by a concrete example. I choose the quaint case of an unlettered man, Stephen H. Bradley, whose experience is related in a scarce American pamphlet. [1]

I select this case because it shows how in these inner alternations one may find one unsuspected depth below another, as if the possibilities of character lay disposed in a series of layers or shells, of whose existence we have no premonitory knowledge.

Bradley thought that he had been already fully converted at the age of fourteen.

"I thought I saw the Saviour, by faith, in human shape, for about one second in the room, with arms extended, appearing to say to me, Come. The next day I rejoiced with trembling; soon after, my happiness was so great that I said that I wanted to die; this world had no place in my affections, as I knew of, and every day appeared as solemn to me as the Sabbath. I had an ardent desire that all mankind might feel as I did; I wanted to have them all love God supremely. Previous to this time I was very selfish and self-righteous; but now I desired the welfare of all mankind, and could with a feeling heart forgive my worst enemies, and I felt as if I should be willing to bear the scoffs and sneers of any person, and suffer anything for His sake, if I could be the means in the hands of God, of the conversion of one soul."

Nine years later, in 1829, Mr. Bradley heard of a revival of religion that had begun in his neighborhood.

"Many of the young converts," he says, "would come to me when in meeting and ask me if I had religion, and my reply generally was, I hope I have. This did not appear to satisfy them; they said they *knew they* had it. I requested them to pray for me, thinking with myself, that if I had not got religion now, after so long a time professing to be a Christian, that it was time I had, and hoped their prayers would be answered in my behalf.

"One Sabbath, I went to hear the Methodist at the Academy. He spoke of the ushering in of the day of general judgment; and he set it forth in such a solemn and terrible manner as I never heard before. The scene of that day appeared to be taking place, and so awakened were all the powers of my mind that, like Felix, I trembled involuntarily on the bench where I was sitting, though I felt nothing at heart. The next day evening I went to hear him again. He took his text from Revelation: 'And I saw the dead, small and great, stand before God.' And he represented the terrors of that day in such a manner that it appeared as if it would melt the heart of stone. When he finished his discourse, an old gentleman turned to me and said, 'This is what I call preaching.' I thought the same; but my feelings were still unmoved by what he said, and I did not enjoy religion, but I believe he did.

"I will now relate my experience of the power of the Holy Spirit which took place on the same night. Had any person told me previous to this that I could have experienced the power of the Holy Spirit in the manner which I did, I could not have believed it, and should have thought the person deluded that told me so. I went directly home after the meeting, and when I got home I wondered what made me feel so stupid. I retired to rest soon after I got home, and felt indifferent to the things of religion until I began to be exercised by the Holy Spirit, which began in about five minutes after, in the following manner:—

"At first, I began to feel my heart beat very quick all on a sudden, which made me at first think that perhaps something is going to ail me, though I was not alarmed, for I felt no pain. My heart increased in its beating, which soon convinced me that it was the Holy Spirit from the effect it had on me. I began to feel exceedingly happy and humble, and such a sense of unworthiness as I never felt before. I could not very well help speaking out, which I did, and said, Lord, I do

---

[1] A sketch of the life of Stephen H. Bradley, from the age of five to twenty-four years, including his remarkable experience of the power of the Holy Spirit on the second evening of November, 1829. Madison, Connecticut, 1830.

not deserve this happiness, or words to that effect, while there was a stream (resembling air in feeling) came into my mouth and heart in a more sensible manner than that of drinking anything, which continued, as near as I could judge, five minutes or more, which appeared to be the cause of such a palpitation of my heart. It took complete possession of my soul, and I am certain that I desired the Lord, while in the midst of it, not to give me any more happiness, for it seemed as if I could not contain what I had got. My heart seemed as if it would burst, but it did not stop until I felt as if I was unutterably full of the love and grace of God. In the mean time while thus exercised, a thought arose in my mind, what can it mean? and all at once, as if to answer it, my memory became exceedingly clear, and it appeared to me just as if the New Testament was placed open before me, eighth chapter of Romans, and as light as if some candle lighted was held for me to read the 26th and 27th verses of that chapter, and I read these words: 'The Spirit helpeth our infirmities with groanings which cannot be uttered.' And all the time that my heart was a-beating, it made me groan like a person in distress, which was not very easy to stop, though I was in no pain at all, and my brother being in bed in another room came and opened the door, and asked me if I had got the toothache. I told him no, and that he might get to sleep. I tried to stop. I felt unwilling to go to sleep myself, I was so happy, fearing I should lose it—thinking within myself

> 'My willing soul would stay
> In such a frame as this.'

And while I lay reflecting, after my heart stopped beating, feeling as if my soul was full of the Holy Spirit, I thought that perhaps there might be angels hovering round my bed. I felt just as if I wanted to converse with them, and finally I spoke, saying, 'O ye affectionate angels! how is it that ye can take so much interest in our welfare, and we take so little interest in our own.' After this, with difficulty I got to sleep; and when I awoke in the morning my first thoughts were: What has become of my happiness? and, feeling a degree of it in my heart, I asked for more, which was given to me as quick as thought. I then got up to dress myself, and found to my surprise that I could but just stand. It appeared to me as if it was a little heaven upon earth. My soul felt as completely raised above the fears of death as of going to sleep; and like a bird in a cage, I had a desire, if it was the will of God, to get released from my body and to dwell with Christ, though willing

to live to do good to others, and to warn sinners to repent. I went downstairs feeling as solemn as if I had lost all my friends, and thinking with myself, that I would not let my parents know it until I had first looked into the Testament. I went directly to the shelf and looked into it, at the eighth chapter of Romans, and every verse seemed to almost speak and to confirm it to be truly the Word of God, and as if my feelings corresponded with the meaning of the word. I then told my parents of it, and told them that I thought that they must see that when I spoke, that it was not my own voice, for it appeared so to me. My speech seemed entirely under the control of the Spirit within me; I do not mean that the words which I spoke were not my own, for they were. I thought that I was influenced similar to the Apostles on the day of Pentecost (with the exception of having power to give it to others, and doing what they did). After breakfast I went round to converse with my neighbors on religion, which I could not have been hired to have done before this, and at their request I prayed with them, though I had never prayed in public before.

"I now feel as if I had discharged my duty by telling the truth, and hope by the blessing of God, it may do some good to all who shall read it. He has fulfilled his promise in sending the Holy Spirit down into our hearts, or mine at least, and I now defy all the Deists and Atheists in the world to shake my faith in Christ."

So much for Mr. Bradley and his conversion, of the effect of which upon his later life we gain no information. Now for a minuter survey of the constituent elements of the conversion process.

If you open the chapter on Association, of any treatise on Psychology, you will read that a man's ideas, aims, and objects form diverse internal groups and systems, relatively independent of one another. Each 'aim' which he follows awakens a certain specific kind of interested excitement, and gathers a certain group of ideas together in subordination to it as its associates; and if the aims and excitements are distinct in kind, their groups of ideas may have little in common. When one group is present and engrosses the interest, all the ideas connected with other groups may be excluded from the mental field. The President of the United States when, with paddle, gun, and fishing-rod, he goes camping in the wilderness for a vacation, changes his system of ideas from top to bottom. The presidential anxieties have lapsed into the background entirely; the official habits are replaced by the habits of a son of nature, and those who knew the man only as the strenuous magistrate would not 'know him for the same person' if they saw him as the camper.

If now he should never go back, and never again suffer political interests to gain dominion over him, he would be for practical intents and purposes a permanently transformed being. Our ordinary alterations of character, as we pass from one of our aims to another, are not commonly called transformations, because each of them is so rapidly succeeded by another in the reverse direction; but whenever one aim grows so stable as to expel definitively its previous rivals from the individual's life, we tend to speak of the phenomenon, and perhaps to wonder at it, as a 'transformation.'

These alterations are the completest of the ways in which a self may be divided. A less complete way is the simultaneous coexistence of two or more different groups of aims, of which one practically holds the right of way and instigates activity, whilst the others are only pious wishes, and never practically come to anything. Saint Augustine's aspirations to a purer life, in our last lecture, were for a while an example. Another would be the President in his full pride of office, wondering whether it were not all vanity, and whether the life of a woodchopper were not the wholesomer destiny. Such fleeting aspirations are mere *velleitates*, whimsies. They exist on the remoter outskirts of the mind, and the real self of the man, the centre of his energies, is occupied with an entirely different system. As life goes on, there is a constant change of our interests, and a consequent change of place in our systems of ideas, from more central to more peripheral, and from more peripheral to more central parts of consciousness. I remember, for instance, that one evening when I was a youth, my father read aloud from a Boston newspaper that part of Lord Gifford's will which founded these four lectureships. At that time I did not think of being a teacher of philosophy: and what I listened to was as remote from my own life as if it related to the planet Mars. Yet here I am, with the Gifford system part and parcel of my very self, and all my energies, for the time being, devoted to successfully identifying myself with it. My soul stands now planted in what once was for it a practically unreal object, and speaks from it as from its proper habitat and centre.

When I say 'Soul,' you need not take me in the ontological sense unless you prefer to; for although ontological language is instinctive in such matters, yet Buddhists or Humians can perfectly well describe the facts in the phenomenal terms which are their favorites. For them the soul is only a succession of fields of consciousness: yet there is found in each field a part, or sub-field, which figures as focal and contains the excitement, and from which, as from a centre, the aim seems to be taken. Talking of this part, we involuntarily apply words of perspective to distinguish it from the rest, words like 'here,' 'this,' 'now,' 'mine,' or 'me'; and we ascribe to the other parts the positions 'there,' 'then,' 'that,' 'his' or 'thine,' 'it,' 'not me.' But a 'here' can change to a 'there,' and a 'there' become a 'here,' and what was 'mine' and what was 'not mine' change their places.

What brings such changes about is the way in which emotional excitement alters. Things hot and vital to us to-day are cold to-morrow. It is as if seen from the hot parts of the field that the other parts appear to us, and from these hot parts personal desire and volition make their sallies. They are in short the centres of our dynamic energy, whereas the cold parts leave us indifferent and passive in proportion to their coldness.

Whether such language be rigorously exact is for the present of no importance. It is exact enough, if you recognize from your own experience the facts which I seek to designate by it.

Now there may be great oscillation in the emotional interest, and the hot places may shift before one almost as rapidly as the sparks that run through burnt-up paper. Then we have the wavering and divided self we heard so much of in the previous lecture. Or the focus of excitement and heat, the point of view from which the aim is taken, may come to lie permanently within a certain system; and then, if the change be a religious one, we call it a *conversion*, especially if it be by crisis, or sudden.

Let us hereafter, in speaking of the hot place in a man's consciousness, the group of ideas to which he devotes himself, and from which he works, call it *the habitual centre of his personal energy*. It makes a great difference to a man whether one set of his ideas, or another, be the centre of his energy; and it makes a great difference, as regards any set of ideas which he may possess, whether they become central or remain peripheral in him. To say that a man is 'converted' means, in these terms, that religious ideas, previously peripheral in his consciousness, now take a central place, and that religious aims form the habitual centre of his energy.

Now if you ask of psychology just *how* the excitement shifts in a man's mental system, and *why* aims that were peripheral become at a certain moment central, psychology has to reply that although she can give a general description of what happens, she is unable in a given case to account accurately for all the single forces at work. Neither an outside observer nor the Subject who undergoes the process can explain fully how particular experiences are able to change one's centre of energy so decisively, or why they so often have to bide their hour to do so. We have a thought, or we perform an act, repeatedly, but on a certain day the real meaning of the thought peals through us for the first time, or the act has suddenly turned into a moral impossibility. All we know is that there are dead feelings, dead ideas, and cold beliefs, and there are hot and live ones; and when one grows hot and alive within us, everything has to re-crystallize about it. We may say that the heat and liveli-ness mean only the 'motor efficacy,' long deferred but now operative, of the idea; but such talk itself is only circumlocution, for whence the sudden motor efficacy? And our explanations then get so vague and general that one realizes all the more the intense individuality of the whole phenomenon.

In the end we fall back on the hackneyed symbol-ism of a mechanical equilibrium. A mind is a system of ideas, each with the excitement it arouses, and with tendencies impulsive and inhibitive, which mutually check or reinforce one another. The collection of ideas alters by subtraction or by addition in the course of experience, and the tendencies alter as the organism gets more aged. A mental system may be undermined or weakened by this interstitial alteration just as a building is, and yet for a time keep upright by dead habit. But a new perception, a sudden emotional shock, or an occasion which lays bare the organic alteration, will make the whole fabric fall together; and then the centre of gravity sinks into an attitude more stable, for the new ideas that reach the centre in the rearrangement seem now to be locked there, and the new structure remains permanent.

Formed associations of ideas and habits are usually factors of retardation in such changes of equilibrium. New information, however acquired, plays an acceler-ating part in the changes; and the slow mutation of our instincts and propensities, under the 'unimaginable touch of time' has an enormous influence. Moreover, all these influences may work subconsciously or half unconsciously. [2] And when you get a Subject in whom the subconscious life—of which I must speak more fully soon—is largely developed, and in whom motives habitually ripen in silence, you get a case of which you can never give a full account, and in which, both to the Subject and the onlookers, there may appear an ele-ment of marvel. Emotional occasions, especially vio-lent ones, are extremely potent in precipitating mental rearrangements. The sudden and explosive ways in which love, jealousy, guilt, fear, remorse, or anger can seize upon one are now to everybody. [3] Hope, happi-ness, security, resolve, emotions characteristic of con-version, can be equally explosive. And emotions that come in this explosive way seldom leave things as they found them.

In his recent work on the Psychology of Religion, Professor Starbuck of California has shown by a statis-tical inquiry how closely parallel in its manifestations the ordinary 'conversion' which occurs in young people brought up in evangelical circles is to that growth into a larger spiritual life which is a normal phase of ado-lescence in every class of human beings. The age is the same, falling usually between fourteen and seventeen. The symptoms are the same,—sense of incomplete-ness and imperfection; brooding, depression, morbid introspection, and sense of sin; anxiety about the here-after; distress over doubts, and the like. And the result is the same,—a happy relief and objectivity, as the con-fidence in self gets greater through the adjustment of the faculties to the wider outlook. In spontaneous reli-gious awakening, apart from the revivalistic examples,

---

[2] Jouffroy is an example: "Down this slope it was that my intelligence had glided, and little by little it had got far from its first faith. But this melancholy revolution had not taken place in the broad daylight of my consciousness; too many scruples, too many guides and sacred affections had made it dreadful to me, so that I was far from avowing to myself the progress it had made. It had gone on in silence, by an involuntary elaboration of which I was not the accomplice; and although I had in reality long ceased to be a Christian, yet, in the innocence of my intention, I should have shuddered to suspect it, and thought it calumny had I been accused of such a falling away." Then follows Jouffroy's account of his counter-conversion, quoted above on p. 147.

[3] One hardly needs examples; but for love, see p. 149; note; for fear, see p. 135; for remorse, see Othello after the murder; for anger, see Lear after Cordelia's first speech to him; for resolve, see p. 148 (J. Foster case). Here is a pathological case in which *guilt* was the feeling that suddenly exploded: "One night I was seized on entering bed with a rigor, such a Swedenborg describes as coming over him with a sense of holiness, but over me with a sense of *guilt*. During that whole night I lay under the influence of the rigor, and from its incep-tion I felt that I was under the curse of God. I have never done one act of duty in my life—sins against God and man, beginning as far as my memory goes back—a wildcat in human shape."

and in the ordinary storm and stress and moulting-time of adolescence, we also may meet with mystical experiences, astonishing the subjects by their sudden-ness, just as in revivalistic conversion. The analogy, in fact, is complete; and Starbuck's conclusion as to these ordinary youthful conversions would seem to be the only sound one: Conversion is in its essence a normal adolescent phenomenon, incidental to the passage from the child's small universe to the wider intellectual and spiritual life of maturity.

"Theology," says Dr. Starbuck, "takes the adolescent tendencies and builds upon them; it sees that the essential thing in adolescent growth is bringing the person out of childhood into the new life of maturity and personal insight. It accordingly brings those means to bear which will intensify the normal tendencies. It shortens up the period of duration of storm and stress." The conversion phenomena of 'conviction of sin' last, by this investigator's statistics, about one fifth as long as the periods of adolescent storm and stress phenomena of which he also got statistics, but they are very much more intense. Bodily accompaniments, loss of sleep and appetite, for example, are much more frequent in them. "The essential distinction appears to be that conversion intensifies but shortens the period by bringing the person to a definite crisis."[4]

The conversions which Dr. Starbuck here has in mind are of course mainly those of very commonplace persons, kept true to a pre-appointed type by instruction, appeal, and example. The particular form which they affect is the result of suggestion and imitation.[5] If they went through their growth-crisis in other faiths and other countries, although the essence of the change would be the same (since it is one in the main so inevitable), its accidents would be different. In Catholic lands, for example, and in our own Episcopalian sects, no such anxiety and conviction of sin is usual as in sects that encourage revivals. The sacraments being more relied on in these more strictly ecclesiastical bodies, the individual's personal acceptance of salvation needs less to be accentuated and led up to.

But every imitative phenomenon must once have had its original, and I propose that for the future we keep as close as may be to the more first-hand and original forms of experience. These are more likely to be found in sporadic adult cases.

Professor Leuba, in a valuable article on the psychology of conversion,[6] subordinates the theological aspect of the religious life almost entirely to its moral aspect. The religious sense he defines as "the feeling of unwholeness, of moral imperfection, of sin, to use the technical word, accompanied by the yearning after the peace of unity." "The word 'religion,'" he says, "is getting more and more to signify the conglomerate of desires and emotions springing from the sense of sin and its release"; and he gives a large number of examples, in which the sin ranges from drunkenness to spiritual pride, to show that the sense of it may beset one and crave relief as urgently as does the anguish of the sickened flesh or any form of physical misery.

Undoubtedly this conception covers an immense number of cases. A good one to use as an example is that of Mr. S. H. Hadley, who after his conversion became an active and useful rescuer of drunkards in New York. His experience runs as follows:—

"One Tuesday evening I sat in a saloon in Harlem, a homeless, friendless, dying drunkard. I had pawned or sold everything that would bring a drink. I could not sleep unless I was dead drunk. I had not eaten for days, and for four nights preceding I had suffered with delirium tremens, or the horrors, from midnight till morning. I had often said, 'I will never be a tramp. I will never be cornered, for when that time comes, if ever it comes, I will find a home in the bottom of the river.' But the Lord so ordered it that when that time did come I was not able to walk one quarter of the way to the river. As I sat there thinking, I seemed to feel some great and mighty presence. I did not know then what it was.

---

[4] E. D. STARBUCK: The Psychology of Religion, pp. 224, 262.

[5] No one understands this better than Jonathan Edwards understood it already. Conversion narratives of the more commonplace sort must always be taken with the allowances which he suggests: "A rule received and established by common consent has a very great, though to many persons an insensible influence in forming their notions of the process of their own experience. I know very well how they proceed as to this matter, for I have had frequent opportunities of observing their conduct. Very often their experience at first appears like a confused chaos, but then those parts are selected which bear the nearest resemblance to such particular steps as are insisted on; and these are dwelt upon in their thoughts, and spoken of from time to time, till they grow more and more conspicuous in their view, and other parts which are neglected grow more and more obscure. Thus what they have experienced is insensibly strained, so as to bring it to an exact conformity to the scheme already established in their minds. And it becomes natural also for ministers, who have to deal with those who insist upon distinctness and clearness of method, to do so too." Treatise on Religious Affections.

[6] Studies in the Psychology of Religious Phenomena, American Journal of Psychology, vii. 309 (1896).

I did learn afterwards that it was Jesus, the sinner's friend. I walked up to the bar and pounded it with my fist till I made the glasses rattle. Those who stood by drinking looked on with scornful curiosity. I said I would never take another drink, if I died on the street, and really I felt as though that would happen before morning. Something said, 'If you want to keep this promise, go and have yourself locked up.' I went to the nearest station-house and had myself locked up.

"I was placed in a narrow cell, and it seemed as though all the demons that could find room came in that place with me. This was not all the company I had, either. No, praise the Lord; that dear Spirit that came to me in the saloon was present, and said, Pray. I did pray, and though I did not feel any great help, I kept on praying. As soon as I was able to leave my cell I was taken to the police court and remanded back to the cell. I was finally released, and found my way to my brother's house, where every care was given me. While lying in bed the admonishing Spirit never left me, and when I arose the following Sabbath morning I felt that day would decide my fate, and toward evening it came into my head to go to Jerry M'Auley's Mission. I went. The house was packed, and with great difficulty I made my way to the space near the platform. There I saw the apostle to the drunkard and the outcast—that man of God, Jerry M'Auley. He rose, and amid deep silence told his experience. There was a sincerity about this man that carried conviction with it, and I found myself saying, 'I wonder if God can save *me*?' I listened to the testimony of twenty-five or thirty persons, every one of whom had been saved from rum, and I made up my mind that I would be saved or die right there. When the invitation was given, I knelt down with a crowd of drunkards. Jerry made the first prayer. Then Mrs. M'Auley prayed fervently for us. Oh, what a conflict was going on for my poor soul! A blessed whisper said, 'Come'; the devil said, 'Be careful.' I halted but a moment, and then, with a breaking heart, I said, 'Dear Jesus, can you help me?' Never with mortal tongue can I describe that moment.

Although up to that moment my soul had been filled with indescribable gloom, I felt the glorious brightness of the noonday sun shine into my heart. I felt I was a free man. Oh, the precious feeling of safety, of freedom, of resting on Jesus! I felt that Christ with all his brightness and power had come into my life; that, indeed, old things had passed away and all things had become new.

"From that moment till now I have never wanted a drink of whiskey, and I have never seen money enough to make me take one. I promised God that night that if he would take away the appetite for strong drink, I would work for him all my life. He has done his part, and I have been trying to do mine." [7]

Dr. Leuba rightly remarks that there is little doctrinal theology in such an experience, which starts with the absolute need of a higher helper, and ends with the sense that he has helped us. He gives other cases of drunkards' conversions which are purely ethical, containing, as recorded, no theological beliefs whatever. John B. Gough's case, for instance, is practically, says Dr. Leuba, the conversion of an atheist—neither God nor Jesus being mentioned.[8] But in spite of the importance of this type of regeneration, with little or no intellectual readjustment, this writer surely makes it too exclusive. It corresponds to the subjectively centered form of morbid melancholy, of which Bunyan and Alline were examples. But we saw in our seventh lecture that there are objective forms of melancholy also, in which the lack of rational meaning of the universe, and of life anyhow, is the burden that weighs upon one—you remember Tolstoy's case.[9] So there are distinct elements in conversion, and their relations to individual lives deserve to be discriminated.[10]

Some persons, for instance, never are, and possibly never under any circumstances could be, converted. Religious ideas cannot become the centre of their spiritual energy. They may be excellent persons, servants of God in practical ways, but they are not children of his kingdom. They are either incapable of imagining the invisible; or else, in the language of devotion, they are

[7] I have abridged Mr. Hadley's account. For other conversions of drunkards, see his pamphlet, Rescue Mission Work, published at the Old Jerry M'Auley Water Street Mission, New York City. A striking collection of cases also appears in the appendix to Professor Leuba's article.

[8] A restaurant waiter served provisionally as Gough's 'Saviour.' General Booth, the founder of the Salvation Army, considers that the first vital step in saving outcasts consists in making them feel that some decent human being cares enough for them to take an interest in the question whether they are to rise or sink.

[9] The crisis of apathetic melancholy—no use in life—into which J. S. Mill records that he fell, and from which he emerged by the reading of Marmontel's Memoirs (Heaven save the mark!) and Wordsworth's poetry, is another intellectual and general metaphysical case. See Mill's Autobiography, New York, 1873, pp. 141, 148.

[10] Starbuck, in addition to 'escape from sin,' discriminates 'spiritual illumination' as a distinct type of conversion experience. Psychology of Religion, p. 85.

life-long subjects of 'barrenness' and 'dryness.' Such inaptitude for religious faith may in some cases be intellectual in its origin. Their religious faculties may be checked in their natural tendency to expand, by beliefs about the world that are inhibitive, the pessimistic and materialistic beliefs, for example, within which so many good souls, who in former times would have freely indulged their religious propensities, find themselves nowadays, as it were, frozen; or the agnostic vetoes upon faith as something weak and shameful, under which so many of us to-day lie cowering, afraid to use our instincts. In many persons such inhibitions are never overcome. To the end of their days they refuse to believe, their personal energy never gets to its religious centre, and the latter remains inactive in perpetuity.

In other persons the trouble is profounder. There are men anæsthetic on the religious side, deficient in that category of sensibility. Just as a bloodless organism can never, in spite of all its goodwill, attain to the reckless 'animal spirits' enjoyed by those of sanguine temperament; so the nature which is spiritually barren may admire and envy faith in others, but can never compass the enthusiasm and peace which those who are temperamentally qualified for faith enjoy. All this may, however, turn out eventually to have been a matter of temporary inhibition. Even late in life some thaw, some release may take place, some bolt be shot back in the barrenest breast, and the man's hard heart may soften and break into religious feeling. Such cases more than any others suggest the idea that sudden conversion is by miracle. So long as they exist, we must not imagine ourselves to deal with irretrievably fixed classes.

Now there are two forms of mental occurrence in human beings, which lead to a striking difference in the conversion process, a difference to which Professor Starbuck has called attention. You know how it is when you try to recollect a forgotten name. Usually you help the recall by working for it, by mentally running over the places, persons, and things with which the word was connected. But sometimes this effort fails; you feel then as if the harder you tried the less hope there would be, as though the name were *jammed*, and pressure in its direction only kept it all the more from rising. And then the opposite expedient often succeeds. Give up the effort entirely; think of something altogether different, and in half an hour the lost name comes sauntering

into your mind, as Emerson says, as carelessly as if it had never been invited. Some hidden process was started in you by the effort, which went on after the effort ceased, and made the result come as if it came spontaneously. A certain music teacher, says Dr. Starbuck, says to her pupils after the thing to be done has been clearly pointed out, and unsuccessfully attempted: "Stop trying and it will do itself."[11]

There is thus a conscious and voluntary way and an involuntary and unconscious way in which mental results may get accomplished; and we find both ways exemplified in the history of conversion, giving us two types, which Starbuck calls the *volitional type* and the *type by self-surrender* respectively.

In the volitional type the regenerative change is usually gradual, and consists in the building up, piece by piece, of a new set of moral and spiritual habits. But there are always critical points here at which the movement forward seems much more rapid. This psychological fact is abundantly illustrated by Dr. Starbuck. Our education in any practical accomplishment proceeds apparently by jerks and starts, just as the growth of our physical bodies does.

"An athlete . . . sometimes awakens suddenly to an understanding of the fine points of the game and to a real enjoyment of it, just as the convert awakens to an appreciation of religion. If he keeps on engaging in the sport, there may come a day when all at once the game plays itself through him—when he loses himself in some great contest. In the same way, a musician may suddenly reach a point at which pleasure in the technique of the art entirely falls away, and in some moment of inspiration he becomes the instrument through which music flows. The writer has chanced to hear two different married persons, both of whose wedded lives had been beautiful from the beginning, relate that not until a year or more after marriage did they awake to the full blessedness of married life. So it is with the religious experience of these persons we are studying."[12]

We shall erelong hear still more remarkable illustrations of subconsciously maturing processes eventuating in results of which we suddenly grow conscious. Sir William Hamilton and Professor Laycock of Edinburgh were among the first to call attention to this class of effects; but Dr. Carpenter first, unless I am mistaken, introduced the term 'unconscious cerebration,' which

[11] Psychology of Religion, p. 117.
[12] Psychology of Religion, p. 385. Compare, also, pp. 137-144 and 262.

has since then been a popular phrase of explanation. The facts are now known to us far more extensively than he could know them, and the adjective 'unconscious,' being for many of them almost certainly a misnomer, is better replaced by the vaguer term 'subconscious' or 'subliminal.'

Of the volitional type of conversion it would be easy to give examples,[13] but they are as a rule less interesting than those of the self-surrender type, in which the subconscious effects are more abundant and often startling. I will therefore hurry to the latter, the more so because the difference between the two types is after all not radical. Even in the most voluntarily built-up sort of regeneration there are passages of partial self-surrender interposed; and in the great majority of all cases, when the will has done its uttermost towards bringing one close to the complete unification aspired after, it seems that the very last step must be left to other forces and performed without the help of its activity. In other words, self-surrender becomes then indispensable. "The personal will," says Dr. Starbuck, "must be given up. In many cases relief persistently refuses to come until the person ceases to resist, or to make an effort in the direction he desires to go."

"I had said I would not give up; but when my will was broken, it was all over," writes one of Starbuck's correspondents.—Another says: "I simply said: 'Lord, I have done all I can; I leave the whole matter with Thee;' and immediately there came to me a great peace."—Another: "All at once it occurred to me that I might be saved, too, if I would stop trying to do it all myself, and follow Jesus: somehow I lost my load."— Another: I finally ceased to resist, and gave myself up, though it was a hard struggle. Gradually the feeling came over me that I had done my part, and God was willing to do his."[14]—"Lord, Thy will be done; damn or save!" cries John Nelson,[15] exhausted with the anxious struggle to escape damnation; and at that moment his soul was filled with peace.

Dr. Starbuck gives an interesting, and it seems to me a true, account—so far as conceptions so schematic can claim truth at all—of the reasons why self-surrender at the last moment should be so indispensable. To begin with, there are two things in the mind of the candidate for conversion: first, the present incompleteness or wrongness, the 'sin' which he is eager to escape from; and, second, the positive ideal which he longs to compass. Now with most of us the sense of our present wrongness is a far more distinct piece of our consciousness than is the imagination of any positive ideal we can aim at. In the majority of cases, indeed, the 'sin' almost exclusively engrosses the attention, so that conversion is *"a process of struggling away from sin rather than of striving towards righteousness."*[16] A man's conscious wit and will, so far as they strain towards the ideal, are aiming at something only dimly and inaccurately imagined. Yet all the while the forces of mere organic ripening within him are going on towards their own prefigured result, and his conscious strainings are letting loose subconscious allies behind the scenes, which in their way work towards rearrangement; and the rearrangement towards which all these deeper forces tend is pretty surely definite, and definitely different from what he consciously conceives and determines. It may consequently be actually interfered with (*jammed*, as it were like the

---

[13] For instance, C. G. Finney italicizes the volitional element: "Just at this point the whole question of Gospel salvation opened to my mind in a manner most marvelous to me at the time. I think I then saw, as clearly as I ever have in my life, the reality and fullness of the atonement of Christ. Gospel salvation seemed to me to be an offer of something to be accepted, and all that was necessary on my part was to get my own consent to give up my sins and accept Christ. After this distinct revelation had stood for some little time before my mind, the question seemed to be put, 'Will you accept it now, to-day?' I replied, 'Yes; *I will accept it to-day, or I will die in the attempt!*'" He then went into the woods, where he describes his struggles. He could not pray, his heart was hardened in its pride. "I then reproached myself for having promised to give my heart to God. . . . The thought was pressing me, of the rashness of my promise that I would give my heart to God that day, or die in the attempt. It seemed to me as if that was binding on my soul; and yet I was going to break my vow. A great sinking and discouragement came over me, and I felt almost too weak to stand upon my knees. Just at this moment I again thought I heard someone approach me, and I opened my eyes to see whether it were so. But right there the revelation of my pride of heart, as the great difficulty that sptood in the way, was distinctly shown to me. An overwhelming sense of my wickedness in being ashamed to have a human being see me on my knees before God took such powerful possession of me, that *I cried at the top of my voice, and exclaimed that I would not leave that place if all the men on earth and all the devils in hell surrounded me.* 'What!' I said, 'such a degraded sinner as I am, on my knees confessing my sins to the great and holy God; and ashamed to have any human being, and a sinner like myself, find me on my knees endeavoring to make my peace with my offended God!' The sin appeared awful, infinite. It broke me down before the Lord." Memoirs, pp. 14-16, abridged.

[14] STARBUCK: Op. cit., pp. 91, 114.

[15] Extracts from the Journal of Mr. John Nelson, London, no date, p. 24.

[16] STARBUCK, p. 64

lost word when we seek too energetically to recall it), by his voluntary efforts slanting from the true direction.

Starbuck seems to put his finger on the root of the matter when he says that to exercise the personal will is still to live in the region where the imperfect self is the thing most emphasized. Where, on the contrary, the subconscious forces take the lead, it is more probably the better self *in posse* which directs the operation. Instead of being clumsily and vaguely aimed at from without, it is then itself the organizing centre. What then must the person do? "He must relax," says Dr. Starbuck,—" that is, he must fall back on the larger Power that makes for righteousness, which has been welling up in his own being, and let it finish in its own way the work it has begun. . . . The act of yielding, in this point of view, is giving one's self over to the new life, making it the centre of a new personality, and living, from within, the truth of it which had before been viewed objectively."[17]

"Man's extremity is God's opportunity" is the theological way of putting this fact of the need of self-surrender; whilst the physiological way of stating it would be, "Let one do all in one's power, and one's nervous system will do the rest." Both statements acknowledge the same fact.[18]

To state it in terms of our own symbolism: When the new centre of personal energy has been subconsciously incubated so long as to be just ready to open into flower, 'hands off' is the only word for us, it must burst forth unaided!

We have used the vague and abstract language of psychology. But since, in any terms, the crisis described is the throwing of our conscious selves upon the mercy of powers which, whatever they may be, are more ideal than we are actually, and make for our redemption, you see why self-surrender has been and always must be regarded as the vital turning-point of the religious life, so far as the religious life is spiritual and no affair of outer works and ritual and sacraments. One may say that the whole development of Christianity in inwardness has consisted in little more than the greater and greater emphasis attached to this crisis of self-surrender. From Catholicism to Lutheranism, and then to Calvinism; from that to Wesleyanism; and from this, outside of technical Christianity altogether, to pure 'liberalism' or transcendental idealism, whether or not of the mindcure type, taking in the mediæval mystics, the quietists, the pietists, and quakers by the way, we can trace the stages of progress towards the idea of an immediate spiritual help, experienced by the individual in his forlorness and standing in no essential need of doctrinal apparatus or propitiatory machinery.

Psychology and religion are thus in perfect harmony up to this point, since both admit that there are forces seemingly outside of the conscious individual that bring redemption to his life. Nevertheless psychology, defining these forces as 'subconscious,' and speaking of their effects as due to 'incubation,' or 'cerebration,' implies that they do not transcend the individual's personality; and herein she diverges from Christian theology, which insists that they are direct supernatural operations of the Deity. I propose to you that we do not yet consider this divergence final, but leave the question for a while in abeyance—continued inquiry may enable us to get rid of some of the apparent discord.

Revert, then, for a moment more to the psychology of self-surrender.

When you find a man living on the ragged edge of his consciousness, pent in to his sin and want and incompleteness, and consequently inconsolable, and then simply tell him that all is well with him, that he must stop his worry, break with his discontent, and give up his anxiety, you seem to him to come with pure absurdities. The only positive consciousness he has tells him that all is *not* well, and the better way you offer sounds simply as if you proposed to him to assert cold-blooded falsehoods. 'The will to believe' cannot be stretched as far as that. We can make ourselves more faithful to a belief of which we have the rudiments, but we cannot create a belief out of whole cloth when our perception actively assures us of its opposite. The better mind proposed to us comes in that case in the form of a pure negation of the only mind we have, and we cannot actively will a pure negation.

There are only two ways in which it is possible to get rid of anger, worry, fear, despair, or other undesirable affections. One is that an opposite affection should over-poweringly break over us, and the other is by getting so exhausted with the struggle that we have to stop,—so we drop down, give up, and *don't care* any longer. Our emotional brain-centres strike work, and we lapse into a temporary apathy. Now there is documentary proof that this state of temporary exhaustion

---

[17] STARBUCK, p. 115.
[18] STARBUCK, p. 113.

not infrequently forms part of the conversion crisis. So long as the egoistic worry of the sick soul guards the door, the expansive confidence of the soul of faith gains no presence. But let the former faint away, even but for a moment, and the latter can profit by the opportunity, and, having once acquired possession, may retain it. Carlyle's Teufelsdröckh passes from the everlasting No to the everlasting Yes through a 'Centre of Indifference.'

Let me give you a good illustration of this feature in the conversion process. That genuine saint, David Brainerd, describes his own crisis in the following words:—

"One morning, while I was walking in a solitary place as usual, I at once saw that all my contrivances and projects to effect or procure deliverance and salvation for myself were utterly in vain; I was brought quite to a stand, as finding myself totally lost. I saw that it was forever impossible for me to do anything towards helping or delivering myself, that I had made all the pleas I ever could have made to all eternity; and that all pleas were vain, for I saw that self-interest had led me to pray, and that I had never once prayed from any respect to the glory of God. I saw that there was no necessary connection between my prayers and the bestowment of divine mercy; that they laid not the least obligation upon God to bestow his grace upon me; and that there was no more virtue or goodness in them than there would be in my paddling with my hand in the water. I saw that I had been heaping up my devotions before God, fasting, praying, etc., pretending, and indeed really thinking sometimes that I was aiming at the glory of God; whereas I never once truly intended it, but only my own happiness. I saw that as I had never done anything for God, I had no claim on anything from him but perdition, on account of my hypocrisy and mockery. When I saw evidently that I had regard to nothing but self-interest, then my duties appeared a vile mockery and a continual course of lies, for the whole was nothing but self-worship, and an horrid abuse of God.

"I continued, as I remember, in this state of mind, from Friday morning till the Sabbath evening following (July 12, 1739), when I was walking again in the same solitary place. Here, in a mournful melancholy state *I was attempting to pray; but found no heart to engage in that or any other duty; my former concern,*

*exercise, and religious affections were now gone. I thought that the Spirit of God had quite left me; but still was not distressed; yet disconsolate, as if there was nothing in heaven or earth could make me happy. Having been thus endeavoring to pray—though, as I thought, very stupid and senseless—*for near half an hour; then, as I was walking in a thick grove, unspeakable glory seemed to open to the apprehension of my soul. I do not mean any external brightness, nor any imagination of a body of light, but it was a new inward apprehension or view that I had of God, such as I never had before, nor anything which had the least resemblance to it. I had no particular apprehension of any one person in the Trinity, either the Father, the Son, or the Holy Ghost; but it appeared to be Divine glory. My soul rejoiced with joy unspeakable, to see such a God, such a glorious Divine Being; and I was inwardly pleased and satisfied that he should be God over all for ever and ever. My soul was so captivated and delighted with the excellency of God that I was even swallowed up in him; at least to that degree that I had no thought about my own salvation, and scarce reflected that there was such a creature as myself. I continued in this state of inward joy, peace, and astonishing, till near dark without any sensible abatement; and then began to think and examine what I had seen; and felt sweetly composed in my mind all the evening following. I felt myself in a new world, and everything about me appeared with a different aspect from what it was wont to do. At this time, the way of salvation opened to me with such infinite wisdom, suitableness, and excellency, that I wondered I should ever think of any other way of salvation; was amazed that I had not dropped my own contrivances, and complied with this lovely, blessed, and excellent way before. If I could have been saved by my own duties or any other way that I had formerly contrived, my whole soul would now have refused it. I wondered that all the world did not see and comply with this way of salvation, entirely by the righteousness of Christ." [19]

I have italicized the passage which records the exhaustion of the anxious emotion hitherto habitual. In a large proportion, perhaps the majority, of reports, the writers speak as if the exhaustion of the lower and the entrance of the higher emotion were simultaneous,[20] yet often again

---

[19] EDWARD'S and DWIGHT'S Life of Brainerd, New Haven, 1822, pp. 45-47, abridged.

[20] Describing the whole phenomenon as a change of equilibrium, we might say that the movement of new psychic energies towards the personal centre and the recession of old ones towards the margin (or the rising of some objects above, and the sinking of others below the conscious threshold) were only two ways of describing an indivisible event. Doubtless this is often absolutely true, and Starbuck is right when he says that 'self-surrender' and 'new determination,' though seeming at first sight to be such different experiences, are "really the same thing. Self-surrender sees the change in terms of the old self; determination sees it in terms of the new." Op. cit., p.160.

they speak as if the higher actively drove the lower out. This is undoubtedly true in a great many instances, as we shall presently see. But often there seems little doubt that both conditions—subconscious ripening of the one affection and exhaustion of the other—must simultaneously have conspired, in order to produce the result.

T. W. B., a convert of Nettleton's, being brought to an acute paroxysm of conviction of sin, ate nothing all day, locked himself in his room in the evening in complete despair, crying aloud, "How long, O Lord, how long?" "After repeating this and similar language," he says, "several times, *I seemed to sink away into a state of insensibility.* When I came to myself again I was on my knees, praying not for myself but for others. I felt submission to the will of God, willing that he should do with me as should seem good in his sight. My concern seemed all lost in concern for others." [21]

Our great American revivalist Finney writes: "I said to myself: 'What is this? I must have grieved the Holy Ghost entirely away. I have lost all my conviction. I have not a particle of concern about my soul; and it must be that the Spirit has left me.' 'Why!' thought I, 'I never was so far from being concerned about my own salvation in my life.' . . . I tried to recall my convictions, to get back again the load of sin under which I had been laboring. I tried in vain to make myself anxious. I was so quiet and peaceful that I tried to feel concerned about that, lest it should be the result of my having grieved the Spirit away." [22]

But beyond all question there are persons in whom, quite independently of any exhaustion in the Subject's capacity for feeling, or even in the absence of any acute previous feeling, the higher condition, having reached the due degree of energy, bursts through all barriers and sweeps in like a sudden flood. These are the most striking and memorable cases, the cases of instantaneous conversion to which the conception of divine grace has been most peculiarly attached. I have given one of them at length—the case of Mr. Bradley. But I had better reserve the other cases and my comments on the rest of the subject for the following lecture.

LECTURE X
CONVERSION—*Concluded*

In this lecture we have to finish the subject of Conversion, considering at first those striking instantaneous instances of which Saint Paul's is the most eminent, and in which, often amid tremendous emotional excitement or perturbation of the senses, a complete division is established in the twinkling of an eye between the old life and the new. Conversion of this type is an important phase of religious experience, owing to the part which is has played in Protestant theology, and it behooves us to study it conscientiously on that account.

I think I had better cite two or three of these cases before proceeding to a more generalized account. One must know concrete instances first; for, as Professor Agassiz used to say, one can see no farther into a generalization than just so far as one's previous acquaintance with particulars enables one to take it in. I will go back, them, to the case of our friend Henry Alline, and quote his report of the 26th of March, 1775, on which his poor divided mind became unified for good.

"As I was about sunset wandering in the fields lamenting my miserable lost and undone condition, and almost ready to sink under my burden, I thought I was in such a miserable case as never any man was before. I returned to the house, and when I got to the door, just as I was stepping off the threshold, the following impressions came into my mind like a powerful but small still voice. You have been seeking, praying, reforming, laboring, reading, hearing, and meditating, and what have you done by it towards your salvation? Are you any nearer to conversion now than when you first began? Are you any more prepared for heaven, or fitter to appear before the impartial bar of God, than when you first began to seek?

"It brought such conviction on me that I was obliged to say that I did not think I was one step nearer than at first, but as much condemned, as much exposed, and as miserable as before. I cried out within myself, O Lord God, I am lost, and if thou, O Lord, dost not find out some new way, I know nothing of, I shall never be saved, for the ways and methods I have prescribed to myself have all failed me, and I am willing they should fail. O Lord, have mercy! O Lord, have mercy!

"These discoveries continued until I went into the house and sat down. After I sat down, being all in confusion, like a drowning man that was just giving up to sink, and almost in an agony, I turned very suddenly round in my chair, and seeing part of an old Bible lying in one of the chairs, I caught hold of it in great haste; and opening it without any premediation, cast my eyes on the 38th Psalm, which was the first time I ever saw

---

[21] A. A. BONAR: Nettleton and his Labors, Edinburgh, 1854, p. 261.
[22] CHARLES G. FINNEY: Memoirs written by Himself, 1876, pp. 17, 18.

the word of God: it took hold of me with such power that it seemed to go through my whole soul, so that it seemed as if God was praying in, with, and for me. About this time my father called the family to attend prayers; I attended, but paid no regard to what he said in his prayer, but continued praying in those words of the Psalm. Oh, help me, help me! cried I, thou Redeemer of souls, and save me, or I am gone forever; thou canst this night, if thou pleasest, with one drop of thy blood atone for my sins, and appease the wrath of an angry God. At that instant of time when I gave all up to him to do with me as he pleased, and was willing that God should rule over me at his pleasure, redeeming love broke into my soul with repeated scriptures, with such power that my whole soul seemed to be melted down with love; the burden of guilt and condemnation was gone, darkness was expelled, my heart humbled and filled with gratitude, and my whole soul, that was a few minutes ago groaning under mountains of death, and crying to an unknown God for help, was now filled with immortal love, soaring on the wings of faith, freed from the chains of death and darkness, and crying out, My Lord and my God; thou art my rock and my fortress, my shield and my high tower, my life, my joy, my present and my everlasting portion. Looking up, I thought I saw that same light [he had on more than one previous occasion seen subjectively a bright blaze of light], though it appeared different; and as soon as I saw it, the design was opened to me, according to his promise, and I was obliged to cry out: Enough, enough, O blessed God! The work of conversion, the change, and the manifestations of it are no more disputable than that light which I see, or anything that ever I saw.

"In the midst of all my joys, in less than half an hour after my soul was set at liberty, the Lord discovered to me my labor in the ministry and call to preach the gospel. I cried out, Amen, Lord, I'll go; send me, send me. I spent the greatest part of the night in ecstasies of joy, praising and adoring the Ancient of Days for his free and unbounded grace. After I had been so long in this transport and heavenly frame that my nature seemed to require sleep, I though to close my eyes for a few moments; then the devil stepped in, and told me that if I went to sleep, I should lose it all, and when I should awake in the morning I would find it to be nothing but a fancy and delusion. I immediately cried out, O Lord God, if I am deceived, undeceive me.

"I then closed my eyes for a few minutes, and seemed to be refreshed with sleep; and when I awoke, the first inquiry was, Where is my God? And in an instant of time, my soul seemed awake in and with God, and surrounded by the arms of everlasting love. About sunrise I arose with joy to relate to my parents what God had done for my soul, and declared to them the miracle of God's unbounded grace. I took a Bible to show them the words that were impressed by God on my soul the evening before; but when I came to open the Bible, it appeared all new to me.

"I so longed to be useful in the cause of Christ, in preaching the gospel, that it seemed as if I could not rest any longer, but go I must and tell the wonders of redeeming love. I lost all taste for carnal pleasures, and carnal company, and was enabled to forsake them." [23]

Young Mr. Alline, after the briefest of delays, and with no book-learning but his Bible, and no teaching save that of his own experience, became a Christian minister, and thence-forward his life was fit to rank, for its austerity and single-mindedness, with that of the most devoted saints. But happy as he became in his strenuous way, he never got his taste for even the most innocent carnal pleasures back. We must class him, like Bunyan and Tolstoy, amongst those upon whose soul the iron of melancholy left a permanent imprint. His redemption was into another universe than this mere natural world, and life remained for him a sad and patient trial. Years later we can find him making such an entry as this in his diary: "On Wednesday the 12th I preached at a wedding, and had the happiness thereby to be the means of excluding carnal mirth."

The next case I will give is that of a correspondent of Professor Leuba, printed in the latter's article, already cited, in vol. vi. of the American Journal of Psychology. This subject was an Oxford graduate, the son of a clergyman, and the story resembles in many points the classic case of Colonel Gardiner, which everybody may be supposed to know. Here it is, somewhat abridged:—

"Between the period of leaving Oxford and my conversion I never darkened the door of my father's church, although I lived with him for eight years, making what money I wanted by journalism, and spending it in high carousal with any one who would sit with me and drink it away. So I lived, sometimes drunk for a week together, and then a terrible repentance, and would not touch a drop for a whole month.

---

[23] Life and Journals, Boston, 1806, pp. 31-40, abridged.

"In all this period, that is, up to thirty-three years of age, I never had a desire to reform on religious grounds. But all my pangs were due to some terrible remorse I used to feel after a heavy carousal, the remorse taking the shape of regret after my folly in wasting my life in such a way—a man of superior talents and education. This terrible remorse turned me gray in one night, and whenever it came upon me I was perceptibly grayer the next morning. What I suffered in this way is beyond the expression of words. It was hell-fire in all its most dreadful tortures. Often did I vow that if I got over 'this time' I would reform. Alas, in about three days I fully recovered, and was as happy as ever. So it went on for years, but, with a physique like a rhinoceros, I always recovered, and as long as I let drink alone, no man was as capable of enjoying life as I was.

"I was converted in my own bedroom in my father's rectory house at precisely three o'clock in the afternoon of a hot July day (July 13, 1886). I was in perfect health, having been off from the drink for nearly a month. I was in no way troubled about my soul. In fact, God was not in my thoughts that day. A young lady friend sent me a copy of Professor Drummond's Natural Law in the Spiritual World, asking me my opinion of it as a literary work only. Being proud of my critical talents and wishing to enhance myself in my new friend's esteem, I took the book to my bedroom for quiet, intending to give it a thorough study, and then write her what I thought of it. It was here that God met me face to face, and I shall never forget the meeting. 'He that hath the Son hath life eternal, he that hath not the Son hath not life.' I had read this scores to times before, but this made all the difference. I was now in God's presence and my attention was absolutely 'soldered' on to this verse, and I was not allowed to proceed with the book till I had fairly considered what these words really involved. Only then was I allowed to proceed, feeling all the while that there was another being in my bedroom, though not seen by me. The stillness was very marvelous, and I felt supremely happy. It was most unquestionably shown me, in one second of time, that I had never touched the Eternal: and that if I died then, I must inevitably be lost. I was undone. I knew it as well as I now know I am saved. The Spirit of God showed it me in ineffable love; there was no terror in it; I felt God's love so powerfully upon me that only a mighty sorrow crept over me that I had lost all through my own folly; and what was I to do? What could I do? I did not repent even; God never asked me to repent. All I felt was 'I am undone,' and God cannot help it, although he loves me. No fault on the part of the Almighty. All the time I was supremely happy: I felt like a little child before his father. I had done wrong, but my Father did not scold me, but loved me most wondrously. Still my doom was sealed. I was lost to a certainty, and being naturally of a brave disposition I did not quail under it, but deep sorrow for the past, mixed with regret for what I had lost, took hold upon me, and my soul thrilled within me to think it was all over. Then there crept in upon me so gently, so lovingly, so unmistakably, a way of escape, and what was it after all? The old, old story over again, told in the simplest way: 'There is no name under heaven whereby ye can be saved except that of the Lord Jesus Christ.' No words were spoken to me; my soul seemed to see my Saviour in the spirit, and from that hour to this, nearly nine years now, there has never been in my life one doubt that the Lord Jesus Christ and God the Father both worked upon me that afternoon in July, both differently, and both in the most perfect love conceivable, and I rejoiced there and then in a conversion so astounding that the whole village heard of it in less than twenty-four hours.

"But a time of trouble was yet to come. The day after my conversion I went into the hay-field to lend a hand with the harvest, and not having made any promise to God to abstain or drink in moderation only, I took too much and came home drunk. My poor sister was heart-broken; and I felt ashamed of myself and got to my bedroom at once, where she followed me, weeping copiously. She said I had been converted and fallen away instantly. But although I was quite full of drink (not muddled, however), I knew that God's work begun in me was not going to be wasted. About mid-day I made on my knees the first prayer before God for twenty years. I did not ask to be forgiven; I felt that was no good, for I would be sure to fall again. Well, what did I do? I committed myself to him in the profoundest belief that my individuality was going to be destroyed, that he would take all from me, and I was willing. In such a surrender lies the secret of a holy life. From that hour drink has had no terrors for me: I never touch it, never want it. The same thing occurred with my pipe: after being a regular smoker from my twelfth year the desire for it went at once, and has never returned. So with every known sin, the deliverance in each case being permanent and complete. I have had no temptation since conversion, God seemingly having shut out Satan from that course with me. He gets a free hand in other ways, but never on sins of the flesh. Since I gave up to God all ownership in my own life, he has guided me in a thousand ways, and has opened my path in a way almost incredible to those who do not enjoy the blessing of a truly surrendered life."

So much for our graduate of Oxford, in whom you notice the complete abolition of an ancient appetite as one of the conversion's fruits.

The most curious record of sudden conversion with which I am acquainted is that of M. Alphonse Ratisbonne, a free-thinking French Jew, to Catholicism, at Rome in 1842. In a letter to a clerical friend, written a few months later, the convert gives a palpitating account of the circumstances. [24] The predisposing conditions appear to have been slight. He had an elder brother who had been converted and was a Catholic priest. He was himself irreligious, and nourished an antipathy to the apostate brother and generally to his 'cloth.' Finding himself at Rome in his twenty-ninth year, he fell in with a French gentleman who tried to make a proselyte of him, but who succeeded no farther after two or three conversations than to get him to hang (half jocosely) a religious medal round his neck, and to accept and read a copy of a short prayer to the Virgin. M. Ratisbonne represents his own part in the conversations as having been of a light and chaffing order; but he notes the fact that for some days he was unable to banish the words of the prayer from his mind, and that the night before the crisis he had a sort of nightmare, in the imagery of which a black cross with no Christ upon it figured. Nevertheless, until noon of the next day he was free in mind and spent the time in trivial conversations. I now give his own words.

"If at this time any one had accosted me, saying: 'Alphonse, in a quarter of an hour you shall be adoring Jesus Christ as your God and Saviour; you shall lie prostrate with your face upon the ground in a humble church; you shall be smiting your breast at the foot of a priest; you shall pass the carnival in a college of Jesuits to prepare yourself to receive baptism, ready to give your life for the Catholic faith; you shall renounce the world and its pomps and pleasures; renounce your fortune, your hopes, and if need be, your betrothed; the affections of your family, the esteem of your friends, and your attachment to the Jewish people; you shall have no other aspiration than to follow Christ and bear his cross till death;'—if, I say, a prophet had come to me with such a prediction, I should have judged that only one person could be more mad than he,—whosoever, namely, might believe in the possibility of such senseless folly becoming true. And yet that folly is at present my only wisdom, my sole happiness.

"Coming out of the café I met the carriage of Monsieur B. [the proselyting friend]. He stopped and invited me in for a drive, but first asked me to wait for a few minutes whilst he attended to some duty at the church of San Andrea delle Fratte. Instead of waiting in the carriage, I entered the church myself to look at it. The church of San Andrea was poor, small, and empty; I believe that I found myself there almost alone. No work of art attracted my attention; and I passed my eyes mechanically over its interior without being arrested by any particular thought. I can only remember an entirely black dog which went trotting and turning before me as I mused. In an instant the dog had disappeared, the whole church had vanished, I no longer say thing, . . . or more truly I saw, O my God, one thing alone.

"Heavens, how can I speak of it? Oh no! human words cannot attain to expressing the inexpressible. Any description, however sublime it might be, could be but a profanation of the unspeakable truth.

"I was there prostrate on the ground, bathed in my tears, with my heart beside itself, when M. B. called me back to life. I could not reply to the questions which followed from him one upon the other. But finally I took the medal which I had on my breast, and with all the effusion of my soul I kissed the image of the Virgin, radiant with grace, which it bore. Oh, indeed, it was She! It was indeed She! [What he had seen had been a vision of the Virgin.]

"I did not know where I was: I did not know whether I was Alphonse or another. I only felt myself changed and believed myself another me; I looked for myself in myself and did not find myself. In the bottom of my soul I felt an explosion of the most ardent joy; I could not speak; I had no wish to reveal what had happened. But I felt something solemn and sacred within me which made me ask for a priest. I was led to one; and there, alone, after he had given me the positive order, I spoke as best I could, kneeling, and with my heart still trembling. I could give no account to myself of the truth of

---

[24] My quotations are made from an Italian translation of this letter in the Biografia del Sig. M. A. Ratisbonne, Ferrara, 1843, which I have to thank Monsignore D. O'Connell of Rome for bringing to my notice. I abridge the original.

which I had acquired a knowledge and a faith. All that I can say is that in an instant the bandage had fallen from my eyes; and not one bandage only, but the whole manifold of bandages in which I had been brought up. One after another they rapidly disappeared, even as the mud and ice disappear under the rays of the burning sun.

"I came out as from a sepulchre, from an abyss of darkness; and I was living, perfectly living. But I wept, for at the bottom of that gulf I saw the extreme of misery from which I had been saved by an infinite mercy; and I shuddered at the sight of my iniquities, stupefied, melted, overwhelmed with wonder and with gratitude. You may ask me how I came to this new insight, for truly I had never opened a book of religion nor even read a single page of the Bible, and the dogma of original sin is either entirely denied or forgotten by the Hebrews of to-day, so that I had thought so little about it that I doubt whether I ever knew its name. But how came I, then, to this perception of it? I can answer nothing save this, that on entering that church I was in darkness altogether, and on coming out of it I saw the fullness of the light. I can explain the change no better than by the simile of a profound sleep or the analogy of one born blind who should suddenly open his eyes to the day. He sees, but cannot define the light which bathes him and by means of which he sees the objects which excite his wonder. If we cannot explain physical light, how can we explain the light which is the truth itself? And I think I remain within the limits of veracity when I saw that without having any knowledge of the letter of religious doctrine, I now intuitively perceived its sense and spirit. Better than if I saw them, I *felt* those hidden things; I felt them by the inexplicable effects they produced in me. It all happened in my interior mind; and those impressions, more rapid than thought, shook my soul, revolved and turned it, as it were, in another direction, towards other aims, by other paths. I express myself badly. But do you wish, Lord, that I should inclose in poor and barren words sentiments which the heart alone can understand?"

I might multiply cases almost indefinitely, but these will suffice to show you how real, definite, and memorable an event a sudden conversion may be to him who has the experience. Throughout the height of it he undoubtedly seems to himself a passive spectator or undergoer of an astounding process performed upon him from above. There is too much evidence of this for any doubt of it to be possible. Theology, combining this fact with the doctrines of election and grace, has concluded that the spirit of God is with us at these dramatic

moments in a peculiarly miraculous way, unlike what happens at any other juncture of our lives. At that moment, it believes, an absolutely new nature is breathed into us, and we become partakers of the very substance of the Deity.

That the conversion should be instantaneous seems called for on this view, and the Moravian Protestants appear to have been the first to see this logical consequence. The Methodists soon followed suit, practically if not dogmatically, and a short time ere his death, John Wesley wrote:—

"In London alone I found 652 members of our Society who were exceeding clear in their experience, and whose testimony I could see no reason to doubt. And every one of these (without a single exception) has declared that his deliverance from sin was instantaneous; that the change was wrought in a moment. Had half of these, or one third, or one in twenty, declared it was *gradually* wrought in *them*, I should have believed this, with regard to *them*, and thought that *some* were gradually sanctified and some instantaneously. But as I have not found, in so long a space of time, a single person speaking thus, I cannot but believe that sanctification is commonly, if not always, an instantaneous work." Tyerman's Life of Wesley, i. 463.

All this while the more usual sects of Protestantism have set no such store by instantaneous conversion. For them as for the Catholic Church, Christ's blood, the sacraments, and the individual's ordinary religious duties are practically supposed to suffice to his salvation, even though no acute crisis of self-despair and surrender followed by relief should be experienced. For Methodism, on the contrary, unless there has been a crisis of this sort, salvation is only offered, not effectively received, and Christ's sacrifice in so far forth is incomplete. Methodism surely here follows, if not the healthier-minded, yet on the whole the profounder spiritual instinct. The individual models which it has set up as typical and worthy of imitation are not only the more interesting dramatically, but psychologically they have been the more complete.

In the fully evolved Revivalism of Great Britain and America we have, so to speak, the codified and stereotyped procedure to which this way of thinking has led. In spite of the unquestionable fact that saints of the once-born type exist, that there may be a gradual growth in holiness without a cataclysm; in spite of the obvious leakage (as one may say) of much mere natural goodness into the scheme of salvation; revivalism has always assumed that only its own type of religious experience can be perfect; you must first be nailed on the cross of natural despair and agony, and then in the twinkling of an eye be miraculously released.

It is natural that those who personally have traversed such an experience should carry away a feeling of its being a miracle rather than a natural process. Voices are often heard, lights seen, or visions witnessed; automatic motor phenomena occur; and it always seems, after the surrender of the personal will, as if an extraneous higher power had flooded in and taken possession. Moreover the sense of renovation, safety, cleanness, rightness, can be so marvelous and jubilant as well to warrant one's belief in a radically new substantial nature.

"Conversion," writes the New England Puritan, Joseph Alleine, "is not the putting in a patch of holiness; but with the true convert holiness is woven into all his powers, principles, and practice. The sincere Christian is quite a new fabric, from the foundation to the top-stone. He is a new man, a new creature."

And Jonathan Edwards says in the same strain: "Those gracious influences which are the effects of the Spirit of God are altogether supernatural—are quite different from anything that unregenerate men experience. They are what no improvement, or composition of natural qualifications or principles will ever produce; because they not only differ from what is natural, and from everything that natural men experience in degree and circumstances but also in kind, and are of a nature far more excellent. From hence it follows that in gracious affections there are [also] new perceptions and sensations entirely different in their nature and kind from anything experienced by the [same] saints before they were sanctified. . . . The conceptions which the saints have of the loveliness of God, and that kind of delight which they experience in it, are quite peculiar, and entirely different from anything which a natural man can possess, or of which he can form any proper notion."

And that such a glorious transformation as this ought of necessity to be preceded by despair is shown by Edwards in another passage.

"Surely it cannot be unreasonable," he says, "that before God delivers us from a state of sin and liability to everlasting woe, he should give us some considerable sense of the evil from which he delivers us, in order that we may know and feel the importance of salvation, and be enabled to appreciate the value of what God is pleased to do for us. As those who are saved are successively in two extremely different states—first in a state of condemnation and then in a state of justification and blessedness—and as God, in the salvation of men, deals with them as rational and intelligent creatures, it appears agreeable to this wisdom, that those who are saved should be made sensible of their Being, in those two different states. In the first place, that they should be made sensible of their state of condemnation; and afterwards, of their state of deliverance and happiness."

Such quotations express sufficiently well for our purpose the doctrinal interpretation of these changes. Whatever part suggestion and imitation may have played in producing them in men and women in excited assemblies, they have at any rate been in countless individual instances an original and unborrowed experience. Were we writing the story of the mind from the purely natural-history point of view, with no religious interest whatever, we should still have to write down man's liability to sudden and complete conversion as one of his most curious peculiarities.

What, now, must we ourselves think of this question? Is an instantaneous conversion a miracle in which God is present as he is present in no change of heart less strikingly abrupt? Are there two classes of human beings, even among the apparently regenerate, of which the one class really partakes of Christ's nature while the other merely seems to do so? Or, on the contrary, may the whole phenomenon of regeneration, even in these startling instantaneous examples, possibly be a strictly natural process, divine in its fruits, of course, but in one case more and in another less so, and neither more nor less divine in its mere causation and mechanism than any other process, high or low, of man's interior life?

Before proceeding to answer this question, I must ask you to listen to some more psychological remarks. At our last lecture, I explained the shifting of men's centres of personal energy within them and the lighting up of new crises of emotion. I explained the phenomena as partly due to explicitly conscious processes of thought and will, but as due largely also to the subconscious incubation and maturing of motives deposited by the experiences of life. When ripe, the results hatch out, or burst into flower. I have now to speak of the subconscious region, in which such processes of flowering may occur, in a somewhat less vague way. I only regret that my limits of time here force me to be so short.

The expression 'field of consciousness' has but recently come into vogue in the psychology books. Until quite lately the unit of mental life which figured most was the single 'idea,' supposed to be a definitely outlined thing. But at present psychologists are tending, first, to admit that the actual unit is more probably the total mental state, the entire wave of consciousness or field of objects present to the thought at any time; and, second, to see that it is impossible to outline this wave, this field, with any definiteness.

As our mental fields succeed one another, each has its centre of interest, around which the objects of which we are less and less attentively conscious fade to a margin so faint that its limits are unassignable. Some fields are narrow fields and some are wide fields. Usually when we have a wide field we rejoice, for we then see masses of truth together, and often get glimpses of relations which we divine rather than see, for they shoot beyond the field into still remoter regions of objectivity, regions which we seem rather to be about to perceive than to perceive actually. At other times, of drowsiness, illness, or fatigue, our fields may narrow almost to a point, and we find ourselves correspondingly oppressed and contracted.

Different individuals present constitutional differences in this matter of width of field. Your great organizing geniuses are men with habitually vast fields of mental vision, in which a whole programme of future operations will appear dotted out at once, the rays shooting far ahead into definite directions of advance. In common people there is never this magnificent inclusive view of a topic. They stumble along, feeling their way, as it were, from point to point, and often stop entirely. In certain diseased conditions consciousness is a mere spark, without memory of the past or thought of the future, and with the present narrowed down to some one simple emotion or sensation of the body.

The important fact which this 'field' formula commemorates is the indetermination of the margin. Inattentively realized as is the matter which the margin contains, it is nevertheless there, and helps both to guide our behavior and to determine the next movement of our attention. It lies around us like a 'magnetic field,' inside of which our centre of energy turns like a compass-needle, as the present phase of consciousness alters into its successor. Our whole past store of memories floats beyond this margin, ready at a touch to come in; and the entire mass of residual powers, impulses, and knowledges that constitute our empirical self stretches continuously beyond it. So vaguely drawn are the outlines between what is actual and what is only potential at any moment of our conscious life,

that it is always hard to say of certain mental elements whether we are conscious of them or not.

The ordinary psychology, admitting fully the difficulty of tracing the marginal outline, has nevertheless taken for granted, first, that all the consciousness the person now has, be the same focal or marginal, inattentive or attentive, is there in the 'field' of the moment, all dim and impossible to assign as the latter's outline may be; and, second, that what is absolutely extra-marginal is absolutely non-existent, and cannot be a fact of consciousness at all.

And having reached this point, I must now ask you to recall what I said in my last lecture about the subconscious life. I said, as you may recollect, that those who first laid stress upon these phenomena could not know the facts as we now know them. My first duty now is to tell you what I meant by such a statement.

I cannot but think that the most important step forward that has occurred in psychology since I have been a student of that science is the discovery, first made in 1886, that, in certain subjects at least, there is not only the consciousness of the ordinary field, with its usual centre and margin, but an addition thereto in the shape of a set of memories, thoughts, and feelings which are extra-marginal and outside of the primary consciousness altogether, but yet must be classed as conscious facts of some sort, able to reveal their presence by unmistakable signs. I call this the most important step forward because, unlike the other advances which psychology has made, this discovery has revealed to us an entirely unsuspected peculiarity in the constitution of human nature. No other step forward which psychology has made can proffer any such claim as this.

In particular this discovery of a consciousness existing beyond the field, or subliminally as Mr. Myers terms it, casts light on many phenomena of religious biography. That is why I have to advert to it now, although it is naturally impossible for me in this place to give you any account of the evidence on which the admission of such a consciousness is based. You will find it set forth in many recent books, Binet's Alterations of Personality [25] being perhaps as good a one as any to recommend.

The human material on which the demonstration has been made has so far been rather limited and, in part at least, eccentric, consisting of unusually suggestible hypnotic subjects, and of hysteric patients. Yet the elementary mechanisms of our life are presumably so uniform that what is shown to be true in a marked degree of

[25] Published in the International Scientific Series.

some persons is probably true in some degree of all, and may in a few be true in an extraordinarily high degree.

The most important consequence of having a strongly developed ultra-marginal life of this sort is that one's ordinary fields of consciousness are liable to incursions from it of which the subject does not guess the source, and which, therefore, take for him the form of unaccountable impulses to act, or inhibitions of action, of obsessive ideas, or even of hallucinations of sight or hearing. The impulses may take the direction of automatic speech or writing, the meaning of which the subject himself may not understand even while he utters it; and generalizing this phenomenon, Mr. Myers has given the name of *automatism*, sensory or motor, emotional or intellectual, to this whole sphere of effects, due to 'uprushes' into the ordinary consciousness of energies originating in the subliminal parts of the mind.

The simplest instance of an automatism is the phenomenon of post-hypnotic suggestion, so-called. You give to a hypnotized subject, adequately susceptible, an order to perform some designated act—usual or eccentric, it makes no difference—after he wakes from his hypnotic sleep. Punctually, when the signal comes or the time elapses upon which you have told him that the act must ensue, he performs it;—but in so doing he has no recollection of your suggestion, and he always trumps up an improvised pretext for his behavior if the act be of an eccentric kind. It may even be suggested to a subject to have a vision or to hear a voice at a certain interval after waking, and when the time comes the vision is seen or the voice heard, with no inkling on the subject's part of its source. In the wonderful explorations by Binet, Janet, Breuer, Freud, Mason, Prince, and others, of the subliminal consciousness of patients with hysteria, we have revealed to us whole systems of underground life, in the shape of memories of a painful sort which lead a parasitic existence, buried outside of the primary fields of consciousness, and making irruptions thereinto with hallucinations, pains, convulsions, paralyses of feeling and of motion, and the whole procession of symptoms of hysteric disease of body and of mind. Alter or abolish by suggestion these subconscious memories, and the patient immediately gets well. His symptoms were automatisms, in Mr. Myers's sense of the word. These clinical records sound like fairy-tales when one first reads them, yet it is impossible to doubt their accuracy; and the path having been once opened by these first observers, similar observations have been made elsewhere. They throw, as I said, a wholly new light upon our natural constitution.

And it seems to me that they make a farther step inevitable. Interpreting the unknown after the analogy of the known, it seems to me that hereafter, wherever we meet with a phenomenon of automatism, be it motor impulses, or obsessive idea, or unaccountable caprice, or delusion, or hallucination, we are bound first of all to make search whether it be not an explosion, into the fields of ordinary consciousness, of ideas elaborated outside of those fields in subliminal regions of the mind. We should look, therefore, for its source in the Subject's subconscious life. In the hypnotic cases, we ourselves create the source by our suggestion, so we know it directly. In the hysteric cases, the lost memories which are the source have to be extracted from the patient's Subliminal by a number of ingenious methods, for an account of which you must consult the books. In other pathological cases, insane delusions, for example, or psychopathic obsessions, the source is yet to seek, but by analogy it also should be in subliminal regions which improvements in our methods may yet conceivably put on tap. There lies the mechanism logically to be assumed,—but the assumption involves a vast program of work to be done in the way of verification, in which the religious experiences of man must play their part. [26]

[26] The reader will here please notice that in my exclusive reliance in the last lecture on the subconscious 'incubation' of motives deposited by a growing experience, I followed the method of employing accepted principles of explanation as far as one can. The subliminal region, whatever else it may be, is at any rate a place now admitted by psychologists to exist for the accumulation of vestiges of sensible experience (whether inattentively or attentively registered), and for their elaboration according to ordinary psychological or logical laws into results that end by attaining such a 'tension' that they may at times enter consciousness with something like a burst. It thus is 'scientific' to interpret all otherwise unaccountable invasive alterations of consciousness as results of the tension of subliminal memories reaching the bursting-point. But candor obliges me to confess that there are occasional bursts into consciousness of results of which it is not easy to demonstrate any prolonged subconscious incubation. Some of the cases I used to illustrate the sense of presence of the unseen in Lecture III were of this order (compare pages 62, 63, 64, 67); and we shall see other experiences of the kind when we come to the subject of mysticism. The case of Mr. Bradley, that of M. Ratisbonne, possibly that of Colonel Gardiner, possibly that of Saint Paul, might not be so easily explained in this simple way. The result, then, would have to be ascribed either to a merely physiological nerve storm, a 'discharging lesion' like that of epilepsy; or, in case it were useful and rational, as in the two latter cases named, to some more mystical or theological hypothesis. I make this remark in order that the reader may realize that the subject is really complex. But I shall keep myself as far as possible at present to the more 'scientific' view; and only as the plot thickens in subsequent lectures shall I consider the question of its absolute sufficiency as an explanation of all the facts. That subconscious incubation explains a great number of them, there can be no doubt.

And thus I return to our own specific subject of instantaneous conversions. You remember the cases of Alline, Bradley, Brainerd, and the graduate of Oxford converted at three in the afternoon. Similar occurrences abound, some with and some without luminous visions, all with a sense of astonished happiness, and of being wrought on by a higher control. If, abstracting altogether from the question of their value for the future spiritual life of the individual, we take them on their psychological side exclusively, so many peculiarities in them remind us of what we find outside of conversion that we are tempted to class them along with other automatisms, and to suspect that what makes the difference between a sudden and a gradual convert is not necessarily the presence of divine miracle in the case of one and of something less divine in that of the other, but rather a simple psychological peculiarity, the fact, namely, that in the recipient of the more instantaneous grace we have one of those Subjects who are in possession of a large region in which mental work can go on subliminally, and from which invasive experiences, abruptly upsetting the equilibrium of the primary consciousness, may come.

I do not see why Methodists need object to such a view. Pray go back and recollect one of the conclusions to which I sought to lead you in my very first lecture. You may remember how I there argued against the notion that the worth of a thing can be decided by its origin. Our spiritual judgment, I said, our opinion of the significance and value of a human event or condition, must be decided on empirical grounds exclusively. If the *fruits for life* of the state of conversion are good, we ought to idealize and venerate it, even though it be a piece of natural psychology; if not, we ought to make short work with it, no matter what supernatural being may have infused it.

Well, how is it with these fruits? If we except the class of preëminent saints of whom the names illumine history, and consider only the usual run of 'saints,' the shopkeeping church-members and ordinary youthful or middle-aged recipients of instantaneous conversion, whether at revivals or in the spontaneous course of methodistic growth, you will probably agree that no splendor worthy of a wholly supernatural creature fulgurates from them, or sets them apart from the mortals who have never experienced that favor. Were it true that a suddenly converted man as such is, as Edwards, says,[27] of an entirely different kind from a natural man, partaking as he does directly of Christ's substance, there surely ought to be some exquisite class-mark, some distinctive radiance attaching even to the lowliest specimen of this genus, to which no one of us could remain insensible, and which, so far as it went, would prove him more excellent than ever the most highly gifted among mere natural men. But notoriously there is no such radiance. Converted men as a class are indistinguishable from natural men; some natural men even excel some converted men in their fruits; and no one ignorant of doctrinal theology could guess by mere every-day inspection of the 'accidents' of the two groups of persons before him, that their substance differed as much as divine differs from human substance.

The believers in the non-natural character of sudden conversion have had practically to admit that there is no unmistakable class-mark distinctive of all true converts. The super-normal incidents, such as voices and visions and overpowering impressions of the meaning of suddenly presented scripture texts, the melting emotions and tumultuous affections connected with the crisis of change, may all come by way of nature, or worse still, be counterfeited by Satan. The real witness of the spirit to the second birth is to be found only in the disposition of the genuine child of God, the permanently patient heart, the love of self eradicated. And this, it has to be admitted, is also found in those who pass no crisis, and may even be found outside of Christianity altogether.

Throughout Jonathan Edwards's admirably rich and delicate description of the supernaturally infused condition, in his Treatise on Religious Affections, there is not one decisive trait, not one mark, that unmistakably parts it off from what may possibly be only an exceptionally high degree of natural goodness. In fact, one could hardly read a clearer argument than this book unwittingly offers in favor of the thesis that no chasm exists between the orders of human excellence, but that here as elsewhere, nature shows continuous differences, and generation and regeneration are matters of degree.

All which denial of two objective classes of human beings separated by a chasm must not leave us blind to the extraordinary momentousness of the fact of his

---

[27] Edwards says elsewhere: "I am bold to say that the work of God in the conversion of one soul, considered together with the source, foundation, and purchase of it, and also th3e benefit, end, and eternal issue of it, is a more glorious work of God than the creation of the whole material universe."

conversion to the individual himself who gets converted. There are higher and lower limits of possibility set to each personal life. If a flood but goes above one's head, its absolute elevation becomes a matter of small importance; and when we touch our own upper limit and live in our own highest centre of energy, we may call ourselves saved, no matter how much higher some one else's centre may be. A small man's salvation will always be a great salvation and the greatest of all facts *for him*, and we should remember this when the fruits of our ordinary evangelicism look discouraging. Who knows how much less ideal still the lives of these spiritual grubs and earthworms, these Crumps and Stigginses, might have been, if such poor grace as they have received had never touched them at all?[28]

If we roughly arrange human beings in classes, each class standing for a grade of spiritual excellence, I believe we shall find natural men and converts both sudden and gradual in all the classes. The forms which regenerative change effects have, then, no general spiritual significance, but only a psychological significance. We have seen how Starbuck's laborious statistical studies tend to assimilate conversion to ordinary spiritual growth. Another American psychologist, Prof. George A. Coe,[29] has analyzed the cases of seventy-seven converts or ex-candidates for conversion, known to him, and the results strikingly confirm the view that sudden conversion is connected with the possession of an active subliminal self. Examining his subjects with reference to their hypnotic sensibility and to such automatisms as hypnagogic hallucinations, odd impulses, religious dreams about the time of their conversion, etc., he found these relatively much more frequent in the group of converts whose transformation had been 'striking,' 'striking' transformation being defined as a change which, though not necessarily instantaneous, seems to the subject of it to be distinctly different from a process of growth, however rapid." [30] Candidates for conversion at revivals are, as you know, often disappointed: they experience nothing striking. Professor Coe had a number of persons of this class among his seventy-seven subjects, and

they almost all, when tested by hypnotism, proved to belong to a subclass which he calls 'spontaneous,' that is, fertile in self-suggestions, as distinguished from a 'passive' subclass, to which most of the subjects of striking transformation belonged. His inference is that self-suggestion of impossibility had prevented the influence upon these persons of an environment which, on the more 'passive' subjects, had easily brought forth the efforts they looked for. Sharp distinctions are difficult in these regions, and Professor Coe's numbers are small. But his methods were careful, and the results tally with what one might expect; and they seem, on the whole, to justify his practical conclusion, which is that if you should expose to a converting influence a subject in whom three factors unite: first, pronounced emotional sensibility; second, tendency to automatisms; and third, suggestibility of the passive type; you might then safely predict the result: there would be a sudden conversion, a transformation of the striking kind.

Does this temperamental origin diminish the significance of the sudden conversion when it has occurred? Not in the least, as Professor Coe well says; for "the ultimate test of religious values is nothing psychological, nothing definable in terms of *how it happens*, but something ethical, definable only in terms of *what is attained.*" [31]

As we proceed farther in our inquiry we shall see that what is attained is often an altogether new level of spiritual vitality, a relatively heroic level, in which impossible things have become possible, and new energies and endurances are shown. The personality is changed, the man *is* born anew, whether or not his psychological idiosyncrasies are what give the particular shape to his metamorphosis. 'Sanctification' is the technical name of this result; and erelong examples of it shall be brought before you. In this lecture I have still only to add a few remarks on the assurance and peace which fill the hour of change itself.

One word more, though, before proceeding to that point, lest the final purpose of my explanation of suddenness by subliminal activity be misunderstood. I do

---

[28] Emerson writes: "When we see a soul whose acts are regal, graceful, and pleasant as roses, we must thank God that such things can be and are, and not turn sourly on the angel and say: Crump is a better man, with his grunting resistance to all his native devils." True enough. Yet Crump may really be the better *Crump*, for his inner discords and second birth; and your once-born 'regal' character, though indeed always better than poor Crump, may fall far short of what he individually might be had he only some Crump-like capacity for compunction over his own peculiar diabolisms, graceful and pleasant and invariably gentlemanly as these may be.

[29] In his book, The Spiritual Life, New York, 1900.

[30] Op. cit., p. 112.

[31] Op. cit., p. 144.

indeed believe that if the Subject have no liability to such subconscious activity, or if his conscious fields have a hard rind of a margin that resists incursions from beyond it, his conversion must be gradual if it occur, and must resemble any simply growth into new habits. His possession of a developed subliminal self, and of a leaky or pervious margin, is thus a *conditio sine qua non* of the Subject's becoming converted in the instantaneous way. But if you, being orthodox Christians, ask me as a psychologist whether the reference of a phenomenon to a subliminal self does not exclude the notion of the direct presence of the Deity altogether, I have to say frankly that as a psychologist I do not see why it necessarily should. The lower manifestations of the Subliminal, indeed, fall within the resources of the personal subject: his ordinary sense-material, inattentively taken in and subconsciously remembered and combined, will account for all his usual automatisms. But just as our primary wide-awake consciousness throws open our senses to the touch of things material, so it is logically conceivable that *if there be* higher spiritual agencies that can directly touch us, the psychological condition of their doing so *might be* our possession of a subconscious region which alone should yield access to them. The hubbub of the waking life might close a door which in the dreamy Subliminal might remain ajar or open.

Thus that perception of external control which is so essential a feature in conversion might, in some cases at any rate, be interpreted as the orthodox interpret it: forces transcending the finite individual might impress him, on condition of his being what we may call a subliminal human specimen. But in any case the *value* of these forces would have to be determined by their effects, and the mere fact of their transcendency would of itself establish no presumption that they were more divine than diabolical.

I confess that this is the way in which I should rather see the topic left lying in your minds until I come to a much later lecture, when I hope once more to gather these dropped threads together into more definitive conclusions. The notion of a subconscious self certainly ought not at this point of our inquiry to be held to *exclude* all notion of a higher penetration. If there be higher powers able to impress us, they may get access to us only through the subliminal door. (See below, p. 387 ff.)

Let us turn now to the feelings which immediately fill the hour of the conversion experience. The first one to be noted is just this sense of higher control. It is not always, but it is very often present. We saw examples of it in Alline, Bradley, Brainerd, and elsewhere. The need of such a higher controlling agency is well expressed in the short reference which the eminent French Protestant Adolphe Monod makes to the crisis of his own conversion. It was at Naples in his early manhood, in the summer of 1827.

"My sadness," he says, "was without limit, and having got entire possession of me, it filled my life from the most indifferent external acts to the most secret thoughts, and corrupted at their source my feelings, my judgment, and my happiness. It was then that I saw that to expect to put a stop to this disorder by my reason and my will, which were themselves diseased, would be to act like a blind man who should pretend to correct one of his eyes by the aid of the other equally blind one. I had then no resource save in *some influence from without.* I remembered the promise of the Holy Ghost; and what the positive declarations of the Gospel had never succeeded in bringing home to me, I learned at last from necessity, and believed, for the first time in my life, in this promise, in the only sense in which it answered the needs of my soul, in that, namely, of a real external supernatural action, capable of giving me thoughts, and taking them away from me, and exerted on me by a God as truly master of my heart as he is of the rest of nature. Renouncing then all merit, all strength, abandoning all my personal resources, and acknowledging no other title to his mercy than my own utter misery, I went home and threw myself on my knees, and prayed as I never yet prayed in my life. From this day onwards a new interior life began for me: not that my melancholy had disappeared, but it had lost its sting. Hope had entered into my heart, and once entered on the path, the God of Jesus Christ, to whom I then had learned to give myself up, little by little did the rest."[32]

It is needless to remind you once more of the admirable congruity of Protestant theology with the structure of the mind as shown in such experiences. In the extreme of melancholy the self that consciously *is* can do absolutely nothing. It is completely bankrupt and without resource, and no works it can accomplish

[32] I piece together a quotation made by W. Monod, in his book la Vie, and a letter printed in the work: Adolphe Monod: I., Souvenirs de sa Vie, 1885, p. 433.

will avail. Redemption from such subjective conditions must be a free gift or nothing, and grace through Christ's accomplished sacrifice is such a gift.

"God," says Luther, "is the God of the humble, the miserable, the oppressed, and the desperate, and of those that are brought even to nothing; and his nature is to give sight to the blind, to comfort the broken-hearted, to justify sinners, to save the very desperate and damned. Now that pernicious and pestilent opinion of man's own righteousness, which will not be a sinner, unclean, miserable, and damnable, but righteous and holy, suffereth not God to come to his own natural and proper work. Therefore God must take this maul in hand (the law, I mean) to beat in pieces and bring to nothing this beast with her vain confidence, that she may so learn at length by her own misery that she is utterly forlorn and damned. But here lieth the difficulty, that when a man is terrified and cast down, he is so little able to raise himself up again and say, 'Now I am bruised and afflicted enough; now is the time of grace; now is the time to hear Christ.' The foolishness of man's heart is so great that then he rather seeketh to himself more laws to satisfy his conscience. 'If I live,' saith he, 'I will amend my life: I will do this, I will do that.' But here, except thou do the quite contrary, except thou send Moses away with his law, and in these terrors and this anguish lay hold upon Christ who died for thy sins, look for no salvation. Thy cowl, thy shaven crown, thy chastity, thy obedience, thy poverty, thy works, thy merits? what shall all these do? what shall the law of Moses avail? If I, wretched and damnable sinner, through works or merits could have loved the Son of God, and so come to him, what needed he to deliver himself for me? If I, being a wretch and damned sinner, could be redeemed by any other price, what needed the Son of God to be given? But because there was no other price, therefore he delivered neither sheep, ox, gold, nor silver, but even God himself, entirely and wholly 'for me,' even 'for me,' I say, a miserable, wretched sinner. Now, therefore, I take comfort and apply this to *myself*. And this manner of applying is the very true force and power of faith. For he died *not* to justify the righteous, but the *un*-righteous, and to make *them* the children of God."[33]

That is, the more literally lost you are, the more literally you are the very being whom Christ's sacrifice has already saved. Nothing in Catholic theology, I imagine, has ever spoken to sick souls as straight as this message from Luther's personal experience. As Protestants are not all sick souls, of course reliance on what Luther exults in calling the dung of one's merits, the filthy puddle of one's own righteousness, has come to the front again in their religion; but the adequacy of his view of Christianity to the deeper parts of our human mental structure is shown by its wildfire contagiousness when it was a new and quickening thing.

Faith that Christ has genuinely done his work was part of what Luther meant by faith, which so far is faith in a fact intellectually conceived of. But this is only one part of Luther's faith, the other part being far more vital. This other part is something not intellectual but immediate and intuitive, the assurance, namely, that I, this individual I, just as I stand, without one plea, etc., am saved now and forever.[34]

Professor Leuba is undoubtedly right in contending that the conceptual belief about Christ's work, although so often efficacious and antecedent, is really accessory and non-essential, and that the 'joyous conviction' can also come by far other channels than this conception. It is to the joyous conviction itself, the assurance that all is well with one, that he would give the name of faith *par excellence.*

"When the sense of estrangement," he writes, "fencing man about in a narrowly limited ego, breaks down, the individual finds himself 'at one with all creation.' He lives in the universal life; he and man, he and nature, he and God, are one. That state of confidence, trust, union with all things, following upon the achievement of moral unity, is the *Faith-state.* Various dogmatic beliefs suddenly, on the advent of the faith-state,

---

[33] Commentary on Galatians, ch. iii. verse 19, and ch. ii. verse 20, abridged.

[34] In some conversions, both steps are distinct; in this one, for example:—

"Whilst I was reading the evangelical treatise, I was soon struck by an expression: 'the finished work of Christ.' 'Why,' I asked of myself, 'does the author use these terms? Why does he not say "the atoning work"?' Then these words, 'It is finished,' presented themselves to my mind. 'What is it that is finished?' I asked, and in an instant my mind replied: 'A perfect expiation for sin; entire satisfaction has been given; the debt has been paid by the Substitute. Christ has died for our sins; not for ours only, but for those of all men. If, then, the entire work is finished, all the debt paid, what remains for me to do?' In another instant the light was shed through my mind by the Holy Ghost, and the joyous conviction was given me that nothing more was to be done, save to fall on my knees, to accept this Saviour and his love, to praise God forever." Autobiography of Hudson Taylor. I translate back into English from the French translation of Challand (Geneva, no date), the original not being accessible.

acquire a character of certainty, assume a new reality, become an object of faith. As the ground of assurance here is not rational, argumentation is irrelevant. But such conviction being a mere casual offshoot of the faith-state, it is a gross error to imagine that the chief practical value of the faith-state is its power to stamp with the seal of reality certain particular theological conceptions.[35] On the contrary, its value lies solely in the fact that it is the psychic correlate of a biological growth reducing contending desires to one direction; a growth which expresses itself in new affective states and new reactions; in larger, nobler, more Christ-like activities. The ground of the specific assurance in religious dogmas is then an affective experience. The objects of faith may even be preposterous; the affective stream will float them along, and invest them with unshakable certitude. The more startling the affective experience, the less explicable it seems, the easier it is to make it the carrier of unsubstantiated notions."[36]

The characteristics of the affective experience which, to avoid ambiguity, should, I think, be called the state of assurance rather than the faith-state, can be easily enumerated, though it is probably difficult to realize their intensity, unless one has been through the experience one's self.

The central one is the loss of all the worry, the sense that all is ultimately well with one, the peace, the harmony, the *willingness to be*, even though the outer conditions should remain the same. The certainty of God's 'grace,' of 'justification,' 'salvation,' is an objective belief that usually accompanies the change in Christians; but this may be entirely lacking and yet the affective peace remain the same—you will recollect the case of the Oxford graduate: and many might be given where the assurance of personal salvation was only a later result. A passion of willingness, of acquiescence, of admiration, is the glowing centre of this state of mind.

The second feature is the sense of perceiving truths not known before. The mysteries of life become lucid, as Professor Leuba says; and often, nay usually, the solution is more or less unutterable in words. But these more intellectual phenomena may be postponed until we treat of mysticism.

A third peculiarity of the assurance state is the objective change which the world often appears to undergo. 'An appearance of newness beautifies every object,' the precise opposite of that other sort of newness, that dreadful unreality and strangeness in the appearance of the world, which is experienced by melancholy patients, and of which you may recall my relating some examples.[37] This sense of clean and beautiful newness within and without is one of the commonest entries in conversion records. Jonathan Edwards thus describes it in himself:—

"After this my sense of divine things gradually increased, and became more and more lively, and had more of that inward sweetness. The appearance of everything was altered; there seemed to be, as it were, a calm, sweet cast, or appearance of divine glory, in almost everything. God's excellency, his wisdom, his purity and love, seemed to appear in everything; in the sun, moon, and stars; in the clouds and blue sky; in the grass, flowers, and trees; in the water and all nature; which used greatly to fix my mind. And scarce anything. among all the works of nature, was so sweet to me as thunder and lightning; formerly nothing had been so terrible to me. Before, I used to be uncommonly terrified with thunder, and to be struck with terror when I saw a thunderstorm rising; but now, on the contrary, it rejoices me."[38]

Billy Bray, an excellent little illiterate English evangelist, records his sense of newness thus:—

"I said to the Lord: 'Thou hast said, they that ask shall receive, they that seek shall find, and to them that knock the door shall be opened, and I have faith to believe it.' In an instant the Lord made me so happy that I cannot express what I felt. I shouted for joy. I praised God with my whole heart. . . . I think this was in November, 1823, but what day of the month I do not know. I remember this, that everything looked new to me, the people, the fields, the cattle, the trees. I was like a new man in a new world. I spent the greater part of my time in praising the Lord."[39]

Starbuck and Leuba both illustrate this sense of newness by quotations. I take the two following from Starbuck's manuscript collection. One, a woman, says:—

---

[35] Tolstoy's case was a good comment on those words. There was almost no theology in his conversion. His faith-state was the sense come back that life was infinite in its moral significance.

[36] American Journal of Psychology, vii. 345-347, abridged.

[37] Above, p. 130.

[38] DWIGHT: Life of Edwards, New York, 1830, p. 61, abridged.

[39] W. F. BOURNE: The King's Son, a Memoir of Billy Bray, London, Hamilton, Adams & Co., 1887, p.9.

"I was taken to a camp-meeting, mother and religious friends seeking and praying for my conversion. My emotional nature was stirred to its depths; confessions of depravity and pleading with God for salvation form sin made me oblivious of all surroundings. I plead for mercy, and had a vivid realization of forgiveness and renewal of my nature. When rising from my knees I exclaimed, 'Old things have passed away, all things have become new.' It was like entering another world, a new state of existence. Natural objects were glorified, my spiritual vision was so clarified that I saw beauty in every material object in the universe, the woods were vocal with heavenly music; my soul exulted in the love of God, and I wanted everybody to share in my joy."

The next case is that of a man:—

"I know not how I got back into the encampment, but found myself staggering up to Rev.—'s Holiness tent—and as it was full of seekers and a terrible noise inside, some groaning, some laughing, and some shouting, and by a large oak, ten feet from the tent, I fell on my face by a bench, and tried to pray, and every time I would call on God, something like a man's hand would strangle me by choking. I don't know whether there were any one around or near me or not. I thought I should surely die if I did not get help, but just as often as I would pray, that unseen hand was felt on my throat and my breath squeezed off. Finally something said: 'Venture on the atonement, for you will die anyway if you don't.' So I made one final struggle to call on God for mercy, with the same choking and strangling, determined to finish the sentence of prayer for Mercy, if I did strangle and die, and the last I remember that time was falling back on the ground with the same unseen hand on my throat. I don't know how long I lay there or what was going on. None of my folks were present. When I came to myself, there were a crowd around me praising God. The very heavens seemed to open and pour down rays of light and glory. Not for a moment only, but all day and night, floods of light and glory seemed to pour through my soul, and oh, how I was changed, and everything became new. My horses and hogs and even everybody seemed changed."

This man's case introduces the feature of automatisms, which in suggestible subjects have been so startling a feature at revivals since, in Edwards's, Wesley's, and Whitefield's time, these became a regular means of gospel-propagation. They were at first supposed to be semi-miraculous proofs of 'power' on the part of the Holy Ghost; but great divergence of opinion quickly arose concerning them. Edwards, in his Thoughts on the Revival of Religion in New England, has to defend them against their critics; and their value has long been matter of debate even within the revivalistic denominations.[40] They undoubtedly have no essential spiritual significance, and although their presence makes his conversion more memorable to the convert, it has never been proved that converts who show them are more persevering or fertile in good fruits than those whose change of heart has had less violent accompaniments. On the whole, unconsciousness, convulsions, visions, involuntary vocal utterances, and suffocation, must be simply ascribed to the subject's having a large subliminal region, involving nervous instability. This is often the subject's own view of the matter afterwards. One of Starbuck's correspondents writes, for instance:—

"I have been through the experience which is known as conversion. My explanation of it is this: the subject works his emotions up to the breaking point, at the same time resisting their physical manifestations, such as quickened pulse, etc., and then suddenly lets them have their full sway over his body. The relief is something wonderful, and the pleasurable effects of the emotions are experienced to the highest degree."

There is one form of sensory automatism which possibly deserves special notice on account of its frequency. I refer to hallucinatory or pseudo-hallucinatory luminous phenomena, *photisms*, to use the term of the psychologists. Saint Paul's blinding heavenly vision seems to have been a phenomenon of this sort; so does Constantine's cross in the sky. The last case but one which I quoted mentions floods of light and glory. Henry Alline mentions a light, about whose externality he seems uncertain. Colonel Gardiner sees a blazing light. President Finney writes:—

"All at once the glory of God shone upon and round about me in a manner almost marvelous. . . . A light perfectly ineffable shone in my soul, that almost prostrated me on the ground. . . . This light seemed like the brightness of the sun in every direction. It was too intense for the eyes. . . . I think I knew something then, by actual experience, of that light that prostrated Paul

---

[40] Consult WILLIAM B. SPRAGUE: Lectures on Revivals of Religion, New York, 1832, in the long Appendix to which the opinions of a large number of ministers are given.

on the way to Damascus. It was surely a light such as I could not have endured long."[41]

Such reports of photisms are indeed far from uncommon. Here is another from Starbuck's collection, where the light appeared evidently external:—

"I had attended a series of revival services for about two weeks off and on. Had been invited to the altar several times, all the time becoming more deeply impressed, when finally I decided I must do this, or I should be lost. Realization of conversion was very vivid, like a ton's weight being lifted from my heart; a strange light which seemed to light up the whole room (for it was dark); a conscious supreme bliss which caused me to repeat 'Glory to God' for a long time. Decided to be God's child for life, and to give up my pet ambition, wealth and social position. My former habits of life hindered by growth somewhat, but I set about overcoming these systematically, and in one year my whole nature was changed, i.e., my ambitions were of a different order."

Here is another one of Starbuck's cases, involving a luminous element:—

"I had been clearly converted twenty-three years before, or rather reclaimed. My experience in regeneration was then clear and spiritual, and I had not backslidden. But I experienced entire sanctification on the 15th day of March, 1893, about eleven o'clock in the morning. The particular accompaniments of the experience were entirely unexpected. I was quietly sitting at home singing selections out of Pentecostal Hymns. Suddenly there seemed to be a something sweeping into me and inflating my entire being—such a sensation as I had never experienced before. When this experience came, I seemed to be conducted around a large, capacious, well-lighted room. As I walked with my invisible conductor and looked around, a clear thought was coined in my mind, 'They are not here, they are gone.' As soon as the thought was definitely formed in my mind, though no word was spoken, the Holy Spirit impressed me that I was surveying my own soul. Then, for the first time in all my life, did I know that I was cleansed from all sin, and filled with the fullness of God."

Leuba quotes the case of a Mr. Peek, where the luminous affection reminds one of the chromatic hallucinations produced by the intoxicant cactus buds called mescal by the Mexicans:—

"When I went in the morning into the fields to work, the glory of God appeared in all his visible creation. I well remember we reaped oats, and how every straw and head of the oats seemed, as it were, arrayed in a kind of rainbow glory, or to glow, if I may so express it, in the glory of God."[42]

The most characteristic of all the elements of the conversion crisis, and the last one of which I shall speak, is the ecstasy of happiness produced. We have already heard several accounts of it, but I will add a couple more. President Finney's is so vivid that I give it at length:—

"All my feelings seemed to rise and flow out; and the utterance of my heart was, 'I want to pour my whole soul out to God.' The rising of my soul was so

---

[41] Memoirs, p. 34.

[42] These reports of sensorial photism shade off into what are evidently only metaphorical accounts of the sense of new spiritual illumination, as, for instance, in Brainerd's statement: "As I was walking in a thick grove, unspeakable glory seemed to open to the apprehension of my soul. I do not mean any external brightness, for I saw no such thing, nor any imagination of a body of light in the third heavens, or anything of that nature, but it was a new inward apprehension or view that I had of God."

In a case like this next one from Starbuck's manuscript collection, the lighting up of the darkness is probably also metaphorical:—

"One Sunday night, I resolved that when I got home to the ranch where I was working, I would offer myself with my faculties and all to God to be used only by and for him. . . . It was raining and the roads were muddy; but this desire grew so strong that I knelt down by the side of the road and told God all about it, intending then to get up and go on. Such a thing as any special answer to my prayer never entered my mind, having been converted by faith, but still being most undoubtedly saved. Well, while I was praying, I remember holding out my hands to God and telling him they should work for him, my feet walk for him, my tongue speak for him, etc., etc., if he would only use me as his instrument and give me a satisfying experience—when suddenly the darkness of the night seemed lit up—I felt, realized, knew, that God heard and answered my prayer. Deep happiness came over me; I felt I was accepted into the inner circle of God's loved ones."

In the following case also the flash of light is metaphorical:—

"A prayer meeting had been called for at close of evening service. The minister supposed me impressed by his discourse (a mistake—he was dull). He came and, placing his hand upon my shoulder, said: 'Do you not want to give your heart to God?' I replied in the affirmative. Then said he, 'Come to the front seat.' They sang and prayed and talked with me. I experienced nothing but unaccountable wretchedness. They declared that the reason why I did not 'obtain peace' was because I was not willing to give up all to God. After about two hours the minister said we would go home. As usual, on retiring, I prayed. In great distress, I at this time simply said, 'Lord, I have done all I can, I leave the whole matter with thee.' Immediately, like a flash of light, there came to me a great peace, and I arose and went into my parents' bedroom and said, 'I do feel so wonderfully happy.' This I regard as the hour of conversion. It was the hour in which I became assured of divine acceptance and favor. So far as my life was concerned, it made little immediate change."

great that I rushed into the back room of the front office, to pray. There was no fire and no light in the room; nevertheless it appeared to me as if it were perfectly light. As I went in and shut the door after me, it seemed as if I met the Lord Jesus Christ face to face. It did not occur to me then, nor did it for some time afterwards, that it was wholly a mental state. On the contrary, it seemed to me that I saw him as I would see any other man. He said nothing, but looked at me in such a manner as to break me right down at his feet. I have always since regarded this as a most remarkable state of mind; for it seemed to me a reality that he stood before me, and I fell down at his feet and poured out my soul to him. I wept aloud like a child, and made such confessions as I could with my choked utterance. It seemed to me that I bathed his feet with my tears; and yet I had no distinct impression that I touched him, that I recollect. I must have continued in this state for a good while; but my mind was too much absorbed with the interview to recollect anything that I said. But I know, as soon as my mind became calm enough to break off from the interview, I returned to the front office, and found that the fire that I had made of large wood was nearly burned out. But as I turned and was about to take a seat by the fire, I received a mighty baptism of the Holy Ghost. Without any expectation of it, without ever having the thought in my mind that there was any such thing for me, without any recollection that I had ever heard the thing mentioned by any person in the world, the Holy Spirit descended upon me in a manner that seemed to go through me, body and soul. I could feel the impression, like a wave of electricity, going through and through me. Indeed, it seemed to come in waves and waves of liquid love; for I could not express it in any other way. It seemed like the very breath of God. I can recollect distinctly that it seemed to fan me, like immense wings.

"No words can express the wonderful love that was shed abroad in my heart. I wept aloud with joy and love; and I do not know but I should say I literally bellowed out the unutterable gushings of my heart. These waves came over me, and over me, and over me, one after the other, until I recollect I cried out, 'I shall die if these waves continue to pass over me.' I said, 'Lord, I cannot bear any more;' yet I had no fear of death.

"How long I continued in this state, with this baptism continuing to roll over me and go through me, I do not know. But I know it was late in the evening when a member of my choir—for I was the leader of the choir—came into the office to see me. He was a member of the church. He found me in this state of loud weeping, and said to me, 'Mr. Finney, what ails you?' I could make him no answer for some time. He then said, 'Are you in pain?' I gathered myself up as best I could, and replied, 'No, but so happy that I cannot live.'"

I just now quoted Billy Bray; I cannot do better than give his own brief account of his post-conversion feelings:—

"I can't help praising the Lord. As I go along the street, I lift up one foot, and it seems to say, 'Glory'; and I lift up the other, and it seems to say 'Amen'; and so they keep up like that all the time I am walking."[43]

One word, before I close this lecture, on the question of the transiency or permanence of these abrupt conversions. Some of you, I feel sure, knowing that numerous backslidings and relapses take place, make of these their apperceiving mass for interpreting the whole subject, and dismiss it with a pitying smile at so much 'hysterics.' Psychologically, as well as religiously, however, this is shallow. It misses the point of serious interest, which is not so much the duration as the nature and quality of these shiftings of character to

---

[43] I add in a note a few more records:—

"One morning, being in deep distress, fearing every moment I should drop into hell, I was constrained to cry in earnest for mercy, and the Lord came to my relief, and delivered my soul from the burden and guilt of sin. My whole frame was in a tremor from head to foot, and my soul enjoyed sweet peace. The pleasure I then felt was indescribable. The happiness lasted about three days, during which time I never spoke to any person about my feelings." Autobiography of DAN YOUNG, edited by W. P. STRICKLAND, New York, 1860.

"In an instant there rose up in me such a sense of God's taking care of those who put their trust in him that for an hour all the world was crystalline, the heavens were lucid, and I sprang to my feet and began to cry and laugh." H. W. BEECHER, quoted by LEUBA.

"My tears of sorrow changed to joy, and I lay there praising God in such ecstasy of joy as only the soul who experiences it can realize."—"I cannot express how I felt. It was as if I had been in a dark dungeon and lifted into the light of the sun. I shouted and I sang praise unto him who loved me and washed me from my sins. I was forced to retire into a secret place, for the tears did flow, and I did not wish my shopmates to see me, and yet I could not keep it a secret."—"I experienced joy almost to weeping."—"I felt my face must have shone like that of Moses. I had a general feeling of buoyancy. It was the greatest joy it was ever my lot to experience."—"I wept and laughed alternately. I was as light as if walking on air. I felt as if I had gained greater peace and happiness than I had ever expected to experience." STARBUCK'S correspondents.

higher levels. Men lapse from every level—we need no statistics to tell us that. Love is, for instance, well known not to be irrevocable, yet, constant or inconstant, it reveals new flights and reaches of ideality while it lasts. These revelations form its significance to men and women, whatever be its duration. So with the conversion experience: that it should for even a short time show a human being what the high-water mark of his spiritual capacity is, this is what constitutes its importance,—an importance which backsliding cannot diminish, although persistence might increase it. As a matter of fact, all the more striking instances of conversion, all those, for instance, which I have quoted, *have* been permanent. The case of which there might be most doubt, on account of its suggesting so strongly an epileptoid seizure, was the case of M. Ratisbonne. Yet I am informed that Ratisbonne's whole future was shaped by those few minutes. He gave up his project of marriage, became a priest, founded at Jerusalem, where he went to dwell, a mission of nuns for the conversion of the Jews, showed no tendency to use for egotistic purposes the notoriety given him by the peculiar circumstances of his conversion,—which, for the rest, he could seldom refer to without tears,—and in short remained an exemplary son of the Church until he died, late in the 80's, if I remember rightly.

The only statistics I know of, on the subject of the duration of conversions, are those collected for Professor Starbuck by Miss Johnston. They embrace only a hundred persons, evangelical church-members, more than half being Methodists. According to the statement of the subjects themselves, there had been backsliding of some sort in nearly all the cases, 93 per cent. of the women, 77 per cent. of the men. Discussing the returns more minutely, Starbuck finds that only 6 per cent. are relapses from the religious faith which the conversion confirmed, and that the backsliding complained of is in most only a fluctuation in the ardor of sentiment. Only six of the hundred cases report a change of faith. Starbuck's conclusion is that the effect of conversion is to bring with it "a changed attitude towards life, which is fairly constant and permanent, although the feelings fluctuate. . . . In other words, the persons who have passed through conversion, having once taken a stand for the religious life, tend to feel themselves identified with it, no matter how much their religious enthusiasm declines."[44]

---
[44] Psychology of Religion, pp. 360, 357.

SECOND SELECTION
To Mrs. James

St. Hubert's Inn,
Keene Valley, *July 9,* 1898.

. . . I have had an eventful 24 hours, and my hands are so stiff after it that my fingers can hardly hold the pen. I left, as I informed you by post-card, the Lodge at seven, and five hours of walking brought us to the top of Marcy—I carrying 18 lbs. of weight in my pack. As usual, I met two Cambridge acquaintances on the mountain top—"Appalachians" from Beede's. At four, hearing an axe below, I went down (an hour's walk) to Panther Lodge Camp, and there found Charles and Pauline Goldmark, Waldo Adler and another school boy, and two Bryn Mawr girls—the girls all dressed in boys' breeches, and cutaneously desecrated in the extreme from seven of them having been camping without a male on Loon Lake to the north of this. My guide had to serve for the party, and quite unexpectedly to me the night turned out one of the most memorable of all my memorable experiences. I was in a wakeful mood before starting, having been awake since three, and I may have slept a little during this night; but I was not aware of sleeping at all. My companions, except Waldo Adler, were all motionless. The guide had got a magnificent provision of firewood, the sky swept itself clear of every trace of cloud or vapor, the wind entirely ceased, so that the fire-smoke rose straight up to heaven. The temperature was perfect either inside or outside the cabin, the moon rose and hung above the scene before midnight, leaving only a few of the larger stars visible, and I got into a state of spiritual alertness of the most vital description. The influences of Nature, the wholesomeness of the people round me, especially the good Pauline, the thought of you and the children, dear Harry on the wave, the problem of the Edinburgh lectures, all fermented within me till it became a regular Walpurgis Nacht. I spent a good deal of it in the woods, where the streaming moonlight lit up things in a magical checkered play, and it seemed as if Gods of all the nature-mythologies were holding an indescribable meeting in my breast with the moral Gods of the inner life. The two kinds of Gods have nothing in common—the Edinburgh lectures made quite a hitch ahead. The intense significance of some sort, of the whole scene, if one could only *tell* the significance; the intense inhuman remoteness of its inner life, and yet the intense *appeal* of it; its everlasting freshness and its immemorial antiquity and decay; its utter Americanism, and every sort of patriotic suggestiveness, and you, and my relation to you part and parcel of it all, and beaten up with it, so that memory and sensation all whirled inexplicably together; it was indeed worth coming for, and worth repeating year by year, if repetition could only procure what in its nature I suppose must be all unplanned for and unexpected. It was one of the happiest lonesome nights of my existence, and I understand now what a poet is. He is a person who can feel the immense complexity of influences that I felt, and make some partial tracks in them for verbal statement. In point of fact, I can't find a single word for all that significance, and don't know what it was significant of, so there it remains, a mere boulder of *impression*. Doubtless in more ways than one, though, things in the Edinburgh lectures will be traceable to it.

In the morning at six, I shouldered my undiminished pack and went up Marcy, ahead of the party, who arrived half an hour later, and we got in here at eight [P.M.] after 10 1/2 hours of the solidest walking I ever made, and I, I think, more fatigued than I have been after any walk. We plunged down Marcy, and up Bason Mountain, led by C. Goldmark, who had, with Mr. White, blazed a trail the year before;[45] then down again, away down, and up the Gothics, not counting a third down-and-up over an intermediate spur. It was the steepest sort of work, and, as one looked from the summits, seemed sheer impossible, but the girls kept up splendidly, and were all fresher than I. It was true that they had slept like logs all night, whereas I was "on my nerves." I lost my Norfolk jacket at the last third of the course—high time to say good-bye to that possession—and staggered up to the Putnams to find Hatty Shaw[46] taking me for a tramp. Not a soul was there, but everything spotless and ready for the arrival today. I got a bath at Bowditch's bath-house, slept in my old room, and slept soundly and well, and save for the unwashable staining of my hands and a certain stiffness in my thighs, am entirely rested and well. But I don't believe in keeping it up too long, and at the Willey House will lead a comparatively sedentary life, and cultivate sleep, if I can. . . .

W. J.

THIRD SELECTION

To James Henry Leuba.

CAMBRIDGE, *Apr.* 17, 1904

. . . My personal position is simple. I have no living sense of commerce with a God. I envy those who have, for I know the addition of such a sense would help me immensely. The Divine, for my *active* life, is limited to abstract concepts which, as ideals, interest and determine me, but do so but faintly, in comparison with what a feeling of God might effect, if I had one. It is largely a question of intensity, but differences of intensity may make one's whole centre of energy shift. Now, although I am so devoid of *Gottesbewustein* in the directer and stronger sense, yet there is *something in me* which *makes response* when I hear utterances made from that lead by others. I recognize the deeper voice. Something tells me, "*thither lies truth*"—and I am *sure* it is not old theistic habits and prejudices of infancy. Those are Christian; and I have grown so out of Christianity that entanglement therewith on the part of a mystical utterance has to be abstracted from and overcome, before I can listen. Call this, if you like, my mystical *germ*. It is a very common germ. It creates the rank and file of believers. As it withstands in my case, so it will withstand in most cases, all purely atheistic criticism, but *interpretative* criticism (not of the mere "hysteria" and "nerves" order) it can energetically combine with. Your criticism seems to amount to a pure *non possumus*: "Mystical deliverances must be infallible revelations in every particular, or nothing. Therefore they are *nothing*, for anyone else than their owner." Why may they not be *some*thing, although not everything?

Your only consistent position, it strikes me, would be a dogmatic atheistic naturalism; and, without any mystical germ in us, that, I believe, is where we all should *unhesitatingly* be today.

Once allow the mystical germ to influence our beliefs, and I believe that we are in my position. Of course the "subliminal" theory is an inessential hypothesis, and the question of pluralism or monism is equally inessential.

I am letting loose a deluge on you! Don't reply at length, or at all. *I* hate to reply to anybody, and will sympathize with your silence. But I had to restate my position more clearly. Yours truly,

WM. JAMES.

---

[45] That is, there was here no path to follow, only "blazes" on the trees.
[46] The housekeeper at the Putnam-Bowditch "shanty."

BALTIMORE CATECHISM NO. 3

1933

PRAYERS

THE LORD'S PRAYER

Our Father, who art in heaven, hallowed be Thy name; Thy kingdom come; Thy will be done on earth as it is in heaven. Give us this day our daily bread; and forgive us our trespasses as we forgive those who trespass against us; and lead us not into temptation, but deliver us from evil. Amen.

THE ANGELICAL SALUTATION

Hail Mary, full of grace! the Lord is with thee; blessed art thou amongst women, and blessed is the fruit of thy womb, Jesus. Holy Mary, Mother of God, pray for us sinners, now and at the hour of our death. Amen.

For millions and millions of Catholics, the **Baltimore Catechism** is hard-wired into the psyche. Even a generation ago it was still widely in use. For American Catholics aged forty and older, the Catechism is often the beginning and the end of the search for God. This edition is from 1933.

THE APOSTLES' CREED

I believe in God, the Father Almighty, Creator of heaven and earth; and in Jesus Christ, His only Son, our Lord; who was conceived by the Holy Ghost, born of the Virgin Mary, suffered under Pontius Pilate, was crucified; died, and was buried. He descended into hell; the third day He arose again from the dead; He ascended into heaven, sitteth at the right hand of God, the Father Almighty; from thence He shall come to judge the living and the dead. I believe in the Holy Ghost, the Holy Catholic Church, the communion of Saints, the forgiveness of sins, the resurrection of the body, and the life everlasting. Amen.

THE CONFITEOR

I confess to Almighty God, to blessed Mary, ever Virgin, to blessed Michael the Archangel; to blessed John the Baptist, to the holy Apostles Peter and Paul, and to all the Saints, that I have sinned exceedingly in thought, word and deed, through my fault, through my fault, through my most grievous fault. Therefore, I beseech blessed Mary, ever Virgin, blessed Michael the Archangel, blessed John the Baptist, the holy Apostles Peter and Paul, and all the Saints, to pray to the Lord our God for me.

May the Almighty God have mercy on me, and forgive me my sins, and bring me to everlasting life. Amen.

May the Almighty and merciful Lord grant me pardon, absolution and remission of all my sins. Amen.

AN ACT OF FAITH

O my God! I firmly believe that Thou art one God in three Divine Persons, Father, Son, and Holy Ghost; I believe that Thy Divine Son became man, and died for our sins, and that He will come to judge the living and the dead. I believe these and all the truths which the Holy Catholic Church teaches, because Thou hast revealed them, who canst neither deceive nor be deceived.

AN ACT OF HOPE

O my God! relying on Thy infinite goodness and promises, I hope to obtain pardon of my sins, the help of Thy grace, and life everlasting, through the merits of Jesus Christ, my Lord and Redeemer.

AN ACT OF LOVE

O my God! I love Thee above all things, with my whole heart and soul, because Thou art all-good and worthy of all love. I love my neighbor as myself for the love of Thee. I forgive all who have injured me, and ask pardon of all whom I have injured.

AN ACT OF CONTRITION

O my God! I am heartily sorry for having offended Thee, and I detest all my sins, because I dread the loss of heaven and the pains of hell, but most of all because they offend Thee, my God, who art all-good and deserving of all my love. I firmly resolve, with the help of Thy grace, to confess my sins, to do penance, and to amend my life.

THE BLESSING BEFORE MEALS

Bless us, O Lord! and these Thy gifts, which we are about to receive from Thy bounty, through Christ our Lord. Amen.

GRACE AFTER MEALS

✠ We give Thee thanks for all Thy benefits, O Almighty God, who livest and reignest forever, and may the souls of the faithful departed, through the mercy of God, rest in peace. Amen.

HOW TO BAPTIZE

✠ In case of necessity (danger of death) anyone can baptize.

In baptizing pour holy- or common water on the forehead or face of the one to be baptized, and while pouring say: "I baptize thee in the name of the Father and of the Son and of the Holy Ghost."

LESSON ONE

ON THE END OF MAN

1. What is a catechism?

A catechism is a book that teaches religion in the form of questions and answers.

2. Why should children study the catechism?

Children should study the catechism because it teaches religion in its simplest form.

3. What is religion?

Religion is the service of love and obedience which we give to God.

4. Is religion necessary for man?

Religion is necessary for man, because he has the duty to love and obey God.

5. Can there be more than one true religion?

There cannot be more than one true religion, because the duties of man to God must be the same for all men.

6. Why must man love and obey God?

Man must love God and obey God, because man belongs to God.

7. Who made the world?

God made the world.

8. Who is God?

God is the Creator of heaven and earth, and of all things.

9. Who is Man?

Man is a creature composed of body and soul, and made to the image and likeness of God.

10. Is this likeness in the body or in the soul?

This likeness is chiefly in the soul.

11. How is the soul like to God?

The soul is like to God because it is a spirit that will never die, and has understanding and free will.

12. Why did God make you?

God made me to know Him, to love Him, and to serve Him in this world, and to be happy with Him forever in the next.

13. What then is the end of Man?

The end of man is to gain everlasting happiness by loving and serving God in this world.

14. Of which must we take more care, our soul or our body?

We must take more care of our soul than of our body.

15. Why must we take more care of our soul than of our body?

We must take more care of our soul than of our body, because in losing our soul we lose God and everlasting happiness.

16. What must we do to save our souls?

To save our souls we must worship God by faith, hope, and charity; that is, we must believe in Him, hope in Him, and love Him with all our heart.

17. Can we find out by ourselves all the things that we should know about God?

We cannot find out by ourselves all the things that we should know about God.

18. From whom do we learn all the things that we should know about God?

We learn from God Himself all the things that we should know about God.

19. To whom did God speak?

God spoke to the patriarchs, prophets and Apostles, but He spoke especially through His Son, our Lord, Jesus Christ.

20. How did the patriarchs, prophets, and Apostles prove that God spoke to them?

The patriarchs, prophets, and Apostles proved that God spoke to them by prophesying and performing miracles.

21. How shall we know the things which we are to believe?

We shall know the things which we are to believe from the Catholic Church, through which God speaks to us.

22. Where shall we find the chief truths which the Church teaches?

We shall find the chief truths which the Church teaches in the Apostles' Creed.

23. Say the Apostles' Creed.

1. I believe in God the Father Almighty, Creator of heaven and earth;
2. And in Jesus Christ, His only Son, our Lord;
3. Who was conceived by the Holy Ghost, born of the Virgin Mary;
4. Suffered under Pontius Pilate, was crucified; died, and was buried;
5. He descended into hell, the third day He arose again from the dead;
6. He ascended into heaven, sitteth at the right hand of God the Father Almighty;
7. From thence He shall come to judge the living and the dead;
8. I believe in the Holy Ghost;

9. The Holy Catholic Church, the communion of saints;

10. The forgiveness of sins;

11. The resurrection of the body;

12. And the life everlasting. Amen.

LESSON TWO

ON GOD AND HIS PERFECTIONS

24. What is God?

God is a spirit, infinitely perfect.

25. Had God a beginning?

God has no beginning; He always was and He always will be.

26. Where is God?

God is everywhere.

27. If God is everywhere, why do we not see Him?

We do not see God, because He is a pure spirit and cannot be seen with bodily eyes.

28. Does God see us?

God sees us and watches over us.

29. Does God know all things?

God knows all things, even our most secret thoughts, words, and actions.

30. Is God all wise?

God is all wise.

31. Can God do all things?

God can do all things, and nothing is hard or impossible to Him.

32. Is God just, holy and merciful?

God is all-just, all-holy, all-merciful, as He is infinitely perfect.

33. Is God truthful and faithful?

God is truthful and faithful.

LESSON THREE

ON THE UNITY AND TRINITY OF GOD

34. Is there but one God?

Yes; there is but one God.

35. Why can there be but one God?

There can be but one God, because God, being supreme and infinite, cannot have an equal.

36. How many Persons are there in God?

In God there are three Divine Persons, really distinct, and equal in all things—the Father, the Son, and the Holy Ghost.

37. Is the Father God?

The Father is God and the first Person of the Blessed Trinity.

38. What works do we ascribe to the Father?

We ascribe to the Father the works of power, especially creation and the forgiveness of sin.

39. Is the Son God?

The Son is God and the second Person of the Blessed Trinity.

40. What works do we ascribe to the Son?

We ascribe to the Son the works of wisdom and order, especially the works of redemption.

41. Is the Holy Ghost God?

The Holy Ghost is God and the third Person of the Blessed Trinity.

42. What works do we ascribe to the Holy Ghost?

We ascribe to the Holy Ghost the works of love, especially the sanctification of man.

43. What do you mean by the Blessed Trinity?

By the Blessed Trinity I mean one God in three Divine Persons.

44. Are the three Divine Persons equal in all things?

The three Divine Persons are equal in all things.

45. Are the three Divine Persons one and the same God?

The three Divine Persons are one and the same God, having one and the same Divine nature and substance.

46. Can we fully understand how the three Divine Persons are one and the same God?

We cannot fully understand how the three Divine Persons are one and the same God, because this is a mystery.

47. What is a mystery?

A mystery is a truth which we cannot fully understand.

48. Why is the knowledge of the Blessed Trinity important to us?

The knowledge of the Blessed Trinity is important to us, because it is the foundation of the Christian faith.

LESSON FOUR

ON CREATION

49. Who created heaven and earth, and all things?

God created heaven and earth, and all things.

50. How did God create heaven and earth?

God created heaven and earth from nothing, by His word only; that is, by a single act of His all-powerful will.

51. In how many days did God create the world?

God created the world in six days.

52. Why did God create the world?

God created the world for His own glory and for the good of His creatures.

DIVINE PROVIDENCE

53. Did God leave the world to itself after He created it?

God did not leave the world to itself after He created it, but He continually preserves and governs it.

54. Can the world exist without God preserving it?

The world cannot exist without God preserving it.

55. Can the world exist without God governing it?

The world cannot exist without God governing it.

56. Who are the chief creatures of God?

The chief creatures of God are Angels and men.

57. What are Angels?

Angels are pure spirits without a body, created to adore and enjoy God in heaven.

58. Were the Angels created for any other purpose?

The angels were also created to assist before the throne of God and minister unto Him; they have often been sent as messengers from God to man; and are also appointed our guardians.

59. Were the Angels, as God created them, good and happy?

The Angels, as God created them, were good and happy.

60. Did all the Angels remain good and happy?

Not all the Angels remained good and happy; many of them sinned and were cast into hell, and these are called devils or bad angels.

61. What do the good Angels do for us?

The good Angels pray for us and protect us from harm to soul and body.

62. What do the bad Angels try to do?

The bad Angels try to harm us by endeavoring to lead us into sin.

LESSON FIVE
ON OUR FIRST PARENTS AND THE FALL

63. Who were the first man and woman?

The first man and woman were Adam and Eve.

64. How did God create Adam?

God created Adam by forming his body from the dust of the earth and breathing into it an immortal soul.

65. Were Adam and Eve innocent and holy when they came from the hand of God?

Adam and Eve were innocent and holy when they came from the hand of God.

66. Did God give any command to Adam and Eve?

To try their obedience God commanded Adam and Eve not to eat of a certain fruit which grew in the Garden of Paradise.

67. What were the chief blessings intended for Adam and Eve had they remained faithful to God?

The chief blessings intended for Adam and Eve, had they remained faithful to God, were a constant state of happiness in this life and everlasting glory in the next.

68. Did Adam and Eve remain faithful to God?

Adam and Eve did not remain faithful to God; but broke His command by eating the forbidden fruit.

69. What befell Adam and Eve on account of their sin?

Adam and Eve, on account of their sin, lost innocence of holiness, and were doomed to sickness and death.

70. What evil befell us on account of the disobedience of our first parents?

On account of the disobedience of our first parents, we all share in their sin and punishment, as we should have shared in their happiness if they had remained faithful.

71. What other effects followed from the sin of our first parents?

Our nature was corrupted by the sin of our first parents, which darkened our understanding, weakened our will, and left in us a strong inclination to evil.

72. What is the sin called which we inherit from our first parents?

The sin which we inherit from our first parents is called original sin.

73. Why is this sin called original?

This sin is called original because it comes down to us from our first parents, and we are brought into the world with its guilt on our soul.

74. Does this corruption of our nature remain in us after original sin is forgiven?

This corruption of our nature and other punishments remain in us after original sin is forgiven.

75. Was any one ever preserved from original sin?

The Blessed Virgin Mary, through the merits of her Divine Son, was preserved free from the guilt of original sin, and this privilege is called her Immaculate Conception.

76. Does free will mean that we may do as we please?

Free will does not mean that we may do as we please.

77. Why may we not do as we please?

We may not do as we please, because God, reason, our own good, and the good of others forbid this.

78. What tells us that we may not do as we please?

Conscience and the laws of God tell us that we may not do as we please.

79. What do we call an act against conscience and the law of God?

We call an act against conscience and the law of God a sin.

LESSON SIX
ON SIN AND ITS KINDS

80. Is original sin the only kind of sin?

Original sin is not the only kind of sin; there is another kind of sin, which we commit ourselves, called actual sin.

81. What is actual sin?

Actual sin is any wilful thought, word, deed, or omission contrary to the law of God.

82. What causes sins in us?

Sins are caused by wilful consent to temptations.

83. How many kinds of actual sin are there?

There are two kinds of actual sin—mortal and venial.

84. What is mortal sin?

Mortal sin is a grievous offense against the law of God.

85. Why is this sin called mortal?

This sin is called mortal because it deprives us of spiritual life, which is sanctifying grace, and brings everlasting death and damnation on the soul.

86. How many things are necessary to make a sin mortal?

To make a sin mortal three things are necessary: a grievous matter, sufficient reflection, and full consent of the will.

87. What is venial sin?

Venial sin is a slight offense against the law of God in matters of less importance, or, in matters of great importance, it is an offense committed without sufficient reflection or full consent of the will.

88. Which are the effects of venial sin?

The effects of venial sin are the lessening of the love of God in our heart, the making us less worthy of His help, and the weakening of the power to resist mortal sin.

89. Which are the chief sources of sin?

The chief sources of sin are seven: Pride, Covetousness, Lust, Anger, Gluttony, Envy, and Sloth; and they are commonly called capital sins.

LESSON SEVEN
ON THE INCARNATION AND REDEMPTION

A. THE PROMISE OF A REDEEMER

90. Did God abandon man after he fell into sin?

God did not abandon man after he fell into sin, but promised him a Redeemer, Who was to satisfy for man's sin and reopen to him the gates of heaven.

91. To whom did God promise the Redeemer?

God promised the Redeemer to the patriarchs Adam, Abraham, Isaac, Jacob, Juda and to King David.

92. Why did not the Redeemer come immediately after the promise?

The Redeemer did not come immediately after the promise so that man might learn through misery and suffering the need of a Redeemer.

93. Did God allow His promise of a Redeemer to be forgotten?

God did not allow His promise of a Redeemer to be forgotten.

94. How could men recognize the Redeemer when He came?

Men could recognize the Redeemer when He came, because He alone would fulfill all the prophecies and types concerning the Redeemer.

B. THE REDEEMER, JESUS CHRIST

95. Who is the Redeemer?

Our Blessed Lord and Saviour Jesus Christ is the Redeemer of mankind.

96. How did Jesus prove that He was the Redeemer?

Jesus proved that He was the Redeemer by fulfilling all the prophecies of the Old Testament concerning the Redeemer.

97. How did Jesus fulfill the prophecies?

Jesus fulfilled the prophecies by leading a holy life and suffering a bitter death, by preaching a holy doctrine, by performing miracles and prophesying, and by establishing an indefectible Church.

98. Could any one have falsified the Gospel story about our Lord?

No one could have falsified the Gospel story about our Lord.

99. What do you believe of Jesus Christ?

I believe that Jesus Christ is the Son of God, the second Person of the Blessed Trinity, true God and true Man.

100. Why is Jesus Christ true God?

Jesus Christ is true God, because He is the true and only Son of God the Father.

101. Why is Jesus Christ true man?

Jesus Christ is true man because He is the Son of the Blessed Virgin Mary and has a body and soul like ours.

102. How many natures are there in Jesus Christ?

In Jesus Christ there are two natures, the nature of God and the nature of man.

103. Is Jesus Christ more than one person?

No, Jesus Christ is but one Divine Person.

104. Was Jesus Christ always God?

Jesus Christ was always God, as He is the second Person of the Blessed Trinity, equal to His Father from all eternity.

105. Was Jesus Christ always man?

Jesus Christ was not always man but became man at the time of His Incarnation.

106. What do you mean by the Incarnation?

By the Incarnation I mean that the Son of God was made man.

107. How was the Son of God made man?

The Son of God was conceived and made man by the power of the Holy Ghost, in the womb of the Blessed Virgin Mary.

108. Is the Blessed Virgin Mary truly the Mother of God?

The Blessed Virgin Mary is truly the Mother of God, because the same Divine Person Who is the Son of God is also the Son of the Blessed Virgin Mary.

109. Did the Son of God become man immediately after the sin of our first parents?

The Son of God did not become man immediately after the sin of our first parents, but was promised to them as a Redeemer.

110. How could they be saved who lived before the Son of God became man?

They who lived before the Son of God became man could be saved by believing in a Redeemer to come, and by keeping the Commandments.

C. THE CHILDHOOD OF CHRIST

111. On what day was the Son of God conceived and made man?

The Son of God was conceived and made man on Annunciation day—the day on which the Angel Gabriel announced to the Blessed Virgin Mary that she was to be the Mother of God.

112. On what day was Christ born?

Christ was born on Christmas day in a stable at Bethlehem, over nineteen hundred years ago.

113. Where did Jesus live after His birth at Bethlehem?

Jesus, after spending the first years of his life in Egypt, lived at Nazareth until He was thirty years old.

114. How did Jesus begin His public life?

Jesus began His public life with His baptism and the forty day fast.

115. What did Jesus do during His public life?

During His public life Jesus taught the people, performed miracles, and gathered seventy-two disciples from which He chose twelve Apostles.

116. How long did Christ live on earth?

Christ lived on earth about thirty-three years, and led a most holy life in poverty and suffering.

117. Why did Christ live so long on earth?

Christ lived so long on earth to show us the way to heaven by His teachings and example.

LESSON EIGHT

ON OUR LORD'S PASSION, DEATH, RESURRECTION, AND ASCENSION

118. What did Jesus Christ suffer?

Jesus Christ suffered a bloody sweat, a cruel scourging, was crowned with thorns, and was crucified.

119. On what day did Christ die?

Christ died on Good Friday.

120. Why do you call that day "good" on which Christ died so sorrowful a death?

We call that day "good" on which Christ died, because by His death He showed His great love for man and purchased for him every blessing.

121. Where did Christ die?

Christ died on Mount Calvary.

122. How did Christ die?

Christ was nailed to the Cross and died on it between two thieves.

123. Why did Christ suffer and die?

Christ suffered and died for our sins.

124. What lessons do we learn from the sufferings and death of Christ?

From the sufferings and death of Christ we learn the great evil of sin, the hatred God bears to it, and the necessity of satisfying for it.

125. Whither did Christ's soul go after His death?

After Christ's death His soul descended into hell.

126. Did Christ's soul descend into the hell of the damned?

Christ's soul did not descend into the hell of the damned, but into a place or state or rest called Limbo, where the souls of the just were waiting for Him.

127. Why did Christ descend into Limbo?

Christ descended into Limbo to preach to the souls who were in prison—that is, to announce to them the joyful tidings of their redemption.

128. Where was Christ's body while His soul was in Limbo?

While Christ's soul was in Limbo His body was in the holy sepulchre.

129. On what day did Christ rise from the dead?

Christ rose from the dead, glorious and immortal, on Easter Sunday, the third day after his death.

130. How long did Christ stay on earth after His resurrection?

Christ stayed on earth forty days after His resurrection to show that He was truly risen from the dead, and to instruct His Apostles.

131. After Christ had remained forty days on earth whither did He go?

After forty days Christ ascended into heaven, and the day on which He ascended into heaven is called Ascension day.

132. Where is Christ in heaven?

In heaven Christ sits at the right hand of God the Father Almighty.

133. What do you mean by saying that Christ sits at the right hand of God?

When I say that Christ sits at the right hand of God I mean that Christ as God is equal to His Father in all things, and that as man He is in the highest place in heaven next to God.

LESSON NINE

ON THE HOLY GHOST AND
HIS DESCENT UPON THE APOSTLES

134. Who is the Holy Ghost?

The Holy Ghost is the third Person of the Blessed Trinity.

135. From whom does the Holy Ghost proceed?

The Holy Ghost proceeds from the Father and the Son.

136. Is the Holy Ghost equal to the Father and the Son?

The Holy Ghost is equal to the Father and the Son, being the same Lord and God as they are.

137. On what day did the Holy Ghost come down upon the Apostles?

The Holy Ghost came down upon the Apostles ten days after the Ascension of our Lord; and the day on which He came down upon the Apostles is called Whitsunday, or Pentecost.

138. How did the Holy Ghost come down upon the Apostles?

The Holy Ghost came down upon the Apostles in the form of tongues of fire.

139. Who sent the Holy Ghost upon the Apostles?

Our Lord Jesus Christ sent the Holy Ghost upon the Apostles.

140. Did the Apostles expect the coming of the Holy Ghost?

The Apostles did expect the coming of the Holy Ghost, because our Lord promised to send Him.

141. Why did Christ send the Holy Ghost?

Christ sent the Holy Ghost to sanctify His Church, to enlighten and strengthen the Apostles, and to enable them to preach the Gospel.

142. Will the Holy Ghost abide with the Church forever?

The Holy Ghost will abide with the Church forever, and guide it in the way of holiness and truth.

LESSON TEN

ON THE EFFECTS OF THE REDEMPTION

143. Which are the two chief effects of the Redemption?

The two chief effects of the Redemption are: the satisfaction of God's justice by Christ's sufferings and death, and the gaining of grace for men.

144. What do you mean by grace?

By grace I mean the supernatural gift of God bestowed on us, through the merits of Jesus Christ, for our salvation.

145. How many kinds of grace are there?

There are two kinds of grace, sanctifying grace and actual grace.

146. What is sanctifying grace?

Sanctifying grace is that grace which makes the soul holy and pleasing to God.

147. When is sanctifying grace first given to us?

Sanctifying grace is first given to us in the sacrament of Baptism.

148. If baptismal grace is lost through sin, how can it be regained?

If baptismal grace is lost through sin it can be regained through the Sacrament of Penance or by an act of perfect contrition.

149. What do you call those graces or gifts of God by which we believe in Him, hope in Him, and love Him?

Those graces or gifts of God by which we believe in Him, and hope in Him, and love Him, are called the Divine virtues of Faith, Hope, and Charity.

150. What is Faith?

Faith is a Divine virtue by which we firmly believe the truths which God has revealed.

151. What is Hope?

Hope is a Divine virtue by which we firmly trust that God will give us eternal life and the means to obtain it.

152. What is Charity?

Charity is a Divine virtue by which we love God above all things for His own sake, and our neighbor as ourselves for the love of God.

153. What is actual grace?

Actual grace is that help of God which enlightens our mind and moves our will to shun evil and do good.

154. Is grace necessary to salvation?

Grace is necessary to salvation, because without grace we can do nothing to merit heaven.

155. Can we resist the grace of God?

We can and unfortunately often do resist the grace of God.

156. What is the grace of perseverance?

The grace of perseverance is a particular gift of God which enables us to continue in the state of grace till death.

LESSON ELEVEN
ON THE CHURCH

157. What are the means instituted by our Lord to enable men at all times to share in the fruits of the Redemption?

The means instituted by our Lord to enable men at all times to share in the fruits of His Redemption are the Church and the Sacraments.

158. What is the Church?

The Church is the congregation of all those who profess the faith of Christ, partake of the same Sacraments, and are governed by their lawful pastors under one visible Head.

159. Did our Lord begin a new religion when He established His Church?

Our Lord did not begin a new religion when He established His Church.

160. What did Christ do to establish His Church?

To establish His Church Christ trained the twelve Apostles, and then gave them the command and the power to teach, govern and administer the sacraments.

161. What is necessary to belong to the Church?

To belong to the Church it is necessary to be baptized and to profess the faith of Christ as the Church teaches it.

162. Who can be a member of the Church?

Every man can and should be a member of the Church.

163. Who is the invisible Head of the Church?

Jesus Christ is the invisible Head of the Church.

164. Who is the visible Head of the Church?

Our Holy Father the Pope, the Bishop of Rome, is the Vicar of Christ on earth and the visible Head of the Church.

165. Why is the Pope, the Bishop of Rome, the visible Head of the Church?

The Pope, the Bishop of Rome, is the visible Head of the Church because he is the successor of St. Peter, whom Christ made the chief of the Apostles and the visible Head of the Church.

THE HIERARCHY OF THE CHURCH

166. Which are the successors of the other Apostles?

The successors of the other Apostles are the Bishops of the Holy Catholic Church.

SALVATION THROUGH THE CHURCH

167. Why did Christ found the Church?

Christ founded the Church to teach, govern, sanctify, and save all men.

168. Can the Church be seen and known?

The Church can be seen and known, for Christ instituted the Church a visible society.

169. Are all bound to belong to the Church?

All are bound to belong to the Church, and he who knows the Church to be the true Church and remains out of it cannot be saved.

LESSON TWELVE
ON THE ATTRIBUTES AND MARKS OF THE CHURCH

A. THE ATTRIBUTES OF THE CHURCH

170. Which are the attributes of the Church?

The attributes of the Church are three: authority, infallibility, and indefectibility.

171. What do you mean by the authority of the Church?

By the authority of the Church I mean the right and power which the Pope and the bishops, as the successors of the Apostles, have to teach and to govern the faithful.

172. What do you mean by the infallibility of the Church?

By the infallibility of the Church I mean that the Church cannot err when it teaches a doctrine of faith or morals.

173. When does the Church teach infallibly?

The Church teaches infallibly when it speaks through the Pope and the bishops, united in general council, or through the Pope alone when he proclaims to all the faithful a doctrine of faith or morals.

174. What do you mean by the indefectibility of the Church?

By the indefectibility of the Church I mean that the Church, as Christ founded it, will last till the end of time.

175. In whom are these attributes found in their fullness?

These attributes are found in their fullness in the Pope, the visible Head of the Church, whose infallible authority to teach bishops, priests, and people in matters of faith or morals will last till the end of the world.

B. THE MARKS OF THE CHURCH

176. Has the Church any marks by which is may be known?

The Church has four marks by which it may be known: it is One; it is Holy; it is Catholic; it is Apostolic.

177. How is the Church One?

The Church is One because all its members agree in one faith, are all in one communion, and are all under one Head.

178. How is the Church Holy?

The Church is Holy because its founder, Jesus Christ, is holy; because it teaches a holy doctrine; invites all to a holy life; and because of the eminent holiness of so many thousands of its children.

179. Why is the Church Catholic or universal?

The Church is Catholic or universal because it subsists in all ages, teaches all nations, and maintains all truth.

180. How is the Church Apostolic?

The Church is Apostolic because it was founded by Christ on His Apostles, and is governed by their lawful successors, and because it has never ceased and never will cease, to teach their doctrine.

181. In which Church are these attributes and marks found?

These attributes and marks are found in the Holy Roman Catholic Church alone.

182. From whom does the Church derive its undying life and infallible authority?

The Church derives its undying life and infallible authority from the Holy Ghost, the Spirit of truth, Who abides with it forever.

183. By whom is the Church made and kept One, Holy, and Catholic?

The Church is made and kept One, Holy, and Catholic by the Holy Ghost, the Spirit of love and holiness, Who unites and sanctifies its members throughout the world.

C. THE CATHOLIC CHURCH AND THE CHURCHES

184. Which are the two large groups of Christians outside the Catholic Church?

The two large groups of Christians outside the Catholic Church are the Greek Orthodox churches and the Protestant churches.

185. Why did the Greek Orthodox Churches separate from the Catholic Church?

The Greek Orthodox churches separated from the Catholic Church because they refused obedience to the Pope.

186. Why did the Protestant Churches separate from the Catholic Church?

The Protestant churches separated from the Catholic Church because they refused to believe all that the Catholic Church teaches.

187. Can Protestants be saved?

Protestants can be saved if through no fault of their own they do not belong to the Church and if they obey God and are in the state of grace.

188. Will all Catholics be saved?

Catholics will be saved only if they do what the Church teaches to be necessary for salvation.

D. THE CHURCH AND THE STATE

189. What is a State?

A State is a society, founded on natural law, to promote the temporal welfare of its members.

190. Has a State the right to interfere with the Church in its mission of salvation?

A State has no right to interfere with the Church in its mission of salvation.

E. THE COMMUNION OF SAINTS

191. What is the communion of saints?

The communion of saints is the spiritual union that exists between the members of the Church militant on earth, and the Church suffering in purgatory and the Church triumphant in heaven.

LESSON THIRTEEN

ON THE SACRAMENTS IN GENERAL

192. What is a Sacrament?

A Sacrament is an outward sign, instituted by Christ to give grace.

193. How many Sacraments are there?

There are seven Sacraments: Baptism, Confirmation, Holy Eucharist, Penance, Extreme Unction, Holy Orders, and Matrimony.

194. Whence have the Sacraments the power of giving grace?

The Sacraments have the power of giving grace from the merits of Jesus Christ.

195. What grace do the Sacraments give?

Some of the Sacraments give sanctifying grace, and others increase it in our souls.

196. Which are the Sacraments that give sanctifying grace?

The Sacraments that give sanctifying grace are Baptism and Penance; and they are called Sacraments of the dead.

197. Why are Baptism and Penance called Sacraments of the dead?

Baptism and Penance are called Sacraments of the dead because they take away sin, which is the death of the soul, and give grace, which is its life.

198. Which are the Sacraments that increase sanctifying grace in our soul?

The Sacraments that increase sanctifying grace in our soul are: Confirmation, Holy Eucharist, Extreme Unction, Holy Orders, and Matrimony; and they are called Sacraments of the living.

199. Why are Confirmation, Holy Eucharist, Extreme Unction, Holy Orders, and Matrimony called Sacraments of the living?

Confirmation, Holy Eucharist, Extreme Unction, Holy Orders, and Matrimony are called Sacraments of the living, because those who receive them worthily are already living the life of grace.

200. What sin does he commit who receives the Sacraments of the living in mortal sin?

He who receives the Sacraments of the living in mortal sin commits a sacrilege, which is a great sin, because it is an abuse of a sacred thing.

201. Besides sanctifying grace do the Sacraments give any other grace?

Besides sanctifying grace the Sacraments give another grace, called sacramental.

202. What is sacramental grace?

Sacramental grace is a special help which God gives, to attain the end for which He instituted each Sacrament.

203. Do the Sacraments always give grace?

The Sacraments always give grace, if we receive them with the right dispositions.

204. Can we receive the Sacraments more than once?

We can receive the Sacraments more than once, except Baptism, Confirmation, and Holy Orders.

205. Why can we not receive Baptism, Confirmation, and Holy Orders more than once?

We cannot receive Baptism, Confirmation, and Holy orders more than once, because they imprint a character in the soul.

206. What is the character which these Sacraments imprint in the soul?

The character which these Sacraments imprint in the soul is a spiritual mark which remains forever.

207. Does this character remain in the soul even after death?

This character remains in the soul even after death: for the honor and glory of those who are saved; for the shame and punishment of those who are lost.

LESSON FOURTEEN
ON BAPTISM

208. What is Baptism?

Baptism is a Sacrament which cleanses us from original sin, makes us Christians, children of God, and heirs of heaven.

209. Are actual sins ever remitted by Baptism?

Actual sins and all the punishment due to them are remitted by Baptism, if the person baptized be guilty of any.

210. Is Baptism necessary to salvation?

Baptism is necessary to salvation, because without it we cannot enter into the Kingdom of heaven.

211. Who can administer Baptism?

The priest is the ordinary minister of Baptism; but in case of necessity any one who has the use of reason may baptize.

212. How is Baptism given?

Whoever baptizes should pour water on the head of the person to be baptized, and say, while pouring the water: I baptize thee in the name of the Father, and of the Son, and of the Holy Ghost.

213. How many kinds of Baptism are there?

There are three kinds of Baptism: Baptism of water, of desire, and of blood.

214. What is Baptism of water?

Baptism of water is that which is given by pouring water on the head of the person to be baptized and saying at the same time: I baptize thee in the name of the Father, and of the Son, and of the Holy Ghost.

215. When should infants be baptized?

Infants should be baptized within one or two weeks after birth.

216. What is baptism of desire?

Baptism of desire is an ardent wish to receive Baptism, and to do all that God has ordained for our salvation.

217. What is Baptism of blood?

Baptism of blood is the shedding of one's blood for the faith of Christ.

218. Is Baptism of desire or of blood sufficient to produce the effects of Baptism of water?

Baptism of desire or of blood is sufficient to produce the effects of the Baptism of water, if it is impossible to receive the Baptism of water.

219. What do we promise in Baptism?

In Baptism we promise to renounce the devil with all his works and pomps.

220. Why is the name of a saint given in Baptism?

The name of a saint is given in Baptism in order that the person baptized may imitate his virtues and have him for a protector.

221. Why are godfathers and godmothers given in Baptism?

Godfathers and godmothers are given in Baptism in order that they may promise, in the name of the child, what the child itself would promise if it had the use of reason.

222. What is the obligation of a godfather and a godmother?

The obligation of a godfather and a godmother is to instruct the child in its religious duties, if the parents neglect to do so or die.

LESSON FIFTEEN

ON CONFIRMATION

223. What is Confirmation?

Confirmation is a Sacrament through which we receive the Holy Ghost to make us strong and perfect Christians and soldiers of Jesus Christ.

224. Who administers Confirmation?

The bishop is the ordinary minister of Confirmation.

225. How does the bishop give Confirmation?

The bishop extends his hands over those who are to be confirmed, prays that they may receive the Holy Ghost, and anoints the forehead of each with holy chrism in the form of a cross.

226. What is holy chrism?

Holy chrism is a mixture of olive oil and balm, consecrated by the bishop.

227. What does the bishop say in anointing the person he confirms?

In anointing the person he confirms the bishop says: I sign thee with the sign of the cross, and I confirm thee with the chrism of salvation, in the name of the Father, and of the Son, and of the Holy Ghost.

228. What is meant by anointing the forehead with chrism in the form of a cross?

By anointing the forehead with chrism in the form of a cross is meant, that the Christian who is confirmed must openly profess and practice his faith, never be ashamed of it, and rather die than deny it.

229. Why does the bishop give the person he confirms a slight blow on the cheek?

The bishop gives the person he confirms a slight blow on the cheek, to put him in mind that he must be ready to suffer everything even death, for the sake of Christ.

230. To receive Confirmation worthily is it necessary to be in the state of grace?

To receive Confirmation worthily it is necessary to be in the state of grace.

231. What special preparation should be made to receive Confirmation?

Persons of an age to learn should know the chief mysteries of faith and the duties of a Christian, and be instructed in the nature and effects of this Sacrament.

232. Is it a sin to neglect Confirmation?

It is a sin to neglect Confirmation, especially in these evil days when faith and morals are exposed to so many and such violent temptations.

LESSON SIXTEEN

ON THE GIFTS AND
FRUITS OF THE HOLY GHOST

233. What are the effects of Confirmation?

The effects of Confirmation are an increase of sanctifying grace, the strengthening of our faith, and the gifts of the Holy Ghost.

234. What are the gifts of the Holy Ghost?

The gifts of the Holy Ghost are Wisdom, Understanding, Counsel, Fortitude, Knowledge, Piety, and Fear of the Lord.

235. Why do we receive the gift of Fear of the Lord?

We receive the gift of Fear of the Lord to fill us with a dread of sin.

236. Why do we receive the gift of Piety?

We receive the gift of Piety to make us love God as a Father and obey Him because we love Him.

237. Why do we receive the gift of Knowledge?

We receive the gift of Knowledge to enable us to discover the will of God in all things.

238. Why do we receive the gift of Fortitude?

We receive the gift of Fortitude to strengthen us to do the will of God in all things.

239. Why do we receive the gift of Counsel?

We receive the gift of Counsel to warn us of the deceits of the devil, and of the dangers to salvation.

240. Why do we receive the gift of Understanding?

We receive the gift of Understanding to enable us to know more clearly the mysteries of faith.

241. Why do we receive the gift of Wisdom?

We receive the gift of Wisdom to give us a relish for the things of God, and to direct our whole life and all our actions to His honor and glory.

242. Which are the Beatitudes?

The Beatitudes are:

1. Blessed are the poor in spirit, for theirs is the kingdom of heaven.
2. Blessed are the meek, for they shall possess the land.
3. Blessed are they that mourn, for they shall be comforted.
4. Blessed are they that hunger and thirst after justice, for they shall be filled.
5. Blessed are the merciful, for they shall obtain mercy.
6. Blessed are the clean of heart, for they shall see God.
7. Blessed are the peacemakers, for they shall be called the children of God.
8. Blessed are they that suffer persecution for justice's sake, for theirs is the kingdom of heaven.

243. Which are the twelve fruits of the Holy Ghost?

The twelve fruits of the Holy Ghost are Charity, Joy, Peace, Patience, Benignity, Goodness, Long-suffering, Mildness, Faith, Modesty, Continency, and Chastity.

LESSON SEVENTEEN

ON THE SACRAMENT OF PENANCE

244. What is the Sacrament of Penance?

Penance is a Sacrament in which the sins committed after Baptism are forgiven.

245. How does the Sacrament of Penance remit sin and restore to the soul the friendship of God?

The Sacrament of Penance remits sin and restores the friendship of God to the soul by means of the absolution of the priest.

246. How do you know that the priest has the power of absolving from the sins committed after Baptism?

I know that the priest has the power of absolving from the sins committed after Baptism, because Jesus Christ granted that power to the priests of His Church when He said: "Receive ye the Holy Ghost. Whose sins you shall forgive, they are forgiven them; whose sins you shall retain, they are retained."

247. How do the priests of the Church exercise the power of forgiving sins?

The priests of the Church exercise the power of forgiving sins by hearing the confessions of sins, and by granting pardon for them as ministers of God and His Name.

248. What must we do to receive the Sacrament of Penance worthily?

To receive the Sacrament of Penance worthily we must do five things:

1. We must examine our conscience.
2. We must be sorry for our sins.
3. We must make a firm resolution never more to offend God.
4. We must confess our sins to the priest.
5. We must accept the penance which the priest gives us.

249. What is the examination of conscience?

The examination of conscience is an earnest effort to recall to mind all the sins we have committed since our last worthy confession.

250. How can we make a good examination of conscience?

We can make a good examination of conscience by calling to memory the commandments of God, the precepts of the Church, the seven capital sins, and the particular duties of our state in life, to find out the sins we have committed.

251. What should we do before beginning the examination of conscience?

Before beginning the examination of conscience we should pray to God to give us light to know our sins and grace to detest them.

LESSON EIGHTEEN

ON CONTRITION

252. What is contrition, or sorrow for sin?

Contrition, or sorrow for sin, is a hatred of sin and a true grief of the soul for having offended God, with a firm purpose to sin no more.

253. What kind of sorrow should we have for our sins?

The sorrow we should have for our sins should be interior, supernatural, universal, and sovereign.

254. What do you mean by saying that our sorrow should be interior?

When I say that our sorrow should be interior, I mean that it should come from the heart, and not merely from the lips.

255. What do you mean by saying that our sorrow should be supernatural?

When I say that our sorrow should be supernatural, I mean that it should be prompted by the grace of God, and excited by motives which spring from faith, and not by merely natural motives.

256. What do you mean by saying that our sorrow should be universal?

When I say that our sorrow should be universal, I mean that we should be sorry for all our mortal sins without exception.

257. What do you mean when you say that our sorrow should be sovereign?

When I say that our sorrow should be sovereign, I mean that we should grieve more for having offended God than for any other evil that can befall us.

258. Why should we be sorry for our sins?

We should be sorry for our sins, because sin is the greatest of evils and an offense against God our Creator, Preserver, and Redeemer, and because it shuts us out of heaven and condemns us to the eternal pains of hell.

259. How many kinds of contrition are there?

There are two kinds of contrition: perfect contrition and imperfect contrition.

260. What is perfect contrition?

Perfect contrition is that which fills us with sorrow and hatred for sin, because it offends God, who is infinitely good in Himself and worthy of all love.

261. What is imperfect contrition?

Imperfect contrition is that by which we hate what offends God, because by it we lose heaven and deserve hell; or because sin is so hateful in itself.

262. Is imperfect contrition sufficient for a worthy confession?

Imperfect contrition is sufficient for a worthy confession, but we should endeavor to have perfect contrition.

263. What do you mean by a firm purpose of sinning no more?

By a firm purpose of sinning no more I mean a fixed resolve not only to avoid all mortal sin, but also near occasions.

264. What do you mean by the near occasions of sin?

By the near occasions of sin I mean all the persons, places, and things that may easily lead us into sin.

LESSON NINETEEN
ON CONFESSION

265. What is confession?

Confession is the telling of our sins to a duly authorized priest, for the purpose of obtaining forgiveness.

266. What sins are we bound to confess?

We are bound to confess all our mortal sins, but it is well also to confess our venial sins.

267. What are the chief qualities of a good Confession?

The chief qualities of a good Confession are three: it must be humble, sincere, and entire.

268. When is our Confession humble?

Our Confession is humble when we accuse ourselves of our sins, with a deep sense of shame and sorrow for having offended God.

269. When is our confession sincere?

Our Confession is sincere when we tell our sins honestly and truthfully, neither exaggerating nor excusing them.

270. When is our Confession entire?

Our Confession is entire when we tell the number and kinds of our sins and the circumstances which change their nature.

271. What should we do if we cannot remember the number of our sins?

If we cannot remember the number of our sins, we should tell the number as nearly as possible, and say how often we may have sinned in a day, a week, or a month, and how long the habit or practice has lasted.

272. Is our Confession worthy if, without our fault, we forget to confess a mortal sin?

If, without our fault, we forget to confess a mortal sin, our Confession is worthy, and the sin is forgiven; but it must be told in Confession if it again comes to our mind.

273. Is it grievous offence wilfully to conceal a mortal sin in Confession?

It is a grievous offence wilfully to conceal a mortal sin in Confession, because we thereby tell a lie to the Holy Ghost, and make our Confession worthless.

274. What must he do who has wilfully concealed a mortal sin in Confession?

He who has wilfully concealed a mortal sin in Confession must not only confess it, but must also repeat all the sins he has committed since his last worthy Confession.

275. Why does the priest give us a penance after Confession?

The priest gives us a penance after Confession, that we may satisfy God for the temporal punishment due to our sins.

276. Does not the Sacrament of Penance remit all punishment due to sin?

The Sacrament of Penance remits the eternal punishment due to sin, but it does not always remit the temporal punishment which God requires as satisfaction for our sins.

277. Why does God require a temporal punishment as a satisfaction for sin?

God requires a temporal punishment as a satisfaction for sin, to teach us the great evil of sin and to prevent us from falling again.

278. What are the chief means by which we satisfy God for the temporal punishment due to sin?

The chief means by which we satisfy God for the temporal punishment due to sin are: Prayer, Fasting, Almsgiving, all spiritual and corporal works of mercy, and the patient suffering of the ills of life.

279. What are the chief spiritual works of mercy?

The chief spiritual works of mercy are seven: To admonish the sinner, to instruct the ignorant, to counsel the doubtful, to comfort the sorrowful, to bear wrongs patiently, to forgive all injuries, and to pray for the living and the dead.

280. What are the chief corporal works of mercy?

The chief corporal works of mercy are seven: to feed the hungry, to give drink to the thirsty, to clothe the naked, to ransom the captive, to harbor the harborless, to visit the sick, and to bury the dead.

LESSON TWENTY
ON THE MANNER OF MAKING A GOOD CONFESSION

281. What should we do on entering the Confessional?

On entering the confessional we should kneel, make the sign of the Cross, and say to the priest, Bless me, Father; then add, I confess to Almighty God and to you, father, that I have sinned.

282. What are the first things we should tell the priest in Confession?

The first things we should tell the priest in Confession are the time of our last Confession, and whether we said the penance and went to Holy Communion.

283. After telling the time of our last Confession and Communion what should we do?

After telling the time of our last Confession and Communion we should confess all the moral sins we have since committed, and all the venial sins we may wish to mention.

284. What must we do when the confessor asks us questions?

When the confessor asks us questions we must answer them truthfully and clearly.

285. What should we do after telling our sins?

After telling our sins we should listen with attention to the advice which the confessor may think proper to give.

286. How should we end our Confession?

We should end our Confession by saying, I also accuse myself of all the sins of my past life, telling, if we choose, one or several of our past sins.

287. What should we do while the priest is giving us absolution?

While the priest is giving us absolution we should from our heart renew the Act of Contrition.

LESSON TWENTY-ONE
ON INDULGENCES

288. What is an Indulgence?

An Indulgence is a remission in whole or in part of the temporal punishment due to sin.

289. Is an Indulgence a pardon of sin, or a license to commit sin?

An Indulgence is not a pardon of sin, nor a license to commit sin; and one who is in a state of mortal sin cannot gain an Indulgence.

290. How many kinds of Indulgences are there?

There are two kinds of Indulgences—Plenary and Partial.

291. What is a Plenary Indulgence?

A Plenary Indulgence is the full remission of the temporal punishment due to sin.

292. What is a Partial Indulgence?

A Partial Indulgence is the remission of a part of the temporal punishment due to sin.

293. How does the Church by means of Indulgences remit the temporal punishment due to sin?

The Church by means of Indulgences remits the temporal punishment due to sin by applying to us the merits of Jesus Christ, and the superabundant satisfactions of the Blessed Virgin Mary and of the saints; which merits and satisfactions are its spiritual treasury.

294. What must we do to gain an indulgence?

To gain an Indulgence we must be in the state of grace and perform the works enjoined.

LESSON TWENTY-TWO
ON THE HOLY EUCHARIST

295. What is the Holy Eucharist?

The Holy Eucharist is the Sacrament which contains the body and blood, soul and divinity, of our Lord Jesus Christ under the appearances of bread and wine.

296. Did our Lord promise us the Sacrament of Holy Eucharist?

Our Lord promised us the Sacrament of Holy Eucharist, when He said that He would give us His flesh to eat and His blood to drink.

297. When did Christ institute the Holy Eucharist?

Christ instituted the Holy Eucharist at the Last Supper, the night before He died.

298. Who were present when our Lord instituted the Holy Eucharist?

When our Lord instituted the Holy Eucharist the twelve Apostles were present.

299. How did our Lord institute the Holy Eucharist?

Our Lord instituted the Holy Eucharist by taking bread, blessing, breaking and giving it to His Apostles, saying: *"Take ye and eat. This is my body"*; and then by taking the cup of wine, blessing and giving it, saying to them: *"Drink ye all of this. This is my blood which shall be shed for the remission of sins. Do this in commemoration of me."*

300. What happened when our Lord said, "This is my body; this is my blood?"

When our Lord said, "This is my body," the substance of the bread was changed into the substance of His body; when He said, "This is my blood," the substance of the wine was changed into the substance of His blood.

301. Is Jesus Christ whole and entire both under the form of bread and under the form of wine?

Jesus Christ is whole and entire both under the form of bread and under the form of wine.

302. Did anything remain of the bread and wine after their substance had been changed into the substance of the body and blood of our Lord?

After the substance of the bread and wine had been changed into the substance of the body and blood of our Lord, there remained only the appearances of bread and wine.

303. What do you mean by the appearances of bread and wine?

By the appearances of bread and wine I mean the figure, the color, the taste, and whatever appears to the senses.

304. What is the change of the bread and wine into the body and blood of our Lord called?

This change of the bread and wine into the body and blood of our Lord is called Transubstantiation.

305. How was the substance of the bread and wine changed into the substance of the body and blood of Christ?

The substance of the bread and wine was changed into the substance of the body and blood of Christ by His almighty power.

306. Does this change of bread and wine into the body and blood of Christ continue to be made in the Church?

This change of bread and wine into the body and blood of Christ continues to be made in the Church by Jesus Christ through the ministry of His priests.

307. When did Christ give His priests the power to change bread and wine into His body and blood?

Christ gave His priests the power to change bread and wine into His body and blood when He said to the Apostles, "Do this in commemoration of me."

308. How do the priests exercise this power of changing bread and wine into the body and blood of Christ?

The priests exercise this power of changing bread and wine into the body and blood of Christ through the words: "This is my body; this is my blood."

LESSON TWENTY-THREE

ON THE ENDS FOR WHICH THE HOLY EUCHARIST WAS INSTITUTED

309. Why did Christ institute the Holy Eucharist?

Christ instituted the Holy Eucharist—

1. To unite us to Himself and to nourish our soul with His divine life.
2. To increase sanctifying grace and all virtues in our soul.
3. To lessen our evil inclinations.
4. To be a pledge of everlasting life.
5. To fit our bodies for a glorious resurrection.
6. To continue the sacrifice of the Cross in His Church.

310. How are we united to Jesus Christ in the Holy Eucharist?

We are united to Jesus Christ in the Holy Eucharist by means of Holy Communion.

311. What is Holy Communion?

Holy Communion is the receiving of the body and blood of Christ.

312. What is necessary to make a good Communion?

To make a good Communion it is necessary to be in the state of sanctifying grace and to be fasting from midnight.

313. Does he who receives Communion in mortal sin receive the body and blood of Christ?

He who receives Communion in mortal sin receives the body and blood of Christ, but does not receive His grace, and he commits a great sacrilege.

314. Is it enough to be free from mortal sin to receive plentifully the graces of the Holy Communion?

To receive plentifully the graces of Holy Communion it is not enough to be free from mortal sin, but we should be free from all affection to venial sin, and should make acts of lively faith, of firm hope, and ardent love.

315. What is the fast necessary for Holy Communion?

The fast necessary for Holy Communion is the abstaining from midnight from everything which is taken as food or drink.

316. Is any one ever allowed to receive Holy Communion when not fasting?

Any one in danger of death is allowed to receive Holy Communion when not fasting.

317. When are we bound to receive Holy Communion?

We are bound to receive Holy Communion, under pain of mortal sin, during the Easter time and when in danger of death.

318. Is it well to receive Holy Communion often?

It is well to receive Holy Communion often, as nothing is a greater aid to a holy life than often to receive the Author of all grace and the Source of all good.

319. What should we do after Holy Communion?

After Holy Communion we should spend some time in adoring our Lord, in thanking Him for the grace we have received, and in asking Him for the blessings we need.

LESSON TWENTY-FOUR
ON THE SACRIFICE OF THE MASS

320. When and where are the bread and wine changed into the body and blood of Christ?

The bread and wine are changed into the body and blood of Christ at the Consecration in the Mass.

321. What is the Mass?

The Mass is the unbloody sacrifice of the body and blood of Christ.

322. What is a sacrifice?

A sacrifice is the offering of an object by a priest to God alone, and the consuming of it to acknowledge that He is the Creator and Lord of all things.

323. Is the Mass the same sacrifice as that of the Cross?

The Mass is the same sacrifice as that of the Cross.

324. Why is the Mass the same sacrifice as that of the Cross?

The Mass is the same sacrifice as that of the Cross because the offering and the priest are the same—Christ our Blessed Lord; and the ends for which the sacrifice of the Mass is offered are the same as those of the sacrifice of the Cross.

325. What were the ends for which the sacrifice of the Cross was offered?

The ends for which the sacrifice of the Cross was offered were: (1) To honor and glorify God; (2) to thank Him for all the graces bestowed on the whole world; (3) to satisfy God's justice for the sins of men; (4) to obtain all graces and blessings.

326. Is there any difference between the sacrifice of the Cross and the sacrifice of the Mass?

Yes; the manner in which the sacrifice is offered is different. On the Cross Christ really shed His blood and was really slain; in the Mass there is no real shedding of blood nor real death, because Christ can die no more; but the sacrifice of the Mass, through the separate consecration of the bread and wine represents His death on the Cross.

327. When did our Lord command the Apostles and their successors to say Mass?

Our Lord commanded the Apostles and their successors to say Mass, when He said at the Last Supper: "Do this in commemoration of me."

328. How should we assist at Mass?

We should assist at Mass with great interior recollection and piety and with every outward mark of respect and devotion.

329. Which is the best manner of hearing Mass?

The best manner of hearing Mass is to offer it to God with the priest for the same purpose for which it is said, to meditate on Christ's sufferings and death, and to go to Holy Communion.

LESSON TWENTY-FIVE
ON EXTREME UNCTION AND HOLY ORDERS

A. EXTREME UNCTION

330. What is the Sacrament of Extreme Unction?

Extreme Unction is the Sacrament which, through the anointing and prayer of the priest, gives health and strength to the soul, and sometimes to the body, when we are in danger of death from sickness.

331. When should we receive Extreme Unction?

We should receive Extreme Unction when we are in danger of death from sickness, or from a wound or accident.

332. Should we wait until we are in extreme danger before we receive Extreme Unction?

We should not wait until we are in extreme danger before we receive Extreme Unction, but if possible we should receive it whilst we have the use of our senses.

333. Which are the effects of the Sacrament of Extreme Unction?

The effects of Extreme Unction are: (1) To comfort us in the pains of sickness and to strengthen us against temptation; (2) To remit venial sins and to cleanse our soul from the remains of sin; (3) To restore us to health, when God sees fit.

334. What do you mean by the remains of sin?

By the remains of sin I mean the inclination to evil and the weakness of the will which are the result of our sins, and which remain after our sins have been forgiven.

335. How should we receive the Sacrament of the Extreme Unction?

We should receive the Sacrament of Extreme Unction in the state of grace, and with lively faith and resignation to the will of God.

336. Who is the minister of the Sacrament of Extreme Unction?

The priest is the minister of the Sacrament of Extreme Unction.

B. HOLY ORDERS

337. What is the Sacrament of Holy Orders?

Holy Orders is a Sacrament by which bishops, priests, and other ministers of the Church are ordained and receive the power and grace to perform their sacred duties.

338. What is necessary to receive Holy Orders worthily?

To receive Holy Orders worthily it is necessary to be in the state of grace, to have the necessary knowledge and a divine call to this sacred office.

339. How should Christians look upon the priests of the Church?

Christians should look upon the priests of the Church as the messengers of God and the dispensers of His mysteries.

340. Who can confer the Sacrament of Holy Orders?

Bishops can confer the Sacrament of Holy Orders.

LESSON TWENTY-SIX
ON MATRIMONY

341. What is the Sacrament of Matrimony?

The Sacrament of Matrimony is the Sacrament which unites a Christian man and woman in lawful marriage.

342. Can a Christian man and woman be united in lawful marriage in any other way than by the Sacrament of Matrimony?

A Christian man and woman cannot be united in lawful marriage in any other way than by the Sacrament of Matrimony, because Christ raised marriage to the dignity of a Sacrament.

343. Can the bond of Christian marriage be dissolved by any human power?

The bond of Christian marriage cannot be dissolved by any human power.

344. Which are the effects of the Sacrament of Matrimony?

The effects of the Sacrament of Matrimony are: (1) To sanctify the love of husband and wife; (2) to give them grace to bear with each other's weaknesses; (3) to enable them to bring up their children in the fear and love of God.

345. To receive the Sacrament of Matrimony worthily is it necessary to be in the state of grace?

To receive the Sacrament of Matrimony worthily it is necessary to be in the state of grace, and it is necessary also to comply with the laws of the Church.

346. Who has the right to make laws concerning the Sacrament of marriage?

The Church alone has the right to make laws concerning the Sacrament of Marriage, though the state also has the right to make laws concerning the civil effects of the marriage contract.

347. Does the Church forbid the marriage of Catholics with persons who have a different religion or no religion at all?

The Church does forbid the marriage of Catholics with persons who have a different religion or no religion at all.

348. Why does the Church forbid the marriage of Catholics with persons who have a different religion or no religion at all?

The Church forbids the marriage of Catholics with persons who have a different religion or no religion at all, because such marriages generally lead to indifference, loss of faith, and to the neglect of the religious education of the children.

349. Why do many marriages prove unhappy?

Many marriages prove unhappy because they are entered into hastily and without worthy motives.

350. How should Christians prepare for a holy and happy marriage?

Christians should prepare for a holy and happy marriage by receiving the Sacraments of Penance and of Holy Eucharist; by begging God to grant them a pure intention and to direct their choice; and by seeking the advice of their parents and the blessing of their pastors.

LESSON TWENTY-SEVEN
ON THE SACRAMENTALS

351. What is a sacramental?

A sacramental is anything set apart or blessed by the Church to excite good thoughts and to increase devotion, and through these movements of the heart to remit venial sin.

352. What is the difference between the Sacraments and the sacramentals?

The difference between the Sacraments and the sacramentals is: (1) the Sacraments were instituted by Jesus Christ and the sacramentals by the Church; (2) the Sacraments give grace of themselves when we place no obstacle in the way; the sacramentals excite in us pious dispositions, by means of which we may obtain grace.

353. Which is the chief sacramental used in the Church?

The chief sacramental used in the Church is the sign of the Cross.

354. How do we make the sign of the Cross?

We make the sign of the Cross by putting the right hand to the forehead, then on the breast, and then to the left and right shoulders, saying, In the name of the Father, and of the Son, and of the Holy Ghost. Amen.

355. Why do we make the sign of the Cross?

We make the sign of the Cross to show that we are Christians and to profess our belief in the chief mysteries of our religion.

356. How is the sign of the Cross a profession of faith in the chief mysteries of four religion?

The sign of the Cross is a profession of faith in the chief mysteries of our religion because it expresses the mysteries of the Unity and Trinity of God and of the Incarnation and death of our Lord.

357. How does the sign of the Cross express the mystery of The Unity and Trinity of God?

The words, in the name, express the Unity of God; the words that follow, of the Father, and of the Son, and of the Holy Ghost, express the mystery of the Trinity.

358. How does the sign of the Cross express the mystery of the Incarnation and death of our Lord?

The sign of the Cross expresses the mystery of the Incarnation by reminding us that the Son of God, having become man, suffered death on the cross.

359. What other sacramental is in very frequent use?

Another sacramental in very frequent use is holy water.

360. What is holy water?

Holy water is water blessed by the priest with solemn prayer to beg God's blessing on those who use it, and protection from the powers of darkness.

361. Are there other sacramentals besides the sign of the Cross and holy water?

Besides the sign of the Cross and holy water there are many other sacramentals, such as blessed candles, ashes, palms, crucifixes, images of the Blessed Virgin and of the saints, rosaries, and scapulars.

LESSON TWENTY-EIGHT

ON PRAYER

362. Is there any other means of obtaining God's grace than the Sacraments?

There is another means of obtaining God's grace, and it is prayer.

363. What is prayer?

Prayer is the lifting up of our minds and hearts to God to adore Him, to thank Him for His benefits, to ask His forgiveness, and to beg of Him all the graces we need whether for soul or body.

364. Is prayer necessary to salvation?

Prayer is necessary to salvation, and without it no one having the use of reason can be saved.

365. At what particular times should we pray?

We should pray particularly on Sundays and holydays, every morning and night, in all dangers, temptations, and afflictions.

366. How should we pray?

We should pray: (1) with attention; (2) with a sense of our own helplessness and dependence upon God; (3) with a great desire for the graces we beg of God; (4) with trust in God's goodness; (5) with perseverance.

367. Which are the prayers most recommended to us?

The prayers most recommended to us are the Lord's Prayer, the Hail Mary, the Apostles' Creed, the Confiteor, and the Acts of Faith, Hope, Love, and Contrition.

368. Are prayers said with distractions of any avail?

Prayers said with wilful distractions are of no avail.

LESSON TWENTY-NINE

ON THE COMMANDMENTS OF GOD

369. Is it enough to belong to God's Church in order to be saved?

It is not enough to belong to the Church in order to be saved but we must also keep the Commandments of God and of the Church.

370. Which are the Commandments that contain the whole law of God?

The Commandments which contain the whole law of God are these two: (1) Thou shalt love the Lord thy God with thy whole heart, with thy whole soul, with thy whole strength, and with thy whole mind; (2) Thou shalt love thy neighbor as thyself.

371. Why do these two Commandments of the love of God and of our neighbor contain the whole law of God?

These two Commandments of the love of God and of our neighbor contain the whole law of God because all the other Commandments are given either to help us to keep these two, or to direct us how to shun what is opposed to them.

372. How do we show our love for God?

We show our love for God by keeping His commandments.

373. Why must we love our neighbor as ourselves?

We must love our neighbor as ourselves because God, who created and redeemed us, commands it.

374. Which are the Commandments of God?

The Commandments of God are these ten:

1. I am the Lord thy God, Thou shalt not have strange Gods before Me.
2. Thou shalt not take the name of the Lord thy God in vain.
3. Remember thou keep holy the Sabbath day.
4. Honor thy father and thy mother.
5. Thou shalt not kill.
6. Thou shalt not commit adultery.
7. Thou shalt not steal.
8. Thou shalt not bear false witness against thy neighbor.
9. Thou shalt not covet thy neighbor's wife.
10. Thou shalt not covet thy neighbor's goods.

375. Who gave the Ten Commandments?

God Himself gave the Ten Commandments to Moses on Mount Sinai, and Christ our Lord confirmed them.

LESSON THIRTY

ON THE FIRST COMMANDMENT

376. What is the first Commandment?

The first Commandment is: I am the Lord thy God: thou shalt not have strange gods before Me.

377. How does the first Commandment help us to keep the great Commandment of the love of God?

The first Commandment helps us to keep the great Commandment of the love of God because it commands us to adore God alone.

378. How do we adore God?

We adore God by faith, hope, and charity, and by prayer and sacrifice.

379. How may the first Commandment be broken?

The first Commandment may be broken by giving to a creature the honor which belongs to God alone; by false worship; and by attributing to a creature a perfection which belongs to God alone.

380. Do those who make use of spells and charms, or who believe in dreams, in mediums, spiritists, fortune-tellers, and the like, sin against the first Commandment?

Those who make use of spells and charms, or who believe in dreams, in mediums, spiritists, fortune-tellers, and the like, sin against the first Commandment, because they attribute to creatures perfections which belong to God alone.

381. Are sins against faith, hope, and charity also sins against the first Commandment?

Sins of faith, hope, and charity are also sins against the first Commandment.

382. How does a person sin against faith?

A person sins against faith: (1) by not trying to know what God has taught; (2) by refusing to believe all that God has taught; (3) by neglecting to profess his belief in what God has taught.

383. How do we fail to try to know what God has taught?

We fail to try to know what God has taught by neglecting to learn the Christian doctrine.

384. Who are they who do not believe all that God has taught?

They who do not believe all that God has taught are the heretics and infidels.

385. Who are they who neglect to profess their belief in what God has taught?

They who neglect to profess their belief in what God has taught are all those who fail to acknowledge the true church in which they really believe.

386. Can they who fail to profess their faith in the true Church in which they believe, expect to be saved while on that state?

They who fail to profess their faith in the true Church in which they believe, cannot expect to be saved while in that state, for Christ has said: "Whosoever shall deny Me before men, I will also deny him before My Father Who is in heaven."

387. Are we obliged to make open profession of our faith?

We are obliged to make open profession of our faith as often as God's honor, our neighbor's spiritual good, or our own requires it. "Whosoever," says Christ, "shall confess Me before men, I will also confess him before My Father who is in heaven."

388. Which are the sins against hope?

The sins against hope are presumption and despair.

389. What is presumption?

Presumption is a rash expectation of salvation without making proper use of the necessary means to obtain it.

390. What is despair?

Despair is the loss of hope in God's mercy.

391. How do we sin against the love of God?

We sin against the love of God by all sin, but particularly by mortal sin.

LESSON THIRTY-ONE
THE FIRST COMMANDMENT—
ON THE HONOR AND INVOCATION OF SAINTS

392. Does the first Commandment forbid the honoring of the saints?

The first Commandment does not forbid the honoring of the saints, but rather approves of it: because by honoring the saints, who are the chosen friends of God, we honor God himself.

393. Does the first Commandment forbid us to pray to the saints?

The first commandment does not forbid us to pray to the saints.

394. What do we mean by praying to the saints?

By praying to the saints we mean the asking of their help and prayers.

395. How do we know that the saints hear us?

We know that the saints hear us, because they are with God, Who makes our prayers known to them.

396. Why do we believe that the saints will help us?

We believe that the saints will help us because both they and we are members of the same Church, and they love us as their children.

397. How are the saints and we members of the same Church?

The saints and we are members of the same Church, because the Church in heaven and the Church on earth are one and the same Church, and all its members are in communion with one another.

398. What is the communion of the members of the Church called?

The communion of the members of the Church is called the communion of saints.

399. What does the communion of saints mean?

The communion of saints means the union which exists between the members of the Church on earth with one another, and with the blessed in heaven, and with the suffering souls in purgatory.

400. What benefits are derived from the communion of saints?

The following benefits are derived from the communion of saints:—the faithful on earth assist one another by their prayers and good works, and they are aided by the intercession of the saints in heaven, while both the saints in heaven and the faithful on earth help the souls in purgatory.

401. Does the first Commandment forbid us to honor relics?

The first Commandment does not forbid us to honor relics, because relics are the bodies of the saints, or objects directly connected with them or with our Lord.

402. Does the first Commandment forbid the making of images?

The first Commandment does forbid the making of images if they are made to be adored as gods, but it does not forbid the making of them to put us in mind of Jesus Christ, His Blessed Mother, and the saints.

403. Is it right to show respect to the pictures and images of Christ and His saints?

It is right to show respect to the pictures and images of Christ and His saints, because they are the representations and memorials of them.

404. Is it allowed to pray to the crucifix or to the images and relics of the saints?

It is not allowed to pray to the crucifix or images and relics of the saints, for they have no life, nor power to help us, nor sense to hear us.

405. Why do we pray before the crucifix and the images and relics of the saints?

We pray before the crucifix and images and relics of the saints because they enliven our devotion by exciting pious affections and desires, and by reminding us of Christ and of the saints, that we may imitate their virtues.

LESSON THIRTY-TWO
FROM THE SECOND TO THE
FOURTH COMMANDMENT

THE SECOND COMMANDMENT

406. What is the second Commandment?

The second Commandment is: Thou shalt not take the name of the Lord thy God in vain.

407. What are we commanded by the second Commandment?

We are commanded by the second Commandment to speak with reverence of God and of the saints, and of all holy things, and to keep our lawful oaths and vows.

What is an oath?

An oath is the calling upon God to witness the truth of what we say.

When may we take an oath?

We may take an oath when it is ordered by lawful authority or required for God's honor or for our own or our neighbor's good.

410. What is necessary to make an oath lawful?

To make an oath lawful it is necessary that what we swear shall be true, and that there shall be a sufficient cause for taking an oath.

411. What is a vow?

A vow is a deliberate promise made to God to do something that is pleasing to Him.

412. Is it a sin not to fulfill our vows?

Not to fulfill our vows is a sin, mortal or venial, according to the nature of the vow and the intention we had in making it.

413. What is forbidden by the second Commandment?

The second Commandment forbids all false, rash, unjust, and unnecessary oaths, blasphemy, cursing, and profane words.

THE THIRD COMMANDMENT

414. What is the third Commandment?

The Third Commandment is: Remember thou keep holy the Sabbath day.

415. What are we commanded by the third Commandment?

By the third Commandment we are commanded to keep holy the Lord's day and the holydays of obligation, on which we are to give our time to the service and worship of God.

416. How are we to worship God on Sundays and holydays of obligation?

We are to worship God on Sundays and holydays of obligation by hearing Mass, by prayer, and by other good works.

417. Are the Sabbath day and Sunday the same?

The Sabbath day and Sunday are not the same. The Sabbath day is the seventh day of the week, and is the day which was kept holy in the Old Law; the Sunday is the first day of the week, and is the day which is kept holy in the New Law.

418. Why does the Church command us to keep Sunday holy instead of the Sabbath?

The Church commands us to keep Sunday holy instead of the Sabbath because on Sunday Christ rose from the dead, and on Sunday He sent the Holy Ghost upon the Apostles.

419. What is forbidden by the third Commandment?

The third Commandment forbids all unnecessary servile work and whatever else may hinder the due observance of the Lord's day.

420. What are servile works?

Servile works are those which require labor rather of body then of mind.

421. Are servile works on Sunday ever lawful?

Servile works are lawful on Sunday when the honor of God, the good of our neighbor, or necessity requires them.

LESSON THIRTY-THREE
FROM THE FOURTH TO
THE SEVENTH COMMANDMENT

THE FOURTH COMMANDMENT

422. What is the fourth Commandment?

The fourth Commandment is: Honor thy father and thy mother.

423. What are we commanded by the fourth Commandment?

We are commanded by the fourth Commandment to honor, love, and obey our parents in all that is not sin.

424. Are we bound to honor and obey others than our parents?

We are also bound to honor and obey our bishops, pastors, magistrates, teachers, and other lawful superiors.

425. Have parents and superiors any duties towards those who are under their charge?

It is the duty of parents and superiors to take good care of all under their charge and give them proper direction and example.

426. What is forbidden by the fourth Commandment?

The fourth Commandment forbids all disobedience, contempt, and stubbornness toward our parents or lawful superiors.

THE FIFTH COMMANDMENT

427. What is the fifth Commandment?

The fifth Commandment is: Thou shalt not kill.

428. What are we commanded by the fifth Commandment?

We are commanded by the fifth Commandment to live in peace and union with our neighbor, to respect his rights, to seek his spiritual and bodily welfare, and to take proper care of our own life and health.

429. What is forbidden by the fifth Commandment?

The fifth Commandment forbids all wilful murder, fighting, anger, hatred, revenge, and bad example.

THE SIXTH COMMANDMENT

430. What is the sixth Commandment?

The sixth Commandment is: Thou shalt not commit adultery.

431. What are we commanded by the sixth Commandment?

We are commanded by the sixth Commandment to be pure in thought and modest in all our looks, words, and actions.

432. What is forbidden by the sixth Commandment?

The sixth Commandment forbids all unchaste freedom with another's wife or husband; also all immodesty with ourselves or others in looks, dress, words, or actions.

433. Does the sixth Commandment forbid the reading of bad and immodest books and newspapers?

The sixth Commandment does forbid the reading of bad and immodest books and newspapers.

LESSON THIRTY-FOUR

FROM THE SEVENTH TO THE END OF THE TENTH COMMANDMENT

THE SEVENTH COMMANDMENT

434. What is the seventh Commandment?

The seventh Commandment is: Thou shalt not steal.

435. What are we commanded by the seventh Commandment?

By the seventh Commandment we are commanded to give to all men what belongs to them and to respect their property.

436. What is forbidden by the seventh Commandment?

The seventh Commandment forbids all unjust taking or keeping what belongs to another.

437. Are we bound to restore ill-gotten goods?

We are bound to restore ill-gotten goods, or the value of them, as far as we are able; otherwise we cannot be forgiven.

438. Are we obliged to repair the damage we have unjustly caused?

We are bound to repair the damage we have unjustly caused.

THE EIGHTH COMMANDMENT

439. What is the eighth Commandment?

The eighth Commandment is: Thou shalt not bear false witness against thy neighbor.

440. What are we commanded by the eighth Commandment?

We are commanded by the eighth Commandment to speak the truth in all things and to be careful of the honor and reputation of every one.

441. What is forbidden by the eighth Commandment?

The eighth Commandment forbids all rash judgments, backbiting, slanders, and lies.

442. What must they do who have lied about their neighbor and seriously injured his character?

They who have lied about their neighbor and seriously injured his character must repair the injury done as far as they are able, otherwise they will not be forgiven.

THE NINTH COMMANDMENT

443. What is the ninth Commandment?

The ninth Commandment is: Thou shalt not covet thy neighbor's wife.

444. What are we commanded by the ninth Commandment?

We are commanded by the ninth Commandment to keep ourselves pure in thought and desire.

445. What is forbidden by the ninth Commandment?

The ninth Commandment forbids unchaste thoughts, desires for another's wife or husband, and all other unlawful, impure thoughts and desires.

446. Are impure thoughts and desires always sins?

Impure thoughts and desires are always sins, unless they displease us and we try to banish them.

THE TENTH COMMANDMENT

447. What is the tenth Commandment?

The tenth Commandment is: Thou shalt not covet thy neighbor's goods.

448. What are we commanded by the tenth Commandment?

By the tenth Commandment we are commanded to be content with what we have, and to rejoice in our neighbor's welfare.

449. What is forbidden by the tenth Commandment?

The tenth Commandment forbids all desires to take or keep wrongfully what belongs to another.

LESSON THIRTY-FIVE

ON THE FIRST AND SECOND COMMANDMENTS OF THE CHURCH

450. Which are the chief commandments of the Church?

The chief Commandments of the Church are six:

1. To hear Mass on Sundays and holydays of obligation.
2. To fast and abstain on the days appointed.
3. To confess at least once a year.
4. To receive the Holy Eucharist during the Easter time.
5. To contribute to the support of our pastors.
6. Not to marry persons who are not Catholics, or who are related to us within the third degree of kindred, nor privately without witnesses, nor to solemnize marriage at forbidden times.

THE FIRST COMMANDMENT OF THE CHURCH

451. Is it a mortal sin not to hear Mass on a Sunday or a holyday of obligation?

It is a mortal sin not to hear Mass on a Sunday or a holyday of obligation, unless we are excused for a serious reason. They also commit a mortal sin who, having others under their charge, hinder them from hearing Mass, without a sufficient reason.

452. Why were holydays instituted by the Church?

Holydays were instituted by the Church to recall to our minds the great mysteries of religion and the virtues and rewards of the saints.

453. How should we keep the holydays of obligation?

We should keep the holydays of obligation as we should keep the Sunday.

454. What do you mean by fast-days?

By fast-days I mean days on which we are allowed but one full meal.

455. What do you mean by days of abstinence?

By days of abstinence I mean days on which we are forbidden to eat flesh-meat, but are allowed the usual number of meals.

456. Why does the Church command us to fast and abstain?

The Church commands us to fast and abstain, in order that we may mortify our passions and satisfy for our sins.

457. Why does the Church command us to abstain from flesh-meat on Fridays?

The church commands us to abstain from flesh-meat on Fridays in honor of the day on which our Saviour died.

LESSON THIRTY-SIX

ON THE THIRD, FOURTH, FIFTH AND SIXTH COMMANDMENTS OF THE CHURCH

458. What is meant by the command of confessing at least once a year?

By the command of confessing at least once a year is meant that we are obliged, under pain of mortal sin, to go to confession within the year.

459. Should we confess only once a year?

We should confess frequently, if we wish to lead a good life.

460. Should children go to confession?

Children should go to confession when they are old enough to commit sin, which is commonly about the age of seven years.

THE FOURTH COMMANDMENT OF THE CHURCH

461. What sin does he commit who neglects to receive Communion during Easter time?

He who neglects to receive Communion during Easter time commits a mortal sin.

462. What is Easter time?

Easter time is, in this country, the time between the first Sunday of Lent and Trinity Sunday.

THE FIFTH COMMANDMENT OF THE CHURCH

463. Are we obliged to contribute to the support of our pastors?

We are obliged to contribute to the support of our pastors, and to bear our share in the expenses of the Church and school.

464. What is the meaning of the commandment not to marry within the third degree of kindred?

The meaning of the commandment not to marry within the third degree of kindred is that no one is allowed to marry another within the third degree of blood relationship.

465. What is the meaning of the command not to marry privately?

The command not to marry privately means that none should marry without the blessings of God's priests or without witnesses.

466. What is the meaning of the precept not to solemnize marriage at forbidden times?

The meaning of the precept not to solemnize marriage at forbidden times is that during Lent and Advent the marriage ceremony should not be performed with pomp or a nuptial Mass.

467. What is the nuptial Mass?

A nuptial Mass is a Mass appointed by the Church to invoke a special blessing upon the married couple.

468. Should Catholics be married at a nuptial Mass?

Catholics should be married at a nuptial Mass, because they thereby show greater reverence for the holy Sacrament and bring richer blessings upon their wedded life.

LESSON THIRTY-SEVEN

ON THE LAST JUDGMENT AND THE RESURRECTION, HELL, PURGATORY, AND HEAVEN

469. When will Christ judge us?

Christ will judge us immediately after our death, and on the last day.

470. What is the judgment called which we have to undergo immediately after death?

The judgment we have to undergo immediately after death is called the Particular Judgment.

471. What is the judgment called which all men have to undergo on the last day?

The judgment which all men have to undergo on the last day is called the General Judgment.

472. Why does Christ judge men immediately after death?

Christ judges men immediately after death to reward or punish them according to their deeds.

473. What are the rewards or punishments appointed for men's souls after the Particular Judgment?

The rewards or punishments appointed for men's souls after the Particular Judgment are Heaven, Purgatory, and Hell.

474. What is Hell?

Hell is a state to which the wicked are condemned, and in which they are deprived of the sight of God for all eternity, and are in dreadful torments.

475. What is Purgatory?

Purgatory is a state in which those suffer for a time who die guilty of venial sins, or without having satisfied for the punishment due to their sins.

476. Can the faithful on earth help the souls in Purgatory?

The faithful on earth can help the souls in Purgatory by their prayers, fasts, alms-deeds; by indulgences, and by having Masses said for them.

477. If every one is judged immediately after death, what need is there of a General Judgment?

There is need of a General Judgment, though every one is judged immediately after death, that the providence of God, which, on earth, often permits the good to suffer and the wicked to prosper, may in the end appear just before all men.

478. Will our bodies share in the reward or punishment of our souls?

Our bodies will share in the reward or punishment of our souls, because through the resurrection they will again be united to them.

479. In what state will the bodies of the just rise?

The bodies of the just will rise glorious and immortal.

480. Will the bodies of the damned also rise?

The bodies of the damned will also rise, but they will be condemned to eternal punishment.

481. What is Heaven?

Heaven is a state of everlasting life in which we see God face to face, are made like unto Him in glory, and enjoy eternal happiness.

HELEN KELLER
1880 - 1968

I count it one of the sweetest privileges of my life to have known and conversed with many men of genius. Only those who knew Bishop Brooks can appreciate the joy his friendship was to those who possessed it. As a child I loved to sit on his knee and clasp his great hand with one of mine, while Miss Sullivan spelled into the other his beautiful words about God and the spiritual world. I heard him with a child's wonder and delight. My spirit could not reach up to his, but he gave me a real sense of joy in life, and I never left him without carrying away a fine thought that grew in beauty and depth of meaning as I grew. Once, when I was puzzled to know why there were so many religions, he said: "There is one universal religion, Helen—the religion of love. Love your Heavenly Father with your whole heart and soul, love every child of God as much as ever you can, and remember that the possibilities of good are greater than the possibilities of evil; and you have the key to Heaven." And his life was a happy illustration of this great truth. In his noble soul love and widest knowledge were blended with faith that had become insight. He saw

> God in all that liberates
> and lifts,
> In all that humbles,
> sweetens and consoles.

Bishop Brooks taught me no special creed or dogma; but he impressed upon my mind two great ideas—the fatherhood of God and the brotherhood of man, and made me feel that these truths underlie all creeds and forms of worship. God is love, God is our Father, we are His children; therefore the darkest clouds will break, and though right be worsted, wrong shall not triumph.

One who might be considered a saint without the canonization, **Helen Keller** was rendered deaf, dumb, and blind by a childhood illness. Despite her awesome obstacles, Keller learned to read and write with the help of her teacher, Anne Sullivan, and eventually graduated from Radcliffe with honors. After completing her education she began a lifelong career in service, working to help others with physical handicaps, and later establishing the Helen Keller Endowment Fund. At the time of her death in 1968, she had traveled to more than twenty-five countries in an effort to create better conditions for the blind. The following excerpt from *Story of My Life* betrays a simple and innocent Christian spirituality rooted in nothing more complicated than love.

I am too happy in this world to think much about the future, except to remember that I have cherished friends awaiting me there in God's beautiful Somewhere. In spite of the lapse of years, they seem so close to me that I should not think it strange if at any moment they should clasp my hand and speak words of endearment as they used to before they went away.

Since Bishop Brooks died I have read the Bible through; also some philosophical works on religion, among them Swedenborg's "Heaven and Hell" and Drummond's "Ascent of Man," and I have found no creed or system more soul-satisfying than Bishop Brook's creed of love.

D. L. MOODY
1837 - 1899

This former shoe salesman is credited with restoring the revivalist tradition to the United States in the nineteenth century. Born in Northfield, Massachusetts, in 1837, **Moody** did not begin life as a preacher. Rather, he found a path to the pulpit through a longtime association with the YMCA: it was on a fundraising tour in Britain that Moody's sermon-making ability made itself apparent. Moody amassed a vast following, and after his return to the U.S., Americans soon followed the example of the British. Although he was never ordained in any specific denomination, he was clearly a devout Christian. Moody was joined in his effort to convert the masses by his songwriting partner Ira Sankey, a gospel writer who wrote, among others, the hymn "Shall We Gather at the River." The preacher not only led hundreds of revival campaigns, he also founded high schools and a seminary with the intent of providing greater opportunity for Christian education for young people. In this excerpt from a biography entitled *D. L. Moody*, the evangelist contemplates conversion and the true feeling of love for God.

Some day you will read in the papers that D. L. Moody of East Northfield is dead. Don't believe a word of it. At that moment I shall be more alive than I am now. I shall have gone higher, that is all; gone out of this old tenement of clay into a house that is immortal; a body that death cannot touch, that sin cannot taint, a body like unto His own glorious body. I was born of the flesh in 1837. I was born of the spirit in 1854. That which is born of the flesh may die. That which is born of the spirit will live forever."

THEODORE ROOSEVELT
1858 - 1919

The most perfect machinery of government will not keep us as a nation from destruction if there is not within us a soul. No abounding material prosperity shall avail us if our spiritual senses atrophy. The foes of our own household shall surely prevail against us unless there be in our people an inner life which finds its outward expression in a morality not very widely different from that preached by the seers and prophets of Judea when the grandeur that was Greece and the glory that was Rome still lay in the future.

In his Farewell Address to his countrymen, Washington said: "Morality is a necessary spring of popular government . . . and let us with caution indulge the supposition that morality can be maintained without religion. Whatever may be conceded to the influence of refined education on minds of peculiar structure, reason and experience both forbid us to expect that national morality can prevail in exclusion of religious principle."

In this excerpt, **Theodore Roosevelt**, youngest man ever to become President and a leader remembered for the protection of thousands of acres of national land, reflects on government and its foundation in the faith. The President served for two terms, losing the election for what would have been a third term to Woodrow Wilson.

Washington lacked Lincoln's gift of words; but not Lincoln himself possessed more robust common sense in the thought that lies back of words. In this case the thought is not new—only a few good thoughts are new; but it was given expression at a time when the European movement with which the American people were in most complete sympathy—the French Revolution—had

endeavored to destroy the abuses of priestcraft and bigotry by abolishing not only Christianity but religion, in the sense in which religion is properly understood. The result was a cynical disregard of morality and a carnival of cruelty and bigotry, committed in the names of reason and liberty, which equalled anything ever done by Torquemada and the fanatics of the Inquisition in the names of religion and order.

Washington wished his fellow countrymen to walk clear of such folly and iniquity. As in all cases where he dealt with continuing causes his words are as well worth pondering now as when they were written. . . .

In this actual world a churchless community, a community where men have abandoned and scoff at or ignore their religious needs, is a community on the rapid down-grade. It is true that occasional individuals or families may have nothing to do with church or with religious practices and observances and yet maintain the highest standard of refined ethical obligation. But this does not affect the case in the world as it now is, any more than the fact that exceptional men and women under exceptional conditions have disregarded the marriage tie without moral harm to themselves interferes with the larger fact that such disregard if at all common means the complete moral disintegration of the body politic. . . .

WOODROW WILSON
1856 - 1924

October 1, 1911

There are great problems, ladies and gentlemen, before the American people. There are problems which will need purity of spirit and an integrity of purpose such as has never been called for before in the history of this country. I should be afraid to go forward if I did not believe that there lay at the foundation of all our schooling and of all our thought this incomparable and unimpeachable Word of God. If we cannot derive our strength thence, there is no source from which we can derive it, and so I would bid you go from this place, if I may, inspired once more with the feeling that the providence of God is the foundation of affairs, and that only those can guide, and only those can follow, who take this providence of God from the sources where it is authentically interpreted. . . .

The happiness of seeing a great company of people like this gathered together in the interest of the Sunday School is the happiness of knowing that there are they who seek light and who know that the lamp from which their spirits can be kindled is the lamp that glows in the Word of God.

The twenty-eighth President of the U.S. comments on the importance of faith and moral values to carry this nation through hard times. Wilson, the son of a Presbyterian minister, was raised in an atmosphere imbued with spirituality. He was a scholar by nature

Every Sunday School should be a place where this great book is not only opened, is not only studied, is not only revered, but is drunk of as if it were a fountain of life, is used as if it were the only source of inspiration and of guidance. No great nation can ever survive its own temptations and its own follies that does not indoctrinate its children in the Word of God; so that as school master and as Governor I know that my feet must rest with the feet of my fellowmen upon this foundation, and upon this foundation only; for the righteousness of nations, like the righteousness of men, must take its source from these foundations of inspiration.

and a politician by practice, remembered for his authorship of the Fourteen Points and his aid in the formation of the League of Nations. He was awarded the Nobel Peace Prize in 1920 for his efforts to achieve peace.

EDITH WHARTON
1862 - 1937

There was, however, one fairy tale at which I always thrilled—the story of the boy who could talk with the birds and hear what the grasses said. Very early, earlier than my conscious memory can reach, I must have felt myself to be of kin to that happy child. I cannot remember when the grasses first spoke to me, though I think it was when, a few years later, one of my uncles took me, with some little cousins, to spend a long spring day in some marshy woods near Mamaroneck, where the earth was starred with pink trailing arbutus, where pouch-like white and rosy flowers grew in a swamp, and leafless branches against the sky were netted with buds of mother-of-pearl; but on the day when Foxy was given to me I learned what the animals say to each other, and to us. . . .

On both sides our colonial ancestry goes back for nearly three hundred years, and on both sides the colonists in question seem to have been identified since early days with New York, though my earliest Stevens forbears went first to Massachusetts. Some of the first Stevens's grandsons, however, probably not

*The author of over fifty books, **Edith Wharton** is best remembered for her ironic and sometimes biting works about the American upper class, into which she was born in 1862. An appreciation for the absurdities of high society propelled many of her novels, and Wharton was never slow to point out the irony of a situation, particularly one involving conflicts between the old aristocracy and nouveau riche.*

Her writing became less critical in later years, and it is those later writings from which I draw, namely from her autobiography, *A Backward Glance*. Wharton's love for language was perhaps the strongest force in her character, and that translated into her relationship with religion as well. She may have cared more for the words of faith than for faith itself.

being of the stripe of religious fanatic or political reformer to breathe easily in that passionate province, transferred their activities to the easier-going New York, where people seem from the outset to have been more interested in making money and acquiring property than in Predestination and witch-burning. I have always wondered if those old New Yorkers did not owe their greater suavity and tolerance to the fact that the Church of England (so little changed under its later name of Episcopal Church of America) provided from the first their prevalent form of worship. May not the matchless beauty of an ancient rite have protected our ancestors from what Huxley called the "fissiparous tendency of the Protestant sects", sparing them sanguinary wrangles over uncomprehended points of doctrine, and all those extravagances of self-constituted prophets and evangelists which rent and harrowed New England? Milder manners, a greater love of ease, and a franker interest in money-making and good food, certainly distinguished the colonial New Yorkers from the conscience-searching children of the "Mayflower". Apart from some of the old Dutch colonial families, who continued to follow the "Dutch Reformed" rite, the New York of my youth was distinctively Episcopalian; and to this happy chance I owe my early saturation with the noble cadences of the Book of Common Prayer, and my reverence for an ordered ritual in which the officiant's personality is strictly subordinated to the rite he performs.

Yet what I recall of those rambles is not so much the comradeship of the other children, or the wise and friendly talk of our guide, as my secret sensitiveness to the landscape—something in me quite incommunicable to others, that was tremblingly and inarticulately awake to every detail of wind-warped fern and wide-eyed briar rose, yet more profoundly alive to a unifying magic beneath the diversities of the visible scene—a power with which I was in deep and solitary communion whenever I was alone with nature. It was the same tremor that had stirred in me in the spring woods of Mamaroneck, when I heard the whisper of the arbutus and the starry choir of the dogwood; and it has never since been still.

F. SCOTT FITZGERALD
1896 - 1940

ABSOLUTION

THERE WAS once a priest with cold, watery eyes, who, in the still of the night, wept cold tears. He wept because the afternoons were warm and long, and he was unable to attain a complete mystical union with our Lord. Sometimes, near four o'clock, there was a rustle of Swede girls along the path by his window, and in their shrill laughter he found a terrible dissonance that made him pray aloud for the twilight to come. At twilight the laughter and the voices were quieter, but several times he had walked past Romberg's Drug Store when it was dusk and the yellow lights shone inside and the nickel taps of the soda-fountain were gleaming, and he had found the scent of cheap toilet soap desperately sweet upon the air. He passed that way when he returned from hearing confessions on Saturday nights, and he grew careful to walk on the other side of the street so that the smell of the soap would float upward before it reached his nostrils as it drifted, rather like incense, toward the summer moon.

Famous for such classics as *The Great Gatsby* and *This Side of Paradise*, **F. Scott Fitzgerald** chronicled the America of the twenties and thirties. Raised in Minnesota as a nonpracticing Catholic, he received his first religious education at the age of fifteen, when he was sent to a Catholic boarding school. "Absolution," his examination of the discomfort felt by young Catholics about confession, will surely ring familiar to many.

But there was no escape from the hot madness of four o'clock. From his window, as far as he could see, the Dakota wheat thronged the valley of the Red River. The wheat was terrible to look upon and the carpet pattern to which in agony he bent his eyes sent his thought brooding through grotesque labyrinths, open always to the unavoidable sun.

One afternoon when he had reached the point where the mind runs down like an old clock, his housekeeper brought into his study a beautiful, intense little boy of eleven named Rudolph Miller. The little boy sat down in a patch of sunshine, and the priest, at his walnut desk, pretended to be very busy. This was to conceal his relief that some one had come into his haunted room.

Presently he turned around and found himself staring into two enormous, staccato eyes, lit with gleaming points of cobalt light. For a moment their expression startled him—then he saw that his visitor was in a state of abject fear.

"Your mouth is trembling," said Father Schwartz, in a haggard voice.

The little boy covered his quivering mouth with his hand.

"Are you in trouble?" asked Father Schwartz, sharply. "Take your hand away from your mouth and tell me what's the matter."

The boy—Father Schwartz recognized him now as the son of a parishoner, Mr. Miller, the freight-agent—moved his hand reluctantly off his mouth and became articulate in a despairing whisper.

"Father Schwartz—I've committed a terrible sin."

"A sin against purity?"

"No, Father . . . worse."

Father Schwartz's body jerked sharply.

"Have you killed somebody?"

"No—but I'm afraid—" the voice rose to a shrill whimper.

"Do you want to go to confession?"

The little boy shook his head miserably. Father Schwartz cleared his throat so that he could make his voice soft and say some quiet, kind thing. In this moment he should forget his own agony, and try to act like God. He repeated to himself a devotional phrase, hoping that in return God would help him to act correctly.

"Tell me what you've done," said his new soft voice.

The little boy looked at him through his tears, and was reassured by the impression of moral resiliency which the distraught priest had created. Abandoning as much of himself as he was able to this man, Rudolph Miller began to tell his story.

"On Saturday, three days ago, my father he said I had to go to confession, because I hadn't been for a month, and the family they go every week, and I hadn't been. So I just as leave go, I didn't care. So I put it off till after supper because I was playing with a bunch of kids and father asked me if I went, and I said 'no,' and he took me by the neck and he said 'You go now,' so I said 'All right,' so I went over to church. And he yelled after me: 'Don't come back till you go' . . . ."

II

"On Saturday, Three Days Ago."

The plush curtain of the confessional rearranged its dismal creases, leaving exposed only the bottom of an old man's old shoe. Behind the curtain an immortal soul was alone with God and the Reverend Adolphus Schwartz, priest of the parish. Sound began, a labored whispering, sibilant and discreet, broken at intervals by the voice of the priest in audible question.

Rudolph Miller knelt in the pew beside the confessional and waited, straining nervously to hear, and yet not to hear what was being said within. The fact that the priest was audible alarmed him. His own turn came next, and the three or four others who waited might listen unscrupulously while he admitted his violations of the Sixth and Ninth Commandments.

Rudolph had never committed adultery, nor even coveted his neighbor's wife—but it was the confession of the associate sins that was particularly hard to contemplate. In comparison he relished the less shameful fallings away—they formed a grayish background which relieved the ebony mark of sexual offenses upon his soul.

He had been covering his ears with his hands, hoping that his refusal to hear would be noticed, and a like courtesy rendered to him in turn, when a sharp movement of the penitent in the confessional made him sink his face precipitately into the crook of his elbow. Fear assumed solid form, and pressed out a lodging between his heart and his lungs. He must try now with all his might to be sorry for his sins—not because he was afraid, but because he had offended God. He must convince God that he was sorry and to do so he must first convince himself. After a tense emotional struggle he achieved a tremulous self-pity, and decided that he was now ready. If, by allowing no other thought to enter his head, he could preserve this state of emotion unimpaired until he went into that large coffin set on end, he would have survived another crisis in his religious life.

For some time, however, a demoniac notion had partially possessed him. He could go home now, before his turn came, and tell his mother that he had arrived too late, and found the priest gone. This, unfortunately, involved the risk of being caught in a lie. As an alternative he could say that he *had* gone to confession, but this meant that he must avoid communion next day, for communion taken upon an uncleansed soul would turn to poison in his mouth, and he would crumple limp and damned from the altar-rail.

Again Father Schwartz's voice became audible.

"And for your—"

The words blurred to a husky mumble, and Rudolph got excitedly to his feet. He felt that it was impossible for him to go to confession this afternoon. He hesitated tensely. Then from the confessional came a tap, a creak, and a sustained rustle. The slide had fallen and the plush curtain trembled. Temptation had come to him too late. . . .

"Bless me, Father, for I have sinned. . . . I confess to Almighty God and to you, Father, that I have sinned. . . . Since my last confession it has been one month and three days. . . . I accuse myself of—taking the Name of the Lord in vain. . . ."

This was an easy sin. His curses had been but bravado—telling of them was little less than a brag.

". . . of being mean to an old lady."

The wan shadow moved a little on the latticed slat.

"How, my child?"

"Old lady Swenson," Rudolph's murmur soared jubilantly. "She got our baseball that we knocked in her window, and she wouldn't give it back, so we yelled 'Twenty-three, Skidoo,' at her all afternoon. Then about five o'clock she had a fit, and they had to have the doctor."

"Go on, my child."

"Of—of not believing I was the son of my parents."

"What?" The interrogation was distinctly startled.

"Of not believing that I was the son of my parents."

"Why not?"

"Oh, just pride," answered the penitent airily.

"You mean you thought you were too good to be the son of your parents?"

"Yes, Father." On a less jubilant note.

"Go on."

"Of being disobedient and calling my mother names. Of slandering people behind their back. Of smoking—"

Rudolph had now exhausted the minor offenses, and was approaching the sins it was agony to tell. He held his fingers against his face like bars as if to press out between them the shame in his heart.

"Of dirty words and immodest thoughts and desires," he whispered very low.

"How often?"

"I don't know."

"Once a week? Twice a week?"

"Twice a week."

"Did you yield to these desires?"

"No, Father."

"Were you alone when you had them?"

"No, Father. I was with two boys and a girl."

"Don't you know, my child, that you should avoid the occasions of sin as well as the sin itself? Evil companionship leads to evil desires and evil desires to evil actions. Where were you when this happened?"

"In a barn in back of—"

"I don't want to hear any names," interrupted the priest sharply.

"Well, it was up in the loft of this barn and this girl and—a fella, they were saying things—saying immodest things, and I stayed."

"You should have gone—you should have told the girl to go."

He should have gone! He could not tell Father Schwartz how his pulse had bumped in his wrist, how a strange, romantic excitement had possessed him when those curious things had been said. Perhaps in the houses of delinquency among the dull and hard-eyed incorrigible girls can be found those for whom has burned the whitest fire.

"Have you anything else to tell me?"

"I don't think so, Father."

Rudolph felt a great relief. Perspiration had broken out under his tight-pressed fingers.

"Have you told any lies?"

The question startled him. Like all those who habitually and instinctively lie, he had an enormous respect and awe for the truth. Something almost exterior to himself dictated a quick, hurt answer. "Oh, no, Father, I never tell lies."

For a moment, like the commoner in the king's chair, he tasted the pride of the situation. Then as the priest began to murmur conventional admonitions he realized that in heroically denying he had told lies, he had committed a terrible sin—he had told a lie in confession.

In automatic response to Father Schwartz's "Make an act of contrition," he began to repeat aloud meaninglessly:

"Oh, my God, I am heartily sorry for having offended Thee . . ."

He must fix this now—it was a bad mistake—but as his teeth shut on the last words of his prayer there was a sharp sound, and the slat was closed.

A minute later when he emerged into the twilight the relief in coming from the muggy church into an open world of wheat and sky postponed the full realization of what he had done. Instead of worrying he took a deep breath of the crisp air and began to say over and over to himself the words "Blatchford Sarnemington, Blatchford Sarnemington!"

Blatchford Sarnemington was himself, and these words were in effect a lyric. When he became Blatchford Sarnemington a suave nobility flowed from him. Blatchford Sarnemington lived in great sweeping triumphs. When Rudolph half closed his eyes it meant that Blatchford had established dominance over him and, as he went by, there were envious mutters in the air: "Blatchford Sarnemington! There goes Blatchford Sarnemington."

He was Blatchford now for a while as he strutted homeward along the staggering road, but when the road braced itself in macadam in order to become the main street of Ludwig, Rudolph's exhilaration faded out and his mind cooled, and he felt the horror of his lie. God, of course, already knew of it—but Rudolph reserved a corner of his mind where he was safe from God, where he prepared the subterfuges with which he often tricked God. Hiding now in this corner he considered how he could best avoid the consequences of his misstatement.

At all costs he must avoid communion next day. The risk of angering God to such an extent was too great. He would have to drink water "by accident" in the morning, and thus, in accordance with a church law, render himself unfit to receive communion that day. In spite of its flimsiness this subterfuge was the most feasible that occurred to him. He accepted its risks and was concentrating on how best to put it into effect, as he turned the corner by Romberg's Drug Store and came in sight of his father's house.

III

Rudolph's father, the local freight-agent, had floated with the second wave of German and Irish stock to the Minnesota-Dakota country. Theoretically, great opportunities lay ahead of a young man of energy in that day and place, but Carl Miller had been incapable of establishing either with his superiors or his subordinates the reputation for approximate immutability which is essential to success in a hierarchic industry. Somewhat gross, he was, nevertheless, insufficiently hard-headed and unable to take fundamental relationships for granted, and this inability made him suspicious, unrestful, and continually dismayed.

His two bonds with the colorful life were his faith in the Roman Catholic Church and his mystical worship of the Empire Builder, James J. Hill. Hill was the apotheosis of that quality in which Miller himself was deficient—the sense of things, the feel of things, the hint of rain in the wind on the cheek. Miller's mind worked late on the old decisions of other men, and he had never in his life felt the balance of any single thing in his hands. His weary, sprightly, undersized body was growing old in Hill's gigantic shadow. For twenty years he had lived alone with Hill's name and God.

On Sunday morning Carl Miller awoke in the dustless quiet of six o'clock. Kneeling by the side of the bed he bent his yellow-gray hair and the full dapple bangs of his mustache into the pillow, and prayed for several minutes. Then he drew off his night-shirt—like the rest of his generation he had never been able to endure pajamas—and clothed his thin, white, hairless body in woollen underwear.

He shaved. Silence in the other bedroom where his wife lay nervously asleep. Silence from the screened-off corner of the hall where his son's cot stood, and his son slept among his Alger books, his collection of cigarbands, his mothy pennants—"Cornell," "Hamlin," and "Greetings from Pueblo, New Mexico"—and the other possessions of his private life. From outside Miller could hear the shrill birds and the whirring movement of the poultry, and, as an undertone, the low, swelling click-a-tick of the six-fifteen through-train for Montana and the green coast beyond. Then as the cold water dripped from the wash-rag in his hand he raised his head suddenly—he had heard a furtive sound from the kitchen below.

He dried his razor hastily, slipped his dangling suspenders to his shoulder, and listened. Some one was walking in the kitchen, and he knew by the light footfall that it was not his wife. With his mouth faintly ajar he ran quickly down the stairs and opened the kitchen door.

Standing by the sink, with one hand on the still dripping faucet and the other clutching a full glass of water, stood his son. The boy's eyes, still heavy with sleep, met his father's with a frightened, reproachful beauty. He was barefooted, and his pajamas were rolled up at the knees and sleeves.

For a moment they both remained motionless—Carl Miller's brow went down and his son's went up, as though they were striking a balance between the extremes of emotion which filled them. Then the bangs of the parent's mustache descended portentously until they obscured his mouth, and he gave a short glance around to see if anything had been disturbed.

The kitchen was garnished with sunlight which beat on the pans and made the smooth boards of the floor and table yellow and clean as wheat. It was the centre of the house where the fire burned and the tins fitted into tins like toys, and the steam whistled all day on a thin pastel note. Nothing was moved, nothing touched—except the faucet where beads of water still formed and dripped with a white flash into the sink below.

"What are you doing?"

"I got awful thirsty, so I thought I'd just come down and get—"

"I thought you were going to communion."

A look of vehement astonishment spread over his son's face.

"I forgot all about it."

"Have you drunk any water?"

"No—"

As the word left his mouth Rudolph knew it was the wrong answer, but the faded indignant eyes facing him had signalled up the truth before the boy's will could act. He realized, too, that he should never have come down-stairs; some vague necessity for verisimilitude had made him want to leave a wet glass as evidence by the sink; the honesty of his imagination had betrayed him.

"Pour it out," commanded his father, "that water!"

Rudolph despairingly inverted the tumbler.

"What's the matter with you, anyways?" demanded Miller angrily.

"Nothing."

"Did you go to confession yesterday?"

"Yes."

"Then why were you going to drink water?"

"I don't know—I forgot."

"Maybe you care more about being a little bit thirsty than you do about your religion."

"I forgot." Rudolph could feel the tears streaming in his eyes.

"That's no answer."

"Well, I did."

"You better look out!" His father held to a high, persistent, inquisitory note: "If you're so forgetful that you can't remember your religion something better be done about it."

Rudolph filled a sharp pause with:

"I can remember it all right."

"First you begin to neglect your religion," cried his father, fanning his own fierceness, "the next thing you'll begin to lie and steal, and the *next* thing is the *reform* school!"

Not even this familiar threat could deepen the abyss that Rudolph saw before him. He must either tell all now, offering his body for what he knew would be a ferocious beating, or else tempt the thunderbolts by receiving the Body and Blood of Christ with sacrilege upon his soul. And of the two the former seemed more terrible—it was not so much the beating he dreaded as

the savage ferocity, outlet of the ineffectual man, which would lie behind it.

"Put down that glass and go up-stairs and dress!" his father ordered, "and when we get to church, before you go to communion, you better kneel down and ask God to forgive you for your carelessness."

Some accidental emphasis in the phrasing of this command acted like a catalytic agent on the confusion and terror of Rudolph's mind. A wild, proud anger rose in him, and he dashed the tumbler passionately into the sink.

His father uttered a strained, husky sound, and sprang for him. Rudolph dodged to the side, tipped over a chair, and tried to get beyond the kitchen table. He cried out sharply when a hand grasped his pajama shoulder, then he felt the dull impact of a fist against the side of his head, and glancing blows on the upper part of his body. As he slipped here and there in his father's grasp, dragged or lifted when he clung instinctively to an arm, aware of sharp smarts and strains, he made no sound except that he laughed hysterically several times. Then in less than a minute the blows abruptly ceased. After a lull during which Rudolph was tightly held, and during which they both trembled violently and uttered strange, truncated words, Carl Miller half dragged, half threatened his son up-stairs.

"Put on your clothes!"

Rudolph was now both hysterical and cold. His head hurt him, and there was a long, shallow scratch on his neck from his father's finger-nail, and he sobbed and trembled as he dressed. He was aware of his mother standing at the doorway in a wrapper, her wrinkled face compressing and squeezing and opening out into new series of wrinkles which floated and eddied from neck to brow. Despising her nervous ineffectuality and avoiding her rudely when she tried to touch his neck with witch-hazel, he made a hasty, choking toilet. Then he followed his father out of the house and along the road toward the Catholic Church.

IV

They walked without speaking except when Carl Miller acknowledged automatically the existence of passers-by. Rudolph's uneven breathing alone ruffled the hot Sunday silence.

His father stopped decisively at the door of the church.

"I've decided you better go to confession again. Go in and tell Father Schwartz what you did and ask God's pardon."

"You lost your temper, too!" said Rudolph quickly.

Carl Miller took a step toward his son, who moved cautiously backward.

"All right, I'll go."

"Are you going to do what I say?" cried his father in a hoarse whisper.

"All right."

Rudolph walked into the church, and for the second time in two days entered the confessional and knelt down. The slat went up almost at once.

"I accuse myself of missing my morning prayers."

"Is that all?"

"That's all."

A maudlin exultation filled him. Not easily ever again would he be able to put an abstraction before the necessities of his ease and pride. An invisible line had been crossed, and he had become aware of his isolation—aware that it applied not only to those moments when he was Blatchford Sarnemington but that it applied to all his inner life. Hitherto such phenomena as "crazy" ambitions and petty shames and fears had been but private reservations, unacknowledged before the throne of his official soul. Now he realized unconsciously that his private reservations were himself—and all the rest a garnished front and a conventional flag. The pressure of his environment had driven him into the lonely secret road of adolescence.

He knelt in the pew beside his father. Mass began. Rudolph knelt up—when he was alone he slumped his posterior back against the seat—and tasted the consciousness of a sharp, subtle revenge. Beside him his father prayed that God would forgive Rudolph, and asked also that his own outbreak of temper would be pardoned. He glanced sidewise at this son, and was relieved to see that the strained, wild look had gone from his face and that he had ceased sobbing. The Grace of God, inherent in the Sacrament, would do the rest, and perhaps after Mass everything would be better. He was proud of Rudolph in his heart, and beginning to be truly as well as formally sorry for what he had done.

Usually, the passing of the collection box was a significant point for Rudolph in the services. If, as was often the case, he had no money to drop in he would be furiously ashamed and bow his head and pretend not to see the box, lest Jeanne Brady in the pew behind should take notice and suspect an acute family poverty. But to-day he glanced coldly into it as it skimmed under his eyes, noting with casual interest the large number of pennies it contained.

When the bell rang for communion, however, he quivered. There was no reason why God should not stop his heart. During the past twelve hours he had committed a series of mortal sins increasing in gravity, and he was now to crown them all with a blasphemous sacrilege.

"*Domine, non sum dignus; ut intres sub tectum meum; sed tantum dic verbo, et sanabitur anima mea. . . .*"

There was a rustle in the pews, and the communicants worked their ways into the aisle with downcast eyes and joined hands. Those of larger piety pressed together their finger-tips to form steeples. Among these latter was Carl Miller. Rudolph followed him toward the altar-rail and knelt down, automatically taking up the napkin under his chin. The bell rang sharply, and the priest turned from the altar with the white Host held above the chalice:

"*Corpus Domini nostri Jesu Christi custodiat animam tuam in vitam aeternam.*"

A cold sweat broke out on Rudolph's forehead as the communion began. Along the line Father Schwartz moved, and with gathering nausea Rudolph felt his heart-valves weakening at the will of God. It seemed to him that the church was darker and that a great quiet had fallen, broken only by the inarticulate mumble which announced the approach of the Creator of Heaven and Earth. He dropped his head down between his shoulders and waited for the blow.

Then he felt a sharp nudge in his side. His father was poking him to sit up, not to slump against the rail; the priest was only two places away.

"*Corpus Domini nostri Jesu Christi custodiat animam tuam in vitam aeternam.*"

Rudolph opened his mouth. He felt the sticky wax taste of the wafer on his tongue. He remained motionless for what seemed an interminable period of time, his head still raised, the wafer undissolved in his mouth. Then again he started at the pressure of his father's elbow, and saw that the people were falling away from the altar like leaves and turning with blind downcast eyes to their pews, alone with God.

Rudolph was alone with himself, drenched with perspiration and deep in mortal sin. As he walked back to his pew the sharp taps of his cloven hoofs were loud upon the floor, and he knew that it was a dark poison he carried in his heart.

V

"Sagitta Volante in Dei"

The beautiful little boy with eyes like blue stones, and lashes that sprayed open from them like flower-petals had finished telling his sin to Father Schwartz—and the square of sunshine in which he sat had moved forward half an hour into the room. Rudolph had become less frightened now; once eased of the story a reaction had set in. He knew that as long as he was in the room with this priest God would not stop his heart, so he sighed and sat quietly, waiting for the priest to speak.

Father Schwartz's cold watery eyes were fixed upon the carpet pattern on which the sun had brought out the swastikas and the flat bloomless vines and the pale echoes of flowers. The hall-clock ticked insistently toward sunset, and from the ugly room and from the afternoon outside the window arose a stiff monotony, shattered now and then by the reverberate clapping of a far-away hammer on the dry air. The priest's nerves were strung thin and the beads of his rosary were crawling and squirming like snakes upon the green felt of his table top. He could not remember now what it was he should say.

Of all the things in this lost Swede town he was most aware of this little boy's eyes—the beautiful eyes, with lashes that left them reluctantly and curved back as though to meet them once more.

For a moment longer the silence persisted while Rudolph waited, and the priest struggled to remember something that was slipping farther and farther away from him, and the clock ticked in the broken house. Then Father Schwartz stared hard at the little boy and remarked in a peculiar voice:

"When a lot of people get together in the best places things go glimmering."

Rudolph started and looked quickly at Father Schwartz's face.

"I said—" began the priest, and paused, listening. "Do you hear the hammer and the clock ticking and the bees? Well, that's no good. The thing is to have a lot of people in the centre of the world, wherever that happens to be. Then"—his watery eyes widened knowingly—"things go glimmering."

"Yes, Father," agreed Rudolph, feeling a little frightened.

"What are you going to be when you grow up?"

"Well, I was going to be a baseball-player for a while," answered Rudolph nervously, "but I don't think that's very good ambition, so I think I'll be an actor or a Navy officer."

Again the priest stared at him.

"I see *exactly* what you mean," he said, with a fierce air.

Rudolph had not meant anything in particular, and at the implication that he had, he became more uneasy.

"This man is crazy," he thought, "and I'm scared of him. He wants me to help him out some way, and I don't want to."

"You look as if things went glimmering," cried Father Schwartz wildly. "Did you ever go to a party?"

"Yes, Father."

"And did you notice that everybody was properly dressed? That's what I mean. Just as you went into the party there was a moment when everybody was properly dressed. Maybe two little girls were standing by the door and some boys were leaning over the banisters, and there were bowls around full of flowers."

"I've been to a lot of parties," said Rudolph, rather relieved that the conversation had taken this turn.

"Of course," continued Father Schwartz triumphantly, "I knew you'd agree with me. But my theory is that when a whole lot of people get together in the best places things go glimmering all the time."

Rudolph found himself thinking of Blatchford Sarnemington.

"Please listen to me!" commanded the priest impatiently. "Stop worrying about last Saturday. Apostasy implies an absolute damnation only on the supposition of a previous perfect faith. Does that fix it?"

Rudolph had not the faintest idea what Father Schwartz was talking about, but he nodded and the priest nodded back at him and returned to his mysterious preoccupation.

"Why," he cried, "they have lights now as big as stars—do you realize that? I heard of one light they had in Paris or somewhere that was as big as a star. A lot of people had it—a lot of gay people. They have all sorts of things now that you never dreamed of."

"Look here—" He came nearer to Rudolph, but the boy drew away, so Father Schwartz went back and sat down in his chair, his eyes dried out and hot. "Did you ever see an amusement park?"

"No, Father."

"Well, go and see an amusement park." The priest waved his hand vaguely. "It's a thing like a fair, only much more glittering. Go to one at night and stand a little way off from it in a dark place—under dark trees. You'll see a big wheel made of lights turning in the air, and a long slide shooting boats down into the water. A band playing somewhere, and a smell of peanuts—and everything will twinkle. But it won't remind you of anything, you see. It will all just hang out there in the night like a colored balloon—like a big yellow lantern on a pole."

Father Schwartz frowned as he suddenly thought of something.

"But don't get up close," he warned Rudolph, "because if you do you'll only feel the heat and the sweat and the life."

All this talking seemed particularly strange and awful to Rudolph, because this man was a priest. He sat there, half terrified, his beautiful eyes open wide and staring at Father Schwartz. But underneath his terror he felt that his own inner convictions were confirmed. There was something ineffably gorgeous somewhere that had nothing to do with God. He no longer thought that God was angry at him about the original lie, because He must have understood that Rudolph had done it to make things finer in the confessional, brightening up the dinginess of his admissions by saying a thing radiant and proud. At the moment when he had affirmed immaculate honor a silver pennon had flapped out into the breeze somewhere and there had been the crunch of leather and the shine of silver spurs and a troop of horsemen waiting for dawn on a low green hill. The sun had made stars of light on their breastplates like the picture at home of the German cuirassiers at Sedan.

But now the priest was muttering inarticulate and heart-broken words, and the boy became wildly afraid. Horror entered suddenly in at the open window, and the atmosphere of the room changed. Father Schwartz collapsed precipitously down on his knees, and let his body settle back against a chair.

"Oh, my God!" he cried out, in a strange voice, and wilted to the floor.

Then a human oppression rose from the priest's worn clothes, and mingled with the faint smell of old food in the corners. Rudolph gave a sharp cry and ran in a panic from the house—while the collapsed man lay there quite still, filling his room, filling it with voices and faces until it was crowded with echolalia, and rang loud with a steady, shrill note of laughter.

Outside the window the blue sirocco trembled over the wheat, and girls with yellow hair walked sensuously along roads that bounded the fields, calling innocent, exciting things to the young men who were working in the lines between the grain. Legs were shaped under starchless gingham, and rims of the necks of dresses were warm and damp. For five hours now hot fertile life had burned in the afternoon. It would be night in three hours, and all along the land there would be these blonde Northern girls and the tall young men from the farms lying out beside the wheat, under the moon.

1924

WILLA CATHER
1873 - 1947

Up in the Negro church one Christmas the congregation were singing the "Peace on Earth." When the plaintive music stopped an old gray-haired Negro in a frock coat and wearing two pairs of glasses arose and began reading the old, old story of the men who were watching their flocks by night and of the babe who as born in the city of David. He became very much excited as he read, and his voice trembled and he unconsciously put the words to measure and chanted them slowly. When he finished he looked up at the ceiling with eager misty eyes as though he could see the light of the heavenly messenger shining in upon him. It is a beautiful story, this of the holiest and purest childhood on earth, beautiful even to those who cannot understand it, as dreams are sweet to men without hope. After all, if we cannot hear the carol and see the heavenly messenger, it is because our ears are deaf and our eyes are blind, not that we turn wilfully away from love or beauty. No one is antagonistic by preference. Almost any of us who doubt would give the little we know or hope to know to go down upon our knees among the lowly and experience a great faith or a great conviction.

The following passage, drawn from one of **Willa Cather**'s youthful columns in the *Nebraska State Journal,* reflects her early appreciation for the beauty of faith. Cather is remembered for her stories of frontier life on the Nebraska prairie, tales such as *My Antonia* and *O Pioneers!* The authoress strove to produce what she called the "unfurnished novel," characterized by a simplicity of language and a poverty of detail. Cather never lost her love for religious ritual; she joined the Episcopal Church after a nervous breakdown, turning to God to heal the illness of the spirit.

JOHN DEWEY
1859 - 1952

SCIENCE, BELIEF AND THE PUBLIC

The old issue between science and religion, or as many preferred to call it between science and theology, has slowly but surely changed its aspect. The operation of four rather than two forces is clearly evident in the current fundamentalist controversy. Instead of an alignment of two opposing tendencies, there is now a quadrilateral situation. The "people" have been called in, so that public opinion and sentiment are a power to be reckoned with; because of this fact the state of general education is a new and decisive factor in shaping the course and outcome of the old struggle.

When a glance is cast upon the earlier conflict between the new science of nature and traditional dogmas, the mass of the people is seen to be indifferent and unconcerned; they are hardly even spectators of the combat. On one side there are a few scientific inquirers, men like Galileo, who in the course of scientific investigations reach results, especially about astronomical matters and the place of the earth in the scheme of things, directly contrary to those contained in the official doctrines of the church. On the other hand, there are the official representatives of the church, aggrieved and insulted by the challenge of a few scientific heretics. Outside of these limited circles, few knew or cared about what was going on. But the printing press, cheap newspapers, mails and telegraph and the extension of schooling have changed all that.

Even in the few years since Darwin published his *Origin of Species* affairs have moved rapidly. The rise of Protestantism and the increased active participation of laymen in matters of religious beliefs had indeed aroused a much wider public concern about the new views regarding the development of life and a naturalistic interpretation of the Descent of Man, than had the older scientific heresies. The issue was no longer wholly between scientific men on one side and established official authorities of the church on the other. Hot debate took place in widely circulated books and magazines, and large numbers were stirred to passionate adherence and more passionate denunciations. But I should guess that the number of daily newspapers was small that concerned themselves with the issue beyond reviews in their literary columns; it would be, I fancy, a safe wager that the controversy did not make the first

Author of such works as *Democracy and Education, Reconstruction in Philosophy* and *Experience and Nature*, **John Dewey** believed that the actions and thoughts of human beings are just as important as their environments. Along with William James, Dewey was at the forefront of the Pragmatist movement, which held that the ultimate test of an idea was whether or not it worked. Pragmatism birthed a generation of reformers and Dewey, no exception, became a leader in educational reform. Here he looks at religion and is obliged to conclude that "educated men" use religion, and not the other way around.

page of newspapers, with glaring headlines, nor cause anything approaching the stir excited today by a single sermon by a well-known clergyman. Certain it is that bills were not introduced in legislatures and parliaments. For geology and biology not being at that time regular parts of even higher schooling, except perhaps for a few, there was nothing for statutes to regulate, unless the state was to emulate the Inquisition in regulating the diffusion of all scientific notions about the world.

These considerations help explain, it seems to me, a fact which has puzzled so many. For a long time it looked as if the conception of continuity of organic development had, in some version or other, become about as firmly entrenched in science and as accepted from science by the public mind as Copernican astronomy. Many of us imagined that a serious attack upon evolutionary views with a revival of pre-Darwinian biology was as improbable as an attack upon the astronomy of Galileo, or a widespread and influential campaign in behalf of the Ptolemaic system. Certainly, from the specialized scientific point of view, the anti-evolutionary campaign comes about three centuries too late. If it were to affect seriously the course of scientific inquiries, a number of persons should have been strangled in their cradles some three hundred years ago. Nevertheless, the issue is for the public actual and vital today, in spite of the elapse of a generation in which we prided ourselves—just as we prided ourselves that a great war was henceforth impossible—upon the advance of the scientific spirit, and the accommodation of the public mind to the conclusions of scientific inquiries.

The moral is inevitable. The public, the popular mass that the enlightened could once refer to as canaille, has taken an active part; but the conditions which have enabled the public actively to intervene have failed in providing an education which would enable the public to discriminate, with respect to the matters upon which it is most given to vehement expression, between opinions untouched by scientific method and attitude and the weight of evidence.

This to my mind is the salient aspect of the present situation. In the large, the controversy between science and dogma in the old sense is over and done with. There are many individuals, believers and others, to whom the question of adjusting their religious conceptions to the conclusions of science is still a vital one. But as a technical and professional cause, science has won its freedom. Scientists in the field and the laboratory may be discommoded at times, individual inquirers and teachers may lose their jobs. But the scientific revolution is nevertheless accomplished; and it is one of the revolutions that do not turn backwards. Inquirers will go on inquiring, and the results of their inquiries will be disseminated at least among their fellow-workers, and will make their way—even if they are as revolutionary as are the discoveries of the last thirty years regarding the constitution of matter and energy, ideas more upsetting of older conceptions in many ways than were those of the intellectual pioneers of the seventeenth century. The real issue is not here. It concerns the growing influence of the general public in matters of thought and belief, and the comparative failure of schooling up to the present time to instil even the rudiments of the scientific attitude in vast numbers of persons, so as to enable them to distinguish between matters of mere opinion and argument and those of fact and ascertainment of fact.

Americans who have been abroad tell of the amused incredulity of educated Europeans over reports of the state of scientific and theological controversy in this country; the reports seem incredible except upon the basis of an almost barbaric state of culture. Yet is may be doubted whether if numbers alone were taken into account, there would not be a larger proportion of persons in this country who could give an intelligent statement of the scientific conceptions involved than in most European countries. The difference is that in those countries those who could not given an intelligent exposition hardly count at all. Here, owing to the spread of democracy in social relations and in education, they count for a great deal. They feel themselves concerned and have channels through which they can make their influence felt.

Naturally such a situation is sport for those hostile to democracy and to universal schooling. They are entitled to chuckle and to make the most of it in their indictments. But, after all, it is a condition and not a theory that confronts us. Defences of democracy are about as much out of place in any scheme of action as are attacks. No social creed produced the present situation. The consequences of the industrialization of affairs in such things as change of population from rural to urban, quick and easy transportation of persons and goods, cheap communications and the rise of cheap printing-matter, have created that state of society which we call democratic, and the democratic creed. Unless the movement of forces is radically altered, attacks upon democracy are about as effective as

shooting paper-wads at a battle-ship—an occupation that may also conceivably relieve the feelings under certain conditions.

The realities of the situation centre about what can be done to ally the forces which create the democratizing of society with the mental and moral attitudes of science. The worst of the predicament is a tendency toward a vicious circle. The forces that compel some degree of general schooling also make for a loose, scrappy and talkative education, and this education in turn reenforces the bad features of the underlying forces. But it is some gain to know where the issue actually lies; to be compelled to face the fact that while schooling has been extended and scientific subjects have found their way into the regular course of studies, little has been accomplished as yet in converting prejudiced and emotional habits of mind into scientific interest and capacity.

This generic diagnosis of the disease may be specified in two particulars. There is a considerable class of influential persons, enlightened and liberal in technical, scientific and religious matters, who are only too ready to make use of appeal to authority, prejudice, emotion and ignorance to serve their purposes in political and economic affairs. Having done whatever they can do to debauch the habit of the public mind in these respects, they then sit back in amazed sorrow when this same habit of mind displays itself violently with regard, say, to the use of established methods of historic and literary interpretations of the scriptures or with regard to the animal origin of man. "Fundamentalism" might have been revived even if the Great War had not occurred. But it is reasonable to suppose that it would have not assumed such an intolerant and vituperative form, if so many educated men, in positions of leadership, had not deliberately cultivated resort to bitter intolerance and to coercive suppression of disliked opinions during the war.

Again, a man may be thoroughly convinced that the spread of certain economic ideas is dangerous to society; but if he encourages, even by passivity, recourse to coercion and intimidation in order to resist the holding and teaching of these ideas, he should not be surprised if others fail to draw the line of persecution and intolerance just where he personally would draw it. The statement that as we sow, so shall we reap, is trite. But there is no field of life in which it applies so aptly and fully as in that of belief and the methods employed to affect belief. Until highly respectable and cultivated classes of men cease to suppose that in economic and political matters the importance of the end of social stability and security justifies the use of means other than those of reason, the intellectual habit of the public will continue to be corrupted at the root, and by those from whom enlightenment should be expected.

The other point concerns the kind of education given in the schools, as that is affected by the temper of actual and professed pillars of society. There are at the best plenty of obstacles in the way of thinking in general, and in particular of using school instruction so as to further discriminating and circumspect thought. The weight of authority, custom, imitation, pressure of time, large numbers, the need of "covering the ground," of securing mechanical skill, of uniformity in administrative matters, of sparing taxpayers, all conspire to depress thinking. These extraneous obstacles are consolidated and held together by the fear entertained by many "best minds" lest the schools promote habits of independent thinking. Fundamentally, fear of the consequences of thought underlies most professions of reverence for culture, respect for quantity of information and emphasis upon discipline. The fundamental defect in the present state of democracy is the assumption that political and economic freedom can be achieved without first freeing the mind. Freedom of mind is not something that spontaneously happens. It is not achieved by the mere absence of obvious restraints. It is a product of constant, unremitting nurture of right habits of observation and reflection. Until the taboos that hedge social topics from contact with thought are removed, scientific method and results in subjects far removed from social themes will make little impression upon the public mind. Prejudice, fervor of emotion, bunkum, opinion and irrelevant argument will weigh as heavily as fact and knowledge. Intellectual confusion will continue to encourage the men who are intolerant and who fake their beliefs in the interests of their feelings and fancies.

AIMEE SEMPLE MCPHERSON
1890 - 1944

It was just a few days after my prayer at the open window of my bedroom that (my Father having come into school for me) we were driving along Main Street on the way home, eagerly talking over and planning my parts in the grand Christmas affairs and concerts in the various churches and halls then looming above us. How pretty the store windows were in their Christmas dress of green and red and tinsel!

But look! Over there on the left-hand side of the street, there was a new sign on a window which I had not seen before, and it read:

PENTECOSTAL MISSION
MEETINGS EVERY NIGHT
ALL DAY SUNDAY

Turning to my Father, I said:

"Daddy, I'd like to go in there tomorrow night. I believe that's the place I have heard about where they jump and dance and fall under the power, and do such strange things. It would be loads of fun to go and see them."

And thus it was that the next evening found us seated in the back seats (where we could see it all) of the little Pentecostal Mission which had recently come to town. We were to have a rehearsal in the town hall for one of our plays, later on in the evening. This had just left me time to come in to the Mission.

They seemed to be a very ordinary lot of people, none of the wealthy or well-known citizens of the town were there, and dressed as I was, with the flowers on my hat, a gold chain and locket, and rings on my fingers, I felt just a little bit above the status of those round about me, and looked on with an amused air as they shouted, danced and prayed.

A man, whom I knew to be one of the town milkmen, shook from head to foot under the power, then fell backward and lay stretched out on the floor praising the Lord. At all these things I giggled foolishly, not understanding it and thinking it all very laughable.

Soon a tall young man, (six feet two), rose to his feet on the platform

---

This Canadian-born evangelist experienced conversion in 1908, at a revival led by her soon-to-be husband, Robert Semple. Involved as a child in the Salvation Army, **McPherson** switched to a Pentecostally oriented faith before her first marriage and was inducted as a regular preacher for the Full Gospel Assembly. After the death of Mr. Semple in China while on a missionary trip, McPherson returned to the U.S. filled with evangelistic fervor. The foundation of the International Church of the Foursquare Gospel soon followed, as McPherson tirelessly preached her way across the country, completing nine transcontinental revivals by 1923. "Sister Aimee" was one of the most renowned evangelists of her day, utilizing the various methods of speaking tours, published sermons, and radio talks.

The "Foursquare" element of the church's name refers to the four parts of Jesus' ministry: Savior of the world, baptizer of the Holy Spirit, healer of illness, and "returning King of kings." The church emphasized the positive, ignoring issues of sin in favor of an all-are-welcome philosophy to salvation. Sister Aimee died in 1944, of an

overdose of barbiturates, later ruled to be accidental. The International Church of the Foursquare Gospel still thrives today, one of the fastest-growing Christian denominations in the country. In this excerpt from her book *This is That*, McPherson relates her early experience with faith, detailing her dramatic childhood conversion to Christian belief.

and taking his Bible in his hand, opened it and began to read. I could not help admiring his frank, open, kindly face, the Irish-blue eyes with the light of heaven in them, and the bushy hair, one brown curl of which would insist on falling down close to his eye, no matter how often he brushed it back with his fingers.

As he spoke with earnest zeal I took him in from head to foot (little knowing that this young man was soon to be my husband). His text was found in the second chapter of Acts, 38th and 39th verses. (There is one thing about a Pentecostal meeting. You cannot go there very long without learning that there is a second chapter to the book of Acts. I learned this in my first meeting.)

The evangelist—Robert Semple, by name—began his discourse with the first word of his text:

"Repent." Oh how he did repeat that word—Repent! REPENT!! R-E-P-E-N-T!!! over and over again. How I did wish he would stop saying that awful word. It seemed to pierce like an arrow through my heart, for he was preaching under diving inspiration and in power and demonstration of the Holy Spirit. He really spoke as through he believed there was a Jesus and a Holy Spirit, not some vague, mythical, intangible shadow, something away off yonder in the clouds, but a real, living, vital, tangible, moving reality dwelling in our hearts and lives—making us His temple—causing us to walk in Godliness, holiness and adoration in His presence.

There were no announcements of oyster suppers or Christmas entertainments or sewing circles made—no appeal for money. Not even a collection was taken. It was just God, God, God from one end to the other, and his words seemed to rain down upon me, and every one of them hurt some particular part of my spirit and life until I could not tell where I was hurt the worst.

"Repent!" The evangelist went on to say that if the love of the world was in us the love of the Father was not there: theaters, moving pictures, dancing, novels, fancy-dress skating rinks (why, it just looked as if somebody had told him I was there, so vividly did he picture

my own life and walk), worldly and rag-time music, etc., he condemned wholesale, and declared that all the people who were wrapped up in this sort of thing were of the devil, and were on their way to hell, and that unless they repented and that right speedily, renouncing the world, the flesh and the devil, they would be lost—eternally damned forever.

I did not do any more laughing, I assure you. I sat up straight in my seat. With eyes and ears wide open I drank in every word he said. After he had finished with the word "Repent," and explained what true salvation meant—the death, burial and resurrection that we would know as we were identified with our Lord, he began to preach on the next verse—

"And ye shall receive the gift of the Holy Ghost. For the promise is unto you, and to your children, and to all that are afar off, even as many as the Lord our God shall call."

Here he began to preach the baptism of the Holy Spirit, declaring that the message of salvation and the incoming of the Spirit should be preached side by side and hand in hand, and that for a Christian to live without the baptism of the Holy Spirit was to live in an abnormal condition not in accordance with God's wishes. He told how the Holy Spirit was received in Bible days and how the recipients of the Spirit had spoken in other tongues—languages they had never learned—as the Spirit gave them utterance.

He put particular emphasis on the "other tongues" spoken of in Acts 2:4, and boldly affirmed that this was the Bible evidence of the baptism of the Holy Spirit.

"Tongues?" said I to myself—"Tongues?—why, I wonder what that is? I never remember having heard of anything like that in the Bible before."

Then, to add still more to my amazement, the speaker himself suddenly broke out talking in tongues, in a loud voice, with his eyes closed and his hands outstretched in my direction.

To me it was the voice of God thundering into my soul awful words of conviction and condemnation, and though the message was spoken in tongues it seemed as though God had said to me—

"YOU are a poor, lost, miserable, hell-deserving sinner!" I want to say right here that I *knew* this was God speaking by His Spirit through the lips of clay. There is a verse in the 14th chapter of I Corinthians which says the speaking in tongues is a sign to the unbeliever. This was certainly true in my case. From the moment I heard that young man speak with tongues to this day I have never doubted for the shadow of a second that there was a God, and that He had shown me my true condition as a poor, lost, miserable, hell-deserving sinner.

No one had ever spoken to me like this before. I had been petted, loved and perhaps a little spoiled: told how smart and good I was. But thank God that He tells the truth. He does not varnish us nor pat us on the back or give us any little sugar-coated pills, but shows us just where we stand, vile and sinful and undone, outside of Jesus and His precious blood.

All my amusement and haughty pride had gone. My very soul had been stripped before God—there was a God, and I was not ready to meet Him. Oh, how could I have looked down upon these dear people and felt that I was better than they? Why, I was not even worthy to black their shoes. They were saints and I was a sinner.

We had to slip out early, before the service was over, and how I got through the rehearsal I can not say, but one thing I knew, and that is the during the next seventy-two hours I lived through the most miserable three days I had ever known up to that time.

Conviction! Oh! I could scarcely eat or rest or sleep. Study was out of the question. "Poor, lost, miserable, hell-deserving sinner" rang in my ears over and over again. I could see those closed eyes and that outstretched hand that pointed to my shrinking, sinful soul that was bared before the eyes of my Maker.

I began enumerating the many things which I would have to give up in order to become a Christian—there was the dancing. I was willing to part with that,—the novels, the theater, my worldly instrumental music. I asked myself about each of them and found that I did not count them dear as compared with the joy of salvation and knowing my sins forgiven.

There was just one thing, however, that I found myself unwilling and seemingly unable to do. I knew that I could not be a Christian and recite those foolish Irish recitations and go through those plays and dialogues. A child of God must be holy and consecrated, with a conversation covered with the blood of Jesus. My Bible said that even for one idle word (let alone foolish words), we should have to give an account before the judgement throne of God. Yet is was too late now to cancel my promises for Christmas, too late to get others to fill my place. Evidently there was nothing to do but wait until after Christmas in order to become a Christian.

But how could I wait? I was desperately afraid. I trembled with conviction. It seemed as though every moment which I lived outside of God and without repentance toward Him was lived in the most awful peril and gravest danger of being cast into hell without mercy. Oh, that every sinner who reads these words might feel the same awful conviction upon his soul!

The second and third day I fell to praying something like this:

"Oh, God, I do want to be a Christian. I want to ever love and serve You. I want to confess my sin and be washed in the blood of Jesus Christ, But oh, please just let me live until after Christmas, and then I will give my heart to You. Have mercy on me, Lord. Oh, don't, don't let me die until after Christmas."

Many people smile now as I testify of that awful terror that seized upon my soul, but the eternal welfare of my souls was at stake—for me it was going to be life or death, heaven or hell forever.

At the end of the third day, while driving home from school, I could stand it no longer. The lowering skies above, the trees, the fields, the very road beneath me seemed to look down upon me with displeasure, and I could see written everywhere—

"Poor, lost, miserable, hell-deserving sinner!"

Utterly at the end of myself—not stopping to think what preachers or entertainment committees or anyone else would think—I threw up my hands, and all alone in that country road, I screamed aloud toward the heavens:

"Oh, Lord God, be merciful to me, a sinner!" Immediately the most wonderful change took place in my soul. Darkness passed away and light entered. The sky was filled with brightness, the trees, the fields, and the little snow birds flitting to and fro were praising the Lord and smiling upon me.

So conscious was I of the pardoning blood of Jesus that I seemed to feel it flowing over me. I discovered that my face was bathed in tears, which dropped on my hands as I held the reins. And without effort or apparent thought on my part I was singing that old, familiar hymn:

Take my life and let it be
Consecrated, Lord to Thee;
Take my moments and my days,
Let them flow in ceaseless praise."

I was singing brokenly between my sobs:

"Take my life and let it be
Consecrated, Lord to Thee."

My whole soul was flowing out toward God, my Father.

"M-Y F-A-T-H-E-R!" Oh, glory to Jesus! I had a heavenly Father! No more need for fear, but His love and kindness and protection were now for me.

When I came to the part in the song that said

"Take my hands and let them move
At the impulse of Thy love"

I knew there would be no more worldly music for me, and it has been hymns from that time forth. And when I sang—

"Take my feet and let them be
Swift and beautiful for Thee"

I knew that did not mean at the dance hall nor the skating rink. Bless the Lord.

"Take my lips and let them sing
Always, only, for my King."

No more foolish recitations and rag-time songs.

"Oh, Jesus, I love Thee,
I know Thou art mine;
For Thee all the follies
Of sin I resign."

Song after song burst from my lips. I shouted aloud and praised God all the way home. I had redeemed!

Needless to say I did not take part in the entertainments, and many in our town through me fanatical and very foolish. Nevertheless the succeeding days were brimful of joy and happiness. How dearly I loved God's Word! I wanted it under my pillow when I went to sleep, and in my hands when my eyes opened in the morning. At school, where I used to have a novel hidden away inside of my Algebra and Geometry, there was now a little New Testament, and I was studying each passage that referred to the baptism of the Holy Spirit.

Of all the promises in which I found comfort, there was none, I believe, that compared with the simple promises of Matthew 7: 7 to 11.

"Ask, and it shall be give you; seek, and ye shall find; knock, and it shall be opened unto you:

"For everyone that asketh receiveth and he that seeketh findeth; and to him that knocketh it shall be opened." Here He assured me that if I asked bread He would not give me a stone, also that He was more willing to give me the Holy Spirit than earthly parents were to give good gifts to their children.

I would get about so far with my reading, and oh, the Bible seemed to me all so new, so living and speaking, (and it was God speaking to me), that unable to wait another moment, I would excuse myself from the room, go down to the basement, fall upon my knees and begin to pray:

"Oh, Lord, baptize me with the Holy Spirit. Lord, you said the promise was unto even as many as were afar off, even as many as the Lord our God should call. Now, Lord, you've called me, the promise is unto me; fill me just now."

The girls found me thus praying and did not know what to make of me so utterly was I changed. No more putting glue in teacher's chair or helping to lock him in the gymnasium, or practicing dance steps in the corridors at noon hour. A wonderful change had taken place—all old things had passed away and all things had become new. I had been born again and was a new creature in Christ Jesus.

Each day the hunger for the baptism of the Holy Spirit became stronger and stronger, more and more intense until, no longer contented to stay in school, my mind no longer on my studies, I would slip away to the tarrying meetings where the dear saints met to pray for those who were seeking the baptism of the Holy Spirit.

What wonderful hours those were! What a revelation to my soul! It was as though heaven had come down to earth. So much of the time was I away from school that I began to fall behind in my studies for the first time, and although the final examinations were near, I could not make myself take any interest in Algebra or Geometry or Chemistry, or anything but the baptism of the Holy Spirit and preparing to meet my soon-coming Savior in the air.

Then came the day when the principal of the High School sent a letter to my Mother which told her that unless I paid more attention to my studies I was certainly going to fail.

And to make matters worse, the same day one of the S. A. officers came to call upon my Mother, saying:

"Now, Sister, we don't mind so much the other people going to that Pentecostal Mission, but we are really surprised and think you do wrong in letting your daughter go. You being connected with the work for so many years, it sets a bad example to other people for you to allow her to be in any way associated with them." They told her also that this so-called power was all excitement or hypnotism and false.

When I went home that night Mother was waiting for me. She gave me a very serious talking to, and wound up by issuing the ultimatum:

"Now, if I every hear of your leaving school and going down to that Mission again, or to the tarrying meetings, I will have to keep you home altogether. I will not have you talked about in this way."

I went to school on the train the next morning as the roads were banked high with snow, and all the way in I was looking out of the window at the falling flakes of snow and praying for the Lord to fix it all some way so that I should be able to knock until He opened or else to baptize me at once.

Walking from the train to High School it was necessary to pass both the Mission and the Sister's home where I often went to tarry for the baptism. As I went past the latter I looked longingly at the windows, hoping that she might be there and that I could speak to her from the sidewalk without going in and thus disobeying Mother's command, but not a sign of her did I see.

I walked slowly past, looking sadly and hungrily back all the way; then finally came to a halt on the sidewalk and said to myself:

"Well, here now, Jesus is coming soon and you know it is more important for you to receive the Holy Spirit than to pass all the examinations in the world. You need the Holy Spirit—oil in your vessel with your lamp—in order to be ready for His appearing.

"As you have to make a choice between going to school and seeking the baptism I guess you won't go to school at all today, but will just go back to the sister's house and make a whole day of seeking the baptism."

With this I turned and walked quickly back to the house, rang the door bell and went in. I told the sister my dilemma, and she said quietly:

"Let's tell Father all about it." So we got down and began to pray. She asked the Lord in her prayer either to baptize me then and there or to arrange it some way that I could stay until I received my baptism.

The Lord heard this prayer, and outside the window the snow which had been falling in light flakes, began to come down like a blinding blizzard. My heavenly Father sent out His angels to stir up some of those big, old, fleecy clouds of His, and down came the snow and—causing the window-panes to rattle, and one of our old-fashioned Canadian blizzards was on.

The entire day was spent in prayer and at night on going to the depot to see about my train home, the ticket agent said, through the window:

"Sorry, Miss, but the train is not running tonight. The roads are blocked with snow. We are not able to get through." Oh, Hallelujah! I was not sorry a bit.

Then the thought came—"This will not do you much good, for you will have to call Mother on the telephone and she will ask you to go to her friend's home to stay, and warn you not to go near the Mission." But when I went to the telephone and gave the number, Central said:

"Sorry, wires all down on account of the storm." This time I did shout "Glory" and ran almost all the way back to the sister's home.

The storm increased, and as fast as the men endeavored to open a pathway, the Lord filled it in with mountains of white snow, until at last all thought of getting through while the storm lasted was abandoned.

Oh, how earnestly I sought the baptism of the Spirit. Sometimes when people come to the altar now and sit themselves down in a comfortable position, prop their heads up on one hand, and begin to ask God in a languid, indifferent way for the Spirit, it seems to me that they do not know what real seeking is.

Time was precious, for while man was working so hard to shovel out the snow, and God had His big clouds all working to shovel it in, I must do my part in seeking with all my heart.

Friday I waited before the Lord until midnight. Saturday morning, rising at the break of day, before anyone was astir in the house, and going into the parlor, I kneeled down by the big Morris chair in the corner, with a real determination in my heart.

My Bible had told me *the kingdom of heaven suffereth violence, and the violent take it by force.* Matt. 11:12. I read the parable again of the man who had knocked for bread and found that it was not because he was his friend, but because of his importunity, that the good man within the house had risen up and given him as many loaves as he had need of. Now Jesus *was* my friend; He had bidden me knock, and assured me that He *would* open unto me. He had invited me to ask, promising that I should receive, and that the empty He would not turn hungry away. I began to seek in desperate earnest, and remember saying:

"Oh, Lord, I am so hungry for your Holy Spirit. You have told me that in the day when I seek with my whole heart you will be found of me. Now, Lord, I am going to stay right here until you pour out upon me the promise of the Holy Spirit for whom you commanded me to tarry, if I die of starvation. I am so hungry for Him I can't wait another day. I will not eat another meal until you baptize me."

You ask if I was not afraid of getting a wrong spirit or being hypnotized, as my parents feared. There was no such fear in my heart. I trusted my heavenly Father implicitly according to Luke 11:11, wherein He assured me that if I asked for bread He would not give me a stone. I knew that my Lord was not bestowing serpents and scorpions on His blood-washed children when they asked for bread. Had He not said, if your earthly fathers know how to bestow good gifts upon their children, *"how much more shall your heavenly Father give the Holy Spirit to them that ask Him?"* Lu. 11:13.

After praying thus earnestly, —storming heaven, as it were, with my pleadings for the Holy Spirit, a quietness seemed to steal over me, the holy presence of the Lord to envelop me. The Voice of the Lord spoke tenderly:

"Now, child, cease your striving and your begging; just begin to praise Me, and in simple, childlike faith, receive ye the Holy Ghost."

Oh, it was not hard to praise Him. He had become so near and so inexpressibly dear to my heart. Hallelujah! Without effort on my part I began to say:

"Glory to Jesus! Glory to Jesus!! GLORY TO JESUS!!!" Each time that I said "Glory to Jesus!" it seemed to come from a deeper place in my being than the last, and in a deeper voice, until great waves of "Glory to Jesus" were rolling from my toes up; such adoration and praise I had never known possible.

All at once my hands and arms began to shake, gently at first, then violently, until my whole body was shaking under the power of the Holy Spirit. I did not consider this at all strange, as I knew how the batteries we experimented with in the laboratory at college hummed and shook and trembled under the power of electricity, and there was the Third Person of the Trinity coming into my body in all His fullness, making me His dwelling, "the temple of the Holy Ghost." Was it any wonder that this poor human frame of mine should quake beneath the mighty movings of His power?

How happy I was, Oh, how happy! happy just to feel His wonderful power taking control of my being. Oh, Glory! That sacred hour is so sweet to me, the remembrance of its sacredness thrills me as I write.

Almost without my notice my body slipped gently to the floor, and I was lying stretched out under the power of God, but felt as though caught up and floating upon the billowy clouds of glory. Do not understand by this that I was unconscious of my surroundings, for I was not, but Jesus was more real and near than the things of earth round about me. The desire to praise and worship and adore Him flamed up within my soul. He was so wonderful, so glorious, and this poor tongue of mind so utterly incapable of finding words with which to praise Him.

My lungs began to fill and heave under the power as the Comforter came in. The cords of my throat began to twitch—my chin began to quiver, and then to shake violently, but Oh, so sweetly! My tongue began to move up and down and sideways in my mouth. Unintelligible sounds as of stammering lips and another tongue, spoken of in Isaiah 28:11, began to issue from my lips. This stammering of different syllables, then words, then connected sentences, was continued for some time as the Spirit was teaching me to yield to Him. Then suddenly, out of my innermost being flowed rivers of praise in other tongues as the Spirit gave utterance (Acts 2:4), and Oh I knew that He was praising Jesus with glorious language, clothing Him with honor and glory which I felt but never could have put into words.

How wonderful that I, even I, away down here in 1908, was speaking in an unknown tongue, just as the believers had in Bible days at Ephesus and at Caesarea, and that now He had come of whom Jesus had said— *"He will glorify Me."*

I shouted and sang and laughed and talked in tongues until it seemed that I was too full to hold another bit of blessing lest I should burst with the glory. The Word of God was true. The promise was really to them that were afar off, even as many as the Lord our God should call. The Comforter had come, lifting my soul in ecstatic praises to Jesus in a language I had never learned. I remember having said:

"Oh, Lord, can you not take me right on up to heaven now? I am so near anyway. Do I have to go back to that old world again?"

"Hypnotism," you say? If so, it is a remarkably long spell and an exceedingly delightful one which has lasted for eleven years, making me love Jesus with all my heart and long for His appearing. Besides this you must take into consideration that there was no one in the room to hypnotize me. I was all alone when I was saved, and all alone when I received the baptism of the Holy Spirit.

"Demon power"—"all of the devil," someone may say. If so the devil must have recently gotten soundly converted, for that which entered into my soul makes me to love and obey my Lord and Savior Jesus Christ, to exalt the blood and honor the Holy Ghost.

"Excitement," you say? Never! It has stood the test too long, dear unbeliever. In sickness, in sorrow, even in the gates of death He has proved Himself to be the Comforter whom Jesus said He would send.

Hearing me speaking in the tongues and praising the Lord, the dear Sister of the home in which I stayed, came down stairs and into the parlor, weeping and praising the Lord with me. Soon Brother Semple and other saints gathered in. What shouting and rejoicing! Oh, hallelujah! And yet with all the joy and glory, there was a stillness and a solemn hush pervading my whole being.

Walking down the street, I kept saying to myself:

"Now you must walk very softly and carefully, with unshod feet, in the presence of the King lest you grieve this tender, gentle dove who has come into your being to make you His temple and to abide with you forever."

The next day was Sunday. The storm had cleared away; the sun was shining down in its melting warmth. Attending the morning services at the Mission, we partook of the Lord's Supper, and as we meditated upon His wonderful love, His blood that was shed for us, His body that was broken on the tree, it was more than I could bear, and I went down to the floor under the power again. Oh, who can describe that exceeding weight of glory as He revealed Himself, my crucified Savior, my resurrected Lord, my coming King!

School-mates and friends were standing up to look over the seats to see what in the world had happened to me, but I was lost again with Jesus whom my soul loved, speaking in tongues and shaking under the power.

One man was so scandalized to see my lying on the floor that he got up and left the meeting, and going to the telephone called my Mother. (The wires which had been down during the storm, unknown to me, had been repaired and were up by this time.) He said:

"You had better come into town and see to that daughter of yours, for she is lying on the floor in the Mission, before all the people, chattering like a monkey."

Poor Mother! She was frantic to think her daughter should so far forget her dignity as to disgrace herself in such a manner. She called me to the 'phone, and I heard her dear voice saying:

"Aimee! What in the world is this that I hear about you lying on the floor in the Mission? What in the world does this all mean?"

I tried to answer, but broke out speaking in tongues again.

"What's that?" she demanded. I tried to explain. Then came her voice, stern and forbidding:

"You just wait 'til I get there, my lady; I will tend to you!"

(Just to relieve the tension on your mind I will run a little ahead of my story and tell you that my dear Mother has her own baptism now, and spoke with other tongues—ON THE FLOOR, TOO!)

Returning to the Sister's home, I sat down at the organ, awaiting in some trepidation and fear, I confess, the coming of my Mother. To keep my courage up I sang over and over that old, familiar hymn:

"I will never leave thee nor forsake thee;
  In my hands I'll hold thee;
  In my arms I'll fold thee;
  I am thy Redeemer; I will care for thee!"

What would Mother say? Would she understand? Why, it had not been so very long since the power of God used to come down in the dear old Salvation Army. Had I not heard her tell how Brother Kitchen (whom they used to call "the Kitchen that God lived in") had shaken as he knelt in prayer, until he had gone clear across the platform and had lain stretched out under the power at the other side? Had I not heard my Father tell me how the old-time Methodist Church used to have this same power? Praying God for strength and wisdom, I sang on—

"E'en though the night
  Be dark within the valley,
  Just beyond is shining,
  An eternal light."

Six o'clock arrived—so did Mother! I heard the jingle of the sleigh-bells suddenly stop in response to my Mother's "whoa!" Then an imperious ring of the bell shivered the tense silence within the house. Slipping down from the organ stool I caught my coat and hat in my hand as I hastened to the door. Mother met me, and with:

"My lady, you come right out and get in here this minute," lost no time in bundling me into the cutter. The Sister and Brother both tried to get a word in edgeways, to reason with and explain to her, but she would hear one of it, and in a moment we were off.

All the way home Mother scolded and cried and almost broke her heart over the daughter that had, as she supposed, been cast under some dire spell by those awful people, who had now been nicknamed by the town, "The Holy Rollers." Oh, praise the Lord! No matter what the devil called them he had to admit that they were holy anyway, and that's more than he could have said of many professing denominations, now, isn't it?

Being an only child, loved and petted, it needed only a word of scolding or remonstrance to bring the tears, but now, when she was scolding me more severely and saying more harsh things than she ever had in my life, for some mysterious reason I couldn't shed a tear. I felt duty bound to squeeze out a few tears, out of respect to her feelings, but I could not do it to help myself. All I could do was sing and sing and sing—all the way—

> *"Joy are flowing like a river,*
> *Since the Comforter has come;*
> *He abides with me forever,*
> *Makes the trusting heart His home."*

The Spirit within rose up and filled me with joy unspeakable and full of glory. Poor Mother would turn to me and say:

"Oh, Aimee! do stop that singing. I can't understand how you can sing; you know your Mother's heart is breaking. Surely you don't call that a fruit of the Spirit." But it did not seem as if I were singing at all: it just seemed to sing itself and came out without any effort.

> *"Blessed quietness, holy quietness,*
> *What assurance in my soul;*
> *On the stormy sea, Jesus speaks to me,*
> *And the billows cease to roll."*

Upon our arrival home we found my Father sitting by the dining-room fire, with his head in his hands, saying:

"Humph! Humph! Humph!" He always did that when he felt very badly over something. Leading me up to him, Mother said:

"Now I want you to tell your Father all about it. Tell him the way you acted and how you lay on the floor before those people." Well, it certainly did look dreadful to tell it, but Oh, that something kept whispering and echoing in my heart:

> *"E'en though the night*
> *Be dark within the valley,*
> *Just beyond is shining*
> *An eternal day.*

When at last they sent me to my room, I kneeled down quickly and began to pray. It happened that I was kneeling beside the stove-pipe hole and could not help overhearing part of the conversation between my parents. It was something like this:

"Oh, what shall we do? Those people have got our girl under their influence, hypnotized her, mesmerized her or something."

"It is perfectly useless to argue with her, for no matter what we say, she only thinks she is being persecuted and will hold it all the more tenaciously."

"Oh, what shall we do?" With this the door closed and I heard no more.

Oh, how can I describe the joy and the glory that had come within my soul? that deep-settled peace, that

knowledge that He would lead and guide and would bring all things out right.

When next my Mother permitted me to go to school she told me of the decision which they had come to, namely, that if I went near those Pentecostal people once more they would take me away from school for good, education or no education. As she told me this the Holy Spirit gave me wisdom to make this reply:

"Mother, the Bible says that children are to obey their parents in the Lord, and if you can show me by the Word of God that what I have received is not in accordance with Bible teaching, or show me any place where we are told that the baptism of the Holy Spirit, with the Bible evidence, speaking in tongues, is not for today, I will never go to the Mission again." I stated my all on the Word.

"Why certainly I can prove it to you," she replied. "Those things were only for the Apostolic days. I will look up the scriptures and prove it to you when you get home tonight."

Dear Mother—she had been a student of the Bible and had taught Sunday School and Bible class for years. Oh, would she be able to prove that all these manifestations of the Holy Spirit's power and presence were only for by-gone days? I was not very well acquainted with the Bible on this subject, yet knew that what I had received was from God.

Assured that Mother would search the Bible honestly, I had pledged myself to stand by the consequences: Whatever the Bible said should stand. Thus it was that we both turned to the Word of God as the final court of appeal to settle the whole matter.

Mother got out her Bible, concordance, pencil and pad, and with heart and mind full of this one thing, immediately sat herself down at the breakfast table, spreading her books out before her, without pausing even long enough to gather up the breakfast dishes for washing—the lamps were not cleaned, and the beds were unmade.

(Oh, if any unbeliever will sit down with an open Bible and an unprejudiced heart, there is no need for us to defend our position, so clear is the Word on God on this subject.)

It was half past eight in the morning when I left home for school. At five-thirty, when I returned, Mother was still seated at the breakfast table, with her Bible and paper before her, and—would you believe it?—the breakfast dishes were still unwashed, the lamps uncleaned, the beds unmade, an unheard-of state of affairs for Mother, ever an excellent housekeeper.

I waited with bated breath for her decision. My heart softened within me as I saw by her reddened eyes that she had been weeping. Oh, what would her answer be? The smile upon her face encouraged me to ask—

"Oh, Mother, what is it?"

Now, dear reader, what do you suppose she said? With shining face she replied—

"Well, dear, I must admit that of a truth, *this is that which was spoken of by the prophet Joel, which should come to pass in the last days!*"

She had found that, away back in Isaiah 28:11, He had said—"*With stammering lips and another tongue will I speak to this people*"—that the prophet Joel had clearly prophesied that in these last days there should be a wonderful outpouring of the Holy Spirit, likened unto the latter rain, wherein the sons and daughters, the servants and the maids were alike to rejoice in this glorious downpour.

With one spring across the room, I threw my arms about my Mother's neck, squeezing her till she declared I had almost broken her neck. How happy we were as we danced around the table—laughing, crying and singing together—

"'Tis the old time religion,
And it's good enough for me—"

If everyone who is skeptical of the reality of the baptism of the Holy Spirit would take the word of God and search from cover to cover, he too, would be convinced without the shadow of a doubt that "This Is That."

GEORGE SANTAYANA
1863 - 1952

For the Greek as for the Jew the task of morals is the same: to subdue nature as far as possible to the uses of the soul, by whatever agencies material or spiritual may be at hand; and when a limit is reached in that direction, to harden and cauterize the heart in the face of inevitable evils, opening it wide at the same time to every sweet influence that may descend to it from heaven. Never for a moment was positive religion entangled in a sophistical optimism. Never did it conceive that the most complete final deliverance and triumph would *justify*

George Santayana, despite his Spanish birthplace, spent about half of his life in the United States. A philosopher who limned the distinction between essence and existence, Santayana viewed religion as a poetic expression of spiritual ideals, not as ultimate truth. He was a prolific author, producing

works such as *Three Philosophical Poets, The Sense of Beauty*, and a rumination on life in America entitled *Character and Opinion in the United States.* This selection is entitled "The Task of Morals."

the evils which they abolished. As William James put it, in his picturesque manner, if at the last day all creation was shouting hallelujah and there remained one cockroach with an unrequited love, *that* would spoil the universal harmony; it would spoil it, he meant, in truth and for the tender philosopher, but probably not for those excited saints. James was thinking chiefly of the present and future, but the same scrupulous charity has its application to the past. To remove an evil is not to remove the fact that it has existed. The tears that have been shed were shed in bitterness, even if a remorseful hand afterwards wipes them away. To be patted on the back and given a sugar plum does not reconcile even a child to a past injustice. And the case is much worse if we are expected to make our heaven out of the foolish and cruel pleasures of contrast, or out of the pathetic obfuscation produced by a great relief. Such a heaven would be a lie, like the sardonic heavens of Calvin and Hegel. The existence of any evil anywhere at any time absolutely ruins a total optimism.

CLARENCE DARROW
1857 - 1938

When I am daringly asked if I can imagine the universe making itself I always frankly admit that I cannot imagine it; but still the question provokes some thought. . . .

How can any one say that there is a God simply because he cannot imagine a universe creating itself? How do we know that the universe could not create itself as well as God could make himself or herself, or itself? How does any one know that the universe could not exist without a cause? Does not the believer mean that he cannot understand or imagine how the universe could exist without a cause? If your senses prove to you that there is a universe, and your reason tells you that there must be a God who made it,

Renowned lawyer **Clarence Darrow** was a defender of evolution. In this excerpt from *The Story of My Life* he discusses his difficulty with believing that God made the world. Darrow, born in Kinsman, Ohio, is best remembered for his defense of

John T. Scopes, the Tennessee teacher who was prosecuted for teaching evolution. He also made headlines for his defense of socialist Eugene Debs.

or, that there must be a maker and you will call him a "God," then, do you stop asking questions? There certainly is one obvious question, so obvious that even a fundamentalist could not avoid thinking of it, and that is,—Where did God come from? The maker is surely bigger than his creation. If not, then the universe may have made God! Is it any more logical for you to tell me that the universe must have had a maker than for me to reply that, by the same logic, God must have had a maker?

Isn't it plain that an already serious question is complicated by bringing in a God? After all, when one is asked where the universe came from, isn't it a bit more modest and less foolish to answer, as I do, that I know nothing about it, rather than to assert that God made it, and, then, when asked where God came from, to suggest that God made himself "in the image of man"? The inhabitant of one of the tiniest of all the numberless planets! To the question of who made God, one might answer that some super-God made God; but this only calls for further questions about who, then, made the super-God, and—but one has to stop somewhere!

H. L. MENCKEN

1880 - 1950

MEMORIAL SERVICE

WHERE is the graveyard of dead gods? What lingering mourner waters their mounds? There was a day when Jupiter was the king of the gods, and any man who doubted his puissance was *ipso facto* a barbarian and an ignoramus. But where in all the world is there a man who worships Jupiter to-day? And what of Huitzilopochtli? In one year—and it is no more than five hundred years ago—50,000 youths and maidens were slain in sacrifice to him. To-day, if he is remembered at all, it is only by some vagrant savage in the depth of the Mexican forest. Huitzilopochtli, like many other gods, had no human father; his mother was a virtuous widow; he

A native of Baltimore, **Henry Louis Mencken** made a career out of words as a newspaper reporter and later as an author and editor. The year 1899 marks the beginning of this writer's sparkling career, when Mencken began reporting for the *Baltimore Morning Herald*. In 1906, Mencken switched newspapers, thus beginning what would be a thirty-five-year tenure at the *Baltimore Sun*. He also published several

was born of an apparently innocent flirtation that she carried on with the sun. When he frowned, his father, the sun, stood still. When he roared with rage, earthquakes engulfed whole cities. When he thirsted he was watered with 10,000 gallons of human blood. But to-day Huitzilopochtli is as magnificently forgotten as Marie Corelli. Once the peer of Allah, Buddha and Wotan, he is now the peer of Father Rasputin, J. B. Planché, Sadi Carnot, General Boulanger, Lottie Collins, and Little Tich.

Speaking of Huitzilopochtli recalls his brother, Tezcatilpoca. Tezcatilpoca was almost as powerful: he consumed 25,000 virgins a year. Lead me to his tomb: I would weep, and hang a *couronne des perles*. But who knows where it is? Or where the grave of Quitzalcoatl is? Or Tialoc? Or Chalchihuitlicue? Or Xiehtecutli? Or Centeotl, that sweet one? Or Tlazolteotl, the goddess of love? Or Mictlan? Or Ixtlilton? Or Omacatl? Or Yacatecutli? Or Mixcoatl? Or Xipe? Or all the host of Tzitzimitles? Where are their bones? Where is the willow on which they hung their harps? In what forlorn and unheard-of hell do they await the resurrection morn? Who enjoys their residuary estates? Or that of Dis, whom Caesar found to be the chief god of the Celts? Or that of Tarves, the bull? Or that of Moccos, the pig? Or that of Epona, the mare? Or that of Mullo, the celestial ass? There was a time when the Irish revered all these gods as violently as they now revere the Pope. But to-day even the drunkest Irishman laughs at them.

But they have company in oblivion: the hell of dead gods is as crowded as the Presbyterian hell for babies. Damona is there, and Esus, and Drunemeton, and Silvana, and Dervones, and Adsalluta, and Deva, and Belisama, and Axona, and Vintios, and Taranuous, and Sulis, and Cocidius, and Adsmerius, and Dumiatis, and Caletos, and Moccus, and Ollovidius, and Albiorix, and Leucitius, and Vitucadrus, and Ogmios, and Uxellimus, and Borvo, and Grannos, and Mogons. All mighty gods in their day, worshipped by millions, full of demands and impositions, able to bind and loose— all gods of the first class, not dilettanti. Men laboured for generations to build vast temples to them—temples

books, including the three-volume autobiography *Newspaper Days, Happy Days, Heathen Days.* Mencken's flair was that of the cultured swordsman, using, of course, the pen for his weapon. Religion was one of his favorite subjects for attack, as the following essay, "Memorial Service," makes clear.

with stones as large as motor-lorries. The business of interpreting their whims occupied thousands of priests, wizards, archdeacons, canons, deans, bishops, archbishops. To doubt them was to die, usually at the stake. Armies took to the field to defend them against infidels: villages were burned, women and children were butchered, cattle were driven off. Yet in the end they all withered and died, and to-day there is none so poor to do them reverence. Worse, the very tombs in which they lie are lost, and so even a respectful stranger is debarred from paying them the slightest and politest homage.

What has become of Sutehl, once the high god of the whole Nile Valley? What has become of:

Resheph	Baal
Anath	Astarte
Ashtoreth	Hadad
El	Addu
Nergal	Shalem
Nebo	Dagon
Ninib	Sharrab
Melek	Yau
Ahijah	Amon-Re
Isis	Osiris
Ptah	Sebek
Anubis	Moloch?

All these were once gods of the highest eminence. Many of them are mentioned with fear and trembling in the Old Testament. They ranked, five or six thousand years ago, with Jahveh himself; the worst of them stood far higher than Thor. Yet they have all gone down the chute, and with them the following:

Bilé	Gwydion
Lêr	Manawyddan
Arianrod	Nuada Argetlam
Morrigu	Tagd
Govannon	Goibniu
Gunfled	Odin
Sokk-mimi	Llaw Gyffes
Memetona	Lleu
Dagda	Ogma
Kerridwen	Mider
Pwyll	Rigantona
Ogyrvan	Marzin
Dea Dia	Mars
Ceros	Jupiter
Vaticanus	Cunina
Edulia	Potina
Adeona	Statilinus

Iuno Lucina	Diana of Ephesus
Saturn	Robigus
Furrina	Pluto
Vediovis	Ops
Consus	Meditrina
Cronos	Vesta
Enki	Tilmun
Engurra	Zer-panitu
Belus	Merodach
Dimmer	U-ki
Mu-ul-lil	Dauke
Ubargisi	Gasan-abzu
Ubilulu	Elum
Gsan-lil	U-Tin-dir-ki
U-dimmer-an-kia	Marduk
Enurestu	Nin-lil-la
U-sab-sib	Nin
U-Mersi	Persephone
Tammuz	Istar
Venus	Lagas
Bau	U-urugal
Mulu-hursang	Sirtumu
Anu	Ea
Beltis	Nirig
Nusku	Nebo
Ni-zu	Samas
Sahi	Ma-banba-anna
Aa	En-Mersi
Allatu	Amurru
Sin	Assur
Abil Addu	Aku
Apsu	Beltu
Dagan	Dumu-zi-abzu
Elali	Kuski-banda
Isum	Kaawanu
Mami	Nin-azu
Nin-man	Lugal-Amarada
Zaraqu	Qarradu
Suqamunu	Ura-gala
Zagaga	Ueras

You may think I spoof. That I invent the names. I do not. Ask the rector to lend you any good treatise on comparative religion: you will find them all listed. They were gods of the highest standing and dignity—gods of civilized peoples—worshipped and believed in by millions. All were theoretically omnipotent, omniscient, and immortal. And all are dead.

1922

COLONEL DONALD S. ROCKWELL

1900 -

The simplicity of Islam, the powerful appeal and the compelling atmosphere of its Mosques, the earnestness of its faithful adherents, the confidence inspiring realization of the millions throughout the world who answer the five daily calls to prayer—these factors attracted me from the first. But after I had determined to become a follower of Islam, I found many deeper reasons for confirming my decision. The mellow concept of life—fruit of the Prophet's combined course of action and contemplation—the wise counsel, the admonitions to charity and mercy, the broad humanitarianism, the pioneer declaration of woman's property rights—these and other factors of the teachings of the Man of Mecca were to me among the most obvious evidence of a practical religion so tersely and so aptly epitomised in the cryptic words of Muhammad, 'Trust in God and tie your camel'. He gave us a religious system of normal action, not blind faith in the protection of an unseen force in spite of our own neglect, but confidence that if we do all things rightly and to the best of our ability, we may trust in what comes as the Will of God.

This American writer discusses his reasons for converting to Islam—explaining that the more deeply he explored the faith, the more drawn he was by its teachings and values. This excerpt is drawn from Islam Our Choice, *a collection of autobiographical writings by Muslim converts.*

The broadminded tolerance of Islam for other religions recommends it to all lovers of liberty. Muhammad admonished his followers to treat well the believers in the Old and New Testaments; and Abraham, Moses and Jesus are acknowledged as Prophets of the One God. Surely this is generous and far in advance of the attitude of other religions.

The total freedom from idolatry... is a sign of the salubrious strength and purity of the Muslim faith.

The original teachings of the Prophet of God have not been engulfed in the maze of changes and additions of doctrinarians. The Qur'an remains as it came to the corrupt polytheistic people of Muhammad's time, changeless as the holy heart of Islam itself.

Moderation and temperance in all things, the keynotes of Islam, won my unqualified approbation. The health of his people was cherished by the Prophet, who enjoined them to observe strict cleanliness and specified fasts and to subordinate carnal appetites... when I stood in the inspiring Mosques of Istanbul, Damascus, Jerusalem, Cairo, Algiers, Tangier, Fez and other cities, I was conscious of a powerful reaction the potent uplift of Islam's simple appeal to the sense of higher things, unaided by elaborate trappings, ornamentations, figures, pictures, music and ceremonial ritual. The Mosque is a place of quiet contemplation and self-effacement in the greater reality of the One God.

The democracy of Islam has always appealed to me. Potentate and pauper have the same rights on the floor of the Mosque, on their knees in humble worship. There are no rented pews nor specials reserved seats.

The Muslim accepts no man as a mediator between himself and his God. He goes direct to the invisible source of creation and life, God, without reliance on saving formula of repentance of sins and belief in the power of a teacher to afford him salvation.

The universal brotherhood of Islam, regardless of race, politics, colour or country, has been brought home to me most keenly many times in my life and this is another feature which drew me towards the Faith.

ANNE MORROW LINDBERGH

1907 -

I can only think of that first week in Hopewell, of you as an ultimate fortress I had, an ultimate source of strength. First: "Well, Mother will be here... when Mother gets here...." Then, morning after morning when there did not seem to be any reason to get up, "Mother is downstairs already," and then those days you went to New York, so terribly long, but "It will be all right tonight, when Mother gets back." And you would always bring back a flurry and breath of life, even in those deathlike days.

I don't know where your ultimate source of strength is, and I feel that I have taken and taken and taken and not given anything back. Perhaps I can't give anything now. It is as though all of us close to

In the selection that follows, **Anne Morrow Lindbergh** *writes of her recovery from grief, recounting the most famous of the Bhudda's teachings on the subject.*

this had lost our faith and once it was smashed we were vulnerable—anything could happen. As though your faith, a beautiful shimmering armor of glass, protected you infallibly as long as it was whole. But it's so fragile—once it's gone to pieces you have nothing. . . .

Then later all day (with a wheeling head and the recurring afterpains) I was blissfully happy, relieved, saying and thinking over and over, "The baby is all right, all right, he is here, he's all right," until C. said, "He has a wart on his left toe," and began teasing me. But I could not get over it. Out of last fall, out of this winter, a perfect baby. It was a miracle.

And I felt years removed from the night before and the months before that night. I felt I had given birth to more than a baby: to new life in myself, in C., in Mother. C., a teasing boy again; Mother, gently, softly gay as she used to be with Charlie. And I felt as if a great burden had fallen off me. I could not imagine the baby would do this for me, but I felt life given back to me—a door to life opened. I *wanted* to live, I felt power to live. I was not afraid of death or life: a spell had been broken, the spell over us that made me dread everything and feel that nothing would go right after this. The spell was broken by this real, tangible, perfect baby, coming into an imperfect world and coming out of the teeth of sorrow—a miracle. My faith had been reborn. . . .

Contrary to the general assumption, the first days of grief are not the worst. The immediate reaction is usually shock and numbing disbelief. One has undergone an amputation. After shock comes acute early grief which is a kind of "condensed presence"—almost a form of possession. One still feels the lost limb down to the nerve endings. It is as if the intensity of grief fused the distance between you and the dead. Or perhaps, in reality, part of one dies. Like Orpheus, one tries to follow the dead on the beginning of their journey. But one cannot, like Orpheus, go all the way, and after a long journey one comes back. If one is lucky, one is reborn. Some people die and are reborn many times in their lives. For others the ground is too barren and the time too short for rebirth. Part of the process is the growth of a new relationship with the dead, the *"véritable ami mort"* Saint-Exupéry speaks of. Like all gestation, it is a slow dark wordless process. While it is taking place one is painfully vulnerable. One must guard and protect the new life growing within—like a child.

One must grieve, and one must go through periods of numbness that are harder to bear than grief. One must refuse the easy escapes offered by habit and human tradition. The first and most common offerings of family and friends are always distractions ("Take her out"—"Get her away"—"Change the scene"—"Bring in people to cheer her up"—"Don't let her sit and mourn" [when it is mourning one needs]). On the other hand, there is the temptation to self-pity or glorification of grief. "I will instruct my sorrows to be proud," Constance cries in a magnificent speech in Shakespeare's *King John*. Despite her words, there is no aristocracy of grief. Grief is a great leveler. There is no highroad out.

Courage is a first step, but simply to bear the blow bravely is not enough. Stoicism is courageous, but it is only a halfway house on the long road. It is a shield, permissible for a short time only. In the end one has to discard shields and remain open and vulnerable. Otherwise, scar tissue will seal off the wound and no growth will follow. To grow, to be reborn, one must remain vulnerable—open to love but also hideously open to the possibility of more suffering.

Remorse is another dead end, a kind of fake action, the only kind that seems possible at the moment. It is beating oneself in a vain attempt to make what *has* happened "*un*-happen." ("If only I had done thus and so, it might not have been.") Remorse is fooling yourself, feeding on an illusion; just as living on memories, clinging to relics and photographs, is an illusion. Like the food offered one in dreams, it will not nourish; no growth or rebirth will come from it.

The inexorably difficult thing in life, and particularly in sorrow, is to face the truth. As Laurens Van der Post has written: "One of the most pathetic things about us human beings is our touching belief that there are times when the truth is not good enough for us; that it can and must be improved upon. We have to be utterly broken before we can realize that it is impossible to better the truth. It is the truth that we deny which so tenderly and forgivingly picks up the fragments and puts them together again."

Undoubtedly, the long road of suffering, insight, healing, or rebirth, is best illustrated in the Christian religion by the suffering, death, and resurrection of Christ. It is also illustrated by the story of Buddha's answer to a mother who had lost her child. According to the legend, he said that to be healed she needed only a mustard seed from a household that had never known sorrow. The woman journeyed from home to home over the world but never found a family ignorant of grief. Instead, in the paradoxical manner of myths and oracles, she found truth, understanding, compassion, and eventually, one feels sure, rebirth. . . .

My own recovery, I realize, was greatly furthered by the love, understanding, and support of those around me. But I was also indebted to many unknown friends who had gone before me and left their testimony to illumine the shadowy path. In return I leave my own record, bearing witness to my journey, for others who may follow.

CARRY A. NATION
1846 - 1911

CHAPTER III

MOVED TO WOODFORD COUNTY, KENTUCKY.—ALSO MOVED TO MISSOURI.— SAVED FROM BEING A THIEF.—MY CONVERSION.—GOING SOUTH AT OPENING OF THE CIVIL WAR.—AN INCIDENT OF MY GIRLHOOD SCHOOL DAYS.—WHY I HAD TO BELIEVE IN REVELATION.—SPIRITUALISM OR WITCHCRAFT.

In 1854, we moved to Woodford County, Kentucky, and bought a farm from Mr. Hibler, on the pike, between Midway and Versailles. Mr. Warren Viley was our nearest neighbor. My father was one of the trustees in building the Orphans' Home at Midway. Here in Midway I attended Sunday school and I had a very faithful teacher who taught me the Word of God. I have forgotten her name but I can see her sweet face now, as she planted seed in my heart that are still bringing forth fruit.

A minister came to our house one day and gave me a book to read, which made a very deep impression on me. As well as I can remember it was called: "The Children of the Heavenly King." This story represented three brothers, one, the youngest, was named Ezra, the other Ulrich, the third I forget. These three were intrusted with watching certain passes in the mountains during the warfare between a great, good king, and a bad one, and in proportion as these boys were faithful, the good king was victorious in battle, but when they

*Born in Garrard County, Kentucky, in 1846, **Carry Nation** devoted her life to a battle against the evils of alcohol. Nation's first husband was Charles Gloyd, an alcoholic who died soon after their wedding. She then married minister David Nation, whose influence caused her religious fervor to grow. She began to see visions and believed she*

neglected their duty, he would suffer loss. The character of little Ezra was a sweet, unselfish one. He tried so hard to help, and have his brothers do right. He would run from his post to wake them up, and tried to make up for their neglect; would do without rest and food for himself, and plead with them to do their duty. At last, when the king came, little Ezra was richly rewarded; Ulrich barely passed, and the unfaithful one was taken out amidst weeping, wailing and gnashing of teeth, and the door was shut. The minister did not know what good he had done.

> *"Only a thought,*
> *but the work it wrought,*
> *Could never by tongue or*
> *pen be taught;*
> *For it ran thro' a life,*
> *like a thread of gold,*
> *And the life bore fruit, an hundred fold.*
> *Only a word, but it was spoken in love,*
> *With a whispered prayer to the Lord above;*
> *And the angels in heaven rejoiced once more*
> *For a new-born soul entered in, at the door."*

I resolved to be like little Ezra as near as I could. When I was a child I fought against my selfish nature. I would often give away my doll clothes and other things that I wanted to keep myself. Some of the strongest characteristics of my life were awakened in my childhood. I would often blush with shame, when committing sins, and I had a great fear of the judgement day; it would terrify me when hearing of Jesus coming to the earth. I would often ask myself: "Where can I hide?" If the public knew of the smashing God gave me the strength to do in my heart, they would not wonder at my courage in smashing the murder-shops of our land. "He that ruleth his own spirit, is greater than he that taketh a city."

In 1855, we moved to Missouri, just a year before the trouble broke out between Kansas and Missouri. Missouri determined to make Kansas a slave state; but Kansas said she would not have a slave upon her soil. Squads of men in Missouri would often go into Kansas and commit depredations. At one time they burned

was divinely inspired to rid the country of drink. Her lifelong quest for temperance sometimes led her to violent means, even going so far as to vandalize saloons in her hometown of Medicine Lodge and liquor establishments in other Kansas cities. She was arrested numerous times for disturbing the peace, particularly in towns where liquor sales were legal.

Lawrence, Kansas, and killed many people. This trouble continued to grow worse until it brought on the great Civil War.

When we moved from Kentucky to Missouri, I took a severe cold on the boat, which made me an invalid for years. I was not a truthful child, neither was I honest. My mother was very strict with me in many ways and I would often tell her lies to avoid restraint or punishment. If there was anything I wanted about the house, especialy something to eat, I would steal it, if I could. The colored servants would often ask me to steal things for them. My nurse Betsy, would say: "Carry get me a cup of sugar, butter, thread or needles," and many other things. This would make me sly and dishonest. I used to go and see my aunts and stay for months. I would open their boxes and bureau drawers and steal ribbons and laces and make doll clothes out of them. I would steal perfumery and would run out of the room to prevent them from smelling it. I am telling this for a purpose. Many little children may be doing what I did, not thinking of what a serious thing it is, and I write this to show them how I was cured of dishonesty: I got a little book at Sunday school and it told the way people became thieves, by beginning to take little things naming them, and some of these were very things I had been taking. I was greatly shocked to see myself a thief; it had never occurred to me that I was as bad as that. I thought one had to steal something of great value to be a thief. My repentance was sincere, and I was made honest by this blessed book, so much so that even after I became grown, if any article was left in my house I would give it away, unless I could find the owner. I was perfectly delighted when I was entirely free. I asked for everything I wanted, even a pin. After that, I could show my doll clothes, and it was not necessary for me to be sly or tell stories any more. It was about this time I was converted. There was a protracted meeting at a place called Hickman's Mill, Jackson County, Missouri. The minister was gray haired and belonged to the Christian or Disciples church, the one my father belonged to. I was at this time ten years old and went with my father to church on Lord's Day morning. At the close of the sermon, and during the invitation, my father stepped to the pulpit and spoke to the minister and he looked over in my direction. At this I began to weep bitterly, seemed to be taken up, and sat down on the front bench. I could not have told any one what I wept for, except it was a longing to be better. I had often thought before this that I was in danger of going to the "Bad place," especially I would be afraid to think of the time that I should see Jesus come. I wanted to hide from Him. My father had a cousin living at Hickman's Mill, Ben Robertson. His wife, cousin Jennie, came up to me at the close of the service, and said: "Carry, I believe you know what you are doing." But I did not. Oh, how I wanted some one to explain to me. The next day I was taken to a running stream about two miles away, and, although it was quite cold and some ice in the water, I felt no fear. It seemed like a dream. I know God will bless the ordinance of baptism, for the little Carry that walked into the water was different from the one who walked out. I said no word. I felt that I could not speak, for fear of disturbing the peace that is past understanding. Kind hands wrapped me up and I felt no chill. I felt the responsibility of my new relation and tried hard to do right.

A few days after this I was at my aunt Kate Doneghy's. Uncle James, or "Jim," we called him, her husband, was not a Christian. He shocked me one day by saying: "So those Campbellites took you to the creek, and soused you, did they 'Cal'?" (A nick name.) What a blow! My aunt seemed also shocked to have him speak thus to me. I left the room and avoided meeting him again. How he crushed me! It had the effect to make me feel like a criminal.

The Protestant Church here makes a fatal error which the Catholics avoid. The ministers of the latter have all young converts come so often to them for instruction. A child may be born, but not being nursed and fed, it will die. God has command them to be fed in the sincere milk of the word. My greatest hindrance has been from the lack of proper Christian teaching. I love the memory of my father, he used to have me read the bible to him, and while I did not enjoy it then, it is a blessed memory. The family altar is essential to the welfare of every home, no other form of discipline is equal to it. The liberty, chivalry, and life of a nation live or die in proportion as the Altar fires live or die.

"And these words which I command thee this day shall be in thine heart and thou shalt teach them diligently unto thy children and shalt talk of them when thou sittest in thine house and when thou walkest by the way and when thou liest down and when thou risest up."

When I was fifteen, the war broke out between the north and the south. My father saw that Missouri would be the battle ground and he, with many others, took their families and negroes and went south, taking what they could in wagons, for there were no railroads then in that section. There was quite a train with the droves of cattle, mules and horses. One wagon had six yoke of oxen to it; had to get into it by a ladder, the kind that was used to freight across the plains. The family went in the family carriage that my father brought from Kentucky. I remember the time when this carriage was purchased, with the two dapple gray horses, and silver mounted harness, and when my mother would drive out she had a driver in broadcloth, with a high silk hat, and a boy rode on a seat behind, to open the gates. This was one of the ways of traveling in Kentucky in those days. My mother was an aristocrat in her ideas, but my father was not. He liked no display. He was wise enough to see the sin and folly of it.

After being on the road six weeks, we stopped in Grayson County, Texas, and bought a farm. As we started from Missouri one of the colored women took sick with typhoid fever. This spread so that ten of the family, white, and black, were down at one time. As soon as we could travel, my father left the colored people south, and took his family back to Missouri. That winter south was a great blessing to me, for I recovered from a disease that had made me an invalid for five years—consumption of the bowels. Poor health had keep me out of school a great deal. My father at one time sent me to Mrs. Tillery's boarding school in Independence, Mo., but I was not in the recitation room more than half of the time.

After I recovered my health in Texas, it was my delight to ride on horseback with a girl friend. The southern boys were preparing to go to war. Many a sewing did we attend, where the mothers had spun and woven the gray cloth that they were now working up so sorrowfully for their sons to be buried in, far away from home. They thought their cause was right. There were many good masters. And again there were bad ones. Whiskey is always a cruel tyrant and is a worse evil than chattel slavery. We were often stopped on our trip by southern troops, in the Territory and Texas, and then again by northerners. We passed over the Pea Ridge battle ground shortly after the battle. Oh! the horrors of war. We often stopped at houses where the wounded were. We let them have our pillows and every bit of bedding we could spare. We went to our home in Cass County, Missouri.

Shortly after this we, with all families living in that country, were commanded by an order from Jim Lane, to move into an army post. This reached several counties in Missouri. It was done to depopulate the country, so that the "Bushwhackers" would be forced to leave, because of not being able to get food from the citizens. This caused much suffering. But such is war. We moved to Kansas City. I was in Independence, Mo., during the battle, when Price came through. I went with a good woman to the hospital to help with the wounded. My duty was to comb the heads of the wounded. I had a pan of scalding water near and would use the comb and shake off the animated nature into the hot water. The southern and northern wounded were in the same rooms. In health they were enemies, but I only saw kindly feeling and sympathy.

Mothers ought to give their daughters the experience of sitting with the sick; of preparing food for them; of binding up wounds. It is a pitiful sight to see a helpless woman in the sick room, ignorant through lack of experience and education, of ways to be useful at the time and place where these characteristics of woman adorn her the most of all others.

After we returned from Texas, being the oldest child and the servants all gone, my mother sick, and the younger children going to school, I had the house work, cooking and most of the washing to do. It was a new experience for me, and it was twice as hard as it ought to have been. I exposed my health; would slop up myself when I washed, and almost ruined my health, because I had not been properly educated. Herein was the curse of slavery. My father saw this, and I don't believe he had a regret when the slaves were free. Mother, it matters not what else you teach your daughters, if they have not an experience in doing the work themselves about a home, they are sadly deficient. It is not the soft, palefaced, painted, fashionable lady we want, for the world would be better without her; but the woman capable of knowing how, and willing to take a place in the home affairs of life. It is an ambition of mine to establish a Preparatory College in Topeka, Kansas, where girls may be taught, as women should be, that they in turn may teach others, how to wash, cook, scrub, dress and talk, to counteract the idea that woman is a toy, pretty doll, with no will power of her own, only a parrot, a parasite of a man. To be womanly, means strength of character, virtue and a power for good. Let your women be teachers of good things, says the Holy Spirit.

The last school I attended was at Liberty, Missouri, taught by Mr. and Mrs. Love. Only went there a year, but it was of untold value to me. I was so eager to get an education. On account of ill health and the war,

I knew but little. I wanted a thorough education. I had read a good many books, and would write sketches; kept a diary part of the time.

I will here relate an incident that will give my readers a little insight into my impulses. At Liberty School we had a class in Smellie's Natural Philosophy." There was an argument among the girls. Some said animals had reasoning faculties. Others said not. Miss Jennie Johnson, our teacher, said: "Have that for a question to debate on in your society." So it was ordered. I was given the affirmative. The Friday came. I was taken by surprise and was in confusion, when I saw the room crowded. The two other societies of the Seminary, "The Mary Lyons" and "Rising Star," also all the teachers, were present. Our Society was the "Eunomian". I had made no preparations. When I was called I know I looked ridiculously blank. The president tried to keep her face straight. I got no farther than, "Miss President". All burst out in uncontrollable laughter. I went to my seat put my face in my arms and turned my back to the audience. I wept with tears of humiliation. I felt disgraced. I thought of what a shame this would be to my parents. How ever after this I must be considered a "Silly" by my schoolmates. These things nerved me. I dried my tears, turned around in my seat, looked up, and the moral force it required to do this was almost equal to that which smashed a saloon. I arose and said: "Miss President, I am ready to state my case." I began in this style: "I know animals have the power to reason for my brothers cured a dog from sucking eggs by having him take a hot one in his mouth, and it was the last egg we ever knew him to pick up. Why? Because he remembered the hot one and reasoned that he might get burned. Why is it that a horse will like one person more than another? Because he is capable of reasoning and knows who is the best to him." I went on in this homely style and spoke with a vehemence which said: "I will make my point," which I did amidst the cheers of the school. I was eighteen at this time and you would say: "You must have been rather green." So I was in some things.

I believe I have always failed in everything I undertook to do the first time, but I learned only by experience, paid dearly for it, and valued it afterwards. My failures have been my best teachers. I see no one more awkward than I once was, but I had determined to conquer. My defects were the great incentives to perseverance, when I felt I was right.

I shall not in this book speak much of my love affairs, but they were, nevertheless, an important part of my life. I was a great lover. I used to think a person never could love but once in this life, but I often now say, I would not want a heart that could hold but one love. It was not the beauty of face or form that was the most attractive to me in young gentlemen, or ladies, but that of the mind. Seeing this the case with myself, I tried to acquire knowledge to make my company agreeable. I see young ladies, and gentlemen, who entertain each other with their silly jokes and gigglings that are disgusting. When I had company I always directed the conversation so that my friend would teach me something, or I would teach him. I would read the poets, and Scott's writings and history. Read Josephus, mythology and the Bible together, and never read a course that taught me as much. I would go the country dances and sometimes to balls in the City. The church did not object to this: I would teach Sunday school at the same time. No one taught me that this was wrong. One thing was a tower of defense to me. I always, when possible, read the Bible and would pray. After retiring would get up and kneel, feeling that to pray in bed only, was disrespectful to God. If the angels in heaven would prostrate themselves before Him, I a poor sinner should. And right here, I believe in "advancing on your knees." Abraham prostrated himself, so did David and Solomon, Elijah, Daniel, Paul, and even our sinless Advocate. Why did the Holy Ghost state the position so often? For our example, of course. There are no space writers in the Scriptures. I often had doubts as to whether the Bible was the work of God or man. I kept these doubts to myself, for I thought infidelity a disgrace. I wanted to believe the Bible the word of God. I early saw that to close the Bible was to shut out all knowledge of the purpose of life. Without its revelations one does not know why we are born, why we live, or where we go after death. We can see the purpose of all nature, but not of this life of ours, and God had, by revelation, to make this known.

The Bible was a mystery to me. It often seemed to be a contradiction. I did not love to read it, but above all things, I did not want to be a hypocrite. I was determined to try to do my part. I would pray for the same thing over and over again, so as to be in earnest, and think of what I was asking. My mind was distracted by thoughts of the world. I said, if there is a God, he will not hear the prayer of those, so disrespectful as not to think of what they ask. I never seemed to get rid of this, unless at times, when I would have some sorrow of heart. "By the sadness of the countenance, the heart is made better."

I do not believe the Bible because I understand it; for there are few things of revelation that I do understand. Creation is a mystery, still we know everything had a beginning. I do not know why things grow out of the earth. Why they are green. Why grass makes wool on a sheep and hair on a cow, but I know these are facts. I cannot understand why or how the blood of Jesus Christ cleanses from sin, neither do I understand that greatest of all mysteries, the new birth, but nothing more positively a fact in my experience.

God is not perceived by the five senses. The things that are seen are temporal, but those that are unseen are eternal. What a sin of presumption to question God in any of His providences. What God says and does is wisdom, righteousness and power.

The book of Psalms condemned me. I said, I never felt like David. I cannot rejoice. Still I felt that I ought to, but instead, a constant feeling of condemnation and conviction. This was torture to me. I would often have been willing to have died, if I thought it would have been an eternal sleep. My childhood and girlhood were not happy; had so many disappointments. I was called "hard headed" by my parents. I never was free to have what I wished; something would come between me and what I wanted. No one understood me so well as my darling aunt Hope Hill, my mother's sister. She seemed to read me and would talk to me of persons and things, answering the very cry of my heart. My mother would often let me stay with her for months. She had five sons, but no daughters and she was very fond of me. This lesson she taught me: A party of ladies came out from Independence to spend the day with her. Mrs. Woodson and a Mrs. Porter, wife of Dr. Porter, I remember the latter, one of the handsomest women I ever saw, beautiful feet, hands, hair, and a woman who knew it, and it was a mater of the greatest pride with her, these charms. I was very much captivated by her splendid appearance and could not keep my eyes from her. Next day Mrs. John Staton, a country neighbor of my aunts, came in to make a visit. She was very plain, wore a calico dress, waist-apron, and she was knitting a sock. After she left aunt said to me: "Carry, you did not seem to like Mrs. Staton's society as you did Mrs. Porter's; but one sentence of Mrs. Staton's is worth all Mrs. Porter said.

Mrs. Porter lives for this world, Mrs. Staton lives for God." This Lesson I did not learn then, but have since. Oh! for the old-fashioned women.

MY EXPERIENCE WITH SPIRITUALISM

Just at the close of the war when we were on a farm in Cass County, Missouri, a colony of spiritualists were near us, Mrs. Hawkins, the medium was about 60 years old, very peculiar, and finely educated. My father had some farms he was selling for other people. He took Mrs. Hawkins and several of her company to look at a farm with a view of selling it. When she saw it from a hill some distance off she said: "That is the place I saw in Connecticut." She bought it for a town site. In writing to Washington to give it a name, the word "Peculiar" was selected, and so it has ever been called. Mrs. Hawkins took a great fancy to me. She would tell me of great things she had done, then say: "Could Jesus Christ have done more?" I had never heard of Spiritualism that I knew of, up to this time. This colony brought mechanics, merchants and musicians with them. I was in great confusion about this matter, not knowing what to think, for she did some superhuman things. Up stairs we had a large safe full of old books. I was looking over them one day, came to a little book called "Spiritualism Exposed". I immediately went to the orchard, sat under a tree, as my custom was, when I wished to read, for there I could be quiet. I read the little book through, before I stopped. This blessed lesson showed me to my entire satisfaction, that modern spiritualism is witchcraft. The writer took the instances in the Bible. God told Moses: "You must not suffer a witch to live;" see it at the court of Pharoah, and that they have "superhuman power." There are two kingdoms. One of darkness, and one of light. God rules in the latter; The Devil in the former. Both have powers above the power of man. The magicians at Pharoah's court were wizards; and the woman of Endor was a witch. The Bible speaks of dealing with "familiar spirits." Manasseh, Saul, and other King, were cursed for such. Gal. 5th has it as one of the "mortal sins." The Devil can do lying miracles to deceive. He will heal the body, or appear to do it, to damn the soul. I find this in "Christian Science." This is the mark of the "Beast" or carnal mind. Man is but a beast without the new birth, or spirit of God. Carnality always seeks to elevate itself. Grace is humble, and sees nothing good outside of God. The mark of the beast, is the number, or mark of a man; that is carnality or the Beast. Rev. 13:18.

GEORGE S. PATTON, JR.

1885 - 1945

Nicknamed "Old Blood and Guts," **George S. Patton** led the U.S. Third Army during World War II. Patton, despite his extreme toughness, had a spiritual side too, although admittedly a spirituality all his own. This prayer, made famous by film, demonstrates this, as General Patton directs the army chaplain to pray for good weather for his troops.

The weather was so bad that I directed all Army chaplains to pray for dry weather. I also published a prayer with a Christmas greeting on the back and sent it to all members of the Command. The prayer was for dry weather for battle.[1]

---

[1] On or about the fourteenth of December, 1944, General Patton called Chaplain O'Neill, Third Army Chaplain, and myself into his office in Third Headquarters at Nancy. The conversation went something like this:

General Patton: "Chaplain, I want you to publish a prayer for good weather. I'm tired of these soldiers having to fight mud and floods as well as Germans. See if we can't get God to work on our side."

Chaplain O'Neill: "Sir, it's going to take a pretty thick rug for that kind of praying."

General Patton: "I don't care if it takes the flying carpet. I want the praying done."

Chaplain O'Neill: "Yes, sir. May I say, General, that it usually isn't a customary thing among men of my profession to pray for clear weather to kill fellow men."

General Patton: "Chaplain, are you teaching me theology or are you the Chaplain of the Third Army? I want a prayer."

Chaplain O'Neill: "Yes, sir."

Outside, the Chaplain said, "Whew, that's a tough one! What do you think he wants?"

It was perfectly clear to me. The General wanted a prayer—he wanted one right now—and he wanted it published to the Command.

The Army Engineer was called in, and we finally decided that our field topographical company could print the prayer on a small-sized card, making enough copies for distribution to the army.

It being near Christmas, we also decided to ask General Patton to include a Christmas greeting to the troops on the same card with the prayer. The General agreed, wrote a short greeting, and the card was made up, published, and distributed to the troops on the twenty-second of December.

Actually, the prayer was offered in order to bring clear weather for the planned Third Army break-through to the Rhine in the Saarguemines area, then scheduled for December 21.

The Bulge put a crimp in these plans. As it happened, the Third Army had moved north to attack the south flank of the Bulge when the prayer was actually issued.

PRAYER

Almighty and most merciful Father, we humbly beseech Thee, of Thy great goodness, to restrain these immoderate rains with which we have had to contend. Grant us fair weather for Battle. Graciously hearken to us as soldiers who call upon Thee that, armed with Thy power, we may advance from victory to victory, and crush the oppression and wickedness of our enemies, and establish Thy justice among men and nations. Amen.

REVERSE SIDE

To each officer and soldier in the Third United States Army, I wish a Merry Christmas. I have full confidence in your courage, devotion to duty, and skill in battle. We march in our might to complete victory. May God's blessing rest upon each of you on this Christmas Day.

G.S. Patton, Jr.
Lieutenant General
Commanding, Third United States Army

Whether it was the help of the Divine guidance asked for in the prayer or just the normal course of human events, we never knew; at any rate, on the twenty-third, the day after the prayer was issued, the weather cleared and remained perfect for about six days. Enough to allow the Allies to break the backbone of the Von Rundstedt offensive and turn a temporary setback into a crushing defeat for the enemy.

We had moved our advanced Headquarters to Luxembourg at this time to be closer to the battle area. The bulk of the Army Staff, including the Chaplain, was still in Nancy. General Patton again called me to his office. He wore a smile from ear to ear. He said, "God damn! look at the weather. That O'Neill sure did some potent praying. Get him up here. I want to pin a medal on him."

The Chaplain came up next day. The weather was still clear when we walked into General Patton's office. The General rose, came from behind his desk with hand outstretched and said, "Chaplain, you're the most popular man in this Headquarters. You sure stand in good with the Lord and soldiers." The General then pinned a Bronze Star Medal on Chaplain O'Neill.

Everyone offered congratulations and thanks and we got back to the business of killing Germans—with clear weather for battle. P.D.H.

FRANKLIN D. ROOSEVELT

1882 - 1945

Storms from abroad directly challenge three institutions indispensable to Americans, now as always. The first is religion. It is the source of the other two—democracy and international good faith.

This brief excerpt from one of many remarks **FDR** made on the subject of religion again underscores how, until very recently, the country's leadership understood the interconnectedness of religion and democracy.

Religion, by teaching man his relationship to God, gives the individual a sense of his own dignity and teaches him to respect himself by respecting his neighbors.

Democracy, the practice of self government, is a covenant among free men to respect the rights and liberties of their fellows.

International good faith, a sister of democracy, springs from the will of civilized nations of men to respect the rights and liberties of other nations of men.

In a modern civilization, all three-religion, democracy, and international good faith—complement and support each other.

Where freedom of religion has been attacked, the attack has come from sources opposed to democracy. Where democracy has been overthrown, the spirit of free worship has disappeared. And where religion and democracy have vanished, good faith and reason in international affairs have given way to strident ambition and brute force.

An ordering of society which relegates religion, democracy and good faith among nations to the background can find no place within it for the ideals of the Prince of Peace. The United States rejects such an ordering, and retains its ancient faith.

ALBERT EINSTEIN

1879 - 1955

Intelligence makes clear to us the interrelation of means and ends. But mere thinking cannot give us a sense of the ultimate and fundamental ends. To make clear these fundamental ends and valuations, and to set them fast in the emotional life of the individual, seems to me precisely the most important function which religion has to perform in the social life of man. And if one asks whence derives the authority of such fundamental ends, since they cannot be stated and justified merely by reason, one can only answer: they exist in a healthy society as powerful traditions, which act upon the conduct and aspirations and judgments of the individuals; they are there, that is, as something living, without its being necessary to find justification for their existence. They come into being not through demonstration but through revelation, through the medium of powerful personalities. One must not attempt to justify them, but rather to sense their nature simply and clearly.

The highest principles for our aspirations and judgments are given to us in the Jewish-Christian religious tradition. It is a very high goal which, with our weak powers, we can reach only very inadequately, but which gives a sure foundation to our aspirations and valuations. If one were to take that goal out of its religious form and look merely at its purely human side, one might state it perhaps thus: free and responsible development of the individual, so that he may place his powers freely and gladly in the service of all mankind. . . .

A person who is religiously enlightened appears to me to be one who has, to the best of his ability, liberated himself from the fetters of his selfish desires and is preoccupied with thoughts, feelings, and aspirations to which he clings because of their super-personal value. It seems to me that what is important is the force of this super-personal content and the depth of the conviction concerning its overpowering meaningfulness, regardless of whether any attempt is made to unite this content with a divine Being, for otherwise it

Albert Einstein was born in Germany in 1879. He rose to fame in 1905, when his theory of relativity was made public. In the same year, Einstein published findings that led to the foundation of modern-day quantum mechanics as well as a paper that proved the atomic theory of matter. By the age of twenty-six, the scientist had already shaped the concept of the world as we know it and did it without the benefit of an academic career. After his discoveries were made public, he was hired as a professor of theoretical physics at the University of Zurich. A number of university positions followed, and Einstein continued his work in Europe until WWII, at which time he emigrated to the United States to escape the Nazis. He became a U.S. citizen in 1940. Einstein went to work for the Institute of Advanced Study in Princeton, New Jersey, where he was employed until his death in 1955.

Although he never claimed membership in a specific congregation, Einstein studied the idea of God with the same thoroughness with which he studied the physical world. Here, in an excerpt from *Out of My Later Years,* he comments on the relationship between science and religion.

would not be possible to count Buddha and Spinoza as religious personalities. Accordingly, a religious person is devout in the sense that he has no doubt of the significance and loftiness of those super-personal objects and goals which neither require nor are capable of rational foundation. They exist with the same necessity and matter-of-factness as he himself. In this sense religion is the age-old endeavor of mankind to become clearly and completely conscious of these values and goals and constantly to strengthen and extend their effect. If one conceives of religion and science according to these definitions then a conflict between them appears impossible. For science can only ascertain what *is,* but not what *should be,* and outside of its domain value judgments of all kinds remain necessary. Religion, on the other hand, deals only with evaluations of human thought and action: it cannot justifiably speak of facts and relationships between facts. According to this interpretation the well-known conflicts between religion and science in the past must all be ascribed to a misapprehension of the situation which has been described.

For example, a conflict arises when a religious community insists on the absolute truthfulness of all statements recorded in the Bible. This means an intervention on the part of religion into the sphere of science; this is where the struggle of the Church against the doctrines of Galileo and Darwin belongs. On the other hand, representatives of science have often made an attempt to arrive at fundamental judgments with respect to values and ends on the basis of scientific method, and in this way have set themselves in opposition to religion. These conflicts have all sprung from fatal errors.

Now, even though the realms of religion and science in themselves are clearly marked off from each other, nevertheless there exist between the two strong reciprocal relationships and dependencies. Though religion may be that which determines the goal, it has, nevertheless, learned from science, in the broadest sense, what means will contribute to the attainment of the goals it has set up. But science can only be created by those who are thoroughly imbued with the aspiration towards truth and understanding. This source of feeling, however, springs from the sphere of religion. To this there also belongs the faith in the possibility that the regulations valid for the world of existence are rational, that is, comprehensible to reason. I cannot conceive of a genuine scientist without that profound faith. The situation may be expressed by an image: Science without religion is lame, religion without science be blind.

Though I have asserted above that in truth a legitimate conflict between religion and science cannot exist I must nevertheless qualify this assertion once again on an essential point, with reference to the actual content of historical religions. This qualification has to do with the concept of God. During the youthful period of mankind's spiritual evolution human fantasy created gods in man's own image, who, by the operations of their will were supposed to determine, or at any rate to influence the phenomenal world. Man sought to alter the disposition of these gods in his own favor by means of magic and prayer. The idea of God in the religions taught at present is a sublimation of that old conception of the gods. Its anthropomorphic character is shown, for instance, by the fact that men appeal to the Divine Being in prayers and plead for the fulfillment of their wishes.

Nobody, certainly, will deny that the idea of the existence of an omnipotent, just and omnibeneficent personal God is able to accord man solace, help, and guidance; also, by virtue of its simplicity it is accessible to the most undeveloped mind. But, on the other hand, there are decisive weaknesses attached to this idea in itself, which have been painfully felt since the beginning of history. That is, if this being is omnipotent then every occurrence, including every human action, every human thought, and every human feeling and aspiration is also His work; how is it possible to think of holding men responsible for their deeds and thoughts before such an almighty Being? In giving out punishment and rewards He would to a certain extent be passing judgment on Himself. How can this be combined with the goodness and righteousness ascribed to Him?

The main source of the present-day conflicts between the spheres of religion and of science lies in this concept of a personal God. It is the aim of science to establish general rules which determine the reciprocal connection of objects and events in time and space. For these rules, or laws of nature, absolutely general validity is required—not proven. It is mainly a program, and faith in the possibility of its accomplishment in principle is only founded on partial successes. But hardly anyone could be found who would deny these partial successes and ascribe them to human self-deception. The fact that on the basis of such laws we are able to predict the temporal behavior of phenomena in certain domains with great precision and certainty is deeply embedded in the consciousness of the modern man, even though he may have grasped very little of the contents of those laws. He need only consider that planetary courses within the solar system may be calculated in advance with great exactitude on the basis of a limited number of simple laws. In a similar way, though not with the same precision, it is possible to calculate in advance the mode of operation of an electric motor, a transmission system, or of a wireless apparatus, even when dealing with a novel development.

To be sure, when the number of factors coming into play in a phenomenological complex is too large scientific method in most cases fails us. One need only think of the weather, in which case prediction even for a few days ahead is impossible. Nevertheless no one doubts that we are confronted with a casual connection whose casual components are in the main known to us. Occurrences in this domain are beyond the reach of exact prediction because of the variety of factors in operation, not because of any lack of order in nature.

We have penetrated far less deeply into the regularities obtaining within the realm of living things, but deeply enough nevertheless to sense at least the rule of fixed necessity. One need only think of the systematic order in heredity, and in the effect of poisons, as for instance alcohol, on the behavior of organic beings. What is still lacking here is a grasp of connections of profound generality, but not a knowledge of order in itself.

The more a man is imbued with the ordered regularity of all events the firmer becomes his conviction that there is no room left by the side of this ordered regularity for causes of a different nature. For him neither the rule of human nor the rule of divine will exists as an independent cause of natural events. To be sure, the doctrine of a personal God interfering with natural events could never be *refuted,* in the real sense, by science, for this doctrine can always take refuge in those domains in which scientific knowledge has not yet been able to set foot.

But I am persuaded that such behavior on the part of the representatives of religion would not only be unworthy but also fatal. For a doctrine which is able to maintain itself not in clear light but only in the dark, will of necessity lose its effect on mankind, with incalculable harm to human progress. In their struggle for the ethical good, teachers of religion must have the stature to give up the doctrine of a personal God, that is, give up that source of fear and hope which in the past placed such vast power in the hands of priests. In their labors they will have to avail themselves of those forces which are capable of cultivating the Good, the True, and the Beautiful in humanity itself. This is, to be sure, a more difficult but an incomparably more worthy task. After religious teachers accomplish the refining process indicated they will surely recognize with joy that true religion has been ennobled and made more profound by scientific knowledge. . . .

The further the spiritual evolution of mankind advances, the more certain it seems to me that the path to genuine religiosity does not lie through the fear of life, and the fear of death, and blind faith, but through striving after rational knowledge. In this sense I believe that the priest must become a teacher if he wishes to do justice to his lofty educational mission.

HARRY S. TRUMAN
1884 - 1972

We have just come through a decade in which forces of evil in various parts of the world have been lined up in a bitter fight to banish from the face of the earth . . . religion and democracy. For these forces of evil have long realized that both religion and democracy are founded on one basic principle, the worth and dignity of the individual man and woman. Dictatorship, on the other hand, has always rejected that principle. Dictatorship, by whatever name, is founded on the doctrine that the individual amounts to nothing; that the State is the only thing that counts; and that men and women and children were put on earth solely for the purpose of serving the State.

In that long struggle between these two doctrines, the cause of decency and righteousness has been victorious. The right of every human being to live in dignity and freedom, the right to worship his God in his own way, the right to fix his own relationship to his fellow men and to his Creator—these again have been saved for mankind.

Harry Truman, who stepped into the Presidency after the death of Franklin Roosevelt, held office during the end of World War II, one of the most turbulent periods of this century. In this excerpt he reminds Americans that we fought for freedom to pray as we like and if we would maintain those tenets of toleration and love, we might avoid another worldwide tragedy.

The fight to preserve these rights was hard-won. The victory took a toll of human life and treasure so large that it should bring home to us forever how precious, how invaluable, is our liberty which we had just begun to take for granted.

Now that we have preserved our freedom of conscience and religion, our right to live by a decent moral and spiritual code of our own choosing, let us make full use of that freedom. Let us make use of it to save a world which is beset by so many threats of new conflicts, new terror, and new destruction. . . .

If men and nations would but live by the precepts of the ancient prophets and the teachings of the Sermon on the Mount, problems which now seem so difficult would soon disappear.

That is the great task for you teachers of religious faith. This is a supreme opportunity for the Church to continue to fulfill its mission on earth. The Protestant Church, the Catholic Church, and the Jewish Synagogue—bound together in the American unity of brotherhood—must provide the shock forces to accomplish this moral and spiritual awakening. No other agency can do it. Unless it is done, we are headed for the disaster we would deserve. Oh for an Isaiah or a Saint Paul to reawaken this sick world to its moral responsibilities!

ELEANOR ROOSEVELT
1884 - 1962

WASHINGTON, JANUARY 27—"I prophesy that if we disobey the law of the final supremacy of spirit over matter, of liberty and love over brute force, in a few years' time we shall have Bolshevism in this land which was once so holy."

This first lady, wife of Franklin Roosevelt, achieved great fame in her own right for her work as a humanitarian. **Eleanor Roosevelt** fought for better conditions for the poor and disenfranchised all over the world, and helped to write the "Universal Declaration of Human Rights." She also served as a delegate to the United Nations General Assembly from 1945 to 1951. This selection is from "My Day," a column that Roosevelt wrote for many years.

What Gandhi said about India is something for every one of us to ponder. Most of us are constantly concerned about material things and yet the people whom we like best to have with us and who make the best impression on those with whom they come in contact are the people who rarely give much thought to material things. Their minds dwell on the deeper questions of life.

Mahatma Gandhi often urged that we "turn the searchlight inward." By this, of course, he meant that we must understand our own weaknesses, our own faults, before we can conquer them. All these teachings of Gandhi are applicable to our modern way of life just as they were in the kind of life he was urging on his people. His inspirational

leadership finally won freedom for his people—and it was achieved without war.

I do not know that Gandhi's plans for living could be applied to modern life, but there is no doubt in my mind that the more we simplify our material needs the more we are free to think of other things. Perhaps what we all need to do is to sit down and think through how this could be accomplished without the loss of gracious living.

I used to think that, of necessity, comfort and beauty cost a great deal of money. I have learned that that is not true. But I still think we encumber our lives with too much, and that perhaps that is the part of Gandhi's teaching that should remain with us today.

ROBERT OPPENHEIMER
1904 - 1967

You put a hard question on the virtue of discipline. What you say is true: I do value it—and I think that you do too—more than for its earthly fruit, proficiency. I think that one can give only a metaphysical ground for this evaluation; but the variety of metaphysics which gave an answer to your question has been very great, the metaphysics themselves very disparate: the bhagavad gita, Ecclesiastes, the Stoa, the beginning of the Laws, Hugo of St. Victor, St. Thomas, John of the Cross, Spinoza. This very great disparity suggests that the fact that discipline is good for the soul is more fundamental than any of the grounds given for its goodness. I believe that through discipline, though not through discipline alone, we can achieve serenity, and a certain small but precious measure of freedom from the accidents of incarnation, and charity, and that detachment which preserves the world which it renounces. I believe that through discipline we learn to preserve what is essential to our happiness in more and more adverse circumstances, and to abandon with simplicity what

Considered by many to be the father of the atom bomb, **J. Robert Oppenheimer** expounds on his feeling about the relationship of the soul to discipline, in this excerpt from one of his letters. From 1943 to 1945 Oppenheimer oversaw the building of the atom bomb—the Manhattan project. He continued his career at the Institute for Advanced Studies after the war's end, working there until his death in 1967.

would else have seemed to us indispensable; that we come a little to see the world without the gross distortion of personal desire, and in seeing it so, accept more easily our earthly privation and its earthly horror—But because I believe that the reward of discipline is greater than its immediate objective, I would not have you think that discipline without objective is possible: in its nature discipline involves the subjection of the soul to some perhaps minor end; and that end must be real, if the discipline is not to be factitious. Therefore I think that all things which evoke discipline: study, and our duties to men and to the commonwealth, war, and personal hardship, and even the need for subsistence, ought to be greeted by us with profound gratitude; for only through them can we attain to the least detachment; and only so we know peace.

PETER MARSHALL
1902 - 1949

THE TAP ON THE SHOULDER

EVERY MAN in public life
every speaker who takes the rostrum
every preacher who mounts the pulpit has certain reticences.

The modern preacher, particularly, hesitates to inject personalities into his preaching.

He is reticent about using illustrations out of his own experience or that of his congregation.

But the apostolic preachers and writers observed no such restraints.

Their sermons were full of their own experiences.

"What we have seen and heard, declare we unto you," they said.

They never tired of telling what the Lord had done for them . . .
    what they had been before . . .
        what they were now . . .
and in the simple telling, there was power—sheer power.

Lately, I have had a feeling of compulsion to tell my own story once again.

I do not know why it was laid on my heart to tell it right now.

I do not need to know.

Nor do I need to offer any apology for doing so, for did not Christ say, "Go home and tell thy friends what great things the Lord hath done for thee."

In my story, Peter Marshall is not glorified, but the Lord.

As a matter of fact, as I think back over the evidences of the Lord's guidance in my own life, I feel ashamed that my faith is not a more radiant, contagious thing.

His hand has very evidently been upon me, and I should be a better man because of it.

It is with the prayer that what I have to say might help others, and at the same time lead me to a more complete surrender, that I tell you the experiences of a boy who was born within nine miles of the city of Glasgow, in the land of John Knox
        Walter Scott
        and Rabbie Burns.

I never knew my father, as other boys, know their father, for he died when I was four, leaving my mother with two children, my sister being only a few months old.

Three years after my father's death, I acquired a stepfather, and my boyhood was profoundly affected by this new relationship.

I soon learned to fear my stepfather, for he was a jealous man with a violent temper.

It was worse when he had been drinking, for he was one of those who felt it necessary, for business reasons, to serve alcoholic beverages at home to business friends and associates.

And yet I know that no business contract
        no order
        or commercial consideration can ever be worth
the happiness of one's home or the peace of one's mind.

I had few toys.

Birthdays came and went unnoticed.

We never had a Christmas tree.

My mother's relatives never visited us, for it was too unpleasant after they left.

Known for the snappy and sometimes pointed wording of his sermons, this Scottish-born Presbyterian minister emigrated to the U.S. in 1927. The son of an insurance agent, **Marshall** was educated first as a mechanical engineer in his native Scotland. After a call from God directed him to move to America, Marshall went to seminary in Georgia. He soon became an ordained Presbyterian minister, eventually preaching at the New York Avenue Presbyterian Church, a church that counted a thousand eight hundred in its congregation. In 1947, the minister was called to the chaplainship of the United States Senate, a position he held until his unexpected death in 1949 at the age of forty-six. In his sermons, Peter Marshall rarely minced words, freely expressing his opinions through the vehicle of prayer. This excerpt from *Mr. Jones, Meet the Master,* a collection of his sermons, is an excellent example of his remarkable oratory.

All references to my father or to my father's family were forbidden.

It was an unnatural situation, in which repressions were the rule.

I was quite unhappy, and began at an early age to think about some escape.

Like every British boy, the sea had a strong appeal.

On a still night one could hear the deep bassoon of ships' sirens as they warped into the docks of Glasgow or slipped down the Clyde for distant ports.

I began to think of the sea and to dream of it.
The books I read were tales of the sea.

With pen and pencil, and later with water colors, I had sketched and scribbled, and always it had been ships.

How I longed to get off to sea . . .
I realize now it was an escape I sought, romanticized in the glamor and the call of the sea.

I had just turned fourteen when I ran off to join the Royal Navy. At that time the Navy signed boys at fifteen and nine months. I said farewell to my friends in high school and to my teachers, and the next morning walked most of the way to the naval recruiting station ten miles away.

My career in the Navy was short-lived, for my parents secured my release because of my age.

And then I very foolishly refused to go back to school, since I had told my friends I was off to sea.

There was nothing left to do but to start working.
I began as an office boy, and enrolled in night school to study mechanical engineering.

I became a junior clerk
    and then a timekeeper.

For two years I worked in an accountant's office.
Then I became a machinist in an iron and steel tube works.

I had six years of night school in technical college, and now had three years' practical engineering experience, operating machines of all kinds.

Then came the climax of an intolerable home life in a harangue and a violent scene when my stepfather, under the influence of drink, gave me an ultimatum to leave the house.

How could I have known, at this time of severe crisis in my life, that even this would work out to the glory of God, and that in the years ahead there was to be a complete reconciliation with my stepfather?

At the time I was earning thirty-eight shillings per week, and the outlook was none too encouraging, for I had given my mother my pay envelope every pay day and had no money saved. I had no financial resources. My mother's faith was simple and strong, and as I made plans to secure lodgings elsewhere, she said,
    "*Dinna* worry, son, the Lord will provide.
    He'll open up the way."
Well do I remember the Monday morning I left home with my overalls under my arm.

That very morning, after I had been at my machine about two hours, I was summoned to the manager's office and informed that I was promoted to be a foreman of a section in another part of the plant, at twice the salary I had.

Thus, from the beginning, God was providing for my material needs.

That fall, a missionary returned from China and spoke in our church to the young people.

He was not seeking money—but volunteers for the mission field.

I volunteered for foreign service.
    I was free.
        I had no responsibilities
and I was obeying some impulse to offer my life.

As I look back upon it, I realize that it might have been the sort of thing youth loves to do, seeking glamorous adventure.

Yet I was born only a few miles from Blantyre, the birthplace of David Livingstone, and the story of that great missionary had inspired me all through Sunday School.

Then too, my own father had tried to go as a missionary, but for some reason had not been able to do so.

Whatever the impulse, from that time on, I knew that my call was for whole-time Christian service.

Correspondence with the London Missionary Society revealed that I would have to go through the university and have years of training.

Now, I had no money
    no family to support me
        no friends able to finance my education
            and no means of borrowing enough.
So we reached an impasse.

The Home Mission Board then persuaded me to consider the ministry at home, but the same difficulties stood in the way.

I had to continue working to support myself, and so they agreed that I should go on and begin studying at night, matriculating at Glasgow or Edinburgh University and save as much as I could, with a view to entering the seminary the following year.

It was a hard grind, and I found that my schooling and travel, books and the other expenses of college ate up all my savings.

Meanwhile I had other troubles with my studies. It is not easy to work ten or twelve hours a day and go to school at night.

I had trouble with French—and twice failed in my examinations. I was majoring in English, French, and mathematics, and suffice it to say that working hard, I was finding the going difficult.

In the midst of my discouragements, a cousin, whom I had not seen for nineteen years, came home from America on business.

He sought me out and told me that it was my father who had helped him to emigrate to the United States. My cousin told me that his life had been remarkably like mine.

He too had a stepfather, who made life miserable for them all.

He too had been forced to leave home.

He too had no resources, but my father had paid his steamship passage to this land of opportunity.

Now he wanted to repay the debt he owed, and since it could not be paid to my father, he wanted to pay it to me, by offering to enable me to come to America.

I told him I had no desire to go to America and informed him of my plans.

He suggested that I could prepare myself as well in America as in Scotland, and pointed out some elements of difference that might make it easier.

For example, he told me how it was possible in this country to work one's way through school,
and how willing people were to help young people with their education.

Furthermore, the seminary course here was only three years as compared with four in Scotland,
and then, too, there were so many more opportunities.

It was an attractive picture.

But I had no desire to come to America.

However, I said I would pray about it and let him know.

I did pray about it, as earnestly as I could.

I prayed for guidance, for the answer.

Day after day, night after night, I thought about it and prayed about it, but no answer came.

The weeks passed, and I could not understand why God did not give me a plain answer.

I was impatient.

Three weeks had gone by, and then one Sunday afternoon the answer came.

I could never describe it to anyone how I knew, but there was no mistaking it.

One moment I was walking along undecided—and the next moment, I *knew* that it was God's will for me to go to America.

I don't think I could describe it any more accurately.

But those of you who have had experience in prayer will understand.

I had to wait a year and a half for a visa, and when finally I sailed, my cousin was still in Europe on business, and I stood alone watching the hills of Scotland sink into the Atlantic Ocean.

I had no idea what lay before me, or how or where or when I would enter the ministry.

That I was willing to leave to Him, who had led me thus far on my way.

I prefer to say as little as possible about the first five months I spent in this country, in New Jersey.

I worked hard for long hours.

I dug ditches.

I wielded spade and shovel.

I was unemployed.

I had three different jobs in five months,
but no contact with any church,
no indication of any possibility of achieving my ambition and following the call.

Then came a letter from Birmingham, Alabama, offering me a position with a newspaper there.

I felt, at once, that this might be the second step in my guidance.

So I made it a matter of prayer.

Should I go South?

Was this the way into the ministry?

Within a week I knew that it was.

My prayers were answered definitely and without doubt.

I borrowed money, and made my way to Birmingham. There I found friends.

I met Dr. Trevor Mordecai of the First Presbyterian Church, to whom I owe more than I shall ever be able to repay.

The first time he saw me, he felt that there was a deep significance in our meeting, and that somehow it was laid upon him to help me.

He knew, before I told him, that I sought to enter the ministry, and he promised to help.

The events of the next few weeks were so amazing and so exciting, that I know it sounds almost unbelievable.

Within the space of a few short weeks, I had joined the First Presbyterian Church

    had been recommended by the Session as a candidate for the gospel ministry,

        had spoken at prayer meeting,

            had been elected president of the young people's league,

                had become interested in the Boy Scouts of that church,

and had been asked to become the teacher of the Men's Bible Class.

All of this took only a few short weeks.

It was agreed, however, that since the seminaries were already in session, it would be well for me to wait until the following year, since I could use the time to become acclimated

to make friends

    and to gain some valuable experience.

It was a happy and a busy year.

My salary with the newspaper was very small, and I was unable to save anything.

When the time came around for me to enter the seminary, some of my friends were quite concerned about how my theological education could possibly be financed, since I still had no money.

Under the spell of all the wonderful things that had already happened to me, I believed implicitly that a way would be provided, although I could not imagine how.

Call it naive if you will, I believed the Lord would provide a way . . .

and so He did.

Just before I left for seminary, the Men's Bible Class assured me of their interest in my going, and that they would follow me through with their prayers.

Understanding the difficulties I might encounter in seminary and in order that I could devote myself wholly to my preparation, they pledged themselves to send me a specified sum every month while I was in seminary.

This they did for two years.

Since I supplied a church in my senior year, I was able to graduate without debt, save that obligation to the Men's Bible Class of the Old First Church, which I can never repay.

My experience with God's guidance did not end there, for in each of my first two pastorates in Georgia, I had clear and unmistakable indications as to where the Lord wanted me to go.

The historic old New York Avenue Presbyterian Church in Washington then called me, and I prayed about the matter for two or three weeks.

I simply could not feel that it was God's will for me to come, and so I declined the call.

Eight months later, the second call arrived, but this time there were factors that made it clear that it was the will of God.

I accepted the call for that reason.

I did not want to leave Atlanta.

I was very happy there, and from every human consideration I wanted to stay.

I came to Washington believing sincerely that that was God's will for me, that He had specific work here that He wanted me to do.

Such has been the case.

During the years in Washington, I have received honors upon honors, all of which have been undeserved and far beyond my fondest dreams.

I have been honored more than any immigrant has any right to expect, even in his most optimistic expectations.

And out of profound gratitude for my adopted country, I can only say that I would like in this land to live and die, and while I live to help other people as much as possible, believing that only in service to other people can I possibly express my gratitude for all that America has done for me.

For the tap on the shoulder that called me to the ministry came to me, and this is the call that brooks no refusal—the call that we cannot ignore, the call that brings us to heel—to fall adoring and wondering at the feet of Christ.

Now if you were walking down the street, and someone came up behind you and tapped you on the shoulder . . . what would you do?

Naturally, you would turn around.

Well, that is exactly what happens in the spiritual world.

A man walks on through life—with the external call ringing in his ears but with no response stirring in his heart, and then suddenly, without any warning, the Spirit taps him on the shoulder.

What happens? He turns round.

The word "repentance" means "turning round."

He repents and believes and is saved.

The "tap on the shoulder" is the almighty power of God acting without help or hindrance upon an elect fallen sinner, so as to produce a new creature, and to lead him into the particular work which God has for him.

God calls men to preach.

How did preaching arise in the first place? By what right does a man stand before his fellows, Bible in hand, and claim their attention?

Not because he is better than they are . . .

Not because he has attended a theological seminary and studied Hebrew . . . Greek . . . and theology.

But primarily because he is obeying a "tap on the shoulder."

Because God has whispered him in the ear and conscripted him for the glorious company of those voices crying in the wilderness of life.

The preacher is conscious of being *called,* as we say, and that means that he is responding to an inward urge that could not be resisted . . .

an urge that grew out of a providential arrangement of his life and his circumstances to the great end that he should become an ambassador of the Chief—an urge that grew into a conviction that only by obeying could he ever find that joy and satisfaction of a life lived according to the plan of God.

God brought Moses from minding the sheep . . .

He took Amos from the herds of Tekoa . . .

He beckoned Peter, James, and John from the fishing boats and their nets . . .

And called Livingstone from the mill in Blantyre, Scotland.

He called Carey from his cobbler's bench . . .

He claimed Moody from the shoe store.

From the mills, the factory, and the farm they come . . .

From the ranks of mediocrity, or the gutters of sin He calls them . . . changes them . . . and makes them His messengers.

The true minister is in his pulpit not because he has chosen that profession as an easy means of livelihood, but because he could not help it, because he has obeyed an imperious summons that will not be denied.

Such was my tap on the shoulder.

The power of the gospel has not lessened with the passing of the years, but has a new significance in this poignantly questioning age, which skeptical of itself,

> of human nature
>> of democracy
>>> skeptical of everything

will yet believe in an old, old story when it is, by the spirit of the living God, applied to the hearts of men and women.

"For . . . it pleased God by the foolishness of preaching to save them that believe."

JUSTICE ROBERT JACKSON
1892 - 1954

IS THERE A FALSE RELIGION?

MR. JUSTICE JACKSON, *dissenting*

I should say the defendants have done just that for which they are indicted. If I might agree to their conviction without creating a precedent, I cheerfully would do so. I can see in their teachings nothing but humbug, untainted by any trace of truth. But that does not dispose of the constitutional question whether misrepresentation of religious experience or belief is prosecutable; it rather emphasizes the danger of such prosecutions.

The Ballard family claimed miraculous communication with the spirit world and supernatural power to heal the sick. They were brought to trial for mail fraud on an indictment which charged that the representations were false and that they "well knew" they were false. The trial judge, obviously troubled, ruled that the court could not try whether the statements were untrue, but could inquire whether the defendants knew them to be untrue; and, if so, they could be convicted.

I find it difficult to reconcile this conclusion with our traditional religious freedoms.

In the first place, as a matter of either practice or philosophy I do not see how we can separate an issue as to what is believed from considerations as to what is believable. The most convincing proof that one believes his statements is to show that they have been true in his experience.

*In this Supreme Court decision, **Robert Jackson** expresses a most uniquely American of viewpoints, upholding the essential right of religious freedom. Justice Jackson, appointed in 1941 by Franklin Roosevelt, expresses the opinion that we cannot possibly put religious beliefs on trial, however unusual or unlikely those beliefs may appear to some. In a country as vast and diverse as ours, such opinions are desperately necessary to the continued existence of religious freedom in this country, to the uninhibited ability of Americans to practice whatever faith they may choose.*

Jackson is remembered for his role as chief prosecutor at the Nuremburg War Trials in 1945. The justice also wrote two books: *The Case Against Nazi War Criminals* and *The Supreme Court in the American System of Government*.

Likewise, that one knowingly falsified is best proved by showing that what he said happened never did happen. How can the Government prove these persons knew something to be false which it cannot prove to be false? If we try religious sincerity severed from religious verity, we isolate the dispute from the very considerations which in common experience provide its most reliable answer.

In the second place, any inquiry into intellectual honesty in religion raises profound psychological problems. William James, who wrote on these matters as a scientist, reminds us that it is not theology and ceremonies which keep religion going. Its vitality is in the religious experiences of many people. "If you ask what these experiences are, they are conversations with the unseen, voices and visions, responses to prayer, changes of heart, deliverances from fear, inflowings of help, assurances of support, whenever certain persons set their own internal attitude in certain appropriate ways." If religious liberty includes, as it must, the right to communicate such experiences to others, it seems to me an impossible task for juries to separate fancied ones from real ones, dreams from happenings, and hallucinations from true clairvoyance. Such experiences, like some tones and colors, have existence for one, but none at all for another. They cannot be verified to the minds of those whose field of consciousness does not include religious insight. When one comes to trial which turns on any aspect of religious belief or representation, unbelievers among his judges are likely not to understand and are almost certain not to believe him.

And then I do not know what degree of skepticism or disbelief in a religious representation amounts to actionable fraud. James points out that "Faith means belief in something concerning which doubt is theoretically possible." Belief in what one may demonstrate to the senses is not faith. All schools of religious thought make enormous assumptions, generally on the basis of revelations authenticated by some sign or miracle. The appeal in such matters is to a very different plane of credulity than is invoked by representations of secular fact in commerce. Some who profess belief in the Bible read literally what others read as allegory or metaphor, as they read Aesop's fables. Religious symbolism is even used by some with the same mental reservations one has in teaching of Santa Claus or Uncle Sam or Easter bunnies or dispassionate judges. It is hard in matters so mystical to say how literally one is bound to believe the doctrine he teaches and even more difficult to say how far it is reliance upon a teacher's literal belief which induces followers to give him the money.

There appear to be persons—let us hope not many—who find refreshment and courage in the teachings of the "I Am" cult. If the members of the sect get comfort from the celestial guidance of their "Saint Germain," however doubtful it seems to me, it is hard to say that they do not get what they pay for. Scores of sects flourish in this country by teaching what to me are queer notions. It is plain that there is wide variety in American religious taste. The Ballards are not alone in catering to it with a pretty dubious product.

The chief wrong which false prophets do to their following is not financial. The collections aggregate a tempting total, but individual payments are not ruinous. I doubt if the vigilance of the law is equal to making money stick by overcredulous people. But the real harm is on the mental and spiritual plane. There are those who hunger and thirst after higher values which they feel wanting in their humdrum lives. They live in mental confusion or moral anarchy and seek vaguely for truth and beauty and moral support. When they are deluded and then disillusioned, cynicism and confusion follow. The wrong of these things, as I see it, is not in the money the victims part with half so much as in the mental and spiritual poison they get. But that is precisely the thing the Constitution put beyond the reach of the prosecutor, for the price of freedom of religion or of speech or of the press is that we must put up with, and even pay for, a good deal of rubbish.

Prosecutions of this character easily could degenerate into religious persecution. I do not doubt that religious leaders may be convicted of fraud for making false representations on matters other than faith or experience, as for example if one represents that funds are being used to construct a church when in fact they are being used for personal purposes. But that is not this case, which reaches into wholly dangerous ground. When does less than full belief in a professed credo become actionable fraud if one is soliciting gifts or legacies? Such inquiries may discomfort orthodox as well as unconventional religious teachers, for even the most regular of them are sometimes accused of taking their orthodoxy with a grain of salt.

I would dismiss the indictment and have done with this business of judicially examining other people's faiths.

EDMUND WILSON
1895 - 1972

THE MESSIAH AT THE SEDER

A middle-aged group of old friends had gathered for the Passover Seder. The host was the son of a rabbi and had studied for ordination in his youth at the Jewish Theological Seminary, but he now worked on the staff of a Jewish magazine. The men guests were a professor of Hebrew; a Viennese psychoanalyst; and a formerly active Marxist, who had fallen back on editing an encyclopedia. The scholar and the Marxist were accompanied by their wives, but the analyst was at present estranged from his, and the hostess's sister made the fourth woman: a handsome vivacious girl, somewhat younger than the others and unmarried. The Seder is designed to be a family affair, but it happened, on this occasion, that no children took part in the ceremony. Those of the host and hostess were under ten and had been put to bed; the Marxist and his wife were childless; the Hebraist's sons were married and living in other cities; and the adolescent son of the analyst had been carried off by his mother. Though parts of the Seder service are especially intended for children and cannot have their full effect without them, it was perhaps on this occasion, in view of what happened, just as well that there were no children present.

A prolific critic and essayist, **Edmund Wilson** was educated at Princeton and began his writing career as a reporter for the *New York Evening Sun*. Reporting was followed by editorships at *Vanity Fair* and *The New Republic*, which were followed by a first critical work entitled *Axel's Castle, a Survey of Symbolist Poets*. The author of over twenty books, Wilson wrote extensively on a myriad of subjects, not the least of which were Judaism and Israel. The following excerpt is drawn from a collection of essays entitled *A Piece of My Mind: Reflections at Sixty*. It describes a Passover Seder in which a young man arrives impromptu, claiming to be the angel Elijah.

None of the company in their ordinary lives conformed with the observances of Orthodox Judaism. Only the professor and his wife practiced a kosher cuisine, and the dinner tonight was not kosher. But most had had some schooling in Hebrew, and all had been brought up in the old way. All enjoyed celebrating this festival, which strengthened the family unit, reënforced the ties among friends, affirmed the solidarity of the Jewish people. In all this it differed much from any feast-day or holy service of their neighbors, either Catholic or Protestant—for it combined a family party like Christmas dinner with a ritual of resurrection that resembled an Easter Mass. The men, although mostly beardless—the professor was the only exception—all wore, for the special occasion, the close-fitting round black caps that made them at home in the Jewish world, and all read aloud from the Haggadah, the traditional Hebrew text, of which each had a copy before him. Two of the wives, who knew no Hebrew, abstained, but the hostess and her sister participated, since they, also, were the children of a rabbi. This text, in its lyrical eloquence, its variety and its flexibility—for it ranges from rhymes for the children to exalted psalms in praise of God—its invocation of sanctions that dignify the meagerest meal, its exultant reawakening of the Jewish sense of consecration, which springs to life among the human actualities of the homeliest Jewish family, was felt by them all as a spell that involved the long dinner table, white-napneried, gleaming with wine glasses and studded with the red and yellow bottles that contained the ceremonial wine; and connected them—there in a modern apartment of uptown West-Side New York—with the legendary past of their people, or rather, with something that was scarcely for them either legendary or even past, since it still lived among them there, and that was not what had happened but what they were living. For, dealing with events that—in terms of our time—must have occurred four thousand years before, composed now in Biblical Hebrew, now in Aramaic of the Exile, now in the dialect of the Talmud, now borrowed from the hymns of the Middle Ages, blending Provence with Babylon, the Haggadah is timeless: excreted, accreted, as it is, by the anonymous processes of centuries, it concentrates in one vibrant poem the despairs and the hopes of millennia.

The celebrants at a Seder are supposed to recline in the manner of a Roman banquet, but today this is only approximated by a cushion or two behind the host. The ritual this evening, to be sure, was a little cavalierly treated, but it is one of the charms of the Seder that it combines the petition and the paean to God with a comfortable informality, and they had not had tonight any intimation that something of importance was due to occur. The Hebrew had been fluent, the singing quite good. Almost all knew the music from childhood, and they could pick up the ancient cadences as readily as the words of a prayer. The sister-in-law of the host had a fresh and silvery voice that caressed and enlivened the spirit. The host had blessed the banquet, and the first cup of wine had been drunk. He had rinsed his hands in a fingerbowl, and the Karpas had been passed around: sprigs of parsley dipped in salt water that represented the bunches of hyssop, dipped in the blood of the Paschal lamb, which, on the eve of the Exodus from Egypt, were used to mark the doorways of the Israelites, so that the Angel of Death would pass by them. The host had then broken the middle Mazzah, a brittle unleavened biscuit, and had stuck away a piece of it in the cushions behind him, and, with the aid of his neighbors on either side, he had held up before him the tray on which lay the egg and the shankbone of lamb: "This is the bread of affliction that our fathers ate in the land of Egypt. All who are hungered—let them come to eat; all who are needy—let them come and celebrate the Passover. Now we are here, but next year may we be in the land of Israel! Now we are slaves, but next year may we be free men!"

The four questions were now asked—failing a child, by the youngest person present, who was the sister-in-law of the host: "How is this night different from other nights?," in respect to the four points of the ritual of dining—which leads to the announcement of the coming-forth from Egypt, with its pleasant little digression, the story of the five rabbis who sat up so late at night telling of this event that their pupils, the next morning, had found them still talking and had to summon them to morning prayer. Then the episode of the four sons: the clever one, the rude one, the simple one and the one who is too young to know how to ask—to each of whom, in suitable terms, the meaning of the ritual must be explained. The goblets had been raised and put down, the Mazzoth covered and uncovered: the promise made to Abraham, the bondage in Egypt, the outcry to God, who remembers—"And God saw the children of Israel, and God knew"; the enumeration of the plagues of Israel, with a drop of wine spilled for each, and the summing-up of these by the strange mnemonic device—"the scorpion stung the uncle"—invented by the Rabbi Judah.

Then, the hymn of Thanksgiving to God, with its trumpet-like refrain "Deyéynu!," which raises the note of rejoicing at His benefits beyond hoping to Israel.

They had eaten of the Mazzah, in remembrance of the bread, baked in haste without leaven, which their fathers had brought with them out of Egypt; of the Bitter Herb—a dish of horseradish—in memory of the bitterness of their misery in bondage, but sweetened by the Haroseth, a relish of chopped apples, raisins and almonds, which stands for the mortar that the Israelite captives were forced to mix for their masters, and which has several other meanings as well. They had drunk the second glass of wine. They had rinsed their fingers in bowls and had listened to the benediction.

The hostess and her sister now brought on the dinner, for which each of the families present had provided one of the dishes. It began with the customary hard-boiled egg served in a bowl of salt water—at once a tongue-whetting hors-d'oeuvre and a reminder, again, of affliction, and went on to a main course of chicken, a permissible substitute for the Paschal lamb. They drank freely now, during dinner, in a non-ritualistic way, and the talk became very lively. They mingled discussion of current events with some effort to keep up the tradition of interpreting and analyzing the service. They criticized the Jewish press, condemning it in all its departments and not sparing the magazine of which their host was an editor. The analyst had some new jokes about Israel. The professor spoke with sharp severity of an eminent Jewish scholar, to whom he referred as "a *yeshiva bochar*." The sister-in-law, next to the analyst, allowed herself to play up to him with dark sidelong glances, and even to propound to him one of her dreams, of which he gave her a frivolous interpretation: "Right off the bat, I'd say that the big black dog was McCarthy, for whom you feel an unconfessed admiration." The wife of the Marxist at one point inquired the origin of the word *Afikoman*, applied to the section of Mazzah that the host hides behind his cushion, and it was explained to her that, according to the Mishnah, this was derived from one or the other of two Greek words meaning, respectively, a festal song and an after-dinner dessert. This piece of unleavened biscuit is eaten at the end of the banquet, and figures as a symbolic substitute for any further form of entertainment. It is forbidden, when the Seder is over, to go on to any other affair.

Now the ritual had been resumed with the comedy of this Afikoman. The fragment of Mazzah is supposed to have been stolen by the youngest child present from the cushions where the father has hidden it, and to be ransomed, at this point in the ceremony, for the minimum price of a quarter. But this evening the part had been played by the handsome sister-in-law, who took an audacious line. When the host had reached for the Afikoman, and had exclaimed that it must have been stolen, and when the sister-in-law had produced it and had been asked what she would take to give it back, she had answered that he could give her in return for it that map of the Middle East, with the names all printed in Hebrew, that he had been showing them before dinner. He managed not to commit himself clearly to this, but she handed him back the Afikoman, which was now broken into bits and handed around the table. Everybody ate a piece. To eat a large amount of the Afikoman is said to prolong life, but though some remembered this, no one did more than nibble. Now the invocation of blessings began again, and the third ritual cup was drunk. "Pour out Thy wrath," they chanted, "upon the heathen that have not known Thee, and upon the kingdoms that have not called upon Thy name: for they have devoured Jacob and have laid waste his dwelling-place. Pour out upon them Thine indignation and let Thy fierce anger overtake them. Pursue them in wrath and destroy them from under the heavens of the Lord."

At this point, the host left the table, went into the hall of the apartment and opened the door into the outer hall. This was done for the Prophet Elijah, who circulates among his people and is present on certain occasions. A chair is set out for Elijah at the ceremony of circumcision, and is left there for three days, till the child is over the worst. At Passover, however, he had never yet come; he was expected—when the hour should arrive—to announce the Messiah's advent. When the fourth cup of wine was poured, a special silver goblet was also filled and set apart on the table for the prophet. This was called the Cup of the Redemption, because it was prepared for the moment when Israel should be redeemed and led back by the Messiah to its home in Jerusalem.

The host had regained his place, and they were proceeding with the chanting of the Haggadah when the professor of Hebrew, who was opposite the door, became aware that someone had entered and, looking up, beheld a tall old man whom he took at first for an Arab. This visitor was dressed in a kind of white cloak that had long sleeves and came to his knees, and a head-dress that was a large folded napkin with the ends crossed under his chin and tied on with a heavy cord. He wore sandals, and his bare legs were sinewy, sunburnt and hairy. His face was as dark as dark leather, and his coarse hair and beard were untrimmed. The

professor stopped reading, and everybody looked up. The old man stopped just inside the door and, throwing back his head, began to declaim in a voice somewhat high and nasal and with heavily marked rhythms that gave almost the effect of singing. It seemed to them that they recognized the language as Hebrew, but they could not make out what he was saying. The guttural sounds suggested to some that the language he was speaking was Arabic. It was only the concluding sentence that they definitely understood, for it contained two of the most familiar Hebrew nouns: "Peace will now come over the whole earth!"

"What a hideous travesty," the Hebraist thought, "of the ancient pronunciation!" He had read that among the Caucasian Jews it was a custom for some young man of the family to appear as a pilgrim come back from Jerusalem to tell them that the Redemption would not now be long, and he was not able to make up his mind whether one ought to resent a prank and say to the visitor, "That isn't funny!" or to accept it as a possible feature of the Seder. In any case, it was up to their host. He remembered that the host's parents came from Southern Russia. He might perhaps himself have arranged this.

But now a second visitor presented himself, putting his hand on the old man's shoulder and making him stand aside. This was a lean but strong-shouldered little man, wearing the black Jewish skull-cap and dressed in a blue double-breasted suit, who had high cheekbones, a vehement chin and a fine sharply beak-like nose. His pale complexion was flushed, and a look of obsessive intensity was sparked from his myopic green eyes, but when he spoke, it seemed plain that he was forcing himself to avoid an exalted tone.

"I don't know whether you got what he said," he began. "This is the Prophet Elijah. He's just announced my coming."

"And who are you?" demanded the scholar.

"The Messiah, believe it or not. You're skeptical. I think that we can soon convince you."

"I should question that," the Hebraist retorted, with a disagreeable smile. "Don't you know that the Messiah does not arrive till three days after Elijah's announcement?"

"If you really want to convince us," said the head of the house, smiling with more amiability, "you'll have to give us the Seven Miracles."

"Talmudic folk-lore!" said the visitor. "We don't need to bother with that. The more we speed things up the better. But you're worrying about credentials. Well, first of all, I'll give you my story." It was evident that he had it on tap. "There was nothing at all out of the ordinary about my early boyhood. I was a run-of-the-mill child prodigy. My father made middle-class furniture in Brooklyn. He was successful but he hadn't had an education, and he wanted to make up for it through me. I had mastered calculus at eight—I played the cello and composed at ten. I graduated from college at thirteen and did advanced work in nuclear physics. But the day I became Bar Mitzvah—the night after I'd been at the synagogue—I was lying in bed—awake—and I heard a voice that called me: 'Shemuel! Shemuel!'—my name is Samuel—and I answered, 'Hineyni.' The Lord first spoke to me then. He told me I was to lead my people back to the land of Israel. Then, on May 14, 1947—just seven years later, and forty-seven, notice—I heard the Voice speak to me again. It told me that a year from that day the big in-gathering would have begun and Israel would be proclaimed a free and independent state. I was just twenty-one at the time, and I was working on Long Island on the atom bomb. The Lord, blessed be He, told me again that I was to lead back my people to Jerusalem—that the nations were to be governed from Zion and peace was to come to the world—just what Elijah was telling you. I threw up my job then and fasted, and then—when I was weak with hunger—I was constantly in touch with the Lord. He told me to work for an organization that was raising money for Israel. That went on for seven years. Then came the final call—last year—the Eve of Passover and the day when Maimonides was born: Nisan 14-May 14, Nisan 14, and both double seven-it bridges the gap between the calendars—and that gave me conclusive proof that it wasn't an hallucination. Note also that, according to our calendar, it was the year 5714—seven and double seven. I was told that a year from that Passover the time would have come to save Israel and for Israel to save the world. I've been working on the project all year. In a sense, we worked it out together. But it's only the upshot that interests you, and that is that the Redemption is at hand—you must get transportation for Israel at the earliest possible moment. The arrangements haven't all been made yet, but there'll be extra planes and boats put on—about that I can be quite positive. Well, there you have the story, and if you don't accept me now, you will a little later on, when the Power behind me begins to work. In the meantime, just to look at our friend here"—and he put his hand on Elijah's shoulder—"ought to say something to you."

The old man, while the Messiah was talking, had been looking around the room with his dark and transfixing eyes, trained like guns from beneath shaggy eyebrows and flanking a magistral Hebraic nose. The young man quickly slipped aside and took down from the dining-room walls a Picasso and a Modigliani, which he set on the floor behind him, with their faces against the wall.

"I didn't want him to be smashing them," he said. "He might think they were Baal or something."

The host's handsome sister-in-law began to feel rather self-conscious. She was wearing large dangling earrings and a bright red damask gown. Personal adornments, of course, were permitted by the Talmud, if properly made, and she remembered that there were earrings in the Bible, but Elijah did look terribly austere. Even if he were not Elijah, but just some insane fanatic, one would hate to be blasted by him! She dropped her eyes to the table: had she really been thinking, she wondered, about having an affair with the analyst?

"Won't you please sit down," said the host. He brought in chairs from another room, and his wife made places for the visitors. He was by no means persuaded of their authenticity but—well versed in rabbinical lore—it came back to him, as the old prophet took his seat and sat erect with one hand on his knee and the other in a kind of pocket that was formed at his breast by a fold of his cloak, that the pious Rabbi Judah of Regensburg had once, at a certain circumcision, been able to perceive that Elijah was absent from his appointed chair, which had augured—it proved, truly—that the child would abandon the Jewish faith. He could not, in any case, but be glad that the visitors had found them at their correct observances. His wife was a little embarrassed at having chicken instead of lamb, and she had hesitated about offering them the non-kosher dinner, but the host now invited them to eat.

"Not for me," said the young man, "but the Prophet might like a snack. This is the first time he's come to a Seder, and I think he'd enjoy eating something." A brief question in Hebrew brought a nod from the old man. The hostess went to heat up something, and in the meantime the formidable visitor, casting his eye about, identified the goblet set out for him and drained it at a single draught. This a little astonished the host, for the time had not yet come in the ceremony when the fourth cup of wine is drunk; but he remembered from Second Kings, 23:22, that between the days of the Judges and the very late reign of Josiah no Passover had ever been celebrated, so that Elijah would not know the ceremony—although wasn't the ritual itself even much later than that?—the four cups of wine, he thought, had been mentioned first in the Mishnah.

But such questions were blurring in his mind. Had he drunk too many glasses at dinner, besides the ceremonial three? Or was he actually feeling the Power of which the young man had spoken, the Power behind him and Elijah? Did they not both have a radiance about them?—did they not, together, create a field in which was intensified and rarefied the yellow electric light? From the moment they sat down at the table, it was impossible not to treat them with deference. They brought silence, imposed themselves. It seemed most difficult to ask them questions. Yet the thought had dawned in every mind that the self-presented Messiah was one of those forced infant prodigies who break down from precocious effort. Had not the nocturnal call of the Lord been suggested by his name, Samuel? The analyst had been watching him shrewdly, had noted that he had left off the glasses without which he was nearly blind in order to make a better impression, that he had had some experience in public speaking, and, physically so unprepossessing, had acquired certain tricks of tone to propitiate and win an audience. Yet the gaze now laid bare by the discarding of his lenses had about it something fervent and gentle that first touched one, then evoked respect; his passion, so determinedly repressed, as he told about his call from God, seemed to burn away a commonness of accent.

The analyst itched to examine him, to lay bare the links of suggestion, the mechanism of instinct and impasse which had braced him to the strength of his delusion. He himself had been very careful not to push his own son too much; but then his wife, once a patient of his, had messed the relationship up, and might, he feared, make the boy another neurotic. The childless wife of the scholar was wondering whether her husband, a despotic and pitiless pedant, would have tried to turn their boy into a prodigy, and, having sometimes indulged herself in the dream of an ambitious son who would become a big business executive, was just as glad she had not had to risk it. The hostess, bringing on the hot plate, had asked the young man again whether he was sure he would not have a snack—she could see he was starving himself. "There's no fasting on Passover," she smiled. But he dismissed it with a negative nod. She thought of her own fat-cheeked children: she would never, she told herself, allow them to go rocketting out of her orbit; but maybe his parents were dead!

A constraint fell upon the whole company. The Marxist was the first to break through it. "Let us ask you a practical question:"—he put it to the Messiah as man to man—"Do you expect all the Jews in the world—all the Jews that aren't in Israel already—to emigrate with you there?"

"In the long run, we certainly expect it, but we're not giving everyone the call tonight."

"May I ask what your principle of selection is?"

"Only those that are holding Seders. We figure that we at least have a chance with *them*. They include, of course, a number of non-believers, or people who think they are, but the fact that they celebrate Passover would indicate that their ties with Judaism are not completely severed."

"Will you have the time to call on every Seder—tonight or tomorrow night?"

"I visit many Seders simultaneously. Between 7 a.m. today and 7 tomorrow morning, I am visiting every Seder from Oslo to Valparaiso."

This stopped the questioner for only a second. "How do you manage that?"

"How do Milt Berle and Monsignor Sheen manage to appear at the same time on every TV screen in New York?"

"That's only a projected photograph, but you're present with us here in this room, and you say that you're also present at a number of other Seders."

"That's correct. You can see me here; you can hear me; I can handle those pictures; but all the time my real basic self is at my headquarters on Ninety-Second Street directing the whole thing."

"I see," said the Marxist.

The analyst took it up: "Can you tell us how this is accomplished?"

"You wouldn't be able to grasp it. It hasn't been worked out by man, so the steps would be unintelligible. I don't understand it myself. It's only the Lord, blessed be He, who makes it possible for me to do all this."

Another queer but apposite reference came back into the mind of the host. The learned Lipmann-Mülhausen, in his *Sepher ha-Nizzahon*, had dealt with precisely the problem of the appearance of the Prophet Elijah simultaneously in different places, and had disposed of practical objections in terms of the pervasion of sunlight and the ubiquity of the Angel of Death.

"But supposing," pursued the Marxist, "that your call is successful tonight. There surely isn't room in Israel for all the dispersed Jews holding Seders."

"We won't be confined to the present area."

"How so?"

"Well, just give a thought to those plagues you've been reading about in the Haggadah. You're going to pick up the paper tomorrow and see that all the Arabs are dropping dead."

The Marxist could not help smiling; the Hebrew scholar sneered. The analyst asked a question in his professional matter-of-fact way: "And how will *that* be accomplished? Bacteriological warfare?"

"You're a long distance behind us again. It's done by a simple vibration—but not, in the crude sense, electrical. Don't worry about the humanitarian angle: death is instantaneous."

"You'll have a disposal problem," suggested the Marxist.

"The bodies crumble to dust. They blow away and mix with the sand."

"Will the other countries," the Marxist inquired, "accept Jewish hegemony? If I understand you, that's what you aim at."

"They will see we have the Lord behind us, and our prestige will rapidly increase."

"You're not afraid," the Marxist pressed him, "that pulverizing all the Arabs will create a bad impression?"

"It'll be the most conspicuous miracle since the crossing of the Red Sea. Who cares about Pharaoh's army?"

"I'm interested"— the host changed the subject— "in the theological aspect. Is there to be a Day of the Lord?"

"There is."

"Would you care to develop that subject? Maimonides tells us that the dead are to rise."

"We can't do anything with that at the present time. We've already got enough mixed elements. And even with the formerly Arab areas, we're not able to accommodate everybody—the dead as well as the living."

"What about reward and punishment?" the hostess's sister asked. She had already had two serious love affairs, one with a married man.

"Yes," said the host: "we read in Saadia that everyone will be steeped in a divine fire, and that this fire will shine for the redeemed without burning them, but eternally burn the unredeemed without shining on them."

"Saadia is not the last word. Maimonides is not the last word," the Messiah replied with assurance.

"But there *will* be reward and punishment?"

"Correct. There will be what I have termed an Assize of Exclusion—exclusion on rigorous principles."

"What will happen to the people excluded?"

"Will they be pulverized?" inquired the analyst.

"Only Arabs will be pulverized," the Messiah replied. "Jews who are unredeemed will not be permitted to live in Israel."

"And you," said the analyst quietly, "are to be the judge of Redemption?"

"With the help of the Lord, yes."

"I am wondering," said the host, "how these things are to be decided. If it is a question of observance of the Law, there is nobody in this room who would qualify."

"So far as observances go, we have, of course, adapted ourselves to the modern developments of Judaism. A good many of the observances, as the Name well knows, have long ago outlived their usefulness; some are unscientific. There's no question of discrimination against members of Conservative or Reformed congregations—or even against good Jews who don't go to the Temple at all. But a minimum of observance we do demand—that's why we begin at the Seder. The Commandments, however, are a different matter. That's where we go along with Maimonides. Grave infractions will be hard to outweigh."

"But of course you will have other criteria?" the Marxist asked a little aggressively.

"Of course: our decisions will be made in accordance with a code of morality which has been formulated by strict definitions."

"It hardly seems fair," said the host, "that we shouldn't have been told about this." His wife, the rabbi's daughter, firmly backed him up: "If we've never been told this code, how could we know that we were violating it?" "And they're asking us to go back," thought her sister, still uneasy on the score of the Seventh Commandment, "with the risk of being thrown out!"

"It's based on the Ten Commandments, and it conforms to the best tradition of Judaism. It's an extension of the Commandments themselves. We interpret them in such a way as to take into account the new conditions that have come to prevail since they were first handed down. That's all I can tell you now."

"Couldn't you give us an idea," asked the analyst, "of the way in which this system of interpretation would work in a specific instance?"

"It's useless to discuss it," the Messiah declared. "You'll be able to learn something about it when you see it applied in practice. But actually you'll never be able fully to comprehend it. The wisdom of the Lord, as you know, passes understanding. Even the greatest prophets could not compass all His aims and methods, and even I, who am admitted to His confidence, fall short of the full revelation. I've helped Him to organize the Judgment in an orderly and practical way, but for difficult decisions I must go to Him."

This seemed to arouse the Marxist, who brusquely, took a bolder line. "You've spoken," he said, "of your training in the mathematical sciences, and also, to some extent, in music. Are we to take it for granted that you're equally at home in all the arts and professions?"

"Potentially, yes; but that's irrelevant. Our judgment in any given case is strictly a moral matter; it doesn't involve the specific skill in which the individual may be proficient."

"I ask because I don't understand how it is possible to judge an individual working in any field without thoroughgoing training in that field, life-long experience of it. Morality that is correct implies correct doctrine. Admittedly, as you were saying, the Torah and the Talmud—including the Commandments—are codes that belong to the earlier phases of social-economic development. They are useless to guide us today among the contradictions of modern society, the mazes of modern politics. And how can social theory, how can political procedure, be judged by a professional physicist? I assume that you are not a Marxist. For a Marxist it would have been quite impossible to work even a day, even an hour, in a laboratory making the bomb!"

"Marx is one of our prophets—"

"Exactly: the greatest of our prophets. But one has to study Marxist theory, to become adept at Marxist practice, in order to know how to discriminate between the true and the false. The false is sometimes subtly disguised: to detect it is not so easy. It is obvious, for example, that Stalinists—Stalinists of whatever complexion, and along with them, the heirs of Stalin—are summarily to be condemned. I should myself be glad to see them destroyed. But we are not to conclude from this that all the adherents of Trotsky are necessarily to be admitted: there are few of them—very few—who could make out a case for themselves as candidates for Redemption—"

"How about the Weinburgites, Harry?" the host interrupted with a mischievous look. "Have we got to let them all in?"

"I am raising a serious question," the Marxist, put out, replied. He had passed, without taking account of it, from an attitude of sophisticated skepticism to an acceptance of the crisis as real.

"I'm in fundamental agreement with Harry," the analyst intervened, "except that I'm an orthodox Freudian instead of belonging to a splinter sect."

"Weinburgism is normative Marxism—"

"All right: well, in just the same way, Freudianism for me is normative Freudianism—correct psychoanalytic theory. Siegmund Freud is another of our prophets. You would agree to that, wouldn't you?" He turned to the Messiah.

"In a sense, yes: I grant you—"

"In the deepest sense. And Freud has been as badly betrayed by those who professed to follow him as Marx or Moses has. I should not care to see any of these betrayers redeemed any more than Harry would the Stalinists." His debonair manner was ebbing and allowing to break through its surface the rock of fundamental conviction. "These loose and sloppy imposters, who disregard the discipline of the Freudian method, who cannot see the inevitability of the fundamental Freudian conceptions—who indulge and ruin their patients, who trifle with them and take their money, who leave them in the moral abasement of their unresolved complications, because they cannot face the problems themselves—these problems that require effort, self-mastery, objective thinking—because they cannot face these problems, which involve unpleasant realities and difficult readjustments, any better than the patients can—such quacks should be treated as criminals! I should be glad to see them all pulverized, beginning with Jung! And here I agree in principle with what my friend has just said. It is impossible to judge of such matters unless one has been a practising analyst."

"You forget," the Messiah retorted, rising to the challenge to combat, "that I have behind me One who has spoken to Marx and Freud, and who can judge the deviations of their followers better than you can do."

"You forget," said the Marxist, "that every good Jew has that One behind him."

"When we get around to the dead," —the Messiah took higher ground— "Freud and Marx will themselves be judged."

"And the Prophets?" cried the Hebraist. "Are *they* to be judged?"

Though the scholar had for a long time been silent, no one of the company present was more resistant than he. He had been scrutinizing Elijah as the old man ate, and the suspicion of his authenticity had seemed to him conclusively confirmed. There is a Biblical word for *knife—m'akhelet—*which is evidently derived from the verb to *eat,* and this has been taken as evidence that the instrument was used at meals. Jealous of the credit of the ancient Jews as pioneers of civilization, the professor was strongly of this opinion, and when he had seen the ninth-century Elijah tearing the chicken apart with his fingers, he had with difficulty repressed his indignation. As the argument grew more heated, this burst. "But this alleged prophet here," he followed up, "it is certainly permitted to judge. I will give you my own judgment. No such Hebrew jargon as his was ever spoken in ninth-century Israel, nor anywhere else then or since. This we know with complete certainty!" He turned on Elijah and addressed him in Yiddish: "Haven't I seen you on the stage at the Yiddish theater?"

Elijah looked up from his plate, then glanced at the Messiah for explanation.

"You mustn't say such things to him," the young man warned the professor. "He's never learned any Yiddish—in spite of all the circumcisions he's been to—but he might think you're not being respectful."

The little professor, however, was unable to contain himself. "Tell me"—he renewed the charge, this time speaking in Hebrew pronounced in accordance with his own system—"did you learn that language from the ravens?"

"Look out!" said the Messiah. "Don't do it!"

"Ravens?" The Prophet repeated, lifting his eyebrows in a piercing smile and stretching out both hands toward the viands. "I have no need of ravens here."

"He thinks you're being hospitable," the young man said. "Now, let it go at that. Have the sense to let him alone."

"I simply want to put it on record," said the Hebraist, speaking to the company in English, "that I do not accept their pretentions. I regard them as barefaced frauds—contemptible blasphemous frauds!"

"Listen!" the Messiah protested. "He still stands high with the Name. Remember what happened to those heathen cultists, when their god let them down on Mount Carmel!"

"Yes: lay off, Lou," intervened the host.

"Well," said the Messiah, rising, "there's no need for us to stay any longer. I'll be seeing you all before long. Any doubts you may still have tonight will, I think, be dispelled tomorrow."

Elijah arose and blessed them. He and the Messiah—in the general silence—left the apartment together, the young man closing the hall door behind them.

"Let's not argue now," said the host. "Let's finish the Seder first."

They took up the Haggadah were they had left it off; went through the thanksgiving hymns punctiliously and rather subduedly. The final words, "To next year in Jerusalem"—familiar though they were—frightened some, put an unexpected question to all. Out of bravado, the Marxist and the analyst—assisted by the vivacious sister-in-law—struck up the children's rhyme, the *Had Gadya,* which parallels *The House That Jack Built,* but this was allowed to peter out.

No one wanted to speak of what had happened. "Well," said the host at last—putting a half-humorous matter-of-fact face on it—"we'll be able to check in the morning whether the Arabs are dropping dead."

But though by this time it was well past midnight, nobody dared to suggest going out to buy a morning paper, and all the guests very soon left.

The Messiah came to himself in his room on East Ninety-Second Street. It was at first an agony of reintegration, of recalling and concentrating in his own single person, the projected multiple selves that had visited the thousands of Seders. Fatigue, incoherence, unbearable strain: gasping from the efforts of self-dispersal, the pangs of organic self-reconstitution, he felt at moments that he could not survive, that he was losing his hold on the world. Then at last he became aware, in the gray early morning light, of the familiar equipment of his room. He was lying on the wooden bed—close to the floor, with no headboard or footboard—that he had had a local carpenter knock together for him; and opposite, against the wall, stood a desk, bought at second-hand, stuffed and piled with his folders and papers. There were also a small bookcase and some second-hand filing cabinets. On the wall were hung a photograph of Zion and, spread out, the embroidered prayer-shawl he had worn at his confirmation. On a chair beside the bed lay a paper bag, a pasteboard container for coffee and the glazed-paper wrapper of a chopped-egg sandwich, with which he had fortified himself just before taking off for his visits. The foody smell of these was now repellent. On a shelf he caught sight of the alarm clock which he had set for seven the night before, in case he should be still in his trance. He could not make out the time. Had it just gone off without his having heard it? Was it still to go off? He shuddered. How it would crash like a rocket-bomb on his already tortured nerves. Yet he did not reach for his glasses.

At this moment the alarm exploded. He made himself rise to his feet, snatched the clock from the shelf and turned it off. He sat a moment on the side of the bed, then he lay down again. Ignorant of the ravages of dissipation, he had known the abysmal depletions that follow intellectual excess. But the recovery from these had been hastened by the sense of accomplishment, triumph; the tissues of the mind soon mended. This morning there was a lesion that did not heal, a horror of failure, of bafflement lay at the back of his aching brain. He shrank from assembling his experiences, reliving them, extracting their meaning. He tried to curb his natural quickness of mind, to lapse into stupor, to dull his wits. But inertia, self-obfuscation were repugnant to him, impossible for him. Spasmodically, with dim fits of fainting, the powers of his mind revived. More and more swiftly and deftly, like one who sifts the contents of an auction room or sorts out a stacked correspondence, he examined, correlated, analyzed his visits of the night before. But below the rapid movements of his mind, the conviction of his mission lay stunned.

Then a deathly collapse engulfed him: "Rejected!" he exclaimed to himself. "Rejected!—I ought to have expected it! They resisted me, repulsed me, mocked me. It's I who am the Suffering Servant of Isaiah, despised and rejected of men!"

But he pulled himself together, sat up, and, summoning, affirming the formulas of prayer, he appealed to the Lord aloud.

"I have failed, my Lord," he said. "Your servant is sick in spirit."

Silence: a terrible fear made the young man sit tense on the edge of the bed, hardly daring to breathe.

Then came the expected Voice, filling, including the room: "You will be made whole again."

"But it hasn't worked out as we thought it would."

Silence: his desperate dread compelled the poor boy to go on, to revert to the self-confident tone with which he had talked to the Deity when he had first unfolded his plans: "Let me give you the picture as I see it. Undoubtedly you can throw more light on it—I beg Thee," he quickly added, lest he seem to qualify Omnipotence, "that Thou wilt aid me to understand Thy will.

"To begin with the Orthodox end: they would give one look at me and throw me out—on account of no earlocks and beard. Well, we more or less anticipated that. I thought—and I believe you approved—that, on the whole, it was more important to make the modernized ones feel at ease, and anyway that was the note we wanted to strike. I was counting on Elijah—though I'd never seen him then—to put it over with the Orthodox, but the trouble is that, begin so first-millennial, so rugged, so much the product of a primitive outdoor life, he doesn't look much more like their idea of a Jew than I do. They thought he was crazy and I was a fake. In fact, that's what most of them thought. But the worst of it is that none of them—or almost without exception—is willing to accept my authority. They will accept their rabbi's authority, but—much as they pretend to adore you—they won't recognize the Over-all Power. That's the trouble about a church with no hierarchy. The Catholics could swing it, but we've got no machine. Those fanatical old-timers in Mea Shearim won't accept the Chief Rabbi of Jerusalem. They set their own rabbi up against him, and they couldn't think of imaging a Day of the Lord in which anyone but themselves would come out on top. Of course, they're the lunatic fringe but it's the same with all the Orthodox as against the Reformed. If we got the emigration started, they'd organize resistance against it; they'd work up a counter-propaganda and denounce me as another Sabbatai Zevi. And even those who have no worship are carrying the same narrow spirit into whatever their department is. The Marxists and the analysts and the scholars of every kind all seem to have their element of Mea Shearim. Every field has its own sects, its own rabbis, and the followers of any rabbi can't face the possibility that the disciples of another rabbi may be counted among the righteous. Why, there's even a music expert—a disciple of the Rabbi Schoenberg—who wants to exclude from Redemption all the modern composers who don't practice the pure twelve-tone system. He told me he would refuse absolutely to recognize the competence of our Final Assize unless I could give him the assurance that neither Bloch nor Milhaud would be passed. There's even a literary critic—a rabbi himself, with his own disciples—who says that he can't run the danger of finding himself assigned to a category which might include certain critics who don't subscribe to his doctrine. The core of that doctrine is that—evaluating in moral terms—there are only five novelists in English whose work can be taken seriously.

"And I'm speaking now only of the people that we thought we could more or less count on! You know how the rest of them are. They don't want to go to

Israel at all, except maybe for a tourist trip. These city lawyers and doctors and men who have built up businesses—half the time they don't care anything about Judaism. They're making good money somewhere or they're good at their work or both, and beyond that they don't want to be bothered. The only group, so far as I can see, that shows any real interest in the project are the unsuccessful small business and professional men who still go to the synagogue and who hope to better themselves. They think that, when the Day of the Lord comes, their piety may get them further than their abilities ever have. They and a few very young people who go to Hebrew-speaking summer camps and are passionately patriotic about Israel. But nobody else is with us. There's nothing like the response we hoped for."

The Voice replied—the young man listened, in spite of his jaunty tone, with anxious and taut attention. "You must not say 'we,'" the Voice chided. "I was never so hopeful as you. I am no longer quite omniscient, as I used to be. Mankind sometimes gets away from me, as I never allowed it to do in the days of Eden and Babel. I have had my forebodings and doubts."

His confidence in his Deity not fortified, the Messiah fell to blaming his people. "The Jews," he came out with it, "could never agree, and why should we—why should *one* expect them to lay off their disputations even in the shadow of the Judgment Day? But the Exile, the Diaspora have aggravated this weakness. I am sure you are fully aware of the harm that has been done them by Protestantism. Living in Protestant countries, they have taken over the Protestant habits of thought: the idea of deciding for oneself, following one's own conscience, setting oneself up as a judge. Even among those who trust in Thee, blessed be Thy Name, each of them wants to feel that he's got his own private line to you. They're getting to be just like the Protestants—they believe in themselves, not you. Yet they got it out of our Bible—in a way its there—and if it's there, you—Thou didst put it there. After all, Thou spakest to all kinds of people—Amos the shepherd or anybody could turn out to be a prophet. You must—Thou needs must have known what would eventually happen."

The Voice did not speak for some time. The young man dropped his face and covered his eyes, assuming a reverent attitude but leaving the point he had made.

Then it answered: "Did it ever occur to you that you yourself are lacking in faith, that you have become disrespectful in addressing Me, that you've taken a good deal into your own hands, and that, now that the result does not satisfy you, you are showing a reprehensible impertinence in attempting to take Me to task?"

It was the turn of the Messiah to be silent.

"I am an unworthy servant, Lord!" he cried. "Forgive me for forgetting that, weak though I am, Thy hand will be strong to uphold me. We'll see how they all feel tomorrow when they read about what's happened to the Arabs."

"The Arabs will be spared," said the Voice.

"They'll be spared? But I've promised they would be destroyed. You can hardly go back on that!"

"That would do no good now. If My people do not believe, this sign would not bring them to Zion. They will simply be convinced that the Middle East is a dangerous place to live."

"But if all the Jews are spared?"

"I have some reputation for justice—though I believe you were implying a moment ago that I had not dealt justly with you. The Arabs, at the hands of My people, have already suffered some injustice, and many of My people know it. Why wipe them all out for no end?"

"Wouldn't the world be better without them?"

"They, too, have learned from my Word—they worship Me, too, in their fashion."

The Messiah curbed himself from retorting: "You're getting entirely too broad-minded!"

"But what a garbling it is of Thy Word!" was what he exclaimed aloud.

"You pity your own disappointment," answered God, partly quoting himself, "and shall I not pity Ishmael, that great people of more than twenty million persons, who hardly know their right hand from their left, and also many camels?"

In the irritation caused by dismay, the young man had the impulse to sneer: "Do you have to give me those old gags?" But what he asked was, "There's not to be a Judgment Day?"

"Not at once."

"Am I still the Messiah?"

"You must live like any other man."

"But I've built my whole life up to this—ever since you first called me, ever since I became Bar Mitzvah!" He had to rein himself in again not to cry out: "You can't do this to me! I might have succeeded in the Gentile world. I could have been a big commercial physicist. I was working on the bomb when you took me away—I was one of the coming men. Now I can never go back: after tonight, I'll be listed as a screwball.

You wouldn't let me make good with the goys, and now I can't lead my people back to Israel. What do you expect me to do?" But what he said was, "My Lord, be blessed to eternity. Thy servant has failed Thee: forgive him, I beg, and direct him to the path of righteousness. Where shall I turn next?"

"Go back to your old work," said the Voice. "Go on raising money for Israel. Maybe some good will come of it."

BISHOP FULTON SHEEN
1895 - 1979

CHARITY is the perfection of Justice. As Aristotle put it so wisely: "When Justice is, there is a further need of friendship; but where friendship is, there is no need of justice." Complementing that last thought, St. Augustine said: "Love God and do whatever you please," for if you love God you will never do anything to offend Him.

It was therefore fitting that the Sixth Word, reflecting the justice of God which fulfilled the will of the Father in its smallest detail, should be followed by the Seventh Word of Charity: "Father, into Thy Hands I commend My Spirit." It was like the seventh day of Creation. During the six words the Son of God labored forgiving enemies, pardoning thieves, solacing a mother, atoning for faithlessness, pleading for love, atoning for injustice, and now He takes His rest and goes back home.

Love is to a great extent a stranger on earth; it finds momentary satisfactions in human hearts, but it soon becomes restless. It was born of the Infinite and can never be satisfied with anything less. In a certain sense, God spoiled us for any other love except Himself, because He made us out of His Divine Love.

Born of His Everlasting Fire, the earthly sparks of affection can but kindle our hearts. We are all kings in exile; prodigals from the Father's House. As flames must mount upward to the sun, so He Who came

Ordained a Catholic priest in 1919, **Fulton Sheen** was born in Texas and raised in Peoria, Illinois. Considered by some at the time to be "probably the most persuasive speaker for Roman Catholicism in America," Sheen was known for his provocative preaching style. Consecrated as a bishop in 1951, Sheen's oratory was so remarkable that he was invited to lecture over the air waves, on the *Catholic Hour* radio broadcasts, a show so popular that the bishop sometimes received as many as six thousand letters a day.

from the Father must go back again to the Father: Love must return to Love. "Father, into Thy Hands I commend My Spirit."

It is noteworthy that He said these words with a loud voice. No one was taking His life away. It was not like the love expressed by a dying parent to his child; such love is begotten of a heart meeting the impact of the inevitable. But in the case of Our Lord, it was completely and absolutely unforced—the deliverance of freedom.

Thus did He teach us that all love on this earth involves choice. When, for example, a young man expresses his love to a young woman and asks her to become his wife, he is not just making an affirmation of love; he is also negating his love for anyone else. In that one act by which he chooses her, he rejects all that is not her.

There is no other real way in which to prove we love a thing than by choosing it in preference to something else. Words and sighs of love may be, and often are, expressions of egotism or passion; but deeds are proofs of love.

When God put Adam and Eve in the garden the preservation of their gifts was conditioned upon fidelity to Him. But how prove fidelity except by choice, namely by obeying God's Will in preference to any other will.

In the freedom of choosing a fruit to a garden was hidden the test of their love. By their decision they proved they loved something else more than God.

After the Resurrection, Our Lord prefaced the conferring of the powers of jurisdiction on Peter as the Rock of the Church by asking the question: "Simon, Son of John, lovest thou Me more than these?" Three times the question is asked, because three times Peter had denied Our Lord—Once again, love is tested by preference.

The beginning and the end of the public life of Our Lord reveals this same basic quality of love. On the Mount of Temptation and on the Mount of Calvary,

Educated at St. Paul's Seminary as well as the Catholic University of America, Bishop Sheen was a prolific writer; he published more than thirteen books as well as innumerable magazine articles. Extremely outspoken and even considered intolerant by some, the ecclesiastic argued passionately against Communism and Freudian psychiatry, using his radio as well as his church pulpit to express his views. Sheen was also the head of the Society for the Propagation of the Faith in the U.S., an organization dedicated to furthering the spread of Catholicism. In this excerpt from *On Being Human*, a collection of sermons, Sheen's talent for preaching is evident, despite the fact that we can only imagine how they must have sounded spoken aloud.

Satan and wicked men throw bribes into the balance to influence His choice. Surveying all the grandeur of earth, Satan in a frightening boast said: "All these kingdoms are mine." He offered them all to Our Lord if falling down He would adore him. Jesus could have the world if He would give up heaven.

Now on the other mount it is satanic men who tempt as they shout: "Come Down and we will believe." "Come Down from your belief in the Heavenly Father." "Come Down from your belief in Divinity." "Come Down from the cross and we will believe." Jesus could have believers if He would give up the Cross, but without the Cross Jesus could not be the Saviour.

But as He did not fall down before Satan, neither did He come down from the cross, for perfect love is the choice of Divine Love. He would choose the Father's Will either to this wealth or His bodily comfort. And that is why: "Greater love than this no man hath. That he lay down His life for his friend."

Now His love was not just declared by word, but proven by deed. He could enjoy the fruit of perfect love: "Father, into Thy Hands I commend My Spirit."

For us, there can be but one conclusion: it is not enough to bear a Christian name, we must also merit the name. "Not everyone that saith 'Lord, Lord' shall enter into the Kingdom of heaven." We can prove we love Our Lord only by choosing Him in preference to anything else, the condition of returning to the Father's hands on the last day is the choice of His Cross and all that it implies.

At any moment of our existence we can test whether we are truly Christian, and that test will be the obedience to His commandments: "He that hath my commandments and keepeth them, he it is that loveth me. And he that loveth me shall be loved of my Father, and I will love him and manifest myself to him. And my Father will love him and we will come to him and make our abode with him" (*St. John* 14:21-23).

This brings us to the second lesson of Charity. In this Seventh Word Our Lord did not express Love of the Father in terms of keeping commandments: it was a personal relationship; that of Father and Son. Even in the text: "He that loveth my commandments and keepeth them, he it is that loveth me," the possessive adjective is to be noted. The commandments are not abstract laws separable from His Person; they are one with Him.

"If you love *Me* keep *My commandments*." Perfect love is therefore quite distinct from obedience to commandments as laws. Laws are for the imperfect; love is for the perfect. Law is for those who want to know the

minimum; love is for those who are interested in the maximum. Laws therefore are generally negative: "Thou shalt not . . ."; love is affirmative: "Love the Lord, thy God, with thy whole heart."

Imperfect Christians are concerned only with keeping the laws of the Church; they want to know how far they can go without committing a mortal sin; how near they can get to hell without falling in; how much wrong they can do short of punishment; how they can please God without displeasing themselves.

The perfect Christian is never interested in borders, or the minimum, because love is never measured. Mary Magdalene did not count out the drops of the precious ointment as she poured them on the feet of Our Divine Saviour. Judas did; he counted the cost.

But Magdalene, because she loved, broke the vessel and gave everything, for love has no limits. St. Paul in like manner could think of no better way of describing the love of Christ for sinners than to say: "He emptied himself."

There is no law to those who love should give gifts to their beloved; there are no laws that mothers should love children. When there is love, there is no law, because love has no limits.

There was no boundary to the cross; the arms outstretched even into infinity portrayed the universal efficacy of Redemption. There was no counting the cost: "Not my will but Thine be done." He even refused to touch a drink which might have dulled His senses, and thus deprive His will of complete self-devotion for men.

Like Magdalene He broke the chalice of His Life, and poured out "plentiful Redemption." Such perfect love could be compensated only by a return to perfect love: "Father, into Thy Hands I commend My Spirit"—

The essence of Christianity is love, yes! But not love as our world understands it; not loving those who love us, but loving even those who hate us. Love is not in the organism, but in the will; not in affection, but in intention; not in satisfaction, but in preference to the choosing of God above everything.

Every soul then, even those who irritate, annoy and hate us must be looked upon as a potential lover of christ, and every Christian must be regarded as a kind of consecrated host.

The most degraded man on the face of the earth is precious, and Christ died for Him. That poor soul may have made the wrong choice, but that is not for us to decide. While he has life, he has hope. He might not seem lovable to us, but he is loved by God.

The perfection of all virtue is charity; love of God and love of our neighbor. Whether or not we, like Christ, shall deliver our souls into the Father's hands on the last day, depends entirely upon the use we make of our freedom.

When we abuse it our conscience tells us that we are our own worst enemy. "Now I know that when I nailed thee to a Cross it was my own heart I slew." All sin is self-mutilation.

Most of us are kept back from a perfect love of God, "fearful lest having Him, we should have naught else beside." There is a fear of losing something by obedience to Him; a hesitation of venturing all on God. Could we but see that when we have the sun we need not the candle, then all would be easy.

God grant us the light to see that in loving Him we have everything, and with that light the grace to die with His words on our lips: "Father, into Thy Hands I commend My Spirit."

ROBERT LOWELL
1917 - 1977

Educated at Harvard and Kenyon, this two-time Pulitzer-prize winning poet wrote ten books of poetry. Born into a family that counted poets James Russell Lowell and Amy Lowell among their number, he wrote both autobiographically and historically, often focusing on religious tradition. The following poem, "After the Surprising Conversions," is an example of **Lowell**'s interest in religious history. It relates the story of Jonathan Edwards's uncle and his experience with religious conversion. Lowell's life was pitted with the obstacles of mental illness and social rebellion. He was a conscientious objector during WWII. Later, in the 1960's, Lowell opposed the Vietnam War, leading protestors in a demonstration against the Pentagon. At the time of his death in 1977, Lowell held a well-deserved rank among the poetic greats of this century.

September twenty-second, *Sir: today*
I answer. In the latter part of May,
Hard on our Lord's Ascension, it began
To be more sensible. A gentleman
Of more than common understanding, strict
In morals, pious in behavior, kicked
Against our goad. A man of some renown,

An useful, honored person in the town,
He came of melancholy parents; prone
To secret spells, for years they kept alone—
His uncle, I believe, was killed of it:
Good people, but of too much or little wit.
I preached one Sabbath on a text from Kings;
He showed concernment for his soul. Some things
In his experience were hopeful. He
Would sit and watch the wind knocking a tree
And praise this countryside our Lord has made.
Once when a poor man's heifer died, he laid
A shilling on the doorsill; though a thirst
For loving shook him like a snake, he durst
Not entertain much hope of his estate
In heaven. Once we saw him sitting late
Behind his attic window by a light
That guttered on his Bible; through that night
He meditated terror, and he seemed
Beyond advice or reason, for he dreamed
That he was called to trumpet Judgment Day
To Concord. In the latter part of May
He cut his throat. And though the coroner
Judged him delirious, soon a noisome stir
Palsied our village. At Jehovah's nod
Satan seemed more let loose amongst us: God
Abandoned us to Satan, and he pressed
Us hard, until we thought we could not rest
Till we had done with life. Content was gone.
All the good work was quashed. We were undone.
The breath of God had carried out a planned
And sensible withdrawal from this land;
The multitude, once unconcerned with doubt,
Once neither callous, curious nor devout,
Jumped at broad noon,
  as though some peddler groaned
At it in its familiar twang: "My friend,
Cut your own throat. Cut your own throat.
  Now! Now!"
September twenty-second, Sir, the bough
Cracks with the unpicked apples, and at dawn
The small-mouth bass breaks water,
  gorged with spawn.

RICHARD WRIGHT
1908 - 1960

It would have been impossible for me to have told him how I felt about religion. I had not settled in my mind whether I believed in God or not; His existence or nonexistence never worried me. I reasoned that if there did exist an all-wise, all-powerful God who knew the beginning and the end, who meted out justice to all, who controlled the destiny of man, this God would surely know that I doubted His existence and He would laugh at my foolish denial of Him. And if there was no God at all, then why all the commotion? I could not imagine God pausing in His guidance of unimaginably vast worlds to bother with me.

In this excerpt from his autobiographical novel, *Black Boy*, **Richard Wright** wrote about his reaction to a conversation with a religious neighbor, explaining that he simply could not accept the idea of an all-powerful force that could not be perceived through the ordinary senses. Wright, author of the seminal work *Native Son*, reasoned that if God does exist, He would simply scoff at the faithlessness of a lone child.

Embedded in me was a notion of the suffering in life, but none of it seemed like the consequences of original sin to me; I simply could not feel weak and lost in a cosmic manner. Before I had been made to go to church, I had given God's existence a sort of tacit assent, but after having seen His creatures serve Him at first hand, I had had my doubts. My faith, such as it was, was welded to the common realities of life, anchored in the sensations of my body and in what my mind could grasp, and nothing could ever shake this faith, and surely not my fear of an invisible power.

MARY MCCARTHY
1912 - 1989

The people I was forced to live with in Minneapolis had a positive gift for turning everything sour and ugly. Even our flowers were hideous: we had golden glow and sickly nasturtiums in our yard. I remember one Good Friday planting sweet peas for myself next to the house, and I believe they actually blossomed—a personal triumph. I had not been an especially pretty child (my own looks were one of my few early disappointments), but, between them, my guardians and my grandmother McCarthy turned me into such a scarecrow that I could not look at myself in the mirror without despair. The reader will see in the photographs that follow the transformation effected in me. It was not only the braces and the glasses but a general leanness and sallowness and lankness.

Looking back, I see that it was religion that saved me. Our ugly church and parochial school provided me with my only aesthetic outlet, in the words of the Mass and the litanies and the old Latin hymns, in the Easter lilies around the alter, rosaries, ornamented prayer books, votive lamps, holy cards stamped in gold and decorated with flower wreaths and a saint's picture. This side of Catholicism, much of it cheapened and debased by mass production, was for me, nevertheless, the equivalent of Gothic cathedrals and illuminated manuscripts and mystery plays. I threw myself into it with ardor, this sensuous life, and when I was not dreaming that I was going to grow up to marry the pretender to the throne of France and win back his crown with him, I was dreaming of being a Carmelite nun, cloistered and penitential, I was also much attracted by an order for fallen women called the Magdalens. A desire to excel governed all my thoughts, and this was quickened, if possible, by the parochial-school methods of education, which were based on the competitive principle. Everything was a contest, our schoolroom was divided into teams, with captains, for spelling bees and other feats of learning, and on the playground we organized ourselves in the same fashion. To win, to skip a grade, to get ahead—the nuns' methods were well adapted to the place and time, for most of the little Catholics of our neighborhood were children of poor immigrants, bent on bettering themselves and

It seems to me that it is rare to find a self-proclaimed atheist who is glad to have been raised firmly in a religious tradition, one who is nothing but pleased to have had years of catechism and convent school. Yet writer **Mary McCarthy**, in her autobiographical memoir, *Memories of a Catholic Girlhood*, is precisely that—a lapsed Catholic who can cite reason upon reason for her childhood fondness for the Catholic Church. McCarthy says, "Looking back I see it was religion that saved me," although it did not save her in the way one might expect. For McCarthy, Catholicism was a path to beauty and intellectual challenge. Her parents died when she was young, and she was forced to live with relatives who were less than aesthetically or intellectually inclined. Religion, but not faith, was her saving grace. She looked to her parochial school for mental challenges that she did not receive at home, regarded the neighborhood church with awed wonder, and considered herself fortunate to have learned Catholic history: "To me it does not matter that this history was one-sided (this can always be remedied later), the important thing was to have learned about the battle and the sovereigns. . . ."

This may seem blasphemous to some, or at the very least unorthodox, but it was hardly out of character for McCarthy. The author of novels like *The Group* and *The Company She Keeps*, McCarthy prided herself on a nonconformist attitude throughout her life. Despite the fact that her novels often revolved around women, she never considered herself a feminist and in fact sneered at the women's movement. McCarthy's iconoclastic attitudes are apparent in this excerpt.

also on surpassing the Protestants, whose children went to Whittier, the public school. There was no idea of equality in the parochial school, and such an idea would have been abhorrent to me, if it had existed, equality, a sort of brutal cutting down to size, was what I was treated to at home. Equality was a species of unfairness which the good sisters of St. Joseph would not have tolerated.

I stood at the head of my class and I was also the best runner and the best performer on the turning poles in the schoolyard, I was the best actress and elocutionist and the second most devout, being surpassed in this by a blond boy with a face like a saint, who sat in front of me and whom I loved, his name, which sounds rather like a Polish saint's name, was John Klosick. No doubt, the standards of the school were not very high, and they gave me a false idea of myself, I have never excelled at athletics elsewhere. Nor have I ever been devout again. When I left the competitive atmosphere of the parochial school, my religion withered on the stalk.

But in St. Stephen's School, I was not devout just to show off, I felt my religion very intensely and longed to serve God better than anyone else. This, I thought, was what He asked of me. I lived in fear of making a poor confession or of not getting my tongue flat enough to receive the Host reverently. One of the great moral crises of my life occurred on the morning of my first Communion. I took a drink of water. Unthinkingly, of course, for had it not been drilled into me that the Host must be received fasting, on the penalty of mortal sin? It was only a sip, but that made no difference, I knew. A sip was as bad as a gallon; I could not take Communion. And yet I had to. My Communion dress and veil and prayer book were laid out for me, and I was supposed to lead the girls' procession, John Klosick, in a white suit, would be leading the boys'. It seemed to me that I would be failing the school and my class, if, after all the rehearsals, I had to confess what I had done and drop out. The sisters would be angry, my guardians would be angry, having paid for the dress and veil. I thought of the procession without me in it, and I could not bear

it. To make my first Communion later, in ordinary clothes, would not be the same. On the other hand, if I took my first Communion in a state of mortal sin, God would never forgive me; it would be a fatal beginning. I went through a ferocious struggle with my conscience, and all the while, I think, I knew the devil was going to prevail: I was going to take Communion, and only God and I would know the real facts. So it came about: I received my first Communion in a state of outward holiness and inward horror, believing I was damned, for I could not imagine that I could make a true repentance—the time to repent was now, before committing the sacrilege; afterward, I could not be really sorry for I would have achieved what I had wanted.

I suppose I must have confessed this at my next confession, scarcely daring to breathe it, and the priest must have treated it lightly: my sins, as I slowly discovered, weighed heavier on me than they did on my confessors. Actually, it is quite common for children making their first Communion to have just such a mishap as mine: they are so excited on that long-awaited morning that they hardly know what they are doing, or possibly the very taboo on food and water and the importance of the occasion drive them into an unconscious resistance. I heard a story almost identical with mine from Ignazio Silone. Yet the despair I felt that summer morning (I think it was Corpus Christi Day) was in a certain sense fully justified: I knew myself, how I was and would be forever, such dry self-knowledge is terrible. Every subsequent moral crisis of my life, moreover, has had precisely the pattern of this struggle over the first Communion, I have battled, usually without avail, against a temptation to do something which only I knew was bad, being swept on by a need to preserve outward appearances and to live up to other people's expectations of me. The heroine of one of my novels, who finds herself pregnant, possibly as the result of an infidelity, and is tempted to have the baby and say nothing to her husband, is in the same fix, morally, as I was at eight years old, with that drink of water inside me that only I knew was there. When I supposed I was damned, I was right—damned, that is, to a repetition or endless re-enactment of that conflict between excited scruples and inertia of will.

I am often asked whether I retain anything of my Catholic heritage. This is hard to answer, partly because my Catholic heritage consists of two distinct strains. There was the Catholicism I learned from my mother and from the simple parish priests and nuns in

Minneapolis, which was, on the whole, a religion of beauty and goodness, however imperfectly realized. Then there was the Catholicism practiced in my grandmother McCarthy's parlor and in the home that was made for us down the street—a sour, baleful doctrine in which old hates and rancors had been stewing for generations, with ignorance proudly stirring the pot. The difference can be illustrated by an incident that took place when I stopped off in Minneapolis, on my way to Vassar as a freshman, in 1929. In honor of the occasion, my grandmother McCarthy invited the parish priest to her house, she wanted him to back up her opinion that Vassar was "a den of iniquity." The old priest, Father Cullen, declined to comply with her wishes and, ignoring his pewholder's angry interjections, spoke to me instead of the rare intellectual opportunities Vassar had in store for me.

Possibly Father Cullen was merely more tactful than his parishioner, but I cannot forget my gratitude to him. It was not only that he took my grandmother down a peg. He showed largeness of spirit—a quality rare among Catholics, at least in my experience, though false magnanimity is a common stock in trade with them. I have sometimes thought that Catholicism is a religion not suited to the laity, or not suited, at any rate, to the American laity, in whom it seems to bring out some of the worst traits in human nature and to lend them a sort of sanctification. In the course of publishing these memoirs in magazines, I have received a great many letters from the laity and also from priests and nuns. The letters from the laity—chiefly women—are all alike, they might almost have been penned by the same person, I have filed them under the head of "Correspondence, Scurrilous." They are frequently full of misspellings, though the writers claim to be educated; and they are all, without exception, menacing. "False," "misrepresentation," "lying," "bigotry," "hate," "poison," "filth," "trash," "cheap," "distortion"—this is the common vocabulary of them all. They threaten to cancel their subscriptions to the magazine that published the memoir; they speak of a "great many other people that you ought to know feel as I do," i.e., they attempt to constitute themselves a pressure group. Some demand an answer. One lady writes: "I am under the impression that the Law forbids this sort of thing."

In contrast, the priests and nuns who have written me, apropos the same memoirs, strike a note that sounds almost heretical. They are touched, many of them say, by my "sincerity"; some of the nuns are praying for me,

they write, and the priests are saying masses. One young Jesuit tells me that he has thought of me when he visited Forest Ridge Convent in Seattle and looked over the rows of girls: "I see that the startling brilliance of a slim orphan girl was fairly matched with fiery resolve and impetuous headlong drive. Nor was it easy for her those days. I suppose I should be thinking that technically you are an apostate, in bad standing, outside the gate. . . ." An older priest writes me that I am saved whether I know it or not: "I do not suggest to you where you will find your spiritual home—but that you will find it—of that I am certain—the Spirit will lead you to it. Indeed for me you have already found it, although you still must seek it." A Maryknoll nun invites me to visit her mission. None of these correspondents feels obliged to try to convert me; they seem to leave that to God to worry about. Some of them have passed through a period of doubt themselves and write me about that, to show their understanding and sympathy. Each of the letters has its own individuality. The only point of uniformity is that they all begin: "Dear Mary."

I am grateful to these priests and nuns, grateful to them for existing. They must be a minority, though they would probably deny it, even among the clergy. The idea that religion is supposed to teach you to be good, an idea that children have, seems to linger on, like a sweet treble, in their letters. Very few people appear to believe this any more, it is utterly out of style among fashionable neo-Protestants, and the average Catholic perceives no connection between religion and morality, unless it is a question of someone *else's* morality, that is, of the supposed pernicious influences of books, films, ideas, on someone else's conduct.

From what I have seen, I am driven to the conclusion that religion is only good for good people, and I do not mean this as a paradox, but simply as an observable fact. Only good people can afford to be religious. For the others, it is too great a temptation—a temptation to the deadly sins of pride and anger, chiefly, but one might also add sloth. My grandmother McCarthy, I am sure, would have been a better woman if she had been an atheist or an agnostic. The Catholic religion, I believe, is the most dangerous of all, morally (I do not know about the Moslem), because, with its claim to be the only true religion, it fosters that sense of privilege I spoke of earlier—the notion that not everyone is lucky enough to be a Catholic.

I am not sorry to have been a Catholic, first of all for practical reasons. It gave me a certain knowledge of the Latin language and of the saints and their stories which not everyone is lucky enough to have. Latin, when I came to study it, was easy for me and attractive, too, like an old friend; as for the saints, it is extremely useful to know them and the manner of their martyrdom when you are looking at Italian painting, to know, for instance, that a tooth is the emblem of Saint Apollonia, patron of dentistry, and that Saint Agnes is shown with a lamb, always, and Saint Catherine of Alexandria with a wheel. To read Dante and Chaucer or the English Metaphysicals or even T. S. Eliot, a Catholic education is more than a help. Having to learn a little theology as an adult in order to understand a poem of Donne or Crashaw is like being taught the Bible as Great Literature in a college humanities course; it does not stick to the ribs. Yet most students in America have no other recourse than to take these vitamin injections to make good the cultural deficiency.

If you are born and brought up a Catholic, you have absorbed a good deal of world history and the history of ideas before you are twelve, and it is like learning a language early, the effect is indelible. Nobody else in America, no other group, is in this fortunate position. Granted that Catholic history is biased, it is not dry or dead; its virtue for the student, indeed, is that it has been made to come alive by the violent partisanship which inflames it. This partisanship, moreover, acts as a magnet to attract stray pieces of information not ordinarily taught in American schools. While children in public schools were studying American history, we in the convent in the eighth grade were studying English history down to the time of Lord Palmerston; the reason for this was, of course, that English history, up to Henry VIII, was Catholic history, and, after that, with one or two interludes, it became anti-Catholic history. Naturally, we were taught to sympathize with Bloody Mary (never called that in the convent), Mary Queen of Scots, Philip of Spain, the martyr Jesuits, Charles I (married to a Catholic princess), James II (married first to a Protestant and then to Mary of Modena), the Old Pretender, Bonnie Prince Charlie, interest petered out with Peel and Catholic Emancipation. To me, it does not matter that this history was one-sided (this can always be remedied later); the important thing is to have learned the battles and the sovereigns, their consorts, mistresses, and prime ministers, to know the past of a foreign country in such detail that it becomes one's own. Had I stayed in the convent, we would have gone on to French history, and today I would know the list of French kings and their wives and ministers, because French history, up to the Revolution, was Catholic history, and Charlemagne, Joan of Arc, and Napoleon were all prominent Catholics.

Nor is it only a matter of knowing more, at an earlier age, so that it becomes a part of oneself; it is also a matter of feeling. To care for the quarrels of the past, to identify oneself passionately with a cause that became, politically speaking, a losing cause with the birth of the modern world, is to experience a kind of straining against reality, a rebellious nonconformity that, again, is rare in America, where children are instructed in the virtues of the system they live under, as though history had achieved a happy ending in American civics.

So much for the practical side. But it might be pointed out that to an American educator, my Catholic training would appear to have no utility whatever. What is the good, he would say, of hearing the drone of a dead language every day or of knowing that Saint Ursula, a Breton princess, was martyred at Cologne, together with ten thousand virgins? I have shown that such things proved to have a certain usefulness in later life—a usefulness that was not, however, intended at the time, for we did not study the lives of the saints in order to look at Italian painting or recite our catechism in order to read John Donne. Such an idea would be atrocious blasphemy. We learned those things for the glory of God, and the rest, so to speak, was added to us. Nor would it have made us study any harder if we had been assured that what we were learning was going to come in handy in later life, any more than children study arithmetic harder if they are promised it will help them later on in business. Nothing is more boring to a child than the principle of utility. The final usefulness of my Catholic training was to teach me, together with much that proved to be practical, a conception of something prior to and beyond utility ("Consider the lilies of the field, they toil not, neither do they spin"), an idea of sheer wastefulness that is always shocking to non-Catholics, who cannot bear, for example, the contrast between the rich churches and the poor people of southern Europe. Those churches, agreed, are a folly; so is the life of a dirty anchorite or of a cloistered, non-teaching nun—unprofitable for society and bad for the person concerned. But I prefer to think of them that way than to imagine them as an investment, shares bought in future salvation. I never really liked the doctrine of Indulgences—the notion that you could say five Hail Marys and knock off a year in Purgatory. This seemed to me to belong to my grandmother McCarthy's kind of Catholicism. What I liked in the Church, and what I recall with gratitude, was the sense of mystery and wonder, ashes put on one's forehead on Ash Wednesday, the blessing of the throat with candles on St. Blaise's Day, the purple palls put on the statues after Passion Sunday, which meant they were hiding their faces in mourning because Christ was going to be crucified, the ringing of the bell at the Sanctus, the burst of lilies at Easter—all this ritual, seeming slightly strange and having no purpose (except the throat-blessing), beyond commemoration of a Person Who had died a long time ago. In these exalted moments of altruism the soul was fired with reverence.

Hence, as a lapsed Catholic, I do not trouble myself about the possibility that God may exist after all. If He exists (which seems to me more than doubtful), I am in for a bad time in the next world, but I am not going to bargain to believe in God in order to save my soul. Pascal's wager—the bet he took with himself that God existed, even though this could not be proved by reasoning—strikes me as too prudential. What had Pascal to lose by behaving as if God existed? Absolutely nothing, for there was no counter-Principle to damn him in case God didn't. For myself, I prefer not to play it so safe, and I shall never send for a priest or recite an Act of Contrition in my last moments. I do not mind if I lose my soul for all eternity. If the kind of God exists Who would damn me for not working out a deal with Him, then that is unfortunate. I should not care to spend eternity in the company of such a person.

THOMAS MERTON
1915 - 1968

FIRST SELECTION

October 6, 1941

Which brings us back to the same conclusion: the first thing to do is to feed the poor and save the souls of men, and in this sense, feeding the poor means feeding them not by law (which doesn't do a damn bit of good), but first of all at the cost of our own appetites, and with our own hands, and for the love of God. In that case, feeding the poor and saving them are all part of the same thing, the love of our neighbor . . .

And when it comes to saving souls, once again writing and talking and teaching come *after* works of love and sanctity and charity, not before. And the first thing of all is our own sanctification, which was the lesson I got out of my retreat at the Trappists, and keep finding out over and over again every day. . .

If I can only make myself little enough to gain graces to work out my sanctification, enough to keep out of hell and make up for everything unpleasant, in time, the lay vocation, as far as I'm concerned, presents no further problems, because I trust God will put in my way ten million occasions for doing acts of charity and if I am smart maybe I can catch seventeen of them, in a lifetime, before they get past my big dumb face.

At this point I realize that this letter is disordered and obscure and badly written and probably extremely uninteresting to everybody. But even if it doesn't make sense, the very fact that I used up so many words talking about lay vocations and writing means that I think I am finding out something about writing and about the lay vocation for me: which is writing over and over as long as I live: when you are writing about God, or talking about Him, you are doing something you were created to do, even if you don't feel like a prince every minute you are doing it, in the end it turns out to be right: but when you are writing or talking about some matter or pride or envy to advance your own self, you feel lousy while you are dong it and worse afterwards and ten times worse when you read the stuff over a week later . . .

Meanwhile, I hope you will come up here again and make some more speeches. The seminarians could do with some ideas about Harlem. I understand the clerics (who have now long ago returned to Washington) are still in a ferment. I'm going to write to one of them and find out, anyway. By the time I get to writing to him, I will probably have thought up another dull and complicated treatise instead of a letter!

But I think a lot of Harlem, and I'll tell you the one reason why: because Harlem is the one place

Sometimes we have to change direction in our lives to find what we are really looking for, turn our back on our prejudices, and throw ourselves wholeheartedly into that fate which is truly meant for us. **Father Thomas Merton** was not raised a Catholic. Indeed, he initially regarded the tradition with more terror than affection. Yet, it was only within the Catholic tradition that Merton was able to find out what "Christians meant by God." And so Thomas Merton, skeptic of Catholicism, became Thomas Merton, devout Catholic, at the age of twenty-four. He did not simply attend church on Sunday mornings: in 1941 he joined Our Lady of Gethsemani, a Trappist monastery, entirely devoting his life to the pursuit of his faith. He remained at the monastery until his trip to the Far East in 1968, which he undertook in search of a greater understanding of Eastern faith and its relationship to his own. That trip proved to be the final chapter of Thomas Merton's amazing life. He met with death on December 10, 1968, accidentally electrocuted by defective wiring in a fan.

Despite his tragically early death, Merton left his mark through his writing. These excerpts, one from his beautifully written autobiography *Seven Storey Mountain*, and one from a letter to his friend, Catherine de Huerck, under whom he had worked in a Harlem ghetto, help to demonstrate in a small way the range and depth of his faith. For a man who initially resisted Catholicism, Merton's words are truly amazing. In his church, he achieved the ultimate goal of all spiritual quests—a home for his soul.

where I have ever been within three feet of anyone who is authentically said to have seen visions—what was the old lady's name? I have forgotten. But believe me when the angels and saints appear among us they don't appear in rich men's houses, and the place I want to be is somewhere where the angels are not only present but even sometimes visible: that is slums, or Trappist monasteries, or where there are children, or where there is one guy starving himself in a desert for sorrow and shame at the sins and injustice of the world. In comparison with all these, St. Bonaventure occasionally takes on the aspects of a respectable golf club, but then again I won't say that either, because the place is, in spite of everything, holy, and when you live under the same roof as the Blessed Sacrament there is no need to go outside looking for anything . . .

I don't know what it is that will help me to serve God better: but whatever it is, it doesn't seem to be here. Something is missing. Whenever I read about the young rich man in the Gospels, who asked the Lord what he should do, beyond keeping the Commandments, and turned away, sad, "because he had great possessions," I feel terrible. I haven't got great possessions, but I have a job, and this ease here, this safety, and some money in the bank and a pile of books and some small stocks my grandfather left me, nothing that the average housemaid or A & P clerk doesn't have, in good times. But I don't feel comfortable at all when I think of that sentence in the Bible. I can't read that and sit still. It makes me very unquiet.

And then when I am filled with that unquietness, I have learned at last that the only thing that will take it away again is to go down into the church and try to tell God that everything I have, I give up to Him, and beg Him to show me how He wants me to give it to Him, in what way, through whom?

Just before you came down here, and I wasn't really thinking of Friendship House at all, I had been saying that prayer and finally started a novena to find out how to give God what He was asking of me: thinking all the time of possessions: maybe some poor person would be brought to my knowledge and I could give him something of what I have received through God's goodness. . . .

However, at least by God's grace I know what to pray for harder and harder every day. Nothing but the strength of His Love, to make me love to deny my fears every time they come up. A nice high ideal. The very thought of how I have always been, under difficulties, makes me so ashamed there is nothing more to do but shut up.

December 6, 1941

You see, I have always wanted to be a priest—that is, ever since my conversion. When someone told me that there was an impediment against my ever being ordained, I was very unhappy, and really, since then, I had been really quite lost, in a way. I knew I wanted to belong to God entirely, but there didn't seem to be any way particularly suited to fill up everything in me that I had hoped would be filled by the priesthood. I tried to get as close to it as possible by coming to Bona's and living just like the priests here, under the same roof as the Blessed Sacrament: but the work itself didn't seem to mean an awful lot, and everything seemed to be a little dead. I simply stayed here, praying and waiting to be shown what I was to do.

SECOND SELECTION

THERE IS A paradox that lies in the very heart of human existence. It must be apprehended before any lasting happiness is possible in the soul of a man. The paradox is this: man's nature, by itself, can do little or nothing to settle his most important problems. If we follow nothing but our natures, our own philosophies, our own level of ethics, we will end up in hell.

This would be a depressing thought, if it were not purely abstract. Because in the concrete order of things God gave man a nature that was ordered to a supernatural life. He created man with a soul that was made not to bring itself to perfection in its own order, but to be perfected by Him in an order infinitely beyond the reach of human powers. We were never destined to lead purely natural lives, and therefore we were never destined in God's plan for a purely natural beatitude. Our nature, which is a free gift of God, was given to us to be perfected and enhanced by another free gift that is not due it.

This free gift is "sanctifying grace." It perfects our nature with the gift of a life, an intellection, a love, a mode of existence infinitely above its own level. If a man were to arrive even at the abstract pinnacle of natural perfection, God's work would not even be half done: it would be only about to begin, for the real work is the work of grace and the infused virtues and the gifts of the Holy Ghost.

What is "grace"? It is God's own life, shared by us. God's life is Love. *Deus caritas est.* By grace we are able to share in the infinitely self-less love of Him Who is such pure actuality that He needs nothing and therefore cannot conceivably exploit anything for selfish ends. Indeed, outside of Him there is nothing, and whatever exists exists by His free gift of its being, so that one of the notions that is absolutely contradictory to the perfection of God is selfishness. It is metaphysically impossible for God to be selfish, because the existence of everything that is depends upon His gift, depends upon His unselfishness.

When a ray of light strikes a crystal, it gives a new quality to the crystal. And when God's infinitely disinterested love plays upon a human soul, the same kind of thing takes place. And that is the life called sanctifying grace.

The soul of man, left to its own natural level, is a potentially lucid crystal left in darkness. It is perfect in its own nature, but it lacks something that it can only receive from outside and above itself. But when the light shines in it, it becomes in a manner transformed into light and seems to lose its nature in the splendor of a higher nature, the nature of the light that is in it.

So the natural goodness of man, his capacity for love which must always be in some sense selfish if it remains in the natural order, becomes transfigured and transformed when the Love of God shines in it. What happens when a man loses himself completely in the Divine Life within him? This perfection is only for those who are called the saints—for those rather who *are* the saints and who live in the light of God alone. For the ones who are called saints by human opinion on earth may very well be devils, and their light may very well be darkness. For as far as the light of God is concerned, we are owls. It blinds us and as soon as it strikes us we are in darkness. People who look like saints to us are very often not so, and those who do not look like saints very often are. And the greatest saints are sometimes the most obscure—Our Lady, St. Joseph.

Christ established His Church, among other reasons, in order that men might lead one another to Him and in the process sanctify themselves and one another. For in this work it is Christ Who draws us to Himself through the action of our fellow men.

We must check the inspirations that come to us in the depths of our own conscience against the revelation that is given to us with divinely certain guarantees by those who have inherited in our midst the place of Christ's Apostles—by those who speak to us in the Name of Christ and as it were in His own Person. *Qui vos audit me audit; qui vos spernit, me spernit.*

When it comes to accepting God's own authority about things that cannot possibly be known in any other way except as revealed by His authority, people consider it insanity to incline their ears and listen. Things that cannot be known in any other way, they will not accept from this source. And yet they will meekly and passively accept the most appalling lies from newspapers when they scarcely need to crane their necks to see the truth in front of them, over the top of the sheet they are holding in their hands.

For example, the very thought of an *imprimatur* on the front of a book—the approbation of a bishop, allowing the book to be printed on the grounds that it contains safe doctrine—is something that drives some people almost out of their minds with indignation.

One day, in the month of February 1937, I happened to have five or ten loose dollars burning a hole in my pocket. I was on Fifth Avenue, for some reason or other, and was attracted by the window of Scribner's bookstore, all full of bright new books.

That year I had signed up for a course in French Medieval Literature. My mind was turning back, in a way, to the things I remembered from the old days in Saint Antonin. The deep, naive, rich simplicity of the twelfth and thirteenth centuries was beginning to speak to me again. I had written a paper on a legend of a "Jongleur de Notre Dame," compared with a story from the Fathers of the Desert, in Migne's *Latin Patrology.* I was being drawn back into the Catholic atmosphere, and I could feel the health of it, even in the merely natural order, working already within me.

Now, in Scribner's window, I saw a book called *The Spirit of Medieval Philosophy.* I went inside, and took it off the shelf, and looked at the table of contents and at the title page which was deceptive, because it said the book was made up of a series of lectures that had been given at the University of Aberdeen. That was no recommendation, to me especially. But it threw me off the track as to the possible identity and character of Etienne Gilson, who wrote the book.

I bought it, then, together with one other book that I have completely forgotten, and on my way home in the Long Island train, I unwrapped the package to gloat over my acquisitions. It was only then that I saw, on the first page of *The Spirit of Medieval Philosophy,* the small print which said: "Nihil Obstat . . . Imprimatur."

The feeling of disgust and deception struck me like a knife in the pit of the stomach. I felt as if I had been cheated! They should have warned me that it was a Catholic book! Then I would never have bought it. As it was, I was tempted to throw the thing out the window at the houses of Woodside—to get rid of it as something dangerous and unclean. Such is the terror that is aroused in the enlightened modern mind by a little innocent Latin and the signature of a priest. It is impossible to communicate, to a Catholic, the number and complexity of fearful associations that a little thing like this can carry with it. It is in Latin—a difficult, ancient and obscure tongue. That implies, to the mind that has roots in Protestantism, all kinds of sinister secrets, which the priests are supposed to cherish and to conceal from common men in this unknown language. Then, the mere fact that they should pass judgment on the character of a book, and permit people to read it: that in itself is fraught with terror. It immediately conjures up all the real and imaginary excesses of the Inquisition.

That is something of what I felt when I opened Gilson's book: for you must understand that while I admired Catholic *culture*, I had always been afraid of the Catholic Church. That is a rather common position in the world today. After all, I had not bought a book on medieval philosophy without realizing that it would be Catholic philosophy: but the imprimatur told me that what I read would be in full conformity with that fearsome and mysterious thing, Catholic Dogma, and the fact struck me with an impact against which everything in me reacted with repugnance and fear.

Now in the light of all this, I consider that it was surely a real grace that, instead of getting rid of the book, I actually read it. Not all of it, it is true: but more than I used to read of books that deep. When I think of the numbers of books I had on my shelf in the little room at Douglaston that had once been Pop's "den"—books which I had bought and never even read, I am more astounded than ever at the fact that I actually read this one: and what is more, remembered it.

And the one big concept which I got out of its pages was something that was to revolutionize my whole life. It is all contained in one of those dry, outlandish technical compounds that the scholastic philosophers were so prone to use: the word *aseitas*. In this one word, which can be applied to God alone, and which expresses His most characteristic attribute, I discovered an entirely new concept of God—a concept which showed me at once that the belief of Catholics was by no means the

vague and rather superstitious hangover from an unscientific age that I had believed it to be. On the contrary, here was a notion of God that was at the same time deep, precise, simple and accurate and, what is more, charged with implications which I could not even begin to appreciate, but which I could at least dimly estimate, even with my own lack of philosophical training.

Aseitas—the English equivalent is a transliteration: aseity—simply means the power of a being to exist absolutely in virtue of itself, not as caused by itself, but as requiring no cause, no other justification for its existence except that its very nature is to exist. There can be only one such Being: that is God. And to say that God exists *a se*, of and by and by reason of Himself, is merely to say that God is Being Itself. *Ego sum qui sum.* And this means that God must enjoy "complete independence not only as regards everything outside but also as regards everything within Himself."

This notion made such a profound impression on me that I made a pencil note at the top of the page: "Aseity of God—God is being *per se.*" I observe it now on the page, for I brought the book to the monastery with me, and although I was not sure where it had gone, I found it on the shelves in Father Abbot's room the other day, and I have it here before me.

I marked three other passages, so perhaps the best thing would be to copy them down. Better than anything I could say, they will convey the impact of the book on my mind.

"When God says that He is being [reads the first sentence so marked] and if what He says is to have any intelligible meaning to our minds, it can only mean this: that He is the pure act of existing."

Pure act: therefore excluding all imperfection in the order of existing. Therefore excluding all change, all "becoming," all beginning or end, all limitation. But from this fulness of existence, if I had been capable of considering it deeply enough, I would soon have found that the fulness of all perfection could easily be argued.

But another thing that struck me was an important qualification the author made. He distinguished between the concepts of *ens in genere*—the abstract notion of being in general—and *ens infinitum*, the concrete and real Infinite Being, Who, Himself, transcends all our conceptions. And so I marked the following words, which were to be my first step towards St. John of the Cross:

"Beyond all sensible images, and all conceptual determinations, God affirms Himself as the absolute act of being in its pure actuality. Our concept of God, a mere feeble analogue of a reality which overflows it in every direction, can be made explicit only in the judgment: Being is Being, and absolute positing of that which, lying beyond every object, contains in itself the sufficient reason of objects. And that is why we can rightly say that the very excess of positivity which hides the divine being from our eyes is nevertheless the light which lights up all the rest: *ipsa caligo summa est mentis illuminatio.*"

His Latin quotation was from St. Bonaventure's *Itinerarium*. The third sentence of Gilson's that I marked in those few pages read as follows:

"When St. Jerome says that God is His own origin and the cause of His own substance, he does not mean, as Descartes does, that God in a certain way posits Himself in being by His almighty power as by a cause, but simply that we must not look outside of God for a cause of the existence of God."

I think the reason why these statements, and other like them, made such a profound impression on me, lay deep in my own soul. And it was this: I had never had an adequate notion of what Christians meant by God. I had simply taken it for granted that the God in Whom religious people believed, and to Whom they attributed the creation and government of all things, was a noisy and dramatic and passionate character, a vague, jealous, hidden being, the objectification of all their own desires and strivings and subjective ideals.

The truth is, that the concept of God which I had always entertained, and which I had accused Christians of teaching to the world, was a concept of a being who was simply impossible. He was infinite and yet finite; perfect and imperfect; eternal and yet changing—subject to all the variations of emotion, love, sorrow, hate, revenge, that men are to prey to. How could this fatuous, emotional thing be without beginning and without end, the creator of all? I had taken the dead letter of Scripture at its very deadest, and it had killed me, according to the saying of St. Paul: "The letter killeth, but the spirit giveth life."

I think one cause of my profound satisfaction with what I now read was that God had been vindicated in my own mind. There is in every intellect a natural exigency for a true concept of God: we are born with the thirst to know and to see Him, and therefore it cannot be otherwise.

I know that many people are, or call themselves, "atheists" simply because they are repelled and offended by statements about God made in imaginary and metaphorical terms they are not able to interpret and

comprehend. They refuse these concepts of God, not because they despise God, but perhaps because they demand a notion of Him more perfect than they generally find: and because ordinary, figurative concepts of God could not satisfy them, they turn away and think that there are no other: or, worse still, they refuse to listen to philosophy, on the ground that it is nothing but a web of meaningless words spun together for the justification of the same old hopeless falsehoods.

What a relief it was for me, now, to discover not only that no idea of ours, let alone any image, could adequately represent God, but also that we *should not* allow ourselves to be satisfied with any such knowledge of Him.

The result was that I at once acquired an immense respect for Catholic philosophy and for the Catholic faith. And that last thing was the most important of all. I now at least recognized that faith was something that had a very definite meaning and a most cogent necessity.

If this much was a great thing, it was about all that I could do at the moment. I could recognize that those who thought about God has a good way of considering Him, and that those who believed in Him really believed in someone, and their faith was more than a dream. Further than that it seemed I could not go, for the time being.

How many there are in the same situation! They stand in the stacks of libraries and turn over the pages of St. Thomas's *Summa* with a kind of curious reverence. They talk in their seminars about "Thomas" and "Scotus" and "Augustine" and "Bonaventure" and they are familiar with Maritain and Gilson, and they have read all the poems of Hopkins—and indeed they know more about what is best in the Catholic literary and philosophical tradition than most Catholics ever do on this earth. They sometimes go to Mass, and wonder at the dignity and restraint of the old liturgy. They are impressed by the organization of a Church in which everywhere the priests, even the most un-gifted, are able to preach at least something of a tremendous, profound, unified doctrine, and to dispense mysteriously efficacious help to all who come to them with troubles and needs.

In a certain sense, these people have a better appreciation of the Church and of Catholicism than many Catholics have: an appreciation which is detached and intellectual and objective. But they never come into the Church. They stand and starve in the doors of the banquet—the banquet to which they surely realize that they are invited—while those more poor, more stupid, less gifted, less educated, sometimes even less virtuous than they, enter in and are filled at those tremendous tables.

When I had put this book down, and had ceased to think explicitly about its arguments, its effect began to show itself in my life. I began to have a desire to go to church—and a desire more sincere and more mature and more deep-seated than I had ever had before. After all, I had never before had so great a need.

The only place I could think of was the Episcopal Church down the road, old Zion Church, among the locust trees, where Father had once played the organ. I think the reason for this was that God wanted me to climb back the way I had fallen down. I had come to despise the Church of England, the "Protestant Episcopal Church," and He wanted me to do away with what there was of pride and self-complacency even in that. He would not let me become a Catholic, having behind me a rejection of another church that was not the right kind of a rejection, but one that was sinful in itself, rooted in pride, and expressed in contumely.

This time I came back to Zion Church, not to judge it, not to condemn the poor minister, but to see if it could not do something to satisfy the obscure need for faith that was beginning to make itself felt in my soul.

It was a nice enough Church. It was pleasant to sit there, in the pretty little white building, with the sun pouring through the windows, on Sunday mornings. The choir of surpliced men and women and the hymns we all sang did not exactly send me up into ecstacy: but at least I no longer made fun of them in my heart. And when it came time to say the Apostles' Creed, I stood up and said it, with the rest, hoping within myself that God would give me the grace someday to really believe it.

The minister sometimes called at our house. Pop addressed him as "Doctor," to his great embarrassment. He did not put himself forward, by any means, as a doctor of divinity. Nevertheless he had read a great deal and we used to get into conversations about intellectual matters and modern literary trends—even about D. H. Lawrence, with whom he was thoroughly familiar.

It seems that he counted very much on this sort of thing—considered it an essential part of his ministry to keep up with the latest books, and to be able to talk about them, to maintain contact with people by that means. But that was precisely one of the things that made the experience of going to his church such a sterile one for me. He did not like or understand what was considered most "advanced" in modern literature and,

as a matter of fact, one did not expect him to; one did not demand that of him. Yet it was modern literature and politics that he talked about, not religion and God. You felt that the man did not know his vocation, did not know what he was supposed to be. He had taken upon himself some function in society which was not his and which was, indeed, not a necessary function at all.

When he did get around to preaching about some truth of the Christian religion, he practically admitted in the pulpit, as he did in private to anyone who cared to talk about it, that he did not believe most of these doctrines, even in the extremely diluted form in which they are handed out to Protestants. The Trinity? What did he want with the Trinity? As for the strange medieval notions about the Incarnation, well, that was simply too much to ask of a reasonable man.

Once he preached a sermon on "Music at Zion Church" and sent me a word that I must be sure to be there, for I would hear him make mention of my father. That is just about typical of Protestant pulpit oratory in the more "liberal" quarters. I went, dutifully, that morning, but before he got around to the part in which I was supposed to be personally interested, I got an attack of my head-spinning and went out into the air. When the sermon was being preached, I was sitting on the church steps in the sun, talking to the black-gowned verger, or whatever he was called. By the time I felt better, the sermon was over.

I cannot say that I went to this church very often: but the measure of my zeal may be judged by the fact that I once went even in the middle of the week. I forget what was the occasion: Ash Wednesday or Holy Thursday. There were one or two women in the place, and myself lurking in one of the back benches. We said some prayers. It was soon over. By the time it was, I had worked up courage to take the train into New York and go to Columbia for the day.

II

Now I come to speak of the real part Columbia seems to have been destined to play in my life in the providential designs of God. Poor Columbia! It was founded by sincere Protestants as a college predominantly religious. The only thing that remains of that is the university motto: *In lumine tuo videbimus lumen*— one of the deepest and most beautiful lines of the psalms. "In Thy light, we shall see light." It is, precisely, about grace. It is a line that might serve as the foundation stone of all Christian and Scholastic learning, and which simply has nothing whatever to do with the standards of education at modern Columbia. It might profitably be changed to *In lumine Randall videbimus Dewey.*

Yet, strangely enough, it was on this big factory of a campus that the Holy Ghost was waiting to show me the light, in His own light. And one of the chief means He used, and through he operated, was human friendship.

God has willed that we should all depend on one another for our salvation, and all strive together for our own mutual good and our own common salvation. Scripture teaches us that this is especially true in the supernatural order, in the doctrine of the Mystical Body of Christ, which flows necessarily from Christian teaching on grace.

"You are the body of Christ and members of one another. . . . And the eye cannot say to the hand: I need not thy help: nor again the head to the feet, I have no need of you. . . . And if one member suffer anything, all the members suffer with it; and if one member glory all the others rejoice with it."

So now is the time to tell a thing that I could not realize then, but which has become very clear to me: that God brought me and a half a dozen others together at Columbia, and made us friends, in such a way that our friendship would work powerfully to rescue us from the confusion and the misery in which we had come to find ourselves, partly through our own fault, and partly through a complex set of circumstances which might be grouped together under the heading of the "modern world," "modern society." But the qualification "modern" is unnecessary and perhaps unfair. The traditional Gospel term, "the world," will do well enough.

All our salvation begins in the level of common and natural and ordinary things. (That is why the whole economy of the Sacraments, for instance, rests, in its material element, upon plain and ordinary things like bread and wine and water and salt and oil.) And so it was with me. Books and ideas and poems and stories, pictures and music, buildings, cities, places, philosophies were to be the materials on which grace would work. But these things are themselves not enough. The more fundamental instinct of fear for my own preservation came in, in a minor sort of a way, in this strange, half-imaginary sickness which nobody could diagnose completely.

The coming war, and all the uncertainties and confusions and fears that followed necessarily from that, and all the rest of the violence and injustice that were in the world, had a very important part to play. All these things were bound together and fused and vitalized and prepared for the action of grace, both in my own soul and in the souls of at least one or two of my friends, merely by our friendship and association together. And it fermented in our sharing of our own ideas and miseries and headaches and perplexities and fears and difficulties and desires and hangovers and all the rest.

I have already mentioned Mark Van Doren. It would not be exactly true to say that he was a kind of nucleus around whom this concretion of friends formed itself: that would not be accurate. Not all of us took his courses, and those who did, did not do so all at the same time. And yet nevertheless our common respect for Mark's sanity and wisdom did much to make us aware of how much we ourselves had in common.

Perhaps it was for me, personally, more than for the others, that Mark's course worked in this way. I am thinking of one particular incident.

It was the fall of 1936, just at the beginning of the new school year—on one of those first, bright, crazy days when everybody is full of ambition. It was the beginning of the year in which Pop was going to die and my own resistance would cave in under the load of pleasures and ambitions I was too weak to carry: the year in which I would be all the time getting dizzy, and in which I learned to fear the Long Island railroad as if it were some kind of a monster, and to shrink from New York as if it were the wide-open mouth of some burning Aztec god.

That day, I did not forsee any of this. My veins were still bursting with the materialistic and political enthusiasms with which I had first come to Columbia and, indeed, in line with their general direction, I had signed up for courses that were more or less sociological and economic and historical. In the obscurity of the strange, half-conscious semi-conversion that had attended my retreat from Cambridge, I had tended more and more to be suspicious of literature, poetry—the things towards which my nature drew me—on the grounds that they might lead to a sort of futile estheticism, a philosophy of "escape."

This had not involved me in any depreciation of people like Mark. However, it had just seemed more important to me that I should take some history course, rather than anything that was still left of his for me to take.

So now I was climbing one of the crowded stairways in Hamilton Hall to the room where I thought this history course was to be given. I looked in to the room.

The second row was filled with the unbrushed heads of those who every day at noon sat in the *Jester* editorial offices and threw paper airplanes around the room or drew pictures on the walls.

Taller than them all, and more serious, with a long face, like a horse, and a great mane of black hair on top of it, Bob Lax meditated on some incomprehensible woe, and waited for someone to come in and begin to talk to them. It was when I had taken off my coat and put down my load of books that I found out that this was not the class I was supposed to be taking, but Van Doren's course on Shakespeare.

So I got up to go out. But when I got to the door I turned around again and went back and sat down where I had been, and stayed there. Later I went and changed everything with the registrar, so I remained in that class for the rest of the year.

It was the best course I ever had at college. And it did me the most good, in many different ways. It was the only place where I ever heard anything really sensible said about any of the things that were really fundamental—life, death, time, love, sorrow, fear, wisdom, suffering, eternity. A course in literature should never be a course in economics or philosophy or sociology or psychology: and I have explained how it was one of Mark's great virtues that he did not make it so. Nevertheless, the material and literature and especially of drama is chiefly human acts—that is, free acts, moral acts. And, as a matter of fact, literature, drama, poetry, make certain statements about these acts that can be made in no other way. That is precisely why you will miss all the deepest meaning of Shakespeare, Dante, and the rest if you reduce their vital and creative statements about life and men to the dry, matter-of-fact terms of history, or ethics, or some other science. They belong to a different order.

Nevertheless, the great power of something like *Hamlet, Coriolanus,* or the *Purgatorio* or *Donne's Holy Sonnets* lies precisely in the fact that they are a kind of commentary on ethics and psychology and even metaphysics, even theology. Or, sometimes, it is the other way 'round, and those sciences can serve as a commentary on these other realities, which we call plays, poems.

All that year we were, in fact, talking about the deepest springs of human desire and hope and fear; we were considering all the most important realities, not indeed in terms of something alien to Shakespeare and to poetry, but precisely in his own terms, with occasional intuitions of another order. And, as I have said,

Mark's balanced and sensitive and clear way of seeing things, at once simple and yet capable of subtlety, being fundamentally scholastic, though not necessarily and explicitly Christian, presented these things in ways that made them live within us, and with a life that was healthy and permanent and productive. This class was one of the few things that could persuade me to get on the train and go to Columbia at all. It was, that year, my only health, until I came across and read the Gilson book.

It was this year, too, that I began to discover who Bob Lax was, and that in him was a combination of Mark's clarity and my confusion and misery—and a lot more besides that was his own.

To name Robert Lax in another way, he was a kind of combination of Hamlet and Elias. A potential prophet, but without rage. A king, but a Jew too. A mind full of tremendous and subtle intuitions, and every day he found less and less to say about them, and resigned himself to being inarticulate. In his hesitations, though without embarrassment or nervousness at all, he would often curl his long legs all around a chair, in seven different ways, while he was trying to find a word with which to begin. He talked best sitting on the floor.

And the secret of his constant solidity I think has always been a kind of natural, instinctive spirituality, a kind of inborn direction to the living God. Lax has always been afraid he was in a blind alley, and half aware that, after all, it might not be a blind ally, but God, infinity.

He had a mind naturally disposed, from the very cradle, to a kind of affinity for Job and St. John of the Cross. And I now know that he was born so much of a contemplative that he will probably never be able to find out how much.

To sum it up, even the people who have always thought he was "too impractical" have always tended to venerate him—in the way people who value material security unconsciously venerate people who do not fear insecurity.

In those days one of the things we had most in common, although perhaps we did not talk about it so much, was the abyss that walked around in front of our feet everywhere we went, and kept making us dizzy and afraid of trains and high buildings. For some reason, Lax developed an implicit trust in all my notions about what was good and bad for mental and physical health, perhaps because I was always very definite in my likes and dislikes. I am afraid it did not do him too much good, though. For even though I had my imaginary abyss, which broadened immeasurably and became ten times dizzier when I had a hangover, my ideas often tended to some particular place where we would hear this particular band and drink this special drink until the place folded up at four o'clock in the morning.

The months passed by, and most of the time I sat in Douglaston, drawing cartoons for the paper-cup business, and trying to do all the other things I was supposed to do. In the summer, Lax went to Europe, and I continued to sit in Douglaston, writing a long, stupid novel about a college football player who got mixed up in a lot of strikes in a textile mill.

I did not graduate that June, although I nominally belonged to that year's class: I had still one or two courses to take, on account of having entered Columbia in February. In the fall of 1937 I went back to school, then, with my mind a lot freer, since I was not burdened with any more of those ugly and useless jobs on the fourth floor. I could write and do the drawings I felt like doing for *Jester*.

I began to talk more to Lax and to Ed Rice who was now drawing better and funnier pictures than anybody else for the magazine. For the first time I saw Sy Freedgood, who was full of a fierce and complex intellectuality which he sometimes liked to present in the guise of a rather suspicious suavity. He was in love with a far more technical vocabulary than any of the rest of us possessed, and was working at something in the philosophy graduate school. Seymour used consciously to affect a whole set of different kinds of duplicity, of which he was proud, and he had carried the *mendacium jocosum* or "humorous lie" to its utmost extension and frequency. You could sometimes gauge the falsity of his answers by their promptitude: the quicker the falser. The reason for this was, probably, that he was thinking of something else, something very abstruse and far from the sphere of your question, and he could not be bothered to bring his mind all that way back, to think up the real answer.

For Lax and myself and Gibney there was no inconvenience about this, for two reasons. Since Seymour generally gave his false answers only to practical questions of fact, their falsity did not matter: we were all too impractical. Besides his false answers were generally more interesting than the truth. Finally, since we knew they were false anyway, we had the habit of seeing all his statements, in the common factual order by a kind of double standard, instituting a comparison between what he had said and the probable truth, and this cast many interesting and ironical lights upon life as a whole.

In his house at Long Beach, where his whole family lived in a state of turmoil and confusion, there was a large, stupid police dog that got in everybody's way with his bowed head and slapped-down cars and amiable, guilty look. The first time I saw the dog, I asked: "What's his name?"

"Prince," said Seymour, out of the corner of his mouth.

It was a name to which the beast responded gladly. I guess he responded to any name, didn't care what you called him, so flattered was he to be called at all, being as he knew an extremely stupid dog.

So I was out on the boardwalk with the dog, shouting: "Hey, Prince; hey, Prince!"

Seymour's wife, Helen, came along and heard me shouting all this and said nothing, imagining, no doubt, that it was some way I had of making fun of the brute. Later, Seymour or someone told me that "Prince" wasn't the dog's name, but they told me in such a way that I got the idea that his name was really "Rex." So for some time after that I called him: "Hey, Rex; hey, Rex!" Several months later, after many visits to the house, I finally learned that the dog was called nothing like Prince nor Rex, but "Bunky."

Moral theologians say that the *mendacium jocosum* in itself does not exceed a venial sin.

Seymour and Lax were rooming together in one of the dormitories, for Bob Gibney, with whom Lax had roomed the year before, had now graduated, and was sitting in Port Washington with much the same dispositions with which I had been sitting in Douglaston, facing a not too dissimilar blank wall, the end of his own blind-alley. He occasionally came in to town to see Dona Eaton who had a place on 112th Street, but no job, and was more cheerful about her own quandary than the rest of us, because the worst that could happen to her was that she would at last run completely out of money and have to go home to Panama.

Gibney was not what you would call pious. In fact, he had an attitude that would be commonly called impious, only I believe God understood well enough that his violence and sarcasms covered a sense of deep metaphysical dismay—an anguish that was real, though not humble enough to be of much use to his soul. What was materially impiety in him was directed more against common ideas and notions which he saw or considered to be totally inadequate, and maybe it subjectively represented a kind of oblique zeal for the purity of God, this rebellion against the commonplace and trite, against mediocrity, religiosity.

During the year that had passed, I suppose it must have been in the spring of 1937, both Gibney and Lax and Bob Gerdy had all been talking about becoming Catholics. Bob Gerdy was a very smart sophomore with the face of a child and a lot of curly hair on top of it, who took life seriously, and had discovered courses on Scholastic Philosophy in the graduate school, and had taken one of them.

Gibney was interested in Scholastic Philosophy in much the same way as James Joyce was—he respected its intellectuality, particularly that of the Thomists, but there was not enough that was affective about his interest to bring about any kind of a conversion.

For three or four years that I knew Gibney, he was always holding out for some kind of a "sign," some kind of a sensible and tangible interior jolt from God, to get him started, some mystical experience or other. And while he waited and waited for this to come along, he did all the things that normally exclude and nullify the action of grace. So in those days, none of them became Catholics.

The most serious of them all, in this matter, was Lax: he was the one that had been born with the deepest sense of Who God was. But he would not make a move without the others.

And then there was myself. Having read *The Spirit of Medieval Philosophy* and having discovered that the Catholic conception of God was something tremendously solid, I had not progressed one step beyond this recognition, except that one day I had gone and looked up St. Bernard's *De Diligendo Deo* in the catalogue of the University Library. It was one of the books Gilson had frequently mentioned: but when I found that there was no good copy of it, except in Latin, I did not take it out.

Now it was November 1937. One day, Lax and I were riding downtown on one of those busses you caught at the corner of 110th Street and Broadway. We had skirted the southern edge of Harlem, passing along the top of Central Park, and the dirty lake full of rowboats. Now we were going down Fifth Avenue, under the trees. Lax was telling me about a book he had been reading, which was Aldous Huxley's *Ends and Means*. He told me about it in a way that made me want to read it too.

So I went to Scribner's bookstore and bought it, and read it, and wrote an article about it, and gave the article to Barry Ulanov who was editor of *Review* by that time. He accepted the article with a big Greek smile and printed it. The smile was on account of the conversion it represented, I mean the conversion in me, as well as in Huxley, although one of the points I tried to make was that perhaps Huxley's conversion should not have been taken as so much of a surprise.

Huxley had been one of my favorite novelists in the days when I had been sixteen and seventeen and had built up a strange, ignorant philosophy of pleasure based on all the stories I was reading. And now everybody was talking about the way Huxley had changed. The chatter was all the more pleasant because of Huxley's agnostic old grandfather—and his biologist brother. Now the man was preaching mysticism.

Huxley was too sharp and intelligent and had too much sense of humor to take any of the missteps that usually make such conversions look ridiculous and oafish. You could not laugh at him, very well—at least not for any one concrete blunder. This was not one of those Oxford Group conversions, complete with a public confession.

On the contrary, he had read widely and deeply and intelligently in all kinds of Christian and Oriental mystical literature, and had come out with the astonishing truth that all this, far from being a mixture of dreams and magic and charlatanism, was very real and very serious.

Not only was there such a thing as a supernatural order, but as a matter of concrete experience, it was accessible, very close at hand, an extremely near, an immediate and most necessary source of moral vitality, and one which could be reached most simply, most readily by prayer, faith, detachment, love.

The point of his title was this: we cannot use evil means to attain a good end. Huxley's chief argument was that we were using the means that precisely made good ends impossible to attain: war, violence, reprisals, rapacity. And he traced our impossibility to use the proper means to the fact that men were immersed in the material and animal urges of an element in their nature which was blind and crude and unspiritual.

The main problem is to fight our way free from subjection to this more or less inferior element, and to reassert the dominance of our mind and will: to vindicate for these faculties, for the spirit as a whole, the freedom of action which it must necessarily have if we are to live like anything but wild beasts, tearing each other to pieces. And the big conclusion from all this was: we must practice prayer and asceticism.

Asceticism! The very thought of such a thing was a complete revolution in my mind. The word had so far stood for a kind of weird and ugly perversion of nature, the masochism of men who had gone crazy in a warped and unjust society. What an idea! To deny the desires of one's flesh, and even to practice certain disciplines that punished and mortified those desires: until this day, these things had never succeeded in giving me anything but gooseflesh. But of course Huxley did not stress the physical angle of mortification and asceticism—and that was right, in so far as he was more interested in striking to the very heart of the matter, and showing the ultimate positive principle underlying the need for detachment.

He showed that this negation was not something absolute, sought for its own sake: but that it was a freeing a vindication of our real selves, a liberation of the spirit from limits and bonds that were intolerable, suicidal—from a servitude to flesh that must ultimately destroy our whole nature and society and the world as well.

Not only that, once the spirit was freed, and returned to its own element, it was not alone there: it could find the absolute and perfect Spirit, God. It could enter into union with Him; and what is more, this union was not something vague and metaphorical, but it was a matter of real experience. What that experience amounted to, according to Huxley, might or might not have been the nirvana of the Buddhists, which is the ultimate negation of all experience and all reality whatever: but anyway, somewhere along the line, he quoted proofs that it was and could be a real and positive experience.

The speculative side of the book—its strongest—was full, no doubt, of strange doctrines by reason of its very eclecticism. And the practical element, which was weak, inspired no confidence, especially when he tried to talk about a concrete social program. Huxley seemed not to be at home with the Christian term "Love" which sounded extraordinarily vague in his contexts—and which must nevertheless be the heart, and life of all true mysticism. But out of it all I took these two big concepts of a supernatural, spiritual order, and the possibility of real, experimental contact with God.

Huxley was thought, by some people, to be on the point of entering the Church, but *Ends and Means* was written by a man Cross and St. Teresa of Avila indiscriminately with less orthodox Christian writers like Meister Eckhart: and on the whole he preferred the Orient. It seems to me that in discarding his family's tradition of materialism he had followed the old Protestant groove back into the heresies that make the material creation evil or itself, although I do not remember enough about him to accuse him of formally holding such a thing. Nevertheless, that would account for his sympathy for Buddhism, and for the

nihilistic character which he preferred to give to his mysticism and even to his ethics. This also made him suspicious, as the Albigensians had been, and for the same reason, of the Sacraments and Liturgical life of the Church, and also of doctrines like the Incarnation.

With all that I was not concerned. My hatred of war and my own personal misery in my particular situation and the general crisis of the world made me accept with my whole heart this revelation of the need for a spiritual life, an interior life, including some kind of mortification. I was content to accept the latter truth purely as a matter of theory: or at least, to apply it most vociferously to one passion which was not strong in myself, and did not need to be mortified: that of anger, hatred, while neglecting the ones that really needed to be checked, like gluttony and lust.

But the most important effect of the book on me was to make me start ransacking the university library for books on Oriental mysticism.

I remember those winter days, at the end of 1937 and the beginning of 1938, peaceful days when I sat in the big living room at Douglaston, with the pale sun coming in the window by the piano, where one of my father's water-colors of Bermuda hung on the wall.

The house was very quiet, with Pop and Bonnemaman gone from it, and John Paul away trying to pass his courses at Cornell. I sat for hours, with the big quarto volumes of the Jesuit Father Wieger's French translations of hundreds of strange Oriental texts.

I have forgotten the titles, even the authors, and I never understood a word of what they said in the first place. I had the habit of reading fast, without stopping, or stopping only rarely to take a note, and all these mysteries would require a great deal of thought, even were a man who knew something about them to puzzle them out. And I was completely unfamiliar with anything of the kind. Consequently, the strange great jumble of myths and theories and moral aphorisms and elaborate parables made little or no real impression on my mind, except that I put the books down with the impression that mysticism was something very esoteric and complicated, and that we were all inside some huge Being in whom we were involved and out of whom we evolved, and the thing to do was to involve ourselves back in to him again by a system of elaborate disciplines subject more or less to the control of our own will. The Absolute Being was an infinite, timeless, peaceful, impersonal Nothing.

The only practical thing I got out of it was a system for going to sleep, at night, when you couldn't sleep.

You lay flat in bed, without a pillow, your arms at your sides and your legs straight out, and relaxed all your muscles, and you said to yourself:

"Now I have no feet, now I have no feet . . . no feet . . . no legs . . . no knees."

Sometimes it really worked: you did manage to make it feel as if your feet and legs and the rest of your body had changed into air and vanished away. The only section with which it almost never worked was my head: and if I had not fallen asleep before I got that far, when I tried to wipe out my head, instantly chest and stomach and legs and feet all came back to life with a most exasperating reality and I did not get to sleep for hours. Usually, however, I managed to get to sleep quite quickly by this trick. I suppose it was a variety of auto-suggestion, a kind of hypnotism, or else simply muscular relaxation, with the help of a little work on the part of an active fancy.

Ultimately, I suppose all Oriental mysticism can be reduced to techniques that do the same thing, but in a far more subtle and advanced fashion: and if that is true, it is not mysticism at all. It remains purely in the natural order. That does not make it evil, *per se*, according to Christian standards: but it does not make it good, in relation to the supernatural. It is simply more or less useless, except when it is mixed up with elements that are strictly diabolical: and then of course these dreams and annihilations are designed to wipe out all vital moral activity, while leaving the personality in control of some nefarious principle, either of his own, or from outside himself.

It was with all this in my mind that I went and received my diploma of Bachelor of Arts from one of the windows in the Registrar's office, and immediately afterwards put my name down for some courses in the Graduate School of English.

The experience of the last year, with the sudden collapse of all my physical energy and the diminution of the brash vigor of my worldly ambitions, had meant that I had turned in terror from the idea of anything so active and uncertain as the newspaper business. This registration in the graduate school represented the first remote step of a retreat from the fight for money and fame, from the active and worldly life of conflict and competition. If anything, I would now be a teacher, and live the rest of my life in the relative peace of a college campus, reading and writing books.

That the influence of the Huxley book had not, by any means, lifted me bodily out of the natural order overnight is evident from the fact that I decided to specialize in eighteenth century English Literature, and to choose my subject for a Master of Arts Thesis from somewhere in that century. As a matter of fact, I had already half decided upon a subject, by the time the last pile of dirty snow had melted from the borders of South Field. It was an unknown novelist of the second half of the eighteenth century called Richard Graves. The most important thing he wrote was a novel called the *Spiritual Quixote,* which was in the Fielding tradition, a satire on the more excited kind of Methodists and other sects of religious enthusiasts in England at that time.

I was to work under Professor Tyndall, and this would have been just his kind of a subject. He was an agnostic and rationalist who took a deep and amused interest in all the strange perversions of the religious instinct that our world has seen in the last five hundred years. He was just finishing a book on D. H. Lawrence which discussed, not too kindly, Lawrence's attempt to build up a synthetic, homemade religion of his own out of all the semi-pagan spiritual jetsam that came his way. All Lawrence's friends were very much annoyed by it when it was published. I remember that in that year one of Tyndall's favorite topics of conversation was the miracles of Mother Cabrini, who had just been beatified. He was amused by these, too, because, as for all rationalists, it was for him an article of faith that miracles cannot happen.

I remember with what indecision I went on into the spring trying to settle the problem of a subject with finality. Yet the thing worked itself out quite suddenly: so suddenly that I do not remember what brought it about. One day I came running down out of the Carpenter Library, and passed along the wire fences by the tennis courts, in the sun, with my mind made up that there was only one possible man in the eighteenth century for me to work on: the one poet who had least to do with his age, and was most in opposition to everything it stood for.

I had just had in my hands the small, neatly printed Nonesuch Press edition of the *Poems of William Blake,* and I now knew what my thesis would probably be. It would take in his poems and some aspect of his religious ideas.

In the Columbia bookstore I bought the same edition of Blake, on credit. (I paid for it two years later.) It had a blue cover, and I suppose it is now hidden somewhere in our monastery library, the part to which nobody has access. And that is all right. I think the ordinary Trappist would be only dangerously bewildered by the "Prophetic Books," and those who still might be able to profit by Blake, have a lot of other things to read that are still better. For my own part, I no longer need him. He has done his work for me: and he did it very thoroughly. I hope that I will see him in heaven.

But oh, what a thing it was to live in contact with the genius and the holiness of William Blake that year, that summer, writing the thesis! I had some beginning of an appreciation of his greatness above the other men of his time in England: but from this distance, from the hill where I now stand, looking back I can really appreciate his stature.

To assimilate him to the men of the ending eighteenth century would be absurd. I will not do it: all those conceited and wordy and stuffy little characters! As for the other romantics: how feeble and hysterical their inspirations seem next to the tremendously genuine and spiritual fire of William Blake. Even Coleridge, in the rare moments when his imagination struck the pitch of true creativeness, was still only an artist, an imaginer, not a seer; a maker, but not a prophet.

Perhaps all the great romantics were capable of putting words together more sensibly than Blake, and yet he, with all his mistakes of spelling, turned out the greater poet, because his was the deeper and more solid inspiration. He wrote better poetry when he was twelve than Shelley wrote in his whole life. And it was because at twelve he had already seen, I think, Elias, standing under a tree in the fields south of London.

It was Blake's problem to try and adjust himself to a society that understood neither him nor his kind of faith and love. More than once, smug and inferior minds conceived it to be their duty to take this man Blake in hand and direct and form him, to try and canalize what they recognized as "talent" in some kind of a conventional channel. And always this meant the cold and heartless disparagement of all that was vital and real to him in art and in faith. There were years of all kinds of petty persecution, from many different quarters, until finally Blake parted from his would-be patrons, and gave up all hope of an alliance with a world that thought he was crazy, and went his own way.

It was when he did this, and settled down as an engraver for good, that the Prophetic Books were no longer necessary. In the latter part of his life, having discovered Dante, he came in contact, through him, with Catholicism, which he described as the only religion that really taught the love of God, and his last years were relatively full of peace. He never seems to

have felt any desire to hunt out a priest in the England where Catholicism was still practically outlawed: but he dies with a blazing face and great songs of joy bursting from his heart.

As Blake worked himself into my system, I became more and more conscious of the necessity of a vital faith, and the total unreality and unsubstantiality of the dead, selfish rationalism which had been freezing my mind and will for the last seven years. By the time the summer was over, I was to become conscious of the fact that the only way to live was to live in a world that was charged with the presence and reality of God.

To say that, is to say a great deal: and I don't want to say it in a way that conveys more than the truth. I will have to limit the statement by saying that it was still, for me, more an intellectual realization than anything else: and it had not yet struck down into the roots of my will. The life of the soul is not knowledge, it is love, since love is the act of the supreme faculty, the will, by which man is formally united to the final end of all his strivings—by which man becomes one with God.

III

On the door of the room in one of the dormitories, where Lax and Sy Freedgood were living in a state of chaos, was a large grey picture, a lithograph print. Its subject was a man, a Hindu, with wide-open eyes and a rather frightened expression, sitting crosslegged in white garments. I asked about it, and I could not figure out whether the answer was derisive or respectful. Lax said someone had thrown a knife at the picture and the knife had bounced back and nearly cut all their heads off. In other words, he gave me to understand that the picture had something intrinsically holy about it: that accounted for the respect and derision manifested towards it by all my friends. This mixture was their standard acknowledgment of the supernatural, or what was considered to be supernatural. How that picture happened to get on that door in that room is a strange story.

It represented a Hindu messiah, a savior sent to India in our own times, called Jagad-Bondhu. His mission had to do with universal peace and brotherhood. He had died not very long before, and had left a strong following in India. He was, as it were, in the role of a saint who had founded a new religious Order, although he was considered more than a saint: he was the latest incarnation of the godhead, according to the Hindu belief in a multiplicity of incarnations.

In 1932 a big official sort of letter was delivered to one of the monasteries of this new "Order," outside of Calcutta. The letter came from the Chicago World's Fair, which was to be held in the following year. How they ever heard of this monastery, I cannot imagine. The letter was a formal announcement of a "World Congress of Religions." I am writing this all from memory but that is the substance of the story: they invited the abbot of this monastery to send a representative to Congress.

I get this picture of the monastery: it is called Sri Angan, meaning "the Playground." It consists of an enclosure and many huts or "cells," to use an Occidental term. The monks are quiet, simple men. They live what we would call a liturgical life, very closely integrated with the cycle of the seasons and of nature: in fact, the chief characteristic of their worship seems to be this deep, harmonious identification with all living things, in praising God. Their praise itself is expressed in songs, accompanied by drums and primitive instruments, flutes, pipes. There is much ceremonial dancing. In addition to that, there is a profound stress laid on a form of "mental prayer" which is largely contemplative. The monk works himself into it, by softly chanting lyrical aspirations to God and then remains in peaceful absorption in the Absolute.

For the rest, their life is extremely primitive and frugal. It is not so much what we would call austere. I do not think there are any fierce penances or mortifications. But nevertheless, the general level of poverty in Hindu society as a whole imposes on these monks a standard of living which most Occidental religious would probably find unlivable. Their clothes consist of a turban and something thrown around the body and a robe. No shoes. Perhaps the robe is only for travelling. Their food—some rice, a few vegetables, a piece of fruit.

Of all that they do, they attach most importance to prayer, to praising God. They have a well-developed sense of the power and efficacy of prayer, based on a keen realization of the goodness of God. Their whole spirituality is childlike, simple, primitive if you like, close to nature, ingenuous, optimistic, happy. But the point is, although it may be no more than the full flowering of the natural virtue of religion, with the other natural virtues, including a powerful natural charity, still the life of these pagan monks is one of such purity and holiness and peace, in the natural order, that it may put to shame the actual conduct of many Christian religious, in spite of their advantages of constant access to all the means of grace.

So this was the atmosphere into which the letter from Chicago dropped like a heavy stone. The abbot was pleased by the letter. He did not know what the Chicago World's Fair was. He did not understand that all these were simply schemes for accumulating money. The "World Congress of Religions" appeared to him as something more than the fatuous scheme of a few restless, though probably sincere, minds. He seemed to see in it the first step towards the realization of the hopes of their beloved messiah, Jagad-Bondhu: world peace, universal brotherhood. Perhaps, now, all religious would unite into one great universal religion, and all men would begin to praise God as brothers, instead of tearing each other to pieces.

At any rate, the abbot selected one of his monks and told him that he was to go to Chicago, to the World Congress of Religions.

This was a tremendous assignment. It was something far more terrible than an order given, for instance, to a newly ordained Capuchin to proceed to a mission in India. That would merely be a matter of a trained missionary going off to occupy a place that had been prepared for him. But here was a little man who had been born at the edge of a jungle told to start out from a contemplative monastery and go not only into the world, but into the heart of a civilization the violence and materialism of which he could scarcely evaluate, and which raised gooseflesh on every square inch of his body. What is more, he was told to undertake this journey *without money*. Not that money was prohibited to him, but they simply did not have any. His abbot managed to raise enough to get him a ticket for a little more than half the distance. After that heaven would have to take care of him.

By the time I met this poor little monk who had come to America without money, he had been living in the country for about five years, and had acquired, of all things, the degree of Doctor of Philosophy from the University of Chicago. So that people referred to him as Doctor Bramachari, although I believe that Bramachari is simply a generic Hindu term for monk—and one that might almost be translated: "Little-Brother-Without-the-Degree-of-Doctor."

How he got through all the red tape that stands between America and the penniless traveller is something that I never quite understood. But it seems that officials, after questioning him, being completely overwhelmed by his simplicity, would either do something dishonest in his favor, or else would give him a tip as to how to beat the various technicalities. Some of them even lent him fairly large sums of money. In any case he landed in America.

The only trouble was that he got to Chicago after the World Congress of Religions was all over.

By that time, one look at the Fair buildings, which were already being torn down, told him all he needed to know about the World Congress of Religions. But once he was there, he did not have much trouble. People would see him standing around in the middle of railway stations waiting for Providence to do something about his plight. They would be intrigued by his turban and white garments (which were partly concealed by a brown overcoat in winter). They observed that he was wearing a pair of sneakers, and perhaps that alone was enough to rouse their curiosity. He was frequently invited to give lectures to religious and social clubs, and to schools and colleges, and he more than once spoke from the pulpits of Protestant churches. In this way he managed to make a living for himself. Besides, he was, always being hospitably entertained by people that he met, and he financed the stages of his journey by artlessly leaving his purse lying open on the living room table, at night, before his departure.

The open mouth of the purse spoke eloquently to the hearts of his hosts, saying: "As you see, I am empty," or, perhaps, "As you see, I am down to my last fifteen cents." It was often enough filled up in the morning. He got around.

How did he run into Sy Freedgood? Well, Seymour's wife was studying at Chicago, and she met Bramachari there, and then Seymour met Bramachari, and Bramachari came to Long Beach once or twice, and went out in Seymour's sailboat, and wrote a poem which he gave to Seymour and Helen. He was very happy with Seymour, because he did not have to answer so many stupid questions and, after all, a lot of the people who befriended him were cranks and semi-maniacs and theosophists who thought they had some kind of a claim on him. They wearied him with their eccentricities, although he was a gentle and patient little man. But at Long Beach he was left in peace, although Seymour's ancient grandmother was not easily convinced that he was not the hereditary enemy of the Jewish people. She moved around in the other room, lighting small religious lamps against the intruder.

It was the end of the school year, June 1938, when Lax and Seymour already had a huge box in the middle of the room, which they were beginning to pack with books, when we heard Bramachari was again coming to New York.

I went down to meet him at Grand Central with Seymour, and it was not without a certain suppressed excitement that I did so, for Seymour had me all primed with a superb selection of lies about Bramachari's ability to float in the air and walk on water. It was a long time before we found him in the crowd, although you would think that a Hindu in a turban and a white robe and a pair of Keds would have been a rather memorable sight. But all the people we asked, concerning such a one, had no idea of having seen him.

We had been looking around for ten or fifteen minutes, when a cat came walking cautiously through the crowd, and passed us by with a kind of a look, and disappeared.

"That's him," said Seymour. "He changed himself into a cat. Doesn't like to attract attention. Looking the place over. Now he knows we're here."

Almost at once, while Seymour was asking a porter if he had seen anything like Bramachari, and the porter was saying no, Bramachari came up behind us.

I saw Seymour swing around and say, in his rare, suave manner: "Ah, Bramachari, how are you!"

There stood a shy little man, very happy, with a huge smile, all teeth, in the midst of his brown face. And on the top of his head was a yellow turban with Hindu prayers written all over it in red. And, on his feet, sure enough: sneakers.

I shook hands with him, still worrying lest he give me some kind of an electric shock. But he didn't. We rode up to Columbia in the subway, with all the people goggling at us, and I was asking Bramachari about all the colleges he had been visiting. Did he like Smith, did he like Harvard? When we were coming out into the air at 116th Street, I asked him which one he liked best, and he told me that they were all the same to him: it had never occurred to him that one might have any special preference in such things.

I lapsed into a reverent silence and pondered on this thought.

I was now twenty-three years old and, indeed, I was more mature than that in some respects. Surely by now it ought to have dawned on me that places did not especially matter. But no, I was very much attached to places, and had very definite likes and dislikes for localities as such, especially colleges, since I was always thinking of finding one that was altogether pleasant to live and teach in.

After that, I became very fond of Bramachari, and he of me. We got along very well together, especially since he sensed that I was trying to feel my way into a settled religious conviction, and into some kind of a life that was centered, as his was, on God.

The thing that strikes me now is that he never attempted to explain his own religious beliefs to me—except some of the externals of the cult, and that was later on. He would no doubt have told me all I wanted to know, if I had asked him, but I was not curious enough. What was most valuable to me was to hear his evaluation of the society and religious beliefs he had come across in America: and to put all that down on paper would require another book.

He was never sarcastic, never ironical or unkind in his criticisms: in fact he did not make many judgements at all, especially adverse ones. He would simply make statements of fact, and then burst out laughing—his laughter was quiet and ingenuous, and it expressed his complete amazement at the very possibility that people should live the way he saw them living all around him.

He was beyond laughing at the noise and violence of American city life and all the obvious lunacies like radio-programs and billboard advertising. It was some of the well-meaning idealisms that he came across that struck him as funny. And one of the things that struck him as funniest of all was the eagerness with which Protestant ministers used to come up and ask him if India was by now nearly converted to Protestantism. He used to tell us how far India was from conversion to Protestantism—or Catholicism for that matter. One of the chief reasons he gave for the failure of any Christian missionaries to really strike deep into the tremendous populations of Asia was the fact that they maintained themselves on a social level that was too far above the natives. The Church of England, indeed, thought they would convert the Indians by maintaining a strict separation—white men in one church, natives in a different church: both of them listening to sermons on brotherly love and unity.

But all Christians missionaries, according to him, suffered from this big drawback: they lived too well, too comfortably. They took care of themselves in a way that simply made it impossible for the Hindus to regard them as holy—let alone the fact that they ate meat, which made them repugnant to the natives.

I don't know anything about missionaries: but I am sure that, by our own standards of living, their life is an arduous and difficult one, and certainly not one that could be regarded as comfortable. And by comparison with life in Europe and America it represents a tremendous sacrifice. Yet I suppose it would literally endanger their lives if they tried to subsist on the standard of living with which the vast majority of Asiatics have to be content. It seems hard to expect them to go around barefoot and sleep on mats and live in huts. But one thing is certain: the pagans have their own notions of holiness, and it is one that includes a prominent element of asceticism. According to Bramachari, the prevailing impression among the Hindus seems to be that Christians don't know what asceticism means. Of course, he was talking principally of Protestant missionaries, but I suppose it would apply to anyone coming to a tropical climate from one of the so-called "civilized" countries.

For my own part, I see no reason for discouragement. Bramachari was simply saying something that has long since been familiar to readers of the Gospels. Unless the grain of wheat, falling in the ground, die, itself remaineth alone: but if it die, it bringeth forth much fruit. The Hindus are not looking for us to send them men who will build schools and hospitals, although those things are good and useful in themselves—and perhaps very badly needed in India: they want to know if we have any saints to send them.

There is no doubt in my mind that plenty of our missionaries are saints: and that they are capable of becoming greater saints too. And that is all that is needed. And, after all, St. Francis Xavier converted hundreds of thousands of Hindus in the sixteenth century and established Christian societies in Asia strong enough to survive for several centuries without any material support from outside the Catholic world.

Bramachari was not telling me anything I did not know about the Church of England, or about the other Protestant sects he had come in contact with. But I was interested to hear his opinion of the Catholics. They, of course, had not invited him to preach in their pulpits: but he had gone into a few Catholic churches out of curiosity. He told me that these were the only ones in which he really felt that people were praying.

It was only there that religion seemed to have achieved any degree of vitality, among us, as far as he could see. It was only to Catholics that the love of God seemed to be a matter of real concern, something that struck deep in their natures, not merely pious speculation and sentiment.

However, when he described his visit to a big Benedictine monastery in the Mid-West he began to grin again. He said they had showed him a lot of work-shops and machinery and printing presses and taken him over the whole "plant" as if they were very wrapped up in all their buildings and enterprises. He got the impression that they were more absorbed in printing and writing and teaching than they were in praying.

Bramachari was not the kind of man to be impressed with such statements as: "There's a quarter of a million dollars' worth of stained glass in this church . . .the organ has got six banks of keys and it contains drums, bells and a mechanical nightingale . . . and the retable is a genuine bas-relief by a real live Italian artist."

The people he had the least respect for were all the borderline cases, the strange, eccentric sects, the Christian Scientists, the Oxford Group and all the rest of them. That was, in a sense, very comforting. Not that I was worried about them: but it confirmed me in my respect for him.

He did not generally put his words in the form of advice: but the one counsel he did give me is some-thing that I will not easily forget: "There are many beautiful mystical books written by the Christians. You should read St. Augustine's *Confessions,* and *The Imitation of Christ.*"

Of course I had heard of both of them: but he was speaking as if he took it for granted that most people in America had no idea that such books ever existed. He seemed to feel as if he were in possession of a truth that would come to most Americans as news—as if there was something in their own cultural heritage that they had long since forgotten: and he could remind them of it. He repeated what he had said, not without a certain earnestness:

"Yes, you must read those books."

It was not often that he spoke with this kind of emphasis.

Now that I look back on those days, it seems to me very probable that one of the reasons why God had brought him all the way from India, was that he might say just that.

After all, it is rather ironical that I had turned, spon-taneously to the east, in reading about mysticism, as if there were little or nothing in the Christian tradition. I remember that I ploughed through those heavy tomes of Father Wieger's with the feeling that all this represented the highest development of religion on earth. The reason may have been that I came away from Hexley's *Ends and Means* with the prejudice that Christianity was a less pure religion, because it was more "immersed in matter"—that is, because it did not corn to use a Sacramental liturgy that relied on the appeal of created things to the senses in order to raise the souls of men to higher things.

So now I was told that I ought to turn to the Christian tradition, to St. Augustine—and told by a Hindu monk!

Still, perhaps if he had never given me that piece of advice, I would have ended up in the Fathers of the Church and Scholasticism after all: because a fortunate discovery in the course of my work on my M.A. thesis put me fairly and definitely on that track at last.

That discovery was one book that untied all the knots in the problem which I had set myself to solve by my thesis. It was Jacques Maritain's *Art and Scholasticism.*

IV

The last week of that school year at Columbia had been rather chaotic. Lax and Freedgood had been making futile efforts to get their belongings together and go home. Bramachari was living in their room, perched on top of a pile of books. Lax was trying to finish a novel for Professor Nobbe's course in novel-writing, and all his friends had volunteered to take a section of the book and write it, simultaneously: but in the end the book turned out to be more or less a three-cornered affair—by Lax and me and Dona Eaton. When Nobbe got the thing in his hands he could not figure it out at all, but he gave us a B-minus, with which we were more than satisfied.

Then Lax's mother had come to town to live near him in the last furious weeks before graduation and catch him if he collapsed. He had to take most of his meals in the apartment she had rented in Butler Hall. I sometimes went along and helped him nibble the various health-foods.

At the same time, we were planning to get a ride on an oil barge up the Hudson and the Erie Canal to Buffalo—because Lax's brother-in-law was in the oil business. After that we would go to the town where Lax lived, which was Olean, up in that corner of New York state.

On "Class Day" we leaned out the window of Lax's room and drank a bottle of champagne, looking at the sun on South Field, and watching the people beginning to gather under the trees in front of Hamilton, where we would all presently hear some speeches and shake hands with Nicholas Murray Butler.

It was not my business to graduate that June at all. My graduation was all over when I picked up my degree in the registrar's office last February. However,

I borrowed the cap and gown with which Dona Eaton had graduated from Barnard a year before, and went and sat with all the rest, mocking the speeches, the edge of my sobriety slightly dulled by the celebration that had just taken place with the champagne in Furnald.

Finally we all got up and filed slowly up the rickety wooden steps to the temporary platform to shake hands with all the officials. President Butler was a much smaller man than I had expected. He looked intensely miserable, and murmured something or other to each student, as he shook hands. It was inaudible. I was given to understand that for the past six or seven years people had been in the habit of insulting him, on these occasions, as a kind of a farewell.

I didn't say anything. I just shook his hand, and passed on. The next one I came to was Dean Hawkes who looked up with surprise, from under his bushy white eyebrows, and growled:

"What are you doing here, anyway?"

I smiled and passed on.

We did not get the ride on the oil barge, after all, but went to Olean on a train, and for the first time I saw a part of the world in which I was one day going to learn how to be very happy—and that day was not now very far away.

It is the association of that happiness which makes upper New York state seem, in my memory, to be so beautiful. But it is objectively so, there is no doubt of that. Those deep valleys and miles and miles of high, rolling wooded hills: the broad fields, the big red barns, the white farm houses and the peaceful towns: all this looked more and more impressive and fine in the long slanting rays of the sinking sun after we had passed Elmira.

And you began to get some of the feeling of the bigness of America, and to develop a continental sense of the scope of the country and of the vast, clear sky, as the train went on for mile after mile, and hour after hour. And the color, and freshness, and bigness, and richness of the land! The cleanness of it. The wholesomeness. This was new and yet it was old country. It was mellow country. It has been cleared and settled for much more than a hundred years.

When we got out at Olean, we breathed its health and listened to its silence.

I did not stay there for more than a week, being impatient to get back to New York on account of being, as usual, in love.

But one of the things we happened to do was to turn off the main road, one afternoon on the way to the Indian reservation, to look at the plain brick buildings of a college that was run by the Franciscans.

It was called St. Bonaventure's. Lax had a good feeling about the place. And his mother was always taking courses there, in the evenings—courses in literature from the Friars. He was a good friend of the Father Librarian and liked the library. We drove in to the grounds and stopped by one of the buildings.

But when Lax tried to make me get out of the car, I would not.

"Let's get out of here," I said.

"Why? It's a nice place."

"It's O.K., but let's get out of here. Let's go to the Indian reservation."

"Don't you want to see the library?"

"I can't see enough of it from here. Let's get going."

I don't know what was the matter. Perhaps I was scared of the thought of nuns and priests being all around me—the elemental fear of the citizen of hell, in the presence of anything that savors of the religious life, religious vows, official dedication to God through Christ. Too many crosses. Too many holy statues. Too much quiet and cheerfulness. Too much pious optimism. It made me very uncomfortable. I had to flee.

When I got back to New York, one of the first things I did was to break away, at last, from the household in Douglaston. The family had really practically dissolved with the death of my grandparents, and I could get a lot more work done if I did not have to spend so much time on subways and the Long Island train.

One rainy day in June, then, I made a bargain with Herb, the colored taximan at Douglaston, and he drove me and all my bags and books and my portable vic and all my hot records and pictures to put on the wall and even a tennis racquet which I never used, uptown to a rooming house on 114th Street, just behind the Columbia library.

All the way up we discussed the possible reasons for the mysterious death of Rudolph Valentino, once a famous movie star: but it was certainly not what you would call a live issue. Valentino had died at least ten years before.

"This is a nice spot you got here," said Herb, approving of the room I was renting for seven fifty a week. It was shiny and clean and filled with new furniture and had a big view of a pile of coal, in a yard by the campus tennis courts, with South Field and the steps of the old domed library beyond. The panorama even took in a couple of trees.

"I guess you're going to have a pretty hot time, now you got away from your folks," Herb remarked, as he took his leave.

Whatever else may have happened in that room, it was also there that I started to pray again more or less regularly, and it was there that I added, as Bramachari had suggested, *The Imitation of Christ* to my books, and it was from there that I was eventually to be driven out by an almost physical push, to go and look for a priest.

July came, with it great, misty heats, and Columbia filled with all the thousands of plump, spectacled ladies in pink dresses, from the Middle-West, and all the grey gents in seersucker suits, all the dried-up high-school principals from Indiana and Kansas and Iowa and Tennessee, with their veins shrivelled up with positivism and all the reactions of the behaviorist flickering behind their spectacles as they meditated on the truths they learned in those sweltering halls.

The books piled higher and higher on my desk in the Graduate reading room and in my own lodgings. I was in the thick of my thesis, making hundreds of mistakes that I would not be able to detect for several years to come, because I was far out of my depth. Fortunately, nobody else detected them either. But for my own part, I was fairly happy, and learning many things. The discipline of the work itself was good for me, and helped to cure me, more than anything else did, of the illusion that my health was poor.

And it was in the middle of all this that I discovered Scholastic philosophy.

The subject I had finally chosen was "Nature and Art in William Blake." I did not realize how providential a subject it actually was! What it amounted to, was a study of Blake's reaction against every kind of literalism and naturalism and narrow, classical realism in art, because of his own ideal which was essentially mystical and supernatural. In other words, the topic, if I treated it at all sensible, could not help but cure me of all the naturalism and materialism in my own philosophy, besides resolving all the inconsistencies and self-contradictions that had persisted in my mind for years, without my being able to explain them.

After all, from my very childhood, I had understood that the artistic experience, at its highest, was actually a natural analogue of mystical experience. It produced a kind of intuitive perception of reality through a sort of affective identification with the object contemplated—the kind of perception that the Thomists call "connatural." This means simply a knowledge that comes about as it were by the identification of natures: in the way that a chaste man understands the nature of chastity because of the very fact that his soul is full of it—it is a part of his own nature, since habit is second nature. Non-connatural knowledge of chastity would be that of a philosopher who, to borrow the language of the *Imitation*, would be able to define it, but would not possess it.

I had learned from my own father that it was almost blasphemy to regard the function of art as merely to reproduce some kind of a sensible pleasure or, at best, to stir up the emotions to a transitory thrill. I had always understood that art was contemplation, and that it involved the action of the highest faculties of man.

When I was once able to discover the key to Blake, in his rebellion against literalism and naturalism in art, I saw that his Prophetic Books and the rest of his verse at large represented a rebellion against naturalism in the moral order as well.

What a revelation that was! For at sixteen I had imagined that Blake, like the other romantics, was glorifying passion, natural energy, for their own sake. Far from it! What he was glorifying was the transfiguration of man's natural love, his natural powers, in the refining fires of mystical experience: and that, in itself, implied an arduous and total purification, by faith and love and desire, from all the petty materialistic and commonplace and earthly ideals of his rationalistic friends.

Blake, in his sweeping consistency, had developed a moral insight that cut through all the false distinctions of a worldly and interested morality. That was why he saw that, in the legislation of men, some evils had been set up as standards of right by which other evils were to be condemned: and the norms of pride or greed had been established in the judgement seat, to pronounce a crushing and inhuman indictment against all the normal healthy strivings of human nature. Love was outlawed, and became lust, pity was swallowed up on cruelty, and so Blake knew how:

The harlot's cry from street to street
Shall weave old England's winding sheet.

I had heard that cry and the echo. I had seen that winding sheet. But I had understood nothing of all that. I had tried to resolve it into a matter of sociological laws, of economic forces. If I had been able to listen to Blake in those old days, he would have told me that sociology and economics, divorced from faith and charity, become nothing but the chains of his aged, icy demon Urizen! But now, reading Maritain, in connection with Blake, I saw all these difficulties and contradictions disappear.

I, who had always been anti-naturalistic in art, had been a pure naturalist in the moral order. No wonder my soul was sick and torn apart: but now the bleeding wound was drawn together by the notion of Christian virtue, ordered to the union of the soul with God.

The word virtue: what a fate it has had in the last three hundred years! The fact that it is nowhere near so despised and ridiculed in Latin countries is a testimony to the fact that it suffered mostly from the mangling it underwent at the hands of Calvinists and Puritans. In our own days the word leaves on the lips of cynical high-school children a kind of flippant smear, and it is exploited in theaters for the possibilities it offers for lewd and cheesy sarcasm. Everybody makes fun of virtue, which now has, as its primary meaning, an affection of prudery practiced by hypocrites and the impotent.

When Maritian—who is by no means bothered by such trivialities—in all simplicity went ahead to use the term in its Scholastic sense, and was able to apply it to art, a "virtue of the practical intellect," the very newness of the context was enough to disinfect my mind of all the miasmas left in it by the ordinary prejudice against "virtue" which, if it was ever strong in anybody, was strong in me. I was never a lover of Puritanism. Now at last I came around to the sane conception of virtue—without which there can be no happiness, because virtues are precisely the powers by which we can come to acquire happiness: without them, there can be no joy, because they are the habits which coordinate and canalize our natural energies and direct them to the harmony and perfection and balance, the unity of our nature with itself and with God, which must, in the end, constitute our everlasting peace.

By the time I was ready to begin the actual writing of my thesis, that is, around the beginning of September 1938, the groundwork of conversion was more or less complete. And how easily and sweetly it had all been done, with all the external graces that had been arranged, along my path, by the kind Providence of God! It had taken little more than a year and a half, counting from the time I read Gilson's *The Spirit of Medieval Philosophy* to bring me up from an "atheist"—as I considered myself—to one who accepted all the full range and possibilities of religious experience right up to the highest degree of glory.

I not only accepted all this, intellectually, but now I began to desire it. And not only did I begin to desire it, but I began to do so efficaciously: I began to want to take the necessary means to achieve this union, this peace. I began to desire to dedicate my life to God, to His service. The notion was still vague and obscure, and it was ludicrously impractical in the sense that I was already dreaming of mystical union when I did not even keep the simplest rudiments of the moral law. But nevertheless I was convinced of the reality of the goal, and confident that it could be achieved: and whatever element of presumption was in this confidence I am sure God excused, in His mercy, because of my stupidity and helplessness, and because I was really beginning to be ready to do whatever I thought He wanted me to do to bring me to Him.

But, oh, how blind and weak and sick I was, although I thought I saw where I was going, and half understood the way! How deluded we sometimes are by the clear notions we get out of books. They make us think that we really understand things of which we have no practical knowledge at all. I remember how learnedly and enthusiastically I could talk for hours about mysticism and the experimental knowledge of God, and all the while I was stoking the fires of the argument with Scotch and soda.

That was the way it turned out that Labor Day, for instance. I went to Philadelphia with Joe Roberts, who had a room in the same house as I, and who had been through all the battles on the Fourth Floor of John Jay for the past four years. He had graduated and was working on some trade magazine about women's hats. All one night we sat, with a friend of his, in a big dark roadhouse outside of Philadelphia, arguing and arguing about mysticism, and smoking more and more cigarettes and gradually getting drunk. Eventually, filled with enthusiasm for the purity of heart which begets the vision of God, I went on with them into the city, after the closing of the bars, to a big speak-easy where we completed the work of getting plastered.

My internal contradictions were resolving themselves out, indeed, but still only on the plane of theory, not of practice: not for lack of good-will, but because I was still so completely chained and fettered by my sins and my attachments.

I think that if there is one truth that people need to learn, in the world, especially today, it is this: the intellect is only theoretically independent of desire and appetite in ordinary, actual practice. It is constantly being blinded and perverted by the ends and aims of passion, and the evidence it presents to us with such a show of impartiality and objectivity is fraught with interest and propaganda. We have become marvelous at self-delusion; all the more so, because we have gone to such trouble to convince ourselves of our own absolute infallibility. The desires of the flesh—and by that I mean not only sinful desires, but even the ordinary, normal appetites for comfort and ease and human respect, are fruitful sources of every kind of error and misjudgment, and because we have these yearnings in us, our intellects (which, if they operated all alone in a vacuum, would indeed register with pure impartiality what they saw) present to us everything distorted and accommodated to the norms of our desire.

And therefore, even when we are acting with the best of intentions, and imagine that we are doing great good, we may be actually doing tremendous material harm and contradicting all our good intentions. There are ways that seem to men to be good, the end whereof is in the depths of hell.

The only answer to the problem is grace, grace, docility to grace. I was still in the precarious position of being my own guide and my own interpreter of grace. It is a wonder I ever got to the harbor at all!

Sometime in August, I finally answered an impulsion that had been working on me for a long time. Every Sunday, I had been going out on Long Island to spend the day with the same girl who had brought me back in such a hurry from Lax's town Olean. But every week, as Sunday came around, I was filled with a growing desire to stay in the city and go to some kind of a church.

At first, I had vaguely thought I might try to find some Quakers, and go and sit with them. There still remained in me something of the favorable notion about Quakers that I had picked up as a child, and which the reading of William Penn had not been able to overcome.

But, naturally enough, with the work I was doing in the library, a stronger drive began to assert itself, and I was drawn much more imperatively to the Catholic Church. Finally the urge became so strong that I could not resist it. I called up my girl and told her that I was not coming out that weekend, and made up my mind to go to Mass for the first time in my life.

The first time in my life! That was true. I had lived for several years on the continent, I had been to Rome, I had been in and out of a thousand Catholic cathedrals and churches, and yet I had never heard Mass. If anything had ever been going on in the churches I visited, I had always fled, in wild Protestant panic.

I will not easily forget how I felt that day. First, there was this sweet, strong, gentle, clean urge in me which said: "Go to Mass! Go to Mass!" It was something quite new and strange, this voice that seemed to prompt me, this firm, growing interior conviction of what I needed to do. It had a suavity, a simplicity about it that I could not easily account for. And when I gave in to it, it did not exult over me, and trample me down in its raging haste to land on its prey, but it carried me forward serenely and with purposeful direction.

That does not mean that my emotions yielded to it altogether quietly. I was really still a little afraid to go to a Catholic church, of set purpose, with all the other people, and dispose myself in a pew, and lay myself open to the mysterious perils of that strange and powerful thing they called their "Mass."

God made it a very beautiful Sunday. And since it was the first time I had ever really spent a sober Sunday in New York, I was surprised at the clean, quiet atmosphere of the empty streets uptown. The sun was blazing bright. At the end of the street, as I came out the front door, I could see a burst of green, and the blue river and the hills of Jersey on the other side.

Broadway was empty. A solitary trolley came speeding down in front of Barnard College and past the School of Journalism. Then, from the high, grey, expensive tower of the Rockefeller Church, huge bells began to boom. It served very well for the eleven o'clock Mass at the little brick Church of Corpus Christi, hidden behind Teachers College on 121st Street.

How bright the little building seemed. Indeed, it was quite new. The sun shone on the clean bricks. People were going in the wide, open door, into the cool darkness and, all at once, all the churches of Italy and France came back to me. The richness and fulness of the atmosphere of Catholicism that I had not been able to avoid apprehending and loving as a child, came back to me with a rush: but now I was to enter into it fully for the first time. So far, I had known nothing but the outward surface.

It was a gay, clean church, with big plain windows and white columns and pilasters and a well-lighted, simple sanctuary. Its style was a trifle eclectic, but much less perverted with incongruities than the average Catholic church in America. It had a kind of a seventeenth-century, oratorian character about it, though with a sort of American colonial tinge of simplicity. The blend was effective and original: but although all this affected me, without my thinking about it, the thing that impressed me most was that the place was full, absolutely full. It was full not only of old ladies and broken-down gentlemen with one foot in the grave, but of men and women and children young and old—especially young: people of all classes, and all ranks on a solid foundation of workingmen and women and their families.

I found a place that I hoped would be obscure, over on one side, in the back, and went to it without genuflecting, and knelt down. As I knelt, the first thing I noticed was a young girl, very pretty too, perhaps fifteen or sixteen, kneeling straight up and praying quite seriously. I was very much impressed to see that someone who was young and beautiful could with such simplicity make prayer the real and serious and principal reason for going to church. She was clearly kneeling that way because she meant it, not in order to show off, and she was praying with an absorption which, though not the deep recollection of a saint, was serious enough to show that she was not thinking at all about the other people who were there.

What a revelation it was, to discover so many ordinary people in a place together, more conscious of God than of one another: not there to show off their hats or their clothes, but to pray, or at least to fulfil a religious obligation, not a human one. For even those who might have been there for no better motive than that they were obliged to be, were at least free from any of the self-conscious and human constraint which is never absent from a Protestant church where people are definitely gathered together as people, as neighbors, and always have at least half an eye for one another, if not all of both eyes.

Since it was summer time, the eleven o'clock Mass was a Low Mass: but I had not come expecting to hear music. Before I knew it, the priest was in the sanctuary with the two altar boys, and was busy at the altar with something or other which I could not see very well, but the people were praying by themselves, and I was engrossed and absorbed in the thing as a whole: the business at the altar and the presence of the people. And still I had not got rid of my fear. Seeing the latecomers hastily genuflecting before entering the pew, I realised my omission, and got the idea that people had spotted me for a pagan and were just waiting for me to miss a few more genuflections before throwing me out or, at least, giving me looks of reproof.

Soon we all stood up. I did not know what it was for. The priest was at the other end of the altar, and, as I afterwards learned, he was reading the Gospel. And the next thing I knew there was someone in the pulpit.

It was a young priest, perhaps not much over thirty-three or -four years old. His face was rather ascetic and thin, and its asceticism was heightened with a note of intellectuality by his horn-rimmed glasses, although he was only one of the assistants, and he did not consider himself an intellectual, nor did anyone else apparently consider him so. But anyway, that was the impression he made on me: and his sermon, which was simple enough, did not belie it.

It was not long: but to me it was very interesting to hear this young man quietly telling the people in language that was plain, yet tinged with scholastic terminology, about a point in Catholic Doctrine. How clear and solid the doctrine was: for behind those words you felt the full force not only of Scripture but of centuries of a unified and continuous and consistent tradition. And above all, it was a vital tradition: there was nothing studied or antique about it. These words, this terminology, this doctrine, and these convictions fell from the lips of the young priest as something that were most intimately part of his own life. What was more, I sensed that the people were familiar with it all, and that it was also, in due proportion, part of their life also: it was just as much integrated into their spiritual organism as the air they breathed or the food they ate worked in to their blood and flesh.

What was he saying? That Christ was the Son of God. That, in Him, the Second Person of the Holy Trinity, God, had assumed a Human Nature, a Human Body and Soul, and had taken Flesh and dwelt amongst us, full of grace and truth: and that this Man, Whom men called the Christ, was God. He was both Man and God: two natures hypostatically united in one Person or suppositum, one individual Who was a Divine Person, having assumed to Himself a Human Nature. And His works were the works of God: His acts were the acts of God. He loved us: God, and walked among us: God, and died for us on the cross, God of God, Light of Light, True God of True God.

Jesus Christ was not simply a man, a good man, a great man, the greatest prophet, a wonderful healer, a saint: He was something that made all such trivial words pale into irrelevance. He was God. But nevertheless He was not merely a spirit without a true body, God hiding under a visionary body: He was also truly a Man, born of the Flesh of the Most Pure Virgin, formed of her Flesh by the Holy Spirit. And what He did, in that Flesh, on earth, He did not only as Man but as God. He loved us as God, He suffered and died for us, God.

And how did we know? Because it was revealed to us in the Scripture and confirmed by the teaching of the Church and of the powerful unanimity of Catholic Tradition from the First Apostles, from the first Popes and the early Fathers, on down through the Doctors of the Church and the great scholastics, to our own day. *De Fide Divina*. If you believed it, you would receive light to grasp it, to understand it in some measure. If you did not believe it, you would never understand: it would never by anything but scandal or folly.

And no one can believe these things merely by wanting to, of his own violation. Unless he receive grace, an actual light and impulsion of the mind and will from God, he cannot even make an act of living faith. It is God Who gives us faith, and no one cometh to Christ unless the Father draweth him.

I wonder what would have happened in my life if I had been given this grace in the days when I had almost discovered the Divinity of Christ in the ancient mosaics of the churches of Rome. What scores of self-murdering and Christ-murdering sins would have been avoided—all the filth I had plastered upon His image in my soul during those last five years that I had been scourging and crucifying God within me?

It is easy to say, after it all, that God had probably foreseen my infidelities and had never given me the grace in those days because He saw how I would waste and despise it: and perhaps that rejection would have been my ruin. For there is no doubt that one of the reasons why grace is not given to souls is because they have so hardened their wills in greed and cruelty and selfishness that their refusal of it would only harden them more. . . . But now I had been beaten into the semblance of some kind of humility by misery and confusion and perplexity and secret, interior fear, and my ploughed soul was better ground for the reception of good seed.

The sermon was what I most needed to hear that day. When the Mass of the Catechumens was over, I, who was not even a catechumen, but only a blind and deaf and dumb pagan as weak and dirty as anything that ever came out of the darkness of Imperial Rome, or Corinth or Ephesus, was not able to understand anything else.

It all became completely mysterious when the attention was refocussed on the altar. When the silence grew more and more profound, and little bells began to ring, I got scared again and, finally, genuflecting hastily on my left knee, I hurried out of the church in the middle of the most important part of the Mass. But it was just as well. In a way, I suppose I was responding to a kind of liturgical instinct that told me I did not belong there for the celebration of the Mysteries as such. I had no idea what took place in them: but the fact was that Christ, God, would be visibly present on the altar in the Sacred Species. And although He was there, yes, for love of me: yet He was there in His power and His might, and what was I? What was on my soul? What was I in His sight?

It was liturgically fitting that I should kick myself out at the end of the Mass of the Catechumens, when the ordained *ostiarii* should have been there to do it. Anyway, it was done.

Now I walked leisurely down Broadway in the sun, and my eyes looked about me at a new world. I could not understand what it was that had happened to make me so happy, why I was so much at peace, so content with life for I was not yet used to the clean savor that comes with an actual grace—indeed, there was no impossibility in a person's hearing and believing such a sermon and being justified, that is, receiving sanctifying grace in his soul as a habit, and beginning, from that moment, to live the divine and supernatural life for good and all. But that is something I will not speculate about.

All I know is that I walked in a new world. Even the ugly buildings of Columbia were transfigured in it, and everywhere was peace in these streets designed for violence and noise. Sitting outside the gloomy little Childs restaurant at 111th Street, behind the dirty, boxed bushes, and eating breakfast, was like sitting in the Elysian Fields.

V

My reading became more and more Catholic. I became absorbed in the poetry of Hopkins and in his notebooks—that poetry which had only impressed me a little six years before. Now, too, I was deeply interested in Hopkins' life as a Jesuit. What was that life? What did the Jesuits do? What did a priest do? How did he live? I scarcely knew where to begin to find out about all such things: but they had started to exercise a mysterious attraction over me.

And here is a strange thing. I had by now read James Joyce's *Ulysses* twice or three times. Six years before— on one of those winter vacations in Strasbourg—I had tried to read *Portrait of the Artist* and had bogged down in the part about his spiritual crisis. Something about it had discouraged, bored and depressed me. I did not want to read about such a thing: and I finally dropped it in the middle of the "Mission." Strange to say, sometime during this summer—I think it was before the first time I went to Corpus Christi—I reread *Portrait of the Artist* and was fascinated precisely by that part of the book, by the "Mission," by the priest's sermon on hell. What impressed me was not the fear of hell, but the expertness of the sermon. Now, instead of being repelled by the thought of such preaching—which was perhaps the author's intention—I was stimulated and edified by it. The style in which the priest in the book talked, pleased me by its efficiency and solidity and drive: and once again there was something eminently satisfying in the thought that these Catholics knew what they believed, and knew what to teach, and all taught the same thing, and taught it with coordination and purpose and great effect. It was this that struck me first of all, rather than the actual subject matter of their doctrine—until, that is, I heard the sermon at Corpus Christi.

So then I continued to read Joyce, more and more fascinated by the pictures of priests and Catholic life that came up here and there in his books. That, I am sure, will strike many people as a strange thing indeed. I think Joyce himself was only interested in rebuilding the Dublin he had known as objectively and vitally as he could. He was certainly very alive to all the faults in Irish Catholic society, and he had practically no sympathy left for the Church he had abandoned: but in his intense loyalty to the vocation of artist for which he had abandoned it (and the two vocations are not *per se* irreconcilable: they only became so because of peculiar subjective circumstances in Joyce's own case) he meant to be as accurate as he could in rebuilding his world as it truly was.

Therefore, reading Joyce, I was moving in his Dublin, and breathing the air of its physical and spiritual slums: and it was not the most Catholic side of Dublin that he always painted. But in the background was the Church, and its priests, and its devotions, and the Catholic life in all its gradations, from the Jesuits down to those who barely clung to the hem of the Church's garments. And it was this background that fascinated me now, along with the temper of Thomism that had once been in Joyce himself. If he had abandoned St. Thomas, he had not stepped much further down than Aristotle.

Then, of course, I was reading the metaphysical poets once again—especially Crashaw—and studying his life, too, and his conversion. That meant another avenue which led more or less directly to the Jesuits. So in the late August of 1938, and September of that year, my life began to be surrounded, interiorly, by Jesuits. They were the symbols of my new respect for the vitality and coordination of the Catholic Apostolate. Perhaps, in the back of my mind, was my greatest Jesuit hero: the glorious Father Rothschild of Evelyn Waugh's *Vile Bodies,* who plotted with all the diplomats, and rode away into the night on a motorcycle when everybody else was exhausted.

Yet with all this, I was not ready to stand beside the font. There was not even any interior debate as to whether I ought to become a Catholic. I was content to stand by and admire. For the rest, I remember one afternoon, when my girl had come in to town to see me, and we were walking around the streets uptown, I subjected her to the rather disappointing entertainment of going to Union Theological Seminary, and asking for a catalogue of their courses which I proceeded to read while we were walking around on Riverside Drive. She was not openly irritated by it: she was a very good and patient girl anyway. But still you could see she was a little bored, walking around with a man who was not sure whether he ought to enter a theological seminary.

There was nothing very attractive in that catalogue. I was to get much more excited by the article on the Jesuits in the *Catholic Encyclopaedia*—breathless with the thought of so many novitiates and tertianship and what not—so much scrutiny, so much training. What monsters of efficiency they must be, these Jesuits, I kept thinking to myself, as I read and reread the article. And perhaps, from time to time, I tried to picture myself with my face sharpened by asceticism, its pallor intensified by contrast with a black cassock, and every line of it proclaiming a Jesuit saint, a Jesuit master-mind. And I think the master-mind element was one of the strongest features of this obscure attraction.

Apart from this foolishness, I came no nearer to the Church, in practice, than adding a "Hail Mary" to my night prayers. I did not even go to Mass again, at once. The following weekend I went to see my girl once again; it was probably after that that I went on the expedition to Philadelphia. It took something that belongs to history to form and vitalize these resolutions that were still only vague and floating entities in my mind and will.

One of those hot evenings at the end of summer the atmosphere of the city suddenly became terribly tense with some news that came out of the radios. Before I knew what the news was, I began to feel the tension. For I was suddenly aware that the quiet, disparate murmurs of different radios in different houses had imperceptibly merged into one big, ominous unified voice, that moved at you from different directions and followed you down the street, and came to you from another angle as soon as you began to recede from any one of its particular sources.

I heard "Germany—Hitler—at six o'clock this morning the German Army . . . the Nazis . . ." What had they done?

Then Joe Roberts came in and said there was about to be a war. The Germans had occupied Czechoslovakia, and there was bound to be a war.

The city felt as if one of the doors of hell had been half opened, and a blast of its breath had flared out to wither up the spirits of men. And people were loitering around the newsstands in misery.

Joe Roberts and I sat in my room, where there was no radio, until long after midnight, drinking canned beer and smoking cigarettes, and making silly and excited jokes but, within a couple of days, the English Prime Minister had flown in a big hurry to see Hitler and had made a nice new alliance at Munich that cancelled everything that might have caused a war, and returned to England. He alighted at Croydon and came stumbling out of the plane saying "Peace in our time!"

I was very depressed. I was beyond thinking about the intricate and filthy political tangle that underlay the mess. I had given up politics as more or less hopeless, by this time. I was no longer interested in having any opinion about the movement and interplay of forces which were all more or less iniquitous and corrupt, and it was far too laborious and uncertain a business to try and find out some degree of truth and justice in all the loud, artificial claims that were put forward by the various sides.

All I could see was a world in which everybody said they hated war, and in which we were all being rushed into a war with a momentum that was at last getting dizzy enough to affect my stomach. All the internal contradictions of the society in which I lived were at last beginning to converge upon its heart. There could not be much more of a delay in its dismembering. Where would it end? In those days, the future was obscured, blanked out by war as by a dead-end wall. Nobody knew if anyone at all would come out of it alive.

Who would be worse off, the civilians or the soldiers? The distinction between their fates was to be abolished, in most countries, by aerial warfare, by all the new planes, by all the marvelous new bombs. What would the end of it be?

I knew that I myself hated war, and all the motives that led to war and were behind wars. But I could see that now my likes or dislikes, beliefs or disbeliefs meant absolutely nothing in the external, political order. I was just an individual, and the individual had ceased to count. I meant nothing, in this world, except that I would probably soon become a number on the list of those to be drafted. I would get a piece of metal with my number on it, to hand around my neck, so as to help out the circulation of red-tape that would necessarily follow the disposal of my remains, and that would be the last eddy of mental activity that would close over my lost identity.

The whole business was so completely unthinkable that my mind, like almost all the other minds that were in the same situation, simply stopped trying to cope with it, and refixed its focus on the ordinary routine of life.

I had my thesis to type out, and a lot of books to read, and I was thinking of preparing an article on Crashaw which perhaps I would send to T. S. Eliot for his *Criterion*. I did not know that *Criterion* had printed its last issue, and that Eliot's reaction to the situation that so depressed me was to fold up his magazine.

The days went on and the radios returned to their separate and individual murmuring, not to be regimented back into their appalling shout for yet another year. September, as I think, must have been more than half gone.

I borrowed Father Leahy's life of Hopkins from the library. It was a rainy day. I had been working in the library in the morning. I had gone to buy a thirty-five-cent lunch at one of those little pious kitchens on Broadway—the one where Professor Gerig, of the graduate school of French, sat daily in silence over a very small table, eating his Brussels sprouts. Later in the afternoon, perhaps about four, I would have to go down to Central Park West and give a Latin lesson to a youth who was sick in bed, and who ordinarily came to the tutoring school run by my landlord, on the ground floor of the house where I lived.

I walked back to my room. The rain was falling gently on the empty tennis courts across the street, and the huge old domed library stood entrenched in its own dreary greyness, arching a cyclops eyebrow at South Field.

I took up the book about Gerard Manley Hopkins. The chapter told of Hopkins at Balliol, at Oxford. He was thinking of becoming a Catholic. He was writing letters to Cardinal Newman (not yet a cardinal) about becoming a Catholic.

All of a sudden, something began to stir within me, something began to push me, to prompt me. It was a movement that spoke like a voice.

"What are you waiting for?" it said. "Why are you sitting here? Why do you still hesitate? You know what you ought to do? Why don't you do it?"

I stirred in the chair. I lit a cigarette, looking out the window at the rain, tried to shut the voice up. "Don't act on impulses," I thought. "This is crazy. This is not rational. Read your book."

Hopkins was writing to Newman, at Birmingham, about his indecision.

"What are you waiting for?" said the voice within me again. "Why are you sitting there? It is useless to hesitate any longer. Why don't you get up and go?"

I got up and walked restlessly around the room. "It's absurd," I thought. "Anyway, Father Ford would not be there at this time of day. I would only be wasting time."

Hopkins had written to Newman, and Newman had replied to him, telling him to come and see him at Birmingham.

Suddenly, I could bear it no longer. I put down the book, and got into my raincoat, and started down the stairs. I went out into the street. I crossed over, and walked along by the grey wooden fence, towards Broadway, in the light rain.

And then everything inside me began to sing—to sing with peace, to sing with strength and to sing with conviction.

I had nine blocks to walk. Then I turned the corner of 121st Street, and the brick church and presbytery were before me. I stood in the doorway and rang the bell and waited.

When the maid opened the door, I said:

"May I see Father Ford, please?"

"But Father Ford is out."

I thought: well, it is not a waste of time, anyway. And I asked when she expected him back. I would come back later, I thought.

The maid closed the door. I stepped back into the street. And then I saw Father Ford coming around the corner from Broadway. He approached, with his head down, in a rapid, thoughtful walk. I went to meet him and said:

"Father, may I speak to you about something?"

"Yes," he said, looking up, surprised. "Yes, sure, come into the house."

We sat in the little parlor by the door. And I said: "Father, I want to become a Catholic."

Norman Vincent Peale
1898 - 1994

My father was a preacher. He served in Cincinnati and in areas round about. When I was a little boy, Father was pastor of what was known as a circuit, five rural churches.

One of the greatest things—perhaps the greatest thing—that ever happened to me occurred in one of those little churches as I sat there one night with my mother. They were holding what were called "protracted meetings"— several meetings that went on for a lengthy time in the winter season.

Dave Henderson was a man in the community, a big fellow, and he was mean. Profane, a drunkard, foul-mouthed, he was known all around the countryside as a tough guy, but he always came to the revival meetings. He would weep and he would sing, but they said in that community that not even God Himself could save Dave.

Then one night when my father gave the invitation to accept Christ, it seemed as though the building shook as a tremendous man walked down the aisle. I turned around, and my mother said, "Glory to God, it's Dave Henderson. He came to the altar and knelt, and people gathered around him and "prayed him through."

I can remember him yet, though I was very young at that time. Dave stood up, raised his arms, and said, "Glory to God! I'm saved!" And he was, too, for he lived in that community for another fifty years, and

Known as the "minister to millions," **Norman Vincent Peale** is most famous for his book *The Power of Positive Thinking*. It sold over fifteen million copies and was translated into forty-two languages—one of the best-selling nonfiction books of all time. Born in Ohio, Peale was the son of a Methodist preacher, and he eventually turned his focus to the ministry as well, serving as senior pastor of the Reformed Church of America for fifty-two years. Peale was unique for his blend of psychology and theology, a personal doctrine that held the goal of helping people as its essential tenet. This excerpt, drawn from an anthology of conversion narratives entitled *He Touched Me*, contains the story of Peale's own conversion. It illustrates his personal vision wonderfully—the unique method of mixing psychology with religion that he employed to help others see the light.

when he died he was by common consent the greatest saint in all the countryside round about.

Well, the next night I asked my mother and father if I could "go forward," and that was the night I found Jesus Christ. But I'm a tough case, and I had to be saved several times! I believe it is perfectly possible for a person to be saved once and for all, but let me tell you that human nature is bad, and the devil is very powerful, and he can get into the mind of anyone who does not have the Spirit in power to ward him off.

But to get back to my father. He was a real person— a forthright, honest, dedicated man. I've had good fortune and been favored, but for my father, year in and year out for the eighty-five years of his life, there were only Jesus Christ and people. He had only one message: that Jesus Christ could save you from sin, that Jesus Christ could change your life, that Jesus Christ could do anything for you.

He was a medical doctor before he became a minister, and I was brought up on a combination of medicine and religion. Heal men's bodies—heal their souls—heal the whole man. When I finally got to working with psychology in my ministry, Father said that it could be used to the glory of God "if you didn't go too far with it"—which I hope I haven't.

Once when I was in theological seminary and bursting with "intellectuality," I came home. My father, then Superintendent of Churches, asked me to preach at a little country church one Sunday when the minister was either sick or away. Father said, "Now remember it's just a simple country church—just farmer people— and don't think you're so smart because you've been to a theological school in Boston!"

All week long I worked on that sermon, and it was heavily packed with theology, as I understood it at the time. On Saturday I sat down again with my father. He always sat in a rocking chair with his feet on a railing, and this time he said, "Read me that sermon." So I read it to him, and when I was through he just sat there rocking.

Finally he asked, "Norman, you want to know what I think you ought to do with that sermon?"

I said, "Yes, Dad, tell me."

He said: "Go out and burn it! In the first place, you wrote it all out. Get rid of the manuscript. Never read a sermon. If you don't feel it in your soul, so that you're burning to tell it, then you shouldn't preach it. If you have to depend upon a manuscript, you'll never get anywhere with it. Go out back and burn it."

Then he went on: "Listen. You found Jesus Christ, didn't you? He helped you overcome your sins, your weaknesses, your inferiority complex. Well, you must go out there in the morning and tell the people about Jesus, and don't talk theoretically—just tell them about Him as you personally know Him."

"But I can't make that last twenty-five minutes," I said.

"Then let it go at five," he said. "The important thing is not how long you preach, but what you say."

So I went the next day to a beautiful little church at the corner of two Ohio cornfields. The corn was knee-high, so it must have been around the Fourth of July. It was one of those sweet-smelling Sundays, peaceful, clear-washed, and quiet. I went into the pulpit to see if everything was all right, and then the people began to come in—the girls all spic and span, starched up like they used to be, pink ribbons, yellow ribbons; the boys sort of abashed; the families all strung out in the pews with father at one end and mother at the other to properly police the children.

They were fine-looking people, the salt of the earth, and I stood up to tell them about Jesus Christ.

I'm sure you have experienced how once in a while, under the power of the Holy Spirit, you get a deep silence in a church, deep but very much alive, as though something great trembles in the air. It happened that morning: the misty look in people's eyes, the expression of longing in their faces. That experience taught me that Jesus Christ is where the people meet.

After the sermon was over I was invited for dinner by some of the folks from that congregation, and a big, heavy-set man came out on the porch to talk to me. He sat down, slapped me on the knee, and began, "Son, you know you've got a powerful lot to learn about preaching, don't you?"

"Yes, sir," I said, "I know that."

"But," he said, "you've got a couple of things right, and the main one is you talked only about Jesus. The second thing is that you talked to people in their own language so that everybody could understand. Just keep doing that—talk in simple language and talk about Jesus, for Jesus is wonderful."

Well, since then I've gone all up and down the land, and I honestly believe that deep down in people's hearts there are love and faith in Jesus Christ. God help us, most of us aren't very faithful to Him, but still we know He is the answer. That has been my spiritual experience.

I also believe that the Bible is the inspired word of God, and I've never found a case where the Bible doesn't work. The older I get and the more difficulties I have to face with myself and with other people, the more I know that the old, basic, fundamental principles of the Christian religion are abundantly right and sound.

The Virgin Birth, the Resurrection, the Holy Spirit—I believe in them all. I believe in the Cross. I have believed in the Cross all my life and have preached that salvation is at the foot of the Cross.

Over the years what I have tried to do in my simple way is to preach the gospel, the old, Christ-centered, church-centered, Holy Spirit-centered gospel. Perhaps I've used a new kind of terminology, but I believe you've got to reach people on their own knowledge-level where they understand, and I think the average American is not·educated in the terminology of the church as people were years ago.

I know a man named Charlie who had many problems. Every time I tried to make suggestions to help him, he would reply, "I have half-a-mind to do that."

Finally, it came to me to say: "Charlie, I believe your trouble is that you are a 'half-a-minder.' You're always telling me you have half-a-mind to do something. You'd like to be strong in your morals and in your faith, and you'd like to be effective in your business. But let me tell you, you'll never in the world reach any of those goals unless you go *all* out instead of *half* out."

He asked, "How can one really get changed?"

Well, I had been doing my best to change this man and was baffled. But just then someone began to play a hymn on a nearby carillon, and the sound floated in at the window. I got up and walked over to look out, and across the way was a church with an illuminated cross on its steeple.

I said: "Come over here, Charlie. Did you ever hear about the Cross when you were a boy and went to church? Haven't you heard that Jesus Christ hung on the Cross for the remission of sins and that you can be saved by faith in the Savior who gave his life on the Cross for you?"

The strangest look came over Charlie's face, and at once he fell to his knees and surrendered his life to the Lord Jesus Christ. He was transformed before my very eyes!

I had applied my theological knowledge and psychological insight to him for two years—and I won't write that off completely, because at least the idea of "half-a-mind to" has some psychological power, but at any rate, it wasn't psychology that saved Charlie. It was the Lord Jesus Christ.

This is my story.

GOLDA MEIR
1898 - 1978

To me, being Jewish means and has always meant being proud to be part of a people that has maintained its distinct identify for more than 2,000 years, with all the pain and torment that have been inflicted upon it. Those who have been unable to endure and who have tired to opt out of their Jewishness have done so, I believe, at the expense of their own basic identify. They have pitifully impoverished themselves.

I don't know what forms the practice of Judaism will assume in the future or how Jews, in Israel and elsewhere, will express their Jewishness 1,000 years hence. But I do know that Israel is not just some small beleaguered country in which 3,000,000 people are trying hard to survive; Israel is a Jewish state that has come into existence as the result of the longing, the faith and the determination of an ancient people. We in Israel are only one part of the Jewish nation, and not even its largest part; but because Israel exists Jewish history has been changed forever, and it is my deepest conviction that there are few Israelis today who do not understand and fully accept the responsibility that history has placed on their shoulders as Jews.

As for me, my life has been greatly blessed. Not only have I lived to see the State of Israel born, but I have also seen it take in and successfully absorb masses of Jews from all parts of the world. When I came to this country in 1921, its Jewish population amounted to 80,000, and the entry of each Jew depended on permission granted by the mandatory government. We are now a population of over 3,000,000 of whom more than 1,000,000 are Jews who have arrived since the establishment of the state under Israel's Law of Return, a law that guarantees the right of every Jew to settle here. I am also grateful that I live

For some, faith has less to do with religion than with culture and shared history. In My Life, *former Israeli Prime Minister* **Golda Meir** *exemplifies just such a sentiment, as she explains that Judaism is to her an issue of identity. In case you are wondering why Meir is included in this book, she grew up in the U.S. after emigrating from Russia in 1906—Milwaukee, to be exact. Meir's faith took the shape of Zionism, an unflagging zeal for a Jewish state, which some would call a political ideology rather than religion. But perhaps this is yet another example of the myriad forms in which faith can appear sometimes; rather than the raiment of religion, it wears a political overcoat.*

in a country whose people have learned how to go on living in a sea of hatred without hating those who want to destroy them and without abandoning their own vision of peace. To have learned this is a great art, the prescription for which is not written down anywhere. It is part of our way of life in Israel.

ELIJAH MUHAMMAD
1897 - 1975

SUBMIT TO ALLAH (GOD) AND FEAR NOT

Islam, the religion of entire submission to the Will of Allah (God). "Nay, whoever submits his whole self to Allah and is a doer of good, he will get his regard with his Lord, on such shall be no fear, nor shall they grieve." (Holy Qur-an 2:112).

That and that alone is Salvation according to the Holy Qur-an. Fear is the number one enemy that is blocking progress and success from coming to the so-called Negroes of America. This fear causes them to grieve. The whole world knows the poor so-called Negroes of America have suffered and still suffer more grief and sorrow than any people on the earth! This fear is the fear of the slave-masters (white man) and what the slave-masters dislike. Let the so-called Negroes submit to Allah (God) and they will not fear anymore, nor will they grieve. As it is written: "The fear of man bringeth a snare." (Proverbs: 29). It has surely snared the so-called Negroes.

Born Elijah Poole in Sandersville, Georgia, **Muhammad** was the leader of the Black Muslims. After moving to Detroit in the 1920's, Muhammad met W. D. Fard, who is considered by him to be the messenger of Allah on earth. He experienced conversion after meeting Fard and changed his name, eventually becoming the movement's leader when Fard disappeared in 1934. Muhammad combined religious faith with a desire for social change, promoting plans for separation of blacks and whites and the formation of an all-black state. He extolled the

The Lord of the world's Finder of we the lost members of the Asiatic Black Nation for 400 years said that the slave-masters put fear in our Fathers when they were babies. Allah is the only one that can remove this fear from us, but he will not remove it from us until we submit to His will, not our will, and fear Him and Him alone. Then, as it is written, "And it shall come to pass in the day that the Lord shall give thee rest from sorrow and from thy fear, and from the hard bondage wherein thou wast made to serve" (Isaiah 14:3). There are so many places that I could point out in the Bible and Holy Qur-an that warn us

of fearing our enemies above or equal to the fear of Allah (God). It is a fool who has greater fear of the devils (white man) than Allah who has the power to destroy the devils and their followers (Rev. 21:8; Holy Qur-an 7:18 and 15:43).

We must remember that if Islam means entire submission to the will of Allah, that and that alone is the True religion of Allah. Do not you and your religious teachers and the Prophets of old teach that the only way to receive God's help or Guidance is to submit to His will!— then WHY NOT ISLAM! It (Islam) is the true religion of Allah and the ONLY way to success.

virtues of thriftiness, industry, and economic independence, encouraging African Americans to start their own businesses and schools. This excerpt from Muhammad's *Message to the Blackman in America*, his textbook of beliefs for Black Muslims, explains some of his ideas and teachings.

MARTIN LUTHER KING, JR.
1929 - 1968

FIRST SELECTION

I had felt the urge to enter the ministry from my latter high school days, but accumulated doubts had somewhat blocked the urge. Now it appeared again with an inescapable drive. My call to the ministry was not a miraculous or supernatural something; on the contrary, it was an inner urge calling me to save humanity. I guess the influence of my father also had a great deal to do with my going into the ministry. This is not to say that he ever spoke to me in terms of being a minister, but that my admiration for him was the great moving factor. He set forth a noble example that I didn't mind following. . . .

Without manuscript or notes, I told the story of what had happened to Mrs. Parks. Then I reviewed the long history of abuses and insults that Negro citizens had experienced on the city buses. "But there comes a time," I said, "that people get tired.

When we look at the history of our country, it becomes instantly apparent that whenever a great fight for freedom was in the works, faith in God was there to strengthen the army. The founders of our country, the early suffragettes, and the Civil Rights activists of the 1960's were all bolstered by their faith in God—and by the strength that such faith offered. **Dr. Martin Luther King, Jr.,** is no exception. A deeply religious man, King was ordained a Baptist minister in 1947. Indivisibly connected to his love of God was his determination to achieve civil rights for African Americans. King fought a battle that began in 1955, a battle fought with nonviolent resistance. The weapons of the Civil Rights activists were bus boycotts and protest marches, church meetings, and inspiring speeches such as the world-famous "I Have a Dream." Although Dr. King did not live to see victory over inequality, he achieved much in his life, winning the Nobel prize in 1964, and helping to establish the Southern Christian Leadership Conference. Throughout all of this, King's faith provided the fuel for the fire, the force that propelled him in his quest for freedom and equality. The words on his tombstone proclaimed, "Free at last, free at last, Thank God Almighty, I'm free at last." In God's eyes, we are all equal, and he believed that in God's house all would find true freedom.

These excerpts, drawn from various collections of King's speeches and writings, illustrate the breadth and depth of his faith. They demonstrate an inextricable link between love for God and the world around us—a world at that time filled with inequality and oppression of black citizens. In Dr. King's own words, "the two cannot be separated: religion for me is life."

We are here this evening to say to those who have mistreated us so long that we are tired—tired of being segregated and humiliated; tired of being kicked about by the brutal feet of oppression." The congregation met this statement with fervent applause. "We had no alternative but to protest," I continued. "For many years, we have shown amazing patience. We have sometimes given our white brothers the feeling that we liked the way we were being treated. But we come here tonight to be saved from that patience that makes us patient with anything less than freedom and justice." Again the audience interrupted with applause.

Briefly I justified our actions, both morally and legally. "One of the great glories of democracy is the right to protest for right." Comparing our methods with those of the white citizens councils and the Ku Klux Klan, I pointed out that while "these organizations are protesting for the perpetuation of injustice in the community, we are protesting for the birth of justice in the community. Their methods lead to violence and lawlessness. But in our protest there will be no cross burnings. No white person will be taken from his home by a hooded Negro mob and brutally murdered. There will be no threats and intimidation. We will be guided by the highest principle of law and order."

With this groundwork for militant action, I moved on to words of caution. I urged the people not to force anybody to refrain from riding the buses. "Our method will be that of persuasion, not coercion. We will only say to the people, 'Let your conscience be your guide.'" Emphasizing the Christian doctrine of love, "our actions must be guided by the deepest principles of our Christian faith. Love must be

our regulating ideal. Once again we must hear the words of Jesus echoing across the centuries: 'Love your enemies, bless them that curse you, and pray for them that despitefully use you.' If we fail to do this our protest will end up as a meaningless drama on the stage of history, and its memory will be shrouded with the ugly garments of shame. In spite of the mistreatment that we have confronted we must not become bitter, and end up hating our white brothers. As Booker T. Washington said, 'Let no man pull you so low as to make you hate him.'" Once more the audience responded enthusiastically.

Then came my closing statement. "If you will protest courageously, and yet with dignity and Christian love, when the history books are written in future generations, the historians will have to pause and say, 'There lived a great people—a black people—who injected new meaning and dignity into the veins of civilization.' This is our challenge and our overwhelming responsibility." As I took my seat the people rose to their feet and applauded. I was thankful to God that the message had gotten over and that the task of combining the militant and the moderate had been at least partially accomplished. The people had been as enthusiastic when I urged them to love as they were when I urged them to protest.

As I sat listening to the continued applause I realized that this speech had evoked more response than any speech or sermon I had ever delivered, and yet it was virtually unprepared. I came to see for the first time what the older preachers meant when they said, "Open your mouth and God will speak for you." While I would not let this experience tempt me to overlook the need for continued preparation, it would always remind me that God can transform man's weakness into his glorious opportunity.

SECOND SELECTION

Now for a more specific phase of my religious development. It was the age of five that I joined the church. I well remember how this event occurred. Our church was in the midst of the spring revival, and a guest evangelist had come down from Virginia. On Sunday morning the guest evangelist came into our Sunday School to talk to us about salvation, and after a short talk on this point he extended an invitation to any of us who wanted to join the church. My sister was the first one to join the church that morning, and after seeing her join I decided that I would not let her get ahead of me, so I was the next. I had never given this matter a thought, and even at the time of {my} baptism I was unaware of what was taking place. From this it seems quite clear that I joined the church not out of any dynamic conviction, but out of a childhood desire to keep up with my sister.

Conversion for me was never an abrupt something. I have never experienced the so called "crisis moment." Religion has just been something that I grew up in. Conversion for me has been the gradual intaking of the noble {ideals} set forth in my family and my environment, and I must admit that this intaking has been largely unconscious.

The church has always been a second home for me. As far back as I can remember I was in church every Sunday. I guess this was inevitable since my father was the pastor of my church, but I never regretted going to church until I passed through a state of skepticism in my second year of college. My best friends were in Sunday School, and it was the Sunday School that helped me to build the capacity for getting along with people.

The lessons which I was taught in Sunday School were quite in the fundamentalist line. None of my teachers ever doubted the infallibility of the Scriptures. Most of them were unlettered and had never heard of Biblical criticism. Naturally I accepted the teachings as they were being given to me. I never felt any need to doubt them, at least at that time I didn't. I guess I accepted Biblical studies uncritically until I was about twelve years old. But this uncritical attitude could not last long, for it was contrary to the very nature of my being. I had always been the questioning and precocious type. At the age of 13 I shocked my Sunday School class by denying the bodily resurrection of Jesus. From the age of thirteen on doubts began to spring forth unrelentingly. At the age of fifteen I entered college and more and more could I see a gap between what I had learned in Sunday School and what I was learning in college. This conflict continued until I studied a course in Bible in which I came to see that behind the legends and myths of the Book were many profound truths which one could not escape.

One or two incidents happened in my late childhood and early adolescence that had tremendous effect on my religious development. The First was the death of my grandmother when I was about nine years old. I was particularly hurt by this incident mainly because of the extreme love I had for her. As stated above, she assisted greatly in raising all of us. It was after this incident for the first time that I talked at any length on the doctrine of immortality. My parents attempted to explain it to me and I was assured that somehow my grandmother still lived. I guess this is why today I am such a strong believer in personal immortality.

The second incident happened when I was about six years of age. From about the age of three up until this time I had had a white playmate who was about my age. We always felt free to play our childhood games together. He did not live in our community, but he was usually around every day until about 6:00; his father owned a store just across the streets from our home. At the age of six we both entered school—separate schools of course. I remember how our friendship began to break as soon as we entered school, of course this was not my desire but his. The climax came when he told me one day that his father had demanded that he would play with me no more. I never will forget what a great shock this was to me. I immediately asked my parents about the motive behind such a statement. We were at the diner table when the situation was discussed, and here for the first time I was made aware of the existence of a race problem. I had never been conscious of it before. As my parents discussed some of the tragedies that had resulted from this problem and some of the insults they themselves had confronted on account of it I was greatly shocked, and from that moment on I was determined to hate every white person. As I grew older and older this feeling continued to grow. My parents would always tell me that I should not hate the white {man}, but that it was my duty as a Christian to love him. At this point the religious element came in. The question arose in my mind, how could I love a race of people {who} hated me and who had been responsible for breaking me up with one of my best childhood friends? This was a great question in my mind for a number of years. I did not conquer this anti White feeling until I entered college and came in contact with white students through working in interracial organizations.

My days in college were very exciting ones. As stated above, my college training, especially the first two years, brought many doubts into my mind. It was at this period that the shackles of fundamentalism were removed from my body. This is why, when I came to Crozer, I could accept the liberal interpretation with relative ease.

It was in my senior year of college that I entered the ministry. I had felt the urge to enter the ministry from my latter high school days, but accumulated doubts had somewhat blocked the urge. Now it appeared again with an inescapable drive. My call to the ministry was not a miraculous or supernatural something, on the contrary it was an inner urge calling me to serve humanity. I guess the influence of my father also had a great deal to do with my going in the ministry. This is not to say that he ever spoke to me in terms of being a minister, but that my admiration of him was the great moving factor; He set forth a noble example that I didn't mine following. Today I differ a great deal with my father theologically, but that admiration for a real father still remains.

At the age of 19 I finished college and was ready to enter the seminary. On coming to the seminary I found it quite easy to fall in line with the liberal tradition there found, mainly because I had been prepared for it before coming.

At present I still feel the affects of the noble moral and ethical ideals that I grew up under. They have been real and precious to me, and even in moments of theological doubt I could never turn away from them. Even though I have never had an abrupt conversion experience, religion has been real to me and closely knitted to life. In fact the two cannot be separated; religion for me is life.

THIRD SELECTION

In recent months I have also become more and more convinced of the reality of a personal God. True, I have always believed in the personality of God. But in past years the idea of a personal God was little more than a metaphysical category which I found theologically and philosophically satisfying. Now it is a living reality that has been validated in the experiences of everyday life. Perhaps the suffering, frustration and agonizing moments which I have had to undergo occasionally as a result of my involvement in a difficult struggle have drawn me closer to God. Whatever the cause, God has been profoundly real to me in recent months. In the midst of outer dangers I have felt an inner calm and known resources of strength that only God could give. In many instances I have felt the power of God transforming the fatigue of despair into the buoyancy of hope. I am convinced that the universe is under the control of a loving purpose and that in the struggle for righteousness man has cosmic companionship. Behind the harsh appearances of the world there is a benign power. To say God is personal is not to make him an object among other objects or attribute to him the finiteness and limitations of human personality; it is to take what is finest and noblest in our consciousness and affirm its perfect existence in him. It is certainly true that human personality is limited, but personality as such involves no necessary limitations.

It simply means self-consciousness and self-direction. So in the truest sense of the word, God is a living God. In him there is feeling and will, responsive to the deepest yearnings of the human heart: thus God both evokes and answers prayers.

The past decade has been a most exciting one. In spite of the tensions and uncertainties of our age something profoundly meaningful has begun. Old systems of exploitation and oppression are passing away and new systems of justice and equality are being born. In a real sense ours is a great time in which to be alive. Therefore I am not yet discouraged about the future. Granted that the easygoing optimism of yesterday is impossible. Granted that we face a world crisis which often leaves us standing amid the surging murmur of life's restless sea. But every crisis has both its dangers and its opportunities. Each can spell either salvation or doom. In a dark, confused world the spirit of God may yet reign supreme.

JOHN F. KENNEDY
1917 - 1963

This country was founded by men and women who were dedicated or came to be dedicated to two propositions: first, a strong religious conviction, and secondly a recognition that this conviction could flourish only under a system of freedom.

Kennedy was, of course, the first Catholic President. His campaign survived fear of a papal puppet on Pennsylvania Avenue. Kennedy addressed the general issue of religion in his proclamation of the National Day of Prayer.

I think it is appropriate that we pay tribute to this great constitutional principle which is enshrined in the First Amendment of the Constitution: the principle of religious independence, of religious liberty, of religious freedom. But I think it is also important that we pay tribute and acknowledge another great principle, and that is the principle of religious conviction. Religious freedom has no significance unless it is accompanied by conviction. And therefore the Puritans and the Pilgrims of my own section of New England, the

Quakers of Pennsylvania, the Catholics of Maryland, the Presbyterians of North Carolina, the Methodists and the Baptists who came later, all shared these two great traditions which, like silver threads, have run through the warp and the woof of American history.

ALAN WATTS
1915 - 1973

Throughout my seminary and ministerial career I was always suspected of pantheism, but with a gift for semantic dexterity I could not be pinned down by people with one-track minds whose thinking was restricted to the linear order of the Book, with its one-way strings of words. For example, my own "pantheistic" view cannot be stated as a proposition, but must be felt as an experience. . . .

Alan Watts, who was once called "the brain and Buddha of American Zen," was always an outlaw in the world of spirituality. Considered the personal guru of the Beats, Watts left his Anglican chaplainship at Northwestern University to found the American Academy of Asian Studies. Born in England and naturalized a U.S. citizen in 1943, he once had his life mission described as that of "interpreting Asian philosophy for Westerners" by the *Dictionary of Literary Biography*. In this excerpt from his autobiography he ruminates on pantheism, God, and the nature of faith.

You cannot be a formal or propositional pantheist if you see that the chart is not the field, if you understand that a separate thing is real only in a system of abstractions. It is not physically or naturally real, for just as there cannot be necks without heads and trunks, there cannot be flowers without environmental fields. The field flows into the flower, and what we call the "thing"—flower—is a wiggle in the flow, while the flow itself, the energy of the universe, admits of no definition. The word "God" is more of an exclamation than a proper name. It expresses astonishment, reverence, and even love for our reality. If you want to put a human face on it, that will do—if you do not take it literally—since we know nothing higher or more mysterious than people, and an energy-field which peoples can hardly be less intelligent than people. Certainly events happen in the field which seem absolutely horrible, but faith is the gamble that there is some way of understanding or at least accepting them. I do not see what other attitude a sane person can take.

MALCOLM X
1925 - 1965

It was the next night, as I lay on my bed, I suddenly, with a start, became aware of a man sitting beside me in my chair. He had on a dark suit. I remember. I could see him as plainly as I see anyone I look at. He wasn't black, and he wasn't white. He was light-brown-skinned, an Asiatic cast of countenance, and he had oily black hair.

I looked right into his face.

I didn't get frightened. I knew I wasn't dreaming. I couldn't move, I didn't speak, and he didn't. I couldn't place him racially—other than that I knew he was a non-European. I had no idea whatsoever who he was. He just sat there. Then, suddenly as he had come, he was gone.

Soon, Mr. Muhammad sent me a reply about Reginald. He wrote, "If you once believed in the truth, and now you are beginning to doubt the truth, you didn't believe the truth in the first place. What could make you doubt the truth other than your own weak self?"

That struck me. Reginald was not leading the disciplined life of a Muslim. And I knew that Elijah Muhammad was right, and my blood brother was wrong. Because right is right, and wrong is wrong. Little did I then realize the day would come when Elijah Muhammad would be accused by his own sons as being guilty of the same acts of immorality that he judged Reginald and so many others for.

But at that time, all of the doubt and confusion in my mind was removed. All of the influence that my brother had wielded over me was broken. From that day on, as far as I am concerned, everything that my brother Reginald has done is wrong. . . .

It's impossible to dream, or to see, or to have a vision of someone whom you never have seen before— and to see him exactly as he is. To see someone, and to see him exactly as he looks, is to have a pre-vision.

This excerpt from *The Autobiography of Malcolm X* exemplifies nothing so much as the difficulties one may face when converting to a new faith. **Malcolm X**, born Malcolm Little in Omaha, Nebraska, converted to Islam during the late forties while in prison. Here the former black leader relates a revelatory experience—a vision of a motionless, silent man sitting beside him in his cell. Malcolm X later became convinced the man was W. D. Fard, whom Nation of Islam founder Elijah Muhammad claimed to be the Messiah. It was this vision that convinced him to invest his heart completely in Islam, despite the misgivings of his brother. This incident is a testament to the strength of faith—a force that can grant visions and empower us to turn our backs even on blood relatives. After his release from prison, Malcolm X became a leader of the Black Muslims—a group that then believed in racial separation. He eventually distanced himself from the organization and attempted to form a rival group, the Organization of Afro-American Unity. He did not live to see the group's formation. Malcolm X was assassinated in 1965, and two Black Muslims were jailed for his murder. Malcolm X is best remembered for his stirring oration and tremendous leadership among the African-American community.

I would later come to believe that my pre-vision was of Master W. D. Fard, the Messiah, the one whom Elijah Muhammad said had appointed him—Elijah Muhammad—as His Last Messenger to the black people of North America.

ISAAC BASHEVIS SINGER

1904 - 1991

Somewhere, I had heard or read the expression "the reappraisal of all values" and it was clear to me that this was what I had to do—reappraise all values. I could not rely on any authority. I still hadn't published a single word and at the Writers Club I was known only as "Singer's brother." Just the same I waged contentions with God, the Prophets, religions, philosophies, as well as with the creators of world literature. Was Shakespeare really the genius he was made out to be? Were Maxim Gorki and Andreyev pillars of literature? Were Mendele Moher Sforim, Peretz, Sholem Aleichem, and Bialik really as great as the Yiddishists and Hebraists wanted them to be? Had Hegel really said anything new in philosophy? Had the species really originated as Darwin claimed they had? Was there any substance to the assertions of Karl Marx, Lenin, Bukharin? Was democracy indeed the best system? Could a Jewish State in Palestine really solve the Jewish question? Did the words "equality" and "freedom" really mean something or were they mere rhetoric? Was it worthwhile to go on living and struggling in this world or were those who spat upon the whole mess right?

I was surrounded on all sides by the faithful who all believed in something: the Orthodox and the Zionists, the Hasidim and the *misnagdim,* the writers of the editorials in the Yiddish press and the anti-Semites

*In this excerpt from A Young Man in Search of Love, America's preeminent Jewish writer ruminates on his difficulties with faith. Born in Poland, **Singer** was the son of a Hasidic scholar and the grandson of rabbis. Despite such spiritual roots, Singer was anything but certain of his faith. The author, who won the Nobel Prize in 1978, is credited with forging an incredibly successful literary career out of a dying language—Yiddish. Singer, though he lived in America for much of his adult life, wrote exclusively in the language of the shtetl. He was the quintessential American immigrant author, bringing the landscape of the Old World to life in that of the new.*

in the Polish press, those who defended the League of Nations and those who opposed it. The brides and grooms who were congratulated in the newspapers apparently believed in the institution of marriage and in bringing forth new generations. I had often heard educators discussing the problems of rearing the young. In his letters to me, my father constantly warned me to live like a Jew and not—God forbid—forget or disgrace my heritage. Mother, on the other hand, pleaded again and again that I guard my health, not catch cold, God forbid, eat on time, go to sleep early, and not overwork. She wished me long life and hoped that I would make a good match and provide her with grandchildren. My sister-in-law Genia, Joshua's wife, often consulted with her sister, Bella, and with neighbors about which would be best for Yosele—to breast-feed him or give him a bottle, to use this formula or that? But something within me asked: "What for? Why? Why slaughter chickens, calves, and kids and bring up people? Why slave and stay up nights so that there would be a Yosele, an Isaac, or a Gina?"

As skillful as Tolstoy was in portraying individual types, so naïve did he seem to me when he tried to give advice on how to solve the agrarian problem in Russia or to expedite the teaching of the Gospel. All this babble about a better tomorrow, a rosier future, a united mankind, or equality was based on wishes, delusions, and sometimes merely on lust for power. It was clear to me that after the First World War there would have to come a second, a third, a tenth. Most faces expressed callousness, supreme egotism, indifference to everything outside their own ken, and, quite often, stupidity. Here they prayed and there they slaughtered. The same priests who preached love on Sunday morning hunted a fox, a hare, or some other helpless creature on Sunday afternoon or tried to hook a fish in the Vistula. The Polish officers who strutted about displaying their medals, brandishing their swords, and saluting each other hadn't the slightest chance of defending their country if it were attacked by Russia or Germany. And it was just as hard to believe that England would surrender her mandate in Palestine or that the Arabs would allow the Jews to establish a nation there. By now, I knew that atheism and materialism were just as unsubstantial as the religions. All my probings led to the same conclusion—that there was some scheme within Creation, someone we call God, but He had not revealed Himself to anyone nor was there even the slightest indication that He desired love, peace, and justice. The whole history of man and beast; all the facts pointed to the very opposite—that this was a God of strength and cruelty Whose principle was: Might makes right.

Oddly enough, this total skepticism or agnosticism led me to a kind of private mysticism. Since God was completely unknown and eternally silent, He could be endowed with whatever traits one elected to hang upon Him. Spinoza had bestowed Him with two known attributes and an endless array of unknown ones. But why couldn't one fantasize many other attributes? Why couldn't creativeness be one of His attributes? Why couldn't beauty, harmony, growth, expediency, playfulness, humor, will, sex, change, freedom, and caprice represent divine attributes too? And where was it written that He was the only God? Maybe He belonged to a whole army of gods, an infinite hierarchy. Maybe He procreated and multiplied and brought forth billions of angels, seraphim, Aralim, and cherubim in His cosmic harem as well as new generations of gods. Since nothing was known about Him and nothing could be known, why not confer upon this divine X all the possible values? The cabalists had done this in their own fashion, the idolators in another, and the Christians and Muslims in another still. I personally was fully prepared to crown Him with all kinds of possible attributes except benevolence and compassion. To ascribe mercy to a God who for millions of years had witnessed massacres and tortures and who had literally built an entire world on the principle of violence and murder was something my sense of justice wouldn't allow me to do. In my mind I created a kind of pecking order between us. I, a dust speck trembling with fear and filled with a sort of sense of right based upon my own silly urges and convictions; He, a universal murderer, a cosmic Genghis Khan or Napoleon—eternal, infinite, omnipotent, so wise and mighty in knowledge and technique that He could keep track of every electron, every atom, every gnat, fly, and microbe. It was even possible that one could phone Him directly with a request through the medium of prayer but with no guarantee whatsoever of an answer. I had actually appropriated Spinoza's God but I had extended Him, anthropomorphized Him, bestialized Him, and reworked Him in my imagination to suit my moods. Incredibly enough, I "phoned" Him my requests and hoped somehow that He *could* answer me if the notion struck Him to do so. At that time my most urgent request was that my stories be printed and that I could have a room of my own. Being together with Gina had begun to grow tiresome for me.

CHARLES COLSON
1931 -

But I was too preoccupied to be good company. My thoughts were not on Watergate but on my visit with Tom Phillips the night before. I had expected to awaken feeling embarrassment for my uncontrolled outburst of emotion. Not so. The sense of freedom in my spirit was still there. Something important was happening, but what? Perhaps I'd find the answer in *Mere Christianity*.

What better place to search for answers than by the ocean. From boyhood when I used to walk the stony beach of Winthrop, Massachusetts, the sea had been important to me. Rejuvenation always came when I lost myself in the sea's vastness, feeling its power as the waves crashed in great sprays of foam onto moss-draped rocks.

When combined exhaustion and anxiety nearly paralyzed me one day late in the 1960 Massachusetts election campaign, I left the campaign office and drove to a favorite spot in Gloucester. There on an overhanging cliff I felt renewed as I watched the raging seas smash against the rocks, then subside into a cluster of small eddies. I'd gone there later to be alone when I was searching for answers about my first marriage. Faced now with a major decision, the sea would again help me find strength and clearness of mind I needed.

After a four-hour drive Patty and I arrived in Boothbay Harbor, a lovely old fishing village and sailing port 180 miles from Boston. The narrow streets of the village are lined with steep-roofed, gray-shingled houses nestled together. Cool breezes from the east fill the air with the briny odor of fish and sea peculiar to New England coastal towns. Old as it is, everything about Boothbay looks freshly scrubbed, even the

This born-again Christian first made headlines for his role in the Watergate scandal and now makes them for his role as a felon-turned-Christian. **Colson**, who was Richard Nixon's special counsel, spent seven months in prison for obstructing justice. It was a result of his experiences that Colson turned to God, finding that faith can be the best comfort when all else seems bleak. He has turned his disaster into a success story, writing a number of books about his experience including the well-known *Born Again* from which this excerpt is drawn. Colson founded Prison Fellowship Ministries in 1976, an evangelical institution that takes religion behind bars to help others who find themselves in the same plight that the author once found himself.

native fishermen who walk through the streets in heavy slickers, high boots, caps shielding their leathery, wrinkled faces from the glare of the sun and sea.

Having made no reservation, we skirted the main part of town, driving along a winding coastal road looking for an out-of-the-way spot. We were twelve miles from town when Patty spotted a small inn at the end of a long, narrow point of land jutting straight out into the Atlantic. "Maybe no one will recognize us there," I agreed, weary of curiosity seekers, autograph collectors, Nixon partisans and adversaries who were always happy to tell me exactly what they thought, often at length and with passion.

Cautiously we drove onto a narrow dirt road atop a man-made causeway built over the sea ten feet below. The causeway connected what was once a small rocky island to the mainland. The innkeeper was a stony-faced young man, tall and gaunt, who gave us the quizzical once-over so typical of cautious Down Easters and then showed us the one cottage which surprisingly was available for the week. It suited us perfectly. One huge room and a great open deck were suspended over the rocks and sea below.

Patty began unpacking, gleeful over our discovery, and I returned to the office. As I signed the register and waited, the innkeeper conferred in a corner with one of his employees. He returned and looked at me curiously. "Colson, eh?"

"That's right."

"From McLean. That near Washington?" He looked suspiciously at the address I'd scribbled. My heart sank; Watergate was following us all the way to this craggy little spit of land.

"Friend here tells me you're famous." He wasn't smiling.

"No, not really."

"You been on TV?"

"Well, yes, a few times. This Watergate business, you know," I admitted. *What was the sense in trying to hide it?*

"Eyuh," followed by a pause and a stare. "Watergate still going on?" The word *eyuh* is generally spoken by Down Easters with a heavy nasal twang and means "Yes," "Maybe," "I don't know," "That's interesting," and scores of other interpretations.

"Yes, it's still going on."

"Well, I'll be—thought t'was over in June. My TV's been busted." With that, still unsmiling, he handed me my key.

I couldn't wait to tell Patty. Hallelujah! We had found a spot where the TV was out of order. And the sea, the beautiful green-blue ocean, was roaring in under our picture window. "What a great time to relax," I told Patty. *What a great time to think about God,* I told myself.

That first night I unpacked Lewis's book and placed a yellow pad at my side to jot down key points, not unlike the way I prepared to argue a major case in court. In a moment of emotion the previous evening I had made a surrender of myself to something—or Someone. Now the habits of a lifetime rose in protest. All my training insisted that analysis precede decision, that arguments be marshaled in two neat columns, pros and cons. I wondered if I could overcome my intellectual obstacles so as to believe in my mind what I had felt in my emotions.

On the top of the pad I wrote: Is there a God?

As I probed back in time, I remembered the night twenty years before when I stared into the vast darkness from the rail of the U.S.S. *Melette,* cruising off the coast of Guatemala. There was no possible explanation for how this whole magnificent universe, the glittering array of galaxies and stars, could remain in such perfect harmony without the direction of some awesome power which created it all in the first instance. That there is such a force greater than man seemed indisputable to me. And I had no trouble calling this force God.

Then I found myself remembering a curious shining moment seven years before. In the summer of 1966 I had bought a fourteen-foot sailboat for my two boys and hauled it to a friend's home on a lake in New Hampshire to teach them to sail. Christian, then ten, was so excited over having his own boat that even though a gentle summer rain was falling the day of our arrival, he was determined to try it out.

As the craft edged away from the dock, the only sound was the rippling of water under the hull and the flapping of the sail when puffs of wind fell from it. I was in the stern watching the tiller, Chris in the center, dressed in an orange slicker, holding the sheet. As he realized that he was controlling the boat, the most marvelous look came over his cherubic face, the joy of new discovery in his eyes, the thrill of feeling the wind's power in his hands. I found myself in that one unforgettable moment quietly talking to God. I could even recall the precise words: "Thank You, God, for giving me this son, for giving us this one wonderful moment. Just looking now into this boy's eyes fulfills my life. Whatever happens in the future, even if I die tomorrow, my life is complete and full. Thank You."

Afterwards, I had been startled when I realized that I had spoken to God, since my mind did not assent to His existence as a Person. It had been a spontaneous expression of gratitude that simply bypassed the mind and took for granted what reason had never shown me. More—it assumed that personal communication with this unproven God was possible. Why else would I have spoken, unless deep down I felt that Someone, somewhere, was listening?

Perhaps, I thought, *it is on this intuitive, emotional level that C. S. Lewis approaches God.* I opened *Mere Christianity* and found myself instead face-to-face with an intellect so disciplined, so lucid, so relentlessly logical that I could only be grateful I had never faced him in a court of law. Soon I had covered two pages of yellow paper with *pros* to my query, "Is there a God?"

On the *con* side were listed the conventional doubts so prevalent in our materialistic, science-has-all-the-answers society—we can't see, hear, or feel God.

Or can we?

What happened to me on Tom Phillips's porch? What was the emotion I had felt? Love? Some unseen force had stirred inside me. And I had always felt that unseen forces were more powerful than visible ones.

A piston engine with 280 horsepower can move a precise number of pounds against the calculated resistance of friction, but not one pound more than known physical laws prescribe. The engine is made of hard steel, its existence evident to every sense. Yet love, which no one sees or touches, moves men and nations in limitless ways. Love caused one man to renounce a kingdom in my lifetime. Another kind of love causes a soldier to hurl his body over a grenade which has fallen into the midst of his buddies. Love has incomparably greater force than any engine of known horsepower.

I struggled on with this thought. A law is tangible in the sense that it is recorded somewhere on a piece of paper, but it exists only to the extent it causes men to do or not to do certain things. Its real force is then beyond the reach of that which we see or touch, made real by the extent people accept and believe.

As a lawyer I was impressed by Lewis's arguments about moral law, the existence of which he demonstrates is real, and which has been perceived with astonishing consistency in all times and places. It has not been man, I saw for the first time, that has perpetuated moral law; it has survived *despite* man's best attempts to defeat it. Its long existence therefore presupposes some other will behind it. Again, God.

I was back with Lewis, my yellow pads, and my questions early the next day. Patty was beginning to eye me a little strangely. Usually when we traveled to new places, I was active, restless, eager to see the sights; here I was sitting quietly engrossed in a book.

If there is a loving God, the automatic next question was, of course, "If He is good, why does He preside over such an evil world?" Again my legal training suggested a useful parallel. In the beginning, God gave to mankind dominion over the earth He created (*see* Genesis 1:26-30). In other words, he made us, in lawyers' parlance, His agents.

The theory of *agency* in the law suggests a freedom of action, something beyond being a servant or mechanical robot. The agent is given the power to act within the *scope*, lawyers say, of authority—within certain set limits. The limits of this authority—the delegation as we call it in the law—God also laid out in Scripture.

But at the same time, He gave us free will. That is the point, of course; give someone less and he is no agent; the giver ends up doing it all himself. With a free will we can defy those limits and His instructions to us as readily as any agent exceeds the scope of his authority in civil law. And that happens each day; there are hundreds of law suits going on to prove it. As with the failure of agency in the law, so man often fails in discharging our Creator's agency.

History supports this view. Down through the years it has been man's abuse of God's authority, his malice toward his fellowmen, which has created the preponderance of human grief. And probably we will go right on abusing it.

To understand this I came back to where Tom Phillips started: pride and ego. As Lewis put it, "The moment you have a self at all, there is a possibility of putting yourself first—wanting to be the centre—wanting to be God. . . ." How devastatingly I now saw that in my own life.

It was during this second day that I was emboldened to begin to tell Patty of the journey I'd begun. "You believe in God, don't you, honey?" I asked. We were both sitting on the deck reading. Patty had inquired once about my little green and white paperback, which I explained merely as a book Tom Phillips had given me.

"You know I do," she answered, with a hint of suspicion in her eyes—the latent, never spoken concern, perhaps, that someday I'd try to talk her out of her Roman Catholicism.

"But have you ever really thought about it—deeply, I mean? Like who is God and how does He watch over each of us and why did He create us, things like that?"

Patty's look of suspicion changed into one of pure bafflement. "What's in that book you're reading?"

In the ten years we'd been married, I realized, we'd never discussed God; religion once in a while, what Patty felt about confession and Communion, the significance of the Mass. But these are procedural points. We'd never gone right to the substance, the living God, the faith down deep inside either one of us. We had done so much together but never touched on the essence of life itself. How much on the surface are even the closest of human relationships!

"I guess I'm looking for something," I continued. "I'm trying to find out what's real and what isn't—who we are—who I am in relation to God." Then I told her something about my evening with Tom Phillips—not the tears, but the dismal self-discovery, all quite clinically, not wanting to admit how much my emotions had been touched. She looked dubious, but was fascinated by the story.

"You see, I'm looking for answers and this little book is terrific."

"Maybe you should talk to a priest," Patty suggested, now wanting (I could see it in the compassion in her eyes) to help me, knowing the struggle was genuine, no flip remark or banter to pass the time. Patty is the gentlest, most caring person I've ever known, taking others' problems as her own, feeling the full weight of every burden I ever had to bear. She hadn't quite expected this one—a search for God—but I sensed she was ready to share it with me.

I checked myself from voicing the critical statement, "No priest or minister these forty years has ever explained any of this to me." Who was I to point an accusing finger? I had never been looking, probably never really listening. Now for the first time, Lewis's explanation and Phillips's example were opening a whole new world.

We talked into the night, while the bell buoy clanged, guiding the lobstermen through the early evening fog, and the waves slapped against the rocks beneath us. It was a relief to have Patty know of my search to find new peace within myself, and to acquire an antidote for the disease inside which had been sucking life out of me, vampire-like, for eight long months ever since election night the year before. We ended by deciding to get out the family Bible when we returned home and begin reading it.

It was during the next morning, as I went on reading, underlining, making notes, that another important question was resolved for me. If God is listening to my prayers, how can He hear those being uttered at the same time by many millions of others?

That is a question which boggles the finite human mind. The difficulty is the same as when we try to understand where the universe ends, and if it does, what is beyond. Lewis shed light on this in a chapter entitled "Time and Beyond Time": "God [is] beyond all space and time." And there is now a respectable body of scientific knowledge to establish that time is indeed relative, not the absolute measure we know.

Since the Creator of an infinite universe has no limitations in terms of hours or days, the fact that He could listen to four billion prayers at once was suddenly not the dazzling feat I with my limited mind had made it out to be. It was hard for me to accept this only so long as I struggled with my finite mind to understand a concept which is beyond finite limits. I can't explain it any better than I can explain what is beyond the stars, but simply knowing that man can't, provides an important answer.

All of this added to my conviction that there is a loving, infinite God, but left unanswered the question of what Tom really meant by the words *accept Christ*. How does Jesus Christ figure into all this? Hindus believe in God and that He can be worshiped in almost any way anyone pleases. All my analyzing so far had only gotten me to Hinduism.

The central thesis of Lewis's book and the essence of Christianity, is summed up in one mind-boggling sentence: *Jesus Christ is God* (see John 10:30). Not just part of God, or just sent by God, or just related to God. *He was* (and therefore, of course, *is*) *God*.

The more I grappled with those words, the more they began to explode before my eyes, blowing into smithereens a lot of comfortable old notions I had floated through life with, without thinking much about them. Lewis puts it so bluntly that you can't slough it off: for Christ to have talked as He talked, lived as He lived, died as He died, He was either God or a raving lunatic.

There was my choice, as simple, stark, and frightening as that, no fine shadings, no gradations, no compromises. No one had ever thrust this truth at me in such a direct and unsettling way. I'd been content to think of Christ as an inspired prophet and teacher who walked the sands of the Holy Land 2,000 years ago—several cuts above other men of His time or, for that matter, any time. But if one thinks of Christ as no more than that, I reasoned, then Christianity is a simple palliative, like taking a sugar-coated placebo once a week on Sunday morning.

On this sunny morning on the Maine coast with fresh breezes picking up off the ocean, it was hard for me to grasp the enormity of this point—that Christ is the living God who promises us a day-to-day living relationship with Him and a personal one at that.

Each of the steps I'd labored through was an essential building block to get to this point, but once I had, the others seemed almost irrelevant. Lewis's question was the heart of the matter. The words—both exciting and disturbing—pounded at me: Jesus Christ—lunatic or God?

Even atheists concede that Christ's coming changed the course of history. The year in which we live, for example, is based upon the date of His birth. He was a man without power in any worldly sense, no money, no armies, no weapons, and yet His coming altered the political alignments of nations. Millions upon millions of men have followed His promises and words. No work of literature has even begun to approach the endurance of the Scriptures which record Christs's life and have the same vitality today as they did nearly two thousand years ago. Magnificent churches, in which are invested centuries of labor and treasure, have been built as altars to Him. Could all this be the result of a lunatic's work, or even the result of one man's work?— The weight of evidence became more overwhelming to me the more I thought of it.

My legal training led me to another parallel. Our system of law is founded on the principle of *stare decisis*, that is, a court decision stands as a precedent with the same force of law as if it had one time been enacted or decreed; the whole system is built on precedents and presumptions which rest upon the foundation of earlier decisions. It is the key to giving stability to the law, a validation of history.

The most important decision of the Supreme Court, for example, studied intensively in law school, is *Marbury* v. *Madison*. Nowhere in the Constitution did the founding fathers give the Supreme Court the right to pass on the constitutionality of acts of Congress. The Court acquired that power years later as a result of this famous case.

Today no one questions the Court's power of judicial review which it has exercised with dramatic effect thousands of times since. Even a neophyte law student would prefer to argue the validity of the case for *Marbury* v. *Madison*. There isn't much going for him with a contrary position, because of the way in which the doctrine has become so well established by its long history of acceptance.

So why should I worry as I once did about being accused of mindlessly following the pack by accepting Christ? And why struggle so hard with concepts about God when I wouldn't question legal principles which have far less historic validity than the one we have laid before our eyes in the life and impact of the Carpenter of Nazareth?

Once faced with the staggering proposition that He is God, I was cornered, all avenues of retreat blocked, no falling back to that comfortable middle ground about Jesus being a great moral teacher. If He is not God, He is nothing, least of all a great moral teacher. For what He taught includes the assertion that He is indeed God. And if He is not, that one statement alone would have to qualify as the most monstrous lie of all time—stripping Him at once of any possible moral platform.

I could not, I saw, take Him on a slightly lower plateau because it is easier to do so, less troublesome to my intellect, less demanding of my faith, less challenging to my life. That would be substituting my mind for His, using Christianity where it helped to buttress my own notions, ignoring it where it didn't.

I realized suddenly that there is less heresy in rejecting Him altogether, dismissing Him as a raving lunatic, to use Lewis's word, than to remake Him into something He wasn't (and isn't). Jesus said take it, all or nothing. If I was to believe in God at all, I had to take Him as He reveals Himself, not as I might wish Him to be.

Patty and I decided to spend Thursday evening in Boothbay Harbor. It was band-concert night on the steps of the town library, a venerable and colorful institution of the New England summer. The music might have sounded to Arthur Fiedler like someone scratching a fingernail across a blackboard, but we loved every discordant note blaring forth with mighty gusto.

The band came in all sizes and shapes—from a tot with a trumpet who couldn't have been more than twelve, to a sweet-faced teenage girl in pigtails on the drums, her face pockmarked with acne, wearing a straight, flowered dress which mostly covered her knobby knees, to a man of eighty or more at the bass trombone, pure-white hair, a wrinkled, unsmiling face, and denim coveralls hanging from his rounded shoulders. Fifteen band members in all were lined along the wide wooden steps of the white clapboard building, the panes of its tall windows etched with century-old swirls and bubbles shimmering in the glow of two big floodlights.

It was a Norman Rockwell *Saturday Evening Post* cover come to life, a priceless piece of rich Americana, unspoiled and untouched by what modern society calls progress. There were tourists sprawled on the green lawn, kids with spun candy on a stick, and a large number of townsfolk for whom the concert is the major outing of the week.

The strains of "As the Saints Go Marching In" mixed with the fresh smell of salt in the night air. As I surveyed the faces in the crowd, something about them looked altogether different. Each one, including the kids with sticky sugar on their cheeks, looked like an individual, a separate human being, a child of God. Always before I'd seen crowds as blurs, a mass of humanity blending into an indistinct mosaic. Perhaps this new perception came from another Lewis passage, one that sent many of my cherished political ideals scattering like tenpins hit by a perfect strike:

And immortality makes this other difference, which, by the by, had a connection with the difference between totalitarianism and democracy. If individuals live only seventy years, then a state, or a nation, or a civilisation, which my last for a thousand years, is more important than an individual. But if Christianity is true, then the individual is not only more important but incomparably more important, for he is everlasting and the life of a state or a civilisation, compared with his, is only a moment.

The lowliest individual was more important than a state or nation! I had to take a lot of deep breaths after that one. Yet I had always thought of myself as a Jeffersonian conservative, one who believed fervently that the state exists only to serve the individual, created and maintained only with the individual's consent. What had happened to me was obvious: everyone who spends time in government becomes to some degree a "statist," dedicated to preserving the institutions of the state, often at all costs. Thus the paramount place of the individual in the scheme of things is gradually, unknowingly subordinated. Law-and-order legislation, for example, is aimed at maintaining the stability of the state—even if a few individuals have their rights trampled on in the process. Then, hard as it was to stomach, I had to admit that Dr. Daniel Ellsberg's rights were more important than preserving state secrets.

The political convictions I had developed from reading Locke and Jefferson had provided pliable guidelines, subject to tempering adjustments as "governmental crises" required, bending in the winds of the moment. But if Christ is real, if that fundamental decision is once made, then I am face-to-face with the very core of life itself, and with that I cannot tinker. Was Christ to change my view of life—and my neighbor, enemy, friend, and stranger alike—so drastically? My mind was whirling. Maybe it was the music, the nostalgia of the moment, the escape from the rest of the world one finds in Boothbay Harbor, Maine. Yet deep down I knew forces were at work which were demanding that I rethink every facet of my life.

Back at the inn doubts about my motives continued to nag at me. Was I seeking a safe port in the storm, a temporary hiding place? Was that what happened in Tom Phillips's driveway? Despite the arrow to the heart and my awakening on the Maine coast to the incredible realization about Jesus Christ, was I somehow looking to religion as a last-gasp effort to save myself as everything else in my world was crashing down about me?

Did I hope that God would keep my world intact? Legitimate doubts, I suppose. Certainly many people would accuse me of copping out in time of trouble. But could I make a decision based on how the world might judge it?

No, I knew the time had come for me: I could not sidestep the central question Lewis (or God) had placed squarely before me. Was I to accept without reservations Jesus Christ as Lord of my life? It was like a gate before me. There was no way to walk around it. I would step through, or I would remain outside. A "maybe" or "I need more time" was kidding myself.

And as something pressed that question home, less and less was I troubled by the curious phrase "accept Jesus Christ." It had sounded at first both pious and mystical, language of the zealot, maybe black-magic stuff. But "to accept" means no more than "to believe." Did I believe what Jesus said? If I did, if I took it on faith or reason or both, then I accepted. Not mystical or weird at all, and with no in-between ground left. Either I would believe or I would not—and believe it all or none of it.

The search that began that week on the coast of Maine, as I pondered it, was not quite as important as I had thought. It simply returned me to where I had been when I asked God to "take me" in that moment of surrender on the little country road in front of the Phillipses' home. What I studied so intently all week opened a little wider the new world into which I had already taken my first halting, shaky steps. One week of study on the Maine coast would hardly qualify, even in the jet age, as much of an odyssey, but I felt as if I'd been on a journey of thousands of miles.

And so early that Friday morning, while I sat alone staring at the sea I love, words I had not been certain I could understand or say fell naturally from my lips: "Lord Jesus, I believe You. I accept You. Please come into my life. I commit it to You."

With these few words that morning, while the briny sea churned, came a sureness of mind that matched the depth of feeling in my heart. There came something more: strength and serenity, a wonderful new assurance about life, a fresh perception of myself and the world around me. In the process, I felt old fears, tensions, and animosities draining away. I was coming alive to things I'd never seen before; as if God was filling barren void I'd known for so many months, filling it to its brim with a whole new kind of awareness.

I wrote to Tom Phillips, telling him of the step I had taken, of my gratitude for his loving concern, and asked his prayers for the long and difficult journey I sensed lay ahead.

I could not possibly in my wildest dreams have imagined what it would involve. How fortunate it is that God does not allow us to see into the future.

ELDRIDGE CLEAVER
1935 -

I returned to the Mediterranean Coast and began thinking of putting an end to it all by committing suicide. I really began to think about that. I was sitting up on my balcony, one night, on the thirteenth floor—just sitting there. It was a beautiful Mediterranean night—sky, stars, moon hanging there in a sable void. I was brooding, downcast, at the end of my rope. I looked up at the moon and saw certain shadows . . . and the shadows became a man in the moon, and I saw a profile of myself (a profile that we had used on posters for the Black Panther Party—something I had seen a thousand times). I was already upset and this scared me.

Born in Depression-era Arkansas, **Eldridge Cleaver** is best known for his involvement with the Black Panther party in the sixties. Cleaver joined the Panthers after an initial stint in prison, at which time he was exposed to the works of thinkers such as Thomas Paine, Karl Marx, and W.E.B. Dubois. Cleaver left prison transformed, energized by his reading and infused with the zeal of a

When I saw that image, I started trembling. It was a shaking that came from deep inside, and it had a threat about it that this mood was getting worse, that I could possibly disintegrate on the scene and fall apart. As I stared at this image, it changed, and I saw my former heroes paraded before my eyes. Here were Fidel Castro, Mao Tse-tung, Karl Marx, Frederick Engels, passing in review—each one appearing for a moment of time, and then dropping out of sight, like fallen heroes. Finally, at the end of the procession, in dazzling, shimmering light, the image of Jesus Christ appeared. That was the last straw.

I just crumbled and started crying. I fell to my knees, grabbing hold of the banister; and in the midst of this shaking and crying the Lord's Prayer and the 23rd Psalm came into my mind. I hadn't thought about these prayers for years. I started repeating them, and after a time I gained some control over the trembling and crying. Then I jumped up and ran to my bookshelf and got the Bible. It was the family Bible my mother had given to me because I am the oldest boy—the oldest son. And this Bible . . . when Kathleen left the United States, she brought with her a very small bag, and instead of grabbing the Communist Manifesto or *Das Kapital*, she packed that Bible. That is the Bible that I grabbed from the shelf that night and in which I turned to the 23rd Psalm. I discovered that my memory really had not served me that well. I got lost somewhere between the Valley of the Shadow of Death and the overflowing cup. But it was the Bible in which I searched and found that psalm. I read through it. At that time I didn't even know where to find the Lord's Prayer. I looked for it desperately. Pretty soon the type started swimming before my eyes, and I lay down on the bed and went to sleep.

That night I slept the most peaceful sleep I have ever known in my life. I woke up the next morning with a start, as though someone had touched me, and I could see in my mind the way, all the way back home,

social revolutionary. It was at this point, in 1967, that the author met Bobby Seale and Huey P. Newton, co-founders of the Black Panthers. Cleaver joined the group and eventually became their information minister, a position he held until his arrest for the murder of Bobby Hutton in 1968. Cleaver jumped bail and fled the country, experiencing religious conversion during his time abroad. After his return to the U.S. in 1975, he condemned the party and announced his sole allegiance to the party of faith. This excerpt from *Soul on Fire* tells the tale of Cleaver's dramatic conversion from politics to God.

just as clear as I've ever seen anything. I saw a path of light that ran through a prison cell. . . . This prison cell was a dark spot on this path of light, and the meaning, which was absolutely clear to me, was that I didn't have to wait on any politician to help me get back home. I had it within my power to get back home by taking that first step, by surrendering; and it was a certainty that everything was going to be all right. I just knew that—that was the solution, and I would be all right if I would take that step. . . .

Many people have looked at what happened and concluded that I must have made a deal with the authorities. This is very intriguing to me: what they are saying is that such things just do not happen, that the whole surrender event was extraordinary and therefore a pay-off was involved. They have to insist on this—otherwise they would have to consider the miracle of salvation involved.

Yes. They are right. I did make a deal; I made a deal with Jesus Christ! Yes, as well as I was able to understand it at that moment, I sold out; I sold out to Jesus! When I surrendered, I was stumbling ahead on faith and a vision, on assurance of the reality and truth of God, but I was still stumbling.

Little did I realize how totally I was surrendering. Nor did I understand that I was surrendering on two levels—to the civil authorities and to God. I am harping on this point, screaming out what seems to me a very vital fact—the act of stepping out on faith—because I clearly did not know what was going to happen. All I had was the assurance that things were going to turn out all right.

But even that assurance was going to be tested in time. The only guarantee I received through my lawyers from the Justice Department was that my security was guaranteed against the California Department of Correction, the Oakland Police Department, and other state and local agencies. Later on I was to regret that the agreement had not also stipulated the name of the Alameda County Sheriff's Department, into whose hands I ultimately fell. . . .

But it was also during this nine months of waiting, locked in a jail cell, that I was to experience the clearest and most open activity of God in my life, as he seemed to send the right person at the right time down to the precise moment. He sent Glenn Morrison and the other brother members of the God Squad—a nickname of an organization called Follow-up Ministries which specializes in bringing the gospel to men and women in jail and prison in the state of California.

Glenn was a regular visitor at the Alameda County Jail, and he gave me a Bible on one of his early visits, which I read avidly. But I was still shy about joining in any of the prayer times Glenn had with some of the other prisoners.

When Glenn and the others would form a circle, close their eyes and hold hands and pray, the hostile guys in the tank would throw bars of soap at them or flick water at them with a brush that had been dipped in the commode. You could see the hate in their eyes, and their obscene comments clashed violently with Glenn's soft-spoken prayers. There was no way then that I could bring myself to be a part of that circle—the tough guys would think I had an angle or was a softy. And I wasn't about to turn my back on them or close my eyes; I'd been in too many jails for that.

But in the lonely and quiet night hours I would sit and think about it all. Tears were close to the surface, and at times I would find myself sobbing uncontrollably. I'd taken some first steps in reaching out to God that moonlight night on the Mediterranean coast, but deep inside lurked the haunting feeling that there was something more to it than I had discovered so far.

Then one day in the second week of February, tired of running away, I joined the circle and listened intently to Glenn's talk and his prayer. He stressed the importance of a personal commitment to Jesus Christ—that it wasn't enough just to know that God exists but that complete freedom comes through inviting Christ into our life. I suppose those same words had fallen on my ears before, but this time I really heard them.

The rest of the day I reflected on what I'd heard and felt. I began to see that I had been focusing intellectually on God and Jesus Christ. Instead of praying, I had just been thinking about God. Now for the first time I saw the difference between that and actually talking to God.

Late that night I confronted the reality of my intense need, and my resistance evaporated. I confessed the name of Jesus Christ. I asked him into my life. I asked him to be my personal Savior. I laid all my sins at the foot of his cross and he set me free.

As I began crying tears of joy, God then began unraveling the mess. In my isolation he sent me brand new friends, brothers and sisters in Christ. My mail exploded. My old friends sent me hate letters, condemning me, calling me a traitor and a turncoat, rejecting me. Some expressed hope that I would rot in jail. But this was more than overbalanced by all of the wonderful people who sent me letters of love and encouragement. Those letters nourished the spiritual embryo that had been planted in my heart, and it was what I call the Christian grapevine that sustained me and kept me going in those dark moments. . . .

During my nine months in Alameda County Jail, well-meaning friends would send me all kinds of books, and I received several copies of Chuck Colson's *Born Again.* At first I would not even look inside the book. Even though I had become a Christian, I still had strong feelings against Colson. But one day when I was just lying around in my cell with nothing to do and absolutely bored to death, I picked up the book and started to read. Much to my amazement, I was strongly attracted to Chuck as I read my way through the book; I became convinced he was a real man and not a phony. And our mutual commitment to a ministry in prisons has cemented a supportive relationship that has been exceptionally helpful to me.

I am just now aware and becoming full of a sense of responsibility in believing that God doesn't waste his time fooling around with people unless he has something for them to do. I believe that God wants me to share the experience I have had in coming to him with others who have turned away from him. The hope of helping bring them back to him is the cause for which I now live.

In my entire life I have never been so happy and never felt so blessed. Many times people ask me if I feel as though I am being used, and I can only tell them that I am happy to be used; the worst thing in the world is to be useless. The only thing I don't like is to be misused, and I look to God to help me keep that from happening. I am thankful that even though it took me forty-one years to come out from beneath all the philosophy and science that I put upon myself, at last I found the bridge between myself and God—between myself and you. I praise the Lord for what happened and for the walk I started. I am two years old as a Christian and the future looks bright. I am here to be used until I am used up. I praise the Lord.

George Foreman

1949 -

I stayed to hear confirmation of the judges' decision, then hurried to my dressing room as Gil Clancy told me I'd been robbed. Though defeated, I felt none of the shame or hurt of the fight in Zaire. I'd given my best and, for the first time, gone the distance.

The dressing room was the usual postfight scene, with managers, trainers, assistants, and stadium officials milling around. Thinking of how racehorses are walked around the track to cool them down after racing, I pace back and forth. Never in my life had I been so hot.

"Man," I said, "where's the window around here?" Somebody cracked the transom, but to no good effect. Not even a hint of a breeze blew in. Out of panic, I started to pace faster.

Maybe it was the heat that made my thoughts come in such a rush. *All right, George. You don't have to worry about this fight anymore. You can retire if you want. You can do television and movies. You just signed a contract with ABC to comment on fights. You're still the world-famous George Foreman. You can always find something to do. And if you don't want to do anything, you don't have to. You've got that fine ranch to live in, and your other houses. You've got money to travel. You've got everything you want. You can retire and die.*

Die?!

How did that get in there? You're not dying. You're not going anywhere. You've got everything to live for—cars, money, houses, safety deposit boxes; things hidden away nobody knows about. You don't have to worry about boxing anymore. If you want to, you can go home and retire and . . . die.

That word again. I didn't understand where it came from or why. In no way was I considering suicide. In fact, I felt more excited about living than ever. But no matter how hard I focused on positives, my thinking was dominated by death. My pacing back and forth was no longer about cooling down; it was about staying alive. Walking soon escalated into calisthenics, and while the deep knee bends and jumping jacks didn't change my

This athlete's career has been so extraordinary one might think that he had received some helpful heavenly intervention. But in reality, pugilist **George Foreman** did not find faith until late in his first boxing career, managing to compile thirty-eight straight wins without the Lord's help. His amazing winning streak was interrupted by the historic knockout by Muhammad Ali in Zaire in 1974, an event that kept him out of the ring for over a decade. In 1987, Foreman realized that the best way he could help raise money for his church was to begin boxing again. At age 46, Foreman took back the title he had lost so many years before—and became the world's oldest heavyweight champion.

Foreman experienced conversion after a defeat in the ring. As he explains in his autobiography, *By George,* his conversion took him completely by surprise, in the form of an unexpected voice in his head inviting him to come to Christ. Often believers are taken by surprise by their Lord. He sneaks up on them when they least expect it, in perhaps their weakest moments, when they have the most trouble remembering who they are and what their place is on this earth. For George Foreman,

that surprise was a life-changing experience, pulling him back from the valueless world of material things and monetary success to the one thing that really matters: the road to faith and kindness.

perspective, they did raise eyebrows. Mine would have been raised, too, if I'd seen a fighter do this twelve brutal rounds. I didn't dare share my reasons with them, nor my thoughts.

My internal struggle went on for—well, I'm not sure whether it was seconds or hours. I considered confiding in someone until I realized that he'd have mistaken my admission for depression. I was fighting for my life, and at that moment understood for the first time how precious life really is.

You've heard of athletes dying after fights. Yeah, but not me, I'm not going to die.

Then a voice interrupted my thoughts. Though it came from inside my head, it definitely wasn't my own: *You believe in God. So why are you scared to die?*

Who was that? I, George Foreman, didn't really, honestly truly believe in God. No one had thought less of religious people than I had. My own voice would have known that about me. Unless of course it was referring to my prayers on the San Juan balcony and at my Marshall bedside. Oh, and there was also that time in Reverend Schuller's church, when I was trying to be liked. But none of those counted as proof of devotion. None of my prayers had ever counted. They had been pretend prayers, for effect only.

Still, the voice insisted: *If you believe in God, then why are you afraid to die?*

I blotted out the words with another recitation of what I had to live for. *I'm still George Foreman. I can still box. I can still give money to charity. And for cancer.* (I'd recently given ten thousand dollars to the American Cancer Society in the name of Dr. Anderson, the man who'd delivered me, who was suffering with the disease.)

As if offended, the voice grew urgent: *I don't want your money, I want you!*

Now I believed I really was dying. The invincibility I'd always felt had been an illusion. Life can end as quickly as a smile.

From somewhere came my own voice, "God, I believe in you—but not enough to die." To this day I don't know whether I said the words aloud or just heard them in my head.

As I fell to the floor of my dressing room, my leg crumpling beneath me, my nostrils filled with the stink

of infection. I recognized it instantly as the smell of absolute despair and hopelessness.

Then I felt myself transported to a far-off place, to an enormous void, to the bottom of the bottom of the bottom. This was the literal idea of nowhere—not someplace you talked about as nowhere, not even a place you could imagine unless you'd been there; but the real nowhere, the place where hope doesn't exist. All I could see was nothing. Nothing but nothing. Over my head and under my feet—just nothing.

A sledgehammer of crushing sadness—the most desperate sadness squared—stopped my breathing at the realization that all the cars, houses, and money for which I'd worked counted for nothing in this nowhere place. They were like ashes that crumble from burned paper when you touch it. When I looked back, I saw it all crumbling behind me. What counted was that I was going to die, and I hadn't told the people I loved how much they'd meant to me. Did I even know? I'd taken them for granted—Mom, my children. I'd not said goodbye. I'd not held them. I'd exchanged harsh words. I'd ignored them. I'd expressed my love mostly through gifts.

One after another, at light speed, my regrets whizzed passed. As they did, the sadness continued to squeeze the life from me. *I'm dead. This is death. This is what it's like to die.*

I said, "I don't care if this *is* death. I still believe there's a God." I had nothing else to lose; this was my last punch. It was as if I'd already died. And I didn't care anymore.

At that, a giant hand lifted and carried me out of that nothingness. Suddenly, feeling blood flowing through my veins again, I was back in the dressing room, lying on the training table. They must have carried me over after my leg crumpled. I looked up at the circle of faces surrounding me—my brothers Roy and Sonny, Gil Clancy, Charley Shipes, my bodyguard Lamar, and my masseur, Perry Fuller, who was crying.

"Hey, I'm dying," I said cheerfully. "But tell everybody I'm dying for God." That great hand has rescued me from a horrible place. I was going to trust it now. I wasn't scared.

They all humored me: "That's all right, George." "You're going to be fine, George." "Don't worry, George." And then: "You're a man, champ. You can get another fight."

As I lay on that dressing room table, I suddenly felt something sucking me from one place to another. In each place, I became a different person, speaking his language, feeling what he felt, worshiping his religion—

living his life. And just as soon as I became comfortable somewhere, I'd get sucked somewhere else. The journey seemed to last a long time, but it probably all happened in a single moment. . . .

Keith West, the doctor who traveled with me, grabbed my head. "Hey, Dr. West," I said, "move your hands, because the thorns on his head are making him bleed." What I saw was blood pouring out of my forehead. And it wasn't from the boxing match.

He didn't say a word. He just smiled wearily.

"Hey, Mr. Fuller," I said, "move your hands. He's bleeding where they crucified him." I saw blood on my hands.

"You're all right, George," he said, tears streaming down his face. Everyone had such pity for me.

"Hey, Jesus Christ is coming alive in me," I yelled.

They humored me some more: "It's okay, George. You'll win another fight. Don't worry."

"I'm not talking about boxing," I said. "Jesus Christ is coming alive in me."

Then Roy came over. I think he was playing around. "Yeah, George," he said, "but you're not clean enough."

"I have to get myself clean," I said.

Pushing them away, I aimed for the shower. Someone called out not to let me in because there was no hot water and the cold water might send me into shock. Everyone grabbed a limb and held on. Before someone got hurt, Dr. West ordered them to let go.

Standing in the water I shouted, "Hallelujah, I'm clean. Hallelujah, I've been born again." Afterward, I didn't towel off. That's when something took possession of me. I felt it below my stomach; I couldn't even control my breathing. I began reciting passages of the Bible I didn't know I knew, and running my mouth. Then I told everyone how much I loved them.

I grabbed Gil Clancy. "Come here," I said. "You're an Irishman, and I love you. You're my brother." I kissed him on the mouth.

"Come here, Mr. Fuller," I said, kissing him on the mouth, too. "I love you."

One by one I did the same to every man in the room. When I got to Sonny, he refused. But I wouldn't accept that. We struggled until Mr. Fuller ordered, "Just do it, Sonny. The man's losing his mind."

They must have figured that my next move was outside, where there were a few thousand people to kiss. That, they couldn't permit, if for no other reason than that I was still naked. I must have understood; I let them lead me to the training table. I lay down.

Then came the voice again: *I come to my brothers, and they don't believe me. I come to my friends, they don't understand me. So now I go to my father in heaven.*

I started to yell again: "Don't let Jesus go. Don't let Jesus go." A loving farewell from the other side. At that moment I was utterly at peace. I'd achieved all the greatness I'd aspired to. I was everything I'd ever wanted to be. The feeling that rocked me was the one I'd never experienced as the world champ. I finally had it all: fulfillment, peace, contentment. And the voice said, *Now I go.*

And just like that, it went. I reached out to grab my experience, but it was like trying to recall a spectacular dream that recedes with every waking second.

Looking up at all those faces I'd just kissed, I was the most embarrassed man on Earth. Now, suddenly, I was an old boxer, naked and wet, who couldn't explain what had just happened.

All I could do was pray and hope that all these witnesses would soon forget what they'd witnessed.

JIMMY CARTER
1924 -

Elected to the Presidency in 1976, **Jimmy Carter** began his political career in his home state of Georgia, where he served both in the state senate and as governor. A devout Baptist, Carter's faith helped him through a difficult Presidency, which was rocked by problems including inflation and severe unemployment at home and the Iranian hostage crisis abroad. Carter is best remembered for his foreign-policy achievements, such as the treaty he helped to seal between Egyptian President Anwar el-Sadat and Israeli prime minister Menachem Begin. In this excerpt, Carter comments first on the gift of religious freedom that we treasure in this country and then cautions that us not to carry such freedom too far. The former president stresses the stabilizing influence that religion can have on lives: "In our rapidly changing world to things that don't change—to truth and justice, to fairness, to brotherhood, to love and to faith. And through prayer, I believe we can find those things."

The leaders of our Nation look with a great deal of concern over the past experiences when kings and princesses had tied themselves to God, to the church, sometimes even in an exalted position relative to God, and had cloaked maladministration and injustice in the protection of the church. So, in our Constitution, we carefully prescribed that there should be no establishment of religion in this country.

So, we worship freely. But that does not mean that leaders of our Nation and the people of our Nation are not called upon to worship, because those who wrote the Declaration of Independence and the Bill of Rights and our Constitution did it under the aegis of, the guidance of, with a full belief in God.

In our rapidly changing world, we need to cling to things that don't change—to truth and justice, to fairness, to brotherhood, to love, and to faith. And through prayer, I believe that we can find those things.

MILES DAVIS
1926 - 1991

I don't like throwing God up into anybody's face and I don't like it thrown in mine. But if I have a religious preference, I think it would be Islam, and that I would be a Muslim. But I don't know about that or any organized religion. I've never been into that, using religion as a crutch. Because I personally don't like a lot of things that are happening in organized religion. It don't seem too spiritual to me, but more about money and power, and I can't go for that.

But I do believe in being spiritual and do believe in spirits. I always have. I believe my mother and father come to visit me. I believe all the musicians that I have known who are now dead do, too. When you work with great musicians, they are always a part of you—people like Max Roach, Sonny Rollins, John Coltrane, Bird, Diz, Jack DeJohnette, Philly Joe. The ones that are dead I miss a lot, especially as I grow older: Monk, Mingus, Freddie Webster, and Fat Girl. When I think about the ones who are dead it makes me mad, so I try not to think about it. But their spirits are walking around in me, so they're still here and passing it on to others. It's some spiritual shit and part of what I am today is them. It's all in me, the things I learned to do from them. Music is

*Arguably the most famous jazz trumpet player in America, **Miles Davis** made musical history every time he lifted his horn to his lips. Born in Alton, Illinois, he played bebop with jazz great Charlie Parker early in his career. Famous for such hit albums as* Kinda Blue *and* Bitches Brew, *Davis was a musical innovator until his death in 1991, helping to create the new jazz trend of fusion. As a musical mentor, he helped protégés such as Chick Corea and Keith Jarrett launch their illustrious careers. The following passage from* Miles Davis, The Autobiography, *contains Davis's reflections on the role of spirituality in his own life. He did not belong to any specific religion, although he asserted a leaning toward Islam. Davis's feelings remind us that faith is a many-colored thing; it comes in all shapes and sizes and is not necessarily constrained by the dictates of church or theology. Here, faith is defined as a helping hand,*

about the spirit and the spiritual, and about feeling. I believe their music is still around somewhere, you know. The shit that we played together has to be somewhere around in the air because we blew it there and that shit was magical, was spiritual.

I used to have these dreams where I thought I could see things, see some other stuff, like smoke or clouds, and my mind would make pictures of them. I do that now when I wake up in the morning and want to see my mother or father or Trane or Gil or Philly, or whoever. I just say to myself, "I want to see them," and they're there and I'm talking to them. Sometimes now when I look in the mirror I see my father there. This has been happening since he died and wrote that letter. I definitely believe in the spirit, but I don't think about death; there's too much for me to do to worry about that.

a source of solace for Davis as he reflects on the sorrows in his life—the loss of his parents and of many beloved fellow musicians. And we should not forget the limitless spirituality of music. Perhaps for Davis, music was his church and jazz his preacher, another example of the individualism that Americans bring to all things, including their quest for faith.

WILLIAM GILLESPIE
1931 -

WHEN YOU THINK YOU HAVE HAD ENOUGH

It is enough.
I Kings 19:4

When I was a boy, poverty for black people was real. Those were the days when there was no television and only a few persons owned radios. Many homes were without the bare necessities such as electricity and running water. Many families in our neighborhood would gather at the home of one of the few neighbors who owned a radio to listen to the broadcast of Joe Louis boxing. I remember listening to the fight in which Max Schmeling defeated Joe Louis. The reaction of all those gathered was one I shall never forget. It was as if their world had come to an end. Joe represented someone to be admired. He was a black man, and the best heavyweight boxer in the world. He epitomized the longing of black people in America to be the best. Each victory for Joe Louis was a victory for black America.

Joe Louis gave hope to blacks in despair. If he could be the best in boxing and make people proud of him, then others could be the best in science, medicine, art, and a thousand other fields of endeavor. But that night Joe Louis was defeated.

In this sermon drawn from his book entitled *Black Preaching*, Presbyterian minister **William Gillespie** addresses the issue of faith in the face of hardship, using the prophet Elijah as an example. Gillespie, who preaches to a primarily black congregation, addresses the difficulties faced by blacks in this country, reminding his audience that discouragement and setbacks are not things unknown even to the great among us, "Elijah, Dr. Martin Luther King— even Jesus Christ."

Little did I know that one day I would experience this feeling of despair among black people again. It came upon the news of the assassination of Dr. Martin Luther King, Jr. Dr. King represented a man of whom all America could be proud. He refused to sacrifice principle for the sake of expediency. He would not close his eyes to the evils of racism and live as though they did not exist. No, he exposed racism, condemned segregation and discrimination of all forms, practiced love for all people—even his enemies. He would not declare that peace and harmony prevailed while he knew that the cancer of racial discrimination was gnawing away at the vitals of the nation. He attacked racism in an effort to destroy it. Dr. King exposed segregation in an effort to remove it from the scene. He opposed violence as a method of solving any problems. Some called him Black Moses. Others looked upon him as a messiah. Still others saw him as the only one with an answer to the American dilemma. But in April, 1968, the news came—"Dr. King is dead!" This shattered the hopes and dreams of us all. Like Elijah, we were ready to cry, "It is enough!"

Life is like that. The very moment your goal is in sight it turns you around and places your goal farther away. Or you become planted in some congenial soil, and along comes a rude gardener who uproots you and moves you on. We have often felt like that writer who declared: "Life is too great a journey; I cannot travel it trustingly. Life is too great a mission; I cannot live it helpfully. Life is too great a contest; I cannot live it victoriously. Life is too great a struggle; I cannot live it successfully. I have had enough."

Life is a journey in which too many of us give up. We begin with great enthusiasm. We trust that we will reach our goal. We have a heart and mind for a successful journey, but soon we are confronted by roadblocks which seem to make that journey impossible. Elijah knew what it meant to be confronted by a roadblock. His was in the form of a woman named Jezebel. This man, tired and spent, had passed through exacting circumstances. Many were his worries prior to his test on Mt. Carmel. Would God vindicate his faith? Would God cause his adversaries to really know that he was His true servant? In other words, would God be on time with His help when it would be needed? Elijah discovered that God was on time. Look at the picture. Ahab has assembled four hundred and fifty prophets of Baal on Mt. Carmel. This was done at the request of Elijah, who wanted the people to make a choice between God and Baal. Almost every student of the Bible can recall his challenge to the people: "How long halt ye between two opinions? if the Lord be God, follow him: but if Baal, then follow him." This was a great moment for both Israel and Elijah. There was silence, no answer when Elijah made his challenge. If silence means consent, then it would appear that the people were pledging their allegiance to the Lord God of Israel. This is not sufficient for Elijah. He wants to hear from their mouths, "The Lord, he is God."

Elijah explains the rules of the contest that is to take place between Baal and God. Following these rules, the prophets of Baal built an altar, killed a bullock, cut it up and laid it on the wood of the altar. They were instructed to put no fire under the altar. The priests of Baal would call upon their god to supply fire, and then Elijah would call upon the God of Israel to do the same. The god who answered by fire would be God. One can almost see the priests of Baal circling the altar, dancing around the sacrifice from morning to noon. They entreat Baal: "Hear us! Hear us!" But Baal is just as silent as the people were to Elijah's challenge. Elijah makes sport of them. He seems to get a thrill from it all, seeing them cut themselves with knives, inflicting physical wounds that would take a long time to heal, trying their best to convince everyone they were doing all they could to make their god hear and answer. But their god remained silent.

Now it is Elijah's turn. He calls the people to come near. Then the prophet with twelve stones repaired a broken-down altar. He dug a trench about the altar and placed the sacrifice, a slain bullock, upon the wood. Four jars of water were poured over the sacrifice upon the wood three times. The water ran around the altar and filled the trench.

It is time for Elijah to call upon God to consume the sacrifice with fire. Listen to his prayer: "O Lord, God of Abraham, Isaac, and Israel, let it be known this day that thou art God in Israel, and that I am thy servant, and that I have done all these things at thy word. Answer me, O Lord, answer me, that this people may know that thou, O Lord, art God, and that thou hast turned their hearts back." Then the fire of the Lord fell, and consumed the burnt offering and the wood, and the stones, and the dust, and licked up the water that was in the trench. When the people saw what had happened, they fell on their faces and said, "The Lord, he is God." After his victory, Elijah had the prophets of Baal seized and killed.

Ahab saw Elijah's prayers for both fire and rain answered. On their return to Jezreel, Elijah was so happy over his victories that he ran before Ahab. When Ahab came into the presence of Jezebel, he told her that all Elijah had done, and how he had slain all the prophets with the sword. Then Jezebel sent a messenger to Elijah saying, "So may the gods do to me, and more also, if I do not make your life as the life of one of them by this time tomorrow."

This threat was something Elijah could not cope with. It took away the sweetness of his victory and filled him with anxiety. He became so fearful of Jezebel that it drove him to madness. He eventually ended up in the wilderness. So frustrating was his experience that it took much of his physical strength away. The Book of First Kings records it this way: "He . . . went a day's journey into the wilderness, and came and sat down under a broom tree; and he asked that he might die, saying, 'It is enough; now, O Lord, take away my life; for I am no better than my fathers.'"

There are times when many of us become weary. We represent causes that are good, but no good comes from our work. We support people who give themselves relentlessly to a good cause and they are killed, imprisoned, or silenced by the forces of evil. We knock on doors that are closed to black people until our knuckles are raw, but the doors remain closed. We prepare ourselves for jobs we never get, for housing we cannot buy, for clubs we cannot enter, for churches where we are unwanted, for dreams that never come true. There are times when we all feel like crying, "I've had enough; I can't take any more." But when you think you have had enough, remember that the race isn't given to the swift, but to him who endures to the end. Remember the words of James, "Happy is the man who remains faithful under trials."

Many of you will recall the movie that was quite popular in the '40s. It was entitled Stormy Weather. One of the stars was Lena Horne, and she sang the title song. In her song she described her discouragement as a result of being separated from the man she loved. Poignant are the words—"keeps on raining all the time. I can't go on; everything I had is gone!" That's the way many felt when Dr. King was assassinated, and when Joe Louis was defeated. Surely this was the feeling of Elijah when he declared, "It is enough."

Elijah felt discouraged because he did not believe that he was a match for Jezebel. This led him to believe that he was inferior in other things. He looked about and lost faith in his fellowman. Elijah did not feel that he could recruit forces strong enough to overcome Jezebel, and he felt that no one else could either.

So many black Americans had this feeling upon King's death. Yet, thank God, it was not King's feeling while he was alive. He said, "I may not get to the promised land with you, but one day we as a people will get there!" He lived with a buoyant optimism. He would not let disappointment, fear, or frustration turn him around. He knew that challenges must be met with our best effort and God's help. He knew that throwing up our hands, walking out on our dreams, screaming, "I've had enough!" would never help one reach his goal. Men must be willing to risk danger, suffer, if it is needful, and even die to achieve some goals. Have we forgotten those blacks faced with discouragement in slavery? They sang such songs of encouragement as "I'll Never Turn Back No More," "Children, Don't You Get Weary," and that comforting spiritual from which these words come:

> There is a balm in Gilead
>> To make the wounded whole,
> There is a balm in Gilead
>> To heal the sin-sick soul.
> Sometimes I feel discouraged,
>> And think my work's in vain,
> But then the Holy Spirit
>> Revives my soul again.

When you think you have had enough, just tell yourself you can take a little bit more. Tell yourself that you are the equal to your discouragement. The words of an old adage declare, "We can't prevent birds from flying over our heads, but we can prevent them from making nests in our hair." Discouragements are sure to come our way, but we need not let them defeat us. Who among us hasn't been discouraged? Our Lord knew discouragement. Surely in the Garden of Gethsemane he was discouraged by his disciples as they slept while he prayed. He expressed it in his words: "Are you still sleeping and taking your rest? Behold, the hour is at hand, and the Son of man is betrayed into the hands of sinners." And yet, how swiftly he challenges even those who had discouraged him. "Rise, let us be going."

Recall again Elijah and his discouragement. Was he defeated by it? What did he do to overcome it? Was he so mesmerized by things that he continued to sit weeping under the broom tree? The words of the writer of the Book of First Kings are these: "And he lay down and slept under a broom tree; and behold, an angel touched him." I like these words. They show us the importance of rest if one is to perform at his best. One who receives adequate rest is better equipped to deal with his problems than those who do not. Elijah was awakened by the touch of an angel. This was indicative of the fact that God was present with him. Elijah now had no need to think himself helpless in the face of his circumstances. He set out on a journey of forty days and nights into a wilderness. Coming to a cave, he heard the voice of God: "What doest thou here, Elijah? Without hesitation, Elijah makes his position known: "I have been very jealous for the Lord God of hosts: for the children of Israel have forsaken thy covenant, thrown down thine altars, and slain thy prophets with the sword; and I, even I only, am left, and they seek my life, to take it away." Recall the Lord's response. It was a great and strong wind that rent the mountains, and broke in pieces the rocks. The Lord was not in the wind nor the earthquake which followed, nor the fire that came after that. God spoke to Elijah in a still, small voice.

The Lord gave him a new perspective on life and a new vision of God. God let Elijah know that all was well as far as Israel's religion was concerned. God put Elijah to work again. He had a great task which needed to be performed, and Elijah was God's man to do it. He spent the remainder of his life doing good—anointing kings, choosing a successor to himself, and, I am sure, praising God.

A number of years ago I came across the story of a young man who lost a leg while serving in the United States Armed Forces. He never lost his beautiful outlook on life. "This is a temporary setback," he wrote his mother. "But I will succeed in spite of it." Each of us is called to make the most of life in whatever circumstances we find ourselves. We must believe we can overcome. We must make all our defeats temporary.

In the beginning I told you of Joe Louis' defeat. He made it a temporary setback. There was a second fight between Louis and Schmeling. Joe won the second fight by a knockout in the first round. From that temporary setback he went on to become one of the greatest heavyweight champions of all time. So often after his victories his words would be similar to these: "I am glad I won. God was on my side." The hymn writer put it this way:

> Be still, my soul: the Lord is on thy side;
> Bear patiently the cross of grief or pain;
> Leave to thy God to order and provide;
> In every change he faithful will remain.
> Be still, my soul: thy God doth undertake
> To guide the future as he has the past.
> Thy hope, thy confidence, let nothing shake;
> All now mysterious shall be bright at last.

Hugh Walpole wrote: "It is not life that matters. It is the courage you bring to it." So, when we come to that point in life where we think we've had enough, we need to reflect on the lines of those who have refused to be defeated by discouragement. Bring a positive attitude into this situation. Don't give way to self-pity. This ultimately leads to failure and defeat. We must not become bitter or resentful for the circumstances in which we find ourselves. Refuse to accept the situation as final and turn your disadvantages into advantages. In other words, make the most of your situation.

Dr. Clarence Macartney told the story of an old man with a bundle of sticks on his back. He sank down by the roadside, and with a groan said he wished he were dead. To his surprise and terror, Death at once made his appearance and asked him what he would have. The old man said quickly, "My bundle on my back, and my feet once more on the road." In his discouragement, what he asked for was not really what he desired. This is true of many of our wishes in the hour of discouragement.

Some will say this all seems to naive. For people who have been waiting so long for a better day, this is understandable. We must live with a long-term faith. Of course, we would like to see things happen now. We must work to make things happen now. All of us want to achieve our goals, realize our dreams while we are here on earth. We must not let a temporary setback stop us. We must keep on keeping on! We must undertake great adventures and challenge others to do the same. Our dreams for justice, equality, and true freedom must remain alive! Jesus lived in this spirit. He spoke of the coming of the kingdom of God. He did not see it. He believed that it would come, and because he believed so

strongly that it would become a reality, he suffered and died on the cross.

Each of us can learn from Jesus' experience. What are your personal discouragements? What makes you want to give up? For each the discouragements are similar—unemployment, soaring death rate from strokes and heart attacks among blacks, repeated failures with our children and sometimes our marriages. But we must continue on. We must continue to work in whatever capacity we find ourselves. Your work is needed. You may not be a senator, representative, state legislator, or mayor. You may not hold any public office—but your work is needed. Your work in your home church and community may be the humblest of all tasks—but it is needed! Put your heart and mind in it. Let nothing stop you or turn you around. This is no time for throwing in the towel. You cannot afford to say, "I've had enough; I can't take any more."

In this sermon I have sought to describe to you how different individuals have handled discouragements, some much greater than any of us would ever encounter. Joe Louis, Dr. Martin Luther King, Jr., Elijah, and even Jesus Christ—all faced discouragement, but each felt his work or cause was so important that he refused to be defeated. With the faith and knowledge that God the Father would see them through, they accomplished what they had to do. With this same faith, we can do it too.

THOMAS HOWARD
1935 -

This is one reason why I find the Incarnation compelling. For in the figure of Jesus the Christ there is something that escapes us. He has been the subject of the greatest efforts at systematization in the history of man. But anyone who has ever tried this has had, in the end, to admit that the seams keep bursting. He sooner or later discovers that he is in touch, not with a pale Galilean, but with a towering, and furious figure who will not be managed. . . .

We had a lively awareness of the points at which all forms of Christianity other than our own failed. We were all adroit at describing how this group and that group

In this excerpt from Christ the Tiger, **Thomas Howard** *examines the figure of Jesus Christ, identifying Him not as a man we can grasp in our hands or an entity we can easily define, but as a huge force, a power unto Himself. Howard, former contributing editor to* Christianity Today,

did not quite measure up. I was once invited to describe the religious life on our campus at a regional conference of student Christian groups. I, of course, felt that the conference was a misnomer in that the other people were not Christian to begin with, since their set of priorities was not mine. In my talk I emphasized frequently what I felt to be the core of Christianity and described it as the thing that bound my group together. I do not remember what I said, but one man, in talking with me afterwards, said, concerning some point that I had made, that it did not show a great deal of self-criticism. "Not at all," I replied blithely. I thought, "Exactly. Why should we indulge in self-criticism? We have the inspired Scriptures on our side, and that's that."

authored a number of books exploring faith. An Anglo-Catholic, Howard was the chairman of English at St. John's Seminary in Massachusetts. He is currently on the faculty of Gordon College. In the following pages, Howard beautifully explores our understanding of Christ, describing Him and canvassing the map of His strength and effect on our lives.

I felt that I had scored a point. I was congratulated by my colleagues afterwards for having given a positive word of "witness" to this misguided conference. I am happy that I do not remember the man's face now, and I hope he has forgotten both me and my remarks.

In this reassessment of my religious posture I wondered in what sense it can be urged that a given segment of Christendom is exempt from the mortal threat of Ichabod. (I found this a useful term: it alluded to the Old Testament story of a woman who named her child Ichabod, because "the glory had departed" from Israel.) Biblical history was full of stories of people who were anointed ones and who finally had had "Ichabod" written over them. How did we know that the glory had not departed from us?

If this was ever suggested, we cited names from our own saints' gallery as witness to God's presence with us, and we pointed out that our people were well intentioned (they were "dear souls," "earnest Christians," and "simple folk") and we cited converts (the implication being that God was drawing the converts, and that He would not be doing this if we had not been satisfactory). We did not care to reflect that you can get converts to anything in the world or that godly forebears do not guarantee godly progeny. Nor did we stop to reflect that what is sauce for the goose is sauce for the gander, ourselves being the gander. That is, we liked the story about the people arriving at the Judgment Seat and pleading that they had done all kinds of good things in God's name only to discover that God had no idea who they were. This applied, of course, to other groups, not to us. We made a career of saying "Lord, Lord" (we are the best extempore pray-ers in the world) but never dreamed that it might be *us* to whom he would turn blankly one fine day and say, "Depart. I never knew you." We liked to tell about the parable of the branches being cut off and thrown into the fire, but we knew quite well who those branches were. We liked the story of Samson, who had been chosen by God and anointed, and who woke up one morning and tried to do great things, and "wist not that Jehovah had departed from him." We, of course, were not Samson, thank God.

We understood Scripture in a highly typological way, and were, therefore, inclined to read all stories as applicable to *somebody*. How we knew that not a word of all this was true of us, I cannot remember. It was, to our mind, not a possibility that we might be massively and tragically wrong in anything. Our patterns for devotion and worship and education and entertainment were as axiomatic as was our creed.

The unconscious assumption of certitude in dogmatic and practical matters had a curious side effect on our response to doubt. It is, of course, common, and probably fashionable, for university students to lose their religious faith. But it was not to my mind legitimate for the elders to throw out the baby (inquiry and real doubt) with the bath water (adolescent exhibitionism or dishonest doubt). At times, the official response to someone's questioning the grounds of our dogma was scandal ("This is heresy!"), or scorn ("Oh, grow up!") or grief ("You have betrayed the faith.").

But it seemed to me that the exercise of actual, as opposed to academic, inquiry, was an important and human exercise, and that the assault of doubt was inevitable upon one whose eyes are open to the ambiguities of existence. But if you attach to your loyalty to your creed the addendum that you thereby know all that is necessary to account for ambiguity and are therefore invulnerable, your faith has changed into presumption. . . .

But I could think that in the figure of Jesus we saw Immanuel, that is, God, that is, Love. It was a figure who, appearing so inauspiciously among us, broke up our secularist and our religious categories, and beckoned us and judged us and damned us and saved us, and exhibited to us a kind of life that participates in the indestructible. And it was a figure who announced the validity of our eternal effort to discover significance and beauty beyond inanition and horror by announcing to us the unthinkable: redemption.

It was a figure we could neither own nor manage. We claimed it as our special possession, and exacted tribute and built shrines and established forms in which to incarcerate it, only to discover that it had fled. It would not be enshrined. It was the figure of a man, and a man must live and walk with other men or die, and this man was alive. He scorned our scruple to shelter him and to prop up his doctrine. What he spoke, he spoke loudly and freely, and his words were their own defense. When we tried to help things by urging sweetness and light, or by interdicting what looked threatening, or by tithing mint, anise, and cummin, or by devising rituals and nonrituals, we found him towering above us, scorching our efforts into clinkers, and recalling us to wildness and risk and humility and love. Just at the moment when we thought we had guaranteed our own standing in his good favor by organizing an airtight doctrine or a flawless liturgy or an unassailable morality, he escaped us, and returned with his hammer to demolish things. Try as we might, we could not own him. We could not protect him. We could not incarcerate him. For he always emerged as our judge, exposing our cynicism and fright by the candor and boldness of his love. He tore our secularist schemes to ribbons by announcing doom and our religious schemes to tatters by announcing love.

He appeared as a man and demonstrated a kind of life wholly foreign to all of our inclinations. For he showed us what a man's life is like when it is energized by *caritas,* and in doing this, he became our judge, because we knew too well that it is that other love, *cupiditas,* that energizes us. He told us of a city, the City of God, in which *caritas* rules. He told us that all who participate in this are citizens of that city.

We experienced this announcement as both death-dealing and life-giving. It was death-dealing because we knew our own incorrigible cupidity—the energy that makes us shriek for the shovel in the sandbox, cut into the ticket line, rush for the subway seat, display our prowess, parade our clothes, and pursue delights regardless of prior considerations.

We remembered our own torrid yearning, for instance, for other bodies, and our insistence that we must seek satisfaction at all costs because this was such an ecstatic bliss. And he said to us, yes, yes, yes, you are quite right, another body *is* the most beautiful thing in the world. This kind of congress *is* ecstatic bliss, but your unexamined pursuit of this will, irony of ironies, dehumanize you, for it is a failure to ask the questions that must be asked—questions about the *imago Dei* in you and your partner, questions about sex as a form of knowledge that requires a high warrant, questions about sex as a metaphor of realities that lie at the heart of everything, and questions about the undying notion in all of us of sex as significant and binding and most holy.

And what is true here is true in all regions of experience. Your mad pursuit is for freedom and intensity and bliss. It is natural. But, by a wry irony at work in the world, the pursuit leads you into a prison where your agony is to become more and more insistent that things shall be as you wish, and less and less able to cope with denial.

But I show you a different way. It is an alien and a frightening one. It is called Love. It asks that you forswear your busy effort to collect the bits of bliss and novelty that lie about. It asks that you disavow your attempt to enlarge your own identity by diminishing that of others. It asks that you cease your effort to safeguard your own claim to well-being by assuming the inferiority of others' claims. It asks, actually, that you die.

For, paradoxically, it offers to you your own best being beyond this apparent immolation of yourself. It says that the cupidity energizing all your efforts is the principle that governs wherever hell is found, and that the dwellers in that realm are a withered host of wraiths, doomed to an eternal hunt for solidity and fulfillment among the shards that lie underfoot. This is not your best being. You were meant to find your home in the City of God, which is among you. Here duty is ecstasy. For that is what is meant by *caritas*: it is the freedom which follows upon the capacity to experience as joy what you are given to do.

But the City is not reached in a moment. It is as remote as the Towers of Trebizond, and as near as your neighbor.

And we experienced his announcement as death dealing again, because it knocked over all the little pickets and wickets that we had tapped carefully into place to guarantee the safety of our religion. He saw our masses and rosaries and prayer meetings and study groups and devotions, and he said yes, yes, yes, you are quite right to think that goodness demands rigor and vigilance and observance, but your new moons and sabbaths and bullocks and altars and vestments and Gospel teams and taboos and Bible studies are trumpery, and they nauseate me because you have elevated *them,* and I alone am the Host. Your incense if foetid, and your annotated Bibles are rubbish paper. Your meetings are a bore and your myopic exegesis is suffocating. Return, return, and think again what I have asked of you: to follow justice, and love mercy, and do your job of work, and love one another, and give me the worship of your heart—your *heart*—and be merry and thankful and lowly and not pompous and gaunt and sere.

But we experienced the announcement as life-giving because it was an announcement, appearing in a dirty barn, and heard among the dry provincial hills and then in the forum of Rome and in the halls of royal princes and in the kitchens and streets of Paris and Calcutta and Harlem and Darien, that Joy and not Havoc is the last word. It announced to us what we could not hope. It saw limitation and contingency and disparity and irrevocability and mutability and decay and death, and it said yes, yes, yes, you are quite right: terror and horror and despair are the only eventually realistic responses . . . *if* this is all there is to it. But it is not.

You have thought of a world free from such conditions. In all your imaginings, and in your myths and your mime and your songs and dances and epics—in your quest for form and significance and beauty beyond fragmentation and inanition and chaos—you have bespoken such a vision. I announce it to you. Here, from this stable, here, from this Nazareth, this stony beach, this Jerusalem, this market place, this garden, this praetorium, this Cross, this mountain, I announce it to you.

I announce to you what is guessed at in all the phenomena of your world. You see the corn of wheat shrivel and break open and die, but you expect a crop. I tell you of the Springtime of which all springtimes speak. I tell you of the world for which this world groans and toward which it strains. I tell you that beyond the awful borders imposed by time and space and contingency, there lies what you seek. I announce to you life instead of mere existence, freedom instead of frustration, justice instead of compensation. For I announce to you redemption. Behold I make all things new. Behold I do what cannot be done. I restore the years that the locusts and worms have eaten. I restore the years which you have dropped away upon your crutches and in your wheel-chair. I restore the symphonies and operas which your deaf ears have never heard, and the snowy massif your blind eyes have never seen, and the freedom lost to you through plunder, and the identity lost to you because of calumny and the failure of justice; and I restore the good which your own foolish mistakes have cheated you of. And

I bring you to the Love of which all other loves speak, the Love which is joy and beauty, and which you have sought in a thousand streets and for which you have wept and clawed your pillow.

CESAR CHAVEZ

1927 - 1993

Cesar Chavez
March 24, 1983

Dear Paul:

Thank you for the letter you wrote to me on February 10, 1983. I am sorry that I could not answer you sooner, but many meetings with farm workers in California and additional engagements made it impossible.

I am pleased that you included me in the survey of people that you respect. My answers to your question will be brief, but I hope they will be satisfactory.

Yes, Paul. I definitely believe in God! The presence of God has been made clear to me first of all by my parents. My father (who died last October at the age of 101!) and my mother were good Catholics and brought us up with great respect for God: They made sure that we learned our prayers, that we respected the teachings of the Church, and that we tried to live justly.

Since I have grown up, the presence of God has been made clear to me in two different ways: through other good people who love God and their brothers and sisters so heroically (Gandhi, St. Francis of Assisi, Rev. Martin Luther King, Jr., Dorothy Day, Mother Teresa) and through my own personal prayer, especially meditation. I find that, if I provide time and silence for God, He will make his presence known to me.

As I said, my answers are quite brief, but I hope they will give you an idea of the presence of God in my life and they will be of use to you in your survey.

Cesar Chavez, born near Yuma, Arizona, in 1927, was a voice for those who could not make themselves heard—the migrant workers of California. He began organizing the grape pickers in 1962, establishing the National Farm Workers Association. Three years later the group merged with the United Farm Workers Organizing Committee. The following year wine grape growers accepted the union as a bargaining agent. In 1970, table grape growers accepted the union. Cesar Chavez's fight to gain rights for workers continued until the end of his life Boycotts, strikes and demonstrations were tools of Chavez's fight—all aspects of nonviolent struggle. This faith in nonviolent battle was surely related to the union organizer's deep faith in God. This excerpt demonstrates Chavez's deep and guiding belief in God.

MUHAMMAD ALI

1942 -

I became a true believer, I'd say, around 1983. Before that, I thought I was a true believer, but I wasn't. I fit my religion to do what I wanted. I did things that were wrong, and chased women all the time. Then, one day, someone I respect asked me, 'Would you go to bed with a woman where your mother could see you? No. Would you go to bed with a woman where your children could see you? No. So why go to bed with a woman where God sees you, because God sees everything all the time.'

The first pilgrimage I made to Makkah [in January 1972] wasn't like a pilgrimage at all. People recognized me and I wished I could have met all of them, but I didn't appreciate where I was. Things weren't Westernized. There was no ice cream, no girls in short dresses, no one listening to Chubby Checker. Now I'm wiser. I've studied more, and each time I make a pilgrimage, it thrills me and makes me humble to be standing where the prophet Muhammad was when he received revelations from God.

Everything I do now, I do to please Allah. I conquered the world, and it didn't bring me true happiness. The only true satisfaction comes from honoring and worshiping God. Time passes quick; this life is short. I see my daughter Maryum. Yesterday she was a baby. Now she's grown and ready to get married. My hair is gray underneath the dye. God doesn't allow you to go back and live your life over again. But the older you get, the wiser you get; and in the time I got left, I'm living right. Every day is a judgment for me. Every night when I go to

This incredible athlete converted to Islam the day after his controversial knockout of Sonny Liston in 1965, a knockout that resulted in his first world championship title. After the fight, he changed his name from Cassius Clay to **Muhammad Ali**. With his legendary defeat of George Foreman in Zaire, in the early 1970's, he won the world title for the second time. Ali's career was unforgettable. As well as winning an Olympic gold medal, he was the only heavyweight champ to hold the world title three times. The boxer who said "Float like a butterfly, sting like a bee" is an internationally recognized figure. He has appeared on the cover of *Sports Illustrated* thirty-two times, one of the most constantly reported-on athletes of all time. He is also remembered for his social impact: his consciousness raising about black issues, his influence on the civil rights movement and his aid in spreading the Islamic faith. Today Ali suffers from Parkinson's disease, but he is more committed to his faith than ever before, traveling the world to spread the word. In Islam he has found what he perhaps now needs most: comfort, guidance, and love. In this excerpt from his autobiography, *Muhammad Ali: His Life and Times*, the boxer describes how he came to faith and how he feels about religion and Islam.

bed, I ask myself, 'If God were to judge me just on what I did today, would I go to heaven or hell?' Being a true Muslim is the most important thing in the world to me. It means more to me than being black or being American. I can't save other people's souls; only God can do that. But I can try to save mine.

RONALD REAGAN

1911 -

I believe that faith and religion play a critical role in the political life of our Nation and always have; and that the church—and by that I mean all churches—has had a strong influence on the state, and this has worked to our benefit as a Nation. Those who created our country—the Founding Fathers and Mothers—understood that there is a Divine order which transcends the human order. They saw the state, in fact, as a form of moral order, and felt that the bedrock of moral order is religion.

From movie star to California governor to two-time President, **Ronald Reagan** is the epitome of an American success story. Religion formed a strong cornerstone in his life, from the former president's upbringing in the Christian Church to his continuing devotion to faith throughout his adult life. According to Lou Cannon, Reagan "quotes Scripture, remembers Bible stories from his childhood days in the Christian Church, and regards Jesus Christ as his personal savior and as a hero of history." Reagan referred to Christ as the man he most admired in all of history. The remarks that follow were made at an Ecumenical Prayer Breakfast in 1984, and they reflect Reagan's concern about the place of religion in modern America.

The Mayflower Compact began with the words, "In the name of God, amen." The Declaration of Independence appeals to "Nature's God," and the "Creator," and "the Supreme Judge of the world." Congress was given a chaplain, and the oaths of office are oaths before God.

James Madison in the *Federalist Papers* admitted that in the creation of our Republic he perceived the hand of the Almighty. John Jay, the first Chief Justice of the Supreme Court, warned that we must never forget the God from whom our blessings flowed.

George Washington referred to religion's profound and unsurpassed place in the heart of our Nation quite directly in his Farewell Address in 1796. Seven years earlier, France had erected a government that was intended to be purely secular. This new government would be grounded on reason rather than the law of God. By 1796, the French Revolution had know the Reign of Terror. And Washington voiced reservations about the idea that there could be wise policy without a firm moral and religious foundation. He said, "Of all the dispositions and habits which lead to political prosperity, Religion and morality are indispensable supports. In vain would that man [call himself a patriot] who [would] labour to subvert these . . . firmest props of the duties of men and citizens. The mere Politician . . . [and] the pious man ought to respect and to cherish [religion and morality]." He added, ". . . let us with caution indulge the supposition, that morality can be maintained without religion."

I believe that George Washington knew the City of Man cannot survive without the City of God; that the Visible City will perish without the Invisible City.

Religion played not only a strong role in our national life, it played a positive role. The abolitionist movement was at heart a moral and religious movement. So was the modern Civil Rights struggle. And throughout this time, the state was tolerant of religious belief, expression, and practice. Society, too, was tolerant.

But in the 1960s, the climate began to change. We began to make great steps toward secularizing our Nation and removing religion from its honored place.

In 1962, the Supreme Court in the New York prayer case banned the compulsory saying of prayers. In 1963, the Court banned the reading of the Bible in our public schools. From that point on, the courts pushed the meaning of the ruling ever outward, so that now our children are not allowed voluntary prayer. We even had to pass a law—pass a special law in the Congress just a few weeks ago—to allow student prayer groups the same access to schoolrooms after classes that a Young Marxist Society, for example, would already enjoy with no opposition.

The 1962 decision opened the way to a flood of similar suits. Once religion had been made vulnerable, a series of assaults were made in one court after another, on one issue after another. Cases were started to argue, against tax-exempt status for churches. Suits were brought to abolish the words "Under God" from the Pledge of Allegiance, and to remove "In God We Trust" from public documents and from our currency.

Today, there are those who are fighting to make sure voluntary prayer is not returned to the classrooms.

And the frustrating thing for the great majority of Americans who support and understand the special importance of religion in the national life—the frustrating thing is that those who are attacking religion claim they are doing it in the name of tolerance and freedom and open-mindedness. Question: Isn't the real truth that they are intolerant of religion? That they refuse to tolerate its importance in our lives?

If all of the children of our country studied, together, all of the many religions in our country, wouldn't they learn greater tolerance of each other's beliefs? And is that not to be desired? If children prayed together would they not understand what they have in common and would this not indeed bring them closer? I submit to you that those who claim to be fighting for tolerance on this issue may not be tolerant at all.

When John Kennedy was running for President in 1960, he said that his church would not dictate his presidency any more than he would speak for his church. Just so—and proper. But John Kennedy was speaking in an America in which the role of religion—and by that I mean the role of all churches—was secure. Abortion was not a political issue; prayer was not a political issue; the right of church schools to operate was not a political issue; and it was broadly acknowledged that religious leaders had a right and a duty to speak out on issues of the day. They held a place of respect; and a politician who spoke to or of them with a lack of respect would not long survive in the political arena. It was acknowledged then that religion held a special place, occupied a special territory in the hearts of the citizenry.

The climate has changed greatly since then. And since it has, it logically follows that religion needs defenders against those who care only for the interests of the state.

There are, these days, many questions on which religious leaders are obliged to offer their moral and theological guidance. And such guidance is a good and necessary thing. To know how a church and its members feel on a public issue expands the parameters of debate. It does not narrow the debate. It expands it.

The truth is, politics and morality are inseparable. And as morality's foundation is religion, religion and politics are necessarily related. We need religion as a guide; we need it because we are imperfect. And our Government needs the Church because only those humble enough to admit they are sinners can bring to democracy the tolerance it requires in order to survive.

A state is nothing more than a reflection of its citizens; the more decent the citizens, the more decent the state. If you practice a religion—whether you are Catholic, Protestant, Jewish, or guided by some other faith—then your private life will be influenced by a sense of moral obligation. So, too, will your public life. One, you see, affects the other.

The churches of America do not exist by the grace of the state; the churches of America are not mere "citizens" of the state. The churches of America exist apart—they have their own vantage point, their own authority. Religion is its own realm; it makes its own claims.

We establish no religion in this country nor will we ever; we command no worship, we mandate no belief. But we poison our society when we remove its theological underpinnings; we court corruption when we leave it bereft of belief. All are free to believe or not to believe, all are free to practice a faith or not. But those who believe must be free to speak of an act on their belief, to apply moral teaching to public questions.

I submit to you that the tolerant society is open to and encouraging of all religions. And this does not weaken us, it makes us strong.

Without God there is no virtue because there is no prompting of the conscience; without God we are mired in the material, that flat world that tells us only what the senses perceive; without God there is a coarsening of the society; without God democracy will not and cannot long endure. And that, simply, is the heart of my message: If we ever forget that we are One Nation Under God, then we will be a Nation gone under.

WALKER PERCY
1916 - 1990

WHY ARE YOU CATHOLIC?

This assignment and the question above (which is sometimes asked in the same context) arouse in me, I'll admit, certain misgivings. One reason, the first that comes to mind, is that the prospect of giving one's "testament," saying it straight out, puts me in mind of an old radio program on which people, mostly show-business types as I recall, uttered their resounding credos, which ended with a sonorous Ed Murrow flourish: *This—I believe.*

Another reason for reticence is that novelists are a devious lot to begin with, disinclined to say any-

Born in Birmingham, Alabama, in 1916, **Percy** studied medicine at Columbia Medical School, but never practiced. Instead he wrote six novels—among them *The Moviegoer*, which won the National Book

Award, and *The Last Gentleman*—and two books of essays. All were primarily about the South. Percy was one of the greatest writers of our century, called by a *Los Angeles Times* obituary "the Faulkner of his generation." And he was a devout Catholic, remaining loyal to his faith despite the anti-religious opinions of many of his contemporaries. In the following essay, "Why Are You Catholic?" Percy explains just that, allowing us as readers to step onto the private ground of another's beliefs.

thing straight out, especially about themselves, since their stock-in-trade is indirection, if not guile, coming at things and people from the side so to speak, especially the blind side, the better to get at them. If anybody says anything straight out, it is apt to be one of their characters, a character, moreover, for which they have not much use.

But since one is obliged by ordinary civility to give a response, the temptation is to utter a couple of sentences to get it over with, and let it go at that. Such as: I am Catholic, or, if you like, a Roman Catholic, a convert to the Catholic faith. The reason I am a Catholic is that I believe that what the Catholic Church proposes is true.

I'd as soon let it go at that and go about my business. The Catholic faith is, to say the least, very important to me, but I have not the least desire to convert anyone or engage in an apologetic or polemic or a "defense of the Faith." But a civil question is entitled to a civil answer and this answer, while true enough, can be taken to be uncivil, even peremptory. And it hardly answers the question.

One justifies the laconicness as a reaction to the current fashion of confessional autobiographies written not only by show-biz types and writers and politicians but by respectable folk as well, confessions which contain not only every sort of sonorous *This—I believe* but every conceivable sexual misadventure as well. The sincerity and the prodigality of the confessions seem to be understood to be virtues.

There is also a native reticence at work here. It has to do with the disinclination of Americans to discuss religion and sex in the company of their peers.

When the subject of religion does arise, at least in the South, the occasion is often an uncivil one, a challenge or a provocation, or even an insult. It happens once in a while, for example, that one finds oneself in a group of educated persons, one of whom, an educated person of a certain sort, may venture some such offhand remark as Of course, the Roman Catholic Church is not only a foreign power but a fascist power. Or, when in a group of less educated persons, perhaps in a small-town barbershop, one of whom, let us say an ex-member of the Ku Klux Klan—who are not bad fellows actually, at least hereabouts, except when it comes to blacks, Jews, and Catholics—when one of them comes out with something like The Catholic Church is a piece of shit, then one feels entitled to a polite rebuttal in both cases, in the one with something like "Well, hold on, let us examine the terms, power, foreign, fascist—" and so on, and in the case of the other, responding in the same tone of casual barbershop bonhomie with, say, "Truthfully, Lester, you're something of a shit yourself, even for white trash—" without in either case disrupting, necessarily, the general amiability.

Yet another reason for reticence in matters religious has to do with the infirmity of language itself. Language is a living organism and, as such, is subject to certain organic ailments. In this case it is the exhaustion and decrepitude of words themselves, an infirmity which has nothing to do with the truth or falsity of the sentences they form. The words of religion tend to wear out and get stored in the attic. The word "religion" itself has a certain unction about it, to say nothing of "born again," "salvation," "Jesus," even though it is begging the question to assume therefore that these words do not have valid referents. And it doesn't help that when religious words are used publicly, at least Christian words, they are often expropriated by some of the worst rogues around, the TV preachers.

So decrepit and so abused is the language of the Judeo-Christian religions that it takes an effort to salvage them, the very words, from the husks and barnacles of meaning which have encrusted them over the centuries. Or else words can become slick as coins worn thin by usage and so devalued. One of the tasks of the saint is to renew language, to sing a new song. The novelist, no saint, has a humbler task. He must use every ounce of skill, cunning, humor, even irony, to deliver religion from the merely edifying.

In these peculiar times, the word "sin" has been devalued to mean everything from slightly naughty excess (my sin was loving you) to such serious lapses as "emotional unfulfillment," the stunting of one's "growth as a person," and the loss of "intersubjective communication." The worse sin of all, according to a book I read about one's growth as a person, is the "failure of creativity."

One reason the poet and novelist these days have a hankering for apocalypse, the end of the old world and the beginning of the new, is surely their sense that only then can language be renewed, by destroying the old and starting over. Things fall apart but words regain their value. A boy sees an ordinary shell on the beach, picks it up as if it were a jewel he had found, recognizes it, names it. Now the name does not conceal the shell but celebrates it.

Nevertheless, however, decrepit the language and however one may wish to observe the amenities and avoid offending one's fellow Americans, sometimes the question which is the title of this article is asked more or less directly.

When it is asked just so, straight out, just so:

"Why are you a Catholic?"

I usually reply,

"What else is there?"

I justify this smart-mouthed answer when I sense that the question is, as it usually is, a smart-mouthed questions.

In my experience, the question is usually asked by two or three sorts of people. One knows quite well what is meant by all three.

One sort is perhaps a family acquaintance or friend of a friend or long-ago schoolmate or distant kin, most likely a Presbyterian lady. There is a certain type of Southern Presbyterian lady, especially Georgian, who doesn't mince words.

What she means is: how in the world can you, a Southerner like me, one of us, of a certain class and background which encompasses the stark chastity of a Presbyterian Church or the understated elegance of an Episcopal Church (but not a Baptist or Methodist Church), a Southern Christian gentleman, that is to say—how can you become one of them, meaning that odd-looking baroque building down the street (the wrong end of the street) with those statutes (Jesus pointing to his heart, which has apparently been exposed by open-heart surgery)—meaning those Irish, Germans, Poles, Italians, Cajuns, Hispanics, Syrians, and God knows who else—though God knows they're fine people and I love them all—but I mean there's a difference between a simple encounter with God in a plain place with one's own kind without all that business of red candles and beads and priest in a box—I mean how can you?

The second questioner is a scientific type, not just any scientist, but the sort who for certain reasons has elected a blunt manner, which he takes to be allowed by friendship and by his scientific mien—perhaps a psychiatrist friend, with their way of fixing the patient with a direct look which seeks to disarm by its friendly directness, takes charming leave to cut through the dross of small talk and asks the smiling direct question: "Why are you a Catholic?" But there's a question behind the question: I mean, for God's sake, religion is all very well, humans in any culture have a need for emotional bonding, community, and even atonement—in the sense of at-one-ment—I myself am a Unitarian Universalist, with some interesting input of Zen lately—but I mean, as if it were not strange enough to elect one of those patriarchal religions which require a Father God outside the cosmos, not only that but that he, this Jewish Big Daddy, elected out of the entire cosmos to enter the history of an insignificant tribe on an insignificant planet, it and no other, a belief for which, as you well know, there is not the slightest scientific evidence—not only that, but of the several hundred Jewish-Christian religions, you pick the most florid and vulgar of the lot—why *that*?

Yet another sort could be a New Age type, an amorphous group ranging from California loonies like Shirley McLaine to the classier Joseph Campbell who, as wildly different as they are, share a common stance toward all credos: that they are to be judged, not by their truth or falsity, sense or nonsense, but by their mythical liveliness. Here the question is not challenging but congratulatory, not: "Why are you a Catholic?" but "So you are a Catholic? How odd and interesting!"

Episcopalians are too polite and gentlemanly to ask the question—and are somewhat inhibited, besides, by their own claim on the word "Catholic."

Jews, whatever they may think of the Catholic Church, are too intuitive to ask the question, having, as they do, a sense of a commonality here which comes of being an exotic minority, which is to say: Never mind what I think of your religion or you of mine; we've both got enough trouble at least to leave each other alone.

So the question remains: "Why are you a Catholic?"

Asked from curiosity alone, it is a civil question and deserves a civil answer.

Accordingly, I will answer here in a cursory, somewhat technical, and almost perfunctory manner which, as unsatisfactory as it may be, will at least avoid the usual apologetic and polemic. For the traditional defense of the Catholic claim, however valid it may be, is generally unavailing for reasons both of the infirmity of language and the inattentiveness of the age. Accordingly, it is probably a waste of time.

My answer to the question, then, has more to do with science and history, science in its root sense of knowing, truth-seeking; history in the sense that, while what is true is true, it may be that one seeks different truths in different ages.

The following statements I take to be common-places. Technically speaking, they are for my purposes axioms. If they are not perceived as such, as self-evident, there is no use arguing about them, let alone the conclusions which follow from them.

Here they are:

The old modern age has ended. We live in a post-modern as well as a post-Christian age which as yet has no name.

It is post-Christian in the sense that people no longer understand themselves, as they understood themselves for some fifteen hundred years, as ensouled creatures under God, born to trouble, and whose salvation depends upon the entrance of God into history as Jesus Christ.

It is post-modern because the Age of Enlightenment with its vision of man as a rational creature, naturally good and part of the cosmos, which itself is understandable by natural science—this age has also ended. It ended with the catastrophes of the twentieth century.

The present age is demented. It is possessed by a sense of dislocation, a loss of personal identity, an alternating sentimentality and rage which, in an individual patient, could be characterized as dementia.

As the century draws to a close, it does not yet have a name, but it can be described.

It is the most scientifically advanced, savage, democratic, inhuman, sentimental, murderous century in human history.

I will give it a name which at least describes what it does. I would call it the age of the theorist-consumer. All denizens of the age tend to be one or the other or both.

Darwin, Newton, and Freud were theorists. They pursued truth more or less successfully by theory—from which, however, they themselves were exempt. You will look in vain in Darwin's *Origin of the Species* for an explanation of Darwin's behavior in writing *Origin of the Species*. Marx and Stalin, Nietzsche and Hitler were also theorists. When theory is applied, not to matter or beasts, but to man, the consequence is that millions of men can be eliminated without compunction or even much interest. Survivors of both Hitler's Holocaust and Stalin's terror reported that their oppressors were not "horrible" or "diabolical" but seemed, on the contrary, quite ordinary, even bored by their actions as if it were all in a day's work.

The denizens of the present age are both sentimental and bored. Last year the Russians and the Americans united to save three stranded whales and the world applauded. It seemed a good thing to do and the boredom lifted for a while. This was not true, unfortunately, of the million Sudanese who died of starvation of the same year.

Americans are the nicest, most generous, and sentimental people on earth. Yet Americans have killed more unborn children than any nation in history.

Now euthanasia is beginning.

Don't forget that the Germans used to be the friendliest, most sentimental people on earth. But euthanasia was instituted, not by the Nazis, but by the friendly democratic Germans of the Weimar Republic. The Weimar Republic was followed by the Nazis.

It is not "horrible" that over a million unborn children were killed in America last year. For one thing, one does not see many people horrified. It is not horrible, because in an age of theory and consumption it is appropriate that actions be carried out as the applications of theory and the needs of consumption require.

Theory supersedes political antinomies like "conservative" versus "liberal," Fascist versus Communist, right versus left.

Accordingly, it should not be surprising that present-day liberals favor abortion, just as the Nazis did years ago. The only difference is that the Nazis favored it for theoretical reasons (eugenics, racial purity), while present-day liberals favor it for consumer needs (unwanted, inconvenient).

Nor should it be surprising that for the same reasons liberal not only favor abortion but are now beginning to favor euthanasia, as the Nazis did.

Liberals understandably see no contradiction and should not be blamed for favoring abortion and euthanasia on the one hand and the "sacredness of the individual," care for the poor, the homeless and oppressed, on the other. Because it is one thing for a liberal editor to see the poor and the homeless on his way to work in his own city and another to read a medical statistic in his own paper about one million abortions. A liberal may act from his own consumer needs (guilt, sentimentality) and the Nazis may act from theory (eugenics, racial purity), but both are consistent in an age of theory and consumption.

The Nazis did not come out of nowhere.

It may be quite true what Mother Teresa said—if a mother can kill her unborn child, then I can kill you and you can kill me—but it is not necessarily horrifying.

America is probably the last and best hope of the world, not because it is not in the same trouble—indeed, the trouble may even be worse due to the excessive consumption in the marketplace and the excessive theorizing in academe—but because, with all the trouble, it preserves a certain innocence and freedom.

This is the age of theory and consumption, yet not everyone is satisfied by theorizing and consuming.

The common mark of the theorist and the consumer is that neither knows who he is or what he wants outside of theorizing and consuming.

This is so because the theorist is not encompassed by his theory. One's self is always a leftover from one's theory.

For even if one becomes passionately convinced of Freudian theory or Marxist theory at three o'clock on a Wednesday afternoon, what does one do with oneself at four o'clock?

The consumer, who thought he knew what he wanted—the consumption of the goods and services of scientific theory—is not in fact satisfied, even when the services offered are such techniques as "personal growth," "emotional maturity," "consciousness-raising," and suchlike.

The face of the denizen of the present ago who has come to the end of theory and consumption and "personal growth" is the face of sadness and anxiety.

Such a denizen can become so frustrated, bored, and enraged that he resorts to violence, violence upon himself (drugs, suicide) or upon others (murder, war).

Or such a denizen may discover that he is open to a search for signs, some sign other than theorizing or consumption.

There are only two signs in the post-modern age which cannot be encompassed by theory.

One sign is one's self. No matter how powerful the theory, whether psychological or political, one's self is always a leftover. Indeed, the self may be defined as that portion of the person which cannot be encompassed by theory, not even a theory of the self. This is so because, even if one agrees with the theory, what does one do then? Accordingly, the self finds itself ever more conspicuously without a place in the modern world, which is perfectly understood by theorizing. The face of the self in the very age which was itself designed for the self's understanding of all things and to please the self through the consumption of goods and services—the face of the self is the face of fear and sadness, because it does not know who it is or where it belongs.

The only other sign in the world which cannot be encompassed by theory is the Jews, their unique history, their suffering and achievements, what they started (both Judaism and Christianity), and their presence in the here-and-now.

The Jews are a stumbling block to theory. They cannot be subsumed under any social or political theory. Even Arnold Toynbee, whose theory of history encompassed all other people, looked foolish when he tried to encompass the Jews. The Jews are both a sign and a stumbling block. That is why they are hated by theorists like Hitler and Stalin. The Jews cannot be gotten around.

The great paradox of the Western world is that even though it was in the Judeo-Christian West that modern science arose and flourished, it is Judeo-Christianity which the present-day scientific set of mind finds the most offensive among the world's religions.

Judaism is offensive because it claims that God entered into a covenant with a single tribe, with it and no other.

Christianity is doubly offensive because it claims not only this but also that God became one man, He and no other.

One cannot imagine any statement more offensive to the present-day scientific set of mind. Accordingly, Hinduism and Buddhism, which have no scientific tradition but whose claims are limited to the self, its existence or nonexistence, which are far less offensive to the present-day scientific set of mind, are in fact quite compatible.

The paradox can be resolved in only two ways.

One is that both the Jewish and the Christian claims are untrue, are in fact nonsense, and that the scientific mind-set is correct.

The other is that the scientific method is correct as far as it goes, but the theoretical mind-set, which assigns significance to single things and events only insofar as they are exemplars of theory or items for consumption, is in fact an inflation of a method of knowing and is unwarranted.

Now that I have been invited to think of it, the reasons for my conversion to the Catholic Church, this side of grace, can be described as Roman, Arthurian, Semitic, and semiotic.

Semitic? Arthurian? This is funny, because what could be more un-Jewish than the chivalric legend of

Arthur? And who could be more un-English than the Old Testament Jews?

Or are they? Or could it in fact have been otherwise? My first hero and the hero of the South for a hundred years was Richard I of *Ivanhoe*, who with his English knights in the First Crusade stormed the gates of Acre to rescue the holy places from the Infidel. But earlier than that, there was the Roman Emperor Marcus Aurelius. If one wished to depict the beau ideal of the South, it would not be the crucified Christ but rather the stoic knight at parade rest, both hands folded on the hilt of his broadsword, his face as grave and impassive as the Emperor's. In the South, of course, he came to be, not the Emperor or Richard, but R. E. Lee, the two in one.

Bad though much of Southern romanticism may be, with Christianity and Judaism and Roman valor seem through the eyes of Sir Walter Scott, how could it have been otherwise with me? After all, the pagans converted by St. Paul did not cease to be what they were. One does not cease to be Roman, Arthurian, Alabamian. One did, however, begin to realize a few things. The holy places which Richard rescued, and whether he thought about it or not, were, after all, Jewish, and he probably did not think about it, because his crusaders killed Jews every which way on the way to the Holy Land. Yet Scott succeeded in romanticizing even the Jews in *Ivanhoe*. But did the European knight with his broadsword at Mont-St.-Michel make any sense without the crucified Jew above him? A modern Pope said it: "Whatever else we are, first we are first of all spiritual Semites." Salvation, the Lord said, comes from the Jews.

In a word, thanks to the Jews, one can emerge from the enchanted mists of the mythical past, the Roman and Arthurian and Confederate past, lovely as it is. For, whatever else the Jews are, they are not mythical. Myths are stories which did not happen. But the Jews were there then and are here now.

Semitic? Semiotic? Jews and the science of signs? Yes, because in this age of the lost self, lost in the desert of theory and consumption, nothing of significance remains but signs. And only two signs are of significance in a world where all theoretical cats are gray. One is oneself and the other is the Jews. But for the self that finds itself lost in the desert of theory and consumption, there is nothing to do but set out as a pilgrim in the desert in search of a sign. In this desert, that of theory and consumption, there remains only one sign, the Jews. By "the Jews" I mean not only Israel, the exclusive

people of God, but the worldwide ecclesia instituted by one of them, God-become-man, a Jew.

It is for this reason that the present age is better than Christendom. In the old Christendom, everyone was a Christian and hardly anyone thought twice about it. But in the present age the survivor of theory and consumption becomes a wayfarer in the desert, like St. Anthony; which is to say, open to signs.

I do not feel obliged to set forth the particular religious reasons for my choosing among the Jewish-Christian religions. There are times when it is better not to name God. One reason is that most of the denizens of the present age are too intoxicated by the theories and goods of the age to be aware of the catastrophe already upon us.

How and why I chose the Catholic Church—this side of grace, which leaves one unclear about who does the choosing—from among the Judeo-Christian religions, Judaism, Protestantism, the Catholic Church, pertains to old family quarrels among these faiths and so such is not of much interest, I would suppose, to the denizens of this age. As for them, the other members of the family, the Jews and the Protestants, they are already all too familiar with the Catholic claim for me to have to repeat it here. It would be a waste of their time and mine. Anyhow, I do not have the authority to bear good news or to proclaim a teaching.

RICHARD J. FOSTER
1942 -

We have come to the end of this study, but only to the beginning of our journey. We have seen how *meditation* heightens our spiritual sensitivity which, in turn, leads us into *prayer*. Very soon we discover that prayer involves *fasting* as an accompanying means. Informed by these three Disciplines, we can effectively move into *study* which gives us discernment about ourselves and the world in which we live.

Through *simplicity* we live with others in integrity. *Solitude* allows us to be genuinely present to people when we are with them. Through *submission* we live with others

In his book *Celebration of Discipline*, **Richard Foster** writes, "The desperate need today is not for a greater number of intelligent people, or gifted people, but for deep people." Foster, a recorded Quaker clergyman who received his education at Fuller Theological Seminary, goes on to tell us that we must acquire that necessary depth and gives us the guidelines to do it. The following excerpt from the conclusion of *Celebration of Discipline* outlines his principles which perhaps originate from the beliefs of the Society of Friends, a religious body with a history that dates from seventeenth-century England and is characterized by a tradition of pacifism, tolerance, and a quiet but very serious pursuit of faith.

without manipulation, and through *service* we are a blessing to them.

Confession frees us from ourselves and releases us to *worship*. Worship opens the door to *guidance*. All the Disciplines freely exercised bring forth the doxology of *celebration*.

The classical Disciplines of the spiritual life beckon us to the Himalayas of the Spirit. Now we stand at timber line awed by the snowy peaks before us. We step out in confidence with our Guide who has blazed the trail and conquered the highest summit.

MAYA ANGELOU

1928 -

Question: *Was religion a major factor in your life then?*

Angelou: Its importance was primarily through music. The church was a central meeting place where one could listen to and participate in the music. Actually, the first poetry I ever knew was the poetry of the gospel songs and the spirituals. I knew that blacks had written that music. I thought it was marvelous stuff! I loved the songs. I also loved the sermons. However, that God with the long hair, the One who sat on a throne in Heaven, He scared me to pieces.

But the music of the sermons inspired me then and still does today.

Question: *Are you a religious person?*

Angelou: Yes, I believe in God. I believe in whatever people call God. I believe in life. I believe in will. I believe in good. I believe that right wins out. It may sound naive, but I believe in those things. . . .

Different people express their faith in different ways. And for some, music is the only way to get the message out—by singing spirituals or hymns. Writer **Maya Angelou** counts herself among that number, explaining that the central influence of religion in her life came through music. In this excerpt from a series of interviews with the author of *I Know Why the Caged Bird Sings*, Angelou explains that her religious feeling is rooted not so much in a doctrine or theology, but in a love for

Question: *Religion has meant a lot to you, hasn't it?*

I have a great attachment—that's such a weak word—a gratitude for the presence of God. (When) we're praying, we are celebrating our existence with God. I grew up in the Baptist church, so I prefer and understand the Baptist ritual, but all roads lead to Rome.

If you know that, you don't put value judgments on (religions). You use the wisdom of all of them. We are a community of children of God, whether we admit it or not, whether we call it God or the Creator or the Source of Nature. We're a community.

church music and in a feeling of "gratitude" for God's existence. This is a simple and joyful faith in the Lord.

SIR JOHN TEMPLETON

1912 -

It's egotistical to think we can comprehend total reality. It's also egotistical for us to think that we are the final product of God's creative process. In these hundred billion other stars in our galaxy and hundred billion other galaxies God may be manifesting himself in something beyond our comprehension. Take that plant in the corner: It might be aware of me—sometimes I water it, sometimes I touch it. The air it breathes is the air I breathe and so forth. So that plant may have some knowledge of me, but it's a tiny bit of knowledge. In the same way maybe God is right here too, and maybe I have a tiny knowledge of God, but it's very tiny.

Throughout history humans have tended to think that religion was an aspect of life. But just the opposite may be true: life may be an aspect of religion. Humans have tended to think that God can be proven to exist or not exist and that God is separate from humans. But more and more the evidence is the other way around—that God is the totality of which each of us and all humanity together is a tiny little part. The simile I've used and like

Sir John Templeton is famous for his enormous wealth. But he has also gained great acclaim for his personal faith, which led him to establish the Templeton Prize, awarded to those who make great achievements in the area of faith. Templeton has sat on the boards of many church and ecumenical councils. He has also authored several books on the subject, including *The God Who Would Be Known* and *Is God the Only Reality?* In this article, culled from *Second Opinion* magazine, the billionaire comments on his life and faith.

best of all is the ocean (although similes don't stand up, as you know, to careful examination). The waves on the ocean are made up of molecules that make up the water, and they form into waves, and the waves have a beginning and an end and an effect. Civilization is like a wave on the ocean. And you are like a molecule in that wave of civilization. But the ocean is God. When the wave is gone, the ocean is still there, and there will be more waves. When your molecule is gone, it isn't gone permanently; it's simply in another situation. I won't carry it as far as without somebody advancing and somebody being left behind. . . .

I think most human beings go through life not really knowing what their calling is. Some of us stumble into one thing, and then we find we're in the wrong place and change it. Many of our students at Princeton Seminary previously had another career. I didn't know that I was right, and young people in general don't know they're right. I always gave it a lot of thought. I thought at one time that the highest calling was to be a Christian minister. I watched the Christian ministers and decided that was not my talent—others were doing it better. I thought about being a missionary, and again the same thing happened. I decided that the best I could hope for in a spiritual way was to be a missionary's helper. When I was 18 I came to believe that the talents that God had given me—not many and not so different from other people's—were elements of judgment and foresight. Where would they be useful? In reading the newspaper I could see the prices of shares fluctuate an average of 100 percent a year. People were losing their money by investing in some company at a time optimism and paying too high a price. They didn't know it was too high a price because they hadn't taken the time to find out what the company was worth in the first place. So I undertook at 18 to educate myself on judging the value of corporations. I thought that would help people and would help religion in the sense that if I were good at it I would be able to do things like what I'm doing now. When I became a trustee of Princeton Seminary their endowments were $3 million. Now they are $ 450 million. Of that, $35 million is just new gifts not spent on buildings, and the rest is profits. So I hope that in some ways I am being a missionary's helper. . . .

It goes back to humility. I don't know what God wants me to do. I don't know why good fortune has come to me more often than bad fortune. I do believe that chance favors the prepared, as it's been said. Opportunity knocks on the door of those people who prepare thoroughly. All the shelves of books written on the problem of evil have explained almost nothing of God's purposes, but I believe this earth is created by somebody far wiser than I and that there's probably some purpose in the things that happened to me and the even sadder things that happen to other people. I doubt if I'll ever understand why it is, but I don't have any trouble believing that the one who created the earth is doing it the right way.

HENRI NOUWEN
1932 -

After I began to write this letter to you something happened that at first seemed rather insignificant to me. In the days following, however, it took on more and more importance. Therefore, I want to tell you about it before I finish this letter. It is a weather story. The weather here in upstate New York was lovely up until ten days ago. The winter was over, the spring had begun. The climate was mild and sunny, and the monks enjoyed walking through the woods and observing the first signs of the new season. Yellow, white, and blue crocuses decorated the yard, and everybody seemed happy that another cold season had come to an end. But not so! On the day I finally got myself organized enough to begin writing you this letter, a violent storm broke over the land, bringing with it heavy rains. Buckets appeared under the leaks in the roof, windows were shut securely, and no one ventured forth from the house. The temperature dropped sharply, and soon the rain turned into snow. The next day we were back in winter. It kept snowing the whole day, and I felt strangely disoriented. My whole body had been

This excerpt from **Henri Nouwen**'s *Letter of Consolation* is a wonderful example of the way in which faith can offer solace when we most need it. Nouwen is wrestling with the death of his mother, painfully searching for a way to relieve his own grief and that of his father (to whom the letter is written). He thinks about the resurrection of Christ and gains strength from it, ruminating over the fact that His rebirth is an event that can offer hope to all of us who are faced with loss: "It [the resurrection] does not make the loss of her less real, but it makes us see and feel that death is part of a much greater and much deeper event, the fullness of which we cannot comprehend, but of which we know is a life-bringing event."

Here faith offers what nothing else seems to—a way to reconcile the death of a loved one, to put it into terms in which the pain and grief seem, if not acceptable, at least bearable. Nouwen is no stranger to pain or hardship in life. A Catholic priest ordained in 1957, he left a position at Yale Divinity School to devote his life to helping people at L'Arche Daybreak in Ontario. In this ecumenical and inter-religious community, which is part of the International Federation of L'Arche, people with mental disabilities live and work with the assistants, who become their friends and family.

anticipating bright flowers, green trees, and songbirds, and this strange new weather felt totally incongruous. When the storm was over, the landscape seemed idyllic, like a Christmas card. The snow was fresh and beautiful and had settled on the green fields and fir trees like a fresh white robe. But I could not enjoy it. I simply kept saying to myself, "Well, one week from now it will be Easter and then it will be spring again." I discovered in myself a strange certainty that Easter would change the weather. And when everything was still pure white on Wednesday of Holy Week, I continued to feel, "Only three more days and everything will be green again!" Well, on Good Friday stormy winds rose up, a miserable rain began to come down, and it poured for the rest of the day. The next morning all the snow was gone. In the afternoon the clouds dissolved and a brilliant sun appeared, transforming everything into a joyous spectacle. When I looked out of my window and saw the fresh, clear light covering the meadows, I had a hard time not breaking the monastic silence. I walked out and went up to the ridge from which I could overlook the valley. I just smiled and smiled. And I spoke out loudly to the skies, "The Lord is risen; he is risen indeed!"

Never in my life have I sensed so deeply that the sacred events that we celebrate affect our natural surroundings. It was much more than the feeling of a happy coincidence. It was the intense realization that the events we were celebrating were the real events and that everything else, nature and culture included, was dependent on these events.

You will probably want to know now what the weather was like on Easter morning. It was gentle and cloudy. Nothing very unusual. No rain, no wind; not very cold, not very warm. No radiant sun, only a gentle, soft breeze. It did not really matter much to me. I would probably have been happy even if there had been snow again. What mattered to me was that I had

come to experience during this holy season that the real events are the events that take place under the great veil of nature and history. All depends on whether we have eyes that see and ears that hear.

This is what I so much want to write to you on this Easter of 1979. Something very deep and mysterious, very holy and sacred, is taking place in our lives right where we are, and the more attentive we become the more we will begin to see and hear it. The more our spiritual sensitivities come to the surface of our daily lives, the more we will discover—uncover—a new presence in our lives. I have a strong sense that mother's death has been, and still is, a painful but very blessed purification that will enable us to hear a voice and see a face we had not seen or heard as clearly before.

Think of what is happening at Easter. A group of women go to the tomb, notice that the stone has been moved away, enter, see a young man in a white robe sitting on the righthand side, and hear him say, "He is not here." Peter and John come running to the tomb and find it empty. Mary of Magdala meets a gardener who calls her by name, and she realizes it is Jesus. The disciples, anxiously huddled together in a closed room, suddenly find him standing among them and hear him say, "Peace be with you." Two men come hurrying back from Emmaus and tell their puzzled friends that they met Jesus on the road and recognized him in the breaking of the bread. Later on, Simon Peter, Thomas, Nathanael, James, and John are fishing on the lake. A man on the shore calls to them, "Have you caught anything, friends?" They call back, "No." Then he says, "Throw the net out to starboard and you'll find something." They do, and when they catch so many fish that they cannot haul in their net, John says to Peter, "It is the Lord." And as these events are taking place, a new word is being spoken, at first softly and hesitatingly, then clearly and convincingly, and finally loudly and triumphantly, "The Lord is risen; he is risen indeed!"

I wonder how this story, the most important story of human history, speaks to you now that you know so well what it means to have lost the one you loved most. Have you noticed that none of the friends of Jesus, neither the women nor the disciples, had the faintest expectation of his return from death? His crucifixion had crushed all their hopes and expectations, and they felt totally lost and dejected. Even when Jesus appeared to them, they kept hesitating and doubting and needing to be convinced, not only Thomas but others as well. There was no trace of an "I-always-told-you-so" attitude.

The event of Jesus' resurrection totally and absolutely surpassed their understanding. It went far beyond their own ways of thinking and feeling. It broke through the limits of their minds and hearts. And still, they believed—and their faith changed the world.

Isn't this good news? Doesn't this turn everything around and offer us a basis on which we can live with hope? Doesn't this put mother's death in a completely new perspective? It does not make her death less painful or our own grief less heavy. It does not make the loss of her less real, but it makes us see and feel that death is part of a much greater and much deeper event, the fullness of which we cannot comprehend, but of which we know that it is a life-bringing event. The friends of Jesus saw him and heard him only a few times after that Easter morning, but their lives were completely changed. What seemed to be the end proved to be the beginning; what seemed to be a cause for fear proved to be a cause for courage; what seemed to be defeat proved to be victory; and what seemed to be the basis for despair proved to be the basis for hope. Suddenly a wall becomes a gate, and although we are not able to say with much clarity or precision what lies beyond that gate, the tone of all that we do and say on our way to the gate changes drastically.

The best way I can express to you the meaning death receives in the light of the resurrection of Jesus is to say that the love that causes us so much grief and makes us feel so fully the absurdity of death is stronger than death itself. "Love is stronger than death." This sentence summarizes better than any other the meaning of the resurrection and therefore also the meaning of death. I have mentioned this earlier in this letter, but now you may better see its full meaning. Why has mother's death caused you so much suffering? Because you loved her so much. Why has your own death become such an urgent question for you? Because you love life, you love your children and your grandchildren, you love nature, you love art and music, you love horses, and you love all that is alive and beautiful. Death is absurd and cannot be meaningful for someone who loves so much.

The resurrection of Jesus Christ is the glorious manifestation of the victory of love over death. The same love that makes us mourn and protest against death will now free us to live in hope. Do you realize that Jesus appeared only to those who knew him, who had listened to his words and who had come to love him deeply? It was that love that gave them the eyes to see his face and the ears to hear his voice when he appeared to them on the third day after his death. Once they had seen and heard him and believed, the rest of their lives became a continuing recognition of his presence in their midst. This is what life in the Spirit of the risen Christ is all about. It makes us see that under the veil of all that is visible to our bodily eyes, the risen Lord shows us his inexhaustible love and calls us to enter even more fully into that love, a love that embraces both mother and us, who loved her so much.

It is with this divine love in our hearts, a love stronger than death, that our lives can be lived as a promise. Because this great love promises us that what we have already begun to see and hear with the eyes and ears of the Spirit of Christ can never be destroyed, but rather is "the beginning" of eternal life.

Today is the third day of Easter. Easter Tuesday. Here in the Trappist monastery it is the last day of the Easter festivities. For three days we have celebrated the resurrection of Jesus Christ, and it has been a real feast. Although the monks speak with each other only when necessary, and although there are no parties or parades, the Easter days have been more joyful than any I have celebrated in the past. The liturgies have been rich and exuberant with their many alleluias; the readings have been joyful and affirmative; the music has been festive; and everyone has been filled with gratitude toward God and each other.

On Easter Sunday I read the Gospel story about Peter and John running to the tomb and finding it empty. There were more than a hundred visitors in the abbey church, some from far away and some from nearby, some young and some old, some formally and some casually dressed. Sitting with forty monks around the huge rock that serves as the altar, they gave me a real sense of the Church. After reading the Gospel, I preached. I had seldom preached on Easter Sunday during my twenty-two years of priesthood, and I felt very grateful that I could announce to all who were present: "The Lord is risen; he is risen indeed." Everyone listened with great attention and I had a sense that the risen Christ was really among us, bringing us his peace. During the Eucharist, I prayed for you, for mother, and for all who are dear to us. I felt that the risen Christ brought us all together, bridging not only the distance between Holland and the United States but also that between life and death. Lent was long, sometimes very hard, and not without its dark moments and tempting demons. But now, in the light of the resurrection of Christ, Lent seems to have been short and easy. I guess this is true for all of life. In darkness we doubt that there will ever be light, but in the light we soon forget how much darkness there was.

Now there is light. In fact, the sun has even broken through and the large stretches of blue sky now visible behind the clusters of clouds remind me again that often what we see is not what is most enduring.

Dear father, this seems the most natural time to conclude not only the Easter celebration but also this letter. For twelve days I have been reflecting on mother's death in the hope of offering you and myself some comfort and consolation. I do not know if I have been able to reach you in your loneliness and grief. Maybe my words often said more to me than to you. But even if this is so, I still hope that the simple fact that these words have been written by your son about her whom we have both loved so much will be a source of consolation to you.

PETER GILLQUIST
1938 -

Not in your lifetime, not in my lifetime, have we ever witnessed such a mass conversion to holy Orthodoxy," announced Metropolitan Philip Saliba as he began his sermon at St. Nicholas Cathedral in Los Angeles that February morning in 1987.

In truth, it was *afternoon*. With the ordination of sixty of us to the deaconate and the priesthood, plus the receiving of nearly two hundred lay people, the service had already taken up over four hours!

Priests and lay leaders had come from all over North America to witness the event. Friends and family came to take part. Bishop Maximos of the Pittsburgh diocese of the Greek Orthodox Church was present and spoke at the banquet which followed.

It had been an entire week of festivity. The receiving of new members and ordinations had begun the week before, February 8, at St. Michael's church in the Los Angeles suburb of Van Nuys. Those to be ordained priests this day, February 15, had been ordained deacons a week earlier. In the Orthodox Church, you do not go from lay status to the priesthood in a single step.

"Last week I said to the evangelicals, 'Welcome home!' the Archbishop continued. "Today I am saying, 'Come home, *America*. Come home to the faith of Peter and Paul.'"

I looked across the large expanse of the altar area at the cathedral and into the eyes of the threescore others who had, with me, just received the grace of ordination to holy orders. The smell of incense lingered from the celebration of the Divine Liturgy, and the candles on the huge marble altar were still aglow.

Many of the Orthodox priests who had come such a great distance to participate had tears in their eyes, as did many of us newcomers to the Church. "Our fathers brought Orthodoxy to America," whispered the veteran priest James Meena of his Arabic Christian forbears. Then he smiled and added, "Now it's your turn to bring America to Orthodoxy."

Why would America need Orthodox Christianity—or even be remotely interested in it? It's so old, so foreign, so "Catholic," so complicated. Could it ever, as we say, play in Peoria?

But second, and of even more immediate concern, whatever would so possess two thousand Bible-believing, blood-bought, Gospel-preaching, Christ-centered, lifelong evangelical Protestants to come to embrace this Orthodox faith so enthusiastically? Is this a new form of religious rebellion? Have vital Spirit-filled Christian people somehow jumped the track to a staid and lifeless, crusty, sacral gloom? Worse yet, is this one of those subtle deceptions of the enemy?

Those of us who led this particular journey met in the 1960s in Campus Crusade for Christ. Though we were products of the Fifties, we must have been something of a tip-off to the turbulent Sixties just ahead: dissatisfied—or better to say, unsatisfied—with the status quo of what we perceived as dull, denominational American Christianity.

Gutsy, outspoken, radical, hopefully maximal—we didn't like the institutional Church and we didn't like the world system, and we were out to change them both.

What great days they were! We wouldn't trade them for anything. And we would not trade where we are now for anything. The one certainly led us to the other.

university to help others come to Christ, to his present position as director of the Department of Missions and Evangelism in the Antiochian Orthodox Archdioces, Gillquist has devoted his life not only to his own spiritual quest, but to the quests of others driven by a calling to preach. In the following passage from *Becoming Orthodox*, Gillquist describes both his passion as a campus leader and his experiences as a convert to the Orthodox tradition.

For many, faith is not just a part of life, it is a driving force behind it, directing all of our plans and actions. Orthodox Christian author **Peter Gillquist** certainly seems to be among the latter, rather than the former. From his days as regional director of the Campus Crusade for Christ, when he spent his time traveling from university to

The Challenge of the Campus

"There's one campus in America you guys can *never* crack," an evangelical businessman friend told me over lunch in Chicago one day in late 1965.

"Which one?" I shot back, already having determined in my mind that I would go there next.

"Notre Dame," he smirked.

"Bet we can," I said. We finished eating over small talk and said goodbye.

I hurried home and telephoned the chaplain's office in South Bend. "I'd like to see him just as soon as possible," I told the secretary after identifying myself.

"I have an appointment for you to see Father at nine tomorrow morning," she said after checking his schedule.

"Good. I'll be there."

That's the way we were. The greater the challenge, the higher the mark on the wall, the better we liked it. And the better we performed. I threw some clothes in a suitcase, said goodbye to my wife and children, pulled out of our snow-packed driveway in Evanston and headed down Outer Drive toward South Bend. I checked into a motel adjacent to the campus with a prayer that the doors to the Irish would somehow be open.

A few months later we had probably twenty-five hundred students from Notre Dame and the adjacent St. Mary's College packed into the brand new Convocation Center on campus, for two nights in a row, to hear Jon Braun and the New Folk, our preaching/singing team. I had promised the chaplain, "We're not coming to make Protestants out of your students, but to call them to a deeper commitment to Jesus Christ." And I meant every word of it.

The response was incredible. In those days, we passed out 3" x 5" cards and asked our listeners to put a check mark by their names if they had prayed with us to open up their lives to Christ. Over two hundred had checked.

We had cracked Notre Dame.

Then came Cal Berkeley. "The Berkeley Blitz," we called it. That was the winter of the 1966-67 school year. We decided we had had enough of the free-speech movement and Betina Apthecker. "Let's hit the campus and shake it to the core," we told each other. Hundreds of students—Berkeley students!—gave up their lunch hour to hear Billy Graham speak in the Greek Theater on campus, following his earlier breakfast meeting with scores of faculty members. Jon Braun spoke on the steps of Sproul Hall the next morning and actually shut down a heckler from the crowd. Nobody else would challenge him, and we won.

Though there were not the ongoing results we had hoped for at Berkeley, at least we had engaged the radicals on their own turf and had succeeded in doing what we had set out to do.

At once, we loved it and we hated it. A shock-troop mentality is thrilling fun, but it can also bring deep disappointment. Though we exhibited some of the same boldness we saw in the early Christians in the Book of Acts, we found nowhere near the long-term staying power in those we reached. Most of the decisions for Christ honestly did not stick.

Our Growing Frustration

Our slogan was "Win the Campus for Christ Today—Win the World for Christ Tomorrow." As much as we loathed to admit it, while we were busy winning the campus, the world was getting worse. We had established Campus Crusade chapters on many of the major campuses in America during the decade of the Sixties, but it was precisely in those same Sixties that our nation's campuses came unglued. They unraveled morally, politically, and culturally. We had done our job, and things got worse, not better. The campus world of 1970 was far, far less culturally Christian than the campus world of 1960.

"What we are doing is not working," we admitted to each other. "We get the decisions, we get the commitments to Christ, we are building the organization and recruiting the staff, but we are not affecting a change. We are a failure in the midst of our own success."

Dr. Jack Sparks couldn't get his mind off Berkeley. He had been a professor teaching statistics and research design at Penn State and at the University of Northern Colorado before he joined the Campus Crusade staff to direct a systematic follow-up program of literature through computerized distribution. Now, after the blitz, he asked for and got a few hard-core Campus Crusade staff people to join him, and he took off for the Berkeley campus.

He out-radicalized all of the rest of us. He swapped his business suits for denim overalls and work shirts, grew a beard, and hit the campus with a higher commitment to Christ than the radicals had ever had to their causes. He even baptized some of his converts in the famous fountain on the Berkeley campus mall!

The style he used, the literature he produced, and the life he and his wife Esther lived crossed over the new counter-culture barriers and began to produce something that gave promise of permanence. It bordered on something you would see in the Book of Acts. It looked less and less like Campus Crusade, and more and more like the beginnings of a Christian community—or dare I say, a Church.

THOMAS KEATING, O.S.C.

1923 -

What is contemplative prayer?

Contemplative prayer is an ancient method of prayer based on the conviction that God resides within us and not way out in the cosmos somewhere. In contemplative prayer we open our minds and hearts to God's presence within us. We accept God's invitation to develop a friendship that will eventually lead to divine union, the full awareness of God's presence in us, in all humanity, and in all human experiences.

Contemplative prayer is the process by which we start to regularly hang out with God, so to speak. We begin to wait on God as one would a friend, and we become more and more familiar with God and ourselves. In contemplative prayer we develop a loving knowledge of God beyond thoughts, feelings, and concepts. This loving knowledge of God's presence within us leads us to establish good habits and makes us sensitive to the inspirations of the Spirit and aware of our own and humanity's basic goodness. Eventually, contemplative prayer leads to the recognition that one is in the abiding state of union with God and is being moved by the Spirit in both prayer and action.

Are there outward signs that someone has reached a contemplative level of prayer?

Although some people who are contemplatives experience psychic and charismatic gifts, such as visions, prophecy, speaking in tongues, or healing, these experiences are not ends in themselves. Charismatic gifts are clearly given for the good of others and are not necessarily signs that someone is holy or in an advanced stage of prayer. In fact, for contemplatives, psychic and charismatic gifts are actually inconveniences because it is not experiences of that kind that they seek on the spiritual journey. They must transcend all that stuff and go to the substance of faith, which is knowledge of the intimate presence of God within them; and that knowledge inspires them to serve God by ministering to other people.

Once a person's consciousness has been raised to a contemplative level of attentiveness toward God, life becomes very ordinary. It is leading ordinary life with extraordinary love that is the triumph of God's grace. In other words, when a person reaches a mature level of contemplative prayer, reality is seen in a new perspective. One discovers a new way of being in the world in which God is present in every experience. A contemplative is motivated by the joyful and sorrowful mysteries of Christ and is moved by the gifts of the Spirit both in prayer and action. These gifts are the gifts of wisdom, understanding, knowledge, counsel, piety, fortitude, and reverence for God.

Is there a scriptural basis for contemplative prayer?

Yes, I think Jesus continually called for a contemplative understanding of his words and actions. By that I mean that, in addition to accepting the literal meaning of the Gospel, one must be open to the contemplative dimension of Scripture.

For example, consider the miracles of Jesus. While they are understood and accepted on a literal level, they go far beyond that level. Jesus' miracles are symbols of the inner healing and awakening of the spiritual senses that occur when people become aware of Christ's interior presence. This inner healing allows one to hear the Gospel at ever deepening levels. The Gospel is addressed not just to our ears. Jesus often complains that people are not hearing him. Jesus' words and actions are addressed to our heart and to our innermost being. It is only when the Gospel reaches this deepest human level—what is called the Stillpoint, or true self—that the Good News has finally been heard. It is out of this deep reception of the

Some traditions teach that God is a remote presence peering down at us from the heavens, an omnipotent force that hovers in the far distance. **Thomas Keating**, a Roman Catholic Cistercian monk, would vigorously disagree. Keating has devoted his life to find a new method of prayer and a means of getting closer to God—a way to "hang out" with God as though He was a neighbor you could invite to come and sit on the stoop. The result is contemplative prayer, a tradition of meditative prayer that originates in the prayer rituals of third-century Christians. Keating, who currently resides at St. Benedict's monastery in Snowmass, Colorado, and spends six months out of every year in a solitude of silence, was prompted in his quest for a new prayer methodology by his interaction with Buddhist monks. After studying Buddhist teachings, Keating became interested in translating Eastern tradition into Catholic practice. He fostered a movement, Contemplative Outreach, that teaches people to spend a period of time each day in silent prayer, speaking directly to God and gradually awakening to a full comprehension of the fact of God's presence inside of us. Keating, who converted to Catholicism while attending Yale University, likens this to friendship with the Maker— a divine union accomplished by quiet, solitary, steady prayer. He has authored four books on the subject and touched thousands of lives, helping people to understand how solitude and prayer can be an aid to ordinary, daily trials and large-scale disasters.

Gospel that the most effective action emerges because it is action under the influence of the Spirit.

How can someone reach a contemplative understanding of a passage in the Bible?

Let's just take one word: rest. It occurs in Jesus' invitation, "Come to me, all you who labor and are heavily burdened, and I will give you rest." There are four levels of hearing that word. Normally, it is heard at the level that reflects where one is in one's developing relationship with God.

The first level of understanding the word "rest" is the *literal* level. When you hear the word "rest" at this level, it means come aside awhile and get some physical and psychological rest. That's what Jesus invited his disciples to do, and Jesus himself took time for this kind of rest. But there's a greater rest for human beings than lying down and taking a nap. It is the rest that comes from not having to sin, from being free from compulsions and habits that trample on the rights of others and stifle our own true goodness. This sense of rest is the *moral* understanding of Scripture. When you hear the Gospel at this level, you feel compelled to put Jesus' teaching and example into practice. This level of understanding the word "rest" is greater than the literal understanding because the Gospel isn't meant just to be read; it's a life to be lived. Insight is the principal purpose of reading Scripture not information.

Beyond the profound rest of freedom from deliberate sin is the even greater rest of freedom from tendency or inclination to sin. This level of scriptural understanding is called the *allegorical* level, and it has two phases. One is the awakening of the personal love of Christ along with an awakening of the spiritual sense of Scripture. The Gospel becomes a mirror of one's own experience of grace. At this level, reading Scripture is like reading your autobiography because your experiences of grace seem very similar to those of Jesus' disciples. Gradually, as your trust in Christ increases, interior purification commences. You begin to recognize and acknowledge the dark side of your personality and face the wounds, repressions, and trauma suffered in early childhood and your methods of coping with them. You finally understand what the so-called consequences of Original Sin really mean, and you acknowledge your selfish tendency to disregard others and your true self.

Interior purification involves the unloading of the emotional damage in the unconscious. When this unloading is complete to some degree, the *unitive* level of Scripture emerges and enables you to rest in God even in the midst of the most intense activity. The monumental illusion that God is absent is finally demolished. You realize that God is your innermost ground, and out of this ground your life emerges at every level.

God's centrality in our lives is what the Gospel is trying to bring home to us. When we reach the unitive level of understanding the Gospel, we finally are certain that God is within us, loving us and embracing us in our uniqueness. We see that our denial or forgetfulness of his presence is what continually gets us into trouble. Through the development of contemplative prayer, Jesus gives us perfect rest—freedom from all that is false in ourselves.

Is this a new method of understanding Scripture?

No, up until the sixteenth century the contemplative dimension of the Gospel was generally recognized; and contemplation was the ultimate goal of every spiritual exercise. The spiritual giants of Catholic tradition, such as the Desert Fathers and Mothers, Augustine, the Cappadocians, Bernard of Clairvaux, Teresa of Avila, and John of the Cross all preached or wrote about the contemplative dimension of the Gospel. The method of prayer for all Christians proposed in the first centuries of Christianity was called *lectio divina,* which literally means "divine reading." This practice involved reading Scripture or, more exactly, listening to it; reflecting and mediating on the words being read or heard; spontaneously responding in prayer to these reflections; and, finally, moving to a state of contemplation, or resting in the presence of God.

Unfortunately, with the onset of the Reformation and the church's efforts to fend off the heresies of the day, believers tended to focus on the doctrinal points of their faith to the exclusion of living the Christian life. Doctrinal points are very important because they point toward the mystery that is embraced in the discipline of prayer, worship, and the sacraments. Yet, the Western model of God that developed in the post-Reformation period was that of a god completely separate from us, sitting in the bleachers and watching us perform and responding with thumbs up or thumbs down. In this worldview, we were supposed to spend our lives on earth gaining merits for the future life. Scripture, however, says that the divine Spirit within us inspires all good thoughts and deeds and we must listen and cooperate. The teaching of the Gospel is to love God and our neighbors in a practical way here and now and to entrust the future to God's mercy. This scriptural model of God has been officially restored by the documents and spirit of Vatican II.

So, although the contemplative approach to Scripture isn't new, it was virtually lost for several centuries. The richness and wisdom of earlier times, such as the stages of the spiritual journey, how contemplative prayer is meant to influence daily life, and the belief that daily life is the arena where transformation takes place—all of these great insights of the early and medieval Christian thinkers got put on the back burner. People were left with a spirituality that was heavily diluted by Cartesian philosophical considerations and the Newtonian worldview. It is only with Einstein's theory of relativity, quantum mechanics, and the new physics that people have moved away from this excessively dualistic and rationalistic worldview and have begun to accept the interrelatedness of everything that exists, which is, of course, what the great saints have been saying all along.

How did you get interested in teaching about contemplative prayer?

After being inspired by Vatican II and the pioneering ecumenical work of Thomas Merton, members of our community got interested in the meditation methods of Eastern religions. We read about them and invited outstanding teachers from other world religions to instruct us in their methods of mediation. Our interest was not only to compare Christian tradition with Eastern spirituality but to see whether we could devise an approach to Christian spirituality that would be comparable to the methods of the East. You see, at that time, literally thousands of young people were visiting India every year to be trained in Eastern meditation practices. Among them was a whole generation of Christians who were starving for spirituality, yet had no idea that a rich, contemplative tradition existed in their own religion. Many of them joined one of the Eastern religions for the sake of the meditative disciplines they did not know existed in Christian tradition. What they were looking for was a discipline of prayer and action rather than a new religion.

What do you mean by discipline?

Discipline is a synonym for asceticism. The original meaning of asceticism was the discipline athletes went through to qualify for the Olympic Games. Gradually, under the influence of Clement of Alexandria, asceticism became a term for the spiritual exercises that a Christian went through to purify the heart. The emphasis was not so much on effort, although there was plenty of that involved, as it was on following a practice that would enable one to cleanse oneself from self-centeredness and

to be more receptive to the divine presence within oneself. The practice, or discipline, involved a lot of effort in the beginning, but the effort was geared toward enduring the divine action of purification and consenting to God's will. It was the passive dimension of spirituality that was lost with the coming of the age of reason.

This practice is what many people in recent years have been trying to revive. Thus, in my community we formulated a discipline based on the spiritual practices of the Christian contemplative tradition. We put together a few simple guidelines that described how to sit down, how to begin, how to end, and how many times a day to pray. This method, which became known as centering prayer, is by no means the only way to reach a contemplative state, but it is one effective way of reducing the obstacles to divine union.

What is the centering-prayer method?

Centering prayer is based on the firm belief that God is not absent but fully present within us. God is so accessible, in fact, that one doesn't have to do a thing to reach God except to consent. When you start the spiritual journey, it makes an enormous difference what your attitude toward God is. If you think that God is a million miles away and you have to climb up to God by means of an infinite number of steps, then when you fall down after climbing the first two or three steps—as usually happens—it's not very encouraging. But if you know that God is already within you and that God loves you first, then you have a point of departure for seeking God that is possible and realistic.

To practice centering prayer we suggest that at least once or preferably twice a day for twenty to 30 minutes you sit in a comfortable position and open yourself in faith and love to the interior presence of God by keeping quiet and letting go of all thoughts and experiences that reinforce the false notion that you are separated from God. Silence is very important. Outward silence is helpful at the early stages of centering prayer to keep free from distractions. Interior silence, where you move beyond conversation in your relationship with God and simply enjoy God's presence, is more important still.

Of course your mind will naturally wander as you try to empty it of thoughts, so you must constantly recenter your attention on God. One way that has proved helpful to many people is to make use of a sacred word—or Christian mantra, if you will—to keep you from dwelling on the stray thoughts or feelings that flow through your consciousness. Some suggestions for the

sacred word include God, Jesus, Abba, love. Whenever you begin to latch on to some thought, you simply recall the sacred word and that recenters you toward God. Gradually, as you move away from routine ways of thinking, reacting, and judging and move deeper into interior silence, you begin to feel rested and refreshed. It's like taking a vacation, only instead of going to Alaska or Hawaii, you take a vacation from your false self, from all that is eating away at you most of the time.

As you regularly practice centering prayer, you develop the capacity to let go of things in daily life that are harmful or upsetting to you. Thus, centering prayer becomes a keystone of a change of consciousness, a true liberation from the false self. It opens you up to the possibility of tasting God's presence if only for a brief moment or two. As you become more assured of God's love for you, the divine therapy begins. You start to unload your unconscious and loosen the emotional weeds that have been choking you.

Once this healing process is established, you are able to keep new emotional weeds from taking root. Your psyche thus gets a regular, even daily, opportunity for deep rest. At this stage things don't get easier, however, because your psyche uses this experience of rest to evacuate the emotional damage of a lifetime; and you are bombarded with all kinds of primitive thoughts and emotions that have been stored or repressed in your unconscious. You may have the painful feeling that you're regressing in the spiritual life. Many people turn back at this stage saying, "This kind of prayer is for the birds!" It is very difficult to let go of the desire for security and certitude. In this situation you don't have the slightest idea where you're going on the spiritual journey, but you're being asked to trust God. If you hang in there, you learn how to give yourself wholly to God. This giving yourself to God out of trust and love is what finally leads to union with God.

Why is reaching union with God so difficult for most people?

It is difficult for us because to reach union we must undermine the illusory view of ourselves that we've been building up since early childhood. Every human being has three instinctual needs in the first years of life: survival/security, affection/esteem/pleasure, and power/control. A child wants prompt fulfillment of these biological necessities. But inevitably some amount of security, affection, or control is withheld from a child because neither parents, peers, nor society on the whole is perfect. When instinctual needs are withheld, the child makes the emotional judgment that he or she is not wanted or is being neglected. The child isn't capable of reasoning or understanding why a particular need isn't being met. For example, if a child is sick with a serious skin disease and his mother can't hold him for several weeks, the child responds with rage because all he knows is that he desperately needs to be held and this need is being ignored. The child's chief form of security, his chief way of bonding with the mother, which is his chief way of being reassured that life in the world is as safe as it was in the womb, is being denied him. It is almost impossible to exaggerate the child's need for physical affection in the first years of life.

Eventually, a child learns to cope with what he or she has perceived as rejection or not being loved by creating defense mechanisms to block out memories that are unbearable. A child begins to make fantastic demands for power as a way to compensate for his or her repressed insecurity. Naturally, because these outrageous demands for compensatory experiences can't be met, a person is constantly feeling in a state of frustration with accompanying feelings of grief, anger, or some other compensatory emotions. Eventually, this entire system of repression and compensation, or what is called the false-self system, hides the true self with its sense of truth and freedom. One is hindered from living in the present moment and from responding to grace. The practice of virtue, then, and the spiritual journey are ways to dismantle the false self with its fantastic demands.

Do you ever reach an end to the spiritual journey?

The spiritual journey is infinite because you are trying to be united with a God who in infinite. In this life there is always more distance to go. But there are significant breakthroughs. The mingling of grace with the false-self system is going on all the time. Even when you accept the values of the Gospel at the conscious level, you still have to deal with the unconscious values that you've invested in emotionally. That is why the heart of asceticism, or spiritual formation, is to confront the false self and dismantle it. The false self can adapt itself to any way of life. Thus, you can study theology, Scripture, spirituality, or engage in a difficult ministry and yet still be under the influence of your false self with its security, affection/esteem, and control needs. Let me give you an example.

Let's take a young man who is very macho. He loves to dominate his peer group. It gives him a great sense of self-exaltation when he drinks all his friends under the table at the local tavern. As he staggers out of the bar, he feels on top of the world and enjoys an enormous sense of satisfaction. What he is doing is compensating for the satisfaction he didn't have as a child because he had a tyrannical parent, or whatever his childhood melodrama was, who put him down all the time. Now, by the mercy of God, he listens to a televangelist and is completely converted. He decides to give up everything and chooses the hardest life he can find to do penance: he enters the Trappists. Now the Trappists don't eat very much, and they fast vigorously—especially during Lent. This young man takes on his Lenten fast with great enthusiasm. Little by little, the older monks are slipping off the fast because of fatigue or illness; but the dutiful young monk faithfully keep up the bread-and-water diet. By Holy Week he is alone in the refectory. When the great bell tolls for the Paschal vigil, he staggers out of the refectory. Suddenly, the same self-exaltation and satisfaction he used to feel coming out of the tavern sweeps over him because now, instead of drinking all his friends under the table, he has fasted all the monks under the table.

What has changed in this young man? Nothing. The same worldliness is there. Worldliness will follow a person anywhere. The false-self system doesn't care if you change your clothes, or change your hairdo, or whatever; it's content as long as you don't ask it to change. But you must change it if you are to grow up and, still more, if you are to be transformed.

The Gospel specifically addresses our desires for excessive security, affection/esteem, and control, particularly in the first three Beatitudes and in the accounts of the first three temptations of Christ. The Gospel asks us to graduate from these emotional desires in order to act as a fully integrated human being—a human being interested in taking personal responsibility in building bridges, in cooperating with others and negotiating disagreements and in showing mercy. Anything less is subhuman. So, the Gospel is calling us into full personhood, full responsibility for our emotional life and for our family, our church, our community, and ultimately for our world and its redemption.

How does Christ fit into the spiritual journey?

Well, he is the spiritual journey. Discovering the true self through prayer is the experience of Christ within us. In other words, Christ is within us but somewhat asleep until faith reaches a certain level. Then, to use Saint John of the Cross' imagery, the giant awakes, the Word of God rolls over and makes us aware of the tremendous reality within us. At first it is scary to feel the giant's presence, especially if the giant wakes up too soon. Who wants to live with God as a member of one's household, so to speak, unless one loves him.

The spiritual journey is gradually getting to know and love Christ within us. We move from acquaintanceship, to friendliness, to friendship, to union. The journey leads to wholeness, to full personhood. We learn to take responsibility for our acceptance of Christ within us and give ourselves to him. This path is the normal Christian way; it's not reserved for saints alone, and it is not meant as a last act before heaven. It's the beginning of a full Christian life and apostolate. The fullness of ministry begins when we act out of total dependence on Christ and his Spirit is able to work in us and through us. In other words, God doesn't go through all the trouble of purifying us for no good reason. God wants us to serve humankind and do something about the human situation.

What's the relationship between contemplative prayer and social action?

Without a spiritual base or contemplative vision for social action, burnout comes quickly. The divine energy that comes with contemplative prayer is the most powerful energy there is, and that is what's required in sustained service to the poor and oppressed and in finding solutions to the great world problems that desperately need attention. To address these problems we must maintain the capacity to show love to everyone, including our oppressors. The more demanding the ministry the more it has to demonstrate the compassion of God who continues, to our great dismay, to love our enemies as well as us. It is very difficult to sustain prophetic witness, prayer, and compassion all together; but that is what the ministry of peace and justice requires. Despite the opposition, persecution, disappointment, and failure we experience or witness, we must continue to witness and serve. The interior peace we find in prayer becomes a reservoir that sustains us in daily life so that we don't give up even in the face of the utmost adversity, the most devastating hardships, or the most inexplicable horrors. Let me give you an example:

A friend of mine had a sister who was raped and murdered. She was a brilliant medical student and the favorite in the family. She was put through gruesome torture before her death. Her brother had to visit the room where she was murdered; and as he sat on her bed amidst the signs of the brutality done to her, he felt the question put to him: "Can you accept her death just as it is?" After praying for a while, he was able to say, "I don't understand it, but I accept it—just as it is." As soon as he opened himself up to the acceptance of the reality, an incredible peace engulfed him; and he sensed her presence in the room as if to reassure him.

This experience is an example of how pain can be transfigured. It is the mystery of Christ's passion. In such an experience we are reminded that the great gift of Christ's passion is that we can never lose God. Christ showed by his death and resurrection that God is present in unbelievable suffering just as much as in the highest enlightenment. Happiness is then understood as being somehow beyond pain and beyond joy but compatible with each; and that means nothing can separate us from the love of Christ.

Do you think this movement among Christians toward contemplative prayer will continue?

It's hard to say. History has seen many wonderful movements in the church come and go. That's why I feel an urgency to do something while the tide is high. There is widespread hunger among people today for a spiritual direction to their lives. The New Age movement addresses this hunger. That is why it is so popular. People need and want the divine in their lives, and it is up to us to minister to this need among Christians. The church has a pretty long history of arriving ten minutes after the train has left the station in nearly all the great spiritual movements in history. If we don't do anything about this hunger, which is one of the greatest signs of renewal in the church today, then the whole agenda for social action will not have a base to hold it together for very long. If the tide goes out without this need being met, I think the Christian religion will be ineffective if not irrelevant in the next century.

Contemplative Outreach, a nationwide prayer-group network, was founded to educate people to their spiritual potential and to offer a way to begin the spiritual journey. Many retreat centers across the country, as well as itinerant teachers, are teaching the method of centering prayer and other contemplative practices. A wide variety of books, tapes, introductory and intensive retreats, and ongoing courses are available. Small contemplative groups are also popping up. Little by little, experienced practitioners are being trained to lead these groups. It is hoped that small, live-in, lay-contemplative communities will be formed, such as Chrysalis House in Warwick, New York, to serve the spiritual needs of the growing contemplative community.

All of this spiritual development is essential if we are to meet the needs of the modern world. The spiritual journey leads to social action, but social action can only be sustained by being grounded in the spiritual base. In other words, if every Christian is called to social action, every Christian is called to be a contemplative.

JANE WAGNER
1935 -

Known best for her authorship of the play *The Search for Signs of Intelligent Life in the Universe*, **Jane Wagner** was born in Morristown, Tennessee, in 1935. Wagner did not start out to be a playwright; it was only after a failed attempt at writing song lyrics that she turned to drama, transforming a rejected song into a teleplay. Lily Tomlin became interested in Wagner after that very teleplay, and a collaboration began that was to lead to huge success. A one-woman play composed of different characters speaking in monologue, *The Search for Signs of Intelligent Life in the Universe* is an anthem to the modern woman's desperate quest for spiritual meaning. Characters include Trudy, a bag lady, and Lynn, a California housewife—both present in the following excerpt and both certainly searching. Wagner has been the recipient of a Peabody award, three Emmy awards, a Tony award and a New York Drama Critics Circle special citation.

One thing I have no worry about is whether God exists.
But it has occurred to me that God has Alzheimer's and has
forgotten
we exist.

ANNIE DILLARD
1945 -

The Cascade range, in these high latitudes, backs almost into the water. There is only a narrow strip, an afterthought of foothills and farms sixty miles wide, between the snowy mountains and the sea. The mountains wall well. The rest of the country—most of the rest of the planet, in some very real sense, excluding a shred of British Columbia's coastline and the Alaskan islands—is called, and profoundly felt to be, simply "East of the Mountains." I've been there.

I came here to study hard things—rock mountain and salt sea—and to temper my spirit on their edges. "Teach me thy way, O Lord" is, like all prayers, a rash one, and one I cannot but recommend. These mountains—Mount Baker and the Sisters and Shuksan, the Canadian Coastal Range and the Olympics on the peninsula—are surely the edge of the known and comprehended world. They are high. That they bear their own unimaginable masses and weathers aloft, holding them up in the sky for anyone to see plain, makes them, as Chesterton said of the Eucharist, only the more mysterious by their very visibility and absence of secrecy. They are the western rim of the real, if not considerably beyond it. If the Greeks had looked at Mount Baker all day, their large and honest art would have broken, and they would have gone fishing, as these people do. And as perhaps I one day shall.

But the mountains are, incredibly, east. When I first came here I faced east and watched the mountains, thinking. These are the Ultima Thule, the final westering, the last serrate margin of time. Since they are, incredibly, east, I must be no place at all. But the sun rose over the snowfields and woke me where I lay, and I rose and cast a shadow over someplace, and thought. There is, God help us, more. So gathering my bowls and spoons, and turning my head, as it were, I moved to face west, relinquishing all hope of sanity, for what is more. . . .

The god of today is rampant and drenched. His arms spread, bearing moist pastures; his fingers spread, fingering the shore. He is time's live skin; he burgeons up

from day like any tree. His legs spread crossing the heavens, flicking hugely, and flashing and arcing around the earth toward night.

This is one world, bound to itself and exultant. It fizzes up in trees, trees heaving up streams of salt to their leaves. This is the one air, bitten by grackles; time is alone and in and out of mind. The god of today is a boy, pagan and fernfoot. His power is enthusiasm; his innocence is mystery. He sockets into everything that is, and that right holy. Loud as music, filling the grasses and skies, his day spreads rising at home in the hundred senses. He rises, new and surrounding; he is everything that is, wholly here and emptied—flung, and flowing, sowing, unseen and flown.

Menachem Mendel Schneerson
1902 - 1992

DEATH AND GRIEVING

What does death really mean?

Death: The very word strikes fear in people's hearts. They consider death as unfathomable as it is inevitable. They are barely able to talk about it, to peer beyond the word itself and allow themselves to contemplate its true implications. This is an understandable reaction, given the fact that so many people think of *life* as nothing more than a state in which the human body is biologically active. But we must ask ourselves: What happens after death, if anything? What does death really mean? How should the surviving loved ones react?

The mystery of death is part of the enigma of the soul and of life itself; understanding death really means understanding life. During life as we know it, the body is vitalized by the soul; upon death, there is a separation between body and soul. But the soul continues to live on as it always has, now unfettered by the physical constraints of the body. And since a person's true

Sidebar (left column):

It has been said that after the churches and synagogues, the temples and mosques, the only really holy thing in this country is the land. Americans always have regarded their landscape with an attitude of worship, imbuing the very ground we walk on with religious seriousness. And so it is no surprise that a person might turn to nature as the last stop on the journey to faith, after the usual inquiries have been made, even after God with a capital "G" seems to have disappeared. In **Annie Dillard**'s *Holy the Firm* this is precisely what happens. Dillard, an essayist and poet presently teaching at Wesleyan University, was frustrated in her search for faith. Looking for reasons to explain tragedies like that of a neighbor child whose face was horribly burned in an accident, she turned to the natural world and found it suffused with spirituality. This is not new ground for Dillard. In her Pulitzer Prize winning book *Pilgrim at Tinker Creek*, the author spent months living in solitude in Virginia's Blue Ridge mountains, learning to live with the rhythm of nature. This can be understood as pantheism of the highest order or no "religion" at all. But Dillard found faith in the mountains of the Cascade Range and the dew on the grass. A kind of modern-day Thoreau, this author went to the mountains to find God, much as that earlier thinker went into the woods to live deliberately.

Sidebar (right column):

The fact of death is one aspect of life that prompts many to turn to religion in the first place, often in search of explanation. **Schneerson**, former leader of the Chabad movement, writes about death in the following excerpt, in an attempt to comfort and explain. Chabad is an Orthodox Jewish sect that claims hundreds of thousands of members around the world. Schneerson, who was known as the Rebbe, was considered by many to be the Messiah. His death in 1992 left thousands saddened and confused, as they struggled both with their grief and with the possibility that he was not the Savior. The Rebbe was born in Russia, eventually fleeing to America during World War II. A man known for his incredible charisma and wisdom, Schneerson spoke ten languages and published 28 books.

character—his goodness, virtue, and selflessness—lies in the soul, he will ascend to a higher state after fulfilling his responsibilities on earth.

Modern physics has taught us that no substance truly disappears, that it only changes form, that matter is another form of energy. A tree, for instance, might be cut down and used to build a house, or a table, or a chair. Regardless of how the form changes, the wood remains wood. And when that same wood is burned in a furnace, it again changes form, becoming an energy that gives off heat and gas. The tree, the chair, and the fire are all merely different forms of the same substance.

If this is the case with a material substance, it is even more so with a spiritual substance. The spiritual life force in man, the soul, never disappears; upon death, it changes from one form to another, higher form. This may be difficult to comprehend at first, since we are so dependent on using our sensory tools to get through life. With wood, for example, it is easier to hold a chair in our hands than to grasp the heat and energy released from burning wood; and yet, the heat is no less real than the wooden chair.

As we become more attuned to the spiritual thinking, we learn to relate to the reality of the spirit, and its elevation upon death and release from the body to a purer form of spiritual energy.

No matter what physical ailments might befall a person, they are just that: *physical* ailments. Nothing that happens to the flesh and blood diminishes in any way the soul's power, which is purely spiritual. It is inappropriate, therefore, to use the term "afterlife" to define what happens after death. "Afterlife" implies that we have entered another, separate place, whereas death is actually a continuation of life as we know it, only in a new, higher form. The chapter in Genesis discussing the death of Sarah, for instance, is called "The Life of Sarah." The chapter discussing the death of Jacob is called "And Jacob Lived."

So before we can truly answer the question "What is death?" we must first ask, "What is life?" By medical definition, life takes place when one's brain and heart are functioning. Yet a person can be biologically alive but not alive at all; breathing and walking and talking are only the manifestations of what we call life. The true source of life, the energy that allows the body to function, is the soul. And the soul, because it is connected to G-d, the giver of life, is immortal. While the manifestations of life may cease upon death, the soul lives on, only in a different form.

How can a mortal human being connect to eternal life? By living a material life that fuses body and soul, thereby connecting to G-d. A person who transforms his or her body into a vehicle for love and generosity is a person who nurtures his or her eternal soul. It is by giving life to others that one becomes truly alive.

To a person for whom life consists of material gains, death indeed represents "the end." It is the time when all fleeting achievements come to a halt. But to a person for whom life consists of spiritual gains, life never ends. The soul is fueled by the inexhaustible energy of the good deeds a person performed on earth, and it lives on materially through his or her children and the others who perpetuate his or her spiritual vitality. As the sages say, "Just as his descendants are alive, he, too, is alive."

We often have a difficult time distinguishing between biological life and spiritual life, or true life. We are distracted by the many material trappings of biological life. Once the soul leaves the body, though, we can clearly see how it lives on, how that soul continues to inspire people to perform good deeds, to educate and help others, to live G-dly and spiritual lives. It is when a righteous person physically departs the earth that he or she begins to exert the most profound influence. . . .

What does death mean for the survivors?

While death represents the soul's elevation to a higher level, it nevertheless remains a painful experience for the survivors. At the same time, it must serve—as must all experiences in life—as a lesson; as a move forward. We must see death not as a negative force, but as an opportunity for growth.

Since death provokes such strong emotions, we must have a clear channel through which to express them, to go about healing in a constructive way. When a loved one dies, powerful and conflicting emotions are aroused: sadness over the loss and confusion about the future. The sages teach us that it would be barbaric not to mourn at all, but that we should not mourn longer than necessary. A week of mourning is sufficient; otherwise, a person's death becomes a presence unto itself, continuously saddening us and impeding our progress in life.

But why should we restrain our natural pain and sadness over a loved one's death? Grief is a feeling, after all, and feelings cannot be controlled, can they? Isn't it wrong to set limits and repress our grief, or to try to channel it in a certain direction?

True, feelings are feelings, but we *can* choose whether to experience them in a destructive or productive light. The key in this case is to understand death for what it is, to celebrate its positive element. A mourner must ultimately come to realize that the soul of his or her loved one has now reached an even greater place than it occupied during its time on earth, and that it will continue to rise. It is the act of reconciling this positive realization with our grief that can turn death from a traumatic experience into a cathartic one.

To diminish our expression of grief is unhealthy and inappropriate, but to allow our grief to overwhelm us is to selfishly overlook the true meaning of death—the fact that a person's righteous soul has found an even more righteous home.

What should we learn from death?

Besides celebrating the elevation of a loved one's soul and expressing our own grief, there is another purpose to mourning: Death is also an opportunity to examine our own lives an evaluate how we are fulfilling our divine mission. As Maimonides writes, a mourner should be "anxious and concerned and evaluate his behavior and repent."

So remembering the soul of a loved one is a most appropriate occasion to gaze into your own soul. We all know how difficult it can be to assess one's own behavior, and we often aren't compelled to do so until a friend or family member has passed on. At that point, we remember the things he accomplished during his life, how he treated his family and friends, how he went out of his way to help strangers. Unfortunately, it is often the blow of a death that shakes us out of our complacency and makes us rethink our own priorities.

Because the true bond between a parent and child or a husband and wife is a spiritual one, it remains intact and strong after death. Mourning also helps us retain this bond, for the soul of a departed person, eternal and intact, watches over the people with whom she was close. Every gracious act gives her great pleasure and satisfaction, particularly when such acts are committed in a manner that she taught, whether by instruction or example.

Her soul is fully aware of what is happening to the friends and relatives she has left behind. The soul is distressed when they experience undue grief or depression, and it rejoices when they move beyond their initial pain and continue to build their lives and inspire those around them.

There is no way to replace a departed loved one, for each person is a complete world. But there is a way to help partially fill the void. When family and friends supplement their customary good deeds with further virtuous acts on behalf of the departed, they continue the work of his or her soul. By performing such acts in the memory of a loved one, we can truly build a living memorial.

Where does one find this extra energy, especially while we are experiencing grief over the death itself? Just as the body reaches into its reservoir of strength when it is under attack, the soul is able to exert hidden strength during times of great trauma, strength that we may not even have been aware of.

What are we to make of all this, this rethinking of the way we look at death? What implications are there for those of us who inhabit a reality defined by our five senses and the laws of nature, a reality in which physical life inevitably yields to a physical death?

For those who continue to look at only the outer layer of life, the physical component as circumscribed by the human body, death indeed seems to be the end of life. But we must learn to peer inside this outer layer and see the human soul, our connection to G-d and to eternity.

Deep in our hearts, we are all aware of this connection. Any thinking person who contemplates the solar system, for example, or the complexities of an atom, must come to the conclusion that our universe did not come about by some freak accident. Nor is it composed merely of physical matter; every fiber of being is pulsating with energy. Wherever we turn, we see design and purpose—the hallmark of our creator. It would follow, therefore, that each human being, too, has a purpose, as does every single event in our lives.

So even death has a purpose in our lives; even death becomes a tool for leading a more meaningful life; and even death is another form of energy.

But after all is said and done, death is still an incomprehensible, devastating experience to those who are left behind. After all the rationalizations, all the explanations, the heart still cries. And it *should* cry.

When friends or relatives are grieving for a loved one, do not try to explain; just be there with them. Soothe and console them, and weep with them. There is nothing one can really say, for no matter how we

might try, we must accept that we often do not understand G-d's mysterious ways.

But we should ask of G-d to finally bring the day when death shall be no more, when "death shall be swallowed up forever and G-d shall wipe the tears from every face."

ISAAC ASIMOV
1920 -

I am sometimes suspected of being nonreligious as an act of rebellion against Orthodox parents. That may have been true of my father, but it was not true of me. I have rebelled against nothing. I have been left free and I have loved the freedom. The same is true of my brother and sister and our children.

Nor, I must add, is it simply that I find Judaism empty and that I must search for something else to fill the spiritual void in my life. I have never, in all my life, not for one moment, been tempted toward religion of any kind. The fact is that I feel no spiritual void. I have my philosophy of life, which does not include any aspect of the supernatural and which I find totally satisfying. I am, in short, a rationalist and believe only that which reason tells me is so.

Mind you, this isn't easy. We are so surrounded by tales of the supernatural, by the easy acceptance of the supernatural, by the thunders of the powers that be who attempt with all their might to convince us of the existence of the supernatural, that the strongest among us may feel himself swaying.

Something like that happened to me recently. In January 1990, I was lying in a hospital bed one afternoon (never mind why—we'll discuss that at the proper time) and my dear wife, Janet, was not with me, but had gone home for a few hours to take care of some necessary chores. I was sleeping, and a finger jabbed at me. I woke, of course, and looked blearily about to see who had awakened me and for what purpose.

My room, however, had a lock, and the lock was firmly closed and there was a chain across the door too. Sunlight filled the room and it was clearly empty. So were the closet and the bathroom. Rationalist though I am, there was no way in which I could refrain from thinking that some supernatural influence had interfered to tell me that something had happened to Janet (naturally, my ultimate fear). I hesitated for a moment, trying to fight it off, and for anyone but Janet I would have. So I phoned her at home. She answered immediately and said she was perfectly well.

Relieved, I hung up the phone and settled down to consider the problem of who or what had poked me. Was it simply a dream, a sensory hallucination? Perhaps, but it had seemed absolutely real. I considered.

When I sleep alone, I often wrap myself up in my own arms. I also know that when I am sleeping lightly, my muscles twitch. I assumed my sleeping position and imagined my muscles twitching. It was clear that my own finger had poked into my shoulder and that was it.

Now suppose that at the precise moment I had poked myself, Janet, through some utterly meaningless coincidence, had tripped and skinned her knee. And suppose I had called and she had groaned and said, "I just hurt myself."

Would I have been able to resist the thought of supernatural interference? I hope so. However, I can't be sure. It's the world we live in. It would corrupt the strongest, and I don't imagine I'm the strongest.

In this excerpt, acclaimed science fiction author **Isaac Asimov** relates his relationship to religion—specifically, that he has none. One of this country's most prolific authors (Asimov wrote over three hundred books in his lifetime), he calls himself a rationalist, a rigid resister to all that which cannot be perceived through ordinary means. However, as Asimov explains, even that faith which amounts to no faith at all can be tested. The author admits that he is sometimes tempted to explain natural phenomena with the existence of the supernatural. Asimov, who was born in Russia and naturalized as an American citizen in 1928, is famous for his Foundation novels, a series of books that depict the possibilities of life in the future.

FREDERICK BUECHNER
1926 -

14. EMMANUEL

MATTHEW 1:23
"Behold, a virgin shall conceive and bear a son, and his name shall be called Emmanuel" (which means, God with us).

For we preach Christ crucified," the Apostle Paul wrote to the church at Corinth, "a stumbling block to Jews and folly to Gentiles." He could as well have written "We preach Christ born" or "We preach Christmas" because the birth presents no fewer problems than the death does both to religious people—"the Jews"—and to everybody else—"the Gentiles." Christmas is not just Mr. Pickwick dancing a reel with the old lady at Dingley Dell or Scrooge waking up the next morning a changed man. It is not just the spirit of giving abroad in the land with a white beard and reindeer. It is not just the most famous birthday of them all and not just the annual reaffirmation of peace on Earth that is often reduced to so that people of many faiths or no faith can exchange Christmas cards without a qualm. On the contrary, if you do not hear in the message of Christmas something that must strike some as blasphemy and others as sheer fantasy, the chances are you have not heard the message for what it is. Emmanuel is the message in a nutshell, which is Hebrew for "God with us." Who is this God? How is he with us? That's where the problem lies.

In this excerpt from *A Room Called Remember*, Christian writer **Frederick Buechner** contemplates the various mysteries of religion, from the Christmas miracle to the obscure origin of faith to the difficulties that many have in believing in any of the above. Buechner, an ordained Presbyterian Minister, has gained acclaim for *The Book of Bebb*, a series of five novels about the experiences of a Bible salesman, as well as other fiction and nonfiction works. Educated at Union Theological Seminary with the likes of Paul Tillich and Reinhold Niebuhr, Buechner has taught at NYU, Harvard and Yale.

God is "the high and lofty One who inhabits eternity," says the prophet Isaiah, and by and large, though they would use different language and symbols to express it, all the major faiths of the world would tend to agree. Judaism calls him Yahweh. Islam calls him Allah. Buddhism and Hinduism use terms like Brahman-Atman or the Void or the One. But whatever they call him, all of them point to the ultimate spiritual Ground of existence as transcendent and totally other. The reality of God is so radically different from anything we know as real that in the last analysis we can say nothing about him except what he is not. *Neti neti* is the Upanishad's famous definition: he is not this, he is not that. "The Tao that can be expressed is not the eternal Tao" says the *Tao Te Ching* of Taoism. The Old Testament says it in characteristically concrete form as a narrative. When Moses asks to see God, God answers by saying, "You cannot see my face, for man cannot see me and live." As a mark of special favor, he hides Moses in the cleft of a rock and only after he has passed by in his glory takes his hand away so that Moses can see his back. According to the Protestant theologian Paul Tillich, you cannot even say that God exists in the same sense that you say a person exists, or a mountain or an idea. God is not a thing among other things. He does not take his place in a prior reality. He is that out of which reality itself arises, and to say that "he is" as we say that "we are" is to use language that is at best crudely metaphoric.

If all this sounds hopelessly abstruse, it nonetheless reflects the common experience of human beings as they contemplate the mystery that surrounds them. When a person looks up at the stars and ponders that which either goes on forever or ends at some unthinkably remote point beyond which there is Nothing; when we pray out of our deepest need to a God whom we can know only though faith; when we confront the enigma of our own life and the inevitability of our own death, all we can do is hold our tongues or say with Job, "Behold, I am of small account. I lay my hand on my mouth. . . . I have uttered what I did not understand, things too wonderful for me, which I did not know."

That is not the end of it, of course. Transcendent as God is—of another quality entirely from the world that he transcends—he nonetheless makes himself known to the world. Many would say that he is known to it because he made it, and from their earliest beginnings, people have looked at the world of nature and claimed to see in its the marks of his handicraft. Where nature is beautiful and beneficent, they have seen the love of God and where it is harsh and terrifying, his wrath. In the orderliness of nature they have seen God as lawgiver, and where this order is interrupted by the unforeseen and chaotic, they have seen miracle. And the same holds true for the world of history. The prosperity of nations or individuals suggests God's favor, and disaster suggests either condemnation or warning. Even the religions of India, which see the world less as the creation of the Ultimate than as a kind of illusory reverberation of it, speak of the law of karma which as inexorably as the law of gravity rewards the good and punishes the evil. Furthermore, though they do not see the world as a book where humankind can read of the nature and will of God but rather as an endless cycle of death and rebirth where our only hope is to escape altogether into the ineffable bliss of Nirvana, the very fact that such escape is available suggests the presence of something not entirely unlike divine intervention. Indeed, great teaching Buddhas and infinitely compassionate Bodhisattvas keep reappearing throughout the ages to show the way to Nirvana just as in the Biblically

based religions of Judaism, Islam, and Christianity, God keeps sending forth prophets, saints, angels.

And in all these traditions, needless to say, God also makes himself known through the mystics. However religions differ in other ways, all of them produce men and women who, by turning their attention inward, encounter him at first hand. As different from one another as Teresa of Avila, Ramakrishna, Thomas Merton, and using language that varies from the Bhagavad Gita to the journals of the Quaker George Fox, they all clearly seem to be trying to express the same ecstatic and inexpressible experience which might best be summarized as, at one and the same time, the total loss and total realization of self in merging with the ultimately Real.

Back then to the essential message of Christmas which is Emmanuel, God with us, and to the questions it raises: Who is this God and how is he with us? "The high and lofty One who inhabits eternity" is the answer to the first. The One who is with us is the One whom none can look upon because the space-and-time human mind can no more comprehend fully the spaceless, timeless Reality of the One than the eyes of the blind can comprehend light. The One who is with us is the One who has made himself known at most only partially and dimly through the pantomime of nature and history and the eloquent but always garbled utterance of prophets, saints, and mystics.

It is the answer to the second question that seems "folly to the Gentiles" and "a stumbling block to the Jews" because the claim that Christianity makes for Christmas is that at a particular time and place God came to be with us himself. When Quirinius was governor of Syria, in a town called Bethlehem, a child was born who, beyond the power of anyone to account for, was the high and lofty One made low and helpless. The One who inhabits eternity comes to dwell in time. The One whom none can look upon and live is delivered in a stable under the soft, indifferent gaze of cattle. The Father of all mercies puts himself at our mercy.

For those who believe in the transcendence and total otherness of God, it radically diminishes him. For those who do not believe in God, it is the ultimate absurdity. For those who stand somewhere between belief and unbelief, it challenges credulity in a new way. It is not a theory that can be tested rationally because it is beyond reason and because it is not a theory, not something that theologians have thought their way to. The claim is, instead, that it is something that has happened,

and reason itself is somehow tested by it, humankind's whole view of what is possible and real. Year after year the ancient tale of what happened is told—raw, preposterous, holy—and year after year the world in some measure stops to listen.

In the winter of 1947 a great snow fell on New York City. It began slowly, undramatically, like any other snow. The flakes were fine and steady and fell straight, with no wind. Little by little the sidewalks started to whiten. Shopkeepers and doormen were out with their shovels clearing paths to the street. After a while the streets began to fill and the roofs of parked cars were covered. You could no longer tell where the curb was, and even the hydrants disappeared, the melted discs over manhole covers. The plows could not keep up with it, and traffic moved more and more slowly as the drifts piled up. Businesses closed early, and people walked home from work. All evening it continued falling and much of the night. There were skiers on Park Avenue, children up way past their bedtime. By the next morning it was a different city. More striking than anything else about it was the silence. All traffic had stopped. Abandoned cars were buried. Nothing on wheels moved. The only sounds to be heard were church bells and voices. You listened because you could not help yourself.

"Ice splits starwise," Sir Thomas Browne wrote. A tap of the pick at the right point, and fissures shoot out in all directions, and the solid block falls in two at the star. The child is born, and history itself falls in two at the star. Whether you believe or do not believe, you date your letters and checks and income tax forms with a number representing how many years have gone by since what happened happened. The world of A.D. is one world, and the world of B.C. is another. Whatever the mystery was that widened the gaze of Tutankhamen's golden head, it was not this mystery. Whatever secret triggered the archaic smiles of Argive marbles or made the Bodhisattvas sit bolt upright at Angkor Vat, it was not our secret. The very voices and bells of our world ring out on a different air, and if most of the time we do not listen, at Christmas it is hard not to.

Business goes on as usual only moreso. Canned carols blast out over shopping center blacktops before the Thanksgiving turkey is cold on the plate. Salvation Army tambourines rattle, and streetcorner Santas stamp their feet against the cold. But if you have an ear for it at all, at the heart of all the hullabaloo you hear a silence, and at the heart of the silence you hear— whatever you hear.

"The Word became flesh and dwelt among us, full of grace and truth," the prologue to the Gospel of John says. A dream as old as time of the God descending hesitates on the threshold of coming true in a way to make all other truths seem dreamlike. If it is true, it is the chief of all truths. If it is not true, it is of all truths the one perhaps that people would most have be true if they could make it so. Maybe it is that longing to have it be true that is at the bottom even of the whole vast Christmas industry—the tons of cards and presents and fancy food, the plastic figures kneeling on the floodlit lawns of poorly attended churches. The world speaks of holy things in the only language it knows, which is a worldly language.

Emmanuel. We all must decide for ourselves whether it is true. Certainly the grounds on which to dismiss it are not hard to find. Christmas is commercialism. It is a pain in the neck. It is sentimentality. It is wishful thinking. With its account of the shepherds, the star, the three wise men, it smacks of a make-believe pathetically out of place in a world of energy crisis and space exploration and economic *malaise.* Yet it is never as easy to get rid of as all this makes it sound because whereas to dismiss belief in God is to dismiss only an idea, an hypothesis, for which there are many alternatives (such as belief in no god at all or in any of the lesser gods we are always creating for ourselves like Science or Morality or the inevitability of human progress), to dismiss Christmas is for most of us to dismiss part of ourselves.

For one thing it is to dismiss one of the most fragile yet enduring visions of our own childhood and of the child that continues to exist in all of us. The sense of mystery and wonderment. The sense that on this one day each year two plus two adds up not to four but to a million. The leap of the heart at waking up into a winter morning which for a while at least is as different from all other mornings as the city where the great snow fell was a different city. "Let all mortal flesh keep silence," the old hymn goes, and there was a time for most of us when it did.

And it is to dismiss a face. Who knows what we would have seen if we had been present there in Quirinius's time. Whether it happened the way Luke says it did, with the angels and the star, is most beside the point because the one thing that believer and unbeliever alike can be equally sure happened is an event that changed the course of human history. And it was a profoundly human event—the birth of a human being by whose humanness we measure our own, of a human being with a face which, though none of us has ever seen it, we would all likely recognize because for twenty centuries it has been of all faces the one that our world has been most haunted by.

More than anything else perhaps, to dismiss this particular birth as no different in kind from the birth of Socrates, say, or Moses or Gautama Buddha would be to dismiss the quality of life that it has given birth to in an astonishing variety of people over an astonishing period of time. There have been wise ones and simple ones, sophisticated ones and crude ones, respectable ones and disreputable ones. There have been medieval peasants and eighteenth-century aristocrats, nineteenth-century spinsters and twentieth-century dropouts. They need not be mystics or saints or even unusually religious in any formal, institutional sense, and there may never have been any one dramatic moment of conversion that they would point to in the past. But somewhere along the line something deep in them split starwise and they became not simply followers of Christ but bearers of his life. A birth of grace and truth took place within them scarcely less miraculous in its way than the one the Magi traveled all those miles to kneel before.

To look at the last great self-portraits of Rembrandt or to read Pascal or hear Bach's B-minor Mass is to know beyond the need for further evidence that if God is anywhere, he is with them, as he is also with the man behind the meat counter, the woman who scrubs floors at Roosevelt Memorial, the high-school math teacher who explains fractions to the bewildered child. And the step from "God with them" to Emmanuel, "God with us," may not be as great as it seems. What keeps the wild hope of Christmas alive year after year in a world notorious for dashing all hopes is the haunting dream that the child who was born that day may yet be born again even in us and our own snowbound, snowblind longing for him.

15. SUMMONS TO PILGRIMAGE

At its heart, religion is mysticism. Moses with his flocks in Midian, Buddha under the Bo tree, Jesus up to his knees in the waters of Jordan: each of them responds to Something for which words like shalom, oneness, God even, are only pallid souvenirs. "I have seen things," Aquinas told a friend, "that make all my writings seem like straw." Religion as institution, ethics, dogma, ritual, scripture, social action—all of this comes later and in the long run maybe counts for less. Religions start, as Frost said poems do, with a lump in the throat, to put it mildly, or with the bush going up in flames, the rain of flowers, the dove coming down out of the sky.

As for the man in the street, wherever his own religion is a matter of more than custom it is apt to because, however dimly, a doorway opened in the air once to him too, a word was spoken, and, however shakily, he too responded. The debris of his life continues to accumulate, the Vesuvius of the years scatters its ashes deep and much gets buried alive, but even under many layers the telltale heart can go on beating still.

Where it beats strong, there starts pulsing out from it a kind of life that is marked by, above all things perhaps, compassion—that sometimes fatal capacity for feeling what it is like to live inside another's skin, knowing that there can never really be peace and joy for any until there is peace and joy finally for all. Where it stops beating altogether, little is left religiously speaking but a good man, not perhaps in Mark Twain's "worst sense of the word," but surely in the grayest and saddest: the good man whose goodness has become cheerless and finicky, a technique for working off his own guilts, a gift with no love in it which neither deceives nor benefits any for long.

Religion as a word points to that area of human experience where in one way or another man comes upon mystery as a summons to pilgrimage; where he senses meanings no less overwhelming because they can be only hinted at in myth and ritual; where he glimpses a destination that he can never know fully until he reaches it.

We are all of us more mystics than we believe or choose to believe—life is complicated enough as it is, after all. We have seen more than we let on, even to ourselves. Through some moment of beauty or pain, some sudden turning of our lives, we catch glimmers at least of what the saints are blinded by; only then, unlike the saints, we tend to go on as though nothing has happened. To go on as though something has happened, even though we are not sure what it was or just where we are supposed to go with it, is to enter the dimension of life that religion is a word for.

Some, of course, go to the typewriter. First the lump in the throat, the stranger's face unfurling like a flower, and then the clatter of the keys, the ting-a-ling of the right-hand margin. One thinks of Pascal sewing into his jacket, where after his death a servant found it, his "since about half past ten in the evening until about half past midnight. Fire. Certitude. Certitude. Feeling. Joy. Peace," stammering it out like a child because he had to. Fire, fire, and then the scratch of pen on paper. There are always some who have to set it down in black and white.

There are poetry books and there are poetic books— the first a book with poems in it, the second a book which may or may not have poems in it but which is in some sense itself a poem—and possibly a similar distinction can be made between religion books and religious books. A religion book is a book with religion in it in the everyday sense of religious ideas, symbols, attitudes, and, if it takes the form of fiction or drama, with characters and setting that to one degree or another have religious associations or implications.

In the field of fiction, there would be *The Scarlet Letter, Billy Budd,* Mann's Joseph tetralogy, Faulkner's *A Fable,* Hesse's *Siddhartha,* much of Graham Greene, much of Mauriac, and so on. And of coarse the element of religion need not dominate as in those but can be just one of many other things that are going on.

Christ symbols are to be found almost anywhere: Hemingway taking his Old Man up Calvary with his mast on his shoulder and his palms lacerated by fishline, the Beatles singing of the Fool on the Hill as "the man of a thousand voices" whom "nobody ever hears."

Characters also talk about religion in novels: old Mr. Hook in John Updike's *The Poorhouse Fair* fumbling through his arguments for the existence of God while the young Perfect, Conner, demolished them one by one until in the process he is himself somehow demolished; Tarrou in *The Plague* asking the question which has in different forms come to preoccupy so many: "Can one be a saint without God?" Explicitly or implicitly, sometimes profoundly, sometimes superficially, a religion book tells us something about religion as a poetry book presents us with poems.

With religious books, we need more than our wits about us, maybe sometimes less. A religious book may or may not have religion in it, but what it does have is a certain openness to Mystery itself, and what it asks of us is also a certain openness, a certain suspension of either belief or disbelief. If we let it, the reading of a religious book can become in itself an experience of what, at its best, a religion book can only tell about. A religion book is a canvas, a religious book a transparency. With a religious book it is less what we see in it than what we see through it that matters.

J.R.R. Tolkien's fairy-tale epic *The Lord of the Rings* helps draw the distinction perhaps. Some of its admirers have tried to make it into a religion book by claiming, among other things, that the Ring of Power which must be destroyed is the hydrogen bomb. Tolkien, on the other hand, denied this unequivocally. But intended or otherwise, there can be little doubt that for many it has become a religious book. The "Frodo Lives" buttons are not entirely a joke, because something at least comes to life through those fifteen hundred pages, although inevitably it is hard to say just what.

It seems to have something to do with the way Tolkien has of making us see the quiddity of things like wood, bread, stone, milk, iron, as though we have never seen them before or not for a long time, which is probably the truth of the matter; his landscapes set deeper echoes going in us than any message could. He gives us back a sense that we have mostly lost of the things of the earth, and because we are ourselves of the earth, whatever else, we are given back too some sense of our own secret. Very possibly again he did not intend it. It may well be axiomatic that, religiously, a writer achieves most when he is least conscious of doing so. Certainly the attempt to be religious is as doomed as the attempt to be poetic is.

The word, I suppose, is *revelation*. Religious books always seem to end up being about ourselves in the sense not simply of illuminating our own experience but of opening up vistas into worlds that, until they were revealed to us, we never knew were home.

There is very little religion in Shakespeare, but when he is greatest, he is most religious. It is curious that the plays that fit this best are, like *The Lord of the Rings*, in their own way fairy tales. There is *The Tempest*, the masque of his old age where all comes right in the end, where like Rembrandt in his last self-portraits Shakespeare smiles up out of his wrinkles and speaks into the night a golden word too absurd to be anything perhaps but true, the laughter of things beyond the tears of things.

And there is *King Lear*, its Cinderella opening with the wicked sisters and the good one. But then the fairy tale is turned on its head, and although everything comes right in the end, everything also does not come right—religion books are usually tidier. Blinded, old Gloucester sees the truth about his sons but too late to save the day. Cordelia is vindicated in her innocence only to be destroyed more grotesquely because more pointlessly than her sisters in their lustful cunning. And Lear himself emerges from his madness to become truly a king at last, but dies then babbling that his dead darling lives and fumbling with a button at his throat.

Maybe fairy tales tend to become religious because if we read them at all, we have our guards up less. We are prepared for mystery. *The Brothers Karamazov*, a religious book par excellence, is among other things a murder mystery, and in murder mysteries too we are ready for the unexpected—ready to believe that it was the butler after all who did it, and when Alyosha kisses the earth and begs its forgiveness, ready to glimpse in ourselves and beyond an abyss of pity and longing deeper than we ever dreamed.

Finally a word about Graham Greene. To list *The End of the Affair* and *The Heart of the Matter* as religion books seems just. They are on the border, perhaps, between the religion book and the religious. But when it comes to *The Power and the Glory*, he seems to cross that border. The art is the same, there is the same concern with the subterranean presence of a grace that can save a man's soul even through his sin, and yet something else is here that is better heard than described.

Trying to escape north out of revolutionary Mexico, the whiskey-priest reaches a peasant village where he meets his bastard daughter for what turns out to be the last time. She is an ancient, malicious dwarf of a child who recoils, sniggering, when he first tries to embrace her. Greene writes:

He said: "I love you. I am your father and I love you. Try to understand that." He held her tightly by the wrist and suddenly she stayed still, looking up at him. He said: "I would give my life, that's nothing, my soul . . . my dear, my dear, try to understand that you are—so important." . . . She stared back at him out of dark and unconscious eyes: he had a sense that he had come too late. He said: "Good-bye, my dear," and clumsily kissed her—a silly infatuated aging man, who as soon as he released her and started padding back to the plaza could feel behind his hunched shoulders the whole vile world coming round the child to ruin her. His mule was there, saddled, by the gaseosa stall. A man said: "Better to north, father," and stood waving his hand. One mustn't have human affections—or rather one must love every soul as if it were one's own child. The passion to protect must extend itself over a world—but he felt it tethered and aching like a hobbled animal to the tree trunk. He turned the mule south.

It is like Alice's looking-glass, I suppose, where we see at first our own homeliness-more than half in love, all of us, with our own sin, silly and doomed and we pad along disheveled ways—and then at last the glass melts away like a mist and opens out, for a moment at least, into looking-glass land. Nothing stays put there for long, and nothing is entirely what it seems. Victory and defeat, love and justice, sin and grace, life and death even—distinctions go dim and contrariwise. Beasts talk and flowers come alive. Both in the reading and in the writing, a religious book is an act of grace—no less rare, no less precious, no less wildly improbable.

18. ALL'S LOST—ALL'S FOUND

"How my mind has changed in the last decade" is the subject to which I was invited to address myself several years ago, and since the invitation seemed to offer a certain amount of leeway, I undertook to produce less of a formal essay than a few rather informal paragraphs under three different headings. To begin with, *How my mind has changed about myself.*

My readings in Buddhism have long since convinced me that when I talk about myself, I don't really know what I'm talking about. "How do I learn to control myself? To understand myself? To live with myself?" the harried Occidental goes to the Buddhist monk to inquire, and after twenty minutes or so of properly inscrutable silence, the monk says something like, "Show me this self you're fretting about. Then maybe I can help you with it." Needless to say, the point seems to be that when you come right down to it, there's nothing to show. I do not have a self. I am a self. As soon as I draw back to scrutinize "it," I have by the very act of drawing back removed from my scrutiny the very thing I seek to know. So instead of trying to talk about who I am, let me simply describe something of what it feels like to live inside my skin now as compared with ten years ago.

In many ways it feels much the same. As much in my fifties as in my forties, I feel much of the time like a child. I get excited about the kinds of things that excite a ten year-old. The first snow of the year, for instance. The smell of breakfast. Buying things, especially books, which, like a child, it is less important for me to read than simply to have. Getting things in the mail. Going to the movies. Having somebody remember my name. Remembering somebody's name. Making a decent forehand in tennis. Being praised. Chocolate ice cream. And so on.

Like a child too I feel uneasy in the presence of people who are more grown-up than I am. I find myself saying to them less what I really feel like saying than what I feel they'd like to have me say. When people are taking me seriously as a grown-up—listening to me lecture or preach or talking to me about one of my books—I think to myself *if they only knew.* If someone were to wake me up in the middle of the night with a flashlight in my eyes and, before I had time to think, ask me who I was, I would not say my grown-up name but my childhood name. If they asked my age, I would say not fifty-six but twenty-six. Maybe even sixteen. Given the choice between having flying saucers, the Loch Ness monster, ghosts, magic and miracles generally proven either true or false, I would choose them to be true without a moment's hesitation. And so on again.

The child in me is very much alive, in other words, and though this involves certain serious disadvantages, I would not have it otherwise. A child is apt to see certain things better than his elders, I think, because, less sure than they of what to *expect,* he is more apt than they to see what, actually though unexpectedly, *is.* By the same token, a child is apt to feel certain things more than his elders too because he is not as good as they at keeping his feelings under control, and even though this makes him vulnerable to some emotional inanities that maturity is relatively safe from, I still would not have it any other way.

All of this was as true of me ten years ago as it is now, but there have been changes too. One instance of this is the word that during the last ten years I find I've started to use for sighing with. Instead of the traditional *oh dear* or *oh well* or any of those, again and again I hear myself saying *child, child* in a tone of voice that seems to be a sort of weary reproof and yet a kind of lament too. Don't be so foolish the grown-up in me says to the child. Don't make such a fuss. Don't let the world get under your skin so. Keep your guard up more. Stay on an evener keel. Grow up. That is the reproof. The lament, I think, stems from knowing that the reproof will be heeded all too well. Already the child *is* keeping his guard up more, keeping the world at arm's length more, starting to see less, feel less. It is a step toward maturity and as such to be rejoiced in. But it is a step away from something in its way equally precious and as such to be lamented too. *Child, child . . .* I feel a state of being, a dimension of selfhood, coming to an end, and it is proper that it should come to an end so that something richer and wiser and in the long run even holier can take its place. But the end of anything is sad because the end of anything foreshadows the end, finally, of everything. And that final end is death, about which also my mind has changed, and hence the second heading: *How my mind has changed about death.*

Even forty years ago, let alone ten, I knew that like everybody else I would die someday, and in my mind I had already died many times. I have never had an ache or pain that wasn't fatal or an illness that wasn't terminal. One of the occupational hazards of being a writer of fiction is to have an imagination as overdeveloped as a blacksmith's right arm. Again and again I have watched the doctor pause for a way to break the tragic news to me. I have lain in a hospital room receiving the final visits of friends. I have said goodbye to my wife and children for the last time. I have attended my own funeral.

There is something to be said for such nonsense. For one thing, to have the doctor tell you that it is not lung cancer after all but just a touch of the flu is in a way to be born again. For another thing, it is to be given back not just your old life again but your old life with a new sense of its pricelessness. At least for a time old grievances, disappointments, irritations, failures, that had cast a shadow over your days suddenly cease to matter much. You are alive. That's all that matters, and the sheer wonder and grace of it are staggering, the sense of life as gift, and the sense of the pricelessness of each moment too, even the most humdrum. The taste of fresh bread. The trip to pick up the laundry. The walk with a friend. They were nearly taken away for good. Someday they will be taken away for good indeed. But in the meantime they are yours. Treasure them for what they will not be forever. Treasure them for what, except by God's grace, they might never have been at all.

All of this was part of what it was like to be me in the 1970s and continues to be so in the 1980s, but at some point during the intervening decade I experienced death in a new way still. I tried to describe the experience in a novel once. There is a scene in which a man goes to visit his sister Miriam's grave in a Brooklyn cemetery. He tries to shed a tear for her, but the tear won't come. Instead, his mind begins to wander until in a sense it wanders off altogether, and he ends up just staring down at the grass so hard that he doesn't even see it. He doesn't have a thought in his head. What follows next he describes like this:

> I was still standing there in this kind of empty-headed trance, and then it was like what happens when, just as you're about to go to sleep at night, you seem to trip over something and can feel the whole bed shake under you. *I came to,* I suppose you would say. Some stirring in the air or quick movement of squirrel or bird brought me back to myself, and just at that instant of being brought back to myself, I knew that the self I'd been brought back to was some fine day going to be as dead as Miriam. I knew it not just in the usual sense of knowing it but knew it in almost the Biblical sense of having sex with it. I knew

> I didn't just *have* a body. I *was* a body. It was like walking into a closed door at night. The thud of it jolted me down to the roots of my hair.

> "The body I was going to be dead. I'd known it before, but here I banged right into it—not a lesson this time but a collision. You might say that there at my sister's grave I finally lost my innocence, saw the unveiling of middle-age's last and most intimate secret. There in Brooklyn I was screwed by my own death."

At some point during the last ten years, in other words, I came, like the narrator in the novel, to know my death in a new way. What I had feared as hypochondriac came to seem by comparison, a small thing or, more accurately, a constellation of small things. I had feared the pain and indignity of disease. I had feared hospitals—the smell, the sterility, the depersonalization. I had dreaded the last farewells. I had dreaded leaving the party while I was still having a good time. I had feared and dreaded the ultimate separation from everything and everybody I held most dear. But behind all these fears, and essential to their fearsomeness, was the presupposition that the self that I am would be in some sense around to experience them, down to and including my own funeral.

What I have come to experience since, and with a degree of immediacy impossible to describe, is the extinction of the self itself. With something more than my imagination I have come at odd moments to experience something more than my death, that is to say something more than my death as an event in which my self will participate. I have come to experience it as a nonevent which I will no longer have or be a self to participate in it with. Call it Nothingness. Call it the End. And the curious thing is that when it comes to this most staggering reality of all, I am no longer afraid.

Dying and dissolution continue to strike fear in me. Death itself does not. Ten years ago if somebody had offered me a vigorous, healthy life that would never end, I would have said yes. Today I think I would say no. I love my life as much as I ever did and will cling on to it for as long as I can, but life without death has become unthinkable to me as day without night or waking without sleep. Which brings me to the third and final heading, which is *How my mind has changed about God.*

Needless to say this is closely related to the other two. The child in me must die so the man in me can be born. Yet the man in me must die too, all of me, the most that I have it in my power to become as well as the least out of whose demise the most emerges. And yet timorous, overimaginative, doom-ridden, life-loving, self-serving and self-centered and sinful as I am, I find that I contemplate this fact with a new and curious absence of fear. Why should this be so?

By way of an answer I find myself drawing again from a novel of mine called *Godric*. It has to do with a medieval hermit-saint who for many years chastened his flesh in the icy waters of the river Wear near the city of Durham in northern England. As a very old man he describes the experience of bathing in it in the dead of winter:

First there's the fiery sting of cold that almost stops my breath, the aching torment in my limbs. I think I may go mad, my wits so outraged that they seek to flee my skull like rats a ship that's going down. I puff. I gasp. Then inch by inch a blessed numbness comes. I have no legs, no arms. My very heart grows still. These floating hands are not my hands. The ancient flesh I wear is rags for all I feel of it.

"'Praise, praise!'" I croak. Praise God for all that's holy, cold, and dark. Praise him for all we lose, for all the river of the years bears off. Praise him for stillness in the wake of pain. Praise him for emptiness. And as you race to spill into the sea, praise him yourself, old Wear. Praise him for dying and the peace of death.

"In the little church I built of wood for Mary, I hollowed out a place for him. Perkin brings him by the pail and pours him in. Now that I can hardly walk, I crawl to meet him there. He takes me in his chilly lap to wash me of my sins. Or I kneel down beside him till within his depths I see a star."

"Sometimes this star is still. Sometimes she dances. She is Mary's star. Within that little pool of Wear she winks at me. I wink at her. The secret that we share I cannot tell in full. But this much I will tell. What's lost is nothing to what's found,

and all the death that ever was, set next to life, would scarcely fill a cup."

At the age of one hundred the old man knows what at my age I am only just beginning to see—that if it is by grace we are saved, it is by grace too that we are lost, or lost at least in the sense of losing our selves, our lives, our all. In the past, when my faith was strong, I always trusted God more or less. I trusted him with my life, which is to say I trusted him but with the presupposition that I would always be in some measure alive to say to him in the words of the *Te Deum*, "Oh Lord, in thee have I trusted; let me never be confounded," in the sense that I would always be around to cajole with him, plead with him, and in general to remind him to be the God of mercy and love I always trusted him to be. The change is that now I begin, at least to trust him with my death. I begin, at least, to see that death is not merely a biological necessity but a necessity too in terms of the mystery of salvation.

We find by losing. We hold fast by not letting go. We become something new by ceasing to be something old. This seems to be close to the heart of that mystery. I know no more now than I ever did about the far side of death as the last letting-go of all, but I begin to know that I do not need to know and that I do not need to be afraid of not knowing. God knows. That is all that matters.

Out of Nothing he creates Something. Out of the End he creates the Beginning. Out of selfness we grow, by his grace, toward selflessness, and out of that final selflessness, which is the loss of self altogether, "eye hath not seen nor ear heard, neither have entered into the heart of man" what new marvels he will bring to pass next. All's lost. All's found. And if such words sound childish, so be it. Out of each old self that dies some precious essence is preserved for the new self that is born; and within the child-self that is part of us all, there is perhaps nothing more precious than the fathomless capacity to trust.

timorous, overimaginative, doom-ridden, life-loving, self-serving and self-centered and sinful as I am, I find that I contemplate this fact with a new and curious absence of fear. Why should this be so?

By way of an answer I find myself drawing again from a novel of mine called *Godric*. It has to do with a medieval hermit-saint who for many years chastened his flesh in the icy waters of the river Wear near the city of Durham in northern England. As a very old man he describes the experience of bathing in it in the dead of winter:

First there's the fiery sting of cold that almost stops my breath, the aching torment in my limbs. I think I may go mad, my wits so outraged that they seek to flee my skull like rats a ship that's going down. I puff. I gasp. Then inch by inch a blessed numbness comes. I have no legs, no arms. My very heart grows still. These floating hands are not my hands. The ancient flesh I wear is rags for all I feel of it.

"'Praise, praise!'" I croak. Praise God for all that's holy, cold, and dark. Praise him for all we lose, for all the river of the years bears off. Praise him for stillness in the wake of pain. Praise him for emptiness. And as you race to spill into the sea, praise him yourself, old Wear. Praise him for dying and the peace of death.

"In the little church I built of wood for Mary, I hollowed out a place for him. Perkin brings him by the pail and pours him in. Now that I can hardly walk, I crawl to meet him there. He takes me in his chilly lap to wash me of my sins. Or I kneel down beside him till within his depths I see a star."

"Sometimes this star is still. Sometimes she dances. She is Mary's star. Within that little pool of Wear she winks at me. I wink at her. The secret that we share I cannot tell in full. But this much I will tell. What's lost is nothing to what's found,

and all the death that ever was, set next to life, would scarcely fill a cup."

At the age of one hundred the old man knows what at my age I am only just beginning to see—that if it is by grace we are saved, it is by grace too that we are lost, or lost at least in the sense of losing our selves, our lives, our all. In the past, when my faith was strong, I always trusted God more or less. I trusted him with my life, which is to say I trusted him but with the presupposition that I would always be in some measure alive to say to him in the words of the *Te Deum,* "Oh Lord, in thee have I trusted; let me never be confounded," in the sense that I would always be around to cajole with him, plead with him, and in general to remind him to be the God of mercy and love I always trusted him to be. The change is that now I begin, at least to trust him with my death. I begin, at least, to see that death is not merely a biological necessity but a necessity too in terms of the mystery of salvation.

We find by losing. We hold fast by not letting go. We become something new by ceasing to be something old. This seems to be close to the heart of that mystery. I know no more now than I ever did about the far side of death as the last letting-go of all, but I begin to know that I do not need to know and that I do not need to be afraid of not knowing. God knows. That is all that matters.

Out of Nothing he creates Something. Out of the End he creates the Beginning. Out of selfness we grow, by his grace, toward selflessness, and out of that final selflessness, which is the loss of self altogether, "eye hath not seen nor ear heard, neither have entered into the heart of man" what new marvels he will bring to pass next. All's lost. All's found. And if such words sound childish, so be it. Out of each old self that dies some precious essence is preserved for the new self that is born; and within the child-self that is part of us all, there is perhaps nothing more precious than the fathomless capacity to trust.

THE
THREE MINUTE
SERMON

SEARCHING
FOR GOD
IN AMERICA

The Three Minute Sermon

(Or Why I Like Writing Songs of Faith)

BY WALT HARRAH

"Let the word of Christ dwell in you richly as you teach and admonish one another with all wisdom, and as you sing psalms, hymns and spiritual songs with gratitude in your hearts to God."

—The Apostle Paul writing to the church at Colossae

"When you come together, everyone has a hymn. . . ."

—The Apostle Paul writing to the church at Corinth

"The Slade brothers with their families and farm hands are singing as they trudge along the country road to attend the little white church on Sunday. The women and children are packed into the ox cart in front, the men walking behind, all singing hymns with strong voices as they walk the four miles to church. It is customary for the village folks to wait in front of the church for the Slades to arrive before ringing the last bell and then to join them as they march into church singing."

— A local tradition in Alstead, New Hampshire, around 1800

America didn't invent hymns, as much as we might like to take partial credit. Hymns didn't even begin with the Wesleys or Watts or even Martin Luther. They preceded Augustine and already existed when the Christian church was born. In fact, the angelic choir sang a hymn of sorts when they announced the birth of Jesus to the shepherds. If you ask me, heaven is the place where hymns started, and we have just picked up on the idea here on earth. It's the next logical step once you discover God. Singing hymns down here is mainly preparation. The main event will take place in eternity, where the singing will be truly unbelievable!

I am fortunate to be a sacred songwriter by profession. Sure, it has its down side, but what doesn't? And because seeking God has become a consuming, lifelong passion for me, my pursuit of God and my art have ended up running into each other a lot, and songs happen. OK, so I'm no Beethoven or Bach or Elton John or Lennon or Dylan. But I can take something that I have found to be true about my search for God, put it in verse form, rhyme the ends of the phrases, write a melody, record it, and then watch the most amazing thing happen. People always hear it, somehow relate to it, and get encouraged by it. No, not everybody, but usually somebody! And sometimes I'm lucky enough to hear about it. A letter made its way to me from Ballymena, Ireland:

"I felt very strongly that I should start a soup kitchen in our home town of Ballymena. I have found it extremely hard work, but some have joined me and God seems to be winning through. I am in my early sixties and wonder sometimes what will happen when I am not here. That is why your tape means so much to me. I have never considered all the people so full of faith who didn't see their work accomplished."

Wow! Is she saying that the songs I wrote have given her a perspective that will help her to keep on going? Will some homeless people get fed and clothed by a warm and friendly woman, in part because of a song that came out of my experience with God? That is an awesome and scary thought!

And there was this recent letter from a man in a hospital:

"I am writing this letter from a 'life management' hospital. I am scheduled to go to a pain clinic in about a week to evaluate my chronic back and leg pain caused by scar tissue wrapped around the nerve roots where they exit the spine. I have been in extreme pain for in excess of seven years. All the specialists have told me that my condition is inoperable, and that the best I could hope for was perhaps maintaining the pain at a tolerable level. The message of perseverance that comes through your composition, NO TURNING BACK, has sustained me through six years of doubt and fear and pain."

You can imagine how it felt, to think that this man I didn't even know had been helped so powerfully by something that had come out of my faith experience! Only, for me the songs were five parts concept and one part experience. For him, these songs were life and death. But that was not all. I would have been thrilled just knowing that he had been helped by the songs. What he went on to describe took the power of truth in song one step farther. I can only imagine the scene.

"I have had the opportunity to sing two of the songs from your work at my local church, and many hearts were touched. We had one lady come forth as I sang, and I was able to come off the stage and finish the song with my arm around her shoulder, and the Lord ministered to her in a very special way. She told me that she was feeling like there was a great conflict inside her and that the song gave her the guidance and release she needed to overcome. She had not been to the church for several months, but is now attending regularly."

Let me see if I get this straight. This man, suffering from chronic back pain, has got his arms around a woman in need and is caring for her? One of the songs he sang in church was "No More Night." Inspired by the Apostle John's vision of the New Jerusalem in the Book of Revelation, it describes what heaven will be like:

No more night
No more tears
No more pain
Never crying again
Praises to the great 'I Am'
We will live in the light of the risen Lamb.

No more pain. Those words coming from that man represented such intense hope. Surely everyone present knew of his struggle to go on living, to be forced to live with pain, knowing there was little hope in this life of any improvement. And yet, there he was, singing a song I had written. Me, who writhes in pain at the least little scratch! I don't know whether he sang the song in tune or if the melody came out the way I intended it, but I know this much—all of heaven must have been rejoicing that day. Job himself probably led the celestial applause when the song was finished!

I guess what is great about a song is that it takes on a life of its own. It starts out meaningful to the writer; but truth being what it is, others soon get caught up in its light as well. In God's economy, songs are like little angelic three-minute messages; and at just the opportune time, we get changed by the truth they contain.

But there's more. My friend mentioned singing two songs, both of which had played a role in his battle with pain. Incredibly, his story grew more riveting:

"The reason I'm in the hospital now is that last Thursday I was contemplating suicide again. Wednesday the thoughts started coming to me as I had not been able to sleep for approximately four days because of the pain! I told the Lord that I couldn't endure the pain, discouragement, radical mood swings, the inability to provide for my family, etc. If I was going to live in this hell, I may as well go there! I felt weak and hopeless. Then I believe the Lord spoke to me and simply said, 'What about Walt?' I asked the Lord why He had to bring you into my thoughts and I believe that He allowed me to understand that the seed you, Walt, have sown is about to spring forth."

These lyrics are the seed that he was referring to:

> *Well I don't care how hard the way might be*
> *He'll lead me there eventually*
> *By faith I choose the road that can't be seen*
> *I'll take the wealth of His great love outpoured*
> *For life with Him is its own reward.*

I'm nothing special. There have been thousands of hymn writers before me, each of whom has left a trail of faith in the lyrics he wrote. Take for instance, Fanny Crosby. Blind from six months old, she wrote over six thousand hymns until she died at ninety-four! Millions have been moved and strengthened by her songs!

The hymns that follow are representative of the legacy of faith that has survived into the latter part of this century. They are beginning to be noticed, because in them lie truths, truths that no longer are fashionable in the spirit of the age, truths that need to be rediscovered. If our search for God in a technological world is to be a successful one, we need all the help we can get.

HOW FIRM A FOUNDATION
Robert Keene

First published in London in 1787, the text of this hymn has more stories attached to it than almost any other. General Curtis Guild, Jr., told the *Sunday School Times* this story at the turn of the century. The Seventh Army Corps was dug in the hills surrounding Havana, Cuba, on Christmas Eve of 1898. A sentinel from the Forty-ninth Iowa called out, "Number ten; twelve o'clock, and all's well." From somewhere a strong voice started singing, "How firm a foundation, ye saints of the Lord." The Sixth Missouri added its voices, and the Fourth Virginia joined in. Soon "on the long ridges above the great city whence Spanish tyranny once went forth to enslave the New World, a whole American army corps was singing:

> "'*Fear not, I am with thee, O be not dismayed,*
> *for I am thy God, and will still give thee aid;*
> *I'll strengthen thee, help thee, and cause thee to stand,*
> *upheld by my righteous, omnipotent hand.'*"

General Guild spoke of the unity that hymn helped to forge on the ridge that Christmas night: "The Northern soldier knew the hymn as one he had learned beside his mother's knee. To the Southern soldier, it was that and something more; as the favorite hymn of General Robert E. Lee, it had been sung at his funeral. Protestant and Catholic, South and North, singing together on Christmas day in the morning—that's an American army!"

One day in his old age, Andrew Jackson, who had become a devout member of the Presbyterian church, was entertaining some visitors. "There is a beautiful hymn that deals with the great promises of God to His people, and it was the favorite hymn of my wife. Perhaps you know it." And as he began to sing the first refrain, the entire room joined in.

"How firm a foundation, ye saints of the Lord,
is laid for your faith in his excellent word!
What more can he say than to you he hath said?,
to you who for refuge to Jesus have fled?

"Fear not, I am with thee, O be not dismayed,
for I am thy God, and will still give thee aid;
I'll strengthen thee, help thee, and cause thee to stand,
upheld by my righteous, omnipotent hand.

"When through the deep waters I call thee to go,
the rivers of sorrow shall not overflow;
for I will be with thee, thy troubles to bless,
and sanctify to thee thy deepest distress.

"When through fiery trials thy pathway shall lie,
my grace, all sufficient, shall be thy supply;
the flame shall not hurt thee, I only design
thy dross to consume, and thy gold to refine.

"The soul that on Jesus still leans for repose,
I will not, I will not desert to its foes;
that soul, though all hell should endeavor to shake,
I'll never, no, never, no, never forsake!"

My Faith Looks Up to Thee

Ray Palmer

As he was reading a brief German poem of only two stanzas, Ray Palmer reflected on the significance of the cross. The last words, "a ransomed soul," summed up for him the entire experience of his faith and he soon found himself crying "abundant tears." The following stanzas are the lasting result of that experience.

My faith looks up to thee,
thou Lamb of Calvary,
Savior divine!
Now hear me while I pray,
take all my guilt away;
O let me from this day
be wholly thine!

May thy rich grace impart
strength to my fainting heart,
my zeal inspire;
as thou hast died for me,
O may my love to thee
pure, warm and changeless be,
a living fire!

While life's dark maze I tread,
and griefs around me spread,
be thou my guide;
bid darkness turn to day,
wipe sorrow's tears away,
nor let me ever stray
from thee aside.

Before one of the terrible battles of the wilderness in the Civil War, eight young Christian soldiers met for prayer in a tent. As they faced the reality of impending death, they decided to commit their thoughts to paper, documenting their courage in the face of death. No doubt they wished to comfort their relatives should the next day's battle be their last. They chose this hymn as a statement of their faith. Seven of the eight met their death in the tragic battle that followed, but the fourth stanza proved to be a more than adequate epitaph.

When ends life's transient dream,
when death's cold, sullen stream
shall o'er me roll;
blest Savior, then, in love,
fear and distrust remove;
O bear me safe above,
a ransomed soul!

STAND UP, STAND UP FOR JESUS
George Duffield

Five thousand persons attended the noon prayer meeting at Jayne's Hall in Philadelphia in the spring of 1858. A revival had been going on for months; and on that particular day the preaching of the young Episcopalian clergyman, Dudley A. Tyng, was so effective that fully one thousand of the hearers responded in a commitment of faith. Tyng had recently been dismissed from the pulpit of the traditional downtown church that he had inherited from his father. It seems that in his youthful vigor he was far too aggressive in addressing the whole issue of slavery and now found himself meeting in a common hall on Sundays with a small crowd of faithful followers.

As he addressed the listeners that noon, he dramatically thundered to emphasize a point: "I would rather my right arm were amputated at the trunk than fail to deliver to you God's message." That statement proved tragically prophetic, for the following week, while in the country observing a corn thrasher at work, he caught his loose sleeve in the machinery, severely mangling his right arm, and with the infection that set in, death became imminent. With several of his pastor friends gathered at his bedside, he was asked for a statement; and his final advice was to "stand up for Jesus."

George Duffield, pastor of the Temple Presbyterian Church in Philadelphia, took those words to heart; and his congregation heard a sermon that Sunday on the text from Ephesians 6:14, "Stand therefore, having your loins girded about with truth. . . ." As he closed the sermon, he read the newly composed text that follows.

Stand up, stand up for Jesus,
ye soldiers of the cross,
lift high his royal banner,
it must not suffer loss.
from victory unto victory
his army shall he lead,
till every foe is vanquished
and Christ is Lord indeed.

Stand up, stand up for Jesus,
the trumpet call obey;
forth to the mighty conflict
in this his glorious day.
Ye that are brave, now serve him
against unnumbered foes;
let courage rise with danger,
and strength to strength oppose.

Stand up, stand up for Jesus,
stand in his strength alone;
the arm of flesh will fail you—
ye dare not trust your own;
put on the gospel armor,
each piece put on with prayer;
where duty calls, or danger,
be never wanting there.

Stand up, stand up for Jesus,
the strife will not be long;
this day the noise of battle,
the next, the victor's song:
to those who conquer evil
a crown of life shall be;
they with the King of glory
shall reign eternally.

MINE EYES HAVE SEEN THE GLORY

Julia Ward Howe

Launched as the Civil War battle song of the Republic, this hymn by Julia Ward Howe first appeared in February of 1862, in the *Atlantic Monthly*. Among her many lifetime achievements, Mrs. Howe was involved in various humanitarian pursuits, and she was an outspoken critic of slavery. As a leader in the Woman's Suffrage Movement, she spearheaded an international crusade of women with the express purpose of halting all war.

President Lincoln attended a large patriotic rally at which this hymn was sung by a soloist. After the tumultuous applause had died down, Lincoln, with "tears in his eyes," requested that it be sung again.

Mine eyes have seen the glory of the coming of the Lord;
he is trampling out the vintage where the grapes of wrath are stored;
he hath loosed the fateful lightning of his terrible swift sword;
his truth is marching on.

REFRAIN
Glory! glory, hallelujah! (3 times)
Our God is marching on.

I have seen him in the watch-fires of a hundred circling camps;
they have builded him an altar in the evening dews and damps;
I can read his righteous sentence by the dim and flaring lamps;
his day is marching on.

He has sounded forth the trumpet that shall never call retreat;
he is sifting out the hearts of men before his judgment seat;
O be swift, my soul, to answer him! Be jubilant, my feet;
Our God is marching on.

In the beauty of the lilies Christ was born across the sea,
with a glory in his bosom that transfigures you and me;
as he died to make men holy, let us live to make men free,
while God is marching on.

IT IS WELL WITH MY SOUL

Horatio G. Spafford

Spafford was a successful Chicago businessman until he invested heavily in real estate on the shore of Lake Michigan just months prior to the Great Fire of 1871. His finances were wiped out in that tragic event. Already reeling from the death of his only son, his faith was sorely tested. Two years later, he planned a trip to London to attend the Moody crusade to be held in that city. Because of a last-minute business interruption, he sent his wife and four daughters on ahead of him, sailing on the S. S. Ville du Havre. Again tragedy struck. In a collision at sea, the ship went down in twelve minutes. The daughters were lost, and his wife cabled him from Wales with the terse message, "saved alone." Quickly he made his way to her side. As the boat steamed across the Atlantic, the pilot called Spafford to the bridge when they passed the approximate spot where his daughters lay in their watery grave. Overwhelmed with emotion, the words to this hymn took form and became the ultimate credo for trusting and hoping in God.

When peace like a river attendeth my way,
when sorrows like sea billows roll,
whatever my lot, thou hast taught me to say,
"It is well, it is well with my soul."

REFRAIN
It is well with my soul,
it is well, it is well with my soul.

Though Satan should buffet, though trials should come,
let this blest assurance control:
that Christ has regarded my helpless estate,
and has shed his own blood for my soul.

My sin— O, the bliss of this glorious thought,
my sin— not in part but the whole,
is nailed to the cross and I bear it no more:
Praise the Lord, praise the Lord, O my soul!

And, Lord, haste the day when my faith shall be sight,
the clouds be rolled back as a scroll,
the trump shall resound and the Lord shall descend:
"Even so"— it is well with my soul.

I Heard the Bells on Christmas Day

Henry Wadsworth Longfellow

Henry Wadsworth Longfellow, Harvard professor and the first American to be honored in the Poet's Corner in Westminster Abbey, penned a poem that has become a mainstay of the Christmas repertoire each year. The hope for the Christian of peace on earth meets head-on with the reality of the Civil War in these verses; but, for Longfellow at least, Christmas bells have a way of piercing through even the din of cannon roar.

"I heard the bells on Christmas Day
Their old familiar carols play,
And wild and sweet
The words repeat
Of peace on earth, good will to men!

"And thought how, as the day had come,
The belfries of all Christendom
Had rolled along
The unbroken song
Of peace on earth, good will to men!

"Till, ringing, singing on its way,
The world revolved from night to day,
A voice, a chime,
A chant sublime
Of peace on earth, good will to men!

"Then from each black accursed mouth
The cannon thundered in the South
And with the sound
The carols drowned
Of peace on earth, good will to men!

"It was as if an earthquake rent
The hearthstones of a continent,
And made forlorn
The households born
Of peace on earth, good will to men!

"And in despair, I bowed my head;
'There is no peace on earth,' I said;
'For hate is strong, and mocks the song
Of peace on earth, good will to men!'

"Then pealed the bells more loud and deep:
'God is not dead; nor doth He sleep!
The wrong shall fail,
The right prevail,
With peace on earth, good will to men!'"

GOD OF OUR FATHERS

Daniel C. Roberts

The small Episcopal parish in Brandon, Vermont, was fortunate to be the place where this hymn was first sung, on July 4, 1876. Their rector, Daniel C. Roberts, had specifically composed the hymn for America's centennial birthday. Later that year, when the adoption of the Constitution was commemorated, his hymn was chosen to be part of that celebration.

God of our fathers, whose almighty hand
leads forth in beauty all the starry band
of shining worlds in splendor through the skies,
our grateful songs before thy throne arise.

Thy love divine hath led us in the past;
in this free land by thee our lot is cast;
be thou our Ruler, Guardian, Guide and Stay,
thy Word our law, thy paths our chosen way.

From war's alarms, from deadly pestilence,
be thy strong arm our ever sure defense,
thy true religion in our hearts increase,
thy bounteous goodness nourish us in peace.

Refresh thy people on their toilsome way;
lead us from night to never-ending day;
fill all our lives with love and grace divine;
and glory, laud, and praise be ever thine.

GREAT IS THY FAITHFULNESS

Thomas O. Chisholm

The log cabin has an honored place in the lore of American history, and the writer of this famous hymn came from such a humble beginning. Thomas O. Chisholm was born in Franklin, Kentucky, in 1866 and after attending the country schoolhouse, he began teaching in that same place at the age of sixteen! Of Chisholm's over twelve hundred poems, this is the one that has lasted. Perhaps it is worth noting that his health was never good. In that context, this poem is a sermon in itself.

Great is thy faithfulness, O God my Father,
there is no shadow of turning with thee;
thou changest not, thy compassions they fail not;
as thou hast been thou forever wilt be.

REFRAIN
Great is thy faithfulness! Great is thy faithfulness!
Morning by morning new mercies I see;
all I have needed thy hand hath provided—
great is thy faithfulness, Lord, unto me!

Summer and winter, and spring-time and harvest,
sun, moon and stars in their courses above
join with all nature in manifold witness
to thy great faithfulness, mercy and love.

Pardon for sin and a peace that endureth,
thy own dear presence to cheer and to guide;
strength for today and bright hope for tomorrow,
blessings all mine, with ten thousand beside!

SOFTLY AND TENDERLY JESUS IS CALLING

Will L. Thompson

Born in the middle of the last century, Will Thompson was trained as a musician, but always wrote with an unsophisticated style. As a publisher as well as a writer, he made a sizable income, but never lost touch with the common person. In his native Ohio, he was known for traveling from town to town by horse and buggy, singing his songs for anyone who would listen. Dwight L. Moody, the famous Chicago evangelist, was a close friend, and this song was one of his favorites. On his deathbed he reportedly whispered to the visiting Thompson, "Will, I would rather have written 'Softly and Tenderly' than anything I have been able to do in my whole life."

Softly and tenderly Jesus is calling,
calling for you and for me;
see, on the portals he's waiting and watching,
watching for you and for me.

REFRAIN
Come home, come home,
ye who are weary, come home;
earnestly, tenderly, Jesus is calling,
calling, O sinner, come home!

Why should we tarry when Jesus is pleading,
pleading for you and for me?
Why should we linger and heed not his mercies,
mercies for you and for me?

O for the wonderful love he has promised,
promised for you and for me!
Though we have sinned, he has mercy and pardon,
pardon for you and for me.

THE WONDER OF IT ALL

George Beverly Shea

The birth of a song is a mystery, with inspiration coming from unlimited sources. Mr. Shea has been the crusade soloist for Billy Graham since the beginning in the fifties, and he has personally watched hundreds of thousands of people respond to the message that the evangelist has preached. In relating this to a passenger on an ocean liner, he said enthusiastically, ". . . if you could just see the wonder of it all!" The man quickly wrote the words down on a piece of paper and handed them to Mr. Shea. "That sounds like a song to me," he said. And a song that has been sung by millions was born.

There's the wonder of sunset at evening,
The wonder as sunrise I see;
But the wonder of wonders that thrills my soul
Is the wonder that God loves me.

REFRAIN (2 TIMES)
O the wonder of it all!
The wonder of it all!
Just to think that God loves me.

There's the wonder of springtime and harvest,
The sky, the stars, the sun;
But the wonder of wonders that thrills my soul
Is a wonder that's only begun.

IN THE GARDEN

C. Austin Miles

Holed up in his dark room, Mr. Miles described being overwhelmed by the light of a portion of Scripture he was reading. The Gospel of John, chapter 20, refers to an encounter between the just-resurrected Jesus and His follower Mary Magdalene. As Miles read the account, he sensed that somehow he was actually there. Characters from the story came and went, just like the narration, until all alone Mary knelt before Jesus and looked into His face, exclaiming "Rabboni." As Miles tells the vision, "I awakened in full light, gripping the Bible, with muscles tense and nerves vibrating. Under the inspiration of this vision, I wrote as quickly as the words could be formed the poem exactly as it has since appeared. That same evening I wrote the music."

I come to the garden alone,
while the dew is still on the roses;
and the voice I hear, falling on my ear,
the Son of God discloses.

REFRAIN
And he walks with me, and he talks with me,
and he tells me I am his own,
and the joy we share, as we tarry there,
none other has ever known.

He speaks, and the sound of his voice
is so sweet the birds hush their singing,
and the melody that he gave to me
within my heart is ringing.

I'd stay in the garden with him
though the night around me be falling,
but he bids me go; through the voice of woe
his voice to me is calling.

THE OLD RUGGED CROSS

George Bennard

I was praying for a full understanding of the cross," Rev. Bennard explained in describing how this hymn came to be. "The Christ of the cross became more than a symbol. The scene pictured a method, outlined a process, and revealed the consummation of spiritual experience. It was like seeing John 3:16 leave the printed page, take form, and act out the meaning of redemption." From this spiritual encounter, only the essence of the song emerged. Trying to finish it, an inner voice seemed to say, "Wait." It wasn't until he had finished a series of evangelistic meetings that the rest of the song was completed; and when the ending came to him, it was with "facility and dispatch." The result has become probably America's best known and loved gospel song.

On a hill far away stood an old rugged cross,
the emblem of suffering and shame;
and I love that old cross, where the dearest and best
for a world of lost sinners was slain.

REFRAIN
So I'll cherish the old rugged cross,
till my trophies at last I lay down;
I will cling to the old rugged cross,
and exchange it some day for a crown.

O that old rugged cross, so despised by the world,
has a wondrous attraction for me;
for the dear Lamb of God left his glory above
to bear it to dark Calvary.

In the old rugged cross, stained with blood so divine,
a wondrous beauty I see;
for 'twas on that old cross Jesus suffered and died
to pardon and sanctify me.

To the old rugged cross I will ever be true,
its shame and reproach gladly bear;
then he'll call me some day to my home far away,
where his glory forever I'll share.

I Belong to the King

Ida L. Reed

At first glance, the life of Ida Reed should have produced cynicism and bitterness. Born and reared in the mountains of West Virginia, she was forced to take care of her invalid and widowed mother. Years of arduous farm work took its toll and broke her health, and she lived out much of her life afflicted and bedridden. The words of this hymn were written from her hospital bed late in life. The American Society of Composers, Authors and Publishers became aware of her financial state and voted her a pension with a monthly allowance.

I belong to the King,
I'm a child of His love,
I shall dwell in His palace so fair;
For He tells of its bliss
in yon heaven above,
And His children its splendors shall share.

REFRAIN
I belong to the King,
I'm a child of His love,
And He never forsaketh His own;
He will call me some day to His palace above,
I shall dwell by His glorified throne.

I belong to the King,
And He loves me I know,
For His mercy and kindness, so free,
Are unceasingly mine, wheresoever I go,
And my refuge unfailing is He.

I belong to the King,
And His promise is sure,
That we all shall be gathered at last
In His Kingdom above, by life's waters so pure,
When this life with its trials is past.

AMERICA, THE BEAUTIFUL

Katherine Lee Bates

The beauty of the world around us has prompted thousands of lines of poetry, and this song is a wonderful example of that inspiration. In 1893, as a teacher of English at Wellesley College, Katherine Lee Bates visited Pike's Peak in the state of Colorado. Overcome by the majesty of what she saw, and reflecting on the people and places that had contributed to this country's greatness, she paid tribute to the grace that God has shown America with this hymn. On that same trip west, she had visited the Columbian Exhibition on Chicago's south side, where "alabaster cities" had been erected to help envision what America's cities of the future might look like. One can't help but wonder what her prayer to God would be if she were to write a fifth stanza today.

O beautiful for spacious skies,
for amber waves of grain,
for purple mountain majesties
above the fruited plain!
America! America!
God shed his grace on thee,
and crown thy good with brotherhood
from sea to shining sea!

O beautiful for pilgrim feet,
whose stern, impassioned stress
a thoroughfare for freedom beat
across the wilderness!
America! America!
God mend thine every flaw,
confirm thy soul in self-control,
thy liberty in law!

O beautiful for heroes proved
in liberating strife,
who more than self their country loved,
and mercy more than life!
America! America!
May God thy gold refine,
till all success be nobleness,
and every gain divine!

O beautiful for patriot dream
that sees beyond the years
thine alabaster cities gleam,
undimmed by human tears!
America! America!
God shed his grace on thee,
and crown thy good with brotherhood
from sea to shining sea!

MY HEART, HOW VERY HARD IT'S GROWN

Cotton Mather

In 1681, while reflecting on a toothache, Cotton Mather penned in his diary: "Have I not sinned with my teeth? By sinful, graceless, excessive eating. And by evil speeches, for there are liberal dentals used in them, from which I have yet been free, for a considerable while. Let me ask then: Have not I of late given way to some old iniquity?"

Another entry discusses his meditation on "the inexpressible evil, which there would be,... if one of my... many and mighty obligations, to the most unspotted Sanctity, would harbour or indulge in myself any wicked Thing in the World." Mather's remorse over his sin is the theme of a hymn that he himself composed.

My heart, how very hard it's grown!
Thickened and stiffened clay
Daily trod by the wicked one,
Of sin the beaten way.

An heart wherein compacted weeds
Of diverse lusts abound,
No entrance for the heavenly seeds
Falling on such a ground!

O my almighty Saviour, come!
Thy word's a wondrous plow,
And let thy spirit drive it home;
This heart, oh break it so!

Lord, let my broken heart receive
Thy truth with faith and love;
May it a just reception give
To what falls from above.

Will my God plow upon a rock?
Change thou the soil, my Lord!
My heart, once by thy plowshare broke,
Will entertain thy word.

ANGEL OF PEACE, THOU HAST WANDERED TOO LONG

Oliver Wendell Holmes

Preacher's kid, Harvard-trained lawyer, physician, poet, popular public speaker, and the father of the famous Supreme Court judge of the same name, Oliver Wendell Holmes contributed a hymn in 1869 that chides heaven to "make good" on the promise that the angels gave the shepherds that first Christmas Eve, making peace on earth a fuller reality.

Angel of Peace, thou hast wandered too long!
Spread thy white wings to the sunshine of love!
Come while our voices are blended in song,
Fly to our ark like the stormbeaten dove!
Fly to our ark on the wings of the dove!
Speed o'er the far sounding billows of song,
Crowned with thine olive leaf garland of love,
Angel of Peace, thou hast waited too long!

Brothers we met, on this altar of thine,
Mingling the gifts we have gathered for thee,
Sweet with the odors of myrtle and pine,
Breeze of the prairie, and breath of the sea,
Meadow and mountain and forest and sea!
Sweet is the fragrance of myrtle and pine,
Sweeter the incense we offer to thee,
Brothers once more round this altar of thine!

Angels of Bethlehem, answer the strain!
Hark! a new birthsong is filling the sky!
Loud as the storm wind that tumbles the main,
Bid the full breath of the organ reply.
Let the loud tempest of voices reply,
Roll the long surge like the earth-shaking main!
Swell the vast song till it mounts to the sky!
Angels of Bethlehem, echo the strain!

A LITTLE KINGDOM I POSSESS

Louisa May Alcott

"Go then, my little Book, and show to all
That entertain and bid thee welcome shall,
What thou dost keep close shut up in thy breast;
And wish what thou dost show them may be blest
To them for good, may make them choose to be
Pilgrims better, by far, than thee or me.
Tell them of Mercy; she is one
Who early hath her pilgrimage begun.
Yea, let young damsels learn of her to prize
The world which is to come, and so be wise;
For little tripping maids may follow God
Along the ways which saintly feet have trod."

Preface to *Little Women*
Adapted from John Bunyan

A little kingdom I possess,
Where thoughts and feelings dwell,
And very hard I find the task
Of governing it well;
For passion tempts and troubles me,
A wayward will misleads,
And selfishness its shadow casts,
On all my will and deeds.

How can I learn to rule myself,
To be the child I should,
Honest and brave, nor ever tire
Of trying to be good?
How can I keep a sunny soul
To shine along life's way?
How can I tune my little heart,
To sweetly sing all day?

Dear Father, help me with the love
That casts out my fear!
Teach me to lean on thee and feel
That thou art very near.
Than no temptation is unseen,
No childish grief too small,
Since thou, with patience infinite,
Dost soothe and comfort all.

I do not ask for any crown
But that which all may win;
Nor try to conquer any world
Except the one within.
Be Thou my guide until I find,
Led by a tender hand,
The happy kingdom in myself
And dare to take command.

Our Bondage, It Shall End

Peter Cartwright

Famous for his camp-meeting exploits in the first half of the 1800's, Peter Cartwright was a "circuit-riding preacher" in Kentucky. During a time when religious revivals were common and expected, he stopped to preach at a farmhouse on the Cumberland River. On that occasion he was preaching to both whites and blacks. "I sung and prayed, took my text, and preached to them about an hour as well as I could. The colored people wept, the white people wept, the man of the house wept; and when I closed he said, 'Do leave another appointment, and come and preach to us, for we are sinners and greatly need preaching.'" The following tune is commonly attributed to Peter Cartwright, around 1835.

Our bondage it shall end,
by and by, by and by,
Our bondage, It shall end, by and by.
From Egypt's yoke set free;
Hail the glorious jubilee,
And to Canaan we'll return,
by and by, by and by,
And to Canaan we'll return, by and by.

Our Deliverer will come,
by and by, by and by,
Our Deliverer, will come, by and by.
And our sorrows have an end,
With our threescore years and ten,
And vast glory crowns the day,
by and by, by and by,
And vast glory crowns the day, by and by.

Though our enemies are strong,
we'll go on, we'll go on.
Though our enemies are strong, we'll go on.
Though our hearts dissolve with fear,
Lo! Sinai's God is near,
While the fiery pillar moves,
we'll go on, we'll go on,
While the firey pillar moves, we'll go on.

And when to Jordan's flood,
we are come, we are come,
And when to Jordan's flood, we are come.
Jehovah rules the tide,
And the waters he'll divide,
And the ransom'd host shall shout,
"We are come, we are come."
And the ransomed host shall shout,
We are come."

Then friends shall meet again
who have loved, who have loved.
Then friends shall meet again who
have loved.
Our embraces will be sweet
At the dear Redeemer's feet,
When we meet to part no more,
who have loved, who have loved.
When we meet to part no more,
who have loved.

I LOVE THY KINGDOM, LORD

Timothy Dwight

Imagine the president of any major university today writing a hymn that declares a love for any kingdom other than the one this world offers! Yet here is Timothy Dwight, president of Yale University at the end of the eighteenth century, letting all the world know where his main loyalties lay. A grandson of the great American preacher Jonathan Edwards, Dwight had been shocked by the lack of faith when he took over as president of Yale. Due largely to his prayers, tears, and vision, a second "great awakening" took place, spreading from that campus to other universities and into the general culture as well. He also authored a number of scholarly books, as well as writing thirty-three hymn texts.

I love thy kingdom, Lord,
the house of thine abode,
the Church our blest Redeemer saved
with his own precious blood.

I love thy Church, O God!
Her walls before thee stand,
dear as the apple of thine eye,
and graven on thy hand.

For her my tears shall fall,
for her my prayers ascend;
to her my cares and toils be given,
till toils and cares shall end.

Beyond my highest joy
I prize her heavenly ways,
her sweet communion, solemn vows,
her hymns of love and praise.

Sure as thy truth shall last,
to Zion shall be given
the brighest glories earth can yield,
and brighter bliss of heaven.

ABIDE IN ME, O LORD, AND I IN THEE

Harriet Beecher Stowe

Is it so surprising that the same person who helped to prick the conscience of a nation by writing *Uncle Tom's Cabin* would also be a preacher's kid, marry a preacher, and have two brothers who followed in their father's footsteps? The book that sold three hundred fifty thousand copies in the first year was written by a person whose private faith in God was intensely personal, honest, and self-abasing, as her hymn from 1855 reveals.

Abide in me, O Lord, and I in thee,
From this good hour, oh, leave me nevermore;
Then shall the discord cease, the wound be healed,
The lifelong bleeding of the soul be o'er.

Abide in me; o'er shadow by thy love
Each half-formed purpose and dark thought of sin;
Quench ere it rise each selfish, low desire,
And keep my soul as thine, calm and divine.

As some rare perfume in a vase of clay,
Pervades it with a fragrance not its own,
So, when thou dwellest in a mortal soul,
All heaven's own sweetness seems around it thrown.

Abide in me; there have been moments blest,
When I have heard thy voice and felt thy power;
Then evil lost its grasp; and passion, hushed,
Owned the divine enchantment of the hour.

These were but seasons beautiful and rare;
Abide in me, and they shall ever be;
Fulfill at once thy precept and my prayer.
Come, and abide in me, and I in thee.

WE LOVE THE VENERABLE HOUSE

Ralph Waldo Emerson

This preacher's kid is said to have undergone an intense religious experience in 1830 or 1831 at the age of twenty-six or twenty-seven. He described it as a "sweet inward burning," bringing to mind a similar experience by the preacher of the Great Awakening, Jonathan Edwards. Sadly, though he was ordained as junior pastor at the church where Increase and Cotton Mather had preached a century earlier, that congregation was now spiritually cold and dead, and Emerson himself would be exposed to the same forces of doubt. Emerson addressed the graduating class of the Divinity College at Harvard in 1838, revealing his awareness of the church adrift, without an anchor. And though much of the controversial speech was a call to navigating without a compass, he also prophetically warned of the results of a "decaying church and a wasting unbelief."

"What greater calamity can fall upon a nation, than the loss of worship? Then all things go to decay. Genius leaves the temple, to haunt the senate, or the market. Literature becomes frivolous. Science is cold. The eye of the youth is not lighted by the hope of other worlds, and age is without honor. Society lives to trifles, and when men die, we do not mention them."

> *We love the venerable house*
> *Our fathers built to God;*
> *In heaven are kept their grateful vows,*
> *Their dust endears the sod.*
>
> *Here holy thoughts a light have shed*
> *From many a radiant face,*
> *And prayers of humble virtue spread*
> *The perfume of the place.*
>
> *And anxious hearts have pondered here*
> *The mystery of life,*
> *And prayed th' Eternal Light to clear*
> *Their doubts and aid their strife.*
>
> *From humble tenements around*
> *Came up the pensive train,*
> *And in the church a blessing found,*
> *That filled their homes again;*
>
> *For faith, and peace, and mighty love,*
> *That from the Godhead flow,*
> *Showed them the life of heaven above*
> *Springs from the life below.*
>
> *They live with God their homes are dust;*
> *Yet here their children pray,*
> *And in this fleeting lifetime trust*
> *To find the narrow way.*

Dear Lord and Father of Mankind

John Greenleaf Whittier

Raised in a Quaker home, John Greenleaf Whittier's poetry is replete with scriptural references, so much so that if comprehension is the goal of the reader, then access to a Bible is a must. Whittier dedicated much of his life to opposing slavery, using his poetry artfully, like a sword. Calling for "an immediate surrender of baneful prejudice to Christian love," he got specific, demanding an immediate practical obedience to the command of Jesus Christ: ". . . Whatsoever ye would that men should do unto you, do ye even so to them."

Dear Lord and Father of mankind,
Forgive our foolish ways;
Reclothe us in our rightful mind;
In purer lives thy service find,
In deeper reverence, praise.

In simple trust like theirs who heard,
Beside the Syrian sea,
The gracious calling of the Lord,
Let us, like them, without a word,
Rise up and follow thee.

O Sabbath rest by Galilee!
O calm of hills above!
Where Jesus knelt to share with thee
The silence of eternity,
Interpreted by love.

Drop thy still dews of quietness,
Till all our strivings cease;
Take from our souls the strain and stress,
And let our ordered lives confess
The beauty of thy peace.

Breathe through the heats of our desire
Thy coolness and thy balm;
Let sense be dumb, let flesh retire;
Speak through the earthquake, wind, and fire,
O still small voice of calm.

WHEN ISRAEL WAS IN EGYPT'S LAND

Anonymous

The spirituals that emerged from the African-American slavery experience never have a composer attached to them; but the truth of those songs is so powerful that they transcend the feelings and emotions of any one individual, becoming instead the collective voice of an entire people. What would the slave have done without faith, without the hope that we worship a God who will someday right all wrongs? In the Bible, suffering became a point of reference, encouraging perseverance in the face of massive injustice. If God is the same yesterday, today, and forever, and if He delivered Daniel from the lions' den, well, can't He deliver again?

When Israel was in Egypt's land,
Let my people go;
Oppressed so hard they could not stand,
Let my people go.

REFRAIN
Go down, Moses,
Way down in Egypt land,
Tell ole Pharaoh,
Let my people go.

Thus saith the Lord, bold Moses said,
Let my people go;
If not, I'll smite your firstborn dead,
Let my people go.

No more shall they in bondage toil,
Let my people go;
Let them come out with Egypt's spoil,
Let my people go.

O let us all from bondage flee,
Let my people go;
And let us all in Christ be free,
Let my people go.

We need not always weep and moan,
Let my people go;
And wear these slavery chains forlorn,
Let my people go.

HIGHER GROUND

Johnson Oatman, Jr.

Samuel Rutherford, the persecuted Scottish preacher jailed in Aberdeen, wrote from prison to the daughter of a friend in 1637:

"Oh that this land were humbled in time, and by prayers, cries, and humiliation, would bring Christ in at the church-door again, now when His back is turned towards us, and He is gone to the threshold, and His one foot is, as it were, out of the door! I am sure that His departure is our deserving—we have brought it with our iniquities; for even the Lord's own children are fallen asleep, and alas! professors [believers] are made all of show and fashions, and are not at pains to recover themselves again. Everyone hath his set measure of faith and holiness, and contented himself with but a stinted measure of godliness, as if that were enough to bring him to heaven. We forget that as our gifts and light grow, so God's gain and the interest of His talents should grow also, and that we cannot pay God with the old use and wont (as we use to speak) which we gave Him seven years ago. O what difficulty there is in our Christian journey, and how often we come short of many thousand things that are Christ's due!"

> I'm pressing on the upward way,
> New heights I'm gaining every day;
> Still praying as I'm onward bound,
> "Lord, plant my feet on higher ground."
>
> REFRAIN
> Lord, lift me up and let me stand
> By faith on heaven's table land,
> A higher plane than I have found;
> Lord, plant my feet on higher ground.
>
> My heart has no desire to stay
> Where doubts arise and fears dismay;
> Though some may dwell where these abound,
> My prayer, my aim is higher ground.
>
> I want to live above the world,
> Though Satan's darts at me are hurled;
> For faith has caught the joyful sound,
> The song of saints on higher ground.
>
> I want to scale the utmost height
> And catch a gleam of glory bright;
> But still I'll pray, 'til heaven I've found,
> "Lord, lead me on to higher ground."

SEVENTY YEARS AGO

Twyla Paris

America's faith is a faith that has been handed down. The people who believed before us have passed on the baton; and though their leg of the journey may have ended, the race is still not over. Twyla Paris is a devout songwriter of the last fifteen years, who in the tradition of all the hymn writers who have preceded her, writes and sings about the personal nature of her faith. With her Oklahoma roots showing up in this ballad, she relates not just the story of her faith, but of generations of belief in her family, honestly admitting the responsibility she feels to live up to the legacy that is now hers to carry on.

Seventy years ago my father's mother's father
led the clan of Nicholson
He and my great grandmother had four lovely daughters
and a strong and honest son
And they traveled Arkansas and Oklahoma
building arbors made of vine
And the people of the town would come at sundown
some to scoff, and some to see what they would find
And the sisters dressed in white
and the family sang and prayed into the night
And they rode in a covered wagon
as they walked in holiness
And they lived and preached the power
and forgiveness of the Lord—seventy years ago

Seventy years ago there wasn't much in preaching
but it never slowed them down
They loved the truth of all the hearts that He was reaching
and their eyes were on the crown
So they traveled Arkansas and Oklahoma
with a burning in their souls
And it drove them to their knees and to the next town
for the sake of a wealth they could not hold
And the sisters dressed in white
and the people sang and prayed into the night
Sometimes I feel like a pale reflection
living in the blessing they passed down
Some of them have held me, some never knew my name
but the secret has been found
I want to give this to my children
And when I am very old
I hope there will be a story worth the telling
seventy years ago

HOPE IN GOD

Walt Harrah

I was stunned, watching helplessly as the rescuers searched the bombed-out Federal Building for any sign of life. Oklahoma City became a collective nightmare for the American citizen, and our deepest suspicions of each other were aroused to the breaking point by that act of terrorism. If God is not relevant at the point of deepest pain and loss, if His presence is hidden or distant, then truly there is no hope. If we can only trust in ourselves and each other, then this world has truly lost its way. But these words come to us as a light in a very dark world:

> "For I know the plans I have for you," declares the LORD, "plans to prosper you and not to harm you, plans to give you hope and a future. Then you will call upon me and come and pray to me, and I will listen to you. You will seek me and find me when you seek me with all your heart."
>
> —JEREMIAH 29:11-13 NIV

Has a future filled with dreams
Just unraveled at the seams?
HOPE, HOPE IN GOD

For the body they may kill
But this truth they never will!
HOPE, HOPE IN GOD

Though it seems that evil triumphs
that the prince of darkness reigns
that it's all a game, and we've become
*   the pawn*

There's a truth to be remembered
this crucible will pass
for joy will accompany the dawn

When you've felt the sting of wrong
Fear and doubt are weighing strong
HOPE, HOPE IN GOD

Though the feeling is not there
Rest assured, you're in His care
HOPE, HOPE IN GOD

Though a part of you is shattered
there's a God who can repair
He can shape the mangled pieces
*   into form*

As a Father to His children
He will hold you in His arms
He's a fortress in the fiercest raging storm

When the pain is hard to bear
And you're given to despair
HOPE, HOPE IN GOD

Every heartache that you feel
Is a pain that God can heal
HOPE, HOPE IN GOD

APPENDICES

SEARCHING
FOR GOD
IN AMERICA

Afterword

HUGH HEWITT

Mark Roberts suggested in the preface that people of faith often flag in their search for God once they find "it." He cautions them. Faith is not a one-minute conversion. It's a lifetime challenge. It's a career. It is, in fact, a daily discovery of the new and the astonishing.

Because of luck and Providence, I was given the most astonishing thing—a job that for nearly a year has involved talking about, reading about, and thinking about God. The best gig in America. And here is what I've discovered.

I could repeat the search each year for the rest of my life, and even if I lived a very long time, I would still be scratching around the surface of that very small portion of the universe entitled "faith in America." There is too much to capture, too much to ponder, and certainly too much ever to understand in a conventional sense.

Recognizing the depth and breadth of Americans' experiences with faith, I cannot imagine anything more exciting or rewarding than continuing the search. To continue reading about others' search for God, to continue talking to others about it, and of course, to continue to pray and try to conform my own life to God's direction. It is that last thought that I suspect holds many people back from searching for God. That search may require action. It may require change. And it may require deep sacrifice and an uncomfortable, indeed painful transition.

In the very first systematic Bible study I ever attended—a comprehensive survey course fairly well known in the U.S., named The Bethel Bible Series—my wife and I met another young couple who became our close friends. Terry and Jill Eastland are models of Christian life lived in both the public and private arenas. Of course they have their faults. Terry is, for example, a Braves fan, and he was decidedly ungenerous toward the Cleveland Indians in the fall of 1995, but our friendship did not founder.

Terry commented in one of those Bethel classes that he had always been wary of "the wild side" of God. There was no telling what God would command the faithful to do. Remember Abraham and Isaac. It's not a fable to believers in Scripture.

And while I don't know of any modern commands of that sort, I am always unsettled by my occasional contacts with missionaries. A young missionary couple spent a year on home leave in my congregation two years ago. And I marveled—I still do—at the faith that compelled them to leave this country and live among a primitive people in a faraway rain forest. "Compel" seems to me the only appropriate word. I genuinely shudder to think what would happen if I felt called to that. My back is bad. I'm in love with creature comforts. I *need* two newspapers a morning. Better not "search" too hard. What if I found that wild side that Terry suspected was there?

And what if you did? Forget missionary calls. What if you found a God who compelled tithing? Or even a mild-mannered God who persistently nudged you to make a few minor but decidedly inconvenient changes?

My friend Walt Harrah is a fairly scary man of faith—a compliment. He's not scary because he ever demands anyone do anything about belief. Rather, he just lives the life, right down to the details. A very troubling example to us baby boomers who want God plus the Volvo and a trip to Maui every year (or more). Walt selected the songs and hymns that appear in this anthology. He's a tremendous musician, but he's awfully direct for the nuanced 1990's. Not long after I gave him the book's first draft, I called to get a reaction. Relieved that this authentic man of faith found the book useful, I was still startled by Walt's conclusion. We were talking about John Woolman, the itinerant Quaker preacher who would not sign a bill of sale for a slave. Walt's conclusion on Christians of today vis-à-vis those of Woolman's era: "We're such wimps."

A couple of points. Walt did not say "they" are such wimps. He was not judging a "them." And, he's right.

Oh, there are exceptions among Christians and among others who deeply believe in a different tradition. The Dalai Lama and his fellow Buddhists are about as far removed from wimpy as possible. And there is Roberta Hestenes, off to Thailand for World Vision a week after a heart attack. Cecil Murray, walking his shooting-plagued streets, and Chuck Colson marching into a South American prison where the local officials would not accompany him.

And so the conviction grows that genuine faith is accompanied by the courage to do very hard things. And to do them with great joy. And to do them with a wholly irrational humility. This recognition is one reason why seekers must pause and say, "There is something here." Because this kind of courage is not normal. This kind of behavior is not *self*-interested. This kind of behavior is *nuts*.

Unless, of course, God exists and He compels believers to act in certain ways. Unless faith is dangerous because God does indeed have a wild side.

I am a little embarrassed to admit it, but I hope this project—the TV series, the book, the audio-cassette—somehow advances God's work. And I'm embarrassed of my embarrassment. How can a believer not have that hope and not nurture that ambition?

And how can a believer not act as God commands?

That is the problem of sin and separateness from God. Why do children who love their parents misbehave? Why do marriages falter and drunks drink and shooters shoot? Why doesn't God just conjure up His wand and fix this mess? A Christian asks: "Why doesn't Jesus come back right now?" A Jew asks: "Where is the Messiah?" And a Muslim asks: "Why is this Allah's will?"

God knows. And we don't. And it matters not a whit as to the day's work ahead. Nor does it obstruct progress in an individual's understanding of and relationship with God.

At the end of this search, I've come to a very simple conclusion: No excuses. There are no excuses for not having a faith. There are many explanations why one ends up in one tradition of religious belief or another. And there's a huge rationale for non-belief that inevitably goes back to pride. But there are no excuses. There's a believer's T-shirt for you: No excuses.

This is my conclusion: Anyone who genuinely searches for God finds God. Period.

Once, when my son was young, he got lost. He had wandered away from a picnic going on in the commons of a rabbit-warren development ringed by busy streets. I and a half dozen other adults scattered without a plan, running and shouting. The risks were very great in our minds, especially from the nearby four-lane divided thoroughfare with cars zipping along at fifty and from the numerous pools. A friend found him in the middle of a parking lot, a wholly unperturbed two-year-old holding aloft a plastic sword. There is nothing like that kind of parent's fear and nothing like that relief.

I have to believe—I do believe—that God views each of us with the same urgency with which I searched for my boy. There is a difference. As Roberta Hestenes and Harold Kushner and many others said, God values freedom so much, He will not compel our rescue. He's not going to pluck us up unless we ask.

Many do ask. But many are like my son. Wandering around, completely unaware of peril, swords held up high.

On the other hand, many are helping others in the search.

All who for a moment genuinely desire God will find God. I believe that. Some sooner than others. And the more active the search, the quicker its conclusion. I hope you take away from this project the lasting impression that this belief of mine is not unique and it's not unusual. It's millennias-old, and it's proved true over and over again.

Search for God in America, and you will find God in America. And then God will say, "Welcome. I am happy. And here's what you are going to do now."

Acknowledgments

Amy Schroeder compiled hundreds of possible excerpts for this book and drafted background papers and compiled biographies. She is an editorial assistant of great humor and talent, without whom this book could not have been written. Amy's hundreds of hours of efforts improved the manuscript immeasurably. Every reader who enjoys it owes her a thank-you.

Marc Goldman is a very diligent and successful law student who also carved out time to collect possible excerpts. He too was invaluable to the search.

Noël Manske and Mike Fairchild diligently proofed the manuscript—a daunting task given the often obscure references and spelling from some of the earliest selections in the anthology. Snow Philip also lent her meticulous eye to help prepare the manuscript for publication.

Lynne Chapman has been my assistant for seven years, but never more than in the six weeks leading up to the completion of the manuscript. No one else could have kept this project organized and moving forward toward stern deadlines. Everyone who works with me knows that Lynne is behind the appearance of competence, and that is especially true on this project. My law partners smiled when I seized the word processing system; and Toki Aya, Camy Townsend, Susan Lockridge, and Dorothy Winkler all pitched in on this very un-legal undertaking.

The entire team at KCET supported the book project as much as the television show. Martin Burns directed and produced the series, but he also kept one eye close on the manuscript as well as one on overlooked sources. Peter Stone was, with Martin, a wonderful friend to the interviews through his commitment to the filming process. He's a quality artist.

Martin Wassell was instrumental in arranging our interview with His Holiness the Dalai Lama. I thank him for his efforts.

Ben Adair worked tirelessly with Amy on the actual production of the interviews, but he also found time to assist in the manuscript. Troy Witt found time in a busy college schedule to assist in the search for good material.

Stephen Kulczycki, Blaine Baggett, and Joyce Campbell are the three senior KCET executives who embraced and sold the idea of the series to PBS. All are wonderful colleagues without whom the project would not have launched.

Sealy Yates and Tom Thompson are responsible for this book finding a home at Word. Kip Jordan and Joey Paul welcomed Sealy's call and committed to the project. Jim Nelson Black lent his great editorial touch. David Koechel and John Peterson designed the cover and layout. They are wonderful artists. I thank them all.

Finally, Dr. Mark Roberts and Walt Harrah contributed the introduction and the chapter on music, respectively. I cannot thank them enough.

And Betsy Hewitt put up with lots of out-of-town filming over weekends and lots of writing at night. She encouraged the effort every day and contributed selections and helpful critiques throughout. It's her book as much as it is mine.

Sources

AMERICA'S SPIRITUAL TREASURY

JOHN ADAMS

"To Thomas Jefferson" 15 Sept. 1813 from *Correspondence of John Adams and Thomas Jefferson,* edited by Paul Wilstach. Copyright © 1925 by The Bobbs-Merrill Company.

LOUISA MAY ALCOTT

From *Louisa May Alcott: Life, Letters and Journals,* edited by Ednah Cheney. Copyright © 1928 Little, Brown.

MUHAMMAD ALI

Reprinted with the permission of Simon & Schuster from *Muhammad Ali: His Life and Times,* by Thomas Hauser. Copyright © 1991 by Thomas Hauser and Muhammad Ali.

MAYA ANGELOU

From *Conversations with Maya Angelou,* edited by Jeffrey M. Elliott. Copyright © 1989 by University Press of Mississippi.

FRANCIS ASBURY

From "To Most Dear and Tender Friends" in *The Armenian Magazine,* Vol. 2, 1790.

ISAAC ASIMOV

From *I, Asimov: A Memoir* by Isaac Asimov.

Copyright © 1994 by The Estate of Isaac Asimov. Used by permission of Doubleday, a division of Bantam Doubleday Dell Publishing Group Inc.

BALTIMORE CATECHISM NO. 3

Baltimore Catechism No. 3. Copyright © 1933 by Rauch & Stoeckel Printing Co., Inc.

BLACK ELK

From *Black Elk Speaks: Being the Story of a Holy Man of the Oglala Sioux as Told to John Neihardt (Flaming Rainbow),* edited by John G. Neihardt. Copyright © 1932 by W. Morrow & Company.

ANNE BRADSTREET

From *The Works of Anne Bradstreet, in prose and verse,* by Anne Bradstreet. Edited by John Harvard. Copyright © 1932 by P. Smith.

FREDERICK BUECHNER

Excerpts from *A Room Called Remember* by Frederick Buechner. Copyright © 1984 by Frederick Buechner. Reprinted by permission of HarperCollins Publishers, Inc.

ANDREW CARNEGIE

From *Autobiography of Andrew Carnegie* by Andrew Carnegie. Copyright © 1920 by Houghton Mifflin Company.

JIMMY CARTER

From "Remarks at the Presidential Prayer Breakfast" 2 Feb. 1978.

WILLA CATHER

From "One Way of Putting It" in *Nebraska State Journal.* 5 Nov. 1893, p. 13.

CESAR CHAVEZ

From *The God Letters,* edited by Paul Rifkin. Copyright © 1986 by Warner Books.

ELDRIDGE CLEAVER

From *Soul on Fire* by Eldridge Cleaver. Copyright © 1978 by Word, Inc., Dallas, Texas. Used with permission.

CHARLES COLSON

From *Born Again* by Charles Colson. Chosen Books, Inc., a division of Baker Book House Company, Grand Rapids, Michigan. Copyright © 1976. Used with permission.

CLARENCE DARROW

From *The Story of My Life* by Clarence Darrow. Copyright © 1932 by Charles Scribner's Sons.

MILES DAVIS

Reprinted with permission of Simon & Schuster for *Miles: The Autobiography* by Miles Davis with Quincy Troupe. Copyright © 1989 by Miles Davis.

JOHN DEWEY

From "Science, Belief and the Public" in *Vol. 15 of The Middle Works, 1899-1924.* Edited by Jo Ann Boydston. Copyright © 1983 by the Board of Trustees, Southern Illinois University Press, reprinted with permission of the publisher.

EMILY DICKINSON

"To Mrs. A. P. Strong" 29 January 1850, from *Life and Letters of Emily Dickinson,* edited by Martha Dickinson Bianchi. Copyright © 1924 by Houghton Mifflin Company.

ANNIE DILLARD

Selected excerpt from *Holy the Firm* by Annie Dillard. Copyright © 1977 by Annie Dillard. Reprinted by permission of HarperCollins Publishers, Inc.

FREDERICK DOUGLASS

From *Life and Times of Frederick Douglass: from 1817-1821, Written by Himself,* edited by John Lobb. Copyright © 1882 by Christian Age Office.

MARY BAKER EDDY

From *Retrospection and Introspection,* by Mary Baker Eddy. Copyright © 1892 by The Christian Science Publishing Society.

JONATHAN EDWARDS

From *The Life and Character of the Late Reverend Mr. Jonathan Edwards, President of the College at New Jersey,* by Samuel Hopkins. Copyright © 1765 by S. Kneeland.

ALBERT EINSTEIN

From *Out of My Later Years,* by Albert Einstein. Copyright © 1950 by Philosophical Library. Used by permission.

RALPH WALDO EMERSON

From *The Heart of Emerson's Journals,* edited by Bliss Perry. Copyright © 1926 by Houghton Mifflin Company.

CHARLES G. FINNEY

From *Memoirs,* by Charles G. Finney. Copyright © 1876 by Fleming H. Revell Company.

F. SCOTT FITZGERALD

From *The Last Tycoon: An Unfinished Novel: Together with The Great Gatsby and Selected*

HELEN KELLER

Excerpt from *The Story of My Life*, by Helen Keller. Copyright © 1923 by Doubleday.

JOHN F. KENNEDY

From "Remarks at the Dedication Breakfast of International Christian Leadership, Inc." 9 Feb. 1961.

MARTIN LUTHER KING, JR.

FIRST SELECTION: Haskins, Jim. *I Have A Dream.* Reprinted by arrangement with The Heirs to the Estate of Martin Luther King, Jr., c/o Writers House, Inc. as agent for the proprietor. Copyright © 1963 by Martin Luther King, Jr., copyright renewed © 1991 by Coretta Scott King.
SECOND SELECTION: From *The Papers of Martin Luther King, Jr.,* edited by Ralph E. Luker, et al. Copyright © 1992 University of California Press. Used with permission.
THIRD SELECTION: From *I Have A Dream,* edited by James M. Washington. Copyright © 1986 by Harper San Francisco.

MOTHER ANN LEE

From *Testimonies of the Revelations of Mother Ann Lee and the Elders With Her.* Copyright © 1888 by Weed, Parsons & Co.

JARENA LEE

From *Religious Experience and Journal of Mrs. Jarena Lee, Giving an Account of Her Call to Preach the Gospel,* by Jarena Lee. Printed and Published for the Author, 1849.

ROBERT E. LEE

"To Mrs. Robert E. Lee" 25 December 1862 in *Recollections of General Robert E. Lee.* Copyright © 1924 by Doubleday, Page & Company.

ABRAHAM LINCOLN

From "*Second Inaugural Address*" 4 March 1865.

ANNE MORROW LINDBERGH

Excerpt from *Hour of Gold, Hour of Lead: Diaries and Letters of Anne Morrow Lindbergh,* copyright © 1973 by Anne Morrow Lindbergh, reprinted by permission of Harcourt Brace & Company.

ROBERT LOWELL

"After the Surprising Conversions" from *Lord Weary's Castle,* copyright © 1946 and renewed 1974 by Robert Lowell, reprinted by permission of Harcourt Brace & Company.

MALCOLM X

From *The Autobiography of Malcolm X* by Malcolm X with Alex Haley. Copyright © 1964 by Alex Haley and Malcolm X. Copyright © 1965 by Alex Haley and Betty Shabazz. Reprinted by permission of Random House, Inc.

PETER MARSHALL

From *Mr. Jones, Meet the Master* by Peter Marshall. Fleming H. Revell, a division of Baker Book House Company, Grand Rapids, Michigan. Copyright © 1949. Used with permission.

THE MAYFLOWER COMPACT

"The Mayflower Compact" in *American Canon,* edited by Daniel Marsh. Copyright © 1939 by Abingdon-Cokesbury Press.

MARY MCCARTHY

Excerpt from "To the Reader" in *Memories of a Catholic Girlhood,* copyright © 1957 and renewed 1985 by Mary McCarthy, reprinted by permission of Harcourt Brace & Company.

RED JACKET

Excerpt from *Native American Testimony,* edited by Peter Nabokov. Copyright © 1979 by Harper & Row Publishers, Inc.

COLONEL DONALD S. ROCKWELL

From *Islam—Our Choice.* Copyright © 1961 by Begum Aisha Bawany Waqf.

ELEANOR ROOSEVELT

From *Vol. 3 of My Day,* edited by David Elmblidge. Copyright © 1991 by Pharos Books.

FRANKLIN D. ROOSEVELT

From "Address at George Rogers Clark Memorial, Vincennes, Indiana" 14 June 1936.

THEODORE ROOSEVELT

From "The World of Micah: The Religion of Service," by Theodore Roosevelt.

MARY ROWLANDSON

From *The Sovereignty and Goodness of God, Together with the Faithfulness of His Promises Displayed, Being a Narrative of the Captivity and Restoration of Mrs. Mary Rowlandson,* by Mary Rowlandson. Copyright © 1682 by Samuel Green.

GEORGE SANTAYANA

From "The Task of Morals," in *The Practical Cogitator,* edited by Charles P. Curtis, Jr., et al. Copyright © 1962 by Houghton Mifflin Company.

MENACHEM MENDEL SCHNEERSON

From *Toward a Meaningful Life: The Wisdom of the Rebbe Menachem Mendel Schneerson.* Adapted by Simon Jacobson. Copyright © 1995 by Vaad Hanochos Hatmimim. By permission of William Morrow & Company, Inc.

JUNIPERO SERRA

Excerpt from *The Last of the Conquistadors—Junipero Serra (1713-1784)* by Omer Englebert, English translation by Katherine Woods, copyright © 1954 by Harcourt Brace & Company, reprinted by permission of the publisher.

BISHOP FULTON SHEEN

From *The Seven Virtues,* by Fulton Sheen. Copyright © 1940 by Garden City Books.

ISAAC BASHEVIS SINGER

From *A Young Man in Search of Love.* Copyright © 1978 by Isaac Bashevis Singer. This usage granted by permission.

JOSEPH SMITH

From *Joseph Smith History. 1:3-75. History of the Church of Jesus Christ of Latter-day Saints.* Copyright © 1967 by Deseret Book Company. Used with permission.

LUTHER STANDING BEAR

From *My People the Sioux,* edited by E. A. Brininstool. Copyright © 1928 by Houghton Mifflin Company.

ELIZABETH CADY STANTON

From *The Woman's Bible, Part One,* by Elizabeth Cady Stanton. Copyright © 1895 European Publishing Co.

HARRIET BEECHER STOWE

"To Frederick Douglass" 9 July 1851 from *Life and Letters of Harriet Beecher Stowe,* edited by Annie Fields. Copyright © 1898 by Houghton, Mifflin and Company.

HENRY DAVID THOREAU

From *Walden; or Life in the Woods,* by Henry David Thoreau. Copyright © 1893 Houghton Mifflin Company.

SIR JOHN TEMPLETON

Templeton, John Mark. 1993. "Bridging Two Worlds: An Interview with Sir John Templeton," *Second Opinion 19 No. 1 (July): 71-80 Magazine.* Used with permission by the Park Ridge Center for the Study of Health, Faith and Ethics (Chicago, Illinois).

ALEXIS DE TOCQUEVILLE

From *Democracy In America,* 3rd ed., by Alexis de Tocqueville. Copyright © 1863 by Sever & Francis.

HARRY S. TRUMAN

From "Address to the Federal Council of Churches" 6 March 1946.

MARK TWAIN

FIRST SELECTION: From *What Is Man? and Other Essays,* by Mark Twain. Copyright © 1917 by Harper and Brothers.
SECOND SELECTION: "Thoughts of God" from *Fables of Man* by Mark Twain. Copyright © 1973 by University of California Press. Used with permission.

JANE WAGNER

From "The Search for Signs of Intelligent Life in the Universe" by Jane Wagner. Copyright © 1986 by Harper & Row.

GEORGE WASHINGTON

From "Farewell Address" 19 September 1796.

ALAN WATTS

From *In My Own Way* by Alan Watts. Copyright © 1972 by Alan Watts. Reprinted by permission of Pantheon Books, a division of Random House, Inc.

MUHAMMAD ALEXANDER RUSSELL WEBB

From *Islam—Our Choice.* Copyright © 1961 by Begum Aisha Bawany Waqf.

EDITH WHARTON

From *A Backward Glance,* by Edith Wharton. Copyright © 1934 by D. Appleton-Century Company, Incorporated.

GEORGE WHITEFIELD

From *George Whitefield's Journals.* Copyright © 1961 by Banner of Truth Trust.

WALT WHITMAN

From *Leaves of Grass,* by Walt Whitman. Copyright © 1867 by W. E. Chapin & Co.

EDMUND WILSON

Wilson, Edmund. *A Piece of My Mind: Reflections at Sixty.* Copyright © 1956 by Edmund Wilson and renewed © 1984 by Helen Wilson, Farrar, Strauss and Cudahy.

WOODROW WILSON

From "Address in Trenton, New Jersey" 1 October 1911.

JOHN WINTHROP

From *Puritan Personal Writings: Autobiographies and Other Writings,* edited by Sacvan Bercovitch. Copyright © 1982 by AMS Press.

JOHN WOOLMAN

From *The Journal and Other Writings,* by John Woolman. Copyright © 1910 by J. M. Dent & Sons, Ltd.

RICHARD WRIGHT

Selected excerpt from *Black Boy* by Richard Wright. Copyright © 1937, 1942, 1944, 1945 by Richard Wright. Copyright renewed 1973 by Ellen Wright. Used by permission of HarperCollins Pub., Inc.

BRIGHAM YOUNG

From *Journal of Discourses,* by Brigham Young. Copyright © 1967 by Deseret Book Co. Used by permission.

HYMNS

"A Little Kingdom I Possess," "Abide in Me, O Lord, and I in Thee," "Angel of Peace, Thou Hast Wandered Too Long," "Dear Lord and Father of Mankind," "Let My People Go," "My Heart, How Very Hard It's Grown," "Our Bondage, It Shall End," and "We Love the Venerable House" from *American Hymns: Old and New,* compiled by Albert Christ-Janer, Charles W. Hughes, and Carleton Sprague Smith. Copyright © 1980 by Columbia University Press.

"America, the Beautiful," "God of Our Fathers," "How Firm a Foundation," "I Love Thy Kingdom, Lord," "In the Garden," "It Is Well With My Soul," "Mine Eyes Have Seen the Glory," "My Faith Looks Up to Thee," "Softly and Tenderly," "Stand Up, Stand Up for Jesus!" and "The Old Rugged Cross" from *The Worshiping Church,* copyright © 1990 by Hope Publishing Co.

From *Great Is Thy Faithfulness,* by Thomas O. Chisholm. Copyright © 1923. Renewal 1951 by Hope Publishing Co., Carol Stream, IL 60188. All rights reserved. Used by permission.

"Higher Ground" and "The Wonder of It All" from *Worship His Majesty.* Copyright © 1987 by Gaither Music Co., Inc.

"Hope in God" by Walt Harrah. Copyright © 1995 by Seedsower Music.

"I Belong to the King" from *Forty Gospel Hymn Stories* compiled by George W. Sanville. Copyright © George W. Sanville. Published by The Rodeheaver-Hall Mac, Co.

"I Heard the Bells on Christmas Day" from *Chats from a Minister's Library* by Wilbur M. Smith. Copyright © 1951 by W. A. Wilde Company.

From *Seventy Years Ago* by Twyla Paris. Copyright © 1993 Ariose Music/Mountain Spring Music. Admin. by EMI Christian Music Publishing. All rights reserved. Used by permission.

From *The Wonder of It All,* by George Beverly Shea. Copyright © 1923 by Word Records and Music. Used by permission.

PHOTOS